The Routledge Handbook of Contemporary English Pronunciation

The Routledge Handbook of Contemporary English Pronunciation provides a comprehensive survey of this field covering both theoretical and practical perspectives on pronunciation. In 35 chapters contributed by leading scholars from around the world, this handbook examines:

- linguistic and historical background of sound systems and theoretical issues linked to sound changes;
- pronunciation acquisition and factors related to speech production;
- pronunciation research and applications to second language pronunciation;
- the link between pronunciation and other language skills including perception and other sociocultural factors;
- pronunciation and its relation to world Englishes.

The Routledge Handbook of Contemporary English Pronunciation will be essential reading for anyone with an interest in pronunciation.

Okim Kang is Associate Professor at Northern Arizona University, USA.

Ron I. Thomson is Professor at Brock University, Canada.

John M. Murphy is Professor at Georgia State University, USA.

Routledge Handbooks in English Language Studies

Routledge Handbooks in English Language Studies provide comprehensive surveys of the key topics in English language studies. Each Handbook focuses in detail on one area, explaining why the issue is important and then critically discussing the leading views in the field. All the chapters are specially commissioned and written by prominent scholars. Coherent, accessible and carefully compiled, *Routledge Handbooks in English Language Studies* are the perfect resource for both advanced undergraduate and postgraduate students.

For a full list of titles in this series visit www.routledge.com/series/RHELS

The Routledge Handbook of Stylistics
Edited by Michael Burke

The Routledge Handbook of Language and Creativity
Edited by Rodney H. Jones

The Routledge Handbook of Contemporary English Pronunciation
Edited by Okim Kang, Ron I. Thomson and John M. Murphy

The Routledge Handbook of Contemporary English Pronunciation

Edited by
Okim Kang, Ron I. Thomson
and John M. Murphy

LONDON AND NEW YORK

First published 2018 by Routledge
2 Park Square, Milton Park, Abingdon, Oxon OX14 4RN

605 Third Avenue, New York, NY 10017

First issued in paperback 2021

Routledge is an imprint of the Taylor & Francis Group, an informa business

Publisher's Note
The publisher has gone to great lengths to ensure the quality of this reprint
but points out that some imperfections in the original copies may be
apparent.

British Library Cataloguing-in-Publication Data
A catalogue record for this book is available from the British Library

Library of Congress Cataloging-in-Publication Data
Names: Kang, Okim, editor. | Thomson, Ron, (Professor of linguistics)
editor. | Murphy, John, 1952– editor.
Title: The Routledge handbook of contemporary English pronunciation /
edited by Okim Kang, Ron Thomson and John M. Murphy.
Description: First edition. | Abingdon, Oxon ; New York, NY :
Routledge, 2018. |
Series: Routledge handbooks in English language studies | Includes
bibliographical references and index.
Identifiers: LCCN 2017025475| ISBN 9781138856882 (hardcover) |
ISBN 9781315145006 (ebook)
Subjects: LCSH: English language – Pronunciation. | English language –
Pronunciation by foreign speakers.
Classification: LCC PE1137 .R65 2017 | DDC 421/.52 – dc23
LC record available at https://lccn.loc.gov/2017025475

ISBN 13: 978-1-03-209614-8 (pbk)
ISBN 13: 978-1-138-85688-2 (hbk)

Typeset in Times New Roman and Stone Sans
by Florence Production Ltd, Stoodleigh, Devon, UK

Printed in the United Kingdom
by Henry Ling Limited

Contents

Contents

Figures and appendices

Figures

Appendices

Tables

Contributors

John Archibald (PhD, Toronto) has been Professor of Linguistics at the University of Victoria since 2010, following 19 years at the University of Calgary. He specializes in second language phonology, and is author or editor of seven books and approximately 30 journal articles and book chapters.

Amanda A. Baker is Coordinator of the TESOL programme at the University of Wollongong in Australia. Amanda's research interests focus on the dynamic relationships that exist between second language (L2) teachers' knowledge, beliefs and practices, especially in the areas of L2 pronunciation, speaking and listening pedagogy.

Donna M. Brinton is an educational consultant based in Beverly Hills, CA. She frequently presents nationally and internationally on the topic of teaching pronunciation and is one of the authors of *Teaching Pronunciation* (Cambridge University Press); she has co-authored and co-edited numerous other resource books for teachers of English as a second/foreign language.

Maxi-Ann Campbell (MA in applied linguistics from Georgia State University) currently teaches academic writing at Duke Kunshan University's Language and Culture Center (Kunshan, China). Her research focuses on improving interactions between native and non-native speakers of English, and best practices for teaching English as a foreign language. She is co-author of the third edition of *More than a Native Speaker* (TESOL International).

Walcir Cardoso is a professor at Concordia University (Canada). His current research focuses on the acquisition of second/foreign language syllable structure within an approach that combines insights from theoretical and applied linguistics.

Richard Cauldwell has taught English in France, Hong Kong, Japan and the UK, where he worked at the University of Birmingham. Since 2001 he has published electronic and print materials for listening and pronunciation. His most recent publication is *Phonology for Listening: Teaching the Stream of Speech*. He is currently working on a book for teachers and textbook authors – *A Syllabus for Listening*.

Graeme Couper, Senior Lecturer at Auckland University of Technology, applies his many years of teaching experience to research into L2 pronunciation teaching and learning. His classroom-based research brings theory and practice together within a Cognitive Linguistics framework that allows for both the cognitive and social nature of language learning.

Catia Cucchiarini is Senior Researcher at the Centre for Language and Speech Technology of the Radboud University in Nijmegen and Senior Consultant at the Dutch Language Union in The Hague. Her research addresses phonetic transcription, speech processing, L2 pronunciation, non-native speech recognition and computer-assisted language learning.

Tracey M. Derwing is Professor Emeritus in the Department of Educational Psychology at the University of Alberta and Adjunct Professor in the Department of Linguistics at Simon Fraser University. Her research interests include L2 pronunciation and issues of immigration and integration.

David Deterding is a professor at Universiti Brunei Darussalam, where he teaches phonetics, translation, forensic linguistics and research methods. His research focuses on the pronunciation of Englishes in South East Asia, including Brunei, Singapore, Hong Kong and China, and also misunderstandings that arise in international communication.

Wayne B. Dickerson is Professor Emeritus in the Department of Linguistics at the University of Illinois at Urbana-Champaign, where he taught courses in English phonology (online and face-to-face) and ESL pronunciation. His research focuses on pedagogical applications of phonetics, pronunciation pedagogy, the value of orthography for learners, phonological variability and pronunciation assessment.

Fred R. Eckman is University Distinguished Professor of Linguistics at the University of Wisconsin-Milwaukee. He has published a number of chapters in anthologies along with articles on second language phonology, second language syntax and second language theory in journals such as *Language Learning*, *Applied Linguistics*, *Studies in Second Language Acquisition*, *Second Language Research* and *Journal of Second Language Pronunciation*.

Jennifer A. Foote is an assistant professor in the English Language School in the Faculty of Extension at the University of Alberta. Her research focuses on second language pronunciation teaching, second language speech perception and comprehensibility.

Ishamina Athirah Gardiner is an adjunct lecturer at the Language Centre, Universiti Brunei Darussalam, and has recently completed her PhD research on misunderstandings and the intelligibility of Brunei English speech in international communication. Much of her research involves analysis of the pronunciation and syntactic features of English in Brunei. She currently teaches academic writing and presentation skills and has taught courses on phonetics and forensic linguistics.

Jette G. Hansen Edwards is Professor of Applied English Linguistics at the Chinese University of Hong Kong. She conducts research on the intelligibility of world Englishes, the relationship between social and linguistic factors in the acquisition of an L2 phonology, and multilingual accents and identity. She is the co-editor of *Phonology and Second Language Acquisition* (2008 and 2011, John Benjamins).

Debra M. Hardison, Michigan State University, conducts research involving auditory-visual integration in spoken language processing, learner variables in oral skills development, co-speech gesture, and the applications of technology in perception and production training of the segmental and suprasegmental aspects of language. She teaches courses on second language phonetics and research methods.

Kirk Hazen is Professor of Linguistics at West Virginia University, where he is the founding director of the West Virginia Dialect Project. His research, teaching and linguistic service are all centred on social and linguistic patterns of language variation. His most recent book is *An Introduction to Language* (Wiley, 2015), and he is co-editor (with Janet Holmes) of *Research Methods in Sociolinguistics* (Wiley, 2014).

Talia Isaacs is a senior lecturer in applied linguistics and TESOL at the UCL Centre for Applied Linguistics, UCL Institute of Education, University College London. A major focus of her work is on assessing pronunciation, particularly human- and technology-mediated assessments and scoring processes and outcomes in formal and informal settings.

Tamara Jones has taught in Russia, Korea, England, Belgium and the United States. She is coordinator of the intensive English programme with the English Language Center of Howard Community College, Maryland. She holds a PhD from the University of Sheffield and is the editor of *Pronunciation in the Classroom* (2016, TESOL International).

Okim Kang is Associate Professor in the applied linguistics programme at Northern Arizona University, Flagstaff, AZ, USA. Her research interests are speech production and perception, L2 pronunciation and intelligibility, L2 oral assessment and testing, automated scoring and speech recognition, world Englishes and language attitude.

Jagdish Kaur is a senior lecturer at the Faculty of Languages and Linguistics, University of Malaya. She conducts research in the areas of English as a lingua franca, intercultural communication and global Englishes. She has published her work in journals such as *World Englishes*, *Journal of Pragmatics*, *Intercultural Pragmatics* and *Text&Talk*.

Alyssa Kermad is a fourth-year PhD student in the applied linguistics programme at Northern Arizona University (NAU). She conducts research in L2 speech perception and production, L2 speech assessment and L2 acquisition. Alyssa has taught English in France and the United States and currently teaches at NAU.

John Levis is Professor of Applied Linguistics and TESL at Iowa State University. He co-edited *Social Dynamics in Second Language Accent* (De Gruyter Mouton), the *Handbook of English Pronunciation* (Wiley-Blackwell), and *Pronunciation: Critical Concepts in Linguistics* (Taylor & Francis). He initiated the Pronunciation in Second Language Learning and Teaching Conference and is founding editor of the *Journal of Second Language Pronunciation*.

Stephanie Lindemann is an associate professor of applied linguistics at Georgia State University. Her research focuses on the role of native speaker listeners in communication with non-native speakers, including their perceptions of non-native speech, their attitudes towards such speech, and ways of improving both their attitudes and comprehension.

Ee Ling Low is Professor of Applied Linguistics and Teacher Learning at the National Institute of Education, Nanyang Technological University, where she is also the chief planning officer. She is the president of the Singapore Association for Applied Linguistics and the series editor for the Routledge-SAAL Series for World Englishes.

Lillian May is a lecturer in the Department of Psychology at the University of British Columbia. Her research has examined speech perception and word learning in infancy, using both behavioural and neuroimaging methods.

Murray J. Munro is Professor of Linguistics at Simon Fraser University in Vancouver. His work in applied phonetics, much of it carried out in collaboration with Tracey M. Derwing, covers speech intelligibility, L2 speech learning and the social evaluation of L2 speech.

John M. Murphy is Professor of Applied Linguistics at Georgia State University. His contributions in research and teaching are informed by sociocognitive and sociocultural understandings of how teachers and learners develop new abilities. His books include *Teaching the Pronunciation of English: Focus on Whole Courses* (editor, University of Michigan Press), *Teaching Pronunciation* (TESOL International) and *Understanding the Courses We Teach: Local Perspectives on English Language Teaching* (co-editor with Pat Byrd, University of Michigan Press).

Jonathan Newton is an associate professor at the School of Linguistics and Applied Language Studies, Victoria University of Wellington, New Zealand. His research and scholarship span language teacher education, task-based language teaching, intercultural perspectives on language education, and communication training for the multicultural workplace.

Lucy Pickering is Professor of Applied linguistics and Director of the Applied Linguistics Laboratory at Texas A&M-commerce. Her research programme is focused on a number of aspects of spoken discourse including prosodic development in L2 learners, intonation in classroom discourse, humour in discourse, talking at work and corpus studies.

Joanna Przedlacka is a research fellow in phonetics at Oxford University. Her interests focus on experimental phonetics. She is currently co-investigator on a project examining how contact between ethnic groups contributes to the diachronic development of intonation in Asia Minor Greek. She is also interested in aspects of nasal co-articulation in Polish and French. Joanna has lectured university-level phonetics for clinical, fieldwork and EFL purposes (UCL, SOAS and De Montfort University) and is also an experienced EFL teacher. Joanna is a co-editor of *English Pronunciation Models: A Changing Scene*. She is involved in organizing the biennial Phonetics Teaching and Learning Conference at University College London.

Nur Raihan is studying for her PhD at the Faculty of Arts and Social Sciences, Universiti Brunei Darussalam. Her research focuses on the pronunciation of school students, undergraduates and English teachers. Her other research areas include language change and the Americanization of Brunei English.

Pamela Rogerson-Revell is Associate Professor in Applied Linguistics at the University of Leicester, UK. She is author of *English Phonology and Pronunciation Teaching* (Bloomsbury) and co-author of *Speaking Clearly with Judy Gilbert* (Cambridge University Press). She has a keen interest in online language learning and has developed an open educational resource (OER) for pronunciation teaching and learning (*Phonology and Phonetics Review*).

Boikanyego Sebina is a lecturer of English language and linguistics at the University of Botswana, Botswana. She holds an MA in English language and linguistics from the University of Botswana. She is currently doing a PhD in English language and applied linguistics at the University of Reading, United Kingdom.

Jane Setter is Professor of Phonetics at the University of Reading, UK. She has worked in the UK, Hong Kong and Japan and publishes mainly on suprasegmental aspects in global Englishes and in atypical populations. She is co-editor of the *Cambridge English Pronouncing Dictionary* (18th Edition, CUP, 2011).

Sinem Sonsaat is a PhD candidate in the applied linguistics and technology programme at Iowa State University, where she supervises ESL listening/reading classes and teaches oral communications, writing and linguistics courses. She is editorial assistant for the *Journal of Second Language Pronunciation*. Her research interests include pronunciation instruction, computer-assisted language learning, and materials evaluation and development.

Helmer Strik is Associate Professor in Speech Science and Technology at the Radboud University in Nijmegen, co-founder and CSO of NovoLanguage, and Chair of the 'International Speech Communication Association' (ISCA) 'Special Interest Group' (SIG) on 'Speech and Language Technology in Education' (SLaTE, http://hstrik.ruhosting.nl/slate/). His research addresses speech processing, automatic speech recognition (ASR), pronunciation variation modelling, spoken dialogue systems and the use of ASR technology in real-life applications for language learning and therapy.

Jolanta Szpyra-Kozłowska is Professor of English Linguistics at Maria Curie-Skłodowska University in Lublin, Poland. Her main research interests concern phonology, phonetics, pronunciation pedagogy and gender linguistics. She has published seven books (including *Pronunciation in EFL Instruction: A Research-Based Approach*, Multilingual Matters, 2015), five edited volumes and over 100 papers. She organizes international biennial conferences entitled Approaches to Phonetics and Phonology (APAP).

Ron I. Thomson is Professor of Applied Linguistics at Brock University. His research focuses on the development of oral skills by L2 English learners. He is also the creator of www.englishaccentcoach.com, a free High Variability Phonetic Training (HVPT) application for learning to perceive English vowels and consonants.

Ivor Timmis is Reader in English Language Teaching (ELT) at Leeds Beckett University, UK. His research interests include the relationship between language research and practice in ELT, particularly in the sociocultural relevance of spoken corpus findings to contemporary language classrooms. He is author of *Corpus Linguistics for ELT* and *Historical Spoken Language Research: Corpus Perspectives* (both Routledge).

Pavel Trofimovich is a professor of applied linguistics in the Department of Education at Concordia University, Montreal, Canada. His research focuses on cognitive aspects of second language processing, second language speech learning, sociolinguistic aspects of second language acquisition and the teaching of second language pronunciation.

Ann Wennerstrom (PhD, JD) is author of *The Music of Everyday Speech* (Oxford) and *Discourse Analysis in the Language Classroom* (University of Michigan Press). Her research interests include intonational meaning, conversation analysis, second language discourse and forensic linguistics. Ann has served as an expert witness in legal cases where limited English proficiency resulted in constitutional violations. She is currently an immigration attorney in Seattle.

Janet F. Werker is a University Killam Professor and Canada Research Chair in the Department of Psychology at the University of British Columbia (UBC), with fellowships in many US and Canadian societies. Her research focuses on understanding the perceptual foundations of language acquisition in infancy. She is a founder and co-director of UBC Language Sciences.

Tania S. Zamuner is Associate Professor of Linguistics at the University of Ottawa. Her research focuses on psycholinguistics, developmental speech perception and production, lexical acquisition and spoken word recognition. She is the director of the Centre for Child Language Research/Centre de recherche sur le langage des enfants.

Acknowledgements

Figure 3.3: Collins, B., & Mees, I. M. (2013). *Practical Phonetics and Phonology* (2nd ed., p. 87). Routledge. Reprinted with permission of Taylor & Francis Books UK.

Figure 3.4: Cruttenden, A. (2014). *Gimson's Pronunciation of English* (8th ed., p. 10). Routledge. Reprinted with permission of Taylor & Francis Books UK.

Figure 3.5: Ashby, P. (2011). *Understanding Phonetics* (p. 37). Routledge. Reprinted with permission of Taylor & Francis Books UK.

Figure 3.7: Ashby, P. (2011). *Understanding Phonetics* (p. 88). Routledge. Reprinted with permission of Taylor & Francis Books UK.

Figure 29.1: Hardison, D. M. (2004). Generalization of computer-assisted prosody training: Quantitative and qualitative findings. *Language Learning & Technology*, 8, 34–52 (Figures 2 and 3). Used with permission.

Figure 29.2: Motohashi-Saigo, M., & Hardison, D. M. (2009). Acquisition of L2 Japanese geminates: Training with waveform displays. *Language Learning & Technology*, 13(2), 29–47 (Figures 1 and 2). Used with permission.

Figure 29.3: Olson, D. J. (2014). Benefits of visual feedback on segmental production in the L2 classroom. *Language Learning & Technology*, 18(3), 34–52 (Figure 3). Used with permission.

Every effort has been made to trace and contact copyright holders. The publishers would be pleased to hear from any copyright holders not acknowledged here so that this acknowledgements list may be amended at the earliest opportunity.

Introduction

Okim Kang, Ron I. Thomson and
John M. Murphy

Until the turn of the twenty-first century, the topic of second language (L2) pronunciation had been marginalized in the larger disciplines of applied linguistics and second language acquisition (SLA) and often treated as a sub-skill of speaking. Examining major refereed journals (e.g. *Applied Linguistics* and *TESOL Quarterly*) for the preceding 30 years, for example, only a limited number of published articles have focused on pronunciation-related topics (with the notable exception of a special issue of *TESOL Quarterly* in 2005). Since 2005, there has been an explosion in research in this area (see Thomson & Derwing, 2015). This has coincided with the inception of the annual Pronunciation in Second Language Learning and Teaching Conference, which began in 2008, and the 2015 launch of the *Journal of Second Language Pronunciation*, the first journal entirely devoted to L2 pronunciation. Even meetings of applied linguistics associations have witnessed a marked increase in the number of papers related to this topic. Despite these significant achievements, Thomson and Derwing (2015) note that much of the recent work is not rigorous enough to use as the basis for strong conclusions about L2 pronunciation and its teaching. A comprehensive understanding of this domain and stronger links between research and practice are needed (Derwing & Munro, 2005) to best meet English language learners' needs (Celce-Murcia, Brinton, Goodwin & Griner, 2010).

The term pronunciation is often applied quite broadly to include the domains of phonetics and phonology, as well as prosodic features of larger speech segments, such as phrases, sentences and texts. Whereas phonetics concerns measurable acoustic and articulatory properties of speech sounds, phonology deals with more abstract features of sound systems in language and how they are represented in the mind during language processing. Historically, research in L2 pronunciation has largely focused on the pronunciation of individual vowels and consonants (known as segmentals), treating the speech stream as a sequence of discrete segments. However, prosodic elements of pronunciation such as stress, rhythm and intonation (known as suprasegmentals) are drawing increasing attention from teachers and researchers alike. Therefore, in more current pronunciation literature, the sound system of English is often described in terms of segmental and suprasegmental features. Furthermore, pronunciation has been described as comprising an increasingly complex building-block structure, for example moving from sounds to syllables to phrases and finally to extended discourse (Goodwin, 2013). Some pronunciation scholars argue that this building-block model of pronunciation does not reflect how learners actually experience language, which is instead perceived as continuous, and rife with ambiguity in boundaries between adjacent segments. The sound–spelling correspondence adds another layer of complexity to the task of teaching English pronunciation since connections between sounds and spelling in English are less transparent in comparison with many other languages (e.g. Spanish) and are often perceived by learners as opaque or seemingly contradictory. Yet, it is not uncommon for L2 pronunciation materials to reference spelling of the language to provide guidance for learners in how to pronounce English words in reading and speaking (Cruttenden, 2008).

Given the long tradition of phonetics and phonology within linguistic circles, it is somewhat surprising that language teachers often lack a basic knowledge of how speech sounds can be described and classified (Thomson, 2013). Beyond this, teachers often have a poor understanding of the role that a first language (L1) pronunciation system plays in acquiring the pronunciation of a second language (L2). Numerous surveys of language instructors have confirmed these concerns (Foote, Holtby & Derwing, 2011). Briefly reviewing historical trends in English pronunciation, practical descriptions of speech sounds, and theoretical issues related to speech perception and production will provide novice and experienced language teachers with important tools for improving learner outcomes.

At the same time, given new directions in the field of L2 pronunciation, even an understanding of phonetics and phonology is now seen as inadequate to inform best practice for teachers. Much more is now known about L2 accented speech. For example, learner improvement in L2 pronunciation is seen as being about more than the speaker getting sounds right. The role listeners play in understanding accented L2 pronunciation is also now seen as pivotal to communication, and complex, involving not only properties of speech but also listeners' interpretations (Kang, Rubin & Lindemann, 2015).

With an increasing focus on pronunciation and speaking research, many researchers now distinguish between complementary but partially distinct dimensions of pronunciation. This is the stance taken by Munro and Derwing (1995), for example, when discussing the constructs of intelligibility, comprehensibility and accentedness. For them, intelligibility refers to the extent to which a speaker's message is understood; comprehensibility refers to listeners' perceptions of how much effort they are expending while listening to a stretch of non-native-accented speech; non-native accent refers to the extent to which a speaker's pronunciation differs from a target language (and dialect) norm (See Thomson, 2017, for a detailed overview of how these constructs are applied and sometimes misapplied to later research). A key consensus of intelligibility, comprehensibility and accentedness research is that the degree of non-native accent is not a perfect predictor of an L2 speaker's intelligibility and comprehensibility. That is, it is possible for a speaker to have a strong non-native accent but still be intelligible. This has led to increasing agreement that pronunciation instruction should focus on what Levis (2005) labels 'the intelligibility principle' rather than the 'nativeness' principle.

The object of some recent research has been to empirically document which features of speech most contribute to intelligibility and comprehensibility vis-à-vis non-native accent (e.g. Field, 2005; Kang, 2010; Trofimovich & Isaacs, 2012). It may be the case that these constructs are too broad in their application and give insufficient attention to individual differences across learners. Uncovering individual differences will help us to determine learner-specific approaches to improving speech intelligibility.

Finally, with the internationalization of English, there are more non-native speakers than native speakers of English (Crystal, 2007; Yano, 2001). Consequently, the nature of pronunciation's role across different varieties of English needs to be addressed. Contemporary issues related not only to major varieties, but also New Englishes (e.g. Indian English, Nigerian English), and the future direction of English pronunciation instruction across such varieties are increasingly a topic of debate.

Overview of the handbook

This *Handbook of Contemporary English Pronunciation* offers a single, comprehensive resource for language teachers, teacher trainers, classroom practitioners, applied linguists and undergraduate and graduate students in pronunciation-related fields. While any particular chapter may contain content that is already understood by a subset of this broader audience, other chapters will address gaps in their knowledge. The text provides an overview of traditional orientations to pronunciation found in theoretical linguistics, clarifies evidence-based constructs in L2 pronunciation, and applies research to suggestions for practice. At the same time, the handbook encourages readers to consult more specialized works on particular aspects of English pronunciation. We have tried to bring together various strands of research and practice with an emphasis on pronunciation. Beginning with a brief overview of historical and linguistic background of speech sounds, the handbook considers theoretical and pedagogical aspects of pronunciation, new ways of teaching pronunciation, factors related to pronunciation acquisition, current research topics and applications on L2 pronunciation, the connection between pronunciation and other language skills, and the place of pronunciation within the emerging paradigm of world Englishes. By integrating theoretical and practical perspectives on English pronunciation, we hope to demystify the construct of pronunciation, which is still viewed as a theoretical puzzle by many language teachers and applied linguists. The handbook offers a thorough overview of both the fundamentals and new directions of English pronunciation.

The handbook's specific aims are to provide:

- a linguistic and historical background of sound systems and theoretical issues related to sound changes, including the practical description of speech sounds;
- pedagogical approaches to pronunciation instruction and research with application to classroom instruction and teacher training;
- discussion of pronunciation acquisition and factors related to speech production;
- pronunciation research and its application to teaching practice and to society;
- description of pronunciation linked to perception and other sociocultural factors;
- interpretation of pronunciation from the perspectives of world Englishes;
- future directions.

The handbook consists of six distinctive sections: (1) historical and theoretical perspectives on pronunciation, (2) descriptions of English pronunciations, (3) varieties of English pronunciation, (4) pronunciation instruction in language teaching, (5) current issues in pronunciation research and (6) future directions of pronunciation. The first section provides a critical foundation for understanding the theoretical and research-oriented sections that follow. Given that the field has faced gradual changes in foci (e.g. from segmentals to suprasegmentals, from accentedness to intelligibility, from controlled classroom practice to more communicative practice), this section introduces various perspectives related to changes in pronunciation teaching and research (e.g. Archibald's transfer, contrastive analysis and interlanguage phonology or Eckman's theoretical L2 phonology). In addition to the historical perspectives, models of pronunciation development are described. Werker, May and Zamuner provide an overview of phonological development in first languages, while Foote and Trofimovich offer a comprehensive discussion of phonological development in second languages.

The second section focuses on the sounds of English as commonly found in English pronunciation literature. The purpose of this section is to describe the speech sounds of English in general and to explain how English sounds are connected to spelling systems. Setter and Sebina, for example, review the current state of research on phonological development in infancy, focusing on how the perception, understanding and knowledge of the sounds of language become increasingly tuned to the properties of the native language over the first years of life with focus on English lexical stress, prominence and rhythm. English pronunciation is further explained by Rogerson-Revell's English vowels and consonants, Cardoso's English syllable structure and, finally, Wennerstrom's intonation and language learning.

The third section looks at varieties of English pronunciation. While different varieties of English or English pronunciation are introduced and described in several other texts (e.g. Jennifer Jenkins's *Phonology of English as an International Language*, or the *Handbook of World Englishes*), they tend to describe English accents (e.g. North American, British, African-American, colonial) in separate entries. In this handbook, however, we touch upon core topics of English pronunciation, such the concept of traditional standard Englishes before examining them in relation to a movement towards world Englishes. This section starts with Hazen's description of standards of English pronunciation and regional accents followed by Raihan and Deterding's discussion of the fallacy of standard English, where Raihan and Deterding show how received pronunciation (RP) is currently undergoing changes in its status by considering the results of surveys on pronunciation preferences. They then consider trends in pronunciation in Singapore and Brunei in particular. In light of this trend, Deterding and Gardiner point out the emergence of new forms of English pronunciation, presenting a case study of interactions between non-native speaker interlocutors. By analysing their pronunciation of polysyllabic words, they illustrate how new pronunciation forms are becoming increasingly acceptable. The section ends with Szpyra's inclusive accounts of instructional models in the global context.

The fourth section deals with how pronunciation has been addressed historically in language classrooms. While prior to the advent of communicative language teaching (CLT) it did receive some focus, with the advent of CLT it lost some of its lustre. Recently, a more balanced approach has emerged. Chapters on the ethics and the business of pronunciation instruction by Foote, teacher training by Murphy and the efficacy of pronunciation instruction by Derwing provide unique perspectives not found in other texts.

Section 5 is of particular importance to a large group of interested parties (e.g. graduate students, novice or established researchers). Current topics of pronunciation research are typically only briefly introduced in pronunciation teaching books (e.g. Celce-Murcia et al., 2010) or completely ignored. The authors of chapters in this section do this important topic justice. Starting with Newton's pronunciation and speaking, research issues are further discussed by Jones's connection between pronunciation and other areas of language, Edwards's individual differences, Lindemann and Campbell's language attitudes, Munro's dimensions of pronunciation and Pickering's pronunciation in discourse contexts. This section will provide those in the field with a much better understanding of the core topics of research, and their research findings and implications for teaching.

The sixth and final section of the handbook focuses on future directions in pronunciation learning, teaching and research. As noted at the beginning of this introduction, as a discipline in its own right the field of pronunciation has been rapidly growing over the last two decades. This section addresses various opinions, approaches and resources that demand further discussion and understanding. Brinton introduces innovative approaches to teaching L2 pronunciation. Couper describes how to apply cognitive linguistic frameworks to L2 pronunciation teaching. Timmis, Low and Kaur respectively offer explicit accounts on pronunciation and intelligibility issues in the contexts of world and New Englishes. Kang and Kermad suggest new directions in pronunciation assessment including validity and reliability of pronunciation assessment, measurement of pronunciation constructs and features, rating scales and criteria, and technology-based pronunciation assessment. This topic of automatic speaking assessment is further described by Cucchiarini and Strik's chapter on automatic speech recognition for L2 pronunciation training and Isaacs's work on fully automated speaking assessments.

References

Celce-Murcia, M., Brinton, D., Goodwin, J., & Griner, B. (2010). *Teaching pronunciation: A reference for teachers of English*, 2nd ed. New York: Cambridge University Press.

Cruttenden, A. (2008). *Gimson's pronunciation of English*, 8th ed. Cary, NC: Oxford University Press.

Crystal, D. (2007). *English as a global language*. Cambridge: Cambridge University Press.

Derwing, T. M., & Munro, M. J. (2005). Second language accent and pronunciation teaching: A research-based approach. *TESOL Quarterly, 3*(3), 379–397.

Field, J. (2005). Intelligibility and the listener: The role of lexical stress. *TESOL Quarterly, 39*, 399–423.

Foote, J. A., Holtby, A. K., & Derwing, T. M. (2011). Survey of the teaching of pronunciation in adult ESL programs in Canada, 2010. *TESL Canada Journal, 29*, 1–22.

Goodwin J. (2013). Teaching pronunciation. In M. Celce-Murcia (Ed.), *Teaching English as a second or foreign language* (pp. 136–152). Boston, MA: Heinle & Heinle.

Jenkins, J. (2000). *The phonology of English as an international language*. Oxford: Oxford University Press.

Levis, J. M. (2005). Changing contexts and shifting paradigms in pronunciation teaching. *TESOL Quarterly, 39*(3), 369–377.

Kang, O. (2010). Relative salience of suprasegmental features on judgments of L2 comprehensibility and accentedness. *System, 38*, 301–315.

Kang, O., Rubin, D., & Lindemann, S. (2015). Using contact theory to improve US undergraduates' attitudes toward international teaching assistants. *TESOL Quarterly, 49*, 681–706.

Munro, M. J., & Derwing, T. M. (1995). Foreign accent, comprehensibility, and intelligibility in the speech of second language learners. *Language Learning, 45*(1), 73–97.

Thomson, R. I. (2013). ESL teachers' beliefs and practices in pronunciation teaching: Confidently right or confidently wrong? In J. Levis & K. LeVelle (Eds), *Proceedings of the 4th Pronunciation in Second Language Learning and Teaching Conference*. August 2012. (pp. 224–233). Ames, IA: Iowa State University.

Thomson, R. I. (2017). Measurement of accentedness, intelligibility and comprehensibility. In O. Kang & A. Ginther (Eds), *Assessment in second language pronunciation* (pp. 11–28). New York: Routledge.

Thomson, R. I., & Derwing, T. M. (2015). The effectiveness of L2 pronunciation instruction: A narrative review. *Applied Linguistics, 36*(3), 326–344.

Trofimovich, P., & Isaacs, T. (2012). Disentangling accent from comprehensibility. *Bilingualism: Language and Cognition, 15*(4), 905–916.

Yano, Y. (2001). World Englishes in 2000 and beyond. *World English, 20*, 119–131.

Section 1

Historical and theoretical perspectives on pronunciation

1

Transfer, contrastive analysis and interlanguage phonology

John Archibald

Introduction

As with any field that has been active for over half a century, the technical terms found within it are both precise and, simultaneously, laden with connotation. In this chapter, I have purposefully used traditional terms in the title because I think they provide a fine vehicle for surveying some of the key issues in both the history and future of the discipline.

Historical and current conceptualizations

As Stern (1983) showed, much of the history of the study of second language learning was, in fact, more focused on second language *teaching*. There was much concern as to which teaching method was the best. Gradually, this emphasis began to shift as the field of *second language acquisition* (SLA) emerged, and more attention was paid to the learner. For the benefit of newcomers to the area, let me begin by setting out the timeline by introducing key terms.

Transfer: It has long been widely recognized (e.g. Gass & Selinker, 1983) that second language (L2) production is influenced by properties of the first language (L1). Surface level elements were the focus of descriptions of L2 production (either spoken or written).

Contrastive analysis: In an effort to determine why some learners were not learning some elements, the method of contrastive analysis (Lado, 1957) attempts to describe or explain what was called 'non-learning'. At this point, it would be worth pointing out that the work in language teaching, or applied linguistics, or educational linguistics, was not isolated from other academic disciplines (such as psychology). At the time when contrastive analysis was first proposed (see Archibald, 1993, for discussion), the dominant theory of learning was behaviourism (an extreme form of empiricist learning theory). Such an account places the emphasis on the *environment* as the driver of learning and highlights the role of feedback as the driver of change in the learner. From this perspective, the goal is to design the best learning environment (i.e. classroom) to ensure that learning takes place. Following a behaviourist paradigm of learning as habit formation within a model of stimulus/response, there was no place in the discipline for what was known as *mentalism*. There was no recourse to a mental representation (or grammar) to explain why the learners were doing what they were doing. It should also be noted that the contrastive analysis hypothesis has little to say about the time course, or developmental path, of L2 learning.

Interlanguage: Selinker (1972), drawing on the work of Nemser's (1971) approximative systems, formalized the notion that there is a systematic representation of linguistic competence for L2 learners. Furthermore, he acknowledges that the interlanguage grammar can contain some features from the L1 *and* some features from the L2 but that the precise mix of features could change over time. In this way, the interlanguage hypothesis introduces a dynamic model for the acquisition process.

Phonology: the final word in the title is *phonology*. I include this perhaps self-explanatory term to highlight some of the changes in the discipline and to illustrate where I think we are now in the field. The study of phonology is concerned with the mental representation and computation of sound structures. It focuses on the notion of phonological competence. Placed in the context of the goals of linguistics (Chomsky, 1988), our tasks are to both describe and explain:

(a) the nature of linguistic competence;
(b) how that knowledge is neurally instantiated;
(c) how that knowledge is used in everyday situations.

But perhaps most central to the discussion in this chapter:

(d) how that knowledge is acquired

In order to understand why I assign primary importance to (d), let me provide a brief discussion of the approach to the study of language known as language *learnability* (Gold, 1967; Wexler & Culicover, 1980; Pinker, 1984). In the early days of generative linguistics, much effort was spent on coming up with a descriptively and explanatorily adequate account of what native speakers of a language knew. In phonology, in particular, this included many abstract rules and representations (such as those found in Chomsky & Halle, 1968). Let us take an example from stress placement. As any learner of English knows, the patterns of English stress placement are complex: *robúst, énter, cínema, Appalàchicóla*. Chomsky and Halle's main stress rule was one of the first successful attempts to find patterns in English stress placement. To paraphrase and simplify (ignoring nouns):

> For verbs or adjectives, assign primary stress to the final vowel of the word if the word ends in a long vowel, or a short vowel followed by a consonant; otherwise stress the penultimate syllable.

As Kaye (1990) pointed out: if this is a possible rule, what isn't? The point to be made here is that, when looking at proposals like the main stress rule, linguists began to realize that grammatical models must be *learnable* based on the input that the learners are exposed to. It was no longer enough to find the patterns in the data. From this point on, linguistic theory began to offer real insights into the study of both first and second language acquisition. The rules proposed give us descriptions of where the L2 learner starts, where they want to end up and what their intermediate system looks like.

| Initial State Grammar | ⟶ | Intermediate State Grammar | ⟶ | Final State Grammar |

Figure 1.1 Development of SLA grammar

Indeed, this is where we find ourselves in the field of SLA today, as represented in Figure 1.1 above. The solid arrows indicate the notion of developmental path. Learners proceed from an initial state grammar (which under models of full transfer (Schwartz & Sprouse, 1996) would be identical to the grammar of their L1). The target of their acquisition is the grammar of the L2, which would be as described by linguistic descriptions of native speakers of that target language. The dashed arrows are meant to indicate that the intermediate grammars may be representations that are neither L1-like nor L2-like, or which may include features of both.

The goal of this chapter, then, is to guide the reader to a better understanding of the field that I have called *second language phonology* through a discussion of the key terms of the title: transfer, contrastive analysis and interlanguage phonology.

Illustrations and examples

Transfer

The term transfer has been central to the field as it captures an obvious aspect of non-native speech insofar as there are properties of the L1 that influence the production and perception of an L2. Weinreich (1953), Nemser (1971), Lado (1957) and Scovel (1988) have all discussed elements of this sort of transfer. Perhaps most obviously, this phenomenon makes its presence felt in the realm of L2 accent. A native speaker of English will be able to recognize that a native speaker of French sounds different from a native speaker of, say, German when they are both speaking English. For example, the English word *have* [hæv] might be pronounced as [haf] by a German speaker and [av] by a French speaker. Both L1s, lacking the [æ] vowel, may substitute [a]; the German speaker might devoice the syllable-final [v] to produce [f] (as would happen in German); the French speaker would not produce a [h] given its absence from the French consonantal inventory. The work of Scovel (1988) and others focuses on the underlying aetiology of this trait and falls within the general rubric of the critical period hypothesis. Treated under the broad category of *age effects in SLA* (Birdsong, 1992; Harley, 1986; Herschensohn, 2000; Hyltenstam & Abrahamsson, 2003; Meisel, 2011; Singleton, 1989), the key questions would be (a) are these accentual patterns correlated with or caused by the age of acquisition, (b) what other components of the grammar are implicated and (c) what function might this trait serve?

Scovel is of the opinion that an L2 accent in production serves an anthropological, or perhaps even evolutionary, function. Across the species, our ability to detect foreign accents is acute, and Scovel suggests that the purpose is to identify in-group and out-group members of a social order. This kind of fascinating speculation reminds us that we can transfer our perceptual properties as well. Transfer does not merely implicate a late production routine. Rochet (1995) provides a nice example when it comes to the perception of the high front rounded vowel [y] by English and Brazilian Portuguese (BP) speakers. English speakers tend to mishear the [y] as [u] while the BP speakers hear it as [i].

Contrastive analysis

Another well-known term in the field is contrastive analysis (Lado, 1957). Though there are strong and weak versions (Wardhaugh, 1970) and even a moderate version (Oller & Ziahosseiny, 1970), the basic assumption is that L2 errors can be predicted based on a comparison of two languages. For phonology, the contrastive analysis hypothesis (CAH) assumes that comparing the sound systems of a learner's L1 and L2 allows us to predict what will be simple to learn and what will be challenging.

There are also complexities involved in determining which elements to compare to make the predictions. While CAH primarily focuses on surface level structures (i.e. language as it is produced, as opposed to underlying mental representations to which rules are applied in order to generate surface structures), there is some acknowledgement of abstract representation in such constructs as allophony (the same sound category pronounced differently in different phonetic environments). In phonology, it was claimed that a difference in behaviour would result depending on whether two sounds were allophonic in the L1 and phonemic in the L2 or vice versa. For example, [d] and [ð] are allophonic (i.e. predictable based on context) in Spanish but phonemic (i.e. separate categories) in English. Following CAH, this predicts that it will be more difficult for the Spanish speakers to set up a new phoneme than for the English speakers to suppress an L1 phoneme. These are what are known as *directionality of difficulty* effects. A theory of L2 phonology has to both predict and explain such directionality effects.

However, it is only fair to acknowledge that CAH does not have a rich linguistic representational framework to work with. Let us take an example from syntax. Surface structures might suggest that Dutch and English word orders are similar (if not identical):

Dutch: Jan hielp zijn moeder.
         Jan helped his mother.

English: John helped his mother.

But the similarity in these main-clause, single-verb examples would obscure the fact that underlyingly (i.e. at deep structure) Dutch has subject–object–verb (SOV) word order. This can be seen in more complex sentences such as:

Jan wilde zijn moeder gaan helpen
Jan wanted his mother to go help

John wanted to go help his mother.

What the L2 learner has to acquire is (a) the underlying word order and (b) the rules of when the verb has to raise higher in the sentence. The point is that a comparison of the *surface* word orders would not illuminate what needed to be acquired by the L2 learner.

White (1992) convincingly demonstrates that approaches to SLA that are built upon generative linguistic theory (e.g. Schwartz and Sprouse, 1996) are not merely notational variants of what we might see under contrastive analysis (which is based more on structuralist linguistic theories as found in Saussure or Bloomfield). Structuralist linguists described the structure of a particular sentence. A structuralist analysis might be familiar to language teachers if asked to underline the direct object of a sentence and circle the indirect object. Generative linguists, by contrast, sought to uncover the rules that generated *all* the grammatical sentences of a language: a much more abstract enterprise – yet one with bene-fits to the study of SLA.

A similar problem arises in L2 phonology if we do not adopt generative models of the target language. Let us consider two examples. The first concerns the L2 acquisition of stress; the second the L2 acquisition of a new segment.

L2 stress

First we need to ask the question *what is stress*? Phonetically, we can look to identify the acoustic correlates of stress prominence (such as intensity, duration, pitch and vowel quality). However, this does not address the question of what the rules of stress placement are in a particular language. Let us consider three hypotheses.

(a) Stress is a property of an individual vowel. Under this assumption, the learner needs to store which vowel is stressed in a word such as *aróma*. One might then expect stress errors to vary considerably from word to word, as the task of the learner is to acquire the correct lexical representation (which includes stress).

(b) Stress is a relative phenomenon. Under this assumption, stress is not viewed as an intrinsic component of the vowel but rather the result of what is called metrical foot structure (e.g. iambic versus trochaic feet). In this model, stress signals relative prominence of a *syllable*. The task of the L2 learner then would be to acquire the target foot type. Learners of French would acquire *iambic* (strong on the right) feet, while learners of English would acquire *trochaic* (strong on the left) feet.

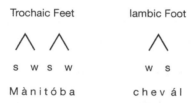

Figure 1.2 Examples of words with trochaic and iambic feet

(c) Stress assignment is governed by a range of what are known in generative linguistics as *parameters*. While the most complex model, this parametric view (Dresher and Kaye, 1990) captures the fact that stress assignment relies on a range of properties such as whether a syllable is light (ending in a vowel) or heavy (closed by a consonant), or whether secondary stresses are allowed. The task of the L2 learner would be to acquire the L2 parameter settings, two of which are listed below as an illustration:

P1: The foot is strong on the [left/right]. English feet are strong on the left; French feet are strong on the right.

P5: Feet are quantity-sensitive (QS) [yes/no]. In QS languages (such as English), syllables closed by a consonant (i.e. heavy) are stressed. Compare the stress placement in *agénda* as opposed to *cínema*. If there is a heavy syllable it gets stressed; if there is none we see the initial stress in *cinema*. French is not QS.

Traditional contrastive analysis would view stress as a surface property of lexical items. There were no abstract theoretical models available at the time that captured the *patterns* of stress assignment.

Early SLA studies, couched in a generative linguistic theory, revealed that stress is, indeed, a complex construct. Polish speakers have to acquire the correct P5 setting for English. Archibald (1991) showed that the values of the *parameters* transferred. Polish learners would transfer their L1 quantity-insensitivity into English. This demonstrates that interlanguage grammars are, in fact, complex mental representations in which the initial state of the L2 grammar is, indeed, what is transferred from the L1 but that the details of that representation are described by generative linguistic theory.

While contrastive analysis focuses on production data and what is likely to cause trouble, this type of study also demonstrates that, because it is the *grammar* that needs to be acquired, not just a production routine, L2 *perception* will also be affected by cross-linguistic transfer. The relationship between language perception and language production is a complex one. Of course, it relates to linguistic competence insofar as we can ask the question 'does non-native-like production result from a non-native-like phonological representation?' This is a question that is familiar from the field of first language acquisition as well. Imagine a child who refers to a fish as a [fɪs]. Is it because they cannot hear the difference between [s] and [ʃ]? Or because they cannot physically generate the gestures which result in a [ʃ]? How could we tell? One way is to look at the perceptual abilities of the learners via perceptual experimentation. Imagine the following conversation:

Parent: What's that?
Child: A [fɪs].
Parent: A fis?
Child: No! It's my [fɪs].

Such a conversation demonstrates that the child identifies an error in the production of the adult. They know that the adult pronounced the word *fish* incorrectly. These data would suggest that the child has the correct (i.e. adult-like) linguistic representation because they can perceive the difference between two linguistically relevant sounds. The question was articulated well by Locke (1983) when he essentially asked whether they are '(a) producing an incorrect representation accurately, or (b) producing a correct representation inaccurately'.

L2 segments

The question of whether learners might have *incorrect* grammatical representations is very familiar in the domains of L2 morphology and syntax. Hawkins and Chan (1997) in the failed functional features hypothesis, argue that if a speaker's L1 is lacking a feature (such as [tense]) then that feature will be unacquirable in the L2. Lardiere (1998, 2007), on the other hand, suggests that L2 learners *can*, in fact, acquire features that are absent from the L1. If learners have incorrect representations then we would expect perception errors, too. However, even if learners have acquired the *correct* mental representation, then there may be errors, just as native speakers occasionally make errors. The errors in this case would be, essentially, performance errors. Let us consider the kinds of factors that might lead to such performance errors in phonology. Imagine an L2 learner who needs to acquire a new segment, say English [θ] or French [ʁ]. Perhaps we would find a learner who would be able to make these sounds in isolation, and perhaps also in simple words or phrases.

Th[θ]ank you.
R[ʁ]ouge.

However, as the complexity of the utterance increases in terms of the phonological environment or the syntactic complexity, we may find errors in production emerging. In all of the following examples, I am indicating the 'error' by including a non-native-like sound (say [t] for [θ], or [r] for [ʁ]).

Math[t] problems
(increased phonetic complexity with 'th' followed by two consonants)

I couldn't say if the archaeologists were th[t]inking of burial grounds.
(increased syntactic complexity)

Chapit[r] deux
(increased phonetic complexity due to word-final 'tr' sequence followed by another consonant)

Il y a plus d'un âne à la foir[r]e qui s'appelle Martin
(increased syntactic complexity in the idiom for 'don't jump to conclusions', literally 'there is more than one donkey in the market named Martin')

All of this can be explained by the fact that humans are limited capacity processors. We cannot pay attention to everything at once.

If the initial state of the L2 grammar consists of the end state of the L1 grammar transferred, then there will be elements in the L2 that are absent from the L1 that need to be acquired. New representations will have to be set up. Some learners, then, on some tasks, will show evidence of having non-target-like representations and show consistent non-native-like performance. Other learners will have acquired the new representations but still evidence variation in their production.

Transfer redux

This leads us to the next big question: if there is an impoverished representation (compared to native-like representations), does this mean that the new representation can *never* be acquired? In the field of morphosyntax, Hawkins and Chan (1997) argued that no new features could be acquired, while Tsimpli and Dimitrakopoulou (2007) argued that some new features could be acquired. In the domain of phonology, Brown (2000) argued that no new features could be acquired, while Archibald (2009) and Gonzalez Poot (2014) argued that new features could be acquired.

Archibald (2005, 2009) outlines two scenarios in which new contrasts can be acquired: (a) when the L1 has the necessary structures that can be *redeployed* to build new representations in the L2; and (b) when the new contrasts to be acquired are signalled by *robust* acoustic cues. Let us look at each of them in turn.

Redeployment

The basic idea of *redeployment* is that new structures can be assembled out of the building blocks found in the L1.

Consider the example of English speakers trying to acquire the Czech alveolar stop [t]/palatal stop [c] contrast found in Czech. English does not make this place distinction in stops but does so in the fricative series ([s]/[ʃ]). Atkey (2001) argues that this distinction is built via the [posterior] place feature. [posterior] is a feature that represents sounds made at or behind the hard palate. So, English [s] would be a [posterior] feature just as Czech [c] is. She demonstrates that the English speakers can take the [posterior] feature, which they use for the fricative ([s]/[ʃ]) contrast and learn to build new stop contrasts when learning Czech as a second language.

Summerell (2007) investigates the acquisition of Japanese long vowels and geminate (i.e. long) consonants by native speakers of English. English does not have a long/short consonant distinction (as can be found in language like Italian, where [fato] and [fatto] contrast in meaning). The long consonants (e.g. [tt]) are referred to as geminates (which means *twin*). However, English does have a distinction between heavy and light syllables (as seen in section on L2 stress) when it comes to stress assignment. Heavy syllables (those with syllables that end in a consonant) tend to attract stress in English, as can be seen in a word like *agénda* (where the closed syllable [dʒɛn] is stressed). The final consonant of a closed syllable projects a unit of weight known as a *mora*, making the closed syllable bimoraic (one mora for the vowel and one for the following consonant). Summerell looked to see whether English speakers could acquire Japanese long segments. Crucially, these Japanese geminate consonants also project a mora (just like English heavy syllables). She found that the intermediate and advanced L2 speakers performed indistinguishably from native speakers in terms of their performance with respect to both consonants and vowels. Thus, the interesting question is *why can they acquire these geminate consonants if their L1 lacks geminates?* The answer lies in the construct of redeployment. Archibald (2005) argues that the English speakers can take the bimoraic structures found in their L1 and use them to acquire both long and short vowels and consonants; they redeploy L1 structures used for stress and build a new segmental contrast for geminates.

More problems for contrastive analysis

As we have seen, traditional contrastive analysis is based on the assumption that L2 elements that are similar to the L1 will be easy to acquire, while L2 elements that are different would be difficult. However, this is a problematic assumption. A well-known example can be drawn from the field of cross-linguistic speech perception, which demonstrates that there are certainly cases where similarity does not result in ease of learning, nor difference with difficulty. One of the most influential models has been Flege's (1992) speech learning model. The critical feature of the model that I would highlight would be the following (and note the difference from contrastive analysis):

Difference = Easy
Similarity = Hard

An extreme example of the first type would be the acquisition of velaric ingressive clicks [ʘ !] by speakers of languages without clicks. These sounds could be argued to be so different from anything in the L1 that they do not cause any confusion. Flege's model also makes subtler predictions, however. Imagine the case of acquiring new vowel phonemes. The vowel inventory on the left in Figure 1.3 below is from Danish, while the vowel inventory on the right is from Spanish.

Imagine further that speakers of each of the languages were learning an L2, which required them to acquire a new vowel, say [ɪ]. Flege's model would predict that there would be greater potential confusion in the acoustic space of Danish to fit in [ɪ] than there would be in the Spanish vowel space. In other words, Spanish speakers would find the new vowel to be very

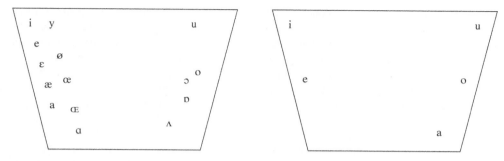

Figure 1.3 Danish and Spanish vowel inventories

different from their L1 vowels, while Danish speakers would find the new vowel to be very similar. This would lead to a difference in difficulty (or ease) in acquisition.

However, it is not just properties of the L1 inventory that affect L2 acquisition. The properties of the L2 acoustic signal are also important. I will illustrate this first with a specific example and then generalize. The specific example is drawn from Escudero (2000), who looked at the acquisition of a tense/lax vowel distinction by Spanish speakers who were exposed to two different dialects of L2 English. Tense vowels are, for example, [i e ɑ o u], while lax vowels (which have less muscular tension) are, for example, [ɪ ɛ æ ɔ ʊ].

She compared Spanish speakers who were exposed to Scottish English with those exposed to British English. Both dialects, of course, have an /i/ɪ/ distinction so why is the dialect difference important? The difference lies in the acoustic *cues* used to implement the contrast. Scottish English uses vowel quality (which can be read off a spectrogram, which measures the frequency of the sounds) primarily to distinguish the vowels; the Scottish [i] is made with the tongue higher in the mouth than [ɪ]. Southern British vowels have less of a vowel quality difference but more of a durational difference; the British [i] is longer (as measured in milliseconds) than the [ɪ]. Spanish lacks durational contrasts in its vowel inventory. As a result, Spanish learners of Scottish English were better able to discriminate the two vowels because they could distinguish them by the spectral cues.

To summarize, we have seen examples which demonstrate that L2 learners can (a) acquire new contrasts when they can redeploy the L1 structures to build new L2 structures (e.g. English speakers acquiring Japanese geminate consonants, or Czech palatal stops); or (b) acquire new contrast when the contrast is signalled in a way that is either cued in the same way as the L1 contrast (e.g. vowel quality). But let me now try to generalize beyond this second exemplar. What I want to argue now is that L2 learners can acquire new features even if they are neither found in the L1 nor cued by L1 acoustic properties. To do this, let me introduce the construct of *intake frequency*.

Intake frequency

There are also cases where L2 learners can acquire contrasts that are not built on features found in their L1. Wright (2004) outlines the construct of *robust* phonetic cues. A robust cue (e.g. the release burst of an aspirated stop [pʰ] as in 'pot') is resistant to environmental masking; it can be heard better in a noisy environment. The robustness of a cue is a property of the acoustic signal but is something that can be used by the learner to acquire the target grammar. Robustness can help us to account for why some segments are processed more accurately than others. It can account for why certain positional variants (sometimes onsets, sometimes codas are processed more accurately). For example, as Brown (2000) demonstrates, Japanese learners of English do better on the [l/r] contrast at the end of syllables (i.e. in codas) than they do at the beginning of syllables (i.e. in onsets). This is because the phonetic properties of certain sounds make them more salient to the learners which, in turn, makes them more accessible to the phonological parser (see Archibald, 2005).

This notion of robustness can help us to account for one of the puzzles of language acquisition, which, following Chomsky, we can label *Orwell's Problem*: in the face of abundant evidence how can we not learn? L2 learners are exposed to much input and evidence of the target language. For example, they hear lots of [r]s or [θ]s or consonant clusters but may remain resistant to acquiring these; they can be difficult to learn. What was traditionally referred to as *fossilization* is a real phenomenon. But, yet, learning *can* take place over time. Whether we are looking at individual consonants, or vowels, or consonantal sequences, we do not acquire everything at once. As Gregg (1993) articulated, we need to provide a *transition* theory of SLA that accounts for why a particular developmental path is followed. There are many factors that have been considered, such as markedness, frequency, orthography and instruction, to name a few. I want to add an additional factor and argue that the developmental path emerges because some input items become *intake* to the processor before others. Let me define the key terms.

Going back to Corder (1967), researchers have distinguished between *input* (the entirety of the linguistic environment; the primary linguistic data) and the *intake* (the subset of the linguistic environment that is processed by a given learner at a given time). Many researchers have looked for correlations between accuracy and environmental frequency (Davidson, 2006). But there are also clear cases where input frequency is not the best explanation for accuracy (e.g. Cardoso, 2008). Archibald (2013) proposed the notion of *intake* frequency as a possible explanation for certain L2 developmental paths. The challenge, of course, is to avoid circularity of the following sort:

Q: Why is it accurate?
A: Because it was intake.

Q: How do you know it was intake?
A: Because it was accurate.

Intake frequency can be difficult to operationalize because, while we may directly observe the input and the output, we need a *theory* of the grammar, and a *theory* for which input becomes intake. Many factors have been proposed to account for the accurate production of L2 sounds:

- L1 transfer (Trofimovich and Baker, 2006)
- amount of experience (Bohn and Flege, 1992)
- amount of L2 use (Guion, Flege, Liu & Yeni-Komshian, 2000)
- age of learning (Herschensohn, 2000)
- orthography (Hayes-Harb et al., 2010; Escudero & Wanrooi, 2010)
- frequency (Davidson, 2006)
- probability (Wilson & Davidson, 2013)
- attention (Guion & Pederson, 2007; Schmidt, 1990)
- training (Wang, Jongman & Sereno, 2003)
- L1 phonological features (Brown, 2000).

In my view, we need to take seriously the learnability perspective (Wexler & Culicover, 1980) and ask ourselves *what is to be acquired?* Then we look at all of the factors that can influence this acquisition. In a representational approach, an L2 learner acquires a grammar. Abstract representations must be acquired and it is critical to remind ourselves that these values cannot always be read directly off the input signal. There are no invariant acoustic cues for the acquisition of verbs, or complementizers, or aspect, or tense. While this lack of direct environmental cueing of linguistic representations may be seen as unsurprising in the domain of morphosyntax or semantics, it is, perhaps, less obvious in the domain of phonology as well. Let us look at a concrete example.

Many languages make contrasts that are often described as involving voicing or aspiration differences. According to the International Phonetic Alphabet, [p] is voiceless while [b] is voiced]. [pʰ] is aspirated while [p] is unaspirated. English has a /p/–/b/ contrast. French has a /p/–/b/ contrast. Thai has a three-way /p/–/pʰ/–/b/ contrast. It has been argued (Iverson & Salmons, 1995), however, that the phonological feature that mentally encodes these contrasts can vary from language to language. Phonetically, English relies primarily on *aspiration* (with /p/ being aspirated and /b/ being unaspirated). French relies primarily on *voicing* with /b/ being pre-voiced before the stop consonant is released in to the following vowel, and with /p/ having voicing start shortly after the consonantal release. An English speaker learning French would have to acquire the [voice] feature while a French speaker learning English would have to acquire the [aspiration] feature, and make this part of their phonological grammar.

The challenge from a learnability perspective is how the learner (either L1 or L2) knows which phonological feature to represent. This is a complex question but the important part at this time is to note that the cue for the feature [voice] or [aspiration] cannot be read directly from the input. English 'voicing' contrast is often suppressed. There may be no actual vocal fold vibration in either the /d/ or the /t/ in 'bead' versus 'beat' (Keyser & Stevens, 2006). The more reliable cue to voicing in English is the length of the preceding vowel. The [i] in 'bead' is longer than the [i] in 'beat'. It goes beyond the mandate of this chapter to spell out the theory but it is clear that for a learner to make a connection between vowel length in the linguistic input and setting up a voicing contrast for the stops at the end of syllables would involve a complicated model. What this demonstrates is that L2 phonological feature acquisition is a *learning* problem not just a *noticing* problem (see Carroll, 2001). The task of the learner is not just to pick up certain acoustic properties in the input and map them directly and deterministically onto phonological features stored in the mind. That being said, the acoustic properties of the input can certainly influence the developmental path of the L2 learner.

Robust input cues are more likely to become intake. What starts as a property of the signal becomes a property of the representation. Segments that are perceived more readily in noisy environments (for example) are more likely to become part of the lexical representation (or phonologized) in the L2.

L2 Yucatec Mayan

One strong example to illustrate this comes from Gonzalez Poot (2014), who investigated the acquisition of Yucatec Mayan ejectives by native speakers of Spanish in Mexico. Ejectives are a class of sound characterized by a forceful glottal release of a voiceless consonant. The phonetic symbol is a following apostrophe as in [p'], or [k'], or [s'].

Spanish does not have ejectives and does not have any contrast that utilizes the phonological feature (let us call it [ejective]) needed for ejectives elsewhere in the phonological inventory. The empirical question is whether the L2 learners can acquire this feature. Gonzalez Poot (2011) used both a discrimination task and a forced-choice picture selection task to probe this question. A discrimination task is designed to determine whether subjects can perceive a contrast in a non-semantic task. For example, subjects would hear sequences such as [p] [b] or [p] [p] and have to indicate whether the two sounds are the same or different. The accuracy of their performance measures their perceptual abilities. A picture selection task is designed to determine whether subjects can lexically store a phonological contrast. An example from English would be to have subjects look at a picture of either a 'rake' or a 'lake' and to hear a single word spoken (either 'rake' or 'lake'). The accuracy of their performance provides clues to their phonological representations.

He found the following:

- Non-native speakers did not perform significantly differently from native speakers at the beginning of syllables.
- However, they *did* perform significantly differently from the native speakers at the ends of syllables.
- The acoustic cues for ejectives are much subtler at the end of a syllable.

Ejectives are robust owing (in part) to their dual release bursts (an oral cavity release of the lips or tongue, and a glottal release in the larynx). However, not all ejective segments were acquired at the same time by the L2 subjects. He noted the following accuracy gradients at the beginning of a syllable (where > is read as 'more accurate than'):

k'/p' > t'/tʃ' > ts'

Now, note the accuracy pattern in at the end of syllables:

tʃ' > ts' > k' > p' > t'

Clearly, not all of the ejectives are processed at the same time by a given learner. At the beginning of a syllable, we note that the non-sibilant stops ([k'], [p'], [t']) are parsed more accurately stemming from the robustness of the release bursts. Here, the non-sibilant ejectives become intake before the sibilant ejectives do. In contrast, at the end of a syllable, the sibilant stops ([tʃ'], [ts']) are more accurate due to *their* phonetic properties, and thus we can say that they become intake before the non-sibilant ejectives in this phonetic environment. Such patterns of behaviour (i.e. at the beginning and end of syllables) are grounded both typologically and phonetically, in that ejective sibilants are more common in the world's languages at the ends of syllables than at the beginning, and that it is easier to perceive a sibilant ejective (e.g. [ts']) at the end of a syllable than to perceive a non-sibilant ejective (e.g. [k']). Perceptual accuracy, as indicated on a discrimination task, paves the way for grammatical restructuring and the phonologicization of the [ejective] feature, as indicated by on a picture selection task.

The converse of the enhanced intake frequency of robust cues can be seen when we look at L2 learners trying to acquire a novel segment that is non-robust. Mah (2012) looks at the acquisition of English /h/ by native speakers of French. Using an event-related potential (ERP) paradigm, she argues that the L2 subjects do not acquire the English /h/. ERPs are used to measure brain activity during language processing.

Mah shows that her subjects do not react exceptionally to sentences like *She has curly air* or *He blurted out the hanswer*. Archibald (2013) argues that it is the non-robust nature of the acoustic cue for [h] which causes the learning delay.

Together, the Yucatec Maya and French L2 data allow us to make the following generalizations. Rather than simple input frequency explaining why some sounds are acquired earlier than other, we can operationalize what I have called intake frequency. More robust input cues receive a boost to intake frequency. Thus, certain input is privileged to become intake. The more robust input items

- are preferentially processed/parsed
- are preferentially preserved in production.

A transition theory of interlanguage phonology is enhanced by the construct of intake frequency.

The phonology/morphology interface

Some more recent approaches look to the role phonology plays in accounting for the omission of certain morphemes in production. The prosodic transfer hypothesis (PTH) assumes that the grammatical representation that transfers to the initial stage of the L2 is the full grammar of the L1. Crucial to our discussion, though, is the notion that these constituent structures (in particular phonological constituents) are what transfers to the L2 learner and which will explain their production (particularly the omission of certain morphemes). Goad and White (2004) and Goad, White and Steele (2003) propose that, if a particular morpheme is not produced, maybe this is because it is composed of sound sequences that are difficult to pronounce, not because the morpheme itself has not been acquired. Thus, morpheme omission is caused by a mapping problem from morpheme to pronunciation, not by a representational failure. Learners would omit morphemes when the L1 prosodic structure (which is transferred into the L2) does not allow particular sequences of sounds. In English, the production of inflectional morphology is confounded with the presence of word-final consonant clusters to mark this morphology. The basic question here is whether what is interpreted as the lack of, say, past tense morphology is, in fact, the inability to produce consonant clusters. So, if someone says, 'Yesterday, I [wɑk] to the store' are they producing a non-past verb or a [+past] marked verb with the final consonant deleted because of L1 transfer? The answer to this question speaks to the explanation of the phenomenon.

All of this reveals that inflectional morphemes are not either 'left out' or 'put in' but, as with other aspects of L2 performance, variable.

New directions and recommendations

We have only begun to scratch the surface when it comes to the breadth and depth of L2 phonology. We have not talked about syllables, or clitics, or intonation, or phrasal stress, or so many other relevant areas of interest. But I hope that the examples we have discussed, and the general principles we have introduced, have illuminated both the history and the current state of L2 phonology.

My goal in this chapter was to present not a comprehensive catalogue of all significant research but rather a document that, by taking an historical perspective, will illuminate the key questions and terminology that frame our discipline. The critical constructs of (a) cross-linguistic transfer, (b) rich description of end-state grammar (target knowledge) and (c) developmental status and path of intermediate grammars, while evolving over the years, have not faded in their utility in describing and explaining the surprisingly broad field of L2 phonology.

References

Archibald, J. (1991). *Language learnability and L2 phonology: The acquisition of metrical parameters.* Dordrecht: Kluwer.

Archibald, J. (1993). Language learnability: an overview of the issues. *TESL Canada Journal, 11*(1), 53–74.

Archibald, J. (2005). Second language phonology as redeployment of L1 phonological knowledge. *Canadian Journal of Linguistics, 50*(1/2/3/4), 285–314.

Archibald, J. (2009). Phonological feature re-assembly and the importance of phonetic cues. *Second Language Research, 25*(2), 231–233.

Archibald, J. (2013). *Reverse engineering the L1 filter: Bagging the elusive construct of intake frequency.* Plenary Talk. New Sounds. Montreal.

Atkey, S. (2001). *The acquisition of non-native segmental contrasts: A look at English speakers' acquisition of Czech palatal stops.* MA thesis, University of Calgary.

Birdsong, D. (1992). Ultimate attainment in second language acquisition. *Language, 68*(4), 706–755.

Bohn, O.-S., & Flege, J. E. (1992). The production of new and similar vowels by adult German learners of English. *Studies in Second Language Acquisition, 14*, 131–158.

Brown, C. (2000). The interrelation between speech perception and phonological acquisition from infant to adult. In J. Archibald (Ed.), *Second language acquisition and linguistic theory* (pp. 4–63). Malden, MA: Blackwell.

Cardoso, W. (2008). The development of sC onset clusters in interlanguage: Markedness vs. frequency effects. In Roumyana Slabakova et al. (Eds), *Proceedings of the 9th Generative Approaches to Second Language Acquisition Conference (GASLA 2007)* (pp. 15–29). Somerville, MA: Cascadilla Proceedings Project.

Carroll, S. (2001). *Input and evidence: The raw material of second language acquisition.* Amsterdam: John Benjamins.

Chomsky, N. (1988). *Language and problems of knowledge: The Managua lectures.* Cambridge, MA: MIT Press.

Chomsky, N., & Halle, M. (1968). *The sound pattern of English.* New York, NY: Harper & Row.

Corder, S. P. (1967). The significance of learners' errors. *International Review of Applied Linguistics, 5*, 160–170.

Davidson, L. (2006). Phonology, phonetics, or frequency: Influences on the production of non-native sequences. *Journal of Phonetics, 34*(1), 104–137.

Dresher, E., & Kaye, J. (1990). A computational learning model for metrical phonology. *Cognition, 34*, 137–195.

Escudero, P. (2000). *Developmental patterns in the adult L2 acquisition of new contrasts: The acoustic cue weighting in the perception of Scottish tense/lax vowels in Spanish speakers.* Unpublished MSc thesis, University of Edinburgh.

Escudero, P., & Wanrooi, K. (2010). The effect of L1 orthography on non-native perception. *Language and Speech, 53*(3), 343–365.

Flege, J. E. (1992). Speech learning in a second language. In C. Ferguson, L. Menn, & C. Stoel-Gammon (Eds), *Phonological development: Models, research & application* (pp. 565–604). Timonium, MD: York Press.

Gass, S. M., & Selinker, L. (1983). *Language transfer in language learning. Issues in second language research.* Rowley MA: Newbury House.

Goad, H., & White, L. (2004). Ultimate attainment of L2 inflection: Effects of L1 prosodic structure. In S. Foster-Cohen, M. Sharwood Smith, A. Sorace & M. Ota (Eds), *Eurosla yearbook volume 4* (pp. 119–145). Amsterdam: John Benjamins.

Goad, H., White, L., & Steele, J. (2003). Missing surface inflection in L2 acquisition: A prosodic account. In B. Beachley, A. Brown, & F. Conlin (Eds), *Proceedings of the 27th Annual Boston University Conference on Language Development* (pp. 264–275). Somerville, MA: Cascadilla.

Gold, E. M. (1967). Language identification in the limit. *Information and Control, 10*(5), 447–474.

Gonzalez Poot, A. (2011). *Conflict resolution in the Spanish SLA of Yucatec ejectives: L1, L2, and universal constraints*. PhD thesis, University of Calgary.

Gonzalez Poot, A. (2014). Conflict resolution in the Spanish L2 acquisition of Yucatec ejectives: L1, L2 and universal constraints. In L. Teddiman (Ed.), *Proceedings of the Canadian Linguistic Association*. Retrieved from http://cla-acl.ca/actes-2014-proceedings.

Gregg, K. (1993). Taking explanation seriously; or, let a couple of flowers bloom. *Applied Linguistics, 14*(3), 276–294.

Guion, S., & Pederson, E. (2007). Investigating the role of attention in phonetic learning. In O. S. Bohn, & M. J. Munro (Eds), *Language experience in second language speech learning: In honor of James Emil Flege* (pp. 57–78). Amsterdam: John Benjamins.

Guion, S. G., Flege, J. E., Liu, S. H., & Yeni-Komshian, G. H. (2000). Age of learning effects on the duration of sentences produced in a second language. *Applied Psycholinguistics, 21*, 205–228.

Harley, B. (1986). *Age in second language acquisition*. Clevedon: Multilingual Matters.

Hayes-Harb, R., Nicol, J., & Barker, J. (2010). Learning the phonological forms of new words: Effects of orthographic and auditory input. *Language and Speech, 53*(3), 367–381.

Hawkins, R., &. Chan, Y.-H. C. (1997). The partial availability of Universal Grammar in second language acquisition: The 'failed functional features hypothesis'. *Second Language Research, 13*, 187–226.

Herschensohn, J. (2000). *The second time around: Minimalism and L2 acquisition*. Amsterdam: John Benjamins.

Hyltenstam, K., & Abrahamsson, N. (2003). Maturational constraints in SLA. In C. J. Doughty & M. H. Long (Eds), *The handbook of second language acquisition* (pp. 539–588). Oxford: Blackwell.

Iverson, G., & Salmons, J. (1995). Aspiration and laryngeal features in Germanic. *Phonology, 12*, 369–396.

Kaye, J. (1990). *Phonology: A cognitive view*. Hillsdale, NJ: Erlbaum.

Keyser, S. J., & Stevens, K. (2006). Enhancement and overlap in the speech chain. *Language, 82*, 33–62.

Lado, R. (1957). *Linguistics across cultures*. Ann Arbor, MI: University of Michigan Press.

Lardiere, D. (1998). Dissociating syntax from morphology in a divergent L2 end-state grammar. *Second Language Research 14*(4), 359–375.

Lardiere, D. (2007). *Ultimate attainment in second language acquisition: A case study*. Mahwah, NJ: Lawrence Erlbaum.

Locke, J. L. (1983). *Phonological acquisition and change*. New York, NY: Academic Press.

Mah, J. (2012). Segmental representations in interlanguage grammars: The case of francophones and English /h/. PhD thesis, McGill University.

Meisel, J. (2011). *First and second language acquisition*. Cambridge: Cambridge University Press.

Nemser, W. (1971). Approximative systems of foreign language learners. *IRAL, 9*,(2), 115–124.

Oller, J., & Ziahosseiny, S. M. (1970). The contrastive analysis hypothesis and spelling errors. *Language Learning, 20*(2), 183–189.

Pinker, S. (1984). *Language learnability language development*. Cambridge, MA: Harvard University Press.

Rochet, B. (1995). Perception and production of second-language speech sounds by adults. In W. Strange (Ed.), *Speech perception and linguistic experience: Issues in cross-language research* (pp. 379–410). Timonium, MD: York Press.

Schmidt, R. (1990). The role of consciousness in second language learning. *Applied Linguistics, 11*, 129–158.

Schwartz, B. D., & Sprouse, R. A. (1996). L2 cognitive states and the full transfer/full access model. *Second Language Research, 12*(1), 40–72.

Scovel, T. (1988). *A time to speak: A psycholinguistic inquiry into the critical period for human speech*. Cambridge: Newbury House.

Selinker, L. (1972). Interlanguage. International Review of Applied Linguistics, *10*, 209–241.

Singleton, D. (1989). *Language acquisition: The age factor*. Clevedon: Multilingual Matters.

Stern, H. H. (1983). *Fundamental concepts of language teaching*. Oxford: Oxford University Press.

Summerell, F. (2007). *The L2 acquisition of Japanese length contrasts*. MA thesis, University of Calgary.

Trofimovich, P., & Baker, W. (2006). Learning second-language suprasegmentals: Effect of L2 experience on prosody and fluency characteristics of L2 speech. *Studies in Second Language Acquisition, 28*, 1–30.

Tsimpli, I. M., & Dimitrakopoulou, M. (2007). The Interpretability hypothesis: Evidence from wh-interrogatives in second language acquisition. *Second Language Research*, *23*(2), 215–242.

Wang, Y., Jongman, A., & Sereno, J. (2003). Acoustic and perceptual evaluation of Mandarin tone production before and after perceptual training. *Journal of the Acoustical Society of America*, *113*, 1033–1044.

Wardhaugh, R. (1970). The contrastive analysis hypothesis. *TESOL Quarterly*, *4*(2), 123–130.

Weinreich, U. (1953). *Languages in contact: Findings and problems*. The Hague: Mouton.

Wexler, K., & Culicover, P. (1980). *Formal principles of language acquisition*. Cambridge, MA: MIT Press.

White, L. (1992). Universal grammar: Is it just a new name for old problems? In S. Gass & L. Selinker (Eds), *Language transfer in language learning* (pp. 217–232). Amsterdam: John Benjamins.

Wilson, C. & Davidson, L. (2013). Bayesian analysis of non-native cluster production. In *Proceedings of NELS 40*. Cambridge, MA: MIT.

Wright, R. A. (2004). A review of perceptual cues and cue robustness. In B. Hayes, R. Kirchner, & D. Steriade (Eds), *Phonetically based phonology* (pp. 34–57). Cambridge and New York, NY: Cambridge University Press.

2

Theoretical L2 phonology

Fred R. Eckman

Introduction

The purpose of this chapter is to give an overview of the field of theoretical second language (L2) phonology, dating from about the middle of the twentieth century until the present. Owing to space limitations, and the fact that this research domain constitutes a large area of investigation, the coverage will necessarily not be complete. The discussion will be limited to the study of L2 pronunciation patterns with English as the target language (TL), and will necessarily be constrained in terms of the number of frameworks treated.

This chapter is structured as follows. The background section will lay out several terms, concepts and assumptions that are relatively uncontroversial across virtually all approaches to L2 phonology, and which are vital to understanding the goals and methods of the field. The following section will then provide some historical perspective by exemplifying two major approaches that have laid much of the basis for current analyses of L2 phonological patterns. We then consider some of the contributions that have been made to several important topics and critical issues in the field.

Background

A good point of departure is the observation that the majority of schools of thought in modern linguistics focus their analyses on spoken, rather than written, language. The view that the spoken language takes precedence over the written language can be supported with several pieces of evidence, including the fact that children learn to speak before they learn to write, that many languages of the world today exist without writing systems, and that writing is a relatively recent development in the evolution of human cultures. Thus, for most linguists, the spoken language reflects a living, linguistic system that is part of the natural world, just as lightning, the rotation of the earth and gravity are. Writing, on the other hand, represents a later, human invention that has been imposed on the language. The spoken language, therefore, constitutes the domain of study for the vast majority of modern linguistic schools of thought.

It is also true that many of the current approaches to linguistics view language as a system that has been acquired by a human being, and which enables that person to produce and comprehend utterances of that language. Linguists term this acquired system a *grammar*, and phonology is the subpart of a grammar that underlies the pronunciation patterns of the language. An important assumption with respect to the acquisition of this language system is that all acquirers of a language must, at a minimum, learn the words (lexical items) of the language. To be sure, a learner must ultimately acquire much more than the lexical items, but at a minimum a learner must internalize an inventory of words in a *mental lexicon* that includes information about what words mean, how they can be used in a sentence and how they are pronounced. This last piece of information is important for our purposes and is called the *lexical representation* of a word.

As the major focus of this chapter will be how linguists analyse and attempt to explain English L2 phonological patterns, let us begin with a well-known example of such a pattern, namely the distribution of the regular past tense ending as in [lækt] *lacked*, [lægd] *lagged*, [pled] *played*, and [læn.dəd] *landed*. These forms show that the regular past tense ending is pronounced in three ways, as [t] after voiceless obstruents, [d] after voiced consonants and vowels or [əd] after alveolar stops or flaps. Linguists account for this regularity by hypothesizing that the pattern is underlain by a system that native speakers of English have acquired. Children must create their own internal grammar on the basis of the surrounding input that they are exposed to, and linguists study this learning process, at least in part, by analysing the intermediate stages of acquisition that learners pass through, thereby gaining insights into the learning process. For example, it has been reported that English-speaking children pass through three stages during the acquisition of the English past tense. The child initially uses the correct form of the irregular past tense at Stage 1, but by Stage 2 the child has not only learned the pattern of the regular past tense but has extended this pattern to irregular verbs, driving out the target-like forms of Stage 1 in favour of non-target-like forms such as *runned* or *ranned*. Finally, at Stage 3 the child is able to sort out the irregular verbs from regular ones, and produces the past tense *ran*.

The linguist's attempt to understand the learning process involves considering the target that the learner is trying to reach, noting where the learner 'lands' relative to the target, that is, determining the error that the learner has made, and then hypothesizing learning strategies that would account for the learner's intermediate stages. This is also the type of thinking linguists use in trying to explain the acquisition of L2 phonological patterns by adult learners. Linguists assume that the learner's patterned, error-ridden performance is underlain by some system, albeit not the target system, and then linguists analyse the stages of learning in order to hypothesize the intermediate system that the learner may be employing in the acquisition process.

Linguistic research in phonological acquisition in general, and in the acquisition of L2 pronunciation patterns in particular, attempts to explain why the learning takes place as it does by seeking to identify and account for the various errors that learners make, and the intermediate stages that they pass through in the course of acquisition.

Historical perspectives

There are at least two major components of a historical perspective on L2 phonology. The first is the framework that hypothesized that the influence of the learner's native language on the acquisition of the TL was paramount. This approach therefore attempted to describe L2 pronunciation patterns in terms of learner difficulty stemming from differences between a learner's native language (NL) and the TL being acquired. The second framework stems from the impact of generative grammar (Chomsky, 1965) on the field of linguistics, and views the utterances of L2 learners as resulting from the acquisition of a set of rules. In this vein it has been argued that the learners have internalized a system that represents their own version of the TL. The fundamental insights of these two early approaches to L2 phonology persist in the principles and methods of current explanations of L2 speech patterns.

Native language influence

One of the most interesting and straightforward explanations for why L2 learners produce errors in pronouncing the target language is the contrastive analysis hypothesis (CAH), the content of which was formulated by Lado (1957), although the name of the hypothesis is from Wardhaugh (1970). The CAH claimed that L2 pronunciations could be explained on the basis of L2 learners' finding it difficult to produce TL patterns that are different from those of the learners' native language. This claim is embodied in the following quotation from Lado (1957).

> We assume that the student who comes in contact with a foreign language will find some features of it quite easy and others extremely difficult. Those elements that are similar to his native language will be simple for him, and those elements that are different will be difficult.
>
> (Lado, 1957, p. 2)

If it is assumed that learning difficulty is reflected in pronunciation errors, then the CAH predicts that learners should err only in the areas of difference between the NL and TL. For example, one aspect of English phonology that has been the focus of a number of L2 studies over the years is the acquisition of the contrast between the English vowels /i/ and /ɪ/, as in *beat* and *bit*, respectively, by native Spanish speakers. Spanish has the vowel /i/, but does not have /ɪ/, and therefore, according to the CAH, the pronunciation of English words containing /ɪ/ are predicted to present difficulties for Spanish learners of English, resulting in pronunciation errors. To the extent that the errors occurred on utterances with /ɪ/, in particular, and on other sounds that differed between Spanish and English, in general, the hypothesis would be supported. Conversely, any systematic pronunciation errors that did not involve Spanish–English differences would be counter to the CAH.

As an example of a test case of the CAH, consider the data in (1) below. These data come from Eckman (1981), and though they constitute only a small subset of the elicited utterances they are representative this learner's TL pronunciation pattern.

(1) *L2 pronunciation*   *TL pronunciation*   *Gloss*

	L2 pronunciation	TL pronunciation	Gloss
a.	[ɾɛt]	[ɹɛd]	red
b.	[rɛðər]	[ɹɛɾəɹ]	redder
c.	[bik]	[bɪg]	big
d.	[bigər]	[bɪgəɹ]	bigger
e.	[pik]	[pɪg]	pig
f.	[pigi]	[pɪgi]	piggy
g.	[fʌsi]	[fʌzi]	fuzzy
h.	[sik]	[sɪk]	sick
i.	[sikəst]	[sɪkəst]	sickest
j.	[wɛt]	[wɛt]	wet
k.	[wɛtər]	[wɛtəɹ]	wetter
l.	[fris]	[fɹiz]	freeze

Several of the learner's utterances in (1) support the predictions of the CAH, in particular the learner's pronunciation of the TL vowel /ɪ/ as /i/ in the words, *big, bigger, sick* and *sickest*. Spanish lacks the vowel /ɪ/, and, according to the predictions of the CAH, the learner making errors on words containing this vowel supports the hypothesis. Several other examples where the NL has apparently influenced the learner's pronunciation in support of the CAH include the use of the alveolar tap, /ɾ/ in place of English /ɹ/ in *red, redder* (both initially and finally), *bigger, wetter* and *freeze*. Likewise, the occurrence of [ð] in *redder*, and [s] for target /z/ in *fuzzy* and *freeze* can both be explained with reference to the NL phonology, in that [ð] is the Spanish allophone (variant) of /d/ that occurs between vowels. Moreover, Spanish has no /z/ phoneme, though [z] and [s] are environmentally conditioned allophones of the phoneme /s/, with [z] occurring before voiced consonants and [s] occurring elsewhere. Thus, there are several aspects of the data in (1) that are supportive of the CAH in that these pronunciation errors can be explained in terms of differences between NL and TL.

Several error types in (1) that cannot be so explained, or at least are ambiguous in this regard, include errors on [ɹɛd] and [bɪg], where a word-final [t] and [k] are produced instead of the target-like [d] and [g], respectively. This error type is at least partially understandable in terms of NL influence, because Spanish does not have words that end in either [d] or [g]. These word-final consonants therefore constitute an area of NL–TL difference, and the learner, in fact, errs on these words by pronouncing the corresponding voiceless stops [t] and [k] for [d] and [g], respectively. On the other hand, it is difficult to see how these pronunciations could be explained in terms of NL influence, since Spanish does not have words that end in word-final voiceless stops such as [t] or [k]. Spanish allows words to end in only five consonant sounds: [n], [ɾ], [l], [s] and [ð], none of which is a stop. Therefore, though both [rɛt] and [bik] constitute non-target-like pronunciations, neither of these productions is NL-like and therefore neither is supportive of an explanation in terms of NL influence.

Over the decades, empirical tests of the CAH have reported mixed findings; some have been supportive of the hypothesis in that learner errors have been attributable to differences between the NL and TL, whereas others have not. Please consult the section below on further readings for a brief account of some of these studies.

The legacy of research done within the CAH/NL influence paradigm is that some L2 phonological error patterns could be explained on the basis of NL–TL differences, whereas others could not. This idea has endured up to the present, in that no serious theory of L2 phonology completely excludes the notion of NL influence on a learner's error patterns.

Rule-based approach to L2 phonologies

With the demise of the contrastive analysis hypothesis and the rise of the generative grammar paradigm in theoretical linguistics (Chomsky, 1965), the goal of the research programme in L2 phonology evolved from one that attempted to explain learning difficulty to one of characterizing the nature of the *learner language* that was hypothesized to be internalized by L2 acquirers.

One of the key proposals that addressed the problems with the CAH and that also led to the concept of a learner language was the attempt to explain L2 error patterns as the result of developmental processes that reflected various strategies that learners used in dealing with the TL system without recourse to the learner's NL. This framework, called *error analysis* (Richards, 1971), attempted to characterize the systematic way in which L2 pronunciations deviated from TL forms. EA did not exclude the possibility of NL–TL differences affecting the learning of the L2 patterns, nor did it claim that such differences are necessary for the explanation of learner errors. The key idea underlying this framework is that the errors produced by L2 learners are systematic.

Examples of how L2 phonological patterns were studied within the EA framework can be illustrated using the data in (1) above. The analysis looks for systematicity in the learner's pronunciation errors and then attempts to characterize these non-target-like forms in terms of generalizations that relate the learner's errors to the target pronunciations. Along this line, the L2 forms [rɛt] *red* and [bik] *big* are both non-TL-like, and are representative of a regularity that, if true in general of this speaker's English utterances, can be characterized as the learner substituting voiceless word-final consonants for word-final voiced ones. In other words, one can say that some of the learner's utterances are missing the target in a way that can be characterized as TL word-final voiced obstruents being pronounced as voiceless. It is important to note at this juncture that the description along these lines attempts to represent the learner's L2 pronunciations as systematic errors. From the idea that L2 learners' systematic errors stemmed from various learning strategies, it was a small step, especially with the rise of the Chomskyan paradigm in linguistics, to postulating that L2 learners internalized their own version of the target language grammar.

The hypothetical construct in second language acquisition theory that could be considered a breakthrough in the overall research programme is the postulation of a 'learner language'. This concept was proposed independently by three different scholars, Corder (1971), Nemser (1971) and Selinker (1972), and labelled *interlanguage*, the term that has endured, by Selinker. The crux of all three proposals is that L2 learners internalize their own version of the TL grammar, which may contain aspects of the NL that have been transferred, along with portions of the TL that have been learned on the basis of the input. The most interesting aspect of an interlanguage is that it may also exhibit patterns that are independent of both the NL and TL. The evidence for the independence of interlanguage is a set of patterns produced by an L2 learner, where those patterns do not stem from the NL, because the NL does not evince those patterns, nor do they come from TL input, because the TL does not have those patterns. Consequently, such regularities must be attributed to some system other than the NL or TL, namely to the system the learner has internalized, the interlanguage (IL).

There are two significant implications of the concept of IL for L2 phonological theory. The first is that the research programme in L2 phonology changed from one of trying to predict learning difficulty to one of testing hypotheses about the nature of IL phonologies. The second implication is that L2 learning now becomes characterized as the acquisition of an interlanguage grammar, rather than the learning of the target language.

An IL grammar may overlap with both the NL and TL, in that the IL can consist in part of elements that have been transferred from the NL, as well as structures that have been learned on the basis of the input from speakers of the TL. The most important claim, however, is that at least some structures of the IL are independent of both the NL and TL. The crucial argument for this claim is an empirical one and requires showing that there are systematic L2 utterances that do not derive from the NL, because the NL does not evidence the regularity in question, nor could the systematicity be tied to TL input, because the TL does not exhibit the relevant pattern either. In other words, neither the NL nor the TL can explain the observed systematicity in the learner's utterances, but because these regularities nevertheless require an explanation, some system other than the NL or TL must be hypothesized to explain the observed regularity.

Within this context, consider a partial interlanguage analysis of the L2 pronunciations in (1). The essential ingredient of an IL analysis is that we consider the L2 pronunciations on their own grounds, just as a linguist would analyse the utterances of a native language speaker. In other words, the linguist treats the IL as a language system independent of the TL, in that one recognizes that the L2 learner has created the IL grammar on the basis of TL input data, but one also realizes that the resultant IL system may differ from the TL grammar in important ways.

As the first step, we again note the regularity that the learner's consonants in word-final position are all voiceless, as in [rɛt], [bik], [sik], [wɛt] and [fris]. And, we also note that the words [rɛt] and [bik] are morphologically related to the suffixed forms of the words, [rɛðɚ] and [bigɚ], respectively, where the final voiceless consonant alternates with a voiced consonant between vowels. Again, given that it is possible to attest a wider set of similar L2 pronunciation types from this learner, the pattern exhibited here is one in which all word-final obstruent consonants are pronounced voiceless, whereas some, though not all, of these words have a voiced consonant between vowels in the suffixed form of the word. One way to account for this regularity is to postulate an IL system containing a phonological rule, as in (2).

(2) Interlanguage Rule
All word-final obstruents are pronounced voiceless.

This interlanguage analysis characterizes the L2 learner's pronunciations in (1) by postulating that the learner has internalized an IL that represents his/her version of the TL. This system is different from both the learner's NL and the TL, English, in that neither the NL nor TL contains the rule in (2).

This IL rule in (2) states a regularity within the learner's IL grammar that is motivated by the alternations between word-final voiceless consonants in [rɛt] and [bik] and intervocalic voiced consonants such as the [ð] in [rɛðɚ] and the [g] in [bigɚ]. Thus, the claim of the IL analysis is that the learner's lexical representations for the words *red* and *big* are, respectively, /rɛd/ and /big/, the same as the TL forms. This is supported by the fact that the IL pronunciations for *redder* and *bigger* are produced with a voiced consonant between vowels. In other words, there is evidence that the L2 learner *knows* that the words *red* and *big* contain a final voiced consonant. The learner simply does not pronounce the final [d] or [g] as voiced because of the IL rule (2).

It is important to note at this point that the alternation between the word-final voiceless sounds [t] and [k] in [rɛt] and [bik] with the voiced intervocalic [ð] and [g] could not be explained by instead positing that the learner's IL contained the lexical representations /rɛt/ and /bik/, along with a rule that made the voiceless /t/ and /k/ become voiced between vowels (with subsequent application of the NL rule that turns intervocalic /d/ to [ð]). Such an analysis could not be maintained because of the IL pronunciations [fʌsi], [sikəst], [wɛtɚ], each of which contains an intervocalic voiceless obstruent, thereby countering any proposed rule to make obstruents voiced between vowels.

One additional point should be made with respect to the above IL analysis. It has already been noted that the rule in (2) is independent of both the NL and TL. It is interesting to note, however, that patterns shown in (1) and rules such as (2) have been motivated for the grammars of a number of languages of the world, including Catalan, German, Polish and Russian, to cite just a few. This finding constitutes one of the most interesting phenomena in L2 phonology, specifically a pattern that is independent of both the NL and TL but that is nevertheless attested in the grammars of other languages of the world. This fact alone would seem to support a strong theoretical and empirical connection between IL phonologies and L1 phonologies, an idea taken up briefly below in the discussion of the structural conformity hypothesis.

There are at least three major points that constitute the legacy of the findings of work done within the earlier research paradigms. The first is that at least some L2 phonological error patterns can be explained on the basis of NL–TL differences. The second is that the errors that L2 learners make are in general systematic. And the third is that L2 learners construct their own version of the TL grammar that can differ in interesting ways from the grammars of the NL and TL.

More recent contributions and research

The focus for this section will be on several frameworks that reflect the efforts of researchers to explain L2 phonologies in terms of some of the theoretical principles and constructs that have been motivated for L1 phonologies. In so doing, L2 researchers attempt to understand second language phonology by relating it to L1 phonology. The discussion concerns four proposals that were designed to explain various aspects of L2 pronunciation patterns in terms of universal principles and generalizations that were postulated on data from native languages.

Universals as explanatory principles

The first proposal addresses the fact that the contrastive analysis hypothesis could not account for some differences between the learner's NL and the TL causing difficulty. It was also clear that some aspects of the TL could represent greater difficulty than others, but this fact could not be explained by the CAH. One proposed solution to these problems was the hypothesis that the concept of *typological markedness* (Greenberg, 1966) could serve as a measure of degree of learning difficulty.

The idea behind typological markedness is that many structural aspects of languages differ from each other systematically and implicationally. An example of a such structural difference is a voice contrast in obstruents. Not all languages exhibit such a contrast, but, where they do, the word-positions in which such a contrast occurs differ systematically and implicationally across languages. For example, some languages such as English have a voice contrast in obstruents both in syllable onset position and coda position, as in, for example, [to] *toe* versus [do] *dough*, and [ot] *oat* versus [od] *ode*, respectively. Other languages, such as Japanese, have this contrast only in onsets, but not in codas, whereas still other languages, such as Mandarin, do not have this contrast in either onsets or codas. Interestingly, there is no known language that exhibits this contrast only in codas. These facts can be represented

Table 2.1 Categorization of language types according to the distribution of a voice contrast

Type	Contrast in onsets	Contrast in codas	Example
A	No	No	Chinese
B	Yes	No	Japanese
C	Yes	Yes	English
D	No	Yes	None (does not occur)

in Table 2.1, showing that the distribution of a voice contrast in obstruents attests only three of the four logically possible language types.

Table 2.1 characterizes the facts that languages differ from each other systematically and implicationally with respect to the syllable positions of a voice contrast. A voice contrast in onsets is privileged across languages in that it occurs more widely, and supports the implicational generalization in (3).

(3) The presence of a voice contrast in obstruents in syllable codas implies the presence of this contrast in syllable onsets, but not vice versa.

Assigning the term *unmarked* to this privileged member of the distinction is a way of giving it special status and indicating that it is considered to be, in some definable way, simpler, more basic and more natural than the less widely occurring member of the distinction, which is designated as being *marked*. Thus, a language may not necessarily exhibit a voice contrast in obstruents, but, if it does, it will always be in onsets.

The first important observation that needs to be made in this context is that typological markedness is a relative notion. A given structure is marked or unmarked not absolutely but relative to some other structure. The second is that the concept of typological markedness is applicable not just to phonological segments or contrasts but also to linguistic representations in other grammatical domains as well, including morphology, the lexicon, syntax and semantics (Battistella, 1990).

There are non-linguistic examples of markedness in everyday life. In most states of the USA, a person who holds a driver's license is not legally authorized to drive public passengers. To transport passengers, one needs a chauffeur's license. However, someone holding a chauffeur's license also has the privileges of a driver's license. Thus, the privileges of a chauffeur's license are marked relative to those of a driver's license.

Returning to the main theme, we note that the markedness differential hypothesis stated in (4) attempted to address some problems with the CAH by including typological markedness as a measure of relative difficulty.

(4) The Markedness Differential Hypothesis (MDH) (Eckman 1977, p. 321)

The areas of difficulty that a language learner will have can be predicted such that (a) those areas of the target language which differ from the native language and are more marked than the native language will be difficult; (b) the relative degree of difficulty of the areas of difference of target language which are more marked than the native language will correspond to the relative degree of markedness; and (c) those areas of the target language which are different from the native language, but are not more marked than the native language will not be difficult.

The claim of the MDH is that differences between the NL and TL are necessary but not sufficient to explain L2 learning difficulty, and therefore it is necessary to incorporate typological markedness into the hypothesis. Within the areas of difference between the NL and TL, marked structures are more difficult than the corresponding unmarked structures.

There are at least three empirical implications that follow immediately from the MDH. The first is that, where there is no markedness relationship between the areas of NL–TL difference, there is no prediction of systematic difficulty. The second is that different structures in a given TL will cause different degrees of difficulty for learners depending on the relative markedness of the structures. And the third is that there will be a 'directionality of difficulty' involved in some language contact situations. Thus, a language learner who is a native speaker of L_x may find it more difficult to acquire aspects of L_y than does a speaker of L_y learning L_x. This difficulty depends on the respective markedness relations. A number of works that have tested the claims of the MDH have been listed below under Further reading.

A second hypothesis incorporating universal principles as an explanation for L2 pronunciation patterns is the similarity differential rate hypothesis (SDRH), formulated by Major and Kim (1996). The SDRH reprises the idea from some earlier work that dissimilar sounds may be easier than sounds that are similar to those in the NL. The SDRH combines this notion with markedness, claiming that dissimilar structures are acquired more quickly than similar structures, and that markedness is a mediating factor. According to this view, *rate of acquisition* is the basis for explaining L2 pronunciation errors, not *difficulty*, as is stated in the CAH and the MDH. The primary argument for this claim is that the learning situation for beginning learners can run counter to that for advanced learners: similar sounds are easier for beginners, because learners can employ L1 transfer, but advanced acquirers often find sounds that are different to be less problematic. Major (2001) developed his theory into the ontogeny phylogeny model, which seeks to reconcile the influence of the NL, the TL, and universal properties on the development of L2 phonologies, by explaining L2 phonology using constructs stemming from all three areas.

The third hypothesis that invoked linguistic universals as an explanation for L2 phonological patterns is the structural conformity hypothesis (SCH) (Eckman 1991), stated as in (5).

(5) The structural conformity hypothesis

The universal generalizations that hold for primary languages hold also for interlanguages.

The rationale behind the SCH is to explain the nature of interlanguage phonologies using universal generalizations that linguists have hypothesized for native languages. The SCH resulted from stripping NL–TL differences from the statement of the MDH, thereby addressing problems encountered by the hypothesis in which learner difficulty patterns did not arise in an area of NL–TL difference and were therefore not explained by the MDH.

The SCH and typological markedness relations can be exemplified by considering once again the data in (1) above. Two points about these data can be addressed in terms of typological markedness. The first is that pronunciations such as [rɛt] *red* and [bik] *big* are not adequately explained in terms of NL influence, because the NL, Spanish, does not have words that end in voiceless obstruents such as [t] and [k]. The second point is that alternations such as [bik] and [bigər] motivate a rule of word-final devoicing for the L2 phonology, where such a rule is not part of the phonology of either the NL or TL.

The SCH claims that IL phonologies should obey the same generalizations as native language phonologies. The relevant generalization is expressed in Table 2.1 above. The TL, English, is a type C language and has a voice contrast in both codas and onsets, whereas the IL data derive from a type B language with a voice contrast in onsets, as in words such as [sikəst] 'sickest' and [bigər] 'bigger', but not in codas, as in [wɛt] 'wet' and [rɛt] 'red'. Thus, the IL data pattern is like neither the NL nor the TL but is nevertheless consistent with the generalization in Table 2.1.

Frameworks that invoked linguistic universals to help explain L2 phonological patterns are tacitly assuming that one of the important similarities between L1 and L2 phonologies is that they both obey linguistic universals. We now describe three additional areas of focus for researchers in L2 phonology, beginning with phonetics.

Speech learning model and perceptual assimilation model

Within the context of addressing problems with NL influence as a satisfactory explanation for L2 pronunciation patterns, two important models of L2 phonetics emerged, claiming that a plausible explanation for L2 learners' difficulty with TL sounds that are different from those of the learners' NL is that the TL sounds are not accurately perceived by the learner. The perceptual assimilation model (PAM), put forth by Best (1995), and the speech learning model (SLM), posited by Flege (1995), hypothesized that L2 learners perceive non-native sounds in terms of their native phonological system, and that the articulatory characteristics of the TL sounds determine the extent to which these sounds will be incorporated into the phonetic categories of the NL system. This, in turn, determines how accurately a non-native sound can be produced. Limitations of space will allow elaboration of only the SLM, which consists of four postulates and seven hypotheses. The fundamental claims of the SLM are that L2 learners perceive TL sounds in terms of the phonetic categories established in the NL sound system, and that learners relate TL sounds to these categories using a mechanism of *equivalence classification* that allows a learner to classify TL sounds as either equivalent to, or different from, the NL categories. A learner will incorporate into NL categories sounds that are classified as similar to those of the NL but will establish a new phonetic category for sounds the learner perceives as different from the native categories. An important empirical consequence of these claims is that an L2 learner may actually pronounce TL sounds more target-like if the learner perceives them as different from the NL categories, because the learners in this case would set up new phonetic categories that the learners would strive to pronounce more accurately. TL sounds that are perceived as equivalent to NL sounds will be incorporated into the existing NL system, even though the TL sounds may not be exactly the same as the NL sounds. This situation results in learners using the NL categories to pronounce these TL sounds in a way that may not be completely target-like.

Within-speaker variation

In our discussion of L2 phonology up to this point, we have abstracted away from the fact that L2 learners exhibit variability in their pronunciation patterns, and may therefore evidence TL-like pronunciations on one occasion only to produce the same or similar words as non-target-like on another occasion. Such within-speaker variation is an example of an issue that arose first in L1 phonology and then became a topic of debate in L2 phonology only a few years later. Some linguists have claimed that it is scientifically justifiable to abstract away from L2 variability, since variation may well be a function of factors that lie outside a speaker's IL grammar. Others have argued that the study of variation in L2 phonology is crucial, because there is a relationship between L2 pronunciation and various social factors, such as speech style, linguistic context and elicitation task. Thus, a number of researchers have proposed that the findings of sociolinguistic studies of L1 variation have important implications for the study of variability in L2 pronunciation.

Constraint-based analyses

The discussion turns now to optimality theory, which has recently made its way into L2 phonology. The major difference between a grammar within optimality theory (OT) and grammars within rule-based frameworks is the way in which well-formedness is described. In rule-based grammars, grammaticality is characterized by positing a set of rules to which utterances must adhere in order to be grammatical. Deviance is depicted by showing that ungrammatical utterances violate at least one of the rules. Within OT, on the other hand, grammars consist not of a set of rules but instead of a set of universal constraints. These constraints can be viewed as criteria for grammaticality, and because no language can satisfy all of these criteria it is accepted that some of the constraints will conflict with each other. In other words, the constraints are violable and conflicts are resolved by the ranking of the constraints in cases of conflict. Grammars of particular languages result from different rankings of the universal constraints, and thus grammars differ from each other not in terms of the presence or absence of the constraints but rather in terms of the rankings of the constraints. Any ranking of the universal constraints must yield a grammar of a language, and any grammar of a language must conform to one of the possible rankings of the constraints.

OT grammars and rule-based grammars accomplish in different ways the aim of specifying all and only the well-formed utterances of a language. Rule-based grammars begin with the lexical representation of an utterance and apply the appropriate rules to the this representation, continuing until all of the applicable rules have been brought to bear and the output is specified. An ill-formed, or ungrammatical, utterance is characterized by showing that its derivation violates one or more of the rules of the grammar. On the other hand, the constraints of an OT grammar are violable, and therefore grammaticality is not characterized on the basis of whether or not an utterance violates one or more of the constraints. Instead, the grammaticality of an utterance is determined by an optimization procedure whereby well-formed utterances are those that conform to the highest ranked constraints in the grammar.

Optimality theory offers an interesting and promising framework for research on L2 phonology. Perhaps the most important implication of this constraint-based approach to L2 phonology is the implicit claim that IL grammars attest the same set of constraint rankings as do L1 grammars. In short, IL grammars differ from each other, and from L1 grammars, in the same way that L1 grammars differ from each other.

Usage-based analyses

So far, our discussions have centred on approaches to L2 phonology that postulate mental grammars consisting of rules or constraints and that have the goal of characterizing the set of utterances that are potentially well formed in the learner's IL. Over the last 20 years or so, a relatively new framework has emerged in which a grammar is viewed not as a set of rules or constraints but as 'the cognitive organization of one's experience with the language' (Bybee, 2008, p. 216). Theories within this school of thought, termed *usage-based theories*, postulate that users of a language create a network of associations of phonological, semantic and syntactic pairings of forms and functions called *constructions* (Goldberg, 1995).

One of the major claims of usage-based approaches is that the frequency with which any form occurs affects the cognitive structure of the grammar. This is particularly important in L2 phonology, because repetition strengthens memory representations and makes these structures more accessible.

Some important work in this framework in L2 phonology has been carried out in a number of papers by Fraser and colleagues in which principles and concepts of phonology have been brought to bear on a number of everyday problems, including preliterate spellings in young children, the role of L2 accent in the determination of nationality, and the training of second language teachers (Eades et al., 2003; Fraser, 2000, 2004; Hannam, Fraser & Byrne, 2007; Derwing, Fraser, Kang & Thomson, 2014).

Future directions

Although it is, of course, nearly impossible to predict what the research focus of L2 phonologists will be in the near future, we would like to speculate on three possible areas of focus that involve new, or new uses of, technology.

The postulation of lexical representations is necessary within most schools of thought in L2 phonology, and the evidence that linguists use for positing these forms is largely indirect. As we saw in our error analysis and IL analysis above, we hypothesized lexical representations on the basis of the occurrence of alternations and whether it was possible to predict the occurrence of one of the alternates. The form that was unpredictable was postulated as the lexical representation. However, using functional magnetic resonance imaging (fMRI) techniques it may be possible in the future to garner neurological evidence on lexical representations, as well as other hypothetical constructs (Schumann, 1997). The challenge would arise in ensuring that the granularity of both kinds of evidence is aligned. Eye tracking methods have also been employed in studies on L2 acquisition (Ellis et al., 2014) to investigate learner attention to various cues in the input. And finally, ultrasound techniques (Davidson, 2005, 2006; Stone, 2005) have been used to measure the tongue positions and movements of L2 participants to investigate why certain TL contrasts were not perceived by native speakers of the TL, as it has been determined that very subtle differences in tongue position can cause large distinctions in acoustic measurements.

Further reading

This section cites a number of additional readings for each of the topics discussed above. For more depth in exploring the contrastive analysis hypothesis and the influence of the learner's native language on TL pronunciation, consult Wardhaugh (1970), Ioup (1984) and Young-Scholten (1985), for starters. Additional readings on error analysis include Altenberg and Vago (1983) and Richards (1971). Further exploration of learner languages is available through the writings of some of the scholars who made the original proposals, such as Corder (1971) and Nemser (1971), as well as an empirical study employing the construct (Tarone, 1980). Descriptions of studies incorporating markedness and other universal principles into the explanation of L2 pronunciation patterns are Anderson (1987), Sato (1984), Broselow and Finer (1991) and Carlisle (1998). An excellent source for an elaboration of the ontogeny phylogeny model is the originator of the framework, Major (2001). This is true also for the phonetic models, namely the perceptual assimilation model and the speech learning model, where the writings of the models' originators would be the most insightful, Best (1995) and Flege (1995), respectively. Classics involving language variation in the acquisition of L2 phonology are W. Dickerson (1976), L. Dickerson (1975) and Beebe (1980). Two influential studies on L2 pronunciation within the Optimality Theory framework are Broselow et al. (1998) and Hancin-Bhatt (2000).

References

Altenberg, E., & Vago, R. (1983). Theoretical implications of an error analysis of second language phonology production. *Language Learning, 33,* 427–447.

Anderson, J. I. (1987). The markednesss differential hypothesis and syllable structure difficulty. In G. Ioup & S. Weinberger (Eds), *Interlanguage phonology: The acquisition of a second language system* (pp. 279–291). Cambridge: Newbury House.

Battistella, E. L. (1990). *Markedness: The evaluative superstructure of language.* Albany, NY: State University of New York Press.

Beebe, L. (1980). Sociolinguistic variation and style shifting in second language acquisition. *Language Learning, 30,* 433–447.

Best, C. (1995). A direct realist view of cross-language speech perception. In W. Strange (Ed.), *Speech perception and linguistic experience: Issues in cross-language research* (pp. 171–204). Baltimore, MD: York Press.

Broselow, E. & Finer, D. (1991). Parameter setting in second language phonology and syntax. *Second Language Research, 7,* 35–59.

Broselow, E., Chen, S., & Wang, C. (1998). The emergence of the unmarked. *Studies in Second Language Acquisition, 20,* 261–280.

Bybee, J. (2008). Usage-based grammar and second language acquisition. In P. Robinson & N. C. Ellis (Eds), *Handbook of cognitive linguistics and second language acquisition* (pp. 216–236). New York, NY: Routledge.

Carlisle, R. S. (1998). The acquisition of onsets in a markedness relationship: A longitudinal study. *Studies in Second Language Acquisition, 20,* 245–260.

Chomsky, A. N. (1965). *Aspects of the Theory of Syntax.* Cambridge, MA: Massachusetts Institute of Technology.

Corder, S. P. (1971). Idiosyncratic dialects and error analysis. *IRAL, 9,* 149–159.

Davidson, L. (2005). Addressing phonological questions with ultrasound. *Clinical Linguistics & Phonetics, 19*(6–7), 619–633.

Davidson, L. (2006). Comparing tongue shapes from ultrasound imaging using smoothing spline analysis of variance. *The Journal of the Acoustical Society of America, 120*(1), 407–415.

Derwing, T., Fraser, H., Kang, O.., & Thomson, R. (2014). L2 accent and ethics: Issues that merit attention. In A. Mahboob & L. Barratt (Eds), *Englishes in Multilingual Contexts* (pp. 63–80). Dordrecht: Springer.

Dickerson, L. (1975). The learner's interlanguage as a system of variable rules. *TESOL Quarterly, 9,* 401–407.

Dickerson, W. (1976). The psycholinguistic unity of language learning and language change. *Language Learning, 26,* 215–231.

Eades, D., Fraser, H., Siegel, J., McNamara, T., & Baker, B. (2003). Linguistic identification in the determination of nationality: A preliminary report. *Language Policy, 2,* 179–199.

Eckman, F. (1977). Markedness and the contrastive analysis hypothesis. *Language Learning, 27,* 315–330.

Eckman, F. (1981). On predicting phonological difficulty in second language acquisition. *Studies in Second Language Acquisition, 4,* 18–30.

Eckman, F. (1991). The Structural Conformity Hypothesis and the acquisition of consonant clusters in the interlanguage of ESL learners. *Studies in Second Language Acquisition, 13,* 23–41.

Ellis, N. C., Hafeez, K., Martin, K., Chen, L., Boland, J., & Sagarra, N. (2014). An eye-tracking study of learned attention in second language acquisition. *Applied Psycholinguistics, 35,* 547–579.

Flege, J. E. (1984). The effect of linguistic experience on Arabs' perception of the English /s/ vs. /z/ contrast. *Folia Linguistica, 18,* 117–138.

Flege, J. E. (1995). Second language speech learning: Theory, findings and problems. In W. Strange (Ed.), *Speech Perception and Linguistic Experience: Issues in Cross-Language Research* (pp. 233–277). Baltimore, MD: York Press.

Fraser, H. (2000). Coordinating improvements in pronunciation teaching for adult learners of English as a second language. Canberra: DETYA (Australian National Training Authority Adult Literacy Project). Retrieved from http://www-personal.une.edu.au/~hfraser/docs/HF_ANTA_REPORT.pdf.

Fraser, H. (2004). Constraining abstractness: Phonological representation in the light of color terms. *Cognitive Linguistics, 15,* 239–288.

Goldberg, A. (1995). *Constructions*. Chicago, IL: University of Chicago Press.

Greenberg, J. H. (1966). *Language universals*. The Hague: Mouton.

Hannam, R., Fraser, H., & Byrne, B. (2007). The sbelling of sdops: Preliterate children's spelling of stops after /s/. *Reading and Writing, 20*, 399–412.

Hancin-Bhatt, B. (2000). Optimality in second language phonology: Codas in Thai ESL. *Second Language Research, 16*, 201–232.

Hancin-Bhatt, B., & Bhatt, R. (1997). Optimal L2 syllables: Interaction of transfer and developmental effects. *Studies in Second Language Acquisition, 19*, 331–378.

Ioup, G. (1984). Is there a structural foreign accent: A comparison of syntactic and phonological errors in second language acquisition. *Language Learning, 34*, 1–18.

Lado, R. (1957). *Linguistics across cultures*. Ann Arbor, MI: University of Michigan Press.

Major, R. (2001). *Foreign accent*. Philadelphia, PA: John Benjamins.

Major, R., & Kim, E. (1996). The similarity differential rate hypothesis. *Language Learning, 46*, 465–496.

Nemser, W. (1971). Approximative systems of foreign language learners. *IRAL, 9*, 115–123.

Richards, J. C. (1971). A non-contrastive approach to error analysis. *English Language Teaching, 25*, 204–219.

Sato, C. (1987). Phonological processes in second language acquisition: Another look on interlanguage syllable structure. In G. Ioup & S. Weinberger (Eds), *Interlanguage phonology: The acquisition of a second language system* (pp. 248–260). Cambridge: Newbury House.

Schumann, J. H. (1997). *The neurobiology of affect in language*. Oxford: Blackwell.

Selinker, L. (1972). Interlanguage. *IRAL, 10*, 209–231.

Stone, M. (2005). A guide to analysing tongue motion from ultrasound images. *Clinical linguistics & Phonetics, 19*(6–7), 455–501.

Tarone, E. (1980). Some influences on the syllable structure of interlanguage phonology. *IRAL, 18*, 139–152.

Wardhaugh, R. (1970). The contrastive analysis hypothesis. *TESOL Quarterly, 4*,123–130.

Young-Scholten, M. (1985). Interference reconsidered: The role of similarity in second language acquisition. *Selecta, 14*, 6–12.

3

An overview of phonetics
for language teachers

Joanna Przedlacka

Introduction

Hearing an unfamiliar language for the first time means perceiving a continuous stream of sounds, some of them resembling those of our native language. Others, previously unheard, appear to an unaccustomed ear exotic and hard to describe. This experience is far removed from the one of listening to and speaking our native language. Using our mother tongue we are able to segment the flow of speech into words, understand their meanings and respond accordingly. This multi-level linguistic processing operates below the level of conscious awareness. Doing so, we do phonetics. Its knowledge in the case of our native language is subconscious and taken for granted.

Phonetics is the science of speech. The goal of descriptive phonetics is to account for all the sounds of human languages. It provides a framework to describe speech at many levels. We can list the vowels and consonants of a language and present their properties. We can also provide an account of the changes in melody of the voice (*intonation*) throughout an utterance and how they may influence meaning. Any variety can be described to a good degree of detail. We can also characterize developing, disordered or learner speech. Phonetics deals with the physical properties of sounds, the possibilities of the human vocal tract and the representation of speech. Phonology is interested in how sounds function as a system, i.e. how they form patterns in languages and which physical properties of sounds contribute to the differences in meaning.

Pronunciation instruction, which finds its place in foreign and second language teaching, is an obvious practical application of phonetic science. Efficient communication in the target language depends on the ability to perceive and distinguish its sounds and making one's own speech intelligible. Studying, classifying and describing speech enable us to learn another language, thus making the transition from perceiving a string of unfamiliar sounds to making sense of them. Phonetic knowledge is necessary to alter pronunciation, an area of L2 learning notoriously resistant to change. It is a precursor to phonetic awareness and, combined with practice, it allows us to produce sounds in the appropriate contexts and consequently communicate efficiently in a language not spoken natively.

In the process of helping learners achieve this goal, teachers tackle several tasks, such as selecting a pronunciation model, setting targets, diagnosing the students' difficulties and designing a syllabus. In their expertise portfolio, teachers need the knowledge of the systemic and phonetic differences between the native and target languages, coupled with an auditory ability to distinguish sounds. The training and maintenance of this skill, key for a phonetician (Ladefoged & Johnson, 2015), is also indispensable for pronunciation instructors.

This chapter discusses key concepts in phonetics indispensable to teaching practice. It begins by setting out the basics of speech production and looks at different levels of organization in a language, such as *segment*, *syllable* and *suprasegmentals*. It is shown how aspects of speech can be represented. Theoretical concepts such as the linguistic status of sounds are placed in the context of second language learning. Finally, the issue of pronunciation model choice is discussed. Examples from English and other languages are used throughout.

An overview of speech production

As we breathe, the air travels from the lungs, moving upwards through the *trachea* (windpipe) and into the oral and nasal cavities on its way out. It is also the building material for speech, being modified at several locations along the vocal tract (Figure 3.4). Those changes influence the final 'shape' of the sounds we hear.

Voicing

The first modification occurs at the *larynx* (voice box), a cartilaginous structure sitting atop the windpipe. Its front wall protrudes more in males due to the sharper angle of the *thyroid cartilage* (Adam's apple). The back wall of the larynx and its floor are formed by the *cricoid cartilage*. On its top sit two further cartilages, called *arytenoids*. The larynx is shown in Figure 3.1.

The larynx houses the *vocal folds* (Figure 3.2), two flaps of soft, fleshy membranes, attached horizontally at the front to the thyroid cartilage and at the back to the arytenoids. The space between the vocal folds is the *glottis*. See the vocal folds in action at www.linguistics.ucla.edu/faciliti/demos/vocalfolds/vocalfolds.htm.

The vocal folds are moved by muscles attached to the arytenoids and can adopt different settings. They contribute to speech in a number of ways. In *voiceless* sounds the folds are held apart, allowing the air to flow freely and producing no sound. In *voiced* sounds they are close together and vibrating when impacted by the lung air. In English we distinguish between pairs such as <*pat–bat*>, <*seal–zeal*>, <*bicker–bigger*>, but a third of the languages surveyed for the *World Atlas of Language Structures Online* do not have the voiced–voiceless contrast (Maddieson, 2013). The difference can be demonstrated by placing your palm on the larynx when articulating sounds such as s–z and feeling the vibration in the latter, or by covering your ears and feeling the sensation of the resonance. In English, vocal folds also contribute to the production of two consonants /h/ and the glottal stop /ʔ/, as in <uh-uh> 'no' and <uh-huh> 'yes'. The vocal folds may vibrate at different frequencies and we perceive those vibrations as *pitch*. Not only does this help distinguish between male, female and children's voices; pitch also has linguistic functions (see section on suprasegmentals).

Nasal and oral airflow

After the air has passed through the larynx, it may flow into both oral and nasal cavities. This is true of the sounds called *nasal*, as at the end of <*whim–win–wing*>. However, in most speech sounds the nasal cavity is cut off by the raised *soft palate* (the *velum*), the soft tissue

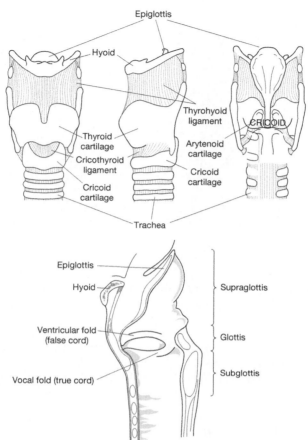

Figure 3.1
The front, side and back views of the larynx (top) and a side view of the larynx, showing the location of the vocal folds (bottom)

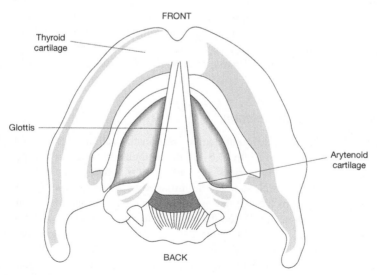

Figure 3.2 The larynx and the vocal folds

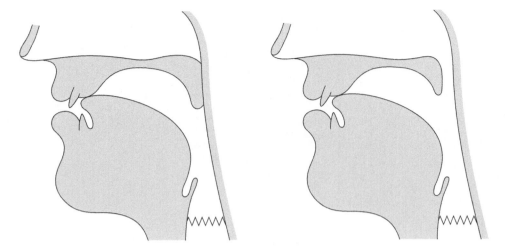

Figure 3.3 The production of an oral and a nasal consonant

Source: A modified version of Figure B2.8 from Collins & Mees (2013)

at the back of the mouth. The velum acts like a valve, directing the airflow only through the oral cavity. Sounds produced in this way are called *oral*. The velum position is responsible for the differences between pairs of otherwise similar sounds such as the final consonants of <*bid–bin*>, shown in Figure 3.3.

Consonants: place of articulation

As the air progresses through the vocal tract, it may be further altered in a number of ways. Most *consonant* sounds involve an obstruction to the airflow through a contact of the parts of the vocal tract called *articulators*. Articulators are of two types: *active*, which move in speech production (tongue tip, tongue body, lower lip) and *passive*, which are stationary (teeth, hard palate, the wall of the pharynx). Consonants are produced along the entire length of the vocal tract, i.e. articulators may approach anywhere along its length. The area of the narrowest constriction is called the *place of articulation* (Figure 3.5), usually named after the passive articulator.

Consonants: manner of articulation

At each place of articulation, different degrees of constriction are described as differences in the *manner of articulation* (Figure 3.6). If the articulators touch, a complete closure is formed. Sounds formed in this manner are called *stops*, because the air is stopped from flowing freely. They can be oral, such as the initial sounds of <*pie–buy*>, or nasal, such as the one in <*my*>. In oral stops the velum is up, directing all air through the mouth and leading to an increase in the air pressure. When the articulators move rapidly apart, the compressed air is explosively released. This auditory effect is called *plosion* and oral stops are also called *plosives*. In nasal stops the lowered velum allows the air to escape through the nasal cavity.

With the articulators close together (*narrow approximation*), the air squeezing through the gap produces audible turbulence, producing *fricatives*, such as the initial sounds of

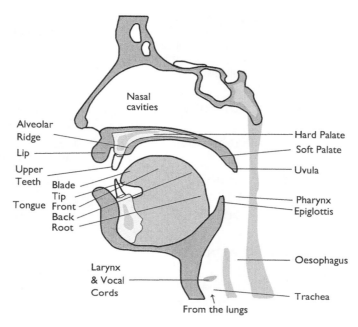

Figure 3.4 The organs of speech

Source: Cruttenden, A. (2014). *Gimson's Pronunciation of English* (8th ed., p. 10)

<fat, thin, van, thick and *hid>*. The fricative /h/ is unusual because there is no narrow approximation. The breath friction results from the air passing through the vocal tract. A subset of fricatives where the air directed at the teeth produces a high-pitched loud noise is called *sibilants*, such as the initial sounds of *<sin, zero, shin, Zsa Zsa>*. In English, sibilants behave differently to other fricatives, i.e. the nouns ending in sibilants form plurals and the third-person present tense with the presence of a vowel in the suffix: compare *<kiss, quiche>* with *<laugh, myth>*.

When the air flows unhindered (the articulators in *wide approximation*), the resulting sounds are *approximants*, such as the initial sounds of *<wed, led, read* and *yet>*. The only source of sound is the vocal fold vibration amplified by the shape of the resonating cavity. Manner of articulation is not confined to vertical distance. In our four approximants other gestures contribute to their quality. Thus, /w/ has two simultaneous strictures (velar and bilabial); during /l/, the only *lateral* approximant in English, the air escapes over the sides of the vocal tract, not the midline and the post-alveolar stricture for /ɹ/ is accompanied by lip rounding.

Sounds involving articulator contact can also differ in the speed of the closure release, as in the initial consonants of the English [t] in *<tongue>* versus German [ts] in *<Zunge>* (stop versus *affricate*). Another difference is the duration of the contact (stop versus *tap*). For example, the middle consonant in the carefully spoken word *<British>* will have a stop. However, in fast speech the contact is shorter, producing a tap. The variant choice is related not only to speech tempo but also to the variety of English. American and Canadian accents will usually have a tap, while in British English both stop and tap are possible.

Manner of articulation can also involve gesture repetition. This difference is absent from English, but is responsible for meaning contrasts in other languages, exemplified by the Spanish

Articulators	Place of articulation	Examples (from MRP unless otherwise stated)
Passive: *Active*:	**BILABIAL**	[m p b] as in *mum, pop, bib*
Passive: upper incisors (front teeth) *Active*: lower lip	**LABIODENTAL**	[f v] as in *fife, viva*
Passive: upper lip *Active*: tongue tip	**LINGUOLABIAL**	Tangoa [t̼] (*Extremely rare sound*)
Passive: upper incisors *Active*: tongue tip	**DENTAL**	[θ ð] as in <u>th</u>ink, <u>th</u>e
Passive: alveolar ridge *Active*: tongue tip and/or blade	**ALVEOLAR**	[n t d s z l] as in *nine, tot, dad, sauce, zoos, loll*
Passive: rear of the alveolar ridge *Active*: tongue tip	**POSTALVEOLAR**	[ɹ] as in <u>r</u>ed <u>r</u>oses
Passive: hard palate *Active*: tongue tip (Note *the tongue tip is stepping out of line here, away from the inherent rest-position relationship between active and passive articulators*)	**RETROFLEX** (Note *This rather impressionistic term is used instead of the literal place names such as:* apico-palatal, sub-apico-palatal, etc.)	[ɻ] (GAm r-sound)
Passive: hard palate + rear of alveolar ridge	**PALATOALVEOLAR** (*Sub-category of Postalveolar*)	[ʃ ʒ tʃ dʒ] as in *sheepish, pleasure, church, judge*
Active: front + tip/blade of tongue *Passive*: front of hard palate + rear of alveolar ridge	**ALVEOLOPALATAL** (*These sounds are represented under 'Other Symbols' on the IPA chart.*)	Polish [ɕ ʑ] Serbian [tɕ] Japanese [dʑ]
Active: front of tongue *Passive*: hard palate *Active*: front of tongue	**PALATAL**	[j] as in <u>y</u>es
Passive: soft palate (velum) *Active*: back of tongue	**VELAR**	[ŋ k g] as in si<u>ng</u>, kick, gag
Passive: uvula (= extreme end of soft palate) *Active*: back of tongue	**UVULAR**	French [ʁ] German [ʀ]
Passive: rear wall of pharynx *Active*: root of tongue	**PHARYNGEAL**	Arabic [ʕ] (the *ayn*)
Passive: aretynoid cartilages *Active*: epiglottis	**EPIGLOTTAL**	Agul [ʜ ʡ] (*Extremely rare sounds*)
The vocal folds	**GLOTTAL**	[h ʔ] as in *ho'*

Figure 3.5 Places of articulation. English examples refer to received pronunciation. Examples of places of articulation not employed in English are from other languages

Source: Ashby, P. (2011). *Understanding phonetics* (p. 37). Oxford: Routledge

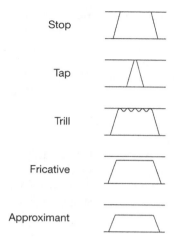

Stop

Tap

Trill

Fricative

Approximant

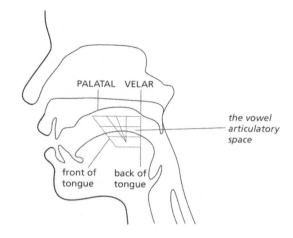

PALATAL   VELAR

the vowel
articulatory
space

front of   back of
tongue   tongue

Figure 3.6
Manners of articulation

Source: Modified from Figure 4.11, Ashby, M. &
Maidment, J. (2005). *Introducing Phonetic Science*
(p. 60). Cambridge: Cambridge University Press

Figure 3.7
An idealized shape of the vowel space

Source: Figure 6.3, Ashby, P. (2011). *Understanding
phonetics* (p. 88). Oxford: Routledge

<*cero*> 'zero' versus <*cerro*> 'hill'. The middle consonant in <*cero*> is a tap, a quick contact of the tongue tip with the tooth ridge. If this contact is repeated in quick succession, this produces <*cerro*> and the middle consonant is a *trill*. Both sounds also appear in some varieties of Scottish English (although the latter is now rare), where they do not contribute to meaning distinctions. We will learn more about this in the section on the liguistic status of sounds.

Vowels

Vowels are produced with the air flowing relatively freely, in contrast to consonants, where the airflow is usually impeded in some way (e.g. blocked in stops or turbulent in fricatives). Vowels are produced in the small area between the hard palate and the velum (Figure 3.7), using the body of the tongue, which lies directly below. Moving the tongue, lips and jaw changes the shape of the vocal tract. Those differences contribute to each vowel sounding different, known as *vowel quality*.

Vowel quality depends on three main factors: how high the tongue is raised towards the roof of the mouth, how far forward or back within the palato-velar area the highest point of the tongue is, and the lip shape. Some vowels have one quality as the exaggerated vowel in <*cheese*> uttered posing for pictures, others change as a result of the tongue and lip movement. They are called *diphthongs*, as exemplified by both words in the phrase <*nice boy*>. In English their starting quality is much longer and slowly decreases in loudness.

In some languages vowels also differ in length. For example English has short and long vowels, the latter indicated by the [ː] diacritic. Vowel duration can be affected by their context in connected speech. Vowels can also be oral (airflow through the mouth) or nasal (airflow through mouth and nose), exemplified by the French pair <*sait*> 'knows' versus <*saint*> 'saint'. Not all languages have nasal vowels.

L2 users of English often find it difficult to distinguish and produce its vowels. One reason for this is that inner circle Englishes, most frequently chosen as models, have rather complex systems with respect to both vowel number and type. For example, American, southern hemisphere and most British accents (except Scottish English) have a contrast between the high vowels of *<pool–pull>*, which differ both in quality and length. However, many languages have only one vowel in that region. A complicating factor is that the exposure to one pronunciation model in the classroom does not prepare the students for a real-life experience of regional accent differences. Ladefoged and Johnson (2015, p. 97) state that many Californian and Midwestern US speakers do not distinguish between the vowels of *<cot–caught>*, while others make contrasts absent from General American (GA).

Another issue is that learners often fail to use reduced vowels, such as schwa, the initial sound in *<above>* which has a central quality and is short. Spoken inner circle Englishes are characterized by the occurrence of schwa in most unstressed syllables. L2 speakers have a tendency to use strong vowels in its place. This may be due to an influence of spelling, with learners believing that the letters <i, e, o, a, u> correspond to full vowels, or simply to a lack of awareness that reduced vowels exist.

Representing speech: the IPA chart and transcription

The International Phonetic Alphabet (IPA) is a notational system used to represent sounds of the world's languages, based largely on the Roman alphabet, with additional symbols. This is necessary, as the number of alphabet letters is far smaller than a variety of sounds in human speech. Any utterance can be represented by a sequence of symbols. This way of representing speech is called *transcription* and is used to convey information about the sounds that have been spoken. There are different kinds of transcription, depending on the degree and kind of detail needed.

While useful, the IPA is a somewhat simplified way of representing spoken language, involving several underlying principles. Primarily, it operates on what is termed *segments*, that is, an assumption that the flow of speech 'can be represented partly as a sequence of discrete sounds or "segments"' (*Handbook of the International Phonetic Association*, 1999, p. 3). They are divided into two categories: vowels and consonants. Each segment is assigned a unique phonetic symbol and referred to by mostly three-part labels describing its articulatory configurations. For consonants, these are *voice*, *place* and *manner*. For example, /p/ in *<pin>* is a voiceless bilabial stop, while /j/ in *<yet>* a voiced palatal approximant. For vowels, there is also a three-way label, representing its articulatory properties, such as tongue height (high–mid–low), frontness–backness (front–central–back) and lip shape (rounded–neutral–spread). For example, our *<cheese>* vowel is high, front and spread. Thus, the division into segments serves to illustrate information, which may be linguistically relevant, but the IPA notation is also used to represent linguistically relevant features of speech above and below a segment. Aspects of speech, such as voice quality, tempo or emotion are not represented by the IPA. A full IPA chart is attached as an appendix to this chapter.

We have said that the IPA uses segments as the basis for sound classification. Indeed, the concept of linear phonetic units that are relatively unchanging (Laver 1994, pp. 112–113) is a convenient way of thinking about sounds and representing their key properties. Additionally, segments have a certain psychological reality for language users brought up with writing systems. However, bear in mind that each sound, even if represented by a single symbol, in fact encompasses a number of dynamic vocal tract configurations. This happens because its production involves a number of articulators, all moving independently. For example the production of the voiceless bilabial plosive /p/ involves the contact of the lips, which causes a blockage in the vocal tract, the build-up of air pressure and finally the rapid parting of the lips and an explosive release. While the mouth is adopting this setting, the vocal folds are apart and the velum blocks the passage to the nasal cavity. This is what would happen if /p/ were pronounced in isolation, which is rarely the case. We need to remember that speech is produced by constant transitions between sounds. It is therefore convenient to think of the IPA labels and symbols as a way of capturing one of the stages of a sound production, in the same way that a photo captures a snapshot of activity. A photograph is informative of what occurred and captures the spirit of the moment but does not tell the whole story.

Another common misconception regards the transcription system. The type of transcription found in dictionaries, textbooks and language teaching materials is *broad* or *phonemic*. Its purpose is to provide a framework for studying a language, indicating the type and number of sounds it has. A dictionary entry clarifies what sounds occur in a word, in what order and which syllable is stressed. For example, the transcription of <*boots*> /buːts/ shows that the word is composed of four sounds. It starts with a b-type sound, has an u-type vowel in the middle and ends with two voiceless consonants. However, this representation does not provide us with information about sound properties, i.e. it does not tell us when or if the vocal folds start vibrating during the first consonant, whether the /uː/ has a back or a central quality and whether the /t/ is dental, alveolar or pre-glottalized.

Therefore, it contains little information how a word would be uttered by a native speaker. This needs to be taught from audio materials and by a teacher who is aware of those details and able to demonstrate them. It is of course possible to include this detailed information in transcription, through the use of diacritics and symbol choice – the word <*boots*> in narrow transcription might be represented as [b̥uːʔts]. This type of representation is called *narrow* or *phonetic* and is often used when collecting field data or working in a speech therapy clinic. However, most of the time it would be impractical to include this level of detail in language instruction materials. In other words, teaching resources employ the IPA to indicate phonemic representation, which does not show phonetic features and is not sufficient to teach pronunciation.

The linguistic status of sounds: contrastiveness, phonemes and allophones

This section looks at two kinds of phonetic differences and their role in communication. In the second section we saw that some physical features of sounds contribute to distinguishing between words, e.g. voicing <*seal–zeal*>, nasality <*bid–bin*> or tongue height <*pool–pull*>. Let us now examine another type of physical difference. For example, comparing the words <*late*> and <*plate*> in Southern British English we can hear that the /l/ sound in <*late*> is voiced, while the one in <*plate*> sounds voiceless and has slight friction. We can represent it as [l̥]. We can find more examples of l-type sounds in the same variety of English, e.g. in <*hell*> and <*health*>. We can observe that the tongue tip has a different position, touching the alveolar ridge in <*hell*> and the teeth in <*health*> because of the adjacent dental fricative. We refer to the place of articulation of the latter as dental and represent it as [l̪]. Now we can make some more observations. Comparing the /l/ in <*late*> with the one in <*hell*>, we also note that they sound different. This is because in the latter the back of the tongue moves towards the velum, resulting in a more constricted vocal tract. We hear this quality as a 'dark' resonance and represent it by a tilde written across the mid-section of the symbol [ɫ]. Many speakers do not have a dark [ɫ] but a back vowel of an [o] quality in those words.

So we see that the /l/ sounds [l][l̥][ɫ][l̪] in <*late, plate, hell, health*> are produced differently, yet a native speaker of Southern British English intuitively recognizes them as 'the same', despite their varied physical characteristics. This is because of their linguistic status. They do not change meaning. They are members of one *phoneme*, which is a linguistic unit of contrast. In other words, a phoneme is how native speakers conceptualize which physical differences between sounds are key to signalling differences in meaning and which are not. The different variants of a phoneme are called *allophones*. We can represent the status of sounds by the use of brackets. A symbol in slant brackets indicates a phoneme /l/ and square brackets indicate its variants (allophones) [l][ɭ][ɫ][ɬ].

Native speakers' intuitions are not the only factor in deciding on the linguistic status of sounds. Grouping them as allophones of the same phoneme or belonging to different phonemes, we primarily take into account their *contrastiveness*. Consider again the /l/ sound in *<late>*. As an experiment, we could substitute [l] for other sounds from the /l/ family: [ɭ], [ɫ] or [ɬ]. As a result, the word sounds different, as if uttered by a speaker of another variety of English or an L2 user, but it is still recognized as the same lexical item.

The way we group sounds into families is therefore more dependent on their role in communication, rather than their physical similarities. This intuitive knowledge forms part of our language competence and tends to be taken for granted. On the one hand, unless linguistically trained, we tend not to pay attention to those physical differences that cause no change in meaning. On the other, we assume that what is contrastive in our mother tongue is also contrastive in other languages. An example is the alveolar lateral approximant [l] and post-alveolar approximant [ɹ], the difference being contrastive in English, as in *<late–rate>* or *<play–pray>*. Japanese also has [l] and [ɹ], yet they are variants of one phoneme, with [l] in all positions and [ɹ] occasionally present (Okada, 1999). Thus, like a native English speaker, a Japanese native speaker has experience of using both sounds and is capable of pronouncing both. The reason they might be unable to hear or produce the difference the English *<late>* and *<rate>* difference in a controlled manner is then not a result of their unfamiliarity with those sounds but their status in their L1. Fraser (2001, p. 20) skilfully illustrates this well-known difficulty using an example of 'two Australian friends, Alison and Bronwyn, travelling in Japan. They found themselves with new names: Arison and Blonwyn!' She advises that teaching the articulation of the sounds that the students can already make perfectly well is unhelpful as the difficulty lies in conceptualizing them differently than in their L1, i.e. in learning to discriminate and organize them in the mind. Thus the teaching of underlying concepts needs to precede production and perception work. There is evidence that high-variability identification training improves perceptual learning (Bradlow, Pisoni, Akahane-Yamada & Tohkura 1997). For classroom practice, this means designing exercises that expose learners to a large amount of tokens (preferably in a variety of accents) containing the problematic sounds and asking students to identify them.

Syllables and phonotactics

Speech is organized on many levels. So far we have looked at the segmental level but sounds are also grouped into *syllables*. In a very basic sense, a syllable is the smallest unit of speech because every utterance contains at least one. It is well recognized that 'there is no agreed phonetic definition of a syllable' (Ladefoged & Johnson, 2015, p. 253). Simultaneously, despite problems in formally defining the concept, it appears to be an important unit of structure. There are several reasons for this. One of them is native speakers' intuitions. If asked to divide a word into syllables, any native (adult or child) user of a language will be able to do so without linguistic training. Second, the construct of the syllable constitutes an important

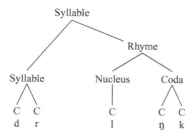

Figure 3.8 A model of syllable structure for the word <drink>

domain for phonological regularities and some allophones are conditioned by their place within a syllable. A syllable is divided into two main parts. The universally adopted convention terms the first part an *onset* and the second a *rhyme*, in turn composed of a *nucleus* and a *coda* (Gussenhoven & Jacobs, 2011). The basic syllable template is shown in Figure 3.8.

There are some universal properties of syllables. It must contain one loud or prominent part, which is almost always a vowel sound. There may optionally be consonants preceding or following the vowel. Thus, consonants are usually found at the syllable edges and with a vowel nucleus in their core. The most common syllable type across languages is CV (consonant–vowel). The exact syllable composition is language-specific.

Phonotactics is the study of the permitted syllable structures, i.e. combinations of sounds within a language. It specifies which consonants can form clusters, how many members a cluster may have and where in the syllable they are allowed to occur. For example, languages differ with respect to the type of clusters in the onset. Some allow only simple ones or none at all.

Let us look at English and Polish. Both allow a *pt- cluster, as in English <opt> or <stopped> and Polish <deptak> 'promenade' and <ptak> 'bird'. An English speaker learning Polish will have no difficulty pronouncing the former word but the latter will usually be problematic. They will either reduce the cluster, saying /tak/ or split it with a vowel, producing /pətak/, thus creating two simpler syllables. The reason for the adoption of those strategies lies in the phonotactic difference between the languages. The *pt- in <ptak> occurs in a syllable-initial position, disallowed in English. English has no syllables (or indeed words) beginning with a *pt-, which is what causes the production difficulty. Pronouncing <deptak> the NES can split the cluster between the two syllables and therefore it is less of an issue when trying to pronounce it. Both languages allow this cluster in syllable-final position, hence an English speaker should have no problems producing Polish words such as <szept> 'whisper'.

Another example is the English word <sport>, which may be pronounced [espɔːt] by Spanish-speaking learners. This will contribute to a perception of a foreign accent but is likely comprehensible. However, inserting vowels to break up a cluster may also result in complete misunderstandings. Thus, when uttered by a Japanese speaker, <sport> may become [supɔːt], and be interpreted as <support>. Coda consonants and clusters are also difficult for many L2 users of English, since many languages permit few or no coda consonants while English permits up to four in this position, as in <strengths>. In contrast, Cantonese allows only a single consonant in the coda and this can only be a stop or a nasal.

Suprasegmentals

In previous sections we looked at segments and how they are organized into syllables. Many features of speech extend beyond the segment, spreading over a syllable, a word or a longer utterance. They are called *suprasegmental* or *prosodic* and, like segments, they contribute to the meaning and organization of the spoken discourse. Suprasegmental aspects of language can be analysed, systematically described and taught to non-native users, although in practice some are more difficult than others. For example, according to Pennington and Ellis (2000), nucleus placement appears to be learnable but pitch movement and the intonation of question tags are not.

Stress

The term *stress* may be used as a theoretical construct or a phonetic property of a syllable. A stressed syllable is more prominent than the adjacent syllables. In terms of its phonetic manifestation, a stressed syllable may be louder and longer and have a more peripheral vowel quality. Most stressed syllables involve some combination of those features. Stress is a relative property and it does not make sense to describe an isolated syllable as stressed or unstressed. Stress may be contrastive as in English noun–verb pairs, such as <*an invite*> and <*to invite*>. Both have the same segment sequence, represented as /ɪnvaɪt/, but the difference lies in *stress* placement; on the first syllable for the noun /ˈɪnvaɪt/ and second for the verb /ɪnˈvaɪt/. In many dictionaries, the location of stress is marked by a raised diacritic before the syllable.

We distinguish two kind of stress, *lexical* and *rhythmic*. The former is a property of an individual word, i.e. the potential of a syllable to become more prominent, as in the example above, where either syllable can attract stress depending on the word's lexical category. This is called the *citation* form, the way the word is pronounced in isolation. In connected speech not all potential stresses are realized. If either of our <*invite*> words were part of a longer utterance the syllable stressed in isolation would likely lose prominence, as in:

> I missed the party because rather than tell me in good time, they sent me a LATE invite.

Rhythmic stress is therefore the degree of syllable prominence within a longer stretch of speech and depends on the structure and intended meaning of the utterance. Stressed syllables act as rhythmic beats in speech. English belongs to a group of languages with *variable* lexical stress, but a description of rules is beyond the scope of this chapter. Languages such as Czech, Polish, French or Welsh have *fixed* lexical stress. Thus stress in Polish always falls on the penultimate syllable of the word and in French on the last one.

(Pitch) accent

In addition to increased length, loudness and strong vowel quality, some stressed syllables also involve a *pitch* movement. Syllables belonging to this subset are called *accents* (also *pitch accents*). Accented syllables are pitch-prominent, i.e. they differ in pitch from the preceding syllable. They can jump up or down in pitch or initiate a pitch movement. Their prominence marks important turning points in intonational tunes.

Intonation

In the flow of utterances our voices continually go up and down. This is true even of the speakers we call monotonous. Those changes are perceived as rises and falls in *pitch*. The articulatory feature responsible for pitch variation is the rate of vibration of the vocal folds, called the *fundamental frequency* of speech. It refers to the number of vibratory cycles per second and is measured in hertz. For example, if the vocal folds vibrate a hundred times per second, the fundamental frequency is 100 Hz. The faster the vibrations the higher the perceived pitch. Male voices in conversational speech have on average a lower fundamental (50–250 Hz) than female ones (120–480 Hz), which in turn are lower-pitched than children's voices (Laver 1994, p. 451). Every speaker has a pitch range, i.e. a scale of pitches they are able to produce. Within their range they also perform pitch movements. When we talk about high or low pitch we do not refer to an absolute frequency value but describe where a given syllable is placed within a speaker's range in relation to other syllables.

Languages use pitch variations to signal meaning differences. For example, <*John*> uttered with a falling pitch is a statement, but spoken with a rising pitch a question. The same is true of longer utterances: <*He's out*> spoken on a fall is a comment on the state of affairs, while if a pitch rises listeners interpret this as a question. Thus, like other aspects of speech, the direction of pitch change may be contrastive, i.e. indicate the grammatical category difference between a declarative and an interrogative. Not every pitch change is linguistically significant.

The parameters of intonation

A common misconception has it that intonation is hard if not impossible to pin down and consequently unteachable. This myth is partly fuelled by another incorrect belief that while segments (vowels and consonants) have clear boundaries, the continuous fluctuations of the pitch are somewhat intangible and cannot be captured within any systematic framework. However, intonation is used in a number of ways to clarify meaning in context. It can in fact be divided into components and described in a systematic manner. This section deals with the framework used to describe intonation within the British School, as applied in Wells (2006). The main variables are the 'three Ts': *tonality*, *tonicity* and *tone*. Those key aspects of intonation play different roles in signalling meaning and each of them makes an independent contribution.

Tonality

One of the functions of intonation is to divide speech into smaller, manageable chunks of information for the listeners to process. Speakers make choices about *tonality*, i.e. how an utterance can be divided into meaningful, coherent units. These are called *intonation phrases* (IPs) (also *thought groups*) and are indicated by '|'. In most cases, speakers are free to make choices about the number of IPs they use. An IP may be a complete sentence, a phrase or even a single word. A story can be told with a different number of IPs:

> *on Saturday | I woke up and didn't know what to do | so I rang my best mate | to see if she wanted to come out | but she was like | oh I don't know what to wear | and said help me choose my outfit | in the end by the time we got into town we were so hungry | that we skipped the shops | and headed for a pizza |*

or

> *on Saturday | I woke up | and didn't know what to do | so I rang my best mate | to see | if she wanted to come out | but she was like | oh | I don't know what to wear | and said help me choose my outfit | in the end | by the time we got into town | we were so hungry | that we skipped the shops | and headed for a pizza |*

Division into IPs can also be used to express differences in meaning. The following sentence, uttered as one IP:

> *I didn't invite him because of Jessica*

means that Jessica was not the reason I invited him. But, divided into two IPs, as in:

> *I didn't invite him | because of Jessica*

means that Jessica was the reason I did not invite him.

Tonicity

Another function of intonation is highlighting the parts of an utterance the speaker considers the most important. Thus, after the division of an utterance into IPs, the next decision regards its focus. Phonetically, this is manifested as the placement of accented syllables within each IP and one of them becoming its *nucleus* or the *tonic* syllable. The nucleus is the last of the many pitch changes within an IP, but not the most prominent one as a widely held misconception has it. Nucleus placement (*tonicity*) reflects the focus of an utterance. There are two main types of focus: *broad* (neutral) and *narrow*.

In broad focus, when the whole utterance constitutes new information, the default position for nucleus is the last content word in the group, illustrated in (a). The nuclear syllable is underlined.

(a) *I've finally finished my <u>home</u>work*

If the utterance focus is narrow, this is reflected in the placement of the nucleus on the stressed syllable of the word that constitutes new information, as in (b–e). Here, the fact that homework is involved is already known to the interlocutors and so the focus is narrow.

(b) *I've finally finished <u>my</u> homework*

(c) *I've finally <u>fin</u>ished my homework*

(d) *I've <u>fin</u>ally finished my homework*

(e) *<u>I've</u> finally finished my homework*

Tone

We have seen that the nucleus is the last change of pitch in an IP. This pitch movement is called the nuclear *tone*. Tones are symbolized by the use of *tonetic marks* (shown below). English uses a number of tones and the most basic distinction (Wells, 2006) is based on the direction of pitch movement: *falling* and *non-falling* tones. The latter are further subdivided into *rise, fall–rise* and *mid-level*. Fall and rise tones are also divided into high and low, i.e.

high fall, *low fall*, *high rise* and *low rise*. This is based on what distance across the speaker's pitch range the pitch movement covers.

Falling	High fall	\Right
	Low fall	ˌRight
	Rise–fall	^Right
Non-falling	High rise	/Right
	Low rise	ˌRight
	Fall–rise	ᵛRight
	Mid-level	>Right

Broadly speaking, the choice of tone is related on the one hand to an utterance type (statement, question); on the other it helps organize discourse, signalling whether information is new or already known. Tone choice may have an attitudinal function, but its use is also motivated by other factors.

Regarding utterance types, Wells (2006, p. 15) points out that 'a popular idea among language students is that statements are said with a fall, questions with a rise'. Indeed, statements more often than not have a fall, but questions differ. The basic principle is:

(a) falling tones: statements, commands and wh-questions:
   What do you want to \underline{\drink}?
   I'd like a glass of \underline{\red}.

(b) rising tones: yes/no questions:
   Do you want a /\underline{drink}?

The choice of tone also helps organize discourse, i.e. it signals either continuity or completeness. Continuity is associated with the rising and level tones. Completeness (finality) is associated with falling tones. Consider the following example, where the rising tone on the final noun <*vodka*> indicates that the list is going to go on.

   Do you want /\underline{wine} |or /beer| or /\underline{gin} |or /\underline{vodka} |

Compare this with the fall on the first syllable of <*vodka*> below, which suggests that the list of drinks is complete. The host does not have any other beverages.

   Do you want /\underline{wine} |or /\underline{beer}| or /\underline{gin} |or \\underline{vodka} |

Third, the choice of tone reinforces the status of information in an utterance, i.e. whether it is new or presupposed by the speakers. Falling tones indicate new information. A fall–rise suggests shared information as in the example below. Note that the order of the phrases does not contribute to the meaning, but the choice of tone does:

   I'm going on ᵛ\underline{holi}day | when I've finished all that \\underline{marking} |
   When are you going on holiday?

   I'm going on \\underline{holi}day | when I've finished all that ᵛ\underline{marking} |
   What are you going to do when you've finished all that marking?

Like other aspects of a language, intonation is subject to L1 interference. Thus, learners will transfer their native patterns to the language they are trying to master. However, lay perceptions of suprasegmentals and segments differ. We readily acknowledge that it takes time to learn L2 vowels and consonants both in terms of phonemic distinctions and the qualities. In contrast, the mastery of intonation is frequently taken for granted. Such views might spring from the fact that intonation has (among others) an attitudinal function and a common assumption is that its learning comes naturally.

Consequently, when an advanced learner uses intonation in a non-native manner, listeners frequently fail to make allowances for the discrepancies between their speech and the expectation. The NNS might be deemed impolite when no such intention existed. For example, the neutral tone in English declaratives is a high fall, while a low fall signals boredom or detachment. However, this would be the default choice in Polish for an unmarked statement. Imagine saying <I'm fine> with a low and a high fall in response to a greeting and think of the impression it gives the interlocutor.

Model choice

Teaching a language necessitates selecting a spoken variety as a model. In the EFL context, this is standard English (the dialect used in media, education and other public life domains), possibly allowing for some regional grammatical, morphological or semantic traits, depending on where in the world the instruction is taking place. The accent of choice is an educated variety. In the Americas and Asia this is usually General American, a broadcast news network accent. In Europe this is primarily received pronunciation (RP), an accent commonly heard in the BBC news broadcasts. Artificially derived varieties such as lingua franca core have been proposed as more suitable alternatives when English is used for communication between non-native speakers.

An accent choice may be open to objections such as that very few people speak it (as is the case for RP) or that it is hard to delimit (for problems in defining GA, see Preston, 2008). However, we have to 'teach *something* after all' (Trudgill, 2001) and the extensively described RP and GA are a practical solution. Second, we need to remember that our choice serves essentially as a reference variety. Primarily, we teach a phonemic framework. In other words, the model serves to point out the type of distinctions the students might not have in their L1, e.g. the RP vowels /æ – ʌ – ɑː/ contributing to the <cat–cut–cart> contrast. This is notoriously hard to grasp for beginners as many languages have one low vowel where English has three. Indeed, while teaching the framework, we also demonstrate and teach a lot of phonetic detail.

However, phonetic accuracy is usually neither the main focus of instruction nor required for successful communication. In the classroom we do not teach what is in lay terms called 'an accent' and should therefore not be afraid of passing on an undesirable one. A native-like pronunciation is never achieved by most L2 learners (owing to factors such as motivation, learning goals, age and individual ability). Indeed, a handful (mainly language professionals) accomplish this feat but it requires exceptional motivation and an intensive input (Bongaerts, van Summeren, Planken & Schils, 1997). It is therefore important to take into account the immediate and long-term needs of our learners and set realistic goals. A model is a vehicle to teach syllable structure, connected speech phenomena and aspects of intonation crucial for intelligibility. If we do find time to focus on phonetic detail, a bigger concern is staying current with empirical research that signals instructional priorities (for a summary see Derwing & Munro, 2015) and keeping up to date with recent developments in English speech.

Future directions

Familiarity with fundamental phonetic concepts will assist teaching professionals in better understanding of learners' problems and facilitate the choice of the most effective teaching techniques and activities. In addition to journal articles there are further professional development opportunities such as conference attendance; two major events on both sides of the Atlantic are the annual Pronunciation in Second Language Learning and Teaching Conference and the biennial Phonetics Teaching and Learning Conference. The *Summer Course in English Phonetics*, held annually in London, has groups specifically aimed at EFL professionals. Teachers might also consider taking the IPA Examination for the Certificate of Proficiency in the Phonetics of English, a formal non-degree certification of phonetic competence recognized by employers. IATEFL has a Pronunciation Special Interest Group, which has its own journal and a range of events. There are numerous online phonetics resources and blogs, compiled on the IPA website. The links are provided below:

> https://speechlab.utah.edu/PSLLT2017.php
> www.ucl.ac.uk/pals/study/cpd/cpd-courses/ptlc/
> www.ucl.ac.uk/pals/study/cpd/cpd-courses/scep
> www.internationalphoneticassociation.org/content/ipa-exam
> http://pronsig.iatefl.org/index.html
> www.internationalphoneticassociation.org/content/links

Further reading

Ashby, P. (2005). *Speech sounds*. London: Routledge.

Bauer, L., & Trudgill, P. (1998). *Language myths*. London: Penguin

Brazil, D. (1997). *The communicative value of intonation in English*. Cambridge: Cambridge University Press.

Collins, B., & Mees, I. (2013). *Practical phonetics and phonology: a resource book for students* (3rd ed.). London & New York, NY: Routledge.

Cruttenden, A. (1997). *Intonation* (2nd ed.). Cambridge: Cambridge University Press.

Deterding, D. (2012). Pronunciation models. In C. A. Chapelle (Ed.). *The encyclopedia of applied linguistics* (pp. 4722–4725). Oxford: Blackwell.

Deterding, D. (2013). *Misunderstandings in English as a lingua franca: An Analysis of ELF Interactions in South-East Asia*. Berlin: De Gruyter.

Grant, L. (2014). *Pronunciation myths. Applying second language research to classroom teaching*. Ann Arbor, MI: Michigan University Press.

Maidment, J., & Lecumberri, M. L. G. (2000). *English transcription course*. London: Arnold.

Ogden, R. (2009). *An introduction to English phonetics*. Edinburgh: Edinburgh University Press.

Rogerson-Revell, P. (2011). *English phonology and pronunciation teaching*. London: Continuum.

Tench. P. (2011). *Transcribing the sound of English: A phonetics workbook for words and discourse*. Cambridge: Cambridge University Press.

References

Ashby, P. (2011). *Understanding phonetics*. Oxford: Routledge.

Ashby, M., & Maidment, J. (2005). *Introducing phonetic science*. Cambridge: Cambridge University Press.

Bongaerts, T., van Summeren, C., Planken, B., & Schils, E. (1997). Age and ultimate attainment in the pronunciation of a foreign language. *Studies in Second Language Acquisition, 19*(4), 447–465.

Bradlow, A. R., Pisoni, D., Akahane-Yamada, R., & Tohkura, Y. (1997). Training Japanese listeners to identify English /r/ and /l/: IV. Some effects of perceptual learning on speech production. *Journal of the Acoustical Society of America, 101*(4), 2299–2310.

Fraser, H. (2001). *Teaching pronunciation. A handbook for teachers and trainers.* Sydney: TAFE NSW Access Division.

Derwing, T. M., & Munro, M. J. (2015). *Pronunciation fundamentals: Evidence-based perspectives for L2 teaching and research.* Amsterdam: John Benjamins.

Gussenhoven, C., & Jacobs, H. (2011). *Understanding phonology.* (3rd ed.). Oxford: Routledge.

Handbook of the International Phonetic Association. A guide to the use of the International Phonetic Alphabet. (1999). Cambridge: Cambridge University Press.

Ladefoged, P., & Johnson, K. (2015). *A course in phonetics* (7th ed.). Stamford, CT: Cengage Learning.

Laver, J. (1994). *Principles of phonetics.* Cambridge: Cambridge University Press.

Maddieson, I. (2013). Voicing in plosives and fricatives. In M. S. Dryer, & M. Haspelmath (Eds), *The world atlas of language structures online.* Leipzig: Max Planck Institute for Evolutionary Anthropology. Retrieved from http://wals.info/chapter/4.

Okada, H. (1999). Japanese. In *Handbook of the International Phonetic Association* (pp. 117–119). Cambridge: Cambridge University Press.

Pennington, M., & Ellis, N. (2000). Cantonese speakers' memory for English sentences with prosodic cues. *The Modern Language Journal, 84*(3), 372–389.

Preston, D. (2008). How can you learn a language that isn't there. In K. Dziubalska-Kołaczyk & J. Przedlacka (Eds), *English pronunciation models: A changing scene* (pp. 37–58). Frankfurt: Lang.

Trudgill, P. (2001). Received pronunciation: Sociolinguistic aspects. *Studia Anglica Posnaniensia, 36,* 3–13.

Wells, J. C. (2006). *English intonation.* Cambridge: Cambridge University Press.

Appendix to Chapter 3

THE INTERNATIONAL PHONETIC ALPHABET (revised to 2015)

CONSONANTS (PULMONIC)

© 2015 IPA

	Bilabial	Labiodental	Dental	Alveolar	Postalveolar	Retroflex	Palatal	Velar	Uvular	Pharyngeal	Glottal
Plosive	p b			t d		ʈ ɖ	c ɟ	k g	q ɢ		ʔ
Nasal	m	ɱ		n		ɳ	ɲ	ŋ	N		
Trill	B			r					R		
Tap or Flap		ⱱ		ɾ		ɽ					
Fricative	ɸ β	f v	θ ð	s z	ʃ ʒ	ʂ ʐ	ç ʝ	x ɣ	χ ʁ	ħ ʕ	h ɦ
Lateral fricative				ɬ ɮ							
Approximant		ʋ		ɹ		ɻ	j	ɰ			
Lateral approximant				l		ɭ	ʎ	L			

Symbols to the right in a cell are voiced, to the left are voiceless. Shaded areas denote articulations judged impossible.

CONSONANTS (NON-PULMONIC)

Clicks		Voiced implosives		Ejectives	
ʘ	Bilabial	ɓ	Bilabial	ʼ	Examples:
ǀ	Dental	ɗ	Dental/alveolar	pʼ	Bilabial
ǃ	(Post)alveolar	ʄ	Palatal	tʼ	Dental/alveolar
ǂ	Palatoalveolar	ɠ	Velar	kʼ	Velar
ǁ	Alveolar lateral	ʛ	Uvular	sʼ	Alveolar fricative

OTHER SYMBOLS

ʍ Voiceless labial-velar fricative
w Voiced labial-velar approximant
ɥ Voiced labial-palatal approximant
ʜ Voiceless epiglottal fricative
ʢ Voiced epiglottal fricative
ʡ Epiglottal plosive

ɕ ʑ Alveolo-palatal fricatives
ɺ Voiced alveolar lateral flap
ɧ Simultaneous ʃ and x

Affricates and double articulations can be represented by two symbols joined by a tie bar if necessary.

t͡s k͡p

VOWELS

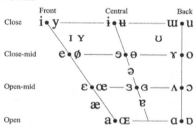

Where symbols appear in pairs, the one to the right represents a rounded vowel.

SUPRASEGMENTALS

ˈ	Primary stress	ˌfoʊnəˈtɪʃən
ˌ	Secondary stress	
ː	Long	eː
ˑ	Half-long	eˑ
̆	Extra-short	ĕ
ǀ	Minor (foot) group	
ǁ	Major (intonation) group	
.	Syllable break	ɹi.ækt
‿	Linking (absence of a break)	

DIACRITICS
Some diacritics may be placed above a symbol with a descender, e.g. ŋ̊

	Voiceless	n̥ d̥		Breathy voiced	b̤ a̤		Dental	t̪ d̪
	Voiced	s̬ t̬		Creaky voiced	b̰ a̰		Apical	t̺ d̺
ʰ	Aspirated	tʰ dʰ		Linguolabial	t̼ d̼		Laminal	t̻ d̻
	More rounded	ɔ̹	ʷ	Labialized	tʷ dʷ	̃	Nasalized	ẽ
	Less rounded	ɔ̜	ʲ	Palatalized	tʲ dʲ	ⁿ	Nasal release	dⁿ
	Advanced	u̟	ˠ	Velarized	tˠ dˠ	ˡ	Lateral release	dˡ
	Retracted	e̠	ˤ	Pharyngealized	tˤ dˤ	̚	No audible release	d̚
	Centralized	ë	̴	Velarized or pharyngealized	ɫ			
	Mid-centralized	e̽		Raised	e̝	(ɹ̝ = voiced alveolar fricative)		
	Syllabic	n̩		Lowered	e̞	(β̞ = voiced bilabial approximant)		
	Non-syllabic	e̯		Advanced Tongue Root	e̘			
˞	Rhoticity	ɚ a˞		Retracted Tongue Root	e̙			

TONES AND WORD ACCENTS

LEVEL			CONTOUR		
e̋ or ˥	Extra high	ě or ˩˥	Rising		
é ˦	High	ê ˥˩	Falling		
ē ˧	Mid	e̋ ˦˥	High rising		
è ˨	Low	e̖ ˩˨	Low rising		
ȅ ˩	Extra low	e̗ ˧˩˧	Rising-falling		
↓	Downstep	↗	Global rise		
↑	Upstep	↘	Global fall		

4

Phonological development in first languages

Lillian May, Tania S. Zamuner
and Janet F. Werker

Introduction

Sensitivity to the sounds and sound structures of the native language (NL) begins early in development, with influences from the ambient linguistic environment beginning even before birth. In this chapter, we review the current state of research on phonological development in infancy. We begin the chapter by briefly noting the range of theoretical approaches to phonological development that exist, and then describe in more depth approaches that have guided empirical attention. We next highlight research on speech sound discrimination, phonotactics and word learning, and explain several of the common research methods used to examine phonological development in infants and children. Finally, we discuss implications for educators, parents and clinicians, as well as some future directions for the field. Throughout, we consider both language comprehension and language production, taking the position that, to get a full picture of phonological development, both aspects of language must be viewed in tandem.

Language can be explored on many different levels. In this chapter, we focus on segmental phonology, the sound (or medium) system. Because we are interested in phonological development, we consider phonology as not only the rule-governed aspects seen in a mature system but also the various aspects of the sound system of a language that an infant becomes sensitive to across the first years of life. Definitions for the terms used to describe the various levels of phonological acquisition are given below.

When we talk about *acoustics*, we will be referring to the characteristics of the sound waves that constitute the audio signal of speech. *Phonetics* refers to the physical description of the individual speech segments – the consonants and vowels (see Chapter 1, this volume). The term *phoneme* will be used to characterize those segments that are used to contrast meaning in the language (see Chapter 1, this volume). For example, the segments /b/ and /p/ are phonemes in English because, when they are part of a word, the meaning of the word changes, such as in <bat> versus <pat>. *Phonotactics* refers to the rules and restrictions for how segments may be sequenced to form words; for example, 'str' is allowed only at the beginning of English words. *Prosody* is loosely the 'melody' of speech. It refers to the pitch, intonation, and rhythmic patterns of language.

For the purposes of this chapter, we will concentrate our review on phonological development within spoken languages, and specifically on segmental phonology. However, there is also a parallel body of research on attunement to the prosodic features of the NL, including a focus on how prosody might bootstrap acquisition of NL grammar (see Gervain & Mehler, 2010, for a review). Finally, while our focus is on oral/aural language, much of what we discuss with regards to segmental phonology has been shown to be similar in both the segmental and prosodic aspects of signed languages as well (see Pettito, 1994; Emmorey, 2001; Bates & Dick, 2002).

Historical perspectives

Any review of phonological development research as it stands today begins with a discussion of speech perception development in infancy. Historically, however, the study of phonological acquisition and that of infant speech perception were quite distinct, and they did not begin to come together until the 1980s. The field of phonological acquisition is much older, established in the early 1900s. The dominant view was that there is a distinction between phonetics (the surface form) and phonology (the rules), and thus that the most primitive unit of study in phonological acquisition was the phoneme (Trubetskoy, 1969). Consistent with this view, in a highly influential manuscript, Jakobson (1941), as described in Waugh (1976), argued that there is a discontinuity between babbling and speech, claiming that only once children began to build a lexicon could one talk about the emergence of a true phonological system. To address those claims, child language researchers of the time systematically documented the productive development of children. In so doing, they amassed sufficient data to challenge the discontinuity view (see Vihman, Macken, Miller, Simmons & Miller, 1985, for an early review), and to convince the field that the foundations of phonology are already apparent in babbling development. While findings from speech perception studies were not considered to be as informative to child language researchers for a very long time as compared to findings from early speech production, discoveries by child language researchers on the importance of babbling research actually set the stage for increasing consideration of prelinguistic speech perception work as informative to phonological acquisition.

Research on infant speech perception was initially motivated to deepen understanding of the linguistic claim that adults show 'categorical perception', that discrimination is limited to only those speech sound differences that can be labelled as members of distinct categories (i.e. as distinct phonemes, such as between /b/ and /p/ sounds) (see Eimas, Siqueland, Jusczyk & Vigorito, 1971). The initial interpretation of the infant data was that they revealed innate knowledge of phonemes. Yet, almost as soon as the first infant speech perception studies were complete, auditory perception researchers – from speech sciences, acoustics and experimental psychology – challenged these claims and designed experiments to test whether it is general auditory sensitivities rather than categorical boundaries that best explains infant speech perception sensitivities. This question dominated the first two decades of infant speech perception studies, leading to the establishment of a rigorous, laboratory-based empirical approach but deflecting the focus from a link to phonological acquisition.

Researchers now study the roots of phonological acquisition, beginning with speech perception in the very youngest infants. Current theoretical approaches explore the relationship between the development of language-specific speech perception and the emergence of phonology.

Critical issues and topics

To acquire the phonology of their NL, infants must learn about many aspects of their language's speech sounds and structure: the speech sounds in their language, what speech sound combinations are allowed in their language and how these sound combinations map on to meaning, in the case of words. In the section below, we review these important achievements in early phonological development, describing some of the most influential research in the field.

Current contributions and research

Speech sound discrimination

Since the classic studies of Eimas and colleagues (1971), it has been known that infants as young as one month of age are better able to detect acoustic differences from two distinct phonetic categories (such as the difference between /b/ and /p/ sounds) than they are to detect within-category differences (such as the difference between two different /p/ sounds, for example the /p/ in the word 'pin' as compared with the /p/ in the word 'spin'). Moreover, this sensitivity extends to non-native, and hence never-before-heard, acoustic-phonetic variation (Werker & Tees, 1984): for example, infants learning English are able to distinguish between sounds that are not present in the English language inventory but that are present in other languages. In the following decades, both behavioural and ERP studies revealed that this organization is evident at birth (Kuhl, 2004; Werker & Gervain, 2013), even in infants born as early as 29 weeks' gestation (Dehaene-Lambertz, Hertz-Pannier, Dubois & Dehaene, 2008), and that cross-category phonetic discrimination (such as between /b/ and /p/ sounds) activates left hemisphere temporal areas of the brain, known to be classic language areas in adults (Dehaene-Lambertz & Gliga, 2004; Mahmoudzadeh et al., 2013). While it is now known that with more subtle measures it is possible for infants to demonstrate sensitivity to within-phonetic category differences as well (such as to two different /p/ sounds) (McMurray & Aslin, 2005), cross-category discrimination is unfailingly the most robust. The meaning of these findings continues to be an area of active debate. The argument, and resulting research, concerns the extent to which initial speech perception reveals evidence of an innate phonetic module (biologically specialized system for speech processing) versus a broadly evolved auditory system that supports speech processing not because it is speech per se but because it favours salient acoustic differences that happen to occur in human language.

There are also clear effects of language experience on speech perception development. During the first year of life, discrimination of non-native phonetic distinctions declines (Werker & Tees, 1984; Maurer & Werker, 2014) and discrimination of native distinctions improves (Kuhl et al., 2006; Sundara, Polka & Genesee, 2006). While in most cases development results in a process of improvement, in the case of speech perception part of development is just the opposite in that young infants demonstrate sensitivity to more speech sound distinctions than do older infants. This process of developmental change from initial sensitivity to both native and non-native speech sound differences to a more circumscribed ability to only discriminate those speech sound differences that are used in the NL is sometimes referred to as 'perceptual narrowing'. This effect was first shown robustly for consonant discrimination: young English infants can discriminate two /d/ sounds that are used to contrast meaning in Hindi, but not English, but by 10–12 months of age – like English-speaking adults – English-learning infants no longer do so (Werker & Tees, 1984). Similar findings have been reported for many other consonant contrasts, for vowels – albeit in some cases at slightly earlier ages (Polka & Werker, 1994; Kuhl, Williams, Lacerda, Stevens & Lindblom, 1992), for lexical tone as used in Chinese languages (Mattock, Molnar, Polka & Burnham, 2008) and even for linguistic hand signs (Baker, Golinkoff & Petitto, 2006; Palmer, Fais, Golinkoff & Werker, 2012). Babies growing up bilingual continue to discriminate the speech sound contrasts of each of their native languages (Albareda-Castellot, Pons & Sebastián-Gallés, 2011; Bosch & Sebastián-Gallés, 2003; Burns, Yoshida, Hill & Werker, 2007).

The most pronounced effects of experience on phonetic perception occur between six and 12 months, suggesting the operation of a critical or sensitive period during which the speech perception system is most open to experience (Werker & Hensch, 2015). In most circumstances the timing of this window seems constrained by maturation (Peña, Werker & Dehaene-Lambertz, 2012). That is, even babies who are born up to 12 weeks premature and are otherwise healthy do not show accelerated perceptual narrowing from their 12 additional weeks of listening experience. Rather, these premature babies attune to the speech sound differences of the NL at the same gestational age (rather than time since birth), as do full-term infants. While the timing of openness to listening experience cannot be accelerated without a biological perturbation to the system (e.g. some maternal antidepressant medication may accelerate attunement: Weikum, Oberlander, Hensch & Werker, 2012), the timing of sensitivity to input can be delayed or be kept open longer under different types of experiential situations. For example, highly engaging social interaction can make infants sensitive to non-native speech sound differences for a longer period of time in development (Elsabbagh et al., 2013; Kuhl, Tsao & Liu, 2003), and exposure to maternal depression can slow down the timing of attunement (Weikum et al., 2012).

An active area of research involves investigating the learning mechanisms that enable infants to establish native phonetic categories. One mechanism that has been identified is distributional learning. To return to the Hindi versus English differences in /d/ sounds, infants who are growing up learning Hindi hear two minimally different common words: the more front (dental) /dal/ means 'lentils' and the more back (retroflex) /Dal/ means 'branch'. Thus, Hindi-learning infants hear a bimodal distribution of front versus back 'd' sounds in different pronunciations of these two words. In contrast, English-learning infants just hear one word like those, 'doll', with variation around that single exemplar. To model this, researchers created a continuum of 'd' sounds that spanned the front, centre, and back oral-acoustic space, and then trained infants with either a bimodal distribution from this continuum with lots of instances towards the ends of the continuum and few in the middle (like a Hindi infant would hear) or a unimodal distribution (many of the central sounds like an English infant would hear and fewer from the ends). Following familiarization, infants of six to eight months change their discrimination patterns. Following bimodal exposure, they discriminate between the front versus back Hindi distinction whereas, following unimodal exposure, they do not (Maye, Werker & Gerken, 2002; Maye, Weiss & Aslin, 2008). By 10 months of age distributional learning is less effective (Yoshida, Pons, May & Werker, 2010), whereas manipulations that pair speech sound distinctions with distinct objects, <e.g.> hearing a front 'd' while seeing one object and a back 'd' while seeing a different object can still facilitate discrimination (Yeung & Werker, 2009). Similarly, hearing the two different non-native speech sounds in a contingent social communicative exchange (Kuhl et al., 2003) can also maintain non-native speech sound discrimination. These studies raise the possibility that while passive listening might contribute to phonetic category development in early infancy, towards infants' first birthdays phonetic category learning becomes more integrated with language acquisition (see Werker, Yeung & Yoshida, 2012). Indeed, computational studies that model the learning of phonetic categories and of meaningful words simultaneously, in an interactive fashion, yield the most robust and generalizable findings (Feldman, Griffiths & Morgan, 2009; Peperkamp, LeCalvez, Nadal & Dupoux, 2006; Swingley, 2009) setting the attunement of phonetic categories within, rather than as prior to, the establishment of phonological categories.

Virtually all of the work reviewed above has focused on perception of syllable-initial phonetic differences. Discrimination and equivalence categorization across medial and final syllables may develop later (Archer, Zamuner, Fais, Engel & Curtin, 2016), and these patterns are also mirrored in learners' omissions in early speech production (Levelt, 2012). While it is still argued that the apex of phonetic/phonological development is the establishment of position independent phonological categories (Ladd, 2011), at least in the early stages of phonological development phonemes may be position-dependent (Pierrehumbert, 2003; Werker & Curtin, 2005). For example, this means that there could be separate representations for word-initial sounds as compared to word-final sounds, which reflect the fact that there are different acoustic realizations of sounds depending on where they occur within a word or syllable.

While phonetic discrimination narrows during infancy, the ability to represent and generalize phonetic categories improves. Research reveals an internal structure to phonetic categories from as young as two to four months (e.g. Kuhl, 1979), and some evidence of perceptual constancy for vowel sounds in the presence of different consonants (Bertoncini, Bijeljac-Babic, Jusczyk, Kennedy & Mehler, 1988). However, it is not until six months that infants have been shown to represent more generalizable consonant categories, e.g. to treat the /b/ in <beat>, <bed>, <boom> etc. as equivalent (Hochmann & Papeo, 2014). This again may be a step along the way towards the establishment of abstract phonological units.

Phonotactics

As infants learn the sounds of their NL(s), they also learn the system that governs how sounds are organized. Because phonotactic patterns vary from language to language, this knowledge is generally thought to be acquired from exposure to language. Infants begin to show sensitivity to the phonotactics of their NL around nine months (Friederici & Wessels, 1993; Jusczyk, Friederici, Wessels, Svenkerud & Jusczyk, 1993). At this time, infants also display sensitivity to the frequency of sound patterns, listening longer to lists of words containing frequent compared to less frequent sound combinations (Jusczyk, Luce & Charles-Luce, 1994), as well as sound combinations that occur in many words compared to fewer words within a language (Archer & Curtin, 2011). Knowledge of the permissible sequencing of sounds may bootstrap word learning by demarcating word onsets and offsets in running speech (Mattys & Jusczyk, 2001). For example, if an English learner has knowledge about the permissible sequences of sounds in English, they can use that knowledge to deduce that the word boundary in a string like 'redcar' must be red.car and not re.dcar because no English words begin with the sequence 'dc'.

While infants show sophisticated knowledge of NL sound patterns, the acquisition of phonotactic knowledge can interplay with other aspects of language, such as where the phonotactic pattern occurs within words or syllables (Zamuner, 2006), the perceptual acoustic salience of the phonotactic pattern (Narayan, Werker & Beddor, 2010) and how frequent the pattern is in the language (Zamuner, 2013). For example, if a phonotactic pattern is perceptually salient (easy to perceive) a potential consequence is that the pattern will be easier to learn compared to a less perceptual salient phonotactic pattern. Infants are able to learn novel phonotactic patterns that do not occur in their NLs (Seidl & Buckley, 2005); moreover, younger infants are more flexible in the types of phonotactic patterns they can learn (Cristià & Seidl, 2008; Cristià, Seidl & Gerken, 2011). Infants are better at learning words that match the permissible phonological patterns of the language (MacKenzie, Curtin & Graham, 2012) and words comprised of frequent sound patterns (Gonzalez-Gomez, Poltrock & Nazzi, 2013; Graf-Estes & Bowen, 2013). For more discussion on phonotactic acquisition see Zamuner and Kharmalov (2016).

Speech production research has also examined how the phonological shape of a word influences how it is pronounced. Children are more accurate and faster at producing words and non-words comprised of frequently occurring sound patterns (e.g. Munson, Edwards & Beckman, 2005; Zamuner, 2009). For example, English-learning children will produce <ged> (comprised of frequent sounds and sound combinations in English) more accurately than <thaff> (with less frequent sounds and sound combinations). These frequency-based effects are argued to reflect phonological and lexical knowledge, language acquisition mechanisms, and/or constraints on memory (Coady & Evans, 2008). What emerges from the literature on phonotactic acquisition is that infants' knowledge of the sound patterns of their NLs impacts how words are learned and pronounced in the first year and beyond.

Word learning

Infants typically produce their first words at around 12 months of age but begin comprehending words much earlier. As young as six to nine months, infants recognize very common words, including labels for body parts, household items and names of familiar individuals (Bergelson & Swingley, 2012; Tincoff & Jusczyk, 1999). This early understanding is impressive (yet normative), as in order to learn words infants must accomplish two difficult feats: segmenting words from continuous speech, which has no consistent demarcations of word boundaries, and mapping words with their correct meanings.

The ability to segment and later recognize individual words from fluent speech is evident by 7.5 months (Jusczyk & Aslin, 1995). If provided with additional cues or further familiarization, success is seen even earlier, at six months (Thiessen & Saffran, 2003; Bortfeld, Morgan, Golinkoff & Rathbun, 2005). One mechanism infants may use to help identify words is the conditional probability of transitions between different syllables. For example, the syllables <pre> and <ty> have a high probability of being heard together, with <pre> preceeding <ty> (making the word <pretty>). Likewise, there is a high likelihood that the syllable <bay> is followed by the syllable <bee> (making the word <baby>). In contrast, the chance that the syllable <ty> is followed by <bay> (as would be the case in the phrase <pretty baby>) is significantly less. By eight months of age, infants are sensitive to such statistical probabilities in language, and are more likely to segment and learn syllable combinations that have high probabilities of occurring together (Aslin, Saffran & Newport, 1998; Saffran, Werker & Werner, 2006; Graf-Estes, Evans, Alibali & Saffran, 2007). Other cues that infants have been shown to use in word segmentation include stress (identifying words based on the common stress pattern used in their language: Jusczyk, Houston & Newsome, 1999), allophonic differences in the pronunciation of phonemes in word-initial versus word-medial or word-final positions (Jusczyk, Hohne & Bauman, 1999) and phonotactics, as described above.

Another aspect of word learning that has been studied in depth is the specificity of infants' early phonological representations of words. When tested on familiar words, young word-learners appear sensitive to phonetic detail: infants look to the correct object when presented with a correct pronunciation of its label (e.g. they look to a picture of a baby versus a picture of a car when presented with the label <baby>), but not when the word is mispronounced (e.g. when presented with the label <vaby>) (Swingley & Aslin, 2000, 2002). However, infants initially seem to have difficulty learning novel similar-sounding labels. When 14-month-old infants are taught two minimally different labels (e.g. <bin> and <din>) in an experimental word learning task, they fail to learn the novel words, even in the same task to which infants of this age can successfully learn non-minimally different labels (e.g. <lif> and <neem>) (Werker, Cohen et al., 1998). Not until 17–20 months do infants successfully learn novel minimally different labels in such a task (Werker, Cohen, Lloyd, Casasola & Stager, 1998). Of interest, if the acoustic differences between minimal words are made more obvious (Curtin, Fennell & Escudero, 2009), the memory demands are decreased (e.g. Fennell, 2011; Yoshida, Fennell, Swingley & Werker, 2009) or the referential intent is made more clear (Fennell & Waxman, 2013), infants of 14 months can succeed, revealing that there are developmental steps even in the transition to the phonological use of native phonetic categories. One explanation for these findings is that it is not until 17–20 months that infants have established more stable NL phonological representations that serve to guide word learning across a variety of circumstances (Werker & Curtin, 2005).

Further evidence that infants have acquired stable NL phonological representations by 17–18 months comes from work investigating infants' willingness to accept non-native language sounds in labels (names for objects, places or things). At 14 months of age, if infants are shown cues that novel labels containing unfamiliar non-native language sounds (i.e. click consonants from African click languages) are intended to refer to an object, infants will accept and successfully learn such non-native labels as names for objects. However, by 20 months, infants appear unwilling or unable to do so, even provided with the same referential cues (May & Werker, 2014). Building upon the previously described work on minimal pair word learning, these findings suggest that by 17–20 months infants have gained sufficient knowledge of the phonology of their NL to support the learning of new words.

To produce a word, a speaker must retrieve stored representations of the word form (the sounds and structure of the sounds) from memory. The research described above based on measures of language comprehension indicates that, by 17–20 months, infants' receptive knowledge of words and their sounds is fairly well developed. However, a striking characteristic of early speech production is that children's pronunciations deviate from the adult form, such as omitting consonants and syllables (<banana> becomes <nana> and <train> becomes <tain>). Child phonology researchers have interpreted these systematic errors in speech production as stemming from an underdeveloped or child specific grammar (Demuth, 2011). Other factors, such as articulatory ease and acoustic salience, are also predictive factors for children's speech productions; however, these factors can also depend on the sounds' frequency or function in a language. For example, while /v/ is acquired late in English (around four years), it is mastered earlier in Swedish (Ingram, 1988). More recently, researchers have begun to examine patterns in children's word productions to study phonological and lexical representations and how these representations are accessed during the process of spoken word production (Munson et al., 2005). Sosa and Stoel-Gammon (2012) found that children produced high-frequency words with less variability than low-frequency words, demonstrating that lexical frequency is a factor in speech production. Anderson (2008) found that children were faster at producing early-acquired words (<hat>, <fish>) compared to late-acquired words (<heart>, <bell>). In addition, rather than considering phonological and word development as independent, it appears there may be a bidirectional relationship between the developing sound system and productive lexical knowledge (Curtin & Zamuner, 2014; Werker & Curtin, 2005; Stoel-Gammon, 2011; Vihman, 2017). Hence, research is now examining how the knowledge of a sound system emerges from the existing lexicon and how the knowledge of the sound system influences what words are acquired in both comprehension and production.

Main research methods

Preferential looking

Many of the methodologies used to examine speech perception utilize infants' looking time as a dependent variable. Unlike adult or child subjects, infants have little or no control over their verbal responses, or many of their physical responses. However, infants will look to a visual display when interested in, or surprised by, a sound. Commonly used procedures thus utilize looking behaviour as a dependent variable, exposing infants to two or more different stimuli or types of stimuli and measuring the time infants look in response. If infants look for different amounts of time, it is taken as evidence that they are able to detect a difference between the stimuli and/or prefer the stimuli on which they look longer.

While the preferential looking method is widely employed, one caveat is that it cannot illuminate *why* infants look longer to one type of stimulus over another. Infants' visual preference may be driven by familiarity, by a lack of familiarity (a surprise response) or by a difference in visual or acoustic complexity. For this reason, results obtained from preferential looking paradigms should be interpreted cautiously.

Habituation

Habituation procedures have been used to test infants' discrimination and learning abilities. The basic premise is that infants are first 'habituated' to a stimulus or type of stimulus until their attention decreases, at which point they are shown a new stimulus and whether their attention recovers (or 'dishabituates') is assessed. If infants have learned and remember what they were exposed to during the habituation phase of the experiment, and can detect the difference between the habituation stimuli and the novel stimuli, it is expected that their attention should increase when exposed to the novel stimuli.

Most commonly, infant habituation studies utilize infants' looking time as a metric of interest. For example, in the 'switch' task (Werker et al., 1998), infants are habituated to two word–object pairings: they are shown these pairings repeatedly until their looking to the target objects decreases a pre-defined amount (typically to 50–65 per cent of their initial looking). Two test trials follow habituation: a 'same' trial, in which one of the same word–object pairings shown during the habituation phase is presented again, and a 'switch' trial, in which a novel pairing of one of the words and one of the objects from the habituation phase is presented (i.e. if infants are exposed to Object A, labelled <lif>, and Object B, labelled <neem>, the 'switch' trial might consist of Object A labelled <neem>). If infants have learned the word–object association, they should show a recovery in looking time to the 'switch' trial as compared to the 'same' trial. Habituation procedures can also utilize metrics other than looking time as a proxy for infants' attention, such as their sucking response (in high amplitude sucking procedures; see Byers-Heinlein, 2014).

Head-turn preference procedure (HPP)

Another common method is the head-turn preference procedure (HPP) (Fernald, 1985) and the modified HPP, which has an additional training phase before the testing phase.

The experiment is contingent on the infants' head-turn behaviour that is being recorded online by an experimenter. Infants' looking behaviour is measured as they listen to different types of stimuli over the course of the experimental trials (see Johnson & Zamuner, 2010, for a discussion of the paradigm). Differences in looking times across the experimental conditions are taken as an indicator that infants can distinguish between the stimuli, and their linguistic preferences and knowledge are inferred from their listening and looking behaviour. To illustrate, one of the first studies to examine phonotactic acquisition used the HPP (Friederici & Wessels, 1993). Nine-month-old infants were presented with different trials comprised of non-words with manipulated phonotactics (lists of phonotactically permissible or phonotactically non-permissible non-words). Infants' mean looking time was significantly longer during trials with phonotactically permissible compared to (non-permissible) non-words. The paradigm has been used to test a variety of issues in phonological development, ranging from infants' sensitivity to lower-level subphonemic cues (Johnson, 2008; McMurray & Aslin, 2005) to higher units such as multi-word phonological phrases (Sonderstrom, Nelson & Jusczyk, 2005).

Neuroimaging methods

In recent years, researchers have increasingly moved beyond using only behavioural techniques to examine speech perception in infants, and have incorporated a variety of neuroimaging methods. The most commonly used methods with infants include electro-encephalogram (EEG)/event-related potentials (ERP), functional magnetic resonance imaging (fMRI), and functional near-infrared spectroscopy (fNIRS).

With EEG/ERP, brain activity is assessed through the measurement of the electrical activity associated with neuronal firing. For both EEG (a continuous measure of electrical activity) and ERP (recordings that are time-locked to the presentation of specific stimulus), electrical sensors that detect voltage changes are placed on an infant's scalp. Advantages of EEG/ERP are that the measurements have excellent temporal accuracy and are relatively easy to collect. However, there is limited spatial accuracy, and EEG/ERP is sensitive to artefacts from movement. Both fMRI and fNIRS measure changes in the hemodynamic response associated with cortical activity. While fMRI assess this response through the use of magnetic fields, fNIRS utilizes near-infrared light. Both methods have good spatial resolution (with fMRI being superior to fNIRS) yet restricted temporal accuracy (see Gervain et al., 2011).

Speech production methods

Among the earliest examinations of speech production were diary studies of children's speech, such as Darwin's (1877) study of his son's development. While rich diary studies can allow for an assessment of language across development, some of the major drawbacks are that they cannot allow for generalizations across large groups of children, and one cannot assess the accuracy of the phonetic transcriptions, as phonetic transcriptions have been shown to change depending on the transcriber's expectations of the speaker's age (Munson, Edwards, Schellinger, Beckman & Meyer, 2010). Large-scale databases such as CHILDES and PHON have made it possible for researchers to investigate phonological development, with access to phonetic transcriptions and audio files (MacWhinney, 2000; Rose & MacWhinney, 2014). However, these large-scale corpora are not suitable for all research questions. For example, a researcher may want to examine how children produce words with a specific phonological structure or they may be interested in looking at how children recall a newly learned word after a specific period of time. When there are not enough data available from spontaneous and naturalistic sources, researchers can use experimental methodologies, such as the picture naming task (PNT) (Brooks, Seiger-Gardner, Obeid & MacWhinney, 2015; Zamuner, Kilbertus & Weinhold, in press) and non-word repetition task (NWRT) (Zamuner & Johnson, 2011). In these tasks, children as young as two to three years name images (PNT) or repeat non-words (NWRT), which are controlled for their phonological properties. Children's accuracy and speech errors are then coded depending on the research question. The systematic errors in children's production are used to investigate a range of issues in phonological development, such as phonological and lexical knowledge, grammars, language acquisition mechanisms, and/or memory. For example, a child may repeat the non-word <thaff> as <taff>. The substitution of 'th' as 't' can stem from multiple sources, such as an error in perception, difficulty in articulation, memory constraints or limited language experience with 'th', which does not occur at the beginning of many English words. Other methods are standardized production tests (review in Eisenberg & Hitchcock, 2010), tasks from laboratory phonology, such as kinetic measurements or lip and jaw movement during production (Heisler, Goffman & Younger, 2010), acoustic analyses (Song, Demuth & Shattuck-Hufnagel, 2012) and ultrasound (Lin & Demuth, 2015). Lastly, a new paradigm in the adult 'production effect' literature has been recently adapted to study child language (Icht & Mama, 2015; Zamuner et al., in press). Participants are trained on a set of words; a subset of the words is repeated aloud by the participants and a subset is heard silently. At test, participants are tested on their recall and recognition of the trained items to determine whether producing the items during training improves later recall and recognition. An advantage for produced items at recall is found when children are trained on real words (Icht & Mama, 2015); however, the opposite pattern is found when children are trained on novel words, such that children recall more items that are heard silently (Zamuner et al., in press). These results, along with findings from the adult literature, show that the effect of speech production on word learning interacts with factors such as attention and task complexity, the linguistic stimuli, and the developmental stage of the learner. We return to the implications of this literature for pronunciation at the end of the following section.

Recommendations for practice

There are many recommendations for practice that follow from the research reviewed above. First and foremost, these studies reveal that infants begin learning about their NL long before they begin to talk; hence it is important to speak to young infants and to do so in a fashion that will engage their interest. Similarly, it is important to ensure that their hearing is intact (e.g. no middle ear infection) so that they can progress according to schedule. The relationship between perception and production shows that listening in infancy is important not only for establishing veridical phonological comprehension categories, but also for guiding speech production. Indeed, longitudinal studies indicate that the precision of native phonetic perceptual categories in infancy predicts vocabulary size at two years (Tsao, Liu & Kuhl 2004) and the use of phonological categories to guide word learning at 14–20 months can help predict phonological awareness, and other pre-reading skills, at three years of age (Bernhardt, Kemp & Werker 2007), particularly among children with low vocabulary in the toddler years (Kemp et al., 2017).

Recommendations for remediation also follow from this review. On the one hand, while phonological acquisition begins early, it takes a long time to complete. Knowing about the steps in phonological development, and the age ranges within which these steps are typically achieved, positions speech pathologists to intervene at earlier ages and to do so in a targeted fashion. Additional research linking these infant skills to the use of reading, spelling, and even the use of narrative in everyday speech, are important directions for further research.

Another recommendation is for the teaching of pronunciation for a second language (L2). When teaching L2 pronunciation to adolescents and adults, learners will already have a fully developed (mature) NL phonology in place. This NL phonological system can act, at least in part, as a powerful perceptual filter when L2 learners are presented with a new phonological system. This is especially relevant when one considers the variety of different language systems that learners acquire. For example, an L2 learner of German who speaks English as an NL will have the most difficulty with the subset of German sounds that do not occur in English, but for the most part, the two languages share many common segmental and prosodic characteristics. However, it will be harder for the same speaker to learn an L2 phonological system that is more unique from the NL, such as learning a tonal language as an L2, because a tonal system was not established during the early language learning years described in this chapter. Thus, it is important for L2 teachers to know that the L2 acquisition system will be different from the acquisition of NL phonology, because a matured and fully developed NL phonological system, which took years to develop, is already in place. The field of L2 cognitive phonology proposes that L2 learners need to be provided with opportunities to develop awareness of the differences between the NL and L2 phonological systems, that mere explaining and practice is not enough, and that time and opportunity is needed because developing this awareness is more difficult than learning an NL (Fraser, 2006, 2010). L2 learners need to begin to notice such differences for themselves (and also that their teachers play essential roles in helping to facilitate such noticing and awareness building). Such awareness is a necessary condition for eventual changes in the L2 intelligibility to take place.

Our last recommendation is to point out that learning pronunciation also interplays with other aspects of word learning. There is a large body of literature on the production effect (MacLeod, Gopie, Hourihan, Neary & Ozubko, 2010; Zamuner, Morin-Lessard, Strahm & Page, 2016), which indicates that adults are better at recalling and recognizing words that are read aloud compared to words read silently. However, a handful of studies have reported that the production effect can be attenuated or reversed (Dahlen & Caldwell-Harris, 2013; Kaushanskaya & Yoo, 2011). When adults are taught novel words that contain phonemes outside their NL repertoire, participants learn the novel words better if they do not overtly produce them during training (Kaushanskaya & Yoo, 2011). Part of the disruption stems from mismatches between the auditory target and adults' non-target-like productions. Thus, practitioners may want to consider the students' NL phonology and the target L2 phonology when combining pronunciation practice and vocabulary learning. Also see Barcroft (2015), who discusses task- and cognitive-related effects in second language learning.

Future directions

Many of the researchers studying phonological development focus exclusively on speech perception and word comprehension, to the exclusion of a full consideration of production. This is in part because the methods are distinct: studies of word comprehension and word learning build on and reflect the empirical methods first developed for speech perception studies and also adapt designs used in adult psycholinguistic studies, while studies of speech production continue to be more contextually situated and descriptive. Throughout this chapter we have attempted to describe research on perception and comprehension as well as research on production. But it is important to note that a complete theory of phonological development that places equal emphasis on perception and production is still lacking. We would argue that this should be the next step for the field of phonological development.

Further reading

Saffran, J. R., Werker, J. F., & Werner, L. A. (2006). The infant's auditory world: Hearing, speech, and the beginnings of language. In R. Siegler & D. Kuhn (Eds), *Handbook of Child Psychology: Vol. 2. Cognition, Perception and Language* (6th ed., pp. 58–108). New York, NY: Wiley. This chapter provides a comprehensive review on early auditory development, speech perception and language learning.

Werker, J. F., & Curtin, S. (2005). PRIMIR: A developmental framework of infant speech processing. *Language Learning and Development*, *1*(2), 197–234. This article provides a framework for speech perception and word learning in infancy.

Zamuner, T. S., & Johnson, E. J. (2011). Methodology in phonological acquisition: Assessing the joint development of speech perception and production. In B. Botma, N. Kula, & K. Nasukawa (Eds), *Continuum handbook to phonology* (pp. 16–29). Amsterdam: Continuum. This chapter describes methodologies used to examine the development of both speech perception and speech production.

Related topics

Phonetics for language teachers; phonology for language teachers; models of L2 speech; intonation.

References

Albareda-Castellot, B., Pons, F., & Sebastián-Gallés, N. (2011). The acquisition of phonetic categories in bilingual infants: new data from an anticipatory eye movement paradigm. *Developmental Science*, *14*, 395–401.

Anderson, J. D. (2008). Age of acquisition and repetition priming effects on picture naming of children who do and do not stutter. *Journal of Fluency Disorders*, *33*(2), 135–155.

Archer, S. L., & Curtin, S. (2011). Perceiving onset clusters in infancy. *Infant Behavior and Development*, *34*(4), 534–540.

Archer, S., Zamuner, T. S., Fais, L., Engel, K., & Curtin, S. (2016). Infants' discrimination of consonants: Interplay between word position and acoustic saliency. *Language Learning and Development*, *12*, 60–78.

Aslin, R. N., Saffran, J. R., & Newport, E. L. (1998). Computation of conditional probability statistics by 8-month-old infants. *Psychological Science*, *9*(4), 321–324.

Baker, S. A., Golinkoff, R. M., & Petitto, L. A. (2006). New insights into old puzzles from infants' perception of soundless phonetic units. *Language Learning and Development*, *2*, 147–162.

Barcroft, J. (2015). *Lexical input processing and vocabulary learning (Vol. 43)*. Amsterdam: John Benjamins.

Bates, E., & Dick, F. (2002). Language, gesture, and the developing brain. *Developmental Psychobiology*, *40*(3), 293–310.

Bergelson, E., & Swingley, D. (2012). At 6–9 months, human infants know the meanings of many common nouns. *Proceedings of the National Academy of Sciences*, *109*(9), 3253–3258.

Bernhardt, B. M., Kemp, N., & Werker, J. F. (2007). Early word-object associations and later language development. *First Language*, *27*, 315–328.

Bertoncini, J., Bijeljac-Babic, R., Jusczyk, P. W., Kennedy, L. J., & Mehler, J. (1988). An investigation of young infants' perceptual representations of speech sounds. *Journal of Experimental Psychology: General*, *117*(1), 21–33.

Bortfeld, H., Morgan, J. L., Golinkoff, R. M., & Rathbun, K. (2005). Mommy and me: Familiar names help launch babies into speech-stream segmentation. *Psychological Science, 16*(4), 298–304.

Bosch, L., & Sebastián-Gallés, N. (2003). Simultaneous bilingualism and the perception of a language-specific vowel contrast in the first year of life. *Language and Speech, 46*, 217–43.

Brooks, P. J., Seiger-Gardner, L., Obeid, R., & MacWhinney, B. (2015). Phonological priming with nonwords in children with and without specific language impairment. *Journal of Speech, Language, and Hearing Research, 58*(4), 1210–1223.

Burns, T. C., Yoshida, K. A., Hill, K., & Werker, J. F. (2007). The development of phonetic representation in bilingual and monolingual infants. *Applied Psycholinguistics, 28*(3), 455–474.

Byers-Heinlein, K. (2014). High amplitude sucking. In E. Brooks & V. Kempe (Eds), *Encyclopedia of language acquisition* (pp. 263–264). Thousand Oaks, CA: Sage.

Coady, J. A., & Evans, J. L. (2008). Uses and interpretations of non-word repetition tasks in children with and without specific language impairment (SLI). *International Journal of Language & Communication Disorders, 43*, 1–40.

Cristià, A., & Seidl, A. (2008). Is infants' learning of sound patterns constrained by phonological features? *Language Learning and Development, 4*, 203–227.

Cristià, A., Seidl, A., & Gerken, L. A. (2011). Learning classes of sounds in infancy. *University of Pennsylvania Working Papers in Linguistics, 17*, 69–76.

Curtin, S., Fennell, C., & Escudero, P. (2009). Weighting of vowel cues explains patterns of word–object associative learning. *Developmental Science, 12*(5), 725–731.

Curtin, S., & Zamuner, T. S. (2014). Understanding the developing sound system: interactions between sounds and words. *Wiley Interdisciplinary Reviews: Cognitive Science, 5*(5), 589–602.

Dahlen, K., & Caldwell-Harris, C. (2013). Rehearsal and aptitude in foreign vocabulary learning. The *Modern Language Journal, 97*(4), 902–916.

Darwin, C. (1877). A biographical sketch of an infant. *Mind* (7), 285–294.

Dehaene-Lambertz, G., & Gliga, T. (2004). Common neural basis for phoneme processing in infants and adults. *Journal of Cognitive Neuroscience, 16*(8), 1375–1387.

Dehaene-Lambertz, G., Hertz-Pannier, L., Dubois, J., & Dehaene, S. (2008). How does early brain organization promote language acquisition in humans?. *European Review, 16*(4), 399–411.

Demuth, K. (2011). The acquisition of phonology. In J. A. Goldsmith, J. Riggle, & A. Yu (Eds), The *handbook of phonological theory* (pp. 571–595). Malden, MA: Blackwell.

Eimas, P. D., Siqueland, E. R., Jusczyk, P., & Vigorito, J. (1971). Speech perception in infants. *Science, 171*, 303–306.

Eisenberg, S. L., & Hitchcock, E. R. (2010). Using standardized tests to inventory consonant and vowel production: A comparison of 11 tests of articulation and phonology. *Language, Speech, and Hearing Services in Schools, 41*(4), 488–503.

Elsabbagh, M., Hohenberger, A., Campos, R., Van Herwegen, J., Serres, J., de Schonen, S., . . . Karmiloff-Smith, A. (2013). Narrowing perceptual sensitivity to the native language in infancy: exogenous influences on developmental timing. *Behavioral Sciences, 3*(1), 120–132.

Emmorey, K. (2001). *Language, cognition, and the brain: Insights from sign language research.* Mahwah, NJ: Lawrence Erlbaum.

Feldman, N., Griffiths, T., & Morgan, J. (2009). Learning phonetic categories by learning a lexicon. *Proceedings of the 31st Annual Conference of the Cognitive Science Society*, 2208–2213.

Fennell, C. T. (2011). Object familiarity enhances infants' use of phonetic detail in novel words, *Infancy, 16*(3), 1–15.

Fennell, C. T., & Waxman, S. R. (2010). What paradox? Referential cues allow for infant use of phonetic detail in word learning. *Child Development, 81*(5), 1376–1383.

Fernald, A. (1985). Four-month-old infants prefer to listen to motherese. *Infant Behaviour and Development, 8*, 181–195.

Fraser, H. (2006). Helping teachers help students with pronunciation: A cognitive approach. *Prospect, 21*, 80-94.

Fraser, H. (2010). Cognitive theory as a tool for teaching second language pronunciation. *Fostering Language Teaching Efficiency through Cognitive Linguistics*, 357–379.

Friederici, A. D., & Wessels, J. M. (1993), Phonotactic knowledge and its use in infant speech perception. *Perception and Psychophysics, 54*, 287–295.

Gervain, J., & Mehler, J. (2010). Speech perception and language acquisition in the first year of life. *Annual Review of Psychology, 61*, 191–218.

Gervain, J., Mehler, J., Werker, J. F., Nelson, C. A., Csibra, G., Lloyd-Fox, S., . . . Aslin, R. N. (2011). Near-infrared spectroscopy: a report from the McDonnell infant methodology consortium. *Developmental Cognitive Neuroscience, 1*(1), 22–46.

Gonzalez-Gomez, N., Poltrock, S., & Nazzi, T. (2013). A 'bat' is easier to learn than a 'tab': Effects of relative phonotactic frequency on infant word learning. *PloS One, 8*(3), e59601– e59601.

Graf-Estes, K., & Bowen, S. (2013). Learning about sounds contributes to learning about words: Effects of prosody and phonotactics on infant word learning. *Journal of Experimental Child Psychology, 114*(3), 405–417.

Graf-Estes, K., Evans, J. L., Alibali, M. W., & Saffran, J. R. (2007). Can infants map meaning to newly segmented words? Statistical segmentation and word learning. *Psychological Science, 18*(3), 254–260.

Heisler, L., Goffman, L., & Younger, B. (2010). Lexical and articulatory interactions in children's language production. *Developmental Science, 13*(5), 722–730.

Hochmann, J. R., & Papeo, L. (2014). The invariance problem in infancy: A pupillometry study. *Psychological Science, 25*(11), 2038–2046.

Icht, M., & Mama, Y. (2015). The production effect in memory: A prominent mnemonic in children. *Journal of Child Language, 42*(5), 1102–1124.

Ingram, D. (1988). The acquisition of word-initial [v]. *Language and Speech, 31*(1), 77–85.

Jakobson, R. (1941). *Child language, aphasia and linguistic universals.* The Hague: Mouton.

Johnson, E. J., & Zamuner, T. S. (2010). Using infant and toddler testing methods in language acquisition research. In E. Blom & S. Unsworth (Eds), *Experimental methods in language acquisition research* (pp. 73–93). Amsterdam: John Benjamins.

Johnson, E. K. (2008). Infants use prosodically conditioned acoustic-phonetic cues to extract words from speech. *The Journal of the Acoustical Society of America, 123*(6), EL144–EL148.

Jusczyk, P. W., & Aslin, R. N. (1995). Infants' detection of the sound patterns of words in fluent speech. *Cognitive Psychology, 29*(1), 1–23.

Jusczyk, P. W., Friederici, A. D., Wessels, J. M., Svenkerud, V., & Jusczyk, A. M. (1993). Infants' sensitivity to the sound patterns of native language words. *Journal of Memory and Language, 32*, 402–420.

Jusczyk, P. W., Hohne, E. A., & Bauman, A. (1999). Infants' sensitivity to allophonic cues for word segmentation. *Perception & Psychophysics, 61*(8), 1465.

Jusczyk, P. W., Houston, D. M., & Newsome, M. (1999). The beginnings of word segmentation in English-learning infants. *Cognitive Psychology, 39*(3), 159–207.

Jusczyk, P. W., Luce, P. A. & Charles-Luce, J. (1994), Infants' sensitivity to phonotactic patterns in the native language. *Journal of Memory and Language, 33*(5), 630–645.

Kaushanskaya, M. & Yoo, J. (2011). Rehearsal effects in adult word learning. *Language and Cognitive Processes, 26*, 121–148.

Kemp, N., Scott, J., Bernhardt, B. M., Johnson, C. E., Siegel, L.S., & Werker, J. F. (2017). Minimal pair word learning and vocabulary size: links with later language skills. *Applied Psycholinguistics, 38*(2), 289–314.

Kuhl, P. K. (1979). Speech perception in early infancy: Perceptual development in the second year of life: a longitudinal study. *Child Development, 75*(4), 1067–1084.

Kuhl, P. K. (2004). Early language acquisition: Cracking the speech code. *Nature Reviews Neuroscience, 5*(11), 831–843.

Kuhl, P. K., Stevens, E., Hayashi, A., Deguchi, T., Kiritani, S. & Iverson, P. (2006). Infants show a facilitation effect for native language phonetic perception between 6 and 12 months. *Developmental Science, 9*(2), F13–F21.

Kuhl, P. K., Tsao, F. M., Liu, H. M. (2003). Foreign-language experience in infancy: Effects of short-term exposure and social interaction on phonetic learning. *Proceedings of the National Academy of Sciences USA, 100*(15), 9096–9101.

Kuhl, P. K., Williams, K. A., Lacerda, F., Stevens, K. N., & Lindblom, B. (1992). Linguistic experience alters phonetic perception in infants by 6 months of age. *Science, 255*(5044), 606–608.

Ladd, D. R. (2011). Phonetics in phonology. In J. Goldsmith, J. Riggle, & A. Yu (Eds), *Handbook of phonological theory* (2nd ed., pp. 348–373). Oxford: Blackwell.

Levelt, C. C. (2012). Perception mirrors production in 14- and 18-month-olds: The case of coda consonants. *Cognition, 123*(1), 174–179.

Lin, S., & Demuth, K. (2015). Children's acquisition of English onset and coda/l: Articulatory evidence. *Journal of Speech, Language, and Hearing Research, 58*(1), 13–27.

MacKenzie, H., Curtin, S., & Graham, S. A. (2012). 12-month-olds' phonotactic knowledge guides their word–object mappings. *Child Development, 83*(4), 1129–1136.

MacLeod, C. M., Gopie, N., Hourihan, K. L., Neary, K. R., & Ozubko, J. D. (2010). The production effect: Delineation of a phenomenon. *Journal of Experimental Psychology: Learning, Memory, and Cognition, 36*(3), 671–685.

MacWhinney, B. (2000). The CHILDES project: Tools for analyzing talk (3rd ed.). Mahwah, NJ: Lawrence Erlbaum.

Mahmoudzadeh, M., Dehaene-Lambertz, G., Fournier, M., Kongolo, G., Goudjil, S., Dubois, J., ... & Wallois, F. (2013). Syllabic discrimination in premature human infants prior to complete formation of cortical layers. *Proceedings of the National Academy of Sciences, 110*(12), 4846–4851.

Mattock, K., Molnar, M., Polka, L., & Burnham, D. (2008). The developmental course of lexical tone perception in the first year of life. *Cognition, 106*(3), 1367–1381.

Mattys, S. L., & Jusczyk, P. W. (2001). Phonotactic cues for segmentation of fluent speech by infants. *Cognition, 78*(2), 91–121.

Maurer, D., & Werker, J. F. (2014). Perceptual narrowing during infancy: A comparison of language and faces. *Developmental Psychobiology, 56*(2), 154–178.

May, L., & Werker, J. F. (2014). Can a click be a word? Infants' learning of non-native words. *Infancy, 19*(3), 281–300.

Maye, J., Weiss, D. J., & Aslin, R. N. (2008). Statistical phonetic learning in infants: Facilitation and feature generalization. *Developmental Science, 11*(1), 122–134.

Maye, J., Werker, J. F., & Gerken, L. (2002). Infant sensitivity to distributional information can affect phonetic discrimination. *Cognition, 82*(3), B101–B111.

McMurray, B., & Aslin, R. (2005). Infants are sensitive to within-category variation in speech perception. *Cognition, 95*(2), B15–B26.

Munson, B., Edwards, J., & Beckman, M. E., (2005). Relationships between nonword repetition accuracy and other measures of linguistic development in children with phonological disorders. *Journal of Speech, Language, and Hearing Research, 48*, 61–78.

Munson, B., Edwards, J., Schellinger, S. K., Beckman, M. E., & Meyer, M. K. (2010). Deconstructing phonetic transcription: Covert contrast, perceptual bias, and an extraterrestrial view of Vox Humana. *Clinical Linguistics & Phonetics, 24*(4–5), 245–260.

Narayan, C., Werker, J. F., & Beddor, P. (2010). The interaction between acoustic salience and language experience in developmental speech perception: Evidence from nasal place discrimination. *Developmental Science, 13*(3), 407–420.

Palmer, S. B, Fais, L., Golinkoff, R. M., & Werker, J. F. (2012) Perceptual narrowing of linguistic sign occurs in the first year of life. *Child Development, 83*(2), 543–553.

Peña, M, Werker, J. F. &, Dehaene-Lambertz, G. (2012). Earlier speech exposure does not accelerate speech acquisition. *Journal of Neuroscience, 32*, 11159–11163.

Peperkamp, S., Le Calvez, R., Nadal, J., & Dupoux, E. (2006). The acquisition of allophonic rules: Statistical learning with linguistic constraints. *Cognition, 101*(3), B31–B41.

Petitto, L. A. (1994). Are signed languages 'real' languages. Evidence from American Sign Language and Langue des Signes Québécoise. Reprinted from: *Signpost (International Quarterly of the Sign Linguistics Association), 7*(3), 1–10.

Pierrehumbert, J. (2003). Phonetic diversity, statistical learning, and acquisition of phonology. *Language and Speech, 46*(2–3), 115–154.

Polka, L., & Werker, J. F. (1994). Developmental changes in perception of nonnative vowel contrasts. *Journal of Experimental Psychology: Human Perception and Performance, 20*(2), 421–435.

Rose, Y., & MacWhinney, B. (2014). The PHONBANK initiative. *The Oxford Handbook of Corpus Phonology*, 380–401.

Saffran, J. R., Werker, J. F., & Werner, L. A. (2006). The infant's auditory world: Hearing, speech, and the beginnings of language. In W. Damon & R. M. Lerner (Series Eds) & R. Siegler & D. Kuhn (Vol. Eds), *Handbook of child psychology: Vol. 2. Cognition, perception and language* (6th ed., pp. 58–108). New York, NY: Wiley.

Sato, Y., Y. Sogabe & R. Mazuka. 2010. Discrimination of phonemic vowel length by Japanese infants. *Developmental Psychology, 46*, 106–119.

Seidl, A., & Buckley, E. (2005). On the learning of arbitrary phonological rules. *Language Learning and Development, 1*(3–4), 289–316.

Soderstrom, M., Nelson, D. G. K., & Jusczyk, P. W. (2005). Six-month-olds recognize clauses embedded in different passages of fluent speech. *Infant Behavior and Development, 28*(1), 87–94.

Song, J. Y., Demuth, K., & Shattuck-Hufnagel, S. (2012). The development of acoustic cues to coda contrasts in young children learning American English. *The Journal of the Acoustical Society of America, 131*(4), 3036–3050.

Sosa, A. V., & Stoel-Gammon, C. (2012). Lexical and phonological effects in early word production. *Journal of Speech, Language and Hearing Research, 55*(2), 596–608.

Stoel-Gammon, C. (2011). Relationships between lexical and phonological development in young children. *Journal of Child Language, 38*(1), 1–34.

Sundara, M., Polka, L., & Genesee, F. (2006). Language-experience facilitates discrimination of / d-/ in monolingual and bilingual acquisition of English. *Cognition, 100*(2), 369–388.

Swingley, D. (2009). Contributions of infant word learning to language development. *Philosophical Transactions of the Royal Society B: Biological Sciences, 364*(1536), 3617–3632.

Swingley, D., & Aslin, R. N. (2000). Spoken word recognition and lexical representation in very young children. *Cognition, 76*(2), 147–166.

Swingley, D., & Aslin, R. N. (2002). Lexical neighborhoods and the word-form representations of 14-month-olds. *Psychological Science, 13*(5), 480–484.

Thiessen, E. D., & Saffran, J. R. (2003). When cues collide: use of stress and statistical cues to word boundaries by 7-to 9-month-old infants. *Developmental Psychology, 39*(4), 706.

Tincoff, R., & Jusczyk, P. W. (1999). Some beginnings of word comprehension in 6-month-olds. *Psychological Science, 10*(2), 172–175.

Trubetskoy, N. S. (1969). *Principles of Phonology.* Berkeley, CA: University of California Press.

Tsao, F. M., Liu, H. M., & Kuhl, P. K. (2004). Speech perception in infancy predicts language development in the second year of life: A longitudinal study. *Child Development,* 1067–1084.

Vihman, M. M. (2017). Learning words and learning sounds: Advances in language development. *British Journal of Psychology.*

Vihman, M. M., Macken, M. A., Miller, R., Simmons, H., & Miller, J. (1985). From babbling to speech: A re-assessment of the continuity issue. *Language, 61*(2), 397–445.

Waugh, L. (1976). *Roman Jakobson's science of language.* Lisse: Peter de Riddler.

Weikum, W. M., Oberlander, T. F., Hensch, T. K., & Werker, J. F. (2012). Prenatal exposure to antidepressants and depressed maternal mood alter trajectory of infant speech perception. *Proceedings of the National Academy of Sciences, 109(Supplement 2),* 17221–17227.

Werker, J. F., Cohen, L. B., Lloyd, V. L., Casasola, M., & Stager, C. L. (1998). Acquisition of word–object associations by 14-month-old infants. *Developmental Psychology, 34*(6), 1289.

Werker, J. F., & Curtin, S. (2005). PRIMIR: A developmental framework of infant speech processing. *Language Learning and Development, 1*(2), 197–234.

Werker, J. F., Fennell, C. T., Corcoran, K. M., & Stager, C. L. (2002). Infants' ability to learn phonetically similar words: Effects of age and vocabulary size. *Infancy, 3*(1), 1–30.

Werker, J. F., & Gervain, G. (2013). Speech perception in infancy: A foundation for language acquisition. *The Oxford Handbook of Developmental Psychology, 1,* 909–925.

Werker, J. F., & Hensch, T. K. (2015). Critical periods in speech perception: New directions. *Annual Review of Psychology, 66*(1), 173–196.

Werker, J. F., & Tees, R. (1984). Cross-language speech perception: Evidence for perceptual reorganization during the first year of life. *Infant Behavior and Development, 7,* 49–63.

Werker, J. F., Yeung, H. H., & Yoshida, K. A. (2012). How do infants become experts at native-speech perception?. *Current Directions in Psychological Science, 21*(4), 221–226.

Yeung, H. H., & Werker, J. F. (2009). Learning words' sounds before learning how words sound: 9-month- olds use distinct objects as cues to categorize speech information. *Cognition, 113,* 234–243.

Yoshida, K. A., Fennell, C. T., Swingley, D., & Werker, J. F. (2009). Fourteen-month-old infants learn similar-sounding words. *Developmental Science, 12*(3), 412–418.

Yoshida, K. A., Pons, F., Maye, J., & Werker, J. F. (2010). Distributional phonetic learning at 10 months of age. *Infancy, 15,* 420–433.

Zamuner, T. S. (2006). Sensitivity to word-final phonotactics in 9- to 16-month-old infants. *Infancy, 10,* 77–95.

Zamuner, T. S. (2009), Phonological probabilities at the onset of language development: Speech production and word position. *Journal of Speech, Language and Hearing Research, 52,* 49–60.

Zamuner, T. S. (2013). Perceptual evidence for young children's developing knowledge of phonotactic probabilities. *Language Acquisition, 20*, 241–253.

Zamuner, T. S., & Johnson, E. J. (2011). Methodology in phonological acquisition: Assessing the joint development of speech perception and production. In B. Botma, N. Kula, & K. Nasukawa (Eds), *Continuum handbook to phonology* (pp. 16–29). Amsterdam: Continuum.

Zamuner, T. S., & Kharlamov, V. (2016). Phonotactics and Syllable Structure. In J. Lidz, W. Synder, & J. Pater (Eds), *Oxford handbook of developmental linguistics* (pp. 27–42). Oxford: Oxford University Press.

Zamuner, T. S., Kilbertus, L., & Weinhold, M. (in press). Game-influenced methodology: Addressing data attrition in child development research. *Interntional Journal of Child-Computer Interaction.*

Zamuner, T. S., Morin-Lessard, E., Strahm, S., & Page, M. P. A. (2016). Spoken word recognition of novel words, either produced or only heard during training. *Journal of Memory and Language, 89*, 55–67.

Zamuner, T. S., Morin-Lessard, E., Strahm, S., & Page, M. (in press). Reverse production effect: Children recognize novel words better when they are heard rather than produced during training. *Developmental Science.*

5

Second language pronunciation learning

An overview of theoretical perspectives

Jennifer A. Foote and Pavel Trofimovich

Introduction

For many second language (L2) learners, pronunciation is 'simultaneously the most difficult of the language skills and the one they most aspire to master' (Fraser, 2010, p. 358). It is then surprising that pronunciation has been historically under-represented and overlooked in comparison to other areas of second language acquisition (SLA) research. This neglect has been widely discussed and documented (e.g. Deng et al., 2009; Derwing & Munro, 2005). Fortunately, pronunciation research is beginning to catch up to research in other language skills. A new journal of L2 pronunciation has recently been launched (Levis, 2015), a steady stream of pronunciation-related research is being published, and an increasing number of evidence-based pronunciation teaching materials and handbooks are appearing on the market (e.g. Derwing & Munro, 2015; Grant, 2014, 2017), all of which led Thomson and Derwing to declare that 'the tide has shifted' in the area of L2 pronunciation (2015, p. 326).

However, one of the most acute problems, which has persisted despite an increase in studies targeting pronunciation, is a lack of theory to guide pronunciation research. Currently, there are no dominant theories, models, or frameworks that have risen to prominence in the study of L2 pronunciation learning. For example, in a recent summary of 75 studies targeting pronunciation instruction, Thomson and Derwing noted that 'researchers tend to ask *what* the consequences of instruction are, but not *why*' (2015, pp. 334–335, original emphasis), with few researchers framing their studies within a theoretical framework. One reason for this is that existing theoretical perspectives are either too limited or instead too broad in scope to have the potential to take a central role as a view of pronunciation development. Another likely reason is that most well-established theories of SLA have rarely been extended to pronunciation, so few pronunciation researchers are aware of what these theories can contribute to pronunciation development.

Therefore, the goal of this chapter is to take an initial step in confronting the problem of theory by exploring how different theoretical perspectives can inform L2 pronunciation learning. We first discuss what a theory of pronunciation should be able to explain and then explore how linguistic, psychological, interactionist, sociocultural, identity and sociocognitive perspectives can be useful for L2 pronunciation research. To conclude, we discuss the role of research in pronunciation pedagogy and suggest possibilities for moving research forward with theory that can address both social and cognitive aspects of learning.

What must be explained?

Successful theory building requires a clear understanding of the phenomena to be explained. VanPatten and Williams (2015) provide the following list of 10 observable phenomena that a viable theory in SLA should be able to handle (pp. 9–11):

(a) Exposure to input is necessary for SLA.
(b) A good deal of SLA happens incidentally.
(c) Learners come to know more than they have been exposed to in the input.
(d) Learner's output (speech) often follows predictable paths with predictable stages in the acquisition of a given structure.
(e) L2 learning is variable in its outcome.
(f) L2 learning is variable across linguistic subsystems.
(g) There are limits on the effects of frequency on SLA.
(h) There are limits on the effect of a learner's first language on SLA.
(i) There are limits on the effects of instruction in SLA.
(j) There are limits on the effects of output (learner production) on language acquisition.

While this list is a good starting point, it may not provide a comprehensive fit for L2 pronunciation or may not capture its characteristics fully. Compared to other language skills, pronunciation is unique. For example, while learners acquire some aspects of L2 pronunciation, such as word-final consonant voicing, along a predictable path (see Eckman, this volume), it is unclear whether other aspects of pronunciation are subject to developmental sequences and what these sequences might be. Similarly, variability in rates and outcomes of learning is arguably more pronounced for pronunciation than for other dimensions of language. Pronunciation may also be unique among language skills, in that it is highly constrained by such individual differences as learners' age, for example, with exposure to an L2 beyond the first six to nine months after birth resulting in non-native perception abilities (Long, 2007). The pervasive influence of age might also make it unlikely that learners acquire L2 pronunciation incidentally (i.e. without intention to learn and largely without awareness), assuming that the learning mechanisms supporting incidental learning are not readily available to adults (DeKeyser, 2013).

In addition, despite a common belief that learners' native language (L1) 'does not have massive effects on either the processes or outcomes, as once thought' (VanPatten & Williams, 2015, p. 11), the influence of learners' L1 on the rate and ultimate success of L2 pronunciation learning is pervasive, which is acknowledged in multiple theoretical views (e.g. Flege, 2003). Pronunciation is also tied to expressions of a speaker's identity (Lybeck, 2002), perhaps more so than any other aspect of language, and pronunciation is intertwined with attitudes, stereotyping and stigma (Lippi-Green, 2012). Yet the identity dimensions of L2 pronunciation learning are largely absent in theoretical perspectives. Last but not least, the physical articulatory component of pronunciation is perhaps the most obvious characteristic distinguishing it from other skills. Its physical component makes pronunciation 'more like gymnastics than linguistics' (Strevens, 1974, p. 182), and pronunciation instructors often focus on teaching articulation (Foote, Holtby & Derwing, 2012) and believe it to be extremely important (Thomson, 2013). However, theoretical models of L2 pronunciation often favour perception over articulation (e.g. Flege, 2003).

In sum, while no single theory is expected to account for all learning phenomena, a viable theory of L2 pronunciation learning should handle at least some of its most crucial characteristics. These include the importance of input in L2 pronunciation development, the pervasive influence of learners' L1, the significant role of individual differences (including age) in L2 pronunciation learning, and the systematicity and variability of pronunciation development. A viable theory of L2 pronunciation learning should also ideally incorporate sociocultural dimensions of pronunciation learning, such as identity, and acknowledge the motor component of pronunciation as a skill.

Theoretical perspectives on L2 pronunciation learning

Linguistic perspective

Some of the most popular theoretical views of L2 pronunciation come from linguistics and its subfields of phonetics and phonology (see Archibald and Eckman, this volume, for other linguistic perspectives). One prominent view of L2 pronunciation – the perceptual assimilation model (PAM) developed by Best (1995) – focuses on how contrasting L2 vowels and consonants (sounds), such as /r/ and /l/ in English words such as *rock* and *lock*, are initially perceived by non-native listeners. This model assumes that listeners' difficulty with perceiving contrasting L2 sounds depends on how listeners associate L2 sounds in relation to the sounds in their L1. According to PAM, there are several patterns of perceptual relationships between L2 and L1 sounds. For example, contrasting L2 sounds may be perceptually identified as – or, in PAM terminology, assimilated to – a single L1 sound, which would make L2 sounds difficult for non-native listeners to discriminate. Alternatively, both contrasting L2 sounds may be assimilated to the same L1 sound, with one judged a better exemplar of this category; the discriminability of these L2 sounds may range from easy to moderately difficult depending on how different they are from each other and from the L1 category in which they are subsumed. It is also possible that each contrasting L2 sound may be perceptually linked to a unique L1 sound, thus rendering these L2 sounds easily discriminable. Other L2 sounds may be termed 'uncategorizable' or 'non-assimilable' to any L1 sound and are therefore predicted to be easy to distinguish. In essence, PAM relies on the notion of cross-language similarity to predict how easily listeners can differentiate L2 sound contrasts. According to PAM, listeners 'compute' cross-language similarity at the articulatory level, such that they actively compare the gestural properties of L2 sounds with gestural properties of potentially similar L1 sounds.

Though PAM has since been extended to explain perceptual difficulties of L2 learners, not just first-time listeners (Best & Tyler, 2007), it is Flege's speech learning model (SLM) that remains a dominant linguistic model of L2 pronunciation learning (Flege, 1995, 2003). SLM assumes that learning L2 sounds involves creating and using long-term memory representations (categories) for sounds. Yet how well and how quickly learners establish such L2 categories depends on their ability to detect phonetic differences between L1 and L2 sounds. For example, when an L2 sound is distinct from perceptually similar L1 sounds, and L2 learners are sensitive to such differences, it is likely that a separate L2 sound category will be established. In contrast, when an L1–L2 sound pair is highly similar perceptually such that an L2 sound is entirely assimilated, or subsumed within, an L1 sound category, it is less likely that a separate L2 sound category will be formed. Most importantly, SLM assumes that the capacity for learners to learn L2 sounds remains intact across an individual's lifespan, and ascribes an important role to input, in terms of its quantity and quality, in enabling learners to perceive crucial cross-language differences which could lead them to establish L2 sound categories (Flege, 2009).

Although both PAM and SLM have generated considerable research output, the two models remain narrow in their scope, targeting only the learning of individual sounds. The two models succeed the most at explaining how a learner's L1 influences the development of L2 perception and production. SLM also accounts for effects of learners' age, by ascribing age-related difficulties in pronunciation learning to non-maturational or input-related factors (Baker, Trofimovich, Flege, Mack & Halter, 2008; Flege, 2009). Unlike SLM, PAM additionally features a prominent focus on the motor component of speech, as it postulates that speech perception is articulatory, not auditory, in nature, such that listeners primarily perceive speech gestures rather than its acoustic properties. However, the models arguably have little to say about the systematicity and variability of L2 pronunciation learning, apart from stipulating that similarities and differences in the paths and outcomes of learning are related to learners' knowledge of prior languages (with their particular sound inventories) and variation in learners' perceptual experiences throughout learning. Further, research within both models has been criticized for oversimplifying the degree to which specific instances of sounds may be perceived as belonging or not belonging to a perceptual category (Thomson, Nearey & Derwing, 2009). Last but not least, the two models lack a social dimension, leaving the role of identity in pronunciation largely unexplained and unexamined. With the view of the future, it would be important for both PAM and SLM to consider the learning of other aspects of L2 pronunciation, such as prosody, which includes word stress, prominence and intonation (see Mennen, 2015), and to incorporate social dimensions of learning (e.g. identity and ethnic group affiliation). This also includes the need to provide a nuanced understanding of linguistic input and interaction, which thus far have been measured rather crudely as length of residence in an L2-speaking environment and amount of self-rated language use (e.g. Flege, Schirru & MacKay, 2003). And, with respect to cross-language similarity, which serves as a measure of phonetic distance in both models, the models would benefit from a clearer definition of what such a perceptual metric entails and what minimum noticing thresholds are required for learners to engage or re-engage L2 pronunciation learning. Put differently, it is unclear which specific features of the speech signal listeners (both native and non-native) detect as being similar or different, how much of a difference could be detected (e.g. in perceptual, acoustic or gestural terms) and whether the perception of differences leads to further learning, especially in naturalistic contexts of language use, where listeners are not just comparing two individual sounds as part of a lab-based testing procedure but are exposed to instances of longer, contextualized spoken discourse in authentic interaction (see Foote & Trofimovich, 2016).

Psychological perspective

One cognitive psychological perspective relevant to L2 pronunciation learning is skill acquisition theory (DeKeyser, 2015), which is a broad view that applies to various human behaviours learned through practice, such as playing the violin or completing Sudoku puzzles (see Couper, this volume, for another perspective). Its main tenet is that learning involves three main stages as it progresses from initial exposure to skilled performance. These stages include acquisition of declarative knowledge, transformation of declarative knowledge into procedural knowledge, and automatization. The first stage involves learning declarative knowledge about a skill – usually in the form of abstract rules and specific examples – by reading books, through observation or from a teacher. The second stage requires that declarative knowledge be deployed procedurally to perform a skill, typically through slow and deliberate training. The final stage includes a large amount of practice for the purpose of achieving effortless and fluid skill performance. This learning sequence is characterized by the power law of practice, which states that practice leads to improvements but that learning gains gradually diminish as the amount of practice increases. Put simply, the learning involved in skill acquisition involves a shift from declarative knowledge (e.g. being able to state a rule for using a verb tense) to procedural knowledge (e.g. being able to actually use the verb correctly when speaking to someone), followed by a gradual process of fine-tuning through practice, which likely results in not just faster but also more efficient performance (DeKeyser, 2007; Segalowitz, 2010).

Some aspects of skill acquisition theory make it a good fit for pronunciation. This theory can account for various constraints on L2 pronunciation learning. According to DeKeyser (2015), the phenomena that relate to effects of frequency, instruction and output, as well as variability and systematicity of learning, can all be explained by whether (and how) language is taught in the declarative stage and whether (and how) it is practised afterwards. Thus, pronunciation learning might be difficult, variable or incomplete in its outcomes because learners do not receive adequate instruction or input, which leads them to form incorrect generalizations about pronunciation, or because they do not engage in (sufficient) language practice. Even if practice occurs, it may not be entirely useful because what gets proceduralized and automatized might be based on incomplete or inaccurate initial knowledge. Skill acquisition theory also accounts for individual differences, as the process of automatization will occur faster or more slowly based on several factors, including learners' age, motivation, willingness to communicate, and aptitude (Carlson, 2003). The practice component of skill acquisition highlights the articulatory dimension of pronunciation. However, skill acquisition has little to say about issues related to identity, other than perhaps to acknowledge that how learners feel about acquiring new pronunciation will impact their motivation to practice it. This theory also makes no specific claims about the role of learners' L1, apart from implying that previously learned languages will likely interact with new declarative and procedural knowledge.

If practice 'gets a raw deal' in the teaching of L2 grammar and vocabulary because it is associated with 'mind-numbing drills in the sweatshops of foreign language learning' (DeKeyser, 2007, p. 1), this is certainly not the case for pronunciation. In fact, many pronunciation specialists embrace the idea that pronunciation requires both explicit instruction (declarative learning) and large amounts of controlled practice (proceduralization) and fluency activities (automatization) (e.g. Celce-Murcia, Brinton & Goodwin, 2010). Skill acquisition theory is also in agreement, with research showing the importance of explicit pronunciation instruction in early stages of learning (e.g. Saito, 2013) and highlighting the role of practice in subsequent proceduralization (e.g. Thomson, 2012). If successful mastery of a skill requires access to unambiguous rules and sufficient examples that then need to be practised through deliberate and sustained effort, then pronunciation learning is largely a matter of receiving proper input and instruction followed by extensive directed practice. This conceptualization of L2 pronunciation learning, which is compatible with communicatively oriented views of L2 teaching (Freeman & Richards, 1993), appears to be promising in explaining many pronunciation phenomena. However, very little research has been conducted within this framework. Future research is therefore needed to clarify which types of instruction are most beneficial in each stage of skill acquisition and what timing and sequence of pronunciation practice are most effective. Future research must also examine how different aspects of pronunciation develop through various stages of skill acquisition and how such learning interacts with learner- and situation-specific variables, such as age, identity or learning context.

Interactionist perspective

The interaction approach, often discussed in reference to the interaction hypothesis (Long, 1996), explains L2 learning 'through the learner's exposure to language, production of language, and feedback on that production' (Gass & Mackey, 2015, p. 181). At the core of this approach is the principle that interaction with interlocutors can help learners determine how their language is similar to or different from the language of their speaking partner, which leads to language development. In particular, language learning is hypothesized to take place when communication is interactively co-constructed during conversational interaction involving L2 learners. When interlocutors encounter communication breakdowns attributable to language, they often make intuitive or conscious efforts to repair the non-target linguistic element, relying on clarification requests, various forms of feedback, or comprehension and confirmation checks to facilitate understanding. This conversational behaviour – termed negotiation for meaning – is considered to be facilitative of L2 development because it draws learners' attention to problematic aspects of language, gaps in understanding or heretofore unnoticed linguistic features.

The interaction approach is appealing as a theoretical view of L2 pronunciation learning because it is fully compatible with the intelligibility principle of L2 pronunciation (Levis, 2005). Unlike the nativeness principle, which highlights near-native, unaccented pronunciation as a desirable learning and teaching goal, the intelligibility principle emphasizes a speaker's ability to be understood, which is possible even in the presence of a noticeable accent. Because interaction-based learning is driven by communication breakdowns, what is likely to be learned through negotiation for meaning and interactional modifications would be those dimensions of pronunciation that are tied to making speech understandable (intelligible and/or comprehensible) to the interlocutor (Saito, Trofimovich & Isaacs, 2016). In fact, there is mounting evidence that learners benefit from such interactional features as feedback targeting pronunciation (Saito, 2015; Saito & Wu, 2014) and that they focus on pronunciation as part of interaction (e.g. Storch & Aldosari, 2013). With its focus on input and communication, an interactionist perspective can also reveal how pronunciation is learned outside of the explicit instruction and controlled practice typical of the pronunciation classroom. This is important because many learners do not receive sufficient amounts of pronunciation-specific instruction (Foote, Trofimovich, Collins & Soler Urzúa, 2016), making it necessary to understand what can or cannot be expected to be learned through interaction alone.

Despite its strengths, the interaction approach does not seem to easily account for the roles of learners' L1, individual differences (including learners' age), systematicity and variability, as well as identity in pronunciation learning, although it certainly does not preclude research that targets these variables as part of interaction (e.g. Mackey & Sachs, 2012). The interaction approach also has little to contribute to the motor component of pronunciation, apart from suggesting that articulatory issues that result in a loss of intelligibility may be noticed owing to feedback or explicit focus on language during interaction. There are also concerns that interaction-driven learning cannot account for the full complexity of pronunciation development. For instance, language users residing in L2-speaking environments often level out or even deteriorate in their pronunciation despite daily opportunities to engage in interaction (Derwing & Munro, 2013) and it might take explicit classroom instruction featuring focused practice to help such speakers improve (e.g. Derwing, Munro, Foote, Waugh & Fleming, 2014). Research in L2 pronunciation would benefit from further studies carried out within the interactionist perspective, investigating, for example, the potential for corrective feedback to address problematic aspects of prosody, the relationship between task design and interactional focus on pronunciation, and the role of such variables as learners' attention capacity, motivation, anxiety or language background and identity in their ability to benefit from interaction.

Sociocultural perspective

Sociocultural theory, an approach to learning rooted in Vygotskian psychology, is predicated on the idea that, while innate biological factors are necessary for mental processes to emerge, it is social and cultural variables that allow those processes to develop (Lantolf, Thorne & Poehner, 2015). Central to this view is the belief that the mind is mediated by way of cultural tools, and that these tools can be both physical and symbolic. Physical tools, such as a shovel or a software app, help people mediate (influence) the outside world. However, it is language – a symbolic tool – that is used to create and transform thought. As speakers develop language through interaction in social activities, they gain control over, or regulate, their own mental activity and become independent (self-regulating) individuals. Language is thus considered to be the most important tool used by humans to establish their connection to the world and to each other.

Within sociocultural theory, much research on language learning has centred on the concept of zone of proximal development (ZPD), which roughly refers to the developmental distance between what individuals can accomplish alone and what they can achieve through assistance and collaboration from others. For instance, L2 research has examined how feedback and collaboration provided within a language learner's ZPD by a teacher or a more expert partner can help learners improve in various L2 skills (e.g. de Guerrero & Villamil, 2000). In order for learning to be successful, the support provided to learners through feedback, interaction or instruction must be appropriate to learners' current ZPD. Put simply, as language skills improve, learners tend to receive fewer instructions or less feedback.

In terms of L2 pronunciation development, sociocultural theory can explain several phenomena. First, within this theory, all learning is embedded in a particular social world, and all development is the result of the learner's mediated experiences in a social context. In essence, sociocultural theory highlights how linguistic input, language output and the learner cannot be separated from a specific sociocultural environment. Sociocultural theory tends to focus on mediated experiences in an instructional context, that is, how learners and teachers co-construct knowledge as teachers help scaffold instruction and create learning opportunities for their learners in the ZPD. In this sense, it is a theory better suited to examining pronunciation in an instructed, rather than naturalistic, context. With respect to systematicity and variability, the paths and outcomes of learning will vary 'depending on the type of mediation [learners] receive and the specific goals for which they use the language' (Lantolf et al., 2015, p. 219). By addressing learner goals, sociocultural theory also highlights issues of motivation and identity, in the sense that a learner may ultimately be more successful if his or her goal is to use an L2 to make friends or become part of a community. However, the account of variability in pronunciation learning outcomes that is solely based on considerations of learning experiences may not be altogether sufficient.

This is because it does not account for the inherent difficulties that may persist for many adult learners even after decades of language use (e.g. Derwing et al., 2014). Furthermore, within sociocultural theory, L1 effects apply mainly to language meanings rather than forms (Lantolf et al., 2015), whereas the L1-related learning challenge in L2 pronunciation is predominantly, if not exclusively, with language form. As with the interactionist approach, the motor component of speech production has no clear place in sociocultural theory, apart from being something that may be resolved through instruction and support appropriate to a particular learner's ZPD.

Despite these issues, sociocultural theory has the potential to make unique contributions to our understanding of pronunciation learning, given that there is currently little research targeting L2 pronunciation within the ZPD. For instance, it might be interesting to see if pairing learners of different levels of intelligibility would result in the 'expert' learner providing pronunciation-related assistance and scaffolding to the 'novice' learner or whether the support provided by the interactants is bidirectional in nature. This line of research might reveal how learners seek, provide, reject and appropriate pronunciation-specific assistance while engaged in culturally and situationally embedded communication, or how teachers scaffold pronunciation teaching on a turn-by-turn basis inside language classrooms. As a result, sociocultural research into L2 pronunciation learning can yield rich, thick descriptions of contextually embedded learning, especially across different learning situations, something that many current studies of L2 pronunciation lack.

Identity perspective

In response to Norton's (2000) call for L2 acquisition theory to account for (often inequitable) social structures manifested through daily social interaction, much of the current research views identity as flexible and dynamic, influenced by context as well as cultural and historic realities (Darvin & Norton, 2015). One prominent branch of identity research focuses on imagined communities, which refer to groups of people who are unavailable to us in an immediate and tangible way but with whom we create affiliations through imagination (Kanno & Norton, 2003). Imagined communities have a powerful influence on language learning, such that 'learners' actual and desired memberships in imagined communities affect their learning trajectories, influencing their agency, motivation, investment, and resistance in [language] learning' (Pavlenko & Norton, 2007, p. 589). Kanno and Norton provide an example of Katrina, previously a teacher from Poland, who was taking an English as a second language (ESL) class in Canada, unable to gain a teaching position. After being told that her English was not good enough for a computer class, Katrina got extremely offended and never returned to her ESL class. This seemingly counterproductive reaction to a commonplace remark makes sense assuming that Katrina's imagined community – being a member of a professional community – was threatened by her teacher. Pavlenko (2003) cited another L2 learner whose view of the imagined community of native speakers influenced her attitudes towards pronunciation: 'I spent a lot of time to take lessons about English pronunciation and intonation in order to imitate native speakers' accents, and to practice them rather than attempted to verbalize my thoughts towards various phenomena around me' (p. 257). These examples highlight how imagined communities, and an investment to enter into them, can have profound implications for how people approach language learning and how it makes them feel.

The concept of imagined communities can offer a theoretical prism for viewing the role of identity and pronunciation learning. Learners' real or desired membership of professional, cultural, social and linguistic communities will impact how they approach pronunciation learning. It will also impact which model(s) of pronunciation they will want to use. For example, a learner in Taiwan acquiring English for career advancement may belong to an imagined community of international business people who use English as a means of communication. If that learner sees the community as truly international, then an English as a lingua franca model may appeal to that learner (see Deterding & Gardiner, this volume). However, if she imagines successful business people to be predominantly from Canada, Great Britain and the USA, then she may strive for the native speaker model, regardless of her chances of mastering such a model. In ESL settings, the importance that learners place on improving their pronunciation may come from how they view their membership in the imagined community of speakers in their immediate environment. It may also be strongly impacted by their sense of loyalty to an imagined community who share their L1, or by how they think their pronunciation will affect their membership in an imagined community in the future (Trofimovich & Turuševa, 2015).

The identity framework of imagined communities can account for some of the observable phenomena of L2 pronunciation learning. It can account for variable paths and outcomes of learning because every learner's imagined communities are different, leading learners to approach pronunciation learning in different ways. Learners' age and their L1 are also factors that will influence how they position themselves in their imagined communities. Clearly, identity theory is not meant to explain cognitive processes that underpin pronunciation learning, including its motor component. Instead, identity theory underscores how language teaching, and especially pronunciation instruction, does not occur in a vacuum. Learners come to language classrooms with their geopolitical, social and personal histories, often shaped by power structures that, in the case of English, are frequently inequitable (see Nur Raihan & Deterding, this volume), and all of these have the potential to influence language development. While identity theory cannot fully explain how pronunciation is learned, there is clearly a need for research and pedagogy that reflect the socio- and geopolitical and personal realities of pronunciation learning and teaching.

Sociocognitive perspective

A relatively recent addition to theories of L2 learning, the sociocognitive approach, combines cognitive and sociocultural perspectives, as its name suggests (Atkinson, 2011, 2014). Underlying this approach is the idea that the human mind cannot be understood separately from the body and the world in which it exists. Sociocognitive learning is something that occurs in the world, not inside our heads, with the consequence that learning cannot be understood fully without reference to the social and physical space in which it takes place. In essence, language is not just a set of internal processes that can be studied indirectly through scores or performance measures; language is a tool used for social interaction. Language can be studied by observing 'the activities of human beings acting-thinking-being-aligning in and to the world' (Atkinson, Churchill, Nishino & Okada, 2007, p. 172), and language learning is a continuous adaptation of the learner to his or her environment through what is known as alignment. The process of alignment is complex, involving multiple dimensions that range from linguistic and non-verbal behaviours, to physical objects and tools (e.g. textbooks), to social conventions and structures, to personal relationships and histories of the participants (Atkinson, 2011, 2014). For example, when people communicate with each other, they might approach each other (i.e. align) or alternatively refrain from doing so in terms of not only facial expression, body posture, gesture, voice quality or eye gaze but also fluency patterns as well as various aspects of language, such as prosody, pronunciation of vowels and consonants, syntactic constructions and vocabulary choice. As part of communication, interlocutors can ostensibly also align to each other (or fail to do so) in terms of their beliefs, motivations and identity expressions.

Compared to sociocultural and identity theories, the sociocognitive approach appears to have more potential to explain various aspects of pronunciation learning. Variability and systematicity in rates and outcomes of learning can be explained through both similarities and also the vast differences in how each individual learner – with his or her own cognitive skill set – approaches the complex task of aligning to his or her interlocutors and educational setting in a specific sociocultural context. Learners' age and L1 could also be viewed as factors that will affect alignment, as can issues relating to a learner's identity. And the articulatory component of pronunciation can be conceptualized as part of a complex task of realigning an already-known set of speech gestures to match the speaking patterns of an interlocutor or a speech community. The sociocognitive approach thus appears to offer sufficient room for pronunciation-specific research that addresses both cognitive and social factors, especially because this view is 'so new and undeveloped that it seems open to the full range of possibilities' (Atkinson, 2011, p. 162).

The sociocognitive approach also allows for a more focused look at pronunciation learning (see Trofimovich, 2016, for a characterization of L2 pronunciation as sociocognitive learning). This perspective comes from the fields of social and cognitive psychology, where alignment (a key component of sociocognitive learning) has been investigated extensively. For instance, sociolinguists have described speakers' use of fluency, prosody and pronunciation as reflecting their attitude towards and desire to connect with their interlocutors. Put differently, speakers converge or diverge in their interaction patterns, which include a variety of speech phenomena, such as pausing, speech rate and the pronunciation of vowels and consonants, because they wish to be liked and accepted by their interlocutors or instead because they want to distance themselves from their listeners (Giles, Coupland & Coupland, 1991; Giles & Ogay, 2007). And cognitive psychologists have discussed alignment as a mechanism by which interlocutors facilitate understanding through interaction. In essence, speakers tend to imitate, reuse and otherwise appropriate each other's language (e.g. words, expressions, structures, pronunciation patterns) and non-linguistic behaviours (e.g. gestures, eye gaze, body posture) because they help speakers understand each other. These processes are often automatic and thus can occur quickly and subconsciously, but may also be associated with conscious and intentional decisions speakers might take (Gambi & Pickering, 2013; Pickering & Garrod, 2013). Seen from this vantage point, then, L2 pronunciation learning can be conceptualized as a complex task requiring learners to align or realign their pronunciation patterns – for instance, in terms of the articulation of individual vowels or the production of fluency and prosody – to their interlocutors, be they teachers or fellow non-native speakers. Depending on learners' cognitive abilities, the frequency and type of interactions they engage in, and their identity orientation, age or L1, some learners might be more successful than others at this kind of sociocognitive alignment.

Although the sociocognitive approach cannot yet account for the full range of observable L2 pronunciation phenomena, the scope of this approach provides room for pronunciation researchers to investigate many factors as part of sociocognitive alignment. For example, learners' imagined communities could determine how they align with other learners or a classroom environment, ultimately influencing their pronunciation development. Researchers could also look at how different pronunciation models used in instruction (e.g. English as a lingua franca or nativist models) affect learner alignment. The sociocognitive approach could reveal detailed information about how learners behave during interaction, with the view of finding evidence of alignment in interaction – through cognitive convergence and/or social accommodation (Gambi & Pickering, 2013) – and of its impact on development. In this respect, a detailed multimodal interaction analysis, carried out within the alignment perspective, can be invaluable in offering a focused look at learner behaviour in communication (Atkinson et al., 2007; Churchill, Okada, Nishino & Atkinson, 2010; Mori & Hayashi, 2006). Last but not least, sociocognitive alignment can be studied across various types of tasks involving non-native speakers (Trofimovich & Kennedy, 2014) and in classroom teaching, as part of learner–learner interaction (Trofimovich, McDonough & Foote, 2014), in order to provide evidence with stronger pedagogical implications. In sum, the socio-cognitive approach may not offer a quick fix to the problem of finding a comprehensive L2 pronunciation theory but it shows more potential to build on existing theoretical frameworks than is currently realized in pronunciation research.

Recommendations and future directions

From theory to pedagogy

As the preceding discussion suggests, there are many interesting perspectives targeting various aspects of L2 pronunciation development. However, to those involved in the practical task of language teaching it is abundantly clear that, although many of these proposals are scientifically sound and engaging, they often have little to contribute to L2 pedagogy, either because they were not designed with practice in mind or because such links have not yet been established. While the utility of theories cannot (and should not) be judged solely based on their contributions to practice, one goal of theory building in L2 pronunciation should be the establishment of best practice, or the idea that research should ultimately inform pronunciation teaching. This is because pronunciation is not simply a fascinating object of inquiry but because pronunciation permeates all spheres of human life, lying at the core of oral language expression and embodying the way in which the speaker and the hearer work together to produce and understand each other's utterances.

Therefore, it is important for theoretical perspectives to also consider the realities of pronunciation teaching. For example, while the ideal language classrooms of today embrace authentic input and communication, with problematic aspects of language form targeted whenever such focus is required, the pronunciation instruction frequently employed by teachers and learners involves a strong focus on form, often by way of repetition, though ideally in a contextualized way (e.g. Gilbert, 2005). There have been attempts to make pronunciation instruction more communicative in nature (for an overview, see Murphy & Baker, 2015), as the influence of communicative language teaching (CLT) has pushed many teachers to try to bring pronunciation within a more CLT-oriented framework. However, there is also an acknowledgement that pronunciation is difficult to address adequately in communicative classrooms (Foote et al., 2016; Levis & Grant, 2003). While there are good reasons to include authentic communication in pronunciation teaching, it is unlikely that the form-focused orientation of pronunciation instruction will shift dramatically, at least in part because the very nature of pronunciation difficulties (which largely reside at level of form and require learners to shift their attentional focus away from communication to attend to language) is not easily amenable to purely meaning-focused pronunciation instruction. In fact, previous research documenting pronunciation learning gains has invariably involved some form of language focus (e.g. Couper, 2006; Saito & Lyster, 2012), although some aspects of speech are more amenable than others to improvement outside of instruction, making the relative roles of instruction versus naturalistic exposure different depending on which aspect of pronunciation is being targeted (e.g. Derwing, Thomson, Foote & Munro 2012; Munro, Derwing & Thomson, 2015). This makes it very difficult to generalize findings from 'typical' communicative language classrooms to pronunciation. Pronunciation is taught, and subsequently learned, differently from other language skills.

Another important consideration pertains to which aspects of pronunciation should be taught and which model(s) should be used when choosing instructional targets. Most pronunciation research today embraces the intelligibility principle, or the idea that what needs to be targeted through instruction involves those aspects of pronunciation that impede successful communication rather than those that make L2 speech non-native (Levis, 2005). However, the very notion of intelligibility raises important questions. One of these questions is 'To what extent should speech be intelligible?' This issue is further complicated when intelligibility is considered in tandem with a companion construct of comprehensibility, which refers to a listener's perception of how easy or difficult an utterance is to understand (Munro & Derwing, 1995). An utterance may be largely intelligible but still require considerable processing effort to understand. At what point, then, would speech be considered to have reached a sufficient threshold of both intelligibility and comprehensibility? This brings up another equally important and no less complex question: 'Who should speech be intelligible to?' In fact, most intelligibility research has assumed that learners' interlocutors will be native speakers (e.g. Isaacs & Trofimovich, 2012). However, recent years have witnessed increased interest in L2 pronunciation as it is used primarily in communication with other non-native speakers (for further discussion of pronunciation models, see Szpyra-Kozłowska, this volume). Pronunciation teaching contexts also vary widely. Learners may be learning in foreign or second language environments, where learning goals and future contexts of use can vary enormously, or in lingua franca contexts, where learners are pursuing a language primarily to use as a means of communication with other L2 speakers. Therefore, theoretical perspectives of L2 pronunciation learning should at minimum account for pronunciation phenomena that apply to a variety of learners in different contexts of language use and cut across different interlocutors, both native and non-native.

Conclusion

Finding a single theory that can rise to prominence in L2 pronunciation research is likely both difficult and unsustainable. Theories of SLA frequently overlook pronunciation, which is partly because pronunciation is not an easy fit, owing to its unique qualities, within broader theories of SLA. However, many current theoretical frameworks do offer the potential for pronunciation researchers to ask questions that can be addressed through research. For instance, there are many ways in which the interactionist and sociocultural perspectives could be used to learn more about pronunciation learning during authentic communication. There are also powerful possibilities offered by the sociocognitive perspective, as it offers a broad framework for researching L2 pronunciation through both a cognitive lens and a sociocultural lens. Finding ways to address the cognitive and linguistic variables traditionally studied in L2 pronunciation research and also to acknowledge and explore sociocultural issues, such as identity, is a serious challenge, not just in pronunciation research but in SLA research in general. However, without bridge building across theoretical and methodological divides, theories of L2 pronunciation learning will be incomplete. Finally, to ensure that research can guide practice, at least some research needs to be tied to classroom practice because the goal of applied research by its very nature is to solve practical problems. While research conducted using theories of SLA can often inform research and pedagogy (see Ellis & Shintani, 2014), it is nonetheless disappointing that, in Long's (2007) words, 'most SLA theories and SLA theorists are not primarily interested in language teaching, and in some cases they are not at all interested' (p. 19). Therefore, in the field of L2 pronunciation learning, there is a need for more evidence that can inform pronunciation pedagogy, and it should be considered a priority for researchers in this domain to provide this evidence.

Further reading

Atkinson, D. (2014). Language learning in mindbodyworld: A sociocognitive approach to second language acquisition, *Language Teaching*, *47*, 467–483. This article outlines the sociocognitive approach and its applications to second language development.

Mennen, I. (2015). Beyond segments: Towards a L2 intonation learning theory. In E. Delais-Roussarie, M. Avanzi, & S. Herment (Eds), *Prosody and language in contact: L2 acquisition, attrition and languages in multilingual situations* (pp. 171–188). Berlin: Springer. This chapter outlines a model of L2 intonation learning.

Trofimovich, P., & Turuševa, L. (2015). Ethnic identity and second language learning. *Annual Review of Applied Linguistics*, *35*, 234–252. This review of research discusses identity issues in L2 pronunciation learning.

Trofimovich, P. (2016). Interactive alignment: A teaching-friendly view of second language pronunciation learning. *Language Teaching*, *49*(3), 411–422. This article discusses applications of sociocognitive principles to L2 pronunciation learning.

Related topics

Transfer, contrastive analysis and interlanguage; instructional models; accent and stereotyping; individual differences; attitudes towards L2 pronunciation; intelligibility in the global context

References

Atkinson, D. (2011). A sociocognitive approach to second language acquisition: How mind, body, and world work together in learning additional languages, In D. Atkinson (Ed.), *Alternative approaches to second language acquisition* (pp. 143–166). New York, NY: Routledge.

Atkinson, D. (2014). Language learning in mindbodyworld: A sociocognitive approach to second language acquisition. *Language Teaching*, *47*, 467–483.

Atkinson, D., Churchill, E., Nishino, T., & Okada, H. (2007). Alignment and interaction in a sociocognitive approach to second language acquisition. *The Modern Language Journal*, *91*, 169–188.

Baker, W., Trofimovich, P., Flege, J. E., Mack, M., & Halter, R. (2008). Child-adult differences in second-language phonological learning: The role of cross-language similarity. *Language and Speech*, *51*, 316–341.

Best, C. T. (1995). A direct-realist perspective on cross-language speech perception. In W. Strange (Ed.), *Speech perception and linguistic experience: Theoretical and methodological issues* (pp. 171–204). Timonium, MD: York Press.

Best, C., & Tyler, M. (2007). Nonnative and second-language speech perception. In O.-S. Bohn, & M. J. Munro (Eds), *Language experience in second language speech learning: In honor of James Emil Flege* (pp. 13–24). Amsterdam: John Benjamins.

Carlson, R. (2003). Skill learning. In L. Nadel (Ed.), *Encyclopedia of cognitive science*. London: Macmillan.

Celce-Murcia, M., Brinton, D., & Goodwin, J., with Griner, B. (2010). *Teaching pronunciation: A course book and reference guide* (2nd ed.). New York, NY: Cambridge University Press.

Churchill, E., Okada, H., Nishino, T., & Atkinson, D. (2010). Symbiotic gesture and the sociocognitive visibility of grammar in second language acquisition. *The Modern Language Journal*, *94*, 234–253.

Couper, G. (2006). The short- and long-term effects of pronunciation instruction, *Prospect*, *21*, 46–66.

Darvin, R., & Norton, B. (2015). Identity and a model of investment in applied linguistics. *Annual Review of Applied Linguistics, 35*, 36–56.

de Guerrero, M. C. M., & Villamil, O. (2000). Activating the ZPD: Mutual scaffolding in L2 peer revision. *The Modern Language Journal, 84*, 51–68.

DeKeyser, R. M. (2007). Introduction: Situating the concept of practice. In R. M. DeKeyser (Ed.), *Practice in a second language: Perspectives from applied linguistics and cognitive psychology* (pp. 1–20). New York, NY: Cambridge.

DeKeyser, R. M. (2013). Age effects in second language learning. In S. Gass, & A. Mackey (Eds), *Handbook of Second Language Acquisition* (pp. 442–460). London: Routledge.

DeKeyser, R. M. (2015). Skill acquisition theory. In B. VanPatten & J. Williams (Eds), *Theories in second language acquisition: An introduction* (2nd ed.) (pp. 94–112). New York, NY: Routledge.

Deng, J., Holtby, A., Howden-Weaver, L., Nessim, L., Nicholas, B., Nickle, K. . . . Sun, M. (2009). *English pronunciation research: The neglected orphan of second language acquisition studies?* Edmonton: Prairie Metropolis Centre.

Derwing, T., & Munro, M. (2005). Second language accent and pronunciation teaching: A research-based approach. *TESOL Quarterly, 39*, 379–397.

Derwing, T. M., & Munro, M. J. (2013). The development of L2 oral language skills in two L1 groups: A seven-year study. *Language Learning, 63*, 163–185.

Derwing, T. M., & Munro, M. J. (2015). *Pronunciation fundamentals: Evidence-based perspectives for L2 teaching and research.* Amsterdam: John Benjamins.

Derwing, T. M., Munro, M. J., Foote, J. A., Waugh, E., & Fleming, J. (2014). Opening the window on comprehensible pronunciation after 19 years: A workplace training study. *Language Learning, 64*, 526–548.

Derwing, T. M., Thomson, R. I., Foote, J. A., & Munro, M. J. (2012). A longitudinal study of listening perception in adult learners of English: Implications for teachers. *Canadian Modern Language Review, 68*, 247–266.

Ellis, R., & Shintani, N. (2014). *Exploring language pedagogy through second language acquisition research.* New York, NY: Routledge.

Flege, J. (2003). Assessing constraints on second-language segmental production and perception. In A. Meyer, & N. Schiller (Eds), *Phonetics and phonology in language comprehension and production: Differences and similarities* (pp. 319–355). Berlin: Mouton de Gruyter.

Flege, J. (2009). Give input a chance! In T. Piske, & M. Young-Scholten (Eds), *Input matters in SLA* (pp. 175–190). Bristol: Multilingual Matters.

Flege, J. E. (1995). Second language speech learning: Theory, findings, and problems. In W. Strange (Ed.), *Speech perception and linguistic experience: Theoretical and methodological issues* (pp. 233–277). Timonium, MD: York Press.

Flege, J. E., Schirru, C., & MacKay, I. R. (2003). Interaction between the native and second language phonetic subsystems. *Speech communication, 40*, 467–491.

Foote, J. A., Holtby, A. K., & Derwing, T. M. (2012). Survey of the teaching of pronunciation in adult ESL programs in Canada, 2010. *TESL Canada Journal, 29*, 1–22.

Foote, J. A., & Trofimovich, P. (2016). A multidimensional scaling study of native and non-native listeners' perception of second language speech. *Perceptual and Motor Skills, 122*, 470–489.

Foote, J. A., Trofimovich, P., Collins, L., & Soler Urzúa, F. (2016). Pronunciation teaching practices in communicative second language classes. *The Language Learning Journal, 44*(2), 181–196.

Fraser, H. (2010). Cognitive theory as a tool for teaching second language pronunciation. In S. De Knop, F. Boers, & A. De Rycker (Eds), *Fostering language teaching efficiency through cognitive linguistics* (pp. 357–379). Berlin: Mouton de Gruyter.

Freeman, D., & Richards, J. C. (1993). Conceptions of teaching and the education of second language teachers. *TESOL Quarterly, 27*, 193–216.

Gambi, C., & Pickering, M. J. (2013). Prediction and imitation in speech. *Frontiers in Psychology, 4*(340), 1–9.

Gass, G. and Mackey, M. (2015). Input, interaction, and output in second language acquisition. In B. VanPatten, & J. Williams (Eds), *Theories in second language acquisition: An introduction* (2nd ed.) (pp. 180–206). New York, NY: Routledge.

Gilbert, J. (2005). *Clear speech: Pronunciation and listening comprehension in American English* (3rd ed.). New York, NY: Cambridge University Press.

Giles, H., Coupland, N., & Coupland, J. (1991). Accommodation theory: Communication, context, and consequence. In H. Giles, J. Coupland, & N. Coupland (Eds), *Contexts of accommodation: Developments in applied sociolinguistics* (pp. 1–68). Cambridge: Cambridge University Press.

Giles, H., & Ogay, T. (2007). Communication accommodation theory. In B. B. Whaley, & W. Santer (Eds), *Explaining communication: Contemporary theories and exemplars* (pp. 293–310). London: Lawrence Erlbaum.

Grant, L. (Ed.). (2014). *Pronunciation myths: Applying second language research to classroom teaching.* Ann Arbor, MI: University of Michigan.

Grant, L. (2017). *Well said: Pronunciation for clear communication* (4th ed.). Boston, MA: Thomson/ Heinle & Heinle.

Isaacs, T., & Trofimovich, P. (2012). Deconstructing intelligibility: Identifying the linguistic influences on listeners' L2 comprehensibility ratings. *Studies in Second Language Acquisition, 34,* 475–505.

Kanno, Y., & Norton, B. (2003). Imagined communities and educational possibilities: Introduction. *Journal of Language, Identity, and Education, 2,* 241–249.

Lantolf, J. P., Thorne, S. L. and Poehner, M. (2015). Sociocultural theory and second language learning. In B. VanPatten, & J. Williams (Eds), *Theories in second language acquisition: An introduction* (2nd ed.) (pp. 207–226). New York, NY: Routledge.

Levis, J. M. (2005). Changing contexts and shifting paradigms in pronunciation teaching. *TESOL Quarterly, 39,* 369–377.

Levis, J. (2015). The Journal of Second Language Pronunciation: An essential step toward a disciplinary identity. *Journal of Second Language Pronunciation, 1,* 1–10.

Levis, J. M., & Grant, L. (2003). Integrating pronunciation into ESL/EFL classrooms. *TESOL Journal, 12,* 13–19.

Lippi-Green, R. (2012). *English with an accent: Language, ideology, and discrimination in the United States* (3rd ed.). New York, NY: Routledge.

Long, M. H. (1996). The role of the linguistic environment in second language acquisition. In W. C. Ritchie, & T. K. Bhatia (Eds), *Handbook of language acquisition: Second language acquisition* (pp. 413–468). New York, NY: Academic Press.

Long, M. H. (2007). *Problems in SLA.* Mahwah, NJ: Lawrence Erlbaum.

Lybeck, K. (2002). Cultural identification and second language pronunciation of Americans in Norway. *Modern Language Journal, 86,* 174–191.

Mackey, A., & Sachs, R. (2012). Older learners in SLA research: A first look at working memory, feedback, and L2 development. *Language Learning, 62,* 704–740.

Mennen, I. (2015). Beyond segments: Towards a L2 intonation learning theory. In E. Delais-Roussarie, M. Avanzi, & S. Herment (Eds), *Prosody and language in contact: L2 acquisition, attrition and languages in multilingual situations* (pp. 171–188). Berlin: Springer.

Mori, J., & Hayashi, M. (2006). The achievement of intersubjectivity through embodied completions: A study of interactions between first and second language speakers. *Applied Linguistics, 27,* 195–219.

Munro, M. J., & Derwing, T. M. (1995). Foreign accent, comprehensibility, and intelligibility in the speech of second language learners. *Language learning, 45,* 73–97.

Munro, M. J., Derwing, T. M., & Thomson, R. I. (2015). Implications of naturalistic segment development for pronunciation teaching technology. *International Review of Applied Linguistics in Language Teaching, 53*(1), 39–60.

Murphy, J. M., & Baker, A. A. (2015). History of ESL pronunciation teaching. In M. Reed, & J. M. Levis (Eds), *The handbook of English pronunciation* (pp. 36–65). Hoboken, NJ: John Wiley & Sons.

Norton, B. (2000). *Identity and language learning: Gender, ethnicity and educational change.* Harlow: Pearson Education.

Pavlenko, A. (2003). 'I never knew I was a bilingual': Reimagining teacher identities in TESOL. *Journal of Language, Identity, and Education, 2,* 251–268.

Pavlenko, A., & Norton, B. (2007). Imagined communities, identity, and English language learning. In J. Cummins, & C. Davison (Eds), *International handbook of English language teaching* (pp. 669–680). New York, NY: Springer.

Pickering, M. J., & Garrod, S. (2013). An integrated theory of language production and comprehension. *Behavioral and Brain Sciences, 36,* 329–392.

Saito, K. (2013). Re-examining effects of form-focused instruction on L2 pronunciation development: The role of explicit phonetic information. *Studies in Second Language Acquisition, 35,* 1–29.

Saito, K. (2015). Communicative focus on L2 phonetic form: Teaching Japanese learners to perceive and produce English /r/ without explicit instruction. *Applied Psycholinguistics*, *36*, 377–409.

Saito, K., & Lyster, R. (2012). Effects of form-focused instruction on L2 pronunciation development of /ɹ/ by Japanese learners of English. *Language Learning*, *62*, 595–633.

Saito, K., Trofimovich, P., & Isaacs, T. (2016). Second language speech production: Investigating linguistic correlates of comprehensibility and accentedness for learners at different ability levels. *Applied Psycholinguistics*, *37*, 217–240.

Saito, K., & Wu, X. (2014). Communicative focus on form and L2 suprasegmental learning: Teaching Cantonese learners to perceive Mandarin tones. *Studies in Second Language Acquisition*, *36*, 647–680.

Segalowitz, N. (2010). *Cognitive bases of second language fluency*. London: Routledge.

Storch, N., & Aldosari, A. (2013). Pairing learners in pair work activity. *Language Teaching Research*, *17*, 31–48.

Strevens, P. (1974). A rationale for teaching pronunciation: The rival virtues of innocence and sophistication. *ELT Journal*, *28*, 182–189.

Thomson, R. I. (2012). Improving L2 listeners' perception of English vowels: A computer-mediated approach. *Language Learning*, *62*, 1231–1258.

Thomson, R. I. (2013). ESL teachers' beliefs and practices in pronunciation teaching: Confidently right or confidently wrong? In J. Levis, & K. LeVelle (Eds), *Proceedings of the 4th Pronunciation in Second Language Learning and Teaching Conference*. August 2012 (pp. 224–233). Ames, IA: Iowa State University.

Thomson, R. I., & Derwing, T. M. (2015). The effectiveness of L2 pronunciation instruction: A narrative review. *Applied Linguistics*, *36*, 326–344.

Thomson, R. I., Nearey, T. M., & Derwing, T. M. (2009). A modified statistical pattern recognition approach to measuring the crosslinguistic similarity of Mandarin and English vowels. *The Journal of the Acoustical Society of America*, *126*, 1447–1460.

Trofimovich, P. (2016). Interactive alignment: A teaching-friendly view of second language pronunciation learning. *Language Teaching*, *49*(3), 411–422.

Trofimovich, P., & Kennedy, S. (2014). Interactive alignment between bilingual interlocutors: Evidence from two information-exchange tasks. *Bilingualism: Language and Cognition*, *17*, 822–836.

Trofimovich, P., McDonough, K., & Foote, J. (2014). Interactive alignment of multisyllabic stress patterns in a second language classroom. *TESOL Quarterly*, *48*, 815–832.

Trofimovich, P., & Turuševa, L. (2015). Ethnic identity and second language learning. *Annual Review of Applied Linguistics*, *35*, 234–252.

VanPatten, B., & Williams, J. (2015). Introduction: The nature of theories. In B. VanPatten, & J. Williams (Eds), *Theories in second language acquisition: An introduction* (2nd ed.) (pp. 1–16). New York, NY: Routledge.

Section 2

Descriptions of English pronunciations

6

English vowels and consonants

Pamela Rogerson-Revell

Introduction

The sound system of most languages is based on individual sounds, typically vowels and consonants, which form the building blocks for larger units, such as syllables, words and phrases. These sound segments, or 'phonemes', are the smallest phonological units that can create a linguistic difference in meaning, such as the vowel phonemes /e/ and /ɪ/ distinguishing the words <pen> and <pin> and the consonant phonemes /t/ and /d/ distinguishing the word <lit> from <lid>.

Vowels and consonants can be described both 'phonetically' (i.e. how they are produced) and 'phonologically' (i.e. how they function within a specific language). We will look at phonetic differences (i.e. how individual sounds are produced) in some detail in this chapter. There is a basic phonetic distinction between how vowels and consonants are formed. Consonants are produced by restricting and narrowing the airflow through the mouth, while for vowels the air flows relatively freely, although the shape of the mouth cavity may change. Phonologically, vowels and consonants perform different functions in language. Vowels typically occur at the centre or 'peak' of a syllable, as 'e' in the word <red>, while consonants occur at the beginning or end of a syllable, as the 's' and the 't' in the word <sit>.

Most languages have a range of vowels and consonant phonemes, some of which are common to many languages and others are distinctive to that particular language. For example, the sound /e/,[1] as in <ten> is common in many languages, while the sound /ɜː/ as in <girl> is relatively uncommon. Also, some phonemes occur more frequently, so, for example, the most frequent consonant (that is, the one appearing most often in speech) in many languages is /m/ and the most frequent vowel is /i/, whereas /n/ is the most frequently occurring consonant in English and /ə/ the most common vowel sound (Cruttenden, 2014, p. 235). Similarly, most languages have many more consonants than vowels, while English is quite unusual in having a larger number of vowels.

The sounds described in this chapter represent a standard, non-regional variety of British English, commonly used in the broadcast media and by educated professionals. The variety will be referred to as 'General British' or 'GB' English, in preference to the term 'received pronunciation' or 'RP', which was formerly used to describe standard Southern British English and which is now seen increasingly as a minority, outmoded variety (Cruttenden,

2014; Roach, 2009). Where relevant, differences will be pointed out between the phonemes of GB and other English varieties, particularly 'North American English' (NAE). Similarly, where there is some variation between specialists in how some symbols and labels are used to describe the phonemes of English, such differences will be indicated.

The chapter will first explain how speech sounds are made and then describe how English vowels and consonants sounds are produced. It will then show how phonemes can vary in context, particularly in different regional and national varieties of English. Finally, it will consider how important phonemes are for intelligibility and conclude with some recommendations for pronunciation learning.

Producing speech sounds

All English sounds are produced by expelling air from the lungs through the mouth and/or nose. The part of the anatomy involved in speech production, from the lungs to the mouth or nose, is called the 'vocal tract' and the different speech organs within the vocal tract are referred to as 'articulators'. The articulators are the different parts of the vocal tract that can change the shape of the air flow as it escapes through either the mouth or nose.

Figure 6.1 shows diagrammatically each of the articulators in the vocal tract.

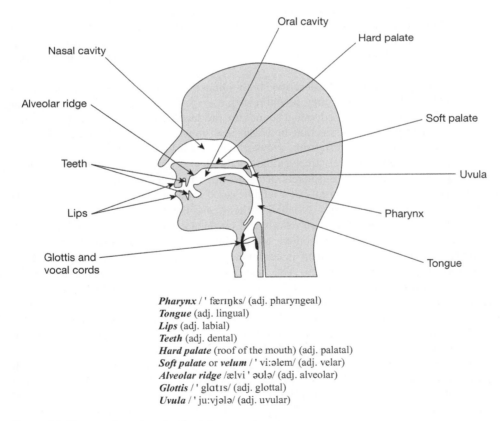

Pharynx / ' færɪŋks/ (adj. pharyngeal)
Tongue (adj. lingual)
Lips (adj. labial)
Teeth (adj. dental)
Hard palate (roof of the mouth) (adj. palatal)
Soft palate or *velum* / ' viːələm/ (adj. velar)
Alveolar ridge /ælvi ' əʊlə/ (adj. alveolar)
Glottis / ' glɑtɪs/ (adj. glottal)
Uvula / ' juːvjələ/ (adj. uvular)

Figure 6.1 The vocal tract and articulators

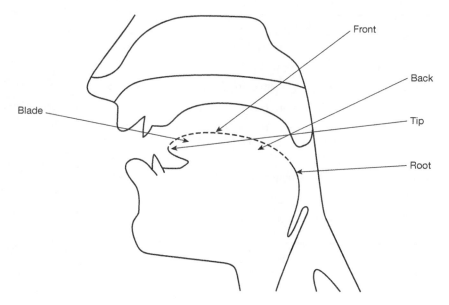

Figure 6.2 Sections of the tongue

The tongue is perhaps the most important of all the articulators and can itself be divided into different sections, as shown in Figure 6.2, which can move to change the shape of the space within the mouth, i.e. 'the oral cavity'.

Consonants

Producing consonants

Generally, we can describe the way consonant sounds are produced in terms of:

(a) *place* of articulation – i.e. *where* the sounds are produced in the vocal tract;
(b) *manner* of articulation – i.e. *how* they are produced;
(c) *voicing* – i.e. whether or not there is vibration of the vocal cords/folds.

Place of articulation

There are eight possible places of articulation for English consonants, as shown in Table 6.1. We will now look at each point of articulation in turn.

1. Bilabial: /b/ /p/ /m/

The upper and lower lips come together, e.g. /p/ as in <pan>; /b/ in <ban>; /m/ in <mat>; /w/ in <wet>.

2. Labio-dental: /f/ /v/

The lower lip makes contact with the upper teeth, e.g. /f/ in <fan>; /v/ in <van>.

Table 6.1 Place of articulation for English consonants

	Place	*Articulation*	*Examples*
1	bilabial	upper and lower lips in contact	/p/ in p̲an, /m/ in m̲at
2	labio-dental	lower lip contacts upper teeth	/f/ in f̲an, /v/ in v̲an
3	dental	tongue tip contacts teeth	/θ/ in t̲h̲in, /ð/ in t̲h̲ese
4	alveolar	tongue contacts alveolar ridge	/t/ in t̲in, /s/ in s̲ip, /d/ in d̲ip
5	Palato-alveolar	tongue contacts alveolar ridge while front of tongue is raised towards hard palate	/ʃ/ in s̲h̲ed, /ʒ/ in leis̲ure
6	palatal	front of tongue contacts hard palate	/j/ in y̲es
7	velar	back of tongue contacts soft palate	/k/ in c̲at /g/ in dog̲, /ŋ/ in sin̲g̲
8	glottal	restricting or narrowing of airflow through glottis	/h/ in h̲ot

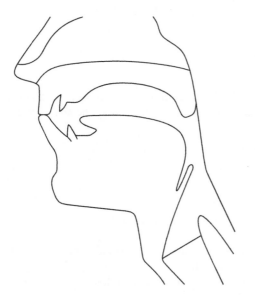

Figure 6.3
Place of articulation for bilabial sounds

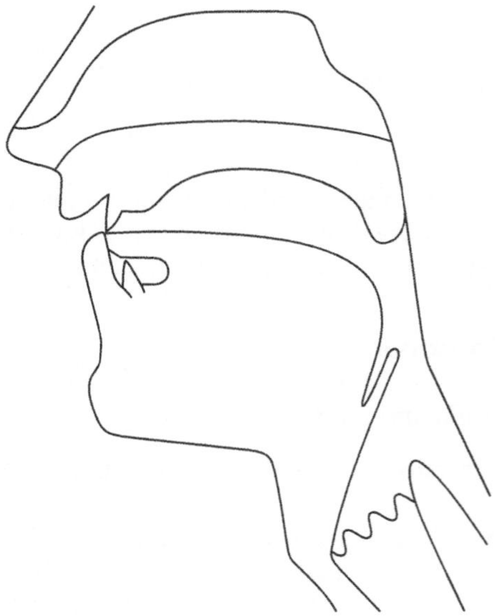

Figure 6.4
Place of articulation for labio-dental sounds

3. Dental: /θ/ /ð/

The tongue tip contacts the upper teeth, e.g. / θ/ in <t̲h̲in>; <wit̲h̲>; and /ð/ in <t̲h̲ese>, <brea*th*e>.

4. Alveolar: /t/ /d/

The tongue contacts the alveolar ridge, e.g. /t/ in <t̲in>, /s/ in <s̲ip>, /d/ in <d̲ip>.

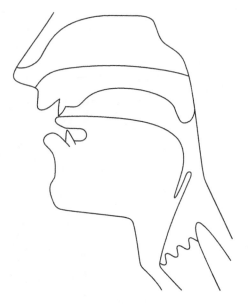

Figure 6.5
Place of articulation for dental sounds

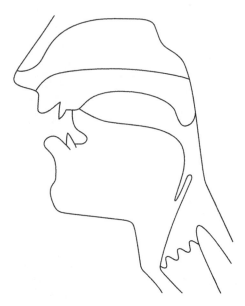

Figure 6.6
Place of articulation for alveolar sounds

Many English consonants are articulated in this position: /t/, /d/, /s/, /z/, /l/, /r/ and /n/. However, in some languages, such as French, Spanish and Italian, these sounds are made in a slightly different position, with the tongue touching the back of the top teeth rather than the alveolar ridge. While this is unlikely to cause comprehension difficulties, it does often account for a noticeable foreign accent.

5. Palato-alveolar: /ʃ/ /ʒ/
The tongue makes near contact with the alveolar ridge and the front of the hard palate, e.g. /ʃ/ in <shed>, /ʒ/ in <leisure>.

6. Palatal: /j/ (though this symbol is frequently replaced by /y/ in North American descriptions)
A mid-section of the tongue presses up towards the hard palate, e.g. /j/ in <yacht>, <yet>.

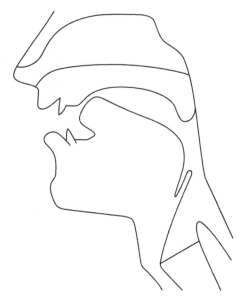

Figure 6.7
Place of articulation for palato-alveolar sounds

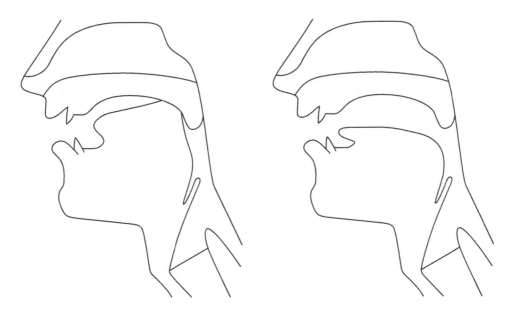

Figure 6.8
Place of articulation for velar sounds

Figure 6.9
Place of articulation for glottal sounds

7. Velar: /k/ /g/

The back of tongue contacts the soft palate, e.g. /k/ in <<u>c</u>at>; /g/ in <do<u>g</u>>.

8. Glottal: /h/

There is no contact between the articulators as air passes under pressure through the open space within the glottis (i.e. between the vocal folds).

Say the words below and feel the position of the underlined consonants. Can you relate these sounds to their place of articulation?

<u>m</u>o<u>p</u>	/m/ /p/	bilabial
<u>f</u>i<u>v</u>e	/f/ /v/	labio-dental
<u>th</u>ese <u>th</u>ings	/ð/ /Θ/	dental
<u>t</u>a<u>n</u>	/t/ /n/	alveolar
<u>sh</u>ort vi<u>s</u>ion	/ʃ/ /ʒ/	palato-alveolar
<u>y</u>our	/j/	palatal
<u>k</u>i<u>ng</u>	/k/ /ŋ/	velar
<u>h</u>ouse	/h/	glottal

We can see then a consonant sound is distinguished by its point of articulation, which is the place in the vocal tract where the airflow is obstructed. The tongue is involved in the production of most English consonant sounds; for example, the tip of the tongue is involved in the articulation of dental, alveolar, post-alveolar and palatal consonant sounds, while the back of the tongue is used to produce velar consonants.

Manner of articulation

Just as there are differences in *where* sounds are made, there are also differences in *how* they are made. So, as well as the 'place' of articulation, we need to be able to describe the 'manner' of articulation for individual consonant sounds.

All consonant sounds involve some degree of narrowing or 'stricture' of the airflow caused by movement of the articulators. There are three possible levels of stricture: (a) complete closure, (b) partial closure and (c) approximation.

(a) *Complete closure* – a complete 'stoppage' of the air flow, producing *plosives*:

    e.g. /p/ ('pan') bilabial plosive
        /k/ ('kit') velar plosive

(b) *Partial closure* – a narrowing of the air stream
    (i)   causing friction between articulators, producing *fricatives*:

        e.g. /f / ('fun') labio-dental fricatives
               /θ / ('think') dental fricatives

    (ii) causing air to 'go round' the closure, producing *laterals and nasals*:

        e.g. /l/ ('lid') alveolar lateral
             /m/ ('men') bilabial nasal

(c) *Approximation* – proximity of the articulators without actual contact, producing *approximants*:

    e.g. /r/ ('run') alveolar approximant
        /w/ ('wet') bilabial approximant
        /j/ ('yes') palatal approximant

To recap, not all consonants are created equal. While all consonants obstruct the airflow to some extent, some do so more than others. The group of consonants with maximum obstruction are the 'plosives', which stop the air stream completely. 'Nasal' consonants impede the airflow from passing through the mouth (the oral cavity) but allow the air to escape through the nose (nasal cavity). 'Fricatives' constrict the airflow considerably, causing friction, but do not block the airflow completely. 'Laterals' divert the air from passing through the centre of the mouth but allow it to pass around the sides of the tongue. Finally, the group of consonants classed as 'approximants' cause such limited obstruction that they could almost be described as vowels, or 'semi-vowels', for example /w/ and /j/ (see below).

Voicing

The third way of classifying consonants is based on the presence or absence of voicing (i.e. the vibration of the vocal folds (cords)). With 'voiceless' sounds, the vocal folds are open and relaxed and air passes freely through the open glottis with no vibration, while with 'voiced' sounds the vocal folds are close together and tightened. So, for example, the consonant /k/ in the word <cot> is voiceless, while the consonant /g/ in <got> is voiced.

Fortis and lenis

The terms voiced and voiceless are sometimes replaced by the terms 'fortis' (Latin for strong) and 'lenis' (Latin for weak). The voiceless consonants /p/, /t/ and /k/ require greater force and articulatory tension than voiced /b/, /d/ and /g/. In English, all fortis consonants are voiceless and lenis consonants can potentially be voiced (although not in some positions).

English consonants

GB and NAE English have 24 common consonants. We have seen that the most important criteria for the classification of consonants in English are their respective places and manners of articulation, together with presence or absence of voicing.

Figure 6.10 presents all of the English consonants, categorized by place of articulation (horizontal axis), manner of articulation (vertical axis) and voicing, i.e. the pairs of phonemes in a single cell represent a voicing contrast (i.e. a minimal pair of voiced/voiceless phonemes). The majority of English consonant phonemes consist of such voiced/voiceless pairs.

Place of articulation		Bilabial	Labiodental	Dental	Alveolar	Palato-alveolar	Palatal	Velar	Glottal
Manner of articulation	PLOSIVE	p b			t d			k g	
	FRICATIVE		f v	θ ð	s z	ʃ ʒ			h
	AFFRICATE					tʃ dʒ			
	NASAL	m			n			ŋ	
	APPROXIMANT	w					r	j	
	LATERAL				l				
	APPROXIMANT								

Figure 6.10 English consonant chart

The consonants /l/ and /r/ are sometimes referred to as 'liquids' in other classification systems. Also, /w/ and /j/ are sometimes referred to as 'semi-vowels'. We will now see how we can use these categories to describe the consonants of English in more detail.

Plosives (or stops)

This group of consonants stop the airflow completely at some point in the vocal tract by the temporary physical contact between articulators, usually involving the lips or the tongue. Consonants that stop the airstream in this way are called 'stops' or 'plosives'. Their articulation has three phases:

(a) closure phase – the articulators come together;
(b) hold phase – air pressure builds up behind the closure;
(c) release phase – articulators come apart and the compressed air is released either rapidly with plosion or more gradually with friction.

Try to make a /p/ sound in slow motion to feel these different phases.

The distinction between plosives and other consonants is sometimes referred to as 'stops' versus 'continuants'. In 'stop' sounds the air is completely blocked off at some point and not allowed to continue before it is released in plosion (e.g. /p/, /t/, /k/). In contrast, with 'continuant' sounds the air flow can continue until you run out of breath (e.g. /f/, /v/, /s/).

There are six plosives in English, in three voiced/voiceless pairs. The point where the airflow is obstructed (place of articulation) is different for the three pairs; the /p/ versus /b/ pair are bilabial plosives with the air stopped by the two lips coming together; /t/ versus /d/ are alveolar plosives with the air stopped by the tongue tip touching the alveolar ridge, and /k/ versus /g/ are velar plosives with the back of the tongue touching the soft palate (i.e. the velum).

	Bilabial	Alveolar	Velar
voiceless	/p/	/t/	/k/
voiced	/b/	/d/	/g/

Another important distinguishing feature between these pairs is that the voiceless plosives are 'aspirated' when they appear at the beginning of a syllable (initial position), for example the initial /p/, /t/, /k/ in <pin>, <tin> and <can>, or at the beginning of a stressed syllable, e.g. <atomic>,<acclaim>. This means there is an additional 'puff of air' or extra energy when the air is released in the plosion phase of the articulation. In contrast, the voiced pairs /b/, /d/ and /g/ are not aspirated in initial position, e.g. <bin>, <din>, <gate>; this difference in aspiration is even more significant than the absence or lack of voicing. Consequently, it is important for learners to be aware of the importance of aspiration of syllable-initial voiceless plosives if this is not present in their first language (e.g. L1 speakers of Arabic).

To illustrate, if you hold a piece of paper in front of your mouth when you say <pat–bat> you will notice the slight puff of air after the release of /p/ but not after /b/. This shows that the fortis consonant /p/ in <pat> has a more energetic, stronger articulation than the lenis /b/ of <bat>.

Neither the voiced nor the voiceless plosives are aspirated at the end of a syllable (final position) and they are often difficult to hear because these sounds are regularly not fully exploded. What mainly distinguishes voiceless /p/, /t/ and /k/ from voiced /b/, /d/ and /g/ in syllable-final position is that vowels appearing immediately before /p/, /t/ and /k/ are generally of much shorter duration than those before /b/, /d/ and /g/, as for example in pairs such as <lap> versus <lab> or <dock> versus <dog>. Intelligibility problems are usually due to learners not lengthening the preceding vowel sufficiently before the voiced plosives, rather than to the lack of clarity of the final consonant phoneme itself. For instance, Chinese learners may pronounce <lid> in a way that it is perceived by first language (L1) English listeners as <lit>.

Fricatives

Fricatives are found in all languages and they form the largest group of consonant phonemes in English (nine). Fricatives are produced by a partial blockage of the airstream as the articulators come together. This narrowing of the airflow creates friction. So, for example, the sounds /t/ and /s/ have the same place of articulation (i.e. the alveolar ridge) but the manner of their articulation is different. Try saying a /s/ and then a /t/ to feel the difference. The /t/ is a stop sound that fully obstructs the air temporarily, while the /s/ stops the air at the sides of the tongue but allows air to flow through a groove along the centre of the tongue, creating a hissing sound. Some fricatives are even more tightly constricted and create more noticeable hissing than others; these are referred to as 'sibilants' (i.e. /s, z, ʃ, ʒ/). The sibilants constitute a four-member subset within the broader category of nine fricative consonants. Unlike plosives, fricatives are continuants (the sound can be prolonged). Try saying /s/ for as long as possible and then try prolonging the stop sound of /t/ (which cannot be done).

There are five voiced/voiceless pairs of fricatives in English, each with a different point of articulation, plus a glottal fricative /h/.

	Place of articulation	Voiceless (-v)		Voiced (+v)	
1	labio-dental	/f/	fat	/v/	vat
2	dental	/θ/	thin	/ð/	this
3	alveolar	/s/	sip	/z/	zip (sibilants)
4	palato-alveolar	/ʃ/	mesh	/ʒ/	measure (sibilants)
5	glottal	/h/	house		

The phoneme /h/ is unusual because phonologically it functions like a consonant (it only occurs before vowels in English) but phonetically it is like a voiceless vowel. It is produced by the airstream creating friction in the glottis but the position of the articulators (e.g. lips, tongue) varies depending upon whatever vowel happens to follow the /h/. In sequence, try saying <heat>, then <hold>, then <head> to feel the difference in the respective articulations of the /h/ sound.

Learners of English may substitute stops for fricatives, for example /t/ for /θ/ ('I tink so' instead of 'I think so'). The opposite is also possible, with a fricative replacing a stop, for example 'de' instead of 'the' (e.g. Sylvester Stallone's movie character Rocky might say, 'Dis is da greatest!'). In fact, the θ/ and /ð/ sounds are uncommon in many other languages and can be quite difficult for learners to master. Learners may therefore substitute a /d/ for the voiced /ð/ and either /f/ or /t/ for the voiceless /θ/.

The /h/ fricative can also be problematic. Learners may replace it with the velar fricative /x/, which is common in many European languages, as well as some English accents, such as the Scottish pronunciation of <loch>. Alternatively, some learners may find /h/ hard to pronounce before a vowel such as in <hotel> if it is not pronounced in this position in their first language (e.g. French).

Affricates

There are two complex consonant sounds in English that might be thought of as a joint articulation of two sounds, a stop and a fricative. These are called 'affricates'. The two English affricates are /tʃ/ and /dʒ/.

Place of articulation	Voiceless (–v)	Voiced (+v)
Palato-alveolar	/tʃ/ chin	/dʒ/ gin
	chop	job
	lunch	lunge

Try saying <shop-chop> and <leisure-ledger>. Can you feel the initial voiceless stop /t/ sound in <chop> and the initial voiced stop /d/ in <ledger>?

Many languages have complex sounds such as /ts/ and /dz/ and learners may substitute this voiceless/voiced pair for the English affricates /ʧ/ and /ʤ/. Another common problem is the substitution of the complex affricate /ʧ/ by the simple fricative /ʃ/, in words such as <muc<u>ch</u>>, <mar<u>ch</u>>, and <<u>ch</u>ur<u>ch</u>>, for example by Vietnamese learners.

Nasals

Nasals belong to the group of sounds classed as continuants although these phonemes are not fricatives. Unlike all other English consonant sounds, for which the air passes through the mouth (i.e. the oral cavity), with nasals the air escapes through the nose. This distinguishing feature of nasals occurs because the velum is lowered as the back of the mouth so that the air passes freely through the nasal cavity.

There are three nasal phonemes in English, /m/, /n/, and /ŋ/, each with a different point of articulation

/m/	voiced *bilabial* nasal	-ru<u>m</u>
/n/	voiced *alveolar* nasal	-ru<u>n</u>
/ŋ/	voiced *velar* nasal	-ru<u>ng</u>

In each case, the back of the tongue and the velum (i.e. the soft palate) are in contact, blocking the air from escaping out of the mouth, as shown in Figure 6.11 for /ŋ/

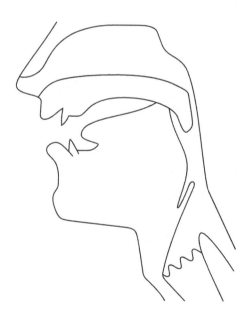

Figure 6.11 /ŋ/

The consonant /ŋ/ is not common in other languages and may cause difficulty for learners, mainly because its place of articulation is so far back within the oral cavity. This consonant never occurs in initial position in English, but does occur in both word-medial (e.g. si<u>ng</u>er,) and word-final positions (e.g. ra<u>ng</u>). Notice that although /ŋ/ is a single phoneme, in the spelling system of English this single consonant is often represented with the orthographic letter combination <n+g>.

Approximants

As with the three nasals, there is another group of English consonant sounds that are also continuants and not fricatives. But with this next set the air escapes through the mouth rather than the nose. For these sounds, the articulators are in close proximity but wide enough apart not to create friction in the airstream. These sounds, called 'approximants', are not archetypical consonants as the articulators get close to, or approximate, each other but do not actually touch. In this sense, they are quite 'vowel-like'. There are four sounds in this category: /l/, /w/, /j/ and /r/. This group of approximants is further distinguished in NAE descriptions as 'liquids' (/l/ and /r/) and 'glides' or 'semi-vowels' (/j/ [or, /y/ in NAE] and /w/).

(a) Lateral: /l/
There is just one lateral in English, the alveolar lateral /l/, as in <low>. For this sound, the tongue blade is in contact with the alveolar ridge but the sides of the tongue are lowered to allow the air to escape around them (i.e. laterally). Try saying /s/ and then /l/ to feel the difference in the air flow and to feel the tongue blade moving up and down.

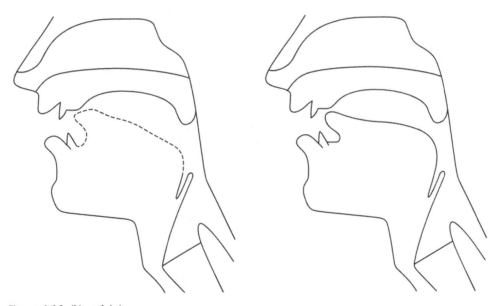

Figure 6.12 /l/ and /s/

(b) Retroflex: /r/
There are many different pronunciations of /r/ in the various accents and dialects of English worldwide. However, we can describe the GB English /r/ (when it occurs in syllable-initial position as in <red>) as a post-alveolar approximant. The /r/ sound in syllable-initial position is made with the sides of the tongue in contact with the back teeth. The tongue tip is also slightly curled back and the lips are typically rounded. It may help to compare word-initial

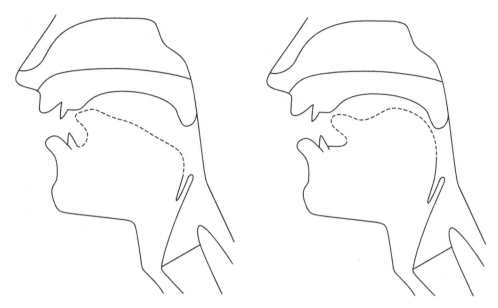

Figure 6.13 /l/ and /r/

/r/ with /l/ where the tip of the tongue is touching the alveolar ridge and the sides of the tongue are lowered. With /r/ these positions are reversed, so that the air passes over the centre of the tongue rather than around its sides. Try saying <led>, <red>, or <lolly> <lorry> to feel the tip of the tongue moving forwards for the /l/ and sides of the tongue touching the back teeth for the /r/.

Many languages contain 'r' sounds but the articulation can vary greatly from language to language and within languages. For instance, 'r' in Polish and Spanish, and similarly in some Scottish accents, is typically produced as a trill, with the tongue tip repeatedly touching the alveolar ridge. Alternatively, the 'r' commonly used in French and German is not alveolar but uvular, i.e. produced at the back of the mouth.

Conversely, 'r' is not a phoneme in Japanese or Mandarin Chinese and learners may have difficulties distinguishing for instance between /r/ and /l/. So, <arrive> may sounds like <alive> and <right> like <light>.

(c) Semi-vowels: /j/ (or /y/ in NAE) and /w/

The two remaining English consonants, /w/ as in <wet> and /j/ as in <yet>, are hard to classify. They function as consonants, i.e. at the edges of syllables, but do not involve very much obstruction of the airflow. In this sense, they are phonetically quite similar to vowels and are, in fact, sometimes referred to as 'semi-vowels' in some classificatory systems. They can be described as:

/j/   voiced, palatal approximant – yes, you, p(j)ure, few, _use
/w/   voiced, labio-velar approximant – wet, when, _one, rewind

However, the articulation of /j/ is very similar to that of the vowel /iː/ in <eat>'. If you say /iː/ and prolong it by holding it for a few seconds you will hear this. In both /j/ and /iː/

the corners of the mouth spread very wide apart. Similarly, /w/ is produced in a very similar way to the vowel /uː/ as in <two>. If you say the word <wet> and prolong the /w/ by holding it for a few seconds you will hear this. In both /w/ and /uː/ the lips are distinctively rounded (note the stark contrast with the spread lips of /j/).

/w/ can be problematic for some learners, again if it is not a separate phoneme in the first language (L1). For instance, German learners of English may substitute /v/ for /w/ (e.g. <vest> for <west>).

Contextual variations in consonants

Obviously, there are slight differences in how consonant phonemes are produced. These small phonetic differences in articulation are referred to as 'allophonic variations'. These differences may be due to individual speaker variation (i.e. no two people will say the /p/ in <pan> exactly the same way) or due to contextual variation. Most phonemes can vary depending on context, i.e. either based on their position in a syllable (i.e. initial, middle, final) or owing to variations in social or regional accent. For consonants, most of these variations are slight and do not, on their own, cause major intelligibility problems. Nevertheless, there are some contextual variations that are significant and these will be described briefly here.

Positional variation

Vowel lengthening before final voiced consonants

English is unusual in having voiced consonants at the end of syllables (e.g. 'dog', 'flies', 'leave') as many languages do not have a lenis/fortis contrast in word-final consonants. For example, in German <wirt> (host) and <wird> (become) are pronounced the same. Some learners may therefore find it difficult to make the contrast in English pairs such as <rice> versus <rise> and <light> versus <lied>. Awareness of the rule to lengthen the vowel immediately before a final voiced consonant is important in such cases. In syllable-final position, all plosives are regularly left unreleased (i.e. unaspirated), e.g. <let>. Again, an awareness of the vowel lengthening rule is helpful to distinguish words such as <led> versus <let>.

Aspiration

Differences in the production of plosives at the beginning of syllables (syllable-initial position) and at the end (syllable-final) are quite noticeable. In particular, the fact that the voiceless plosives /p/, /t/ and /k/ are aspirated in initial position with a characteristic puff of air [ʰ], e.g. /pʰet /. If this aspiration is not present, the listener is likely to hear the sound as the voiced equivalent (e.g. /bet/).

Dark or light /l/

Even apparently identical sounds can vary depending on their position within a syllable or word. For instance, the /l/ in <lip> is phonetically slightly different from the /l/ in <pill>. To make the /l/ in <lip> the tongue tip is touching the alveolar ridge but the sides of the tongue are lowered. To make the /l/ of <pill> the tongue tip is in the same position but the back of the tongue is raised towards the soft palate or velum. We call the first type of /l/ a 'light or clear' /l/ and the second type a 'dark' /l/. In English, the clear /l/ allophone occurs before vowels (as in <lift>), while dark /l/ occurs in other positions, most noticeably in word-final position as in <fill>. Using the different allophones in inappropriate locations of a word would not necessarily cause a loss of intelligibility or misunderstanding but would probably sound strange or 'accented' to L1 English listeners.

Dialect variation

Some variations in the production of consonants are mainly due to accent or dialect differences. While there is less regional variation in consonants than vowels, we will consider the most obvious ones here.

Flapping

Many NAE speakers pronounce the /t/ or /d/ in the middle of word in the same way, so that, for example, <putting> would sound the same as <pudding>. The sound is voiced like a /d/ but is shorter than a /d/ when it occurs at the beginning of a word. This is referred to as a 'flap' sound in which the tip of the tongue briefly strikes the alveolar ridge as it passes to the place of articulation of the next sound. However, this only happens immediately following a stressed vowel or across word boundaries if the following word starts with a vowel. The flap allophone is transcribed as [ɾ] in the International Phonetic Alphabet.

So, the following would be homophones (words that sound the same) in NAE.

latt(ɾ)er	ladd(ɾ)er
bitt(ɾ)er	bidd(ɾ)er
putt(ɾ)ing	pudd(ɾ)ing

In informal speech, the 't's' in italics would be flapped (before a word beginning with a vowel):

I go*t* a new car
Shu*t* up
Ge*t* ou*t* of there

This use of flaps (in informal connected speech) is common for some GB speakers as well.

'Rhotic' versus 'non-rhotic' accents

The production of /r/ varies greatly across different English accents and dialects, ranging from a post-alveolar approximant /r/ in General British English to an alveolar tap (a single rapid beat with the tongue) in many Scottish and Welsh varieties. However, a much more significant difference is the split of accents into two groups according to where in a word the /r/ occurs.

In General British (GB) English, the /r/ phoneme is only pronounced preceding a vowel (pre-vocalic position) and in <red>, <arrive> and <hearing> but not after a vowel (i.e. post-vocalic position) as in <hear>, <her> and <bird>. Therefore, we classify GB English as a 'non-rhotic' accent, while many other varieties of English, including NAE, Canadian, Scottish and Irish have 'rhotic' accents.

Glottalization

A 'glottal stop', represented by the symbol [ʔ], is a plosive caused by obstructing the airflow in the glottis (i.e. by rapidly closing the space between the vocal folds). Glottal stops are found in many accents of English, particularly in British English. This addition of a glottal stop is referred to as 'glottalization'. In some accents, the glottal stop actually replaces the voiceless alveolar plosive [t] when it follows a stressed vowel:

e.g.: witness ['wɪʔnəs] sit down [sɪʔ daʊn]

Similarly, many accents of English replace [t] with [ʔ] when it precedes a weak syllable with a final [l] or [n].

e.g.: bottle [bɒʔl] and button [bʌʔn]

Glottal stops also affect a small number of high-frequency words, such as <get>, <it>, <that>, <got>, <not>, <quite> and <right>. This can confuse learners who are expecting to hear clear final consonants.

In some cases it is not always easy to distinguish between allophonic variation that is positional and that which is regional. For instance, the aspiration of initial voiceless plosives is common to most varieties of English, but not all. Further, Indian speakers typically will not aspirate initial /p/, /t/ and /k/, so that words like <beer> and <pier> may be hard to distinguish for some GB and NAE listeners. Similarly, glottalization is more common in some accents than others. Its use, however, is generally increasing in certain positions, such as mid-word and to replace final voiceless plosives, regardless of accent (e.g. butter [bʌʔə], what [wɒʔ], lot[lɒʔ]).

Vowels

Most of the world's languages have many more consonants than vowels so English is unusual in having almost as many vowels (up to 19) as consonants (24). There is also a lot of variation in the production of vowels among speakers) of English, both within a regional variety of English (for instance, differences in how the vowel in <bath> or <grass> is pronounced in GB accents) and between varieties (for instance, how the vowel in <pen> is pronounced by NAE and South African speakers of English). These complexities can make the English vowel system quite challenging for language learners.

The vowels described here are those of GB English but key accent variations will be considered. It is important to remember that there very well may be variations between your own vowel system and the one described here.

Producing vowels sounds

Vowels cannot be described in the same way as consonants. With vowels, unlike consonants, there is considerable space between the articulators and the air flows relatively unobstructed between them. Vowels are voiced and, also, all of them are continuants, as the sound can be lengthened and continued. As vowels are louder or more 'sonorous' than consonants and can be prolonged, they typically form the core (i.e. the 'nucleus') of syllables in languages.

Vowel sounds are classified in terms of:

(a) vowel quality
(b) quantity – duration of the sound.

Quality

The quality of different vowel sounds is described mainly in relation to the position of the tongue and lips.

Tongue position and shape

The tongue, lips and jaw are the main articulators involved in producing vowels. The tongue is a very strong, mobile muscle and its different parts can be raised or lowered or pulled forwards or back to produce different sounds. In the production of all but a few vowels, the tongue is usually convex in the mouth.

Vowels are classified, along a vertical axis, as 'close', 'mid' or 'open' (NAE specialists employ the terms 'high', 'mid' or 'low'), depending on the position of the jaw and how close the tongue is to the roof of the mouth. Along a horizontal axis, vowels are classified as 'front', 'central' or 'back', depending on which part of the tongue is raised highest in the mouth.

If you say the word <tea> followed by the word <tan>, for example, you should feel the tongue and jaw lowering for <tan>, as in Figure 6.14. When the tongue and jaw are lowered, it creates a wide-open mouth cavity with the tongue far away from the roof of the mouth. Vowels produced in this position are called 'open vowels'.

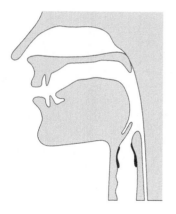 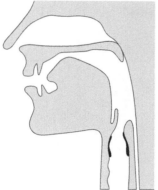 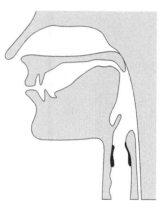

Figure 6.14 'tan'   *Figure 6.15 'tea'*   *Figure 6.16 'too'*

If you reverse the order, saying <tan> and then <tea>, you should feel the tongue and jaw rising for <tea>. This makes the oral cavity relatively closed with the top side of the tongue close to the roof of the mouth. We call vowels produced in this position 'close vowels'. Vowels where the front part of the tongue is raised (as in <tea>) are called 'front vowels'. Figure 6.15 depicts the front of the tongue raised close to the roof of the mouth for the sound /iː/ in <tea>.

Vowels where the back part of the tongue is raised (as in <too>) are called 'back vowels'.

Figure 6.16 shows that the back of the tongue is raised up and back towards the roof of the mouth for /uː/ in <too>.

Obviously, there are vowels that fall mid-way on both dimensions and we refer to these as 'central' (between 'front' and 'back') and 'mid' (between 'close' and 'open'). So, we have the following possibilities:

	front	*central*	*back*
close	tea /iː/	—	too /uː/
mid	ten /e/	ton	torn
open	tan /æ /	turn	tar

Practise saying <tea> and <tan> to feel the tongue and jaw moving from raised to lowered (from a close /iː/, then mid /e/, then open /æ / vowel). Then say <tan>, <turn>, <tar>, to feel the tongue moving gradually backwards (from a front /æ/ then central /ɜː/then a back /ɑː/ vowel). Finally, say <tar>, <torn> and <too> to feel the back of the tongue rising from an open-back /ɑː/ then mid-back /ɔː/ and then close-back /uː/. These articulations are not easy to describe to language learners but can be illustrated in a vowel chart, as in Figure 6.16.

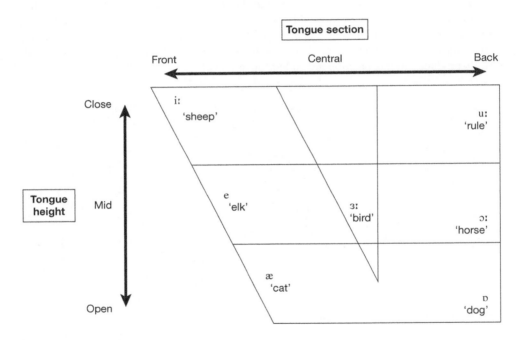

Figure 6.17 Vowel chart

This chart illustrates two dimensions: (a) tongue height, i.e. how high (close) or low (open) the tongue is in relation to the roof of the mouth, and (b) tongue section, i.e. whether the front, central or back part of the tongue is involved.

To understand the location of vowel articulations, it is helpful to illustrate how the vowel chart relates to the space within the oral cavity, as in Figure 6.18.

However, it should be remembered that it is very difficult to be exact about the position of the articulation of vowels as there is so much variation between speakers and accents. Nevertheless, the front/back and open/close distinction is important.

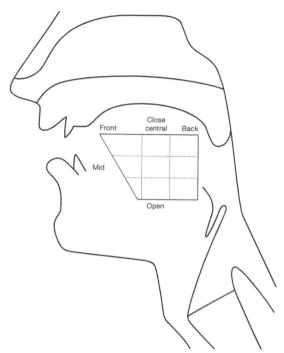

Figure 6.18 Vowel space

Lip shape

Another important factor in the production of vowels is the position of the lips, as a change in lip shape modifies the shape of the oral cavity and hence the resonance of the sound being produced. In particular, the degree of lip rounding creates different vowel qualities. We can describe vowels according to whether the lips are 'rounded', 'spread' or 'neutral', as shown in Figure 6.19.

Typically, in English and many of the world's languages, front and open vowels have spread to neutral lips and back vowels have rounded lips. For example, feel the difference in lip shape between the paired vowels of <see> versus <Sue> and <pet> versus <port> as the lips move from spread to a more rounded position.

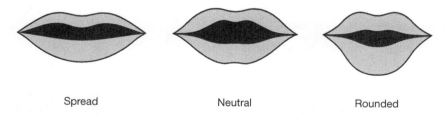

Spread   Neutral   Rounded

Figure 6.19 Lip shapes

Duration

In many languages, some vowels are of longer temporal duration than others. This is true of English, where a distinction is often made between short and long vowels, e.g. <bid> versus <bead> and <hut> versus <hurt>, although the actual duration of the vowels can vary depending on the degree of prominence given to a word in context. In British English the distinction is typically shown in transcriptions by using length marks for long vowels, e.g. /iː/ /uː/, while in NAE descriptions the difference is more often referred to as a contrast between 'tense' and 'lax' vowel sounds, reflecting the fact that short vowels are produced with less muscular tension than long vowels.

Tense	Lax
(long vowels)	*(short vowels)*
/iː/ beat	bit /ɪ/
/uː/ boot	book /ʊ/
/eɪ/ bait	bet /e/
	or NAE /ɛ/

Figure 6.20 Tense/lax vowels

In Figure 6.20, the vowels in the left-hand column, which require more musculatory effort, are sometimes called *tense* vowels, while the right-hand vowels are called *lax* vowels. It is possible to feel that the facial muscles are more tense when we say <beat> than when we say <bit>. Both length and quality help to distinguish the vowel phonemes in English.

The classification of English vowels

English is a Germanic language and characteristically this group of languages has a relatively large number of vowels. Many languages, such as Russian, Spanish or Japanese, only have five vowels. However even within English, the number of vowels varies, depending on the variety of English we describe, so for example GB is usually described as having 19 vowels while NAE is often described as having 15. We will look at the vowels of GB here. They include seven short vowels, five long vowels and seven diphthongs.

five long vowels:	/iː/ /uː/ /ɑː/ /ɔː/ /ɜː/
seven short vowels:	/ɪ/ /e/ /ə/ /æ/ /ɒ/ /ʌ/ /ʊ/
seven diphthongs:	/eɪ/ /aɪ/ /ɔɪ/ /ɪe/ /ʊə/ /əʊ/ /aʊ/

'Long' and 'short' vowels

The distinction between long and short vowels can be useful for learners of English pronunciation. However, the variation in length between vowels such as /ɪ/ in <bin> and /iː/ in <bean> depends on phonological context, even though there are also very real differences in quality between the two vowels, which is why different symbols are used to represent the vowels as well as a length marking.

Short vowels in English

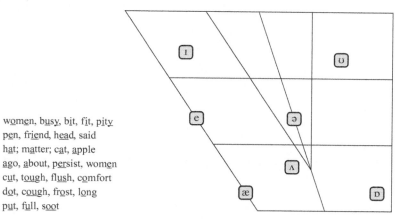

/ ɪ /	wom<u>e</u>n, b<u>u</u>s<u>y</u>, b<u>i</u>t, f<u>i</u>t, p<u>i</u>t<u>y</u>
/ e /	p<u>e</u>n, fr<u>ie</u>nd, h<u>ea</u>d, said
/ æ /	h<u>a</u>t; m<u>a</u>tter; c<u>a</u>t, <u>a</u>pple
/ ə /	<u>a</u>go, <u>a</u>bout, p<u>e</u>rsist, wom<u>e</u>n
/ ʌ /	c<u>u</u>t, t<u>ou</u>gh, fl<u>u</u>sh, c<u>o</u>mfort
/ ɒ /	d<u>o</u>t, c<u>ou</u>gh, fr<u>o</u>st, l<u>o</u>ng
/ ʊ /	p<u>u</u>t, f<u>u</u>ll, s<u>oo</u>t

Figure 6.21 Short vowels in English

The seven short vowels include three front vowels /ɪ/, /e/ and /æ/; two central vowels, /ə/ and /ʌ/; and two back vowels, /ɒ/ and /ʊ/.

Practice saying the three front vowels, <pin>, <pen> and <pan>, to feel the difference between the front-close vowel /ɪ/, then the front-mid vowel /e/ and then the front-open vowel /æ/. For all three front vowels, the lips are slightly spread. The /e/ vowel is similar to the North American vowel /ɛ/ but with /e/ the front of the tongue is slightly more raised towards the roof of the mouth. Learners may have difficulties distinguishing between the three front short vowels. In particular, if they have been taught the now 'old-fashioned' pronunciation of <pan>which was more like <pen> /pɛn/ and not so 'open' as the modern-day /æ/. This sound can also be confusing if the learner's L1 has this /ɛ/ vowel, as in German or Cantonese, which is half way between /e/ and /æ/.

The central vowels, /ə/ and /ʌ/, are quite similar but the tongue is slightly lower for /ʌ/. The lips are relaxed or neutral for both sounds. The main difference between these two vowels is that /ə/ only occurs in unstressed syllables (e.g. as '<u>a</u>nnoy', 'b<u>a</u>nan<u>a</u>') and /ʌ/ only occurs in stressed syllables (e.g. sh<u>u</u>t, r<u>ou</u>gh). /ə/ is called 'schwa' and is the most common vowel sound in English. Students may have problems with these sounds if there are no short-central vowels in their L1 (e.g. French, Arabic) but also the concept of having a reduced vowel /ə/ in unstressed syllables may be foreign to some learners.

Practise saying the two back vowels, <pot> <put>, to feel the difference in tongue height between them. /ɒ/ is a back, open vowel, while /ʊ/ is a close, back vowel. The lips are more rounded for /ʊ/ than for /ɒ/.

English has more short vowels than many languages, which can cause confusions for some learners. In particular, the front-close vowel, /ɪ/, and the central vowel, /ə/, may be new to many learners.

The five long vowels include one front vowel, /iː/; one central vowel, /ɜː/; and three back vowels, /ɑː/, /ɔː/ and /uː/.

/iː/ is a close-front vowel made with the lips slightly spread. It is more close and more front than the short vowel /ɪ/. Try saying <beat> then <bit> to feel the tongue lower slightly and the lips relax when you move from /iː/ in <beat> to /ɪ/ in <bit>.

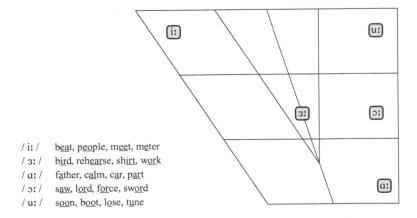

/ iː /	b<u>ea</u>t, p<u>eo</u>ple, m<u>ee</u>t, m<u>e</u>ter
/ ɜː /	b<u>ir</u>d, reh<u>ea</u>rse, sh<u>ir</u>t, w<u>or</u>k
/ ɑː /	f<u>a</u>ther, c<u>a</u>lm, c<u>a</u>r, p<u>ar</u>t
/ ɔː /	s<u>aw</u>, l<u>or</u>d, f<u>or</u>ce, sw<u>or</u>d
/ uː /	s<u>oo</u>n, b<u>oo</u>t, l<u>o</u>se, t<u>u</u>ne

Figure 6.22 Long vowels in English

/ɜː/ is a central vowel made with lips in a neutral position, as in words such as <heard> and <word>. Many English speakers use this sound when they hesitate ('er . . .').

/ɑː/ is the vowel sound in words such as <hard> or <palm>. It is an open-back vowel, made with lips in a neutral position and the tongue very low in the mouth (which is why doctors may ask you to say 'ah' when they need to look at your throat).

/ɔː/ is a mid-back vowel with rounded lips, as in words such as <call> or <lawn>.

/uː/ is the third short, back vowel, as in words such as <two> or <blue>. A posterior region of the tongue is raised close to the roof of the mouth for this sound, so it is a close vowel with rounded lips. Try saying <tar>, <turn> and <two> to feel the tongue gradually raising and the lips rounding further when you move from <tar> to <two>.

The general distinction between long and short (or tense and lax) vowels may be difficult for some learners to perceive or make, as, for instance, in the contrasts 'beat' /iː/ versus 'bit' /ɪ/; 'boot' /uː/ versus 'book' /ʊ/; and 'pat' /æ/ versus /ɑː/ 'part'.

Diphthongs

The vowels described above are single sounds, sometimes referred to as 'monophthongs' or 'pure vowels'. However, there are other English vowels that are composed of two sounds, called 'diphthongs'. Diphthongs consist of a central sound or 'nucleus', which is the core of the vowel and a transient 'off-glide' sound. In English the nucleus always comes before the off-glide, for instance <here> /hɪə/ and <how> /haʊ/, but in some languages the order is reversed. Diphthongs are all at least as long in duration as the long vowels discussed above and the nucleus (core) is their longest, strongest element.

GB English has seven diphthongs (many other English accents, including NAE, have fewer). These include:

- two centring diphthongs – where the sound glides towards the central /ə/ sound;
- three fronting diphthongs – where the sound glides towards the close vowel /ɪ/;
- two backing diphthongs – where the sound glides towards the close vowel /ʊ/.

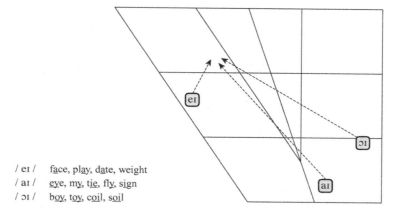

/ eɪ /   f<u>a</u>ce, pl<u>ay</u>, d<u>a</u>te, w<u>eigh</u>t
/ aɪ /   <u>eye</u>, m<u>y</u>, t<u>ie</u>, fl<u>y</u>, s<u>ig</u>n
/ ɔɪ /   b<u>oy</u>, t<u>oy</u>, c<u>oi</u>l, s<u>oi</u>l

Figure 6.23 Fronting diphthongs – gliding towards /ɪ/:

/eɪ/   This vowel begins at with the mid-front vowel /e/, as in <t<u>e</u>n>, and then glides to the more close-front vowel /ɪ/, as in <b<u>ay</u>>.

/aɪ/   The vowel's dynamic glide to a close position is more pronounced with this diphthong as it moves from an central-open vowel of /a/ towards the close-front vowel of /ɪ/, as in <buy>.

/ɔɪ/   This glide moves from the half-close-back position of /ɔː/ to /ɪ/, as in <boy>.

Practise saying <bay>, <buy> and <boy>. As you do, you will feel how the top side of the tongue ends up close to the roof of the mouth for the vowel in each word.

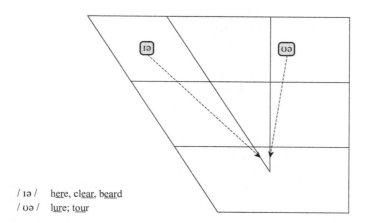

/ ɪə /   h<u>e</u>re, cl<u>ea</u>r, b<u>ea</u>rd
/ ʊə /   l<u>u</u>re; t<u>ou</u>r

Figure 6.24 Centring diphthongs – gliding towards /ə/

/ɪə/   This glide begins with the close-front vowel /ɪ/, as in 'p<u>i</u>t', and moves towards the central schwa /ə/, as in <pier>.

/ʊə/   The diphthong begins with the rounded, close-back vowel /ʊ/ and glides towards schwa /ə/, as in <cure>.

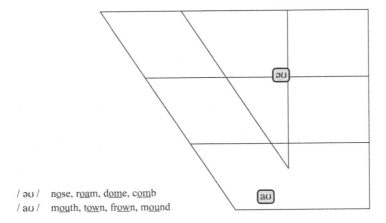

/ əʊ /   nose, roam, dome, comb
/ aʊ /   mouth, town, frown, mound

Figure 6.25 Backing diphthongs – gliding towards /ʊ/

/əʊ/   The nucleus of this diphthong is the central vowel, schwa /ə/, as in the first syllable of the word <ago>. It glides back and up with the top, back part of the tongue raised close to the roof of the mouth for the final /ʊ/ sound. The glide is accompanied by quite pronounced lip rounding.

/aʊ/   The tongue raises from the more central, open /a/ position and glides towards the more lip rounded back vowel /ʊ/.

Diphthongs plus /ə/

The five fronting and backing diphthongs can be followed by a schwa /ə/. For example:

eɪ+ə   =   eɪə   (player, layer)
aɪ+ə   =   aɪə   (hire, drier)
ɔɪ+ə   =   ɔɪə   (soil, royal)
əʊ+ə   =   əʊə   (lower, mower)
aʊ+ə   =   aʊə   (our, shower)

In traditional descriptions, these are referred to as 'triphthongs', composed of a nucleus and two glides. So the word <player>, for instance, would be /pl e+ɪ+ə/. However, many people intuitively hear a word like <player> as two syllables, with a semi-vowel /j/ in the middle (i.e. /pleɪjə/) rather than a single syllable with a triphthong /pleɪə/.

Diphthongs may be problematic to language learners who do not have any in their first language (e.g. French, Japanese, Polish) or where the sounds exist but spelling may cause confusion; for example, Spanish has the /aɪ/ and /eɪ/ diphthongs but L1 Spanish speakers of English may mispronounce the word <main> as /maɪn/.

Contextual variations in vowels

As mentioned earlier, there is a lot more variation in the production of vowels than consonants but most of this relates to accent variations, i.e. between individuals or between varieties of English rather than positional variations.

Positional variation

The most noticeable positional variations relate to vowel length and vowel reduction.

Vowel length

As mentioned earlier, vowels are of longer temporal duration before syllable-final voiced consonants, /b/, /d/, /g/, /z/ and /dʒ/. Vowels are also more fully lengthened at the end of a word, for example:

Short vowel	Long vowel	Even longer vowel
write	ride	rye
neat	need	knee

Vowel reduction

Vowels are frequently reduced in unstressed, weak syllables; typically to schwa /ə/ (which is why this is the most common vowel in English).

e.g.   mother   /mʌːðə/
e.g.   'banana'   /bənɑːnə/

Some varieties of English (e.g. many African English varieties) and some language learners, make much less use of vowel reduction. This does not necessarily have a negative impact on intelligibility but it can lead to perceptions of a noticeable 'accent'.

Dialect variation

Compared with consonants, there is less similarity between the vowel systems of different varieties of English. Some common differences are described here:

'bath', 'bat'

Some accents of British English (particularly northern ones) and most NAE speakers would say all of the following words with a single front vowel /æ/:

e.g.   bath, grass, after, sat, stand

However, GB English speakers would use a different vowel, i.e. the open-back vowel /ɑː/, for the first three words, /bɑːθ/, /grɑːs/ and the initial syllable of /ɑːftə/.

'pen', 'pin'

Many English speakers from New Zealand, South Africa and the southern states of the USA would use the same vowel sound for the two words <pen> and <pin>, i.e. the close-front-mid vowel /ɪ/.

'cut', 'foot'

The /ʌ/ phoneme is not used by a lot of Northern English speakers, so the same vowel /ʊ/ is used in words such as <cut> and <foot> for example, <He's cut /kʊt/ his foot /fʊt/> Similarly, for instance, the word <shut> might be pronounced /ʃʌt/ in GB English and /ʃʊt/ in northern varieties.

'cot', 'caught'

Most British speakers would use different vowels in <cot> and <caught> (i.e. /kɒt/ and /kɔːt/) but for a large minority of NAE speakers (approximately 25 per cent) throughout both Canada and the United States their vowels would sound the same (i.e. [kɔt]).

Post-vocalic /r/

The vowels in words like <sought> and <sort> would be the same for GB English speakers, i.e. a back, mid-open rounded vowel /ɔː/. However, rhotic accents (those that employ a post-vocalic /r/), including Scottish English and NAE, would pronounce the /r/ in <sort>. It has been suggested that the post-vocalic /r/, although not used in GB English, 'may indeed reflect a majority pronunciation among the total number of native speakers and will ease learning for many learners' (Cruttenden, 2008, p. 326).

Diphthongs

Many varieties of English have pure vowels, while a characteristic feature of both NAE and GB English is the pervasive use of diphthongs; for example, the word <no> can be pronounced as /nəʊ / in GB English and /noː/ in many Northern English, Scottish and NAE varieties.

In fact, only the three closing diphthongs /aʊ/, /aɪ/ and /ɔɪ/ are common across all native speaker varieties. Many diphthongs either vary considerably across regional dialects or are changing across generations. In particular, the /ʊə/ of <poor> is increasingly replaced by /ɔː/. Similarly, the /eə/ of <square> is increasingly being replaced by /ɛː/.

Recommendations for practice

Phonemes and intelligibility

Obviously, a level of accuracy is essential in the production and perception of individual sounds to ensure intelligibility. However, research also suggests that segmental errors seem to have a much greater impact on intelligibility between non-native English speakers of different L1 backgrounds who are using English as a shared lingua franca rather than between native English speakers (Derwing & Munro, 2015; Jenkins & Setter, 2005; Leather, 1999; Walker, 2010). It is also a common belief that a foreign accent, often noticeable at the segmental level, is the cause of a lack of intelligibility. This obviously can be the case, depending on the degree of accent and the context, as an L1 regional accent can be. However, research has shown that the relationship between accent and intelligibility is not straight-forward and there are cases in which heavily accented speech is clearly intelligible (Derwing & Munro, 2015; Munro & Derwing, 2006). The issue is deciding if and when an accent can be problematic with respect to intelligibility.

Because there is relatively little contextual variation in consonant phonemes, it has been argued that tolerance of errors is quite low and therefore there is a greater need for learner accuracy with respect to the consonant system (Rogerson-Revell, 2011). Consequently, the majority of the GB consonants are considered essential for intelligibility with L1 speakers of English, although some contrasts (e.g. /θ/ and /ð/; /ʃ/ and /ʒ/) are seen as unimportant for English as a lingua franca (ELF) contexts (Jenkins, 2000; Cruttenden, 2014). This is based on the concept of 'functional load', which refers to the importance of phoneme contrasts to distinguish meaning between word pairs or 'minimal pairs' such as 'bit' and 'beat'. So, for example, the phonemes /ʃ/ and /ʒ/ distinguish relatively few words and therefore carry a lower functional load than contrasts such as /s/ and /ʃ/, which distinguish many words (e.g. <<u>s</u>in > versus <<u>sh</u>in > or <me<u>ss</u>> versus <me<u>sh</u>>).

Unlike consonants, there is substantial variation in English vowels, so we could conclude that there will be greater tolerance of non-standard forms. Thus, vowel contrasts appear to play a less crucial role in intelligibility than consonant contrasts. Indeed, some researchers suggest a minimum ELF core of 10 vowels that are sufficient for international intelligibility. Notably the most frequently occurring English vowel, /ə/, is not included in this core vowel list, which is a matter of some debate among language teachers.

Key aspects of consonants and vowels for L2 learning and teaching

Throughout this chapter, reference has been made to segmental features, both consonants and vowels, which may be particularly difficult for L2 learners of English or may be problematic to particular groups of learners. Typically, difficulties can arise if a sound is 'new' to the learner, i.e. there is no equivalent phoneme in the L1 (for instance, the interdental /θ/ does not exist in French). Alternatively, if the sound, or a similar sound exists but is an allophone rather than a discrete phoneme (for instance, [v] is an allophone of /f/ in Arabic). The key aspects of English consonants and vowels that learners need to be aware of are summarized below.

Consonants

- The majority of consonant phonemes are important for intelligibility when interacting with L1 speakers of English.
- Aspiration is an important cue to distinguishing the voiceless plosives /p/, /t/ and /k/ from voiced plosives /b/, /d/ and /g/, in word-initial position (e.g. /pɪn/ versus /bɪn/), rather than voicing.
- Lengthening of the preceding vowel distinguishes voiced plosives from unvoiced plosives in syllable-final position (e.g. <right> /raɪt/ versus <ride> /raɪd/).
- Syllable-final voiced consonants (e.g. /d/, /g/ and /z/) are more common in English than most languages. So contrasts such as <ri<u>ce</u>> versus <ri<u>se</u>> and <ligh<u>t</u>> versus <lie<u>d</u>> can be difficult for learners whose L1 does not make this distinction.
- Word-final fricatives and affricates (e.g. <wi<u>se</u>> /waɪz/, <ri<u>ch</u>> /rɪtʃ/) are relatively rare across languages and can be a source of difficulty for many L2 learners of English.
- It may be easier to produce /r/ in all positions, as in NAE (i.e. a rhotic accent) rather than restricting the production of /r/ to pre-vocalic positions (i.e. non-rhotic accent), as in GB English. Rhotic accents are also spoken by a larger number of English speakers (Cruttenden, 2014).
- Other consonant contrasts that carry a high functional load and are therefore a high priority for learners aiming to use English either with L1 speakers or in English as a lingua franca contexts include: /r/ and /l/, /w/ and /v/, /tʃ/ and /dʒ/, and /tr/ and /dr/. The contrasts /θ/ versus /ð/ and /ʃ/ versus /ʒ/), in contrast, are seen as unimportant for ELF contexts (Jenkins, 2000; Walker, 2010).

Vowels

- All 20 vowel phonemes of GB English are necessary, if the learner target is a near-native English accent (Cruttenden, 2014).

- If the learner target is intelligibility in ELF contexts, five short vowels (/ɪ/, /e/, /æ/, /ʊ/ and /ɒ/) and five long vowels (/ɑː/, /iː/, /uː/, /ɔː/ and /ɜː/) may be sufficient (Jenkins, 2000; Walker, 2010).
- The /ʊ/ versus /ʌ/ contrast carries a low functional load (e.g. <l<u>u</u>ck> and <l<u>oo</u>k> are pronounced similarly in many northern GB accents).
- The schwa /ə/ phoneme plays an important role in the production of weak forms, word stress and rhythm and is therefore considered a high intelligibility priority for communications with L1 speakers. However, its importance in ELF communication is a subject of continuing debate (Jenkins, 2000; Cruttenden, 2014; Walker, 2010).
- The contrasts between / ɪ / versus / iː / (i.e. <sh<u>i</u>p > versus <sh<u>ee</u>p >); /æ/ versus /ʌ/ (i.e. <h<u>a</u>t> versus <h<u>u</u>t>); and /ɜː/ versus /ɑː/ (i.e. <c<u>ur</u>tain> versus <c<u>ar</u>ton>) should have high priority for all learners of English as they have a high functional load, distinguishing many minimal pairs.
- Only the three closing diphthongs /aʊ/, /aɪ/ and /ɔɪ/ are common across all native speaker varieties of English (Jenner, 1995). That is, <h<u>e</u>re> is usually pronounced as /hɪə/ in GB English, as /hiːr/ in Scottish varieties and as /hɪr/ in NAE. So, the teaching and learning of such diphthongs is less of a priority as long as vowel length considerations are maintained (Cruttenden, 2014; Jenkins, 2000).

Conclusion

As discussed at the beginning of the chapter, vowels and consonants constitute the sound segments of speech and form the building blocks of pronunciation. We have looked at how these sounds are made and shown the complexity of the English sound system in comparison with those of many other languages.

As with many aspects of language, individual sounds evolve and change. This is particularly the case with vowels since they have historically been subject to a great deal of variation and change. Currently, one of the more noticeable changes relating to vowels is the 'smoothing' of diphthongs as mentioned earlier, and, with consonants, the increasing use of glottalization, particularly by younger GB speakers

It should be remembered that most L1 speakers are either unaware of or unconcerned by segmental variations and changes in their own language. Also, despite the variations in the production of vowels and consonants, some of which have been outlined here, different varieties of English have high degrees of similarity and educated speakers of English generally manage to communicate with each other with reasonable ease (i.e. mutual intelligibility is maintained).

Note

1   In North America, the epsilon symbol /ɛ/ is used for the mid-front-lax vowel of <ten>.

References

Cruttenden, A. (2008). *Gimson's Pronunciation of English* (7th ed.). Oxford: Routledge.
Cruttenden, A. (2014). *Gimson's Pronunciation of English* (8th ed.). Oxford: Routledge.
Derwing, T. M., & Munro, M. (2015). *Pronunciation fundamentals: Evidence-based perspectives for L2 teaching and research*. Amsterdam: John Benjamins.
Jenkins, J. (2000). *The phonology of English as an international language*. Oxford: Oxford University Press.

Jenkins, J., & Setter, J. (2005). State of the art review article: pronunciation. *Language Teaching, 38*, 1–17.

Jenner, B. (1995). On dipthongs. *Speak Out!, 15*, 15–16.

Leather, J. (1999). *Second-language speech research*: An introduction. *Language Learning, 49*, 1–37.

Munro, M., & Derwing, T. (2006). Foreign accent, comprehensibility, and intelligibility in the speech of second language learners. *Language Learning, 45*, 73–97.

Roach, P. (2009). *English phonetics and phonology: A practical course* (4th ed.). Cambridge: Cambridge University Press.

Rogerson-Revell P. (2011). *English phonology and pronunciation teaching*. London: Continuum.

Walker, R. (2010). *Teaching the pronunciation of English as a Lingua Franca*. Oxford: Oxford University Press.

7

English syllable structure

Walcir Cardoso

Introduction and definitions

An article published by Livingstone (2014) in the British newspaper *The Guardian* entitled 'Do syllables exist?' stated poetically in its conclusion that

> [t]he syllable is an invisible thing, something that we can only really perceive and count when we say something out loud. It is hard to grasp scientifically and yet the basis for the most elegant things that humans have dreamed up out of the subtle alchemy of language use.

Although not conceptualized to define the syllable, this statement epitomizes some of the concerns encountered when one attempts to describe and investigate this elusive domain, which inhabits the intersection of sounds (concrete, *parole* in a Saussurean sense) and their prosodic organization (abstract, *langue*). From a purely phonetic perspective, Rogerson-Revell (2012, p. 115) defines the syllable as

> an alternation between vowel-like and consonant-like states . . . moving from a centre which has little or no obstruction to the airflow and which sounds relatively loud to the beginning and end of syllables where there is great obstruction to airflow and/or less loudness.

A simpler and clearer definition is provided by Bernhardt and Stemberger (1998, p. 110), for whom the syllable constitutes '[t]he smallest major grouping of segments that all phonologists agree on', or, phonologically speaking, an overarching prosodic unit that organizes segments of speech into the units of articulation that make part of our phonological system (Bybee, 2001).

Despite its hard-to-define nature, knowledge of English syllable structure is invaluable in the teaching and learning of pronunciation (Jenkins, 2002; Major, 2001). As documented in the literature, language learners have difficulties in perceiving and producing syllabic constituents such as onsets and codas (syllable-initial and syllable-final consonants, respectively; e.g. Cardoso, 2011a, 2011b; Carlisle, 2006). To complicate the matter, English has one of the world's most complex syllable structure systems (Yavaş, 2006), allowing up to three consonants in the onset and up to four segments in the coda position. A good example is the word 'strengths' (pronounced [strɛŋkθs] = CCCVCCCC, where C denotes a consonant and V a vowel), which contains a single syllable with three onsets and four codas (the longest syllable in English). Brazilian Portuguese, Farsi, Japanese, Mandarin Chinese, Spanish, Turkish and many other languages, on the other hand, impose restrictions on the number of constituents that can syllabify as onsets and codas, as well as the types of consonants that can syllabify within these two constituents. Japanese, for example, allows only one consonant in the onset (CV) and no codas, unless the latter is a nasal /n/ or part of a geminate. As can be anticipated, speakers of these languages have problems in pronouncing and identifying English complex onset clusters and codas in general: they modify the challenging segments either by deleting them (e.g. 'dog' becomes d[ɑ] in Mandarin Chinese) or by inserting a vowel, a process known as vowel epenthesis (e.g. 'dog' becomes dog[u] in Japanese; 'stop' become [ɛ]stop in Spanish). In perception, the inserted vowel is referred to as an 'illusory vowel' (see Cardoso (2011a), and Berent, Steriade, Lennertz & Vaknin (2007) for perceptual illusions in L2 syllabification).

Without receiving training or materials that explain how syllables work and their role in second or foreign language (L2) development, language instructors and non-native English speakers are unlikely to fully recognize the extent to which these constituents may be affecting L2 phonological acquisition. For instance, instructors may incorrectly believe that their students are struggling with a particular consonant (e.g. the onset /g/ in 'good') when, in fact, the problem relates to the perception and/or production of that sound in a not-yet-acquired syllable position (e.g. when /g/ syllabifies as a coda, as in 'dog'). Surprisingly, research on this suprasegmental component is rarely transferred to pronunciation texts (including teacher-oriented publications), despite being a highly investigated topic in L2 phonology (e.g. Cardoso, 2011a, 2011b; Carlisle, 2006; Major, 2001), an influencing factor (along with segments and other prosodic elements) in determining a foreign accent (Major, 2001), and one of the features that affect mutual intelligibility according to Jenkins's (2002) lingua franca core.

This chapter introduces the English syllable structure and its constituents, reviews the literature on the subject from both theoretical and applied standpoints, and argues for a more prominent place for the syllable in the L2 pronunciation curriculum, one that emphasizes current research on the acquisition of the L2 syllable in production and perception. These include: (1) the effects of first language (L1) and L2 phonotactics (the rules that govern the order in which segments appear in a language), (2) manner of articulation (the way in which the airstream from the lungs is affected by parts of the vocal tract, e.g. the release of airstream through the nose produces a nasal sound), (3) place of articulation (the location where speech organs approach or come together to produce a sound, e.g. the contact of the tongue between the upper and lower teeth to produce the interdental 'th'), (4) word size (i.e. the number of segments or syllables within a word), (5) saliency (the quality of being particularly noticeable by listeners) and (6) frequency (based on the assumption that the higher the frequency of a given form in the language, the easier it is to acquire it). The chapter ends with a discussion of the pedagogical implications for materials development and some of the challenges and directions for future research, with the aim of motivating the investigation of this prosodic constituent in L2 pronunciation studies.

Syllable structure: constituents, organization and its psychological reality

The standard and most common way of illustrating syllable structure is via a hierarchical branching structure (traditionally called a 'tree' diagram), composed of four constituents, as illustrated in Figure 7.1. Onsets are optional elements composed of consonants or glides (semi-vowels). For example, in the word 'pen', /p/ is syllabified in the onset, an optional constituent (indicated by parentheses) that precedes the vowel. It is optional because most languages (including English) allow the occurrence of onset-less syllables such as 'egg' and 'arm'. The rhyme consists of both the nucleus and the coda. The nucleus (usually a vowel) is the only obligatory component of a syllable and, as such, it may appear alone (e.g. the definite article 'a'), be preceded by an onset (e.g. 'so') or be followed by a coda (e.g. 'at'). Finally, the last constituent, the coda, can be occupied by consonants or glides, as illustrated by /n/ in Figure 7.1.

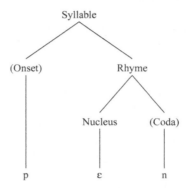

Figure 7.1 Syllable structure: a tree diagram

An important theoretical notion that governs the organization of sounds into syllables is sonority (one of the attributes of manner of articulation). Despite its wide use as a tool to explain phenomena that revolve around the syllable, the concept is notoriously difficult to define, as it can be characterized from a variety of perspectives that include amplitude (acoustically defined as intensity and perceptually as loudness or prominence), openness of the vocal tract, propensity for voicing, and acoustic energy (for a comprehensive discussion, see Parker, 2008). Based on these features, a sonority hierarchy has been established in which vowels are ranked as the most sonorous class of segments (adapted from Selkirk, 1982): (9) Vowels >> (8) Liquids >> (7) Nasals >> (6) Voiced fricatives >> (5) Voiceless fricatives >> (4) Voiced affricates >> (3) Voiceless affricates >> (2) Voiced stops >> (1) Voiceless stops (where >> denotes 'are more sonorous than'). This concept and related hierarchy are important because they serve to define the syllable in a more precise way: a unit comprised of an obligatory head, which constitutes the peak of sonority (usually a vowel), and surrounded by segments of decreasing sonority (usually consonants or glides). This sequencing of sonority within the syllable has been formalized as the sonority sequencing principle (Clements, 1990; Selkirk, 1982).

The concept of sonority is important not only for defining the syllable, as discussed above, but also for explaining certain L1 and L2 acquisition phenomena. For example, the difficulty in acquiring /s/ + stop onset clusters such as /st/ in 'stop' [stɑp] is often attributed to the violation of sonority sequencing within the syllable, as the fricative /s/ + stop /t/ + vowel /a/ sequence does not constitute a pattern of 'a peak of sonority surrounded by segments of *decreasing* sonority', as /s/ is more sonorous than /t/, thus constituting a case of sonority reversal (see Cardoso, John & French (2009) and Carlisle (2006) for similar analyses). The same applies to the acquisition of stop + /s/ coda clusters found in words such as 'fix' (pronounced [fɪks]), in which sonority does not progressively decrease; instead, it decreases and increases due to the presence of the stop + fricative sequence (/ks/; see Yavaş, 2006). Another ramification of sonority's importance is the generalization that, while onsets favour segments of lower sonority such as voiceless stops, the preference of codas is for comparatively high-sonority segments such as liquids and nasals (Clements, 1990). In the context of complex onsets, this generalization holds that higher-sonority distances are preferred among the members of the cluster (e.g. /tr/ in 'trip' is preferred over /dr/ in 'drip' because the former set constitutes a higher-sonority distance between the two elements, seven and six levels of sonority, respectively, based on the hierarchy discussed above).

The organization of segments into syllables is also governed by a set of (often intuitive) rules that determine what is permissible or illicit in the language. These rules comprise what is known as the phonotactics of the language. In the context of English, for example, its native speakers are aware of the restrictions that the language imposes on syllable well-formedness, allowing them to reject illicit onsets such as /ng/ in 'ngurt' but accept forms such as /pl/ in 'plick' in pseudowords. As expected, the knowledge of a target language's phonotactics is not easily acquired and, as a consequence, it is more likely to be subjected to L1 transfer (Archibald, 1998; Major, 2001). From an acquisition perspective, learning an L2 thus entails deciphering these phonotactic restrictions and fine-tuning one's L1 phonotactic knowledge to minimize its transfer into the target language.

As is the case with any theoretical construct, the concept of the syllable, particularly related to its constituency, has been challenged in the literature. For example, while Chomsky and Halle (1968) ignore its existence in their seminal work, others dispute the elements of its constituency (e.g. Harris's 1994 government phonology debates the existence of the coda constituent). Despite the controversy that surrounds the syllable, there are many intuitive and experimental arguments for its existence. Focusing on English, these include: (1) speakers' ability to count syllables (Derwing & Eddington, 2014; e.g. that 'book' and 'Canada' consist of one and three syllables, respectively); (2) speakers' ability to intuitively reject violations of the language's phonotactics (e.g. that 'gmo' is not a possible syllable in English); (3) metrical systems in poetry (e.g. the iambic pentameter, where each line consists of exactly 10 syllables); (4) language games (e.g. pig Latin, which transfers the onset of each word to the end of that word and adds [ej] such that 'banana' is pronounced 'ananab[ej]; see also verlan, a French language game that consists of reversing syllables such that 'Paris' is pronounced as 'Ripas'); (5) sonority-driven onset-coda asymmetries, as discussed above (e.g. while onsets favour segments low in sonority such as voiceless stops, codas prefer high-sonority consonants such as nasals; Clements, 1990); and (6) empirical evidence suggesting that young children are better equipped to count syllables, not phonetic segments (Lieberman, Shankweiler, Fisher & Carter, 1974). These arguments confirm that syllables are real and, accordingly, assumed to constitute parts of our phonological system.

Historical perspectives

The notion of the syllable has existed for over three millennia, when human writing shifted from pictograms to a syllabary system in which sequences of sounds were represented on tablets as onset–rhyme units (i.e. as syllables). According to Daniels and Bright (1996), this shift constitutes 'the most important advance in the history of writing' (p. 8) and, accordingly, it predates the appearance of the first letters used in the alphabet.

Although the syllable is one of the oldest constructs in linguistics, it only began to receive considerable attention in the field in the 1800s, when linguists attempted to uncover the Indo-European language family and realized that certain segments were systematically transcribed in different ways depending on their location within a certain sound stream. In the context of English, for example, this would be the equivalent of noticing that, while the word-initial /p/ in 'pop' is aspirated in (stressed) onset position, the same segment is realized differently as a coda: here, the /p/ is either unaspirated or unreleased. Later in the nineteenth century, with the advent of the International Phonetic Alphabet (IPA) and consequently an emphasis on segments and not syllables, an interesting and enduring dichotomy was established, with each side emphasizing its importance as the basis for linguistic analysis (Cairns & Raimy, 2011).

In the late nineteenth century, an important contribution to syllable studies was the development of the notion of sonority and related features, and their effects on syllabification. Initially proposed by Jespersen (1899), the idea was revisited by the American structuralist Bloomfield (1935) and Heffner (1949), and was further refined by Clements (1990), as mentioned in the context of the sonority sequencing principle in the preceding section. In 1939, Trubetzkoy proposed that syllables have an internal structure (roughly resembling what the representation in Figure 7.1 illustrates) and that they constitute domains for stress assignment, as is the case for English. Based on Trubetzkoy's proposal, Fudge (1969) presented the first theory of syllable structure in which the domain was decomposed into the four constituents illustrated in Figure 7.1: onset, rhyme, nucleus and coda. This idea was further developed by the proponents of prosodic phonology (Selkirk, 1982; Nespor & Vogel, 1986), for whom the syllable constitutes the locus for a variety of phonological phenomena (e.g. the English rule that causes /t/ to be pronounced as the glottal stop [ʔ] in coda position, as in 'wai[tʔ]' and 'a[tʔ]las', which many L2 learners perceive as t-deletion; note that [tʔ] indicates a glottalized /t/). Finally, one of the most recent and innovative proposals to define and explain syllable-related phenomena can be found in optimality theory (OT), a framework that combines traditional proposals such as sonority and syllable constituency with constraint interaction. Briefly, OT assumes that tendencies observed across language such as the avoidance of codas can be captured by the interaction of two constraints, one that favours its appearance (BeFaithful), and one that bans it (NoCoda). Languages such as English position BeFaithful more prominently in their phonology, resulting in the proliferation of codas in their phonological inventories, while languages such as Japanese and Mandarin avoid them due to their strong reliance on the NoCoda constraint (for an introduction to syllables in OT, see Féry & van de Vijver (2003)).

The current literature on phonological L2 acquisition, which only began seriously in the 1970s (Major, 2001), reinforces and reflects these developments in syllable studies and, as such, attempts to explain L2 phenomena by appealing to sonority, syllable constituency and constraint interaction. Some of the critical issues and topics from this research will be discussed in the following section.

Critical issues and topics

As is the case with other aspects of L2 pronunciation and phonology in general, one of the core problems in analysing the English syllable is how to describe and explain the variation observed in its L2 acquisition accurately and systematically. Consider the learning of English consonant clusters such as /tr/ and /dr/, where the former is acquired earlier and more easily (/tr/ >> /dr/; Yildiz, 2016). As discussed earlier, phonological theory attributes this behaviour to the sonority distance between the members of the cluster, favouring the sequence with the higher-sonority gap (i.e. /tr/ over /dr/). While this analysis provides an elegant and theoretically grounded explanation for the observed pattern, many questions remain. Are the results also triggered by the frequency of these forms in the target English language (L2 frequency/input effect) or in the L1 (where the cluster may occur as a coda-onset sequence; an L1 frequency effect), thus indirectly impacting learners' performance? Are they influenced by the better perceptibility of one form over the other? How do other, less abstract constructs such as ease of articulation influence their acquisition? What are the effects of extralinguistic factors (e.g. age of acquisition, gender) on the learning of these forms?

With respect to the asymmetries observed in onset and coda positions (e.g. onsets prefer segments of low sonority while codas favour segments high in sonority; onsets have little or no restrictions regarding place of articulation while codas prefer alveolar segments such as /n/ and /t/ – see forthcoming discussion), why are codas more prone to modifications such as substitution, deletion and epenthesis? Are these asymmetries caused by sonority and place of articulation restrictions, as they have been traditionally explained (see forthcoming discussion), or are they also triggered by cognitive factors or a combination of both? These are some of the critical issues and topics being addressed in the literature regarding the L2 syllable, as will be discussed in the next section.

Current contributions and research

Due to the nature of L2 acquisition, in which the learner's initial state includes knowledge of at least one first language, and the fact that one-member (singleton) onsets are found in all languages, studies on the L2 English syllable have traditionally focused on problematic onset clusters (stop + liquid sequences such as /tr/ in 'trip' and /s/ + consonant clusters such as /st/ in 'stop') and on the typologically rare codas. As expected, English speakers and learners produce and identify features in the onset more accurately than in syllable codas (e.g. Winters, 2003). This section reviews some of the research on these topics and their contribution to L2 research.

The acquisition of onset clusters

The bulk of L2 acquisition research on onset clusters in English has focused on the production of /s/ plus consonant sequences (sC henceforth). However, there are important generalizations that may be derived from studies involving other types of onset clusters, such as those by Yildiz (2016) involving stop + liquid sequences (CC; e.g. /tr/, /dr/ and /kr/). Briefly, these studies reveal that the acquisition of these onsets is influenced by both sonority and the place of articulation of the members of the cluster. For sonority, for example, it has been found that voiceless stop + liquid sequences (e.g. /tr/) are more accurately produced than voiced stops + liquid clusters (e.g. /dr/) because the former incur in a higher-sonority distance between the two members (see earlier discussion for more details about this analysis). As for place of articulation, these studies indicate that English learners produce clusters that differ in place of articulation (e.g. the velar + alveolar sequence /kr/ in 'cream' and the bilabial + alveolar cluster /br/ in 'bread') more accurately than those that do not (e.g. the alveolar + alveolar sequence /tr/ in 'trip'). The presence of the same places of articulation in alveolar + alveolar clusters such as /tr/ violates a principle that disfavours such a succession of phonemes: the obligatory contour principle (OCP), formalized by McCarthy (1986). This principle, which constitutes a modern version of Posner's (1961) dissimilation principle, is responsible for many phonological phenomena in English, including the epenthesis of schwa [ə] or [ɪ] in past tense marking for forms that end in /t/ and /d/ as in 'wanted' and 'added', to avoid the co-occurrence of identical places of articulation (e.g. /td/ becomes [təd] or [tɪd] in 'wanted').

The prolific literature on the analysis of another type of complex onsets, sC clusters, has revealed a number of interesting facts about its L1 and L2 acquisition. For example, there seems to be a developmental sequence in its acquisition such that /s/ + liquids are more accurately produced than /s/ + nasals and /s/ + stops, in that order. Explanations for this behaviour are based on sonority sequencing and the sonority distance between cluster members: for example, /sl/ and /sn/ are favoured because the gradual increase in sonority towards the nucleus is obeyed; /st/, on the other hand, violates this principle owing to a reversal in the order of sonority. The /sl/ >> /sn/ acquisition order is established by appealing to the sonority distance of the former (i.e. three levels between /s/ and /l/, as opposed to two for /s/ and /n/), which is higher and therefore less marked, and consequently easier to acquire. For similar analysis involving a variety of L1s, see Cardoso (2011b), Carlisle (2006) and Rauber (2006).

Another factor that may influence the acquisition of sC is place of articulation, as discussed at the outset of this section in the context of non-sC clusters such as /tr/. Research indicates that sC sequences that differ in place of articulation, such as alveolar + bilabial /sm/ and alveolar + bilabial /sp/, are more easily acquired because the places of articulation of the two sC members differ, while sequences that share the same places of articulation, such as alveolar + alveolar /sn/ and /st/, are comparatively more difficult to acquire. As discussed above, the explanation for this pattern is usually attributed to OCP or dissimilation effects, highlighting the universality of this principle that disfavours sequences of identical places of articulation. This pattern has been observed in a number of L2 syllable studies, including those of Carlisle (2006) and Yildiz (2016).

Finally, the acquisition of sC structure is also influenced by the cluster's length, supporting the hypothesis that longer constituents correspond to relative increases in markedness (Carlisle, 2006). Roughly defined, markedness refers to the state of standing out as rare or difficult (marked) in comparison to more common/easier-to-produce forms (unmarked). In a marked–unmarked relation, the unmarked (or least marked) form is assumed to be more frequent and easier to produce and, consequently, more easily acquired. In practice, Carlisle's findings suggest that longer (and rarer) trilateral onsets such as /str/ in 'strength' are more marked and, consequently, they are harder to acquire than shorter sequences such as /st/ in 'stop' (Anderson, 1987; Carlisle, 2006).

Concerning the perception of complex onsets, the field is still in its infancy, with a dearth of studies addressing the issue. Targeting a small number of sC clusters that share place of articulation (/sl/, /sn/, /st/), however, Cardoso et al.'s (2009) findings suggest that the frequency with which these sequences occur in the L2 input best captures their perceptual development in target English (contra a sonority analysis, as hypothesized, or perceptual salience, following Goldschneider and DeKeyser's (2001) proposal that forms that are harder to perceive are more difficult to acquire). Being the most frequent sC form in the target language, /st/ is more likely to be recognized as such, without an illusory (L1-transferred) epenthetic vowel, than the less frequent /sn/ and /sl/ clusters. This pattern contradicts the findings for production in which /st/ is the most difficult to acquire, as discussed earlier.

The acquisition of codas

Research on the acquisition of codas has yielded results relatively similar to those obtained for onset clusters inasmuch as they highlight the effects of place of articulation, manner of articulation (i.e. sonority) and length of the constituent (e.g. one versus two elements), as well as other coda-specific restrictions. As has been the tradition in phonology, the vast majority of these studies focus on the production of the constituent.

Starting with the effects of place of articulation on coda production, one of the main generalizations is the constituent's preference for alveolar segments (particularly n, r, l, t, d) in contrast to bilabials/labiodentals (/m, p, b, f, v/) and velars (ŋ, k, g), as observed in English and in the vast majority of languages. This means that, in L2 coda development, alveolars are more easily acquired than bilabials/labiodentals and velars. In phonological theory, this pattern is usually attributed to the markedness of bilabials/labiodentals and velars vis-à-vis alveolars as codas, thus suggesting that the latter are also mastered first in L1 acquisition and, consequently, are typologically more frequent (e.g. Cardoso, 2007; Wang, 1995).

Another important construct commonly used in explaining L2 coda acquisition is sonority, as the development of this constituent is characterized by a preference for highly sonorous segments. Based on the sonority hierarchy discussed earlier, the ideal codas in English are therefore liquids and nasals (i.e. /l, r, n, m and ŋ/, which form the class of sonorants), while the least preferred are fricatives, affricates and stops (e.g. /s, f, tʃ, t and g/, the obstruents). Findings that confirm this generalization abound in L2 syllable literature and can be found in the seminal works of Broselow, Chen and Wang (1998) and Tropf (1987). A sonority-based analysis, however, fails to explain the behaviour within the class of obstruents, where less sonorous codas such as /t/ and /p/ are preferred over their respective more sonorous voiced counterparts /d/ and /b/.

Finally, the production of codas is also affected by size constraints, such as the length of the constituent and the size of the word containing the coda. For the former, research confirms that the more constituent phonemes the coda has (e.g. [ŋkθs] in 'strengths'), the more likely it is modified by deletion or epenthesis (e.g. Anderson, 1987; Hansen, 2004). For word size, on the other hand, the reverse is observed: word-final codas are more accurately produced if they occur in words with more than one syllable (e.g. the word 'attack' is more likely to be produced accurately with the coda /k/ than 'tack' because the former word is longer – it has two syllables). The cause for this preference is usually attributed to a universal word minimality requirement that is also found across languages and in L1 acquisition (e.g. Bernhardt & Stemberger, 1998). Evidence for this phenomenon in English L2 acquisition can be found in Broselow et al. (1998) and Cardoso (2011a).

As was the case for onset clusters, research on L2 coda perception is comparably less common. In addition, the existing studies have overlooked many of the factors that play a role in coda production, including the effects of sonority, place of articulation, cluster length and word size. Although it is premature to make generalizations owing to insufficient evidence, the available findings provide some interesting insights. For example, while the perceptual salience of bilabials/labiodentals is higher than that of velars and alveolars, respectively (Winters, 2003; velars /k, g/ > bilabials /p, b/ > alveolars /t, d/, where > denotes 'are more perceptible than'), findings in Cardoso (2011a) suggest that the actual perceptibility of L2 English codas (i.e. alveolars and bilabials /t, d; p, b/ > velars /k, g/) requires a multidimensional explanation that must include a combination of perceptual salience, input frequency and constraints on place of articulation.

Effects of instruction

Although there have been a number of empirical investigations regarding the effects of instruction on the acquisition of segments and suprasegmentals (see Saito & Lyster (2012) and Saito & Saito (2017), respectively, for more recent research), the area concerning the effects that teaching may have on the acquisition of syllable constituents remains unexplored. This is surprising because, as indicated above, the learning of syllable structure is characterized by a developmental sequence phenomenon in which items are acquired in a piecemeal, sequential order. Consider the acquisition of sC clusters, in which the /sl/ sequence is acquired first and the most marked, /st/, last: /sl/ >> /sn/ >> /st/. From a pedagogical perspective, this raises an interesting question with regard to instructional intervention: will the effects of a focus on the form that is acquired later (and assumed to be more difficult) lead to the learning of forms that are usually acquired early (and assumed to be easy)? Or will the reverse lead to a more successful mastery of developmental sequences, as is usually implied in the design of L2 instructional materials in which these sequences are often introduced starting with more easily acquired forms (e.g. Ellis, 2002)? Second language literature contains a number of studies that show the effects of either (or a combination) of these two views on the teaching of different aspects of morphosyntax (e.g. Spada & Lightbown, 1999), but, surprisingly, there is only one study that has looked at instructional effects on the acquisition of syllable structure, involving the same sC set described above: /st/, /sn/ and /sl/ (see Cardoso, 2011b). Results show that the group that was taught exclusively the more difficult /st/ had the best overall performance in the acquisition of all three sC clusters, supporting Zobl's (1983) recommendation for the teaching of forms that follow a developmental sequence. Pedagogical implications of these findings and potential directions for further research on the topic will be discussed later in this chapter.

Main research methods

As suggested by the highly technical and sometimes complex ways to describe and explain L2 syllable-related phenomena, the focus of the majority of research on the subject has been purely descriptive and/or theoretical in nature. For instance, while some propose theoretical models for the analysis of L2 phenomena and the representation of syllable structure (e.g. Young-Scholten & Archibald, 2000), others examine well-established notions such as sonority sequencing and other intricate constructs for explaining interlanguage phenomena within this domain (e.g. Carlisle, 2006). In sum, the field of L2 syllable studies and associated research methods remain attached to this tradition of theoretical speculation, with little empirical evidence to substantiate highly abstracts proposals about phonological representations. For a critique of the traditional methods of investigating the syllable and an appeal for more experimental psycholinguistic approaches to the subject, see Derwing and Eddington (2014).

Recommendations for practice

Knowledge of syllable structure is important to make L2 learners mutually intelligible in English (e.g. Jenkins, 2002; Major, 2001) and to improve their overall pronunciation (see Rogerson-Revell (2012) for similar claims). Based on the findings discussed in this chapter and assuming that the primary focus of pronunciation teaching should be on improving learners' intelligibility (Derwing & Munro, 2005) and eventually lead them to an increase in fluency and impact (i.e. to make an impression on the audience; Rogerson-Revell, 2012), a number of recommendations for teaching syllable constituents can be put forward. Following a simplified version of Celce-Murcia, Brinton, Goodwin & Griner's (2010) framework for teaching pronunciation, the proposed suggestions respect a perception-before-production approach to L2 pedagogy in which the teaching of pronunciation begins with the development of sound awareness, is followed by controlled practice and culminates with communicative interactions involving both productive (speaking) and receptive (listening) skills.

The first recommendation concerns the teaching of consonants that appear in the coda position in English. Because these are particularly difficult to acquire in both perception and production, this constituent should be emphasized so that the form is easily perceived by language learners (e.g. via clear articulation of the consonant as if it appears in an onset: 'cat', pronounced as a disyllabic [kæ.t], anticipating one of the intermediate stages in coda development in which the consonant sounds like an onset – Cardoso, 2011c). The same constituent could then be emphasized in production activities using the same exaggerated pronunciation via choral repetitions. There are also a number of tongue twisters that can be used for controlled practice (see Celce-Murcia et al. (2010) and Linse (2005) for the rationale behind the use of tongue twisters in L2 pronunciation instruction). Consider, for example, the target codas in 'A bi[g] blac[k] bu[g] bit a bi[g] blac[k] bear. Where's the bi[g] blac[k] bear the bi[g] blac[k] bu[g] bi[t]?' An interesting aspect of this tongue twister is that it contains hard-to-acquire codas (i.e. stops, bilabials and velars) in environments that make them difficult to perceive and produce (i.e. preceding other stops, in monosyllabic words). Finally, learners can engage in communicative practice involving the target syllable constituent (e.g. creating a story containing a set of syllabic minimal pairs such as cop/copy, old/oldie, pick/picky, presenting it to the class, and providing peer feedback with the teacher's support).

Similar procedures can be followed for the teaching of onset clusters such as sC. An interesting feature of these clusters is that the first element, the segment /s/, is a 'continuant', indicating that its production can be easily sustained over time, just like a vowel. This characteristic allows the production of /s/ in isolation so that words such as 'speak' can be pronounced as two syllables: [s:.pik] (where ':' denotes a lengthened segment and '.' a syllable boundary). This way, teachers can develop learners' phonological awareness of sC by over-pronouncing the cluster as two syllables, as described above, and asking them to do the same via choral repetition and other controlled practice activities. The following tongue twister illustrates a sentence in which the target sC is one that poses the biggest problems for L2 learners: /s/ + stop sequences (Cardoso, 2011b; Carlisle, 2006; Rauber, 2006): '[st]ewart [st]arted [st]udying the [st]ory for the test'. For the development of meaningful com-municative practice, teachers could ask students to prepare a set of instructions, advice or recipes in which a number of pre-specified sC words must be used (e.g. 'start', 'smell', 'sleep', ensuring that the target sC is preceded by a pause or consonant so that the original sC sequence is not resyllabified as [s.C], a coda-onset cluster: th[is.t]ory for 'the story'). This activity could be followed by group or individual presentations to the class, accompanied by teacher and/or peer feedback on the observed pronunciation problems.

Regarding the items that follow a development sequence, findings from current research (Cardoso, 2011b) and scholars such as Doughty and Williams (1999) and Eckman and Iverson (1997) recommend that they be taught starting with and emphasizing the hardest and latest acquired element of the hierarchy. Regardless of one's preferred approach to teaching these sequences (an alternative is to follow their order of acquisition, as proposed by Ellis (2002), going from the easiest to the most difficult), the summary provided in Table 7.1 may be useful for determining teaching priorities based on the instructor's views or preferences on the subject. This table also summarizes the main findings discussed in this chapter.

Table 7.1 Syllable constituents and their order of acquisition in L2 English: a summary

	Order of acquisition		
Feature	*Acquired first: easy*	>>	*Acquired last: hard*
Syllable constituent	*Onsets*		*Codas*
Onsets			
Stop + liquid	Bilabial/labiodental/velar + liquid		Alveolar + liquid
sC: sonority	/s/ + liquid	/s/ + nasal	/s/ + stop
sC: place	Alveolar + bilabial/velar		Alveolar + alveolar
sC: length	Shorter clusters		Longer clusters
sC: perception	/st/		/sn/, /sl/
Codas			
Codas: place	Alveolars		Bilabials, labiodentals, velars
Codas: sonority	Sonorants		Obstruents
Codas: voicing	Voiceless		Voiced
Codas: length	Shorter clusters		Longer clusters
Codas: word length	Longer words		One-syllable words
Codas: perception	Alveolars, bilabials		Velars

Note: If not specified under 'order of acquisition', sC refers to all /s/ + consonant clusters in English.

Future directions

This chapter has introduced the English syllable structure, reviewed some of the relevant literature on the subject and highlighted the implications of what is known about this prosodic constituent for L2 pronunciation research and teaching. However, as indicated in parts of the chapter, there are still many issues that need to be investigated and/or corroborated in future research. This section presents three of these issues with the goal of motivating the investigation and teaching of the English syllable, and ends with an appeal for a more prominent position for this constituent in L2 pronunciation texts.

First, there is a clear need for research on the effects that syllable constituents and their attributes have on the development of L2 pronunciation (these include traditional features such as sonority, place of articulation and markedness, as well as psycholinguistic factors such as perceptual salience and L1/L2 frequency effects), particularly in perception. Because of the multifaceted nature of L2 phonological acquisition, discussed here in the context of the syllable, these studies should adopt analytical approaches that recognize that the learning process is constrained by multiple factors (Bayley, 2007) and, accordingly, that its explanation must be multidimensional in scope (Goldschneider & DeKeyser, 2001). This shift in focus is also likely to address Derwing and Eddington's (2014) demand for more empirical evidence to substantiate claims about the abstractness of phonological knowledge, particularly relating to the L2 syllable.

Another topic in need of further investigation relates to the effects of instruction on the acquisition of onset clusters and codas, as our knowledge about the impact that teaching has on the development of these constituents is rather limited. Some of the key related questions include: will the effects of a focus on the form that is acquired later (and assumed to be more difficult) lead to the forms that are usually acquired early (and assumed to be easy), as Eckman and Iverson (1997) recommend, but without empirical evidence? Or will the reverse lead to a more successful mastery of developmental sequences, as is usually implied in the design of instructional materials in which these sequences are often introduced starting from the easy end of the hierarchy (e.g. Ellis, 2002)? As discussed earlier, the empirical findings in Cardoso et al. (2009) suggest that an instructional focus on hard-to-acquire forms is sufficient to trigger the learning of relatively easier forms in a given developmental sequence, but these findings need to be corroborated by research involving other L1s, a wider variety of onset clusters, and other syllable constituents such as codas.

Finally, the third direction is an appeal for a more comprehensive coverage of syllable structure in pronunciation texts (e.g. teacher training materials, student textbooks), emphasizing current research on its acquisition in perception and production (i.e. the effects of L1 and L2 phonotactics, place and manner of articulation, word size, sonority, perceptual salience, frequency and instruction). Despite the longevity of the syllable as a phonological unit (Goldsmith, 2011), the relevance of its production to intelligible and non-accented speech (Jenkins, 2002, and Major, 2001, respectively), and the fact that its study has been an essential part of the development of phonological theories and phonological representations (Goldsmith, 2011), it is surprising that this prosodic constituent remains conspicuously absent from many pronunciation texts. When references to syllabic elements are present in pronunciation materials (usually using inadequate terms such as 'final consonants' or 'initial consonants'), they are often relegated to a chapter dedicated to consonants. Examples of this observation include popular pronunciation texts for in-training and experienced English teachers (e.g. Celce-Murcia et al. (2010); Kelly (2000); Kentworthy (1987) – but see Prator & Robinett (1985) and Rogerson-Revell (2012) for exceptions) and ESL learners (e.g. Baker (1982); Esarey (1997); Underhill (2005)). In addition, these texts provide no information on what is known about the English syllable and related effects on learning, including the perception and production of its constituents, as summarized in Table 7.1.

Figure 7.2 illustrates a general proposal for displaying, presenting and addressing syllable structure in pronunciation texts, one that assigns the constituent as much prominence as segments and other suprasegmental features. This suggestion thus demands a dedicated chapter for syllables so that its constituents and related restrictions are fully covered and, more importantly, so that instructors can become better equipped to address their students' syllable-related pronunciation problems. This proposed 'features of pronunciation' (or what to teach in an L2 pronunciation curriculum) reinforces the idea that the syllable inhabits the intersection of segments/sounds (concrete, *parole*) and their prosodic organization (abstract, *langue*).

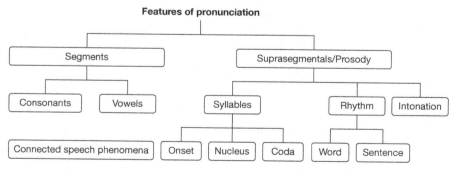

Figure 7.2 Features of pronunciation: the syllable as a suprasegmental constituent

Further reading

Cairns, C., & Raimy, R. (Eds). (2011). *Handbook of the syllable*. Leiden: Brill. This edited volume investigates the syllable from a variety of theoretical, empirical and methodological perspectives with the goal of addressing some of the concerns and challenges in defining this prosodic constituent. The book aims to answer the question 'what does the syllable do?'

Carlisle, R. (2001). Syllable structure universals and second language acquisition. *International Journal of English Studies, 1*(1), 1–19. The article reviews research that examines the influence of language universals on the development of L2 syllable structure. The discussion includes relevant concepts such as the preference for CV structures and the effects of sonority, frequency and constituent length.

Derwing, B., & Eddington, D. (2014). The experimental investigation of syllable structure. *The Mental Lexicon 9*(2), 170–195. Contrasting with standard research on syllables (often based on descriptions or theoretical in nature), this article reports on issues related to the use of experimental methods to investigating syllable structure in first and second language speech.

Goldsmith, J. (2011). The syllable. In J. Goldsmith, J. Riggle, & A. Yu (Eds), *The handbook of phonological theory*. Oxford: Blackwell. This chapter provides a succinct, albeit theoretical, introduction to the syllable. It covers many of the concepts discussed in this chapter, from a variety of perspectives for analysing the constituent.

Taylor, D. S. (1995). Vowels, consonants and syllables: An English teaching perspective. *International Review of Applied Linguistics in Language Teaching, 33*(1), 1–8. This article provides a basic, pedagogically oriented introduction to the English syllable by contrasting it with vowels and consonants.

Related topics

Transfer, contrastive analysis and interlanguage phonology; theoretical research in L2 phonology; English vowels and consonants

References

Anderson, J. (1987). The markedness differential hypothesis and syllable structure difficulty. In G. Ioup & S. Weinberger (Eds), *Interlanguage phonology: the acquisition of a second language sound system* (pp. 279–291). Cambridge, MA: Newbury House.

Archibald, J. (1998). *Second language phonology*. Amsterdam: John Benjamins.

Baker, A. (1982). *Ship or sheep? An intermediate pronunciation course*. Cambridge: Cambridge University Press.

Bayley, R. (2007). Second language acquisition: A variationist perspective. In R. Bayley & C. Lucas (Eds), *Sociolinguistic variation: Theories, methods and applications* (pp. 133–144). Cambridge: Cambridge University Press.

Berent, I., Steriade, D., Lennertz, T., & Vaknin, V. (2007). What we know about what we have never heard: Evidence from perceptual illusions. *Cognition, 104*(3), 591–630.

Bernhardt, B., & Stemberger, J. (1998). *Handbook of phonological development: From the perspective of constraint-based nonlinear phonology*. San Diego, CA: Academic Press.

Bloomfield, L. (1935). The stressed vowels of American English. *Language, 11*, 97–116.

Broselow, E., Chen, S-I., & Wang, C. (1998). The emergence of the unmarked in second language phonology. *Studies in Second Language Acquisition, 20*, 261–280.

Bybee (2001). *Phonology and language use*. Cambridge: Cambridge University Press.

Cairns, C., & Raimy, R. (Eds). (2011). *Handbook of the syllable*. Leiden: Brill.

Cardoso, W. (2007). The variable development of English word-final stops by Brazilian Portuguese speakers: A stochastic optimality theoretic account. *Language Variation and Change, 19*, 1–30.

Cardoso, W. (2011a). The development of coda perception in second language phonology: A variationist perspective. *Second Language Research, 27*(4), 1–33.

Cardoso, W. (2011b). Teaching foreign sC onset clusters. In K. Dziubalska-Kołaczyk, M. Wrembel, & M. Kul (Eds), *Achievements and perspectives in second language acquisition of speech* (pp. 29–40). Frankfurt: Peter Lang.

Cardoso, W. (2011c). Onset-nucleus sharing and the acquisition of second language codas: A stochastic optimality theoretic account. *Studia Linguistica, 65*(2), 198–231.

Cardoso, W., John, P., & French, L. (2009). The variable perception of /s/ + coronal onset clusters in Brazilian Portuguese English. In B. Baptista, A. Rauber, & M. Watkins (Eds), *Recent research in second language phonetics/phonology: Perception and production* (pp. 203–233). Newcastle Upon Tyne: Cambridge Scholars.

Carlisle, R. (2006). The sonority cycle and the acquisition of complex onsets. In B. Baptista & M. Watkins (Eds), *English with a Latin beat: Studies in Portuguese/Spanish English interphonology* (pp. 105–138). Amsterdam: John Benjamins.

Celce-Murcia, M., Brinton, D., Goodwin, J., & Griner, B. (2010). *Teaching pronunciation: A course book and reference guide* (2nd ed.). Cambridge: Cambridge University Press.

Chomsky, N., & Halle, M. (1968). *The sound pattern of English*. New York, NY: Harper and Row.

Clements, N. (1990). The role of the sonority cycle in core syllabification. In J. Kingston & M. Beckman (Eds), *Between the grammar and physics of speech* (pp. 283–333). Cambridge: Cambridge University Press.

Daniels, P., & Bright, W. (Eds). (1996). *The world's writing systems*. New York, NY: Oxford University Press.

Derwing, B., & Eddington, D. (2014). The experimental investigation of syllable structure. *The Mental Lexicon, 9*(2), 170–195.

Derwing, T., & Munro, M. (2005). Second language accent and pronunciation teaching: A research-based approach. *TESOL Quarterly, 39*(3), 379–397.

Doughty, D., & Williams, J. (1999). Pedagogical choices in focus on form. In C. Doughty & J. Williams (Eds), *Focus on form in classroom second language acquisition* (pp. 197–262). New York, NY: Cambridge University Press.

Eckman, F. R., & Iverson, G. K. (1997). Structure preservation in interlanguage phonology. In S. Hannahs & M. Young-Scholten (Eds), *Focus on phonological acquisition*. Philadelphia, PA: John Benjamins.

Esarey, G. (1997). *Pronunciation exercises for English as a second language*. Ann Arbor, MI: University of Michigan Press.

Ellis, N. (2002). Frequency effects in language processing. *Studies in Second Language Acquisition, 24*(2), 143–188.

Féry, C., & van de Vijver, R. (Eds). (2003). *The syllable in optimality theory*. Cambridge: Cambridge University Press.

Fudge, E. (1969). Syllables. *Journal of Linguistics, 5*, 253–287.

Goldschneider, J., & DeKeyser, R. (2001). Explaining the 'natural order of L2 morpheme acquisition' in English: A meta-analysis of multiple determinants. *Language Learning, 51*, 1–50.

Goldsmith, J. (2011). The syllable. In J. Goldsmith, J. Riggle, & A. Yu (Eds), *The handbook of phonological theory*. Oxford: Blackwell.

Hansen, J. (2004). Developmental sequences in the acquisition of English L2 syllable codas. *Studies in Second Language Acquisition, 26*, 85–124.

Harris, J. (1994). *English Sound Structure*. Oxford: Blackwell.

Heffner, R-M. S. (1949). *General phonetics*. Madison, WI: University of Wisconsin Press.

Jenkins, J. (2002). A sociolinguistically based, empirically researched pronunciation syllabus for English as an international language. *Applied Linguistics, 23*(1), 83–103.

Jespersen, O. (1899). *Fonetik. En systematisk fremstilling af laeren om sproglyd*. Copenhagen: Det Schubotheske Forlag.

Kelly, G. (2000). *How to teach pronunciation*. Harlow: Pearson.

Kentworthy, J. (1987). *Teaching English pronunciation*. New York, NY: Longman.

Lieberman, I., Shankweiler, D., Fisher, F., & Carter, B. (1974). Reading and awareness of linguistic segments. *Journal of Experimental Child Psychology, 18*, 201–212.

Linse, C. (2005). *Practical English language teaching: Young learners*. New York, NY: McGraw-Hill.

Livingstone, J. (25 June 2014). Do syllables exist? *The Guardian*. Retrieved from www.theguardian.com/education/2014/jun/25/english-do-syllables-exist-linguists.

McCarthy, J. (1986). OCP effects: Gemination and antigemination. *Linguistic Inquiry, 17*, 207–263.

Major, R. (2001). *Foreign accent. The ontogeny and phylogeny of second language phonology*. New York, NY: Routledge.

Nespor, M., & Vogel, I. (1986). *Prosodic phonology*. Dordrecht: Foris.

Parker, S. (2008). Sound level protrusions as physical correlates of sonority. *Journal of Phonetics*, *36*, 55–90.

Prator, C., & Robinett, B. (1985). *Manual of American English pronunciation* (4th ed.). New York, NY: Holt, Rinehart & Winston.

Posner, R. (1961). *Consonantal dissimilation in the Romance languages*. Oxford: Blackwell.

Rauber, A. (2006). Production of English initial /s/-clusters by speakers of Brazilian Portuguese and Argentine Spanish. In B. Baptista & M. Watkins (Eds), *English with a Latin beat: Studies in Portuguese/Spanish English interphonology* (pp. 155–167). Amsterdam: John Benjamins.

Rogerson-Revell, P. (2012). *English phonology and pronunciation teaching* (2nd ed.). London: Bloomsbury.

Saito, K., & Lyster, R. (2012). Effects of form-focused instruction and corrective feedback on L2 pronunciation. *Language Learning*, *62*, 595–633.

Saito, Y. & Saito, K. (2017). Differential effects of instruction on the development of second language comprehensibility, word stress, rhythm, and intonation: The case of inexperienced Japanese EFL learners. *Language Teaching Research*. Advance online publication.

Selkirk, E. (1982). The syllable. In H. Van der Hulst & N. Smith (Eds), *The structure of phonological representations* (pp. 337–385). Dordrecth: Foris.

Spada, N., & Lightbown, P. M. (1999). Instruction, first language influence and developmental readiness in second language acquisition. *Modern Language Journal*, *83*, 1–22.

Tropf, H. (1987). Sonority as a variability factor in second language phonology. In A. James & J. Leather (Eds), *Sound patterns in second language acquisition* (pp. 173–191). Providence, RI: Foris.

Trubetzkoy, N. (1939). Grundzuege der Phonologie. In *Travaux du Cercle Linguistique de Prague 7*. Gottingen: Vandenhoeck & Ruprecht.

Underhill, A. (2005). *Sound foundations: Learning and teaching pronunciation*. Oxford: MacMillan.

Wang, C. (1995). The acquisition of English word-final stops by Chinese speakers. PhD thesis, State University of New York, Stony Brook.

Winters, S. J. (2003). Empirical investigations into the perceptual and articulatory origins of cross-linguistic asymmetries in place assimilation. PhD Thesis, Ohio State University, Columbus.

Yavaş, M. (2006). *Applied English phonology*. Oxford: Blackwell.

Yildiz, Y. (2016). *Age effects in the acquisition of English onset clusters by Turkish learners: An optimality-theoretic approach*. Newcastle Upon Tyne: Cambridge Scholars.

Young-Scholten, M., & Archibald, J. (2000). Second language syllable structure. In J. Archibald (Ed.), *Second language acquisition and linguistic theory* (pp. 64–101). Oxford: Blackwell.

Zobl, H. (1983). Markedness and the projection problem. *Language Learning*, *33*, 293–313.

8

English lexical stress, prominence and rhythm

Jane Setter and Boikanyego Sebina

Introduction/definitions

Lexical stress, prominence and rhythm are very much intertwined in speech and pronunciation. They are suprasegmental elements, 'suprasegmental' referring to units larger than the individual sound segment, phoneme or speech sound. Lexical stress in English relates to individual syllables in words and can be defined as 'the force of articulation with which a syllable is uttered' (Arnold, 1957, p. 222) and the auditory effect this has on the listener. This force makes certain syllables more prominent than others, i.e. it makes them stand out more in the stream of speech. These syllables are referred to as being stressed or accented.

At the individual word level, stress begins to manifest itself in words of two or more syllables, one-syllable words being intrinsically stressed if spoken on their own in their citation form. Lexical stress rules, therefore, concern which syllable in a di- or multisyllabic word is pronounced with the greatest force of articulation. However, the rules are somewhat cumbersome and not easily learned.

Syllables in English words are made prominent by manipulating a combination of syllable length (duration), loudness (intensity), changes in pitch, and vowel quality (Roach, 2009). Stressed syllables tend to be longer than unstressed ones, louder than unstressed ones, often have a higher pitch than unstressed ones – or there is an audible pitch difference – and must have a full vowel rather than a reduced/weak vowel such as schwa (/ə/). It should be noted that 'pitch' here is used to refer to both the articulation and the auditory effect. For example, in the noun <desert>, the vowel in the first syllable is stressed and will sound longer, louder and higher in pitch than the second syllable. It will contain a full vowel, whereas the second syllable will not. In the General British accent (see Cruttenden, 2014), we can give the transcription /ˈdezət/, with the diacritic /ˈ/ indicating that the first syllable is stressed. Compare this with the noun <dessert>, which can be transcribed /dəˈzɜːt/, in which the vowel in the second syllable is stressed, i.e. it is longer, louder and pitch-prominent, and contains a full vowel. Acoustic displays of these words spoken by the first author indicate the differences (see Figures 8.1 and 8.2).

Speech rhythm in English arises from the placement of stressed syllables in utterances normally greater than individual words and from the listener's perception of the placement

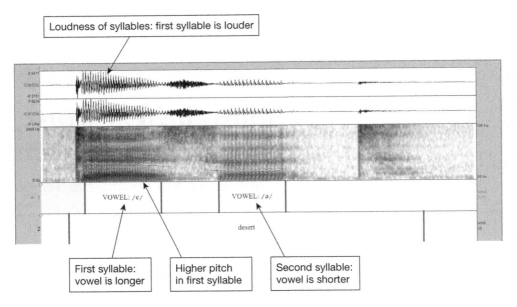

Figure 8.1 Annotated acoustic display of <desert>

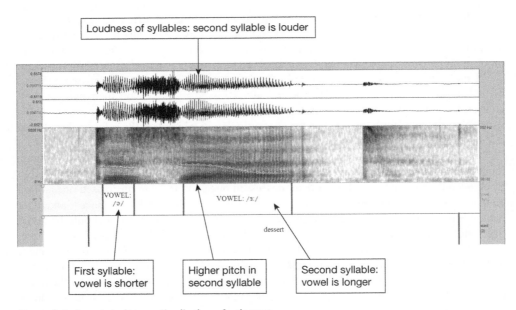

Figure 8.2 Annotated acoustic display of <dessert>

of these syllables. We are now, therefore, describing rhythmic stress – or 'sentence stress' – rather than lexical/word stress. Prominent syllables may be in single-syllable or multi-syllabic words dependent on the communicative message the speaker wishes to convey, and tend to be in lexical (content) words, such as nouns, main verbs, adverbs and adjectives, rather than functional (grammar) ones, such as determiners, prepositions, conjunctions, auxiliary verbs and pronouns.

For example, in the utterance <tell me she likes desserts made with icecream>, the lexical words are <tell>, <likes>, <desserts>, <made> and <icecream>. Theoretically, the rhythmic stresses are likely to fall on the following syllables (1):

(1)　'tell me she 'likes de'sserts 'made with 'icecream

We can divide this utterance into groups known as the 'foot', each foot beginning with the onset of a stressed syllable. This utterance, therefore, has five feet (2):

(2)　|'tell me she |'likes de |'sserts | 'made with | 'icecream

In addition, according to the theory of stress-timing, the time the speaker takes to produce each foot – i.e. the syllables between each stress – will be equal; that is, it will take the same amount of time to say the three syllables <tell me she> from the onset of the first syllable <tell> as it will to say the two syllables <likes de-> from the onset of the syllable <likes> and the single-syllable <-sserts>. This is known as 'isochrony' (Abercrombie, 1967).

However, in actual speech, it is entirely possible to produce this utterance with three rhythmic stresses, for example (3), or even fewer:

(3)　|'tell me she likes de |'sserts made with | 'icecream

In (3), it will theoretically take the same amount of time to say <tell me she likes de-> (five syllables) as to say <-sserts made with> (three syllables).

We refer to the lexical words in this utterance as 'stressable', i.e. it is likely that the lexical words will be rhythmically stressed rather than the function words (1), but it is not necessary that they all are (3). However, it is also possible for the non-lexical words to become prominent, depending on prior context and the intentions of the speaker.

(4)　|'tell me | 'she likes de |'sserts made with | 'icecream

In (4), <she> is made prominent to draw the listener's attention to that word, in contrast with another person implicated in the discourse, for example. This will have an effect on the rhythm of the utterance in that we now have the feet <tell me> (two syllables) and <she likes de-> (three syllables) but, in theory, it should not affect the stress-timing; i.e. theoretically, the time it takes to say each foot will still be equal.

Anderson-Hsieh (1992, p. 51) writes: 'Suprasegmentals provide the framework for utterances, they direct the listener's attention to important information in the discourse, and they help to establish cultural harmony between the speaker and listener.' Speakers of varieties of English that use lexical stress and speech rhythm in the way described above will therefore expect stresses and rhythm to be reliable indicators of meaning in an utterance. Deviation from the expected forms can have serious consequences for intelligibility, comprehensibility and cultural harmony. However, how one predicts lexical stress in new words and whether English really is stress-timed are problematic issues.

Historical perspectives

Lexical stress

Historically, definitions of lexical stress in English centre on the fact that, in multisyllabic words, some syllables have greater force of articulation than others. Intensity, or loudness, is usually given as a salient feature. For example, Bloomfield (1933), Bloch and Trager (1942) and Pike (1947) all mention intensity or loudness; Jones (1949) and Arnold (1957) refer to the force of utterance of a syllable. This is often followed by a discussion of levels of stress; Jones (1956, p. 142) explains that it is possible to distinguish 'up to four degrees of stress', but notes that it is adequate to refer to three or even two levels. In Jones's *English Pronouncing Dictionary* (EPD), first published in 1917 (current 18th edition, 2011), two levels of stressed syllable are indicated: primary and secondary stress, although this could be counted as three if one takes 'unstressed' to be a level of stress. Similarly, Kenyon and Knott's *Pronouncing Dictionary of American English* (1953) indicates primary and secondary stress, using the term 'accent' in preference to 'stress' (p. xviii). The first edition of Wells's *Longman Pronunciation Dictionary* (1990) indicates tertiary stress, but this was later dropped.

The main stress in a word is associated with 'pitch prominence' (Arnold 1957, p. 225), i.e. there is a noticeable change in pitch when a stressed syllable is uttered. We will refer to this type of stress as primary stress.

As an example, let us consider the words <photograph>, <photography> and <photographic>, as given in (5):

(5) (a) 'photograph
    (b) pho'tography
    (c) ,photo'graphic

The stress mark (') on <photograph> (5a) indicates that primary stress is on the first syllable. This is likely to be pitch-prominent in comparison with the others and, if spoken in citation form, will normally be the onset of a falling intonation pattern. The stress mark on the second syllable of <photography> (5b) indicates the first syllable is unstressed and the linguistically prominent material begins on the second syllable; similarly, this syllable will be the onset of a falling intonation pattern if spoken in citation form. See the chapters on intonation for more information about tone choice.

The stress pattern in <photographic> (5c) is different in that both primary (') and secondary (,) stress are indicated. Arnold (1957, p. 225) argues that secondary stress 'lacks the pitch prominence always associated with a principle stress'. Therefore, the first syllable of <photographic> is likely to be louder than the unstressed syllables, but not stand out as much as the third syllable, which is indicated to be primary and pitch-prominent. In general, one can also expect stressed syllables to be greater in length than unstressed ones, and incrementally so; we can therefore expect the third syllable of <photographic> to be the longest in the word, followed by the first.

Lexical stress is also linked intrinsically to vowel quality in English; a stressed syllable must contain a full vowel, not a weak one. An unstressed syllable, however, may contain a full vowel or a reduced/weak vowel. There is a lengthy discussion of this in Arnold (1957), where he refers to 'LENIS' and 'FORTIS' vowels (small capitals in the original). LENIS vowels are those 'which are *normally* rhythmically weak' (Arnold, 1957, p. 235, italics in the original): /i, ə, u, o/; FORTIS vowels are those 'which are *normally* rhythmically strong' (Arnold, 1957, p. 235, italics in the original): /iː, e, æ, ɑː, ɔ, ɔː, uː, ʌ, əː, ei, əu, ai, au, ɔi, ɛə/ (vowel symbols from the original). Arnold then covers the rules of assignation of stress to syllables in words, based on word type and whether a syllable contains a FORTIS or a LENIS vowel; this complex exposition continues from page 237 to page 441, i.e. 205 pages. Jones (1949) comments on the lack of useful rules for English lexical stress and indicates that foreign learners must simply learn the stress of a word when they learn the word.

Rhythm

The first thorough treatment of the notion that English has stressed syllables that are equally spaced in time is attributed to Steele, 'who in 1775 [tried] to represent speech rhythm by means of musical notation, dividing stretches of speech into "cadences" equivalent to musical bars, each of them beginning with a strong syllable' (Knowles, 1987, p. 144). Although later work on rhythmic grouping in English dispensed with the musical notation, the idea of dividing up groups of syllables beginning with a strong stress (i.e. a foot) has persevered.

Classe investigated the reality of isochronous stress in English prose, commenting that, in normal speech, 'the realisation of a perfectly isochronous rhythm would sometimes produce ludicrous results' (Classe, 1939, p. 70). What is viewed as permissible is the idea of English speech being composed of 'more or less isochronous groups' (1939, p. 133). He concludes in one section that 'perfect isochronism can only be realised when very definite conditions are fulfilled . . . similarity of phonetic structure of the groups, including number of syllables' and 'similarity of grammatical structure of the groups, and similarity of connexion between the groups' (Classe, 1939, p. 100).

As Classe notes, these conditions are not commonly met in ordinary speech but are found in poetry. The controversial terms 'stress-timed' and 'syllable-timed' first appear in Pike (1945). Using what he calls the 'rhythm unit' as a basis for analysis, Pike states:

> The timing of rhythmic units produces a rhythmic succession which is an extremely important characteristic of English phonological structure. The units tend to follow one another in such a way that the lapse of time between the beginning of their prominent syllables is somewhat uniform.
>
> (Pike, 1945, p. 34)

It is this uniformity of spacing of stressed syllables that gives rise to 'the obscuring of vowels' (Pike, 1945, p. 35), i.e. the tendency of unstressed vowels to weaken.

Pike's rhythm unit conforms to what some phoneticians have called the tone unit (see e.g. Roach, 2009, p. 144; Brazil, 1994, p. 3). In his examples, each rhythm unit is given only one stress that is tonic/nuclear. The focus is on grammatical phrases or clauses, which links rhythm strongly to the way that grammatical relationships are expressed in the language and is a view held by others (e.g. Lehiste, 1977; Cutler & Isard, 1980; Pisoni, 1981; Halliday, 1989). Pike's main claim concerning stress-timing seems to be that the tonic syllables of rhythm units are equally spaced, and that the nature of a stressed-timed language is that it contains rhythm units that themselves contain one main stress. He refers to this as a stress-timed unit (Pike, 1945, p. 35). It is noted, however, that all the stressed syllables in a possible rhythm unit containing more than one stressed syllable have 'equal lapses of time' between them (Pike, 1945, p. 34). This is the more usual interpretation of stress-timing.

By contrast, syllable-timing is defined by Pike as follows:

> a rhythm which is more closely related to the syllable; . . . it is the syllables, instead of the stresses, which tend to come at more or less evenly recurrent intervals.
>
> (Pike, 1945, p. 35)

Pike asserts that the syllables are 'less likely to be shortened and modified' (1945, p. 35), giving Spanish as an example of a syllable-timed language.

Abercrombie (1967, p. 97) claims that, '[a]s far as is known, every language in the world is spoken with one kind of rhythm or with the other', and attributes differences between the rhythms of French, Telugu and Yoruba (syllable-timed) on the one hand and English, Russian and Arabic (stress-timed) on the other to the way the pulmonic airstream mechanism is utilized during speech. Following work by Stetson (1957, in Kelso & Munhall 1988), later discredited by Ladefoged (1967), Abercrombie (1967) claims that, in syllable-timed languages, it is the chest pulses producing the airstream for the syllables that are equally spaced, which leads to the isochrony of syllables in these languages. Conversely, in stress-timed languages it is 'the stress-pulses, and hence the stressed syllables' that are isochronous (Abercrombie, 1967, p. 97), leading to the necessity to adjust the length and/or speech rate of successive syllables. Abercrombie (1967, p. 98) uses the following sentence to demonstrate the variation:

| Which is the | train for | Crewe, | please?

Tapping one's finger for each individual syllable, the syllables would be unequally spaced; however, if one taps just the initial syllable, which is stressed, the taps are equally spaced. Abercrombie concludes that

> there is considerable variation in syllable-length in a language spoken with a stress-timed rhythm, whereas in a language spoken with a syllable-timed rhythm the syllables tend to be of equal length.
>
> (Abercrombie, 1967, p. 98)

He notes that few learners of English succeed in mastering stress-timed rhythm without training.

Halliday states that English is a foot-timed language, in which 'all *feet* are more or less the same length' (Halliday 1989, p. 50; emphasis in the original). This is in comparison with French and Hindi, which are examples of languages in which 'all *syllables* are more or less the same length' (Halliday, 1989, p. 50). Although basically seeming to uphold the notion of isochrony in English, Halliday (1989, p. 50) draws our attention to the phrase 'more or less'. In some contexts, he says, it is possible to have feet which are exactly the same length. In most contexts in ordinary conversation, however, the lengths of the feet are not likely to be the same, with a two-syllable foot being slightly longer than a one-syllable foot, 'but nothing like twice as long' (Halliday, 1989, p. 50). In addition, he claims that 'the relative duration of syllables in the foot is also entirely systematic; it is determined by a combination of grammatical and phonological factors' (Halliday, 1989, p. 51).

To end his treatment of English speech rhythm, like Abercrombie (1967), Halliday notes the difficulties faced by learners of English in 'getting the rhythm right' (1989, p. 52), especially for those from a syllable-timed language background, commenting that it can cause unintelligibility.

Critical issues and topics

Lexical stress

Various psychological studies of speech perception demonstrate that deviations from typical English stress patterns can cause difficulty in the correct parsing of a message. This is in comparison with speakers of languages with fixed stress, as lexical stress may not be stored in the mental lexicon; see, e.g. Peperkamp and Dupoux (1992, cited in Field 2005).

Cutler (1984) explains that English 'word stress patterns are an integral part of the phonological representations of words in the mental lexicon' (1984, p. 78) and that something that comes close to that representation must be produced by the speaker. It is, therefore, crucial that this close approximation to the mental representation has correct stressing. If this is not achieved, the listener will at the very best have difficulty reconstructing the message. Cutler & Norris (1988) suggest that lexical access is initiated by the occurrence of a stressed syllable, claiming that the high frequency of English content words starting with stressed syllables means that this strategy works very well in English. This is also supported by Grosjean and Gee (1987), who claim that 'stressed syllables (and only they) are used to initiate lexical search' (1987, p. 144), and Fear, Cutler and Butterfield (1995), who highlight the role of strong and weak syllables in speech perception.

If the stressed syllables in a stream of English speech are incorrectly placed, native speakers may process the message as something completely different. Field (2005) discovered that altering the lexical stress in English disyllabic words had a negative effect on both native and non-native listeners, but that this effect was lessened if the syllables each contained a full vowel. He further discovered that moving the stress to the left – i.e. earlier – in words that normally had stress on the second syllable had a lesser impact than moving it to the right on words normally stressed on the first syllable. He gives the example of <followed> stressed on the second syllable rather than the first, suggesting that, if the listener perceived <load> or <flowed>, this would 'shape [their] expectations as to what was likely to follow' in a way that could seriously impede overall intelligibility (Field, 2005, p. 418).

Rhythm

The notion of stress-timing in English has been disputed, both in terms of whether there is such a thing as a stress-timed versus syllable-timed distinction in languages, and also whether English is, in fact, stress-timed at all. Crystal (1996, p. 8) claims that the distinction 'is an extremely crude one, and in its bare form almost certainly wrong'; Marks (1999, p. 194) concludes 'that stress-timing is something of a myth'; Faber (1986, p. 206) refers to it as 'extremely suspect'; Cauldwell (2002) describes English as 'irrhythmical'. Knowles (1987) claims that listeners are 'willing to treat considerably different intervals as perceptually equal' (p. 145).

Reporting on inconclusive experiments designed to measure the presence or absence of stress-timing in metric feet, Lehiste (1977) found inconclusive support for isochrony. However, she explains that, in English, 'the listener expects isochrony' (Lehiste, 1977, p. 262). She concludes that isochrony is an integrated part of the grammar of English by demonstrating that speakers use it to disambiguate ambiguous sentences, and reports that similar findings were made by O'Malley, Kloker and Dara-Abrams (1973), who looked at how sections in parentheses in algebraic expressions are indicated in speech – e.g. <a + (b × c) versus (a + b) × c>.

Roach (1982) examined spontaneous speech recordings of speakers of Abercrombie's (1967) six languages to see whether it is possible to clearly assign them to one category or the other. Two of Abercrombie's claims are tested:

(i) there is considerable variation in syllable length in a language spoken with stress-timed rhythm whereas in a language spoken with syllable-timed rhythm the syllables tend to be equal in length

(ii) in syllable-timed languages, stress pulses are unevenly spaced.

(Abercrombie, 1967, p. 98)

Concerning (i), Roach measured the standard deviation of the syllable durations in milliseconds and found that the claim was not supported. He also dismissed claim (ii). Hypothesizing that, in order for the claim to be valid, 'syllable-timed languages would exhibit a wider range of percentage deviations in inter-stress intervals than would stress-timed (the latter being more nearly isochronous)' (1982, p. 77), Roach finds that the so-called stress-timed languages demonstrate the greater range of deviance, concluding that one cannot assign languages to either category solely by measuring the time intervals. Like Lehiste (1977), he concludes that 'a language is syllable-timed if it *sounds* syllable-timed' (Roach, 1982, p. 78), and that 'all languages display both sorts of timing' (Roach, 1982, p. 78). This is supported by Miller (1984), whose experiment on the perception of the timing of different languages by groups of French and English phoneticians and non-phoneticians leads her to conclude that 'each language displays features of both types [of timing] in different proportions' (Miller, 1984, p. 82). Roach (1982) also notes that the same speaker may demonstrate different types of timing, with perhaps more formal language being more rhythmical. If one listens to well-known and, often, rehearsed speeches, such as Martin Luther King's <I have a dream> (delivered on 28 August 1963 – see www.youtube.com/watch?v=n82rgdbM9G4 for an excerpt), there is certainly a strongly rhythmic, almost poetic quality to many of them. This type of speech is referred to by Cauldwell (2002) as having 'elected' rhythmicality (see below).

Comparing English, Thai, Spanish, Italian and Greek speakers producing continuous speech, as in Roach (1982), Dauer (1983) finds that inter-stress intervals in English are no more isochronous than those in Spanish, and that the rhythmic difference between the two languages 'has nothing to do with the durations of inter-stress intervals' (Dauer, 1983, p. 54). To account for the fact that, e.g., English and Spanish sound different rhythmically, Dauer (1983) looks at syllable structure, vowel reduction and stress/accent. She finds that there is 'a greater variety in permissible syllable types' in stress-timed languages (Dauer, 1983, p. 55) and that open syllables (CV, where C stands for 'consonant' and V for 'vowel') are found to predominate in Spanish and French, whereas in English there is much more variation among different syllable types. Dauer also finds that 'there is a strong tendency for "heavy" syllables . . . to be stressed and "light" syllables . . . to be unstressed' in stress-timed languages (1983, p. 55); 'light' syllables are those structured CV or V, whereas heavy syllables have a consonantal coda (i.e. one or more consonants at the end, including a glide) and may contain consonant clusters (e.g. <stray> /streɪ/ has a cluster of three consonants at the beginning). She notes that the two most common syllable types in English are CVC and CV, with stressed syllables tending to be CVC. Unstressed CV syllables often contain one of a small set of shortened weakened vowels. These features are similar in Arabic and Thai, also considered to be stress-timed. Spanish, however is different, with CV syllables

Figure 8.3 Dauer's stress-based continuum (1983, p. 60)

predominating, 'whether stressed or unstressed' (Dauer, 1983, p. 56), and fewer variations in syllable duration. Concerning stress, Dauer (1983) claims that syllable-timed languages tend to have no lexical stress, whereas stress-timed languages do.

Preferring the term 'stress-based' (as used by both Allen (1975) and O'Connor (1973)), like Roach (1982), Dauer suggests a continuum on which languages may be placed depending on how stress-based their rhythm is. Her suggestion is as shown in Figure 8.3.

As instrumental studies of rhythm in speech cannot be relied upon when assigning languages to a rhythmic group, Ramus, Nespor and Mehler (1999) refer to Dauer's account of how several factors contribute independently 'the phonological account of rhythm' (Ramus et al., 1999, p. 269). However, this phonological account 'does not explain how rhythm is extracted from the speech signal by the perceptual system' (Ramus et al., 1999, p. 269). Ramus et al. (1999) took instrumental measurements based on consonant and vowel segmentation for eight languages (English, Polish, Dutch, French, Spanish, Italian, Catalan and Japanese) and showed that the phonological properties mentioned by Dauer (1983) have 'reliable phonetic correlates that can be measured in the speech signal, and that these correlates predict the rhythm classes' (Ramus et al., 1999, p. 275). They conclude that the more complex a language's syllable structure is, the more likely it is to be nearer the stress-based end of the continuum.

Current contributions and research

Lexical stress and prominence

Recent research into lexical stress and prominence has looked at how speakers realize lexical stress in Lombard speech, i.e. speech produced in noisy environments (see Lombard, 1911). Arciuli, Simpson, Vogel and Ballard (2014), for example, found that English speakers increase lexical stress contrasts rather than producing all syllables more loudly, although there is an overall increase in speech intensity in noisy conditions. This indicates that speakers place greater importance on prominent syllables in speech production.

Rhythm

As mentioned earlier, Cauldwell's (2002) view is that English is functionally irrythmical. While he does not dispute the occurrence or salience of prominent syllables – in fact, they are the core to the approach presented in *Phonology for Listening* (Cauldwell, 2013) – he refers to regularities in speech rhythm as 'elected', as in poetry, or 'coincidental', i.e. 'the side effects of other higher-order choices made by speakers' (Cauldwell, 2002, p. 1). This is largely because spontaneous speech does not contain long enough units to be perceptually rhythmical. It is Cauldwell's contention that elected regular rhythms occur for a social purpose; although he does not explain what that social purpose could be, Martin Luther King's famous speech could be an example of that phenomenon. Asserting that a 'lack of a regular rhythm in speech production is essential for effective communication' (Cauldwell, 2002,

p. 20), he also claims that, were English truly stress-timed, this would distract the speaker and the listener from the meaningful content of the utterance as too much attention would be paid to producing or perceiving formal elements.

As well as contributing to intelligibility, work by Couper-Kuhlen and colleagues demonstrates that speech rhythm is important in conversational turn-taking (e.g. Couper-Kuhlen 1991, 1993; Auer, Couper-Kuhlen & Müller 1999); interlocutors time their responses to fit with the rhythmic pattern of the preceding turn to the extent of leaving short pauses at the start of a turn, if necessary, to match the rhythmic stress of prominent syllables. This could be an example of Cauldwell's (2002) social purpose, or Anderson-Hsieh's (1992) 'cultural harmony'. Szczepek Reed (2010) shows that, in interactions in English between speakers of so-called stress-timed and syllable-timed languages, syllable-timed language speakers harmonize with stress-timed speakers mainly for the first few turns before moving back to syllable-timing. Her 2012 paper considers the implications of rhythm and turn-taking for learners of English.

Main research methods

The main research methods in lexical stress and prominence largely involve measurements of syllable duration, intensity, pitch change and vowel weakening, and the effect of relocation of the stressed syllable on intelligibility, i.e. on how well a speaker's message is understood by a listener. A selection of studies using these methods has been cited above. In this section, the focus will be on rhythm metrics.

Rhythm metrics are mathematical formulas used to classify languages into rhythmic classes (Arvaniti, 2012). Ramus et al. (1999) could be said to be the pioneers of rhythm metrics as they were the first to devise mathematical equations that could quantify languages into rhythmic classes. Ramus et al. (1999) and others after them (Arvaniti, 2012; Dellwo, 2006; Grabe & Low, 2002; Low, Grabe & Nolan, 2000; White & Mattys, 2007) were largely influenced by language acquisition research. In particular, they were influenced by the finding that newborn babies were able to discriminate between their mothers' language and a language with a different rhythm such as English and Spanish but unable to distinguish between their mothers' language and a language with the same rhythm, e.g. English and Dutch (Nazzi, Bertoncini & Mehler, 1998). The conclusion drawn from the finding was that language acquisition is to some extent dependent on speech rhythm. For this reason, Ramus et al. (1999) set out to find out how languages can be classified based on rhythmic classes.

Ramus and colleagues' approach moved away from isochrony; instead, they concentrated on the acoustic-phonetic element of rhythm. Their rhythm metric required segmentation of an utterance into successive vocalic and consonantal intervals, and measurement involved the duration of each of these intervals. An example phrase from Ramus et al. (1999, p. 272) is <next Tuesday on>, phonetically transcribed in the original as /nɛkstjuzdeiɔn/ and with the following vocalic and consonantal intervals: /n/ /ɛ/ /kstj/ /u/ /zd/ /eiɔ/ /n/. Measurements were then subjected to further calculations, as follows (Ramus et al., 1999, p. 270):

- the proportion of vocalic intervals in the utterance, i.e. the sum of vocalic intervals divided by the total duration of the utterance (%V);
- the standard deviation of vocalic intervals within the utterance (ΔV);
- the standard deviation of consonantal intervals within the utterance (ΔC).

These rhythm metrics were applied to short declarative sentences in eight languages, largely drawn from a multi-language corpus, which were considered stress-, syllable- and mora-timed. Results indicated that the so-called stressed-timed languages (English, Polish and Dutch) exhibited a low %V and a high ΔC, whereas languages considered syllable-timed (Spanish, Italian, Catalan and French) displayed a high %V and a low ΔC. Japanese, a 'mora-timed' language, did not cluster with either stress or syllable-timed languages. The findings demonstrated that languages do indeed fall into different rhythm classes, contrary to the findings of Roach (1982) and Dauer (1983). Ramus et al. (1999) concluded that the measurements that successfully distinguish languages into rhythm classes are %V and ΔC.

A possibly much better known metric is that developed by Low, Grabe and Nolan (2000), later expanded in Grabe and Low (2002). Like Ramus et al. (1999), Low and colleagues measured the acoustic-phonetic component of rhythm by dividing utterances into vocalic and consonantal intervals, and developed a pairwise variability index (PVI), which reflected the level of variability in consecutive vocalic and consonantal intervals. Unlike Ramus et al., they used constructed sentences such as <Grace works through huge mounds each Friday>, in which each syllable is likely to be pronounced with a full vowel, and <Grace was tired of Matthew Freeman>, in which only <Grace>, <tired>, and the first syllables of <Matthew> and <Freeman> are likely to have full vowels in so-called stress-timed languages. Low and colleagues argued that, unlike the rhythm metric in Ramus et al. (1999), the PVI would not show spurious variability caused by speaker rate variation within and across sentences.

The PVI is expressed as both raw PVI (rPVI) and normalized PVI (nPVI). The rPVI is normalized to nPVI by dividing each absolute difference between successive intervals by their mean. The total is multiplied by 100 to yield values comparable to rPVI. Grabe and Low (2002) asserted that languages that are considered stress- and syllable-timed contrasted in the durational variability of vowels and thus proposed that nPVI should be reserved for vowels and rPVI for consonants. They subjected the languages used in Ramus et al. (1999) to nPVI. Their classification of English, Spanish and French agreed with Ramus et al. (1999). However, whereas Ramus et al. (1999) did not group Japanese with either stress-timed or syllable-timed languages, Grabe and Low (2002) grouped it with syllable-timed languages.

Many studies have been carried out that use this metric or slightly modified versions and, in most cases, use it to classify languages as either stress- or syllable-timed. For example: Gibbon and Gut (2001) show that the Nigerian language Ibibio is considered syllable-timed; Mok and Dellwo (2008) use the PVI to show that Cantonese and Mandarin are syllable-timed. Nolan and Asu (2009) indicate that a foot-based PVI measurement may be more successful in capturing rhythmic differences among languages and, looking at Estonian, English, Mexican Spanish and Castilian Spanish, suggest that a language can be both stress- and syllable-timed. Arvaniti (2012) and Bunta and Ingram (2007) establish that nPVI is more successful in distinguishing the speech rhythm of monolingual English speakers than the rPVI is.

Other metrics that have been developed include the 'rate-normalised interval measures of vocalic interval variation' Varco Vowel (VarcoV) and Varco Consonant (VarcoC) (White & Mattys 2007, p. 501). Among other things, it has been shown that VarcoV is particularly successful at showing rhythmic differences among speakers switching between their first and second languages (White & Mattys, 2007). See White and Mattys (2007) for a review and comparison of all the measures mentioned in this section.

Recommendations for practice

Lexical stress

Although lexical stress rules for English are somewhat cumbersome, there have been attempts to teach it using simplified rules, by analogy with other words with similar stress patterns, or by focusing on predictable patterns in words containing (usually) stress-attracting suffixes.

Stress-attracting suffixes either attract the primary stress on to a predictable syllable in the suffix or predictably affect the placement of the primary stress elsewhere within a word. For example, the suffix <-ation> is predictably stressed on the first syllable. In a word such as <harmonize> /ˈhɑːmənaɪz/, the rhythmic stress on the first syllable stays in place as a secondary stress once the suffix is added to form <harmonization>, but the primary stress moves to the suffix: /ˌhɑːmənaɪˈzeɪʃn̩/. By comparison, the suffix <-ic> attracts the primary stress to the syllable preceding it. In, e.g., <demon> /ˈdiːmən/, the primary stress is on the first syllable, but in <demonic> it moves to the second syllable, which is the one now preceding the suffix: /dɪˈmɒnɪk/. It is possible to train learners encountering words formed using stress-attracting suffixes to identify them as such and apply the appropriate rule (see e.g. Hewings, 2004, p. 122–123).

This is used to good effect in Hancock's (1995) pronunciation game 'Happy Families' (pp. 27–31). In the traditional game, players have to collect four members of a number of families by asking each other for specific family members until all cards are collected. In Hancock's variant, the families are four cards comprising a non-complex lexeme that acts as a stem, followed by three words formed using the suffixes <-ity>, <-ize> and <-ization>. Both <-ity> and <-ization> are stress-attracting, <-ity> by moving the primary lexical stress to the syllable preceding it and <-ization> by attracting the stress on to the second syllable of the affix. <-ize> is stress-neutral, i.e. it does not affect the stress in the stem. Players must collect the word families by asking opposing players for cards in a particular family, pronouncing them correctly, by saying: '[Name], can I have [word], please?' For example, if a player had been dealt <civil> and <civilize>, the remaining family members <civility> and <civilization> must be collected by asking, e.g. 'Murat, can I have *civility* please?' (Hancock 1995, p. 27, italics and underlining in the original). This game is preceded by a class activity that demonstrates how affixes affect the stress placement in words using the three affixes in the game.

Approaches using simplified rules, such as those in Kelly (2000), Hancock (2003) and Hewings (2004), often focus on the differences between two-syllable nouns and verbs – e.g. IMport (n.) and imPORT (v.) – and 'core vocabulary' (Kelly, 2000, p. 69), before moving on to 'rule of thumb' suggestions for compound and complex words.

Examples of approaches in which learners match words with similar lexical stress patterns include Kelly's 'Find a partner' (2000, p. 77), using the following commonly seen convention of a string of letters 'o' to represent syllables, with large 'O' denoting primary stress, as visual reinforcement (6):

(6) Politician   ooOo
      It's important   ooOo

Learners are given a set of words and phrases, asked to find the stressed syllable, and are then required to match the words and phrases to those with similar patterns. Hancock (1995) has a number of pronunciation games that use the same basic approach but with filled circles and, as Kelly (2000, p. 76) notes, 'some teachers like to use boxes'.

There are also approaches that teach learners how to produce prominent syllables in comparison with weak syllables, most of which focus on syllable length as an indicator. Gilbert (2012) and Hewings (2004), for example, recommend the kinaesthetic reinforcement of stretching an elastic band between one's thumbs simultaneously with producing the prominent syllable in order to make it tangibly longer than surrounding syllables.

Rhythm

One of the most common basic approaches to teaching English speech rhythm involves starting with a sentence in which all words are single-syllable stressed words and gradually adding increasing numbers of weak or unstressed syllables. Learners produce the sentences by beating time or clapping a regular rhythm only on the words that appeared in the first sentence. For example (7):

> (7) DOGS CHASE CATS
> the DOGS CHASE the CATS
> the DOGS are CHASing the CATS
> the DOGS will have CHASED the CATS
> all the DOGS will have CHASED all the CATS

Assuming the regular rhythm is maintained, this encourages the compression of syllables between the stresses, resulting in a stress-timed rhythm.

Chela-Flores (1998) uses a 'Morse code' approach, recommending each dot be spoken as 'ti', representing a weak syllable, and each dash be spoken as 'TA' or 'TAA' to represent a stressed syllable, with 'TAA' indicating the main stress in the utterance, placed on the last stressed syllable.

For example, a three-syllable pattern would look like this (8a):

> (8a) _ . _   TA ti TAA
>   . _ .   ti TAA ti

Phrases which match these two patterns are as follows (8b):

> (8b) What's your name?   _ . _
>   She's going.   . _ .
>   He couldn't.   . _ .
>   Believe it.   . _ .
>   Twice a day.   _ . _

This builds up to patterns as long as the following (9):

> (9) . _ . . _ . . _   (ti TA ti ti TA ti ti TAA)
>   e.g.   It's time I was having my lunch.
>
>   . _ . . . _ . . .   (ti TA ti ti ti TAA ti ti ti)
>   e.g.   He took it to the railway station.

Learners are first trained on the patterns, then on matching sentences to the patterns, then on trying to produce sentences with the patterns.

Hewings (2004), in a series of exercises, focuses on the functional aspect of identifying and producing prominent words in sentences. He includes work on contrastive stress in sentences. There is also guidance for teachers in Kelly (2000). Hancock (2003) has a number of exercises on sentence stress, including noticing that function words <a>, <of> and <or> are produced with a much reduced vowel in connected speech.

Cauldwell's teacher-oriented text (2013), focusing on teaching the listening process and the identification of stressed syllables in speech, looks at what happens when words get squeezed together in rapid speech produced by English native speakers, as this can lead to unintelligibility. He highlights areas of speech referred to as 'squeeze zones', i.e. the places where it is difficult to understand a word because the spontaneous speech stream has caused the 'sound shapes' to be compressed so much that the output does not resemble citation forms of that word very closely. If you are familiar with the excellent *Streaming Speech* (Cauldwell, 2001), you will know that these zones were animated so they squashed together to give a visual representation of what happens in rapid speech. Cauldwell's position is that '[s]tress-timing theory is (or should be) dead' (2013, p. 141). He admits, however, that the notion of stress-timing is useful from a pronunciation teaching and learning point of view, as exercises such as (7) above, which aim at the learner trying to squash more and more words in between stressed syllables, encourage learners to practice producing words in squeeze zones.

Finally, Coniam (2002) recommends using speech technology to train teachers to recognize the difference between English of different rhythmic types. Using the waveform element of a speech display (see Figures 8.1 and 8.2 above) and recordings of native and non-native speakers, he encourages teachers to notice the difference between English spoken with a stress- and syllable-timed rhythm. Teachers reported that being able to see the visual information 'had given them a clearer perspective of syllable-timed speech' (Coniam, 2002, p. 39).

Future directions

Global Englishes and New Varieties of English (NVEs) do not necessarily demonstrate lexical stress, prominence or rhythmic patterns in the same way as Older Varieties of English (OVEs). However, as we have seen, unexpected word stress can lead to extreme difficulty in lexical retrieval. It is also important that speakers make prominent syllables in words stand out in a stream of speech so a listener can catch the meaning. At discourse level, making certain words prominent is also crucial, and this is discussed elsewhere in this volume.

We would like to suggest, therefore, that where classroom work on stress-timed rhythm may fall out of favour – fun though it can be – more focus will be placed on harmonizing lexical stress placement across speakers of English in order to support intelligibility in international contexts. This should be practised in multicultural interactive contexts, where possible, preferably between speakers from different rhythmic language backgrounds in order to experience as much as possible the variance in stress and rhythm in different speaker groups. Work could be on improving accommodation strategies in this respect among learners, not only in interactions between learners of English and speakers of NVEs, but also among OVE speakers, whose language is not always the most easily understood.

In addition, the focus in longer stretches of speech should be in making the prominent, information-bearing syllables stand out more, but not in generating strict stress-timed rhythms. From the research, it is apparent that rhythm of this kind does not occur very often in spontaneous speech anyway.

Further reading

Arnold, G. F. (1957). Stress in English words. *Lingua*, *6*, 221–441. A thorough and comprehensive account of lexical stress in English.

Cauldwell, R. (2013). *Phonology for listening*. Birmingham: speechinaction. Teachers of English pronunciation will fully understand the issues described in this text and the frustration that can occur when the patterns in real speech do not match with what the textbooks tell us.

Roach, P. (2001). *Phonetics* (Chapter 5). Oxford: Oxford University Press. This chapter on suprasegmentals includes an excellent short introduction to lexical stress, prominence and rhythm, written in Roach's engaging prose.

White, L., & Mattys, S. L. (2007). Calibrating rhythm: First language and second language studies. *Journal of Phonetics*, *35*(4), 501–522. An overview of rhythm metrics currently used in research.

Related topics

Syllable structure; intonation.

References

Abercrombie, D. (1967). *Elements of general phonetics*. Edinburgh: Edinburgh University Press.

Allen, G. D. (1975). Speech rhythm: its relation to performance universals and articulatory timing. *Journal of Phonetics*, *3*, 75–86.

Anderson-Hsieh, J., & Venkatagiri, H. (1994). Syllable duration and pausing in the speech of Chinese ESL speakers. *TESOL Quarterly*, *28*(4), 807–812.

Arciuli, J., Simpson, B. S., Vogel, A. P., & Ballard, K. J. (2014). Acoustic changes in the production of lexical stress during Lombard speech. *Language and Speech*, 0023830913495652.

Arnold, G. F. (1957). Stress in English words. *Lingua*, *6*, 221–441.

Arvaniti, A. (2012). The usefulness of metrics in the quantification of speech rhythm. *Journal of Phonetics*, *40*(3), 351–373.

Auer, P., Couper-Kuhlen, E., & Müller, F. (1999). *Language in time. The rhythm and tempo of spoken interaction*. Oxford: Oxford University Press.

Bloch, B., & Trager, G. L. (1942). *Outline of linguistic analysis*. Baltimore, MD: Linguistic Society of America at the Waverly Press.

Bloomfield, L. (1933). *Language*. New York, NY: Taylor & Francis.

Brazil, D. (1994). *Pronunciation for advanced learners of English*. Cambridge: Cambridge University Press.

Bunta, F., & Ingram, D. (2007). The acquisition of speech rhythm by bilingual Spanish-and-English-speaking 4-and 5-year-old children. *Journal of Speech, Language, and Hearing Research*, *50*(4), 999–1014.

Cauldwell, R. (2001). *Streaming speech*. Birmingham: speechinaction.

Cauldwell, R. (2002). The functional irrhythmicality of spontaneous speech: A discourse view of speech rhythms. *Apples – Journal of Applied Language Studies*, *2*(1), 1–24. Available from http://apples.jyu.fi.

Cauldwell, R. (2013). *Phonology for listening*. Birmingham: speechinaction.

Chela-Flores, B. (1998). *Teaching English rhythm: from theory to practice*. Caracas: Fondo Editorial Tropykos.

Classe, A. (1939). *The rhythm of English prose*. Oxford: Basil Blackwell.

Coniam, D. (2002).Technology as an awareness-raising tool for sensitising teachers to features of stress and rhythm in English. *Language Awareness*, *11*(1), 30–42.

Couper-Kuhlen, E. (1991). A rhythm-based metric for turn-taking. In *Proceedings of the 12th International Congress of Phonetic Sciences* (Vol. 1, pp. 275–278).

Couper-Kuhlen, E. (1993). *English speech rhythm. Form and function in everyday verbal interaction*. Amsterdam: Benjamins.

Cruttenden, A. (2014). *Gimson's pronunciation of English* (8th ed.). New York, NY: Routledge

Crystal, D. (1996). The past, present and future of English rhythm. *Speak Out*, *18*, 8–13.

Cutler, A. (1984). Stress and accent in language production and understanding. In D. Gibbon & H. Richter (Eds), *Intonation, accent and rhythm: Studies in discourse phonology* (pp. 77–90). Berlin: Library of Congress Cataloging.

Cutler, A., & Isard, S. D. (1980). The production of prosody. In B. Butterworth (Ed.), *Language production volume 1: Speech and Talk* (pp. 245–269). London, New York, NY, Toronto, Sydney & San Francisco: Academic Press.

Cutler, A., & Norris, D. (1988). The role of strong syllables in segmentation for lexical access. *Journal of Experimental Psychology: Human perception and performance, 14*(1), 113–121.

Dauer, R. M. (1983). Stress timing and syllable timing reanalysed. *Journal of Phonetics, 11*, 51–62.

Dellwo, V. (2006). Rhythm and speech rate: A variation coefficient for ΔC. *Language and language-processing*, 231–241.

Faber, D. (1986). Teaching the rhythms of English: A new theoretical base. *IRAL-International Review of Applied Linguistics in Language Teaching, 24*(3), 205–216.

Fear, B. D., Cutler, A., & Butterfield, S. (1995). The strong/weak syllable distinction in English. *The Journal of the Acoustical Society of America, 97*(3), 1893–1904.

Field, J. (2005). Intelligibility and the listener: The role of lexical stress. *TESOL Quarterly, 39*(3), 399–423.

Gibbon, D., & Gut, U. (2001). Measuring speech rhythm. In *INTERSPEECH* (pp. 95–98).

Gilbert, J. (2012). *Clear speech from the start* (2nd ed.). Cambridge: Cambridge University Press.

Grabe, E., & Low, E. L. (2002). Durational variability in speech and the rhythm class hypothesis. *Papers in Laboratory Phonology, 7*, 515–546.

Grosjean, F., & Gee, J. P. (1987). Prosodic structure and spoken word recognition. *Cognition, 25*, 135–155.

Halliday, M. A. K. (1989). *Spoken and written language* (2nd ed.). Oxford: Oxford University Press.

Hancock, M. (1995). *Pronunciation games*. Cambridge: Cambridge University Press.

Hancock. M. (2003). *English pronunciation in use*. Cambridge: Cambridge University Press.

Hewings, M. (2004). *Pronunciation practice activities*. Cambridge: Cambridge University Press.

Jones, D. (1949). *An outline of English phonetics*. Cambridge: Heffer.

Jones, D. (1956). *The pronunciation of English*. Cambridge: Cambridge University Press.

Jones, D. (2011). *Cambridge English pronouncing dictionary* (18th ed.). Edited by P. Roach, J. Setter, & J. Esling. Cambridge: Cambridge University Press.

Kelly, G. (2000). *How to teach pronunciation*. Harlow: Pearson Education.

Kelso, J. A. S., & Munhall, K. G. (1988). *RH Stetson's Motor Phonetics: a retrospective edition*. Boston, MA, Toronto & San Diego, CA: College-Hill Press. (Originally published as Stetson, R. H. (1928). *Motor phonetics, a study of speech movements in action*. The Hague: Archives Néerlandaises de Phonétique Experimentale (Vol. III); and (1951). *Motor phonetics* (2nd ed.). Amsterdam: North Holland.).

Kenyon, J. S., & Knott, T. A. (1953). *A pronouncing dictionary of American English*. Springfield, MA: Merriam-Webster.

Knowles, G. (1987). *Patterns of spoken English*. Harlow: Longman.

Ladefoged, P. (1967). Stress and respiratory activity. *Three areas of experimental phonetics*. London: Oxford University Press.

Lehiste, I. (1977). Isochrony reconsidered. *Journal of Phonetics, 5*, 253–263.

Lombard, E. (1911). Le signe de l'elevation de la voix. *Annals Maladiers Oreille. Larynx, Nez Pharynx, 37*, 101–119.

Low, E. L., Grabe, E., & Nolan, F. (2000). Quantitative characterizations of speech rhythm: Syllable-timing in Singapore English. *Language and speech, 43*(4), 377–401.

Marks, J. (1999). Is stress-timing real? *ELT Journal, 53*(3), 191–199.

Miller, M. (1984). On the perception of rhythm. *Journal of Phonetics, 12*, 75–83.

Mok, P. P., & Dellwo, V. (2008, May). Comparing native and non-native speech rhythm using acoustic rhythmic measures: Cantonese, Beijing Mandarin and English. In *Proceedings Speech Prosody* (pp. 423–426).

Nazzi, T., Bertoncini, J., & Mehler, J. (1998). Language discrimination by newborns: toward an understanding of the role of rhythm. *Journal of Experimental Psychology: Human Perception and Performance, 24*(3), 756–766.

Nolan, F., & Asu, E. L. (2009). The pairwise variability index and coexisting rhythms in language. *Phonetica, 66*(1–2), 64–77.

O'Connor, J. D. (1973). *Phonetics*. Harmondsworth: Penguin.

O'Malley, M. H., Kloker, D. R., & Dara-Abrams, B. (1973). Recovering parentheses from spoken algebraic expressions. *IEEE Transactions on Audio and Electro-acoustics AU, 21*, 217–220.

Peperkamp, S., & Dupoux, E. (1992). A typological study of stress 'deafness'. In C. Gussenhoven & N. Warner (Eds), *Laboratory phonology 7* (pp. 203–240). Berlin: Mouton de Gruyter.

Pike, K. L. (1945). *The intonation of American English*. Ann Arbor, MI: University of Michigan Press.

Pike, K. L. (1947). *Phonemics*. Ann Arbor, MI: University of Michigan Press.

Pisoni, D. B. (1981). Some current theoretical issues in speech perception. *Cognition, 10*, 249–259.

Ramus, F., Nespor, M., & Mehler, J. (1999). Correlates of linguistic rhythm in the speech signal. *Cognition, 73*(3), 265–292.

Roach, P. (1982). On the distinction between 'stress-timed' and 'syllable-timed' languages. In D. Crystal (Ed.), *Linguistic controversies: essays in linguistic theory and practice in honour of F R Palmer* (pp. 73–79). London: Edward Arnold.

Roach, P. (2009). *English phonetics and phonology* (4th ed.). Cambridge: Cambridge University Press.

Szczepek Reed, B. (2010). Speech rhythm across turn transitions in cross-cultural talk-in-interaction. *Journal of Pragmatics, 42*(4), 1037–1059.

Szczepek Reed, B. (2012). A conversation analytic perspective on teaching English pronunciation: The case of speech rhythm. *International Journal of Applied Linguistics, 22*(1), 67–87.

Wells, J. C. (1990). *Longman pronunciation dictionary*. Harlow: Pearson Education.

White, L., & Mattys, S. L. (2007). Calibrating rhythm: First language and second language studies. *Journal of Phonetics, 35*(4), 501–522.

9

Intonation and language learning

Ann Wennerstrom

Introduction

Intonational meaning is an essential component of spoken English. The pitch during speech – and its association with certain words and phrases – conveys linguistic meaning beyond the words themselves. Intonational meaning plays a role at the discourse level, as speakers organize their thoughts into units, distinguish new versus old ideas, make contrasts and shift from one topic to the next. In interaction, intonation is central to turn-taking as participants indicate their intention to retain or relinquish the floor. Matters of attitude, emotion and self-expression are also conveyed in intonation. Thus, in any speech event, participants are continuously providing meaningful information about the discourse through their own intonation while attending to the intonation of others. Given that intonation is central to communication, it should factor into educational programmes and materials for learners of English.

Nevertheless, teachers who wish to incorporate intonation into their ESL classes may face certain frustrations. ESL textbooks have traditionally ignored intonation or presented it separately from other speaking activities. Even language theorists do not agree upon a complete description of the English intonation system, nor a common set of terminology. Little research exists about how intonation is acquired by adult learners or the extent to which cognitive constraints play a role during the acquisition process. There remain many open questions on these topics.

This chapter provides a framework to understand the basic components of intonational meaning in English. The author recommends that intonation be introduced as an integral part of the English language in stages throughout the acquisition process with the major meaningful intonation categories as a starting point. The cognitive constraints of the language acquisition process itself affects the intonation produced at early stages of language development: if a language learner is attempting to articulate ideas with limited vocabulary and grammar, it may be that only a single word or memorized language chunk can constitute the thought group of each intonation contour. However, L2 learners can be encouraged to produce simple intonation patterns even at early stages. Later, the more complex subtleties of intonation may be acquired.

Current conceptualizations of intonation

Challenges with the current research

The task of synthesizing the details of previous intonation research is complicated by the fact that neither the scholarship nor the research results have been entirely consistent. Over the years, several theorists have developed models of intonational meaning for standard varieties of English, each model having its own terminology and inventory of meaningful intonation components. Each theoretical model makes different assumptions about the nature of intonation. For example, many scholars believe that pitch movements form the basic meaningful units (Bolinger, 1986, 1989; Brazil, 1985, 1997; Halliday, 1967; Wichmann, 2000; and others). Other scholars, following Pierrehumbert and Hirschberg (1990), assign meaning to an even smaller unit, the individual tone. In their model, a system of meaningful high and low tones forms the phonological skeleton of each intonational phrase. The surface intonation contour that we hear is the result of phonetic processes that link the pitch of the underlying tones together.

The variation among specialist approaches also leads to inconsistent terminology. There are no set terms for intonation such as <noun> and <verb> as used in discussions of syntax. For example, the high pitch that is usually associated with the main idea of the phrase has been labelled the *high pitch accent* (Pierrehumbert & Hirschberg, 1990), *tonic syllable* (Brazil, 1985), *sentence stress* (Hahn, 2004), *focus* (Chomsky & Halle, 1968), and others. Overall, it is difficult to interpret and synthesize the results of research on L2 intonation when different scholars use different models, assumptions and labelling systems. A further complication is that it is often impossible to discern whether one study's finding is in any practical sense comparable to another's.

Another issue that makes some research studies difficult to interpret is methodological. Measurements are not taken in a standardized way from study to study. For example, Wennerstrom (1994) measured pitch peaks at the pitch maximum for a particular syllable, while Kang (2010) measured pitch peaks at the midpoint of the vowel. Furthermore, intonation measurements may be based on averages or other holistic calculations that are not analysed in detail. For example, overall pitch range is relevant to intonation, but based on the range alone it is not clear where the highest pitch peaks are occurring from one phrase to the next. However, for those researchers who seek to measure and interpret the placement of high pitch on particular words in each phrase, a laborious microanalysis is required, which leads to yet another problem: many detailed intonation studies have relied on individual cases or small subject pools. The point is not that these research choices are flawed but rather that, because the work on intonation is pioneering, researchers are still in the process of testing out methodologies, making it difficult to synthesize the results into broader conclusions.

This chapter's purpose is to present a simple framework for language teachers to understand the major components of intonational meaning common to most standard varieties of English. Rather than attempting to chronical every research study of L2 intonation, the chapter reviews only studies that relate specifically to those aspects of intonation found to be most problematic in the language learning process.

Components of intonational meaning

Despite the array of theoretical perspectives, it is possible to draw together some conclusions about intonational meaning for the purpose of language teaching. Rather than strictly adopting a theory-driven labelling system, I will use simple orthography and arrows to illustrate intonation patterns depicted in the chapter, so that no specialized knowledge is required on the reader's part (see Appendix). The starting point will be an overview of certain universal aspects of intonation in the organization of thought. This will be followed by an explanation of categories of intonational meaning in English that have been recognized as problematic for L2 learners. Wherever possible, examples from actual L2 learners' speech will be given to show how intonation can interfere with communicative competence. The chapter ends with a brief commentary on how cognitive processes constrain acquisition and suggestions for teaching.

Universals of intonation

Virtually all scholars agree that speech is divided into short units, each with its own intonation contour. These correspond to units of information, often called *thought groups*. As participants converse in any language, they build an ongoing mental representation of the discourse in progress. They keep track of the topic and the ideas that have been introduced, and they integrate each new idea with what has come before. This is known as the *information structure* of discourse. According to Chafe (1994), each intonation contour reflects 'one new idea' – what is active in the speaker's consciousness as each utterance is produced. The intonation contour is the optimal length to hold each new idea in short-term memory. A new idea may be expressed in a single word or more than one. Although pitch naturally declines throughout the intonational phrase (Klatt, 1975), the speaker can make certain elements within the phrase more or less prominent using higher pitch, loudness and duration to call attention to what is most important. As the speaker moves from one intonational phrase to the next, listeners can process the language in manageable increments of information and focus attention on each new idea from phrase to phrase.

Although the division of intonation into idea-based units is universal, the phonology and phonetics of intonation differ from language to language. Phonology refers to the meaningful pitch patterns within each intonational phrase assigned to important words and phrase boundaries. Basic phonological errors can occur for L2 learners whose native languages have different ways of using intonation. The phonetic details of intonation can also be challenging for L2 learners. A pitch peak may be associated phonologically with a word or phrase but the precise alignment of that pitch peak with a particular point in a syllable may vary from language to language (Mennen, 1998; Trofimovich & Baker, 2006). English exploits pitch range to a greater degree than many other languages, resulting in steeper slopes on the rises and falls in the use of intonation (Jilke, 2007, p. 91). Next we will consider in more detail the major phonological components of the English intonation system, presented in a format designed to be easily accessible to non-specialists.

Intonation and the information structure of English discourse

One use of intonation in English is to show how the words in the current phrase are related to previous information. As we converse, we build a mental model of the discourse in progress and integrate each new idea with what has come before. The new idea (its stressed syllable) is the most prominent part of the intonational phrase and tends to have a relatively higher pitch than surrounding text. Although the content words (nouns, verbs, adjectives and adverbs) tend to be slightly more prominent than function words (prepositions, articles, auxiliaries, copulas etc.), a speaker may raise the pitch of any word to make it more prominent. The following example illustrates an utterance with three content words, of which only one is the new idea in each case (see Appendix for transcription system):

I'd LIKE a CUP of <u>COFFEE</u>.

The content words presented here in capital letters all have higher pitch, but <coffee> is the most prominent new idea. The first syllable of this two-syllable word coincides with the highest pitch of all.

If a new idea is being contrasted with a prior one, the stressed syllable of that word will have a steeply rising pitch peak. In fact, almost any word can be singled out for contrast.

I'd LIKE a CUP of **<u>COFFEE</u>**. (. . . not tea.)

I'd LIKE a **<u>CUP</u>** of COFFEE. (. . . not a thermos.)

I'd **<u>LIKE</u>** a CUP of COFFEE. (. . . but I won't have one – too much caffeine!)

<u>I'D</u> LIKE a CUP of COFFEE. (. . . even if you wouldn't).

As the conversation continues, what was formerly new information becomes given information, usually deemphasized with a lowered pitch. This allows the hearer to focus attention on each new idea rather than trying to process information that is already accessible in context. Even if the exact words change, the given idea is deemphasized:

I've ALREADY had <u>ENOUGH</u> _{COFFEE}. (<coffee> is now given information)

I've ALREADY had <u>ENOUGH</u> _{CAFFIENE}. (<caffeine> is given in the context of coffee)

It is important to remember that *word stress* is a property of individual words or compound words. A word such as <cóffee> has primary stress on its first syllable. This will remain true regardless of the information structure, whether <cóffee> is new, contrastive or given information.

A variety of complications can occur for L2 learners using these intonation patterns. First, the intonation may be flat so that no particular words stand out. The result is that listeners' attention is not directed to the important information. A related issue is that some learners produce word-by-word speech in which all words are equally prominent, including the less important function words. This is shown in the following sample of learner speech, uttered by a Japanese woman in conversation about how the lifestyle in modern Japan is similar to that of the US (Wennerstrom, 2000, p. 116):

I <u>WANT</u>- . . . -<u>TED</u> to <u>SAY</u> <u>THE</u> . . . <u>JAPANESE</u> <u>LIFE</u> . . . IS <u>SIMILAR</u> to <u>YOURS</u>.

Here, we notice emphasis on almost every word, including function words such as <the> and <is> and even the past tense syllable <ted> at the end of <wanted>. This makes it difficult for a native English listener to recognize which ideas the speaker intends to prioritize within the utterance. Also the contrast between <Japanese> and <yours> is the central idea of the phrase, but this meaning is obscured when every single word is emphasized. A more native-like version of the same speech sample might be:

I WANTed to SAY the **<u>JAPANESE</u>** LIFE is SIMILAR to **<u>YOURS</u>**.

Another challenge for L2 speakers is that pitch peaks may be misplaced with respect to the information structure. The following example comes from a Japanese learner trying to make a contrast with misaligned intonation. She is telling a funny story from her teenage years about a time she mistakenly called her best friend's mother instead of her own mother after dialling the wrong number by accident. This led to a mix up and eventually an argument when each thought she was talking to her own family member. Although the main contrast in the excerpt below is meant to be between <**HER** mother> versus <**MY** mother>, the speaker places the contrastive intonation on <**MOTHER**> instead (Wennerstrom, 2007):

> So I started to talk with her mother. And her mother and my best friend uh two of them sometime had a bad arguments. And this time, I didn't notice she was her **MOTHER**; I thought she was my **MOTHER** . . .

Because the pitch peaks are aligned with <**MOTHER**>, the contrast between <**HER**> and <**MY**> is obscured and the whole message is more difficult to understand.

Another error is to associate high pitch with given information in the discourse. Here is an example drawn from a short lecture on the topic of <wood> by a speaker of Mandarin. Notice that the speaker makes the word <wood> prominent repeatedly even when it has the status of given information (Wennerstrom, 2007) (<wood> is the only intonation marked here.)

> In this course, we will- basically we will cover structure of <u>WOOD</u>, and <u>WOOD</u> cell. And the mechanical property of <u>WOOD</u>. And the third part is <u>WOOD</u> products. Ahh, we know we deal with the <u>WOOD</u> every day. We use <u>WOOD</u> to make, ah, build house, ah, make furniture, and even use <u>WOOD</u> make paper. So, ah, there's a lotta uses about <u>WOOD</u>.

In this excerpt, the repeated high pitch on <wood> seems to introduce a new idea or contrast each time it is used. A clearer use of the intonation might be to deemphasize <wood> and place the high pitch on the new ideas. This intonation is illustrated using a short segment:

> . . . We use _{WOOD} to make, ah, build <u>HOUSE</u>, ah, make <u>FURNITURE</u>, and EVEN use _{WOOD} make <u>PAPER</u>. . .

Statistical studies have confirmed that the types of errors shown above are not isolated examples. Several scholars have documented a general tendency for a narrow pitch range and flat delivery by L2 speakers (Kang, 2010; Kormos & Dénes, 2004; Pickering, 2004; Wennerstrom, 1994). Others have found the placement of high pitch on almost every word regardless of whether it is important to the information structure (Juffs, 1990; Pickering, 1999; Wennerstrom, 2000). Such misuses of intonation may not guide listeners' attention to the important parts of the speaker's intended message.

As to the specific placement of pitch peaks, Wennerstrom (1994) asked subjects from Thai, Spanish, Japanese and native speaker backgrounds to read a passage in English that was constructed to require specific high-pitched contrasts on certain words. There was also a free speech description task designed to compare the pitch of content versus function words. In the oral reading the L2 speakers tended to misplace or omit high pitch peaks instead of associating them with the main ideas and contrasts. For example, the reading passage contained a contrast between Seattle, being a rainy city, and other sunnier cities:

> In spring, Seattle is usually **WET**. Meanwhile, other cities are having **SUN**.

While the native speakers all raised their pitch on <sun>, the non-native speakers did not use intonation to the same extent to mark the contrast. As a group, the 10 Thai speakers averaged an even lower pitch on <sun> than they did on <having> because many dropped their pitch to the bottom of the pitch range at the end of the sentence. Another result was that in the free speech task the L2 speakers did not use pitch to distinguish content from function words to nearly the degree of the native speakers.

Such errors in alignment of intonation and information structure have been shown to have a negative effect on ratings of comprehensibility (i.e. how hard it is for listeners to understand a speaker). Hahn (2004) conducted a study in which 90 US undergraduate students were placed into three groups, each of which listened to a different version of a lecture in English delivered by a Korean speaker with highly proficient English. One version had the high pitch correctly aligned with the new ideas and contrasts. The second version had high pitch placed incorrectly. The third version had very little pitch contrast whatsoever. The statistically significant result was that the American students had an easier time recalling the main ideas of the lecture with the conventional intonation than for the other two. Additionally, in a survey of attitudes about the lecture, the students preferred the lecture version with the more standard uses of intonation.

Fluency studies have also found that intonation plays a role. Kormos and Dénes (2004) measured the intonation of low- and high-level Hungarian learners of English who were rated by experienced language teachers. One interesting result of the study was that 'pace', the number of prominent words per minute, showed a strong correlation with fluency ratings. We can interpret this result to mean that the ability to mark the main idea of each phrase with high pitch increased fluency. As Kormos and Dénes point out, 'if a speaker utters a lot of unstressed words with a high speed, he or she is not necessarily perceived to be very fluent' (2004, p. 158).

Intonation boundaries and the relationship between phrases

As explained above, speech is divided into intonational phrases, each of which usually contains one new idea. The pitch associated with the final boundary of each phrase indicates how the speaker intends that phrase to be related to the next one. Intonation boundaries are perceived as having a direction, and five distinct boundaries are discussed here: falling, partially falling, low-rising, high-rising and plateau. Generally, when a boundary falls to the bottom of the speaker's pitch range it signals closure – the end of an idea or a series of ideas, whereas all of the other boundaries signal that the current phrase will be followed by a related idea, either from the same or another speaker. Consider a dieter after dinner:

I never have dessert↓ (end of discussion!)

I never have dessert↗ (. . . but maybe this time I'll make an exception).

In the first example, the *falling boundary* indicates that the decision is made and there is no invitation for further discussion. In the second, the *low-rising boundary* indicates that a dedicated host might press on.

A *partially falling boundary* (which does not reach the bottom of the speaker's range) is often used in fast speech to signal continuation by the same speaker, as shown here after the word <dessert>:

I never have dessert↘ and I won't now.↓

For the *plateau boundary* the final syllable of a phrase is extended into a long, flat shape in the middle of the pitch range to signal the intent to continue. This boundary is often used in listing or in hesitating while thinking.

Dessert?↑ We:::::ll→ (I'm definitely thinking about it)

We have pie:::→ ca:::ke→ ice-crea:::m→ (a list of choices)

A *high-rising boundary* tends to anticipate a response and is typical in open-ended yes/no questions:

Would you like some dessert?↑

In interaction, participants are attuned to these meanings and can usually anticipate the end of a speaker's turn and take the floor appropriately (Ford & Thompson, 1996; Wennerstrom & Siegel, 2003). For example, in conversation, a high or low-rising boundary can be used to solicit feedback that the listener is following the thread of the conversation.

I got this recipe for coconut pie↑ (are you following?)

Uh huh↗ (yes, go on)

And it tastes incredible . . . (conversation continues)

Finally, an intonational phrase may be cut off without any boundary in an interruption or false start.

Would you like- (Oh, never mind).

A common error for L2 speakers is a tendency to insert falling intonation boundaries in the middle of a series of related phrases. The following is a naturally occurring example of a Chinese teaching assistant giving a short lecture about lenses, in which falling pitch boundaries dominate (Wennerstrom, 2007):

Any lens- any lens that is thicker at the center↓ than at its edg- than at its edges↓ is called converging lens↓ It can make parallel light↓ focus↓ to a point↓

The result is that the talk seems disconnected despite the ideas being related. A more native-like rendition might have low-rising or partially falling boundaries between related ideas:

It can make parallel light↗ focus↘ to a point↓

Moreover, an overuse of falling intonation boundaries can convey a sense of social distance. Pickering (2001), who also analysed the presentations of Chinese teaching assistants, concluded that, whereas rising boundaries helped establish common ground with the audience, falling boundaries conveyed little room for negotiation and left students with the impression that their teaching assistant did not care very much about their learning.

A number of other research studies have documented this tendency to insert a falling pitch boundary in mid-stream. Hewings (1995) provided Greek, Korean and Indonesian speakers of English with a series of two-part sentences to be read aloud, structured to prompt the participants to connect the two closely related phrases with a low-rising pitch boundary after the first phrase. Instead, many subjects used falling boundaries. Wennerstrom (1994) found few rising boundaries in the speech of Japanese and Thai speakers describing a picture in their own words. Instead, there was a prevalence of falling pitch boundaries at the ends of phrases, even closely related ones. However, the tendency to use falling pitch in mid-stream is apparently language-specific because in the same study, Spanish speakers were very similar to native English speakers in their use of rising boundaries to connect related ideas. In conversation, the result of mid-stream falling boundaries may be an interruption by an inter-locutor who interprets the fall as a sign of finality and takes it as an appropriate opportunity to start talking (see Davies & Tyler (1994) for microanalysis).

Turning to larger-scale statistical studies, Isaacs and Trofimovich (2012) measured the influence of 19 linguistic variables on ratings of comprehensibility for 40 French learners of English. One measure was the use of intonation boundaries in the context of the discourse. Based on ratings by 60 novice native speaker raters, this measure was found to have a significant positive correlation with ratings (p. 485). That is, the more appropriate the inton-ation boundaries, the higher the comprehensibility ratings. Likewise, Kang, Rubin and Pickering (2010) measured intonation boundaries in their study of 26 non-native speakers' use of 29 different suprasegmental variables. The L2 speech was rated by 166 novice raters for comprehensibility and oral proficiency. Overall the higher the percentage of mid-rising and high-rising boundaries in a speaker's discourse sample, the higher the ratings (pp. 561–562). Intonation boundaries may also influence fluency ratings. It is uncontroversial that length and frequency of pauses correspond to fluency judgements, particularly when the pauses are placed inappropriately (Riggenbach, 1991). However, Isaac (1997) and Wennerstrom (2000) both found data suggesting that the intonation prior to the pause plays a role in fluency. In the following example, an L2 speaker was rated as extremely fluent in conversation despite frequent long pauses. Prior to the pauses, however, he used plateau intonation boundaries, which conveyed an impression of thoughtful consideration rather than lack of fluency (pause length is in parentheses) (Wennerstrom, 2000, p. 119):

NNS: Okay↘ what do you think abou:::t→ (1.6) the actua:::l→ (1.0) politics of the
         Sta:::tes→ (.7) a:::s→ (2.0) guardians of the world↓

NS: Huh↓ um:::→ I see it as being↘ ... (continues)

The American conversation partner waited without interruption during the pauses and answered only after the final falling boundary. In other words, pauses may seem 'inappropriate' owing not to their sheer frequency and length but to the preceding intonation boundary.

Intonation and the organization of topics

Another meaningful aspect of intonation is to signal the hierarchical organization of topics. An initial high pitch can mark a topic shift in what has been called a <*paratone*> (Yule, 1980; see Wichmann, 2000, for overview). Correspondingly, utterances that are meant as asides, when the speaker is 'going off on a tangent' are often presented in a low and narrow pitch range, as a kind of intonational parentheses (Bing, 1985; Wichmann, 2000). These larger intonational groupings and shifts provide an organizational framework for the discourse.

The following example is from a native English speaker giving a lecture in which she discusses data plots drawn on a board. The excerpt begins as she is moving from one data plot (about ducks) to the next. Her pitch goes up by a vast 165 Hertz between topics (Wennerstrom, 2001, p. 102):

> ... Ducks that had a lower plumage rating tended also to have a lower behavioural rating↓ (175 Hz.)
>
> ⇑ (340 Hz.) Let's skip for right now, onto the next plot ...

This dramatic intonation shift, or paratone, clearly signals the introduction of the new topic. For an L2 speaker who omits such signals of topic transition in a lecture or work presentation, the result may be seemingly disorganized because listeners are attuned. Consequently, listeners who are attuned to intonational paragraphing may lose the speaker's organizational thread. An opposite problem can occur if there is a sudden shift from low to high pitch in mid-sentence, which could send a confusing signal of a new topic where none was intended (Tyler, 1992, p. 722).

The topic marking function of intonation has been studied empirically in L2 groups. Wennerstrom (1994) constructed an oral reading passage to contain a topic shift, marked with an indented paragraph starting on a separate line of text. After the L2 and native English speakers read the text aloud, the average pitch range of the sentences before and after the paragraph shift were compared. Spanish and native English speakers both introduced this topic shift with a higher pitch (a paratone), while Thai and Japanese speakers did not make a significant difference in their pitch at this point.

A more general finding has been that greater pitch range correlates with higher ratings on language ability measures. Kang (2010) measured accent ratings for L2 speakers from various countries, rated by 58 American undergraduate students. Overall pitch range accounted for 24 per cent of the variance in the ratings: the greater the pitch range overall, the less the perceived foreign accent (p. 301). Wennerstrom (1998) measured the intonation of 18 Chinese graduate students giving short lectures and compared the pitch range before and after the first 10 major topic shifts. Each lecture was rated by three experienced teachers as a part of an assessment of each student's readiness to assume teaching responsibilities. The results were statistically significant: those who demarcated the major topic shifts with paratones received the higher ratings on this high-stakes test.

In a phenomenon related to the paratone, <*key*> refers to the level of pitch at the onset of any intonational phrase, relative to a speaker's overall pitch range: high, mid or low (Brazil, 1985, 1997). Key encompasses not just topic shifts but all phrase onsets, indicating the current speaker's stance towards what has come immediately before. In interaction, a conversation partner can show social affiliation by matching the key at the onset of a new turn with the pitch level at the termination of the prior speaker's turn. On the other hand, a mismatch in key can show disagreement, or in Brazil's words, people switch to a different key 'at moments when there is a discrepancy between the ways the two parties assess the context of interaction' (p. 86). Here are two examples of mismatch in key at points of social discord:

> A: →I'm taking scuba lessons.↓
> B: ↱You are?↑ (But that's dangerous!)

B's use of a high key shows surprise and disapproval. The following example shows a different type of mismatch in key in a phone call (adapted from Schegloff, 1998, p. 245):

1/A: (answering the phone) →Hello↑
2/B: ↳Hi   (said without enthusiasm or connection)
3/A: ↱HI::::::   (said with surprise and excitement)
4/B: ↳How are you   (said with little enthusiasm)
5/A: ↳Fine↓   (matching B's low enthusiasm).

The low key by B in line 4 following A's initial high-keyed enthusiasm in line 3 shows less social engagement, a stance to which A then acquiesces in line 5. In interaction, these subtle intonational signals are continuously attended to as participants respond to each other.

Key alignment may not be a language universal. Pickering, Hu and Baker (2012) measured key in the conversations of three pairs of Chinese L2 speakers of English compared to three native speaker pairs. Participants viewed a picture of cars and were instructed to reach an agreement about their favourites. Transcripts of the conversations were analysed for disagreements and key was measured from turn to turn. For the native speakers, a mismatch of key was a common feature at points of disagreement, while the L2 participants did not use key consistently in this way. Pickering (2001) conducted a microanalysis of the interactions of Chinese teaching assistants in one-on-one lab sessions with American undergraduate students. She found that sudden high key by a teaching assistant in mid-dialogue had the effect of disrupting and even shutting down the interaction. Pickering's interpretation was that the mismatched key could be heard as critical and distancing to the students, although this was not the teaching assistant's intent. These studies suggest that the L2 speakers did not have this particular intonation category in their native phonological systems.

Intonation provides expressive and pragmatic meaning

The prior discussion notwithstanding, it is important to remember that there is vast variation and nuance in intonation. Whatever the basic phonological structure of an intonational sequence may be, it can also be exaggerated or minimized owing to emotional delivery or other pragmatic factors, as in shouting to be heard at a distance, murmuring a snide remark under one's breath or mimicking another's style. In such cases, an entire sequence may be uttered in an altered pitch range. Distinctive intonational patterns may characterize particular spoken genres, such as anecdote, prayer and news reading (Tench, 1991). A speaker can also delineate an individual word intonationally for a dramatic effect.

Other social factors govern many aspects of intonation. Chun (2002) points out that intonation is one of the features that affects hearers' perceptions of age, sex, regional background and occupation, as well as foreign accent, with resulting stereotypes about the speaker (pp. 66–67). Social identity may play a role in acquisition: L2 learners may claim to want to sound native but resist changing the fundamental intonation patterns of their speech (Pickering & Baker, 2014).

Clearly, the major meaningful components of intonation outlined herein form merely a starting point for understanding the complexity and variation of intonation.

New conceptualizations

So far, several studies have been cited showing statistically significant relationships between ratings of English language ability and measurements of intonational patterns. One rather underemphasized group of participants in these studies is one at the high-proficiency end of the spectrum: those whose intonation was nearly native-like. These successes are encouraging because they imply that non-native speakers can and do acquire English intonation, at least in part.

Yet, the question of exactly how learners acquire intonation is an elusive one. The lack of agreement among researchers about which intonation units are meaningful and how those units should be measured makes it hard to synthesize the past studies and draw 'meta conclusions' about acquisition. Further, longitudinal studies are limited by the logistical difficulties of obtaining measurements of intonation from multiple learners at different stages of their language development. To approach the question of acquisition, a promising idea is to look at how the cognitive processes of adult language development might apply to intonation.

Phonological and phonetic processes

So far, I have discussed the phonology of intonation (the broad categories of intonational meaning and how they associate with important discourse elements). However, the phonetics (the actual manifestation of these phonological elements in the intonation stream) are distinct from the phonology and may be more challenging for L2 learners. Such phonetic details might involve the alignment of a pitch peak in a syllable, the steepness of a rise or fall, fluctuation in pitch range and others.

Trofimovich and Baker (2006) looked specifically at how pitch peaks were aligned with syllables for Korean and American speakers of English. The Koreans tended to align the pitch peak later in the syllable than the Americans, regardless of their English experience or age of arrival. Mennen (1998) found similar errors in peak alignment for advanced Dutch speakers of Greek. Concerning intonation boundaries, Jilke (2007) found that, although both German and English have a low-rising intonation boundary as a meaningful phonological category, the slope and curvature of the boundary differ. For the Germans, the pitch rises more gradually and within a narrower range than for the Americans, which can contribute to a perception of a foreign accent for either group speaking the other's language (p. 85).

The implication of these findings is that the phonology and phonetics of intonation are acquired in separate cognitive processes. Therefore, it would make sense for practitioners to teach intonational phonology at lower levels, raising awareness of the major meaningful components while saving the finer phonetic subtleties for the advanced levels.

Cognitive load and the intonational phrase

It is also likely that the language learning process itself limits the intonation produced at early stages of language development owing to the significant cognitive load that burdens the beginning learner. If a language learner is attempting to articulate ideas with limited vocabulary and grammar, it may be that only a single word or short memorized phrase can be held in consciousness at a given time while preparing to speak. The result may be one-word intonation contours.

Segalowitz and colleagues' discussions of the role of automaticity in L2 fluency are enlightening. According to Segalowitz (2000), beginners' low fluency is explained as the result of controlled, rather than automatic, processing of the new language. Attention is consumed in articulatory planning and other decisions about how to organize the basic linguistic elements of speech: the lexical content of the message, the syntax, morphology and phonology. Controlled processing uses up limited cognitive resources, in competition with higher-order processing of the discourse, resulting in a less fluent delivery. According to Segalowitz and Hulstijn (2005):

> Given the fact that humans have a limited capacity for information processing, it is obvious that language users cannot pay attention to all information at all linguistic levels simultaneously to the same high degree. In most communicative situations, the processing of information at the higher levels – that is information concerning the content and the course of the communication – consumes much of this limited capacity.
>
> (p. 381)

As learners become more proficient, these processes become more automatic, freeing up their attention for higher-order ideas and resulting in greater fluency.

These facts about language processing are relevant to the process of intonation acquisition as well. We have seen that the intonation contour is the site of each new idea that the speaker intends to convey (Chafe, 1994). Because of the attention demanded in L2 processing, new learners are more likely to produce one- or two-word utterances. It may be that for such L2 speakers each lexical item is a 'new idea' to occupy a contour, even if it is merely a function word. This explains the word-by-word speech of prior examples in which intonational phrases were short and even function words were high-pitched. As L2 learners become more proficient, linguistic planning and retrieval processes become more automatic and frequently used language chunks may become 'routinized', which, in turn, leads to more fluent speech (Segalowitz & Hulstijn, 2005, p. 372). Automaticity results in the inclusion of more linguistic content within each intonation contour. Therefore, there is no point in telling a beginner, who can only process one lexical item or phrase at a time, to utter a long well-formed intonational phrase. The shorter intonational phrases common to new learners are a natural result of controlled processing and will necessarily differ from native-like phrasing.

A new learner would also experience cognitive processing constraints for those aspects of intonation associated with the information structure and topic organization of the discourse. These complex uses of intonation may simply be beyond the reach of a beginner who is limited in the ability to track the ideational content of the discourse in progress.

Implications for instruction

As with other aspects of language structure, instruction can play a role in improving learners' awareness and production of intonation. Derwing and Rossiter (2003) conducted a controlled study of ESOL students who were rated in comprehensibility and fluency after receiving instruction in three different settings, one that emphasized pronunciation of segments, a second that emphasized prosody (including intonation) and a third control setting with no special pronunciation instruction. While there were some advantages associated with all three research conditions, the prosody group had higher ratings in comprehensibility and fluency than did the group that received segmental instruction alone.

Despite the challenges discussed above, intonation need not be ignored at lower levels and may be introduced in stages, consistent with learner ability. Early on, perception activities can help learners raise their awareness of the most common meaningful categories of intonation: listening for and underlining prominent words in a printed worksheet, circling pictures corresponding to ideas uttered with high pitch or observing pitch changes using speech technology can all be useful. As for production, beginners can be taught even in one-word phrases to raise their pitch on new information and to direct the final boundary in a meaningful way. They can also learn the intonation contours of common language chunks. Activities such as mimicking, mirroring and echoing models of speech can help develop the ability to consciously monitor intonation (Wremble, 2007).

For intermediate learners, for whom the basic language elements have become more automatic, the discourse-level concepts of intonation can be introduced in more detail. Activities on intonation are best presented in the context of paragraphs or dialogues to allow learners to make judgements about information structure, topic shifts and links between phrases and turns. Any speaking activity can be adapted to highlight intonational meaning in the task. Learners' own monologues or dialogues can be recorded and transcribed to provide compelling and comprehensible texts for intonation learning: after identifying new versus given ideas, contrasts, related phrases, topic shifts and so on, learners can choose the appropriate intonation.

Finally, for advanced learners whose goal is to reduce the subtleties of foreign accent, the phonetic details, such as the alignment of pitch peaks and the slope and range of various rises and falls can be emphasized, especially with the aid of speech technology.

Conclusion

Although all languages apparently divide speech into thought groups that coincide with intonational phrases, the association of high and low pitch with components of discourse differs from language to language. While studies have shown that L2 learners struggle with English intonation, the same studies include successful participants who have made good progress in acquiring intonation. This chapter advocates teaching intonation in a simple manner, starting with the most predictable phonological categories of intonational meaning while taking into account each learner's level of proficiency. For advanced students, there is seemingly limitless room for exploration of the subtle details of intonation. Acquiring intonation to whatever extent can have a significant impact on a learner's communicative competence and on how his or her accent may be perceived.

Appendix: Transcription symbols

TODAY	Content word (upper case)
from	Function word (lower case)
<u>TODAY</u>	New idea
<u>TODAY</u>	Contrasting idea
TODAY	Given idea
today↑	High-rising intonation boundary
today↗	Low-rising intonation boundary
toda:::y→	Flat (plateau) intonation boundary
today↘	Partially falling intonation boundary
today↓	Falling intonation boundary
toda-	Cut-off speech (no intonation boundary)
⇑Today	High paratone
⇓ Today	Low paratone
↾ Today	High key
→ Today	Mid key
↳ Today	Low key
Today↘ (.4) we. . .	Pause duration in seconds
Todáy, TODÁY	Stressed syllable in a word

References

Bing, J. (1985). *Aspects of English prosody*. New York, NY: Garland.

Bolinger, D. (1986). *Intonation and its parts*. Stanford, CA: Stanford University Press.

Bolinger, D. (1989). *Intonation and its uses*. Stanford, CA: Stanford University Press.

Brazil, D. (1985). *The communicative value of intonation*. Discourse Analysis Monograph 8. Birmingham: University of Birmingham English Language Research.

Brazil, D. (1997). *The communicative value of intonation in English*. London: Cambridge University Press.

Chafe, W. (1994). *Discourse, consciousness, and time: The flow and displacement of conscious experience in speaking and writing*. Chicago, IL: University of Chicago Press.

Chomsky, N., & Halle, M. (1968). *The sound pattern of English*. New York, NY: Harper and Row.

Chun, D. (2002). *Discourse intonation in L2: From theory and research to practice*. Amsterdam: John Benjamins.

Davies, C., & Tyler, A. (1994). Demystifying cross-cultural (mis)communication: Improving performance through balanced feedback in a situated context. In C. Madden and C. Myers (Eds), *Discourse and performance of international teaching assistants* (pp. 201–220). Alexandria, VA: TESOL.

Derwing, T., & Rossiter, M. (2003). The effects of pronunciation instruction on accuracy, fluency, and complexity of L2 accented speech. *Applied Language Learning, 13*(1), 1–17.

Ford, C., & Thompson, S. (1996). Interactional units in conversation: Syntactic, intonational, and pragmatic resources for the management of turns. In E. Ochs, E. Schegloff, and S. Thompson (Eds), *Interaction and grammar* (pp. 134–184). Cambridge: Cambridge University Press.

Hahn, L. D. (2004). Primary stress and intelligibility: Research to motivate the teaching of suprasegmentals. *TESOL Quarterly, 38*, 201–223.

Halliday, M. (1967). *Intonation and grammar in British English*. The Hague: Mouton.

Hewings, M. (1995). Tone choice in the English intonation of non-native speakers. *International Review of Applied Linguistics, 33*(3), 251–265.

Isaac, A. (1997). *Critical factors in native speaker perceptions of nonnative speaker fluency*. Paper presented at the American Association of Applied Linguistics annual convention, Orlando, FL, March 1997.

Isaacs, T., & Trofimovich, P. (2012). Deconstructing comprehensibility: Identifying the linguistic influences on listeners' L2 comprehensibility ratings. *Studies in Second Language Acquisition, 34*, 475–505.

Jilke, M. (2007). Different manifestations and perceptions of foreign accent in intonation. In J. Trouvain & U. Gut (Eds), *Non-native prosody: Phonetic description and teaching practice* (pp. 77–96). Berlin: Mouton de Gruyter.

Juffs, A. (1990). Tone, syllable structure and interlanguage phonology: Chinese learners' stress errors. *International Review of Applied Linguistics, 28*(2), 99–117.

Kang, O. (2010). Relative slience of suprasegmental features on judgments of L2 comprehensibility and accentedness. *System, 38*, 301–315.

Kang, O., Rubin, D., & Pickering, L. (2010). Suprasegmental measures of accentedness and judgments of English language learner proficiency in oral English. *Modern Language Journal, 94*, 554–566.

Klatt, D. (1975). Vowel lengthening is syntactically determined in a connected discourse. *Journal of Phonetics, 3*, 129–140.

Kormos, J., & Dénes, M. (2004). Exploring measures and perceptions of fluency in the speech of second language learners. *System, 32*, 145–164.

Mennen, I. (1998). Second language acquisition of intonation: the case of peak alignment. *Chicago Linguistic Society, 34*, 327–341.

Pickering, L. (1999). *The analysis of prosodic systems in the classroom discourse of NS and NNS teaching assistants*. Unpublished doctoral dissertation, University of Florida, Gainesville, FL.

Pickering, L. (2001). The role of tone choice in improving ITA communication in the classroom. *TESOL Quarterly, 35*(2), 233–255.

Pickering, L. (2004). The structure of intonational paragraphs in native and nonnative speaker instructional discourse. *English for Specific Purposes, 23*, 19–43.

Pickering, L., & Baker. A. (2014). Suprasegmental measures of accentedness. In J. Levis, & A. Moyer (Eds), *Social influences on pronunciation acquisition* (pp. 75–94). New York, NY: Oxford University Press.

Pickering, L., Hu, G., & Baker, A. (2012). The pragmatic function of intonation: Cueing agreement and disagreement & implications for ELT. In J. Romeo (Ed.), *Pragmatics, Prosody and ELT* (pp. 199–218). Berlin: Springer-Verlag.

Pierrehumbert, J., & Hirschberg, J. (1990). The meaning of intonational contours in discourse. In P. Cohen, J. Morgan, & M. Pollack (Eds), *Intentions in communication* (pp. 271–311). Cambridge, MA: MIT Press.

Riggenbach, H. (1991). Toward an understanding of fluency: A microanalysis of nonnative speaker conversations. *Discourse Processes, 14*, 423–441.

Schegloff, E. (1998). Reflections on studying prosody in talk-in-interaction. *Language and Speech 41*(3–4), 235–263.

Segalowitz, N. (2000). Automaticity and attentional skill in fluent performance. In H. Riggenbach (Ed.), *Perspectives on fluency* (pp. 200–219). Ann Arbor, MI: University of Michigan Press.

Segalowitz, N., & Hulstijn, J. (2005). Automaticity in bilingualism and second language learning. In J. F. Kroll & A. M. B. De Groot (Eds), *Handbook of bilingualism: Psycholinguistic approaches* (pp. 371–388). New York, NY: Oxford University Press.

Tench, P. (1991). The stylistic potential of intonation. In W. van Peer (Ed.), *The taming of the text* (pp. 50–82). London: Routledge.

Trofimovich, P., & Baker, W. (2006). Learning second language suprasegmentals: Effect of L2 experience on prosody and fluency characteristics of L2 speech. *Studies in Second Language Acquisition 28*, 1–30.

Tyler, A. (1992). Discourse structure and the perception of incoherence in international teaching assistant's spoken discourse. *TESOL Quarterly, 26*(4), 713–729.

Wennerstrom, A. (1994). Intonational meaning in English discourse: A study of nonnative speakers. *Applied Linguistics, 1*(4), 399–420.

Wennerstrom, A. (1998). Intonation and second language acquisition: A study of Chinese speakers. *Studies in Second Language Acquisition, 20*(1), 1–25.

Wennerstrom, A. (2000). The role of intonation in second language fluency. In H. Riggenbach (Ed.), *Perspectives on fluency* (pp. 102–127). Ann Arbor, MI: University of Michigan Press.

Wennerstrom, A. (2001). *The music of everyday speech: Prosody and discourse analysis*. New York, NY: Oxford University Press.

Wennerstrom, A. (2007). *Intonation in the discourse of second language learners*. Paper presented at Information Structure in Adult and Child Language workshop, Max Planck Institute for Psycholinguistics, Nimejen, the Netherlands, 29–31 March 2007.

Wennerstrom, A., & Siegel, A. (2003). Keeping the floor in multiparty conversations: Intonation, syntax, and pause. *Discourse Processes, 36*(2), 77–107.

Wichmann, A. (2000). *Intonation in text and discourse: Beginnings, middles, ends*. Harlow: Pearson Education.

Wremble, M. (2007). Metacompetence-based approach to the teaching of L2 prosody: Practical implications. In J. Trouvain & U. Gut (Eds), *Non-native prosody. Phonetic description and teaching practice* (pp. 189–209). Berlin: Mouton de Gruyter.

Yule, G. (1980). Speakers' topics and major paratones. *Lingua, 52*, 33–47.

10

English orthography as a resource for learners of English

Wayne B. Dickerson

Introduction

One of my students did not understand a word mentioned after class and asked, 'How do you spell that?' As I replied, the student used her index finger to trace the letters on her palm. When she finished visualizing the word, she replied, 'Oh, pen-gOO-een. I understand! Thank you!'

This student, like many others, was attempting to use orthography as a pronunciation resource. In this case, she had some success. She recognized the word <penguin>, although on reading it back from her hand she gave it three syllables rather than two, misplaced the stress to the middle syllable, mispronounced <ng> as /ng/, misinterpreted the <u> after <g> as a vowel and rhymed the last syllable with 'wean'.

My intent for this chapter is to help teachers discover value in spelling to share with their students whenever discussing the pronunciation of words. For this, we reach beyond phonics and hand-me-downs from the past. We tap into the relative new frontier of linguistic spelling research for perspectives, models, strategies of analysis and description, and even rules that, once converted into pedagogical prediction patterns, can make our orthography truly useful to learners (see Dickerson, 2006, 2015).

While students are primed to see the benefit of our spelling, many teachers are not. Therefore we begin with the nature of our spelling system and its implications for teachers. We then demonstrate how linguistics can reveal the sound system through the orthographic conventions of English, and how these insights can be translated into simple pedagogical forms for ESL instruction. Since my personal experience has been with university-level learners, my orientation will be to adult students beyond beginning-level instruction.

Historical and current conceptualizations of English orthography

A prevailing bias

I start with conventional wisdom about our orthography, which is decidedly negative. Complaints, ridicule and scathing denunciations, most poignantly from spelling reformers, are the norm. Dickerson (2006) provides a history of our alphabet; Carney (1994) covers the circuitous history of spelling reform.

Reformers have focused primarily on two areas of vowel orthography: (a) the retention of different spellings for the same vowel sounds, e.g. beat, beet; pain, pane; and (b) the use of the same spelling for different vowel sounds, e.g. now, snow; soup, found; -ea- spellings (beat, great, wealth, heart, heard); and -ough spellings (enough, trough, thorough, through, bough). Examples like these motivated reformers such as Mort Follick (1965, p. 1) to call our spelling system 'a chaotic concoction of oddities without order or cohesion'. Those in the public at large who have struggled with spelling, including many ESL teachers, continue to side with Follick in their opinion of our spelling.

Minority voices such as Noam Chomsky and Morris Halle contrast sharply with those above. After a thorough study of the English sound system, they concluded 'that English orthography, despite its often cited inconsistencies, comes remarkably close to being an optimal orthographic system for English' (Chomsky & Halle, 1968, p. 49). The distance between these understandings is so great it cannot be dismissed.

Chaos or order?

How one regards English orthography depends on one's interpretation of the alphabetic principle. The genius of those who created the first alphabet around 2000 BCE was to pick from the hundreds of Egyptian hieroglyphs available just those representing single sounds (Sacks, 2003, pp. 24–25). When arranged to match the order of phonemes in a word, the symbols gave sounds a graphic form. These unknown innovators were the first to implement the alphabetic principle: written letters (graphemes) connect predictably to sounds (phonemes). The crux of the matter – chaos or order – is the nature of this connection.

Direct symbol–sound correlation: On the one hand, if we believe that letters should tell us how to pronounce words because one grapheme should represent one phoneme directly (the 'phoneme principle'), then we will not be satisfied at all with English spelling. Our spellings seem to ignore this ideal, leading some spelling reformers to give up on our alphabet and start fresh with new symbols and symbol–sound associations (e.g. Ivins, 1947).

Indirect symbol–sound correlation: On the other hand, if we are open to a systematic link between graphemes and phonemes that is indirect, then our spelling system fares better. Some of the earliest reformers, the orthoepists, took this point of view (Carney, 1994). For example, they reasoned that if the word-final <e> and the doubling of consonant letters were applied more broadly, readers could distinguish tense from lax vowels more confidently. By improving spelling patterns, they understood that the same vowel letter in different surroundings could suggest different sounds.

A spelling pattern is a rule that is intended to state the prerequisites for selecting one interpretation of a letter over another. Collectively, these prerequisites – such as the spelling of the target grapheme, neighbouring letters, their position in a word – compose the 'environment' of the rule. That is, an environment consists of specific parts of the word where the grapheme is used. The linguistic name for a word or its parts (such as a prefix or suffix) is 'morpheme'. When information from a morpheme is needed to judge the phonemic value of the letter, the letter and sound are in a 'morphophonemic' relationship. A spelling pattern is an effort to express the morphophonemic principle, to relate symbols to sounds indirectly.

To illustrate, consider these common words: *man, mantle, main, mane*. The <a> after <m> in these words signals nothing about sound except that it is a vowel. How do we know that the first two words have the lax vowel /æ/ and that the next two the tense vowel /ey/? In a lightning-fast decoding process, experienced readers recognize <a> in familiar spelling patterns. We demonstrate a basic, if counterintuitive, truth about our spelling system: letters do not tell us how to pronounce words; words – from which spelling patterns are fashioned – tell us how to pronounce their letters.

It may seem strange that our spelling system should signal sound indirectly until we understand what the system signals directly, namely, the identity of morphemes. For example, everywhere the regular past tense morpheme is written it is spelled uniformly as *-ed*, whether it is pronounced /t/, /d/ or /əd/; *-ed* is a 'morphograph' – a spelled morpheme. A writing system that spells the same morpheme in the same way from word to word (e.g. *-ed*), and uses different spellings for different morphemes (e.g. *write, wright, rite, right*) is called 'morphographic' writing. It communicates meaning directly to the eye, bypassing the sound system. Such writing is possible only if sound is communicated indirectly via rules.

The elegance of our spelling system was not planned. It arose from the convergence of a particular stage in the development of English, the nature of our earliest orthography, the timing of its codification and the regularity of sound change.

The scenario starts at a time in English history when morphemes, particularly borrowings from Latin through French, were pronounced the same in all derivative forms. For example, the *defin-* part of *define, definite, definitive* and *definition* was spoken the same in each word. At this time, the orthography was largely phonemic (Francis, 1958, p. 446) so a morpheme would be spelled the same wherever it occurred, e.g. <defin->, because it was pronounced the same wherever it occurred. Then certain highly conservative forces – like the introduction of the printing press into England in 1476 – froze the orthography in time while the language continued to change. This accident of history made our orthography more reader-friendly, signalling meaning directly via morphographs, than pronouncer-friendly, as the <defin-> examples illustrate. Finally, since language change is regular, a description of the phonological changes that have taken place since the orthography was codified, framed as spelling-based rules and then applied to that ancient orthography, yield today's pronunciation of the derivatives.

This is how the morphographic principle came to dominate a still-frozen orthography, and why the morphophonemic principle reveals the sounds of words. The critical involvement of sound change in this scenario is why linguistic sound change tools are especially appropriate for examining our writing system. Prima facie evidence of this is Chomsky and Halle's 1968 analysis of the English sound system, in which their alternation rules mirror sound change. The similarity between their hypothesized underlying representation of words and standard orthography is what led them to claim that our orthography is nearly optimal for English. Other, non-trivial benefits of an orthography based on morphographic and morphophonemic principles are discussed in Dickerson (2004, pp. 141–146).

When we understand how our orthography works and why, the answer to the initial question – chaos or order? – becomes clearer. Nevertheless, considerable chaos remains in the spelling of our oldest, most common, and largely Anglo-Saxon vocabulary, enough to keep spelling reform movements from going out of fashion. ESL teachers would do well to acknowledge the localized messiness without losing sight of the exceptional regularity that characterizes the system as a whole; it is here they will find the benefits their ESL students crave.

Rule quality and rule use: Rules are the primary means of extracting cues to sound from written words. To be effective for learners of English, pedagogical rules must meet high standards both in descriptive power and ease of use (Dickerson, 2013). A good learner rule must:

(a) adhere to the no prior knowledge assumption (NPKA); it requires no knowledge of English beyond that generally available to learners who are expected to use it;
(b) require a minimum of background information in order to execute;
(c) apply unambiguously; the trigger implicating it is well defined;
(d) operate mechanically; its output does not rely on guessing;
(e) yield a single, unitary output, except where acceptable variation exists;
(f) generate a pronounceable output in one pass; cyclic rules are too burdensome;
(g) be productive; a rule for a handful of words is not worth the bother;
(h) be accurate; the larger the word group, the higher the predictive accuracy should be because of the exceptions to be learned. Common exceptions must be listed;
(i) be memorable; it must be brief, simple, template-like for segmentals, and in a form that can be practised easily.

Pedagogical pointers: To appreciate the role of rules in pronunciation pedagogy, it is important to understand the goals of instruction. Goals arise from an assessment of learners' needs. We frame those needs as improvement in three skill areas – perception, prediction and production – the 3Ps (Dickerson, 2004). Better perception is the ability to draw more meaning from a spontaneous speech stream by listening. Better prediction is the ability to make better judgements about the segmentals and prosody of speech before speaking. Better production is the ability to speak spontaneously so that listeners can understand more easily. Within this framework, the study of patterns in spelling can increase learners' prediction skills to guide the accuracy of their production.

When focusing on meaning during conversation, it is difficult for speakers to attend to the formal linguistic details of their communication. Yet, without a concerted focus on form, learners are less likely to gain the skills needed for comfortable oral interaction. We solve this dilemma in part through classroom instruction, but more importantly by promoting a proven routine of private out-of-class self-instruction we call 'covert rehearsal'. This strategy chain involves speaking aloud to oneself, inspecting one's production vis-à-vis one's knowledge of oral patterns, modifying one's production accordingly and practising one's modifications to a high level of fluency (Dickerson, 1984; Sardegna, 2009). Patterns in spelling are valuable tools that learners can use to monitor and correct their production during covert rehearsal.

This groundwork prepares the way to examine three areas of word-level phonology where spelling-based rules can help learners – word stress placement, vowel choice and consonant selection. Attention to consonant patterns, the most straightforward of our spellings, will be minimized in order to focus more on less well known benefits of the English spelling system.

Illustrations and examples

Word stress prediction

For 15 minutes I listened to an international teaching assistant make her presentation on '/ɛnəməl/ testing'. The topic seemed to be about *animal* testing, but nothing she said matched the topic. I was lost until the TA finally wrote the key word on the board: *enamel*! The identity of the mystery word was surprising but so was the fact that the TA could not pronounce her research topic after several years in an American university.

This incident illustrates the crucial contribution of word stress to communication; the misplaced stress altered vowel qualities to a degree that prevented me from identifying her topic. While a catastrophic failure of understanding does not result from every mis-stressed word, mis-stressing is not trivial. Even if words are not lost, misplaced stresses can slow comprehension enough that listeners are unable to keep up with incoming messages.

English has a large polysyllabic vocabulary – 85 per cent of all dictionary entries (Teschner & Whitley, 2004, p. 27). Pronunciation textbook writers, acknowledging the importance of accurate word stress, have offered a variety of pedagogical suggestions (Dickerson, 2015). The most productive rely on spelling.

Some authors note that stress placement tends to correlate with particular endings. Two issues make this approach problematic. First, authors associate a single stress position with each ending (Woods, 1978), even when some endings guide stress to two different positions, depending on other factors in the word (e.g. *équitable*, *deléctable*). Words stressed on the other position are deemed exceptions when they are not. Second, not all polysyllabic words have a suffix (e.g. *cholesterol*, *maverick*). Others say: to stress a word composed of several morphemes, use the stress of the independent morpheme (e.g. *develop*) for the derivative (e.g. *development*) (Prator & Robinett, 1985). This approach, too, faces difficulties. First, the need to recognize internal free stems and then to stress them accurately violates the NPKA on both counts. Second, many polysyllabic words have no stand-alone stems (e.g. *indefatigable*). Third, some endings shift the major stress from where it is on its stand-alone stem (e.g. *preside*, *président*, *presidéntial*). Without knowing which endings do and do not cause stress shifts, the learner is stymied. Still other textbook authors combine approaches (Dauer, 1992). While better than any single approach, no combination provides comprehensive coverage of English word stress.

Only two ESL textbook writers attempt to develop a language-wide word stress system using linguistic-based rules applied to spelling (Guierre, 1970, 1984; Dickerson, 2004). Guierre's texts offer good coverage of the English lexicon. However, he proliferates stress rules and fails to draw them into a cohesive system. He also uses different methods to assign stress to words with the same ending. In our texts, we pay attention to the structure of the stress system and to the design of its four stress rules to ensure that they adhere to the criteria for good learner rules.

Our approach begins with these fundamental observations.

- Major stress of a polysyllabic word, regardless of length, will fall on only one of two possible syllables, called the key syllable (key) or the left syllable (left).
- Every polysyllabic word belongs to a word group defined by some combination of ending, part of speech and number of syllables.
- The position of the key syllable is defined for each word group using spelling criteria. The left syllable is immediately to the left of the key.
- A stress rule operates mechanically, based on the spelled characteristics of the word, to remove guesswork from the stress decision.

The four stress rules (SR) are non-overlapping, applying to well-defined word groups. The four rules start with the key syllable. They place the stress directly on the key syllable (key SR) or the left syllable (left SR) or require some evaluation of the key syllable (V/VC SR)

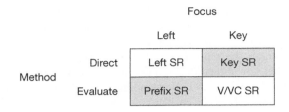

Figure 10.1 Rules in the word stress system

or left syllable (prefix SR) to determine which of the two to stress. A two-by-two table shows these possibilities (Figure 10.1).

To show how to select and use the rules, one example below illustrates the direct method of stress assignment, focusing on the key syllable – the key stress rule – and another illustrates the evaluation method, focusing on the left syllable – the prefix stress rule. For pedagogical materials that present these and the remaining two stress rules to ESL learners, see Hahn & Dickerson (1999a, 1999b).

The key stress rule (KSR): The KSR places the major stress directly on the key syllable, which is located just to the left of an iV-ending. An iV-ending begins with the letter <i> and continues immediately with <a>, <o>, <u> or <enC> (the letters <en> followed by a consonant letter C). In the following examples, a subscripted stroke divides the iV-ending from the remainder; the key is underlined. The rule is the epitome of simplicity.

In a KSR word, stress the key.

ia	io	iu	ienC
cylopéd‚ia	téd‚ious	prém‚ium	expéd‚ient
trív‚ial	stúd‚io	pód‚ium	sál‚ience

The KSR also governs the stress of words in which the iV-ending is followed by certain other recognizable endings – *-able, -al, -ary, -ate, -er, -or, -ory, -ive, -ist, -ism, -ize, -alist, -alism, -alize, -y*. In the examples below, two subscripted strokes mark off the iV-ending and the following ending. The key is underlined. This simple extension of the rule greatly expands the scope of words learners can stress accurately.

lén‚ienc‚y	emót‚ion‚al	opín‚ion‚ated
unmént‚ion‚able	iní t‚ial‚ize	méd‚iat‚or
díct‚ion‚ary	péns‚ion‚er	preservát‚ion‚ist

The prefix stress rule (PSR): The second rule is different on two dimensions, the syllable in focus and the method of assigning stress. The PSR requires the user to evaluate the composition of the left syllable to determine which syllable will receive the major stress. The major stress falls on the left if there is no prefix in the left: *sáliv‚ary*. In all other cases (no left syllable, or a prefix in the left syllable), the major stress falls on the key: *líbr‚ary*, *dispéns‚ary*.

In a PSR word:
Stress left but not a prefix.
If you can't stress left, stress key.

In the main, word groups stressed by the PSR contain words with one of the following endings: *-able, -age, -ary, -er, -ery, -ible, -ish$_{adj}$, -ive, -or, -ory, -ure, -ative, -atory, -ature*, where the key is just left of the ending. The morphographic principle ensures that these endings are visually stable, making them easy to identify. To see examples, note the list of prefixes below.

The PSR violates the NPKA since it requires learners to recognize Anglo-Saxon and Latinate prefixes. To overcome this challenge, we introduce learners to the spelled form of common prefixes. At the level appropriate to introduce the PSR, learners have encountered these prefixes many times because they abound in English writing. Thanks to the orthoepists' reforms, doubled letters cuing Latin-origin prefixes have been preserved, e.g. *attack, illegible* (Carney 1994), and many Anglo-Saxon prefixes are familiar words, e.g. *up-, down-, over-, under-, out-*. Prefix identification is a non-issue. Furthermore, their skill recognizing prefixes serves learners in other ESL instruction, e.g. vowel predictions (below) and vocabulary development. The following presents the most useful prefixes (Hahn & Dickerson, 1999a, pp. 152–159). One- and two-syllable neutral prefixes are explained below.

Neutral 2-syl: over- under- counter- / countra- inter- / intra- extra- retro- super-

Neutral 1-syl: fore- un- up- down- mis- out- non- post- trans- de- re- pre-
  pro- per- ad- ab- ob- sub- con- com- in- ex- dis-

Alternative forms of ad-, ob-, sub-, con-, in-, dis-, ex-

ac+c	af+f	ag+g	al+l	ap+p	at+t
as+s	of+f	op+p	suc+c	sup+p	col+l
cor+r	il+l	im+p	ir+r	dif+f	ef+f

In the following words, the key syllable is underlined.

dispútable	delívery	mónitor	admínistrative
párentage	invísible	cátegory	mándatory
heréditary	outlándish	expósure	cáricature

Pedagogical pointers: Students are surprised that word stress can be predicted, and that they can find the stress themselves for about 10,000 KSR words and about 8,000 PSR words. The following practice opportunities help them master the rules (Dickerson & Hahn, in press).

On the day the instructor introduces a rule, students do three things in class. First, as a check of their predictive skills, they mark the major stress on a dozen less common printed words, making their best guess, e.g. *evidentiary, palliative, octogenarian* (for KSR). Second, they listen to the instructor read each word then circle 'Yes' or 'No' in answer to the question 'Did you place the stress correctly?' Since students are typically not totally accurate, this activity serves to motivate them. Third, they identify by ear which rhythm pattern each word illustrates. This emphasizes that making clear contrasts between the major-stressed syllable and others is as important for clear word rhythm as placing the major stress correctly. We end this preview by covering the stress rule briefly.

For homework we assign pencil-and-paper practice with the rule and oral practice with their predictions. Here we note common stress exceptions. On returning to class, students use the target vocabulary in a variety of discourse activities. We call attention to the stress rule only to encourage learners to correct stress placement themselves. For homework they search their academic terms – vocabulary chosen at the start of the semester as challenging for them – to find examples of the stress rule at work. They list these and mark their stress. As a wrap-up activity, they rehearse and record a short passage to practise the target vocabulary in a discourse context.

Vowel prediction

What is /rˀzˀn/ – *raisin, resign, resin, Roseanne, reason, rezone, rosin, risen*? Even when we know the stress – /rˀzˀn/ – it narrows the options but not enough to identify the word. Every vowel quality in a word – tense, lax and reduced – is important for word recognition. Standard orthography can help with vowel quality. To see how, the oldest patterns, *orthographic* spelling patterns, are discussed first, then the newest, *linguistic* spelling patterns. Lessons in Dickerson 2004 illustrate how both types of spelling patterns are presented and practised in an ESL context.

Orthographic spelling patterns: The poor fit between the five vowel letters, A, E, I, O, U, of the Latin alphabet and a language with three times as many vowel phonemes spurred early English writers to devise various means to signal phonemes with graphemes. All are still in use today. In these examples, V stands for any vowel letter, C for any consonant letter and # for end of word. The first two patterns suggest a lax vowel; the second two a tense vowel.

VC#	ban
VCC	banned, band
VV	bait/bay
VCe#	bane

Orthographic spelling patterns employ man-made conventions that do not reflect the actual structure of syllables, e.g. to double or not double a letter, to treat the end-of-word position as relevant in one place but not in another, to use an 'empty' letter <e> to suggest the value of another letter, to use <i> and <u> for word internal VV spellings and <y> and <w> as vowel letters for word-final VVs. Had these devices been implemented widely and consistently, they would have circumvented the concerns of many spelling reformers.

To be of language-wide use to ESL learners, vowel prediction patterns must take into account this fact about English: no vowel spelling can predict a vowel's quality without access to its stress. For example, the following formulas suggest the quality of the last vowel in only the first word of each pair because, without saying so, the formulas are for stressed vowels only.

VC#	=	lax	Japan versus human
VCC	=	lax	invest versus harvest
VV	=	tense	contain versus captain
VCe#	=	tense	undermine versus determine

From the above, one might assume that the learner must predict word stress before predicting vowel quality. As explained in *Pedagogical pointers* below, this is not an accurate assumption; in fact, it is best not to do so. Before going deeper into pedagogical matters, it is important to understand vowel prediction patterns better.

Stressless patterns are only for native users whose intuitions and vocabulary supply what is missing in patterns. They are not for ESL learners who have no such resources; they violate the NPKA. Nevertheless, textbook authors, although well intentioned and undoubtedly modelling phonics for native speakers, teach stressless vowel patterns as if they were generally applicable (Prator & Robinett, 1985, pp. 221–227; Gilbert, 2001, p. x; Dale & Poms, 2005, p. 73).

Vowel quality patterns: Without stress, spelling patterns have almost no predictive value for learners. With stress, they become prediction patterns. A prediction pattern for a vowel is a 'vowel quality pattern' or VQP. Notice the pattern pairs. (Pedagogical patterns are discussed below.)

Descriptive patterns	Last-syllable prediction	Pedagogical patterns
$\acute{V}$C# = lax	Japán: /æ/	$\acute{V}$C# = shape
$\check{V}$C# = reduced	humăn: /ə/	$\check{V}$C# = reduced
$\acute{V}$CC = lax	invést : /ɛ/	$\acute{V}$CC = shape
$\check{V}$CC = reduced	harvĕst: /ə/	$\check{V}$CC = reduced
$\acute{V}$V = tense	contáin: /ey/	$\acute{V}$V = name
$\check{V}$VC = reduced	captăin: /ə/	$\check{V}$VC = reduced
$\acute{V}$C+E = tense	propóse: /ow/	$\acute{V}$C+E = name
$\check{V}$C+E = reduced	purpŏse: /ə/	$\check{V}$C+E = reduced

One unstressed pattern above, VVC, is not a perfect counterpart of the nearest stressed pattern. The exact counterpart, an unstressed word-final VV spelling, predicts a tense vowel, e.g. *vallĕy, follŏw*. Inside a word, an unstressed VV spelling predicts a reduced vowel only if a consonant letter in the same morpheme follows, e.g. *forfĕit, camŏuflage*. This explains the $\check{V}$VC = reduced pattern above.

Linguistic spelling patterns: A second source of prediction patterns is linguistics. Each linguistic pattern describes a bit of language behaviour or recapitulates a bit of language history when applied to our ancient orthography. Guierre (1984) pursued this strategy. His vowel rules, however, are so complex that only the very brightest students could benefit from them. We take the same linguistic rules and recast them as learner rules that are easy to understand and practice. Two examples will suffice.

The following words will look familiar. They all have iV-endings spelled with the letter <i> followed by either <a>, <o>, <u> or <enC> and are stressed by the KSR.

ia	io	iu	ienC
cylopéd̩ia	téd̩ious	prém̩ium	expéd̩ient
áv̩ian	stúd̩io	pód̩ium	resíl̩ience

When learners stress the key syllable (underlined above), they can also predict the key vowel. If it is spelled with the letters <a>, <e>, <o> or <u> followed by one consonant letter, the vowel will be tense. The general pattern is V́C+iV = tense. If the vowel letter is spelled with <i> before a single consonant letter, as in the last example, *resilience*, the prediction is lax, íC+iV = lax. This second pattern applies first to filter out the iC cases before the general pattern applies. These learner patterns exactly match the output of the technical tensing rules that describe sound changes in English (Chomsky & Halle, 1968, p. 241).

The second group of words should also look familiar. Each is stressed by the PSR. The key syllable is immediately to the left of the ending, as underlined. In these words, the major stress is on the left syllable.

návig̲ able	élig̲ ible	cáteg̲ ory	commúnic̲ ative
herédit̲ ary	attríbut̲ ive	pédic̲ ure	júdic̲ atory
depósit̲ er	mónit̲ or	législ̲ ature	lúmin̲ ary

When we stress left, a stressed <u> vowel letter followed by a single consonant letter predicts a tense vowel; the specific úC ← = tense pattern applies (column 4). In other left syllables, other vowel letters fit the general pattern V̆C ← = lax (columns 1–3). These simple patterns (Dickerson, 1980) predict the same output as technical rules (Chomsky & Halle, 1968, p. 241).

Making vowel (symbol) predictions: Vowel quality predictions are not vowel predictions. To see where vowel prediction enters the process, follow the steps (see Figure 10.2). Stress heads the list; it distinguishes a full vowel prediction from a reduced vowel prediction. Reduced converts directly to /ə/. Spelling patterns sort full vowels into tense and lax vowel qualities. Tense and lax plus the spelling of the target vowel convert to symbols for specific vowel sounds.

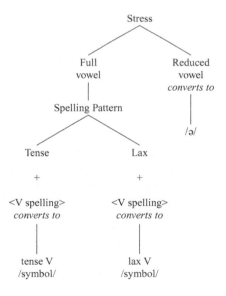

Figure 10.2 Tense and lax vowel qualities for spelling patterns

The phrase 'converts to' refers to a mechanical process that generates a vowel symbol from a vowel quality and a vowel letter, namely, the name–shape translator (Dickerson, 2013). It captures these observations: first, the predicted tense vowel sounds like the *name* of the letter used to spell it. Second, the predicted lax vowel looks like the *shape* of the letter used to spell it. The 'name' and 'shape' connections to vowel symbols are the following.

name of				shape of			
<a>	→	/ey/		<a>	→	/æ/	
<e>	→	/iy/		<e>	→	/ɛ/	
<i>/<y>	→	/ay/		<i>/<y>	→	/ɪ/	
<o>	→	/ow/		<o>	→	/ɔ ~ ɑ/	
<u>	→	/uw/		<u>	→	/ʌ/	

By relabelling vowel qualities as 'name' for tense, and 'shape' for lax (and keeping the label 'reduced'), we give learners a way to predict specific vowels symbols. Recast VQPs, originating as orthographic spelling patterns, are listed above under *Pedagogical patterns* (see p. 177). Those originating as linguistic spelling patterns are recast as follows:

íC+iV	=	shape		úC ←	=	name
V́C+iV	=	name		V́C ←	=	shape

The translator starts with a vowel quality prediction – name, shape or reduced – for the target vowel. If the prediction is name, then the predicted vowel symbol matches the name of the target vowel letter (e.g. *rád͜ius* → V́C+iV = name → /ey/; *tútor͜ed* → úC ← = name → /uw/). If the prediction is shape, then the predicted vowel symbol is closest in shape to the spelled vowel (e.g. *expréss* → V́CC = shape → /ɛ/; *inít͜iate* → íC+iV = shape → /ɪ/). In VV patterns, the name of the first vowel letter identifies the specific target vowel phoneme (*repéat* → V́V = name → /iy/). (A stressed VV pattern for which the translator cannot predict the correct vowel sound consistently becomes a specific VQP, e.g. éu = /uw/, *Europe*.) Unstressed patterns predicting reduced uniformly point to /ə/ (e.g. *hárvest͜ing* → V̌CC = reduced → /ə/).

Pedagogical pointers: There is no single, right or best way to present prediction patterns to learners. Some like the big picture first, e.g. V́C+iV = name; others learn best by starting with the details, e.g. áC+iV = /ey/, éC+iV = /iy/ etc. Our strategy has been to accommodate both preferences (Hahn & Dickerson, 1999a, pp. 188–189). Some students start with the specific patterns and then move to the general pattern because it entails less of a memory load when used with the name–shape translator. Others continue with specific patterns.

Regardless of one's approach, VQPs require knowledge of word stress. As noted above, this does not mean that we introduce VQPs only after presenting stress rules. In fact, it is better that learners begin using VQPs before they learn any stress rules. At this stage, they practise with stressed words. Then, when students learn each stress rule later they can focus on stress prediction and use their stress results with VQPs they already know.

Vowel quality-stress patterns

The major stress of a word is a pivot point. From this point and to the right, learners must know the stress of vowels to predict their qualities. VQPs apply, as illustrated. To the left of the major stress, however, the learner can predict both the stress as well as the vowel quality by the position of the target vowel, its spelling and whether it is in a prefix. VQSPs, vowel quality-stress patterns, from the 'positional stress system' apply. VQSPs are linguistic spelling patterns. For an example of how these patterns are taught to ESL learners, see Dickerson (2004).

Three positions: A target vowel (■) left of the major stress is in one of three positions, under-lined in the examples below. We identify each position starting with a stressed syllable (■) and moving to the left. The symbol ■ identifies another syllable. The term 'prestress' describes the position 'immediately left of the stressed syllable'. 'Initial' means 'at the start of a word' and is symbolized by #. 'Medial' means 'not at the start of a word'; this position is between two other syllables. 'Non-prestress' is the position 'two syllables left of the stressed syllable'.

IP	Initial prestress	Initial syllable just left of a stressed syllable	# ■ ■
		e.g. D<u>a</u>kóta, W<u>i</u>scónsin	
MP	Medial prestress	Syllable between stressed and NP syllables	■ ■ ■
		e.g. Cal<u>i</u>fórnia, Miss<u>i</u>ssíppi	
NP	Non-prestress	Two syllables left of a stressed syllable	■ ■ ■
		e.g. C<u>a</u>lifórnia, M<u>i</u>ssissíppi	

Stress and vowel quality in the three positions of non-prefixed words: In non-prefix syllables, IP syllables can have tense, lax or reduced vowels, depending on their spelling. The <u> in a uC spelling is stressed and tense. If two different consonant letters (C_1C_2) follow the vowel letter, the vowel is stressed and lax. Any of the following spellings will have an unstressed and reduced vowel: VC, VC2, VCl, VCr. C2 refers to two identical consonant letters. The VCl and VCr spellings are explicitly not cases of VC_1C_2.

Initial prestress		Spelling	Pattern	Examples
IP	spelled {	uC	IPùC = tense	T<u>u</u>nésia → Tùnésia
		VC_1C_2	IPV̀C_1C_2 = lax	<u>A</u>lbérta → Àlbérta
		others	ĬP = reduced	D<u>a</u>kóta → Dăkóta
				others: gr<u>ă</u>mmátical, Ătlántic, Nĕbráska

An MP syllable is always unstressed. To be reduced, this vowel letter must be followed by at least one consonant letter in the same morpheme.

Medial prestress	Spelling	Pattern	Examples
MP	any spelling before a C	M̆P = reduced	Penns<u>y</u>lvánia → Pennsўlvánia

In non-prestress position, the vowel is always tertiary-stressed. The <u> in a uC spelling will be tense. All other vowel spellings will be lax regardless of their spelling.

Non-prestress	Spelling	Pattern	Examples
NP	uC	NPùC = tense	ru̱daméntary → rùdaméntary
	all others	ǸP = lax	Pe̱nnsylvánia → Pènnsylvánia

These linguistic spelling patterns produce the same results as the technical rules for vowels left of the major stress (Chomsky & Halle, 1968, pp. 242, 245).

Stress and vowel quality in the three positions of prefixed words: English prefixes are of two types, merged and neutral. 'Merged' prefixes have lost their original meaning; they have merged with the meaning of the whole word. What does the *be-* of *bereave* mean? What does the *de-* of *decide* mean? Since students learned to recognize Anglo-Saxon and Latinate prefixes for the prefix stress rule, they are prepared to recognize prefixes left of the major stress.

Merged prefixes follow the MP and NP patterns as presented above, e.g. *represénted* → M̆P = reduced → /ə/; *repre̱sénted* → ǸP = shape → /ɛ/. In IP position, however, all merged prefixes behave alike; all are unstressed, regardless of their spelling: e.g. *rĕspónd, cŏntórted*. Since the consonant letters after the prefix vowel make no difference, the pattern is different from the IP pattern for non-prefixes. This pattern is IPP (initial prestress prefix) and predicts an unstressed, reduced vowel: IP̆P = reduced.

Neutral prefixes, on the other hand, contribute a distinct meaning to a word. Left of the major stress, they keep the same pronunciation and stress regardless of position, e.g. *dèpópulate, dècompóse*. *De-* means explicitly 'the opposite of'. Neutral prefixes are not subject to positional patterns. That is, we us the IP/IPP, MP, and NP patterns as if the neutral prefix were not present. In *dècompóse*, for example, *com-* is in IPP position, not MP position. The top two rows above (under *The prefix stress rule*, p. 175) contain one- and two-syllable Anglo-Saxon and Latinate prefixes; they are all neutral prefixes. All one-syllable neutral prefixes of Latin origin have the same shape as merged prefixes but have an explicit meaning attached: *de-* 'opposite of', *in-* (all forms) 'not', *sub-* 'secondary, under', *trans-* 'across' etc.

Pedagogical pointers: The positional stress system is a particularly valuable adjunct to teaching vocabulary. Once familiar with the patterns, students become adept at making on-target predictions for all the vocabulary they encounter. One important suggestion to start with: we have learned that a larger-than-normal sans serif font at the start aids syllable identification.

The presentation begins by introducing the IP, MP and NP positions and giving students practice identifying them in a wide variety of words with the major stress given. Next come the IP patterns in words having only one syllable left of the major stress. Students practise using 'name', 'shape' and 'reduced' patterns to solidify the three-way distinction in vowel quality. MP and NP patterns are presented together because an MP syllable is impossible without a preceding NP syllable. Finally, patterns for prefix vowels and for vowels outside the positional system, e.g. *au, eu, ou*, are introduced. Throughout these materials, students are encouraged to practise saying their predictions aloud, to link prediction with production and to hear vowel alternation.

Few TESL professionals pay attention to vowels left of the major stress. One who does is Murphy (2004). Students enumerate the syllables of a word then identify the syllable carrying the major stress by any means at hand. Next, they identify by ear which syllable, if any, carries a tertiary stress. Murphy's technique raises students' awareness of word stress and word rhythm and gives them practice producing them. The positional system suggested here has a different purpose, namely, to give learners the skill to predict vowels left of the major stress after predicting the major stress on their own; articulation practice follows.

Consonant prediction

In the spelling system of English, there are fewer alternative spellings for consonant sounds than for vowel sounds. The Latin alphabet gave English writers more to work with from the start, and sound change touched fewer consonants than vowels. Loanwords have been the single most disruptive force on the original grapheme–phoneme links. Even so, consonant pronunciations remain easier to predict than vowel pronunciations.

Difficult cases: The worst distortion from borrowings affected the interpretation of <ch>, originally /ʧ/ in the oldest stratum of English, e.g. *chat, reach*. French contributed /ʃ/ words spelled <ch>, e.g. *chic, machine*. Greek loanwords compounded the trouble with <ch> pronounced as /k/, e.g. *choir, mechanic*. Although word origin is a good clue to the pronunciation of <ch>, such information is unavailable to ESL learners. Lacking anything better, it is impossible for ESL learners to predict the sound value of <ch> with confidence.

Beyond <ch>, grapheme–phoneme correspondences for consonants improve despite borrowings. Noted here are only a few consonant targets that ESL textbook writers have struggled with and some useful resources.

Virtually unmentioned in ESL materials is the notoriously troublesome 'invisible /y/', the unwritten /y/ in words like *few, value, Europe*. The full system and associated variability can be found in Dickerson (1985, 2004).

Early pronunciation teachers taught that English has two high-back vowels, /uw/ and /yuw/ (Trager & Henderson, 1956, p. 26). That was not as helpful as learner rules that predict the presence (e.g. *feud, fuel*), absence (e.g. *ruin, secluded*) and optional presence (e.g. *tune, news* and *feature, graduate*) of the /y/ 99 per cent of the time (see also Hahn & Dickerson, 1999b, pp. 189–190).

Overly simplified patterns for predicting the sounds of <th> abound (e.g. Grant, 2001, p. 163). Four easy rules in Dickerson (2015) have a 98 per cent accuracy rate for the approximately 800 <th> words in English.

The letters <ng> are also poorly addressed in ESL materials. Dauer (1992, p. 209) is one of the few who tries. Old English <ng> was uniformly pronounced /ŋg/, eventually simplifying to /ŋ/ in final position, e.g. *English language* but *wing, song*. In the oldest French borrowings, the practice of rendering <g> as /ʤ/ before <e i y> introduced words like *strange, engine, mangy*, where <ng> is pronounced as /nʤ/. Later French borrowings like *lingerie* gave English a less common variant for <ng>, namely, /nʒ/. Reliable rules to sort out these variants are presented in Dickerson (2006).

Since many textbooks miss the generalization that unites iV-endings (e.g. four different categories in Dauer (1992, p. 63)), it is not surprising that they also fail to notice generalizations about palatals before these endings (pp. 176–184). When the preceding consonant letter is <c g t s x>, a palatal output is common (Hahn & Dickerson, 1999b, pp. 188–189).

c+iV	=	/ʃ/	magician, special
g+iV	=	/dʒ/	prestigious, allegiance
st+iV	=	/tʃ/	digestion, Sebastian
Vs+iV	=	/ʒ/	explosion, revision
rs+iV	=	/ʃ, ʒ/	conversion, Persian
Cs+iV	=	/ʃ/	commission, expulsion
x+io	=	/kʃ/	retroflexion, crucifixion

The rs+iV pattern illustrates again how we accommodate language change with external rules without touching the orthography. In British English, rs+iV predicts /ʃ/, whereas in American English, rs+iV predicts /ʒ/.

Pedagogical pointers: An ideal point at which to introduce consonant spelling patterns is when working on the associated consonant articulations. For example, the highly reliable <th> patterns mentioned above can help learners sort out which consonant, /ð/ or /θ/, is required in words. Similarly, since palatal consonants are often challenging, palatal patterns with <c g t s x> noted above are useful to tell learners which particular palatal is needed in a word.

Another point at which consonant patterns can be brought up profitably is when presenting new vocabulary. Even though vocabulary is not typically organized by spelling, it is often possible to use the vocabulary in the lesson with extra words to illustrate different pronunciations of similar spellings. For example, if the new words are *triangle, triangular, angle, angular* (illustrating the <ng> pattern predicting /ŋg/), they can be contrasted with *bang/banging, clang/clanged*, which follow the patterns for /ŋ/.

In all such cases, patterns previewed in class can be exercised at home using worksheets. During covert rehearsal learners practise their predictions aloud. On returning to class, the focus turns to producing the target sounds in discourse contexts. If learners mispronounce, the teacher calls attention to the spelling patterns they have learned to encourage self-correction.

Conclusion

It has been my intention in this chapter to offer a glimpse of what linguistic research has to offer orthographic research and what pedagogical applications for ESL learners look like. The conclusion of linguistics is that the spelling system of English is not as flawed as many feared nor as ideal as it could be. As it is, with the accretions of centuries, it still retains some remarkable characteristics that make it a valuable resource for learners of English. Two features stand out, both arising from the fact that English spelling so faithfully captured the language as it was spoken centuries ago, when morphemes were pronounced the same way in their various derivatives and were therefore spelled in the same way.

First, although English is not written as it is spoken today, it is nevertheless written in a way that communicates meaning directly through meaning units that tend to be spelled alike from word to word regardless of how they are pronounced. That makes English spelling 'reader-considerate'. Second, while meaning is more directly accessible to readers, the connection between English spellings and English sounds is not lost. A reader of English orthography can predict the modern-day pronunciation of words indirectly by applying orthographic and linguistic spelling patterns to this ancient writing. In short, even though imperfect, the English spelling system gives readers access to meaning and sound.

This two-part insight from linguistics suggests two directions forward for spelling researchers and those who want to show ESL learners the value of English orthography for pronunciation purposes. First, no progress can be made by insisting that English spelling represents (or should represent) contemporary speech directly and that letters have sounds; these untenable positions retard understanding and impede progress. Further, all hope that spelling reform will institute this supposed ideal is unfounded and should be abandoned. The linguistic perspective described above must be accepted as the foundation for ongoing spelling research and second language applications of that research.

Second, this scientific basis for progress makes explicit the indirect connection of letters to sounds via morphophonemic rules. Therefore, spelling researchers and TESOL practitioners hoping to use spelling as a pronunciation resource for ESL learners need to accept that access to sound through spelling will not be an easy, one-step process and that rules with environmental requirements are a necessary and unavoidable means to this end; there is no shortcut to prediction. If symbol–sound patterns are to find their way into curricula for linguistically naïve ESL learners, the patterns must be easy to use, easy to practise and easy to remember. The focus of research and application for ESL learners should therefore be on devising patterns that more adequately meet the criteria for learner rules presented above. Orthographic spelling patterns have value, but, since they were never implemented consistently, research with a view to help ESL learners should concentrate on simplifying linguistic spelling patterns as illustrated in this chapter.

Related topics

English vowels and consonants; lexical stress; pronunciation teaching

Further reading

Chomsky, C., 1970. Reading, writing, and phonology. *Harvard Educational Review 40*, 287–309. In this classic paper, Chomsky articulates the linguistic point of view and its relevance to the decoding task of reading.
Lehnert, M., 1971. *Reverse dictionary of present-day English*. Leipzig: Veb Verlag Enzyklopadie. This tool spells each word from right to left, grouping words with like endings. It is ideal for spelling researchers and teachers developing ESL materials based on word endings.

References

Carney, E. (1994). *A survey of English spelling*. London: Routledge.
Chomsky, N., & Halle, M. (1968). *The sound pattern of English*. New York, NY: Harper & Row.
Dale, P., & Poms, L. (2005). *English pronunciation made simple*. White Plains, NY: Pearson Education.
Dauer, R. (1992). *Accurate English: A complete course in pronunciation*. Englewood Cliffs, NJ: Regents/Prentice Hall.
Dickerson, W. (1980). Bisyllabic laxing rule: Vowel prediction in linguistics and language learning. *Language Learning, 30*, 317–329. (Erratum, *Language Learning* 31: 283.)
Dickerson, W. (1984). The role of formal rules in pronunciation instruction. In J. Handscombe, R. Orem & B. Taylor (Eds), *On TESOL '83* (pp. 135–148). Washington, DC: TESOL.
Dickerson, W. (1985). The invisible y: A case for spelling in pronunciation learning. *TESOL Quarterly, 19*, 303–316.
Dickerson, W. (2004). *Stress in the speech stream, The rhythm of spoken English*. Urbana, IL: University of Illinois Press. [CD-ROM] (Original work published 1989).
Dickerson, W. (2006). A is for is for alphabet . . . Roman letters and their use in written English. *Educators and Education Journal, 21*, 1–21.

Dickerson, W. (2013). Prediction in pronunciation teaching. *Encyclopedia of Applied Linguistics*. Hoboken, NJ: Blackwell. doi:10.1002/9781405198431.wbeal0950.

Dickerson, W. (2015). Using orthography to teach pronunciation. In J. Levis & M. Reed (Eds), *Handbook of English pronunciation* (pp. 488–504). Hoboken, NJ: Wiley-Blackwell.

Dickerson, W., & Hahn, L. (in press). *Speechcraft: Discourse pronunciation for advanced learners*. Ann Arbor, MI: University of Michigan Press.

Follick, M. (1965). *The case for spelling reform*. London: Pitman.

Francis, W. (1958). *The structure of American English*. New York, NY: Ronald.

Gilbert, J. (2001). *Clear speech from the start*. Cambridge: Cambridge University Press.

Grant, L. (2001). *Well said* (2nd ed.). Boston, MA: Heinle & Heinle.

Guierre, L. (1970). *Drills in English stress-patterns*. London: Longman.

Guierre, L. (1984). *Drills in English stress-patterns*. Paris: Armand Colin-Longman.

Hahn, L., & Dickerson, W. (1999a). *Speechcraft: Discourse pronunciation for advanced learners*. Ann Arbor, MI: University of Michigan Press.

Hahn, L., & Dickerson, W. (1999b). *Speechcraft: Workbook for academic discourse*. Ann Arbor, MI: University of Michigan Press.

Ivins, S. (1947). The Deseret alphabet. *Utah Humanities Review, 1*, 223–239.

Murphy, J. (2004). Attending to word-stress while learning vocabulary. *English for Specific Purposes, 23*, 67–83.

Prator, C., Jr., & Robinett, B. (1985). *Manual of American English pronunciation* (4th ed.). New York, NY: Holt, Rinehart and Winston.

Sacks, D. (2003). *Language visible*. New York, NY: Broadway.

Sardegna, V. (2009). Improving English stress through pronunciation learning strategies. Unpublished doctoral dissertation, University of Illinois, Urbana, IL.

Teschner, R., & Whitley, M. (2004). *Pronouncing English: A stress-based approach with CD-ROM*. Washington, DC: Georgetown University Press.

Trager, E., & Henderson, S. (1956). *Pronunciation drills for learners of English*. Washington, DC: English Language Services.

Woods, H. (1978). *Syllable stress*. Hull: Public Service Commission of Canada.

Section 3

Varieties of English pronunciations

11

Standards of pronunciation and regional accents[1]

Kirk Hazen

Introduction

Variation is part of nature, and, within language, humans create variation as part of its basic fabric. For both spoken and signed language, it is impossible to put our articulators in exactly the same place every time we express ourselves. A sound like [i] in <*beat*> can be made in the high front part of the mouth, yet it will vary within a range of space, limited just enough to distinguish it from other sounds, such as [e] in <*bait*>.

This type of variation is true for every sound we make and hear. Yet humans also love patterns. Different pronunciations coalesce into patterns resulting from both linguistic factors and social influences. For example, the /t/ of <*steak*> will be different from the /t/ of <*teak*> for most English speakers. Usually the /t/ of <*teak*> will have a small puff of air with it, [tʰik], whereas the /t/ of <*steak*> will just have [t]; this aspiration of the /t/ in <*teak*> is due to its surrounding phonetic environment, a linguistic factor. Such language variation happens when our minds weave together the many sounds we produce in a day. Few speakers of English would notice the difference between [t] and [tʰ] in a regular conversation. However, the social effects on sounds are usually more noticeable. For example, North American speakers of English readily notice an [ɑ] vowel in a British pronunciation of <*bath*>; it is farther back in the mouth, and the British variation pricks the interest of American ears. For British speakers themselves, this vowel in the <*bath*> word class is a regional marker in England, where southern speakers have [ɑ] and northern speakers have [a] (Upton, 2004). Humans have a passion for making associations between pronunciation patterns and their social attributes.

Just as the vowel in the <bath> word class serves as a regional marker in England, many other variations in pronunciation coalesce into local patterns. Sets of such patterns are traditionally called *regional accents*. For almost everyone, the term *accent* refers to the speech of people who use different sets of patterns (Wolfram & Schilling, 2016). In other words, people most often assume that others who speak like them do not have an accent, but people who sound different do have an accent. For linguists, the term *accent* specifically refers to every speaker's phonological patterns (Hazen, 2015). Everyone who has a language, sounded or signed, has an accent for that language. Most often, when people talk about accents, they refer to an accent of a region, such as a Boston accent, or a certain social group, such as a

Yankee or Latino accent. Such named accents are loose sets of phonological features, and individuals vary widely along any social accent's spectrum. This chapter focuses on regional accents, but some of these variations may trigger other social associations.

Standard accents are those phonological patterns associated with more powerful social groups in any given country. In England, the traditional standard has been received pronunciation (RP), a prestige variety spoken natively by few (Trudgill, 2002) but strongly associated with money and power. In the United States, standard accents are designated differently; they are defined by not being vernacular (Hazen, 2015), meaning that they do not contain stigmatized phonological features. No global prestige variety exists in the United States, but instead regional standard accents exist in different parts of the nation (Wolfram & Schilling, 2016). All standard accents rise to prominence for social reasons, not historical precedence; linguistically, they develop in regular ways just as any of the other regional accents that do not happen to rise to power.

With the naturalness and inevitability of language variation, regional pronunciations are part of every vibrant, living language on Earth. Accents are not something to be eliminated; they are to be celebrated as an integral part of humanity, language and society. This chapter will explain how standard pronunciations are socially preferred accents and highlight regional divides in usage in order to illustrate the importance of local pronunciations for differentiating insiders and outsiders. The chapter cannot encompass the totality of the thousands of regional, non-standard accents of English around the world. Instead, it attempts to illustrate the kinds of current and long-term variation that develop in accents.

The development of regional accents through diachronic variation

The clearest evidence of language variation is the diversity of languages around the world, of which there are approximately 7,469 (www.ethnologue.com). Even within English, there are many different varieties, from Indian English to Newfoundland English, from Guyanese English to Welsh English, from Thailand English to South African English. Furthermore, within these varieties, there are many opportunities for even further variation. For example, within India, conservative estimates put the number of native English speakers at 350,000 and speakers of English as a second language (ESL) at 200,000,000 (www.ethnologue.com). With that many speakers developing English every day, many opportunities arise for different ways of saying the same thing.

When we examine language variation like this at a single point in time, it is called synchronic variation. With all of these speakers of English in different places, they necessarily have different local, social constraints. Speakers produce synchronic variation daily, for example an [u] vowel that is further front in the mouth or an [l] that happens to be produced more like a vowel. This synchronic variation gets pushed in various directions by those different social forces. As synchronic variation cumulatively heads in different directions, the varieties of English grow less like each other and more diverse. Social groups seize on language variation as badges of identity, and these new patterns begin to be perceived as regional variation. This process is how different regions of any nation end up with certain vowels that mark those speakers, such as speakers in the US South making the /aɪ/ vowel in words like *mine* [maɪ̃n] into a single-part vowel [mãːn], popularly represented in writing as *<mahn>*.

As time marches on, some of the synchronic variation leads to lasting language change, also known as *diachronic variation*. No cataclysmic events are required to create diachronic variation; people just need to talk and listen to each other. The impulse towards language variation is a natural by-product of the human mind, and the resulting forms simply accumulate over time. All living languages are in continuous variation because, at its core, the connection between form and meaning in language is arbitrary. In Old English, for example, the form [klud] meant 'large rock or hill'; through the accumulation of regular synchronic variation, the vowel changed in two different directions, creating the forms <clod> [klad] and <cloud> [klaʊd]. Both the meanings and forms were able to shift over time because they had no inherent connection to each other. This quality of arbitrariness is basic to human language and, given time, many variations accrue.

For English, the time depth is sizeable. What we might first call English came to the isle of Britain around 450 CE and consisted of three Germanic dialects. Since then, that collection of dialects has diversified and grown, through both contact with other languages and regular synchronic variation. For certain national varieties of English, the time depth is considerably more shallow. US English, for example, is younger than the English of England and demonstrates less diversity despite the larger geographic expanse of the United States (Wolfram & Schilling, 2016). The Origins of the New Zealand English (ONZE) project, directed by Jennifer Hay at the University of Canterbury, studies an even younger national variety, as English settlement only began after 1840; the group has been able to examine a relatively ambitious history through audio recordings: www.nzilbb.canterbury.ac.nz/onze. shtml. Yet, despite its relative youth, New Zealand English demonstrates healthy synchronic variation today. For example, the vowel in words such as <kit> has traditionally been in the front of the mouth, but since the middle of the twentieth century New Zealanders have moved the pronunciation of this vowel to the centre of the mouth, making it sound more like the vowel in <cut> (Langstrof, 2003). The key ingredient for diachronic variation is time, which allows for dramatic changes.

The process of diachronic variation can be illustrated on a national scale by reviewing the synchronic and diachronic variation of R sounds. The R sounds in words such as <red>, <dear> and <soaring> can be illustrated in various ways with phonetic symbols but will collectively be referred to here as R sounds. R and L sounds are classified as liquids because they flow relatively unimpeded out of the mouth (i.e. relative to other consonant sounds) and their places of articulation range between the front and back of the mouth. The name 'liquids' captures the fluid nature of these sounds, especially in contrast to 'stop' consonants such as [t] and [b] (Hazen, 2015). Liquids have relatively more expansive envelopes of variation, and any particular pronunciation of R or L depends on what sounds are around it and what the trends are in that particular geographic region. Earlier English speakers in England started off with more consonantal Rs in both contexts such as <red> and <core>. But in the 1700s some varieties of English in southern England began to loosen up the constriction of the tongue against the roof of the mouth, resulting in more vowel-like Rs at the ends of syllables in words like <core> and <hard>. For linguists, this process is called *vocalization* because the consonant sound is made more vocalic (i.e. more like a vowel). For the rest of the world, it is called R-dropping: The R sounds simply have a lower degree of constriction in the oral cavity while speakers' productions of these words maintain the same degree of temporal duration.

R-dropping was regionally distinct in England by the mid-1700s (Burchfield, 1994), yet in only some areas of the United States. Specifically, those areas most socially connected to England in the second half of the eighteenth century adopted this innovative change. As the American colonies became more distanced from England, they had no compelling social reason to adopt this new trend of R-dropping (Wolfram & Schilling, 2016). People in New England and the US South maintained greater British connections at the time of the American

Revolution, and speakers in those areas continue to employ patterns of R-dropping even today. Part of the diversity in regional American accents results from the synchronic variation at the time (Wolfram & Schilling, 2016).

Diachronic variation has resulted in modern accents. Two historical examples illustrate how change over time creates regional pronunciations. The first example involves the sound associated with the letters <gh> in words like <right>, <light> and <knight>. This sound was [x], a voiceless velar fricative, which can be made by either moving an [h] (as in <hot>) forwards in the mouth to the place where [k] is pronounced or by moving the [s] (as in <sin>) back in the mouth to that [k] place. If you know the native pronunciations of <Bach> or <van Gogh>, it is the last sound in those names. Speakers of English pronounced the <gh> of <right> with the [x] sound for centuries, but eventually synchronic variation slipped in and its constriction got loosened up so that it disappeared for more and more people over time. Yet not all dialects of English lost this sound. Some towns in Scotland, such as Buckie, retain the [x] pronunciation (Smith, 2000). Through diachronic variation, what used to be the norm for everyone has now become a regional pronunciation. Neither RP in the UK nor the standard forms in the US retained this sound, but standard varieties do not need to contain all the sounds of a language.

All dialects of English have adopted some newer pronunciations, but the difference between regional dialects sometimes comes down to the range of linguistic environments for the newer patterns. In this second example of diachronic variation, Old English (450–1100) forms for <nut>, <raven> and <loaf> used to be <hnutu>, <hræfn> and <hlaf> (Millward & Hayes, 2012). Over time, speakers of English eventually lost the H sound before consonants. You may notice that this is the same process that caused the K sound to be lost before consonants, as in <knight> and <know>. For some modern-day English varieties in England and southern Wales, the H sound is also dropped before vowels, as in <'istory> for <history>, extending the pattern first used to transform <hnutu> into <nut> (Wells, 1982). There is nothing linguistically extravagant about extending H-dropping to all possible environments, but it is one of the more telling social differences in England today (with H-droppers marked as more working class), although it is widely used across the country (Milroy, 1983; Upton & Widdowson, 2006).

Some diachronic variation comes to completion without any difference in regional pronunciations. As an example, take the split of the fricatives [f] and [v]. Speakers of Old English heard the sounds of [f] and [v] as variations of the same sound (i.e. these two sounds never triggered a difference in meaning). But they did show up in different spots in a word: [v] came between voiced sounds, as in <give> [gɪvə], and [f] was everywhere else, as in <gift> [gɪft]. Only later did the English language pick up contrasts, such as <vase> and <face>, where the [v] and [f] triggered different meanings. Other diachronic variations slip under the social radar. For example, the voiceless and voiced sounds of TH (e.g. voiceless [θ] in <thin> and voiced [ð] in <there>) also split apart between Old and Middle English, much in the same way as [f] and [v]. Our modern divide in the pronunciation of <bath> versus <bathe> results from their early divide. Yet, for many modern speakers, voicing fluctuates for these two interdental forms. At the ends of frequent words like <with>, English speakers oscillate between [θ] and [ð]. There is no orthographic distinction to solidify one form over the other, and there is rarely any meaning distinction based on the variation between [θ] and [ð]. But, as with most cases of perception variation, exceptions persist throughout language. Some regional variation does exist for [θ] and [ð]: for example, the *Oxford English Dictionary* reports that <with> [wɪð] is the standard but that [wɪθ] is chiefly found in northern England.

The same basic sociolinguistic processes will result in the variation of regional accents in the future. In looking across the landscape of English in the twenty-first century, national varieties will diversify across the globe (Kortmann & Schneider et al., 2004). Along with each national variety, numerous dialects will continue to flourish. Synchronic variation is the everyday status for language, and people use it productively and receptively for social distinction.

The slow march of consonants

Although vowels are more often used to distinguish one region's pronunciation from another's, consonant distinctions are well noted. One of the earliest stories for consonants in regional accents involves the hissing sibilant sound at the beginning of the Hebrew word <shibboleth>. The term <shibboleth> itself meant 'ear of corn' in the Old Testament story of Judges (7:4–6), but its social meaning depended on different pronunciations of its initial consonant. In this story, soldiers of Gilead were defending the fords of the Jordan River against deserting Ephraimites. To check for disguised Ephraimites trying to sneak through their defences, the Gileadites tested a particular dialect feature:

> Whenever one of the fugitives of Ephraim said, 'Let me go over,' the men of Gilead would say to him, 'Are you an Ephraimite?' When he said: 'No,' they said to him, 'Then say Shibboleth,' and he said, 'Sibboleth,' for he could not pronounce it right. Then they seized him and killed him at the fords of the Jordan. Forty-two thousand of the Ephraimites fell at that time.
>
> (Judges 7:4–6)

The linguistic difference between <shibboleth> and <sibboleth> is in the two sounds [ʃ] and [s], the same as that between <shoe> and <sue>. This story contains the fundamentals of all accent differences. First, there are separate groups; in this case, the groups were two Semitic tribes, but the separation could just as easily be ethnic, socio-economic, tribal or some other form. Second, the basis for judgement is social, not linguistic, meaning the Ephraimites were not killed because <s> sounds were painful to hear; certainly the Gileadites had <s>s in their own dialect of the language. The Ephraimites were killed because they were Ephraimites, and the pronunciation of <shibboleth> with an initial <s> was simply a dialect feature used to identify them as a social group. The connection between regional divides and place illustrates the importance of local pronunciations in differentiating insiders and outsiders.

Consonant variation is a much slower process than vowel variation, but it still can be used for group distinctions, including regional accent distinctions. Consider the case of θ → f. This consonant variation happenss when a word that historically had a /θ/ develops a pronunciation with [f], as in <birthday~bir[f]day>. For some nations, such as Australia, the UK and the US (Hazen, 2015; Wood, 2003), this alternation can be said to be a regional feature. For example, in Warren County, North Carolina, native speakers commonly have this feature word medially and finally (e.g. <bath>~<ba[f]>), regardless of ethnicity or socio-economic status (Hazen, 2000). The Great Migration, which was the movement of about six million African-Americans from the US South to other parts of the US (Grossman, 1991; Wilkerson, 2010), changed the perception of this regional pronunciation feature. When southern African-Americans settled in northern areas such as Detroit, Michigan, the previously regional feature came to be seen as an ethnic feature of these African-Americans. It was reinterpreted as a highly stigmatized ethnic marker. Although famous white personalities such as the English former professional footballer David Beckham and the late 'Crocodile Hunter' TV personality

Steve Irwin have used θ → f in commercials and television shows with no editing or backlash from audiences (Hazen, 2015), many US speakers react with laughter and derision when African-Americans use this feature. What marks a pronunciation as regional is not any certain inherent linguistic quality. Instead, it is simply the association of some sound patterns with people from a particular region.

When considering regional variation in accents, consider the source of variation. The ING variable (e.g. <walki[n]> and <sleepi[n]>) is an alternation between the velar nasal [ŋ] (as in the last sound in <ring>) and the alveolar nasal [n] (Fisher, 1958; Hazen, 2006). A series of investigations by Houston (1985) and Labov (1989) demonstrated that the main linguistic influence is the grammatical context of the word. When the –ing suffix is on a gerund, such as <_sleeping is my favourite past time_>, the velar nasal [ŋ] shows up more often. When the –ing suffix is on a verb, such as <she was _sleeping_>, the alveolar nasal [n] shows up more often. Before 1500, these two were independent suffixes with separate spellings and apparently different pronunciations: the one that made gerunds was spelled –inge and the one that made verbal participles was spelled –ende. Following widespread use of the printing press, they became homographs, and people eventually came to expect that they would be pronounced the same. Now, ING variation is marked as vernacular and informal, although this pattern used to be the standard for centuries. Such an example highlights the arbitrary nature of social marking on accent variation.

Some accent variations might be part of a region's repertoire while still not being widely noted or identified with that region. Z devoicing is an increasingly common feature in US English. Word-final Z devoicing (e.g. when <bu_zz_> sounds more like <bu_s_>) occurs in regions throughout the US. Perhaps because the envelope of variation for Z contains so many possible elements, different qualities exist in different regions. In the Appalachian region of the US, specifically West Virginia, speakers have a wide range of glottal pulsing for word-final Z. In addition, they do not differentiate the vowel's length before S and Z (Hazen, Lovejoy, Daugherty & Vandevender, 2016). This kind of complexity can be part of what differentiates regional accents, but only some of the linguistic variation might be overtly noted by native speakers.

When a standard feature wanes through diachronic variation, it might begin to mark some regions more than others. In Old English, the initial sounds of <_wh_ich> and <_w_itch> were distinct from each other, with the <wh> (originally spelled <hw>) pronounced as a voiceless W. For most of the history of English, pairs such as <which~witch> were not homophones. As these two consonants began to merge into [w], some regions adopted the change sooner than others. Kurath and McDavid (1961, Map 174) show that, by the middle of the twentieth century, parts of eastern Pennsylvania and New Jersey had lost the initial /h/ in the words <_wh_eelbarrow>, <_wh_inny> and <_wh_ip> but most of the rest of the east coast of the United States retained it. Speakers from the US South held on to this distinction longer than others. Today, some see the voiceless W as a Southern feature. Yet many younger speakers, even in the South, view it as an oddity and sometimes a point of derision (Hazen et al., 2016). Although voiceless W used to be part of the standard accent for words like <_wh_ich> and <_wh_ip>, it has become a vernacular feature, and it is losing its social preference among younger speakers.

The modern development of R-dropping, discussed earlier, is perhaps the best illustration of how regional pronunciations can follow different social tracks. In cities such as New York, R-dropping was a stigmatized feature by the second half of the twentieth century (Labov, 2006). In Boston, however, R-dropping has continued much longer, with varying levels of local pride (Nagy & Irwin, 2010), but it has been receding in New England's rural areas

(Stanford, Severance & Baclawski, 2014). In the rural South, R-dropping is no longer part of upper- or middle-class urban speech. Instead, R-dropping has become a rural feature in that region. It is also a regular feature of African-American English throughout the US, as most varieties of African-American English emanated from the southern US. It is revealing to note that the social and regional divide in the US is in sharp contrast to R-dropping's prestige and normalcy in Great Britain and British-derived dialects. The story of R-dropping is an important lesson about language variation and regional pronunciations: the very same dialect feature that is stigmatized in the speech of one region or social group (e.g. R-dropping in much of the US) might well be the prestige variety elsewhere (e.g. R-dropping in Great Britain). The social judgement of language variation depends on social factors, not the linguistics of the pronunciation. Sounds do not a stigma make.

The range and impact of vowel variation

For regional pronunciations, the rapidity of vowel change is an important quality. Vowels have less constriction in the mouth than consonants and therefore shift more frequently. What linguists mean by 'vowel shift' requires an explanation, as scholars use the label 'vowel' for two different things. On the one hand, the 'vowel' label can be used for historical word class. For example, when we say the /ē/ in Middle English moved up in the mouth, we are referring to the set of words that had /ē/ in it at the time, such as <meet>, <fleet> and <sheep>. On the other hand, the label 'vowel' is also used for the pronunciation of non-consonants in a word: For example, the vowel for <meet> in most modern English dialects is [i]. In the discussion of the vowel shifts below, both senses of 'vowel' are being employed.

The Great Vowel Shift is estimated to have taken place in England primarily between the years of 1400 and 1600, and it resulted in eliminating the English language's long/short vowel system (Millward & Hayes, 2012). Much of the disparity between modern pronunciations and modern spellings can largely be blamed on the period of the Great Vowel Shift. Consider the spellings of <meet> and <boot>. Before the Great Vowel Shift, those two words would have been pronounced with the vowels that <mate> and <boat> have today, respectively. Generally, vowels before Early Modern English were divided into long and short sets (which, to the best of our knowledge, actually differed in temporal duration); vowels after Early Modern English are usually considered to be divided into sets of tense and lax vowels (e.g. <beet> [i] versus <bit> [ɪ]). Before the Great Vowel Shift, the long [e] sound was spelled with two <ee>s and the long [o] sound was spelled with two <oo>s. By the time both vowels had moved up in the mouth, the technical demands of the printing press had already frozen spelling in its place, which is why the spelling system has not kept up with the subsequent changes in pronunciation.

It is worth noting that the Great Vowel Shift did not progress at the same rate in all regions. As diachronic variation unfolds, not all areas adopt changes at the same time or to the same extent. During the Great Vowel Shift, /u/ shifted to the diphthong /aʊ/ in a word like <house> (note that, with this particular shift, modern spelling does capture the change) (Millward & Hayes, 2012). But parts of Scotland did not embrace changes in the back region of vowel space, and some Scottish speakers in the twentieth century still had [hus] for <house>, while most of the rest of the English-speaking world had [haʊs]. This example demonstrates how regional differences from the standard form can be created through natural language change occurring at different rates in multiple regions.

A similar situation with the Great Vowel Shift and regional differentiation of accents exists in Canada (Boberg, 2010). Some of the distinctive qualities of Canadian English are the vowel differences for words such as <right/ride> and <bout/loud>. Many Canadians participate in what is called Canadian Raising, where the first part of the diphthongs in <right> and <bout> is pronounced in the centre of the mouth: [ɹəɪt] and [bəʊt]. This distinction only happens when the following sound is voiceless. In a geographic divide, it could also be found in some areas along the North Carolina/Virginia border in the twentieth century (Kurath and McDavid, 1961). Modern /aɪ/ and /aʊ/ vowels come from Middle English /i/ and /u/, which first lowered in the mouth to the diphthongs /əɪ/ and /əʊ/ while on the way to becoming modern /aɪ/ and /aʊ/. Canadians seem to have completed this process, except for the phonological environment of following voiceless consonants. As before, a historical change is implemented differently in different places, leading to greater regional variation.

There are at least three major vowel shifts in the US today. The major import of these changes is that vowel systems across the United States are growing more diverse. The complete details of these shifts cannot be explored here, but a few reference vowels will be discussed to illustrate how regional accents are differentiating themselves from the standard. Remember, the definition of 'standard accent' in the US simply means that it does not contain any stigmatized dialect features. Whatever is not stigmatized is included in the standard for a region. To study these vowel shifts, the most complete reference book is *The Atlas of North American English* (Labov, Ash & Boberg, 2006), but it may be slightly daunting for the uninitiated. Shorter works such as *Investigating Chain Shifts and Mergers* (Gordon, 2013) and *Phonetic Analysis in Sociolinguistics* (Thomas, 2014) would be better introductions for non-linguists. Keep in mind that when vowels shift in the mouth they follow natural patterns. 'Natural' here refers to how and where they move in the mouth, as there are similar patterns around the world.

In a region stretching from upstate New York through parts of Wisconsin and Illinois, a major vowel change is being propagated by millions of US speakers: the Northern Cities Vowel Shift. One vowel that has been changing since World War II is the /ɛ/ vowel in words such as <bed> and <bet>. In the Northern Cities Vowel Shift, the pronunciation of this vowel is moving farther back in the mouth, towards the centre. The result is that the word <bed> might sound more like <bud> for some speakers. This particular change is not highly stigmatized, nor is it unusual as language change goes. Yet a nearby vowel does get a great deal more social attention: the /æ/ vowel in the words <bad> and <bat>. This vowel was traditionally pronounced in the lower front region of the mouth, but as the vowels rotate in the Northern Cities Vowel Shift, /æ/ is rising up higher in the front of the mouth, so that <bat> might sound more <bet> or even <bait>. This change is well noted in cities like Chicago and Buffalo, and TV shows have used it for comic effect in skits such as *Saturday Night Live*'s 'Bill Swerski's Superfans', with words like <January> and <basketball> (see YouTube clips).

In a different venture, the Southern Vowel Shift takes place in non-urban areas of the traditional US South. In the Southern Vowel Shift, the /ɛ/ vowel is partially moving up and forwards in the mouth, pushing /e/ out of the way. In turn, the /e/ vowel is moving inward and down, so that <bail> sounds like <bell>. While the /ɛ/ starts closer to the outer edge of the mouth, it also has become a diphthong for many Southern US speakers, with its off-glide stretching up to [ɪ]. For a word such as <bed>, speakers with the Southern Vowel Shift will have [beɪd] instead of the traditional form, [bɛd]. The same kind of switching places is happening between the /ɪ/ in <bid> and the /i/ in <bead>. To date, the shifted lax vowels /ɛ/ and /ɪ/ are the most stigmatized of the shifted vowels as they are more closely associated with rural speakers. In all, the vowel system resulting from the Southern Vowel Shift will not resemble the system from the Northern Cities Vowel Shift.

In the California Vowel Shift, which is taking place also in other regions of the US and Canada, the [ɛ] vowel is shifting down to the low, front part of the mouth where the vowels of <bad> and <bat> have traditionally been pronounced (see www.pbs.org/speak/ahead/change/changin). So a younger Californian might pronounce <bed> more like <bad>. Speakers with the California Vowel Shift are changing the vowel /æ/ in different ways than the other two vowel shifts. Whereas speakers in the Northern Cities Shift and Southern Vowel Shift are moving their pronunciation for all the /æ/ vowels in the same direction (up, though to different extents), speakers in the California Vowel Shift are splitting the set of words with /æ/ vowels in two parts and shifting them in opposite directions (Podesva, 2011). When the /æ/ vowel is before a nasal, as in <band>, the vowel is raised and made into more of a diphthong, as in [beînd]. In all other words, the /æ/ vowel is lowered along the front of the mouth and moved farther back in the mouth. For these speakers, a word like <hat> sounds more like a traditional <hot>, and <rack> would sound more like a traditional <rock>. Note that this split involves nasals, and nasals are a motivator for many changes in language: they affect preceding vowels because nasals themselves are in many ways similar to vowels (Thomas, 2011). For example, owing to its following nasal, the vowel in <bin> is not the same as the vowel in <bit>. Sometimes, those different patterns stick, and the various parts of the word class diverge (Labov, 1994).

One of the frequent regional differences that arise with vowels involves the merger (i.e. neutralization of differences) of two word classes rather than the splitting of one. When a vowel merger happens, two previously distinct word classes collapse together and are pronounced with the same vowel. To illustrate the process of vowel mergers, the following subsection will review two vowel mergers in the US that cover vast regions but only geographically overlap in certain areas (Hazen, 2005; Labov et al., 2006). One of them has carried varying levels of social stigma, while the other holds no social meaning. The first is the <pin~pen> merger, while the other is the <caught~cot> merger.

The <pin~pen> merger is native to the US South, but independently takes place in parts of Australia and New Zealand as well. It is also called the front-lax merger, as both the /ɪ/ and /ɛ/ vowels are lax vowels produced in the front of the mouth. In the US, this merger takes place before nasal consonants, as in <pin~pen>. In some communities, this merger has led to lexical innovations to distinguish between what are now homophonous words, such as <ink pen> and <stickpin>. For non-Southerners, and even in some Southern communities, having this merger has been stigmatized because it has been identified as 'Southern' in the US and, historically, Southerners have been looked down upon by the rest of the nation (Preston, 1996; Wolfram & Schilling, 2016).

That stigma is in sharp contrast with the social situation for the <cot~caught> merger. This merger is also called the *low-back merger* by linguists and is hardly ever stigmatized in North America (Gordon, 2013; Wolfram & Schilling, 2016). The vowels /a/ and /ɔ/ overlap in the back corner of the mouth. The /a/ vowel (the one historically in <cot>) has been in the low-central part of vowel space; the /ɔ/ vowel (the one historically in <caught>) has been a mid-back lax vowel. Speakers who produce this merger range from the areas of Pennsylvania and West Virginia all the way west to California and north through most of Canada. Because it covers such a large portion of North America, it is not linked with any one region and does not receive any social or regional stigma. Like the merger of the vowels in words such as <horse> and <hoarse>, the merger of /a/ and /ɔ/ has become part of standard speech for many people in North America.

For most of West Virginia and eastern Kentucky, both the <pin~pen> and <cot~caught> mergers are increasingly normal for natives born after 1980. What used to be regional markers are no longer reliable indicators, as it seems that the <cot~caught> merger will expand ever farther in the southern United States. Although it does not happen in all cases, vowel mergers often expand to encompass larger areas. What began as a regional pronunciation difference in western New England has now spread throughout most of North America.

A special realm of pronunciation: place names

A special realm of pronunciation that fits within regional divides is that of place names. Although the lexical quality of place names can trump phonological patterns, their pronunciations can serve as a regional divide. The general rule of thumb is that however natives of an area pronounce a place name should be considered the norm, even if it is not the statistical majority in the nation as a whole. Consider the case of a university in South Carolina. The spelling of <Clemson> would hint at [klɛmzɔ̃n] as the likely pronunciation, and people not familiar with the university do say either [klɛmzɔ̃n] or [klɛmsɔ̃n]. Yet locals, including the university's students, insert an epenthetic [p] after the /m/ and before the /s/. As a result of this normal phonological process, the local, and hence authoritative, pronunciation is [klɛmpsɔ̃n], with the caveat that the first vowel varies between [ɪ] and [ɛ] because of the <pin-pen> merger in the US South.

Take the case of these duelling town names: Beaufort, North Carolina, and Beaufort, South Carolina. Most people approach unfamiliar words with pronunciations built off the orthography of the word; therefore, for those with any knowledge of French, the letter combination of <Beaufort> would correspond to sounds like <bow-fort>. For the North Carolina beach town with this name, that is indeed the correct pronunciation. But for the South Carolina coastal town, it is pronounced [bjufəɹt] (often conveyed orthographically as <byou-furt>). Both towns were established early (1711 and 1709, respectively), and both were named after Henry Somerset, the second Duke of Beaufort. The North Carolina town is closest to the Duke's pronunciation, but for the South Carolina town the standard is [bjufəɹt], and tourists adjust to the difference. As with these two different pronunciations, local place names can become a point of pride, and new residents are often quick to learn which place names distinguish insiders from outsiders (Anzilotti, 2016).

There are many examples of mispronounced place names. Locals complain about such pronunciations, and correcting outsiders becomes either a game or a mission. Some places take pronunciation difficulties even further and transform them into a publicity opportunity. Bangor, Maine, has created a music video (https://youtu.be/K_q9hAAIS-c) to explain how to pronounce the city's name. The prevalent orthographic interpretation leads outsiders to equate <Bangor> with the American pronunciation of <banger>. To demonstrate the local pronunciation, the city created a song set to the tune of 'We Are The World', and part of it goes: 'There are people, all across this USA, and they all say the name of our city wrong . . . We are [bæŋgoɹ]'. With over 200,000 views, they hope to flip the rest of the world from 'Banger' to 'Bang gore'.

In some regions, a place name might have variable pronunciations, even by natives of the region. The word <Appalachia> is one such case. Although the word <Appalachia> is widely used in scholarly circles and is a federally designated region in the US (a large region stretching from southern New York to eastern Mississippi), it is not a term many natives grow up using as a badge of identity. Because it is not commonly used by natives, speakers have developed several different pronunciations for it. These include [æpəlætʃə], [æpəleʃə], and occasionally [æpəleʃiə] from speakers new to the term. There is no agreement for natives of the region, but because it carries little social meaning for most of them the different pronunciations are not associated with subregions or social groups.

Future directions

Owing to improving audio recording, statistics and mapping technologies, the study of standard and non-standard pronunciations will see positive growth, more coordinated efforts and a wealth of data in the coming years. People are interested in how their accents differ from others and how their region differs from other regions: be it fictional characters such as Francis Underwood in HBO's *House of Cards* (www.youtube.com/watch ?v=mgCeH3xovDw) or real political figures such as the Brooklyn born US Senator from Vermont Bernie Sanders (www.youtube.com/watch?v=waeXBCUkuL8), people want to know why other people sound different. With popular social media enterprises such as Twitter, the broad swatches of language variation can be seen with data (and immediacy of timing) unprecedented in scholarship before this modern age. For example, Twitter NYC: A Multilingual Social City (http://ny.spatial.ly/) displays the language of tweets for New York City.

At the start of the twentieth century, phonetic transcriptions were the best that people could hope for to record the sounds of voices far away. A century later, both audio and video recording for spoken and signed languages are readily available. The resulting avalanche of data can be sorted, counted and displayed with computers by researchers around the world. The result is more knowledge about more varieties than ever before. Whether we can make sense of it all is a pressing question. Can we ask the right questions about accent differences between regions and between people in the same region, to better understand how language works and the role it plays in society? For example, Grieve (2016) has created mapping tools that allow for massive data analysis of Internet searches to show lexical and pronunciation variation across the continental US.

With larger datasets, and hopefully more comprehensive analysis, scholars can better explain the continuum between standard and regional accents for the general public. The desire to distinguish people from each other, to notice language differences, will continue unabated in the future. It is a basic part of the human species. Yet scholars can help people understand language variation and the ubiquity of accents: everyone has one, but only some are stigmatized. If scholars can increase awareness about the process of stigmatization and its motivations, they can bolster moments of social justice surrounding language variation.

Further reading

There are several online sources available to explore regional accents. A few of them include audio recordings of speakers reading the same texts so that speakers from different areas can be compared and direct contrasts can be made. These include the Speech Accent Archive (www.accent.gmu.edu), the Dialect Archive (www.dialectsarchive.com) and more specialized archives such as the American Folklife Center (www.loc.gov/folklife). The field of dialectology takes up the scholarly investigation of such regional variation: see Hazen (2014) for a bibliography of dialectological readings.

A modern milestone for large-scale research into regional pronunciation patterns is *The Atlas of North American English* (Labov et al., 2006) (www.atlas.mouton-content.com). It is a tremendous resource for linguists, as its criteria for regional divisions rely on quantitative acoustic phonetics. For standard and regional accents, a wide variety of academic books exist that can be perused by non-academic audiences. The most comprehensive for world Englishes is Kortmann et al.'s *Handbook of Varieties of English* (2004); the first volume covers phonological variation for all major varieties around the world and many smaller varieties, including the British Isles, the Americas and Caribbean, the Pacific and Australasia, Africa, and Asia.

The six volume *Dictionary of American Regional English* is a monumental achievement for lexical and pronunciation variation in the United States. Its focus is on words not traditionally found in more standard dictionaries (Cassidy and Hall, 1985–2013). In England, prominent accounts of regional and standard accents include Wells's three-volume *Accents of English*. This work provides a thorough description of English in the British Isles as well as variation in North America, the West Indies, India, the Southern Hemisphere and Africa.

Conclusion

The clearest statement concerning regional pronunciations is that they are a normal development of human language. Pronunciation differences, whether consonant changes such as <birfday> or vowel changes such as the <pin~pen> merger, arise from variation that is pushed in different directions by social forces. With a language as wide-ranging as English, national varieties around the world are themselves reflections of regional pronunciations. Within those countries where English is learned natively or widely as a second language, speakers are developing other regional pronunciations. English is becoming more diverse, just as Latin diversified into French, Italian, Spanish, Portuguese and other Romance languages during the Middle Ages. A movement away from standard pronunciation might eventually be adopted as the new norm, as is the case with R-dropping in England from the end of the 1700s until today. Yet, in other regions, the same development might remain a regional feature, as is the case with R-dropping in the United States. With such twists and turns for regional pronunciations, the linguistic constraints are rarely the deciding factor; instead, it is a matter of who uses the regional forms and how those people are perceived in society. Perhaps the most important point to take away from this reflection on regional variation is that there are many standard pronunciations, and, while some of them are more privileged than others owing to the happenstance of sociolinguistic phenomena, they are all engaged in a process of vying for supremacy within their local contexts.

Note

1 I would like to thank Isabelle Shepherd for her engaging dialogue and astute editing of this chapter. Much of my research underlying this chapter comes from NSF grants (BCS-0743489, BCS-1120156) and I thank the NSF for providing that assistance.

References

Anzilotti, E. (19 February 2016). Don't get mad when transplants copy how you talk. www.citylab.com/navigator/2016/02/linguistics-new-city-transplants-regional-accent/470016.

Boberg, C. (2010). *The English language in Canada: Status, history and comparative analysis*. New York, NY: Cambridge University Press.

Burchfield, R. (Ed.). (1994). *English in Britain and overseas: Origins and developments. The Cambridge history of the English language* (Vol. 5). Cambridge: Cambridge University Press.

Cassidy, F. G., & Hall, J. H. (Eds). (1985–2013). *Dictionary of American regional English*. Six volumes. Cambridge, MA: Belknap Press of Harvard University Press.

Fisher, J. L. (1958). Social influences on the choice of a linguistic variant. *Word, 14*(1), 47–56.

Gordon, M. (2013). Investigating chain shifts and mergers. In J. K. Chambers & N. Schilling (Eds), *The handbook of language variation and change* (2nd ed., pp. 203–219). Malden, MA: Wiley-Blackwell.

Grieve, J. (2016). *Regional variation in written American English*. New York, NY: Cambridge University Press.

Grossman, J. R. (1991). *Land of hope: Chicago, Black southerners, and the Great Migration*. Chicago, IL: University of Chicago Press.

Hazen, K. (2000). *Identity and ethnicity in the rural south: A sociolinguistic view through past and present 'be'*. Publications of the American Dialect Society No. 83. Durham, NC: Duke University Press.

Hazen, K. (2005). Mergers in the mountains: West Virginia division and unification. In *English world-wide* (Vol. 26:2, pp. 199–221). Amsterdam: John Benjamins.

Hazen, K. (2006). 'IN/ING Variable.' In K. Brown (Ed.), *Encyclopedia of language and linguistics* (2nd ed., pp. 581–584). Oxford: Elsevier.

Hazen, K. (2014). Dialectology. In M. Aronoff (Ed.), *Oxford bibliographies: Linguistics*. New York, NY: Oxford University Press. doi:10.1093/obo/9780199772810–0163.

Hazen, K. (2015). *An introduction to language*. Malden, MA: Wiley-Blackwell.

Hazen, K. Lovejoy, J., Daugherty, J., & Vandevender, M. (2016). Continuity and change for English consonants in Appalachia. In W. Schumann and R. A. Fletcher (Eds), *Appalachia revisited: Cross-disciplinary perspectives on regional continuity and change* (pp. 157–174). Lexington, KY: University Press of Kentucky.

Houston, A. (1985). *Continuity and change in English morphology: The variable (ING)*. Doctoral thesis, University of Pennsylvania. Retrieved from ProQuest. Paper AAI8515390. http://repository.upenn.edu/dissertations/AAI8515390.

Kortmann, B, & Schneider, E. W., with Burridge, K., Mesthrie, R., & Upton, C. (Eds). (2004). *A handbook of varieties of English: A multimedia reference tool* (Vols. 1–2 and CD-ROM). New York, NY: Mouton de Gruyter.

Kurath, H., & McDavid, R. I., Jr. (1961). *The pronunciation of English in the Atlantic states*. Ann Arbor, MI: University of Michigan Press.

Labov, W. (1989). The child as linguistic historian. *Language Variation and Change, 1*, 85–97.

Labov, W. (1994). *Principles of language change: Internal factors*. Malden, MA: Wiley-Blackwell.

Labov, W. (2006). *The social stratification of English in New York City*. Cambridge: Cambridge University Press.

Labov, W., Ash, S., & Boberg, C. (2006). *The atlas of North American English: Phonetics, phonology and sound change: A multimedia reference tool*. Berlin: Mouton de Gruyter.

Langstrof, C. (2003). The short front vowels in NZE in the Intermediate Period. *New Zealand English Journal, 17*, 4.

MacNeil/Lehrer Productions. (2005). Vowel Shifting. Retrieved from www.pbs.org/speak/ahead/change/changin.

Milroy, J. (1983). On the sociolinguistic history of H-dropping in English. In M. Davenport, E. Hansen & H. Nielsen (Eds), *Current topics in English historical linguistics*. Odense: Odense University Press.

Millward, C. M., & Hayes, M. (2012). *A biography of the English language* (3rd ed.). Boston, MA: Cengage Learning.

Nagy, N., & Irwin, P. (2010). Boston (r): Neighbo(r)s nea(r) and fa(r). *Language Variation and Change, 22*(2), 241–278.

Podesva, R. J. (2011). The California vowel shift and gay identity. *American Speech, 86*(1), 32–51.

Preston, D. R. (1996). Where the worst English is spoken. In E. Schneider (Ed.), *Varieties of English around the world* (Vol. 16: Focus on the USA, pp. 297–360). Amsterdam: John Benjamins.

Smith, J. (2000). *Synchrony and diachrony in the evolution of English: Evidence from Scotland*. Unpublished PhD thesis, University of York.

Stanford, J. N., Severance, N. A., & Baclawski, K. P. (2014). Multiple vectors of unidirectional dialect change in eastern New England. *Language Variation and Change, 26*(1), 103–140.

Thomas, E. R. (2011). *Sociophonetics: An introduction*. Basingstoke: Palgrave Macmillan.

Thomas, E. R. (2014). Phonetic analysis in sociolinguistics. In J. Holmes & K. Hazen (Eds), *Research methods in sociolinguistics* (pp. 119–135). Malden, MA: Wiley-Blackwell.

Trudgill, P. (2002). The sociolinguistics of modern RP. In *Sociolinguistic variation and change* (pp. 171–180). Edinburgh: Edinburgh University Press.

Upton, C. (2004). Synopsis: Phonological variation in the British Isles. In E. W. Schneider, K. Burridge, B. Kortmann, R. Mesthrie, & C. Upton (Eds), *A handbook of varieties of English*. New York, NY: Mouton de Gruyter.

Upton, C., & Widdowson, J. D. A. (2006). *An atlas of English dialects: Region and dialect* (2nd ed.). New York, NY: Routledge.

Wells, J. C. (1982). *Accents of English* (Vols. 1–3). New York, NY: Cambridge University Press.

Wood, E. (2003). TH-fronting: The Substitution of f/v for θ/ð in New Zealand English. *New Zealand English Journal, 17*, 50–56.

Wilkerson, I. (2010). *The warmth of other suns: The epic story of America's Great Migration*. New York, NY: Random House.

Wolfram, W., & Schilling, N. (2016). *American English: Dialects and variation*. Malden, MA: Wiley-Blackwell.

12

The fallacy of standard English

Nur Raihan and David Deterding

Introduction

Standard English is often a focus of debate. Is there really a standard? Or are there multiple standards? Pronunciation, in particular, demonstrates that a single standard for English does not exist because no language is static. Even people who believe in the continued primacy of inner circle Englishes (to use terminology from the three circles model of Kachru (1985)) must acknowledge the existence of two competing norms, one based on the speech of educated people in the south of England and the other linked to the pronunciation of the social elite in North America. Received pronunciation (RP) emerged as the standard for British English dictionaries and textbooks as it was a prestigious accent used by the upper middle class in and around London (Mugglestone, 2003). General American (GA), on the other hand, had a number of influences including language contact between various settlers in North America and some cultural influences from Native Americans (Kretzschmar, 2010).

However, Trudgill and Hannah (2008, p. 5) have suggested that RP is probably only spoken by between 3 per cent and 5 per cent of the population of England, and Preston (2005) suggests that the existence of GA is a myth, as there is actually substantial variation throughout the United States. Both accents have changed over the years and they continue to evolve today. Furthermore, even if we accept the existence of these two standards, many scholars such as Brown (1991) have considered whether alternative standards might be appropriate in the modern world.

One increasing influence on the pronunciation of English might be from various world Englishes as people in a globalized world interact with a wide range of different speakers. It has been suggested that some features commonly found in the pronunciation of world Englishes might serve to enhance intelligibility in international settings (Deterding, 2010), particularly when English is being used as a lingua franca (Jenkins, 2007). Some of these pronunciation features include the use of syllable-based rhythm and also the avoidance of reduced vowels in function words such as <of>, <as> and <than> and in the unstressed first syllable of polysyllabic words like <computer> and <advice>.

This chapter will provide a historical background for the emergence of standards of pronunciation for English. Then it will analyse some of the ongoing pronunciation changes documented for British English in Wells (2008) as well as by speakers of English in Singapore and Brunei. It will conclude with a discussion about the emergence of new norms of pronunciation and what the implications are for teachers.

Historical perspectives

All languages undergo change, and English is no exception. In fact, it has seen huge shifts in all areas, including lexis, syntax and pronunciation, as it evolved from Old English (500–1100) to Middle English (1100–1500), and now to Modern English (mid-sixteenth century onwards). Here some of the major changes that have affected the pronunciation of English will be outlined before the emergence of a standard pronunciation is considered.

Changes over time

Old English had a richer set of initial clusters than we find today, so the pronunciation of the cluster /hl/ occurred at the start of <leap>, /hn/ was pronounced at the start of <nut>, /kn/ was at the start of <knight> and <knee>, and /gn/ occurred at the start of <gnat>. /hl/ and /hn/ were lost first, but /kn/ and /gn/ survived into the Early Modern English period, which is reflected in the fact that 'kn' and 'gn' still exist at the start of the written form of some words (Schreier, 2005, p. 61).

A far-reaching change in English pronunciation was the Great Vowel Shift, which occurred between the fourteenth and seventeenth centuries. It coincided with the shift from Middle English to Early Modern English, and it involved the close long vowels turning into diphthongs while all the other long vowels became less open (Davis, 2010, p. 30). For example, the vowel in <night> shifted from [i] in Middle English to [aɪ] (so it became a diphthong) while <meat> originally had a mid-open [ɛ] vowel but now it has [iː] (so it became more close). The Great Vowel Shift partly explains why English spelling is perceived by many as being somewhat haphazard, as the sounds were shifting at the same time as the process of standardizing the spelling was taking place. This can be seen in the different vowels in words such as <tough> and <through> as well as <lose> and <nose> even though the spelling suggests that they should rhyme, and also words such as <does> (female deer) and <does> (the verb) that are homographs but not homophones.

Two relatively recent changes that affected RP British English were the loss of /r/ in words such as <four> and <farm> and the occurrence of a back vowel /ɑː/ instead of /æ/ in words such as <past> and <class>. These changes in RP were only completed in the nineteenth century, and many settlers to North America had already left by that time, which is why North American English is mostly rhotic.

Initially the absence of /r/ in words such as <morn> and the use of /ɑː/ in <past> were regarded as vulgar (Mugglestone, 2003). This illustrates how standards of pronunciation are constantly subject to change, and furthermore that they can be quite arbitrary: what is perceived as crude or slovenly today might in a few years' time become regarded as elegant. It is a fundamental fallacy that some sounds are inherently beautiful while others are ugly.

The emergence of a standard

Though it was not originally invented in England, the early adoption and extensive use of the printing press in England in the 1470s made way for standardization in spelling, as it facilitated the dissemination of written language (Mugglestone, 2003, p. 29). Printed documents using a single variety of written English, usually chosen based on the dialect of writers in London, were distributed all over the country and eventually spread worldwide. In England, English became the standard written language, though French and Latin continued to be used for certain purposes for some time. However, initially there were no attempts to create a standard for spoken English. In 1755, Samuel Johnson published *A Dictionary of the English Language*, and, though it promoted a more stable spelling system than had previously existed, Johnson did not try to fix pronunciation. Accordingly, even though spelling, the lexicon and grammar were becoming standardized, pronunciation continued to be variable (Mugglestone, 2003, p. 23).

However, not long after, Thomas Sheridan included pronunciation in his *General Dictionary of the English Language*, published in 1780, and in 1791 John Walker published his *Critical Pronouncing Dictionary* (Hickey, 2014). The work of these two writers reflects increasing efforts to promote a standardized English pronunciation in the late eighteenth century. These two dictionaries offered a reference model for pronunciation which enabled people to avoid sounding 'ridiculous', and Mugglestone (2003, pp. 12–13) notes that the existence of a standard along with the notion of correctness also created perceptions of non-standard and sub-standard English. In England, the English spoken by the highly educated and the upper middle class in London was preferred, and this emerged as a standard pronunciation for British English.

Initially the speech of the social elite in the major cities of New York, Boston and Philadelphia, who followed the British norms, was considered the standard in the United States during the colonial era and leading up to the American Revolution, and their speech was not far from the British standard that was developing. However, in 1812 Noah Webster published *The American Dictionary of the English Language* (Hickey, 2014, p. 344) and he encouraged the emergence of an independent American standard that separated it from its British counterpart. From then on, two standards (received pronunciation and General American) for English pronunciation developed, though, as noted above, it is debatable whether there really exists a norm that can be regarded as General American (Preston, 2005).

Nowadays, most people in Australia and New Zealand no longer refer to the pronunciation of Britain for their norms, as their languages have become fully mature varieties of English (Schneider, 2007). An Australian variant of the English language was first recognized between the late seventeenth and early eighteenth centuries, while New Zealand English was distinguished in the early nineteenth century.

We can say, therefore, that there are now multiple standards of English throughout the world. Indeed, new norms of pronunciation in places such as India and Singapore are now developing, and this serves to weaken the dominance of the two original standards even further. However, at the same time, most learners of English in places such as Germany, Japan and China continue to refer to one of the two traditional standards, so it seems that their influence is not entirely over. One might also note that, in the modern world with hundreds of millions of second and foreign language learners of English, the dominance of British and American English may even be increasing in many places, even though this is sometimes condemned as a form of continued imperialism (Phillipson, 1992).

The standard of the UK

The term received pronunciation was first used by Alexander Ellis in the middle of the nineteenth century (Heselwood, 2013, p. 111), and its popularity was established by Daniel Jones in the late nineteenth and early twentieth centuries. Though originally based on the pronunciation of south-eastern England, RP is actually a non-localized accent that was and still to a certain extent is widely regarded as a model for correct British English pronunciation for educated, formal speech (Mugglestone, 2003). Cruttenden (2014, p. 326) explains that received pronunciation may be set as a target for any L2 learners of English who are in contact with native (British) speakers while those who have been traditionally influenced by the US may aim for General American. In addition, other models include Australian English, Caribbean English and Standard Scottish English.

In the media, received pronunciation was traditionally used by BBC newsreaders and it has been labelled as BBC English (Roach, 2009). Other names such as Oxford English and the Queen's English have also been suggested (Cruttenden, 2014, p. 79), but Cruttenden (2014, p. 80) concurs with Gimson (1980, p. 303) that the best term for the accent might be General British, partly because this term parallels its American counterpart. However, the term General British does not (yet) seem to have been widely adopted by others.

Furthermore, documented ongoing changes in RP (Wells, 1999; Przedlacka, 2005) call for a reappraisal of its definition and status as it is falling out of use due to its decreasing number of speakers, while Estuary English (Rosewarne, 1994) has been claimed by some people to be the new standard English. Current changes in RP will be discussed later in this chapter.

The standard of the US

GA is an accent that is often encountered because of the large number of speakers, as it is widely spoken by American people who do not have a recognizably local accent (Brown, 1991, p. 34), even if some scholars have questioned whether it really exists (Preston, 2005). Brown (1991) further notes that it acts as a standard model for pronunciation for ESL learners in countries such as the Philippines and Mexico, where it is more appropriate to acquire a North American accent than a British one mainly due to the historical influence of the USA, as well as other factors including geography, the economy and popular culture. This leading variety of English is sometimes referred to as Network English, in parallel with how RP can similarly be referred to as BBC English (Cruttenden, 2014, p. 87), and its use has spread because of the influence of American political power, media and culture and advanced communications technology (Kirkpatrick, 2007, p. 55).

Critical issues and topics

One of the main issues involving standard languages, models of pronunciation and native speakers is to define them. Indeed, when attempting to provide a meaning for 'standard', it makes one question whether a standard really exists if it is constantly undergoing change, while at the same time there are a range of competing standards. Similarly, it is difficult to define a native speaker of English (McKay, 2002, p. 28) as it is unclear if speakers who acquire two languages simultaneously should be considered native speakers. For example, in Brunei many speakers learn both English and Malay equally fluently. Does that mean that they are native speakers of both?

Despite this problem, many native speakers of British and American English undoubtedly exist, and some of them are perceived to speak with a standard accent. Here a brief description of differences between RP and GA will be offered before some misconceptions about the two standards are discussed and alternative standards are considered.

Differences between British and American English

It is important to understand that the two varieties influence each other by borrowing features, especially via the media and the Internet (Algeo, 2006), and, as will be discussed, such influences may be increasing. Even so, there remain some obvious differences between RP and GA as both varieties have continued to evolve in different ways since the colonial period due to political, social and geographical distances. Perhaps the most salient difference involves rhoticity, as in RP /r/ is only pronounced before a vowel in words such as <red> and <carry> and as a linking sound in phrases such as <far away>, while in GA it occurs wherever there is an 'r' in the spelling, including in <four> and <farm>. As a result, the diphthongs /ɪə/, /ɛə/ and /ʊə/ of RP are absent from the inventory of GA vowels, as each one is a monophthong followed by /r/ (Trudgill & Hannah, 2008, p. 44). For example, <here> is pronounced as [hɪə] in RP while GA speakers tend to say it as [hɪr]. Other differences include: the absence of /ɒ/ in America; the use of /æ/ rather than /ɑː/ in words such as <path>, <laugh> and <grass>; the use of a flapped /t/ in words such as <better> and <matter>; and the pronunciation of /l/ as dark [ɫ] in all positions by Americans while speakers in England usually have clear [l] before vowels (Trudgill & Hannah, 2008, pp. 43–45).

Finally Kövecses (2000, p. 26) shows that British and American English differ in stress patterns. For instance, words such as <formidable> and <inquiry> differ, as many British speakers pronounce them as <forMIDable> and <inQUIry> while American speakers tend to stress the first syllable and say <FORmidable> and <INquiry>. However, one might also note that Wells (2008, p. 318) reports that 46 per cent of British speakers actually prefer stress on the first syllable of <formidable>, while 32 per cent of Americans opt for stress on the second syllable of this word, illustrating that patterns of pronunciation in both varieties are not fixed. Furthermore, by comparing young speakers with older ones, one can surmise that the trend in both varieties seems to be the same, with stress on the second syllable of <formidable> apparently winning out, suggesting that the two varieties may be influencing each other. In addition, Wells (2008, p. 415) reports that 26 per cent of Americans actually prefer stress on the second syllable of <inquiry>, which once more reflects the fact that a single pronunciation is not used by all people in the USA.

There are also lexical and spelling differences between British and American English. For example, an American would probably talk about using the <elevator>, eating <candy> and signing a <check>, while most speakers in Britain would use a <lift>, eat <sweets> and sign a <cheque> (Crystal, 1995, p. 307). However, this chapter will just focus on pronunciation.

Established misconceptions

There is a misconception among many learners of English that most people in England speak with an RP accent. As a result, those who travel to London from elsewhere are often stunned to arrive and find that the overwhelming majority of people do not sound like the recordings in their textbooks. In fact, as mentioned above, only a tiny percentage of people in England actually speak RP.

Furthermore, there is also substantial variation within RP. Gimson (1980) described differences between General RP, Conservative RP and Advanced RP; and, more recently, Cruttenden (2014, p. 81) has suggested a distinction between posh-sounding Conspicuous General British (CGB) and geographically varying Regional General British (RGB). There has been a decline in the number of speakers of CGB in the last 50 years, but it is still spoken by some upper-class people, even though it is nowadays sometimes subject to ridicule. Features of CGB include: a mid /ɪ/ vowel at the end of words such as <happy>; an open quality at the end of the /ɪə/ diphthong in words such as <here>; and a front starting point for the /əʊ/ diphthong in words such as <bone>.

In contrast to CGB, which is a class-based accent, RGB reflects an element of regional variation. Features of RGB include: use of a vowel in place of dark /l/, especially in London, where <held> may be [heʊd] and <ball> may be [bɔʊ]; and use of a front vowel in words such as <after>, <bath> and <past>, especially in the north of England. Given that it has regional variation, Cruttenden (2014, p. 81) notes that there are actually many separate varieties of RGB, so it should really be referred to in the plural: RGBs.

There are also several other misconceptions about RP. Brown (1991, p. 31) observes that it is often believed to be the most prestigious and most intelligible accent of English spoken by people in England. However, over the years, RP has lost much of its original status, due partly to its declining number of speakers, and this has led to a reassessment of its suitability as a model of pronunciation. Indeed, there are now proposals to use alternative models for teaching ESL and EFL, something that will be discussed in the sections below. Furthermore, it is not necessarily true that an RP accent is the most intelligible way of speaking in many parts of the world, as clearly articulated English in countries such as India and Singapore produced by well-educated speakers is probably more easily intelligible in many places.

One other misconception about RP involves the belief that it closely reflects English spelling. Even after orthographic conventions became established, linguistic changes still occurred in the spoken form, and Brown (1991, p. 33) notes that rhotic accents of English actually reflect the spelling more closely than RP, in which 'r' in the spelling is often not present in the pronunciation. Similarly, we might note that omission of word-final /t/ and /d/ in phrases such as <drift by>, <mashed potatoes>, <old man> and <moved back> is common in Britain (Cruttenden, 2014, p. 314), and omission of /t/ in <Christmas> is obligatory, so it is simply not true that RP speakers carefully produce all the sounds suggested by the spelling.

Finally, there is a misconception among some learners of English that their use of RP pronunciation will engender respect. In fact, Brown (1991, p. 33) notes that many native speakers have unfavourable reactions to the use of RP by foreigners, and similarly Preston (2005, p. 56) observes that people sometimes show discomfort towards learners who try too hard to sound like a native speaker.

With regard to the American standard, Preston (2005) asserts that the existence of GA English is itself a myth, claiming that nobody speaks it, not even newsreaders. Furthermore, he observes that young, educated northerners and southerners sound more different now than they did a century ago, despite universal education and media access (2005, pp. 39–42), and he further notes that there are distinctive varieties of American English such as African-American English, Spanish-influenced Englishes, and Native American Englishes, due to ethnic diversity in the USA.

One further misconception about GA is that diversity is limited to the East Coast areas and the pronunciation of older speakers. Preston (2005) counters this by illustrating the distinctive vowels of young people living in the north of the United States as a result of the Northern Cities Vowel Shift (Labov, 1994). This change in pronunciation is happening in the large cities around the Great Lakes, and it results in the vowels in <hut> and <bit> becoming [ɔ] and [ɛ] respectively, which confirms that most people in places such as Chicago and Philadelphia do not actually speak GA.

Changes in the pronunciation of RP and GA

The two standards of English pronunciation, as with all accents and languages, are far from static. Wells (1999) surveyed pronunciation preferences of native British English speakers for words such as <either> and <forehead>, and the results show that there is a tendency for younger people to pronounce these words differently from older ones. This suggests that there is a change in progress, as has always been the case in the history of English, and younger speakers are shifting their pronunciation away from the traditional norms of RP. Further details and analysis of his study will be discussed below.

Przedlacka (2005, pp. 19–21) also discusses changes within RP in the late twentieth century. She reports on the recent tendency in RP for a tense vowel to be used at the end of words such as <study> (the happy vowel), the lowering of /æ/ (the TRAP vowel), the fronting of /uː/ (the GOOSE vowel), and the increasing use of a glottal stop in place of /t/ when it precedes a sonorant or across a word boundary, such as in <what now>.

Cruttenden (2014, pp. 83–85) documents some shifts in RP under three categories: 'changes almost complete', 'changes well established' and 'recent trends'. The first of these includes: the loss of a distinction between words such as <paw> and <pour>; the omission of /j/ before /uː/ in <luminous> and <suit>; and the use of /tʃ/ rather than /tj/ in <culture> and /dʒ/ instead of /dj/ in <soldier>. For the second category, in addition to the changes reported by Przedlacka (2005) and discussed above, Cruttenden notes the following well-established changes: the pronunciation of the vowel in words such as <fare> and <where> as a long monophthong [ɛː]; the occurrence of /ʒ/ rather than an anglicized /dʒ/ in imported words such as <beige>, <rouge> and <genre>; and a high-rise tone at the end of statements, perhaps influenced by the speech of people from Australia and New Zealand. The third category suggested by Cruttenden includes the most recent changes that can be heard, though they may not yet be typically found among the majority of speakers. Some examples in this category are: the realization of the vowels in words such as <beer> and <sure> as [ɪː] and [ʊː] respectively; the use of a labio-dental approximant [ʋ] at the start of words such as <red>; and the vocalization of dark [ɫ] to [ʊ] in words such as <ball> and <field>. Clearly, substantial changes are taking place in the pronunciation of speakers in Britain, and it is a myth that RP remains static.

For American English, Preston (2005, pp. 40–41) uses the Northern Cities Vowel Shift and the Southern Vowel Shift to assert his claim that GA does not exist, as the vowel systems resulting from these two shifts show substantial deviation from the textbook representation of GA vowels. The former shift results in <bat> being pronounced as [bɛət], <bet> is [bʌt] and <bit> is becoming [bɛt]. These pronunciations were taken from young, educated speakers in large cities such as Detroit and Chicago. As a result of the Southern Vowel Shift, speakers in the south of the United States pronounce <bit> as [biət], <beet> as [bɛɪt], <bet> as [beət] and <bait> as [bɑit]. These two vowel shifts, among other dialect patterns in the USA, underscore the distinction between the speech of northerners and southerners in the country, which supports the assertion by Preston (2005, p. 39) that GA English is not very general at all.

Alternative standards

One controversial issue is whether a style of pronunciation used by native speakers in countries such as England and the USA is appropriate as a standard for speakers elsewhere, especially in ESL and EFL countries (Kirkpatrick, 2007, p. 28). Jenkins (2000) notes that native speakers of English are far outnumbered by speakers of ESL and EFL. Furthermore, she challenges the practice of the accent of a minority being used as a pronunciation standard for vast numbers of language learners, many of whom succeed in speaking the language extremely competently. For this reason, some scholars have suggested alternative models.

Rosewarne (1994) suggests that Estuary English, the pronunciation of speakers in south-east England that is influenced by the London accent, is preferred by many younger speakers throughout England and might become the new RP. However, Mugglestone (2003, pp. 282–288) doubts whether this alternative will become adopted as a standard, because it merely reflects trends that already exist in the dynamics of RP and so it is just part of the process of dialect levelling that is taking place throughout England; and Przedlacka (2005, p. 30) suggests that, instead of constituting an emergent standard for the pronunciation of English, Estuary English acts as 'a vehicle for criticising or celebrating socially salient phonetic features'.

Cruttenden (2014, p. 327) offers two alternative models: Amalgam English and International English. The former is similar to the hybrid model suggested by Gimson (1980) in a sense that it is a mixture of American and British varieties, but this proposed updated version would incorporate some features from varieties in the southern hemisphere as well as the Caribbean. In contrast, the International English suggested by Cruttenden aims for minimal intelligibility, and it aims to convey a message efficiently from a native English listener's standpoint in international lingua franca situations.

The International English proposal is similar to that of Jenkins (2000, 2007) for ELF communication. Her lingua franca core (LFC) lists features of pronunciation that she claims are essential for maintaining intelligibility in international settings, and she contends that speakers should be free to choose how to pronounce sounds that are not part of the LFC. Features of pronunciation that are not in the LFC and so do not need to be taught include: the dental fricatives /θ/ and /ð/; consonant clusters in word-final position; small differences in vowel quality; lexical stress placement; and the specific tones associated with intonation. Her research was based on just 40 tokens of misunderstanding between speakers from Switzerland and Japan, but more recent research based on a larger corpus confirms that most misunderstandings do indeed involve core features, such as confusion between /r/ and /w/ and also between initial clusters such as /pr/ and /pl/ (Deterding, 2013), though further research is clearly needed to establish exactly which features of pronunciation are most important for maintaining intelligibility. In some other perception studies, lexical stress is deemed important in intelligibility (Field, 2005), but this may mostly relate to native speaker listeners from places such as the UK and the USA.

In conclusion, even though there are a number of possible replacements for RP, Przedlacka (2005, p. 29) maintains that it still remains the best pronunciation model of English, and attempts at replacing it are currently impractical.

Current contributions and research

Current research shows how the pronunciation of English is changing throughout the world. Here we will first discuss how it is changing in Britain and then consider accents in South East Asia, specifically Singapore and Brunei.

Current changes in Britain

In 1988, John Wells carried out a survey to study pronunciation preferences of native speakers of British English. He investigated 90 words with variable pronunciation such as <ate>, <issue> and <zebra>, and Table 12.1 shows the results for these three words. By comparing the preferences indicated by older and younger speakers, one can predict how the pronunciation is undergoing change (Wells, 1999, p. 38). The final column of Table 12.1

Table 12.1 Pronunciation preferences by British respondents for <ate>, <issue> and <zebra>

	Old pronunciation	New pronunciation	Overall preference for new pronunciation (%)
<ate>	[et]	[eɪt]	45
<issue>	[ɪsjuː]	[ɪʃ(j)uː]	70
<zebra>	[ziːbrə]	[zebrə]	83

Source: J. C. Wells (2008)

shows that, in 1988, the overall preference for the new pronunciation of <ate> was still under 50 per cent, but the process of change was more complete for <issue> and <zebra>.

Both <ate> and <zebra> involve changes influenced by the orthography: the pronunciation of the words has shifted to reflect how the words are spelled. Hickey (2014, p. 297) adopts a more restricted definition of spelling pronunciation, suggesting it is concerned with the pronunciation of a word in which the spelling diverges from its etymology, so for example the /l/ in <fault> is now pronounced even though historically there was never an /l/ in the word; but here we use the broader definition suggested by Algeo (2005, p. 46), including words for which the modern pronunciation is reverting to an earlier form. For example, for 65 per cent of British speakers nowadays, <forehead> has a medial /h/ (Wells, 2008, p. 317), and this is how it was originally pronounced before it became [ˈfɒrɪd].

In contrast to the influence of spelling that seems to be affecting <ate> and <forehead>, the change in the pronunciation of <issue> involves coalescence, as the /s/ merges with /j/ to become /ʃ/ (Wells & Colson, 1971, p. 55).

Other words apparently undergoing a shift in pronunciation in Britain include <harass>, with younger people preferring stress on the second syllable, and <schedule>, for which there is a tendency for younger speakers to use /sk/ rather than /ʃ/ at the start. Both these words may reflect the influence of American pronunciation on British English (Wells, 1999, p. 48).

Wells subsequently conducted further surveys about words with uncertain pronunciation, and the results are shown in the third edition of his dictionary (Wells, 2008). Here, the data from the 2008 dictionary is analysed to gain a snapshot about some of the changes in pronunciation among native British English speakers. There are a total of 69 words for which Wells (2008) includes a chart showing a clear shift in pronunciation in British English. Of these 69 words, 29 primarily involve vowel changes, 21 are due to changes in consonants and 19 involve shifts in stress. Table 12.2 includes one word illustrating each of these issues: <either>, <longitude> and <debris>.

Wells (2008) lists the preferred pronunciation of words in both British and American English, and, for the 69 words mentioned above, 27 of the shifts in pronunciation in British English seem to reflect American influence. For example, in addition to those listed in Table 12.2, <migraine> is increasingly pronounced by people in Britain with /aɪ/ rather than /iː/ in its first syllable, and <primarily> is often stressed on its second syllable.

Finally, 15 words were found in which spelling pronunciation seems to be a factor. For example, in addition to the words already discussed, <nephew> increasingly has a medial /f/ rather than /v/, and <scallop> nowadays tends to have /æ/ rather than /ɒ/ in its first syllable. Although spelling pronunciation is therefore probably a factor in less than one-quarter of the words, it is clearly evident in some cases. Furthermore, it is quite a widespread phenomenon in Englishes around the world, something that will be considered in the next sections.

Table 12.2 The changes in pronunciation for <either>, <longitude> and <debris>

	Old pronunciation	New pronunciation	Class	American influence?	Spelling pronunciation?
<either>	[ˈaɪðə]	[ˈiːðə]	Vowel	✓	✓
<longitude>	[ˈlɒndʒɪtjuːd]	[ˈlɒŋgɪtjuːd]	Consonant		✓
<debris>	[ˈdebriː]	[dəˈbriː]	Stress	✓	

Source: J. C. Wells (2008)

Vowels in Singapore English

To investigate a new standard of Singapore English pronunciation that is emerging, Deterding (2005) recorded 38 trainee English teachers reading a list of 12 sentences. One goal of this research was to describe Singapore English as an independent variety that does not depend on an external variety such as British English. The vowels were analysed by plotting the first two formants to provide an estimate of their quality (Ladefoged & Johnson, 2011, p. 212).

It was found that most of the speakers rhyme <egg> with <vague> and not with <peg>, and furthermore that many of them do not differentiate <red> and <raid>. Other findings include the tendency to use /ʌ/ in <one> while /ɒ/ occurs in <won>, and for most speakers /ʊə/ occurs in <tour> and <poor>, while /ɔː/ is found after a preceding /j/ in words such as <cure> and <pure>. These developments reflect the reverse of the emergent trends in British English, where <one> nowadays is often [wɒn] and <tour> is generally [tɔː], which shows that Singapore English is developing its own style of speech that is quite distinct from the way that people in Britain speak. This is unsurprising as other varieties of English such as Australian English and Jamaican English have also evolved naturally to make themselves distinct from the historical link with British English (Schneider, 2007).

Brunei English

Although Brunei is small, with a population of only about 400,000, the way English is used can provide valuable insights into some of the ways that English is evolving in an outer circle context (Deterding & Salbrina, 2013). Some of the features of the pronunciation of Brunei English are: the use of /t/ at the start of words such as <thought> and <third>; the occurrence of rhoticity, as about 50 per cent of young university students in Brunei now have a rhotic accent, even though historically Brunei English was based on British English because it was a British protectorate from 1888 to 1984 (Hussainmiya, 1995); the avoidance of reduced vowels in function words such as <of> and <as> and in the first syllable of <Japan>; and the widespread use of spelling pronunciation.

A small-scale study was conducted to investigate this last issue and see if spelling pronunciation may be becoming more widespread among Bruneian speakers. Two groups were recorded: 10 teachers (seven females, three males) aged between 30 and 35 years old; and 10 undergraduates (nine females, one male) aged between 20 and 25. All of the speakers were ethnically Malay and they read the following eight sentences:

(a) I would love to try their *buffet*.
(b) The *salmon* is very good here.
(c) A knight is brave and *honest*.

(d) I do not go out *often*.

(e) I *doubt* it will rain.

(f) He plans to expand his *company*.

(g) I think it was a *theatre*, not a cafe.

(h) *Either* one will do.

The words in italics are the ones of principal interest (they were not italicized in the sentences read by the participants). In particular, it was hoped to find out how extensive spelling pronunciation might be, so the investigation considered whether <buffet> has a final /t/, if <salmon> has /l/, if <honest> has initial /h/, if <often> has /t/ and whether <doubt> has /b/. In addition, <company> may have /ɒ/ rather than the expected /ʌ/ in its first syllable, <theatre> may start with /t/ and <either> may have /aɪ/ or /iː/ in its first syllable.

The first five of these words all involve the possible insertion of a consonant. The results are shown in Table 12.3. It can be seen that insertion of /l/ in <salmon> is the normal pronunciation for both groups of speakers, /t/ occurs in <often> with just over half of the teachers but less frequently among the undergraduates, and that insertion of a consonant is more common among the teachers for all five words.

Given that the undergraduates are younger than the teachers, the results seem to suggest that spelling pronunciation for all these words is actually becoming less common in Brunei. However, there may be other factors involved, and far more data is needed from a wide range of different speakers before any firm conclusions can be drawn. Although this small-scale study provides no evidence that spelling pronunciation is increasing in Brunei, it does confirm that it is quite widespread, especially for <salmon>.

The results for the other three words are shown in Table 12.4. (One undergraduate used /eɪ/ at the start of <either>, so this token is omitted.) As with the results from Table 12.3, the undergraduates are more likely to use the more standard pronunciations: /ʌ/ in <company>; and /θ/ in <theatre>. However, there is little difference in the use of an American pronunciation for <either> between the two groups.

One major influence on the pronunciation of English in Brunei is likely to be from Malay, the first language of all the speakers. The pronunciation of Malay is mostly predictable from the spelling (Clynes & Deterding, 2011), and one might predict that this would encourage the use of spelling pronunciation in English. However, the data considered here

Table 12.3 Results for the insertion of consonants

	<buffet>		<salmon>		<honest>		<often>		<doubt>	
	/t/	Ø	/l/	Ø	/h/	Ø	/t/	Ø	/b/	Ø
Teachers	3	7	7	3	3	7	6	4	2	8
Undergraduates	2	8	6	4	1	9	2	8	0	10

Table 12.4 Results for the vowel in the first syllable of <company>, the sound at the start of <theatre> and the vowel at the start of <either>

	<company>		<theatre>		<either>	
	/ɒ/	/ʌ/	/t/	/θ/	/iː/	/aɪ/
Teachers	5	5	4	6	5	5
Undergraduates	1	9	2	8	4	5

gives no evidence for increasing incidence of spelling pronunciation in Brunei English, and it might even be declining. One possibility is that young people are growing up with greater access to international English in movies and via the Internet, and they may therefore be participating in an emerging global style of English, so in fact their English is not as influenced by Malay as that of their elders. Further data from a wider range of speakers is needed to investigate this further.

Recommendations for practice

Teachers often believe that they need a stable model of pronunciation for the basis of their teaching, and consequently Jenkins (2007) reports that they are frequently reluctant to abandon reliance on standard accents. So what can they do when the two most prominent models of English pronunciation, RP and GA, are unstable?

Inevitably, for many years to come these two models will continue to be used as norms for teaching purposes because of the extensive materials available for them. However, Preston (2005, p. 55) questions why learners continue to try so hard to sound exactly like native speakers when the best model should actually be a person who has successfully learned the language. Furthermore, as we have seen, speaking like someone from the UK or USA is not necessarily the best way of making oneself intelligible or gaining respect in an international setting.

Another issue is an over-reliance on RP or GA and a lack of exposure to other ways of speaking. If learners are only able to understand people who speak 'standard' accents, then they are ill prepared to interact with a range of different speakers in the real world. Learners must first understand that all languages or varieties are constantly changing due to a number of factors including geographical distance, political and social influences and language contact. Consequently, teachers of English should expose their students to many varieties of the language to enable them to grasp the fallacy of a single standard and also to cope successfully with speakers who use different accents.

Language teachers should also be open to shifting norms in pronunciation. Even the so-called standard varieties are constantly subject to change, and teachers need to acknowledge this and not cling to outdated modes of speaking. Furthermore, in emergent varieties of English the use of non-standard forms such as consonant cluster simplification or lack of vowel reduction should not be condemned as errors when mutual intelligibility is achieved among speakers in an international setting (Jenkins, 2006; McKay, 2002).

As seen in the previous section, Singapore English and Brunei English are emerging with their own norms of pronunciation, and these new standards pose issues for the representation of speech. If words such as <day> and <rose> have monophthongs in the speech of a majority of speakers, why should they be represented in dictionaries as diphthongs? In addition, should the sound in the onset of <thin> be represented as the dental fricative /θ/ when so many speakers around the world have /t/ or /f/ instead? One solution to this is the proposal by Wells (1982) to use upper-case letters for consonants (for example referring to the voiceless TH sound) and lexical keywords in small caps to represent vowels (so the vowels in <day> and <rose> are FACE and GOAT, respectively). It would be useful for students of English to be familiar with issues such as this, and thereby to appreciate that there is no single standard for the pronunciation of English. In addition, teachers should be tolerant of diversity, so long as their students achieve a high level of intelligibility (Deterding, 2013). Jenkins (2000) asserts that teachers should become aware of which issues in pronunciation have an impact on intelligibility and which do not, and they should not waste time trying to teach aspects of pronunciation that have little impact on making oneself easily understood.

Though helpful in representing many of the sounds of English, the proposals of Wells (1982) do not solve all the problems. For example, as we have seen, in Singapore, <egg> rhymes with <vague> and not with <peg>; so should the vowel in <egg> be represented as FACE or DRESS? It is not clear if it is possible to offer an updated set of lexical keywords that can accommodate all the emerging new varieties of pronunciation.

Teachers should also be aware of the needs of learners and the changing trends of the pronunciation models used for teaching. Przedlacka (2005, p. 30) states that language students consider young, native speakers to be good models for pronunciation teaching, even if they do not necessarily speak with a traditional RP accent. Furthermore, as the number of RP speakers is declining while the burgeoning demand for English teachers seems set to continue into the foreseeable future, it is not possible for all teachers to be native speakers of some optimal pronunciation model. So there should be greater acceptance of local teachers who speak with their own educated, internationally intelligible varieties of English (Kirkpatrick, 2007; Murphy, 2014).

Another approach to consider is to look at the differences between American and British English and to investigate the causes of the divergence. Kövecses (2000, pp. 10–11) suggests that the different perspectives from historical events and cultural traditions may help both teachers and students to abandon the prejudices reflected in the two standards. Moreover, it is easier to see what is uniquely American about American English and specifically British about British English by analysing their differences.

Future directions

This chapter has shown that a single standard of English is a fallacy, and it has documented some of the changes in RP and GA over the years. However, it remains uncertain what the future holds for these two pronunciation models. One possibility is that, with the convenience of travel in the modern world and also the ease of communication over the Internet, the differences between RP and GA will slowly disappear. We can see some signs of this in the trends documented by Wells (2008), as the pronunciation of words such as <either> and <debris> in Britain is apparently being influenced by American speech. How extensive will such influence be?

In addition, we can note the emergence of alternative norms of pronunciation around the world that frequently seem to use spelling pronunciation, such as the widespread occurrence of /l/ in <salmon>, just as /t/ in <often> is becoming more common in Britain and the USA. Furthermore, the tendency to avoid vowel reduction in function words such as <of> and <as> and in the unstressed first syllable of words such as <computer> and <advice> are examples of features occurring in emergent new varieties of English. It remains uncertain whether these changes will become widely acceptable internationally and therefore constitute features of developing international norms of pronunciation. If that happens, then the traditional accents such as RP and GA may become anachronistic reminders of a historical style of pronunciation. Only time will tell if that occurs.

Further reading

Brown, A. (1991). *Pronunciation models*. Singapore: Singapore University Press. Useful for English language teachers, learners and linguists, this book focuses on what to teach in class rather than the methodologies of teaching.

Cruttenden, A. (2014). *Gimson's pronunciation of English* (8th ed.). London & New York, NY: Routledge. This classic book, now in its eighth edition, continues to provide an authoritative and invaluable account of the current pronunciation of English in Britain.

Dziubalska-Kołaczyk, K., & Przedlacka, J. (Eds). (2005). *English pronunciation models: A changing scene*. Bern: Peter Lang. A compilation of scholars' perspectives on current challenges to the continued dominance of RP and GA as models of pronunciation.
Mugglestone, L. (2003). *Talking proper: The rise of accent as social symbol*. New York, NY: Oxford University Press. A detailed account of how a standard English accent emerged and came to be associated with prestige.

Related topics

Standardization; world Englishes; English as a lingua franca; intelligibility; spelling pronunciation

References

Algeo, J. (2005). *The origins and development of the English language* (6th ed.). Boston, MA: Wadsworth Cengage.
Algeo, J. (2006). *British or American English? A handbook of word and grammar patterns*. Cambridge: Cambridge University Press.
Brown, A. (1991). *Pronunciation models*. Singapore: Singapore University Press.
Clynes, A., & Deterding, D. (2011). Standard Malay (Brunei). *Journal of the International Phonetic Association*, *41*(2), 259–268.
Cruttenden, A. (2014). *Gimson's pronunciation of English* (8th ed.). London & New York, NY: Routledge.
Crystal, D. (1995). *The Cambridge encyclopedia of the English language*. Cambridge: Cambridge University Press.
Davis, D. R. (2010). Standardized English: The history of the earlier circles. In A. Kirkpatrick (Ed.), *The Routledge handbook of world Englishes* (pp. 17–36). London & New York, NY: Routledge.
Deterding, D. (2005). Emergent patterns in the vowels of Singapore English. *English World-Wide*, *26*, 179–197.
Deterding, D. (2010). Norms for pronunciation in Southeast Asia, *World Englishes*, *29*(3), 364–367.
Deterding, D. (2013). *Misunderstandings in English as a lingua franca: An analysis of ELF interactions in South-East Asia*. Berlin: De Gruyter.
Deterding, D., & Salbrina, S. (2013). *Brunei English: A new variety in a multilingual society*. Dordrecht: Springer.
Field, J. (2005). Intelligibility and the listener: The role of lexical stress. *TESOL Quarterly*, *39*(3), 399–423.
Gimson, A. C. (1980). *An introduction to the pronunciation of English* (3rd ed.). London: Edward Arnold.
Heselwood, B. (2013). *Phonetic transcription in theory and practice*. Edinburgh: Edinburgh University Press.
Hickey, R. (2014). *A dictionary of varieties of English*. Malden, MA: Wiley Blackwell.
Hussainmiya, B. A. (1995). *Sultan Omar Ali Saifuddin III and Britain: The making of Brunei Darussalam*. Kuala Lumpur: Oxford University Press.
Jenkins, J. (2000). *The phonology of English as an international language*. Oxford: Oxford University Press.
Jenkins, J. (2006). Global intelligibility and local diversity: Possibility or paradox? In R. Ruby & M. Saraceni (Eds), *English in the world: Global rules, global roles* (pp. 32–39). London: Continuum.
Jenkins, J. (2007). *English as a lingua franca: Attitude and identity*. Oxford: Oxford University Press.
Kachru, B. B. (1985). Standards, codification and sociolinguistic realism: The English language in the outer circle. In R. Quirk & H. Widdowson (Eds), *English in the world: Teaching and learning the language and literatures* (pp. 11–30). Cambridge: Cambridge University Press.
Kirkpatrick, A. (2007). *World Englishes: Implications for international communication and English language teaching*. Cambridge: Cambridge University Press.
Kövecses, Z. (2000). *American English: An introduction*. Ontario: Broadview.
Kretzschmar, W. (2010). The development of Standard American English. In A. Kirkpatrick (Ed.), *The Routledge handbook of world Englishes* (pp. 96–112). London & New York, NY: Routledge.

Labov, W. (1994). *Principles of linguistic change (vol. 1): Internal factors*. Oxford: Blackwell.

Ladefoged, P., & Johnson, K. (2011). *A course in phonetics* (6th ed.). Boston, MA: Wadsworth Cengage.

McKay, S. L. (2002). *Teaching English as an international language: An introduction to the role of English as an international language and its implications for language teaching*. Oxford: Oxford University Press.

Mugglestone, L. (2003). *Talking proper: The rise of accent as social symbol*. New York, NY: Oxford University Press.

Murphy, J. (2014). Intelligible, comprehensible, non-native models in ESL/EFL pronunciation teaching. *System, 42*, 258–269.

Phillipson, R. (1992). *Linguistic imperialism*. Oxford: Oxford University Press.

Preston, D. (2005). How can you learn a language that isn't there? In K. Dziubalska-Kołaczyk & J. Przedlacka (Eds), *English pronunciation models: A changing scene* (pp. 37–58). Berlin: Peter Lang.

Przedlacka, J. (2005). Models and myth: Updating the (non)standard accents. In K. Dziubalska-Kołaczyk & J. Przedlacka (Eds), *English pronunciation models: A changing scene* (pp. 17–26). Berlin: Peter Lang.

Roach, P. (2009). *English phonetics and phonology: A practical course* (4th ed.). Cambridge: Cambridge University Press.

Rosewarne, D. (1994). Estuary English: Tomorrow's RP? *English Today*, 10, 3–8.

Schneider, E. W. (2007). *Postcolonial English: Varieties around the world*. Cambridge: Cambridge University Press.

Schreier, D. (2005). *Consonant change in English worldwide: Synchrony meets diachrony*. Basingstoke: Palgrave Macmillan.

Trudgill, P., & Hannah, J. (2008). *International English: A guide to the varieties of Standard English*. London: Hodder Education.

Wells, J. C. (1982). *Accents of English*. Cambridge: Cambridge University Press.

Wells, J. C. (1999). British English pronunciation preferences: A changing scene. *Journal of the International Phonetic Association, 29*(2), 33–50.

Wells, J. C. (2008). *Longman pronunciation dictionary* (3rd ed.). Harlow: Longman.

Wells, J. C., & Colson, G. (1971). *Practical phonetics*. London: Pitman.

13

New Pronunciation en route to world Englishes

David Deterding and Ishamina Athirah Gardiner

Introduction

Since English is the dominant choice of language in international settings, there are now more non-native speakers (NNS) of English than native speakers (NS) (Seidlhofer, 2011, p. 8). Previously, learners of English as a second or foreign language generally opted for British or American English as the standard model, but it can now be questioned whether this is appropriate. A large proportion of NNS interactions do not involve a NS (Jenkins, 2007), and NS styles of pronunciation are not necessarily the most intelligible in international settings.

This chapter first looks at historical aspects of standardization and the emergence of new varieties of English. It then discusses crucial issues concerning intelligibility, giving examples from a case study involving conversations between non-native speakers. The chapter finally summarizes the current status of standards for pronunciation in world Englishes, considers the challenges that are faced in a globalized world, and attempts to speculate briefly on what the future might hold.

Historical perspectives

The standard variety of a language is generally promoted in the classroom and in society. The dominant standard varieties for the pronunciation of English have in the past been received pronunciation (RP) for British English and General American (GA) for American English, but newer standard varieties have emerged in countries such as Australia and New Zealand (Schneider, 2007). Before looking into the emergence of new varieties of English, this section will briefly describe the historical process of standardization in spoken English.

The emergence of norms for English began with the standardization of writing. In the early fifteenth century, official documents were written in English in the variety known as Chancery Standard, which was based on London usage (Beal, 2012, p. 70). The introduction of the printing press in Britain by William Caxton in the late fifteenth century accelerated the process of standardization, as written conventions became more established once the language was widely printed (Fennell, 2001, p. 157). However, during the sixteenth and seventeenth centuries, there still continued to be a great deal of variation in terms of morphology and syntax, and also in spelling, which reflected regional differences in pronunciation.

A standard type of spoken English only emerged in the late eighteenth century, when pronunciation began to be codified. Dictionaries showing pronunciation were published by Thomas Sheridan in 1780 and John Walker in 1791 (Hickey, 2014), both of whom selected the speech of educated Londoners as their model. This is not surprising as London was the political, legal, administrative, commercial and cultural centre of Britain (Mugglestone, 2003, p. 13). Baugh and Cable (2002, p. 314) further note that RP in British English is spoken 'with a fair degree of uniformity by cultivated people in all parts of the country' and that it is class-based rather than a regional dialect. Differences between British and American English were reinforced with the publication of Noah Webster's *American Dictionary of the English Language* in 1812 (Hickey, 2014, p. 344), which asserted that the two varieties are distinct in terms of spelling, pronunciation and lexis.

The nineteenth and twentieth centuries saw the emergence of varieties such as Australian English and New Zealand English, and they have now become established as mature varieties (Schneider, 2007). This can be seen, for example, in the publication of dictionaries of each variety to assert its distinctiveness from other varieties of English (Butler, 2002; Deverson, 1999).

Today, English is the world's leading international language and it is used in many countries in politics, business, education, technology and the media (Jenkins, 2009, p. 38). Crystal (2003, p. 59) states that the status of English as the world's primary global language is mainly due to the expansion of British colonial power towards the end of the nineteenth century and the emergence of the United States as a leading economic power in the twentieth century. The use of English worldwide has resulted in the emergence of new varieties of English as the language has become indigenized in many non-native English-speaking countries (Schneider, 2011). The term 'world Englishes' is used to refer to these newly emergent varieties, and the most influential model to represent them is the three circles of English, in which the circles 'represent the types of spread, the patterns of acquisition, and the functional allocation of English in diverse cultural contexts' (Kachru, 1992, p. 356). The inner circle represents the traditional base of English where it is spoken as the mother tongue, including countries such as Britain, the USA, Canada, Australia and New Zealand. The outer circle involves the spread of English in former colonies, where English may be used in the administration and it plays a second language role, including places such as Singapore, India and Nigeria. The expanding circle includes countries where English is a foreign language and has no official status, such as China, Japan and Germany.

English today is also used as a lingua franca throughout the world, and the term English as lingua franca (ELF) can be defined as 'English as it is used as a contact language among speakers from different first languages' (Jenkins, 2009, p. 143). Jenkins (2009, p. 147) proposes a set of essential pronunciation features called the lingua franca core (LFC), which aims at ensuring mutual intelligibility in international communication. Some of the features included in the LFC are:

- all consonant sounds except /θ/, /ð/, and dark /l/;
- contrasts between long and short vowels;
- avoidance of consonant deletion in word-initial clusters, and only certain deletions permissible in word-medial and final positions;
- placement of nuclear (tonic) stress.

Excluded from the LFC are /θ/ and /ð/, vowel quality, reduced vowels, word stress, rhythm and intonational tones. Jenkins (2000) asserts that students should be allowed to choose how to realize these features of pronunciation, and this gives rise to substantial variation in English around the world without compromising intelligibility. Indeed, Pakir (2001, p. 84) suggests that ELF represents multiple identities because of nativization of the language as it is used in different geographical speech communities. Deterding and Kirkpatrick (2006) note that a number of distinct regional varieties seem to be emerging rather than one global English lingua franca, so the English lingua franca spoken in South East Asia may be distinct from that used across Africa (Gramley & Pätzold, 2004). However, Kirkpatrick and Deterding (2011, p. 375) also suggest that some phonological features seem to occur in many new varieties of English throughout the world, including the substitution of dental fricatives, the reduction of final consonant clusters, the avoidance of vowel reduction and the use of syllable-based rhythm.

In summary, the emergence of varieties of English involves new ways of speaking that deviate from the traditional standards. One key issue is whether these emergent styles of pronunciation lead to loss of intelligibility in international settings. This question is addressed in the next section.

Critical issues

Trudgill (1999) states that the standard of spoken English is hard to define, and Gupta (2006, p. 97) suggests that this is partly because it is not established by government bodies or academies but by 'a loose consensus of writers'. However, there exist pronunciation dictionaries such as Wells (2008) and Jones, Roach, Hartman and Setter (2003) that provide pronunciation guidelines for RP and GA, and also comprehensive reference works such as Cruttenden (2014), who prefers the term General British (GB) instead of RP to refer to the standard variety of British English.

In the past, learning English as a second or foreign language generally involved adopting either RP or GA as a model, and there was an expectation for interlocutors to try to speak like a NS in order to be easily understood. In reality, however, as a large proportion of interactions in English in international settings nowadays do not involve a NS, imitation of NS English is increasingly regarded as inappropriate. This is not just because many NNS do not want to sound like someone from the UK or the USA, but also because some features of NS pronunciation fail to enhance the intelligibility of speech in international contexts (Smith & Nelson, 1985). In an early study on the intelligibility of NNS and NS English spoken by people from nine countries (Hong Kong, India, Japan, Korea, Malaysia, Nepal, the Philippines, Sri Lanka and the USA), ratings show that the NS from the USA was judged to be one of the least intelligible speakers by listeners from Bangladesh, China, Hong Kong, India, Indonesia, Japan, Korea, Malaysia, Nepal, the Philippines and Thailand (Smith & Rafiqzad, 1979). It was thus concluded that NS pronunciation is not necessarily more intelligible than that of NNS varieties.

Smith and Nelson (1985, p. 333) also note that it is important to consider the listener's expectations of the speaker in influencing their perception of how intelligible the speaker is. In fact, the listeners' negative attitudes and low expectations of speakers can influence their perception of the pronunciation of the speakers as incomprehensible (Derwing, Rossiter & Munro, 2002; Munro, Derwing & Morton, 2006). For example, Lindemann (2010) looked at ratings by native US English speakers about the intelligibility of non-native Korean-accented English, and the results show that those who had a negative attitude towards the non-native speakers beforehand rated their interactions as 'unsuccessful' even though most of them actually were successful.

Many NNS varieties of English have distinctive ways of pronouncing words that are different from NS varieties. For example, the first syllable of words such as <advance> and <concern> tends to have a reduced vowel in most NS accents, but many speakers of new varieties of English use a full vowel instead. Similarly, in much of South East Asia, <salmon> is pronounced with an /l/, so, when talking to people in the region, pronouncing the word as [sælmɒn] is probably more intelligible than the standard pronunciation (Deterding, 2013, p. 73). This illustrates how new styles of pronunciation are becoming increasingly acceptable, though it must be acknowledged that many challenges remain. These challenges and the implications for pedagogy will be discussed in the following sections.

In this chapter, the term 'new pronunciation' is used to refer to the speech of new varieties of English, and it is often quite distinct from NS speech. When it is used for communication between people with different first language backgrounds, it can be considered as ELF pronunciation. According to Kirkpatrick (2010, p. 80), discussion of distinctive pronunciation features of varieties of English or of ELF must address the extent to which their features affect intelligibility, as ensuring mutual intelligibility across linguistic and cultural boundaries is essential. This chapter therefore discusses the impact of new pronunciation on intelligibility, focusing on conversations between speakers of Brunei English (the variety of English spoken in Brunei, a small country located in the north of the island of Borneo in South East Asia) and NNS speakers from elsewhere.

Current contributions and research

This section provides a case study to illustrate new pronunciation in ELF interactions, focusing in particular on the impact of certain features of new pronunciation on intelligibility. Data analysis is based on recorded conversations between speakers of Brunei English with people from elsewhere, to provide insights into new pronunciation in naturally occurring speech. Because of the extensive range of pronunciation features in conversational speech, the analysis will focus only on polysyllabic words, considering just the following features: spelling pronunciation; vowel reduction; stress placement; yod-dropping (omission of the palatal approximant /j/ in words such as <museum>); and the distinction between nouns and verbs.

Research methodology

The corpus used in this case study consists of 10 audio recordings collected at Universiti Brunei Darussalam (UBD) in Brunei over a period of six months in late 2013 and early 2014. Each recording consists of a conversation in English between two participants, a Bruneian and a non-Bruneian, who do not share the same L1. Seventeen participants took part in the study, eight Bruneians and nine non-Bruneians, and they are identified by their gender (F or M), followed by a two-letter code representing their country of origin.

The Bruneians are identified as FBr1, FBr2, FBr3, FBr4, FBr5, MBr1, MBr2, and MBr3. Of the non-Bruneian participants, four are from China (FCh1, FCh2, FCh3, FCh4), one from Korea (MKo), one from France (MFr), one from the Maldives (FMd), one from Oman (FOm), and one from Vietnam (FVn). Sixteen of the participants were students at UBD and one, MFr, was a visiting researcher at the university. All of them listed English as either their second or foreign language, and when asked to rate their fluency and proficiency in English they gave a range from 'very good' to 'fair'. Brunei English can be categorized under Kachru's outer circle, and all the non-Bruneians represent speakers from expanding circle

Table 13.1 Recordings

Code	Interviewee	Interviewer	Duration (min:sec)
MBr2+FCh1	MBr2	FCh1	20:48
FBr3+FCh2	FBr3	FCh2	22:46
FBr4+FCh3	FBr4	FCh3	20:56
FBr5+FCh4	FBr5	FCh4	20:27
MBr3+MFr	MBr3	MFr	22:28
MBr3+MKo	MBr3	MKo	21:04
FBr1+FMd	FBr1	FMd	21:45
MBr1+FMd	MBr1	FMd	21:31
MBr1+FOm	MBr1	FOm	22:29
FBr2+FVn	FBr2	FVn	25:12
		Total	3:39:26

countries. Although Jenkins, Cogo and Dewey (2011) have acknowledged that NS may be included in ELF data, this study does not include any speakers from the inner circle, as it seeks to gain insights into NNS–NNS interactions. It is believed that NNS tend to feel more comfortable speaking with other NNS, as they can speak naturally without fear of criticism by a NS. The participants were also selected partly because they were all able to meet the researchers to help clarify any speech that was unclear and give feedback about misunderstandings.

In the recordings, the Bruneian participants were being interviewed by the non-Bruneians, who mainly asked questions about the culture and history of Brunei. Altogether, the 10 recordings last just over 3 hours and 39 minutes, with each recording lasting an average of about 22 minutes, ranging from just under 21 minutes to a little over 25 minutes. Details are shown in Table 13.1. Most participants participated in one recording, except for three participants who took part in two separate recordings: MBr3 in MBr3+MFr and MBr3+MKo; FMd in FBr1+FMd and MBr1+FMd; and MBr1 in MBr1+FMd and MBr1+FOm.

The recordings were conducted in a quiet room at UBD, using a Handy H4n recorder, and they were saved in WAV format. When transcribing the conversations, any problems involving unclear speech were resolved by asking the participants for clarification. Indeed, Deterding (2013, p. 25) notes that it is important to be able to obtain feedback from participants, because it allows researchers to correct transcription that is uncertain, and it also facilitates the identification of occurrences of misunderstandings that are not signalled in the recordings. In fact, the majority of misunderstandings in ELF communication do not result in any obvious communication breakdown, as speakers in ELF interactions have a tendency to adopt a 'let-it-pass' strategy in the hope that failure to understand a few words will not matter in the long run (Firth, 1996; Mortensen, 2013, p. 35).

When considering new pronunciation in polysyllabic words, it is important to investigate whether they are intelligible or not. In obtaining feedback from the participants, instances were identified where misunderstandings might have occurred by selecting short extracts from the recordings, playing them to the participants and asking them to transcribe what they heard. This dictation task is one of the most common methods of assessing intelligibility of speech (Munro et al., 2006, p. 112). However, although this method is reported to be reliable in assessing objective intelligibility, a disadvantage of the methodology is that it does not take

Table 13.2 Tokens of polysyllabic words (121) involving new pronunciation

Classification	Total	Per cent
Spelling pronunciation	72	58.7
No vowel reduction	61	50.4
Stress placement	36	29.8
No yod	13	10.7
Noun/verb distinction	4	3.3

into account the context of the situation, and that understanding individual words does not always indicate a general understanding (Osimk, 2011, p. 66). Furthermore, it must be admitted that it is not possible to be certain that a misunderstanding actually occurred in all instances based on this kind of subsequent feedback. Nonetheless, it provides useful insights about the listeners' comprehension (Munro et al., 2006, p. 113).

The term 'token' is used to refer to a polysyllabic word involving new pronunciation. A total of 121 tokens of polysyllabic words involving innovative pronunciation have been identified from the corpus of a total of 48,727 words. In cases where a speaker repeated a word, only one token is counted; in cases below in which two tokens are listed (e.g. <separate>), they involve different speakers.

The tokens are classified in terms of the pronunciation features: spelling pronunciation, vowel reduction, stress placement, no yod, and lack of distinction between nouns and verbs. The frequency of the classified tokens is summarized in Table 13.2. Many of the tokens involve cross-classification, so the percentages add up to more than 100 per cent. It can be seen that most of the tokens involve spelling pronunciation followed by no vowel reduction.

Of the 121 tokens involving new pronunciation of polysyllabic words, only five were misunderstood by the listeners. These five tokens are included in the total of 152 instances of misunderstanding that have been identified in the corpus, many of which arose from other features of pronunciation and use of unfamiliar lexis. Two of the instances of misunderstandings were evident from the recordings, as the listeners signalled a misunderstanding by asking for clarification, but the other three were identified from the transcription by the listeners in which words or phrases were transcribed inaccurately, and also from the listeners' feedback.

It is important to note that although the linguistic features that may have contributed to the problems can be suggested, the real cause of the misunderstandings cannot be determined with certainty. Indeed, Pitzl, Breiteneder and Klimpfinger (2008) note that it is often hard to determine what the precise cause of a misunderstanding is, and multiple factors are regularly implicated. This study will only look at the 121 tokens, including the five tokens that are misunderstood, and it will not consider the rest of the tokens of misunderstanding as they do not involve new pronunciation of polysyllabic words under the categories identified.

Data analysis

The analysis of the tokens presented in this study will provide one or two examples to illustrate each category. They are presented in separate subsections based on their classification. Brief discussions of the five instances of misunderstanding and their possible causes will also follow, to show how new pronunciation can sometimes cause problems in an international setting.

Spelling pronunciation

One way in which language undergoes change is a shift in the pronunciation of a word to reflect its spelling (Algeo, 2005, p. 46). For instance, the word <forehead> was once pronounced as [fɒrɪd] but nowadays it is increasingly pronounced with /h/ in the middle, reflecting its spelling and also its etymology, and Wells (2008, p. 317) reports that 65 per cent of people in Britain prefer the latter pronunciation, including 80 per cent of younger speakers, indicating that use of /h/ is becoming the norm. Similarly, although <often> is usually pronounced as [ɒfən] without /t/, Wells (2008, p. 560) shows that some speakers in both Britain and America now prefer a pronunciation with /t/. These examples reflect a changing trend in NS varieties, but spelling pronunciation is even more common in new varieties of English around the world. Deterding and Salbrina (2013, p. 42) report that the pronunciation of <salmon> with /l/ is widespread in South East Asia and it seems to be more intelligible in the region than the standard pronunciation without /l/. However, Wells (2008, p. 708) does not list a variant with /l/, even with a symbol to suggest it is a pronunciation that is considered incorrect.

In the corpus in the current case study, 72 out of the 121 tokens of new pronunciation for polysyllabic words involve spelling pronunciation. In one example, MBr1 produced the first syllable of <comfortable> with /ɒ/ rather than the expected /ʌ/, and in another example, FVn pronounced <usually> with /z/ rather than /ʒ/. There is no indication by the listeners, FOm and FBr2, that either of these tokens caused a problem for understanding.

However, two tokens were found where spelling pronunciation may have played a part in a misunderstanding. In the first instance, MBr1 pronounced the word <turrets> with /ʊ/ in the first syllable, probably influenced by its spelling, and also maybe reflecting the pronunciation of his first language, Malay, in which 'u' is always pronounced as /u/. However, although subsequent feedback from FMd indicated that she did not understand the word, she told the authors that she was not familiar with <turrets>, so even if MBr1 had said it as ['tʌrɪts], she still would not have understood him. Although <turrets> seems to be a low-frequency word, it is listed as occurring 393 times in the online Corpus of Contemporary American English (COCA, 2016). The main cause of the misunderstanding is therefore actually lexical, and the conclusion should be that pronunciation only played a secondary role.

In the second instance, MBr3 pronounced the word <counsellor> with /ɒ/ in the first syllable rather than with the expected /aʊ/. This caused a misunderstanding that MKo signalled by repeating the first syllable [kɒn] with a rising tone, seeking clarification. Perhaps MBr3's pronunciation is influenced by the letter 'o' in the spelling after the initial consonant, though this remains uncertain as 'ou' is only pronounced as /ɒ/ in a few words of English such as <cough>, <trough> and <Gloucester> (Cruttenden, 2014, p. 126).

In his investigation of misunderstandings in ELF interactions in South East Asia, Deterding (2013, p. 74) reported that four out of 183 tokens of misunderstandings involved spelling pronunciation. However, he concluded that two of the tokens, <Berlitz> and <niche>, involved unfamiliar lexis, and spelling pronunciation probably played a major part in causing the misunderstanding for just the other two, <tubers> pronounced as [tʌbʊs] and <virgin> pronounced as [vɪədʒɪn]. His findings therefore confirm that spelling pronunciation can be problematic, but only occasionally.

Overall, most of the tokens in this study involving spelling pronunciation did not seem to cause any problems in intelligibility in ELF communication. The examples therefore illustrate spelling pronunciation as a feature of New Englishes, and some examples may become standard in all accents, just as spelling is influencing the pronunciation of <forehead> and <often> in Britain and America and <salmon> with /l/ is widespread throughout the world.

Absence of vowel reduction

In standard English, vowels are commonly reduced to schwa when they occur in weak forms of function words and the unstressed syllables of polysyllabic words. However, it has been reported that there is a lack of vowel reduction in many new varieties of English (Deterding, 2010). According to Kirkpatrick (2010, p. 79), the absence of vowel reduction is presumably influenced by many Asian and African languages that have syllable-based rhythm, because when English is produced with syllable-based rhythm there tends to be equal prominence on each syllable, and this leads to a lack of reduced vowels. In contrast, most NS varieties of English have stress-based rhythm, so there is an alternation between prominent syllables with a full vowel and unstressed syllables that often have a reduced vowel such as a schwa.

In the corpus of the current study, 61 tokens of polysyllabic words were found in which there is no vowel reduction where a reduced vowel such as a schwa would be expected in traditional varieties of English. Some examples include the use of /ɒ/ in the first syllable of <polite> by FOm, and the occurrence of /ʌ/ in the first syllable of <sustains> by FBr5.

Just two tokens were misunderstood, <Atlantis> and <police>. <Atlantis> was pronounced with a full vowel at the start by MBr1, and FOm heard it as <Atlantic City>. However, it turns out that she did not know about the mythical underwater city of Atlantis, so this token should be classified as a lexical issue, and the lack of vowel reduction played no part in the misunderstanding. The pronunciation of <police> by FBr4 with a full vowel in the first syllable will be discussed in the section on stress placement.

The conclusion that the absence of vowel reduction in new pronunciations rarely causes a problem is consistent with the findings of Deterding (2013, p. 71), who found just two tokens out of 183 that may have been caused by lack of vowel reduction: <attend> and <agenda>, both of which had a full vowel in the first syllable.

Stress placement

There are two kinds of stress: word stress, or the syllables in a polysyllabic word that receive most prominence; and utterance stress, which refers to placement of the intonational nucleus within an utterance. This section will only look at word stress since the focus is on polysyllabic words.

Because the rhythm of many new varieties of English has been described as syllable-based, many of them have unpredictable word stress or no clear stress placement. Thirty-six tokens with unexpected stress were identified. For example, FBr1 pronounced <chaotic> as [ˈkæɒtɪk], even though stress would be on the second syllable in RP or GA (Wells, 2008, p. 137); and FMd produced <challenging> with even stress on all three syllables. There is no indication that these tokens were misunderstood.

However, two instances of misunderstanding were identified that may have involved stress placement. In the first, FBr4 said <police> as [ˈpɒlɪs] with stress on the first syllable instead of the expected [pəˈliːs] (Wells, 2008, p. 624), and FCh3 subsequently stated in her feedback that she heard <policy>, a word that does have initial stress. In addition to the unexpected stress, one might note the use of a full vowel rather than a schwa in the first syllable, so this token can be classified under lack of vowel reduction as well as shifted stress. In the second instance of misunderstanding, FCh3 produced <business> with even stress in both syllables instead of the expected [ˈbɪznəs] (Wells, 2008, p. 112), and FBr4 signalled that she did not understand the word by repeating the first syllable, apparently seeking clarification. Although it is probable that unusual stress may be the main cause of the misunderstanding in <police>, it remains uncertain whether the even stress on <business> was the cause of the problem. Perhaps this was just a case of unclear speech.

Overall, a misunderstanding was found in just these two out of the 36 tokens involving stress placement, so it is suggested that unusual word stress is not an important feature for mutual intelligibility in new pronunciation. This concurs with the proposal of Jenkins (2009, p. 148) that word stress be excluded from the LFC, as it rarely causes misunderstandings in ELF settings. Deterding (2013, p. 76) further suggests that word stress placement may only be important with native speaker listeners.

Yod-dropping

Yod-dropping involves the omission of /j/ after a consonant, something which typically occurs in American English after the alveolar consonants /t, d, n/. For example, <new> is pronounced as [njuː] in RP British English, but Wells (2008, p. 538) reports that 86 per cent of Americans prefer the pronunciation [nuː]. Similarly, in America, <tune> is generally pronounced as [tuːn], but in this case a shift seems to be taking place in British English, as older speakers prefer [tjuːn] while younger speakers tend to opt for [tʃuːn] (Wells, 2008, p. 845). This combination of /t/+/j/ to result in /tʃ/ can be described as coalescence (Wells & Colson, 1971, p. 55).

Thirteen tokens in the current study involve yod-dropping with no coalescence. Some examples include <articulated> pronounced as [ʌrtɪkʊleɪtəd] by MBr1, in which /j/ is omitted from the third syllable, and <museum> with no /j/ after the initial /m/ by FBr3. In both these examples, /j/ would be expected in both RP and GA. None of the 13 tokens was misunderstood.

Historical coalescence mostly involves the pronunciation of the affricates /tʃ/ and /dʒ/ in words spelled with 'tu' as in <actual>, 'ti' as in <question>, or 'du' as in <gradual>, and occasionally also 'di' as in <soldier> (Cruttenden, 2014, p. 190). Several tokens in the current study exhibit neither yod nor coalescence after /t/ and /d/, including <situate> and <graduate> with /t/ and /d/ respectively and no following /j/. In these words, /tʃ/ and /dʒ/ would occur in American English, though Wells (2008, p. 745) notes that pronunciation of <situation> with medial /t/ and no /j/ occurs in 'BrE non-RP' pronunciation in Britain (which he indicates using the symbol §), and it was the preferred pronunciation of 1 per cent of his respondents. In the current study, there were three tokens involving /t/ and no following /j/: <situation> (two tokens) and <situated>; and there were six tokens involving /d/: <graduate>, <graduating>, <graduated> (two tokens), <educated> and <educational>.

It is possible that omission of yod could be a feature of Brunei English. However, it does not seem to have much impact on intelligibility. In addition, one may note that the spelling of the words may have an influence on the way they were pronounced, and for this reason they might also be classified under spelling pronunciation.

Noun/verb distinction

In native speaker Englishes, some words with the same spelling involve pronunciation differences to distinguish whether they function as verbs or as nouns or adjectives (Cruttenden, 2014, p. 253). In many words, the verb is distinct from the noun and/or adjective based on the location of stress, so when <digest> functions as a noun, stress falls on the first syllable, but when it is a verb stress is on the second syllable. In other cases, only the quality of a vowel is affected, so <graduate> is a verb if it ends with [eɪt] but a noun if it ends with [ət].

It seems that there is a tendency of failing to distinguish verbs from nouns and adjectives in this way in some new pronunciations. In one token in the current study, MFr used the noun <rebel>, but instead of the expected ['rebəl], he pronounced it as [rɪ'bel], which would be the verb form in standard pronunciation (Wells, 2008, p. 671). However, MBr3 understood him with no problem. In another token, FMd used the word <separate> as an adjective, but instead of the expected ['sepərət] she said ['sepəreɪt], which is the standard pronunciation for the verb form. This token also did not cause any misunderstanding. In total, four tokens were included in this category: <rebel>, <graduate> and <separate> (two tokens).

One can therefore suggest that these few instances of lack of a distinction in pronunciation to indicate word classes do not seem to cause a problem in an ELF setting. One could investigate whether it might be more likely to cause misunderstandings in conversations with NS.

Misunderstandings

In total, there were five instances of misunderstanding in the tokens analysed in the current study: <turrets>, <Atlantis>, <police>, <counsellor> and <business>. The first two of these should actually be classified as lexical, as the listeners did not know the words. <police> misunderstood as <policy> was probably caused by the unexpected stress on the first syllable as well as lack of vowel reduction. For <counsellor>, the occurrence of /ɒ/ in the first syllable seems to have been the problem. And for <business>, it is unclear what the problem was, but uncertain stress placement might have been an issue. The conclusion is therefore that spelling pronunciation, lack of vowel reduction, unexpected stress placement, absence of /j/, and failure to distinguish nouns and adjectives from verbs are rarely problematic in new pronunciations in ELF interactions between NNS speakers.

Recommendations for practice

This case study has investigated some features of new pronunciation in cross-cultural interactions, specifically those that occur in polysyllabic words, and it seems that these features are generally not problematic for intelligibility, though there were a few exceptions. It is acknowledged that general conclusions cannot be made based on the analysis of only a few features of ELF speech, but it does seem that at least some aspects of distinctive new pronunciations do not generally result in communication breakdown in international settings. In fact, one could argue that avoiding vowel reduction can in many cases enhance intelligibility, as for example <vacation> with a full vowel in the first syllable would never be misheard as <vocation>; and speakers who have a full vowel in the auxiliary <have> would never write 'could of' instead of 'could have', an error that is rather common among NS writers. Furthermore, <computer> and <consider> with a full vowel in the first syllable seem to be the preferred pronunciation in many parts of the world, and if this enhances intelligibility in an international setting, there seems little reason for teachers to seek to discourage it.

When discussing the use of English in cross-cultural communication, there seems to be an assumption that a NS is likely to be more intelligible than an NNS, however well-educated the latter might be, even though research has shown that this is not necessarily true (Smith & Rafiqzad, 1979). If NS are not more intelligible than NNS, this raises fundamental questions about the continued use of NS styles of speech as the model for learners of English as a second or foreign language.

Another key issue involves teachability, as it is unrealistic to expect all learners to develop perfect NS pronunciation (Walker, 2010, p. 20). Indeed, attainment of native speaker pronunciation is not possible for the overwhelming majority of ESL and EFL learners, especially those who learn the language in adolescence or adulthood (Moyer, 1999; Derwing & Munro, 2005; Levis, 2005; Ortega, 2009), and so there seems to be little reason to try and insist on it. If learners are set unattainable goals, this can be highly demotivating, and it should therefore be avoided (Murphy, 2014).

As a consequence, it is questionable whether continued use of NS standards is appropriate. Because speakers in the international speech community come from different language backgrounds, most of them speak with their own accents, and these new ways of speaking are gradually gaining acceptance. Furthermore, the goal of teaching pronunciation should be to achieve intelligibility while at the same time retaining the identities of the speakers through their distinctive accents (Brown, 1991, p. 41), and in the future teaching is likely to focus more on enhancing intelligibility than adhering to irrelevant NS norms (Munro, 2008, p. 213).

In order to achieve intelligibility in international settings, some people have proposed that there should be a single universal standard that can be shared by all speech communities. In fact, Crystal (2003, p. 185) suggests that a single standard he terms World Standard Spoken English (WSSE) might arise to cater for the demands of international communication. However, such proposals for WSSE do not seem to have been widely accepted internationally. In contrast, ELF-based teaching envisages substantial diversity in pronunciation, reflecting the varying backgrounds of the speakers, rather than a single standard.

Instead of promoting a single standard, we should focus more on what is required in order to achieve intelligibility in international situations, and Jenkins (2000) has laid the foundation for this with her LFC, particularly for ELF speakers who do not necessarily want to sound like a native speaker. Adopting an ELF approach for pronunciation teaching has many benefits, as outlined by Walker (2010, pp. 61–69):

(a) It lightens the workload for both teachers and learners because the pronunciation syllabus for ELF does not include features of speech such as vowel reduction and word stress that are excluded from the LFC.

(b) It generates a sense of achievement for ELF learners who are able to gain new skills such as accommodating to the speech of their interlocutors and dealing with accent variation.

(c) It allows NNS to retain their own accents and take pride in their national or linguistic identities while at the same time they become highly intelligible.

(d) It accepts the influence of the learner's first language as a positive feature, for example in allowing teachers to use the pronunciation of the learner's first language to help them attain a good command of the LFC features.

(e) It acknowledges that NNS are often the best instructors for ELF teaching because they provide an excellent example of the kind of internationally intelligible accent that their learners aspire to, and because they share a common learning experience with their pupils, which allows them to empathize with them and help them overcome their problems.

Although it makes sense to allow some NNS features in the teaching of pronunciation in an ELF setting, this concept has yet to be accepted by the majority of teachers and education policymakers, so there are still many challenges to face. Indeed, there have been concerns about adopting a new model that is not based on clearly defined standards, and there is also a worry that the use of new models will lead to an increased diversity of NNS varieties of English that might result in speakers being unintelligible to listeners from elsewhere. Walker

(2010, pp. 51–52) adds that there have also been concerns that an ELF approach will lower standards if what are perceived to be errors in native speech are regarded as acceptable.

Furthermore, there is a lack of reference materials for the newly emergent styles of speech. Indeed, Firth (2009) questions whether ELF can be codified, and he contests this on two bases: first, he suggests that there is too much variability in ELF, both linguistically and pragmatically, as ELF interactions demand a wide range of conventions in phonology, grammar, lexical range and pragmatics to suit the proficiency of interactants in diverse interactional settings; and, second, he argues that there are no established theoretical foundations for ELF, as scholars are still exploring its concepts and pedagogical implications. Svartvik and Leech (2006, p. 234) suggest that it will take a long time to overcome the widespread preference for standard native speaker norms, especially in pedagogy, and they question if the concept of ELF will ever gain general acceptance.

Although it has been suggested that the main aim of learning English as a second or foreign language should be for NNS to achieve maximum intelligibility in international communication, one must also accept that some learners have other motivations for trying to achieve NS proficiency, including gaining respect when engaging in international forums. Furthermore, there are also some learners, such as people working in the burgeoning call centre industry in the Philippines and in India, who need to sound like native speakers, and for them new styles of pronunciation are not advisable even when they are highly intelligible. The conclusion should be that ELF-based teaching is only appropriate in some language teaching contexts, and teachers and educational planners should always assess the needs of their pupils.

Future directions

Despite NS varieties still being preferred in most teaching contexts, new styles of pronunciation will continue to emerge, allowing speakers to emphasize their distinctive identity while at the same time endeavouring to maintain intelligibility for listeners from elsewhere. And it seems likely that ELF-based teaching will become increasingly accepted in the future as teachers focus on ensuring that their students achieve intelligible pronunciation while not worrying too much whether they sound like native speakers or not. However, it is unlikely that dependence on traditional NS norms will disappear in the immediate future.

Further research on misunderstandings is needed to establish more clearly which aspects of pronunciation are key to maintaining international intelligibility; and, when the outcome of this research becomes widely disseminated, perhaps the argument for accepting new styles of pronunciation will be accepted by more teachers. One possibility with the development of new pronunciations is that speakers in many parts of the world may adopt shared features that serve to enhance the intelligibility of their speech, regardless of what native speakers do. For example, if the majority of speakers in the outer and expanding circles tend to avoid vowel reduction in the unstressed syllables of polysyllabic words and they find that this makes them more intelligible in international contexts, perhaps this will emerge as the de facto standard for world English. It will then be NS who find that others cannot understand them, and new pronunciations will truly have emerged from continued domination by the traditional inner circle standards.

Further reading

Crystal, D. (2003). *English as a global language* (2nd ed.). Cambridge: Cambridge University Press. This book discusses the global status and role of English and predicts some of its future directions.

Jenkins, J. (2000). *The phonology of English as an international language*. Oxford: Oxford University Press. This seminal work introduced the LFC and explained the rationale behind it.

Jenkins, J. (2009). *World Englishes: A resource book for students* (2nd ed.). London: Routledge. This book outlines some key topics for world Englishes from their historical contexts and development up to their present status, and it introduces students to the concept of ELF. It also discusses current debates in world Englishes and provides examples of emerging varieties of New Englishes.

Schneider, E. W. (2007). *Postcolonial English: Varieties around the world*. Cambridge: Cambridge University Press. This book gives a detailed account of how New Englishes emerged and explains the processes involved in their development.

Walker, R. (2010). *Teaching the pronunciation of English as a lingua franca*. Oxford: Oxford University Press. This book provides welcome guidelines to teachers on ways to teach ELF pronunciation based on the LFC. It additionally describes how the learner's L1 can benefit from the ELF pronunciation approach in the classroom.

Related topics

Pronunciation teaching; world Englishes; intelligibility; English as a lingua franca (ELF); the lingua franca core (LFC)

References

Algeo, J. (2005). *The origins and development of the English language* (6th ed.). Boston, MA: Wadsworth Cengage.

Baugh, A. C., & Cable, T. (2002). *A history of the English language* (5th ed.). Upper Saddle River, NJ: Prentice Hall.

Beal, J. (2012). A national language. In P. Seargeant & J. Swann (Eds), *English in the world: History, diversity, change* (pp. 49–99). Abingdon: Routledge.

Brown, A. (1991). *Pronunciation models*. Singapore: Singapore University Press.

Butler, S. (2002). Language, literature and culture – and their meeting place in the dictionary. In A. Kirkpatrick (Ed.), *Englishes in Asia: Communication, identity, power & identity* (pp. 143–167). Melbourne: Language Australia.

COCA (2016). Corpus of Contemporary American English. Retrieved from http://corpus.byu.edu/coca (accessed 1 July 2016).

Cruttenden, A. (2014). *Gimson's pronunciation of English* (8th ed.). London: Routledge.

Crystal, D. (2003). *English as a global language* (2nd ed.). Cambridge: Cambridge University Press.

Derwing, T. M., Rossiter, M. J., & Munro, M. J. (2002). Teaching native speakers to listen to foreign-accented speech. *Journal of Multilingual and Multicultural Development, 23*, 245–259.

Derwing, T. M., & Munro, M. J. (2005). Second language accent and pronunciation teaching: A research-based approach. *TESOL Quarterly, 39*, 379–397.

Deterding, D. (2010). Variation across Englishes: Phonology. In A. Kirkpatrick (Ed.), *The Routledge handbook of world Englishes* (pp. 385–399). London: Routledge.

Deterding, D. (2013). *Misunderstandings in English as a lingua franca: An analysis of ELF interactions in South-East Asia*. Berlin: De Gruyter.

Deterding, D., & Kirkpatrick, A. (2006). Emerging South-East Asian Englishes and intelligibility. *World Englishes, 25*(3/4), 391–409.

Deterding, D., & Salbrina S. (2013). *Brunei English: A new variety in a multilingual society*. Dordrecht: Springer.

Deverson, T. (1999). Handling New Zealand English lexis. In A. Bell & K. Kuiper (Eds), *New Zealand English* (pp. 23–39). Amsterdam: John Benjamins.

Fennell, B. A. (2001). *A history of English: A sociolinguistic approach*. Oxford: Blackwell.

Firth, A. (1996). The discursive accomplishment of normality: On 'lingua franca' English and conversational analysis. *Journal of Pragmatics, 26*, 237–259.

Firth, A. (2009). The *lingua franca* factor. *Intercultural Pragmatics, 6*(2), 147–170.

Gramley, S., & Pätzold, K-M. (2004). *A survey of modern English* (2nd ed.). London: Routledge.

Gupta, A. F. (2006). Standard English in the world. In R. Rubdy & M. Saraceni (Eds), *English in the world: Global rules, global roles* (pp. 95–109). London: Continuum.

Hickey, R. (2014). *A dictionary of varieties of English*. Malden MA: Wiley Blackwell.

Jenkins, J. (2000). *The phonology of English as an international language*. Oxford: Oxford University Press.

Jenkins, J. (2007). *English as a lingua franca: Attitude and identity*. Oxford: Oxford University Press.

Jenkins, J. (2009). *World Englishes: A resource book for students* (2nd ed.). London: Routledge.

Jenkins, J., Cogo, A., & Dewey, M. (2011). Review of developments in research into English as lingua franca. *Language Teaching, 44*(3), 281–315.

Jones, D., Roach, P., Hartman, J., & Setter, J. (2003). *Cambridge English pronouncing dictionary* (16th ed.). Cambridge: Cambridge University Press.

Kachru, B. B. (1992). Teaching world Englishes. In B. B. Kachru (Ed.). *The other tongue: English across cultures* (2nd ed.) (pp. 355–365). Chicago, IL: University of Illinois Press.

Kirkpatrick, A. (2010). *English as a lingua franca in ASEAN: A multilingual model*. Hong Kong: Hong Kong University Press.

Kirkpatrick, A., & Deterding, D. (2011). World Englishes. In J. Simpson (Ed.), *The Routledge handbook of applied linguistics* (pp. 373–387). London: Routledge.

Levis, J. M. (2005). Changing contexts and shifting paradigms in pronunciation teaching. *TESOL Quarterly, 39*, 369–378.

Lindemann, S. (2010). Who's 'unintelligible'? The perceiver's role. *Issues in Applied Linguistics, 18*(2), 223–232.

Mortensen, J. (2013). Notes on English used as a lingua franca as an object of study. *Journal of English as a Lingua Franca, 2*(1), 25–46.

Moyer, A. (1999). Ultimate attainment in L2 phonology: The critical factors of age, motivation and instruction. *Studies in Second Language Acquisition, 21*, 81–108.

Mugglestone, L. (2003). *Talking proper: The rise of accent as social symbol* (2nd ed.). Oxford: Oxford University Press.

Munro, M. J. (2008). Foreign accent and speech intelligibility. In J. Hansen Edwards & M. Zampini (Eds), *Phonology and second language acquisition* (pp. 193–218). Amsterdam: John Benjamins.

Munro, M. J., Derwing, T. M., & Morton, S. L. (2006). The mutual intelligibility of L2 speech. *Studies in Second Language Acquisition, 28*, 111–131.

Murphy, J. M. (2014). Intelligible, comprehensible, non-native models in ESL/EFL pronunciation teaching. *System, 42*, 258–269.

Ortega, L. (2009). *Understanding second language acquisition*. London: Hodder Arnold.

Osimk, R. (2011). Decoding sounds: An experimental approach to intelligibility in ELF. *Vienna English Working Papers, 18*(1), 64–89.

Pakir, A. (2001). English as a cross-cultural lingua franca: Multiforms, multimedia, multidisciplines. In E. Thumboo (Ed.), *The three circles of English: Language specialists talk about the English language* (pp. 77–90). Singapore: UniPress.

Pitzl, M., Breiteneder, A., & Klimpfinger, T. (2008). A world of words: Processes of lexical innovation in VOICE. *Vienna English Working Papers, 17*(2), 21–46.

Schneider, E. W. (2007). *Postcolonial English: Varieties around the world*. Cambridge: Cambridge University Press.

Schneider, E. W. (2011). *English around the world: An introduction*. Cambridge: Cambridge University Press.

Seidlhofer, B. (2011). *Understanding English as a lingua franca*. Oxford: Oxford University Press.

Smith, L. E., & Nelson, C. L. (1985). International intelligibility of English: Directions and resources. *World Englishes, 4*(3), 333–342.

Smith, L. E., & Rafiqzad, K. (1979). English for cross-cultural communication: The question of intelligibility. *TESOL Quarterly, 13*(3), 371–380.

Svartvik, J., & Leech, G. (2006). *English: One tongue, many voices*. London: Palgrave Macmillan.

Trudgill, P. (1999). Standard English: what it isn't. In T. Bex & R. Watts (Eds), *Standard English: The widening debate* (pp. 117–128). London: Routledge.

Walker, R. (2010). *Teaching the pronunciation of English as a lingua franca*. Oxford: Oxford University Press.

Wells, J. C. (2008). *Longman pronunciation dictionary* (3rd ed.). Harlow: Pearson Education.

Wells, J. C., & Colson, G. (1971). *Practical phonetics*. London: Pitman.

14

Instructional models in the global context

Jolanta Szpyra-Kozłowska

Introduction

The global expansion of English in the last decades and its undeniable status as a lingua franca of the contemporary world have led many scholars and practitioners to question not only the traditional goal of pronunciation teaching, i.e. attaining native-like pronunciation (a shift away from the so-called 'nativeness principle' to the 'intelligibility principle'; see Levis 2005), but also the appropriateness of adopting native English speaker models in teaching this language to millions of its international learners. This means that many core assumptions of pronunciation instruction have been challenged as no longer adequate and in need of urgent revision, as evidenced by a heated debate in many publications (e.g. papers in Dziubalska-Kołaczyk and Przedlacka's 2005 volume; Dauer 2005; Szpyra-Kozłowska 2015).

The spread and the use of English in the world is often discussed in reference to Kachru's (1986) well-known model of concentric circles, with the inner circle representing those areas where English is spoken as a native language (e.g. the British Isles, the United States, Canada, Australia and New Zealand); the outer circle comprising post-colonial countries, such as India and parts of Africa and Asia, where English has an official or semi-official status and is used in education, administration, business and politics; and expanding circle countries such as Japan, Brazil or Spain, where English is learned as a foreign language.

For years such differences in the use of English across regions have considerably influenced the type of English pronunciation adopted for teaching and learning purposes. Thus, immigrants who settled in an inner circle country were usually assumed to aspire to the accent of their hosts. In the outer circle some firmly established local models of English, such as Indian English in India or Nigerian English in Nigeria (i.e. the so-called New Englishes) have been employed in teaching, along with native pronunciation models, predominantly those of the former colonial empire. In the expanding circle, native models, usually received pronunciation (RP) or North American English (NAE), have been adopted. Other varieties, for example Australian English or South African English, have also served as accent models in the regions where they are spoken. Nevertheless, RP and NAE have undoubtedly dominated the English teaching scene worldwide.

After years of relative stability in the area of English pronunciation teaching and instructional models, the beginning of the twenty-first century may be characterized as a period of theoretical debate and controversy. As argued by Levis (2005), pronunciation theory, research and practice are in transition and many widely accepted assumptions such as the supremacy of inner circle models, the primacy of suprasegmentals and the need for native English-speaking instructors have been challenged. These changes have been triggered by the growing realization that English, by becoming a global language, serves millions of non-native English speakers (NNESs) as a means of communication with other NNESs. Consequently, if native English speakers (NESs) are not involved in many international exchanges in English, the value of their linguistic and cultural norms as reference points may be questioned (Jenkins, 2000). Moreover, if we assume that what matters in international contexts is the mutual intelligibility of interlocutors, then achieving native-like pronunciation is unnecessary to attain this goal. Beginning with Abercrombie (1949), such reasoning has been voiced for a long time and many attempts have been made to devise a simplified pronunciation agenda for NNESs (e.g. Jenner, 1989; Cruttenden, 2008). Nevertheless, it was the publication of Jenkins's (2000) provocative study that revived contemporary attention to the pronunciation of English as a lingua franca (ELF). Her contributions have played a major role in challenging the appropriateness of NES models in English pronunciation pedagogy.

The present chapter addresses the issue of current English pronunciation models and the controversies that surround them by discussing strengths as well as limitations of competing proposals. First, four types of models suggested in the literature are presented and critically evaluated: native, nativized, non-native and multiple models. Next, I deal with theory/practice differences and connections before examining instructional models currently employed in the inner circle, outer circle and expanding circle of English language use.

Before discussing various instructional models for NNESs, it is necessary to clarify certain common misunderstandings connected with the very notion of a pronunciation model. Here we will define it as an (idealized) accent of English, an existing and codified phonetic variety, which can serve as a point of reference and guidance to teachers and learners as well as be used as an aspiration model by NNESs. This definition implies that a pronunciation model concerns both perception (as input) and production (output, i.e. learner's speech), and has some phonetic properties that are (or can be) codified and presented in course books, recordings and pronunciation dictionaries. The latter condition is necessary because both teachers and learners need appropriate materials upon which to base the teaching/learning process. I will further assume that in instructional settings a model is provided mainly by the recordings meant to be imitated (in typical 'listen-and-repeat' tasks) and the teacher whose pronunciation often serves as a primary model to which learners are exposed. A similar view is expressed, for instance, by Kelly (2000, 14), who regards the 'model' as 'the pronunciation characteristics of the language a teacher presents to learners in the classroom'.

Not all scholars subscribe to the above definition (although it is often not clear what definition they adopt), as seen in diversified uses of the term 'model'. A frequent confusion concerns instructional models and pronunciation priorities for learners. The former concept concerns a global accent and all its phonetic features, whereas the latter involves selecting some aspects of an accent (or several accents) and prioritizing them when teaching pronunciation. For example, in her discussion of ELF, Jenkins (2000) proposes the lingua franca core (LFC), which she characterizes as a set of instructional priorities meant to safeguard intelligibility between NNESs when NESs are not present, and not as a model since there is no accent of English that contains all and only LFC features. This characterization is explicitly stated by Jenkins (2000, 158), who maintains that 'the Lingua Franca Core is neither a pronunciation model nor a restricted, simplified core in the style of Quirk's Nuclear

English'. Jenkins's stance is corroborated by Walker (2010) in his discussion of appropriate accent models for ELF learners, which, in his view, can be provided either by NNESs or NESs who use the features specified in the LFC and can suppress those features that do not belong to the LFC (for a detailed analysis of ELF and the LFC as well as a discussion of problems involved in adopting this approach, see Szpyra-Kozłowska (2015)). Yet the LFC is often regarded incorrectly as an (artificial) pronunciation model (e.g. Dauer, 2005; Kirkpatrick, 2006). Similarly, other proposals of simplified English pronunciation, such as, for example, Cruttenden's (2008) Amalgam English and International English, constitute sets of pronunciation priorities for learners and are not intended as models for imitation or approximation.

Furthermore, the concept of a model is often confused with that of goals of pronunciation instruction. This confusion follows from a frequent conviction that the aim of pronunciation teaching/learning is to master all the phonetic features of a model accent, in which case the two notions overlap to a large extent. If we assume, however, that not all features of the model can be acquired (see below), this means that with one model different objectives may be pursued (e.g. achieving native-like pronunciation to communicate with NESs as in traditional instruction), or attaining comfortable intelligibility or basic intelligibility in communication with other speakers of English (as in more recent approaches). In other words, the selection of a pronunciation model does not determine the goal the learner might want to strive for. Rogerson-Revell (2011, p. 8) also maintains that

> there is a difference between the reference points or model we use for guidance in pronunciation teaching and learning and the target we set as an achievable goal or aim. The 'goal' is the level which a learner's pronunciation aims to reach in order to facilitate effective communication.

While different pronunciation models have been suggested, there seems to be a consensus that a clear, well-defined and consistent instructional model is needed for learners (Rogerson-Revell, 2011). As argued by Walker (2010, p. 53), 'without a stable model, learners will have nothing on which to base their attempts at pronunciation', which is 'an unacceptable situation'. It is evident, however, that no model is capable of fulfilling all learners' needs and expectations and that no single variety of English is well suited to serve such a purpose. There is also general agreement that for the purposes of comprehension learners should be exposed to a variety of accents in order to be able to understand other users of English (e.g. Rogerson-Revell, 2011; Thomson, 2012).

Types of instructional models

This section introduces four types of English pronunciation models proposed by various scholars, with most attention devoted to native speaker models, commonly used in English instruction around the world. We examine their major strengths and weaknesses, together with their potential functions within the global context.

Native models

Native speaker pronunciation models, the most obvious choice for NNESs for decades and traditionally used in English instruction worldwide, in recent years have been subject of much criticism and even rejection. Below we examine the most frequent arguments voiced against them as well as provide some, nowadays unfashionable, reasons for their continued use in pronunciation teaching.

The strongest criticism of employing NES accent models for purposes of English language instruction has been expressed by the proponents of ELF (e.g. Jenkins, 2000, 2006; Walker, 2010; Seidlhofer, 2011), who contrast the 'old' and 'outdated' English as a foreign language (EFL) approach with the 'new' and 'progressive' concept of ELF. They argue that native pronunciation models are both unrealistic and inappropriate for the majority of L2 learners since very few of them ever achieve native-like pronunciation (e.g. Levis, 2005; Moyer, 1999). From this perspective, setting unrealistic goals can lead to both teachers' and learners' frustration. Moreover, native accent models are claimed to be inappropriate for international learners who use English mainly in contacts with other NNESs, in which case native norms of correctness are irrelevant. What is needed is a form of English pronunciation that would be intelligible to its users, even if such a form differs from traditional standards. In many authentic contexts of English language use, what matters most is the effectiveness of communication and not strict adherence to native linguistic norms. Further, for many ELF supporters the very concept of native speakers and their accents has become outdated. According to Setter (2010, p. 449), 'it has become unfashionable to assert that RP or GenAm [General American, i.e. NAE] should be used as a pronunciation model in this era of global English'. In brief, ELF advocates call for an end to what they call the 'tyranny of inner circle models', 'linguistic imperialism' and the hegemony of NESs both as teachers and language users.

A frequently voiced argument in this debate is that one's accent is inextricably linked to one's national and individual identity, which learners want to express also in a foreign language, and that adopting any native speaker model goes against this desire (Seidlhofer 2011). According to Walker (2010, p. 13), 'whatever accent we have, native speaker or non-native speaker, standard or regional, it is a part of our identity, and for some people losing their accent is the same as losing part of their identity'. It has even been suggested that imposing someone else's accent on learners is morally wrong and harms them emotionally (Porter & Garvin, 1989). Moreover, in countries such as India, Pakistan and Nigeria, in which English is used intranationally, the local accent expresses the local culture in a way that cannot be achieved with a NES style of English pronunciation representative of the inner circle.

Furthermore, Jenkins (2006) argues that an EFL approach, which she refers to as standard language ideology, creates an unrealistic ideal that diminishes those who do not fit the model. According to Jenkins, the more traditional EFL approach breeds prejudice, language insecurity and feelings of linguistic and social inferiority. NNES teachers are in a particularly awkward position as they are forced to teach an English accent that they themselves do not speak. As maintained by Rajadurai (2006, pp. 46–47), 'imposing native-speaker norms circumscribes teacher autonomy and robs non-native teachers of any sense of confidence, forcing them to perform on an unequal playing field; the same is true for the L2 learner'.

While some of the above arguments are convincing, others are highly problematic. First, the claim that NES models are unrealistic because native-like pronunciation is practically impossible to achieve confuses the notion of a pronunciation model with instructional goals. It is both possible and seems reasonable to take an NES accent as a reference point while aiming not at its faithful imitation but its approximation with an attempt to mediate those mispronunciations that hinder intelligibility most. Second, the fact that many NNESs use English as a lingua franca in communication with other NNESs does not necessarily render NES instructional models inappropriate if they can safeguard interlocutors' intelligibility. Third, the wish to retain a foreign accent in English in order to express one's cultural and/or

L1 linguistic identity does not exclude adopting NES accent models. As argued by Szpyra-Kozłowska (2015), in light of the general unlikelihood of achieving native-like pronunciation in L2, the overwhelming majority of NNESs retain in their English speech many L1 traces. Thus, willingly or unwillingly, their L1 linguistic identity is maintained. It is the suppression of one's native accent in L2 that is by far a greater challenge than a hypothesized search for trying to find ways to express it.

With regard to NNES teachers' alleged inferiority complex and lack of confidence caused by their incomplete mastery of English phonology, more effective teacher preparation should be able to offer prospective instructors sufficient (theoretical and practical) training as well as sufficient knowledge of language acquisition processes and pronunciation teaching techniques to equip them with the necessary tools and skills to boost their confidence. A well-prepared, competent teacher should, in turn, be able to cope with their students' language anxieties and insecurities. Though descriptions of a relevant level of pronunciation attainment may be difficult to determine, a person with unintelligible/incomprehensible English pronunciation should not be a language teacher, just as someone who does not know human anatomy well should not be practising medicine as a medical doctor.

Let us now point to some obvious, but often neglected and forgotten, advantages of employing NES pronunciation models in English language instruction. First of all, NES models are well-known, thoroughly described and codified varieties, with a long teaching tradition behind them matched by numerous teaching resources. Moreover, owing to their common instructional use around the world, they successfully serve the function of a lingua franca, for instance in various international organizations. Despite those who try to disassociate English from the pronunciation styles of NESs, such models are considered by many learners to be the only relevant forms of English they know and may view other varieties as inferior in quality. This bias towards NES models is shown in many studies of English accent preferences carried out in different parts of the world (e.g. in Europe by Henderson et al., 2012; in Japan by Matsuda, 2003; in China and Singapore by Goh, 2009; in Argentina by Friedrich, 2003; see also Timmis, 2002). In all of these studies a majority of the study participants voiced a preference for NES models. It is interesting that the proponents of ELF, who argue for the right of learners to choose the type of pronunciation they want to use, tend to ignore such empirical results. As argued by Szpyra-Kozłowska (2015), in the majority of educational contexts the choice of a pronunciation model is not realistic. Moreover, students usually want to learn a form of English pronunciation that would allow them to communicate with all speakers of English, both NES and NNESs, without having to predetermine who their prospective interlocutors might be. Finally, giving up native models in English instruction in favour of other, less precisely defined proposals can lead to learner confusion and loss of intelligibility in international communication via English. As argued by Prodromou (2006), the major advantages of traditional models are that they already exist, are codified and can serve as the basis for an acceptable and accessible international lingua franca. Moreover, they provide uniformity and stability.

It seems that there are two issues surrounding the use of NES models critics find most objectionable: the issue of achieving native-like pronunciation, which, as shown above, confuses the idea of a model with targets of pronunciation instruction, and the issue of adopting the cultural baggage of inner circle countries of little or no relevance to many international learners. Szpyra-Kozłowska (2015) argues, however, that some NES models (see below) can be employed for the purposes of international communication, but should be regarded as a convenient, pragmatically oriented tool, taught without necessarily subscribing to the cultural aspects of the source accents (e.g. as when High German serves as a lingua franca for all

German-speaking, but culturally diversified, regions and countries). Following this reasoning, Szpyra-Kozłowska proposes the concept of native English as a lingua franca (NELF), which she defines as using some inner circle (i.e. NES) models for purposes of pronunciation teaching while leaving ample space for the inclusion of both NES and NNES cultures and norms as integral parts of instructional design.

If NES models continue to be used when teaching English to NNESs, the issue of selecting suitable varieties should be considered since different suggestions have been made in this respect. With regard to British English, Crystal (1995), for example, has argued that Scottish English is a good alternative to RP since it has a smaller vowel inventory and is therefore simpler to learn. Other scholars have suggested Estuary English as a replacement of RP as a prestige accent for the young, devoid of the elitist associations of RP. As argued by Szpyra-Kozłowska (2015), such proposals cannot be regarded as realistic as they fail to recognize the fact that a model accent should satisfy a number of important criteria, which are provided below.

- It should be a standard variety. Non-standard accents are restricted to specific groups of users (regional or social) and are often unintelligible to other speakers of English. Some of them might also be socially stigmatized (e.g. Liverpool English, Appalachian English, African-American vernacular). Moreover, usually only standard types of pronunciation enjoy high social prestige and provide their learners with transparent benefits.
- It should be intelligible to many users of English, both within a given country and outside it. This means many standard varieties that are, however, generally unfamiliar outside their regions or countries, such as Scottish, Appalachian or New Zealand varieties of English, are not suitable candidates.
- The model accent should provide learners with increased chances of an educational and professional career, both within their own country and beyond it. It is doubtful whether this requirement can be satisfied by non-standard or regional varieties.
- It should be a variety for which teaching resources (textbooks, learner dictionaries, recordings) are readily available. Clearly, teachers need appropriate materials and their availability is of primary importance to them.
- It should be an accent that English teachers use (or that they try to approximate). It is rather obvious that we can teach only what we know, and it would be unrealistic to expect instructors to do otherwise.

The above arguments make it clear that there are very few varieties of English that fulfil the above conditions. Scottish, Appalachian and Aboriginal English certainly do not. As a matter of fact only two of them appear to do so in the European context, namely RP and NAE.

RP has become known internationally due to the availability of BBC channels and because of its use as a pronunciation model in EFL in many countries, particularly in Europe, which have close cultural and economic ties with Great Britain. This makes RP intelligible to numerous users of English. In spite of the recent decline in its status (only 3 to 5 per cent of the British use it (Crystal 1995)), RP is still very often positively associated with good education, prestigious professions and economic success. Moreover, RP is the most thoroughly described English accent, with numerous teaching resources available. It is still very often used in BBC radio and television broadcasts, providing phonetic input to learners. Finally, many teachers have received training in RP and try to approximate this accent.

NAE as a model accent also satisfies all the conditions specified above. It has been made popular throughout the world through music, films, the Internet and other media, which helps to ensure its availability to many learners. Moreover, NAE enjoys a high international prestige owing to the economic and political power of the country of its origin. Using it can be beneficial in communication with North Americans (including Canadians) as well as learners from those regions of the world (such as South America and some parts of Asia) in which it is the major accent of classroom instruction.[1] Furthermore, there are numerous NAE teaching resources. Its sound system is somewhat simpler than that of RP since, owing to rhoticity, it is closer to spelling and lacks central diphthongs. Finally, NAE carries no negative connotations of social elitism of RP. In addition, NAE has many millions of native speakers.[2]

The arguments provided above in favour of RP and NAE as realistic pronunciation models should also be considered from the perspective of a specific local educational situation as in various contexts other accents of English might fulfil the presented criteria more adequately than the two varieties discussed above. For instance, Australian, New Zealand and South African English might be more suitable models in such regions as Indonesia, the South Pacific and southern Africa.

Nativized models

In many post-colonial countries, often referred to as the outer circle, English is an institutionalized second language used in higher education, business, administration, entertainment and politics. In such regions, new, indigenized varieties of English have developed, known as New Englishes, which include, for example, Indian English, Nigerian English and Singaporean English. They often serve for the purposes of intranational communication in countries such as Nigeria, in which over 400 other languages are also used (Josiah, Bodunde & Robert, 2012).

New Englishes, for a long time considered to be corrupt versions of native English, after a campaign for a formal recognition led by such linguists as Kachru (1986), now enjoy the status of fully legitimate varieties. Consequently, they can serve as instructional models for learners in the countries where they are widely used. For example, it is estimated that about 60 million people speak Indian English, which makes India one of the countries with the highest number of English speakers.

There are several advantages for adopting nativized instructional models in outer circle countries. First of all, nativized models appear to be firmly established and in common use in their places of origin. Second, they have their roots in the local languages and culture. Unlike inner circle NES models, they are not imposed from the outside. This means, in consequence, that any other models might appear unnatural to the users of the varieties under discussion, interfering with their linguistic habits and cultural identity. Moreover, as argued by Brown (1991, p. 112),

> From the pedagogical point of view, a local form of speech containing interference features is likely to be much easier for its speakers to learn than any externally imposed model: a local model does not represent any radical departure from existing speech habits, thus making maximally efficient use of class time. Such a model is also likely to correspond closely to local teachers' pronunciation.

On the other hand, New Englishes are local/regional varieties, little known outside their countries of origin. This might create problems for their speakers in communication with those who employ other accents of English, both native and non-native. As argued by Rubdy and Saraceni (2006, p. 7),

> Concern has also been expressed about the uncontrolled spread of nativized forms of English on the grounds of linguistic fragmentation. Arguably, if everyone communicates in their local varieties, the language will diverge to the point of mutual incomprehensibility, thus cancelling out its value as a lingua franca.

Furthermore, even many speakers of New Englishes consider them to be of lower prestige than native accents.

Non-native models

Several scholars (e.g. Cook, 1999; Prodromou, 2006; Murphy, 2014) propose that multicompetent, intelligible, comprehensible, non-native-accented English language speakers may serve as pronunciation models for learners of English. According to Murphy, there are two major advantages of such models: their transparency as aspirational models and their relevance to learners' pronunciation needs. He argues (p. 259) that 'more accessible models are more likely to resonate with [students'] own experiences as ESL/EFL learners'.

This proposal can be understood in two ways: an intelligible, comprehensible, non-native-accented model can be provided by a proficient NNES who shares the first language with the learners (Cunningham 2009) or it can be supplied by a successful NNES who, however, does not share learners' L1 (Walker, 2010; Murphy, 2014). The first type of situation involves speakers whose pronunciation is based on native English, but which has some degree of a non-native accent as it, naturally, preserves some features of their L1 (in addition to interlanguage features associated with their developing L2 system). Consequently, this variety of English is phonetically and culturally close to the learners who feel comfortable with it and allows them to express their L1 cultural, linguistic and national identity. According to Cunningham (2009), such a model is the basis for realistic targets. It is currently employed in numerous countries where the majority of teachers are NNESs who share an L1 with the students and who are familiar with such learners' pronunciation challenges. However, if this is the only version of English provided to students, a potential danger is that they might either be unaware of some of the ways in which their pronunciation departs from NES varieties or, if this fact becomes widely known within the study body, learners might regard the quality of instruction as a flawed educational offer. Cunningham (2009, p. 126) poses an important question: 'What if the learner aspires to sound less [non-native] accented than their teacher, more native-like or in some way different? Then their options have been limited by such a model.' Moreover, a heavily L1-accented English might be unintelligible to international users of English.[3] As Murphy (2014) points out, since numerous factors affect intelligibility, 'it is [as yet] impossible to describe a particular NNE speech sample as being intrinsically intelligible or comprehensible' (p. 259).

When a pronunciation model is supplied by a NNES who comes, however, from a different linguistic background than the learners, alternative complications may also arise. First of all, students might observe that the instructor's pronunciation departs from that of NESs and might consider it inferior in quality. Second, the teacher who does not share the learners' L1 might be unable to cope with their particular pronunciation problems. Finally, as pointed out by Szpyra-Kozłowska (2015), such an NNES accent model might create an obstacle to expressing students' national identity through their English pronunciation. For example, if Spanish learners are given samples of Japanese-influenced English to imitate, they may learn to speak English with a Japanese accent (mixed with elements of their L1 and English), which will apparently make signalling their own cultural identity more difficult than in the case of solely L1-influenced speech.

Multiple models

An implicit assumption made in the discussion above has been that language learners are provided with one pronunciation model to approximate. The notion of multiple models, hardly ever discussed in the literature, implies that not one but more accents can be employed in English instruction to a single group of learners. This can mean either using several NES varieties, some NNES varieties or both NES and NNES varieties. The first case concerns instruction involving NES teachers who, however, use different accents. In the second type of situation all instructors are NNESs from different L1 backgrounds. Finally, multiple models can be provided by a mixture of NES and NNES varieties supplied by the teachers and/or by recordings. It is important, however, to employ only a limited number of accent models since too much variation is undesirable as it introduces too much ambiguity in both comprehension and production.

A significant advantage of providing multiple models is that no decision has to be made with regard to which specific accent should be selected, which, as shown above, is a controversial issue. Moreover, this approach prepares learners for a variety of English accents they may encounter in real-life situations. Employing multiple models, as noted by Cunningham (2009), 'will likely mean that the learner will have features of many Englishes in their pronunciation alongside the substrate of their first language(s)' (p. 126). An immediate objection that can be raised against this approach is that the process of exposing language learners to different pronunciation models early on might result in confusion and frustration; if learning one variety is an enormous challenge, then coping with several models might be too heavy a burden.

This complication is exemplified by Kang (2010), whose study set in New Zealand involved learners from many countries who were taught English pronunciation by teachers using different English accents. The respondents evaluated their pronunciation instruction critically, expressed their annoyance with multiple versions of English offered by different teachers and were of the opinion that their English pronunciation would have improved more in their home countries, probably because they would not have encountered the distracting experience of needing to cope with several different unfamiliar versions of English, but could have focused on just one version. As pointed out by Kang (2010), 'learners [in her study] built up a negative perspective on poly-models' (p. 114).[4]

Instructional models in teaching practice around the world

As the discussion in the section above has been largely theoretical, below I examine the use of pronunciation models in current teaching practices in three types of context: the inner circle, the outer circle and the expanding circle.

The inner circle

In inner circle parts of the world, numerous learners attempt to acquire English in naturalistic settings, but some do so also in instructed settings (e.g. in various English language schools and courses). Traditionally referred to as learners of English as a second language (ESL), they include immigrants who have settled in a given country and need to learn or improve their English to be able to function effectively in the target language society. Many international students and scholars on shorter visits may also be classified as ESL learners. The relevant question concerns the model(s) of English pronunciation adopted in English language classes offered to such learners.

While limited information is available on this issue, it can be assumed that in many English-speaking countries in which some accent has the status of standard pronunciation, this prestige variety is likely to be employed as a model for pronunciation teaching. However, such a prestige variety will often compete with whatever might be the local accent learners are exposed to in daily interactions beyond the classroom and which the majority of teachers speak at school. Moreover, in the place of living and in the workplace, many students will hear different varieties of English from other immigrant inhabitants and co-workers, some elements of which they might imitate.

Complications arise in such settings when there is no single, generally accepted standard pronunciation or when a local variety departs considerably from whatever the region's standard might be. A case in point is the situation in the British Isles, where no accent has the status of representative standard, even though RP is considered by many to serve this role. In order to find out what types of pronunciation are employed in English language schools, for the purposes of this chapter I carried out an informal survey in 10 such institutions located in nine different towns in various regions of England.[5] In answer to the question of what pronunciation varieties are taught in these schools, in most cases the answer was that it was either RP and some local accent (such as Midlands English, Geordie or Scottish English) or diversified accents of the UK (used by the teachers). Moreover, in nine out of 10 cases the schools in question employed international teachers, which means that the learners were being exposed to NNES-accented English.[6] Evidently, in all 10 schools multiple models are used. This also holds true of the many language schools in Ireland that took part in D. Murphy's (2011) survey. 36 teachers were asked which model of English pronunciation they presented for their learners to approximate. Of the respondents, 47.2 per cent answered that it was both British English[7] (BE) and Irish English (IE), 19.4 per cent indicated BE, 11.1 per cent IE and 2.7 per cent AE.

An interesting issue concerns learners' views regarding pronunciation models offered to them in English language courses. For example, 95 per cent of Derwing's (2003) immigrant respondents in Canada indicated that they would like to speak like NESs. Kang (2010) carried out a study in which she examined students' opinions on pronunciation instruction in two inner circle countries: New Zealand and the US. The results differed considerably: the learners in New Zealand were dissatisfied with the provided accent models, whereas those in the US accepted them without any major reservations. Kang (p. 112) concludes that 'the results suggest that learners' preference and attitude towards inner circle accents vary among the types of models'.

The outer circle

In outer circle contexts two pronunciation models vie for attention in instructional settings: local nativized varieties belonging to the so-called New Englishes and more traditional NES accents. After a long campaign for the recognition of nativized varieties of English as fully legitimate dialects of the language, it appears that the competition between these two models is still in progress.

According to Chan and Evans (2011),

> In the Asian context, the choice of a pedagogical model is still controversial due largely to the question of local acceptance among the general public and other major stakeholders such as educators, professionals and government officials. In many outer circle contexts (e.g. Singapore and Malaysia), it has been found that the tension between linguistic identity and economic pragmatism is often more a political issue than a purely educational matter.
>
> (p. 4)

A similar view is expressed by Jayapalan and Pillai (2011), who discuss the conflict over instructional pronunciation models in Malaysia:

> The teachers' preference is for a Malaysian accent but at the same time . . . accepting the use of a Standard British English model suggests a conflict between what they are comfortable with (*Our* English) and what they deem to be the correct variety (*Their* English).
>
> (p. 77)

The same dilemma is present in Cameroon, where, according to Ngefac (2011),

> In spite of Kachru's recommendation and the efforts made by scholars from different parts of the world to defend the status, acceptability and equality of Englishes in the three concentric circles, some Outer Circle speakers continue to think that traditional native English norms are superior to those of their indigenized English, despite the positive attitude they show towards their local English.
>
> (p. 41)

Josiah, Bodunde and Robert (2012), who examined pronunciation models in Nigeria, point to a discrepancy between requirements of educational authorities and the learners' pronunciation. They claim that at the university level, Nigerian students' pronunciation performance is evaluated according to the British standard, which the students do not use:

> Most Nigerians, no matter how highly educated, do not approximate closely to the SBE [Southern British English, often used synonymously with RP]. Even if they wished to do so, the exonormative [NES] model sounds quite affected and socially unacceptable to the majority of Nigerians.
>
> (p. 114)

While some researchers, such as those quoted above, opt for teaching nativized varieties, others are in favour of employing NES models. For example, Sethi and Jindal (2006) argue that RP should be taught to Indian learners:

> In India there are many accents of English, some of them diverging so widely from one another (e.g. Assamese English and Malayalee English) that, for a good part, they may be mutually unintelligible. We cannot recommend any of these Indian accents [as models for pronunciation teaching] since none can function as an efficient tool for oral communication across regional boundaries.
>
> (p. 6)

They maintain further that their choice of RP for instructional purposes is motivated by practical considerations as this accent, for historical reasons, is better understood in India that any other English variety and enjoys considerable prestige.

Chan and Evans (2011) present a study carried out in Hong Kong that examines over 500 secondary school students' attitudes towards Hong Kong English (HKE) as a suitable pronunciation model in the local English language classroom. They conclude that '[t]he survey findings reveal that local students have a generally negative attitude towards the existence of HKE as a variety and the adoption of HKE as a teaching model', which suggests that they prefer a native English accent (p. 1). Moreover, as often reported, in many East Asian countries ministries of education insist on native models and even forbid the use of local varieties in English instruction. It can be concluded that in the outer circle settings usually multiple pronunciation models (native and nativized) are used for purposes of language instruction.

The expanding circle

The expanding circle comprises numerous countries on different continents and many millions of learners of English outnumbering those of all of the inner and outer circle English speakers combined. It is the least homogeneous group of English language users as, in various parts of the world, they differ with respect to their ties with English-speaking countries, purposes for learning English, the amount of exposure to spoken English, its use in contacts with NESs and NNESs, the similarity of their L1 phonological systems with inner circle varieties of English, etc.

Such diversity is clearly shown by Cunningham (2009), who compares the role of English in two very different expanding circle countries: Vietnam and Sweden. Cunningham argues (p. 116) that the process of learning English pronunciation is very difficult for the Vietnamese as the two sound systems differ considerably. English is not widely spoken in Vietnam and an international visitor cannot rely on it in daily communication. It is, however, the language of international communication in the East Asian countries. In Sweden the situation is entirely different. 'Although English has no official status in Sweden, it fills in many respects the role of a second language in the country' (Cunningham, 2009, p, 116). For example, it is commonly used in tertiary education. As many Swedes speak fluent English, an international visitor can communicate with them in this language. Moreover, English poses less learning difficulty to Swedes in comparison with the Vietnamese as Swedish is a Germanic language related to English. Owing to such differences, teaching English pronunciation has to be adjusted to the local situation and cannot proceed in exactly the same fashion everywhere.

In the expanding circle two pronunciation models appear to dominate: RP and NAE, depending on the part of the world and the historical and current political and economic ties with the countries in which these dialects originated. Thus, in Europe RP appears to be commonly taught, while in South America NAE is more popular. In Asia the situation is not uniform in this respect, with some countries opting for RP and others for NAE. In the southern parts of this region, Australian English is also used. In many cases several instructional models are employed. For instance, in various European countries (e.g. Holland, Sweden, Poland) RP and NAE are adopted for teaching purposes, while in Indonesia, apart from RP and NAE, Australian English is also often taught, depending on the particular dialect spoken by the teacher. Moreover, learners are usually exposed to different dialects of English through films, music, TV channels and the Internet, which commonly results in mixing elements of several varieties in their speech.

In addition to native models (usually provided in the form of recordings and, less frequently, by NES teachers), in the expanding circle learners are exposed to the speech of non-native instructors. According to Celce-Murcia et al. (2010), 'nonnative English-speaking teachers constitute up to 80 percent of all English teachers globally' (p. 42). This means that multiple models are employed: NES and NNES-accented English of the instructors, who are (or are supposed to be) proficient and intelligible speakers of this language. However, as teachers' English is the major source of language input in the classroom, their pronunciation usually serves as the primary model of instruction.[8]

Conclusion

In view of the considerable diversity of English pronunciation, both native and non-native, and the current climate of acceptance of variety, it is evident that no one-size-fits-all policy can be applied to instructional models in the global context. Consequently, no uniformity can be expected in this respect.

Presently, two opposite tendencies seem to affect the choice of instructional pronunciation models. On the one hand, with the growing number of users of English worldwide and the resulting formation of new localized varieties, one type of pressure is to recognize such varieties as legitimate teaching models. On the other hand, in view of the pervasive use of English for purposes of international communication, there is a strong need to adopt teaching models which would guarantee a sufficient degree of phonetic uniformity to maintain mutual intelligibility between English users of different L1 backgrounds. There is no agreement on how to reconcile these two forces pulling in opposite directions, the first of which supports decentralization and the right of English varieties to differ and be modified by their users without restrictions, the other requiring the minimization of pronunciation differences needed to maintain the emerging role of English as an international lingua franca. Two major options appear to serve the latter purpose: either to promote some varieties as educational models whose approximation will make international learners of English mutually intelligible, or to prioritize those pronunciation features that help to safeguard intelligibility once they are firmly established. It is difficult to predict which of these two approaches will prevail in the future.

Academic discussions notwithstanding, this chapter has shown that in current teaching practices multiple pronunciation models are employed in all of the examined contexts. In the inner circle learners in instructed settings often have teachers who speak different (native and sometimes non-native) accents. In the outer circle, the local indigenized varieties compete with standard native English, while in the expanding circle NES models are employed in language classroom settings alongside forms of NNES-accented English used by the majority of local, non-native teachers. Multiple instructional pronunciation models are thus a pedagogic reality, and one not likely to change in the near future.

Notes

1   However, in some parts of the world an American accent might be met with hostility.
2   It is often claimed (e.g. Preston, 2005), that NAE pronunciation does not exist and is an artificial idealization, which is, however, convenient for pedagogical purposes (see Celce-Murcia, Brinton & Goodwin, 2010).
3   Similar objections can be raised with respect to the proposed local instructional models such as Chinese English and Japanese English (Kirkpatrick, 2007).
4   Multiple models should not be confused with the concept of polymodel. The latter term refers to an approach (e.g. Kirkpatrick, 2006) in which a different pronunciation model is employed in each linguistic, educational and cultural context.

5   The schools are in Norwich, Brighton, Swansea, Newcastle, Worthing, Maidenhead, Margate and Hove.

6   The usual comment in the questionnaires was that the instructors must have a clear and easily comprehensible pronunciation and that these are the teachers' qualifications that matter and not their accents. Many schools consider it beneficial for learners to be exposed to a variety of regional and non-native accents.

7   It seems that in D. Murphy's study the term 'British English' is synonymous with RP.

8   It has also been suggested that local NNES-accented varieties of English could serve as instructional models. Thus, Hu (2004) argues for the recognition of Chinese English and Jordan (2011) of Japanese English as appropriate models in the school systems of China and Japan, respectively.

References

Abercrombie, D. (1949). Teaching pronunciation. *English Language Teaching, 3*, 113–122.

Brown, A. (1991). *Pronunciation models*. Singapore: Singapore University Press.

Celce-Murcia, M., Brinton, D. M., & Goodwin, J. (2010). *Teaching pronunciation: A course book and reference guide*. Cambridge: Cambridge University Press.

Chan, J. Y. H., & Evans, S. (2011). Choosing an appropriate pronunciation model for the ELT classroom: A Hong Kong perspective. *The Journal of Asia TEFL, 8*(4), 1–24.

Cook, V. (1999). Going beyond the native speaker in language teaching. *TESOL Quarterly, 33*, 185–209.

Cruttenden, A. (2008). *Gimson's pronunciation of English* (7th ed.). London: Hodder Education.

Crystal, D. (1995). *The Cambridge encyclopedia of language*. Cambridge: Cambridge University Press.

Cunningham, U. (2009). Models and targets for the pronunciation of English in Vietnam and Sweden. *Research in Language, 7*, 113–128.

Dauer, R. (2005). The lingua franca core: A new model for pronunciation instruction. *TESOL Quarterly, 39*(3), 543–550.

Derwing, T. (2003). What do ESL students say about their accents? *Canadian Modern Language Review, 59*, 547–567.

Dziubalska-Kołaczyk, K., & Przedlacka, J. (Eds). (2005). *English pronunciation models: A changing scene*. Bern: Peter Lang.

Friedrich, P. (2003). English in Argentina: Attitudes of MBA students. *World Englishes, 22*(2), 173–184.

Goh, C. (2009). Perspectives on spoken grammar. *ELT Journal, 63*(4), 303–312.

Henderson, A., Frost, D., Tergujeff, E., Kautzsch, A., Murphy, D., Kirkova-Naskova, A., . . . Curnik, L. (2012). The English pronunciation teaching in Europe survey: Selected results. *Research in Language, 10*(1), 5–28.

Hu, X. G. (2004). Why China English should stand alongside British, American and other 'World Englishes'. *English Today, 20*(2), 26–33.

Jayapalan, K., & Pillai, S. (2011). The state of teaching and learning English pronunciation in Malaysia: A preliminary study. *Malaysian Journal of ELT Research, 7*(2), 63–81.

Jenkins, J. (2000). *The Phonology of English as an international language*. Oxford: Oxford University Press.

Jenkins, J. (2006). Points of view and blind spots: ELF and SLA. *International Journal of Applied Linguistics, 16*(2), 137–162.

Jenner, B. (1989). Teaching pronunciation: The common core. *IATEFL PronSIG Newsletter, 1*, 2–4.

Jordan, E. (2011). Japanese English pronunciation – issues of intelligibility, achievability and perception in the context of world Englishes. *Journal of English as an International Language, 6*(1), 81–90.

Josiah, U., Bodunde, H., & Robert, E. (2012). Patterns of English pronunciation among Nigerian university undergraduates: Challenges and prospects. *International Journal of Business, Humanities and Technology, 2*(6), 109–117.

Kachru, B. (1986). *The alchemy of English: The spread, functions and models of non-native Englishes*. Oxford: Pergamon.

Kang, O. (2010). ESL learners' attitudes toward pronunciation instruction and varieties of English. In J. Levis & K. LeVelle (Eds), *Proceedings of the 1st Pronunciation in Second Language Learning and Teaching Conference* (pp. 105–118). Ames, IA: Iowa State University.

Kelly, G. (2000). *How to teach pronunciation*. Harlow: Longman.

Kirkpatrick, A. (2006). Which model of English: Native-speaker, nativized or lingua franca? In R. Rubdy and M. Saraceni (Eds), *English in the world: Global rules, global roles* (pp. 71–83). London: Continuum.

Kirkpatrick, A. (2007). *World Englishes*. Cambridge: Cambridge University Press.

Levis, J. (2005). Changing contexts and shifting paradigms in pronunciation teaching. *TESOL Quarterly*, *39*(3), 369–377.

Matsuda, A. (2003). The ownership of English in Japanese secondary schools. *World Englishes*, *22*(4), 483–496.

Moyer, A. (1999). Ultimate attainment in L2 phonology: The critical factors of age, motivation and instruction. *Studies in Second Language Acquisition*, *21*, 81–108.

Murphy, D. (2011). An investigation of English pronunciation teaching in Ireland. *English Today*, *27*, 10–18.

Murphy, J. (2014). Intelligible, comprehensible non-native models in ESL/EFL pronunciation teaching. *System*, *42*, 258–269.

Ngefac, A. (2011). When the blind lead the blind: The fallacy of promoting standard British English accent in Cameroon. *Journal of Language Teaching and Research*, *2*(1), 40–44.

Porter, D., & Garvin, S. (1989). Attitudes to pronunciation in EFL. *Speak Out!*, *5*, 8–15.

Preston, D. R. (2005). How can you learn a language that isn't there. In K. Dziubalska-Kołaczyk & J. Przedlacka (Eds), *English pronunciation models: A changing scene* (pp. 37–58). Bern: Peter Lang.

Prodromou, L. (2006). Defining the 'successful bilingual speaker' of English. In R. Rubdy and M. Saraceni (Eds), *English in the world: Global rules, global roles* (pp. 51–70). London: Continuum.

Rajadurai, J. (2006). Pronunciation issues in non-native contexts: A Malaysian case study. *Malaysian Journal of ELT Research*, *2*, 42–59.

Rogerson-Revell, P. (2011). *English phonology and pronunciation teaching*. London and New York, NY: Continuum.

Rubdy, R., & Saraceni, M. (Eds). (2006). *English in the world: Global rules, global roles*. London: Continuum.

Seidlhofer, B. (2011). *Understanding English as a lingua franca*. Oxford: Oxford University Press.

Sethi, J., & Jindal, D. V. (2006). *A Handbook of pronunciation of English words*. New Delhi: Rekha.

Setter, J. (2010). Theories and approaches in English pronunciation. Retrieved from www.um.es/lacell/aesta/contenido/pdf/3/setter.pdf.

Szpyra-Kozłowska, J. (2015). *Pronunciation in EFL instruction: A research-based approach*. Bristol, Buffalo, NY, and Toronto: Multilingual Matters.

Thomson, R. I. (2012). Improving L2 listeners' perception of English vowels: A computer-mediated approach. *Language Learning*, *62*, 1231–1258.

Timmis, I. (2002). Native-speaker norms and international English: A classroom view. *ELT Journal*, *56*(3), 240–249.

Walker, R. (2010). *Teaching the pronunciation of English as a lingua franca*. Oxford: Oxford University Press.

Section 4

Pronunciation instruction in language teaching

15

Pronunciation teaching in the pre-CLT era

Amanda A. Baker

Introduction

This chapter provides an overview of the history of pronunciation teaching, focusing specifically on the pre-communicative language teaching (CLT) era, in a way that should help teachers to better understand modern pronunciation practices. Although current pronunciation teaching and learning generally embrace a communicative approach, the fundamentals of pre-CLT approaches continue to have lasting influence on how pronunciation is taught today. Understanding these earlier approaches highlights a variety of different techniques and practices that continue to be foundational in many contemporary language classrooms.

Concentrating mainly on the classical period (pre-1850s), the first wave (1850s–1880s) and the second wave (1880s–early 1980s) out of the four 'waves' of pronunciation teaching identified by Murphy and Baker (2015), the chapter examines the nitty-gritty of pronunciation pedagogy from a classroom teacher's perspective: what were the tools of the trade and what did they actually look like in the classroom? Whenever possible, the chapter provides reports of pronunciation teaching from historical literature or from excerpts from language methodology textbooks to illustrate pronunciation instruction as situated in its historical context. This is a challenge, as relatively little empirical documentation beyond such sources remains. The chapter's focus is on typical classroom practices, not on experimental work or practices of specialists. The listing below provides a historical timeline and chapter overview.

An overview of pronunciation teaching in the pre-CLT era

Classical approaches (pre-1850s): intuitive-imitative practices

- Oral repetition
- Minimal pairs
- Imitated pronunciation
- Reading aloud

First wave (1850s–1880s): intuitive-imitative practices and emerging innovations

* Continuation of classical approaches
* Introduction of a vowel numbering system

Second wave (1880s–1980s): emergence of analytic-linguistic approaches

* Continuation of classical and first wave approaches
* The Direct Method
* The reform movement: teaching learners about phonology
* Naturalistic approaches: focus on listening
* Audiolingualism and Situational Language Teaching
* Linguistic/scientific study and classroom application
* Focus on intelligibility
* Meaningful practice
* Phonological hierarchies
* Pronunciation teaching philosophies

Classical approaches to pronunciation teaching (pre-1850s)

The first few centuries of English language instruction paid relatively little attention to pronunciation within language teaching. For the language learner of this period, the focus of language education centred primarily on written communication and, only to a limited extent, on general oral communication (listening/speaking) and finally pronunciation. A quote from Palmer illustrates the situation quite well: 'The ancient school said: First learn how to form words, then learn how to form sentences, then pay attention to the 'idiomatic' phenomena, and lastly learn to pronounce and to speak' (Palmer, 1921, p. 28). Pronunciation was a relatively minor component of language instruction during this era (Howatt & Widdowson, 2004).

Although few accounts of pronunciation instruction during this period exist, those that do demonstrate the origins of what we might term 'intuitive-imitative practice' that is still in use today. Intuitive-imitative practices require no special skills in phonetics or speech pathology on the teacher's part, relying mainly on: (a) the teacher's pronunciation and the student's ability to mimic the teacher's speech or, alternatively, (b) discerning pronunciation from a written text. Oral repetition, minimal pair work, oral reading and also what was referred to as 'imitated pronunciation' in dictionaries or texts are emblematic of the classical approaches to pronunciation instruction and are discussed in further detail below.

Oral repetition

What language teacher does not employ oral repetition in their classroom? And why not? As illustrated below, even simple correction of a mispronounced sound involves the teacher repeating the word, and not necessarily isolating the problematic sound. The teacher expected the learner to hear the difference and reproduce the entire word correctly. The following illustration of a pronunciation lesson is probably one of the earliest 'recordings' available. A scene from Shakespeare's *Henry V*, written around 1599, provides some evidence of the typical ESOL classroom of the time. In this scene, Alice provides Katherine with a lesson on parts of the body.

Katharine: Je te prie, m'enseignez: il faut que j'apprenne à parler. Comment appelez-vous <u>la main</u> en Anglais?

Alice: <u>La main</u>? Elle est appelée de <u>hand</u>.

Alice subsequently says the names of several body parts, which then Katharine repeats. In the exchange that follows, Katharine lists all of the words that she has learned. These words have been underlined in the text below. There is no underlining in the original text. The double underlined words below indicate where Katharine has mispronounced a particular word and Alice has immediately corrected her pronunciation of that word. In the final part of the exchange, Katherine asks Alice to provide the English word for several other body parts.

Katharine: [. . .] Je m'en fais la répétition de tous les mots que vous m'avez appris dès à présent. [. . .] écoutez: d'<u>hand</u>, de <u>fingre</u>, de <u>nails</u>, de <u>arma</u>, de <u>bilbow</u>.

Alice: D'<u>elbow</u>, madame.

Katharine: O Seigneur Dieu, je m'en oublie! de <u>elbow</u>. Comment appelez-vous le <u>col</u>?

Alice: De <u>neck</u>, madame.

Katharine: De <u>nick</u>. Et le <u>menton</u>?

Alice: De <u>chin</u>.

Katharine: De <u>sin</u>. Le <u>col</u>, de <u>nick</u>; de <u>menton</u>, de <u>sin</u>.

Alice: Oui. Sauf votre honneur, en vérité, vous prononcez les mots aussi droit que les natifs d'Angleterre.

(III.iv.3–34)

Although this scene is not set in a classroom, it is likely illustrative of typical classroom practice of the time. Teachers tend to teach as they themselves were taught, a process that Lortie (1975) describes as an 'apprenticeship of observation', and thus they would be inclined to teach a second language (L2) similarly to how they learned one (p. 61).

Centuries later, oral repetition still plays a strong role in pronunciation development. As Strevens (1974) notes 'Exhortation, imitation, and mimicry will take care of a large proportion of the pronunciation learning task, and these techniques should normally be used first . . . (they have the advantage of requiring little or no specialised training on the teacher's part)' (p. 189). With relatively few teachers of English to speakers of other languages (ESOL) receiving adequate training in pronunciation pedagogy today (Foote, Holtby & Derwing, 2011; Murphy, 2014), the frequent use of oral repetition in the modern classroom is not surprising.

Minimal pairs

Minimal pairs – pairs of words that differ by only a single sound (such as <ship/sheep>, <loose/goose> or <bear/pear>) – also emerged as a classical technique and continue to be used in many language classrooms today. One of the earliest mentions of minimal pair practice can be found in Cooper's *Grammatica anglicana*, published in London in 1685 (cited in Kelly, 1971, p. 127). This book, written in Latin, was used to teach English pronunciation using minimal pairs to a certain extent; however, although the technique was certainly employed in Cooper's book, the technique was likely introduced much earlier to English-specific language education (Kelly, 1971).

Imitated pronunciation

As the written word dominated language education at the time, it also played an equally prominent role in pronunciation instruction. Dictionaries, language grammars and even language textbooks typically used written approximations of the learner's native language to guide replication of pronunciation in the L2 (Abercrombie, 1949; Bowen, 1972). This technique was referred to as imitated pronunciation and had been employed for more than 400 years (Abercrombie, 1949). However, with the introduction of a phonetic alphabet in the first wave, which continued to receive increasing recognition and use in the second wave of pronunciation teaching, imitated pronunciation gradually diminished in popularity.

Reading aloud

Reading aloud is a technique as old as the written word itself and is naturally an integral component of any historical language classroom and even many contemporary classrooms. 'There comes a time in almost every foreign language class when the instructor says: "Now open your books to today's lesson. Please begin reading [aloud. . .]"' (Meiden, 1963, p. 65). It is a technique that is highly discussed in the literature, with numerous texts giving advice on how it should be done (Jespersen, 1904) or conversely why it should not be done (Hill, 1961/1967; Meiden, 1963). Jesperson (1904) provides a depiction on how reading aloud lessons might best be conducted.

> At the beginner-stage, the teacher must read each sentence by itself and then get the pupils to repeat it while they have the teacher's pronunciation fresh in mind. Later on the teacher may take larger sections, which may be parceled [*sic*] out to the pupils in not too small portions. And one cannot be too particular with the way in which this reading is done; such stuttering, with pauses between words belonging closely together, and neglect of natural and necessary pauses, which used to be the rule, ought never to be tolerated, not even as an exception. Even the first beginners ought to be required to read each sentence connectedly with natural expression; the teacher will not regret any trouble taken on this account, even if it involves ever so much repetition.
>
> (pp. 86–87)

Repetition and a strict focus on fluent, natural reproduction of chunks of 'expressive' speech are considered key, and should start from the earliest stages of language learning. All of this is to be done after learners have examined the meaning of the text to avoid practising sentences just to repeat 'meaningless sounds' (p. 91).

Methodologists of the early twentieth century also highlighted the importance of choral reading as part of oral reading (Jespersen, 1904). Yet, that said, 'There are few things more dreary than for twenty-four pupils to follow with both eye and ear while the twenty-fifth reads a prepared text with which they are familiar or expected to be' (Hervey, 1916, p. 82). For this, Hervey recommended incorporating practice that involves active listening, in which students who are listening to the reader are expected to 'correct errors and answer questions at any moment' (p. 82).

First wave of pronunciation teaching (1850s–1880s)

The first wave of pronunciation teaching marked the beginning of change as a number of innovations to language teaching were introduced by pedagogues such as Marcel, Gouin and

Berlitz in various countries around the world, yet the impact of their ideas remained confined to specialist circles, achieving little or no recognition in most language classrooms (see Murphy & Baker, 2015, for further discussion), at least not during the period of the first wave itself. Although they advocated increased emphasis on the development of speaking skills in the classroom, the focus on reading and writing skill development continued to dominate events in language classrooms. Oral communication skills were not completely neglected, however. The emblems of the classical approach to teaching pronunciation, namely imitative-intuitive practices, permeated classroom practices. Oral repetition, reading aloud, minimal pair drills and imitated pronunciation remained foundational to the first wave, but a few innovations began to surface in L2 classrooms. Perhaps the most prominent of these was a vowel numbering system that began to experience significant usage in language textbooks of the time.

Introduction of a vowel numbering system

Many textbook authors and classroom teachers today use a numbering system to represent the different vowel sounds of the English language (e.g. Goodwin, 2014; Morley, 1991b; Murphy, 2003), but it is during the first wave that we see the origins of this system. In Rensselaer Bentley's *The Pictorial Spelling Book*, different types of vowels (specifically different types of simple, long and diphthongal sounds) are assigned a number. The following excerpt provides a brief description of how the use of pictures is claimed to enhance learner enjoyment while supporting the learning process by associating each word (vowel sound) with a number (Bentley, 1849, p. 18).

Easy words of three letters

In order to make study interesting to children from the beginning, and bring everything within their comprehension; pictures, representing objects with which they are familiar, are inserted at the beginning of several sections, to assist the little learner in pronouncing words. After calling the letters, by a single glance of the eye he sees the picture, and being assisted at the same time both by *sight* and *sound*, he is enabled to pronounce the word without the least difficulty. In this manner he becomes pleased with the exercise, and considers it as an *amusement*, rather than a *task*.

Figure 15.1 Excerpt from Rensselaer Bentley's *The Pictorial Spelling Book*

A decade later, authors of English textbooks appear to modify this system, assigning separate numbers for each of the vowel sounds, a system that was already used to teach French to speakers of English (De Laporte, 1845). The image shown in Figure 15.2 is from Ormsby's (1860, p. 15) *Vermont Speller; Or Progressive Lessons in the English Language*.

> dóve, nòt—túbe, tǔb, bǔll, rúle—ôĭl, pôŭnd—thin, ᴛʜis.
>
> ## LESSON V.
> ### *Easy words of three and four letters.*
>
> | | | 1 | 2 | 3 |
> |---|---|---|---|---|
> | 2 **Arm.** | | age | tuft | gilt |
> | | | ere | belt | milt |
> | | | ode | felt | tilt |
> | | | içe | melt | hilt |
> | | | ale | pelt | wilt |
> | 4 **Axe.** | | ate | welt | gift |
> | | | ore | far | lift |
> | | | 2 | 2 | 1 |
> | 4 **Cat.** | | bent | went | bide |
> | | | dent | lint | hide |
> | | | lent | dint | lide |

Figure 15.2 Excerpt from Ormsby's *Vermont Speller*

The use of a numbering system continued into the second wave of pronunciation teaching with the introduction of mnemonic lines, as we can see from the excerpt shown in Figure 15.3 from Shearer's (1914, p. 22) *A Pronouncing Speller for Foreigners*.

No. 1. SHORT VOWEL SOUNDS.

* Thàt	hėn	will	nŏt	lŏvę	pǔss.
à	ė	ĭ	ŏ	ŏ	ǔ
＼	I	:	V	‿	)
à	ė	ĭ	ŏ	ǔ	ů
àt	pėn	ĭf	ŏx	ǔp	pǔt
àx.	tėn	ĭt	ŏn	ǔs	pǔll
àm	hėn	ĭş	ŏf	sǔn	bǔll
àn	mėn	ĭn	nŏt	rǔn	fǔll

> * The marks underneath the vowels in this mnemonic line indicate the vowel sounds heard in the words above. The manner of finding them is given in Section 19 of the Introduction. The *sounds* are the names of the marks.

Figure 15.3 Excerpt from Shearer's *A Pronouncing Speller for Foreigners*

Today, the use of numbering systems continues to be used in conjunction with increasingly innovative ways to teach pronunciation. Acton, for example, uses haptic techniques (gestures involving hand movement and touch) along with a numbering system when teaching the vowel system in mirror image to a class (e.g. Acton, Baker, Burri & Teaman, 2013). Numbering systems are also used in the teaching of word stress (see Murphy & Kandil, 2004; Murphy, 2004) as a precusor to working with the vowel system.

Second wave of pronunciation teaching (1880s–early 1980s)

The second wave of pronunciation teaching represents a marked break from the strictly imitative-intuitive approaches of the classical era and first wave. For the first time, analytic-linguistic approaches to pronunciation pedagogy were introduced to the language classroom and were merged with imitation-intuitive practices. Many of these imitation-intuitive practices were also packaged as part of new teaching methods of the time.

Direct method

In line with imitation-intuitive approaches, the direct method focused on developing 'correct pronunciation' by following and imitating a model. Drilling and repetition of problematic sounds for a few minutes each day formed part of this approach. An excerpt from Wren's *The Direct Teaching of English in Indian Schools* provides instructions on how to pronounce the word 'boy'.

> *Boy.* Directly the *bi* sound is heard, commence a drill in which each pupil first rounds his lips into a circle and then ejaculates, *oy, oy, oy, oy*, until told to stop. Let the whole class then practise the *oy* sound until it is correctly made. Next have the plain *i* sound made, and draw the attention of the class to the opened and elongated shape of the mouth necessary to the *i* pronunciation, and contrast it with the smaller circle shape required for the *oi*. . . . 'Now say *oi* six times' – 'Now say *i* six times,' and so on. At a later stage practise such sentences as 'Did the b*oy* buy a t*oy*' or 'J*oi*n the l*i*ne'.
>
> (Wren, 1912, p. 62)

The direct method, along with other naturalistic[1] approaches that followed, subscribed to a contrasting philosophy to that of classical approaches, namely 'First learn to form sounds, then memorize sentences, then learn systematically how to form sentences, and lastly learn how to form words' (Palmer, 1921, p. 28), thus emphasizing a shift away from the focus on written communication in the classical era to the focus on oral communication in more modern times.

Thus, in the language of the times, the goals of these approaches were at least from an early 1920s perspective:

- To understand what is said in the foreign language when it is spoken rapidly by natives.
- To speak the foreign language in the manner of natives.
- To understand the language as written by natives.
- To write the language in the manner of natives.

(Palmer, 1921, p. 24)

The reform movement: teaching learners about phonology

> New things always frighten people; they think with terror that here the pupils are to be burdened with an entirely new and difficult science and with a new kind of writing; we had trouble enough with the old kind, they say, and now we are to be bothered with this new alphabet with its barbarous letters!
>
> (Jespersen, 1904, p. 142)

The reform movement marked a pivotal moment in the historical timeline of pronunciation instruction. For the first time, scientific study of linguistic knowledge, specifically of phonetics, began to have an impact on the L2 classroom. The International Phonetic Alphabet (IPA) was first developed in 1886 to encourage the scientific study of phonetics, but it wasn't until more than a decade later that it started to gain wider acceptance in L2 classrooms. Sweet (1899) and other phoneticians introduced the scientific study of phonetics to the language classroom and, ever since the time of its introduction, it has been widely used in L2 classrooms around the world, a practice that certainly continues today (Celce-Murcia, Brinton, Goodwin & Griner, 2010; Setter & Jenkins, 2005). In essence, the analytic-linguistic approach to pronunciation teaching observed the emergence of teachers beginning to share linguistic knowledge about phonology with their students, encouraging students to make connections between sounds, symbols, articulatory descriptions of sounds and movements. An analytic-linguistic approach incorporates all or at least some of the following:

- distinct symbols to represent each of the sounds in a language;
- articulatory descriptions of the movements of different articulators in the vocal tract for the production of each of these sounds;
- visual diagrams depicting the movement of each of these articulators within the vocal tract to aid the teaching of spoken language; and
- the use of a mirror to observe the parts of the mouth in action and a tactile method that involved using your hand to feel the vibration made by sounds produced in the naval cavity, larynx, etc.

(Orlow, 1951)

The following excerpt from Jespersen's text provides an illustration of a teacher using articulatory description to help a student pronounce the word 'Papa'.

> *Teacher*: John, can you say papa? Papa. – How do you go about it? Say it once more. – Papa. First, I open my mouth, and then I open it once again. – Yes, and in the meantime you must, of course, have closed it. Look at me, all of you, and see if I too go about it in that way – Papa. What did I do, William? – First you opened your mouth, then closed it, then opened it again. – What did I close it with? – With the lips. – Now, when I say op, ap, ep, what do I do? – Close the lips every time, and then open them again. – Then I do that every time I say p. Robert can you find any other sounds where I close my lips? No. – Try the word mama. – Yes, in m. – Now, say baby and bib. – Also in b. – Good; then we have three sounds now where the lips are closed, p, b, m. Let us write them in a row on the blackboard.
>
> (Jespersen, 1904, p. 146)

MacCarthy (1952, 1953) also published a series of mini-case studies that he claimed were based on real classroom experiences in which teachers used physiological descriptions to modify students' pronunciation. Here's one that focused on the old chestnut of learner difficulties: the interdental 'th' sound.

> Teacher. . . . there are various points that will need attending to, but I think one of the most obvious things to me, and I imagine to the average English hearer, concerns your way of articulating the English *th*. At the moment it's quite unacceptable! Are you aware of that, I wonder?
>
> Miss D. (mystified). – Nooo. S!, S! (S stands for a faulty sound). Is that wrong? S!
>
> T. – Yes; it's too much like s. Any English person would think it *was* s you were trying to say. Would you mind just pronouncing for me the [word] spelt T-H-I-N-K?
>
> Miss D. – Siŋk!
>
> T. – Quite so. I get the impression that you're saying the word spelt S-I-N-K! Never mind: we can probably begin to put that right straight away. Your tongue isn't far enough forward. Try holding the tip of your tongue between your teeth and a look in this mirror – you'll be able to see what you're doing. There, that's better; now blow!
>
> Miss D. – θS!
>
> T. – Ah! Did you see what happened? As soon as you started to blow, the tip slipped back again. . . . Try again. Mind you keep the tip right forward – where you can see it. Now try.
>
> (MacCarthy, 1952, pp. 112–113)

Along with physiological descriptions, phonetic symbols were integral to phonetic training in the language classroom. After more than 50 years into the development of using the phonetic alphabet to teach pronunciation, the integration of a phonetic alphabet eventually became a foundational component of pronunciation instruction. Orlow (1951, p. 389) published the following 'Steps to Teaching Pronunciation' [full stops added to original text below], which outlines how the phonetic training may have been conducted in classrooms.

1. First of all foreign sounds must be studied carefully *in isolation*. In some cases a [set of] special exercises for lips, tongue, soft palate and jaw must be given to the student in this period.

2. This is followed by the study of *phonetic syllables* which are a combination of a consonant and a vowel. Phonetic syllables actually represent the beginning or the ending of a regular foreign word. They help to fix a new sound pattern which can be reproduced with ease. Those consonants on which drill is desired should be used in succession of initial, final and medial position, the latter being generally the most difficult for pronunciation.

3. *Phonetic words* which are simple one-syllable words formed from the phonetic syllables are the next step.

4. After phonetic words follow *common familiar words*. A list of them should be prepared by the instructor. Here again attention must be called to initial, final and medial position of a sound which is drilled.

5. By this time the student should be ready to use correctly the foreign sounds in *short phrases*. These phrases may be either 'catchy,' humorous expressions or original lines contributed by the instructor.

6. Further the sounds may be used in *short sentences* taken from books or made by the teacher.
7. The final test of achievement is sounds in selections of *prose and poetry*. Attention to intonation must be given during this phase of teaching. In every language intonation is a very important feature of pronunciation.
8. *Informal conversation* is the goal to which all previous work must lead.

Focus on listening: ear training

Integral to naturalistic approaches to language learning was the emphasis on oral communication in general, and listening in particular. This view aligned with the experience of learning a first language, contending that the first exposure a newborn baby has to language is typically the spoken words of the child's care givers. This focus on oral comprehension first was intertwined with the notion of ear training, which is a theme that spans the entirety of the twentieth century and beyond. Active listening and time dedicated to training the ear to hear the sounds produced by others as well as those they produce themselves (self-monitoring) was considered an important element of language learning (Goddard, 1945; Gullette, 1932; Kreidler, 1972; MacCarthy, 1976; Orlow, 1951), and in the communicative period of contemporary times continues to be strongly emphasized, especially in relation to prosody (Gilbert, 2001; Morley, 1991a, 1991b). But the focus on ear training was not merely limited to learners of the language but pertained to teachers as well. Gullette argued that both students and teachers lacked sufficient ear training and that they needed to:

> strive continuously and consistently to listen to the sounds made or heard, in order to tell if they are correct or, should they be wrong, to diagnose whether the fault is caused by too great a jaw opening, by improper position of the lips, by a relaxation of the jaw which permits a glide to enter in by a location too far forward or too far back in the mouth, etc.
>
> (Gullette, 1932, p. 335)

In a round robin discussion published as a co-authored journal article decades later, Morley further highlighted the notion that teachers require an in-depth knowledge of and practice in 'speech analysis, articulation analysis, and error analysis' (Stevick, Morley & Robinett, 1975, p. 85). Furthermore, as Abercrombie noted,

> On the practical side he [sic] needs an ear sufficiently trained to diagnose mistakes, and vocal organs sufficiently under control to produce isolated English sounds and imitations of pupils' mispronunciations; and some acquaintance with those tricks of the phonetic trade which provide short cuts in correcting mistakes.
>
> (Abercrombie, 1949, p. 115)

One of the teacher's resource books of the time, Harold Palmer's (1921) *The Principles of Language Study*, provided teachers with an 'ideal' sequence of study to best support students in learning a language efficiently and effectively.

1. Ears before eyes
2. Reception before reproduction
3. Oral repetition before reading

4. Immediate memory before prolonged memory
5. Chorus-work before individual-work
6. Drill-work before free work.

(pp. 23–24)

Audiolingualism and Situational Language Teaching

The 1940s to the 1950s gave rise to two prominent methods in language teaching, namely what was referred to as Audiolingualism in North America and as Situational Language Teaching in Great Britain. Situational language teaching found its roots in the Direct Method, whereas the audiolingual method drew upon structural linguistics and behavioural psychology for its conceptual support (Richards & Rodgers, 1986), yet they shared much in common and there was considerable overlap between them. Oral communication, first, and written communication, second, were fundamental principles to both, with pronunciation playing a significant role in each (Celce-Murcia et al., 2010). Based on language typically taken from a dialogue or situational text, specific features of pronunciation or fluency were targeted and explicitly corrected as problems arose (Richards & Rodgers, 1986). Frequently, pronunciation drills focused on the use of oral repetition and practice with minimal pairs. Richards and Rodgers summarize the first set of procedures in a typical audiolingual lesson below. It is in this first set where pronunciation instruction is most prominent:

> Students first hear a model dialogue (either read by the teacher or on tape) containing the key structures that are the focus of the lesson. They repeat each line of the dialogue individually and in chorus. The teacher pays attention to pronunciation, intonation, and fluency. Correction of mistakes of pronunciation or grammar is direct and immediate. The dialogue is memorized gradually, line by line. A line may be broken down into several phases if necessary. The dialogue is read aloud in chorus, one half [of the class] saying one speaker's part and the other half responding. The students do not consult their book throughout this phase.

(p. 58)

Linguistic/scientific study and classroom application

The early 1950s witnessed the introduction of some measure of empirical research in classroom contexts to further fine-tune pronunciation pedagogy. The *Manual of American English Pronunciation* comprised four editions, spanning three decades (Prator, 1951, 1957; Prator & Robinett, 1972, 1985), and is representative of this innovation in language teaching. The manual was claimed to be developed based on linguistic principles from both American and British phoneticians as well as knowledge gained from the foreign language classroom. It drew on the experiences of language teachers and speech pathologists at the University of California, Los Angeles. Materials in the book were reported to have been tested in language classrooms and targeted to address the needs of learners from a variety of first language (L1) backgrounds, as is common in most ESL classroom situations. That is, the manual's content and design was informed by a frequency count of pronunciation difficulties derived from speech data collected from university-level ESL students over a period of three years, particularly students from the following L1 backgrounds: Spanish, Northern Chinese, Iranian, Arabic, Germanic, French and Scandinavian.

We believe we have thus avoided two undesirable extremes: (1) a text organized solely in accordance with the subjective intuition of the author, and (2) one which logically and with equal emphasis treats all the elements of the English sound system without taking into consideration the special needs of the student group.

(Prator, 1957, p. xii)

The third (1972) and fourth (1985) editions of the manual are largely consistent with the original but use a modified form of the IPA, which Robinett reports as having been adapted from a combination of Trager-Smith notation system and Fries-Pike's version of the IPA (Prator & Robinett, 1972). For example, the first lesson on the phonetic alphabet begins with a phonetic alphabet symbol, English examples, and approximate equivalents in four major languages as follows (p. 4)

		Approximate equivalents in			
Symbol	English examples	French	German	Japanese	Spanish
/ š /	ship / šIp/	*chez*	*sch*ön	*sh*uppatsu	(none)

The student begins by reading a diagnostic passage and later the teacher analyses the students' pronunciation difficulties according to the 'check list of errors' made available in the manual's provided 'accent inventory'.

Focus on intelligibility

It is important to highlight here that the strong focus on achieving intelligible English is by no means restricted to the contemporary communicative era. A focus on intelligibility has been advocated by scholars for over a century, despite continuous student demand for 'correct' or 'native speaker' pronunciation even in the modern classroom (Drewelow & Theobald, 2007; Timmis, 2002). As early as 1904, Jesperson, although focusing on oral reading, discussed the need for learners to be able to speak 'intelligibly and intelligently' (p. 87). Of course, it is important to note that Jesperson's use of the term 'intelligibly' likely differs from how specialists employ the same term today (e.g. Munro & Derwing, 2011); nevertheless, its usage represents a possible beginning for change. Throughout the decades that followed, numerous scholars began to question the need for 'correct pronunciations' or native speaker-accented speech (Kenyon, 1928; McCutcheon, 1939; Wilson, 1937). Morley, as part of the same round robin discussion mentioned earlier, posited that 'intelligibility for communication is the minimum and beyond that, it is up to the students to continue to perfect their spoken English to the point which they need in order to function to their own satisfaction' (Stevick et al., 1975, p. 85). Hill (1961/1967) argued for a focus on 'internationally intelligible' (p. 77) English for both teachers and students. Bowen (1972) appeared to support these ideas in his argument that the goal should be 'to achieve a competence in pronunciation' but without expecting the student 'to conceal their own different language background' (pp. 84–85), thus enabling learners to maintain their sense of cultural and linguistic identity. Ultimately, greater acceptance of non-native-accented speech has been strongly advocated.

Yet, although pre-communicative era scholars focused on intelligibility as the goal for classroom instruction, the classroom reality focused, nonetheless, on the native speaker as the ideal target. 'The ideal is to be able to pronounce and speak with native-like competence, though in most classrooms and with most students this remains an ideal, a goal to shoot at, the approximation to which serves as a measure of student achievement' (Bowen, 1972, p. 84). It was not until later in the communicative era, through initiatives such as Catford's (1987) relative functional load[2] and Jenkins' lingua franca core (2000, 2002), that the teaching of certain features of pronunciation over others began to be prioritized in the classroom, based on the identification of those features that have the greatest impact on intelligibility.

Meaningful practice

Perhaps in response to this increased focus on learner intelligibility, a focus on meaningful pronunciation practice gained momentum through two notions that appeared to emerge in the 1970s and early 1980s, namely meaningful minimal pair practice and integrating pronunciation into the teaching other skill areas.

Meaningful minimal pairs and contextualization

Bowen (1972), another innovator of the second wave of pronunciation teaching, introduced a series of analytic-linguistic techniques to support contextualized language learning. He advocated placing greater emphasis on contextualizing pronunciation practice for students, moving away from earlier approaches, which depended heavily on decontextualized drills. Instead he targeted 'communicative competence', thus focusing on introducing minimal pair drills (at levels of whole sentences and phrases) in a more meaningful way. Bowen describes the following pronunciation lesson, which exemplifies this idea. First the teacher draws a picture of a horse on the board and has students guess what the drawing depicts. Next, the teacher does the same for fire, horseshoe and hammer. The class then establishes that a blacksmith is the person who fits a heated metal horseshoe to a horse's hoof. Once this background is established, he asks the class to indicate how a blacksmith carries out the following two tasks, in which the statement and rejoinder from a meaningful drill:

> He's heating the shoe.   With a fire.
>
> He's hitting the shoe.   With a hammer.

(p. 88)

The following excerpt illustrates the remainder of the lesson, with its continued focus on pronunciation.

> After I've produced the full sentences several times, He's heating the shoe with a fire. He's hitting the shoe with a hammer, I then give just the first part of the sentence and ask the class to give the final phrase as a rejoinder. If, as often happens, there is disagreement, I stop and ask for a show of hands: 'How many say fire? How many say hammer?' Then I announce which one I said by indicating which response I expected. As confidence builds I get a volunteer to come to the front of the room and work with me. I make my statement and he offers his rejoinder. Then I ask how many in the class agree with him, then announce what my intention was. Then I ask the class to produce the statement in chorus, following my cue as I point alternately to the pictures of the fire and the hammer. . . . Finally I ask for another volunteer, who comes to the front of the room. I mark a figure 1 over the fire and a figure 2 over the hammer. Then I go to the back of the room where only the volunteer can face me. I insist that other students face front, away from me. Then with arms folded or extended I briefly signal an intention to the

volunteer. If I flash one finger, he is to say 'He's heating the shoe'; if two fingers, 'He's hitting the shoe.' The class is to respond with the appropriate rejoinder.

(pp. 89–90)

Integration with other skills

A second major theme that further supported meaningful pronunciation practice was integration of pronunciation instruction with the teaching of other skill areas. Morley was one of the first to raise this point in the round robin discussion that took place in *TESOL Quarterly* (Stevick et al., 1975). She posed the question 'Should pronunciation be isolated from other aspects of language practice?' (p. 86). Although she was referring specifically to the listening/speaking class at the University of Michigan, she stressed that the goal of the oral communication class should include a focus on both fluency and accuracy and that 'meaningful practice in context is the primary concern throughout' (p. 86). To achieve this type of instruction, she outlined the following four activities:

- structured listening practice;
- 'spontaneous' listening practice;
- structured speaking practice (which includes work with prosodics, vowels, and consonants, student-written dialogues and responses, and special oral reading);
- 'spontaneous' speaking practice.

(p. 86)

Since then, and with increasing emphasis throughout the communicative era, numerous scholars have continued to argue for pronunciation to be integrated throughout the curriculum (Levis & Grant, 2003; Murphy, 1991) and gradually classrooms have demonstrated the integration of pronunciation as in courses dedicated to oral communication (Baker, 2011, 2014; Jones 2016).

Emergence of phonological hierarchies into pronunciation instruction

Another concept that emerged towards the end of the second wave was the introduction of phonological hierarchies into pronunciation curriculum. These hierarchies shifted the traditional classroom focus from segmentals (vowels and consonants) towards suprasegmentals (stress, rhythm, intonation, tone groups etc.) and provided a theoretical rationale for this change. Catford (1966, p. 606) and Halliday, whom Catford cites as co-developer, established a model of English phonology using a simplified four-level hierarchy for use in the classroom:

(a) Tone-group (e.g. //The cat chased the mouse / into the green house // = two tone groups or information units with each having a pitch movement);
(b) Foot (also referred to as stress-groups and has contrastive stress, such as //The cat chased the mouse// (The cat didn't watch the mouse; he chased it));
(c) Syllable;
(d) Phoneme.

Catford argued that such a hierarchy provided a curriculum for a pronunciation course, with each unit devoted to one of these four elements. He explained that he has 'found it pedagogically desirable to start with the *foot*, and then work upwards to the *tone-group* and downwards to the *phoneme*' (p. 612).

What started with Catford and Halliday has continued on into the communicative era with the use of phonological hierarchies becoming increasingly prominent in course curricula. One of the more well-known of these is Gilbert's booklet-length discussion of a 'prosody pyramid' (2008), which is freely available online and includes a comprehensive set of notes on how to use this model in the classroom.

Emergence of 'practical' pronunciation teaching philosophies

The final years of the second wave witnessed the advent of pronunciation-specific 'practical' teaching philosophies, as embodied in the published positions of Parish (1977) and Stevick (1978) towards the end of the 1970s. Parish's 'practical philosophy of pronunciation' comprised four key statements:

(a) Everything the teacher does co-involves pronunciation;
(b) Correction of the student's aberrant pronunciation is a continual, ongoing process, not something reserved for lessons or exercises in pronunciation;
(c) The ability of students to absorb and process is a slowly-developing one;
(d) The amount of time that an instructor puts into specific pronunciation explanation and exercise is rarely directly proportionate to and productive of the desired student behaviour: a two-minute articulatory description and modelled list of words containing the target sound may produce unexpected results, and a 10-minute description and exercise may produce little or no results;
(e) Contrastive analysis offers facts about contrast and similarity between segments and structures of two given languages, and the teacher's ear will indeed confirm the facts of contrast;
(f) The knowledge that instructors have about the phonology of at least the target language will enable them to be both accurate and economical in their work with student pronunciation.

(Parish, 1977, pp. 312–313)

In response to Parish's publication, Stevick countered with his own perspective:

(a) Pronunciation is the primary medium through which we bring our use of language to the attention of other people;
(b) People who have normal physiological equipment can mimic new sounds, and will do so, unless (a) they overlook something, or (b) they sound bad to themselves when they mimic well, or (c) they become anxious about the process of making the sound;
(c) Permanent change comes about (a) to an extent that is consistent with the student's self-image, (b) through work that is done by the student, (c) as a part of his or her developing relationship (real and/or imaginary) with speakers of the language;
(d) Therefore, with regard to pronunciation, the essential functions of the teacher are (a) to provide suitable models, and (b) to make it easy for students to find out how their efforts compare with the pronunciation that is taken as the standard for the course.

(Stevick, 1978, pp. 145–147)

One notion in particular that merits mention from these two perspectives is the focus on the learner in Stevick's philosophy and how elements such as 'self-image' and 'anxiety' and 'relationships' play an integral role in pronunciation development. These are all concepts that have gained increasing attention in the communicative era.

Conclusion: shift towards the third wave – communicative styles of pronunciation teaching

The second wave in the history of pronunciation teaching marked an era of significant innovation and pedagogical change in how pronunciation instruction had been transformed in the classroom. In essence, the changes that occurred during this period provided the foundation on which pronunciation teaching in the communicative era has been constructed. These changes were often inspired by theoretical notions but rarely validated by empirical, classroom-based research.

The next chapters in this volume illuminate what pronunciation teaching looks like in the era of communicative language teaching (Levis & Sonsaat, Chapter 16), and reject the outdated model of isolating the teaching of pronunciation from other areas of language and content. Rather, pronunciation is best conceptualized as an integral component of the teaching of all skill areas, including speaking (Newton, Chapter 20), listening (Cauldwell, Chapter 21) and other areas of language (Jones, Chapter 22).

Notes

1 Naturalistic approaches refer to approaches that are similar to how a child learns his/her first language. There is typically an emphasis first on oral communication, especially aural comprehension, and later a focus might be placed on written communication.
2 Relative functional load placed primary importance on learners being able to differentiate, either in listening or speaking, between segmentals that have the greatest impact on comprehensibility.

References

Abercrombie, D. (1949). Teaching pronunciation. *ELT Journal, 3*(5), 113–122.

Acton, W., Baker, A., Burri, M., & Teaman, B. (2013). Preliminaries to haptic-integrated pronunciation instruction. In J. M. Levis & K. LeVelle (Eds), *Proceedings of the 4th Pronunciation in Second Language Learning and Teaching Conference, August 2012* (pp. 234–244). Ames, IA: Iowa State University.

Baker, A. (2011). Discourse prosody and teachers' stated beliefs and practices. *TESOL Journal, 2*(3), 263–292. doi:10.5054/tj.2011.259955.

Baker, A. (2014). Exploring teachers' knowledge of L2 pronunciation techniques: Teacher cognitions, observed classroom practices and student perceptions. *TESOL Quarterly, 48*(1), 136–163. doi:10.1002/tesq.99.

Bentley, R. (1849). *The pictorial spelling book: Containing an improved method of teaching the alphabet, and likewise spelling and pronunciation, by the use of pictures*. New York, NY: Pratt, Woodford.

Bowen, J. D. (1972). Contextualizing pronunciation practice in the ESOL classroom. *TESOL Quarterly, 6*(1), 83–94. doi:10.2307/3585862.

Catford, J. C. (1966). English phonology and the teaching of pronunciation. *College English, 27*(8), 605–613.

Catford, J. C. (1987). Phonetics and the teaching of pronunciation: A systemic description of English phonology. In J. Morley (Ed.), *Current perspectives on pronunciation: Practices anchored in theory* (pp. 83–100). Washington, DC: TESOL.

Celce-Murcia, M., Brinton, D. M., Goodwin, J. M., & Griner, B. (2010). *Teaching pronunciation: A reference for teachers of English to speakers of other languages* (2nd ed.). Cambridge: Cambridge University Press.

De Laporte, C. (1845). *A self-teaching reader, for the study of the pronunciation of the French language: After a plan entirely new; which will enable the American or English student to acquire with facility a correct pronunciation, with or without the assistance of a teacher*. Cambridge: Metcalf.

Drewelow, I., & Theobald, A. (2007). A comparison of the attitudes of learners, instructors, and native French speakers about the pronunciation of French: An exploratory study. *Foreign Language Annals*, *40*(3), 491–520.

Foote, J. A., Holtby, A. K., & Derwing, T. M. (2011). Survey of the teaching of pronunciation in adult ESL programs in Canada, 2010. *TESL Canada Journal*, *29*(1), 1–22.

Gilbert, J. B. (2001). *Clear speech from the start: Basic pronunciation and listening comprehension in North American English* (3rd ed.). New York, NY: Cambridge University Press.

Gilbert, J. B. (2008). Teaching pronunciation: Using the prosody pyramid. Retrieved from www.tesol.org/docs/default-source/new-resource-library/teaching-pronunciation-using-the-prosody-pyramid.pdf?sfvrsn=0.

Goddard, E. R. (1945). A lesson plan for teaching French pronunciation. *The Modern Language Journal*, *29*(3), 187–197. doi:10.2307/318731.

Goodwin, J. (2014). Teaching pronunciation. In M. Celce-Murcia, D. M. Brinton, & M. A. Snow (Eds), *Teaching English as a second or foreign language* (4th ed), 138–154. Boston, MA: National Geographic Learning/Cengage Learning.

Gullette, C. C. (1932). Ear training in the teaching of pronunciation. *The Modern Language Journal*, *16*(4), 334–336.

Hervey, W. A. (1916). Oral practice: Its purpose, means and difficulties. *The Modern Language Journal*, *1*(3), 79–91.

Hill, L. A. (1961/1967). *Selected articles on the teaching of English as a second language*. New York, NY: Oxford University Press. (Reprinted from *Teaching English*, 6(4), August 1961).

Howatt, A. P. R., & Widdowson, H. G. (2004). *A history of English language teaching* (2nd ed.). Oxford: Oxford University Press.

Jenkins, J. (2000). *The phonology of English as an international language*. Oxford: Oxford University Press.

Jenkins, J. (2002). A sociolinguistically based, empirically researched pronunciation syllabus for English as an international language. *Applied Linguistics*, *23*(1), 83–103.

Jespersen, O. (1904). *How to teach a foreign language* (S. Y.-O. Bertelsen, Trans.). London: George Allen & Unwin.

Jones, T. (2016). *Pronunciation in the classroom: The overlooked essential*. Alexandria, VA: Tesolpress.

Kelly, L. G. (1971). English as a second language: An historical sketch. *ELT Journal*, *25*(2), 120–132.

Kenyon, J. S. (1928). Correct Pronunciation. *American Speech*, *4*(2), 150–153.

Kreidler, C. W. (1972). Teaching English spelling and pronunciation. *TESOL Quarterly*, *6*(1), 3–12. doi:10.2307/3585857.

Levis, J. M., & Grant, L. (2003). Integrating pronunciation into ESL/EFL classrooms. *TESOL Journal*, *12*(2), 13–19.

Lortie, D. C. (1975). *School-teacher: A sociological study*. Chicago, IL: University of Chicago Press.

MacCarthy, P. A. D. (1952). Pronunciation teaching: Theory and practice. *ELT Journal*, *6*(4), 111–117. doi:10.1093/elt/VI.4.111.

MacCarthy, P. A. D. (1953). Pronunciation Teaching: Theory and Practice (II). *ELT Journal*, *7*(3), 91–95. doi:10.1093/elt/VII.3.91.

MacCarthy, P. A. D. (1976). Auditory and articulatory training for the language teacher and learner. *ELT Journal*, *30*(3), 212–219.

McCutcheon, R. J. (1939). 'Correct Pronunciations'. *American Speech*, *14*(2), 159–160.

Meiden, W. (1963). A device for teaching pronunciation-the reading of the lesson of the day. *The Modern Language Journal*, *47*(2), 65–69. doi:10.2307/321348.

Morley, J. (1991a). The pronunciation component in Teaching English to Speakers of Other Languages. *TESOL Quarterly*, *25*(3), 481–520.

Morley, J. (1991b). *Rapid review of vowels and prosodic contexts*. Ann Arbor, MI: University of Michigan Press.

Munro, M. J., & Derwing, T. M. (2011). The foundations of accent and intelligibility in pronunciation research. *Language Teaching, 44*, 316–327.

Murphy, J. M. (2003). Pronunciation. In D. Nunan (Ed.) *Practical English language teaching* (pp. 111–128). New York, NY: McGraw-Hill.

Murphy, J. M. (1991). Oral Communication in TESOL: Integrating speaking, listening and pronunciation. *TESOL Quarterly, 25*(1), 51–75.

Murphy, J. M. (2004). Attending to word-stress while learning new vocabulary. *English for Specific Purposes, 23*(1), 67–83. doi:10.1016/S0889–4906(03)00019-X.

Murphy, J. M. (2014). Myth 7: Teacher training programs provide adequate preparation in how to teach pronunciation. In L. Grant (Ed.), *Pronunciation myths: Applying second language research to classroom teaching* (pp. 188–224). Ann Arbor, MI: University of Michigan Press.

Murphy, J., & Baker, A. A. (2015). History of ESL pronunciation teaching. In J. M. Levis & M. Reed (Eds), *Handbook of English pronunciation* (pp. 36–65). New York, NY: Wiley-Blackwell.

Murphy, J., & Kandil, M. (2004). Word-level stress patterns in the academic word list. *System, 32*, 61–74.

Orlow, P. F. (1951). Basic principles of teaching foreign pronunciation. *The Modern Language Journal, 35*(5), 387.

Ormsby, R. (1860). *Vermont speller; or, progressive lessons in the English language* (5th ed.). Bradford, VT: R. Farnham, JR.

Palmer, H. E. (1921). *The principles of language study*. Yonker-on-Hudson, NY: World Book.

Parish, C. (1977). A practical philosophy of pronunciation. *TESOL Quarterly, 11*(3), 311–317.

Prator, C. H. (1951). *Manual of American English pronunciation for adult foreign students*. Berkeley, CA: University of California Press (2nd edition 1957, New York, NY: Rinehart & Company).

Prator, C. H., & Robinett, B. W. (1972). *Manual of American English pronunciation* (3rd ed.). New York, NY: Holt, Rinehart & Winston (4th edition 1985).

Prator, C. H., & Robinett, B. W. (1985). *Manual of American English pronunciation* (4th ed.). New York, NY: Holt, Rinehart & Winston.

Richards, J. C., & Rodgers, T. S. (1986). *Approaches and methods in language teaching*. Cambridge: Cambridge University Press.

Setter, J., & Jenkins, J. (2005). State-of-the-art review article: Pronunciation. *Language Teaching, 38*(1), 1–17. doi:10.1017/S026144480500251X.

Shearer, J. W. (1914). *A pronouncing speller for foreigners. A combination of method of instruction for quickly teaching English pronunciation to foreigners*. New York, NY: William R. Jenkins.

Stevick, E. W. (1978). Toward a practical philosophy of pronunciation: Another view. *TESOL Quarterly, 12*(2), 145–150.

Stevick, E. W., Morley, J., & Robinett, B. W. (1975). Round robin on the teaching of pronunciation. *TESOL Quarterly, 9*(1), 81–88.

Strevens, P. (1974). A rationale for teaching pronunciation: The rival virtues of innocence and sophistication. *ELT Journal, 28*(3), 182–189.

Sweet, H. (1899). *The practical study of languages*. New York, NY: Henry Holt.

Timmis, I. (2002). Native-speaker norms and international English: A classroom view. *ELT Journal, 56*(3), 240–249. doi:10.1093/elt/56.3.240.

Wilson, G. P. (1937). Standards of correct pronunciation. *Quarterly Journal of Speech, 23*(4), 568–576.

Wren, P. C. (1912). *The 'direct' teaching of English in Indian schools*. Bombay: Longmans, Green.

16

Pronunciation teaching in the early CLT era

John Levis and Sinem Sonsaat

Introduction

Communicative Language Teaching (CLT) dates from the early 1970s (Widdowson, 1972; Wilkins, 1972). Its general approach developed from the recognition that teaching language form did not invariably result in success at using language for communication (Berns, 1984; Widdowson, 1972). The dominant teaching methods of the 1960s, oral-situational and the audio lingual method (ALM), correspondingly lost influence over time (Richards & Rodgers, 2001) as language teaching moved from a focus on linguistic competence (knowledge of the language and its formal characteristics) to communicative competence, or ability to use the language for purposes of genuine communication (Littlewood, 2011).

With the rise of CLT from the early 1970s to the early 1990s came the decline of pronunciation in language teaching. Pronunciation had been a central element of ALM and oral-situational teaching, but this centrality was lost in the 1970s, 1980s and beyond. Fewer teacher preparation programmes included pronunciation in their curricula, and fewer teachers were being trained, resulting in teachers not feeling adequately prepared to teach pronunciation (Breitkreutz, Derwing & Rossiter, 2001; Burgess & Spencer, 2000; Burns, 2006; Derwing & Munro, 2005; Macdonald, 2002; Murphy, 1997, 2014).

Why was pronunciation, in the words of Kelly (1969), 'the Cinderella of language teaching' (p. 87)? This image of a stepchild who is unfairly oppressed and unappreciated has been one of the most repeated images for pronunciation teaching in the past four decades (e.g. Celce-Murcia, Brinton & Goodwin, 1996; Dalton, 1997; Seidlhofer, 2001) since Kelly (p. 87) wrote:

> It will be obvious that pronunciation has been the Cinderella of language teaching, largely because the linguistic sciences on which its teaching rests did not achieve the sophistication of semantics, lexicology, and grammar until the 19th century.

Several elements of this quote are important. First is its verb tense – *has been*. Kelly's statement looks back in time from the vantage point of 1969. Kelly's statement, far from saying pronunciation is Cinderella, indicates that pronunciation is not, and that it then had (at least in 1969) the linguistic sophistication to merit an equal seat at the language teaching table.

Second is the time period in which it was written. 1969 was pre-CLT by any estimation, and pronunciation is described as having *been* 'the Cinderella of language teaching'. This tells us that CLT cannot be the original reason for pronunciation's Cinderella status, and that pronunciation's weakened role in CLT reflected a new state of affairs.

There is plenty of anecdotal evidence that those advocating CLT had difficulty fitting pronunciation teaching into the new approach, even by the early 1990s. A colleague of ours provided one example.

> This was around 1990. When I worked at a university in East Asia, I asked if we had any pronunciation activities or materials that we could use in our classes. I was told that we followed principles of communicative language teaching, which had shown that students learn through communication and that pronunciation activities were a waste of time. The senior instructors who were responsible for curriculum decisions believed that students would slowly improve their pronunciation by using English, but students would not improve their pronunciation by using pronunciation activities. . . . I went to a large language learning conference. While at the book fair, I asked one of the publishers about pronunciation materials (a book accompanied with cassette tapes). I was told that there was little interest in pronunciation activities since most teachers adhered to communicative language teaching principles.
>
> (Gary Ockey, personal communication, February 2016)

Such sentiments raise a question of whether CLT proponents in the early years were deliberately and openly negative towards pronunciation, which only recently had been granted an equal place with grammar in language teaching, or was the neglect of pronunciation an unintended consequence of a broad based paradigm shift in language teaching related to the rise of CLT? While the first explanation has anecdotal evidence to recommend it, it is our contention that the second explanation fits the historical facts more closely than the first. The neglect of pronunciation associated with the early CLT era was a result of many factors that reflected a paradigm shift in language teaching and the changes associated with such a shift. In this chapter, we first discuss how pronunciation was situated in second language (L2) teaching during the early CLT era (early 1970s–early 1990s). Then we examine some of the CLT principles that help explain why pronunciation seemed to decline in importance in early CLT. Next, we show why those same principles led to a renewal of pronunciation's role starting around the mid-1980s. Following this, we look at the evidence for CLT's influence from journal articles. Finally, we look at pronunciation-centred ESL classroom textbooks to examine how CLT principles were realized.

Paradigm shift during the development of CLT

The future dominance of CLT was uncertain in the 1970s. Originally a European innovation, CLT was only one among many new ways of teaching during this period. Designer methods such as Counselling Learning, Silent Way and Suggestopedia, where pronunciation was important, also competed for attention in the changing landscape. In addition, American comprehension-based approaches such as total physical response and the natural approach gave little attention to explicit teaching of language form, whether grammar or pronunciation. CLT approaches varied and changed forms quickly, from the somewhat form-based functional-notional approach of Wilkins (1976), in which communication was the result of having a communicative product (e.g. language greetings) to the more radical recommendations of Widdowson (1972), in which teaching involved a communicative process (e.g. classroom procedures should themselves be communicative and use-oriented), which deeply influenced the English for specific purposes movement (e.g. Hutchison & Waters, 1987). A decade into the CLT era, language instruction specialists such as Harmer (1982) were still in the process of elaborating the precise characteristics of CLT. Indeed, Harmer argued that there was no communicative method, only communicative activities. Such a view recognizes that CLT was not a traditional method but rather an approach that allowed much greater flexibility in pedagogy than earlier L2 methods (Richards & Rodgers, 2001). An indirect influence on pronunciation teaching during this time was Krashen (1982), who dominated discussion of the second language acquisition research agenda in the minds of many classroom teachers. Krashen's position was that L2 learning involved two processes, 'learning' and 'acquisition'. Learning was the result of explicit instruction, typically in a classroom. Acquisition, on the other hand, was the result of implicit learning, much like what transpires during first language acquisition. Acquisition resulted from sufficient comprehensible input, and accuracy in grammar and pronunciation was thought to follow from naturalistic acquisition processes. The knowledge gained through learning, in contrast, was subject to conscious control by a monitor, a kind of internal arbiter of correct language use. In Krashen's view, learning could not become acquisition, that is, automatically available in the stream of speech. The effects of Krashen's views on the teaching of language form in classrooms were dramatic and widespread. Teaching formal aspects of language was seen as encouraging 'learning' rather than 'acquisition', and explicit teaching of language form was deemphasized.

Pronunciation during the early CLT era

Questions of the value of pronunciation instruction triggered numerous discussions during the early CLT era, yet explicit written claims that pronunciation should not be taught were rare. Instead, the shifting paradigm left little room for pronunciation teaching as it had been practised. For example, the lack of certainty about the value of error correction, suggestions that errors be skipped during communicative activities (Brown & Yule, 1983), or not corrected at all for certain proficiency levels (Krashen & Terrell, 1983) seemed to imply that pronunciation teaching was incompatible with CLT practice. Another issue was that, with few notable exceptions, almost no one knew what it would be like to teach pronunciation communicatively (Murphy & Baker, 2015). Celce-Murcia (1983, 1987) noted that teaching pronunciation communicatively was entering uncharted waters, especially for supra-segmentals. Writers such as Pica (1984), Morley (1987) and Kenworthy (1987) explored what it meant to teach pronunciation communicatively, but what communicative pronunciation teaching would look like remained uncertain. The paradigm had shifted, and not knowing how pronunciation could be integrated made CLT look like the evil stepmother of this 'Cinderella' story. In reality, there was no villain, just a product (pronunciation) that had lost its relevance in a new type of language teaching market. What had been essential now seemed extraneous, as Brown and Yule (1983, p. 53) described it:

> We have not paid attention in this book to the teaching of pronunciation and intonation. This is partly because our aim here is to focus on developing the student's ability to use English to communicate with someone in long transactional turns. . . . In this stressful task the student needs all the support he can get from the teacher, not criticism of relatively *extraneous features* [emphasis added] like pronunciation.

It should also be noted that Brown and Yule did not say pronunciation should not be taught. On the same page, the authors advised teachers to note down any pronunciation errors that need to be addressed and deal with them once students had completed the communicative task. Thus, they limited pronunciation teaching to cases where communication breakdowns occurred. In this, they represent a dilemma presented by pronunciation in CLT. It does not seem to fit, but it cannot be dispensed with. In a retrospective view of pronunciation and early CLT, Hammond (1995) stated that none of the CLT-oriented methods dictated that pronunciation not be taught; however, he also said that none made an effort to integrate pronunciation into communicative teaching. (Similar things were also being said about grammar teaching; see Thompson, 1996.)

In response to our question about how pronunciation was affected by the rise of CLT, Wayne Dickerson (personal communication, 3 November 2014) noted that pronunciation remained visible during the CLT era, specifically giving credit to influential journals such as *TESOL Quarterly*. The importance given to pronunciation compared to the other skills was deeply affected by changes in language teaching, including the increasing emphasis on integrated skills books in the CLT era. Dickerson thinks that this was an important factor because it was not clear how to integrate pronunciation into communicatively oriented materials, and so it was left out altogether. Dickerson also believes that pronunciation 'suffered' more than grammar (whose role was also questioned) since pronunciation is more challenging to teach because it requires more varied types of knowledge, and improvement may be less immediately noticeable than with grammar because pronunciation is not only cognitive but involves motor skills.

Dickerson pointed out another (unintended) impact of the rise of CLT and the shift in how language teaching was viewed. The number of pedagogical phonology courses decreased in many MATESL programmes during the CLT era (see also Murphy, 1997), leaving pronunciation teaching with fewer educators able to prepare teachers to teach pronunciation. Unfortunately, this loss was far-reaching.

The loss of pedagogical phonology specialists in teacher preparation programmes did not mean that fewer faculty were being hired. Instead, experts in many new, valuable areas (such as L2 reading, L2 writing, sociolinguistics and second language acquisition) quickly found homes in teacher education programmes while pronunciation was becoming less of a priority. However, pronunciation remained important at some influential TESL programmes. Marianne Celce-Murcia (personal communication, 3 December 2014) points out that pronunciation was always important at UCLA because of Clifford Prator's and Donald Bowen's influence. Communicative needs raised by new groups of learners also kept pronunciation from being completely ignored. For example, the oral communication skills of international teaching assistants (ITAs) were given attention because of the difficulties undergraduate students expressed in understanding these teachers. Their difficulties were overwhelmingly tied to pronunciation. Likewise, specialists at other universities, such as Wayne Dickerson (University of Illinois), Joan Morley (University of Michigan), Clifford Hill and Leslie Beebe (Columbia University) and others also argued for the importance of pronunciation in language pedagogy.

CLT principles that help explain the decline of pronunciation

Despite not having an agreed-upon definition of CLT in the 1970s and 1980s (Bax, 2003; Harmer, 2003; Spada, 2007) or about whether it was a method or an approach, the following features characterized CLT, according to Richards (2003):

- The goal of language learning is communicative competence.
- Learners learn a language through using it to communicate.
- Authentic and meaningful communication should be the goal of classroom activities.
- Fluency and accuracy are both important dimensions of communication.
- Communication involves the integration of different language skills.
- Language is a gradual process that involves trial and error.

(p. 21)

Some of these principles help explain the decline of pronunciation in the shifting paradigm in language teaching, especially communicative competence as the ultimate goal of language learning and focus on fluency rather than accuracy.

Communicative competence

Hymes (1992, p. 32) developed the concept of 'communicative competence' in 1966 as a response to Noam Chomsky's emphasis on competence. In Chomskyan linguistics, competence is the knowledge that ideal speaker-hearers have of their native language. It involves intuitive knowledge of grammar (syntax, morphology, phonology) that allows speakers to evaluate whether something is a possible representation of the formal language system. In contrast, performance was the actual use of the language and was at best an imperfect reflection of competence. Hymes disagreed, arguing that a speaker-hearer's knowledge not only involved competence (what Hymes called *linguistic* competence) but also knowledge of appropriate use of the language in normal interaction (i.e. *communicative* competence). Communicative competence was appropriated by language teaching theorists in the 1970s and 1980s to express the appropriate goal of language learning and teaching (Savignon, 1983; Canale & Swain, 1980; Canale, 1983).

Applied to language teaching, communicative competence involved not only grammatical competence (Chomsky's 'competence') but also sociolinguistic competence (appropriate use of language), discourse competence (knowledge of how to put sentences together in discourse) and strategic competence (how to use strategies to communicate when linguistic strategies are not available). In language teaching, the three additional competences of Hymes's more expanded analysis overwhelmed grammatical competence, which was often thought to result from attention to the other categories. A regrettable impact on the wider field of L2 teaching was that pronunciation, a central part of grammatical competence, became viewed as being non-essential.

Accuracy versus fluency

Brown and Yule (1983) proposed that one of the greatest hindrances to the improvement of fluency was constant error correction. They explained that, if there is a misunderstanding in what a student is saying, requests for clarification should come from another student, not the teacher. This approach seemed to exclude the teacher from correcting errors at the time of speaking. However, Brown and Yule did not mean to stop correcting errors completely. They anticipated that teachers, and especially those dedicated to pronunciation teaching, would not be able to avoid correcting errors. They thus recommended that teachers wait until the completion of tasks to address errors.

A year before Brown and Yule, Harmer (1982) raised similar concerns about the potential for pronunciation work to block fluency development in the L2. He noted that students must have the right to speak without intervention by teachers. He further explained, 'by intervene, I mean tell the students they have made mistakes in their English, correct their pronunciation, etc. (p. 166)' Similarly, when Krashen and Terrell (1983) commented 'we do not place undue emphasis in early stages on perfection in the students' pronunciation', they were not exiling pronunciation from language teaching but highlighting its modest level of importance at the beginning of learning (p. 89). The same writers even encouraged teachers who wanted to correct pronunciation errors by saying that pronunciation habits can be changed after the first years of L2 learning. Similarly, Savignon (1987), a well-known CLT specialist, advocated that 'overt correction of pronunciation or verb tenses' might cause the students discomfort in class (p. 239).

However, the push against error correction in CLT was based on an under-appreciation of the complex relationship between feedback and improvement, knowledge of which would come later. Arguments against correction were criticized not only for its effect on pronunciation. Higgs and Clifford (1982) claimed that a communicative approach might trigger fossilization of grammatical errors. In a similar vein, Allen and Waugh (1986) warned that teacher experience indicates that errors do not disappear when they are left to take care of themselves despite exposure to and experience with grammatical structures. Although error correction may not be necessary at the beginning levels, higher levels of student accuracy may be important 'as the fine tuning necessary to refine communication skills' (p. 195). Grammar and pronunciation errors garnered the greatest attention because they are easily noticed. However, the effect of error correction on grammar attracted considerably more research attention than did pronunciation.

Error correction has remained controversial in CLT because of the distinction between form-focused instruction (FFI) and meaning-focused instruction (MFI). For many specialists, MFI is more consistent with principles of communicative language teaching, along with its descendants, task-based and content-based language teaching, as it proposes that language is not an object but a means for communication (Loewen, 2011). FFI, however, is designed to call learners' attention to linguistic forms either implicitly or explicitly during meaning-focused activities (Spada, 1997). Today these questions seem to be settled. Spada and Lightbown (2008) suggest that 'the most engaging questions and debates in L2 pedagogy are no longer about whether CLT should include FFI but rather how and when it is most effective' (p. 184). This more recent conceptual stance represents a change in the perceptions of CLT proponents about errors and the possibly facilitative role of error treatments. Such changes in specialists' perceptions have also led to important changes in pronunciation teaching.

The renewal of attention to pronunciation in L2 teaching

Pronunciation's renewal started with changes in assumptions. First, nativeness (i.e. the attainment of native-like pronunciation) was no longer seen as essential, and was replaced with intelligibility (Levis, 2005), a goal that today remains central to pronunciation teaching (Munro & Derwing, 2011). Pronunciation teaching's contribution to intelligibility and its integration into CLT were a theme of the 1985 TESOL Convention, later published in Morley (1987). In the book's foreword, Morley situates pronunciation firmly in discussions of communicative competence, and calls for a reassessment of learner needs, goals, teaching objectives and methodologies, specifically calling for:

- pronunciation's integration into oral communication as an essential component rather than a separate one;

- prioritizing suprasegmentals and their role in communication;
- specific attention on syllable structure, linking, thought groups, phrasal stress, and rhythm patterns;
- learner-centred teaching by raising learners' awareness about their own speech production and by having them monitor it;
- input coming from natural and contextual speech;
- meaningful tasks that are in line with real-life purposes.

(Preface)

Even early in the CLT era, the importance of pronunciation was noted (e.g. Celce-Murcia, 1983; McGroarty, 1984; Pica, 1984), but specifying an optimal level of pronunciation for communication was elusive. Hinofotis and Bailey (1981) called for a 'threshold level of intelligibility' in pronunciation (p. 124). Their findings, relying on their study of college students' perceptions of ITA teaching, indicated that a degree of pronunciation mastery was essential even if native-like attainment was unlikely.

Intelligibility became the desired goal not only for ITAs. Many researchers defined other groups of non-native speakers for whom pronunciation teaching was a necessity. These include long-term residents in English-speaking countries, including those with vocational needs for pronunciation, refugees, non-native speakers struggling with building relationships at school, in the neighbourhood or workplace, students who wanted to study using English as the medium of communication, and international businesspersons (Anderson-Hsieh, 1989; Celce-Murcia, 1991; McGroarty, 1984; Morley, 1987, 1988; Wong, 1986).

Intelligibility's importance during the early CLT era was also connected to suprasegmental features' being prioritized more than ever before, especially in the early to mid-1980s. For example, in 1986 Wong argued for the importance of correct use of suprasegmental features of pronunciation. She cited Gumperz (1982), in which Indian cafeteria workers' ways of asking whether British workers wanted gravy (with falling intonation) was seen as impolite. This analysis, Wong argued, illustrated that stress, rhythm and intonation were crucial components of communication. She also criticized the view that pronunciation would take care of itself if adequate input were provided by noting that many long-term residents in the US were still in need of pronunciation instruction owing to the many communication problems they continued to encounter due to pronunciation-related challenges. In so doing, Wong emphasized the importance of explicit pronunciation instruction.

Along the same lines, Huckin and Olsen (1984) called attention to people doing technical work in industry. They asserted that technical workers needed to communicate with people inside and outside the field; however, most, who had lived in the US at least for 10 years, had problems during oral communication owing to segmental, suprasegmental and/or discoursal challenges. These early illustrations of how pronunciation was important to the teaching of English for specific purposes helped change views of pronunciation's place in CLT.

Though pronunciation teaching fell into a period of decline during the CLT era, there really never was a time when pronunciation was completely neglected in the field of ELT. An important piece of evidence for the attention pronunciation continued to receive is the number of professional publications that continued to include pronunciation articles throughout the CLT era. In the next section, we present the frequency and distribution of pronunciation-related publications in six journals.

Journal articles in the CLT era

If CLT was the source of pronunciation's decline, as sometimes implied by the Cinderella imagery, there should be evidence of decreasing numbers of professional articles published about pronunciation and/or its teaching over time. Journal articles, however, are subject to a lag in publishing. As a result, we look not only at the early CLT era in question but also at the time before CLT as well as the time after the early CLT era to provide a sense of the long-term effects of the CLT paradigm shift. To this aim, we examined the degrees to which pronunciation-oriented articles were represented in six different journals, three of which were established before 1960 (*Modern Language Journal*, *ELT Journal*, *Language Learning*) and three of which were established in the 1960s (*Foreign Language Annals*, *TESOL Quarterly*, *International Review of Applied Linguistics in Language Teaching* (*IRAL*)).

The first journal in each group represents what specialists of the Anglo-centric world have traditionally referred to as foreign language teaching (e.g. French, Spanish, German, Latin etc.). The *Modern Language Journal* (MLJ) is the premier journal of foreign language teaching in North America, while *Foreign Language Annals*, the journal of the American Council of Teachers of English as a Foreign Language (ACTFL), serves a similar audience. The second pair of journals are the central journals for English as a second language teaching worldwide. *ELT Journal* reflects more British-oriented approaches to ESL/EFL. *TESOL Quarterly*, on the other hand, remains the flagship journal for ESL/EFL research and teaching in North America. Finally, the third pair are best described as general applied linguistics journals. *Language Learning* is dedicated to a broad scientific understanding of the mechanisms of language learning. *IRAL*, a European-based journal, represents a broad scope of language-related research similar in scope to *Language Learning*.

In each pair of journals, we examined titles of articles from all the issues of the journal from 1960–2009 and from 1970–2009. All articles (but not individual book reviews or announcements) were counted, as were the articles featuring pronunciation centrally. If we were not certain about whether an article was about pronunciation from the title, we skimmed the article to make our decision. Some pronunciation-oriented articles were more pedagogical, while others where more phonetically oriented. The nature of the journals ensured that articles were not written for linguistic specialists in phonetics or phonology. Counting articles was not always straightforward. Almost all journals at some point included articles that were not traditional research-oriented articles (e.g. short reports, forum responses to other research etc.). In addition, *Language Learning* began to include supplemental issues in the 1990s. Sometimes these issues were simply reprints of previously published articles, and sometimes they were book-length projects written by a single author. We did not count these in our calculations. Over the course of 40 (1970–2009) or 50 (1960–2009) years, depending on the journal, the calculations provide a comparison of general trends in each journal.

Table 16.1 shows the results for the two mainstream foreign language journals. The number of pronunciation articles in *MLJ* dropped somewhat after 1960–1969, but pronunciation was never a frequent topic, even in the 1960s. From 1980 to 2009, readers had to wait almost two years on average for an article on pronunciation. In *Foreign Language Annals*, on the other hand, pronunciation was almost non-existent since the inception of the journal. The influence of CLT cannot be seen because almost no articles existed during the era of CLT's pre-eminence, and almost none after the early 1990s. In summary, pronunciation in these two journals was and continued to be a topic of cursory interest. It should be no surprise that pronunciation is neglected in the teaching of foreign languages in North America in light of the place it finds in these prominent professional journals.

Table 16.1 Pronunciation articles in *Modern Language Journal* and *Foreign Language Annals*

Modern Language Journal

	Articles	Pron. articles	Percentage	Articles/year
1960–69	536	16	2.98	1.6/year
1970–79	427	11	2.58	1.1/year
1980–89	284	6	2.11	0.6/year
1990–99	264	6	2.27	0.6/year
2000–09	389	5	1.28	0.5/year
Total	1900	44	2.31	

FL Annals

	Articles	Pron. articles	Percentage	Articles/year
1970–79	281	2	0.71	0.2/year
1980–89	423	2	0.47	0.2/year
1990–99	356	0	0	0/year
2000–09	396	5	1.26	0.5/year
Total	1456	9	0.62	

Table 16.2 presents the publication history of the two top English language teaching journals, *English Language Teaching Journal* and *TESOL Quarterly*. These results signal different ways of approaching pronunciation. *ELT Journal* reflects the predicted effect of CLT, with a large drop in publications during the 1980s that continues through 2009. Whether this was a reflection of CLT or not, it is clear that pronunciation has become a much less frequent topic in *ELT Journal* over time. *TESOL Quarterly*, on the other hand, shows a large drop only in the 1990s but a rebound in the first decade after the new century. A special issue in 2005 boosted the number of published articles, but even without the special issue the numbers would have been above the percentage of 1980–89.

Table 16.3 displays the results for the two general applied linguistics journals. In both, pronunciation research has been consistently robust, with ups and downs, but always with more representation of pronunciation than in the four journals depicted in Tables 16.1 and 16.2 (i.e. those more directly focused on language teaching). The representation of pronunciation in *Language Learning*, a dominant presence in applied linguistics research, has ebbed and flowed in no recognizable pattern over the past five decades. However, pronunciation has always maintained a presence above 6.7 per cent, a percentage surpassed only by *ELT Journal* in the 1960s and *TESOL Quarterly* in the 2000s.

The first drop preceded the dominance of CLT and the second was long after its dominance had been established. During the 1980s, the percentage of pronunciation articles attained a peak during the period 1960–69. On average, almost 1/8 of all articles over during the 50-year span of our review have included pronunciation as a central topic. In several decades, readers could expect to see a pronunciation-oriented article in almost every issue. *IRAL* articles reflect a similar level of frequency, with every decade being above 10 per cent. In both of these journals, pronunciation has had a consistently strong presence.

For these six journals, the percentage of published articles on pronunciation decreased from 1960–99, with a modest increase after 2000 (Table 16.4). This decrease, though real, does not reflect a particularly deleterious effect of CLT. It is just as likely that competition

Table 16.2 Pronunciation articles in *ELT Journal* and *TESOL Quarterly*

ELT Journal

	Articles	Pron. articles	Percentage	Articles/year
1960–69	331	26	7.85	2.6/year
1970–79	498	33	6.62	3.3/year
1980–89	442	13	2.9	1.3/year
1990–99	375	10	2.66	1/year
2000–09	362	10	2.76	1/year
Total	2008	92	4.58	

TESOL Quarterly

	Articles	Pron. articles	Percentage	Articles/year
1970–79	302	17	5.62	1.7/year
1980–89	450	20	4.4	2/year
1990–99	475	8	1.68	0.8/year
2000–09	454	32	7.05	3.2/year
Total	1681	77	4.58	

Table 16.3 Pronunciation articles in *Language Learning* and *International Review of Applied Linguistics in Language Teaching* (IRAL)

Language Learning

	Articles	Pron. articles	Percentage	Articles/year
1960–69	207	35	16.9	3.5/year
1970–79	194	13	6.7	1.3/year
1980–89	248	39	15.72	3.9/year
1990–99	187	21	11.22	2.1/year
2000–09	203	17	8.37	1.7/year
Total	1039	125	12.03	

IRAL

	Articles	Pron. articles	Percentage	Articles/year
1970–79	224	33	14.73	3.3/year
1980–89	232	24	10.34	2.4/year
1990–99	187	25	13.37	2.5/year
2000–09	178	19	10.67	1.9/year
Total	821	101	12.3	

Table 16.4 Overall article publications for six journals

	1960–69	1970–79	1980–89	1990–99	2000–9	Total
All articles	1074	1926	2079	1844	1982	8905
Pron. Articles	77	109	104	70	88	448
Percentage	7.2	5.7	5.0	3.8	4.4	5

from other worthy topics such as sociolinguistics, language acquisition and corpus analysis of language were responsible for the decrease. Such competition did not exist in the 1960s. The 1960–69 decade, with a larger number of pronunciation-related articles, included many descriptive treatments of errors from specific language groups (e.g. Bengali, Serbian, Sinhalese etc.). Such studies are now absent from high-impact research journals. In addition, the fluctuation in the number of pronunciation articles varies across journals. The mainstream foreign language journals have never emphasized pronunciation; the ESL-oriented journals show mixed emphasis on pronunciation, with one showing long-term neglect and the other a healthy but inconsistent number of articles across decades; and the applied linguistics journals, despite decreases over time, have always featured pronunciation as a central topic for empirical research. Thus, based on our analysis, we find no compelling evidence of a negative CLT effect within the six journals.

Pronunciation teaching in stand-alone pronunciation course books

In this section, we examine pronunciation teaching techniques in stand-alone pronunciation course books published in 1993 or before to examine the degree of presence of CLT principles. We first analysed the books in light of certain criteria based on the recurring themes that were discussed by pronunciation specialists during the CLT era. Below are our criteria:

- Intended proficiency level of learners;
- Fluency and accuracy;
- Ultimate attainment goal as native-like versus intelligibility;
- Focused on segmentals or suprasegmentals;
- Error correction and monitoring.

Only two of the books (Gilbert, 1984; Prator & Robinett, 1985) set a specific proficiency level for the target audience, but the rest seem to be appropriate for more than one level of students. These books are reported to be appropriate for the learners from low-intermediate to advanced levels. Three of these books (Chan, 1987; Morley, 1979; Prator & Robinett, 1985) state explicitly that they are not intended for absolute beginners. This seems true for most of the books we examined, a reflection of the analytic-wave of pronunciation that began in the late nineteenth century and dominated pronunciation teaching for nearly 100 years (Murphy & Baker, 2015). Pronunciation books explicitly designed for beginners were not available until 2001.

In every book we examined, the authors appealed to fluency and accuracy explicitly or implicitly. Of these seven books, four (Chan, 1987; Dauer, 1993; Grant, 1993; Morley, 1979) state that both accuracy and fluency are desired skills, while one of the books (Hagen & Grogan, 1992) takes a stance more in line with fluency. In Prator and Robinett (1985), the authors present a goal to have learners use pronunciation features they have learned automatically in communicative settings. In none of the books was there a statement of the priority of accuracy over fluency. One thing that is noticeable in some of these books mentioning fluency is that they also highlight the importance of meaningful practice for the sake of real communication. Two books (Grant, 1993; Hagen & Grogan, 1992) also prepare students for various speaking tests that were well known at their time of publication.

Intelligibility is mentioned in almost all the books. Six (Chan, 1987; Dauer, 1993; Hagen & Grogan, 1992; Gilbert, 1984; Grant, 1993; Morley, 1979) state that intelligibility is the ultimate attainment goal, and in only one of the books (Dauer, 1993) is 'near-native accent' the desirable goal for learners. Suprasegmental features are covered to a greater or lesser extent in all of the books. Some (Chan, 1987; Grant, 1993) explicitly prioritize suprasegmental features more as a necessity for intelligibility. In Prator and Robinett (1985), the authors discuss the importance they give to 'the whole stream of speech' as one of the most salient changes from their previous edition (p. xv).

For error correction, the books do not usually include an explicit statement articulating their conceptual stance. However, Grant (1993) reminds teachers and students that errors are to be expected. Grant even proposed that the existence of errors signals learning. Gilbert (1984) recommends dictation tasks on the board since it helps learners notice errors immediately. In most books, error correction is connected to the concept of 'self-monitoring' or 'peer-monitoring'. In five books (Chan, 1987; Dauer, 1993; Hagen & Grogan, 1992; Morley, 1979; Prator & Robinett, 1985), monitoring is explicitly recommended either by students listening to each other and taking notes or listening to themselves via audio recordings. Prator and Robinett (1985) underscore the role of self-monitoring by stating that learners first need to notice their habits and then break them in order to lead to the formation of new habits.

Even though the authors do not explicitly identify CLT as a motivation for their pedagogical principles, most speak about issues consistent with CLT principles. In some books (e.g. Grant, 1993), the authors talk about a progression from form-centred to meaning-centred practice. Some authors underscore that isolated words are not enough to help learners use language in genuinely communicative settings (Prator & Robinett, 1985). But, in general, most authors think that pronunciation learning starts with a controlled context, transferring what has been learned to more communication-oriented contexts.

Pronunciation's shift to accommodate CLT principles

The change from an accuracy-oriented approach to a communicative approach in the teaching of pronunciation did not come quickly, as illustrated by Celce-Murcia (1983, 1987) and Pica (1984). A feature shared by their separate, early discussions of how to teach pronunciation communicatively was the proposal for teachers and materials developers to create contexts for interactive communication in which targeted features occur frequently and meaningfully. Thus, most of Celce-Murcia's (1983, 1987) and Pica's (1984) proposed activities provided learners with practice that was more communicative than mechanical drills but progress to a stage of more extemporaneous communicative interaction was missing.

Another significant change in pronunciation teaching that further advanced communicative ways of teaching pronunciation was increased attention to the role of suprasegmentals. In two influential pronunciation books published during the CLT era (Prator & Robinett, 1985; Wong, 1987), the authors emphasized prosodic features of pronunciation. Wong based her book on (a) learner-centred teaching, (b) instruction reinforcing communicative effectiveness, (c) minimal intelligibility of the learners and (d) rhythm and intonation as part of essential contributors to intelligibility.

Prator and Robinett (1985), whose fourth edition was published in the midst of the early CLT era, presented three steps to learning pronunciation, starting with identifying and discriminating the sounds in native speakers' speech, producing speech by focusing on pronunciation and developing automaticity that allows for pronunciation to function while meaning is under focus. The authors specifically noted that the third step deserves more attention in pronunciation instruction, writing:

The most significant kind of change in the new edition, however, is the result of effort we have made in various lessons to introduce more use of language for real communicative purposes in the learning activities suggested for students to carry out.

(p. xvi)

Pronunciation proponents were aware of the growing influence of communicative approaches, and yet explicit guidelines did not exist for teaching pronunciation communicatively until the mid-1980s (Murphy & Baker, 2015). Celce-Murcia (1983, 1987) came up with the following steps to teach pronunciation communicatively:

- Identify your students' problem areas (different group of students may have different problems).
- Find lexical/grammatical contexts with many natural occurrences of the problem sound(s).
- Develop communicative tasks that incorporate the word.
- Develop at least three or four exercises so that you can recycle the problem and keep practicing the target sound(s) with new contexts

(p. 10)

Pica (1984), another specialist suggesting classroom activities and guidelines to teach pronunciation communicatively, noted that the activities should give students the chance to use pronunciation features in meaningful communication, and she added that the comprehensibility of the students in the given activities depended on their accurate production of the key words. Pica suggests the following steps for activities:

- The teacher introduces a pronunciation point and models representative examples for the class to repeat.
- The teacher gives the class directions on the communication activity that incorporates the pronunciation rule.
- Students then meet in pairs or small groups to work on the activity while the teacher circulates among them, monitoring their activities and answering their questions.
- The class reunites to hear the individual pairs or groups present their decision or report on their activity.

(p. 333–334)

The early CLT era included experimentation with communicative pronunciation materials and a developing view of how to combine the traditional accuracy-oriented approach with the new paradigm. The guidelines developed by early specialists were a necessary step to a future communicative approach to pronunciation teaching.

Conclusions

Looking back, some have argued that the cruel stepmother of the children's fable (i.e. an implicit characteristic of CLT itself, or, what we believe is more likely, specialists' underappreciations for the possibility of making better connections between CLT and pronunciation teaching) resulted in Cinderella (pronunciation) being ignored yet again after she had finally been invited to the language teaching ball. While there may be some truth to this interpretation, we believe the bulk of the evidence points to another interpretation. The decline of pronunciation teaching during the CLT era was the result of a more broadly based paradigm shift in language teaching. As interest in CLT first grew and then expanded, language skills that were form-based no longer seemed compatible with then-contemporary values and beliefs about language teaching. The nature of the ball to which the Cinderella of our story had been invited had changed and, at least for a while, L2 pronunciation teaching once again was on the outside looking in.

Journal publications on pronunciation-related topics show there was no clear drop of pro-nunciation-focused articles during the CLT era. Our analysis of six journals reveals that pronunciation-related publications never disappeared, though their numbers have rarely been satisfying to those interested in pronunciation and pronunciation teaching. This was the case even before the CLT era.

CLT has not actually decreased the importance given to pronunciation in the long run, but it affected how we conceive of pronunciation teaching. The paradigm shift changed the ultimate attainment goal from native to intelligible pronunciation, it changed its content to include a greater emphasis on suprasegmentals, and it called attention to the pronunciation needs of special populations such as international teaching assistants and long-term residents of inner circle countries (Celce-Murcia, Brinton, Godwin, & Griner, 2010; Wong, 1986).

Future directions

Celce-Murcia et al. (2010) provides an extensive list of traditional pronunciation teaching techniques that are evident in early CLT era pronunciation books: listen and imitate, phonetic training, minimal pair drills, contextualized minimal pairs, visual aids, tongue twisters, devel-opmental approximation drills, practice of vowel shifts and stress shifts related by affixation, reading aloud/recitation, and recordings of learners' production. However, the authors also state that most of these techniques have been generally used to promote accuracy, not fluency. Several researchers have expressed the view that there is nothing wrong with using such traditional techniques whenever they are helpful and are being used for a clearly defined purpose (e.g. to foster automaticity) (Harmer, 1982). However, pronunciation cannot be restricted to such techniques if the purpose is to enhance learners' fluency.

Celce-Murcia (C-M) et al. (2010) also propose a communicative framework to teach pronunciation relying on CLT principles but recognizing a concurrent need for accuracy. The C-M framework includes five steps in progress from controlled to extemporaneous language use: description and analysis, listening discrimination, controlled practice, guided practice and communicative practice (p. 44). The rationale for the framework is to scaffold learners in gradually learning to use targeted pronunciation features for more genuinely commun-icative purposes once they have attained sufficient control of the feature(s) being taught. Indeed, the first three steps of the C-M framework embrace accuracy-oriented pronunciation teaching techniques. The framework's final steps carry learners from accuracy-focused practice to fluency and meaning-focused use.

In the books of the early to mid CLT era we analysed, the most frequently used techniques and tasks included phonetic training, listening discrimination, listening and imitation, and read aloud tasks. Only two (Chan, 1987; Grant, 1993) had a good number of guided or communicative practices. In most of the books, guided or communicative exercises are used primarily for suprasegmental features. Our materials analysis looked only at materials during the 1980s–1990s period of transition to a CLT paradigm. A careful and thorough analysis of current pronunciation-centred classroom textbooks (e.g. Grant, 2017) may show a larger change towards including guided and extemporaneous practice activities in pronunciation instructional materials.

Further reading

As a field, pronunciation teaching is radically different from what it was at the beginning of the CLT era. Its research base has become far richer with growing numbers of empirical articles and the publication of books (e.g. Derwing & Munro, 2015; Grant, 2014; Reed & Levis, 2015) tying research and teaching together. Such resources will help to ensure that the future of the field, both in research and teaching, will continue to move in profitable directions.

In addition, textbooks meant to teach pronunciation skills are also changing and include far greater numbers of guided and communicative activities (e.g. Hewings & Goldstein, 1998; Grant, 2017; Miller, 2000) than were evident in earlier instructional materials. There is clearly more than adequate guidance now for how to teach pronunciation communicatively, and materials developers are demonstrating a greater emphasis on guided and communicative tasks. Even with better materials, there will always be a need to go beyond controlled practice and to employ evidence-based practices in the teaching of pronunciation.

References

Allen, W., & Waugh, S. (1986). Dealing with accuracy in communicative language teaching. *TESL Canada Journal, 3*, 193–205.

Anderson-Hsieh, J. (1989). Approaches toward teaching pronunciation: A brief history. *Cross-Currents, 16*, 73–78.

Bax, S. (2003). The end of CLT: A context approach to language teaching. *ELT Journal, 57*(3), 278–787.

Berns, M. (1984). Functional approaches to language and language teaching: Another look. In S. Savignon & M. Berns (Eds), *Initiatives in communicative language teaching II* (pp. 3–22). Reading, MA: Addison-Wesley.

Breitkreutz, J., Derwing, T., & Rossiter, M. (2001). Pronunciation teaching practices in Canada. *TESL Canada Journal, 19*(1), 51–61.

Brown, G., & Yule, G. (1983). *Teaching spoken language: An approach based on the analysis of conversational English*. New York, NY: Cambridge University Press.

Burgess, J., & Spencer, S. (2000). Phonology and pronunciation in integrated language teaching and teacher education. *System, 28*, 191–215.

Burns, A. (2006). Integrating research and professional development on pronunciation teaching in a national adult ESL program. *TESL Reporter, 39*(2), 34–41.

Canale, M. (1983). From communicative competence to communicative language pedagogy. In J. C. Richards & R. Schmidt (Eds), *Language and communication* (pp. 2–27). New York, NY: Routledge.

Canale, M., & Swain, M. (1980). Theoretical bases of communicative approaches to second language teaching and testing. *Applied Linguistics, 1*(1), 1–47.

Celce-Murcia, M. (1983). Teaching pronunciation communicatively. *MEXTESOL Journal, 1*(7), 10–25.

Celce-Murcia, M. (1987). Teaching pronunciation as communication. In J. Morley (Ed.), *Current perspectives on pronunciation* (pp. 1–12). Washington. DC: TESOL.

Celce-Murcia, M. (1991). *Teaching English as a second or foreign language* (2nd ed.). New York, NY: Newbury House.

Celce-Murcia, M., Brinton, D., & Goodwin, J. (1996). *Teaching pronunciation: A course book and reference guide*. New York, NY: Cambridge University Press.

Celce-Murcia, M., Brinton, D., Goodwin, J., & Griner, B. (2010). *Teaching pronunciation: A course book and reference guide*. New York, NY: Cambridge University Press.

Chan, M. (1987). *Phrase by phrase*. Englewood Cliffs, NJ: Prentice-Hall.

Dalton, D. F. (1997). Some techniques for teaching pronunciation. *The Internet TESL Journal, 3*(1). Retrieved from http://iteslj.org/Techniques/Dalton-Pronunciation.html.

Dauer, R. (1993). *Accurate English*. London: Prentice-Hall.

Derwing, T. M., & Munro, M. J. (2005). Pragmatic perspectives on the preparation of teachers of English as a second language: Putting the NS/NNS debate in context. In E. Llurda (Ed.), *Non-native language teachers: Perceptions, challenges and contributions to the profession* (pp. 179–191). Philadelphia, PA: Springer.

Derwing, T. M., & Munro, M. J. (2015). *Pronunciation fundamentals: Evidence-based perspectives for L2 teaching and research*. Amsterdam: John-Benjamins.

Gilbert, J. (1984). *Clear speech: Pronunciation and listening comprehension in American English.* (1st ed.). New York, NY: Cambridge University Press.

Grant, L. (1993). *Well said*. Boston, MA: Heinle & Heinle.

Grant, L. (Ed.). (2014). *Pronunciation myths*. Ann Arbor, MI: University of Michigan Press.

Grant, L. (2017). *Well said: Pronunciation for clear communication* (4th ed.). Boston, MA: Thomson/ Heinle & Heinle.

Gumperz, J. (1982). *Discourse strategies*. New York, NY: Cambridge University Press.

Hagen, S. A., & Grogan P. E. (1992). *Sound advantage: A pronunciation book*. Englewood Cliffs, NJ: Prentice-Hall.

Hammond, R. M. (1995). Foreign accent and phonetic interference: The application of linguistic research to the teaching of second language pronunciation. In F. Eckman, D. Highland, P. Lee, J. Mileham, & R. Rutkowski Weber (Eds), *Second language acquisition theory and pedagogy* (pp. 293–303). Mahwah, NJ: Lawrence Erlbaum.

Harmer, J. (1982). What is communicative? *ELT Journal, 36*(3), 164–168.

Harmer, J. (2003). Popular culture, methods, and context. *ELT Journal, 57*(3), 288–294.

Hewings, M., & Goldstein, S. (1998). *Pronunciation plus: Practice through interaction*. Cambridge: Cambridge University Press.

Higgs, T. V., & Clifford, R. (1982). The push toward communication. In *Curriculum, competence and the foreign language teacher* (pp. 57–79). Skokie, IL: National Textbook Company.

Hinofotis, F. B., & and Bailey, K. M. (1981). American undergraduates' reactions to the communication skills of foreign teaching assistants. In J. Fisher, M. Clarke, & J. Schachter (Eds), *On TESOL '80: Building bridges* (pp. 120–133). Washington, DC: TESOL.

Hutchison, T., & Waters, A. (1987). *English for specific purposes*. New York, NY: Cambridge University Press.

Huckin, T. N., & Olsen, L. A. (1984). The need for professionally oriented ESL instruction in the United States. *TESOL Quarterly, 18*(2), 273–294.

Hymes, D. (1992). The concept of communicative competence revisited. In M. Pütz (Ed.), *30 years of linguistic evolution* (pp. 31–57). Philadelphia, PA: John Benjamins.

Kelly, L. (1969). *25 centuries of language teaching*. Rowley, MA: Newbury House.

Kenworthy, J. (1987). *Teaching English pronunciation*. Harlow: Longman.

Krashen, S. (1982). *Principles and practice in second language acquisition*. Oxford: Pergamon.

Krashen, S., & Terrell, T. (1983). *The natural approach*. Hayword, CA: Allemany.

Levis, J. (2005). Changing contexts and shifting paradigms in pronunciation teaching. *TESOL Quarterly, 39*(3), 369–377.

Littlewood, W. (2011). Communicative language teaching: An expanding concept for a changing world. In E. Hinkel (Ed.), *Handbook of research in second language teaching and learning Volume II* (pp. 541–557). New York, NY: Routledge.

Loewen, S. (2011). Focus on form. In E. Hinkel (Ed.), *Handbook of research in second language teaching and learning, Volume II* (pp. 576–592). New York, NY: Routledge.

MacDonald, S. (2002). Pronunciation – Views and practices of reluctant teachers. *Prospect, 17*(3), 3–18.

McGroarty, M. (1984). Some meanings of communicative competence for second language students. *TESOL Quarterly, 18*(2), 257–272.

Miller, S. (2000). *Targeting pronunciation: The intonation, sounds, and rhythm of American English.* New York, NY: Houghton Mifflin.

Morley, J. (1979). *Improving spoken English*. Ann Arbor, MI: Michigan University Press.

Morley, J. (1987). *Current perspectives on pronunciation: Practices anchored in theory*. Washington, DC: TESOL.

Morley, J. (1988). How many languages do you speak? Perspectives on pronunciation-speech-communication in EFL/ESL. *Nagoya Gakuin University Roundtable on Linguistics and Literature Journal, 19*, 1–35.

Munro, M. J., and Derwing, T. M. (2011). Research timeline: The foundations of accent and intelligibility in pronunciation research. *Language Teaching*, *44*(3), 316–327.

Murphy, J. (1997). Phonology courses offered by MATESOL programs in the U.S. *TESOL Quarterly*, *31*(4), 741–764.

Murphy, J. (2014). Myth 7: Teacher preparation programs provide adequate preparation in how to teach pronunciation, In L. Grant (Ed.), *Pronunciation myths*, 188–223. Ann Arbor, MI: University of Michigan Press.

Murphy, J., & Baker, A. A. (2015). History of ESL pronunciation teaching. In Marnie Reed and John Levis (Eds), *Wiley-Blackwell handbook of English pronunciation*, 36–65. Chichester, West Sussex, UK: Blackwell Handbooks in Linguistics Series.

Pica, T. (1984). Pronunciation activities with an accent on communication. In A. Brown (Ed.) (1991), *Teaching English pronunciation* (pp. 332–342). New York, NY: Routledge.

Prator, C., & Robinett, B. (1985). *Manual of American English pronunciation* (4th ed.). New York, NY: Holt, Rinehart & Winston.

Reed, M., & Levis, J. M. (Eds). (2015). *The handbook of English pronunciation*. Malden, MA: Wiley Blackwell.

Richards, J. C., & Rodgers, T. S. (1986). *Approaches and methods in language teaching*. Cambridge: Cambridge University Press.

Richards, J. C. (2003). 30 years of TEFL/TESL: A personal reflection. *TEFLIN Journal*, *14*(1), 14–57.

Richards, J. C., & Rodgers, T. S. (2001). *Approaches and methods in language teaching* (2nd ed.). Cambridge: Cambridge University Press.

Savignon, S. J. (1983). *Communicative competence: Theory and classroom practice*. Reading, MA: Addison-Wesley.

Savignon, S. (1987). Communicative language teaching. *Theory into Practice*, *26*(4), 235–242.

Seidlhofer, B. (2001). Pronunciation. In R. Carter & D. Nunan (Eds), *The Cambridge Guide to Teaching English to speakers of other languages* (pp. 56–65). Cambridge: Cambridge University Press.

Spada, N. (1997). Form-focused instruction and second language acquisition: A review of classroom and laboratory research. *Language Teaching*, *30*, 73–87.

Spada, N. (2007). Communicative language teaching: Current status and future prospects. In J. Cummins & C. Davidson (Eds), *International handbook of English language teaching* (pp. 271–288). Boston, MA: Springer Science & Business Media.

Spada, N., & Lightbown, P. M. (2008). Form-focused instruction: Isolated or integrated? *TESOL Quarterly*, *42*, 181–207.

Thompson, G. (1996). Some misconceptions about communicative language teaching. *ELT Journal*, *50*(1), 9–15.

Widdowson, H. G. (1972). The teaching of English as communication. *ELT Journal*, *27*(1), 15–19.

Wilkins, D. (1972). The linguistics and situational content of the common core in a unit/credit system. MS, Strasbourg: Council of Europe.

Wilkins, D. (1976). *Notional syllabuses*. Oxford: Oxford University Press.

Wong, R. (1986). Does pronunciation teaching have a place in the communicative classroom? In D. Tannen, & J. Alatis (Eds) *Georgetown University roundtable on languages and linguistics* (pp. 226–236). Washington, DC: Georgetown University Press.

Wong, R. (1987). *Teaching pronunciation: Focus on English rhythm and intonation*. London: Prentice-Hall.

17

Ethics and the business of pronunciation instruction

Jennifer A. Foote

Introduction

Ethics are an important consideration in any type of education or training. Therefore, it may not seem immediately obvious what makes the teaching of second language (L2) pronunciation instruction unique enough to warrant its own chapter in this handbook. It is unlikely anyone will write an chapter entitled 'Ethics and the business of vocabulary instruction' for an L2 vocabulary handbook. This is not to say that ethical issues do not feature in other areas of English language training; however, pronunciation is one area where considerations around ethical practice are particularly critical, especially in relation to the booming industry surrounding it. In recent years, issues of ethical practice in the teaching of pronunciation instruction have begun to receive an increasing amount of attention (e.g. Derwing & Munro, 2015; Thomson, 2014). It is important that attention to this topic continue in order to help curb unethical practice in our field and to help learners avoid becoming victims of such training.

A lot of money can be made in the business of pronunciation instruction. Research has established that for the vast majority of people who learn English as adults a detectable foreign accent will be a feature of their L2 speech (Scovel, 2000). Fortunately, even having a very noticeable accent does not necessarily make someone difficult to understand. However, while a foreign accent may not impair communication, L2 speakers may have reasons for wanting to change the way they speak. Because it is especially salient, pronunciation is often blamed for communication difficulties, despite not being the culprit (Derwing, Fraser, Kang & Thomson, 2014). Further, as Sikorski (2005) notes, even for first language (L1) English speakers who speak with a regional dialect, the consequences of speaking with a noticeable accent can be serious:

> [t]hose with accents are vulnerable to stereotyping. Whether the difficulties are real or perceived, the end product is very real: such individuals may suffer the same social and professional 'handicap' – the Glass Ceiling – that we freely admit exists for other working adults like the older employee, the severely overweight, the woman vying for the male-only positions, and so on.
>
> (p. 120)

Fear of being treated differently owing to their accent may lead second language (L2) speakers to try to change their pronunciation. When a speaker's pronunciation difficulties are such that they cause serious difficulties with communication, the desire to find effective pronunciation instruction can become urgent. For these individuals, traditional language classes may offer little in the way of help. Pronunciation is often overlooked in language classrooms (e.g. Foote, Trofimovich, Collins & Soler Urzúa, 2016) and many instructors do not feel prepared to teach pronunciation in L2 classes (e.g. Foote, Holtby & Derwing, 2011; Henderson et al., 2012; MacDonald, 2002). All of this can lead L2 speakers to seek paid help to alter their pronunciation, and, for those who do, there are many individuals and businesses willing to take their money. While some of the services being offered are effective, affordable and based on current research, many are not. There is no required certification to teach pronunciation and, as a result, the types of services available vary enormously, as do the qualifications of those offering such services. As with almost anything that offers potential economic gain, when there is demand supply will follow. In the unregulated area of L2 pronunciation instruction, it is easy for individuals to fall victim to overpriced 'miracle cures' that offer dubious methods for often exorbitant prices.

This chapter will discuss some of the most important ethical issues facing the booming business of pronunciation instruction. It will begin with a description of key terms related to L2 pronunciation, particularly in regards to the respective roles of accent, comprehensibility and intelligibility in helping learners communicate effectively. It will then move onto an overview of historical perspectives, including a description of Derwing and Munro's (2009) tripartite categorization of pronunciation teaching into a medical view, a business view and an educational view. This will be followed by a discussion of a number of critical issues in the area of ethics and pronunciation instruction that relate to these three perspectives, including the professional qualifications of those providing instruction, the cost of instruction, and the advertising claims made by those selling pronunciation instruction. Issues of learner identity and discrimination add to the complexity of ethics and pronunciation instruction and will also be discussed. Recommendations for practice are given in the form of a series of guiding principles for ethical pronunciation instruction to serve as a resource for language teachers, teacher trainers, classroom practitioners and applied linguists wanting to foster ethical pronunciation instruction in a wide range of contexts. The chapter concludes with a discussion of what can be done to curb unethical pronunciation instruction in the future, as well as ways that emerging technologies present both opportunities and challenges to ethical business practices.

Definitions

As was mentioned in the previous section, having a noticeable foreign accent does not necessarily make a person difficult to understand. Even in the absence of research evidence, it is not hard to think of people who speak with a strong accent but who have no difficulties communicating in a wide range of contexts. A robust body of research has explored the relationship between three distinct but related concepts: accentedness, comprehensibility and intelligibility. Accentedness has been defined in a number of ways. Derwing and Munro (2009) define it as 'the degree to which a speech sample differs from the local variety' (p. 476). In their work, Derwing and Munro (2015) emphasize the role of the listener when discussing accent, noting that while accent is tied directly to a speaker's L1, it is, 'by definition, something that is noticed by listeners' (p. 8). It is important to note that accentedness denotes differences in phonology but does not distinguish between whether or not those differences make a speaker harder for an interlocutor to understand. On this dimension, the terms comprehensibility and intelligibility are used. Comprehensibility is a measure of how easy or difficult an utterance is to process by listeners. Because comprehensibility refers to perceived difficulty, it is possible that an utterance could be low in terms of comprehensibility but still, ultimately, be fully understood. The term intelligibility differs from comprehensibility in that it is used to measure how much of an utterance is ultimately understood, regardless of how much effort was required to reach that understanding.

It is common in teaching materials, assessment instruments and even research studies to conflate accentedness with comprehensibility and intelligibility. However, research has consistently found that these constructs are partially independent; while someone who has low intelligibility and comprehensibility scores will likely also have high accentedness scores, the reverse isn't always true; people can be highly accented and still be easily understood. Awareness of the differences between these constructs is important because pronunciation instruction that focuses only on accent may result in a learner spending a lot of time and energy trying to change aspects of his or her accent without actually becoming noticeably easier to understand. As will be seen in later sections of this chapter, a focus on accentedness rather than intelligibility and comprehensibility is common, particularly in profit-driven pronunciation instruction.

Historical perspectives

The nativeness principle and the intelligibility principle

The differences between accentedness, comprehensibility and intelligibility are important to consider when looking at shifts in how pronunciation instruction has been approached over time. Levis (2005) describes pronunciation pedagogy and research as operating under one of two broad principles: the 'nativeness principle' or the 'intelligibility principle'. For those operating under the nativeness principle, the goal is to eliminate, as much as is possible, all aspects of a foreign accent. This has implications for the business side of pronunciation, as Levis notes: 'popularly, the principle drives the accent reduction industry, which implicitly promises learners that the right combination of motivation and special techniques can eliminate a foreign accent'. (p. 370) The nativeness principle has been increasingly viewed as both an unrealistic and inappropriate goal in the teaching of L2 pronunciation. Instead, the intelligibility principle has gained prominence. Proponents of the intelligibility principle argue that the goal of pronunciation instruction should be speech that is more easily understood. This means that the aspects of speech that are most important to focus upon are not necessarily those that are most salient, but rather those that are most likely to impede successful communication. As well as being a more realistic and attainable goal, the intelligibility principle is also far less prescriptive than the nativeness principle in that it does not automatically demean the presence of a foreign accent. Having a foreign accent is seen as a natural and expected outcome for adult L2 learners and deviations from native speaker pronunciation norms are perceived as problematic only if they make speech difficult for interlocutors to understand.

Three perspectives on L2 pronunciation instruction

Historically, pronunciation instruction has not been the sole domain of language instructors and programmes. Derwing (2003) noted the growth of pronunciation instruction activities by businesses and speech-language pathologists (SLPs). Later, Derwing and Munro (2009) delineated three different views on pronunciation, which are influenced primarily by the professional backgrounds of the providers: the pedagogical view, the medical view and the business view (see Derwing and Munro (2015) for a comprehensive overview). The pedagogical view is typically found in traditional language classes and reflects the view of most L2 instructors. This is the perspective likely to be found throughout this handbook, and, in fact, by using the term *pronunciation instruction* this chapter aligns itself with a pedagogical approach to pronunciation instruction. Within the pedagogical perspective, there has been a shift in how pronunciation is viewed, as language instruction moved through audiolingualism (in which pronunciation was a prominent part of classroom teaching and learners were expected to minimize mistakes as much as possible) to communicative language teaching (in which pronunciation was seen as unimportant and was very much marginalized) and current practice (in which pronunciation has begun to receive increased practitioner and research attention). The recent resurgence of interest in pronunciation is largely due to a realization that some learners still struggle with attaining intelligible pronunciation even after extended naturalistic exposure to their L2 (see Chapter 1, this volume, for a more detailed description of this history). This shift in language teaching methods and approaches is reflected in a transition from the nativeness principle to the intelligibility principle. Historically, audiolingualism was inherently more in line with the nativeness principle (e.g. its focus on preventing errors), while communicative teaching and task-based language teaching are more naturally aligned with the intelligibility principle (e.g. their focus on meaningful exchanges of information).

A medical view of pronunciation may sound strange to readers who come from a pedagogical background. However, many individuals currently offering 'accent modification' instruction are SLPs rather than language instructors. Seeing L2 accent as a disorder is not uncommon among SLPs, despite both the American and Canadian SLP professional associations stating that accent should not be considered a disorder (Derwing & Munro, 2015, p. 162). SLPs refer to the training (or, depending on the view of the practitioner, the treatment) they offer as accent modification, and many SLPs work in this area. In fact, an article in the *American Speech-Hearing Association (ASHA) Leader* (a publication for SLPs) cited accent modification as their field's 'best kept secret' (Kuster, 2010). While both language instructors and SLPs have been in the business of providing help with L2 pronunciation for many years, Sikorski (2005, p. 121) notes that 'the research and the experts cited rarely overlap from one discipline to another'. However, there is some evidence that this may be improving, as applied linguistics research on pronunciation issues, such as the relationships between accentedness, comprehensibility and intelligibility are increasingly being cited in SLP publications (e.g. Fritz & Sikorski, 2013; Levy & Crowley, 2012). In fact, a professional issues statement from the ASHA uses such research to argue for supporting SLP students who have foreign accents (ASHA, 2011). Nonetheless, it remains surprising how little interaction there is between those working on pronunciation within a language instruction paradigm and those working in speech-language pathology contexts.

The business view of pronunciation instruction is found among those who are primarily offering their services for profit, often with little in the way of qualifications. It is with this type of instruction that the term 'accent reduction' is most commonly associated. Thomson (2014) notes that the term accent reduction 'carries with it certain negative connotations about accent that are advantageous for marketing purposes' (p. 165). When discussing the differences between the three groups there can be a significant amount of overlap. Both ESL instructors and SLPs often treat pronunciation instruction as a business (Thomson, 2014).

In fact, articles in prominent SLP publications promote accent modification in the corporate sector (e.g. Christensen, 2006; Feinstein-Whittaker, 2012) and even a cursory search of the Internet using the terms *pronunciation instruction, accent modification* and *accent reduction* will reveal a vast number of for-profit enterprises offering the services of both SLPs and language instructors (see Thomson (2014) for an analysis of websites offering pronunciation instruction using these three search terms). Throughout this chapter, the term pronunciation instruction will be used to refer to all three perspectives unless otherwise specified. Offering pronunciation instruction for profit is not in and of itself unethical. However, as there is no one agreed-upon certification or qualification for offering pronunciation instruction, there are ample opportunities for unethical practices. There is also a difference, ethically speaking, between language instructors trying to address pronunciation instruction as best they can within a larger ESL classroom and those making profit by offering specialized classes or programmes (Derwing, Fraser et al., 2014). The next section will discuss some of the more critical issues facing the business side of pronunciation instruction.

Critical issues and topics

Qualifications and training

Pronunciation instruction should only be offered by people who are qualified to do so. On its face, this statement may seem so readily apparent as to not require discussion. However, it *has* repeatedly been discussed by experts in the field. For example, Thomson (2014) argued that 'when an instructor desires to specialize in pronunciation training, ethical practice demands that they be minimally prepared' (p. 179) and Derwing, Fraser et al. (2014) stated that they 'believe it is unethical for someone who lacks basic knowledge of L2 pronunciation and L2 speech research to provide pronunciation instruction for a profit' (p. 5). Instructor qualifications are a problematic issue in pronunciation instruction for two main reasons. First, some of the people currently selling pronunciation instruction are not qualified to do so and, second, determining what it actually means to be qualified to teach pronunciation is not as simple as it may appear.

Thomson (2014) investigated the educational backgrounds and qualifications of individuals and companies with websites offering English pronunciation instruction, accent modification, or accent reduction. He found that many websites did not provide any information about the educational backgrounds of the providers, and that in a number of cases language teaching experience, rather than actual training, was cited. This is clearly a cause for concern. However, many of the providers did have either a degree in TESL (teaching ESL) or, more commonly, in SLP. Determining instructor credentials might seem an obvious way of determining qualifications. However, it is not clear that a degree in either TESL or SLP necessarily provides the level of knowledge required to sell expert services in pronunciation instruction.

A number of researchers have investigated degrees of L2 instructor preparation for teaching pronunciation. Murphy (2014) analysed 13 studies in this area to determine whether or not TESL training programmes sufficiently prepare instructors to teach pronunciation. He concluded 'that if you feel underprepared to teach pronunciation, you are in good company because the research documents that many ESL and EFL teachers feel this way' (p. 207). In fact, surveys of instructors from a wide range of contexts (e.g. Europe, Canada, Australia and Brazil) have found that instructors feel a need for better training in how to teach pronunciation (e.g. Breitkreutz, Derwing & Rossiter, 2001; Burns, 2006; Buss, 2015; Foote et al., 2011; Henderson et al., 2012).

Rather than simply asking instructors about their level of knowledge and confidence when teaching pronunciation, Thomson (2013) investigated how well English L2 instructors were able to critically evaluate pronunciation materials. He argued that the ability to critically assess such materials is important to ensure that instructors are 'less susceptible to adopting the inaccurate beliefs and practices that are increasingly prevalent in the marketplace' (p. 226). To do this, Thomson took statements from existing online sources (websites and YouTube videos) offering pronunciation instruction, accent modification or accent reduction. He found that there was a lack of agreement among the instructors in relation to questionable and false statements, suggesting that instructors needed more training about pronunciation instruction.

This lack of adequate training is not so surprising when pronunciation is situated within the broader context of L2 teaching. While pronunciation is not completely distinct from other language skills, there are a number important ways in which it does differ from other aspects of language (see Foote & Trofimovich, this volume, for an overview). Perhaps more importantly, the techniques used to effectively teach pronunciation often fall beyond the scope of what is typical of a modern-day communicative classroom. Generally, contemporary language classrooms prioritize authentic communication, often initiated by way of a language task. While there may be some focus on form, it tends to be secondary to the focus on meaning (Ellis, 2001, 2005). It could be argued that pronunciation instruction is often the exact opposite. There is a strong focus on form, often by way of repetition, and, while there is some attention to authentic communication, it is secondary to form (e.g. Gilbert, 2005; Grant, 2010; Hewings, 2004). There have been some attempts to make pronunciation instruction more communicative (e.g. Celce-Murica, Brinton & Goodwin, 1996, 2010; Isaacs, 2009); nonetheless, it often remains difficult to address pronunciation adequately in a communicative classroom (Levis & Grant, 2003). Unfortunately, despite the distinct nature of pronunciation in relation to other aspects of language learning, many TESL degree programmes do not offer specialized training in pronunciation (Murphy, 2014). For example, Foote et al. (2011) found that, of all of the accredited TESL programmes being offered at Canadian universities, only six offered any pronunciation-specific courses.

In contrast to efforts to examine the preparation of ESL instructors to offer pronunciation instruction, there has been far less research investigating how prepared SLPs are in this domain. Accent modification is explicitly defined as part of an SLP's scope of practice in both the United States and Canada. However, accent modification is, in many ways, not a compatible fit for SLPs, since accent is *not* a pathology, and, as such, not something that requires treatment. As Gould (2009) notes,

> for those who do consider accent reduction to be within the scope of speech-pathology professional practice, it would appear that their view of communication impairment differs from the generally accepted norm to include linguistic variation which does not have a biological deficit at its core.
>
> (p. 68)

This lack of compatibility within speech-language pathology led Müller, Ball and Guendouzi (2000) to make a case against SLPs offering such instruction:

> We would argue then that speech-language pathologists, unless they have a dual qualification in applied linguistics or TEFL/TESOL, are unlikely to be the best equipped to deal with foreign accent reduction as they will lack the knowledge base and the

teaching methods to deal with a population that is very different from the phonologically disordered one they are trained to deal with.

(p. 124)

It should be noted Müller et al. were not arguing that SLPs should never offer accent modification, but rather that before SLPs offer such services they should obtain additional training in TESL.

This call for more training is also not meant to imply that SLPs do not have any transferable skills for helping L2 speakers improve their pronunciation. Sikorski (2005) argues that '[s]peech pathologists are ideally suited to carry out regional or foreign accent improvement programs' partially because of SLPs' 'perspectives on sensitivity and inclusion' (p. 120). It should be acknowledged that SLPs have skills that could aid in the teaching of pronunciation that many language instructors do not have. As Thomson (2014) observes, 'many ELTs would benefit from additional training in articulatory phonetics – something most SLPs already have' (p. 178) and Schmidt and Sullivan argue that ESL instructors and SLPs engaged in accent modification could learn from each other. Nonetheless, even Sikorski (2005) states that 'the SLP's professional background does not typically include sufficient perspective on teaching pronunciation as a second language/second dialect' (p. 121). This is particularly true given that the amount of training and clinical practice SLPs receive may be quite limited in some programmes. A survey by Schmidt and Sullivan (2003) found that not all speech-language pathology programmes include accent modification as part of students' clinical experience. So, while SLP training could be seen as containing some useful foundational elements for work with clients on L2 pronunciation, as with a TESL degree, it should not be considered as automatically sufficient to qualify an individual as an L2 pronunciation expert.

Cost

There is no doubt that a key issue at the heart of the discussion ethics and pronunciation instruction is the cost of services offered. As has already been discussed in the previous section, there is no standard qualification for offering pronunciation instruction, and there is no type of regulating body that certifies programmes or services for pronunciation. As Derwing and Munro (2015) point out, 'anyone with a lot of hubris who can come up with a website and make arrangements for credit card payments has the basis for an accent reduction business' (p. 155). As a result, the types of services offered and the costs associated with those services are so varied as to be completely overwhelming to someone searching for help. Thomson (2014) investigated the prices of services being sold under the terms *accent reduction, accent modification* and *pronunciation instruction*. The average price for pronunciation instruction ($116) was much lower than accent modification ($454) and accent reduction ($958). However, more interesting than the average prices in each category was how much price variability there was overall, with services being offered for as little as $6 and up to as much as $10,620. Of course, the length of treatment and/or the materials being provided is reflected in many fees, but if an L2 speaker is going to invest hundreds or even thousands of dollars for help with pronunciation, one would expect that the methods and results of that programme would have to be exceptional indeed in order to offer a potential customer sufficient return on investment; charging large amounts of money for methods that are neither research-based nor proven to work is, at best, ethically questionable.

Advertising

Of course, it could be argued that cost is irrelevant in a free market where nobody is being forced to purchase expensive services. This is where questions around ethics and advertising become critical. A number of different sources (e.g. Derwing, Fraser et al., 2014; Derwing & Munro, 2015; Müller et al., 2000; Thomson, 2014) have critiqued advertising for pronunciation instruction. One does not need to spend much time searching the Internet to find a wealth of advertising for pronunciation-related services that raise red flags. Ethics in advertising is difficult to address because effective advertising leads purveyors of goods to spin their message in such a way as to make their products appear desirable. As Thomson (2014) notes, there are two main ways in which pronunciation advertising often appears to cross an ethical line: (a) making claims about the efficacy of the training/treatment offered that are exaggerated or untrue, and (b) using fear as a motivating factor for selling services. The following are two recent examples, taken from the Internet, that show the types of advertising that are sometimes used to sell pronunciation instruction.

(a) The fastest way to improve your spoken English and lose your accent. Guaranteed!

(b) Are you frustrated that people are always asking you to repeat yourself? Are you tired of people asking you where you are from, instead of listening to what you have to say? Do your colleagues lose interest or 'switch off' when you're talking to them? Are you sick of getting noticed only because of the way you sound?

Any website that claims to be able to make dramatic changes to a person's accent in a very short period of time should be viewed with extreme suspicion, and claims of being able to completely eliminate an accent are almost surely false. As Munro (2003) states, 'no ethical teacher or researcher would claim that foreign accents can be routinely eliminated, no matter what type of pedagogy or speech therapy is used' (p. 40). I would argue, and others (e.g. Thomson, 2104) have made similar cases, that it is also unethical to use advertising that preys on clients' fears of losing employment opportunities or having difficultly forming social relationships with native speakers because of the presence of a foreign accent.

Unfortunately, there are reasons why fear-based advertising is effective for selling pronunciation instruction. There is no doubt that discrimination owing to the presence of a foreign accent is a very real problem (Lippi-Green, 2012; Munro, 2003). Perhaps more important in a discussion about advertising is that L2 speakers themselves often feel that they are treated differently because of their accents (Derwing, 2003; Gluszek & Dovidio, 2010; Levis, 2015). For example, in a survey of 100 language learners in Canada, Derwing (2003) found that a third of participants believed that they were discriminated against because of their accents, and 53 percent agreed that they would be more respected if their English pronunciation were better. In a United States-based study, Levis (2015) interviewed 12 L2 English-speaking graduate students who were receiving pronunciation tutoring, to see how they viewed their own pronunciation in terms of their personal and professional goals and identities. He found that the participants saw pronunciation as being one of their main roadblocks in terms of their professional advancement. For example, one of Levis's participants stated 'I think when I speak English because I have that strong accent, my feeling like people think that I am non-educated person' (p. 46). Interestingly, that same participant had been told by her boss that he (i.e. the boss) thought her accent made her sound intelligent, but still she felt insecure about how she spoke at work. While accent discrimination is a problem, most people who have an accent are able to communicate successfully. Advertising that makes learners feel that they cannot be successful unless they are able to get rid of their accents is preying on the learners' fears and insecurities. Ultimately, it is contributing to the problem rather than helping to resolve it.

Pronunciation and identity

All of the critical issues and topics discussed thus far essentially come down to whether the people and businesses offering pronunciation instruction are doing so in ways that are honest and effective. However, it merits mentioning that there is debate around whether it is ethical to offer pronunciation instruction at all, regardless of cost, qualifications or effectiveness, because asking a person to change their pronunciation may be perceived as being tantamount to asking them to give up part of their identity (e.g. Porter & Garvin, 1989). This is an issue worthy of serious consideration given the strong link people see between accent and identity. As Matsuda (1991) states, 'your accent carries the story of who you are' (p. 1329). This connection between identity and accent is one of the reasons for the decline of the nativeness principle and ascent of the intelligibility principle. However, there are some who believe that, even with a focus on intelligibility, pronunciation instruction is, by its very nature, unethical. Unfortunately, this viewpoint overlooks the consequences of having speech that is very difficult to understand. Derwing and Munro (2015) clarify that 'if an individual is unable to communicate in the L2 in a way that interlocutors can understand, the expression of personal identity is threatened far more than by any changes pronunciation instruction may bring about' (p. 153).

Many learners themselves would agree with Derwing and Munro's position on this issue. In Derwing's (2003) interviews of 100 L2 learners, participants were asked if they would want to speak like a native speaker if they could; ninety-five per cent of participants agreed that they would. Levis's (2015) interviews with L2 speaking graduate students probed how much learners felt their identities were connected to their L2 accents. He found that there was a 'weak or nonexistent connection of identity and pronunciation in the students' comments' (p. 48). For the most part, the participants did not see their identities from their L1 backgrounds as being tied to their accents when speaking their L2, and, in fact, many seemed surprised that the interviewer would even ask such as question. The issue of identity and accent is complex and difficult to fully understand using surveys and interviews. Further, context likely plays a strong role in how L2 learners perceive accent and identity. For example, there is a major difference between learners in an ESL context and learners in an EFL or lingua franca context. Even with participants giving such adamantly negative answers, Levis acknowledged that there was likely more of a link between L2 accent and identity than the participants realized. However, while there certainly are ethical issues if one is forcing students to try to reduce their accents, it seems equally unethical to deny assistance to learners who wish to make their speech more intelligible due to an a priori assumption that doing so would damage their identity.

Current contributions and research

If, as was argued in the previous section, advertising often makes exaggerated or false claims about the efficacy of pronunciation services, then an important question research can address would be what would constitute a reasonable claim. Is it possible that some accent reduction programmes actually are eliminating L2 accents in their clients? As was mentioned in the introduction, it is unlikely that an adult language learner will ever sound like a native speaker of their target language. Whether a critical period for phonological development, or a broader sensitive period, as suggested by Flege, Munro and Mackay (1995), it has been widely observed that accent is the one aspect of language that is uniquely sensitive to the effects of age. However, anecdotally, many people claim to know someone who has achieved a native-like accent. In fact, there is some research that supports that, at least in certain conditions, some learners do overcome the constraints of critical period to achieve native-like or near-native-like speech (e.g. Bongaerts, Van Summeren, Planken & Schils, 1997; Ioup, Boustagui, El Tigi & Moselle, 1994). Bongaerts, Mennen & Silk (2000) conclude, however, that, typically, such individuals likely speak a language closely related language to their L1; further, Abrahamsson and Hyltenstam (2009) found that learners who can pass as native speakers past adolescence are still relatively young learners (i.e. between 10–17 years) and that when tested rigorously it is extremely rare for a late L2 language learner to truly be indistinguishable from a native speaker. Perhaps most importantly, while there may be some exceptional learners (e.g. Moyer, 2014), there is no known *exceptional treatment* that research has found to eliminate a foreign accent. In fact, pronunciation is such a challenge for many adult L2 learners that research has been more interested in whether pronunciation instruction can lead to noticeable changes at all, rather than investigating whether it can lead to native-like speech.

Fortunately, while there may not be any known instructional method that can enable an L2 speaker to quickly and easily lose all traces of his or her accent, there is now a wealth of evidence that indicates that pronunciation can be improved through instruction. Thanks to the rise in the number of intervention-based pronunciation studies in the past several years, Lee, Jang and Plonsky (2015) were able to conduct a statistical meta-analysis on the effects of pronunciation instruction. After analysing 86 studies, the researchers found a large effect size, indicating that instruction can indeed lead to genuine improvements in pronunciation. However, in a narrative review of the same studies, Thomson and Derwing (2015) noted that many of these studies did not use measures of comprehensibility or intelligibility. Encouragingly, a study by Derwing, Munro, Foote, Waugh and Fleming (2014) found that pronunciation instruction was able to lead to improvements in comprehensibility even in learners who had been speaking English as an L2 for an average of 19 years, a point at which many learners are considered to be *fossilized* in terms of their phonology. Taken as a whole, studies of pronunciation instruction would suggest that it is not unreasonable to assume that at least some pronunciation instruction can lead to improvement, but that it is highly unlikely that treatments will lead to native-like or near-native-like speech.

Recommendations for practice

This chapter has identified a number of ethical challenges facing for-profit pronunciation instruction providers. Despite the issues raised, the goal of this chapter is not to bring an end to all commercial pronunciation instruction. Rather, it is hoped that information provided here can help language instructors warn their students about what to look for when considering such services. It is also hoped that anyone contemplating entering the business end of pronunciation instruction will consider what constitutes ethical practice in the area and endeavour to provide instruction in an ethical way. To these ends, the following guidelines for providing ethical language instruction are offered.

(a) Pronunciation instruction should focus on making learners more intelligible, not on reducing the degree of their accentedness.

(b) When teaching pronunciation, an L2 accent should be viewed as a natural aspect of L2 development, not a speech disorder.

(c) People who are selling pronunciation instruction should have specialized training in pronunciation pedagogy; a degree in TESL or speech-language pathology may not, in and of itself, be sufficient to qualify someone as a pronunciation expert.

(d) Businesses and schools offering pronunciation instruction should not make exaggerated claims about the efficacy of the instruction they offer.

(e) Businesses and schools offering pronunciation instruction should not use fear-based advertising that demonizes the presence of an L2 accent.

(f) Pronunciation teaching methods should, wherever possible, be based on research findings rather than intuition.

While this list is neither detailed nor exhaustive, it covers many of the key issues related to pronunciation instruction and provides a good starting point for ensuring that people who profit from pronunciation instruction do so in a way that is ethical.

Future directions

Both pronunciation research and pedagogy are changing rapidly. This is partially due to a resurgent interest in pronunciation over the past 15 years in both classrooms and research, and partially due to advances in technology that have led to a wave of new pronunciation products in the form of apps and websites. This new technology offers great opportunities for learners who are hoping to improve their pronunciation but it also creates several concerns. For learners looking for an affordable and convenient way to improve their pronunciation, there are a wide range of apps to choose from. However, as Foote and Smith (2013) noted in a survey of pronunciation teaching apps, many are limited in what they provide to learners and may use dubious methods. For example, some apps use synthetic voices as speech models, and others use voice recognition software to offer questionable feedback on learner output. As technology improves, the possibilities of receiving meaningful feedback and customized instruction will undoubtedly improve. Unfortunately, it can be difficult for teachers and learners to know how much they can rely on the promises of slick-looking products. For example, if a programme offers a score on a learner's pronunciation, and identifies a problem word, it is very difficult for the user to know if that computer analysis actually reflects how a human listener would perceive the same utterance. Because these products are often reasonably cheap and convenient to purchase, it is easy to waste money and time on apps, websites or other software that are unlikely to lead to genuine improvements.

Unfortunately, there is little that can be done to assess the quality of new apps, websites and software. Equally, unless a regulatory body steps in, it is unlikely that there is any way to prevent unqualified people from selling pronunciation instruction or from employing unethical advertising methods. For this reason, it is important that instructors help make learners aware of what to look for and avoid when seeking help with their pronunciation. A big step forward for our field would be an increase in the number of TESL programmes offering pedagogical training in L2 pronunciation. The benefits of this would be twofold: instructors would be better prepared to offer effective research-based instruction themselves, and they would be better able to make students aware of how to critically evaluate services that claim to improve speakers' productions in their L2.

Related topics

Pronunciation; speech perception; ethics; computer-assisted pronunciation instruction; accent; comprehensibility; intelligibility; identity

Further reading

Derwing, T. M., Fraser, H., Kang, O., & Thomson, R. I. (2014). L2 accent and ethics: Issues that merit attention. In A. Mahboob & L. Barratt (Eds), *Englishes in multilingual contexts*. Berlin: Springer. This article provides an overview of ethical issues related to L2 accent, focusing on both pronunciation instruction and language analysis for determination of origin (LADO).

Derwing, T. M., & Munro, M. J. (2015). *Pronunciation fundamentals: Evidence-based perspectives for L2 teaching and research*. Amsterdam: John Benjamins. This book provides a general introduction to L2 pronunciation. One chapter focuses specifically on issues related to ethics and pronunciation.

Levis, J. (2015). Learners' views of social issues in pronunciation learning. *Journal of Academic Language and Learning*, 9(1), A42–A55. This article presents research examining issues around identity and L2 accent, and also provides a succinct and useful overview of literature on L2 accent and identity.

Müller, N., Ball, M. J., & Guendouzi, J. (2000). Accent reduction programmes: Not a role for speech-language pathologists? *Advances in Speech-Language Pathology*, 2, 119–129. This article explains some of the issues and concerns around accent modification and speech-language pathology. It gives more information about issues surrounding pronunciation instruction that follows the medical view of pronunciation discussed earlier in this chapter.

Thomson, R. I. (2014). Myth 6: Accent reduction and pronunciation instruction are the same thing. In L. Grant (Ed.), *Pronunciation myths: Applying second language research to classroom teaching* (pp. 160–187). Ann Arbor, MI: University of Michigan. This book chapter explains many of the issues surrounding ethics and accent reduction. It also presents an analysis of the types of services currently being advertised on the Internet using the terms pronunciation instruction, accent modification and accent reduction.

References

Abrahamsson, N., & Hyltenstam, K. (2009). Age of onset and nativelikeness in a second language: Listener perception versus linguistic scrutiny. *Language Learning*, 59(2), 249–306.

American Speech-Language-Hearing Association. (2011). *The clinical education of students with accents* [Professional Issues Statement]. Retrieved from www.asha.org/policy.

Bongaerts, T., Mennen, S., & Slik, F. V. D. (2000). Authenticity of pronunciation in naturalistic second language acquisition: The case of very advanced late learners of Dutch as a second language. *Studia linguistica*, 54(2), 298–308.

Bongaerts, T., Van Summeren, C., Planken, B., & Schils, E. (1997). Age and ultimate attainment in the pronunciation of a foreign language. *Studies in Second Language Acquisition*, 19(04), 447–465.

Breitkreutz, J., Derwing, T. M., & Rossiter, M. J. (2001). Pronunciation teaching practices in Canada. *TESL Canada Journal*, 19(1), 51–61.

Burns, A. (2006). Integrating research and professional development on pronunciation teaching in a national adult ESL program. *TESL Reporter*, 39, 34–41.

Buss, L. (2015). Beliefs and practices of Brazilian EFL teachers regarding pronunciation. *Language Teaching Research*, Advance online publication. doi:10.1177/1362168815574145.

Celce-Murcia, M., Brinton, & D. Goodwin, J. (1996). *Teaching pronunciation: A reference for teachers of English to speakers of other languages*. New York, NY: Cambridge University Press.

Celce-Murcia, M., Brinton, & D. Goodwin, J., with Griner, B. (2010). *Teaching pronunciation: A course book and reference guide* (2nd ed.). New York, NY: Cambridge University Press.

Christensen, B. (January, 2006). Corporate speech-language pathology: Is It right for you? *The ASHA Leader*, 11, 14–25. Retrieved from http://leader.pubs.asha.org/article.aspx?articleid=2278238.

Derwing, T. (2003). What do ESL students say about their accents? *Canadian Modern Language Review*, 59(4), 547–567.

Derwing, T. M., & Munro, M. J. (2009). Putting accent in its place: Rethinking obstacles to communication. *Language Teaching, 42,* 476–490.

Derwing, T. M., & Munro, M. J. (2015). *Pronunciation fundamentals: Evidence-based perspectives for L2 teaching and research.* Amsterdam: John Benjamins.

Derwing, T. M., Fraser, H., Kang, O., & Thomson, R. I. (2014). L2 accent and ethics: Issues that merit attention. In A. Mahboob & L. Barratt (Eds), *Englishes in multilingual contexts* (pp. 63–80). Berlin: Springer.

Derwing, T. M., Munro, M. J., Foote, J. A., Waugh, E., & Fleming, J. (2014). Opening the window on comprehensible pronunciation after 19 years: A workplace training study. *Language Learning, 64*(3), 526–548.

Ellis, R. (2001). Introduction: Investigating form-focussed instruction. *Language Learning, 51*(S1), 1–46.

Ellis, R. (2005). Principles of instructed language learning. *System, 33*(2), 209–224.

Feinstein-Whittaker, M. (March, 2012). A growing niche in corporate America, *The ASHA Leader, 17,* 28–31. Retrieved from http://leader.pubs.asha.org/article.aspx?articleid=2280165.

Flege, J. E., Munro, M. J., & MacKay, I. R. (1995). Factors affecting strength of perceived foreign accent in a second language. *The Journal of the Acoustical Society of America, 97*(5), 3125–3134.

Foote, J. A., Holtby, A. K., & Derwing, T. M. (2011). Survey of the teaching of pronunciation in adult ESL programs in Canada, 2010. *TESL Canada Journal, 29*(1), 1–22.

Foote, J. A., & Smith, G. (2013, September). *Is there an App for that?* Paper presented at the Pronunciation in Second Language Learning and Teaching conference, Ames, IA.

Foote, J. A., Trofimovich, P., Collins, L., & Soler Urzúa, F. (2016). Pronunciation teaching practices in communicative second language classes. *The Language Learning Journal, 44*(2), 181–196.

Fritz, D. R., & Sikorski, L. D. (2013). Efficacy in accent modification services: Quantitative and qualitative outcomes for Korean speakers of American English. *SIG 14 Perspectives on Communication Disorders and Sciences in Culturally and Linguistically Diverse (CLD) Populations, 20*(3), 118–126.

Gilbert, J. (2005). *Clear speech: Pronunciation and listening comprehension in American English* (3rd ed.). New York, NY: Cambridge University Press.

Gluszek, A., & Dovidio, J. F. (2010). Speaking with a nonnative accent: Perceptions of bias, communication difficulties, and belonging in the United States. *Journal of Language and Social Psychology, 29*(2), 224–234.

Gould, J. (2009). There is more to communication than tongue placement and 'show and tell': Discussing communication from a speech pathology perspective. *Australian Journal of Linguistics, 29*(1), 59–73.

Grant, L. (2010). *Well said* (3rd ed.). Boston, MA: Heinle & Heinle.

Henderson, A., Frost, D., Tergujeff, E., Kautzsch, A., Murphy, D., Kirkova-Naskova, A., & Curnick, L. (2012). The English pronunciation teaching in Europe survey: Selected results. *Research in Language, 10*(1), 5–27.

Hewings, M. (2004). *Pronunciation practice activities.* Cambridge: Cambridge University Press.

Isaacs, T. (2009). Integrating form and meaning in L2 pronunciation instruction. *TESL Canada Journal, 27,* 1–12.

Ioup, G., Boustagui, E., El Tigi, M., & Moselle, M. (1994). Reexamining the critical period hypothesis. *Studies in Second Language Acquisition, 16*(1), 73–98.

Kuster, M. K. (2010, Apr 27). Accent modification cited as 'Best-Kept Secret'. *The ASHA Leader.* Retrieved from www.asha.org/leaderarticle.aspx?id=10737440471.

Lee, J., Jang, J., & Plonsky, L. (2015). The effectiveness of second language pronunciation instruction: A meta-analysis. *Applied Linguistics, 36*(3), 345–366.

Levis, J. M. (2005). Changing contexts and shifting paradigms in pronunciation teaching. *TESOL Quarterly, 39*(3), 369–377.

Levis, J. (2015). Learners' views of social issues in pronunciation learning. *Journal of Academic Language and Learning, 9*(1), A42–A55.

Levis, J. M., & Grant, L. (2003). Integrating pronunciation into ESL/EFL classrooms. *TESOL Journal, 12*(2), 13–19.

Levy, E. S., & Crowley, C. J. (2012). Policies and practices regarding students with accents in speech language pathology training programs. *Communication Disorders Quarterly, 34,* 59–68.

Lippi-Green, R. (2012). *English with an accent: Language, ideology, and discrimination in the United States* (2nd ed.). London: Routledge.

MacDonald, S. (2002). Pronunciation: Views and practices of reluctant teachers. *Prospect, 17*, 3–18.

Matsuda, M. J. (1991). Voices of America: Accent, antidiscrimination law, and a jurisprudence for the last reconstruction. *Yale Law Journal, 100*(5), 1329–1407.

Moyer, A. (2014). Exceptional outcomes in L2 phonology: The critical factors of learner engagement and self-regulation. *Applied Linguistics, 35*(4), 418–440.

Müller, N., Ball, M. J., & Guendouzi, J. (2000). Accent reduction programmes: Not a role for speech-language pathologists? *Advances in Speech-Language Pathology, 2*, 119–129.

Munro, M. J. (2003). A primer on accent discrimination in the Canadian context. *TESL Canada Journal, 20*(2), 38–51.

Murphy, J. (2014). Myth 7: Teacher training programs provide adequate preparation in how to teach pronunciation. In L. Grant (Ed.) *Pronunciation myths: Applying second language research to classroom teaching* (pp. 188–224). Ann Arbor, MI: University of Michigan.

Porter, D., & Garvin, S. (1989). Attitudes to pronunciation in EFL. *Speak Out, 5*, 8–15.

Schmidt, A. M., & Sullivan, S. (2003). Clinical training in foreign accent modification: A national survey. *Contemporary Issues in Communication Science and Disorders, 30*, 127–135.

Scovel, T. (2000). A critical review of the critical period research. *Annual Review of Applied Linguistics, 20*, 213–223.

Sikorski, L. D. (2005). Regional accents: A rationale for intervening and competencies required. *Seminars in Speech and Language, 26*, 118–125.

Thomson, R. I. (2013). ESL teachers' beliefs and practices in pronunciation teaching: Confidently right or confidently wrong? In J. Levis & K. LeVelle (Eds). *Proceedings of the 4th Pronunciation in Second Language Learning and Teaching Conference*, August 2012. (pp. 224–233). Ames, IA: Iowa State University

Thomson, R. I. (2014). Myth 6: Accent reduction and pronunciation instruction are the same thing. In L. Grant (Ed.) *Pronunciation myths: Applying second language research to classroom teaching* (pp. 160–187). Ann Arbor, MI: University of Michigan.

Thomson, R. I., & Derwing, T. M. (2015). The effectiveness of L2 pronunciation instruction: A narrative review. *Applied Linguistics, 36*(3), 326–344.

18

Teacher training in the teaching of pronunciation[1]

John M. Murphy

Purpose

The chapter's purpose is to guide and support teacher educators charged with preparing L2 teachers to teach the pronunciation of English. For most teachers, professional forums such as regional, national and international conferences afford opportunities to meet and interact with potential mentors who specialize in this area. For reasons discussed below, such opportunities are less available within most teacher development courses and language programmes. To address this disciplinary gap, the chapter discusses ways of designing and offering a certificate, undergraduate or graduate applied linguistics/MATESOL course in teaching the pronunciation of English as a second language (ESL), English as a foreign language (EFL) or English as an (international) lingua franca (ELF). Because the chapter is designed to support both current and prospective teachers, it may serve as a basis for designing a teacher development course or for purposes of self-study. Topics featured include what pronunciation teachers need to know (i.e. knowledge about phonetics and phonology), what teachers need to know how to do (i.e. pedagogical content knowledge[2]), alternative structures for a teacher development course, application tasks designed for pre-service teachers, a synthesis of research-based implications for teaching, professional development resources, teaching resources, and where to turn to learn more.

Historical perspective

As signalled in Murphy and Baker's (2015) recent history of L2 pronunciation teaching and reiterated by Derwing in this volume (see Derwing's chapter, titled 'The efficacy of pronunciation instruction') and Levis (2016), empirical investigations in support of pronunciation teaching only 'began in earnest' in the mid-1990s (Derwing & Munro, 2015, p. 14). The findings and implications of this increasingly important research tradition have been recently summarized and reviewed in book-length treatments by Derwing and Munro (2015) and Grant (2014) and in separate journal articles by Lee, Jang and Plonsky (2015), Levis (2016) and Thomson and Derwing (2015). Though not necessarily appropriate as required readings in L2 teacher development settings, these publications constitute the types of source materials L2 teacher educators should draw from when designing a pronunciation-centred teacher preparation course. For ease of presentation, connections between empirical research findings, pronunciation teaching and teachers' developments of pedagogical content knowledge will be discussed throughout the chapter.

With respect to knowledge of the phonological system itself, Table 18.1 offers a prioritized listing of fourteen core knowledge about phonetics and phonology topics that research suggests L2 teachers need to know about to be able to teach the pronunciation of English. More important items (i.e. those meriting early and sustained attention when preparing novice teachers; those with greater impact on the intelligibility of NNESs) appear earlier in the list. Table 18.1 is organized to reflect contemporary research findings as summarized by Derwing and Munro (2015), Grant (2014), Lee et al. (2015) and Thomson and Derwing (2015), while also taking into consideration several specialist recommendations for preparing language teachers in this area (e.g. Brinton, 2014; Dickerson, 2010; Gilbert, 2008; Goodwin, 2014; Murphy, 2013, 2017).

Table 18.1's listing of core topics in phonetics and phonology serves a dual purpose since it may also inform teacher decision-making when it comes to sequencing priorities for teaching pronunciation to NNESs. When time is limited for pronunciation teaching in an ESL, EFL or ELF course, the first few items listed in Table 18.1 might be prioritized (e.g. items 1–3 or 1–5). In settings where more time is available, more of the topics may be introduced. Fuller coverage of the entire list might only happen in language courses specifically dedicated to pronunciation. Likewise, a full course dedicated to preparing pronunciation teachers might feature more extensive coverage of all 14 topics, while a single teacher training workshop or instructional unit might introduce just the first few.

While Table 18.1 serves as a preliminary road map for what pronunciation teachers need to know about phonetics and phonology, it does not shed any light on how they might go about teaching pronunciation in language classrooms. This distinction reinforces the theme that (declarative) knowledge about phonetics and phonology and (procedural) pedagogical content knowledge are complementing, though separable, domains of teacher knowledge. As discussed by Baker and Murphy (2011), together they comprise a knowledge base for pronunciation teaching. A theme missing from many discussions of how to prepare

Table 18.1 A prioritized listing of 14 core topics in phonetics and phonology

What pronunciation teachers need to know		
1	The process of thought grouping	8	Consonant phonetics (e.g. word endings, clusters)
2	Prominence (sentence-level stress)	9	Vowel phonetics (e.g. high- and low-frequency vowels, vowel reductions)
3	Word stress	10	Connected speech phenomena (e.g. assimilation, linking, palatalization, deletion, compression)
4	Consonant phonemes (the basic inventory)	11	Construction stress (e.g. how affixation impacts word stress)
5	Vowel phonemes (the basic inventory)	12	Rhythm
6	Sound–spelling correspondence	13	Intonation (e.g. how 'tone choices' impact listener perceptions)
7	Variable nature of spoken language	14	Discourse meaning

Table 18.2 What pronunciation teachers need to know how to do: pedagogical content knowledge

Teachers need to know how to:

(a) identify NNESs' likely areas of pronunciation challenge (e.g. thought grouping, prominence, word endings, volume, tempo, intonation) (see Swan & Smith, 2001)

(b) design and implement needs analysis techniques

(c) identify pedagogical priorities (e.g. phonological elements that impact intelligibility; functional load)

(d) describe, explain and illustrate pronunciation topics in accessible ways

(e) provide students with experiential opportunities to apply what they are learning about the pronunciation of English while speaking extemporaneously

(f) develop and implement a wide range of teaching techniques that may be grouped under the broad categories of listening discrimination, controlled production, guided practice, self-monitoring and extemporaneous practice (see Celce-Murcia et al. 2010; Marks and Bowen 2012)

(g) structure, sequence and pace the inclusion of all five categories of teaching techniques listed in item (f)

(h) design and implement pronunciation assessment techniques (see Celce-Murcia et al., 2010; Isaacs, 2014)

(i) teach the listening process in general, listening for comprehension, and listening for pronunciation (see Cauldwell, 2013; Field, 2008)

(j) differentiate between the teaching of spoken fluency and pronunciation

(k) work productively with:

    (i) pronunciation-centred ESL classroom textbooks (e.g. Grant, 2017a)

    (ii) other pedagogical resources constructed to support pronunciation teaching (e.g. activity recipe collections, Internet sites)

    (iii) resources designed to teach other language skills as potential supports for pronunciation teaching (see Jones, 2016)

    (iv) non-pedagogical realia, gadgets, and props to support pronunciation learning (e.g. kazoos, mirrors, smart phones, tablets) (see Gilbert, 1991)

    (v) non-pedagogical Internet sources (e.g. TedTalks, Three Minute Thesis) to support pronunciation learning

    (vi) breathing and relaxation techniques

    (vii) kinesthetic techniques (e.g. speech-synchronized gestures such as hand claps, handshakes, high fives) (see Acton, 1984; Murphy, 2013)

    (viii) fluency-building techniques (see Klippel, 2004)

    (ix) multisensory reinforcement techniques (see Samuel, 2010)

    (x) corrective feedback techniques (see Lyster, Saito & Sato, 2013)

    (xi) drama techniques (Galante & Thomson, 2016)

    (xii) mirroring and shadowing techniques (see Meyers, 2013; Rosse, 1999)

    (xiii) print media (e.g. strip cartoons from newspapers, comic books, and graphic novels)

    (xiv) audio & video recordings (e.g. textbooks' accompanying CDs, DVDs and digital files)

    (xv) peer interactive techniques (e.g. games, role plays, simulations)

    (xvi) jokes and riddles (see Wong, 1987)

    (xvii) punctuation-free samples of written discourse (see Murphy, 2013, 2015)

    (xviii) poetry, rhymes, jazz chants, songs

    (xix) pronunciation software and Internet sites (e.g. Thomson, 2012; English Accent Coach, www.englishaccentcoach.com/index.aspx)

pronunciation teachers (e.g. workshops, conference papers, courses, journal articles) is that neither domain is sufficient on its own. However, it is important to recognize that knowledge about phonetics and phonology has served as the traditional focus, all too often the sole focus, of teacher preparation endeavours. A sign of this historical imbalance is that teacher educators have a wider array of phonetics/phonology-centred resources at their disposal in comparison with resources and theory to support the development of procedural knowledge about how to teach pronunciation. A result of this imbalance is that resources centred on knowledge about phonetics and phonology tend to dominate the content featured in most teacher preparation courses and programmes in this area (Burgess & Spencer, 2000; Murphy, 1997).

To address this imbalance, Table 18.2 complements Table 18.1 by providing a listing of core pedagogical content knowledge topics that pronunciation teachers need to be able to act upon when teaching the pronunciation of English. Although Table 18.2's listing of pedagogy related topics is not intended to be comprehensive, it is inspired by pronunciation teacher development resources such as Avery and Ehrlich (1992), Celce-Murcia, Brinton, Goodwin and Griner (2010), Gilbert (2008), Lane (2010) and Rogerson-Revell (2011); journal articles and book chapters such as Brinton (2014), Gilbert (1991), Goodwin (2014), Isaacs (2009), Levis and Grant (2003), and Morley (1994); and classroom activity recipe collections such as Brown (2012), Hewings (2004), Laroy (1995) and Marks and Bowen (2012).

Beyond the development of knowledge about phonetics and phonology through participation in certificate and degree programmes, and in addition to opportunities to read and discuss articles and book chapters designed to engender pedagogical knowledge (e.g. Barrera-Pardo, 2008; Isaacs, 2009), pronunciation teachers also need opportunities to try things out for themselves through guided micro-teaching, tutoring of L2 learners, practice teaching opportunities, and other first-hand experiential learning-to-teach activities (Johnson, 2009; Murphy, 2014b). In an ideal world, practice-focused guidance and support of this kind would continue once novice teachers begin their teaching careers (Johnson & Golombek, 2016) although, as Farrell (2016) discusses, on-site guidance of L2 teaching rarely occurs in the workplace.

Critical issues and topics

Why does the teaching of pronunciation merit a specialized course? As in most professional fields, novice teachers expect to be well prepared for future teaching assignments through the teacher preparation programmes they attend, the resources made available to them, and the teacher educators they meet. Preparation in how to serve as a competent teacher of pronunciation is no exception. Beyond the necessity of reliable background supports, Baker (2014) documents that once they begin to teach, those new to pronunciation teaching benefit from mentoring opportunities provided by supportive colleagues on the job. A complication is that many certificate and degree programmes in applied linguistics/TESOL devote limited attention to this area (Burgess & Spencer, 2000; Foote, Holtby & Derwing, 2011). Also, in most teacher preparation programmes topics in phonetics and phonology vie for attention in more broadly focused courses (e.g. introduction to linguistics, general linguistics, teaching methods), where even less attention is given to implications for pronunciation teaching (Burgess & Spencer, 2000; Murphy, 1997). Further, a recurring theme that Baker (2014), Burns (2006), Foote et al. (2011), Henderson et al. (2012) and MacDonald (2002) document is that large numbers of contemporary L2 teachers feel both ill prepared and reluctant to teach pronunciation. As a result, potential mentors for those interested in developing expertise in teaching the pronunciation of English are, all too often, unavailable.

Learning objectives

A starting point for designing a pronunciation-centred teacher preparation course is to identify learning objectives for prospective teachers. The overarching objective is that by the end of the course students will be ready to serve as competent pronunciation teachers. Such competence means they will possess requisite levels of both knowledge about phonetics and phonology and pronunciation-specific pedagogical content knowledge, and that they will be able to apply what they know in language classrooms. In the language of measurable learning objectives, by the end of the period of study successful course participants will be able to:

(a) conduct needs analysis;
(b) specify learning priorities for L2 learners;
(c) design either pronunciation-centred or pronunciation-inclusive courses;
(d) assess the quality of relevant classroom textbooks and related instructional materials;
(e) implement pronunciation-focused activities featured in such resources;
(f) modify found activities and materials to fit local contexts of pronunciation teaching;
(g) generate original instructional materials and activities;
(h) monitor and continue to assess learner progress;
(i) interpret and apply empirical findings of relevant research;
(j) use emerging technologies in ways compatible with learners' needs and abilities;
(k) revise and adapt teaching practices as needed; and,
(l) continue to learn more (e.g. through reading; collaborations with colleagues; professional development opportunities).

Learning opportunities, application tasks, assessment procedures and assessment rubrics can be designed for each of the objectives listed above. The remainder of the chapter will focus on ways of preparing novice teachers to meet these learning objectives. Also, several of the objectives receive generous attention in other chapters of this book.

Text resources to support teacher training in this area

As already mentioned, there is a wide assortment of books available to support the development of knowledge about phonetics and phonology, and new ones appear regularly. The sources of information featured in such texts have a long history of continual improvement that stretches at least as far back as the reform movement of the 1890s (Derwing, this volume; Murphy & Baker, 2015). In general terms, contemporary applied linguistics texts that feature topics in phonetics and phonology may be divided into two broad genres:

(a) texts centred on information about phonetics and phonology (i.e. ones that are content knowledge focused), and
(b) texts that integrate information about phonetics and phonology with related pedagogical content knowledge discussions and illustrations.

In the genre of texts centred on information about phonetics and phonology, the description and analysis of the sound system of English dominates. Three classic examples (all of which are available in recently updated and expanded editions) are Collins and Mees (2013), Roach (2009) and Ladefoged and Johnson (2014). Even if only as reference materials, information-centred texts of this kind are indispensable sources for teacher educators to examine. Up until the twentieth century's final decades, these were the only types of resources available to support the preparation of pronunciation teachers. A complication is that, since their primary purpose is to develop declarative knowledge about phonetics and phonology, limited attention is devoted to developing procedural knowledge about the process of teaching pronunciation. Although not a strategy advocated in this chapter, it might be possible to select a text centred on knowledge about phonetics and phonology as required reading if more pedagogically focused materials and discussions, or a more practice-oriented course were also available to the participating teachers. However, both Burgess and Spencer (2000) and Murphy (1997) document that few programmes in applied linguistics/TESOL offer even a single course, much less two, dedicated to either knowledge about phonetics and phonology or pronunciation-focused pedagogical content knowledge. Further, programmes with a required practicum in which prospective teachers gain classroom experience rarely focus on pronunciation teaching (see Crookes, 2003). Also of concern, over two decades of teacher development research signals how uncommon it is for novice L2 teachers to be able to apply declarative knowledge about language, including knowledge about phonetics and phonology, unless the preparation programmes they attend not only feature, but immerse novice teachers in frequent discussions and illustrations of L2 teaching in conjunction with practice teaching opportunities (Bartels, 2009; Borg, 2003; Gregory, 2005; Johnson, 2009). Given these concerns, a complicating factor with resources of the first genre is their failure to go beyond information about phonetics and phonology by fostering insights into practices of pronunciation teaching.

Teacher preparation texts that integrate knowledge about phonetics and phonology with pedagogical content knowledge

A compelling reason to move away from texts centred on information about phonetics and phonology is that, fortunately, there is an even more promising genre of possible core texts to use in teacher preparation courses. The defining characteristic of the second genre is that these texts feature generous attention to information about phonetics and phonology but go well beyond declarative knowledge by offering frequent discussions and explicit illustrations of how to teach the pronunciation of English (Murphy, 2014b). Beginning with Kenworthy (1987), over a dozen teacher development texts that integrate substantive information about phonetics and phonology with generous attention to implications for classroom pedagogy have appeared. Some notable ones include Avery and Ehrlich (1992), Celce-Murcia et al. (2010), Lane (2010), Murphy (in press for 2017) and Rogerson-Revell (2011), as well as the current volume. All of them could serve as a core text in a teacher development course or for purposes of self-study. It is also worth mentioning that Dalton and Seidlhofer (1994) is a text of this genre specifically designed for self-study.

Teacher preparation texts focused on teaching practices

In addition to the first two genres, there are a few high-quality texts that illustrate yet a third, and even more practice-focused, resource category. Texts of this third genre are targeted to teachers who already possess requisite knowledge about phonetics and phonology since they focus even more exclusively on illustrations of pronunciation teaching pedagogy. Termed 'activity recipe collections' by Murphy (2014b, p. 211), some interesting examples are Bowen and Marks (1992), Brown (2012), Hancock (1996), Hewings (2004), Jones (2016), Laroy

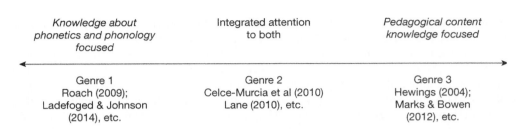

Knowledge about phonetics and phonology focused	Integrated attention to both	Pedagogical content knowledge focused
Genre 1 Roach (2009); Ladefoged & Johnson (2014), etc.	Genre 2 Celce-Murcia et al (2010) Lane (2010), etc.	Genre 3 Hewings (2004); Marks & Bowen (2012), etc.

Figure 18.1 Continuum of possible texts types to feature in a teacher preparation course

(1995) and Marks and Bowen (2012). These represent another useful type of support for pronunciation teaching. Of the ones listed, Marks and Bowen (2012) is particularly accessible to those completely new to this area of L2 teaching; Brown (2012) focuses specifically on ways of teaching compressed speech phenomena (e.g. linking, vowel reduction); and Jones (2016) is a genre hybrid since it mixes activity recipe descriptions with more extended discussions of somewhat broader pedagogical content knowledge themes. Resources of the third genre meet the needs of language teachers interested in connections between knowledge about phonetics and phonology and L2 pedagogy. Figure 18.1 places the three L2 teacher development genres identified so far along a continuum from texts focused on developing knowledge about phonetics and phonology to those focused on developing pedagogical content knowledge.

Now that core themes in the preparation of pronunciation teachers have been introduced (e.g. definitions of key terms, the chapter's central purpose, some historical perspective, listings of what teachers need to know and know how to do, learning objectives, three types of text resources), the remainder of the chapter presents nine recommendations to L2 teacher educators charged with preparing prospective pronunciation teachers (PPTs). Substantive discussion follows each of the recommendations.

Recommendations for preparing PPTs

Distinguish between teaching the pronunciation of ESL, EFL and ELF

Since the publication of Jenkins's (2000, 2007) early research on the phonology of English when it is used as an international lingua franca, it has become increasingly important for teacher educators, classroom teachers, researchers and materials developers to be explicit about the form of pronunciation reflected in their work (Seidlhofer, 2011; Walker, 2010). At a minimum, teachers should be conversant with differences between teaching the pronunciation of ESL, EFL and ELF. Contrasts and areas of overlap between them pivot on two foundational concerns: (a) the ultimate level of pronunciation attainment expected of learners, and (b) the features of the English phonological system considered to be the most important to teach. With respect to these dual concerns, ESL, EFL and ELF styles of pronunciation teaching lead to alternative purposes, goals, supporting resources, models of pronunciation and research traditions (Derwing & Munro, 2015; Seidlhofer, 2011). To avoid confusion between them, it is important that all three styles be introduced and discussed openly in teacher development courses. Although ESL, EFL and ELF styles of pronunciation teaching share many areas of overlap (e.g. the process of thought grouping; most of the consonant system; word stress; prominence; some of the more common instructional techniques classroom teachers typically employ), a foundational theme is that most students' needs reside primarily with just one of the three styles.

As discussed by Pickering (2001), NNES international teaching assistants (ITAs) who are charged with teaching university students in English dominant parts of the world have compelling reasons for learning the pronunciation of ESL. An ESL focus also meets the needs of many NNESs who are long-term residents of countries where English is the majority language, as well as NNES residents of other parts of the world in business, education, entertainment and government whose professional activities involve frequent interactions with native English speakers (NESs) (e.g. call centre employees).

While ESL norms and purposes have long dominated most discussions of pronunciation teaching, Szpyra-Kozłowska (2015) offers a research-based account of how teaching the pronunciation of EFL differs from the teaching of both ESL and ELF pronunciation. Szpyra-Kozłowska explains that an EFL focus prepares NNESs to communicate with both NESs and other NNESs (see also Szpyra-Kozłowska's chapter in this volume). She proposes that relevant EFL teaching processes should feature both NES and NNES sociocultural norms as well as NES and NNES cultural elements in instructional materials and pronunciation learning tasks.

At present, much of the controversy surrounding different purposes for pronunciation teaching may be traced to researchers', teachers', curriculum designers' and materials developers' failures to be consistent in clearly distinguishing between teaching the pronunciation of ESL, EFL and ELF. An example is when ELF research-based proposals for teaching a lingua franca core of pronunciation features (see Jenkins, 2000, 2007; Walker, 2010) are adopted and applied in classrooms populated by more ESL-oriented learners. Comparable confusions arise whenever there is a mismatch between the ESL, EFL or ELF population being served and the principles, teaching decisions and instructional materials employed to support pronunciation learning. When this happens, connections between learners' needs, pedagogical goals and instructional practices are not only weakened but the teacher's credibility may suffer. A resolution is for all parties involved to be explicit concerning the focus of their work.

It is also useful to keep these distinctions in mind when reading or discussing the research and pedagogic literature of the field. Even when authors fail to make ESL, EFL and ELF distinctions clear, their focus can usually be inferred by examining the discussion's underlying premises (e.g. the participant population of a research study; the research questions being asked). Pickering's (2001) previously mentioned study reveals an overriding ESL focus given its setting (a large state university in the USA), participant population (L1 Mandarin ITAs) and culminating implication to teach ITAs to make more appropriate 'tone choice' when addressing NES undergraduates (p. 252). By way of contrast, Walker (2005) is an explicitly ELF-focused discussion since it is designed to engender a style of pronunciation teaching tailored to the needs of NNESs in communication with other NNESs of different L1 backgrounds *when NESs are not present*. Two complications are: (1) when an author's focus cannot be determined (this may reveal a problem with the quality of the work), and (2) when a reader, such as a prospective pronunciation teacher, fails to make connections to a relevant style of pronunciation instruction or who infers flawed connections.

With respect to the latter, opportunities to support and assess teacher reasoning on these topics should be included in teacher development courses. For example, following a unit on ELF teaching, those preparing to serve as pronunciation teachers can be asked to review a set of pedagogical materials focused on the teaching of *stress-timing* (i.e. the way that NESs 'appear to "squash" syllables together so that stress syllables in the speech flow can come at more or less regular intervals' (Walker, 2010, p. 40)). Course participants who have already learned about ELF instructional priorities should recognize that a focus on stress-timing is incompatible with ELF pronunciation teaching since ELF specialists not only downplay its importance but stress-timing is beyond even the periphery of the lingua franca core.

In short, those new to pronunciation teaching need to learn about the respective instructional priorities in ESL, EFL and ELF settings. Once aware of their differences, teachers are better equipped to make relevant teaching decisions based on (a) the populations of English speakers with whom learners will be communicating in the future, (b) the settings in which their communications will be taking place and (c) students' purposes for using spoken English. A reason for gathering such information is to match as well as possible learners' needs with pronunciation teaching priorities, resources, processes and goals while treating the constructs of ESL, EFL and ELF pronunciation teaching as distinct entities with some areas of overlap.

Introduce broader topics first

When designing a sequence of topics to present through assigned reading, lecture-discussion and application tasks, it is important to include core knowledge about phonetics and phonology topics (e.g. definitions and illustrations of phonemes; voice, place and manner of articulation for consonants etc.; see Table 18.1). The traditional trajectory for introducing them (e.g. Collins & Mees, 2013; Roach, 2009) begins with the constructs of phones, phonemes and allophones, and then builds upon these preliminary topics with an expanding micro- to macro-level sequencing of attention to consonant phonetics, vowel phonetics, spelling connections, variability principles, word stress, primary stress, construction stress, phrase rhythm, prominence, intonation and even broader discourse-level considerations. In contrast to this traditional sequencing, Dickerson (2010) recommends a principled reordering of topics in phonetics and phonology to permit earlier introduction of broader discourse considerations first. As depicted in Table 18.1, such a reordering makes it easier to understand how the sound system of English operates by starting at the macro level (e.g. thought grouping, prominence, word stress) and later introducing mezzo-level and micro-level topics. An advantage of such a revised course trajectory is that it circumvents a familiar complication many of those new to pronunciation teaching voice of 'not being able to see the forest for the trees'.

In alignment with Dickerson's recommendations, Brazil (1994), Cauldwell (2013), Gilbert (2008) and Murphy (2013) also suggest a macro-, mezzo- to micro-level sequencing of topics in phonetics and phonology when preparing PPTs. Again, their reasoning is that once PPTs perceive the landscape of how the phonological system of English operates within broader stretches of discourse, they find it easier to make sense of more narrowly focused knowledge about phonetics and phonology topics. To cite an example, many PPTs find it difficult to recognize the role and importance of vowel phonemes and to distinguish between them, unless they already have some insight into the pivotal role vowels play as markers of prominent locations within thought groups and of their impacts on both word stress and rhythmic structure. While Dickerson's proposed reordering of topics in phonetics and phonology may seem reminiscent of 'whole language' versus 'phonics' controversies in the teaching of first language literacy (see Adams, 1994), Brazil, Cauldwell, Dickerson and Gilbert agree that the full range of macro-, mezzo- and micro-level knowledge about phonetics and phonology topics eventually needs to be introduced to PPTs. As specialists in pronunciation teaching, they recognize the dynamic interplay across all three levels. Their recommendation is for teacher educators to re-envision where to begin when preparing PPTs (see Table 18.1). In contrast to the whole language versus phonics debate of earlier decades, once initial understanding of macro-level topics is established (e.g. though grouping, prominence, word stress), these specialists advocate a positon of inclusion with respect to eventual coverage of the full range of knowledge about phonetics and phonology topics when sufficient time is available.

To begin at the macro level while offering a teacher development course calls for selective reordering of required readings (i.e. book chapters, chapter sections, journal articles, activity illustrations) when working with most of the higher quality PPT preparation textbooks on the market today. Just as language teachers often find it necessary to rearrange the sequence of textbook chapters to be covered in a language course, teacher educators can resequence assigned readings from the text(s) selected for teacher training purpose. By doing so, assigned readings, classroom mini-lectures, discussions and illustrations of classroom pedagogy may be reorganized to prioritize broader dimensions of phonology early on. This principled reordering also permits spiralling back to topics in phonetics and phonology frequently and building upon them as touch stones for coverage of later course themes.

Select a core course text

Most teacher preparation courses depend upon a high-quality text as a foundation for private study, in-class discussion and practice teaching. Undeniably, course design is greatly strengthened with the adoption of a suitable text. Teacher educators are well positioned to survey what's available, to select a course text that gives attention to both knowledge about phonetics and phonology and *pedagogical content knowledge*, and to discern which text is more compatible with local contexts of teacher preparation. The most interesting teacher preparation texts currently available include Avery and Ehrlich (1992), Cauldwell (2013), Celce-Murcia et al. (2010), Dalton and Seidlhofer (1994), Derwing and Munro (2015), Fraser (2001), Gilbert (2008), Kelly (2000), Kenworthy (1987), Lane (2010), Murphy (in press for 2017), Reed and Levis (2015), Rogerson-Revell (2011), Underhill (1994) and Walker (2010). Particularly for language teachers who will be operating within a North American sphere of influence, Celce-Murcia et al. (2010) is, arguably, the most useful one on the market today. First published in 1996, its present version is a revised and expanded second edition. Though not a perfect text (e.g. for even more useful discussions of the teaching of intonation, see Cauldwell (2013), Levis (1999) and Levis and Wichmann (2015); for more current discussions of research to support pronunciation teaching, see Derwing and Munro (2015) and Grant (2014)), it serves as a solid foundation for integrated attention to knowledge about phonetics and phonology and pedagogical content knowledge. To compensate for any gaps associated with its dominant ESL focus, Celce-Murcia et al. (2010) may be supplemented with excerpts from EFL-oriented sources such as Szpyra-Kozłowska (2015) and from ELF-oriented sources such as Walker (2010). In contrast, one of these other two texts might serve as the core course text in a teacher development setting more clearly centred on either EFL or ELF pronunciation teaching.

Exercise your central role as course instructor and mentor

Although required reading materials play an important role, they are merely a starting point for developing and offering a teacher preparation course. PPTs' experiences as learners of pronunciation teaching pivot upon the leadership efforts of their course instructor and the quality of the discussions and experiential activities they, their classmates, and their instructor are able to collaboratively construct together. Any assigned readings need to be complemented by additional resources (e.g. journal articles, book chapters, lab and workbook materials, Internet sites), and fleshed out with relevant applications tasks and activities (e.g. lectures, large and small group discussions, exercises in phonological problem-solving, panel discussions, micro-teaching, guided student research, practice teaching projects, reflection tasks, tutoring opportunities), along with sustained instructor engagement. The adoption of even an optimally balanced set of assigned readings is never enough since processes of L2 teacher development pivot upon the inventiveness and professional guidance of the course instructor (Johnson & Golombek, 2016, p. 163). Commenting on this last point from the perspective of sociocultural theory, Johnson (2015) explains that an essential dimension of the teacher educator's role is to act upon their specialist insights of discernment to guide PPTs 'toward more theoretically and pedagogically sound instructional practices and greater levels of professional expertise' (p. 526). Reading assignments and planned activities certainly matter a lot, but the dynamic interactions that arise between everyone in the course room – coupled with experiential activities beyond the course room guided by the L2 teacher educator – matter even more.

Assign contemporary journal articles and book chapters

Along with selecting and assigning a core teacher preparation text to develop both knowledge about phonetics and phonology and pedagogical content knowledge, the nature and structure of the course should provide PPTs with a thirst for always wanting to learn more. To this aim, another part of a teacher educator's role is to introduce PPTs to whatever might be the most relevant examples of past and recent scholarship and to guide them on where to go to learn more. Particularly at the graduate level, degree candidates expect to examine and discuss both pedagogical scholarship and empirical research reports. Most university courses provide sufficient time for a manageable number of such reading-for-discussion assignments in addition to readings from a core course text. Teacher educators need to be skilful in identifying and selecting readings that are conceptually sound, of high quality, and accessible to newcomers. The search for the latter type of supplementary readings calls for a discerning eye since not all specialist discussions are readily accessible to those new to pronunciation teaching. A principle for selecting them is to find a balance between three types of contemporary and historically relevant scholarship. These are empirical research reports, conceptual discussions (e.g. think pieces, state-of-the-art articles) and practical illustrations of pronunciation pedagogy. Though recommended items will change over time as the scholarship of pronunciation teaching continues to mature, the core genres from which items may be drawn are likely to remain stable. Though the major applied linguistics/TESOL journals are all useful as sources for relevant journal articles, the recently inaugurated *Journal of Second Language Pronunciation* (Levis, 2015) has already begun to function pivotally in this regard (p. 1). Table 18.3 offers a few reliable illustrations from each of three genres mentioned as of 2017.

When structuring a syllabus plan, an option is to select at least one item from either of Table 18.3's first two columns (i.e. either a 'research report' or a 'think piece') to serve as a required weekly reading-for-discussion assignment in addition to a chapter from the selected core course text. Because readings from the third column tend to be both shorter and less conceptually complex, one of these may also be included as a reading-for-discussion assignment every other week or more often. Also, readings from any of the columns may be

Table 18.3 Illustrations of journal articles, chapters and textbook units to assign for in-class discussion (all items are mentioned elsewhere in the chapter)

Empirical research reports	Conceptual discussions (think pieces)	Illustrations of classroom pedagogy
Baker (2014); Derwing (2003); Field (2005); Foote et al. (2011); Galante and Thomson (2016); Henderson et al. (2012); Lee et al. (2015); Murphy (2014a); Pickering (2001); Saito (2012); Sifakis and Sougari (2005); Zielinski (2008). Also, Derwing and Munro (2015) and Grant (2014) feature chapters that synthesize recent research on a variety of topics in pronunciation teaching.	Baker and Murphy (2011); Barrera-Pardo (2008); Brinton (2014); Cauldwell (2013); Derwing (2010); Dickerson (2010); Fraser (2006); Gilbert (1991); Isaacs (2009); Jenkins (2005); Levis (1999, 2016); Morley (1994); Morgan (1997); Murphy (1991, 2014b); Murphy and Baker (2015); Thomson and Derwing (2015); Walker (2010). Also, the dozens of individual chapters featured in Reed and Levis (2015) and chapters featured in the present book.	Acton (1984); Firth (1992); Gilbert (1991, 2008); Jones (2016); Levis and Grant (2003); Meyers (2013); Murphy (2004; in press for 2017); Rosse (1999); Samuel (2010); Sicola and Darcy (2015); Walker (2005). Also, sections from activity recipe collections such as: Brown (2012); Hewings (2004); Marks and Bowen (2012). In addition, chapters from ESL classroom textbooks such as Brazil (1994), Gilbert (2012a, 2012b), Grant (2017a, 2017b), Lane (2005), Marks (2007), Miller (2006), Reed and Michaud (2005).

divvied up between class members depending upon students' areas of interest and need. These may serve as bases for additional discussion and/or in-class reports. Some readings might serve as starting points for individual students' more extensive reading in specialist areas beyond the topic areas suggested in Table 18.3. Ideally, opportunities for more extensive reading-for-discussion and private reading activities of this kind may be planned to facilitate continued exploration of specific themes (e.g. corrective feedback, functional load, gender differences, effectiveness of instruction, intelligibility). Such activities should be structured with an eye towards encouraging PPTs to follow through with either tutoring-focused, teaching-focused or research-focused final course projects (e.g. analyses of practice teaching, literature reviews, annotated bibliographies, reviews of instructional materials, book reviews), and in-class reports (e.g. action research, more formal research).

Work with a pronunciation-centred activity recipe collection

To help ensure that the course has a strong pedagogical component, reliable supports are available that relieve teacher educators from having to reinvent the wheel. In addition to the discussions of instructional pedagogy featured in Table 18.3's second and third columns, there are several notable classroom activity recipe collections (ARCs) already published and additional examples of this practice-focused genre continue to appear. ARCs are book-length collections, each containing many dozens of hands-on descriptions of classroom activities (i.e. language learning tasks) originally designed by specialists who are seasoned pronunciation teachers. Currently, the highest quality ARCs are Brown (2012), Bowen and Marks

(1992), Hancock (1996), Hewings (2004), Jones (2016), Laroy (1995) and Marks and Bowen (2012). Murphy (2014b) offers guidelines for how language teachers might make productive use of ARC resources. His central message is that on their own the activity descriptions featured in ARCs are never enough, nor should teachers expect them to be. Because processes of L2 teaching and learning are always tied to a local setting and the needs of a particular group of learners (Murphy, in press for 2017; Murphy & Byrd, 2001), activity recipe descriptions always need to be fine-tuned by the language teachers working with them. When doing so, it is a teacher's responsibility to build upon found activity descriptions to generate even better ways (e.g. more context-sensitive ways; more research-informed ways) of matching the interests, needs and expectations of the language learners with whom the teacher is working.

With these principles of application in mind, activity recipes included in an ARC are especially useful when they serve as springboards for discussion, analysis and modification in a teacher development setting. In fact, these sorts of discussions between PPTs result in some of the more memorable and rewarding experiences teacher preparation courses afford. This is another area in which a teacher educator serves a pivotal role as discussion moderator, guide and facilitator of the insights that commonly arise during discussions between novice teachers. In addition, ARCs are especially helpful as a basis for PPTs to begin to micro-teach within teacher development courses and teaching practica. PPTs may examine ARCs for ideas and inspiration and as reference points for making comparisons to the findings of contemporary research and other related course themes.

Work with pronunciation-centred ESL classroom textbooks

Another recommended strategy for developing pronunciation teaching skills is to familiarize PPTs with contemporary pedagogical materials. As of the time of writing, there are at least 17 pronunciation-centred ESL classroom textbooks of high quality. These include Beisbier (1994, 1995), Brazil (1994), Cauldwell (2012), Dauer (1993), Gilbert (2012a, 2012b), Gorsuch, Meyers, Pickering and Griffee (2013), Grant (2017a, 2017b), Hahn & Dickerson (1999), Hancock (2003), Hewings (2007), Lane (2005), Marks (2007), Miller (2006) and Reed and Michaud (2005). It would be a missed opportunity for PPTs to complete their period of training unacquainted with resources of this kind. Not surprisingly, Levis (2016) identifies gaps in the coverage of textbooks such as these when their substance is compared with contemporary research in support of pronunciation teaching (see also Derwing, Diepenbroek & Foote, 2013). Most notably, published materials tend to overemphasize the teaching of compressed speech phenomena and suprasegmentals (over segmentals) to degrees as yet lacking empirical research support. As Levis explains, 'in both cases, pedagogical emphasis outstrips what is justifiable based on research findings. It may be that future research will justify the emphases these practices enjoy, but we are far from that point.' While acknowledging these concerns, PPTs are better prepared when they are familiar with available pedagogical materials, especially if they are asked to analyse with a critical eye the quality of what they find. An option is for teacher educators to make available as many pronunciation-centred ESL classroom textbooks as possible. This can be accomplished by including one or more as required reading in the course, sharing personal desk copies and/or setting up library reserve procedures.

Having implemented each of these options over recent years, students regularly comment how useful it is (a) to compare how different writers treat similar pronunciation topics in different ways; (b) to discuss ways of modifying and improving upon ideas for pronunciation teaching featured in published materials; (c) to identify areas of L2 students' pronunciation needs missing from published materials; and (d) to trace the impact and/or lack of connections to contemporary empirical research. Guided exposure to contemporary teaching materials also informs and enriches the quality of culminating course papers/projects and, looking to long-term professional growth, encourages PPTs to begin to see themselves as potential material developers of the future. Such procedures help to ensure that PPTs complete the course already familiar with pedagogical resources and an expanded repertoire of teaching techniques. Further, PPTs are better able to assess the quality of teaching resources that may become available in the future.

Set up frequent small group and whole-class discussions

Because certificate and degree candidates typically reveal differences in learning styles and preferences, a shifting of classroom configurations for in-class presentations and discussions is important. To cite an example, whole-class lectures can be either followed, preceded or straddled by student review and discussion of scheduled course topics in twos or small groups. The following illustrates a less familiar option for structuring guided discussion of assigned readings. It combines the principle of exposing PPTs to the wider scholarship of the field with opportunities for peer collaborations.

The first step is to divide the class into medium-size groups. In a class of 18 PPTs, for example, three discussion groups may be created with six students per group. In anticipation of what will be a multi-direction information-gap activity, the syllabus is designed so three different journal articles are available for the targeted day of class. A week ahead of time, different groups might be asked to read and prepare to discuss journal articles such as Fraser (2006), Levis and Grant (2003) and Morgan (1997), for example (see Table 18.3 for listings of possible options). Under this arrangement, all six members of a single group read the same article in preparation for student-led discussions. As part of the lead up to the targeted day of class, students prepare to be able to discuss the content of their assigned reading with their five classmates who have read the same article and, later, with other members of the class who have read one of the other items. An option is for one member of each group to assume responsibility for generating and distributing a handout that summarizes the article's key themes. To initiate in-class discussion, I first provide time for the members of each group to work in a collaborative study circle. Through discussion with those who have read the same material, students share and compare what they have gleaned from the reading. At this point, their charge is to support each other since all of them will be responsible for introducing the article's major themes to members of the class beyond their initial study circle. Depending upon the composition of the class, this initial phase of article summary and discussion usually takes 15–20 minutes.

Once everyone in the initial group feels adequately prepared, the 18 students are then rearranged into six new groups of three students each. These smaller groups are constituted so each of the three readings is represented by one member of the group. At this point, students take turns summarizing, explaining and answering questions about their respective readings to their two groupmates who have not read the same material. It usually takes another 25–30 minutes for everyone to contribute and for this phase of the three-way information-gap exchanges to run its course. At the end, some additional options are for the course instructor to:

- lead a whole-class discussion about one or more of the three readings;
- initiate a panel discussion at the front of the room about implications for classroom teaching between one to two representatives from each of the initial groups;
- ask everyone to stand and participate in cocktail party or speed-dating format so that one-on-one conversations about the assigned readings may continue in an even less formal, interactive setting.

At any point throughout these various lesson phases, the teacher has the option to participate within any of the groups, move between them, intervene from time to time to address any emerging concerns, provide a mini-lecture or clarification if needed, etc.

Teach how to gather and analyse NNES language samples and, if possible, engage PPTs in opportunities to serve as pronunciation tutors

An essential course objective is for PPTs to be able to identify and assess language learners' needs. To do so, they need guided practice in how to gather language samples from NNESs first-hand as a basis for conducting needs analysis. To meet this objective, a term-long project is for the PPTs to produce and analyse original audio recordings of NNES speech. Using whatever technology is accessible (e.g. preferably digital audio recordings, or audio plus video), PPTs are guided in the production of original recordings. A recommended option is to secure permission to produce audio recordings of NNESs in advance. NNESs the course participants work with might be ESL students in a local intensive English programme, tutees, learners in language courses they either teach or are associated with in some other way, or NNES contacts arranged by others. On this theme, Tracey M. Derwing (personal email communication, 7 July 2016) advises as follows:

> When I originally started to use this [needs assessment] assignment, I thought it was fine to let the TESL students locate and make arrangements to record NNESs on their own. Unfortunately, my hands-off strategy ended up not being a very good idea, because the TESL students would often pick a NNES who didn't really need much in the way of pronunciation training. They tended to pick NNESs who were simply available and willing. In later offerings of the course, I made all the arrangements for the tutees with a local language program. I contacted the coordinator, who in turn, contacted the classroom teachers, who identified NNES students who had intelligibility challenges and who were willing to spend at least an hour a week for eight weeks being assessed and tutored by one of the TESL students. Also, although I completely agree with Zielinski and Yates [2014] that pronunciation instruction should start from the very beginning of L2 instruction for learners who need it, I restricted the tutees the TESL teachers in training might work with to just intermediate and advanced level NNESs. I set these constraints because I wanted the TESL teachers to be able to identify suprasegmental [broader] errors as well as segmental [narrower] errors. In earlier iterations of the course, when the TESL students chose their own tutees, some people picked very low proficiency NNESs who were at a one-word-at-a-time level of speaking in English – and that was very limiting in terms of meeting the PPTs' professional development needs.

For this course component, participants' charge is to produce a few recorded samples of L2 learner speech. Each sample should be at least several minutes in length and may be excerpted from longer recordings. Firth's (1992) brief book chapter offers guidelines on how to collect recorded samples of L2 learner speech, how to use contrastive analysis information to compare the phonological system of English and with those of other languages, and how to conduct formal and informal data collection both within and outside a classroom setting. Celce-Murcia et al.'s (2010) teacher resource text (see pp. 312–315, 481–486), Grant's (2017b) lower-level ESL classroom textbook (see pp. 1–6), Grant's (2017a) higher-level ESL classroom textbook (see pp. 2–6) and Morley's (1994) book chapter (see pp. 76–79) feature similarly useful guidelines.

As Celce-Murcia et al. (2010), Grant (2017b) and Morley (1994) recommend, it is best if language samples of three different discourse types are collected: a recording of a NNES simply reading aloud from a relatively short and proficiency level-appropriate written text; a recording of the NNES enacting the script of a written dialogue along with someone else (e.g. the PPT or an NNES peer); and a recording of the same NNES engaged in spontaneous conversation. Of the three discourse types, the spontaneous speech sample is likely the most challenging to produce. Grant (2017a) offers several useful prompts for gathering a more extemporaneous speech sample (e.g. 'Please describe the place where you grew up and an experience you had while growing up there'), or the learner might be asked to describe the stages of a familiar process such as doing laundry, making coffee or washing dishes (p. 3) (see Derwing, Rossiter, Munro and Thomson (2004) for additional suggestions).

Once the language samples have been recorded, the PPTs can take turns (e.g. one person each time the course meets; or several PPTs working collaboratively in separate small groups) introducing and presenting their recordings to the class. Because each participant's charge is to produce and bring to class an authentic recording of NNES speech and not necessarily to complete an analysis of the speech sample ahead of time, at least 30 minutes should be dedicated to having everyone listen to several recordings multiple times each week to learn to identify areas of L2 pronunciation challenge. Derwing (personal email communication, 7 July 2016) further advises that PPTs who have opportunities to begin tutoring NNESs need even more intensive guided listening practice of this kind within the first few weeks of their training. She recommends at least three hours of guided practice in learning to identify learners' needs through listening to such recordings before PPT tutoring of NNESs begins.

For the NNES needs identification component of the course, the PPTs' application tasks are to discern, analyse and discuss the pronunciation challenges captured in their own and their peers' recordings and how the information gleaned may inform priorities for pronunciation teaching. As they listen to and analyse the recordings, another benefit is that PPTs can attend to and describe the characteristics of whatever might be the phonological foci of that week's class. For example, at the start of the teacher development course PPTs might listen for the NNES' control of thought grouping and prominence as revealed in an audio recording. Later in the course, they might listen for the L2 speaker's control of other pronunciation features such as sound assimilations, enunciation of final consonants, palatalization, vowel reductions etc.

In settings where access to language learners is problematic, another option is for PPTs to work with recordings of NNESs accessible through the Internet (see Murphy, 2014a). The International Dialects of English Archive (IDEA) (www.dialectsarchive.com) and George Mason University's Accent Archive (http://classweb.gmu.edu/accent) are useful resources for this purpose, as are the many recordings of NNESs featured in sites unrelated to the study of linguistics such as Three Minute Thesis (http://threeminutethesis.org/3mt-showcase) and TedTalks (www.ted.com/talks). Though time-consuming, needs-identification activities of this kind enrich the quality of a teacher preparation course.

As already suggested, the experience of learning to identify NNESs' needs is vastly enhanced when PPTs have opportunities to act upon what they are learning as either pronunciation tutors or novice teachers. Just listening to NNES language samples and identifying the pronunciation challenges they notice with peers has benefits with respect to engendering awareness, but for more profound development of pedagogical content knowledge and teaching abilities, awareness building activities are insufficient. Without the follow-through of having to deal with some of the pronunciation challenges they have learned to identify, most PPTs find it difficult to develop the understanding, skills and teaching strategies they will need to serve as competent pronunciation teachers (Derwing, ibid., 7 July 2016). For this reason, when possible it is even more useful to couple PPT experiences in the type of course being described in this chapter with first-hand experiential opportunities to either tutor, practice teach, classroom assistant teach, or regularly teach the pronunciation of English while working with NNESs under the guidance of a more experienced teacher.

Conclusion

This chapter has focused on ways of offering an L2 teacher development course designed to prepare language teachers to teach the pronunciation of English in either ESL, EFL or ELF settings. On completing the chapter, readers should have a clearer sense of how to structure a teacher preparation course of this kind, what some of the more useful resource materials are, what might serve as core course components and where to go to learn more. The chapter's central theme is the importance of distinguishing between knowledge about phonetics and phonology and pedagogical content knowledge. Both domains of teacher knowledge need to be given balanced, integrated attention in a teacher development course. To this aim, the chapter discusses how to make efficient use of the following resources:

(a) textbooks specifically designed to prepare pronunciation teachers;
(b) journal articles and book chapters of three types (empirical research reports, conceptual discussions, ones focused on instructional techniques);
(c) activity recipe collections;
(d) pronunciation-centred classroom textbooks;
(e) opportunities for PPTs to tutor or teach the pronunciation of English to NNESs.

The chapter offers underlying rationale and suggestions for working with each of the resources listed above. Also featured is a discussion of what language teachers need to know to serve as effective teachers of pronunciation as well as practical strategies for engendering such knowledge. As an aid for syllabus design, the chapter includes a concise listing of measurable learning outcomes for a teacher development course. Extending the work of several contemporary specialists (e.g. Dickerson, 2010), the chapter calls for a principled restructuring of how to sequence topics in phonetics and phonology when training teachers. It recommends early attention to the more macro-level processes of thought grouping, prominence and word stress as requisite starting points before giving subsequent attention to more mezzo-level and micro-level concerns such as phonemes, sound assimilations, features of connected speech, sound–spelling correspondences and the other knowledge about phonetics and phonology topics listed in Table 18.1. The chapter's final sections suggest ways of providing PPTs with opportunities to read and discuss contemporary scholarship; to review, analyse and compare notes on the quality of pedagogical materials; to learn how to gather and analyse their own recorded samples of NNES speech; and to tutor or teach the pronunciation of English to NNESs. Current and prospective language teachers who are conscientious in completing a course along the lines described in the chapter should be well positioned to serve as effective pronunciation teachers in ESL, EFL and ELF settings.

Notes

1　Some less familiar acronyms used in the chapter are: ELF (English as a lingua franca), NESs (native English speakers), NNESs (non-native English speakers), and PPTs (prospective pronunciation teachers).

2　Though the related term 'personal practical knowledge' is sometimes used as a label for more personalized forms of pedagogical knowledge of an individual teacher, it is not this chapter's focus (Golombek, 2009, p. 155).

References

Acton, W. (1984). Changing fossilized pronunciation. *TESOL Quarterly*, *18*(1), 71–85.

Adams, M. J. (1994). *Beginning to read: Thinking and learning about print*. Cambridge, MA: MIT Press.

Avery, P., & Ehrlich, S. (1992). *Teaching American English pronunciation*. New York, NY: Oxford University Press.

Baker, A. (2014). Exploring teachers' knowledge of second language pronunciation techniques: Teacher cognitions, observed classroom practices, and student perceptions. *TESOL Quarterly*, *48*, 136–163.

Baker, A., & Murphy, J. (2011). Knowledge base of pronunciation teaching: Identifying a research agenda. *TESL Canada Journal*, *28*, 29–50.

Barrera-Pardo, D. (2008). The reality of stress-timing. *English Language Teaching*, *62*, 11–17.

Bartels, N. (2009). Knowledge about language. In A. Burns & J. C. Richards (Eds), *The Cambridge guide to second language teacher education* (pp. 125–134). New York, NY: Cambridge University Press.

Beisbier, B. (1994). *Sounds great: Low-intermediate pronunciation for speakers of English*. Boston, MA: Heinle & Heinle.

Beisbier, B. (1995). *Sounds great: Intermediate pronunciation for speakers of English*. Boston, MA: Heinle and Heinle.

Borg, S. (2003). Teacher cognition in language teaching: A review of research on what language teachers think, know, believe and do. *Language Teaching*, *36*, 81–109.

Bowen, T., & Marks, J. (1992). *The pronunciation book*. New York, NY: Longman.

Brazil, D. (1994). *Pronunciation for advanced learners of English*. New York, NY: Cambridge University Press.

Brinton, D. (2014). Epilogue to the myths: Best practices for teachers. In L. Grant (Ed.), *Pronunciation myths*, 225–242. Ann Arbor, MI: University of Michigan Press.

Brown, J. D. (2012). *New ways in teaching connected speech*. Alexandria, VA: TESOL.

Burgess, J., & Spencer, S. (2000). Phonology and pronunciation in integrated language teaching and teacher education. *System*, *28*, 191–215.

Burns, A. (2006). Integrating research and professional development on pronunciation teaching in a national adult ESL program. *TESL Reporter*, *39*(2), 34–41.

Cauldwell, R. (2012). *Cool speech: Hot listening, cool pronunciation*. [iPad application]. Birmingham: Speech in Action.

Cauldwell, R. (2013). *Phonology for listening*. Birmingham: Speech in Action.

Celce-Murcia, M., Brinton, & D. Goodwin, J., with Griner, B. (2010). *Teaching pronunciation: A course book and reference guide* (2nd ed.). New York, NY: Cambridge University Press.

Collins, B., and Mees, I. M. (2013). *Practical phonetics and phonology* (3rd ed.). New York, NY: Routledge.

Crookes, G. (2003). *A practicum in TESOL*. Cambridge: Cambridge University Press.

Dalton, C., & Seidlhofer, B. (1994). *Pronunciation*. New York, NY: Oxford University Press.

Dauer, R. (1993). *Accurate English: A complete course in pronunciation*. Englewood Cliffs, NJ: Regents Prentice-Hall.

Derwing, T. M. (2003). What do ESL students say about their accents? *Canadian Modern Language Review, 59,* 545–564.

Derwing, T. M. (2010). Utopian goals for pronunciation teaching. In J. M. Levis & K. LeVelle (Eds), *Proceedings of the 1st Pronunciation in Second Language Learning and Teaching Conference* (pp. 24–37). Ames, IA: Iowa State University.

Derwing, T., Diepenbroek, L., & Foote, J. (2013). How well do general-skills ESL textbooks address pronunciation? *TESL Canada Journal, 30*(1), 22–44.

Derwing, T. M., & Munro, M. J. (2015). *Pronunciation fundamentals: Evidence-based perspectives for L2 teaching and research.* Philadelphia, PA: John Benjamins.

Derwing, T. M., Rossiter, M. J., Munro, M. J., & Thomson, R. I. (2004). Second language fluency: Judgements on different tasks. *Language Learning, 54*(4), 655–679.

Dickerson, W. (2010). Walking the walk: Integrating the story of English phonology. In J. M. Levis & K. LeVelle (Eds), *Proceedings of the 1st Pronunciation in Second Language Learning and Teaching Conference* (pp. 10–23). Ames, IA: Iowa State University.

Farrell, T. S. (2016). *From trainee to teacher: Reflective practice for novice teachers.* Sheffield: Equinox.

Field, J. (2005). Intelligibility and the listener: The role of lexical stress. *TESOL Quarterly, 39,* 399–423.

Field, J. (2008). *Listening and the language classroom.* New York, NY: Cambridge University Press.

Firth, S. (1992). Pronunciation syllabus design: A question of focus. In P. Avery and S. Ehrlich (Eds), *Teaching American English pronunciation* (pp. 173–181). New York, NY: Oxford University Press.

Foote, J. A., Holtby, A. K., & Derwing, T. M. (2011). 2010 survey of pronunciation teaching in adult ESL programs in Canada. *TESL Canada Journal, 29,* 1–22.

Fraser, H. (2001). *Teaching pronunciation: A handbook for teachers and trainers.* Ames, NSW: Department of Education Training and Youth Affairs. Retrieved from http://helenfraser.com.au/downloads/HF%20Handbook.pdf.

Fraser, H. (2006). Helping teachers help students with pronunciation: A cognitive approach. *Prospect, 21,* 80–96.

Galante, A., & Thomson, R. I. (2016). The effectiveness of drama as an instructional approach for the development of second language oral fluency, comprehensibility, and accentedness. *TESOL Quarterly, 51,* 115–142.

Gilbert, J. B. (1991). Gadgets: Non-verbal tools for teaching pronunciation. In A. Brown (Ed.), *Teaching English pronunciation: A book of readings.* London: Routledge.

Gilbert, J. B. (2008). *Teaching pronunciation: Using the prosody pyramid.* Cambridge: Cambridge University Press.

Gilbert, J. B. (2012a). *Clear speech from the start* (2nd ed.). New York, NY: Cambridge University Press.

Gilbert, J. B. (2012b). *Clear speech* (4th edition). New York, NY: Cambridge University Press.

Golombek, P. (2009). Personal practical knowledge in L2 teacher education. In A. Burns & J. C. Richards (Eds), *The Cambridge guide to second language teacher education* (pp. 155–162). New York, NY: Cambridge University Press.

Goodwin, J. (2014). Teaching pronunciation. In M. Celce-Murcia, D. M. Brinton, & M. A. Snow (Eds), *Teaching English as a second or foreign language* (4th ed., 138–154). Boston, MA: National Geographic Learning/Cengage Learning.

Gorsuch, G., Meyers, C., Pickering, L., & Griffee, D. (2013). *English communication for international teaching assistants* (2nd ed.). Long Grove, IL: Waveland Press.

Grant, L. (Ed.). (2014). *Pronunciation myths.* Ann Arbor, MI: University of Michigan Press.

Grant, L. (2017a). *Well said: Pronunciation for clear communication* (4th edition). Boston, MA: Thomson/Heinle & Heinle.

Grant, L. (2017b). *Well said intro: Pronunciation for clear communication* (2nd ed.). Boston, MA: Thomson/Heinle & Heinle.

Gregory, A. (2005). What's phonetics got to do with language teaching? Investigating future teachers' use of knowledge about phonetics and phonology. In N. Bartels (Ed.), *Applied linguistics and language teacher education* (pp. 201–220). Dordrecht: Kluwer.

Hahn, L., & Dickerson, W. (1999). *Speech craft: Discourse pronunciation for advanced learners.* Ann Arbor, MI: University of Michigan Press.

Hancock, M. (1996). *Pronunciation games*. Cambridge: Cambridge University Press.

Hancock, M. (2003). *English pronunciation in use (intermediate)*. Cambridge: Cambridge University Press.

Henderson, A., Frost, D., Tergujeff, E., Kautzsch, A., Murphy, D., Kirkova-Naskova, A., & Curnick, L. (2012). The English pronunciation teaching in Europe survey: Selected results. *Research in Language, 10*(1), 5–27.

Hewings, M. (2004). *Pronunciation practice activities*. Cambridge: Cambridge University Press.

Hewings, M. (2007). *English pronunciation in use (advanced)*. Cambridge: Cambridge University Press.

Isaacs, T. (2009). Integrating form and meaning in L2 pronunciation instruction. *TESL Canada Journal, 27*(1), 1–12.

Isaacs, T. (2014). Assessing pronunciation. In A. J. Kunnan (Ed.), *The companion to language assessment* (Vol. 1, pp. 140–155). Hoboken, NJ: Wiley-Blackwell.

Jenkins, J. (2000). *The phonology of English as an international language*. Oxford: Oxford University Press.

Jenkins, J. (2005). Implementing an international approach to English pronunciation: The role of teacher attitudes and identity. *TESOL Quarterly, 39*, 535–543.

Jenkins, J. (2007). *English as a lingua franca: Attitude and identity*. Oxford: Oxford University Press.

Johnson, K. E. (2009). *Second language teacher education: A sociocultural perspective*. New York, NY: Routledge.

Johnson, K. E. (2015). Reclaiming the relevance of L2 teacher education. *Modern Language Journal, 99*, 515–528.

Johnson, K. E., & Golombek, P. R. (2016). *Mindful L2 teacher education: A sociocultural perspective on cultivating teachers' professional development*. New York, NY: Routledge.

Jones, T. (Ed.) (2016). *Pronunciation in the classroom: The overlooked essential*. Alexandria, VA: TESOL.

Kelly, G. (2000). *How to teach pronunciation*. Harlow: Pearson Education.

Kenworthy, J. (1987). *Teaching English pronunciation*. London: Longman.

Klippel, F. (2004). *Keep talking: Communicative fluency activities*. New York, NY: Cambridge Handbook for Language Teaching.

Ladefoged, P., & Johnson, K. (2014). *A course in phonetics* (7th ed.). Stamford, CT: Cengage Learning.

Lane, L. (2005). *Focus on pronunciation (books 1, 2, & 3)*. White Plains, NY: Pearson Longman.

Lane, L. (2010). *Tips for teaching pronunciation: A practical approach*. White Plains, NY: Pearson Longman.

Laroy, C. (1995). *Pronunciation*. New York, NY: Oxford University Press.

Lee, J., Jang, J., & Plonsky, L. (2015). The effectiveness of second language pronunciation instruction: A meta-analysis. *Applied Linguistics, 36*(3), 345–366.

Levis, J. (1999). Intonation in theory and practice, revisited. *TESOL Quarterly, 33*(1), 37–62.

Levis, J. (2015). The journal of second language pronunciation: An essential step toward a disciplinary identity. *Journal of Second Language Pronunciation, 1*, 1–10.

Levis, J. (2016). Research into practice: How research appears in pronunciation materials. *Language Teaching, 49*, 423–437.

Levis, J., & Grant, L. (2003). Integrating pronunciation into ESL/EFL classrooms. *TESOL Journal, 12*, 13–19.

Levis, J. M., & Wichmann, A. (2015). English intonation: Form and meaning. In M. Reed & J. Levis (Eds), *Wiley-Blackwell handbook of English pronunciation* (pp. 139–155). Chichester: Wiley-Blackwell.

Lyster, R., Saito, K., & Sato, M. (2013). Oral corrective feedback in second language classrooms. *Language Teaching, 46*, 1–40.

Macdonald, S. (2002). Pronunciation views and practices of reluctant teachers. *Prospect, 17*, 3–18.

Marks, J. (2007). *English pronunciation in use (elementary)*. Cambridge: Cambridge University Press.

Marks, J., & Bowen, T. (2012). *The book of pronunciation*. Peaslake: Delta.

Meyers, C. (2013, August). Mirroring project update: Intelligible accented speakers as pronunciation models. TESOL Video News (the newsletter of the TESOL Video and Digital Media Interest Section). Teachers of English to Speakers of Other Languages. Retrieved from http://newsmanager. commpartners.com/tesolvdmis/ issues/2013–07–27/email.html#3 (accessed 30 December 2013).

Miller, S. F. (2006). *Targeting pronunciation* (2nd ed.). New York, NY: Houghton Mifflin.

Morgan, B. (1997). Identity and intonation: Linking dynamic processes in an ESL classroom. *TESOL Quarterly*, *31*, 431–449.

Morley, J. (1994). A multidimensional curriculum design for speech-pronunciation instruction. In J. Morley (Ed.), *Pronunciation pedagogy and theory: New views, new directions* (pp. 64–91). Alexandria, VA: TESOL.

Murphy, J. M. (1991). Oral communication in TESOL: Integrating speaking, listening & pronunciation. *TESOL Quarterly*, *25*(1), 51–75.

Murphy, J. (1997). Phonology courses offered by MATESOL programs in the United States. *TESOL Quarterly*, *31*, 741–764.

Murphy, J. M. (2004). Attending to word-stress while learning new vocabulary. *English for Specific Purposes Journal*, *23*(1), 67–83.

Murphy, J. (2013). *Teaching pronunciation*. Alexandria, VA: Teachers of English to Speakers of Other Languages.

Murphy, J. (2014a). Intelligible, comprehensible, nonnative models in ESL/EFL pronunciation teaching. *System*, *42*, 258–269.

Murphy, J. (2014b). Teacher preparation programs provide adequate preparation in how to teach pronunciation (pp. 188–223). In L. Grant (Ed.), *Pronunciation myths*. Ann Arbor, MI: University of Michigan Press.

Murphy, J. (2015). Clearer speech through the process of thought grouping. In M. Lewis and H. Reinders (Eds), *New ways in teaching adults* (pp. 121–123). Alexandria, VA: TESOL.

Murphy, J. (Ed.). (in press for 2017). *Teaching the pronunciation of English: Focus on whole courses*. Ann Arbor, MI: University of Michigan Press.

Murphy, J., & Baker, A. A. (2015). History of ESL pronunciation teaching. In John Levis and Marnie Reed (Eds), *Wiley-Blackwell handbook of English pronunciation* (pp. 36–65). Chichester: Blackwell.

Murphy, J. & Byrd, H. P. (Eds). (2001). *Understanding the courses we teach: Local perspectives on English language teaching*. Ann Arbor, MI: University of Michigan Press.

Pickering, L. (2001). The role of tone choice in improving ITA communication in the classroom. *TESOL Quarterly*, *35*, 233–255.

Reed, M., & Levis, J. (Eds). (2015). *Wiley-Blackwell handbook of English pronunciation*. Chichester: Blackwell.

Reed, M., & Michaud, C. (2005). *Sound concepts: An integrated pronunciation course*. New York, NY: McGraw-Hill.

Roach, P. (2009). *English phonetics and phonology: A practical course* (4th ed.). Cambridge: Cambridge University Press.

Rogerson-Revell, P. (2011). *English phonology and pronunciation teaching*. London: Continuum.

Rosse, M. (1999). Tracking – A method for teaching prosody to ESL learners. *Prospect*, *14*(1), 53–61.

Saito, K. (2012). Effects of instruction on L2 pronunciation development: A synthesis of 15 quasi-experimental intervention studies. *TESOL Quarterly*, *46*(4), 842–854.

Samuel, C. (2010). Pronunciation pegs. *TESL Canada Journal*, *27*(2), 103–113.

Seidlhofer, B. (2011). *Understanding English as a lingua franca*. Oxford: Oxford University Press.

Sicola, L., & Darcy, I. (2015). Integrating pronunciation into the language classroom. In M. Reed and J. Levis (Eds), *The handbook of English pronunciation* (pp. 471–487). Chichester: Wiley-Blackwell.

Sifakis, N. and Sougari, A-M. (2005). Pronunciation issues and EIL pedagogy in the periphery: A survey of Greek state school teachers' beliefs. *TESOL Quarterly*, *39*(3), 467–488.

Swan, M., & Smith, B. (Eds). 2001. *Learner English: A teacher's guide to interference and other problems* (2nd ed.). Cambridge: Cambridge University Press.

Szpyra-Kozłowska, J. (2015). *Pronunciation in EFL instruction: A research-based approach*. Bristol, Buffalo, NY, and Toronto: Multilingual Matters.

Thomson, R. I. (2012). Improving L2 listeners' perception of English vowels: A computer-mediated approach. *Language Learning*, *62*, 1231–1258.

Thomson, R. I., & Derwing, T. M. (2015). The effectiveness of L2 pronunciation instruction: A narrative review. *Applied Linguistics*, *36*(3), 326–344.

Underhill, A. (1994). *Sound foundations: Learning and teaching pronunciation*. London: Macmillian.

Walker, R. (2005). Using student-produced recordings with monolingual groups to provide effective, individualized pronunciation practice. *TESOL Quarterly*, *39*, 550–558.

Walker, R. (2010). *Teaching the pronunciation of English as a lingua franca*. Oxford: Oxford University Press.

Wong, R. (1987). *Teaching pronunciation: Focus on English rhythm and intonation.* Englewood Cliffs, NJ: Prentice Hall Regents.

Zielinski, B. (2008). The listener: No longer the silent partner in reduced intelligibility. *System 36*(1), 69–84.

Zielinski, B., & Yates, L. (2014). Pronunciation instruction is not appropriate for beginning-level learners (pp. 56–79). In L. Grant (Ed.), *Pronunciation myths*. Ann Arbor, MI: University of Michigan Press.

19

The efficacy of pronunciation instruction

Tracey M. Derwing

Introduction/definitions

Although pronunciation instruction (PI) has existed for centuries, the last decade has seen a dramatic increase in research studies devoted to its effects. For instance, Lee, Jang and Plonsky (2015) conducted a meta-analysis of 86 studies, most of which were very recent, and found that the majority showed changes in L2 speakers' productions directly linked to the intervention they received. At first glance, this is a positive finding, but as Thomson and Derwing (2015) pointed out in a narrative analysis of many of the same studies, most researchers used a measure of accent reduction (or accuracy) as opposed to a change to comprehensibility or intelligibility (for definitions of these terms, please see Table 19.1) to determine outcomes. Thomson and Derwing identified only seven studies (of 75) that demonstrated significant improvement in either comprehensibility or intelligibility as a result of PI. Given this finding, it is important to consider the limitations of many of the existing studies. The value of PI, surely, should be determined by the extent to which it can improve communication. Of course, it is conceivable that a more accurate rendition of a single segment or suprasegmental feature may indeed render an L2 speaker's speech more intelligible and/or comprehensible, but that depends on many factors. Did the rest of the word or phrase remain intact, or did the effort expended in changing the target result in distortions elsewhere in the word? Did a focus on changing a suprasegmental feature interfere with the clarity of some other aspect of the utterance? Did the aspect of pronunciation in question actually interfere with listener understanding in the first place? Was the change measured in connected speech or in isolated citation forms? These may seem like esoteric questions, but, in fact, more accurate pronunciation of some features of a word or phrase can indeed result in less comprehensible productions overall (Derwing & Munro, 2015), as was the case for Joanna Tam, a visual artist who explored the concepts of accent, identity, displacement and standardization (Tam, 2012). Joanna received PI from an accent coach that made her both less comprehensible and less intelligible. Fortunately, the changes brought about by the interventions of her accent coach were not maintained.

Ideally, PI should result in both increased and lasting intelligibility and comprehensibility, but an improvement of one or the other alone is still a positive outcome. However, a change to accent with no change to intelligibility and comprehensibility (or, worse, decreased

Table 19.1 Definition of key terms

Term	Definition
Accentedness	Degree of difference between a speaker's productions and those of the interlocutor, usually measured using scalar responses.
Intelligibility	Degree to which a speaker's intended meaning is actually understood by the listener, typically measured using dictation tasks, summaries, comprehension questions and/or true/false sentences. Retrospective interviews with videos or recordings of a given conversation also shed light on intelligibility. Micro measures include identity tasks in which listeners indicate which phoneme they heard.
Comprehensibility	Degree of effort required to understand accented speech, usually measured using scalar responses from listeners.
Fluency	The flow, fluidity, or smoothness of speech (entails factors such as speech rate, mean length of run between pauses (usually measured in syllables), hesitation forms etc.), often measured using scalar responses, but temporal measures are common as well (e.g. syll/s).

comprehensibility and/or intelligibility) is of little or no use (Munro & Derwing, 2015b). The value of PI is completely determined by whether it improves overall communication or not.

Historical perspectives

Pronunciation instruction has had a roller coaster ride in L2 curricula over the years. Murphy and Baker (2015) outline four waves of pronunciation teaching, documenting its progress from the 1850s on (see Chapters 15 and 16 in this volume), starting with the precursors, who broke with traditional approaches to teaching foreign languages by focusing on oral skills. The second wave, or the reform movement, included phoneticians such as Henry Sweet (1900), who called for English PI with a focus on intelligibility. Since then, influential personages have made the point that helping L2 students to become comfortably understood should be the goal of language teachers (e.g. Abercrombie, 1949). However, during the audiolingual era, Lado and Fries (1958) and others advocated a heavy emphasis on accurate pronunciation, to prevent the transfer of 'errors' from the L1; in other words, they wanted to eradicate accents. Audiolingualism was characterized by 'listen-and-repeat' both in chorus and individually. The language lab was a prominent feature of audiolingual programmes, because it allowed extensive practice outside class. This approach to language teaching was embraced in most of North America for an extensive period of time, and it spread to several 'outer' and 'expanding' circle countries as well. It was viewed as a scientific method for teaching languages, and was significantly influenced by behaviourism (particularly the notion that learning is, in part, a matter of developing habits) and Bloomfieldian linguistics, which focused on the importance of oral/aural language.

Other mid-twentieth-century approaches to L2 teaching also focused on pronunciation, most notably Gettegno's (1963) silent way, in which learners acquired a highly controlled, extremely limited set of vocabulary at the beginning stages, with attention directed almost exclusively on accurate pronunciation, or native-like accent. Colour-coded sound charts were designed to create associations for the students to enhance their oral productions. However, the implementation of methods such as this were limited, in part because of the specialized training required to teach in such classrooms, and in part because they seemed so removed from mainstream language education.

The advent of communicative language teaching (CLT), which was at least as influential in North America as audiolingualism, signalled a change in focus on pronunciation. Theories such as Krashen's input hypothesis (1985) suggested that pronunciation would simply develop over time with adequate exposure to the L2. The ethos was that pronunciation would take care of itself with sufficient natural conversation. Aside from a few proponents such as Judy Gilbert, Clifford Prator and Joan Morley, who argued that pronunciation was a necessary skill requiring intervention in some instances, most practitioners did their best to develop tasks that would encourage close-to-authentic language to give L2 students opportunities for acquiring new grammatical structures and vocabulary in context, without concern for pronunciation.

It eventually became clear, however, that there is no one-to-one correspondence between the development of accuracy of L2 accent (or, more importantly, intelligibility and comprehensibility) with proficiency levels, as measured by syntax and the lexicon. Some individuals, despite a great deal of exposure to their L2, and ample opportunities to interact, still exhibited aspects of pronunciation that made them difficult to understand. In response, the third wave of PI (Murphy & Baker, 2015) appeared in the mid-1980s and 1990s. ESL classroom textbooks, 'recipes' for activities collections, and teacher preparation textbooks appeared. However, despite the growth in publications to support PI, a majority of teachers in communicative classrooms lacked the training and confidence to teach in this area (Breitkreutz, Derwing & Rossiter, 2001; Burns, 2006); consequently, many programmes continued to ignore the needs of those students whose speech was difficult to understand (Foote, Holtby & Derwing, 2011). Moreover, the goal of attaining a native-like accent seemed unreachable for most learners. Since the general philosophy at the time leaned towards accuracy rather than intelligibility and comprehensibility, teaching pronunciation appeared to be relatively futile (Pica, 1994).

Pronunciation research in the latter half of the twentieth century tended to focus on aspects of L2 productions that did not involve pedagogy. Topics such as the effects of alcohol and other consciousness-affecting substances on pronunciation (Guiora, Acton, Erard & Strickland, 1980), the impact of familiarity with accented speech on the listener (Gass & Varonis, 1984) and stereotypical attitudes towards certain L2 accents were explored (e.g. Ryan, Carranza & Moffie, 1977) – all valuable areas of investigation, but most did not have immediate implications for the classroom. However, empirical pedagogical studies first started to appear in the early 1980s, when de Bot and Mailfert (1982) and de Bot (1983) conducted studies on the effects of visual feedback on the production of English intonation. Perlmutter (1989) carried out what was likely the first classroom-based study to investigate the role of PI, with immigrants learning English in the USA during their first six months in the country. She concluded that the PI had been effective when she compared ratings of read speech samples from the outset of the study to ratings collected at the end. Unfortunately, a control group was not included; thus the improvement observed could have been caused by exposure to the L2 during the 'window of maximal opportunity' (WMO). Derwing, Munro, Foote, Waugh and Fleming (2014) have described the first six months of massive exposure to the L2 as the WMO because it appears to be the time when learners are most aware of and can best adapt to many features of the new phonological system. Another relatively early study was Champagne-Muzar, Schneiderman and Bourdages (1993), who examined the effects of perception and production training on the pronunciation of learners of French. The researchers included a control group in their study. Their findings constitute the first empirical evidence of PI having a positive effect in language classrooms, corroborating the long-held intuitions of teachers.

Murphy and Baker's (2015) fourth wave of PI – the emergence of empirical research – began in earnest in the mid-1990s. One of the first studies of that period was that of MacDonald, Yule and Powers (1994), who compared three types of PI to determine whether one was more effective than the others, using a measure of accentedness. The interventions lasted between 10 and 30 minutes. Listeners heard speech samples taken both immediately before and after the interventions, as well as a delayed recording made two days later. Although the results were disappointing (not surprisingly, given the short time span allotted), this study sparked considerable interest in the empirical examination of classroom-based PI.

Derwing, Munro and Wiebe's (1998) classroom-based study of the efficacy of PI employed a control group, a group of ESL students who were given segmental training, and another group who had suprasegmental instruction, 20 minutes daily for 10 weeks. The researchers collected both extemporaneous and read speech samples pre- and post-intervention, which they played to listeners who assessed them for comprehensibility. In the sentence reading condition, both instructed groups showed significant improvement in comprehensibility, whereas the control group's productions did not change over time, but in the extemporaneous speech condition (taken from a picture narrative) only members of the suprasegmental group showed significantly improved comprehensibility following PI. Derwing et al. concluded that both suprasegmental and segmental PI are warranted in language classrooms. Suprasegmental instruction seemed to be valuable in facilitating the general comprehensibility of natural speech, and segmental instruction may assist learners who have become aware of their errors and have the time to focus on a repair.

In 2006, Couper published a study in which he measured the long-term effects of PI, 12 weeks after the intervention. Although his measures were of accuracy (accent) rather than comprehensibility or intelligibility, he showed conclusively that several features of an accent can change as a result of PI and that some of those changes appear to be maintained over time, suggesting that the learners' phonological representations can be altered relatively permanently.

In another accentedness study, Saito and Lyster (2012) examined the role of feedback in PI, in training sessions involving Japanese learners of English who had difficulty with the /l/–/ɹ/ distinction. They compared recasts used in conjunction with form-focused instruction of /ɹ/ with form-focused instruction of the same segment in the absence of feedback. Listeners responded to a nine-point rating scale of 'very good English /ɹ/' to 'very poor English /ɹ/' (basically an accent rating); the researchers also conducted acoustic analyses to identify changes to F3 values. They concluded that corrective feedback was effective in bringing about changes to the learners' productions; but, again, this study was concerned with accuracy rather than intelligibility or comprehensibility.

Isaacs and Trofimovich (2012) deconstructed comprehensibility in an exploratory study in which they compared rating data with teachers' comments about the same English productions (made by Quebec French speakers). They identified several features of speech that were correlated with comprehensibility ratings, but the strongest features were lexical type frequency, word stress error, mean length of run (a fluency measure) and grammatical accuracy. These linguistic factors all contributed to comprehensibility ratings, illustrating that how easy or difficult an L2 speaker is to understand is not limited to phonological aspects of speech but can be perceived as such (echoing Gass and Varonis's 1982 finding that the weaker the speaker's grammar, the worse L2 pronunciation is perceived). The implications are that rating scales for formal assessments of oral productions should not be limited to 'accent' or 'pronunciation', and that teachers should consider very carefully what it is about their own learners' productions that could be problematic for listeners.

In an innovative comparison study, Galante and Thomson (2016) conducted research in Brazilian EFL classrooms in which they contrasted the use of drama techniques versus traditional CLT. All the learners received the same laboratory instruction, involving recording and listening to their own speech, focusing on segmental and prosodic factors known to be difficult for some Portuguese speakers, and shadowing recorded passages. The students in the drama condition undertook several scenarios and role plays; they also did some scripted works, performing dramatic scenarios at the end of their course. The students who received CLT participated in pair and group work to develop presentations on topics of interest to them, which they gave at the end of the course. Raters were engaged to judge the fluency, comprehensibility and accentedness of five oral tasks that each of the speakers performed both at the outset and end of the study. The drama group made more gains than the CLT group in both fluency and comprehensibility, leading the authors to conclude that the inclusion of drama activities in L2 classrooms may lead to improved pronunciation, reinforcing some of the explicit instruction received in the lab. This study is one of the first to compare techniques for efficacy of PI using comprehensibility as the determiner.

Each of the studies reviewed in this section represents a milestone in PI of one sort or another, but some also indicate that both the Nativeness and the Intelligibility Principles are alive and well. Levis (2005) described the former as the view that 'it is possible and desirable to achieve native-like pronunciation in a foreign language' (p. 370), while the intelligibility principle 'holds that learners simply need to be understandable' (p. 370). Indeed, as mentioned above, Thomson and Derwing (2015) found that 63 per cent followed the nativeness principle, in that they assessed the effects of PI through a measure of accentedness or accuracy, as opposed to comprehensibility and/or intelligibility measures. This puts into question the value of much of the PI that has been carried out thus far, because merely changing one's accent does not necessarily lead to improved communication.

Critical issues and topics

Among the several issues important to any consideration of the value of PI, those that are most crucial have to do with language teachers' reluctance to teach pronunciation, what the foci of PI should be, when PI should be introduced, and factors that affect the nature of PI research study outcomes.

Reluctance to teach pronunciation

A critical issue facing our field is the fact that many L2 teachers are reluctant to engage in PI because of the complexity of issues facing them, such as the substantial degree of variation across students, not only from different L1 backgrounds but even among those who share the same L1. Several surveys of teachers in ESL settings (e.g. Macdonald, 2002; Foote et al., 2011) have shown that, although teachers acknowledge the importance of pronunciation, in many instances they lack confidence in their own ability to provide knowledgeable support. Moreover, some teachers in EFL settings are also uncomfortable with PI, as Buss indicated in a study of pre-service EFL instructors:

[I]t is possible to say that the pre-service EFL teachers generally attended to pronunciation and possibly understood the importance and purpose of its teaching. Nonetheless, they did not appear to be fully prepared for this task for two main reasons. First, most of the time they could not appropriately diagnose and explain very common pronunciation errors made by Brazilian EFL learners. Second, their teaching seemed to be restricted to an intuitive-imitative approach, with no use of more explicit, awareness-raising activities.

(Buss 2013, p. 262)

A related issue is the fear many non-native English language teachers have that their own pronunciation will be an inadequate model for learners (Levis, Sonsaat, Link & Barriuso, 2016, Llurda & Huguet, 2003).

As Murphy (2014) has pointed out with regard to English language programmes in North America, it is often the case that teachers do not have ready access to professional development opportunities to augment their knowledge of PI. Henderson et al. (2012) made a similar argument in a survey of English teachers in Finland, France, Germany, Macedonia, Poland, Spain and Switzerland: 'Our findings suggest that teacher training in relation to the teaching of English pronunciation is woefully inadequate, according to the majority of participants' (p. 23). Without adequate education in this particular area, teachers tend to refrain from doing more than correcting individual words as they come up in class. However, when L2 students do not get the pronunciation support they perceive to be necessary, they will often turn to other options, including accent coaches, who, in some cases, have even less expertise than language teachers (Thomson, 2014).

Focus of PI

On the surface, the value of pronunciation teaching for learners who have difficulty making themselves understood is obvious. Most speakers, most of the time, want their intended message to be transmitted successfully. However, this basic requirement is not the only benefit of clear speech; pronunciation is also important in the sense that even if an individual can be understood through considerable effort and close listening on the part of the interlocutor, people generally prefer to interact with others who are easy to understand, where little or no effort is involved, regardless of the strength of an accent (Derwing & Munro, 2009). As Dragojevic and Giles (2016) have demonstrated, the more difficult it is for listeners to process speech, the more negative their attitudes towards the speaker will be '*independent* of stereotyping. . . . [O]ne reason foreign-accented speakers tend to be evaluated more negatively than native-accented speakers is simply because they are harder to understand' (p. 19). It is extremely difficult to make social connections if there are perceived barriers such as difficult-to-understand speech, or a lack of shared interests or values. Easy-to-understand speech is often highly conventional, not only in terms of phonology but also lexical choice, grammatical structures and pragmatic usages. This suggests that comprehensibility should be a chief goal of the instructor, and that PI should be integrated into all aspects of L2 teaching.

This brings us to a critical issue in the field of PI: the focus of instruction. Merely changing some aspects of an L2 accent does not necessarily mean that either intelligibility or comprehensibility will improve. In fact, sometimes changes to more native-like features of accent can result in less comprehensible speech. For instance, Gordon and Darcy (2016) compared three classes of ESL students under three pedagogical conditions: explicit suprasegmental instruction, explicit segmental instruction and non-explicit listen-and-repeat exercises.

Although the students who received explicit segmental instruction (focusing on four vowels) produced more native-like vowels as measured acoustically after instruction, they were perceived to be significantly more difficult to understand than at the outset of the study. Gordon and Darcy's approach, to obtain both comprehensibility ratings and acoustical measures, is helpful in that it demonstrates clearly that, even if some aspects of accent become more native-like, listeners will not necessarily perceive the changes to be important. Critically, the learners who were given explicit suprasegmental instruction were perceived to be significantly more comprehensible at the end of the study, whereas the listen-and-repeat non-explicit instruction group did not make significant comprehensibility gains.

To provide PI of value to the learner, the teacher must have a good understanding of the basics of pronunciation and what seems to interfere with both intelligibility and comprehensibility. Currently research offers some overall suggestions of matters that have influenced listeners in the past (e.g. lexical stress; Field, 2005; Zielinski, 2008). However, in light of the wide range of variability among students, it is up to the instructor to identify each individual's features of speech that most affect comprehensibility, a skill that takes considerable practice and guidance, in addition to an understanding of the sound system of the version of English to be taught, including prosodic elements.

When to start pronunciation instruction

Another critical issue has to do with when to start PI. Zielinski (2012) analysed interview data from 26 Australian migrants (beginners and intermediates) about their feelings towards their own pronunciation. Negative comments were made by 92 per cent, positive comments by only 27 per cent. The negative comments for both beginners and intermediates were heavily linked to having difficulty being understood: 84.6 per cent for beginners and 81.8 per cent for intermediates. Furthermore, 23 per cent of the beginners said that they had experienced decreased confidence to speak.

> [F]or some, bad experiences where someone had laughed at their pronunciation had seriously affected their confidence to speak. If pronunciation difficulties lead to such a loss of confidence to interact in spoken English, it is likely that these participants will have limited opportunities for practice, which in turn can impact their further language development, and ultimately affect many aspects of their lives.
>
> (Zielinski 2012, p. 24)

Zielinski and Yates (2014) have demonstrated that introducing PI with beginners to give them self-confidence and to enhance their intelligibility is not the daunting task that many teachers think. They cite several activities from Springall (2002), who taught pronunciation to beginners in Australia, both raising awareness and providing the learners with an understanding of metalanguage to discuss pronunciation issues.

Clearly, it is ideal to start pronunciation instruction as early as possible, not only to ensure that learners do not experience so many communication breakdowns that their confidence is shaken but also to take advantage of the WMO. However, it is often the case that L2 speakers struggle with pronunciation for years because they did not get sufficient help when they initially learned English. In workplace contexts, especially, employees can be negatively affected by pronunciation barriers. Fortunately, though, the maxim *better late than never* applies for improving comprehensibility. Derwing et al. (2014) conducted an intervention with native speakers of Vietnamese and Khmer whose performance at work was hindered by difficulties with intelligibility and comprehensibility. The speakers had been living and working in an English-speaking environment for an average of 19 years, and none of them had ever received any formal pronunciation training. PI targeting their needs resulted in significant and lasting improvement in both their own perception and their comprehensibility. The participants' employers also noted an improvement in the participants' emails and other written documents, partly attributable to the awareness-raising of plural endings and other sound–orthography correspondences.

Ultimately, the issue of when to start pronunciation instruction is tied to the needs of L2 speakers, regardless of where they are in their L2 learning trajectory. If their speech causes communication breakdowns, then they should be able to access pronunciation training that will result in improved communicative success.

Factors that affect the nature of PI research study outcomes

Up to this point, we have examined issues that affect whether pronunciation is taught, what the focus should be and when PI should be introduced. Another critical issue has to do with the design of PI research studies and how and what they contribute to our understanding of effective PI. Lee et al. (2015) raise several matters for consideration. First, they noted that larger effects were obtained for PI when interventions were longer; they also observed that most PI studies used read stimuli rather than extemporaneous or spontaneous speech, which is more ecologically valid. In addition, the sample size in most studies is small, and very few studies in Lee et al.'s meta-analysis reported effect sizes, thus potentially giving a misleading impression of the overall effect of any changes identified. Few researchers conducted delayed post-tests, making it difficult to determine whether PI had a lasting effect. Lee et al. also observed that PI involving technology evidenced smaller effects than PI offered by teachers.

Thomson and Derwing (2015) also noted several limitations of much of the extant PI research they reviewed, including the fact that few studies address both perception and production. In addition, 53 per cent of the studies they examined dealt with segmentals, but, in most cases, issues such as functional load were not taken into account. More problematic, though, is the fact that, when a single segment was taught, accuracy (or accentedness) was almost exclusively the dimension used to measure progress, as opposed to comprehensibility, which is a far more important judgement for communication purposes.

However, although the comprehensive reviews of PI studies conducted by Lee et al. (2015) and Thomson and Derwing (2015) have identified significant limitations in existing PI research, they also provide ample advice for future PI studies, in which at least some if not all of these limitations can be addressed.

Current contributions and research

In this section we will examine some aspects of using technology, particularly high-variability phonetic training (HVPT), for teaching pronunciation, and we will also consider research involving L2 instructors.

The studies discussed above have largely focused on production, but Thomson's (2012) study focused on improving perception. Using high-variability phonetic training, or HVPT, where students are exposed to multiple voices producing the same segments, Thomson was able to enhance learners' perception skills for a set of 10 vowels, and at the delayed post-test, a month after the post-test, the findings held: there was a significant improvement in perception of the vowels. Not only that, the learners' production improved as a result of the perceptual training. But what is really important for teaching is that Thomson extended his research into practice by developing a software tool that is readily available to any learners of English who have access to the Internet: *The English Accent Coach* (www.englishaccent-coach.com). This is a boon to learners who have difficulty with English segments, and to teachers, who can recommend individual study to their learners and monitor it by having the students send their results to the instructor.

The use of technology for PI has been advocated for a long time because of its (largely unfulfilled) promise of individualized teaching (Derwing & Munro, 2015). Although Lee et al. (2015) found that interventions using technology were less effective than interventions provided by teachers, many of the studies they examined did not involve teacher supervision. When Ferrier, Reid and Chenausky (1999) compared two groups of learners using technology for pronunciation purposes, they found that the monitored group outperformed those who were working without a teacher's guidance. Technology could provide considerable benefits to learners, as a supplement to teacher-led PI, but only if teachers have a good sense of what their students need, and if they use tools that have been shown to be effective. Even very simple technology can be utilized to improve pronunciation. Bueno Alastuey (2010) had learners of English conduct information exchange tasks in English on Skype under three different conditions: a shared L1 (Spanish), different L1s (Spanish and Turkish) and tasks with native speakers of English. She found an improvement in pronunciation at the end of the test period in all three groups, but there was more negotiation between the Spanish and Turkish groups because they encountered more pronunciation problems that they had to solve.

Ted Talks and YouTube videos have also been the subject of PI research and teaching. These resources are accessible, easy to use and suitable for shadowing/mirroring activities to both raise awareness and facilitate improved productions (Meyers, 2013).

Another area of current research that addresses a concern of many teachers who are L2 speakers of English themselves is the study of Levis et al. (2016), in which they demonstrated that a highly proficient L2 speaker with good pronunciation performed as well as a trained native speaker, in the sense that their students, carefully matched for PI needs, showed similar levels of improvement.

Main research methods

Research methods for investigating the value of PI have been discussed above. The point should be reiterated, however, that human listeners represent the gold standard for assessing comprehensibility and intelligibility. Acoustic and other measures have a role to play in L2 research, but they are an inadequate proxy for the two most important speech dimensions for successful communication (see Munro, this volume, and Munro & Derwing, 2015a).

Currently, a great deal of PI research is being conducted, and, in fact, a new journal, the *Journal of Second Language Pronunciation*, has appeared on the scene. This journal, and the *Proceedings of the Pronunciation in Second Language Learning and Teaching Conference*, are both key resources to inform PI, and good repositories of research using a range of approaches.

Recommendations for practice

Encouraging instructors to teach pronunciation

Clearly, the primary recommendation for ensuring high-quality PI is to focus on enhancing intelligibility and/or comprehensibility, rather than aiming for native-like accents. To do this, language instructors need enough training to determine which aspects of their learners' speech are interfering with their communication skills. This not only requires a good understanding of the sound system of English (including prosodic factors) but also an ability to distinguish grammatical and discourse-level issues from pronunciation difficulties. Obviously, teacher training programmes are implicated here, in that instructors should have relatively easy access to sufficient professional development (see Murphy, this volume). With appropriate preparation, L2 teachers' resistance to PI can be overcome. Resources such as Grant's (2014) *Pronunciation Myths* book and Derwing and Munro's (2015) *Pronunciation Fundamentals*, among others, are suitable for teacher preparation courses on pronunciation or self-study, especially since they advocate evidence-based practices.

Approaches to PI

Several areas of focus for PI, both suprasegmental and segmental, have been identified in research studies. Speech rate has been shown to be a factor that affects comprehensibility, but, contrary to common intuition, many learners need to speed up rather than slow down (Munro & Derwing, 2001). Hahn (2004) conducted research indicating that primary sentence stress is important to intelligibility, and both Field (2005) and Zielinski (2008) demonstrated that word stress is important to intelligibility. Sicola and Darcy (2015) and Murphy (2004) have argued that learners should be able to learn the stress pattern of a word when they learn the meaning; in other words, they advocate the incorporation of pronunciation into vocabulary and grammar lessons.

When focusing on segmentals, the concept of functional load (the extent to which two phonemes differentiate minimal pairs) should be taken into account (Munro & Derwing, 2006). There have been several studies examining the production of the interdental fricatives in English, but, given that these are rare contrasts that make very little difference to intelligibility and comprehensibility, it becomes clear that functional load is a crucial consideration, in terms of both research and the selection of segmentals for teaching.

A useful technique that focuses attention on phonology alone is the accent imitation approach taken by Everitt (2015). In a study comparing learners' performance in English after conventional pronunciation instruction versus imitating an English accent in the L1 (Spanish), the imitators showed more improvement in their pronunciation than the other group. Rojczyk (2015) proposed a similar technique. He examined voice onset time (VOT) in voiceless stops. Learners increased their VOTs when using an English accent in Polish words. These two studies suggest that learners can activate their knowledge of accents in their L1 to enhance their productions in their L2.

The timing of pronunciation instruction

It is never too early to offer PI, either in terms of proficiency level (Zielinski & Yates, 2014) or in terms of the first massive exposure to L2 speech (Derwing et al., 2014). The only consideration should be whether the learners need help with PI; if they are clear speakers who are easy to understand, then PI is unnecessary.

Future directions

We are now entering a golden age for PI, so it is incumbent upon us, researchers and instructors alike, to get it right. The last thing our students need is another roller coaster dip, when pronunciation difficulties that interfere with communication are ignored. First, increased collaboration among researchers and language teachers could lead to a better understanding of the constraints faced by both groups, and improved sharing of insights. John Levis' nascent website, www.pronunciationforteachers.com, is a step in the right direction. There are thousands of websites, YouTube videos etc. that purport to assist both teachers and learners with pronunciation issues, but many of them are incredibly ill-informed. A trustworthy repository of information for teachers such as Levis's promises to be an invaluable resource that, with the contributions of other experts, could become a go-to site providing helpful support for classroom instructors. One individual cannot do it all, but, ideally, several respected researchers and practitioners could populate the site with classroom videos, guest lectures or answers to specific questions about pronunciation teaching. Of course, if we want better-trained teachers, there is a need for university TESOL programmes to offer credit courses in teaching pronunciation, an area that is sorely lacking at present (Foote et al., 2011).

Because it is still such a young field, and because so many of the studies carried out so far have been too small to be generalizable (Lee et al. 2015), the possibilities for future pronunciation research are wide open. Analyses of the relative contributions of different PI tasks (e.g. role-playing, HVPT, shadowing, explicit explanation etc.) to determine their relative efficacy would be extremely helpful, along the lines of Galante's and Thomson's (2016) research.

In future intervention studies, it is incumbent upon researchers to determine whether there has been a lasting effect. Delayed post-tests, difficult as they are, given that participants are not always easy to locate, should be planned from the beginning. In classroom and workplace settings, perception and production tasks could be carried out at least three times (pre- post- and delayed post-tests) to determine whether any changes were maintained, and interviews could be conducted with L2 speakers and their interlocutors long after the instruction has taken place to gain their reflections on the value of the instruction and whether real-life interactions are perceived to have improved. Learning what was retained and what was not would be useful in the design of future experiments.

The role of technology and PI should be explored to a far greater degree. Although Lee et al. (2015) found that interventions using technology were less effective than those with instructors, technology still offers the possibility of instruction tailored specifically to the needs of individual students. Furthermore, an under-utilized feature of technology is the possibility of adaptive training that automatically adjusts to an individual's needs in response to his/her performance. Many of the studies investigating technology in Lee et al.'s analysis took a one-size-fits-all approach, and generally did not determine whether the outcomes had an effect on comprehensibility.

The logistics may prove difficult, but the relative efficacy of PI within the WMO should be explored, in comparison with a matched group of L2 speakers who have been immersed in English for a relatively long time. Theoretically, earlier intervention should be more effective, regardless of the proficiency level of the individuals. If, in fact, PI allows for greater comprehensibility and intelligibility gains in the early stages of massive exposure to English, fewer individuals will require remedial support to address heavily entrenched pronunciation patterns later on.

Finally, it is relatively common for teacher trainers to suggest that instructors conduct research themselves. I have attended several plenary talks in which the speakers (usually textbook writers) tend to minimize the benefits of refereed, published research (especially the use of statistics), suggesting that teachers know their students better than anyone else. They encourage instructors to conduct research themselves, regardless of their skill set. I view this advice as a great disservice to teachers and researchers alike. Instead, I recommend far more collaborations of researchers and teachers in which both parties play a significant role. Most teachers of my acquaintance already have incredibly full days, preparing for class, teaching in the moment, focusing on the needs of individual learners, dealing with issues from outside the classroom that affect student performance, assessing progress and so on (in addition to administrative duties associated with their employment). Serious teachers generally make an effort to squeeze in professional development, but they are restricted by what is available to them. Unless the language programme in which they work offers the time and resources necessary for them to conduct studies (normally within university or college settings), and the teachers have the necessary background to do so, to ask them to add to their load the task of conducting research is both unfair and inefficient. On the other hand, researchers are usually trained in methodology appropriate to the research questions being posed. They are more likely than instructors to have access to funding to compensate participants, and if the study entails a listening experiment, for instance, they are better placed to recruit them. Recent years have witnessed an increase in researchers who have taught in language classrooms, and who are well aware of the constraints faced by educational institutions and their staff. It makes sense for researchers and instructors to collaborate in meaningful ways, bringing their separate skill sets to the task of designing interesting questions, the answers to which will enhance our field's knowledge and will influence pedagogical decisions going forwards.

Acknowledgements

I am grateful to my colleague and friend, Murray Munro, with whom I have conducted many pronunciation studies over the years. I thank Beth Zielinski, Bruce Derwing, Ron Thomson and John Murphy for useful feedback. Any errors or omissions are my own.

Further reading

Derwing, T. M., & Munro, M. J. (2015). *Pronunciation fundamentals: Evidence-based perspectives for L2 teaching*. Amsterdam: John Benjamins.
Murphy, J., & Baker, A. (2015). History of English pronunciation teaching. In M. Reed & J. M. Levis (Eds), *The handbook of English pronunciation* (pp. 36–65). Chichester: Wiley Blackwell.
Thomson, R. I., & Derwing, T. M. (2015). The effectiveness of L2 pronunciation instruction: A narrative review. *Applied Linguistics, 36*, 326–344.
Zielinski, B., & Yates, L. (2014). Myth 2: Pronunciation instruction is not appropriate for beginning-level learners. In L. Grant (Ed.), *Pronunciation myths: Applying second language research to classroom teaching* (pp. 56–79). Ann Arbor, MI: Michigan University Press.

Related topics

Pronunciation teaching; teacher training in the teaching of pronunciation; computer-assisted pronunciation teaching

References

Abercrombie, D. (1949). Teaching pronunciation. *English Language Teaching, 3*(5), 113–122.

Breitkreutz, J., Derwing, T., & Rossiter, M. (2001). Pronunciation teaching practices in Canada, *TESL Canada Journal, 19*(1), 51–61.

Bueno Alastuey, M. C. (2010). Synchronous-Voice Computer-Mediated Communication: Effects on Pronunciation. *CALICO Journal, 28*, 1–20.

Burns, A. (2006). Integrating research and professional development on pronunciation teaching in a national adult ESL program. *TESL Reporter, 39*, 34–41.

Buss, L. (2013). Pronunciation from the perspective of pre-service EFL teachers: An analysis of internship reports. In J. Levis & K. LeVelle (Eds), *Proceedings of the 4th Pronunciation in Second Language Learning and Teaching Conference* (pp. 255–264), Iowa State University, Ames, IA.

Champagne-Muzar, C., Schneiderman, E. I., & Bourdages, J. S. (1993). Second language accent: The role of the pedagogical environment. *IRAL, 31*, 143–160.

Couper, G. (2006). The short and long-term effects of pronunciation, instruction. *Prospect, 21*(1), 46–66.

De Bot, K. (1983). Visual feedback of intonation I: Effectiveness and induced practice behavior. *Language and Speech, 26*, 331–350.

De Bot, K., & Mailfert, K. (1982). The teaching of intonation: Fundamental research and classroom applications. *TESOL Quarterly, 16*, 71–77.

Derwing, T. M., & Munro, M. J. (2009). Comprehensibility as a factor in listener interaction preferences: Implications for the workplace. *The Canadian Modern Language Review, 66*(2), 181–202.

Derwing, T. M., & Munro, M. J. (2015). *Pronunciation fundamentals: Evidence-based perspectives for L2 teaching*. Amsterdam: John Benjamins.

Derwing, T. M., Munro, M. J., & Wiebe, G. E. (1998). Evidence in favor of a broad framework for pronunciation instruction. *Language Learning, 48*, 393–410.

Derwing, T. M., Munro, M. J., Foote, J. A., Waugh, E., & Fleming, J. (2014). Opening the window on comprehensible pronunciation after 19 years: A workplace training study. *Language Learning, 64*, 526–548.

Dragojevic, M., & Giles, H. (2016). I don't like you because you're hard to understand: The role of processing fluency in the language attitudes process. *Human Communication Research*. Advanced online publication. doi:10.1111/hcre.12079.

Everitt, C. (2015). *Accent imitation on the L1 as a task to improve L2 pronunciation*. Unpublished master's thesis, Universitat de Barcelona, Spain.

Ferrier, L. J., Reid, L. N., & Chenausky, K. (1999). Computer-assisted accent modification: A report on practice effects. *Topics in Language Disorders, 19*(4), 35–48.

Field, J. (2005). Intelligibility and the listener: The role of lexical stress. *TESOL Quarterly, 39*, 399–423.

Foote, J. A., Holtby, A. K., & Derwing, T. M. (2011). Survey of the teaching of pronunciation in adult ESL programs in Canada, 2010. *TESL Canada Journal, 29*, 1–22.

Galante, A., & Thomson, R. I. (2016). The effectiveness of drama as an instructional approach for the development of second language oral fluency, comprehensibility, and accentedness. *TESOL Quarterly*, Advanced online publication. doi:10.1002/tesq.290.

Gass, S., & Varonis, E. M. (1984). The effect of familiarity on the comprehensibility of nonnative speech. *Language Learning, 34*, 65–89.

Gettegno, C. (1963). *Teaching foreign languages in schools: The silent way*. Reading: Educational Explorers.

Gordon, J., & Darcy, I. (2016). The development of comprehensible speech in L2 learners: A classroom study on the effects of short-term pronunciation instruction. *Journal of Second Language Pronunciation, 2*, 57–93.

Grant, L. (Ed.) (2014). *Pronunciation myths: Applying second language research to classroom teaching*. Ann Arbor, MI: Michigan University Press.

Guiora, A. Z., Acton, W. R., Erard, R., & Strickland, F. W. (1980). The effects of benzodiazapene (valium) on permeability of language ego boundaries. *Language Learning, 30*, 351–361.

Hahn, L. D. (2004). Primary stress and intelligibility: Research to motivate the teaching of suprasegmentals. *TESOL Quarterly, 38*(2), 201–223.

Henderson, A., Frost, D., Tergujeff, E., Kautzsch, A., Murphy, D., Kirkova-Naskova, A., . . . Curnick, L. (2012). The English pronunciation teaching in Europe survey: Selected results. *Research in Language, 10*, 5–27.

Isaacs, T., & Trofimovich, P. (2012). 'Deconstructing' comprehensibility: Identifying the linguistic influences on listeners' L2 comprehensibility ratings. *Studies in Second Language Acquisition, 34,* 475–505.

Krashen, S. D. (1985). *The input hypothesis: Issues and implications.* London: Longman.

Lado, R., & Fries, C. C. (1958). *English pronunciation: Exercises in sound segments, intonation, and rhythm* (Vol. 3). Ann Arbor, MI: University of Michigan Press.

Lee, J., Jang, J., & Plonsky, L. (2015). The effectiveness of second language pronunciation instruction: A meta-analysis. *Applied Linguistics, 36,* 345–366.

Levis, J. M. (2005). Changing contexts and shifting paradigms in pronunciation teaching. *TESOL Quarterly, 39,* 369–377.

Levis, J. M., Sonsaat, S., Link, S., & Barriuso, T. A. (2016). Native and nonnative teachers of L2 pronunciation: Effects on learner performance. *TESOL Quarterly.* Advance online publication. doi:10.1002/tesq.272.

Llurda, E., & Huguet, A. (2003). Self-awareness in NNS EFL primary and secondary school teachers. *Language Awareness, 12,* 220–233.

MacDonald, D., Yule, G., & Powers, M. (1994). Attempts to improve English L2 pronunciation: The variable effects of different types of instruction. *Language Learning, 44*(1), 75–100.

Macdonald, S. (2002). Pronunciation: Views and practices of reluctant teachers. *Prospect, 17*(3), 3–18.

Meyers, C. (2013, August). Mirroring project update: Intelligible accented speakers as pronunciation models. TESOL Video News (the newsletter of the TESOL Video and Digital Media Interest Section). Teachers of English to Speakers of Other Languages. Retrieved from http://newsmanager. commpartners.com/tesolvdmis/ issues/2013–07–27/email.html#3 (accessed 30 December 2013).

Munro, M. J., & Derwing, T. M. (2001). Modeling perceptions of the accentedness and comprehensibility of L2 speech. *Studies in Second Language Acquisition, 23,* 451–468.

Munro, M. J., & Derwing, T. M. (2006). The functional load principle in pronunciation instruction: An exploratory study. *System, 34,* 520–531.

Munro, M. J., & Derwing, T. M. (2015a). A prospectus for pronunciation research in the 21st century: A point of view. *Journal of Second Language Pronunciation, 1,* 11–42.

Munro, M. J., & Derwing, T. M. (2015b). Intelligibility in research and practice. In M. Reed & J. M. Levis (Eds), *The handbook of English pronunciation* (pp. 378–396). Chichester: Wiley Blackwell.

Murphy, J. M. (2004). Attending to word-stress while learning new vocabulary. *English for Specific Purposes Journal, 23*(1), 67–83.

Murphy, J. (2014). Myth 7: Teacher training programs provide adequate preparation in how to teach pronunciation. In L. Grant (Ed.) *Pronunciation myths: Applying second language research to classroom teaching* (pp. 188–224). Ann Arbor, MI: Michigan University Press.

Murphy, J., & Baker, A. (2015). History of English pronunciation teaching. In M. Reed & J. M. Levis (Eds) *The handbook of English pronunciation* (pp. 36–65). Chichester: Wiley Blackwell.

Perlmutter, M. (1989). Intelligibility rating of L2 speech pre-and post-intervention. *Perceptual and Motor Skills, 68*(4), 515–521.

Pica, T. (1994). Questions from the language classroom: Research perspectives. *TESOL Quarterly, 28,* 49–79.

Rojczyk, A. (2015). Using FL accent imitation in L1 in foreign-language speech research. In E. Waniek-Klimczak & M. Pawlak (Eds), *Teaching and researching pronunciation of English* (pp. 223–233). Cham: Springer.

Ryan, E. B., Carranza, M., & Moffie, R. W. (1977). Reactions towards varying degrees of accentedness in the speech of Spanish-English bilinguals. *Language and Speech, 20*(3), 267–273.

Saito, K., & Lyster, R. (2012). Effects of form-focused instruction and corrective feedback on L2 pronunciation development: The case of English /ɹ/ by Japanese learners of English. *Language Learning, 62,* 595–633.

Sicola, L., & Darcy, I. (2015). Integrating pronunciation into the language classroom. In M. Reed & J. Levis (Eds), *Handbook of English pronunciation* (pp. 471–487). Chichester: Wiley Blackwell.

Springall, J. (2002). *Pronunciation project.* Unpublished manuscript.

Sweet, H, 1900, *The practical study of languages: A guide for teachers and learners.* New York, NY: Henry Holt.

Tam, J. (2012). *Reduction study: Installation with videos and sound.* Boston, MA: Tufts University.

Thomson, R. I. (2012). Improving L2 listeners' perception of English vowels: A computer-mediated approach. *Language Learning, 62,* 1231–1258.

Thomson, R. I. (2014). Myth 6: Accent reduction and pronunciation instruction are the same. In L. Grant (Ed.), *Pronunciation myths: Applying second language research to classroom teaching* (pp. 160–187). Ann Arbor, MI: Michigan University Press.

Thomson, R. I., & Derwing, T. M. (2015). The effectiveness of L2 pronunciation instruction: A narrative review, *Applied Linguistics, 36,* 326–344.

Zielinski, B. (2008). The listener: No longer the silent partner in reduced intelligibility. *System, 36,* 69–84.

Zielinski, B. (2012). The social impact of pronunciation difficulties: Confidence and willingness to speak. In J. Levis & K. LeVelle (Eds), *Proceedings of the 3rd Annual Pronunciation in Second Language Learning and Teaching Conference* (pp. 18–26), Iowa State University, Ames, IA.

Zielinski, B., & Yates, L. (2014). Myth 2: Pronunciation instruction is not appropriate for beginning-level learners. In L. Grant (Ed.), *Pronunciation myths: Applying second language research to classroom teaching* (pp. 56–79). Ann Arbor, MI: Michigan University Press.

Section 5

Current issues in pronunciation research

20

Pronunciation and speaking

Jonathan Newton

Introduction

Pronunciation has often been overlooked as a skill in its own right in well-established communicative teaching approaches that emphasize learning through communicative practice and focus on the goal of oral fluency. Such approaches often appear to work on the implicit assumption that pronunciation will naturally develop through communicative practice. Consequently, teachers are often reluctant to teach pronunciation (Foote, Trofimovich, Collins & Urzúa, 2016) and commercial textbooks similarly have often failed to provide systematic materials for pronunciation teaching (Derwing, Diepenbroek & Foote, 2012). However, there is growing recognition of the value of instruction focused on developing speaking skills (Goh & Burns, 2012; Newton, 2017) and, with this, attention has naturally turned to pronunciation.

In concert with a growing interest in pronunciation, globalization has generated a growing demand for proficiency in spoken, communicative English. English is increasingly used as an international language/lingua franca (Leitner, Hashim & Wolf, 2016), especially in work contexts, and English language learners have access to an ever-widening range of opportunities for communication in English through study mobility and online interaction. Not surprisingly, as speaking skills in English become increasingly important for work and study, the spotlight falls on issues of mutual intelligibility and comprehensibility and on how the pronunciation needs of English language learners can be met.

This chapter primarily focuses on the role that pronunciation plays in second language acquisition research on speaking and on the pedagogic implications of this research. It begins with a brief historical survey that highlights the roles of speaking and pronunciation in language teaching over the past century. It then looks at how pronunciation has been addressed in research on four aspects of speaking: speaking in task-based language teaching, negotiation of meaning, language-related episodes in classroom interaction, and corrective feedback. Drawing on this discussion, the chapter proposes recommendations for incorporating pronunciation into speaking skills instruction and concludes by identifying future directions for research.

Historical perspectives

Celce-Murcia, Brinton and Goodwin (2010) offer a useful heuristic for understanding historical trends in teaching pronunciation and speaking. Drawing on a distinction made by Kelly (1969), they identify two broad approaches to teaching pronunciation: an intuitive-imitative approach and an analytic-linguistic approach. As the name suggests, an intuitive-imitative approach harnesses the learner's ability to learn through imitation of models (invariably native speaker models, with a corresponding emphasis on native speaker standards). An analytic-linguistic approach, on the other hand, emphasizes deliberate teaching and learning of phonemic information about the sound system and articulatory settings. The phonetic alphabet is often used to assist in the learning of discrete, often decontextualized aspects of pronunciation.

Intuitive-imitative and analytic-linguistic approaches are of course not binary opposites; methods for teaching pronunciation often draw on both. But, nevertheless, there has been a historical tendency to move back and forth between these approaches, emphasizing one more strongly than the other. For example, an intuitive-imitation approach is seen in the direct method, a naturalistic learning method that emerged in the late nineteenth century in Europe and became well established in the Berlitz method. Both the direct and Berlitz methods focus on everyday spoken language and on learning through imitation and immersion in the target language in the classroom. Learning correct pronunciation is viewed as important, but is seen to happen through careful imitation rather than explicit instruction.

In contrast, the audiolingual method (ALM), which emerged around the middle of the twentieth century, displays core features of an analytic-linguistic approach. While it also emphasizes learning through imitative speaking practice, ALM foregrounds direct instruction and rote, mechanical practice, mostly focused on segmental features. Imitative speaking practice is typically preceded by explicit analysis of sound distinctions (for example, minimal pairs) and by extensive non-communicative practice involving various kinds of pattern practice and drills. Accuracy in replicating native speaker pronunciation is a central goal of learning.

English language teaching since the 1980s–1990s is broadly seen as being in a post-method era (Adamson, 2006), although one characterized by CLT in its many guises, including task-based language teaching (TBLT) and content and language integrated learning. In CLT, the relationship between pronunciation and speaking has been somewhat in tension. On the one hand, the emphasis on communicative speaking reenergized pronunciation teaching as seen in the work of early CLT proponents of systematic pronunciation teaching such as (listed chronologically): Bowen (1972), Brazil, Coulthard and Johns (1980), Pica (1984), Pennington and Richards (1986), Celce-Murcia (1987) and Morley (1994). On the other hand, in rejecting the explicit instruction and non-communicative drills typical of ALM, CLT practitioners often overlooked systematic pronunciation teaching, not least because of its association with discredited behaviourist learning theory. Indeed, pronunciation teaching was often neglected altogether – the baby having been thrown out with the bathwater. The shift in emphasis in CLT away from accuracy for its own sake and towards intelligibility only exacerbated this issue.

Despite a resurgence of interest in pronunciation in recent decades, the neglect of pronunciation in the teaching of speaking is by no means a thing of the past. Recent surveys of pronunciation content in commercial English language teaching textbooks have found that pronunciation content is often non-systematic and presented as add-ons in the margins of lessons (Derwing, Diepenbroek & Foote, 2012). Similarly, in an analysis of English second language (ESL) lessons in Quebec, Canada, Foote et al. (2016) found pronunciation teaching to be infrequent in classroom practice, and when it did occur, to mostly involve incidental, unplanned corrective feedback. Pronunciation has been equally neglected in scholarship on speaking, a theme addressed in following sections. One example will suffice. In his book which provides an extensive review of task-based language teaching (TBLT), Ellis (2003) does not include the terms *pronunciation* and *phonology* as indexable items despite the fact that the vast majority of TBLT research involves speaking. This is not to fault Ellis so much as to show how little attention pronunciation has received in what is now a very large body of TBLT research on speaking.

Critical issues and topics

With the current flourishing of research on and interest in pronunciation teaching and learning, a range of critical issues on the relationship between pronunciation and speaking have received attention. Following is a representative sample of these issues:

(a) the place of pronunciation teaching in communicative classrooms (Foote et al., 2016);
(b) the role of explicit focus on form and deliberate pronunciation practice (Hamada, 2016; Trofimovich & Gatbonton, 2006);
(c) incidental focus on form and its role in pronunciation learning through speaking (Mackey, 2007a & b);
(d) the effectiveness of corrective feedback for pronunciation learning (Lyster, Saito & Sato, 2013);
(e) the relationship between fluency and pronunciation (Derwing & Rossiter, 2003);
(f) accentedness, and the social and ethical implications of instruction focused on accent reduction (Derwing & Munro, 2005, 2013);
(g) the related issue of the spread of English as an international language (EIL) and the implications of this shift for identifying appropriate pronunciation targets (Jenkins, 2002);
(h) the role of pronunciation in employability (Pilott, 2016; Timming, 2016).

Although by no means exhaustive, this list illustrates the range of themes inherent in the relationship between pronunciation and speaking, including pedagogically oriented themes (points a–d), theoretical themes (point e) and socially oriented themes (points f–h), although there is considerable overlap between these categories. This chapter focuses mainly on themes related to speaking pedagogy.

Current contributions and research

How has pronunciation been addressed (or not) in research on the role of speaking in classroom language learning? Speaking is such a broad topic that to address this question necessarily requires a selective focus. Here, I focus on four overlapping research areas within which pronunciation might be expected to feature, namely (1) task-based oral language production, (2) negotiation of form and meaning, (3) language-related episodes (LREs) in classroom communicative interaction, and (4) corrective feedback. The section concludes by turning to a topic that connects pronunciation and speaking to the world beyond the classroom; that is, the impact of pronunciation and speaking on employability.

Pronunciation and task-based language teaching

We turn first to pronunciation and task-based speaking, and specifically to research into how tasks push spoken language production by language learners and the implications for language learning through speaking. Surprisingly, despite this being a highly productive area of research, pronunciation is under-represented. Research in this area seeks to identify how factors such as different types of tasks, different levels of task complexity and different task implementation variables (e.g. planning time) push learners to attend to different aspects of language production and, in so doing, to develop their L2 linguistic resources and processing capacities (e.g. Robinson, 2011; Skehan, 2014). Following Skehan (1998), spoken language production is seen to consist of three main dimensions: fluency, accuracy and complexity. One might expect pronunciation to be represented in measures of spoken accuracy and fluency. And yet this is largely not the case. Accuracy is mostly defined in relation to morphosyntactic and lexical features, while prosodic features are not included in measures of fluency beyond measures of speech rate and pausing (e.g. Skehan, 2009; Michel, Kuiken & Vedder, 2007; cf. Derwing & Rossiter, 2003). Why is this? One likely explanation is that this research is largely cognitivist in orientation and so focuses on how task factors influence the conceptualization and formulation stages of speech production rather than on the details of articulation and prosody. This is a gap that warrants closer scrutiny in future research and in the development of measures of spoken language production.

Outside the task literature, only one study of which I am aware, Derwing and Rossiter (2003), has drawn on the complexity–accuracy–fluency framework and Skehan's trade-off hypothesis (Skehan, 1998) to inform research on pronunciation instruction. Derwing and Rossiter investigated the impact of three different approaches to teaching pronunciation on the comprehensibility of elicited production by adult learners in an ESL programme in Canada. The first instructional approach focused on segmental features (i.e. individual phonemes), the second on suprasegmentals (e.g. intonation, word and sentence stress, rhythm and projection) and the third contained no planned instruction on pronunciation. In a comparison of pre- and post-course elicited production, the study found that, while learners in the segmental condition reduced the number of phonological errors they made over the duration of the programme, their performance on comprehensibility and fluency measures declined, while that of learners in the suprasegmental condition improved significantly on both. The authors ascribe these results to a number of factors including a trade-off effect (Skehan, 1998), in which the focus in the segmental condition on accurate production of vowels and consonants drew the attentional resources of these learners away from attending sufficiently to the complexity and fluency of their speech. In contrast, because of the close relationship between the content/communicative meaning of speech and prosodic features, learners in the suprasegmental group appeared better equipped to attend to both complexity and fluency in mutually supportive ways. Consequently, their elicited production at the end of the course achieved higher comprehensibility ratings than the segmental instruction group. These results, the authors argue, do not suggest that segmental instruction is of no value. On the contrary, they note that the segmental group made substantial gains in phonological accuracy. However, they conclude that, on the basis of these results, pronunciation instruction should include a stronger emphasis on prosodic features than has traditionally been the case.

Two other studies (Derwing, Thompson & Munro, 2006; Derwing & Munro, 2013) looked at the development of accent, comprehensibility and fluency by first language (L1) Slavic and Mandarin language-speaking immigrants to Canada in relation to factors including contact with English speakers, L1 background and age of arrival. Among the results of these studies, L1 background was found to have a significant impact on fluency and comprehensibility, with the L1 Mandarin speakers making much fewer or no gains over time while the L1 Slavic speakers continued to improve in comprehensibility and fluency. Of relevance to the current chapter, the authors of the second study draw on the willingness to communicate framework (MacIntyre, 2007) to explain these findings. As they argue, 'The Mandarin speakers overall showed greater ties to their L1 community, more reluctance to initiate conversations as a result of lower self-confidence in their English abilities, and fewer opportunities to interact in English' (Derwing & Munro, 2013, p. 179). However, when they asked the most proficient of the Mandarin speakers at the end of the seven years of the study what advice he would give to newcomers, he replied, 'I think first, always talk, talk with people. If you have any time, any chance' (p. 179). For this person at least, speaking was perceived to be a key to learning pronunciation.

Pronunciation, classroom interaction and negotiation of meaning

A second major strand of speaking research investigates the role of interaction and negotiation of meaning in language learning (Mackey, 2007a), and here again we might expect pronunciation to be a prominent topic of research. However, this is not the case. In studies in this area, the extent to which pronunciation issues arise during interaction and trigger negotiation of meaning/form sequences is often not addressed (e.g. Adams, 2007), and, where it is, it is generally shown to play a minor role. For instance, in a qualitative study of native speaker/non-native speaker interactions on a series of information-gap and discussion tasks, Nakahama, Tyler and Van Lier (2001) found that, from a total of 217 triggers of negotiation sequences in the data set, only 15 involved pronunciation issues. In contrast, Newton (2013) found that misheard, unfamiliar or mispronounced words accounted for a substantial number of negotiation sequences in task-based interaction between non-native speakers. However, these three types of trigger were not distinguished in the analysis and so the extent to which pronunciation errors were involved is not clear. In sum, as Mackey (2007b) notes, 'there has been very little interaction research to date that has focused on the acquisition of phonological features . . . although there is no reason to suspect that these areas would not be impacted by interaction' (p. 3).

Pronunciation and language-related episodes (LREs)

Interaction research also includes studies that investigate incidental focus on form and LREs as they occur in naturally occurring classroom discourse or in interactions recorded in quasi-experimental studies. From a pronunciation perspective, a problem with studies in this area is that the coding frameworks used to categorize LREs often subsume pronunciation LREs in larger categories alongside LREs focused on other linguistic features such as spelling or morphology, thus making it difficult to disentangle pronunciation from other language issues. Swain and Lapkin (1998), for example, distinguish lexical from form-based LREs and in so doing categorize pronunciation LREs as form-based LREs alongside spelling, morphology and other aspects of language form. Still other studies such as Kim and McDonough (2008), Leeser (2004), and McDonough and Sunitham (2009) include pronunciation within lexical LREs, which they distinguish from grammatical LREs.

These classification issues aside, overall research in this area shows pronunciation to be a relatively minor focus of LREs in classroom interaction in comparison to vocabulary and grammar (cf. Kim & McDonough, 2008). For example, in comparing the task-based interaction between EFL students at an Indonesian university working in either pairs or small groups of three, Lasito and Storch (2013) found pronunciation LREs to constitute only 6 per cent of LREs generated by pairs, and 16 per cent of those generated by the small groups. Similarly, in a study investigating LREs in naturally occurring classroom interaction in New Zealand ESOL classrooms, Ellis, Basturkmen and Loewen (2001) found pronunciation LREs to occur much less frequently than LREs focused on grammar and vocabulary. Notably, though, they found that, even though pronunciation LREs were infrequent, when they did occur they were more likely to result in successful uptake than LREs with a grammatical or lexical focus. (Successful uptake refers to instances in which a learner demonstrates that they have understood or can use a linguistic feature correctly.) Similarly, Aubrey (2015) found that, for Japanese tertiary EFL students, spelling and pronunciation LREs led to self-reported learning at higher rates than other linguistic foci.

Pronunciation and corrective feedback

Research on the impact of oral corrective feedback (CF) on pronunciation errors shows a similar pattern of low rates of occurrence but high rates of uptake when CF is given. That said, as Lyster et al. (2013) point out in their comprehensive review of CF research, few of the many CF studies published in recent decades have actually addressed the value of CF for pronunciation development.

A question widely addressed in CF research is what aspects of language do teachers attend to in their CF. A consistent finding is that CF is more concerned with grammatical errors than with other kinds of errors (Lyster et al., 2013; Mackey, Gass & McDonough, 2000). However, the types of errors that teachers typically give feedback on are not necessarily those that learners notice and/or successfully repair the most. In fact, while research shows that morphosyntactic errors receive proportionally more CF, learners have been shown to be more successful at repairing lexical and phonological errors, and better at accurately perceiving CF that targets such errors (Kim & Han, 2007). To explain this finding, Lyster et al. (2013) reiterate the suggestion from Mackey et al. (2000) that learners are likely to be more sensitive to CF on lexical and phonological errors than on morphosyntactic errors because these former error types are more likely to seriously interfere with understanding and so to be important for successful L2 communication (see also Isaacs & Trofimovich, 2012). This finding suggests a promising role for CF in pronunciation development.

A second topic of CF research concerns type of CF. Much of the CF research has focused on recasts (i.e. a reformulation of a previous utterance in which an error in the original utterance is repaired or *recast*) and explicit corrections, although only a small number of these studies have investigated pronunciation development. In a notable exception, Saito and Lyster (2012) conducted a quasi-experimental classroom study into the effectiveness of recasts for acquisition of /ɹ/ by adult Japanese learners of English. They found that learners who received recasts of instances of mispronunciation of the target form made demonstrable gains while those in an experimental group in which the target form was highlighted and practised but without recasting made no such gains. Notably, the gains were present in controlled *and* spontaneous speech although only for familiar items that learners had met in instruction. CF in which recasting is supported by the provision of explicit phonetic information has also been shown to be effective. In a follow-up study, Saito (2013) found that presenting students with explicit phonetic information in the form of teachers' exaggerated models of pronunciation of /ɹ/ and instruction on articulatory settings before they performed form-focused tasks enhanced the effectiveness of recasts. Students who received both recasts and explicit information made marked improvements in their production of /ɹ/ for both familiar and unfamiliar lexical items. In regard to these studies on recasting and pronunciation, Lyster et al. (2013) conclude:

> Though few in number, these studies suggest that short pronunciation-focused recasts can play an important role in L2 pronunciation development, arguably because students benefit from the opportunities afforded by such recasts, first, to notice the negative evidence directed at the intelligibility of their output and, second, to practise the correct form in response to their teachers' model pronunciation (positive evidence).
>
> (p. 24)

In sum, pronunciation is under-represented in research on speaking and, likewise, in classroom interaction it appears to be a less frequent target for negotiation of meaning/form, LREs and CF than morphosyntax. However, in both the LRE and CF studies, evidence suggests that when incidental focus on form addresses pronunciation issues, it has a positive impact on pronunciation development.

Pronunciation and employability

The final topic appropriately concludes this section by looking beyond the classroom at the relationship between pronunciation, speaking and the world of work. English communication skills, including aspects of pronunciation such as accent and intelligibility, have moved into the spotlight in employment contexts as a consequence of migration patterns and globalization, which have dramatically increased the multicultural mix in the workplace in many countries (Newton & Kusmierczyk, 2011). Recent research has shown that pronunciation errors and accentedness have a strong influence on employability and promotion opportunities. Timming (2016) used simulated telephone interviews to investigate how a non-native accent influenced the employability ratings of applicants in the USA. He found clear evidence of accent-based discrimination by the managers who took part in the telephone-based job interviews. Their rating of the prestige of different accents displayed statistically significant patterns, with Chinese, Indian and Mexican accents all rated lower than North American accents, and, within these three non-native accents, Indian and Mexican accents rated lowest, with Indian accents in the middle. Voices with these different accents were also rated significantly lower for customer-facing jobs compared to non-customer-facing jobs. As an aside, Timming also found that applicants with a British accent fared at least as well as and sometimes better than those with an American accent. (See Gluszek and Dovidio (2010) for a discussion of research on native speakers' attitudes towards accented speech.)

Also on the topic of pronunciation and employment, Pilott (2016) investigated the extent to which employers perceived pronunciation variables to influence the employability of migrants from non-English-speaking backgrounds to New Zealand. Using survey data, he found that, while fluency (comprised of the variables of speed, smoothness, fluidity, variety, co-articulation and pausing) was the strongest predictor of perceived suitability for employment, accuracy with segmentals and quality of intonation were also both significant predictors. Pilott developed a subjective global measure of pronunciation called *acceptability*, which is defined as the extent to which pronunciation is 'good enough for a defined purpose'. (p. 55). Acceptability is distinct from employability since the latter includes a range of other criteria (e.g. legal ability to work in a country, physical capacity to do the job, availability, attitude etc.), while acceptability is a context-dependent global measure of pronunciation. Pilott argued on the basis of his findings that acceptability, which encompasses segmental, prosodic and fluency variables, is a more ecologically valid and statistically robust measure of the effect of pronunciation on perceived employability. Pilott concludes that workplace-oriented ESOL instruction should focus on acceptability as an important learning goal.

Recommendations for practice

As noted in the earlier discussion of historical trends, two contradictory trends in pronunciation teaching have been evident in the CLT era. On the one hand, CLT opened up opportunities for innovative pronunciation teaching practice beyond the reliance on imitation, drilling and segmental practice so common in the field in earlier methods. The work of Brazil (1994), Brazil et al. (1980), Celce-Murcia et al. (2010) and Morley (1994) are noteworthy examples of scholarship that pioneered principled, innovative CLT approaches to pronunciation teaching. However, these cases aside, the de-emphasis on systematic teaching of linguistic structures in CLT often led to the formal teaching of pronunciation disappearing or, at best, being moved to the margins. Concurrently, the international demand for native speaker EFL teachers frequently outstripped supply and consequently many native speakers joined the profession underqualified (often with the sole qualification being their status as a 'native speaker') and especially lacking in the expertise to teach pronunciation. Today, pronunciation teaching expertise continues to be a problem for the ESL/EFL profession even for teachers who are otherwise qualified and experienced (Couper, 2016; Foote et al., 2016).

To help address this gap, we can glean a number of recommendations for practice from research on pronunciation and speaking. First, it is worth noting that, despite the obvious relationship between speaking and pronunciation, speaking practice isn't necessarily the first step in teaching pronunciation. Before learners engage in intensive productive practice, there is general consensus that learners benefit from perceptual training and from awareness-raising focused on metacognition (Vandergrift & Goh, 2012) on the way that sounds are made in the case of segmental features (Trofimovich & Gatbonton, 2006) and on the nature of supra-segmental features and their functional weight in conveying meaning in English (Cauldwell, 2013). On this basis, Nation and Newton (2009) propose a simple four-step heuristic to address pronunciation issues: survey, analyse, hear and produce. The survey step involves identifying which pronunciation features a learner or group of learners need to work on. This pronunciation needs analysis helps the learner(s) and teacher set learning priorities (e.g. Couper, 2006). The second step involves the teacher guiding learners through an analysis *of* the target features in order to raise conscious awareness of articulatory settings (Saito, 2013). Learning about the sound system of English is intended to aid attention and noticing (Schmidt, 2001) rather than being an endpoint in itself. The third step is to engage in listening practice, both focused and global, in order to tune in the perceptual systems to the sounds, patterns or prosodic features being targeted by instruction. The final step is to move to production practice, transitioning from imitative practice to guided practice and finally to independent practice (Morley, 1994).

In considering how these steps can be put into practice, now more than ever, teachers and learners have access to readily available, highly mobile and often free technologies to expand and enrich their pedagogic options (Godwin-Jones, 2012). For example, software such as Cool Speech (Cauldwell, 2016) provides learners with intensive guided opportunities to analyse natural speech, to record their voice and compare their recording to a model and to do intensive pronunciation practice. Other software, including Praat and Visipitch, provides visual displays of wave forms and pitch contours and so offered a useful way to draw learners' attention to prosody. Animations showing the placement and movement of articulatory organs for different phonemes are also available through websites and programmes such as the SoundsofSpeech website developed by the University of Iowa. However, Derwing and Munro (2015) caution that the effectiveness of technology depends on how it is designed and implemented, concluding that, in the foreseeable future, teachers will continue to play a role in pronunciation teaching; technology, they argue, is a tool to be used with reference to evidence-based pedagogic principles rather than as a substitute for teacher-led instruction.

While there is an obvious sequence in the four steps (survey, analyse, hear, produce) of moving from perception to production, in reality these steps often overlap or reoccur in recursive cycles. Nevertheless, teachers should ensure that perceptual training and awareness-raising are not neglected as is often the case when pronunciation teaching is dominated by imitative production practice. Couper (2006) designed and evaluated an instructional intervention that nicely illustrates this principle. Couper's study investigated the impact of pronunciation instruction on the errors made by ESL learners (migrants attending ESL classes in New Zealand) on two segmental targets: epenthesis (addition of a sound) and absence (inappropriate omission of a consonant). Learners in an experimental group received instruction on these two errors in 12 short weekly teaching sessions while learners in a control group did not. In these sessions, the instructor identified common epenthesis and absence errors in recordings made by the learners, which were then discussed. Next, learners listened to and discussed a collated set of segments from the recordings, including target- and non-target-like examples of the targeted features. Only after this intensive analysis and perceptual training was structured practice carried out. A comparison of pre-post-tests (scripted production tests) showed that learners in the experimental group produced significantly fewer errors in both the post and delayed post-tests, with no such change found in the performance of the control group.

Having argued that pronunciation teaching practices should emphasize awareness-raising and perceptual training, one particular *imitative* speaking technique known as shadowing has been shown to improve learners' phoneme perception skills (Hamada, 2016). Shadowing involves learners immediately vocalizing the speech they hear. As Hamada notes, shadowing is distinct from oral reading or rote repetition in that it is an *online* process which requires immediate vocalization of speech without time to access meaning; learners' focus is solely on phonology (p. 36). Hamada argues that this online feature of shadowing strengthens the functioning of the phonological loop. In so doing it creates a virtuous cycle in which improvements in phoneme perception from shadowing lead to improved word recognition, which in turn enhances listening comprehension skills. There is a substantial body of research on shadowing, most of which has been carried out in Japan, where shadowing is popular, and with a primary focus on listening skill development rather than pronunciation. Hamada's 2016 study is therefore important for including a measure of phoneme perception. In the study, 43 Japanese tertiary-level EFL students in two proficiency groups (low and intermediate proficiency) took part in nine shadowing lessons over a month. Prior to and following the shadowing intervention they took a dictation cloze test designed to reveal improvements in phonemic perception. Results showed that, regardless of proficiency, both groups improved their phonemic perception to a similar extent. While productive dimensions of the learners' pronunciation were not measured, the findings nevertheless suggest a promising role for shadowing in helping to build the cognitive foundations for improved pronunciation. What is interesting about this finding for the role of speaking in pronunciation is that the productive speaking practice involved in shadowing led to improvements in receptive/perceptual competence.

The discussion so far concerns *how* to teach pronunciation. Of course, *what* to teach is equally important. The construct of functional load (FL) is one example of a principled approach to prioritizing instructional targets (Brown, 1991), although there is as yet limited research on its application to the classroom. FL refers to the 'importance of linguistic phenomena in distinguishing meanings in a language' (Derwing & Munro, 2015, p. 74). Two examples provided by Derwing and Munro are the /p/–/b/ distinction in English, which has a high FL because of the many minimal pairs it discriminates, and, in contrast, the /ə/–/ð/ distinction, which is involved in relatively few such pairings. In a study that investigated the value of the FL construct for setting instructional targets, Munro and Derwing (2006) had native English listeners rate Cantonese-accented speech samples, which had been created to reflect graded permutations of FL. They found high FL errors to have a significantly greater impact on comprehensibility and concluded that FL provides a useful framework for identifying which segmental errors deserve priority, albeit one that needs further research.

Of course the sound system is much more than sound segments – it also involves pitch, stress, intonation, elision, rhythm, pulse, pause and other prosodic, suprasegmental features that play a vital role in shaping meaning and conveying the pragmatics of oral communication and so warrant systematic, planned attention by teachers (Celce-Murcia et al., 2010; Pickering, 2001). As Munro and Derwing (1999) note, '[e]ven heavily accented speech is sometimes perfectly intelligible and prosodic errors appear to be a more potent force in the loss of intelligibility than phonetic errors' (p. 285). This conclusion was confirmed by Zielinski (2007) in a small-scale exploratory study that investigated the impact of L2 speech characteristics on intelligibility as perceived by native listeners. She found that an L2 speaker's syllable stress pattern had the greatest impact on intelligibility, but with an important secondary effect for segmental features when they occurred in strong syllables. As discussed earlier in this chapter, Derwing and Rossiter (2003) found that a classroom focus on global aspects of pronunciation such as word and sentence stress and intonation proved more beneficial than a focus on segments (i.e. phonemes) for the development of the fluency and comprehensibility of learners' spoken language. (A classroom focus on segments did however substantially reduce the rate of segmental errors.)

More recently, Galante and Thomson (2016) came to a similar conclusion concerning the benefits of instruction on paralinguistic features of communication. In this study, which involved early teenage Brazilian EFL learners at a private language institute in Brazil, the authors investigated the impact on pronunciation learning (and on fluency) of drama-based instruction compared to a traditional communicative approach to instruction. While both approaches dealt with segmental and suprasegmental features, the drama-based approach also included instruction on paralinguistic features such as vocal projection and expressing emotion. Galante and Thomson found a large effect for fluency development from the drama-based instruction compared to the traditional approach. They also found a smaller effect for comprehensibility and no effect for accent from either approach. They conclude that, '(e)xplicit instruction that helps L2 learners gain greater control over global functions of language, including vocal projection, stress, rhythm, and the ability to be easily understood, can be more beneficial than those with an exclusive focus on global accent' (p. 21).

One way to strengthen learners' control over suprasegmental aspects of their pronunciation is to incorporate pronunciation into word learning (cf. Trofimovich & Gatbonton, 2006). In this regard, Murphy (2004) argues that attention needs to be given to word stress in the process of learning a word, especially in English for academic purposes (EAP) contexts, in which systematic learning of academic vocabulary is an important component. He points out that awareness of word-level stress is a central dimension of what it means to know the spoken form of a word (see also Nation, 2013). Murphy proposes a three-digit numerical coding system for developing learners' awareness of word stress, in which the first digit represents the number of syllables in the word, the second the location of the word's primary stressed syllable and, where needed, the third represents the location of a secondary stressed syllable. Learners are encouraged to tap words out, to find the strongest syllable and to code a word accordingly. Using classroom survey data, Murphy found that most of a group of 36 ESL learners at a North American university who had been trained in this approach perceived it as useful and recommended that it be continued.

Finally, an important instructional principle is that any classroom speaking activity can be adapted to include a focus on pronunciation (Kaltenböck & Seidlhofer, 1999). In this way, pronunciation can be a small but consistent focus throughout speaking lessons in addition to whatever dedicated instructional space is devoted to it elsewhere. As Burns and Seidlhofer (2010) express it, 'every lesson involving the spoken language is (also) a pronunciation lesson' (p. 212). But this does not happen automatically. Speaking lessons need to be tailored by thoughtful teachers to include the kinds of pronunciation components relevant to the needs of learners. Such an approach goes some way to addressing the challenge teachers face of needing to address learners' pronunciation needs without compromising opportunities to develop communicative confidence and fluency. Ultimately, the goal of pronunciation teaching is to help learners to make themselves understood. Comprehensibility and intelligibility rather than NS-like pronunciation or accent reduction are widely acknowledged as appropriate goals of pronunciation teaching (Munro & Derwing, 1999; Derwing & Munro, 2015).

Future directions

As noted earlier, pronunciation has tended to be neglected in second language acquisition research on speaking and classroom interaction in favour of a prevailing emphasis on morphosyntactic development, vocabulary learning and fluency. Research on speaking from a TBLT perspective is a case in point. Few studies in this area mention pronunciation, let alone treat it as a variable of interest. In the TBLT literature for teachers, there is also little in the way of advice and resources to guide pronunciation teaching within a task-based curriculum, a notable exception being Kaltenböck and Seidlhofer (1999). Given that English as a foreign language (EFL) teachers cite concerns that learners will practise mistakes as a disincentive for teaching with tasks (e.g. Carless, 2007), this is a gap in need of attention. In a study which offers a useful model for TBLT research, Jenkins (2002) shows how a small corpus of learner–learner conversational data can be analysed to explore the potential for communicative speaking to draw learners' attention to pronunciation issues that impact on the comprehensibility of their spoken English.

Research on the role of corrective feedback (CF) in language learning is another case where pronunciation-focused research is under-represented. And again, given that teachers often appear to rely on CF to address pronunciation issues (e.g. Foote et al., 2016), we need more research on the impact of CF on different aspects of pronunciation development, research conducted in a wider range of contexts/education sectors, with different types of learners and, importantly, with teachers who are themselves second language speakers of English. This research might fruitfully include descriptive studies of teaching practices, learner action, and teacher and learner cognition with respect to pronunciation, balanced alongside experimental studies designed to provide more fine-grained evidence for the effect of particular combinations of instruction and CF on targeted pronunciation features. We especially need research on CF and on pronunciation teaching and learning in primary/ elementary and secondary school EFL contexts that cater for millions of young EFL learners worldwide and yet are under-represented in research.

More research from a pronunciation perspective is also needed on techniques for form-focused instruction, with Hamada's (2016) study on the effect of shadowing on phonemic perception being a good example. Indeed, shadowing is one technique that deserves more attention for its pronunciation learning potential. It is especially in need of research in a wider range of contexts beyond Japan, where most of the current research has been carried out, owing to the widespread popularity of this technique among Japanese EFL teachers.

To conclude, while this chapter has focused on instructional dimensions of the relationship between pronunciation and speaking, there is plenty of evidence that L2 pronunciation is consequential to a raft of social well-being outcomes, especially those concerning work and employment (e.g. Pilott, 2016; Timming, 2016). Not surprisingly, then, just as pronunciation is inextricably linked to issues of social justice, so too does pronunciation instruction require language education professionals to engage with the social, political and ethical issues bound up with accent, with varieties of English and with the implications of reframing English as an international language.

Further reading

Goh, C., & Burns, A. (2012). *Teaching speaking: A holistic approach*. Cambridge: Cambridge University Press. This book provides a general overview of the teaching of speaking within which pronunciation is approached from a discourse perspective. Particularly useful is the authors' outline of how to foster learners' metacognitive awareness with respect to developing the various dimensions of L2 speaking including pronunciation.

Derwing, T. M., & Munro, M. J. (2015). *Pronunciation fundamentals: Evidence-based perspectives for L2 teaching and research*. New York, NY: John Benjamins. This book provides a comprehensive, accessible and practical discussion of research on L2 pronunciation teaching and learning. It provides an extended treatment of many of the topics discussed in this chapter.

Related topics

Pronunciation teaching; new ways of thinking about teaching pronunciation; instructional models in the global context

References

Adams, R. (2007). Do second language learners benefit from interacting with each other? In A. Mackey (Ed.), *Conversational interaction in second language acquisition* (pp. 29–52). New York, NY: Oxford University Press.

Adamson, B. (2006). Fashions in language teaching methodology. In A. Davies & C. Elder (Eds), *The handbook of applied linguistics* (pp. 604–622). Malden, MA: Blackwell.

Aubrey, S. (2015). *Effect of inter-cultural contact on L2 motivation and L2 learning: A process product study*. Unpublished PhD thesis, University of Auckland, Auckland, New Zealand.

Bowen, D. (1972). Contextualizing pronunciation practice in the ESOL classroom. *TESOL Quarterly*, *6*, 83–94.

Brazil, D. (1994). *Pronunciation for advanced learners of English*. Cambridge: Cambridge University Press.

Brazil, D., Coulthard, M., & Johns, C. (Eds). (1980). *Discourse intonation and language teaching.* Harlow: Longman.

Brown, A. (1991). Functional load and the teaching of pronunciation. In A. Brown (Ed.), *Teaching English pronunciation: A book of readings* (pp. 211–224). London: Routledge.

Burns, A., & Seidlhofer. B. (2010). Speaking and pronunciation. In N. Schmitt (Ed.). *An introduction to applied linguistics* (2nd ed., pp. 96–214). London: Hodder Education.

Carless, D. (2007). The suitability of task-based approaches for secondary schools: Perspectives from Hong Kong. *System*, 35, 595–608.

Cauldwell, R. (2013). *Phonology for listening.* Birmingham: Speech in Action.

Cauldwell, R. (2016). *Cool speech* [Online]. Retrieved from www.speechinaction.org/cool-speechhot-listening-fluent-pronunciation.

Celce-Murcia, M. (1987). Teaching pronunciation as communication. In J. Morley (Ed.), *Current perspectives on pronunciation: Practices anchored in theory* (pp. 5–12). Washington, DC: TESOL.

Celce-Murcia, M., Brinton, D. M., & Goodwin, J. M. (2010). *Teaching pronunciation: A reference for teachers of English to speakers of other languages* (2nd ed.). Cambridge: Cambridge University Press.

Couper, G. (2006). The short- and long-term effects of pronunciation instruction. *Prospect*, *21*(1), 46–66.

Couper, G. (2016). Teacher cognition of pronunciation teaching amongst English language teachers in Uruguay. *Journal of Second Language Pronunciation*, *2*(1), 29–55.

Derwing, T. M., Diepenbroek, L., & Foote, J. (2012). How well do general-skills ESL textbooks address pronunciation? *TESL Canada Journal*, *30*(1), 23–44.

Derwing, T. M., & Munro, M. J. (2005). Second language accent and pronunciation teaching: A research-based approach. *TESOL Quarterly*, *39*(3), 379–397.

Derwing, T. M., & Munro, M. J. (2013). The development of L2 oral language skills in two L1 groups: A 7-year study. *Language Learning*, *63*(2), 163–185.

Derwing, T. M., & Munro, M. J. (2015). *Pronunciation fundamentals: Evidence-based perspectives for L2 teaching and research.* New York, NY: John Benjamins.

Derwing, T. M., & Rossiter, M. (2003). The effects of pronunciation instruction on the accuracy, fluency, and complexity of L2 accented speech. *Applied Language Learning*, *13*(1), 1–17.

Derwing, T. M., Thomson, R., & Munro, M. J. (2006). English pronunciation and fluency development in Mandarin and Slavic speakers. *System*, *34*, 183–193.

Ellis, R. (2003). *Task-based language learning and teaching.* Oxford: Oxford University Press.

Ellis, R., Basturkmen, H., & Loewen, S. (2001). 'Learner uptake in communicative ESL lessons'. *Language Learning*, 51, 281–318.

Foote, J. A., Trofimovich, P., Collins, L., & Urzúa, F. S. (2016). Pronunciation teaching practices in communicative second language classes. *The Language Learning Journal*, *44*(2), 181–196.

Galante, A., & Thomson, R. I. (2016). The effectiveness of drama as an instructional approach for the development of second language oral fluency, comprehensibility, and accentedness. *TESOL Quarterly*. doi:10.1002/tesq.290.

Gluszek. A., & Dovidio, J. F. (2010). The way they speak: A social psychological perspective on the stigma of nonnative accents in communication. *Personality and Social Psychology Review*, *14*(2),214–237.

Godwin-Jones, R. (2012). Emerging technologies for language learning. In C. Chapelle, *The encyclopedia of applied linguistics* (pp. 1882–1886). London: Blackwell.

Goh, C., & Burns. A. (2012). *Teaching speaking.* Cambridge: Cambridge University Press.

Hamada, Y. (2016). Shadowing: Who benefits and how? Uncovering a booming EFL teaching technique for listening comprehension. *Language Teaching Research*, *20*(1), 35–42.

Isaacs, T., & Trofimovich, P. (2012). Deconstructing comprehensibility: Identifying the linguistic influences on listeners' L2 comprehensibility ratings. *Studies in Second Language Acquisition*, *34*(3), 475–505.

Jenkins, J. (2002). A sociolinguistically based, empirically researched pronunciation syllabus for English as an international language. *Applied Linguistics*, *23*(1), 83–103.

Kaltenböck, G., & Seidlhofer, B. (1999). Task-based teaching: What's in it for pronunciation? *IATEFL Speak Out!*, 24, 9–15.

Kelly, G. (1969). *25 centuries of language teaching.* Rowley, MA: Newbury House.

Kim, J., & Han, Z. (2007). Recasts in communicative EFL classes: Do teacher intent and learner interpretation overlap?. In A. Mackey (Ed.), *Conversational interaction in second language acquisition: A collection of empirical studies* (pp. 269–297). Oxford: Oxford University Press.

Kim, Y., & McDonough, K. (2008). The effect of interlocutor proficiency on the collaborative dialogue between Korean as a second language learners. *Language Teaching Research, 12*(2), 211–234.

Lasito L., & Storch, N. (2013). Comparing pair and small group interactions on oral tasks. *RELC Journal, 44*(3), 279–302.

Leeser, M. (2004). Learner proficiency and focus on form during collaborative dialogue. *Language Teaching Research, 8*(1), 55–81.

Leitner, G., Hashim, A., & Wolf, H-G. (2016). *Communicating with Asia: The future of English as a global language*. Cambridge: Cambridge University Press.

Lyster, R., Saito, K., & Sato, M. (2013). Oral corrective feedback in second language classrooms. *Language Teaching, 46*, 1–40.

MacIntyre, P. D. (2007). Willingness to communicate in a second language: Understanding the decision to speak as a volitional process. *Modern Language Journal, 66*, 739–758.

Mackey, A. (Ed.) (2007a). *Conversational interaction in second language acquisition*. New York, NY: Oxford University Press.

Mackey, A. (2007b). Introduction. In A. Mackey (Ed.). *Conversational interaction in second language acquisition* (pp. 1–3). New York, NY: Oxford University Press.

Mackey, A., Gass, S., & McDonough, K. (2000). How do learners perceive interactional feedback? *Studies in Second Language Acquisition, 22*(4), 471–497.

McDonough, K., & Sunitham, W. (2009). Collaborative dialogue between Thai EFL learners during self-access computer activities. *TESOL Quarterly, 43*(2), 231–254.

Michel, M., Kuiken, F., & Vedder, I. (2007). The influence of complexity in monologic versus dialogic tasks in Dutch L2. *International Review of Applied Linguistics, 45*, 241–259.

Morley, J. (1994). A multidimensional curriculum design for speech-pronunciation instruction. In J. Morley (Ed.), *Pronunciation pedagogy and theory* (pp. 64–91). Bloomington, IN: TESOL.

Morley, J. (Ed.). (1994). *Pronunciation pedagogy and theory*. Bloomington, IN: TESOL.

Munro, M. J., & Derwing, T. M. (1999). Foreign accent, comprehensibility, and intelligibility in the speech of second language learners. *Language Learning, 49*(1), 285–310.

Munro, J. M., & Derwing, T. M. (2006). The functional load principle in ESL pronunciation instruction: An exploratory study. *System, 34*(4), 520–531.

Murphy, J. (2004). Attending to word-stress while learning new vocabulary. *English for Specific Purposes, 23*(1), 67–83.

Nakahama, Y., Tyler, A., & Van Lier, L. (2001). Negotiation of meaning in conversational and information gap activities: A comparative discourse analysis. *TESOL Quarterly, 35*(3), 377–405.

Nation, I. S. P. (2013). *Learning vocabulary in another language* (2nd ed.). Cambridge: Cambridge University Press.

Nation, I. S. P., & Newton, J. (2009). *Teaching ESL/EFL listening and speaking*. New York, NY: Routledge.

Newton, J. (2013). Incidental vocabulary learning in classroom communication tasks. *Language Teaching Research, 17*(2), 164–187.

Newton, J. (2017). Learning-to-speak and speaking-to-learn: Five categories of learning opportunity. In E. Hinkel (Ed.), *Handbook of research in second language teaching and learning (Volume 3)* (2nd ed.). New York, NY: Routledge.

Newton, J., & Kusmierczyk, E. (2011). Teaching second languages for the workplace. *Annual Review of Applied Linguistics, 31*, 1–19.

Pennington, M., & Richards, J. (1986). Pronunciation revisited. *TESOL Quarterly, 20*(2), 207–225.

Pica, T. (1984). Pronunciation activities with an accent on communication. *English Teaching Forum, 22*, 2–6.

Pickering, L. (2001). The role of tone choice in improving ITA communication in the classroom. *TESOL Quarterly, 35*, 233–255.

Pilott, M. (2016). *Migrant pronunciation: What do employers find acceptable?* Unpublished doctoral thesis, Victoria University of Wellington, New Zealand.

Robinson. P. (2011). Second language task complexity, the cognition hypothesis, language learning and performance. In P. Robinson (Ed.), *Second language task complexity: Researching the cognition hypothesis of language learning and performance* (pp. 3–37). Amsterdam: John Benjamins.

Saito, K. (2013). Re-examining effects of form-focused instruction on L2 pronunciation development: The role of explicit phonetic information. *Studies in Second Language Acquisition, 35*(1), 1–29.

Saito, K., & Lyster, R. (2012). Effects of form-focused instruction and corrective feedback on L2 pronunciation development of /ɹ/ by Japanese learners of English. *Language Learning, 62*(2), 595–633.

Schmidt, R. (2001). Attention. In P. Robinson (Ed.), *Cognition and second language instruction* (pp. 3–32). Cambridge: Cambridge University Press.

Skehan, P. (1998). *A cognitive approach to language learning*. Oxford: Oxford University Press.

Skehan, P. (2009). Modelling second language performance: Integrating complexity, accuracy, fluency, and lexis. *Applied Linguistics, 30*(4), 510–532. doi:10.1093/applin/amp047.

Skehan, P. (Ed.). (2014). *Processing perspectives on task performance*. Amsterdam: John Benjamins.

Swain, M., & Lapkin, S. (1998). Interaction and second language learning: Two adolescent French immersion students working together. *Modern Language Journal, 82*(3), 320–337.

Timming, A. (2016). The effect of foreign accent on employability: A study of the aural dimensions of aesthetic labour in customer-facing and non-customer-facing jobs. *Work, Employment & Society, 31*, 409–428. doi:10.1177/0950017016630260.

Trofimovich, P., & Gatbonton, E. (2006). Repetition and focus on form in processing L2 Spanish words: Implications for pronunciation instruction. *Modern Language Journal, 90*, 519–535.

Vandergrift, L., & Goh, C. (2012). *Teaching and learning second language listening: Metacognition in action*. New York, NY: Routledge.

Zielinski, B. (2007). The listener: No longer the silent partner in reduced intelligibility. *System, 36*, 69–84.

21

Pronunciation and listening

The case for separation

Richard Cauldwell

Close links between listening and pronunciation can be found in theories of perception (Liberman & Mattingly, 1985), in teacher training axioms (e.g. 'if you can say it you can hear it'; 'you need to hear the difference before you can say it'), and in textbook materials ('listen and repeat'). They are also linked in that they are both susceptible to avoidance in discussions of English language teaching (ELT). Research has shown that teachers avoid teaching pronunciation (Breitkreutz, Derwing & Rossiter, 2001; Macdonald, 2002; Murphy, 2014) and when teaching listening they avoid direct encounters with the sound substance of English (Field, 2008), the characteristic acoustic blur of spontaneous speech (Brown, 1990; Cauldwell, 2013). There is a further link in that they have both been referred to as the 'Cinderella' skills of both second language (L2) and foreign language (FL) instruction (Kelly, 1969; Nunan, 2002; Thanasoulas, 2003; Vandergrift 1997).

Although they are closely linked, I shall treat the constructs of pronunciation and listening as separable. Indeed, my position is that they need to have separate goals, language models and classroom activities. Justification for their separation finds support in Celce-Murcia, Brinton and Goodwin's (2010) statement that for listening and pronunciation 'the goals for mastery are different' (p. 370). Celce-Murcia et al.'s (2010) position is that 'our goal as teachers of listening is to help our learners understand *fast, messy, authentic speech*' (p. 370, emphasis added). They caution that there are sharp differences between the language we encourage learners to speak, and that which they have to decode and understand:

> The spoken language our learners need to comprehend is *much more varied and unpredictable* than what they need to produce in order to be intelligible.
>
> (p. 370, emphasis added)

On the one hand, the language model that commonly serves as the basis for L2 pronunciation instruction is stable (much less varied) and predictable. On the other, the language model that needs to serve as a basis for L2 listening instruction should incorporate the wildness, messiness and unpredictability of spontaneous speech. These conflicting instructional requirements for the teaching of pronunciation and listening speak to the need for two separate models of speech, to achieve their different respective goals. This chapter explores the different requirements of L2 pronunciation and L2 listening and argues that their inter-relatedness – long taken for granted – should now be replaced by a productive separation in ELT.

For the purposes of pronunciation and listening instruction, most teachers and materials developers employ a model of English speech we may refer to as the careful speech model (CSM). The CSM is perhaps best typified in audio recordings made for beginning- and intermediate-level ELT course texts but also in many teacher training materials, and sometimes in a specialized speaking style of classroom teachers known as teacher talk (Sinclair & Brazil, 1982). The CSM is often characterized by an over-reliance on the conventions of the written language, and an almost exclusive focus on a pronunciation-centric orientation that values clarity over reality. An unfortunate effect of this over-reliance on phonological clarity is that, throughout the history of ELT, the listening needs of L2 learners have been poorly met (Cauldwell, 2013; Field, 2008). The field's focus on the CSM has set up conditions for L2 listening instruction in which learners are not provided with opportunities to learn how to deal with the speeds, messiness and compressions of normal, everyday speech.

In contrast, and a central purpose of this discussion, is that we need a conceptual separation between pronunciation and listening in terms of L2 instructional goals, language models and classroom activities. In the terms of a metaphor to be described below, we need to add a 'Jungle' dimension (Cauldwell, 2013) to conventional classroom activities (p. 260). To achieve this, we need to construct an alternative model of speech production, the spontaneous speech model (SSM), which can accommodate and embrace the realities of speed, transience and messiness of the sound substance of everyday normal speech. Clues to the nature of what I am calling the SSM model can be found in standard instructional materials, but many of these clues need fuller interpretation and amplification. The chapter ends with a detailed description of a classroom activity designed to familiarize students, and make them comfortable, with the messiness (i.e. lack of clarity) and unruliness of normal everyday speech.

Terminology: not 'pronunciation' but 'sound shapes'

The use of the term 'pronunciation' in discussions of L2 listening is common. Swan (2012, p. 21), for example, writes of 'receptive pronunciation', and Hancock and McDonald (2014, p. 16 and passim) present nine chapters under the title 'Pronunciation for listeners'. From the L2 listening point of view, such employments of the word 'pronunciation' are unfortunate due to very strong connotations of clarity, precision and accuracy, which are reflected in two of the most frequent questions L2 learners ask about pronunciation:

(a) What is the correct pronunciation of this word?

(b) How should I pronounce it?

To these questions, most language teachers readily provide relatively fixed answers, which may be traced back to the CSM. With the term 'pronunciation' thus being so strongly associated with notions of correctness and tidiness, I propose, following Cauldwell (2013) to use the term 'sound shapes' to refer to the wide variety of ways in which individual words can occur in the stream of everyday spontaneous speech. Having adopted this terminology, we can now present two questions tied to L2 listening that are parallel to those offered above in connection with pronunciation:

(a) What different sound shapes of a particular word am I likely to encounter?

(b) How should I prepare myself as an L2 listener to handle such alternative sound shapes?

This chapter answers these L2 listening-specific questions. But, before continuing, there are three preliminary issues that need to be addressed in order to establish a foundation for what is to follow. The first issue concerns the status of the sound substance of English.

Inspection of the written language is the preferred mode

The sound substance of spoken language is – in its normal form as everyday spontaneous speech – invisible, ephemeral, fast-moving and stream-like. This sound substance must be handled both orally (through speaking/pronunciation) and aurally (while listening) by English language learners in order to communicate effectively. However, the ephemeral nature of the sound substance conflicts with long-established traditions in the history of L2 materials development. These traditions demand that the language samples used as the focus for instruction be written – that thus they are visible, static, brick-like and open to close inspection. As a consequence, most language teachers and learners bring to the L2 learning process an assumption that 'words' are what you can see on the page, where they can be inspected for spelling and looked up within reference materials for meaning and pronunciation. Detailed inspection of the graphic substance (i.e. orthographic forms, the written language) is the preferred mode of L2 teaching and learning. As a result, static, visible, brick-like *graphic* shapes of written words and phrases take precedence over and serve to dominate the transient stream-like *sound* shapes of the spoken language. Thus, a major complication when treating listening and pronunciation together is that there is a temptation for teachers to feel that they have dealt with both skills in tandem, when in fact they have only dealt with the spelling and pronunciation of a word. Even if the teacher employs sound files, this complication persists if the audio contains an overabundance of citation forms. Rather, pronunciation and listening are best viewed as two identifiably separate ways of handling the sound substance of language. From this perspective, pronunciation may be defined as the encoding (production) of meanings in fluent streams of intelligible speech, while L2 listening involves the decoding (interpretation) of these fluent streams of speech by L2 listeners.

The careful speech model

The careful speech model (CSM) consists of the citation forms of words, rules for variations in pronunciation both within and across word boundaries (e.g. assimilation, elision, epenthesis, linking, palatalization), and rules about prosodic shapes when they occur in sentences (e.g. stress-timing, question intonation, placement of nuclear stress).

As such, the CSM is tidy, rule-governed and optimized for traditional models of English language instruction in that its rules are amenable to being presented in detail and inspected in writing. Additionally, CSM rules illustrate for learners the conventional units most familiar to teachers and learners (i.e. printed words, phrases and sentences). A major force that serves to shape, define and in some ways limit the CSM is the requirement to teach connections between pronunciation and spelling. Thus Windsor-Lewis (2009) argues that, if the editor or author of a pronunciation dictionary has to choose between two sound shapes,

There can surely be little argument that, if there are two fully common variants in existence, recommending the one which is not antagonistic to the spelling is beneficial to the learner.

(p. 239)

Windsor-Lewis articulates what seems to be a very reasonable principle. It favours helping learners to master relationships between spelling (orthographic forms) and pronunciation. But there is another viable perspective that pronunciation-centred specialists such as Windsor-Lewis may be failing to acknowledge. If there are 'two fully common variants' (i.e. two alternative soundshapes), the one that merits more instructional attention is the one that L2 learners are most likely to hear (based on frequency of occurrence) and/or the one most likely to present perceptual difficulties to L2 listeners (based on relative degree of perceptual challenge). Further, the standpoint adopted in this chapter is, since all words have many more than merely two sound shapes, at least some of these alternative pronunciations need to be featured as integral parts of L2 listening instruction.

A theme consistent in the work of contemporary specialists in L2 listening (e.g. Brazil, 1994, 1997; Cauldwell, 2013; Field, 2008) is that few if any of the analytic rules of the CSM are consistent with everyday, normal speech phenomena. Such CSM analyses may more accurately be classified as register-specific hypotheses, many of which (e.g. stress-timing, question intonation, the relationship between attitude and intonation) simply do not hold true for spontaneous, everyday, normal speech production. Since the CSM regularly fails to represent the acoustic reality of everyday speech, it is therefore both inadequate and inappropriate for teaching L2 listening. Currently, however, the CSM dominates the field of ELT, as revealed in the pages of teacher training handbooks and other resource materials, which either overtly or covertly tend to deprecate (e.g. 'this only happens in fast casual speech') the authentic speech phenomena that should be central to L2 listening instruction. The next section introduces a third preliminary issue, a metaphor that will help facilitate subsequent discussion.

The Greenhouse, the Garden, and the Jungle

It is useful to think of the sound substance of speech as residing along a continuum consisting of three domains: the Greenhouse, the Garden, and the Jungle. The *Greenhouse* is the domain of CSM citation forms where individual words – like individual plants in their separate pots – are carefully isolated from other words, preceded and followed by a pause, and every syllable and segment is carefully attended to.

The *Garden* is the domain of connected speech rules – of linking, elision, stress-timing, question intonation – where words may come into relatively genteel contact with each other, in a pleasing patterned way similar to an orderly arrangement of a well-tended, mature flowerbed. There is contact between flowers (just as there is acoustic contact between spoken words), although the nature of the contact is tidy, controlled, predictable and patterned.

The *Jungle*, in contrast, is the domain of normal spontaneous speech, where just about anything can happen at any time, where the sound substance of speech may be characterized as unpatterned, unruly, often unpredictable, and messy. In the Jungle of spontaneous speech, words are transformed into new, unfamiliar and unanticipated sound shapes. The clean regularities we may find in the Greenhouse and even in the Garden occur only rarely in the Jungle, where such regularities would require the coincidental alignment of particular language features. The Jungle is the domain of 'fast messy authentic speech' (Celce-Murcia et al., 2010), the understanding of which is one of the primary goals of L2 listening instruction (p. 370).

A crucial point is this: the traditional and widely influential CSM includes both the Greenhouse and the Garden but it largely excludes consideration of the Jungle. This exclusion is problematic in itself, but it is doubly so because CSM rules that may usefully serve as a basis for pronunciation instruction are treated (in the absence of an SSM) as an equally relevant basis for L2 listening instruction. It is unfortunate that many if not most contemporary approaches to ELT are premised on the assumption that the CSM encompasses all facets of the botanic continuum introduced in this discussion, including the Jungle. The fact is that the CSM is very limited in scope and its limitations are insufficiently acknowledged in ELT. This is a blind spot in our profession that complicates the lives of English language learners because once they begin to participate in settings of spontaneous speech, they are entering into the Jungle, a communicative arena of verbal interaction for which the vast majority of learners have been very poorly prepared.

Our traditional practice – our blind spot – has been to promote a model of speech, well suited for pronunciation work, which rarely encroaches on the Jungle. The CSM promotes a view of speech – genteel, predictable, Garden-like – which continues to serve as an obstacle to effective L2 listening. Students learn ideal sound shapes for words (citation forms) and the tidy rules for their combination (connected speech rules) but do not learn the wide range of sound shapes that a word can have when embedded within normal streams of speech.

Attempts to accommodate the messiness of the SSM within the confines of the CSM can be found in lists of 'weak forms' (e.g. Cruttenden, 2014, pp. 273–277), but such lists are far from comprehensive. Lists of weak forms are typically restricted to 'the most common' words of the language (ibid, p. 273). Unfortunately, such lists are often interpreted by teachers and materials developers as being something close to comprehensive. A consequence is that lists of this kind have the effect of deafening ELT practitioners to the much larger set of alternative pronunciations for particular words, and for the much larger set (literally all words) that have multiple sound shapes, even within the spontaneous speech of a single speaker. As we will see below, words take on different sound shapes according to their position in the variety of patterns of speech unit that are found in spontaneous speech. (Although this chapter employs the term 'speech units', alternative terms for the same construct include breath groups, thought groups, intonation units, tone units, pause groups etc.). These sound shapes vary according to speed, volume, whether the words are prominent or not and whether or not they coincide with tone locations.

Additionally, traditional conceptions of the CSM assume that there is a one-to-one relationship between prosodic/intonational shape and sentence types (e.g. yes/no questions have rising intonation; high fall means surprise). But in the Jungle of the SSM there is a many-to-many relationship between prosodic shapes and sentence types, which means that any question can have a wide range of intonation contours; any intonation contour can go with a wide range of different emotions. Thus, when teachers overlook the Jungle in the teaching of L2 listening, they are neglecting what should be the central component of the listening classroom, i.e. the nature of the sound substance of normal everyday speech.

Instead of addressing the sound substance in anything approaching a systematic way, most L2 listening lessons typically devote considerable time and energy to admittedly useful activities focused on 'top-down' contextual factors, and the promotion of (useful) communicative strategies. Many specialists recommend that these L2 listening strategies should be employed in the absence of understanding, even though lack of understanding is often caused by an inability to decode. But such inabilities are commonly caused by a lack of knowledge of the sound substance of the spoken language, and a lack of skill training in how to handle it. For well over two decades, strategy training and practice have dominated the L2 listening classroom (e.g. Mendelsohn, 1994), and the nature of the sound substance typically remains ignored – not least because of dubious teacher training mantras such as 'Native listeners do not listen for every word when seeking to understand speech, therefore L2 learner listeners should not listen for every word'.

Listening question 1 – sound shapes in squeeze zones

Listening question 1 is 'What different sound shapes of a particular word am I likely to encounter?' You may feel that no learner is likely to pose a question quite this formally. But here's how one learner, Ying, actually formulated the question on her own as reported by Goh (1997):

> I believe I need to learn what the word sounds like when it is used in the sentence. Because sometimes when a familiar word is used in a sentence, I couldn't catch it. Maybe it changes somewhere when it is used in a sentence.

> (p. 366)

Ying refers to the problem of hearing a word in a sentence, a word that she previously believed that she knew, but finds she cannot 'catch it' when it occurs in a spoken sentence. This is what Cauldwell (2013) refers to as 'Ying's dilemma' (p. 15). The dilemma is that Ying believes herself to be very familiar with the word in question, but cannot recognize it when it occurs in spontaneous speech. She also refers to the notion of a 'sentence' – a concept relevant to discussions of the written language that may be preventing her from engaging more deeply with the realities of the spoken language. These are issues sorely in need of instructional attention.

In everyday spontaneous speech words occur in speech units (variously referred to as breath groups, thought groups, tone units etc.), which may be characterized as alternating, multi-word, rhythmic trickles and bursts of sound substance. The sound substance both consists of and contains the sound shapes of words, along with the sound shapes of more extraneous 'drafting phenomena' such as a speaker's use of conversational fillers (e.g. *uh, you know, how shall I put it, and that kind of thing*) (Cauldwell, 2013, p. 81ff). These speech units vary in speed dramatically, to an extent generally underestimated and underreported in ELT literatures and teaching resources. Speech units are also transient and invisible and, being so, they pass by very quickly. Further, they are inaccessible to close inspection. Within the sound substance of speech units, words occur in an incredible variety of different acoustic shapes (i.e. sound shapes), which the CSM accounts for only inadequately. As illustrated in Table 21.1, words are particularly vulnerable to a dramatic transformation of sound shape when they occur prior to, and between, prominences.

Table 21.1 displays a double prominence speech unit (Cauldwell, 2013, p. 113) in which the prominent syllables occur in columns 4 and 2 and non-prominent syllables occur in columns 5, 3 and 1. Note that the columns are numbered from right to left. The syllables that occur before prominences (e.g. column 5) and between prominences (e.g. column 3) are called squeeze zones because, relative to the prominent syllables located in the even numbered columns, their enunciations are compressed and indistinct.

Table 21.1 Double prominence speech unit

5	4	3	2	1
this is	**ONE**	I'm going to be looking at in slightly more	**DE**	tail in fact

This table is available as Extract 8.13 from the www.speechinaction.com website – *Phonology for Listening* downloads. The columns are numbered from right to left for reasons explained in Cauldwell (2013, p. 26).

This particular speech unit was produced within the context of an academic seminar by a British man named Geoff at 9.3 syllables per second (approximately 400 words per minute). Such a rate of speech is extremely fast. Analysing Geoff's production within this five-part structure signals that columns 5 and 3 are compressed squeeze zones in which words take on a great variety of Jungle soundshapes.

In contrast to the squeeze zones, there are two prominent syllables in the even numbered columns (4 and 2): the single-syllable word <ONE> and the first syllable of the word <DEtail>. All of the remaining syllables of columns 5, 3 and 1 are non-prominent. What follows is a description of some of the features of the soundshapes in the squeeze zone of column 3, a squeeze zone bounded by the prominent syllables Geoff employed:

- *I'm* has a final consonant |ŋ|, thus |aɪŋ|
- *going* loses its final syllable, thus |gəʊ|
- *to* and *be* are inaudible in the recording
- *looking* loses |k| and . . .
- the two vowels of *looking* merge into |ʊ|, thus we get monosyllabic |lʊŋ|
- *at* acquires |j| thus |jæt|
- the vowel of *more* is close to |u| thus |mu| – *moo*

These alternative soundshapes demonstrate some of the rather extreme results that can occur when words are squeezed, between two prominences, at the speed of 9.3 syllables per second (sps) or approximately 430 words per minute (wpm).

Less extreme, and perhaps more representative is the following sequence of speech units, from a British (Estuary English) speaker named Dan:

```
01 || and I just STARTed ||
02 || and my VOICE just went [creak] ||
03 || and NOTHing came OUT ||
04 || and Everyone just WENT ||
05 || [SIGH] ||
06 || oh POOR YOU ||
07 || and then THAT was THAT ||
08 || and WE ||
08 || didn't get THROUGH ||
```

The sound file of this extract is readily accessible on the Internet at www.speechinaction.com as Cauldwell's (2013) extract 8.2. Its transcription follows the conventions of discourse intonation (Brazil, 1997), as adapted by Cauldwell, in which upper-case letters denote prominent syllables and lower-case letters denote non-prominent syllables.

In the extract presented above, the word <and> occurs at the beginning of six of the eight speech units, before the first prominences, and are thus very susceptible to being squeezed into different sound shapes, as indeed they are. The soundshapes of <and> that occur her can be represented in folk spellings as <an>, , <im>, <on>, <an> and <um>. The sound shape <an> occurs twice, but there are four other sound shapes (, <im>, <on>, <um>) that are left unmentioned in Cruttenden's (2014) canonic set of six associated weak forms (see pp. 273–275). So, a more complete answer to question 1's 'What different sound shapes of a particular word am I likely to encounter?' is 'Many different sound shapes for virtually every word you might hear'.

Finding the SSM – adding the Jungle dimension

As represented in the ELT literature, the rules of connected speech are firmly rooted in the Garden – they are part of the CSM. Such rules of connected speech are useful for teaching pronunciation because they promote the production of intelligible, clear speech. However, such rules are much less applicable, and frequently do not apply at all, within the Jungle. When teaching L2 listening, we can compensate for at least some of the missing elements by adding a Jungle dimension to discussions and illustrations of the rules of the CSM. By way of illustration, we will look at some examples of how this can be accomplished with what are commonly referred to as linking rules. Table 21.2, adapted from Celce-Murcia et al. (2010, p. 172), shows the linking rule, which explains the phonological conditions under which word-final /t/ and /d/ deletions/elisions occur. The top row provides the target rule, and the second and third rows depict examples consisting of adjective–noun pairs.

Table 21.2 Linking rules derived from Celce-Murcia et al.

Deletion of /t, d/	No deletion before /h, y, w, r/	Resyllabification
East side	East Hill	Eas/t-end
Old boyfriend	Old rags	Ol/d-age

Source: Adapted from Celce-Murcia et al. (2010, p. 172)

Column 1 signals that before certain (but not all) consonants, the /t/ of 'east' will be deleted; column 2 signals that there will be no deletion in front of the four consonants listed at the top of the column; and column 3 shows that, in front of vowels, the /t/ and /d/ will not be deleted/elided, but will instead will be shifted over (i.e. across their respective word boundaries) and attach themselves to the following syllable.

This is a typical presentation of a CSM rule for purposes of teaching pronunciation. It is conveyed in writing, it focuses on the genteel contact between the phonological 'edges' of two words, it can be inspected at leisure, and it can be vocalized slowly by teachers and learners. Such demonstrations serve a useful purpose in leading teacher trainees and L2 learners along a path from the Greenhouse to the Garden. But it is a path that never makes it into the Jungle of L2 listening instruction. By way of contrast, an example of making our way into the Jungle is depicted in Table 21.3 – itself derived from Table 21.2. Column 3 presents alternatives for each row in the form of the Jungle forms 'eassend' and 'ol'age'. Such a presentation combines the pedagogical benefits of Garden illustrations with some of the sound substance realities of the Jungle.

Table 21.3 Adding the Jungle dimension to linking rules

	Greenhouse	Garden	Jungle
1	east end	eas/t-end	eassend
2	old age	ol/d-age	ol'age

Note the considerable differences between the sound shapes of the words depicted in Table 21.2's resyllabification column and those of Table 21.3's Jungle column.

As we will see in what follows, tables such as these can be used in both teacher training and classroom activities to present words in the three domains of the Greenhouse, the Garden and the Jungle. The format illustrated in Table 21.3 is not intended to be comprehensive; it is just one way in which depictions of different sound shapes might be accomplished. A point worth emphasizing is that, within the domain of the Jungle, the traditional rules of linking (as featured in most pronunciation-centred classroom textbooks, instructional resource materials and teacher training programmes) may not be all that useful for purposes of L2 listening instruction. This is a gap in existing resources better addressed through discussion of the SSM.

Finding the spontaneous speech model (SSM) – extremes of speed

Owing to the continuing tenacity of the CSM, most ELT specialists and classroom teachers underestimate both typical speaking speeds of native English speakers (NESs) and the relationship between speed of speech and speaking style. Cauldwell (2013) surveyed the research literature on NES speed of speech in order to derive a set of benchmarks about what constitutes 'slow', 'average' and 'fast' speech. Table 21.4 summarizes these findings. The speaking speeds are displayed in both words per minute and syllables per second.

Table 21.4 Average speaking speeds in words per minute and syllables per second

	Slow	Average	Fast
Words per minute (wpm)	90	180	240
Syllables per second (sps)	2.0	4.0	5.3

Each column provides a notional centre of the three different speeds, 'slow', 'average' and 'fast'. Thus the numeric figures for slow speech (90 wpm/2.0 sps) denote the centre of what are a spread of speeds, which might be located along a continuum of 'extremely slow' through 'slow-ish' to 'slow to average'. Of course, what counts as 'slow' will vary from person to person, and with the register/speaking style, and so these numeric values should be interpreted flexibly. Another important consideration is that the values one gets for speed of speech will depend very much on the size of the units of analysis. If you measure speeds of speech units, which typically have durations of two seconds or less, one gets a great variety of speeds, including extreme variations in neighbouring units. On the other hand, if you measure larger units of a minute in length these extremes tend to be ironed out.

For the purposes of constructing the SSM, it is necessary to account for the extremes and to prioritize a finer-grained speech unit analysis. Almost all speech styles contain brief bursts of fast speech that go well beyond the 240 wpm/5.3 sps listed in Table 21.4. Below is an eight-second extract spoken by Jess, from New Mexico, USA. It consists of 10 speech units – including a 'mmHMM' from Jess's interlocutor in unit 05. Our focus is the speed of each unit, which is given in syllables per second at the end of each line.

```
01 || UM || 1.9
02 || FOR || 1.7
03 || aBOUT || 2.6
04 || two YEARS || 2.9
05 || mmHMM || 7.2
06 || and then they FInally bought a BIG house || 7.5
07 || a BIgger house for US || 6.5
08 || to be Able to LIVE in || 8.8
09 || so we MOVED || 4.6
10 || for THAT REAson || 7.6
```

The average speed for the eight seconds of these 10 units is 4.8 sps, which is 'average to fast' according to Table 21.4. However, there are also slow units (01–04: speeds between 1.7 and 2.9 sps) followed by extremely fast units (06–08: speeds between 6.5 and 8.8 sps) featured in the extract. To help learners decode spontaneous speech, we need to prepare them for such intermittent short bursts of extreme speeds.

However, Jungle speeds already encroach on the scripted speech of ELT instructional materials. In the speech unit below, from Brazil (1994), the speech unit goes at 5.0 sps/300 wpm, but the three words <where there were> are realized at over twice that speed, at a Jungle speaking rate of 12 sps/720 wpm.

```
01 || where there were STREET LIGHTS || 5.0
```

These kinds of sudden bursts of speed cause real perceptual difficulties for learners (i.e. Ying's dilemma) even when the words captured in the speech sample are 'known' by the listener. They also demonstrate that momentary flashes of Jungle phenomena can intrude even within CSM/Garden conditions. Thus, another feature of the Jungle is that speeds of speech (when measured moment by moment) are considerably more extreme than typically depicted in the CSM.

Finding the SSM – it's out there

Many of our standard textbooks about speech contain information about the SSM, but we are warned to downplay such information, because the author's focus tends to be pronunciation. Cruttenden (2014), the eighth edition of a classic text titled *Gimson's Pronunciation of English* is a clear example. It aims to describe a slow but casual style of speech:

> The style generally described in this book is slow but casual, i.e. it is not rapid and it is not careful.

> (p. 305)

This statement seems to position the essence of Cruttenden's presentation somewhere between the Garden ('slow') and the Jungle ('casual', 'not careful'). But the clause 'it is not rapid' is the key here, particularly since Cruttenden (2014) goes on to explain that 'a rapid style will produce many more changes from citation forms than are described [in this book]' (p. 305). This latter statement makes it clear that – generally – Jungle phenomena are excluded from the author's consideration. So, from our point of view, this is a book centred on Garden rules of speech.

Although Cruttenden mentions Jungle phenomena occasionally, when he does they are usually accompanied by the word 'rapid' (e.g. p. 333). When 'rapid' is employed as a qualifier in this way, it is used to remove Jungle phenomena from central consideration, and to imply that we need not bother with them because they are rare. The following is a fairly typical example from Cruttenden (2014):

> there are some <u>uncommon</u> reduced forms which are heard <u>only in rapid speech</u>. . . . and <u>these should not be imitated by foreign learners</u>. The use of |jə| or |mə| in such phrases as *your mother*, *my father* will sound slangy and, if employed inappropriately by a learner, could appear comically incongruous.
>
> (p. 333, emphasis added)

The key words in this quotation are underlined: two of them are statements of frequency ('uncommmon' and 'only in') and the other is a piece of advice ('these should not. . .').

Once we add the Jungle perspective to our considerations, and the fact that we are seeking to assemble an SSM, statements of frequency such as 'uncommon' and 'only' should be taken to mean 'can happen at any time in the Jungle' and 'very likely to happen in normal speech', respectively. In other words, such statements of frequency and of restriction are obstacles to more effective L2 listening instruction that the pronunciation-centric CSM perspective inflicts on conceptions of ELT. Cruttenden also advises that 'these [Jungle phenomena] should not be imitated by foreign learners'. The orientation towards pronunciation (in contrast to L2 listening instruction) is apparent in this advice. In our terms, Cruttenden's advice needs to be reinterpreted to mean something along the lines of 'these are not appropriate for the goal of pronunciation instruction (in contrast to the goals of listening instruction), but they are essential to master *when the L2 learner's purpose is to learn to perceive and understand*'.

The good news is that there is increasing evidence that L2 teachers and materials developers are becoming more observant of, and open to using Jungle phenomena. In J. D. Brown's (2012) edited ELT classroom activity recipe collection, the contributors are largely content to stay within the CSM but there are several instances in which they present some intriguing Jungle forms. In one of the editor's own contributions (pp. 205–207), Brown presents three possible sound shapes for the phrase <he gave me> that are well aligned with the botanic metaphor. James Cassidy (ibid. p. 94) provides a Garden illustration along with two Jungle forms for the phrase <will have been>. Arthur Nakano (ibid.,

Table 21.5 Illustrations of the SSM in Brown (2012)

	Greenhouse	Garden	Jungle
1	higevmi	higebmi	higemi
2	wɔləvbɛn	ələvbɛn	ələbn̩
3	dɪ ju	dɪdʒu	dʒə

p. 248) gives Greenhouse, Garden and Jungle forms for the very high frequency phrase <did you>.

Thus, some information about the Jungle and components of the SSM can be found in contemporary teacher training/resource textbooks, though this is an area of L2 instruction that needs to be more fully embraced by a larger number of classroom teachers, teacher educators, researchers and materials developers.

Finding the SSM – tones and meaning – stress-timing

Up to this point we have looked at the sound shapes of single words and groups of words. But the CSM also includes rules about the prosodic shape of longer stretches of speech, such as statement intonation, question intonation and stress-timing.

Statements and questions

It is commonly asserted in ELT circles, and in related instructional materials, that statements in English have falling intonation, and questions have rising intonation. But, interestingly, major authors of teacher training books disagree. Wells (2006) begins his chapter on the relationship between sentence type and tone:

> In English . . . statements may have a fall – but they may also have a non-falling tone. . . . In general there is no simple predictable relationship between sentence type and tone choice.
>
> (p. 15)

This seems to be a direct rebuttal of the CSM view of statement and question (cf. also Cruttenden, 2014, p. 335). However, Wells mitigates the impact of his rebuttal by inserting an escape clause that posits the existence of a 'default tone', as follows: 'Nevertheless, it is useful to apply the notion of a *default* tone (=unmarked tone, neutral tone) for each sentence type' (p. 335; emphasis in original). This appeal to a default tone allows us to continue believing that the CSM level of analysis is reliable (i.e. true), and that we have the academic support of a specialist in English phonology for believing so. Having invoked the notion of a 'default' tone, Wells feels that he has to defend it, and does so in a footnote, 76 pages later:

> It is not necessarily the case that the default tones, as described here, are statistically the most frequent. Nevertheless, it is at the very least pedagogically useful to assume that there are default tones.
>
> (p. 91)

Here again we witness a sidestepping of a fuller engagement with the realities of spontaneous speech of English since Wells seems to be admitting that there is no statistical evidence to justify the notion of default tones. It is also noteworthy that while doing so Wells invokes the notion of pedagogic usefulness. That is, Wells is proposing that the analytic fiction he provides is useful in the L2 classroom for promoting clear, intelligible pronunciation. But we need to recognize that this pronunciation-centric view of ELT interferes with more realistic depictions of both the SSM in general and Jungle phenomena in particular. Considerably more realistic analyses and characterizations of the realities of spontaneous speech of English will be required for the purpose of more effective L2 listening instruction.

Stress-timing

Another widely accepted foundation of the CSM is that English rhythm is stress-timed, as opposed to languages such as French, which are said to be syllable-timed. But research by Dauer (1983) and Roach (1982) documented decades ago that the stress-timed character-ization of spoken English is not much more than another analytic fiction (Cauldwell, 2002). It is a long-discredited belief, but one that is very difficult to dislodge because it has come to mean something else in ELT (e.g. Barrera-Pardo, 2008). Stress-timing has come to serve as a short-hand way of referring to rhythmic differences between languages. Part of the reason for the continued belief in stress-timing is that occasionally spontaneous speech contains a triple prominence unit such as the following:

|| a a CERtain proPORtion of THAT || 5.2

This speech unit can be heard as stress-timed, because the three prominences (CER-, -POR-, THAT) may be heard as bounding two equal intervals of time each containing pairs of syllables <-tain pro-> and <-tion of->. But each interval contains two syllables, and therefore one could just as easily conclude even from this seemingly convincing example of stress-timing that such a perception may be traced to the equal number of non-prominent syllables, and that English, therefore, is syllable-timed.

A challenge to the widespread belief in the stress-timed nature of spoken English is that, in the Jungle, instances of triple prominence speech units are very rare. By way of illustration, the one cited above occurs at the end of the following extract, in which the speed varies from slow to fast (2.4 sps to 5.9 sps). There are only two triple prominence speech units: unit 11, already presented above, and unit 08, which does not have equal numbers of syllables between the prominences. Rather, the intervals between the prominences contain one and three syllables respectively – <-ty> and <-venty five> – , and the unit therefore does not sound 'stress-timed' at all.

```
01 || it's PRObably || 4.1
02 || i MEAN || 4.1
03 || MILEagewise || 2.4
04 ||. . .square mile . . . || 5.2
05 ||. . .i mean . . . || 3.6
06 || it's PRObaBLY || 4.4
07 || the COUNty is like maybe || 3.9
08 || FIFty SEventy five MILES wide || 3.9
09 || AND || 2.4
10 || the CIty is ONly || 5.9 [pause]
11 || a a CERtain proPORtion of THAT || 5.2
```

In total, there are five single prominence units, two incomplete speech units (04 and 05) and two double prominence units and none of them is sufficiently patterned to sound stress-timed. All of these features make the extract – which is entirely characteristic of NES spontaneous speech – anything but timed. In sum, the SSM needs to embrace the rhythmic complexity of the Jungle, and resist the temptation to regard it, or refer to it, as 'stress-timed'.

Listening question 2 – vocal gymnastics

Listening question 2 was 'How should I prepare myself as an L2 listener to handle such alternative sound shapes?' A relevant answer to this question at conceptual and curriculum development levels will lead classroom teachers to treat pronunciation and listening as separate goals requiring separate models of spoken English. With respect to classroom teaching, it is necessary to conceive of pronunciation activities serving a listening goal. To avoid confusion we will refer to such activities as vocal gymnastic exercises. These exercises cover the full range of sound shapes along a continuum from the CSM/Greenhouse to the SSM/Jungle, and will involve imitating and producing the messiness and lack of clarity of the Jungle. To help in the conceptual task of keeping the notions of 'pronunciation' and 'vocal gymnastics' separate, it will be useful to remind ourselves of the distinction between *classroom activities* and *goals of learning*.

A classroom activity is an observable behaviour – what we might call 'a doing' – so that an observer sitting at the back of a classroom could say 'they are doing a reading activity' or 'they are doing a listening activity'. A reading *activity* involves students attending to a piece of writing while a listening activity involves their attending to audio inputs of sound substance – typically from teacher talk or from an audio or video recording. In contrast, a *goal* is a purpose for learning – a learning target that students strive towards. A goal is what the students are referring to when they say things such as, 'I want to improve my listening'. This difference between a listening activity and a listening goal is depicted concisely by Wilson (2008, p. 135) when he distinguishes between 'the listening *lesson*' and 'listening *in* the lesson'.

In principle, any activity may serve any goal as there is no fixed relationship between the two constructs. For example, it is common for a reading activity to serve as a basis for the goal of writing a particular type of text (e.g. a job application, a short-answer essay exam). Therefore it may be that the activity a classroom observer witnesses ('they are doing reading') may be in pursuit of a goal tied to another skill – 'they are reading the transcript of a recording in order to improve their listening'. In the case of vocal gymnastics, the teacher's and learners' classroom behaviours may seem to an uninformed observer to have a pronunciation goal, whereas teachers and learners are working towards a listening goal.

Vocal gymnastics – an example

Vocal gymnastic exercises are designed to lead learners along a path that starts at the Greenhouse, continues through the Garden and enters the Jungle. While traversing this path, the goal is to support L2 students as they work to become increasingly familiar and comfortable with everyday spontaneous speech. The exercises described below involve savouring and handling the messiness and unruliness of spontaneous speech in order to help L2 students learn to listen spontaneous speech.

Savouring the sound substance

Here is an example of a simple vocal gymnastic activity. It involves placing three pictures representing the three parts of the botanic metaphor – the Greenhouse, the Garden and the Jungle – at the front of the class, and the teacher going through a series of 'listen-and-repeat' drills as exemplified in Table 21.6.

Table 21.6 Using <Did you enjoy . . .> to go from the
Greenhouse to the Garden to the Jungle

Greenhouse	Garden	Jungle
did you enjoy	dijew wenjoy	dinjoy
	did you enJOY your TIME there			

An essential point both to recognize and to discuss with students is that the goal of the lesson is to enhance their L2 listening abilities. Once the Greenhouse, Garden, and Jungle metaphors have been successfully introduced, the teacher stands in front of the Greenhouse picture and says each of the six words separately and clearly (i.e. DID || YOU || enJOY || YOUR || TIME || THERE). It helpful to do this with exaggerated facial expressions that convey a visual sense of relishing and savouring the sounds and words being produced. The idea is to do so as if you were experiencing the enjoyment savouring some particularly tasty foods (e.g. combining your facial expressions and theatrical abilities to persuade a dubious child that mouthfuls of broccoli are especially delicious!).

The next stage is for the teacher to position herself in front of the picture of the Garden while producing an exaggerated blending of the words together. For example, the word group <did you enjoy> may be repeated several times, speeding it up slightly each time. While doing so, the idea is for the teacher to continue to maintain, as well as s/he can, a set of facial expressions that conveys intense enjoyment of the words and phrases being savoured as part of the process. The next step is to involve everyone in the room in the process by getting them to repeat the word group along with their teacher, while the teacher gently but firmly encourages all to join in. Eventually, these processes are repeated with the full speech unit, while continuing to gradually speed things up:

|| dijewwenJOY your TIME there ||

Lastly, the teacher moves in front of the picture of the Jungle and, again, repeats the process. The teacher asks everyone to listen and then repeat the phrase <did you enjoy>, which by now is likely to have become something more like <din joy>, and eventually expands the challenge by asking everyone to attempt the full speech unit at a gradually increasing tempo. In essence, the instructional process of 'savouring' starts at an unnaturally slow tempo and shifts to a moderate speed, and the teacher gradually speeds things up until everyone in the room is saying the speech unit as fast as they possibly can. A related challenge is for everyone to try to maintain facial expressions of savouring/relishing – though this may be difficult to accomplish once the tempo really takes off (a point worth sharing with the class).

Following the teacher-led phase of the lesson as outlined above, the next step is to get learners to practise in pairs what the whole class has been practising under the direct leadership of the teacher. Once reconfigured into pairs, Student A begins by saying the word <Greenhouse> to prompt Student B who should begin saying the individual words slowly and clearly, in citation form, several times. While attending to Student B's pronunciations, Student A's role is to work to ensure that there are many repetitions ('say it again') and monitors for signs of relishing ('enjoy it!'). Then Student A, says <Garden> and Student B performs the exaggerated linking version of the language sample (e.g. <dijew wenjoy>). Student A continues to work to ensure that there are many repetitions and also monitors for both speed ('now faster') and relishing ('you should be savouring this!'). On the third round, Student A says <Jungle> and Student B begins to produce the fastest, messiest versions possible (e.g. <dinjoy>), while Student A continues to monitor for speed ('faster! As fast as you can!') and facial expressions ('enjoy yourself!'). Eventually, the students switch roles.

Following the pair work phase, the teacher solicits student feedback on the procedures introduced thus far. Typically, students voice comments such as 'I cannot do obvious facial gestures when I am speaking fast'. The teacher then tries to elicit from the class what they believe has happened to the first three syllables of phrase <Did you enjoy your time there> as they moved from the Garden to the Jungle. For example, in the Jungle the three syllables <Did you en-> are likely to have coalesced into the single-syllable <din> losing the final |d| of the word <did> in the process. Also, the personal pronoun <you> is likely to have disappeared entirely, along with the initial mid-front-lax vowel of the word <enjoy>. An essential principle to convey before completing the activity is to remind learners that the purpose of savouring fast-speech (i.e. compressed) forms of words and phrases is to help them become familiar and comfortable with Jungle characteristics of the sound substance of English, explicitly for the purpose of improving their L2 listening abilities.

Activities such as 'savouring' help answer listening question 2, and help the learners internalize the feel of (a) the different sound shapes words may have, (b) the rhythmic groups that contain such words and (c) the variations and extreme speeds of spontaneous speech.

Conclusion – the need for separation

Pronunciation and listening need to be thought of as separate skills that have different goals, require different models of speech and need carefully differentiated classroom activities. Currently, the pronunciation-centric view (i.e. the careful speech model – CSM) dominates the field, and it does so because it dovetails with the conventional view that ELT instructional practices need to be grounded in the written language. The CSM has many useful features. It contains a long-established set of conventions that materials developers, teacher educators and language teachers have turned into rules and activities that are teachable, learnable and testable, and which can be relatively easily explained using a mixture of the written language and phonetic symbols. But the dominant role of the CSM also carries the disadvantage of not allowing conceptual space for a model of speech that is more appropriate for handling the reality of everyday spontaneous speech, and for informing the teaching of listening (i.e. the spontaneous speech model – SSM).

The CSM persists despite the fact that ELT materials increasingly feature recordings of authentic speech and more and more teachers introduce L2 learners to authentic speech samples through the Internet (e.g. TEDTalks, Three Minute Thesis) and other multimedia sources. The availability of such resources and the more authentic speech styles they contain should serve the function of challenging the status of the CSM as an instructional norm, because the rules of the CSM are inadequate to cope with the realities of spontaneous speech. But the CSM is so embedded in teacher training and in instructional materials that it is difficult for the field to take the necessary leap of faith that might lead to long-overdue conceptual changes. These changes do not require abandoning the CSM. It simply means recognizing its limitations and seeking to compensate for them by allowing conceptual space for the spontaneous speech model (SSM). By conceptual space, I mean that it should receive attention (e.g. as an instructional module) in applied linguistics and TESL/TESOL degree courses, in teacher training courses and manuals, and in ESL classroom instructional materials.

In some ways, the SSM is already available. Phoneticians and phonologists have documented that the realities of spontaneous speech are considerably wilder and messier (e.g. Brown, 1990; Lass, 1984; Cauldwell, 2013) than is typically reflected in ESL classroom textbooks (Derwing, Diepenbroek & Foote 2012) and in instructional practice (Baker, 2014). But the examples of the SSM that are currently available need to be gathered together and treated more coherently. We need to encourage researchers, materials developers, corpus designers and other ELT specialists who have written so well about the CSM to give comparable attention to the SSM (Cauldwell, 2014).

Over a quarter of a century ago, Nolan and Kerswill (1990) defined connected speech as 'the fluent continuous speech performance of everyday life' (p. 295). But, these many years later, instruction in the L2 listening component 'of everyday life' is being held back by a model of speech production (i.e. the CSM) out of step with the realities of everyday speech. The CSM will continue to merit ELT instructional attention as it meets two requirements of the field: it is pronunciation centred and written language friendly. At the same time, part of its baggage is that the CSM is neither listening centred or spontaneous speech friendly. It is for this reason that – if we want to improve the teaching of L2 listening – we need to give separate consideration to the goals, language models and classroom activities we employ for the teaching of listening. Our immediate challenge as teachers, researchers and materials developers is that we need to enter into, and learn to embrace, the Jungle.

References

Baker, A. (2014). Exploring teachers' knowledge of L2 pronunciation techniques: Teacher cognitions, observed classroom practices and student perceptions. *TESOL Quarterly, 48*, 136–163.

Barrera-Pardo, D. (2008). The reality of stress-timing. *ELT Journal, 62*(1), 11–17.

Breitkreutz, J. A., Derwing, T. M., & Rossiter, M. J. (2001). Pronunciation teaching practices in Canada. *TESL Canada Journal, 19*, 51–61.

Brazil, D. (1994). *Pronunciation for advanced learners of English*. Cambridge: Cambridge University Press.

Brazil, D. (1997). *The communicative value of intonation in English* (2nd ed.). Cambridge: Cambridge University Press.

Brown, G. (1990). *Listening to spoken English* (2nd ed.). Harlow: Longman.

Brown, J. D. (2012). *New ways in teaching connected speech*. Alexandria, VA: TESOL.

Cauldwell, R. T. (2002). The functional irrhythmicality of spontaneous speech: A discourse view of speech rhythms. *Apples, 2*(1), 1–24.

Cauldwell, R. T. (2013). *Phonology for listening: Teaching the stream of speech*. Birmingham: Speech in Action.

Cauldwell, R. T. (2014). An impertinent question: What happens in spontaneous speech? *Speak Out!, 48*, 4–7.

Celce-Murcia, M., Brinton, D. M., & Goodwin, J. M. (2010). *Teaching pronunciation: A course book and reference guide*. New York, NY: Cambridge University Press.

Cruttenden, A. (2014). *Gimson's pronunciation of English* (8th ed.). Cambridge: Cambridge University Press.

Dauer, R. (1983). Stress-timing and syllable-timing reanalyzed. *Journal of Phonetics, 11*, 51–62.

Derwing, T. M., Diepenbroek, L. G., & Foote, J. A. (2012). How well do general-skills ESL textbooks address pronunciation? *TESL Canada Journal, 30*(1), 23–44.

Field, J. (2008). *Listening in the language classroom*. Cambridge: Cambridge University Press.

Goh, C. (1997). Metacognitive awareness and second language listeners. *ELT Journal, 51*(4), 361–369.

Hancock, M., & McDonald, A. (2014). *Authentic listening resource pack*. Peaslake: Delta.

Kelly, L. G. (1969). *25 centuries of language teaching*. Rowley, MA: Newbury House (cited in Celce-Murcia et al., p. 2).

Lass, R. (1984). *Phonology*. Cambridge: Cambridge University Press.

Liberman, A. M., & Mattingly, I. G. (1985). The motor theory of speech perception revised. *Cognition, 21*(1), 1–36.

Macdonald, S. (2002). Pronunciation views and practices of reluctant teachers. *Prospect, 17*, 3–18.

Mendelsohn, D. (1994). *Learning to listen: A strategy based approach for the teaching of listening comprehension*. San Diego: Dominie.

Murphy, J. (2014). Myth 7: Teacher preparation programs provide adequate preparation in how to teach pronunciation, In L. Grant (Ed.), *Pronunciation myths* (pp. 188–223). Ann Arbor, MI: University of Michigan Press.

Nolan, F., & Kerswill, P. E. (1990). The description of connected speech processes. Studies in the pronunciation of English. In S. Ramsaran (Ed.) *A commemorative volume in honour of A.C. Gimson* (pp. 295–316). London: Routledge.

Nunan, D. (2002). Listening in language learning. In J. C. Richards & W. A. Renandya (Eds), *Methodology in language teaching: An anthology of current practice* (pp. 238–241). Cambridge: Cambridge University Press.

Roach, P. (1982). On the distinction between 'stress-timed' and 'syllable-timed' languages. In D. Crystal (Ed.), *Linguistic controversies*. London: Edward Arnold.

Sinclair, J. M., & Brazil, D. (1982). *Teacher talk*. Oxford: Oxford University Press.

Swan, M. (2012). Grammar and pronunciation. *Speak Out!*, *47*, 21–23.

Thanasoulas, D. (2003). Pronunciation: the 'Cinderella' of language teaching here. Retrieved from http://developingteachers.co.uk/articles_tchtraining/pron3_dimitrios.htm (accessed 23 February 2016).

Vandergrift, L. (1997). The Cinderella of communication strategies: Reception strategies in interactive listening. *The Modern Language Journal*, *81*(4), 494–505.

Wells, J. C. (2006). *English intonation: An introduction*. Cambridge: Cambridge University Press.

Wilson, J. J. (2008). *How to teach listening*. Harlow: Pearson Education.

Windsor Lewis, J. (2009, August). Jack Windsor Lewis's review of LPD. *Journal of the International Phonetic Association*, *39*(2), 238–240.

22

Pronunciation with other areas of language

Tamara Jones

Introduction and definitions

Although English as a second language (ESL) and English as a foreign language (EFL) learners are motivated by a wide range of academic, employment and social goals, at the most basic level they all want to communicate more easily and comprehensibly in English. To this end, many of them register for grammar and vocabulary classes. However, even though they may spend hours mastering grammatical structures and memorizing vocabulary words, 'when people – including our learners – refer to "second language ability," their primary goal seems to be speaking. . . . Almost all of my ESL/EFL students dream of the day when they can finally say, "I speak English well"' (Folse, 2006, p. 3–4).

One of the most crucial aspects of second language (L2) communication is comprehensible pronunciation. After all, it doesn't matter how large students' personal word banks may be or how accurate and complex their grammatical structures are if their pronunciation is difficult to understand. Simply put, while other linguistic inadequacies may make an exchange difficult, incomprehensible pronunciation will literally stop the conversation. It is for this reason that most language teachers and students agree that acquiring intelligible pronunciation is a vital part of learning a new language (Levis and Grant, 2003).

Despite the central role that intelligible pronunciation plays in successful communication, it is often sidelined in ESL and EFL classrooms. Teachers devote curricular space to the study of grammar and vocabulary, while pronunciation continues to be marginalized (Foote, Trofimovich, Collins & Soler-Urzua, 2013; Gilbert, 2010). Some reasons for this include the lack of consistent attention to pronunciation in ESL and EFL textbooks (Derwing, Diepenbroek & Foote, 2012), the inadequacy of pronunciation preparation in teacher training programmes (Baker, 2011; Murphy, 2014b) and the dearth of stand-alone pronunciation courses available to many ESL and EFL students (Foote, Holtby & Derwing, 2011). However, this challenging situation provides an interesting opportunity in English language teaching (ELT) to approach pronunciation as an integral component of communication rather than as an afterthought.

A survey of current popular ELT instructional materials reveals that most are organized by content themes and grammatical features. Pronunciation, if present at all, is usually related to the target grammar point featured in the chapter (Derwing et al., 2012) and, perhaps as a result, teachers tend to make grammar a priority in their lessons (Kelly, 2000; Rimmer, 2013). Thus, as general skills textbook authors have discovered, linking pronunciation to grammar and vocabulary lessons can result in the more effective integration of pronunciation within ELT curricula. Another feature is that these texts tend to revisit key grammar points at various levels. This recycling can provide the much-needed repeated exposure to related pronunciation features, specifically prosody, which Gilbert (2008) describes as 'rhythmic and melodic signals [which] serve as "road signs" to help the listener follow the intentions of the speaker' (p. 2). Prosody can be broken down into manageable chunks that can be easily taught, practised and recycled within existing lesson plans (Miller & Jones, 2016) by being paired with appropriate instruction in grammar and lexis at all levels. In this way, general skills ESL and EFL classes can become more systematically pronunciation-inclusive.

Historical perspectives

For many years, grammar, vocabulary and pronunciation held important roles in ELT. In particular, practitioners of the direct method and audiolingual method valued accuracy above fluency and drilled students on lexical and grammatical features with a focus on the 'eradication of deviant first language (L1) tendencies' (Isaacs, 2009, p. 2). Instructors presented students with rules, models, drills and controlled practice, often taking on the presentation–practice–production lesson format. With many of these traditional approaches, lexical, grammatical and pronunciation (specifically segmental) accuracy was paramount even at low levels, as it was feared that student errors could easily fossilize (Richards, 2006).

However, beginning in the 1970s, the teaching of all three fell out of favour with the advent of communicative language teaching (CLT). Faced with the linguistic needs of a burgeoning group of new immigrants and influenced by social democratic values of individual empowerment, the Council of Europe promoted principles of language teaching focused on developing L2 learners' communicative competence, i.e. what learners could *do* with the language (Savignon, 2002). Proponents of CLT focused on the use of language for genuine purposes of interpersonal communication and, consequently, a focus on accuracy was no longer at the core of ESL and EFL curricula. 'Perhaps as a reaction to over reliance on meaning-free minimal pair drilling, pronunciation as a whole was dumped overboard' (Gilbert, 2016, p. vi) in the vast majority of language programmes.

For the few who continued to teach pronunciation, CLT had some interesting effects. First, the emphasis placed on communicative competence prompted some educators to consider the importance of suprasegmentals (e.g. stress, rhythm, intonation) in the teaching of pronunciation (Celce-Murcia, Brinton & Goodwin, 2010). Second, because pronunciation advocates understood that intelligible pronunciation is essential to successful communication, they sought ways to teach pronunciation communicatively (Celce-Murcia, 1987). In other words, they wanted activities that engaged learners in meaningful tasks that required intelligible pronunciation for messages to be effectively communicated (Pica, 1984).

Soon following the advent of CLT, the early 1980s witnessed the emergence of Krashen and Terrell's (1983) natural approach (cover page), which promotes the position that grammar, vocabulary and pronunciation are acquired as a result of receiving comprehensible input and not through explicit instruction (Jones, 2002). In fact, advocates of the natural approach contend that 'focused instruction is at best useless and at worst detrimental' (Jones, 2002, p. 179). According to Krashen (1985), anything *learned* (explicitly), as opposed to *acquired* (subconsciously), such as grammar rules or pronunciation features, is never exploited during spontaneous speech acts. Therefore, teachers were encouraged to provide input so students could naturally acquire English as their pronunciation and grammar challenges naturally disappeared. Partly as a result of the impact of Krashen's influence on ELT, accuracy-based skills, such as grammar and especially pronunciation, fell out of favour in many ELT classrooms during this period (Gilbert, 2010; Isaacs, 2009). 'Pronunciation was so strongly associated with the "drill and kill" methods that it was deliberately downplayed [and] phonetics and phonology courses were gradually dropped from many teacher training programs' (Fraser, 2000, p. 33).

Recent years have witnessed the rise of a more balanced approach to the integration of grammar, vocabulary and pronunciation in ELT (e.g. Celce-Murcia et al., 2010). A great many studies have demonstrated that grammar instruction affects students' ultimate level of proficiency attainment and how quickly they progress (Cowan, 2008). Similarly, many educators acknowledge that explicit instruction coupled with ample practice opportunities can help students acquire the vocabulary they need to communicate (Folse, 2004). Pronunciation, too, has experienced a renaissance, of sorts (e.g. Reed and Levis 2015), and today's pronunciation curriculum 'seeks to identify the most important aspects of both suprasegmentals and segmentals and integrate them appropriately in courses that meet the needs of any given group of learners' (Celce-Murcia et al., 2010, p. 11).

Critical issues and topics

Despite the resurgence of interest in pronunciation instruction (e.g. Derwing & Munro, 2015; Grant, 2014; Reed and Levis, 2015), several challenges persist for teachers who want to integrate pronunciation into language lessons. First, teachers often feel ill prepared to teach pronunciation. Research conducted by Baker (2011), Breitkreutz, Derwing and Rossiter (2001) and Foote, Holtby and Derwing (2011) suggests that, while many teachers believe that pronunciation is an important aspect of communication, they lack confidence in their abilities to teach it. The same researchers describe a lack of training opportunities, both in their pre-service teacher training and through professional development opportunities. These reported feelings of teacher insecurity are even more clearly documented with non-native English speaker (NNES) teachers despite their potential strengths as pronunciation teachers, including their first-hand experience as learners of English pronunciation. Due to their first-hand lived experiences, NNESs represent attainable models of English pronunciation with which language learners may more easily identify (Murphy, 2014a).

This reported lack of language teacher self-confidence when it comes to pronunciation teaching may be one the main reasons why pronunciation is under-represented in many ESL and EFL classes, as documented by Foote et al. (2013). These researchers found that teachers tend to focus on pronunciation only 10 per cent of the time, much less than either grammar or vocabulary. Moreover, 'teachers often address pronunciation unsystematically, applying it primarily as a corrective measure' (Levis & Grant, 2003, p. 13). In addition, a myth persists that pronunciation should not be taught to beginning-level learners because it is deemed too complicated, too intimidating and too difficult to explain (Marks, 1986; Zielinski & Yates, 2014), though it is unlikely that language teachers would avoid teaching grammar or vocabulary for those reasons. Unfortunately, when explicit pronunciation instruction is avoided at lower levels, intelligibility suffers along with a loss of confidence in speaking abilities (Zielinski, 2012). Therefore, just as the teaching of vocabulary and grammar begin at the lowest levels, so should pronunciation instruction.

Current contributions and research

The integration of pronunciation instruction into speaking and listening lessons makes a lot of sense from the standpoint of ELT pedagogy. After all, pronunciation is an integral part of both communicating comprehensibly and understanding what others are saying. In addition, these lessons contain the kind of communicative activities into which practice with segmentals and suprasegmentals can be naturally interwoven because they promote a *focus on form* approach by drawing learners' attention to target grammar and vocabulary items as they come up in interaction (Long, 1991). However, such approaches may result in sporadic error treatment, which is problematic because 'without instruction that first guides students to notice a targeted aspect of pronunciation, students are not always going to recognise that they are receiving feedback' (Foote et al., 2013, p. 3).

In contrast, grammar and vocabulary lessons offer the opportunity for a *focus on forms*, which means that grammar items are introduced discretely and with increasingly communicative follow-up practice (Sheen 2002). This 'presentation, practice, production' approach (Lindsay, 2000, p. 314) has natural links with pronunciation instruction as well, and allows for a more systematic, proactive approach. In other words, grammar and vocabulary lessons can provide convenient pedagogical pegs on which to hang targeted pronunciation instruction. One example of such a pedagogic peg that has already been exploited in several sets of ELT instructional materials (e.g. Azar & Hagen, 2014; Schoenberg, 2011) is the issue of syllable count and the regular past tense. However, although textbooks often include a note on relevant pronunciation, it tends to be a topic covered just once, relegating the teaching of pronunciation to the periphery of language teaching. Moreover, by neglecting a more systematic integration of pronunciation matters within grammar and vocabulary textbooks, materials developers are missing potential benefits of offering students multiple engagements with the target language structures that the added dimension of pronunciation practice would afford. In addition to being 'mutually reinforcing' (Chela-Flores, 2001, p. 87), the inclusion of pronunciation lessons within a grammar- and vocabulary-focused syllabus would serve to expand the scope of pronunciation instruction to students (e.g. lower-level learners) who traditionally have not been provided with such opportunities. Unfortunately, when such learners are eventually provided with pronunciation instruction a higher level, the instruction usually takes the form of remedial training (Chela-Flores, 2001). The integration of pronunciation instruction into grammar and vocabulary lessons from the onset of language learning affords repeated exposure to target structures and allows teachers to 'bring learners gradually from controlled, cognitively based performance to automatic, skill-based performance' in keeping with the goal of a *focus on forms* approach (Pennington and Richards, 1986, p. 219).

Recommendations for practice

Teach the pronunciation of derivational morphology

L2 learners have long been aware that developing a robust vocabulary is an essential part of using another language (Folse, 2004). Researchers such as Schmitt and Meara (1997), Paribakht and Wesche (1999) and Zhang and Koda (2012) agree that an efficient way for students to enlarge their word banks is by learning about prefixes and suffixes and how to manipulate the morphological structure of words (i.e. derivational morphology).

Accordingly, if students learn the meaning of lexemes, for example <vary>, and English prefixes and suffixes, they are better positioned to recognize and eventually productively use lexical items within the same word family such as <variety>, <various>, <variable> and <invariably>, thereby expanding their vocabulary exponentially. However, as learners transform words with affixes, they also need to be aware that related items within the same word family (e.g. different parts of speech) tend to differ phonologically. By way of illustration, notice the changes in word stress and associated vowel productions within the same word family of <electric>, <electrify>, <electrician>, <electricity> and <electrification>.

Many words in English are multisyllabic, especially those reflecting the more Latinate- and French-influenced vocabulary of both written and spoken academic genres. Two key elements to understanding, learning and learning to use multisyllabic words as part of one's active vocabulary are knowing how many syllables the new word contains and the location of its primary stressed syllable (Murphy, 2004). For instance, the lexeme <PHOto> has two syllables and the first is stressed, but the word <photoGRAPHic> has four syllables and the word's primary stress shifts to the third syllable. Learning about the word stress of a word family is essential for L2 learners because as the word changes from noun to verb to adjective to adverb, so the stress may also change (e.g. <His CONduct is terrible> but <The maestro conDUCTS the orchestra>). Moreover, English speakers store words in their minds as phonological chunks, and the stressed syllable of a word provides an access code for retrieval (Grosjean & Gee, 1987). As a result, 'we find it difficult to interpret an utterance in which a word is pronounced with the wrong stress pattern – we begin to "look up" [in our internal mental lexicon] possible words under this wrong stress pattern' (Brown, 1990, p. 51).

Students may run into a variety of challenges when learning about word stress in English. First, they may have trouble identifying the correct number of syllables in a word. In some more orthographically transparent languages, if a letter appears in a word it is pronounced, but the written conventions of the English orthographic system have followed a different historical trajectory. As Mackay (1987) explains, English language spelling/orthographic conventions are tied more firmly to morphophonemic principles than to alphabetic principles. That is, words that look alike (e.g. <atom>, <atomic>, <atomized>; <electric>, <electrician>, <electrification>) tend to be related in meaning. Consequently, morphemes in English tend to maintain recognizable orthographic identities even when their pronunciation changes. One of the impacts of related historical developments in the English orthographic system is that the spelling conventions of English are more reading-based and reader-friendly than either speaking-based or listener-friendly (J. Murphy, personal communication, 15 January 2015).

Furthermore, even if students pronounce a word with the correct number of syllables, they may struggle to identify its stressed syllable accurately. For instance, a speaker whose first language places equal stress on every syllable may attempt to say the vowel sound of each syllable very clearly, operating under the false impression that the sound system of English works similarly. They may not realize that L1 speakers of English are more likely to stress one syllable in particular within a word and reduce the others.

Finally, though L2 speakers may produce a word's correct number of syllables and identify the stressed syllable accurately, a learner may still be misunderstood if the peak vowel sound is produced incorrectly. It is challenging for NNESs to gain firmer control of the English vowel system. Many NNESs are from L1 backgrounds in which words contain between five and eight vowel sounds (Celce-Murcia et al., 2010), while most dialects of English contain a core vowel inventory of at least 14 items. NNESs struggle to perceive differences between vowels they believe to be similar, such as the high-front-lax vowel /ɪ/ in <ship> and the high-front-tense vowel /iʸ/ in <sheep>. Moreover, pronouncing vowel sounds correctly is also a daunting task for English learners owing to the fact that vowels in general lack many of the more readily perceived characteristics of consonant sounds (e.g. voicing distinctions (all vowels are voiced); contact of articulation (for vowel production the tongue does not actually touch the teeth, tooth ridge or other easily felt places of articulation); and the modification of air flow (air flow for vowel production is relatively open and unobstructed)). Unfortunately, if students aren't exposed to word stress when they learn target vocabulary two problems arise: (a) they may not recognize even the words they think they know when they hear them, and (b) they may not be understood when they use the new words they have been learning while reading when occasions to use them while speaking arise (Gilbert, 2008).

It is essential that when NNESs study derivational morphology their teachers provide systematic instruction in word stress locations of polysyllabic words. Fortunately, this can be fairly easily integrated into existing vocabulary materials. As learners are exposed to new morphological combinations, the teacher can read the words aloud, one by one, and have the students indicate how many syllables they hear by holding up fingers, tapping their pencils on their desks or calling out syllable tallies. Such procedures provide students with practice hearing syllables and it gives teachers immediate feedback about whether or not students are able to identify the correct number of beats (i.e. syllables) in the target vocabulary. As word stress can sometimes begin to feel arbitrary and confusing to NNESs unfamiliar with this facet of the phonological system of English, it is helpful to explicitly teach some of the more productive stress pattern conventions associated with prefixes and suffixes.

- Prefixes are not usually stressed in English.
- Words ending in *-ion, -ic, -ical, -ity, -ify, -ial, -ious, -al, -able, -ible, -ium, -imum, -ian, -graphy* and *-logy* are usually stressed on the syllable before the suffix (e.g. organiZAtion, acaDEmic, PRACtical, liaBILity, JUStify, fiNANcial, deLIcious, DENtal, dePENdable, SENsible, audiTORium, MAXimum and muSIcian).
- Words ending in two consonants + *-ive* are also stressed on the syllable before the suffix (e. g. disTINCtive).
- Words ending in *-ee, -eer, -ese, -ette, -esque, -eer* and *-ique* are usually stressed on the suffix (e.g. employEE, enginEER, chinESE, cassETTE, kafkaESQUE, auctioNEER and unIQUE).
- Words ending in *-ate* and *-ary* are usually stressed on the syllable that is two syllables before the suffix (e.g. parTIcipate and VOluntary).

As students learn to manipulate affixes, it can be helpful for them to notice that the stress can shift within word families as the form of the word changes (illustrated previously with the word family of <PHOtograph>, <phoTOGrapher>, <photoGRAphic>). Because speakers of many languages do not alternately lengthen and reduce vowel sounds the way English speakers do (Gilbert, 2008), it can be helpful for students to practise listening for the contrast between stressed and reduced vowels in the new vocabulary they are learning. For example, the teacher may need to direct learners' attention to the way the initial vowel sound /o^w/ is particularly clear and fully enunciated in the stressed syllable of <PHOtograph>, but the vowel of same initial syllable reduces to the less distinct schwa sound /ə/ in the word <phoTOgrapher>. As students are learning these words, the teacher could say them aloud and have learners mark the stress pattern by drawing circles above the syllables or beside the words, small circles for the reduced syllables and a bigger circle for the stressed syllable, as in *photograph* (O o o) and *photographer* (o O o o).

Once students demonstrate that they can hear the stressed syllable, they need to work on saying the words while applying the correct placement of word stress. Kjellin (1999) recommends whole-class choral repetition as an effective technique for practising patterns of word stress. It is especially valuable when the teacher models the correct pronunciation for the students first, and then has them say it along with their teacher in unison, so the sound of the teacher's voice serves to scaffold the repetition. As documented empirically by researchers such as Baddeley, Gathercole and Papagno (1998), when a student learns a new word it needs to be repeated aloud in order for sounds to be assigned to the word. Such classroom routines facilitate the transfer of the word to the student's long-term memory (LTM). If students aren't given the opportunity to chorally repeat new vocabulary several times, they run the risk of either assigning incorrect sounds before it is transferred to LTM or not assigning any sounds to the word and, therefore, not relocating the word into LTM at all (Woo & Price, 2016).

Moreover, integrating movement into choral practice, for example clapping, snapping the fingers or raising the eyebrows in coordination with a word's rhythmic pattern, can help students internalize the pronunciation of new words. Gilbert (2008) suggests giving each student a rubber band, the thicker the better, and having them repeat the target vocabulary while stretching the rubber band on the word's primary stressed syllable. In this way, students really feel the length of the stressed syllable, which, according to Brown (1990), is the easiest characteristic of word stress for students to master. By combining physical movements such as these with choral repetition, students are not only given a physical gesture that anchors the pronunciation of the word mentally, but they are also given yet another opportunity to create a physical memory for the word, or, as Folse (2004) puts it, 'to "touch" the word in a different way, which can result in better retention of the vocabulary' (p. 144).

However, simply lengthening the vowel sound of a stressed syllable may not be enough to ensure that learners can comprehensibly pronounce a new word. An important facet of vowel clarity lies in pronouncing the actual vowel sound itself correctly, a notoriously difficult task. In order to help students accurately produce the appropriate vowel sound of a peak syllable, it can be helpful to introduce students to either the Color Vowel Chart (CVC), a visual aid developed by Taylor and Thompson (2009), or a comparable vowel chart such as the International Phonetic Alphabet (see Celce-Murcia et al., 2010, p. 116). The CVC assigns each of the 14 core vowel phonemes of English to a colour and noun (e.g. <red dress> for the mid-front-lax vowel /ɛ/ and <blue moon> for the high-back-tense vowel /uʷ/.) The positioning of symbols and key words on both the CVC and an IPA vowel chart corresponds with a side view of how individual vowel phonemes are produced within the human mouth and in relation to each other within the larger vowel field. These are useful tools for the study of vocabulary because they provide easy, visual reference points for teachers and learners while talking about and practising the production of vowel sounds.

Thus, although learning about affixes can be an effective way for students to build their English word banks, the pronunciation norms associated with morphology also need to be explicitly taught as students are exposed to prefixes and suffixes. Without this instruction, students may feel insecure and reticent to use more complex vocabulary when speaking (Dunn, 1989; Murphy, 2004) and the time invested in mastering English derivational morphology may be wasted.

Teaching the pronunciation of inflectional morphology

In addition to lexical processes that build words from lexemes and affixes, English users also attach grammatical endings to words, a process known as inflectional morphology.

There are eight regular morphological inflections in English: plural, possessive, third-person singular present tense, regular simple past tense, present participle, past participle, comparative and superlative. These word endings are typically addressed in the grammar curriculum, often from the beginning level. Unfortunately, the morphophonemic impact of adding an *-s*, *-ed*, *-ing*, *-er* or *-est* ending to a word is often ignored within ELT classrooms.

This lack of integration between morphology and pronunciation can affect other areas of language proficiency, such as listening, speaking and writing. For example, if learners are unaware of the three phonological realizations of the regular past tense ending, they are likely to confuse present- and past-tense utterances. In addition, these markers may be missing from their speech and writing. Thus, it is clearly an area where teachers and textbook writers, especially at the beginning level, need to give greater attention to pronunciation (Celce-Murcia et al., 2010).

The morphological inflections that are perhaps the most difficult for students to master involve word-final <-s>, and it is not uncommon to hear students dropping it entirely when they speak (Folse, 2009). In fact, if students have learned English in a context that places emphasis on fluency at the expense of accuracy, even advanced students may drop the final <-s> long after they have studied the grammar rules if this feature of their spoken English has fossilized. Likewise, even advanced-level learners often struggle with the pronunciation of the <-ed> ending, most frequently by pronouncing all <-ed> endings as full syllables. These errors, however, do not usually cause breakdowns in communication (Richards, 2008), so learners may notice them less frequently than other errors. Since the articulation of the final <-s> and final <-ed> are pronunciation issues and not grammatical issues, it is essential that students be explicitly taught how to pronounce these inflectional endings as they learn the relevant grammar points before fossilization sets in.

Exposure to and practice with the different pronunciations of the <-s> ending can be accomplished fairly quickly in a lesson in which the target grammar is either the third-person singular of the simple present tense, the possessive or the regular plural, as the pronunciation rules are the same in each instance. Specifically, if the word ends with a voiced consonant (e.g. /d/ as in <grade>), or a vowel sound, the final <-s> to be added is pronounced with the voiced sibilant /z/. If the word ends with a voiceless consonant sound (e.g. /f/ as in <laughs>), the final <-s> to be added is pronounced with the voiceless sibilant /s/. A third possibility is that if the word ends with a final consonant sound that is already a sibilant such as /s/, /z/, /ʃ/, /tʃ/ or /dʒ/, in order to maintain a perceptible contrast for listeners the sound to be added is combined with the insertion of a vowel and is pronounced as an added syllable /ɪz/. As mentioned previously, the same phonological rules apply for several of the morphological inflections listed above. Similar rules govern the pronunciation of <-ed> endings associated with the simple past tense and regular past participles, as well (see Celce-Murcia et al., 2010, pp. 398–400). Grammar texts tend to cover the transformation of regular verbs briefly, focusing on the spelling changes associated with adding the <-ed> ending. Perhaps as a result, 'teachers often believe the irregular past to be the trickiest aspect of mastering past tenses; however, using regular past tenses in conversation creates pronunciation challenges that can impede communication' (Miller & Jones, 2016, p. 93). As with the <-s> ending, how the <-ed> ending is articulated depends on the sound that comes before. When such rules are being elicited, the teacher should read the words in three groups so students can more easily deduce the three distinct pronunciations. Once the rule has been introduced, students might work in pairs or small groups to categorize the words based on the pronunciation of the ending. Students could be given sets of verb index cards and instructed to sort the cards into three categories: /t/, /d/ and /ɪd/, for instance. Alternately, the teacher could list words on the board and have students write them on a handout in the appropriate category.

Finally, to ensure that students are pronouncing the final consonant sound with more intelligible pronunciation, the teacher can assign each student a verb to read aloud. It can be beneficial to give students a minute or two to determine for themselves what the pronunciation of the ending should be before they say it aloud. Once the student says the word, the rest of the class should then indicate which sound they heard by holding up a designated number of fingers. For instance, if the target structure is the regular simple past tense, students would hold up one finger for /d/, two fingers for /t/ and three fingers for /ɪd/. This activity also works very well as a pair activity with the teacher circulating to address any pronunciation problems.

The accurate pronunciation of the final consonant sounds of morphological inflections is important because words are not usually produced in isolation. Therefore, in addition to mastering the pronunciation of these endings, teachers also need to expose students to the concepts of linking and assimilation. Teachers may balk at the notion of encouraging students to speak in what they perceive to be an overly informal or casual manner; however, if students are not introduced to the characteristics of connected speech, their own speech may be choppy and, even worse, they may have trouble comprehending the discourse of proficient English speakers (Field, 2003). For these reasons, practising the pronunciations of the <-s> and <-ed> endings in alternative contexts (e.g. short phrases, thought groups, whole sentences, dialogues, role plays) and extemporaneous speech is crucial.

Thus, it is helpful for students to become aware of the norms associate with linking and assimilation as connected to <-s> and <-ed> endings. They need to know that when words ending in consonant sounds are followed by words beginning with vowel sounds within the same thought group, they are usually linked. Therefore, in the phrase <*gets a cat*> the final sibilant of the word <*gets*> links to the following word <*a*> to sound like one word, /ɡɛtsə/. Similarly, when a word ends in a consonant sound and the following word begins with either the same or a similar consonant sound within a thought group, they are usually linked. For instance, in the phrase <*wanted dogs*> the two /d/ sounds assimilate to form a single /d/ sound, so the phrase sounds like /wantədɔgz/. Teachers may also want to draw more advanced-level students' attention to the regressive assimilation that occurs when a word ends with the consonant sibilant sound /s/ or /z/ and the following word begins with /ʃ/, as in the phrase <*one's shirt*>. In this case, the preceding sound, the /s/ or /z/, is assimilated into the following sound, so that <*one's shirt*> may sound like /wʌnʃɜrt/, making it difficult to differentiate from the phrase <*one shirt*> unless the listener has also learned to attend to related contextual cues. Finally, higher-level students may also benefit from learning that the final <-ed sounds> /t/ and /d/ may assimilate to following /p/, /k/, /b/ or /g/ sounds, respectively. For instance, <*helped Tom*> might sound like /hɛlptɔm/ and <*loved baseball*> might sound like /lʌvbeʸsbɔl/.

To help students learn about these norms, Field (2003) suggests using dictations and dicto-comps. During a lesson featuring attention to the final <-s> or <-ed> endings, teachers can read several sentences aloud containing the target linking or assimilation and ask students to write out what they hear. Students are often startled to realize that what they think they hear is not what the teacher is actually saying. Similarly, Cauldwell (2013) makes the related point that L1 speakers of English, including many ESL and EFL teachers, are often surprised as they begin to realize that the sounds they produce in their own connected speech are commonly modified in sometimes surprising ways and often differ from what they believe themselves to be saying.

Once students have been introduced to the most common instances of linking and assimilation associated with targeted word endings, they can be asked to chorally repeat phrases with the teacher. As with word stress, it is useful to use body movements, in particular hooking the two index fingers together when uttering the linked or assimilated sounds. Grammar lessons that focus on one of the eight regular morphological inflections, specifically the third-person singular in the simple present tense, regular plurals, possessives, the simple past tense or the past participle, benefit from the integration of pronunciation. By focusing students' attention on both the segmental pronunciation of the word-final endings and the linking and assimilation that can occur across word boundaries, teachers are better preparing learners to communicate more intelligibly both as speakers and as listeners.

Future directions

With conceptual roots dating back to the 1960s, contemporary approaches to L2 teaching such as CLT and task-based language teaching (TBLT) continue to serve as the preferred approaches to ELT in most programmes worldwide (Brown & Lee 2015; Richards 2006). Although many language teachers believe that pronunciation teaching is incompatible with principles of CLT and TBLT (Isaacs 2009), they are mistaken. The past three decades reveal a vibrant specialist tradition that has illustrated both communicative and task-based ways of teaching the pronunciation of English. As early as the mid-1980s, specialists such as Celce-Murcia (1983, 1987) and Pica (1984) were already well along this path. Murphy and Baker (2015) document the contributions of the large number of specialists who have successfully built upon and extended Celce-Murcia's and Pica's early illustrations with an impressive number of high-quality teacher preparation texts (e.g. Celce-Murcia et al., 2010; Lane, 2010; Rogerson-Revell, 2011), additional teacher resource materials (e.g. Brown, 2012; Marks & Bowen, 2012) and ESL classroom textbooks (e.g. Gilbert 2012/1984; Grant, 2017/1993), which integrate pronunciation instruction with principles and procedures of CLT and TBLT. Further, researchers have continued to document what many ELT classroom instructors have long realized, that a significant number of students will continue to struggle with intelligibility if they do not receive explicit instruction and supportive, corrective feedback in pronunciation (Derwing & Munro, 2015).

Moving forwards, other key prosodic features should be featured in the teaching of grammar and other language skills at all levels of L2 proficiency. For example, in addition to word stress and connected speech, thought groups and prominence can also easily be assimilated into existing lessons. An essential theme is that proficient English speakers group words together, so that listeners can process the message more easily. These words, phrases or clauses are separated by brief pauses, something like the way punctuation separates written English (Murphy, 2013). For instance, a spoken utterance such as *<After she left I made a sandwich and watched TV>* would probably be divided into two or even three thought groups, as in, *<After she left / I made a sandwich / and watched TV>*. Thought groups are important for students to learn for two reasons. First, students who are able to distinguish pause-bounded units of language hear and remember more of what they are listening to (Harley, 2000). Second, speakers who divide their own streams of speech into thought groups are easier to understand (Levis & Grant, 2003; Murphy, 2013). In addition to becoming better speakers and listeners, students who have opportunities to practise the target structures they are learning aloud will have firmer control of both grammar structures and phonological phenomena.

The most obvious point at which to introduce the process of thought grouping is when teaching complex and compound sentences; however, even beginners can benefit from practice chunking their speech, as they can make accented speech more intelligible. To build awareness about thought groups, teachers need not create new materials. Rather, the recordings that accompany many textbooks provide an excellent foundation for this dimension of pronunciation practice. Once students have read and listened to the recording, and identified the key grammar point, the teacher can play the conversation once more while challenging students to draw slash marks (/) whenever they hear a pause (i.e. between thought groups). Then, they can be encouraged to perform the conversation aloud with a partner, taking care to pause slightly at thought group boundaries. In this way, attention to thought groups can be integrated into a grammar-focused lesson.

Prominence is another core pronunciation feature that can be easily integrated into grammar lessons. Within every thought group, one word is pronounced more clearly and loudly and its primary stressed vowel sound is held a little longer and enunciated more clearly. Although the focus word generally is the last content word of a thought group, the speaker may emphasize another word in order to communicate a particular message in the context of an interactive conversation. For instance, in the sentence <*That's my book*> the speaker could say any of the three words with prominence, but the meaning would be slightly different for each iteration.

(a) THAT'S my book.
    (Of the various books in front of us that we are both looking at, the specific book that I am pointing at now is mine. None of the others belongs to me.)

(b) that's MY book.
    (The book is mine. It is not yours, his or hers.)

(c) that's my BOOK.
    (You are probably wondering what that is. It's not a box; it's a book.)

In addition to being said more clearly, more loudly and longer, the focus word is also the recipient of the pitch contour. In other words, the speaker's voice usually rises on the stressed syllable of a prominent word and either falls or continues to rise immediately after it. For instance, in the sentence <*My sister is taller than my mother*> the speaker would probably rise and fall on the last word, <*mother*>. However, if a speaker wanted to demonstrate that he or she was surprised about this information, he or she might continue to rise after the stressed syllable of the word <*mother*>. Prominence is an important pronunciation feature for students to learn because English language learners need to be aware that *how* speakers say things has the 'power to reinforce, mitigate, or even undermine the words spoken' (Wichmann, 2005, p. 22). Otherwise, they risk not hearing information other listeners have grasped. However, because prominence is a broader, discourse-level feature, illustrations at sentence-level (such as those above) are notoriously challenging for language learners to appreciate. Therefore, Levis (1999) suggests providing discourse-level rather than sentence-level illustrations.

As with thought groups, prominence can be easily integrated into existing grammar lessons. When listening to recordings that accompany many general skills text books, teachers can take a few minutes to play the recording a second or multiple times and have students highlight or circle the prominent word within each thought group. This is especially important when it comes to teaching modals, such as <*can*> and <*can't*>. Proficient speakers tend to put focus on the main verb (as in <*i can GO*>) in an affirmative sentence, but on the contracted modal (as in <*i CAN't go*>) in a negative sentence. As with all pronunciation skills, the more opportunities for controlled (e.g. choral repetition), guided and (eventually) more spontaneous language practice, the better. Therefore, it is imperative that students have multiple opportunities to practise the target language while paying special attention to the pitch contours on focus words within thought groups.

There are numerous opportunities to integrate pronunciation into vocabulary and grammar lessons. In fact, by using the target language from a grammar or vocabulary lesson in pronunciation practice, teachers are providing students with much-needed review of the vocabulary or grammar items as well as reinforcing the characteristics of intelligible speech. Although this approach would clearly benefit students, the onus continues to be on classroom teachers to integrate pronunciation with other areas of language. Gilbert's (2010) suggestions for the incorporation of pronunciation, including that curriculum designers and materials developers address pronunciation skills in a more integrated way, have yet to be met. In a utopian world of ELT, pronunciation would be so thoroughly integrated into instructional materials that every time students speak they would be practising pronunciation skills in tandem with target grammar and vocabulary. Unfortunately, there remains a long way to go before anything approaching such a utopia becomes the instructional norm.

Further reading

Gilbert, J. (2008). *Teaching pronunciation: Using the prosody pyramid.* Cambridge: Cambridge University Press. This free booklet introduces the prosody pyramid, an accessible visual depiction of the rhythm and melody of English.

Grant, L. (Ed.). (2014). *Pronunciation myths.* Ann Arbor, MI: University of Michigan Press. This book debunks seven commonly held myths about how students acquire comprehensible English pronunciation. By connecting real world examples with a review of related research, its chapters discredit many of the most persistent misconceptions about pronunciation and follow up with practical teaching recommendations.

Jones, T. (Ed.). (2016). *Pronunciation for the classroom: The overlooked essential.* Alexandria, VA: TESOL. This book contains practical suggestions for integrating pronunciation into a variety of skill areas: vocabulary, listening, speaking, reading, spelling and grammar. The chapters balance theory with practice and cover a wide variety of pronunciation features, both segmental and suprasegmental.

References

Azar, B. S., & Hagen, S. A. (2014). *Basic English grammar* (4th ed.). White Plains, NY: Pearson.

Baddeley, A., Gathercole, S., & Papagno, C. (1998). The phonological loop as a language learning device. *Psychological Review, 105*(1), 158–173.

Baker, A. A. (2011). Discourse prosody and teachers' stated beliefs and practices. *TESOL Journal, 2*(3), 263–292.

Breitkreutz, J., Derwing, T. M., & Rossiter, M. J. (2001). Pronunciation teaching practices in Canada. *TESL Canada Journal, 19*, 51–61.

Brown, G. (1990). *Listening to spoken English.* London: Longman.

Brown, H. D., & Lee, H. (2015). *Teaching by Principles: An interactive approach to language pedagogy* (4th ed.). Englewood Cliffs, NJ: Prentice-Hall Regents.

Brown, J. D. (2012). *New ways in teaching connected speech.* Alexandria, VA: TESOL.

Cauldwell, R. (2013). *Phonology for listening: Teaching the stream of speech.* Birmingham: Speech in Action.

Celce-Murcia, M. (1983, May). Activities for teaching pronunciation communicatively. *CATESOL News*, 10–11.

Celce-Murcia, M. (1987). Teaching pronunciation as communication. In J. Morley (Ed.), *Current perspectives on pronunciation* (pp. 1–12), Washington, DC: TESOL.

Celce-Murcia, M., Brinton, D., & Goodwin, J. (2010). *Teaching pronunciation: A course book and reference guide* (2nd ed.). New York, NY: Cambridge University Press.

Chela-Flores, B. (2001). Pronunciation and language learning: and integrative approach. *International Review of Applied Linguistics in Language Teaching, 39*(2), 85–101.

Cowan, R. (2008). *The teacher's grammar of English with answers: A course book and reference guide.* Cambridge: Cambridge University Press.

Derwing, T. M., Diepenbroek, L. G., & Foote, J. A. (2012). How well do general-skills ESL textbooks address pronunciation? *TESOL Canada Journal / Revue TESOL du Canada, 31*(1), 22–44.

Derwing, T. M., & Munro, M. (2015). *Pronunciation fundamentals: Evidence-based perspectives for L2 teaching and research.* Amsterdam: John Benjamins.

Dunn, J. R. (1989). How-to-do-it: Are pronunciation exams effective in developing biology students' vocabulary? *The American Biology Teacher, 51*(3), 176–178.

Field, J. (2003). Promoting perception: Lexical segmentation in L2 listening. *ELT Journal, 57*(4), 325–334.

Foote, J. A., Holtby, A. K., & Derwing, T. M. (2011). Survey of the teaching of pronunciation in adult ESL programs in Canada, 2010. *TESOL Canada Journal / Revue TESOL du Canada, 29*(1), 1–22.

Foote, J. A., Trofimovich, P., Collins, L., & Soler-Urzua, F. (2013). Pronunciation teaching practices in communicative second language classes. *The Language Learning Journal* (online 16 April 2013). doi:10.1080/09571736.2013.784345.

Folse, K. (2004). *Vocabulary myths.* Ann Arbor, MI: University of Michigan Press.

Folse, K. (2006). *The art of teaching speaking.* Ann Arbor, MI: University of Michigan Press.

Folse, K. (2009). *Keys to teaching grammar to English language learners,* Ann Arbor, MI: Michigan University Press.

Fraser, H. (2000). *Coordinating improvements in pronunciation teaching for adult learners of English as a second language.* Canberra: DETYA.

Gilbert, J. B. (2008). *Teaching pronunciation: Using the prosody pyramid.* Cambridge: Cambridge University Press.

Gilbert, J. B. (2010). Pronunciation as orphan: what can be done? *SpeakOut: The Newsletter of the IATEFL Pronunciation Special Interest Group, 43,* 3–7.

Gilbert, J. B. (2012). *Clear speech: Pronunciation and listening comprehension in North American English* (4th ed.; 1st edition 1984). New York, NY: Cambridge University Press.

Gilbert, J. B. (2016). Foreword. In T. Jones (Ed.), *Pronunciation in the classroom: The overlooked essential* (pp. v–ix). Alexandria, VA: TESOL.

Grant, L. (Ed.). (2014). *Pronunciation myths.* Ann Arbor, MI: University of Michigan Press.

Grant, L. (2017). *Well said: Pronunciation for clear communication* (4th ed.; 1st ed. 1993). Boston, MA: Thomson/Heinle & Heinle.

Grosjean, F., & Gee, J. (1987). Prosodic structure and spoken word recognition. *Cognition, 25,* 135–155.

Harley, B. (2000). Listening strategies in ESL: Do age and LI make a difference? *TESOL Quarterly, 34*(4), 769–777.

Isaacs, T. (2009). Integrating form and meaning in L2 pronunciation instruction. *TESOL Canada Journal / Revue TESOL du Canada, 27*(1), 1–12.

Jones, R. H. (2002). Beyond 'listen and repeat': Pronunciation teaching materials and theories of second language acquisition. In J. C. Richards & W. L. Renandya (Eds), *Methodology in language teaching: An anthology of current practice* (pp. 178–187). Cambridge: Cambridge University Press.

Kelly, G. (2000). *How to teach pronunciation.* Harlow: Pearson Education.

Kjellin, O. (1999). Accent addition: Prosody and perception facilitates second language learning. In O. Fujimura, B. D. Joseph, & B. Palek (Eds), *Proceedings of LP'98 Linguistics and Phonetics Conference: Vol. 2* (pp. 373–398). Columbus, OH: Karolinum.

Krashen, S. D. (1985). *The input hypothesis: Issues and implications.* New York, NY: Longman.

Krashen, S., & Terrell, T. (1983). *The natural approach.* Hayward, CA: Alemany.

Lane, L. (2010). *Tips for teaching pronunciation: A practical approach.* White Plains, NY: Pearson/Longman.

Levis, J. (1999). Intonation in theory and practice, revisited. *TESOL Quarterly, 33*(1), 37–62.

Levis, J., & Grant, L. (2003). Integrating pronunciation into ESL/EFL classrooms, *TESOL Journal, 12*(2), 13–21.

Lindsay, P. (2000). *Teaching English worldwide: A new practical guide to teaching English*. Provo, UT: Alta.

Long, M. H. (1991). Focus on form: A design feature in language teaching methodology. In K. de Bot, R. Ginsberg & C. Kramsch (Eds), *Foreign language research in cross-cultural perspective* (pp. 39–52). Amsterdam: John Benjamins.

Mackay, I. (1987). *Phonetics: The science of speech production* (2nd ed.). Boston, MA, Toronto and San Diego, CA: Little, Brown.

Marks, J. (1986). All language teaching is phonology teaching. *IATEFL Phonology Special Interest Group Newsletter, 1*, 8–9.

Marks, J., & Bowen, T. (2012). *The book of pronunciation: Proposals for a practical pedagogy*. Peaslake: Delta.

Miller, S. F., & Jones, T. (2016). Taking the fear factor out of integrating pronunciation and beginning grammar. In T. Jones (Ed.) *Pronunciation in the classroom – The overlooked essential* (pp. 89–102). Alexandria, VA: TESOL.

Murphy, J. M. (2004). Attending to word-stress while learning new vocabulary. *English for Specific Purposes Journal, 23*(1), 67–83.

Murphy, J. (2013). *Teaching pronunciation*. Alexandria, VA: TESOL.

Murphy, J. (2014a). Intelligible, comprehensible, non-native models in ESL/EFL pronunciation teaching. *System, 42*, 258–269.

Murphy, J. M. (2014b). Myth 7: Teacher training programs provide adequate preparation in how to teach pronunciation. In L. Grant (Ed.), *Pronunciation myths* (pp. 188–234). Ann Arbor, MI: University of Michigan Press.

Murphy, J., & Baker, A. A. (2015). History of ESL pronunciation teaching. In M. Reed and J. Levis (Eds), *Wiley-Blackwell handbook of English pronunciation* (pp. 36–65). Chichester: Blackwell.

Paribakht, T. S., & Wesche, M. (1999). Reading and 'incidental' L2 vocabulary acquisition: An introspective study of lexical inferencing. *Studies in Second Language Acquisition, 21*, 195–224.

Pennington, M. M., & Richards, J. C. (1986). Pronunciation revisited. *TESOL Quarterly, 20*(2), 207–225.

Pica, T. (1984). Pronunciation activities with an accent on communication. *English Teaching Forum, 22*(3), 2–6.

Reed, M., & Levis, J. (Eds). (2015). *Wiley-Blackwell handbook of English pronunciation*. Chichester: Blackwell.

Richards, J. (2006). *Communicative language teaching today*. New York, NY: Cambridge University Press.

Richards, J. (2008). *Moving beyond the plateau*, New York, NY: Cambridge University Press

Rimmer, W. (2013). Will we be using them in 60 years time? The future as a matter of course-books. *Ih Journal*. Retrieved from http://ihjournal.com/will-we-be-using-them-in-§60-years%E2%80%99-time-the-future-as-a-matter-of-course-books-by-wayne-rimmer (accessed 27 December 2015).

Rogerson-Revell, P. (2011). *English phonology and pronunciation teaching*. London: Continuum.

Savignon, S. J. (2002). Communicative language teaching: Linguistic theory and classroom practice. In S. Savignon (Ed.), *Interpreting communicative language teaching: Contexts and concerns in teacher education* (pp. 1–28). New Haven, CT: Yale University Press.

Schmitt, N., & Meara, P. (1997). Researching vocabulary through a word knowledge framework: Word associations and verbal suffixes. *Studies in Second Language Acquisition, 19*, 17–36.

Schoenberg, I. E. (2011). *Focus on grammar: An integrated skills approach* (4th ed.). White Plains, NY: Pearson.

Sheen, R. (2002). 'Focus on form' and 'focus on forms'. *ELT Journal, 56*(3), 303–305.

Taylor, K., & Thompson, S. (2009). The Color Vowel™ Chart. Retrieved from www.colorvowel chart.org (accessed 26 April 2015**).**

Wichmann, A. (2005). Please – from courtesy to appeal: The role of intonation in the expression of attitudinal meaning. *English Language and Linguistics, 9*(2), 229–253.

Woo, M., & Price, R. (2016). The pronunciation-reading connection. In T. Jones (Ed.), *Pronunciation in the classroom – The overlooked essential* (pp. 129–141). Alexandria, VA: TESOL.

Zhang, D., & Koda, K. (2012). Contribution of morphological awareness and lexical inferencing ability to L2 vocabulary knowledge and reading comprehension among advanced EFL learners: Testing direct and indirect effects. *Reading and Writing, 25*(5), 1195–1216.

Zielinski, B. (2012). The social impact of pronunciation difficulties: Confidence and willingness to speak. In J. Levis & K. LeVelle (Eds) *Proceedings of the 3rd Pronunciation in Second Language Learning and Teaching Conference* (pp. 18–26). Ames, IA: Iowa State University. Retrieved from https://apling.engl.iastate.edu/alt-content/uploads/2016/06/Proceedings.

Zielinski, B., & Yates, L. (2014). Myth 2: Pronunciation instruction is not appropriate for beginning-level learners. In L. Grant (Ed.), *Pronunciation myths* (pp. 56–79). Ann Arbor, MI: University of Michigan Press.

23

Pronunciation and individual differences

Jette G. Hansen Edwards

Introduction

The study of individual differences in second language (L2) learning and, in particular, L2 learning *outcomes*, has been a dominant focus of second language acquisition (SLA) research for nearly 70 years. Although individual differences have been variously defined and researched (see Dörnyei & Skehan, 2003), researchers generally focus on factors such as motivation, aptitude, age, learning styles and learning strategies. In the area of individual differences in L2 pronunciation attainment, researchers have also focused on length of residence (LOR), extent of L1 and L2 use, language learning context, gender and ethnic/peer identification in the attempt to understand why some learners are able to attain native or native-like pronunciation ability in the L2, while others are not. These factors are the focus of the current chapter.

Before moving into this discussion, it is important to note a few caveats. Although most current thinking is that the most realistic goal and outcome of pronunciation teaching is intelligibility (Derwing & Munro, 2009), and that *degree* of accent in the L2 is not as directly related to intelligibility as some traditionally have assumed (after all, *all* spoken language is accented), the majority of studies examine individual differences in the attainment of native or near-native pronunciation of the target language. Therefore, the focus of individual differences research may not match the goals of pronunciation teaching. Another caveat is the frequent assumption that the learner wants to attain native or near-native accent; however, as this chapter will demonstrate, learners are 'active agents in their language use, language choices, and targets for acquisition . . . they are not passive recipients of the target language' (Hansen Edwards, 2008, p. 251). The social context of language learning may impact what the learner chooses to use of the L2. Not all learners (Derwing, 2003; Smit & Dalton, 2000) may wish to sound like a native or near-native speaker of the L2. Another caveat is that, in measuring learners' pronunciation against native attainment, measurement is usually made against a monolingual norm, based on a standard variety of the language. This learning situation does not reflect the linguistic realities of many language learners in the real world, and particularly English users for whom English is one of multiple languages learned and used. For example, recent survey and interview research (Cavallaro, Ng & Seilhamer, 2014; Hansen Edwards, 2015, 2016) in the outer circle settings of Singapore and Hong Kong indicate that a localized variety of English is gaining acceptance and is used as a marker of identity by some speakers of English in these contexts.

With these caveats in mind, this chapter will provide an overview of current conceptualizations and research findings into individual differences in pronunciation. It focuses on the main factors found to affect L2 pronunciation, namely age, aptitude, affective variables, learning strategies, learning context, length of residence, gender and ethnic/peer/ social group identifications, as these are the factors most commonly researched for L2 pronunciation. Each of these will be discussed in turn, followed by recommendations for practice and future directions.

Current conceptualizations and research into individual differences

Age

First proposed by Penfield and Roberts (1959), and developed in more detail by Lenneberg (1967), the question of a whether a critical or sensitive period exists for the learning of languages has received a significant amount of research attention from both first language (L1) and second language (L2) researchers and in no domain is this more prevalent than L2 pronunciation. There is a widespread belief that age is a significant barrier to ultimate attainment in L2 pronunciation, and that native or near-native mastery is nearly impossible unless the learner acquires the language before the age of five, by some accounts (Granena & Long, 2012).

The effect of age has typically been investigated within an L2 context, as it was conceptualized first as age of arrival (AOA) to the target language setting and then later as age of 'meaningful L2 exposure' (Granena & Long, 2012, p. 311), also referred to as age of onset (AO) of meaningful L2 learning, owing to the recognition that AOA in an L2 setting did not guarantee actual exposure to the L2. There is a wealth of studies (e.g. Moyer, 2014; Thompson, 1991) that confirm that earlier age of acquisition is related to accentedness ratings.

What is not known is what accounts for these age effects; numerous proposals have been suggested, including quality and quantity of input differences to children versus adults, biological maturational effects and affective differences, though none of these explanations has been universally accepted (Granena & Long, 2012). Cases of 'exceptional' learners – learners who appear to defy age limitations in L2 pronunciation as they are judged to have a native accent in the L2 – as well as cases of learners who begin the L2 acquisition process in early childhood and yet fail to attain a native-like accent, complicate the issue. It is also worth noting that research on 'exceptional' learners has typically been carried out with participants whose L1 has a similar origin as the L2, which may promote positive transfer in L2 acquisition. Additionally, these studies typically employ controlled rather than spontaneous speech samples, which may not completely represent the learner's natural language use. While it is clear that age has a powerful impact on L2 pronunciation attainment, it is also apparent that other factors can override age effects for some learners. In a recent review of the AO literature, Granena and Long (2012) conclude that attainment of a native-like pronunciation is optimal if L2 acquisition occurs before the age of five, suggesting that there is a 'sensitive' period for L2 pronunciation acquisition; this claim contrasts with the widely cited conclusion by Flege, Munro and MacKay (1995) that there is no sensitive period but rather a linear relationship between age and accent. Granena and Long suggest that age effects increase as AO increases, with ultimate attainment in L2 pronunciation decreasing sharply after the age of five, while attainment in other areas, such as syntax or morphology, may have a longer sensitive period. After the close of a sensitive period, factors such as instruction, motivation, aptitude, L1 and L2 exposure and use may be more important in affecting ultimate attainment in the L2. In fact, aptitude may be the key factor in mitigating age effects, owing to the belief that aptitude is important for explicit learning and the hypothesis that explicit learning is more important in adolescent or adulthood language learning, as it may replace or support the ability for incidental/implicit learning, which declines with age. This suggests that explicit pronunciation teaching may be key to pronunciation attainment in the L2 and able to mitigate age effects.

Indeed, the numerous accounts of 'exceptional learners' who are able to pass for a native speaker (Moyer, 2004, 2011) indicate age of acquisition can be overridden by other factors such as professional motivation, an earlier age of instruction, type of instruction (explicit instruction with segmental and suprasegmental feedback), desire to sound like a native speaker and to culturally and linguistically assimilate with and have contact with native speakers. Conversely, other studies (Flege, Frieda & Nozawa, 1997; Thompson, 1991) have found cases of young learners – with AO below the sensitive period – who fail to attain native-like attainment in L2 pronunciation, indicating that native-like pronunciation is not guaranteed, even with an early AO. In particular, strong identification with the L1 community and/or extensive L1 use may also mitigate the favourable effects of an early AO. More research on both these phenomena is needed to more fully understand AO effects and how they can be alleviated via instruction in the L2 classroom.

Aptitude

Aptitude is defined as a special talent or ability in a particular area; interest in whether there was a special aptitude for language learning began in the 1960s by researchers such as Carroll (1962) and Pimsleur (1966), who operationalized aptitude for language learning as encompassing special abilities in phonemic coding ability (PCA), grammatical sensitivity, associative memory and inductive language learning ability. Several test batteries have been developed to assess aptitude as a predictor of L2 achievement including the modern language aptitude test (MLAT) and the Pimsleur language assessment battery (PLAB) (Carroll & Sapon, 1959; Pimsleur, 1966). While both of these test batteries include PCA, and while overall aptitude may possibly be the strongest predictor of L2 achievement (Baker Smemoe & Haslam, 2013), there have only been a few studies that directly examined the relationship between aptitude and L2 pronunciation attainment, although it has been hypothesized that learners with low PCA have more difficulty learning and remembering phonetic material as well as mimicking speech sounds (Hu et al., 2013).

Recent empirical work suggests that language aptitude is a general (not L2-specific) ability, and that individuals who exhibit L2 aptitude by implication have L1 aptitude in the same skill areas. Granena and Long (2012) investigated the role of language aptitude and found that aptitude effects may be interconnected with age effects, as learners who had an AO of three to six years of age had higher aptitude scores than learners who arrived between the ages of seven and 15, suggesting that early language training (or early bilingualism) may help increase language aptitude skills in general. The authors also found that aptitude became more important for L2 pronunciation attainment for older AO (particularly between the ages of 16 and 39). Taken together, these results suggest that early childhood language learning may help the development of language aptitude skills but conversely, that later adolescent/adult language learning success is increasingly dependent upon language aptitude.

In research on adult L1 German learners of English, Helmke and Wu (1980) found that the type of aptitude learners exhibited affected the impact of different types of instruction: learners who had high auditory discrimination scores benefited the most from pronunciation drills (multiple types of minimal pairs), whereas learners who had low auditory discrimination skills benefited more from single pronunciation exercises (a single type of minimal pairs).

Researchers (Hu et al., 2013; Milovanov, Huotilainen, Valimaki, Esquef & Tervaniemi, 2008) have also investigated the relationship of musical aptitude and L2 pronunciation attainment, with the finding that musical aptitude is correlated with higher productive and perceptive accuracy of L2 sounds for both children and adults. A study by Milovanov et al. (2008) on Finnish children learning English phonemes found that those children who scored higher on a pronunciation skills test also had higher scores on all subcomponents of a musical aptitude test, specifically in the areas of pitch, timbre, rhythm, tonality, time, loudness and general musical aptitude. As the authors state,

> It is possible that the participants with less-advanced pronunciation skills overlook the musical components of language, while those participants with advanced pronunciation skills have found the key to successful foreign language learning by also paying attention to the musical [i.e. melodic] components of speech.
>
> (p. 85)

Recent research (Hummel, 2009; Hu et al., 2013) on language aptitude has focused on phonological working memory (PWM), a part of working memory (see Badderly, 2003), as a special cognitive talent that has not been measured in traditional aptitude tests. PWM is considered to be responsible for speech and/or acoustic memory and maintenance (Hummel, 2009); research has found that there is an overlap between PWM and other brain networks involved in speech production and perception (Hu et al., 2013). Research suggests that the importance of PWM declines with age of learning for child L1 learners, and with vocabulary development for all L2 learners, as other factors such as long-term vocabulary and phonological knowledge play a greater role, suggesting that PWM is a more powerful predictor of learning at lower rather than advanced levels of proficiency. Research (e.g. Hu et al. 2013) has also found that PCA, as measured by the MLAT, and not PWM, was significantly correlated with English pronunciation aptitude, as measured by segmental accuracy on reading passage, suggesting that PCA and PWM represent different cognitive processes.

Affective variables: motivation, attitudes, anxiety, and willingness to communicate

Motivation can be defined as 'why humans behave and think as they do. . . . In broad terms, motivation is responsible for why people decide to do something, how long they are willing to sustain the activity, and how hard they are going to pursue it' (Dörnyei & Skehan, 2003, p. 614). L2 motivation research began in the late 1950s and was popularized by the socio-psychological work by Gardner, Lambert and Clements and colleagues (Gardner, 1985). This work pioneered the enduring binary constructs of instrumental and integrative motivation, which perceived motivation to be either linked to professional (instrumental) or social/personal (integrative) gains, while more recent research has expanded upon these constructs by adding components such as identity and willingness to communicate (WTC) to the formulation of motivation (MacIntyre, Dörnyei, Clément & Noels, 1998).

Studies of L2 pronunciation on 'exceptional' learners who are able to attain native-like L2 pronunciation cite motivation as one of the strongest factors impacting the learners' success. Moyer (2014) posits that type and extent of motivation is important: '*intensity* of one's drive to acquire the L2 – and even more, the *consistency* of that drive over time – is what matters for ultimate attainment in accent' (p. 431).

While learners may display motivation to learn L2 pronunciation, they may not necessarily be motivated to sound like a native or near-native speaker of the L2. Smit and Dalton (2000) researched the motivation of advanced learners of English in Austria who wanted to become English specialists. Results indicate that motivation was important for pronunciation learning. However, while the participants were motivated to learn the L2, they wanted to sound like themselves – and not like near-native speakers of British or American English.

WTC is defined as the 'probability of engaging in communication when free to choose to do so' (MacIntyre et al., 1998) and is influenced by many factors, including motivation, attitudes and the communicative situation (p. 546). Derwing, Munro and Thomson (2007) suggest that WTC may be more important in L2 rather than a FL context. The researchers found that L2 English participants who were more willing to communicate with native and non-native speakers of English made greater gains in comprehensibility and fluency over a 10-month period.

Several studies (Elliot, 1995; Kissling, 2014; Moyer, 2007) have also examined attitudes to the L2. Elliot (1995) developed the pronunciation attitude inventory (PAI) to assess L2 learners' attitudes towards acquiring the L2. In an examination of attitudes as a predictor of Spanish L2 pronunciation accuracy, Elliot found that the strongest predictor of L2 accuracy was the speaker's concern about acquiring native or target-like Spanish pronunciation. Moyer (2007) found attitudes towards the language itself, rather than the culture of the L2 speakers, is more powerful in predicting L2 pronunciation scores though both are significant. Neither of these types of attitudes, however, outweighed AO or LOR (see below) for predicting L2 pronunciation attainment. Attitudes may not have an equal effect on all features of the L2: Kissling's (2014) study of Spanish L2 learners' gains on consonants found that attitude was a signification predictor of both gains in perception and production of [d] [ð], though not other consonants investigated in the study.

Language learning strategies

Language learning strategies refers to 'the conscious actions that learners take to improve their language learning' (Anderson, 2005, p. 757). Research has often focused on documenting the strategies that advanced or successful L2 learners of pronunciation use frequently to repair communication breakdowns (Derwing & Rossiter, 2002; Osburne, 2003). Osburne (2003, p. 137) found that the most common strategies used by the successful learners in her study were, in order of frequency:

(a) focus on memory or imitation;
(b) focus on paralanguage (speed, volume, clarity);
(c) local articulatory gesture or single sound;
(d) focus on individual words;
(e) global articulatory gesture (mouth posture etc.);
(f) focus on prosodic structure;
(g) focus on individual syllables;
(h) clusters/focus on sounds below the syllable level.

Derwing and Rossiter (2002) found that paraphrase was the most frequently used strategy for repairing communication breakdowns, followed by self-repetition. The researchers conclude that paraphrasing may be a useful strategy for segmental and suprasegmental problems; teaching it may be beneficial.

Research has also examined the relationship between strategy use and L2 pronunciation achievement, finding that both quantity and type of strategies are important for pronunciation gains. Peterson (2000) researched the strategy use of adult learners of L2 Spanish and found that cognitive strategies (practising naturalistically, practising formally and analysing the sound system) were the most commonly used by her participants. Pawlak (2010), in a review of the pronunciation learning strategies (PLS) literature, also notes that cognitive, rather than memory or communicative strategies, may play a larger role in learning L2 pronunciation – which means that learners who use these types of strategies may perform better in the classroom than those who do not. Robins (2010), in research on the relationship between strategy use and segmental gains by L2 Japanese learners of English, found that pronunciation gains were correlated with *type* of strategy usage. One strategy – think of benefits to be gained by improving pronunciation (motivation) – was used the most frequently by the high-gain group, suggesting that strategy use is connected with motivation.

Other research suggests that quantity of strategy use may impact L2 pronunciation attainment (Rokoszewska, 2012), and that the use of one strategy is correlated with the use of other strategies. Finally, benefits of strategy use may be mediated by proficiency level: Ingels (2011) examined gains on suprasegmental features across three types of strategy use: (a) listening only, (b) listening and transcribing, (c) listening, transcribing and annotating and (d) rehearsal. She found that strategy use benefits differed by proficiency level: for lower-proficiency learners, greater gains were made if a combination of listening and transcribing as well as rehearsal strategies were used. For higher-proficiency learners, the combination of the strategy of listening, transcribing and annotating as well as rehearsal was more effective. Lower-proficiency learners also made greater gains from using strategies than higher-proficiency learners, and these self-monitoring strategies also affected aspects of suprasegmentals differently: overall, thought groups, linking and function words showed greatest improvements.

Language learning context

What do we mean by language learning context? A typical definition has been the physical context of learning, e.g. the difference between a foreign and a second language setting. Researchers have suggested that affective variables such as motivation and WTC may be more important in bilingual/L2 rather than FL learning contexts (Derwing, Munro & Thomson, 2007). This may not be the case for language learning strategies, as Baker Smemoe and Haslam (2013) did not find any differences in language learning context on the use of pronunciation strategies, perhaps because language learners have increasing access to the target language through the media. Such research may indicate that differences in FL versus L2 learning contexts are becoming obsolete.

Another way of examining the effect of language learning context is to examine studying abroad (SA) versus in a university at home (AH). A study by Díaz-Campos (2004) on L1 English learners of Spanish L2 investigated the linguistic gains in the acquisition of different phonemes by students AH versus those who were SA. Overall, Díaz-Campos found that improvement on some sounds was stronger for the AH group. Díaz-Campos also found that use of Spanish outside classroom during the semester had a significant effect on pronunciation accuracy. Finally, gender was a factor with women having a more native-like pronunciation than men.

Lord (2010) also examined the effect of SA on the acquisition of Spanish voiced stops and fricatives by contrasting two groups of SA: one group that had had explicit pronunciation instruction prior to the SA and one group that had had no explicit pronunciation instruction prior to SA. While Lord found that both groups gained in accuracy on some segmental features, the group that had instruction before the SA had greater gains, particularly on spirantization (e.g. pronouncing the intervocalic voiced consonant 'g' of 'agua' as a fricative), after the SA experience. This suggest that meaningful gains can best be made for an SA experience if the learners have previously been taught explicit pronunciation rules, so that they notice how these features are used in the input and thereby increase their own accuracy. Learners who do not have this instruction may still benefit from SA, but may not be as aware of how particular linguistic features are used by the speakers unless they have been explicitly taught such pronunciation rules.

Length of residence/extent of L1-L2 use/L2 experience

LOR was initially operationalized as the number of years the learner(s) had been living in the target language context; LOR has often been confounded with age of arrival (AOA) as learners who have a longer LOR have typically arrived in the target culture at an earlier age than those with a shorter LOR. As researchers note (e.g. Granena & Long, 2012), LOR is not a strong predictor of pronunciation attainment, even after age affects have been removed from the analysis. The major reason for this is that living in a target language region of the world does not in and of itself guarantee (or promote) greater L2 exposure and use; learners can have a long LOR in a region of the world in which the target language and culture are widely represented (e.g. the USA for English; Colombia for Spanish) and have primarily L1 networks and language use.

In more recent research, LOR has been redefined as: (a) extent of L1/L2 use and (b) L2 experience. A series of studies by Flege and colleagues (e.g. Flege, Frieda & Nozawa, 1997) have examined the impact of self-reported L1 and L2 use on L2 accent ratings, with the findings that not only increased L2 use and contact with native speakers but also decreased L1 use may positively impact L2 accentedness ratings.

The most recent reconceptualization of the LOR construct has been 'L2 experience' – the level of the actual engagement the learner has with the L2 in the L2 culture. Research suggests that different elements of L2 pronunciation may be affected differently by L2 experience. Trofimovich and Baker (2006) examined the acquisition of suprasegmental features and found that stress-timing was affected by amount of L2 experience, whereas peak alignment, speech rate, pause frequency and duration did not appear to be affected. AO also significantly affected speech rate and pause frequency and duration, however, though it did not affect stress-timing or peak alignment.

Derwing, Munro and Thomson (2007) examined the pronunciation changes of Slavic and Mandarin speakers across an L2 English context for over 10 months and found that the participants who reported greater contact with speakers of English had greater gains in fluency. Neither of the groups, however, had significant changes in accentedness, indicating that experience in the L2 may promote development in certain aspects of pronunciation such as fluency and intelligibility, important dimensions of oral communication, but not in segmental accuracy, which may require explicit instruction.

Moyer's (2011) research on L2 experience, which she defines as 'active language practice and use' (p. 194), focuses both on *quantity* of L2 experience (amount of type and quantity of modes) and *quality* of L2 experience (the extent to which the learner engages in L2 use in 'functionally significant ways') (p. 195). Moyer examined accuracy ratings on a number of segmental and suprasegmental features as well as LOR, AO, L2 experience and gender. Moyer found that age of immersion, age of instruction and AO were all highly significant, as was LOR. Interestingly, Moyer did not find that either marriage or cohabitation with a native speaker resulted in more native-like accent ratings; neither did length of instruction (though age of instruction did, suggesting that *when* you begin instructed L2 learning is more important than *how long* you receive it). Similar to previous research, Moyer also found that extent of L1 use was positively correlated with L2 accent – the greater the L1 use, the greater the L2 accent; however, *quantity* of L2 use was not significant. Quality of L2 use was significantly, and particularly, exposure to the L2 via multiple modes (e.g. not just speaking and listening but also reading and writing) and use of English in more *personal* modes such as home and social use rather than more formal modes such as with classmates or instructors and in academic settings. In particular, interaction with native-speaking friends as well as LOR were the strongest predictors of more native-like accentedness ratings. Conversely, Kissling (2014), in research on Spanish L2 learners, found that the effectiveness of explicit pronunciation instruction on Spanish consonants was improved by less contact with Spanish speakers outside the classroom, particularly if the speakers used a non-standard variety of Spanish. Kissling hypothesizes that this is because:

> The learners who used Spanish outside class reported that they interacted frequently with co-workers or friends. Some of their interlocutors may have had non-target-like pronunciations of the target sounds, or the learners may have been practicing their own non-target-like pronunciation of the sounds in these interactions, thereby becoming more entrenched in their pronunciation routines for some consonants during the study period.
> (p. 549)

As this research suggests, what learners do outside the classroom – who they interact with, what language they interact in, the types of contact with the language in the form of media etc. – has an impact on how native-like their L2 speech is perceived to be and what and how much of the L2 they learn.

Gender

Early research conceptualized this construct as a biological factor and used gender as a predictor variable for pronunciation accuracy, with mixed results (see Piske, MacKay and Flege (2001) for a review of these studies). Later research has examined gender as a socially constructed factor and acknowledges that gender, identity and social networks are connected in affecting what the L2 learner targets for acquisition and use.

L1 research has consistently found that women are more likely to use prestige/standard forms (Coates, 1986). Since L2 pronunciation attainment research typically compares learners' speech based on 'standard' L1 forms, it is plausible that women may appear to be better L2 learners because of differences in how the L2 is used, rather than differences in how it is acquired. To be specific, women have been found to use more prestige forms as they are targeting the gendered speech norms of the community in which they live. This pattern is evidenced by a range of research studies: Adamson and Regan (1991), for example, in their research on Vietnamese and Cambodian refugees to the US, found that the men had a greater usage of the non-standard [ɪn] variant of the {-ing} morpheme, while the women had a greater use of the prestige, standard [ɪŋ], reflecting the gendered usage of these variants by the larger L1 community in which the learners were living. This suggests that the women and men in Adamson and Regan's study had different (and gender-based) targets for acquisition, based on local speech norms and social/peer group networks. This is confirmed by research by Major (2004) on the acquisition of four American English naturalistic fast speech phenomena (informal speech variants) by L1 speakers of Japanese and Spanish; Major also found that the women consistently used more formal variants than the men, leading him to conclude that 'gender differences [in language] are acquired before stylistic [differences]' (p. 178). Díaz-Campos (2004) (discussed above) also found the women had more native-like pronunciation than men.

L1 and L2 gender roles may also impact what and how much of the L2 a learner is exposed to. Polat and Mahalingappa (2010) explored gender roles, identity and attainment of an L2 accent by Kurdish students learning L2 Turkish in Turkey. The researchers studied both middle (ages 13–14) and secondary (ages 16–18) school students and found that, similar to previous studies, girls had significantly more accurate pronunciation ratings than boys. The researchers investigated the participants' levels of identification with either the Turkish-speaking or Kurdish-speaking communities and found that the girls had higher levels of identification with the L2 Turkish community than boys, and that identification with the Turkish-speaking community is positively related to more native-like L2 accent scores. The researchers found that both family and non-family networks (likely peer and social groups) differed, with girls having more Turkish-speaking family and non-family networks than boys. Girls also had many more same-gender networks than boys, indicating that gender roles may be restricting the social networks the Kurdish girls were able to develop, leading to more Turkish networks than boys, hence greater exposure to the L2 than boys. A number of other studies (Hansen, 2006; Kouritzin, 2000) found also that L1 gendered norms may impact L2 access and opportunities for L2 use.

Gender and identity are also inextricably connected, with a learner's L1 identity at times conflicting with the gender identity portrayed by features of the L2, particularly in the acquisition of languages that may have gendered features that differ from the learner's L1 norms. Both Siegal (1996) and Ohara (2001) examined the resistance to use of particular L2 features by Western women learning Japanese; in both studies, some participants felt that the use of highly gendered features projected a humble and 'cute' identity at odds with their L1 identity. Though they knew how to and were able to use these features in the appropriate contexts, the participants rejected their usage, preferring to sound 'inappropriate' or as though they had failed to acquire these features, rather than using them and projecting a false and conflicting identity.

Identity: ethnic, peer and social group identifications

There is ample evidence that learners are aware of the differences in how the L2 is used by different groups of speakers in the L2 community and actively target or resist using different features due to ethnic, peer and social group affiliations. There has been a great deal of research on the relationship between use of different pronunciation features and ethnic identity. As a series of studies by Gatbonton and Trofimovich and colleagues (e.g. Gatbonton, 1975; Gatbonton, Trofimovich & Segalowitz, 2011) have investigated ethnic group affiliation (EGA) and L2 pronunciation among French–English bilinguals in Quebec, Canada. In an early study, Gatbonton (1975) found that greater English interdental fricative use was found for the French–English bilinguals in her study who had a stronger non-nationalistic (i.e. pro-English) stance than those who had strong nationalistic, and therefore pro-French stance. A later study by Gatbonton et al. (2011) on EGA and the use of the voiced interdental fricative by Francophone learners of English in Quebec found that different EGA types effected pronunciation accuracy, with participants who had higher political aspirations for their group and stronger beliefs in the role of language in group identity having fewer interdental fricative realizations. In research on American women learning Norwegian in Norway, Lybeck (2002) found that the use of an American versus a Norwegian /r/ was related to the level of cultural identification of the women to Norwegian culture, as well as their willingness to project a Norwegian rather than an American identity in Norway. This is confirmed by research by Gluszek, Newheiser and Dovidio (2011) on L2 learners in the US; the researchers found that the more the learner identified with the L2 culture, the more accurate the accent ratings.

Learners may also target non-standard variants if these are perceived to have 'covert' prestige within their social and peer groups. Anisman (1975), for example, found that peer identification impacted use of three phonological variables: schwa, /aɪ/ and the voiced dental fricative, for the male Puerto Rican study participants. The males with Black peer group contacts used more Black English variants, while the males with more Puerto Rican group contacts used more Spanish variants. Finally, those males who were targeting mainstream norms and values had the most standard English variants. Slomanson and Newman (2004), examined the use of light /l/ in onsets and dark /l/ in codas as well as /ey/ and /ow/ as monophthongs by New York Latino English speakers and found the usage of these features was related to the students' peer group identifications with hip-hoppers versus skaters. As these and the studies on gender suggest, the use of non-standard variants may appear to signify lack of acquisition of the 'target' form; for some learners, however, the non-standard variant *is* the target, and it is not that they have failed to acquire or are unable to acquire the standard form. They have simply chosen not to, based on gender, ethnic and peer identifications and affiliations.

Recommendations for practice

The major conclusion one can draw from this chapter is that individual differences in learner performance in the classroom are based on a myriad of interrelated factors, and not one factor alone. Additionally, not all pronunciation features may be affected in similar ways as some features may be more difficult to acquire due to markedness and/or L1 transfer. It is also important to recognize that learners have different aims, motives and goals for L2 learning, and that these may sometimes differ from instructional priorities. Based on these findings, I offer the following observations and suggestions to English language teachers:

- Despite an age-related decline in ultimate attainment of L2 pronunciation, pronunciation teaching matters and explicit pronunciation training has a facilitative, positive effect on development of a more native-like accent.
- There is a difference between what the learners *know* of the L2, and how they actually use it. Deleting word-final /l/ may not be due to lack of acquisition but rather a signal of in-group membership.
- There is no *one* correct accent. Everyone speaks with an accent, native English speakers and non-native English speakers alike. Whether the accent is *intelligible* in the contexts in which the learner uses the TL is what matters the most.

- Teach students to use a broad range of pronunciation learning strategies, and particularly cognitive strategies.
- Encourage learners to use the L2 in a variety of modes both inside and outside the classroom. Research suggests that using the L2 in a wide range of modes – including reading and writing – benefits L2 pronunciation.
- Provide learners with strategies and linguistic tools (e.g. samples of extemporaneous speech) to engage in naturalistic, personal communication with speakers of the L2 outside the classroom.
- Assist learners in determining their goals and targets for L2 pronunciation learning and develop realistic tasks and assessments based on these goals.
- Be aware of how L1 cultural norms affect how learners use the L2 within and beyond the classroom.
- Incorporate melodic (musical) training for pitch, tone, stress, as well as segmental features.
- Build awareness of sociolinguistic differences in how the L2 is used in the learner's local community.
- Provide a range of models (pronunciation features) for learners to choose from and explain when each may be used.
- Provide explicit pronunciation training for students going on SA before the SA sojourn.
- Aim for intelligibility, not accent reduction.

Future directions

An important question that has not always been asked in research on individual differences in L2 pronunciation attainment is, 'What do learners want to sound like? Is their preference to sound like a native speaker, to be intelligible to native speakers or to be intelligible to other L2 speakers from other backgrounds?' As was discussed in the chapter's introduction, the majority of research on individual differences has evaluated learners' pronunciation in reference to native or monolingual, 'inner circle' (Kachru, 1985) norms. For the many language learners, this is not the linguistic reality of their L2 learning nor may it be a desired or attainable goal. While we know a great deal about how individual differences affect native-like pronunciation attainment, we know very little about how these differences affect the *intelligibility* of L2 speakers. Future research on individual differences should shift gears and focus on intelligibility, and not ultimate attainment of L2 pronunciation. It should also be grounded in learners' linguistic realities – based on an L1-influenced multilingual model and localized varieties of the L2, which may, in some contexts, attain the status of an L1 for some speakers (e.g. Singapore English in Singapore, as discussed by Davies (2005)). Rather than asking 'Why aren't the learners attaining a native-like accent in the L2?', we should ask 'What are their actual contexts of English language use?'

Additionally, research on individual differences should be longitudinal as factors may shift across time. For example, motivation may change across time, language attitudes may change and speakers may also have changed social/peer groups. Finally, this chapter has not raised questions about issues such as *whose* judgement of accuracy and/or intelligibility is most relevant to the process of pronunciation learning.

Previous research has placed the burden of communicative success on the L2 learner, rather than focusing on the communication dynamic that exists between the speaker and listener, implying that the speaker must be 'accurate' in order to be understood. Future research on individual differences needs to expand from the research lab into the 'real' language classroom – the outside world – to examine how individual differences (personality, age, motivation, use of strategies, use of particular speech features to mark or resist identity) of both the speaker and the listener impact intelligibility.

References

Adamson, H. D., & Regan, V. M. (1991). The acquisition of community speech norms by Asian immigrants learning English as a second language. *Studies in Second Language Acquisition, 13*, 1–22.

Anderson, N. J. (2005). L2 learning strategies. In E. Hindle (Ed.), *Handbook of research in second language teaching and learning* (pp. 757–772). Mahwah, NJ: Lawrence Erlbaum.

Anisman, P. H. (1975). Some aspects of code switching in New York – Puerto Rican English. *Bilingual Review, 2*, 56–85.

Badderly, A. (2003). Working memory: Looking back and looking forward. *Nature Reviews Neuroscience, 4*, 829–839. doi:10.1038/nrn1201.

Baker Smemoe, W., & Haslam, N. (2013). The effect of language learning aptitude, strategy use and learning context on L2 pronunciation learning. *Applied Linguistics, 34*(4), 435–456.

Cavallaro, F., Ng, B. C., & Seilhamer, M. F. (2014). Singapore colloquial English: Issues of prestige and identity. *World Englishes, 33*(3), 378–397.

Carroll, J. B. (1962). The prediction of success in intensive foreign language training. In R. Glaser (Ed.), *Training research and education* (pp. 87–136). Pittsburgh, PA: University of Pittsburgh Press (ERIC Document Reproduction Service No. ED 038 051).

Carroll, J. B., & Sapon, S. M. (1959) [2002]. *Modern language aptitude test*. Bethesda, MD: Second Language Testing.

Coates, J. (1986). *Women, men and language: A sociolinguistic account of gender differences in language*. London: Longman.

Davies, A. (2005). The native speaker in applied linguistics. In A. Davies, & C. Elder, *The handbook of applied linguistics*. Oxford: Blackwell.

Derwing, T. M. (2003). What do ESL students say about their accents? *The Canadian Modern Language Journal/La Revue des langues vivantes, 59*(4), 547–566.

Derwing, T. M., & Munro, M. J. (2009). Putting accent in its place. Rethinking obstacles to communication. *Language Teaching, 42*(4), 476–490.

Derwing, T. M., Munro, M. J., & Thomson, R. I. (2007). A longitudinal study of ESL learners' fluency and comprehensibility development. *Applied Linguistics, 29*(3), 359–380.

Derwing, T. M., & Rossiter, M. J. (2002). ESL learners' perceptions of their pronunciation needs and strategies. *System, 30*, 155–166.

Díaz-Campos, M. (2004). Context of learning in the acquisition of Spanish second language phonology. *Studies in Second Language Acquisition, 26*, 249–273.

Dörnyei, Z., & Skehan, P. (2003). Individual differences in second language learning. In Doughty, C., *The handbook of second language acquisition* (pp. 589–630). Oxford: Blackwell.

Elliot, A. R. (1995). Field independence/dependence, hemispheric specialization, and attitude in relation to pronunciation accuracy in Spanish as a foreign language. *The Modern Language Journal, 79*(3), 356–371.

Flege, J. E., Frieda, E. M., & Nozawa, T. (1997). Amount of native-language (L1) use affects the pronunciation of an L2. *Journal of Phonetics, 25*, 169–186.

Flege, J. E., Munro, M. J., & MacKay, I. R. A. (1995). Factors affecting strength of perceived foreign accent in a second language. *Journal of the Acoustical Society of America, 97*(5), 3125–3134.

Gardner, R. C. (1985). *Social psychology and second language learning: The role of attitudes and motivation*. London: Edward Arnold.

Gatbonton, E. (1975). *Systematic variations in second language speech: A sociolinguistic study*. Unpublished doctoral dissertation, McGill University.Gatbonton, E., Trofimovich, P., & Segalowitz, N. (2011). Ethnic group affiliation and the development of a phonological variable. *The Modern Language Journal, 95*(2), 188–204.

Gluszek, A., Newheiser, A.-K., Y. Dovidio, J. H. (2011). Social psychological orientations and accent strength. *Journal of Language and Social Psychology, 30*(1), 28–45.

Granena, G., & Long, M. H. (2012). Age of onset, length of residence, language aptitude, and ultimate L2 attainment in three linguistic domains. *Second Language Research, 29*(3), 311–343.

Hansen, J. G. (2006). *Acquiring a non-native phonology: Linguistic constraints and social barriers*. London: Continuum.

Hansen Edwards, J. G. (2008). Social factors and variation in production in L2 phonology. In J. G. Hansen Edwards and M. L. Zampini (Eds), *Phonology and second language acquisition* (pp. 251–279). Amsterdam: John Benjamins.

Hansen Edwards, J. G. (2015). Hong Kong English: Attitudes, identity, and use. *Asian Englishes, 17*(3), 184–208.

Hansen Edwards, J. G. (2016). The language of politics and identity: Attitudes towards Hong Kong English pre- and post- the Umbrella Movement. *Asian Englishes, 18*(2), 157–164.

Helmke, B., & Wu, Y. S. (1980). Individual differences and foreign language pronunciation achievement. *Revue de phonétique appliquee, 53*, 25–34.

Hu, X., Ackermann, H., Martin, J. A., Erb, M., Winkler, S., & Reiterer, S. M. (2013). Language aptitude for pronunciation in advanced second language (L2) learners: Behavioural predictors and neural substrates. *Brain & Language, 127*, 366–376.

Hummel, K. M. (2009). Aptitude, phonological memory, and second language proficiency in nonnovice adult learners. *Applied Psycholinguistics, 30*, 225–249.

Ingels, S. A. (2011). *The effects of self-monitoring strategy use on the pronunciation of learners of English*. Unpublished doctoral dissertation, University of Illinois at Urbana-Champaign.

Kachru, B. (1985). Standards, codification, and sociolinguistic realism: The English language in the outer circle. In R. Quirk and H. Widdowson (Eds), *English in the world: Teaching and learning the language and the literature*. Cambridge: Cambridge University Press.

Kissling, E. M. (2014). What predicts the effectiveness of foreign-language pronunciation instruction? Investigating the role of perception and other individual differences. *The Canadian Modern Language Review/La revue canadiennes des langues vivantes, 70*(4), 532–558.

Kouritzin, S. (2000). Immigrant mothers redefine access to ESL classes: Contradictions and ambivalence. *Journal of Multilingual and Multicultural Development, 21*(1), 14–32.

Lenneberg, E. (1967). *Biological foundation of language*. New York, NY: Wiley.

Lord, G. (2010). The combined effects of immersion and instruction on second language pronunciation. *Foreign Language Annals, 43*(3), 488–503.

Lybeck, K. (2002). Cultural identification and second language pronunciation of Americans in Norway. *The Modern Language Journal, 86*(ii), 174–191.

MacIntyre, P. D., Dörnyei, Z., Clement, R., & Noels, K. A. (1998). Conceptualizing willingness to communicate in a L2: A situational model of L2 confidence and affiliation. *The Modern Language Journal, 82*(4), 545–562.

Major, R. C. (2004). Gender and stylistic variation in second language phonology. *Language Variation and Change, 16*(3), 169–188.

Milovanov, R., Huotilainen, M., Valimaki, V., Esquef, P. A. A., & Tervaniemi, M. (2008). Musical aptitude and second language pronunciation skills in school-aged children: Neural and behavioral evidence. *Brain Research, 1194*, 81–89.

Moyer, A. (2004). *Age, accent, and experience in second language acquisition*. Clevedon: Multilingual Matters.

Moyer, A. (2007). Do language attitudes determine accent? A study of bilinguals in the USA. *Journal of Multilingual and Multicultural Development, 28*(6), 502–518.

Moyer, A. (2011). An investigation of experience in L2 phonology: Does quality matter more than quantity? *The Canadian Modern Language Review/La Revue canadienne des langues vivantes, 67*(2), 191–216.

Moyer, A. (2014). Exceptional outcomes in L2 phonology: The critical factors of learner engagement and self-regulation. *Applied Linguistics, 35*(4), 418–440.

Ohara, Y. (2001). Finding one's voice in Japanese: A study of the pitch levels of L2 users. In A. Pavlenko, A. Blackledge, I. Piller, and M. Teutsch-Dwyer (Eds), *Multilingualism, second language learning, and gender* (pp. 231–256). Berlin: Mouton de Gruyter.

Osburne, A. G. (2003). Pronunciation strategies of advanced ESOL learners. *IRAL 41*, 131–143.

Pawlak, M. (2010). Designing and piloting a tool for the measurement of the use of pronunciation learning strategies. *Research in Language, 8*, 189–202.

Penfield, W., & Roberts, L. (1959). *Speech and brain mechanisms*. Princeton, NJ: Princeton University Press.

Peterson, S. S. (2000). *Pronunciation learning strategies: A first look*. Unpublished research report.

Pimsleur, P. (1966) [2003]. *The Pimsleur language aptitude battery*. Bethesda, MD: Second Language Testing.

Piske, T., MacKay, I. R. A., & Flege, J. E. (2001). Factors affecting degree of foreign accent in an L2: A review. *Journal of Phonetics, 29*, 191–215.

Polat, N., & Mahalingappa, L. J. (2010). Gender differences in identity and acculturation patterns and L2 accent attainment. *Journal of Language, Identity, and Education, 9*(1), 17–35.

Robins, S. (2010). *Examining the effects of pronunciation strategy usage on pronunciation gains by L2 Japanese learners*. Unpublished manuscript. BYU ScholarsArchive.

Rokoszewska, K. (2012). The influence of pronunciation learning strategies on mastering English vowels. *Studies in Second Language Learning and Teaching, 2*(3), 391–413.

Siegal, M. (1996). The role of learner subjectivity in second language sociolinguistic competency: Western women learning Japanese. *Applied Linguistics, 17*(3), 356–382.

Slomanson, P., & Newman, M. (2004). Peer group identification and variation in New York Latino English laterals. *English World-Wide, 25*(2), 199–216.

Smit, U., & Dalton, C. (2000). Motivational patterns in advanced EFL pronunciation. *IRAL, 38*, 229–246.

Thompson, I. (1991). Foreign accents revisited: The English pronunciation of Russian immigrants. *Language Learning, 41*(2), 177–204.

Trofimovich, P., & Baker, W. (2006). Learning second language suprasegmentals: Effect of L2 experience on prosody and fluency characteristics of L2 speech. *Studies in Second Language Acquisition, 28*, 1–30.

24

Attitudes towards non-native pronunciation

Stephanie Lindemann and Maxi-Ann Campbell

Introduction

Listeners often feel comfortable making non-linguistic judgements about speakers, including drawing conclusions about their education, economic status and personality based on their pronunciation. This is particularly true of reactions to non-native speakers (NNSs), whose pronunciation is often measured against native speaker (NS) norms.[1] However, there are also several other factors that affect listeners' evaluations, such as where they believe, or are told, the speaker is from and what this person looks like. Educators, researchers and NNSs themselves may wish to take an understanding of such factors into account when deciding how to respond to negative evaluations of non-native pronunciation. The first part of this chapter introduces key terms and approaches used to investigate attitudes towards NNS pronunciation and the findings from studies that employed these methods. The chapter's second part looks at other social factors that affect how people evaluate NNSs. Finally, future directions for teachers and researchers to address the issue of listeners' attitudes towards non-native pronunciation in teaching and research are suggested.

Investigating listeners' attitudes towards pronunciation

Key terms and approaches

Attitudes towards non-native pronunciation have been investigated in a variety of fields, including social psychology and applied linguistics. Studies in the field of social psychology, beginning with groundbreaking work by Lambert and colleagues (Lambert, Hodgson, Gardner & Fillenbaum, 1960) have overwhelmingly used *matched-guise* and *verbal guise* techniques to ascertain a listener's evaluation of accents in different contexts. In these techniques, listeners rate speakers who are all saying the same thing, usually reading a script with lexical and grammatical choices kept constant, allowing a focus on reaction to accent without explicitly alerting the listener to that focus. The matched-guise technique involves having listeners unknowingly evaluate the same speaker who is employing different 'guises', in this case speaking in different accents. This technique can help to control for the natural variance in vocal quality between speakers, such as one speaker perhaps sounding more 'nasal' than another, because the listeners are evaluating the same speaker(s) under different guises. However, it is difficult to find people who are truly multidialectal in terms of their pronunciation of the same language. Therefore, many studies employ the verbal guise technique. The verbal guise technique is similar to the matched-guise technique in that the listener is evaluating different accents but different speakers produce these accents; ideally speakers are otherwise well matched in terms of other factors such as gender, voice quality, speed, intonation patterns and the like.

The scales for evaluating the speaker have traditionally fallen into the categories *status* and *solidarity*, with some studies also including *dynamism* and/or *language-focused traits*. Status traits are associated with the speaker's perceived social and economic status in society and may involve rating the speaker's intelligence or education level. Solidarity traits relate to that person's character, including whether or not they seem kind or friendly. Dynamism refers to 'how active, confident, and energetic the speaker sounds' (Cargile & Giles, 1998, p. 341). Finally, language-focused traits offer insight into the listeners' perception of how well the speaker speaks, such as judging whether the speaker is 'nice to listen to' (Lindemann, 2003). Participants in these studies are typically asked to rate each speaker on a number of such traits on a five- or seven-point scale from 'agree strongly' to 'disagree strongly' or the like. Furthermore, the key dimensions discussed here have some variation among studies in how they are labelled; for example, solidarity is sometimes referred to as *attractiveness*. However, these terms serve as a good starting point for the following discussion on how NSs and NNSs evaluate non-native pronunciation.

A more recent approach to studying attitude in social psychology has been the implicit association test (Greenwald, McGhee & Schwartz, 1998), which aims to give insight into subconscious or unstated attitudes. These tests ask participants to sort variables and attributes as quickly as possible, with one variable sorted into the same category with positive attributes and the other with negative attributes. One would then complete the sorting task again where the variables and attributes were reversed. For example, Dasgupta, McGhee, Greenwald and Banaji (2000) asked their participants to sort Caucasian in the same category as pleasant concepts and African-American with unpleasant concepts. The participants were then asked to complete the tasks again, but categorizing African-American with pleasant concepts and Caucasian with unpleasant. The participant's speed in each version of the task is compared, interpreted with the assumption that people will react faster to associations that they frequently make and slower when they are making connections that go against their usual attribution. In this case, participants tended to sort faster when Caucasian was associated with pleasant attributes and African-American with negative attributes, indicating a bias against African-Americans that the participants themselves would likely not have expressed more directly and might not even have been aware of. This technique can also be utilized in assessing listeners' attitudes towards different accents. As Pantos and Perkins (2013, p. 13) note, 'listeners can hypercorrect their explicit attitude reporting if they suspect their implicit attitudes might reveal a socially unacceptable bias'; therefore, having an implicit measure of attitudes can offer a more accurate picture of a person's attitudes towards an accent.

Finally, linguists such as Niedzielski and Preston have pursued similar questions under the general category of *folk linguistics* (Niedzielski & Preston, 2003, 2009; Preston, 2011). Folk linguistics refers to non-linguists' beliefs about language, including pronunciation, which may be different than a linguist's beliefs about or descriptions of language. For example, the term *accent* when used by non-linguists often means 'not sounding like me' or 'mispronounced', as opposed to a specific set of pronunciation features that generally characterize the way a group of people sound when they speak. Folk beliefs or attitudes can be investigated through a variety of approaches, including more direct methods such as asking participants to rate or describe different accents, either in paper-and-pencil surveys or through interview methods.

These folk beliefs about language are sometimes related to or include *standard language ideology* (Milroy & Milroy, 1998). Standard language ideology is the belief that there exists a set of core English features or rules that are inherently correct and that could at least in principle be uniquely identified (such that one way of speaking is 'right' and that another is 'wrong', even if a group of speakers cannot agree on which is which). The people who follow these rules closely are considered 'well-spoken', 'educated' and the like, while the opposite is true for those who diverge from these rules. In actuality, there is nothing inherently better about the variety considered 'standard', and the rules (or pronunciations) themselves are simply based on those that happen to be used natively by social groups who have greater political power, either currently or historically. In other words, what is considered 'correct', including 'correct pronunciation', is based on the power of the speakers who use it, rather than inherent characteristics of the pronunciation itself. In addition, there is considerable variation in what is considered 'standard', especially since standards of pronunciation change over time and from place to place. Thus, what is called 'standard' is not actually standard in the sense of uniform. Given the controversial and unclear definition of 'standard', the term will be used in quotes throughout this chapter. Standard language ideologies have been investigated using several of the methods already mentioned as well as discourse analysis (e.g. Jenkins, 2007; Subtirelu, 2015); more recent studies have also utilized corpus linguistic approaches (e.g. Subtirelu, 2015).

Findings

One common finding from studies using all of the above approaches is that 'standard' native accents are consistently evaluated more favourably on status traits than are non-native accents. For example, Ryan and Bulik (1982) utilized a verbal guise technique to investigate listeners' evaluations of German-accented and US-accented English. They found that listeners evaluated the German-accented speakers more negatively not only on status traits but also on solidarity and language-focused traits. Lindemann (2003) explored attitudes towards Korean-accented speakers, finding that they were also evaluated more negatively on status traits than the NSs and were evaluated even more negatively on language-focused traits, although they were rated equally on solidarity traits. Overall, results from verbal guise studies have demonstrated that native English listeners regularly rate non-native accents more negatively than 'standard' NS accents on status and language traits, whereas results for solidarity traits have been more mixed (Cargile, 1997; Cargile & Giles, 1998; Ryan, Carranza & Moffie, 1977; Ryan & Sebastian, 1980).

Interestingly, more negative evaluations for a non-native accent are also found among NNSs themselves (e.g. Scales, Wennerstrom, Richard & Wu, 2006). Such negative evaluations even extend to rating NNSs from one's own language background more negatively than NSs on status traits such as intelligence and education. For example, McKenzie (2008) investigated English-learning Japanese university students' attitudes towards multiple English accents (e.g. Glasgow Standard and Midwest US) and Japanese-accented English, finding that these students rated NSs significantly higher than NNSs on competence (parallel to status) traits. Dalton-Puffer, Kaltenböck and Smit (1997) had similar findings in Austria, as did Xu, Wang and Case (2010) in China, and Yook and Lindemann (2013) in Korea, all for non-native English speakers' ratings of their own accents. Given these findings, it is perhaps unsurprising that English learners frequently express a preference for acquiring a native-like accent over an intelligible but identifiably non-native one (Timmis, 2002), in spite of the low likelihood of their being able to acquire such an accent (Moyer, 1999).

The implicit association test (IAT) has only recently begun to be used to assess attitudes towards non-native pronunciation, but the one study that applied this technique found more negative attitudes towards non-native speech than found with a verbal guise task. Specifically, Pantos and Perkins (2013) found that their participants, who were from diverse backgrounds and included native and non-native English speakers, preferred a US as opposed to a Korean-accented English speaker in the IAT results, although the explicit measure of their attitudes (the verbal guise task) showed more positive views of the Korean-accented speaker. This might suggest that evaluations of non-native speech may be more negative than is captured in many of the studies using explicit attitudes approaches.

Nevertheless, folk linguistic studies that ask for explicit ratings of non-native speech also find that both native and non-native respondents are quite willing to provide negative descriptions or ratings of non-native speech. For example, when Lindemann (2005) asked native US English-speaking participants to rate the Englishes of undergraduate students from different countries on how correct, pleasant and friendly they sounded, participants not only rated the native varieties as the most correct but also as the most pleasant and friendly. Similarly, Jenkins (2007) found that NNSs completing a similar task also rated native varieties the highest on all traits (in this case, correctness, acceptability for international communication, and pleasantness). Further, when discussing an alternative (non-NS-based) approach to teaching pronunciation for English as a lingua franca users, Jenkins (2007) found that both NS and NNS MA students who were also language teachers initially thought it would be 'a lowering of standards' (p. 124) and 'the watering down of the pronunciation system as it exists' (p. 125). This highlights that language teachers, in addition to laypeople, may view non-native accents as in some ways inferior to native accents.

These attitudes are not only manifested when researchers elicit them as in the studies above; negative attitudes towards non-native accents have also been found in real-world situations in studies that focus on standard language ideology. Lippi-Green (2012) discusses several examples in which people either lost their jobs or were denied a promotion owing to their accent. For example, Phanna Xieng, a banker, was denied a promotion because of his superiors' concerns about his 'accent', despite his stellar work record and the fact that he was already successfully doing the job to which he was denied promotion. On a somewhat different level, Shuck (2004) found in her interviews of US undergraduates about their experiences with people who 'didn't speak English very well' (p. 197) that descriptions frequently included claims that one 'couldn't understand a word he/she said' (p. 196). As Subtirelu (2015) pointed out in his analysis of how undergraduate students evaluated their maths professors on the site RateMyProfessor.com, 'this formulaic strategy uses the social acceptability of hyperbole in complaints or narratives to erase [non-native English-speaking] instructors' English competency' (p. 52). Further, he found that students frequently commented on the language of instructors with common Asian last names but rarely ever spoke about the language ability of instructors with US last names. Students rarely ever offered high praise to their 'Asian' instructors, though they frequently did so for US instructors. Given the importance of student evaluations in an instructor's teaching portfolio, these students' focus on the instructor's accent as a seemingly justified means of negatively evaluating the instructor's maths teaching abilities clearly has harmful consequences for Asian instructors.

Ironically, such negative attitudes towards non-native accents are perpetuated even in the language teaching industry, with systematic and in some cases entirely overt hiring biases against teachers who are NNSs (Clark & Paran, 2007; Kubota & Lin, 2006; Mahboob, Uhrig, Newman & Hartford, 2004; Methitham, 2011). For example, Mahboob et al. (2004) found that NNS English teachers only made up about 7.9 per cent of teachers employed in the 118 intensive English programmes surveyed, though data have suggested that NNSs make up approximately 40 per cent of the student population of TESOL, applied linguistics and language education programmes in North America, Britain and Australia (Liu, 1999). Clark and Paran (2007) conducted a similar study in the UK and found that hiring practices were the same, with NNS English teachers being less likely to be employed by institutions that believed that native speaker status is either moderately or very important, which made up 72.3 per cent of the respondents. While other factors are also considered in the hiring process, the importance of native speaker status to recruiters of language teachers can put NNS English teachers at an immediate and significant disadvantage.

In many cases such hiring practices may be based on or at least justified by pointing to learners' demands for teachers who are NSs themselves (Medgyes, 2003). However, Watson Todd and Pojanapunya (2009) found a disparity in their Thai participants' explicit and implicit preferences for native and NNS English teachers. These English language learners explicitly stated a preference for NS English teachers, but their implicit evaluations (measured through an IAT) showed no significant preference for either. Furthermore, they expressed having more 'warm' feelings towards Thai English teachers. These findings suggest that language learners may consciously state or believe native speakers are the best role models for effective language teaching even when they do not have an implicit preference, or use other criteria for teacher preference (e.g. teaching style).

To summarize, both native and non-native speakers tend to evaluate NNSs, as identified by their pronunciation, more negatively on status traits, though ratings of NNSs on solidarity traits are more mixed. Language-focused traits are also evaluated negatively, sometimes even more so than status traits. This is often the case even when evaluating one's own non-native accent. These attitudes are then realized in the job market, with an NNS's accent being cited as problematic in relationship to whether or not they can do their job as effectively as an NS. This is seen in the language teaching industry as well, with English programme recruiters citing NS status as an important criterion in their hiring practice. However, these attitudes and resulting behaviours are not only based on pronunciation, as the next section will illustrate.

Attitudes towards social groups, not language

One reaction to the research discussed in the preceding section may be to suggest that learners should focus on achieving a native-like accent in order to avoid negative attitudes. In fact, there is evidence that more native-like accents are rated more positively than less native-like ones (Beinhoff, 2013; Bresnahan, Ohashi, Nebashi, Liu & Morinaga Shearman, 2002; Ryan et al., 1977). It is also quite plausible that when listeners have difficulty understanding a speaker they are more likely to rate them negatively (although negative attitudes can also lead to poorer comprehension, making it more complicated to determine the root prob-lem). Thus, individual NNSs may decrease the negativity of attitudes directed towards their accents if they are able to adopt more native-like pronunciation, especially if the starting point is an accent that is hard for a wide range of listeners to understand. However, there are several problems with this as a comprehensive approach to addressing negative attitudes towards non-native pronunciation. First, many researchers have noted that native-like pronunciation is an unrealistic goal for most learners (e.g. Moyer, 1999). Second, the difficulty of understanding an accent is not necessarily correlated with how far it is from native-like (Munro & Derwing, 1995). A third issue, related to the main focus of this section, is that where there is discrimination against some accents it is unjust to place the onus on the victim of that discrimination.

Indeed, the negative ratings of non-native speech described in the previous section extend beyond issues of intelligibility and comprehensibility into assessments of a speaker's intelligence and other unrelated factors. Such ratings are best understood as attitudes towards the social or political groups associated with the speech, rather than towards non-native speech itself. The remainder of this section examines some of the evidence for this claim by looking at how listeners' perception of speakers' social groups (whether defined by ethnicity, race, nationality or other factors) appear to influence their attitudes towards their speech. Specifically, there is evidence that (a) attitudes towards NNSs appear to show patterns based on factors that are irrelevant to language proficiency, such as race, (b) ratings of the same speakers may change depending on how those speakers are presented and (c) the same linguistic features may be evaluated differently depending on who is perceived as using them.

In terms of the first point, that attitudes towards NNSs appear to show patterns based on factors that are irrelevant to their proficiency, Lippi-Green (2012) has pointed out in reference to negative attitudes to non-native speech in the US that 'it is not all foreign accents, but only accent linked to skin that isn't white, or which signals a third-world homeland, which evokes such negative reactions' (p. 253). She also notes that the varieties spoken by large recent immigrant groups tend to be viewed particularly negatively, such that the specific varieties that occasion the most negative reactions change over time with immigration patterns.

In fact, a folk linguistic study in which participants were asked to rate the correctness, pleasantness and friendliness of the English of US college students who came from various countries of the world found that the most positively rated countries were in Western Europe and did not include any with large populations of recent immigrants – indeed, with respondents distinguishing between the English of college students from Spain and those from Mexico, with the latter rated more negatively (Lindemann, 2005). Political relationships between the US and the students' countries of origin also appeared to explain participants' ratings in some cases. Specifically, the lowest-rated countries included Eastern European countries and the Middle East, with Iraq and Afghanistan – both of which the US had recently been in conflict with when the data were collected – at the very bottom of the list of 58 countries. The fact that the study participants made these sorts of distinctions although they were asked to rate the imagined speech of college students in the US suggests that their ratings are not likely based on the language proficiency of the speakers but on the speakers' imagined social groups.

Further evidence of the role of non-linguistic factors in attitudes to pronunciation comes from the second point noted above, the fact that the same speech may be rated differently depending on how the speaker is identified to listeners. For example, Buckingham (2014) had Omani university students rate five NNS English teachers, each in two different guises: once when they were identified by their actual nationality, and a second time when they were identified as a different nationality that was plausible for their accent. Speakers from Iran, Pakistan and Syria were rated significantly lower when they were identified by their actual nationality than when they were identified as being from the US (in the case of the Irani) or the UK. (On the other hand, the Kenyan speaker was rated no higher when he was identified as Canadian; the fifth speaker, an Omani, was rated no differently in Omani and Philippine guises.)

Apparent race can also play a role in perceptions of speech, as seen in studies that found that listeners who hear a recorded lecture and see a picture of either an Asian or a Caucasian apparently delivering the lecture provide different ratings depending on the face they see (Kang & Rubin, 2009; Rubin, 1992). In these studies, both perception of accent and recall of the lecture content were affected, with seeing an Asian linked to perceiving more of a non-native accent and poorer recall. Such findings complicate the link between poor comprehension and negative attitudes; in this case, more negative attitudes led to poorer comprehension rather than the reverse (Kang & Rubin, 2009).

In other cases, the same speakers have been rated differently depending on whether or not their background was revealed to listeners. Yook and Lindemann (2013) found that Korean listeners expressed a preference for US English when they were directly asked what variety they thought Korean speakers should learn. However, in a verbal guise task with five accents presented, they rated a British speaker the highest on competence traits when they were not told anything about the speaker's origin. When participants were told speakers' origins, they rated the British speaker (and an African-American speaker) lower than when they were not told, while they rated a European-American speaker and a Korean-accented speaker more highly in that condition. In other words, their ratings of speakers' competence was influenced by what they were told about the speakers' national and ethnic background rather than only their actual pronunciation, with ratings of speakers lining up more with their stated accent preferences when they had this information. In Japan, NSs of Southern US English, Midwestern US English and Glaswegian English were all rated as significantly more competent when listeners could accurately identify what country the speakers were from (McKenzie, 2008).

Other background information about the speaker may interact with accent in its effects on listener ratings. Ryan and Sebastian (1980) found that native English-speaking undergraduates rated the same Spanish-accented speakers more negatively on solidarity traits as well as status traits when they were presented as lower-class than when they were presented as middle class, while the difference between ratings of NS accents in the same class guises was smaller. In other words, explicit information about a speaker's social class had less impact on ratings of an NS than it did on ratings of a Spanish-accented speaker.

Similarly, a study investigating 'interviewer' judgements of job applicants found an interaction between cues based on name and accent (Segrest Purkiss, Perrewé, Gillespie, Mayes & Ferris, 2006). Undergraduate students enrolled in basic management courses rated a video-recorded highly qualified job applicant speaking English in one of four guises, including all combinations of Hispanic versus Anglo name and Spanish accent versus native accent. The guise in which the applicant had a Hispanic name with a native accent was rated most highly, while the Hispanic name and Spanish accent guise was rated most negatively. Both Anglo name guises fell in between, with no such effect of accent. Thus, in this case, the impact of accent on ratings was dependent on whether the speaker's name also identified him as Hispanic.

Summing up evidence for this second point, that ratings of the same speakers may change depending on how those speakers are presented, we see that listeners may demonstrate positive attitudes towards non-native speech when the speaker belongs to or is perceived as belonging to a more favourably viewed group. Anecdotal evidence suggests that more positive attitudes towards non-native speech may also occur when the speaker is viewed as personally attractive in some other way. For example, although an analysis of the use of the term 'broken English' in the Corpus of Contemporary American English (Davies, 2008) and on the Internet found that it was largely used to describe marginalized or highly negative people, it was in rare cases used to demonstrate a more positive feature, as in Fabio's 'charmingly broken English' or Sammy Sosa's 'delightful broken English' (Lindemann & Moran, 2010). The few examples of this positive usage were mostly applied to famous people; in all such cases the people were presented very positively in terms of their non-language-related qualities as well.

While 'broken English' cannot be identified as a specific linguistic feature, this leads to the third point, that the same linguistic features may be evaluated differently depending on who is perceived as using them. Some participants in Lindemann's (2005) study described German and Russian accents together as 'harsh, broken, hard' and as 'very throat-like, tough' (p. 203). Although we do not have more information about the sounds these participants had in mind, anecdotally US students sometimes produce something like a velar fricative as an example of the 'harsh sound' of German accents. However, although this sound occurs in German, it does not usually occur in a German accent in English. On the other hand, a very similar sound, produced farther back (and therefore more 'throat-like') does commonly occur in French accents, which were not described as 'harsh' in Lindemann's data at all and were rated more highly on pleasantness.

One study that explicitly addressed this issue by investigating the role of consonant pronunciation in attitudes towards the speaker found that more native-like consonants were rated higher, but the speaker's native language may be a more important factor. Specifically, Beinhoff (2013) investigated the pronunciation of specific consonants produced by German and Greek speakers in words that otherwise did not vary greatly in consonant pronunciation (e.g. *bill*, *pool* and *call* for /l/), and also asked British, German and Greek listeners to rate the accents on friendliness, intelligence and reliability based on pronunciation of these individual words. Interestingly, the Greek speakers' pronunciation of post-vocalic /l/ (for example) fell between the velarized (sometimes called 'dark l') pronunciation of British speakers and the unvelarized ('clear l') pronunciation of the German speakers, yet the average ratings of Greek speakers on intelligence and reliability based on words with this /l/ were nevertheless lower than those of German speakers. In other words, even where the Greek accent was more native-like than the German accent, the Greek accent was still rated more negatively. Beinhoff concludes that general stereotypes of the speaker's social (in this case, national) group influence the overall ratings of accents, and that adjustments to accents could only alter such attitudes within certain boundaries, 'given that German accents were never rated significantly more negatively on reliability and intelligence than Greek accents no matter how much their consonants varied' (p. 232).

Thus, although certain pronunciations may be cited as being the justification for negative attitudes towards an accent, such examples may well be after-the-fact rationalizations (in the case of participants in Lindemann's 2005 study) or secondary to other factors (as in Beinhoff's 2013 study). On the other hand, we see clear examples where presumably irrelevant information such as information about the speaker's race or nationality affects listener perceptions of their speech, including evaluations of the speaker. In the following section we consider how knowledge of such factors in attitudes towards non-native pronunciation may be addressed in teaching.

Recommendations for practice

As indicated thus far, teaching students pronunciation based on NS norms does not guarantee that these learners will be evaluated more positively. Furthermore, while students might explicitly state a preference for NS models or teachers, this may not match their implicit preferences (Watson Todd & Pojanapunya, 2009, discussed in the findings section), especially when the language they are studying is not a dominant language in the students' context. Therefore, a focus on learners' intelligibility rather than nativeness of accent (Levis, 2005) is warranted not only for reasons of practicality but also based on the attitudes research discussed in the previous section. Teachers should also consider the use of comprehensible and intelligible NNSs as pronunciation models in the classroom (Murphy, 2014). While it is true that materials that incorporate non-native pronunciation models are not as readily available as materials that use NS models presently, publishers will respond to the change in teachers' materials needs if they notice a shifting trend in pronunciation models used in the classroom. In any case, Murphy (2014) suggests that teachers can direct students in how to use the Internet to find and utilize intelligible and comprehensible – but still identifiably non-native – models from the students' own language backgrounds, and provides links to several specific examples, such as Felipe Calderon, Jehan Sadat and Tu Wei-Ming.

In addition to including NNS models, teachers are in a good position to change the way their students think and talk about their pronunciation. Specifically, teachers can highlight variation in pronunciation in the students' native language in order to raise students' awareness that variation in pronunciation is also likely in the language they are studying. Chavez (2009) argues in her folk linguistic account of learners' description of German pronunciation, vocabulary and grammar that

> instructional practices lure learners into the mistaken assumption that the way in which linguists, textbooks, and teachers describe language, i.e. in the form of rules which together shape a 'system,' accurately reflects how we use and how we learn languages and, in fact, represents a comprehensive account of language itself.
>
> (p. 14)

In other words, sometimes instruction can give the impression that the language has been fully explained in the pages of the textbook or context of the classroom. It is admittedly easier to teach one 'correct' way to pronounce a phoneme, word or phrase without including any discussion of the natural variation in pronunciation that happens even among NSs of a language. Müller (2013) refers to the former teaching method as '*pronunciation-in-isolation*', and she suggests that teachers include discussions of '*pronunciation-as-language*' (p. 216, italics in original). Pronunciation-as-language involves discussing variation in accents, raising awareness that variation in pronunciation is normal and engaging students in reflective discussions about their attitudes towards their own and others' accents.

Finally, it is important in teaching language, especially English given its current lingua franca status, to acknowledge that the present system puts NNSs, particularly non-Anglo NNSs, at an immediate disadvantage to 'standard' NSs. For example, when miscommunication occurs between native and non-native speakers, the onus is often placed on the NNS, although the NSs' reaction could be a result of their own negative attitudes (Lindemann, 2002), inexperience with non-native speech (Gass & Varonis, 1984) or assumptions about the speaker (Rubin, 1992). The findings from the research discussed in this chapter could be used to empower language learners by making them aware that negative reactions to their pronunciation are not necessarily indicative of insufficient study or practice. This could help students to maintain their motivation when they have difficulty communicating, as Subtirelu (2014) found that learners were more willing to communicate in their second language if they did not immediately assume blame for any communication breakdowns. The ability to identify other reasons why an interaction might not have been successful can also help students to develop strategies for engaging with others who are potentially unfamiliar with their accent or have negative attitudes towards NNSs.

Future directions

Further research can help us interpret how the research findings thus far relate to the daily experiences of NNSs, as well as refine ways of addressing attitudes towards pronunciation in language teaching. As we have seen, negative attitudes towards non-native pronunciation are pervasive and well-documented. We have also seen that non-native pronunciation can interact with other non-linguistic speaker factors such as identification of that speaker's ethnicity or nationality, although much more research is needed on how such factors interact. Such research can lead to a much more nuanced understanding of the factors involved in how people may react to non-native accents in more everyday situations, when they are not merely presented with decontextualized (and often repetitive) recordings. Besides factors such as ethnicity and how the speaker is identified, more individual factors such as a speaker's (non-linguistic) attractiveness or personal charisma may complicate attitudes towards non-native pronunciation; such factors remain to be investigated.

Future research should also consider how pronunciation interacts with other speaker linguistic factors, as well as with listener factors. In terms of speaker linguistic factors, we know relatively little about how attitudes may relate to specific aspects of pronunciation, as opposed to how they relate to globally and nebulously defined non-native accents (or participants' claims about those accents, which may or may not correspond with the actual pronunciation used). In many studies, accents are simply identified by the speaker's native language, with no further information about specific features of pronunciation. Very few studies have systematically manipulated aspects of pronunciation to determine their effect on attitude, although Beinhoff's (2013) study is a start in this direction. Another attitudes study that systematically manipulated speech rate and pitch variation found that these features were more relevant than accent to listeners' attitudes (Ray & Zahn, 1999). However, the only accents investigated were those of different native English varieties; it would be interesting to discover whether the same pattern holds for non-native accents.

Other linguistic factors may also impact listener attitudes towards accent. For example, an NNS's focus on producing a native-like accent may result in lower fluency (Thomson, 2015), which may trigger more negative evaluations than a less native-like accent spoken more fluently; to our knowledge, the effect of this trade-off on the listener's attitude has not been tested. In addition, as noted above, most language attitudes studies have also controlled for lexicon and grammar. However, such features may well interact with accent. Interestingly, one matched-guise study investigating attitudes towards Japanese-accented English found no difference in listener attitudes towards a 'heavy' accent compared to a 'heavy' accent using simplified vocabulary and non-native grammatical features (Cargile & Giles, 1998). In fact, listeners rated the 'heavy' accent guise that did not include these features more negatively on grammar and vocabulary than they rated a 'moderate' accent guise, although these two guises did not differ along those particular dimensions. In other words, NNSs with accents that are more strongly influenced by their native language may be perceived as also having weaker vocabulary and grammatical skills than they actually do.

On the other hand, increased grammatical accuracy and lexical richness have both been found to be related to judgements of higher comprehensibility in non-scripted speech (Trofimovich & Isaacs, 2012). Thus, it is possible that attitudes towards accent could be influenced by lexical choice and grammar, with more varied combinations of grammatical and lexical choices with different accents showing different results than Cargile and Giles's (1998) study, which only included non-native grammatical features and simplified vocabulary in one guise.

In addition, it is worth noting that language attitudes studies have seldom investigated how easily or how well listeners actually understand the accents in question. In fact, this issue is usually rendered less relevant because participants hear the same text spoken by all speakers. Thus, while we know that negative attitudes can lead to lower comprehension (Kang & Rubin, 2009), it is less clear as to what degree lower comprehension may contribute to more negative attitudes. Recent evidence suggests that greater difficulty processing speech can lead to more negative attitudes, even where that greater difficulty is due to speaker-external factors such as background noise (Dragojevic & Giles, 2016). Additional investigation may discover whether listeners who have more positive attitudes towards speakers' social groups are less likely to be affected by speaker-external factors in this way. Indeed, it is possible that those with very positive attitudes are more likely to distinguish between any failures to understand a speaker and their evaluations of the speaker's intelligence and other unrelated factors usually measured in language attitudes studies.

Most language attitudes studies have also tended to control for listener factors or simply average across listeners in order to focus on speaker factors. However, listener factors such as experience with non-native varieties and experience as an NNS are also clearly relevant. Kang & Rubin (2009) investigated how listeners' comprehension of a lecturer who was presented as an NNS, as well as ratings of his teaching and the 'standardness' of his accent, were related to several listener background variables, including experience with other languages and experience with NNSs. Further study of this nature would put more of the focus on attitudes concerning non-native accents on the more relevant parties: those who actually hold such attitudes. Ultimately, it may help inform efforts to improve negative attitudes towards non-native pronunciation (Subtirelu & Lindemann, 2014).

Note

1   We use 'native' to refer to a speaker who has acquired a variety naturalistically from an early age, whether it is their first or second (or beyond second) language. So a speaker from India who speaks Hindi as a first language but also has English as an early-acquired second language would be considered an NS of English as well as of Hindi. In reality, language attitudes studies have seldom compared evaluations of varieties such as Indian English to British or American English.

Further reading

Jenkins, J. (2007). *English as a lingua franca: Attitude and identity*. Oxford: Oxford University Press. This book analyses attitudes toward English, especially pronunciation, used primarily between NNSs and not driven by NS norms; it provides suggestions for how negative attitudes can be addressed through language materials and teacher education.

Lippi-Green, R. (2012). *English with an accent: Language, ideology, and discrimination in the United States* (2nd ed.). New York, NY: Routledge. This is a classic book in which Lippi-Green discusses the ways that language, especially pronunciation, has been used as a means of discriminating against groups of people based on their racial and socio-economic backgrounds. Three chapters focus on non-native accents in particular, with individual chapters each addressing stereotypes of Spanish speakers and Asians in the US.

Müller, M. (2013). Conceptualizing pronunciation as part of translingual/transcultural competence: New impulses for SLA research and the L2 classroom. *Foreign Language Annals, 46*, 213–229. This article looks at pronunciation through the lens of communicative competence and introduces the concept of 'pronunciation-as-language' as a means of engaging students in critical reflection on their attitudes towards accents. The discussion offers specific activities teachers can employ in the classroom to foster critical reflection.

Subtirelu, N. C. (2014). A language ideological perspective on willingness to communicate. *System*, *42*, 120–132. This article provides an accessible definition of two competing language ideologies that can affect learners' willingness to communicate. It then provides pedagogical approaches that can be taken to develop the language ideology that increases learners' willingness to communicate.

Related topics

Accent and stereotyping

References

Beinhoff, B. (2013). *Perceiving identity through accent: Attitudes towards non-native speakers and their accents in English*. Bern: Peter Lang.

Bresnahan, M. J., Ohashi, R., Nebashi, R., Liu, W. Y., & Morinaga Shearman, S. (2002). Attitudinal and affective response toward accented English. *Language and Communication*, *22*, 171–185.

Buckingham, L. (2014). Attitudes to English teachers' accents in the Arabian Gulf. *International Journal of Applied Linguistics*, *24*(1), 50–73. doi:10.1111/ijal.12058.

Cargile, A. C. (1997). Attitudes toward Chinese-accented speech: An investigation in two contexts. *Journal of Language and Social Psychology*, *16*(4), 434–444.

Cargile, A. C., & Giles, H. (1998). Language attitudes toward varieties of English: An American-Japanese context. *Journal of Applied Communication Research*, *26*, 338–356.

Chavez, M. (2009). Learners' descriptions of German pronunciation, vocabulary, and grammar: A folk linguistic account. *Die Unterrichtspraxis/Teaching German*, *42*(1), 1–18. doi:10.1111/j.1756-1221.2009.00031.x.

Clark, E., & Paran, A. (2007). The employability of non-native-speaker teachers of EFL: A UK survey. *System*, *35*, 407–430. doi:10.1016/j.system.2007.05.002.

Dalton-Puffer, C., Kaltenböck, G., & Smit, U. (1997). Learner attitudes and L2 pronunciation in Austria. *World Englishes*, *16*(1), 115–128. doi:10.1111/1467–971X.00052.

Dasgupta, N., McGhee, D. E., Greenwald, A. G., & Banaji, M. R. (2000). Automatic preference for white Americans: Eliminating the familiarity explanation. *Journal of Experimental Social Psychology*, *36*(3), 316–328. doi:10.1006/jesp.1999.1418.

Davies, M. (2008). *The corpus of contemporary American English: 400 million words, 1990-present.* Retrieved from http://corpus.byu.edu/coca/.

Dragojevic, M., & Giles, H. (2016). I don't like you because you're hard to understand: The role of processing fluency in the language attitudes process. *Human Communication Research*, *42*, 396–420. doi:10.1111/hcre.12079.

Gass, S., & Varonis, E. M. (1984). The effect of familiarity on the comprehensibility of nonnative speech. *Language Learning*, *34*(1), 65–89.

Greenwald, A. G., McGhee, D. E., & Schwartz, J. L. K. (1998). Measuring individual differences in implicit cognition: The implicit association test. *Journal of Personality and Social Psychology*, *74*(6), 1464–1480.

Jenkins, J. (2007). *English as a lingua franca: Attitude and identity*. Oxford: Oxford University Press.

Kang, O., & Rubin, D. L. (2009). Reverse linguistic stereotyping: Measuring the effect of listener expectations on speech evaluation. *Journal of Language and Social Psychology*, *28*(4), 441–456. doi:10.1177/0261927X09341950.

Kubota, R., & Lin, A. (2006). Race and TESOL: Introduction to concepts and theories. *TESOL Quarterly*, *40*, 471–493. doi:10.2307/40264540.

Lambert, W. E., Hodgson, R. C., Gardner, R. C., & Fillenbaum, S. (1960). Evaluational reactions to spoken languages. *Journal of Abnormal and Social Psychology*, *60*(1), 44–51.

Levis, J. (2005). Changing contexts and shifting paradigms in pronunciation teaching. *TESOL Quarterly*, *39*(3), 369–377. doi:10.2307/3588485.

Lindemann, S. (2002). Listening with an attitude: A model of native-speaker comprehension of non-native speakers in the United States. *Language in Society*, *31*(3), 419–441.

Lindemann, S. (2003). Koreans, Chinese, or Indians? Attitudes and ideologies about non-native English speakers in the United States. *Journal of Sociolinguistics*, 7(3), 348–364.

Lindemann, S. (2005). Who speaks 'broken English'? US undergraduates' perceptions of non-native English. *International Journal of Applied Linguistics*, 15(2), 187–212.

Lindemann, S., & Moran, K. (2010). *What is 'broken English'? Using corpora to examine folk beliefs about non-native language.* Paper presented at the American Association for Applied Linguistics, Atlanta, GA.

Lippi-Green, R. (2012). *English with an accent: Language, ideology, and discrimination in the United States* (2nd ed.). New York, NY: Routledge.

Liu, D. (1999). Training non-native TESOL students: Challenges for TESOL teacher education in the West. In G. Braine (Ed.), *Non-native educators in English language teaching* (pp. 197–210). Mahwah, NJ: Erlbaum.

Mahboob, A., Uhrig, K., Newman, K. L., & Hartford, B. S. (2004). Children of a lesser English: Status of nonnative English speakers as college-level English as a second language teachers in the United States. In L. D. Kamhi-Stein (Ed.), *Learning and teaching from experience: Perspectives on non-native English-speaking professionals* (pp. 100–120). Ann Arbor, MI: University of Michigan Press.

McKenzie, R. M. (2008). The role of variety recognition in Japanese university students' attitudes towards English speech varieties. *Journal of Multilingual and Multicultural Development*, 29(2), 139–153.

Medgyes, P. (2003). Native or non-native: Who's worth more? *ELT Journal*, 46(4), 340–349. doi:10.1093/elt/46.4.340.

Methitham, P. (2011). White prestige ideology and its effects on ELT employment in Thailand. *International Journal of the Humanities*, 9(4), 145–156.

Milroy, J., & Milroy, L. (1998). *Authority in language: Investigating language prescription and standardisation* (3rd ed.). London: Routledge.

Moyer, A. (1999). Ultimate attainment in L2 phonology: The critical factors of age, motivation, and instruction. *Studies in Second Language Acquisiton*, 21, 81–108.

Müller, M. (2013). Conceptualizing pronunciation as part of translingual/transcultural competence: New impulses for SLA research and the L2 classroom. *Foreign Language Annals*, 46(2), 213–229. doi:10.1111/flan.12024.

Munro, M. J., & Derwing, T. M. (1995). Foreign accent, comprehensibility, and intelligibility in the speech of second language learners. *Language Learning*, 45(1), 73–97.

Murphy, J. M. (2014). Intelligible, comprehensible, nonnative models in ESL/EFL pronunciation teaching. *System*, 42, 258–269. doi:10.1016/j.system.2013.12.007.

Niedzielski, N., & Preston, D. R. (2003). *Folk linguistics.* Berlin and New York, NY: Mouton de Gruyter.

Niedzielski, N., & Preston, D. R. (2009). Folk pragmatics. In J. Östman, J. Verschueren & G. Senft (Eds), *Culture and language use* (pp. 146–155). Philadelphia, PA: John Benjamins.

Pantos, A. J., & Perkins, A. W. (2013). Measuring implicit and explicit attitudes toward foreign accented speech. *Journal of Language and Social Psychology*, 32(1), 3–20. doi:10.1177/0261927X12463005.

Preston, D. R. (2011). Methods in (applied) folk linguistics: Getting into the minds of the folk. *AILA Review*, 24, 14–39.

Ray, G. B., & Zahn, C. J. (1999). Language attitudes and speech behavior: New Zealand English and Standard American English. *Journal of Language and Social Psychology*, 18(3), 310–319.

Rubin, D. L. (1992). Nonlanguage factors affecting undergraduates' judgments of nonnative English-speaking teaching assistants. *Research in Higher Education*, 33(4), 511–531.

Ryan, E. B., & Bulik, C. M. (1982). Evaluations of middle class and lower class speakers of standard American and German-accented English. *Journal of Language and Social Psychology*, 1(1), 51–61.

Ryan, E. B., Carranza, M. A., & Moffie, R. W. (1977). Reactions toward varying degrees of accentedness in the speech of Spanish–English bilinguals. *Language and Speech*, 20, 267–273.

Ryan, E. B., & Sebastian, R. J. (1980). The effects of speech style and social class background on social judgements of speakers. *British Journal of Social and Clinical Psychology*, 19, 229–233.

Scales, J., Wennerstrom, A., Richard, D., & Wu, S. H. (2006). Language learners' perceptions of accent. *TESOL Quarterly*, 40(4), 715–738.

Segrest Purkiss, S. L., Perrewé, P. L., Gillespie, T. L., Mayes, B. T., & Ferris, G. R. (2006). Implicit sources of bias in employment interview judgments and decisions. *Organizational Behavior and Human Decision Processes*, 101, 152–167.

Shuck, G. (2004). Conversational performance and the poetic construction of an ideology. *Language in Society*, *33*, 195–222.

Subtirelu, N. C. (2014). A language ideological perspective on willingness to communicate. *System*, *42*, 120–132. doi:10.1016/j.system.2013.11.004.

Subtirelu, N. C. (2015). 'She does have an accent but. . .': Race and language ideology in students' evaluations of mathematics instructors on RateMyProfessors.com. *Language in Society*, *44*(1), 35–62. doi:10.1017/S0047404514000736.

Subtirelu, N. C., & Lindemann, S. (2014). Teaching first language speakers to communicate across linguistic difference: Addressing attitudes, comprehension, and strategies. *Applied Linguistics*, *37*(6), 765–783. doi:10.1093/applin/amu068.

Thomson, R. I. (2015). Fluency. In M. Reed & J. M. Levis (Eds), *The handbook of English pronunciation* (pp. 209–226). Malden, MA: Wiley Blackwell.

Timmis, I. (2002). Native-speaker norms and international English: A classroom view. *ELT Journal*, *56*(3), 240–249.

Trofimovich, P., & Isaacs, T. (2012). Disentangling accent from comprehensibility. *Bilingualism: Language and Cognition*, *15*(4), 905–916. doi:10.1017/S1366728912000168.

Watson Todd, R., & Pojanapunya, P. (2009). Implicit attitudes towards native and non-native speaker teachers. *System*, *37*, 23–33. doi:10.1016/j.system.2008.08.002.

Xu, W., Wang, Y., & Case, R. E. (2010). Chinese attitudes towards varieties of English: A pre-Olympic examination. *Language Awareness*, *19*(4), 249–260.

Yook, C., & Lindemann, S. (2013). The role of speaker identification in Korean university students' attitudes toward five varieties of English. *Journal of Multilingual and Multicultural Development*, *34*(3), 279–296. doi:10.1080/01434632.2012.734509.

25

Dimensions of pronunciation

Murray J. Munro

Introduction

Current thinking in second language (L2) speech research is converging on the view that pronunciation is best considered in terms of several partially independent dimensions, each providing a window on communicative effectiveness. Nevertheless, agreement on the nature of such dimensions, their relative importance and the ways they should be operationalized is incomplete. This chapter focuses on the tripartite approach to L2 speech analysis described by Munro and Derwing (1995a, 1995b) and Derwing and Munro (1997) in which *accentedness*, *comprehensibility* and *intelligibility* are primary considerations. As discussed by Munro (2008, 2011), such phenomena do not reside exclusively in the speech signal itself but instead arise from perceivers' responses to spoken utterances. Consequently, it is redundant to refer to them as 'perceived' accentedness, 'perceived' comprehensibility or 'perceived' intelligibility, since they are all, by definition, 'perceived' phenomena and, at least for teaching and learning purposes, cannot be meaningfully considered in any other way. Moreover, their significance is not restricted to L2 speech, since L1 speakers also vary in all three, owing to regional dialects, choice of register, disorders of production, degree of articulatory clarity and speaking rates. To complicate matters, speech judged highly on any of these dimensions may be perceived differently as a result of changes in context, mode of communication, listener affect and many other factors.

This chapter synthesizes findings on dimensions of pronunciation in the ESL contexts of Canada and the United States, with likely relevance for other immigrant-receiving areas. It highlights current criticisms, some pointing to issues needing deeper exploration and others resulting from misunderstandings. In addition, new data are reported to shed light on the nature of the least-investigated of the three dimensions – comprehensibility – and to clarify its relationship with the other two.

Definitions

In most L2 speech studies, *accentedness* denotes the degree of difference between the pronunciation of an utterance and a listener's internalized representation of it: the greater the divergence, the greater the accentedness. Often listeners make their assessments with respect to their native speech community, and it is sometimes asserted that the perceptions of L2 listeners have been ignored; however, the latter is a misrepresentation. In fact, a number of studies from the past 25 years have reported judgements from non-native listeners (Crowther, Trofimovich & Isaacs, in press; Derwing & Munro, 2013; Flege 1988; Matsuura, Chiba & Fujieda, 1999; Munro, Derwing & Morton, 2006; Riney, Takagi & Inutsuka, 2005, among others), and at least one has included listeners having no familiarity at all with the language at issue (Major, 2007). Accentedness conveys indexical information, a component of speech that is widely referenced in the sociophonetics literature (e.g. Thomas, 2011), and which concerns the phonetic properties of utterances from which listeners may infer characteristics of a speaker such as gender, age and physical size, among others. Indexical aspects of speech may have powerful effects on interactions. Interlocutors, for instance, may evaluate 'foreign-sounding' speakers positively or negatively because of their presumed ethnicity, or because their accents are regarded as attractive or unattractive (Munro, 2008). Moreover, deducing a speaker's place of origin from speech patterns may activate internalized stereotypes and lead to discriminatory behaviour (Munro, 2003). For these reasons, the relationship between accentedness and social judgement is important from both theoretical and practical perspectives.

In contrast, *intelligibility* is tied to the listener's understanding of the speech material. The present discussion assumes Schiavetti's (1992, p. 13) broad definition as 'the match between the intention of the speaker and the response of the listener to speech passed through the transmission system'. Possible means of operationalizing will be discussed below. From a functional standpoint, intelligibility is the most important requirement in an interaction. Without it, communication fails, with consequences for interlocutors ranging from minor inconvenience in casual encounters to risk of death in high-stakes situations, such as aircraft-to-ground communications (Munro, 2011). Unsurprisingly, then, speech scientists have discussed intelligibility extensively in the study of normal and disordered language, of speech perception in adverse listening conditions, such as noise or distortion, and of synthetic speech. The resulting benefits are legion and include such applications as remediation of disordered speech, improved classroom acoustics, enhancement of radio communications in high-risk contexts and improved accessibility for disabled users through assistive technologies (Cook & Polgar, 2012; Klatte, Lachmann & Meis, 2010; Marshall & Jones, 1971; Molesworth & Estival, 2015). Arguably, then, intelligibility is an unimpeachable theoretical concept with far-reaching ramifications, not only in day-to-day interactions but also in human health, safety and quality of life.

The importance of intelligibility has been discussed in second language, foreign language and lingua franca research (Bent & Bradlow, 2003; Hayes-Harb & Watzinger-Tharp, 2012; O'Brien, 2014; Pickering, 2006; Walker, 2010). In much recent work, emphasis has been placed on a bidirectional understanding of the construct, according to which both speaker and listener play roles in determining communicative success (Munro, 2008). On that view, loss of intelligibility sometimes occurs because of characteristics of the speech itself, but it may also be due to the perceiver's imperfect listening skills or to bias against the speaker. Speech specialists have occasionally been accused of failing to acknowledge the listener's contribution. However, this claim is doubtful and is probably due to a misreading of the literature. For example, Lindemann and Subtirelu (2013) incorrectly cite Tajima, Port and Dolby (1997) as having treated intelligibility as an 'inherent' property of L2 speech. In fact, Tajima et al. (1997) make no such assumption; rather, they take pains to emphasize the role of such factors as listener experience and context in determining intelligibility (p. 4). Nonetheless, Tajima et al. (1997) provide solid evidence that L2 speech properties *can be causal factors* in the loss of intelligibility. In particular, they demonstrate that an utterance produced by a particular L2 speaker can be rendered intelligible or unintelligible through controlled manipulation of speech properties alone. Contrary to what Lindemann and Subtirelu (2013) seem to assume, such an outcome cannot be explained by 'listener bias' against the talker because the talker's identity is obviously the same in both manipulated and unmanipulated conditions.

Empirical studies show that intelligibility and accentedness are distinct but partially related (Derwing & Munro, 1997; Munro & Derwing, 1995a, 1995b; Winters & O'Brien, 2013). Although heavily accented speech is sometimes not understood by listeners, fully intelligible utterances may exhibit *any* degree of accentedness, ranging from none at all to very strong. Furthermore, reducing the accentedness of utterances through pedagogical intervention or digital manipulation may have no effect on intelligibility and, in some cases, may even decrease it. For example, Derwing, Munro & Wiebe (1997) identified several learners whose post-instruction speech was judged significantly less accented but whose intelligibility remained unchanged. In another study, in which native-like prosodic patterns were imposed on non-native utterances through resynthesis, Winters & O'Brien (2013) found a significant reduction in listeners' accentedness judgements. However, the intelligibility of the same utterances was actually *lower* after modification. This seemingly paradoxical outcome is logically predicted by Munro & Derwing's (1995a, 1995b, 2001) modelling of accentedness and intelligibility as quasi-independent features. Moreover, it suggests that different aspects of an accent may interact in unexpected ways. In Winters & O'Brien (2013), the non-nativeness of the talkers' prosody appears to have counteracted other non-native features of the speech in such a way as to enhance listener comprehension.

When an L2 user's speech is fully intelligible during an interaction, the main (and perhaps only) important effect of an accent may be to index the speaker as non-native. In recognition of this, the absence of a straightforward correspondence between accentedness and intelligibility has been emphasized for decades (Abercrombie, 1949; Gimson 1970; Munro & Derwing, 1995a; Rajadurai, 2007; Sweet, 1900), and an influential movement favouring the 'intelligibility principle' over the 'nativeness principle' has emerged in L2 pedagogical circles (Levis, 2005). Nonetheless, confusion about the distinction has occasionally occurred (Munro & Derwing, 2015), perhaps because of unfamiliarity with specialists' use of the terminology and inconsistent usage in the literature. Smith & Rafiqzad (1979, p. 371), for example, defined intelligibility as the 'capacity for understanding a word or words when spoken/read in the context of a sentence being spoken/read at natural speed'. However, Smith and Nelson (1985) equated it with 'word recognition', a quite different conceptualization that emphasizes actual behaviour as opposed to 'capacity' for achieving something. The latter is closer to the definition used by Munro and Derwing, but such inconsistency may account for Golombek and Rehn Jordan's (2005) unexpected argument *against* a focus on intelligibility in L2 classrooms, which seems bizarre since deemphasizing intelligibility would have the effect of inhibiting communication. Likewise Rajagopalan (2010) may simply have been unaware of intelligibility's conceptual and empirical significance in phonetics when he asserted that experiencing speech as 'intelligible' or not is analogous to judging it as 'beautiful' or 'ugly'. In fact, he provided no definition of the term and failed to cite any of the literature that systematically evaluates the construct. To reconcile the wide acceptance of intelligibility in the speech sciences with the suspicion it has received by some (a minority of) applied linguists, we must assume a lack of common understanding of the concept. Since it is not possible to police usage, researchers should always be clear to their audiences about the definition they intend.

In addition to and distinct from both accentedness and intelligibility is *comprehensibility*, defined by Varonis and Gass (1982, p. 125) as 'how easy it is to interpret the message'.

Subsequent research (Derwing & Munro, 1997; Derwing, Munro & Thomson, 2008; Derwing, Munro & Wiebe 1998; Munro & Derwing, 1995a, 1995b) adopted the Varonis and Gass (1982) definition while operationalizing it differently. Elaboration of this concept was prompted by evidence that two equally intelligible productions of the same utterance could differ in the processing effort required of the listener. For instance, listeners might, in both cases, arrive at a complete grasp of content (full intelligibility), yet find that one production required considerably more cognitive 'work' to comprehend. Such a case exemplifies a difference in *processing fluency*, the degree of effort exerted in any cognitive task (Alter & Oppenheimer, 2009). Processing fluency in speech is a metacognitive experience that figures prominently in human interaction (Lev-Ari & Keysar, 2010). Not only do listeners notice their own level of difficulty in understanding speech but they can report it reliably (Munro & Derwing, 1995b). Furthermore, they may become fatigued or irritated because of low-comprehensibility experiences (Dragojevic & Giles, 2016).

Just as accentedness and intelligibility are partially independent, so are accentedness and comprehensibility. Munro and Derwing (1995a) and Derwing and Munro (1997) reported mainly moderate to weak correlations between the two. Additional evidence comes from Saito, Trofimovich and Isaacs (2015), who found that accentedness correlated with a different combination of linguistic measures (vowels, consonants and word stress) than did comprehensibility (fluency, lexis and grammar, as well as vowels consonants and stress). A different line of evidence comes from research showing increased processing time for varieties of speech that differ from the listener's variety (Bürki-Cohen, Miller & Eimas, 2001; Clarke & Garrett, 2004; Floccia, Butler, Goslin & Ellis, 2009). Not only do these findings point to the relevance of processing difficulty to L2 pronunciation, but Munro and Derwing's (1995b) finding that comprehensibility was related to processing time but that accentedness was not supports the distinction between the two constructs. It is also striking that comprehensibility can improve owing to instruction or L2 experience, even while accentedness remains unchanged (Derwing, Munro & Wiebe, 1998; Saito & Akiyama, in press). Finally, a repeatedly observed tendency towards leftward skewing of accentedness scores (i.e. proportionately fewer ratings at the lower end of the accent scale) indicates that listeners more often judge utterances to be heavily accented than hard to understand (Munro & Derwing, 1995a, 1995b).

Empirical evidence of the partial independence of comprehensibility and intelligibility is also abundant. The weak to moderate correlations between the two are comparable to those between accentedness and intelligibility (Derwing & Munro, 1997; Matsuura et al., 1999; Munro & Derwing, 1995a). In some cases, listeners have indeed judged utterances as difficult to understand even though intelligibility is high, and the reverse scenario – relatively high comprehensibility ratings when intelligibility is low (Matsuura et al., 1999) – occurs when speakers mistakenly believe that they have easily processed and understood an utterance, though in fact they have failed to comprehend it (Munro, 1998). The fact that listeners sometimes do not realize their own misunderstandings illustrates why intelligibility should not be evaluated with rating scales (presumably anchored at one end with 'completely understood' and at the other with 'not understood at all'). In short, listeners sometimes cannot tell whether or not they have understood. (See Schiavetti (1992) for further coverage of the problems of intelligibility scaling.)

Because poor comprehensibility entails different consequences than a loss of intelligibility, grasping the distinction is as important as understanding the intelligibility/accentedness difference. Although the widely used Munro & Derwing (1995a) definition of comprehensibility has been reiterated throughout 20 years of the literature (Derwing & Munro, 1997;

Kennedy & Trofimovich, 2008; Munro & Derwing, 1995a, 1995b, 2006; O'Brien, in press), serious misinterpretations still arise. For instance, in a review of listener factors in speech perception, Lindemann and Subtirelu (2013) conflate intelligibility and comprehensibility into a single notion (referred to by them as 'I/C') and treat comprehensibility as a 'subjective' analogue of intelligibility. They then attempt to argue that the absence of strong correlations between the two dimensions calls into question the validity of the comprehensibility concept. As already noted, research long predating their review demonstrates that the two dimensions exhibit different data distributions, correlate with different aspects of the speech signal and cannot logically be measured on the same type of continuum. Conflating them is therefore inconsistent with both theoretical conceptualizations and extensive empirical data. Furthermore, moderate to weak correlations are precisely what should be expected if the two dimensions capture different aspects of listeners' responses, with comprehensibility reflecting processing effort and intelligibility indicating actual comprehension. Ultimately, then, the weak relationships cited by these writers actually help to confirm the validity of the comprehensibility/intelligibility distinction rather than to disconfirm the meaningfulness of the constructs, as the authors incorrectly represent.

Historical perspectives

L2 speech measurement

In speech research, the need for reliable and valid measurement of spoken utterances is uncontroversial. To a great extent, the twentieth-century development of such instruments as the oscilloscope, Visipitch, and the sound spectrograph helped address measurement needs in phonetics, though advanced hardware was initially available only in well-funded laboratories. More recently, the ubiquity of computers and of sophisticated open-source software has made acoustic-phonetic analysis widely accessible. Despite the benefits for researchers, the usefulness of acoustic speech data is closely tied to their application to aspects of speech perception. For instance, the phonetic importance of timing differences in stop consonants, the spectral and temporal properties of vowels and the pitch component of intonation patterns must be interpreted by reference to listeners' perceptions. Specifically, voice onset time and vowel formant frequencies are worthy of close study because manipulations of these features greatly affect listeners' perceptions. By the same token, other measureable properties of utterances may be of only secondary importance to speech perception, or not relevant at all. Hillenbrand, Clark and Houde (2000), for example, observed a reliable duration difference in *productions* of the American /i/–/ɪ/ distinction, yet found the difference to have minimal importance for *perception*. Their study relied on audio-perceptual (AP) assessment, an approach in which listeners provide ratings, categorical judgements or transcriptions, thus enabling researchers to pinpoint the properties of speech that are relevant to phonetic processing.

In L2 research, AP is a well-established tool, and, given that pronunciation dimensions are defined in terms of listeners' responses, they clearly must be assessed in AP terms. Further insights into their nature can be gained by relating AP data to expert transcriptions and acoustic measurements. Among early L2 studies of value of AP assessment was Brennan, Ryan and Dawson (1975), who examined scalar judgements of the 'amount of accentedness' in L2 speakers' productions. Their data showed high inter-rater reliability and appeared valid because speakers' scores were predictable from independently assessed speech properties. In other words, the listeners had based their ratings on verifiable phenomena in the stimuli rather than on idiosyncratic biases. Subsequent studies have confirmed the reliability of accentedness ratings, comprehensibility ratings and intelligibility scores, and their connection with the speech signal (Derwing & Munro, 1997; Kang, 2010; O'Brien, 2014; Riney, Takagi & Inutsuka, 2005; Saito, Trofimovich & Isaacs, 2015, inter alia). However, more definitive evidence of causal relationships between particular L2 speech properties and listener responses is that controlled speech manipulations can cause utterances to be more or less native-like or more or less intelligible (e.g. Magen, 1998; Munro & Derwing, 2001; Winters & O'Brien, 2013).

Operationalizing accentedness and comprehensibility

Since accentedness is a continuum, scalar assessment is needed. Direct magnitude estimation (DME), in which listeners assign their own preferred number to a speech sample by comparing it with a reference stimulus (modulus) was found reliable by Brennan, Ryan and Dawson (1975) for phonetically unsophisticated listeners. However, Likert-type scaling, in which listeners select one number from a particular range, are more convenient and have been used more extensively. Scale sizes have varied to cover five points (Isaacs & Thomson, 2013), seven points (Southwood & Flege 1999) and nine points (Munro & Derwing, 1995a). Sometimes a quasi-continuous scale has been used, with only the endpoints labelled. Flege (1988), for instance, used a sliding potentiometer, which could be positioned anywhere along an unnumbered scale. Listeners confirmed ratings with a button press, and the system returned a number with eight-bit resolution (effectively a 255-point scale). In still another reliable approach, Brennan, Ryan and Dawson (1975) had listeners squeeze a hand dynamometer to register accent strength.

Comprehensibility has been evaluated using essentially the same techniques, typically with seven- or nine-point scales having endpoints labelled 'easy to understand' and 'very difficult to understand'. Numerous studies attest to the high reliability of scalar comprehensibility ratings (see Munro, 2008). Recently, Saito, Trofimovich and Isaacs (2015) and Crowther, Trofimovich, Saito and Isaacs (2015) obtained reliable comprehensibility ratings using an updated slider technique on a computer screen that offered 1,000 points of resolution.

Despite widespread use of these scales, relatively few studies have focused specifically on methodological issues. One concern, for instance, is whether listeners are able to partition pronunciation scales such that the distance between '2' and '3' on the scale, for instance, corresponds to the same degree of difference as that between '5' and '6'. A comparison of seven-point ratings with DME judgements by Southwood and Flege (1999) indicated that listeners did indeed treat foreign-accentedness as a linear, equal-interval scale. However, there appear to be no parallel studies of comprehensibility ratings. To address this gap, the present chapter reports an investigation in which DME and nine-point ratings of comprehensibility were compared.

With respect to optimal scale size, no clear consensus exists. Southwood and Flege (1999) proposed that seven points may be too few to capture listeners' sensitivity to accentedness differences, and when Isaacs and Thomson (2013) compared five-point and nine-point ratings the latter yielded slightly more consistent results in terms of intraclass correlations. However, listeners had some difficulty distinguishing among ratings near the middle of the scale. Moreover, a 'gap' between the ratings of L1 productions and those of L2 speech was reflected in an absence of L2 ratings at the positive end. These findings suggest that the appropriateness of a particular scale size may depend on the properties of the elicited speech material. Specifically, if none of the L2 talkers exhibits extremely high proficiency, no productions are likely to be judged 'extremely good', and if the utterances pose little phonological challenge no 'extremely poor' productions may be identified.

Still another under-researched issue is the stability of ratings across multiple speech samples. By this, I mean the degree to which ratings remain consistent across different utterances. While clearly dependent on listener reliability, stability is probably also influenced by the length and phonological content of the speech samples rated. At present no accepted standards exist to cover these concerns.

Operationalizing intelligibility

Since intelligibility is the match between the speaker's intention and the listener's response, assessment of it requires measurement of the degree of correspondence between the two. Commonly, listeners are presented with utterances for transcription in standard orthography, and the percentage of correctly transcribed words is computed. Although recognizing the words in an utterance is not always equivalent to understanding its full meaning, the relationship between the two is known to be close. In particular, Schiavetti (1992) discusses evidence supporting the use of words-correct counts from contextual speech, concluding that the approach is reliable and has external validity as a measure of intelligibility in communicative contexts. Nevertheless, it is noteworthy that L2 researchers have measured intelligibility in other ways, including comprehension questions, cloze tests, true/false sentence verifications and detailed interviews with listeners (see Munro, 2008). No evidence has emerged, however, that any of these approaches offers an advantage over word counts in terms of practicality, reliability or validity.

Applications in L2 pronunciation research

AP-based assessment can be applied in several areas of pronunciation research. For one, error gravity studies can pinpoint aspects of speech that impede intelligibility and comprehensibility, and that are therefore good targets for instruction. Munro and Derwing (2006), for instance, found that segmental errors involving high functional load distinctions affected comprehensibility additively and more adversely than low functional load errors. In another vein, a longitudinal examination of changes in intelligibility and comprehensibility can highlight aspects of speech that are learned more readily than others and that therefore require less instructional attention (Derwing & Munro, 2015). Still another application is intervention studies, in which pre- and post-instructional AP assessments reveal whether or not a pedagogical technique enhances intelligibility and comprehensibility (Derwing, Munro & Wiebe, 1998).

The use of pronunciation ratings in high-stakes language assessment requires a more refined approach than does 'low-stakes' research (Harding, 2012; Isaacs, 2008). In particular, Isaacs and Thomson (2013, p. 154) observed that 'in the absence of a criterion-referenced standard and rigorous rater training using purposeful benchmarking, ratings are interpretable only within a specific study, not across studies'. To illustrate, the fact that a speaker in a particular study receives a mean comprehensibility rating of '6' prior to an intervention but improves to a rating of '4' post-intervention may indicate that the intervention has been successful. However, because they are not criterion-referenced, the specific ratings of '4' and '6' say little, if anything, about the speaker's actual proficiency.

Critical issues and topics

The preceding discussion has identified several critical issues in pronunciation research that require further examination. Three of these will receive special attention in the remainder of this chapter, in which an empirical study will be presented.

1. How amenable is comprehensibility to equal-interval scaling?

As noted earlier, no previous research appears to have evaluated the appropriateness of equal-interval scaling for comprehensibility in the way that Southwood and Flege (1999) examined accentedness. Their technique, based on Schiavetti, Metz and Sitler (1981), entailed a comparison of DME and interval ratings for the same items. In DME, listeners make judgements of each target item in relation to a single 'modulus' (e.g. twice as accented as the modulus, half as accented and so on). A linear relationship between DME and interval ratings indicates that both techniques give much the same information. On the other hand, a curvilinear relationship (or a lack of a clear relationship at all) suggests that interval scaling is inappropriate because perceived differences between sequential points of the scale are not of equal size. In the present study, Southwood and Flege's (1999) work will be replicated and extended. Both accentedness and comprehensibility ratings will be collected and a comparison of DME and nine-point ratings for identical items will be carried out.

2. Is a nine-point scale satisfactory for evaluating comprehensibility?

Southwood and Flege (1999) suggested that a scale of at least nine points may be needed to optimize reliability for accentedness ratings, while Isaacs and Thomson (2013) pointed to listener difficulties with a nine-point scale. The present study will probe this issue by examining listeners' actual use of different rating values. In particular, DME reveals listeners' scaling preferences in that they must choose not only the numbers they assign as ratings but also the scale resolution (i.e. the number of numbers). A strong preference for fewer than nine distinct ratings would argue for a smaller scale, whereas a larger number of choices might indicate greater resolution capabilities on the part of the listeners.

3. How stable are comprehensibility ratings of a particular talker across different sentence-length utterances?

Although it is important to consider how well the ratings of one particular utterance represent the talker's pronunciation in general, little work has looked specifically at the stability of ratings across multiple utterances. In this study, the degree of stability, referring here to 'consistency of ratings', across short (sentence-length) utterances will be examined.

Current contribution

Methods

Talkers

The L2 talkers, recruited from among Canadian post-secondary students, were 19 native Mandarin (MA) speakers (12 female, 7 male). All were from China and had moved to Canada after the age of 16. In the researcher's opinion, they exhibited foreign accents ranging from mild to strong. For perceptual anchoring purposes, utterances from two native speakers (one female, one male) of General Canadian English (NE) were also used.

Recordings

Stimuli were high-quality recordings (22.05 kHz, 16 bits pcm), normalized for peak amplitude. In a sound-treated room, each talker read aloud a list of 40 single-clause statements from related work (see Munro & Derwing, 1995b). In case of lexical errors or dysfluencies, items were repeated until a fluent version was produced. Six sentences (Table 25.1) were selected for the ratings because of their similar lengths. Three were arbitrarily assigned to the comprehensibility rating set and three to the accentedness set.

Table 25.1 Stimulus sentences

Set	Sentence
Accentedness	S23. Some roses have a beautiful smell.
	S27. You can start a fire with a match. (Modulus)
	S32. Many people drink coffee for breakfast.
Comprehensibility	S13. Exercise is good for your health. (Modulus)
	S20. Some people love to eat chocolate.
	S41. The Canadian flag is red and white.

Stimuli were screened by the experimenter to identify a single utterance with a moderate foreign accent that would serve as the modulus in the DME accentedness task. The same (female) voice uttering a different sentence was the modulus for the DME comprehensibility ratings. Each of the two final sets consisted of 63 items (21 talkers × 3 sentences). For DME ratings, one of these items was the modulus.

Listeners

Listeners were 21 native speakers of Canadian English (14 female, 7 male) recruited from among students in linguistics courses. Their mean age was 29 years (range: 20 to 49) and all reported normal hearing.

Procedure

Ratings were collected during small group sessions in an acoustically-treated room. Each listener was assigned to one of two cohorts. The order of the DME and nine-point ratings was counterbalanced for the DME-first cohort (nine listeners) and the nine-point first cohort (12 listeners). Stimuli were presented in random order through loudspeakers on each side of the room, and an assistant controlled playback to keep the listeners in step.

Each listening session comprised four blocks. For the DME-first cohort, the listeners evaluated DME accentedness followed by nine-point accentedness, and then DME comprehensibility followed by nine-point comprehensibility. The nine-point first cohort rated nine-point accentedness, followed by DME accentedness, nine-point comprehensibility and DME comprehensibility.

The DME sessions began with an instruction to evaluate the strength of the talkers' accents. Each judgement was to be made by comparing the stimulus to a modulus, which would be played several times during the task and which was always to be given a score of 100. If listeners judged the target to be twice as accented as the modulus, they should give it a score of 200; for a target half as accented they should use a score of 50, and so on. They were instructed to use numbers greater than zero with no upper limit, but to assign values both above and below 100. The modulus was presented twice for familiarization, and a 10-item practice session (with non-test items) was administered. During testing, the modulus was played at the outset and after every tenth stimulus, for a total of seven presentations. A female voice announced either the number of the test item or 'modulus'. Listeners responded in a booklet with stimulus numbers next to blanks for writing their ratings. For DME comprehensibility, the same procedure was used, except that the listeners judged how difficult each target was to understand, with numbers greater than 100 indicating greater difficulty than for the modulus, and numbers less than 100 signalling less difficulty.

In the nine-point rating blocks, the listeners circled their ratings in the booklet. For accentedness, the scale was labelled from 'No Accent' on the left to 'Very Strong Accent' on the right. For comprehensibility, the labels were 'Very Easy to Understand' and 'Very Difficult to Understand'. The listeners were instructed to use the full scale, and a 10-item practice session was provided. Each block required about 12 minutes, and the entire session, including short breaks, lasted about one hour.

Results

Raters' use of the scales

For the two DME blocks, all listeners correctly followed the instructions to assign a value of 100 to the modulus each time it was played and to avoid ratings lower than 1. All but one listener (L07) assigned some scores above 100 for accentedness, and all but one (L11) did so for comprehensibility. The count of unique numbers assigned for accentedness averaged 16 (range: 7 to 31, with only one listener using fewer than 9), while for comprehensibility unique scores averaged 15 (range: 5 to 26, with three listeners using fewer than 9).

For nine-point accent scaling, 16 of the 21 listeners used either eight or nine of the available points, while one used only five points. For comprehensibility, 19 listeners used either eight or nine of the points. However, L07 used only three points and rated all but one of the MA talkers '1' or '2'. One stimulus, for instance, was rated '2' by L07 but '6' or higher by 18 other listeners.

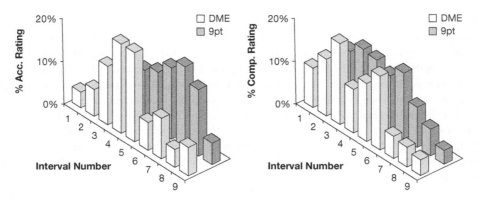

Figure 25.1 Data distributions for DME and nine-point scaling of accentedness (left) and comprehensibility (right). Higher interval numbers indicate greater accentedness and greater difficulty in understanding

Histograms (MA stimuli only) comparing DME with nine-point ratings appear in Figure 25.1. Outliers from both DME sets (> 2 SDs from the mean) were trimmed, and the binning was set to 9. For accentedness, the two rating sets are not especially well matched, with DME scores positively skewed and nine-point ratings skewed leftward. The comprehensibility ratings, however, show very similar distributions, with peaks at bins 3 and 6 in both cases.

Reliability

Average measures intraclass correlations (two-way random) are shown in Table 25.2 (Shrout & Fleiss, 1979). Inter-rater reliability was high, with the lowest value (.921) for the accentedness DME ratings and all other values equal to or exceeding .95. In comparison, Southwood and Flege (1999) reported lower values for accentedness ratings: .69 and .68 for DME, and .85 and .58 for seven-point scaling.

Table 25.2 Intraclass correlations for the four rating sets

Rating	DME	Nine-point
Accentedness	.921***	.950***
Comprehensibility	.953***	.957***

Note: ***p <.001

Comparison of MA and NE talker ratings

The overlap between the MA and NE talkers in accentedness ratings was minimal. For NE, 55 per cent of the DME ratings were 1, and no NE speech sample was rated higher than 25, while 94 per cent of the MA ratings exceeded 25. On the nine-point scale, 94 per cent of the NE ratings, but only 2 per cent of the MA ratings, were 1.

For comprehensibility, the degree of overlap was slightly greater. Of the NE group's DME ratings, 58 per cent were 1, and no talker was rated higher than 50. Of the MA ratings, 63 per cent exceeded 50. On the nine-point scale, 90 per cent of NE ratings and 8 per cent of the MA ratings were 1.

Talker variability in nine-point scaling

Figure 25.2 shows the mean nine-point scores, pooled over listeners and sentences for each talker, with means ordered from lowest to highest. Mean accentedness ranged from 2.8 to 6.9, thus spanning slightly more than five units. For comprehensibility, the range was greater, from about 1.9 to 6.5, or 5.6 units. The data illustrate a fairly smooth progression in both cases, except for a discontinuity between the means for Talker 14 (rated least accented and easiest to understand) and the other talkers. On average, the 95 per cent confidence intervals extend .45 point on either side of the mean for both dimensions, for a total span of slightly less than one scalar point. For comprehensibility, slightly wider intervals can be seen near the middle of the set (Talkers 6, 7 and 19).

Stability of ratings within talkers (and across sentences)

Mean accentedness and comprehensibility scores for each utterance were used to compute intercorrelations among sentences (Table 25.3). Because of the small number of data points and non-normal distributions, non-parametric (Kendall's Tau) tests were used. The low to moderate pairwise correlations tended to be parallel for DME and nine-point scaling. Overall, ratings of any one sentence never correlated very highly with ratings of any other.

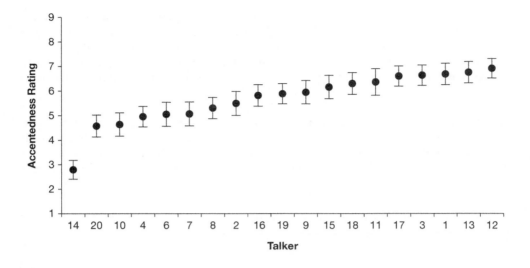

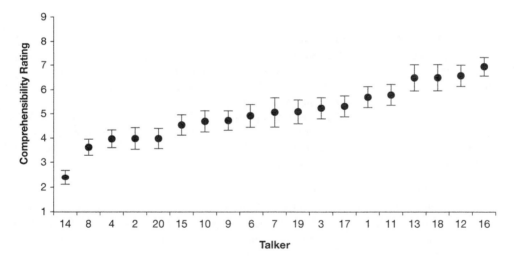

Figure 25.2 Mean talker accentedness (top) and comprehensibility (bottom) with 95 per cent confidence intervals. Ratings are pooled over listeners

Comparison of DME with nine-point scaling

Following Schiavetti et al. (1981), the DME data were reduced by computing the geometric means of the ratings (the *n*th root of the product of *n* ratings) on each item. This technique serves as a type of normalization to facilitate comparing a large number scale (DME) with a smaller one (nine-point). Figure 25.3 illustrates the relationship between the resulting values and the arithmetic means of the nine-point scores. In terms of nine-point scaling, the moduli were somewhat more accented (6.5) and somewhat harder to understand (6.6) than average.

Table 25.3 Intercorrelations (Kendall's Tau) among ratings for different sentences

Accentedness					Comprehensibility				
	S27		S32			S20		S41	
	DME	Nine-pt	DME	Nine-pt		DME	Nine-pt	DME	Nine-pt
S23	.325	.346*	.534**	.484**	S13	.396*	.459**	.434*	.404*
S27	—	—	.165	.22	S20	—	—	.366*	.334

Note: *p < .05; **p < .01

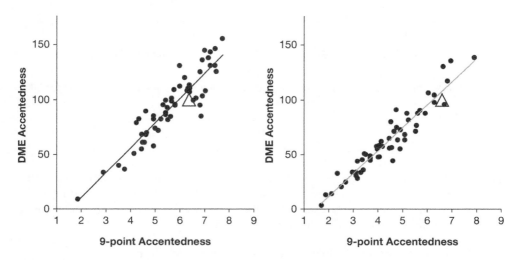

Figure 25.3 The relationship between DME (geometric mean) and nine-point ratings of accentedness (left) and comprehensibility (right). Triangles denote modulus ratings

Strong linear relationships emerged in both sets of scores, with Pearson $r = .915$ for accentedness and $r = .957$ for comprehensibility, $p < .001$ in both cases. Thus 84 per cent and 92 per cent, respectively, of the variance (r^2) in the data from one rating method could be accounted for by scores from the other. Regression analyses indicated that the amount of further variance that would be explained by adding a second order (i.e. curvilinear) term to the models was negligible (<1 per cent in either case).

Relationship between accentedness and comprehensibility ratings

Because the raters assigned accentedness and comprehensibility scores to two different sets of utterances, it is not possible to directly compare the two dimensions. However, pooling ratings over the three sentence productions allows an indirect comparison of global accentedness and comprehensibility as shown in Figure 25.4. The magnitudes of the correlation coefficients were moderate and very similar for the two rating types, with Kendall's Tau = .531 for the DME scores and .541 for nine-point scaling, $p = .002$ in both cases.

425

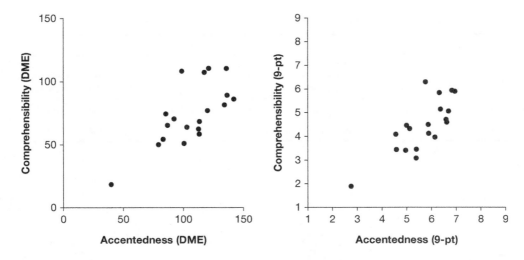

Figure 25.4 Mean accentedness and comprehensibility ratings assigned to each talker for DME (left) and nine-point scaling (right)

Discussion

These results add further evidence to work verifying the appropriateness of comprehensibility measurement in L2 speech research (see Isaacs & Trofimovich, 2012). Nonetheless, as explained below, caution must be exercised in the administration of comprehensibility rating tasks, given some limitations of the findings.

Critical issue 1: Is comprehensibility amenable to equal-interval scaling?

In general, the data support Southwood and Flege's (1999) finding that accentedness is amenable to equal-interval scaling and extend that finding to comprehensibility, which has not previously been examined using their approach. First, both DME and nine-point ratings were reliable, with intraclass correlations higher than those reported by Southwood and Flege (1999). The difference may be partly due to the use of nine-point, as opposed to seven-point, scales in the present work. Second, the two rating types (DME, nine-point) evinced high linear correlations, suggesting that they were largely interchangeable, at least for controlled sentence readings in which pronunciation, but not grammatical or lexical accuracy, was at issue. However, since other work has shown that comprehensibility can be influenced by the latter factors (Saito et al., 2015), further comparisons using extemporaneous speech are needed to develop a more complete picture of the relationship between the scaling types.

Critical issue 2: Is a nine-point scale satisfactory for evaluating comprehensibility?

In the DME block in which listeners could select as many different numbers as desired for comprehensibility ratings, a mean of 15 choices were used. The fact that all but three listeners used nine or more unique numbers suggests that most were comfortable in partitioning the scale into at least that many points, though intra-listener reliability in doing so has not been addressed here. The wide range in the number of choices also suggests considerable variability in listeners' resolution preferences, and possibly their capabilities. Identifying factors that account for such differences may prove to be a fruitful area for further study that could shed additional light on the processing of L2 speech input.

The DME findings were paralleled in the nine-point scaling block, in which 19 of 21 listeners used at least eight of the nine points. Those who did not use the full scale tended not to select the highest numbers (worst ratings), as can be seen in Figure 25.1. Although this tendency might reflect a bias against assigning extreme ratings, it might also indicate sampling limitations in the speech stimuli. It is possible that the included speech material did not adequately represent the full range of comprehensibility found in actual L2 utterances. It appears, for instance, that a 'gap' in representation existed between the most comprehensible talker (Talker 14) and the others, a phenomenon also observed by Isaacs & Thomson (2013). This gap may reflect the decision to sample only from learners who had arrived in Canada after age 16. In fact, ample evidence indicates that the least accented L2 speakers tend to be those who arrived in their L2-speaking countries in childhood (see Derwing & Munro (2015) for an extensive review), and the same may well be true for comprehensibility. To evaluate this possibility, future work might include a mix of 'early' and 'late' learners, with respect to age, to determine whether such inclusion will more fully represent the range of possible comprehensibility ratings for L2 talkers. At the same time, it is possible that the relative rarity of talkers at the high end of the scale reflects an actual characteristic of the L2-speaking population: low-comprehensibility L2 talkers may simply be uncommon, especially in cases of intermediate to advanced L2 proficiency.

Critical issue 3: How stable are comprehensibility ratings assigned to a particular talker?

A comparison of ratings for the same talkers across different utterances indicated that ratings of any one sentence were poor to moderately-successful predictors of ratings of any other, irrespective of rating type (DME or nine-point). That outcome suggests that comprehensibility ratings of a single short utterance do not necessarily capture the talkers' general comprehensibility. This may be unsurprising, since short samples could be expected to under- or over-represent a talker's L2 phonological difficulties. However, it raises the question of how much speech material must be elicited from a talker in order to adequately characterize the talker's general performance. That concern has yet to receive sufficient attention in the pronunciation literature. It is not known, for instance, whether utterances of a specified length drawn from a single speech sample would give the most valid results, or whether listeners should rate multiple, independent speech samples from a talker, followed by computation of a mean value.

Other issues

The outcomes of several previous studies have pointed to only a moderate relationship between accentedness and comprehensibility. In the current study it was not possible to directly compare the two; however, scores pooled over listeners and sentences correlated with accentedness ratings at only slightly above .5, in line with previous indications that listeners can distinguish talkers' accentedness from their comprehensibility.

Recommendations for practice

These results suggest that a nine-point comprehensibility scale is at least as easy for raters of L2 speech to use as a nine-point accentedness scale, and yields results that are equally reliable. Moreover, the data provide no support for the use of DME over equal-interval ratings. While all AP-based techniques have weaknesses, the balance of the evidence supports the use of comprehensibility scaling as a reliable and valid approach to L2 speech evaluation for research purposes. Comprehensibility judgements appear well suited to examining pronunciation error gravity, evaluating the effects of teaching interventions and investigating longitudinal speech learning phenomena. Although this study has focused closely on nine-point scaling, evidence from other research suggests that alternative techniques, such as quasi-continuous judgements on unnumbered scales, may be satisfactory as well.

Future directions

The body of research using accentedness, comprehensibility and intelligibility to identify positive and negative influences on L2 speech perception is growing rapidly. Munro (2008) proposed that these factors could be categorized in terms of properties of the speech itself, listener characteristics and contextual influences. Understanding the role of all three types through systematic implementation of AP tasks is key both to satisfactory theoretical accounts of listeners' responses to speech and also to effective pedagogy. For example, despite sincere efforts, listeners sometimes fail to understand L2 utterances. When this results from pronunciation errors, a speaker's willingness to modify production patterns may be essential to improved success in interactions. Other evidence, however, shows that interlocutors sometimes fail to attend adequately to speech, possibly because of negative stereotyping, such as when seeing a 'foreign-looking' face (see Kang & Rubin, 2014). In such cases, adjusting listeners' attitudes about L2 speakers may be the only possible route to better communication.

However, emerging evidence points to a need for restraint in attributing particular motivations and biases to raters in speech studies, and to interlocutors in real-word communication. Blame for communicative breakdowns cannot be assigned in simple 'either/or' fashion. Dragojevic and Giles (in press), for instance, found that decreased processing fluency (lower comprehensibility) played a *causal* role in listeners' language attitudes, rather than the reverse. Likewise, McGowan's (2016) work calls for a re-evaluation of stereotyping accounts in which listeners fail to pay adequate attention. When he presented Chinese-accented speech to listeners while showing either a Caucasian or Chinese face, intelligibility improved in the latter condition. That finding might be explained in terms of exemplar theory, which assumes that listeners store and access indexical information about speech that facilitates comprehension when faces and voices are congruent, or detract from it when they are not. In view of such findings, applied linguists must be careful in interpreting AP data. Just as it would be ill-advised to take at face value *any* judgement that a speaker's productions are inherently incomprehensible or unintelligible, it is also unsatisfactory to automatically dismiss negative judgements of L2 speech as instances of bias or racism.

Further reading

Derwing, T. M., & Munro, M. J. (2015). *Pronunciation fundamentals: Evidence-based perspectives for L2 teaching*. Amsterdam: John Benjamins. A comprehensive overview of pronunciation research that includes considerable coverage of dimensions of pronunciation and their role in pedagogy.

References

Abercrombie, D. (1949). Teaching pronunciation, *English Language Teaching, 3*, 113–122.

Alter, A. L., & Oppenheimer, D. M. (2009). Uniting the tribes of fluency to form a metacognitive nation. *Personality and Social Psychology Review, 13*, 219–235.

Bent, T., & Bradlow, A. R. (2003). The interlanguage speech intelligibility benefit. *Journal of the Acoustical Society of America, 114*, 1600–1610.

Brennan, E. M., Ryan, E. B., & Dawson, W. E. (1975). Scaling of apparent accentedness by magnitude estimation and sensory modality matching. *Journal of Psycholinguistic Research, 4*, 27–36.

Bürki-Cohen, J., Miller, J. L., & Eimas, P. D. (2001). Perceiving non-native speech. *Language and Speech, 44*, 149–169.

Clarke, C. M., & Garrett, M. F. (2004). Rapid adaptation to foreign-accented English. *Journal of the Acoustical Society of America, 116*, 3647–3658.

Cook, A. M., & Polgar, J. M. (2012). *Essentials of Assisted Technologies*. St Louis, MO: Elsevier Mosby.

Crowther, D. Trofimovich, P., & Isaacs, T. (in press). Linguistic dimensions of second language accent and comprehensibility: Nonnative listeners' perspectives. *Journal of Second Language Pronunciation*.

Crowther, D., Trofimovich, P., Saito, K., & Isaacs, T. (2015). Second language comprehensibility revisited: Investigating the effects of learner background, *TESOL Quarterly, 49*, 814–837.

Derwing, T. M., & Munro, M. J. (1997). Accent, intelligibility, and comprehension: Evidence from four L1s. *Studies in Second Language Acquisition, 19*, 1–16.

Derwing, T. M., & Munro, M. J. (2013). The development of L2 oral language skills in two L1 groups: A 7-year study, *Language Learning, 63*, 163–185.

Derwing, T. M., & Munro, M. J. (2015). *Pronunciation fundamentals: Evidence-based perspectives for L2 teaching*. Amsterdam: John Benjamins.

Derwing, T. M., Munro, M. J., & Thomson, R. I. (2008). A longitudinal study of ESL learners' fluency and comprehensibility development. *Applied Linguistics, 29*, 359–380.

Derwing, T. M., Munro, M. J., & Wiebe, G. E. (1998). Evidence in favor of a broad framework for pronunciation instruction. *Language Learning, 48*, 393–410.

Derwing, T. M., Munro, M. J., & Wiebe, G. E. (1997). Pronunciation instruction for 'fossilized' learners: Can it help? *Applied Language Learning, 8*, 185–203.

Dragojevic, M., & Giles, H. (2016). I don't like you because you're hard to understand: The role of processing fluency in the language attitudes process. *Human Communication Research, 42*, 396–420.

Flege, J. E. (1988). Factors affecting degree of perceived foreign accent in English sentences. *Journal of the Acoustical Society of America, 84*, 70–79.

Floccia, C., Butler, J., Goslin, J., & Ellis, L. (2009). Regional and foreign accent processing in English: Can listeners adapt? *Journal of Psycholinguistic Research, 38*, 379–412.

Gimson, A. C. (1970). *An introduction to the pronunciation of English* (2nd ed.). London: Edward Arnold.

Golombek, P., & Rehn Jordan, S. (2005). Becoming 'black lambs' not 'parrots': A poststructuralist orientation to intelligibility and identity. *TESOL Quarterly, 39*, 513–533.

Hayes-Harb, R., & Watzinger-Tharp, J. (2012). Accent, intelligibility, and the role of the listener: Perceptions of English-accented German by native German speakers. *Foreign Language Annals, 45*, 260–282.

Harding, L. (2012). Pronunciation assessment. In Chapelle, C. (Ed.), *The encyclopedia of applied linguistics*. Hoboken, NJ: Wiley-Blackwell.

Hillenbrand, J., Clark, M. J., & Houde, R. A. (2000). Some effects of duration on vowel recognition. *Journal of the Acoustical Society of America, 108*, 3013–3022.

Isaacs, T. (2008). Towards defining a valid assessment criterion of pronunciation proficiency in non-native English-speaking graduate students. *Canadian Modern Language Review, 64*, 555–580.

Isaacs, T., & Thomson, R. (2013). Rater experience, rating scale length, and judgments of L2 pronunciation: Revisiting research conventions. *Language Assessment Quarterly, 10*, 135–159.

Isaacs, T., & Trofimovich, P. (2012). Deconstructing comprehensibility: Identifying the linguistic influences on listeners' L2 comprehensibility ratings. *Studies in Second Language Acquisition, 34*, 475–505.

Kang, O. (2010). Relative salience of suprasegmental features on judgments of L2 comprehensibility and accentedness. *System, 38*, 301–315.

Kang, O., & Rubin, D. (2014). Reverse linguistic stereotyping. In J. Levis and A. Moyer (Eds), *Social dynamics in second language accent* (pp. 239–254). Boston, MA: Walter De Gruyter.

Kennedy, S., & Trofimovich, P. (2008). Intelligibility, comprehensibility and accentedness of L2 speech: The role of listener experience and semantic context. *Canadian Modern Language Review, 64,* 459–489.

Klatte, M., Lachmann, T., & Meis, M. (2010). Effects of noise and reverberation on speech perception and listening comprehension of children and adults in a classroom-like setting. *Noise and Health, 12,* 270–282.

Lev-Ari, S, & Keysar, B. (2010). Why don't we believe non-native speakers? The influence of accent on credibility. *Journal of Experimental Social Psychology, 46,* 1093–1096.

Levis, J. M. (2005). Changing contexts and shifting paradigms in pronunciation teaching. *TESOL Quarterly, 9,* 369–377.

Lindemann, S., & Subtirelu, N. (2013). Reliably biased: The role of listener expectation in the perception of second language speech. *Language Learning, 63,* 567–594.

Magen, H. S. (1998). The perception of foreign-accented speech. *Journal of Phonetics, 23,* 381–400.

Major, R. C. (2007). Identifying a foreign accent in an unfamiliar language. *Studies in Second Language Acquisition, 29,* 539–556.

Marshall, R. C., & Jones, R. N. (1971). Effects of a palatal lift prosthesis upon the speech intelligibility of a dysarthric patient. *The Journal of Prosthetic Dentistry, 25,* 327–333.

Matsuura, H., Chiba, R., & Fujieda, M. (1999). Intelligibility and comprehensibility of American and Irish Englishes in Japan. *World Englishes, 18,* 49–62.

McGowan, K. B. (2015). Social expectation improves speech perception in noise. *Language and Speech, 58,* 502–521.

Molesworth, B. R. C., & Estival, D. (2015). Miscommunication in general aviation: The influence of external factors on communication errors. *Safety Science, 73,* 73–79.

Munro, M. J. (1998). The effects of noise on the intelligibility of foreign-accented speech. *Studies in Second Language Acquisition, 20,* 139–154.

Munro, M. J. (2003). A primer on accent discrimination in the Canadian context. *TESL Canada Journal, 20*(2), 38–51.

Munro, M. J. (2008). Foreign accent and speech intelligibility. In J. G. Hansen Edward & M. L. Zampini (Eds), *Phonology and second language acquisition* (pp. 193–218). Amsterdam: John Benjamins.

Munro, M. J. (2011). Intelligibility: Buzzword or buzzworthy? In J. Levis & K. LeVelle (Eds), *Proceedings of the 2nd Pronunciation in Second Language Learning and Teaching Conference* (pp. 7–16). Ames, IA: Iowa State University.

Munro, M. J., & Derwing, T. M. (1995a). Foreign accent, comprehensibility, and intelligibility in the speech of second language learners. *Language Learning, 45,* 73–97.

Munro, M. J., & Derwing, T. M. (1995b). Processing time, accent, and comprehensibility in the perception of native and foreign-accented speech. *Language and Speech, 38,* 289–306.

Munro, M. J., & Derwing, T. M. (2001). Modelling perceptions of the comprehensibility and accentedness of L2 speech: The role of speaking rate. *Studies in Second Language Acquisition, 23,* 451–468.

Munro, M. J., & Derwing, T. M. (2006). The functional load principle in ESL pronunciation instruction: An exploratory study. *System, 34,* 520–531.

Munro, M. J., & Derwing, T. M. (2015). A prospectus for pronunciation research in the 21st century: A point of view. *Journal of Second Language Pronunciation, 1,* 11–42.

Munro, M. J., Derwing, T. M., & Morton, S. L. (2006). The mutual intelligibility of L2 speech. *Studies in Second Language Acquisition, 28,* 111–131.

O'Brien, M. G. (2014). L2 learners' assessments of accentedness, fluency and comprehensibility of native and nonnative German speech. *Language Learning, 64,* 715–748.

O'Brien, M. G. (in press). Methodological choices in rating speech samples. *Studies in Second Language Acquisition.*

Pickering, L. (2006). Current research on intelligibility in English as a lingua franca. *Annual Review of Applied Linguistics, 26,* 219–233.

Rajadurai, J. (2007). Intelligibility studies: a consideration of empirical and ideological issues. *World Englishes, 26,* 87–98.

Rajagopalan, K. (2010). The soft, ideological underbelly of the notion of intelligibility in discussions of 'World Englishes'. *Applied Linguistics, 31,* 465–470.

Riney, T., Takagi, N., & Inutsuka, K. (2005). Phonetic parameters and perceptual judgments of accent in English by American and Japanese listeners. *TESOL Quarterly, 39*, 441–466.

Saito, K., Trofimovich, P., & Isaacs, T. (2015). Using listener judgments to investigate linguistic influences on L2 comprehensibility and accentedness: A validation and generalization study. *Applied Linguistics, 38*(4), 439–462. doi:10.1093/applin/amv047.

Saito, K., & Akiyama, Y. (in press). Video-based interaction, negotiation for comprehensibility, and second language speech learning: A longitudinal study. *Language Learning*.

Schiavetti, N. (1992). Scaling procedures for the measurement of speech intelligibility. In R. E. Kent (Ed.) *Intelligibility in speech disorders* (pp. 11–34). Philadelphia, PA: John Benjamins.

Schiavetti, N., Metz, D. E., & Sitler, R. W. (1981). Construct validity of direct magnitude estimation and interval scaling of speech intelligibility: Evidence from a study of the hearing impaired. *Journal of Speech and Hearing Research, 24*, 441–445.

Shrout, P. E., & Fleiss, J. L. (1979). Intraclass correlations: Uses in assessing rater reliability. *Psychological Bulletin, 2*, 420–428.

Smith, L. E., & Nelson, C. (1985). International intelligibility of English: Directions and resources. *World Englishes, 4*, 333–342.

Smith, L. E., & Rafiqzad, K. (1979). English for cross-cultural communication: The question of intelligibility. *TESOL Quarterly, 13*, 371–380.

Southwood, M. H., & Flege, J. E. (1999). Scaling foreign accent: direct magnitude estimation versus interval scaling. *Clinical Linguistics & Phonetics, 13*, 335–349.

Sweet, H. (1900). *The practical study of languages: A guide for teachers and learners*. New York, NY: Henry Holt.

Tajima, K., Port, R., & Dalby, J. (1997). Effects of temporal correction on intelligibility of foreign-accented English. *Journal of Phonetics, 25*, 1–24.

Thomas, E. (2011). *Sociophonetics: An introduction*. Basingstoke: Palgrave Macmillan.

Varonis, E., & Gass, S. (1982). The comprehensibility of nonnative speech. *Studies in Second Language Acquisition, 4*, 114–136.

Walker, R. (2010). *Teaching the pronunciation of English as a lingua franca*. Oxford: Oxford University Press.

Winters, S., & O'Brien, M. G. (2013). Perceived accentedness and intelligibility: The relative contributions of F0 and duration. *Speech Communication, 55*, 486–507.

26

Pronunciation in discourse contexts

Lucy Pickering

Introduction

Historically, presentations of English pronunciation patterns have focused on phonetic distinctions that by their nature prompted consideration of smaller units of speech such as syllables or words. Teaching materials have typically prioritized segmental production and limited their representation of larger contexts to discussion of co-articulation processes in connected speech (e.g. elision, linking, assimilation or palatalization) and minimal coverage of utterance-level word stress and intonation patterns. This chapter begins with a historical perspective on pronunciation instruction that exemplifies this approach. It then examines current discourse-pragmatic conceptualizations of speech production that prioritize supra-segmental features including temporal features of oral production such as pause structure and speech rate. A comprehensive list of these features and how they can be operationalized is proposed. As these features are difficult to reproduce in standard pronunciation teaching models, these innovations have encouraged a number of changes within pronunciation teaching in terms of materials development and classroom practice. Following a discussion of pedagogical applications, the chapter concludes with a discussion of future directions in this area with the addition of discourse pronunciation features in the contexts of world Englishes and English as a lingua franca. The chapter focuses on features of discourse pronunciation in English as consideration of additional languages would require more space.

Historical perspectives

During the first part of the twentieth century, the field of linguistics was characterized by an emphasis on descriptive linguistics and a focus on structuralist approaches. The study of phonetics formed an important part of the work at this time, in both the European and American traditions (Bloomfield, 1933; Pike, 1945; Trubetzkoy, 1969). Sample pronunciation texts for English language teaching from the mid-twentieth century continued to reflect these priorities. They focused on articulatory phonetics and phoneme recognition, and activities primarily comprised work with minimal pairs (i.e. Trim, 1975). Discussion of co-articulation patterns in speech was minimal, and there were no examples of larger phonological patterns such as speech paragraphs or paratones.

Consideration of such a narrow environment precluded analysis of discourse-level suprasegmental features. Within the European tradition, intonologists such as Palmer (1970) and O'Connor and Arnold (1973) investigated the composition of individual tone groups (i.e. thought groups, sense groups or tone units). Where intonation appeared in pronunciation teaching texts, it comprised lists of attitudinal or grammatical patterns. At this time, intonation was regarded as a system that primarily served the linguistic systems of syntax and semantics (Halliday, 1967).

The study of suprasegmentals in discourse thrived even less well in the American tradition. Although Bloomfield (1933) extended principles of phonemic analysis to the study of intonation and stress, he regarded them as 'secondary phonemes' and continued to be ambiguous regarding their precise status. Work on pitch phonemes reached its peak in the work of Pike (1945), who was concerned with cementing the status of stress and intonation as distinctive linguistic features that could be described as phonemic. He posited four pitch phonemes and two pause phonemes as the basic building blocks for intonation contours, although he continued to view intonation as strictly attitudinal in nature, and the focus continued to be on the meaning of individual contours as opposed to structures or patterns that might occur in a discourse environment.

The publication of *The Sound Pattern of English* (Chomsky & Halle, 1968) and the rise of generative grammar shifted the focus from phonetics to phonological rules and representations (Kenstowicz, 1994). Intonation is purposely omitted from the Chomsky & Halle text, and readers are referred to Stockwell (1964) and Lieberman (1966), who were attempting to generate intonation contours via transformational rules. This was naturally problematic as it was not possible to incorporate the attitudinal function of intonation into the types of transformational rules of interest to Chomsky and Halle. Thus, researchers attempted to separate out linguistic and non-linguistic aspects of intonation and, once again, the status of intonation as a system was called into question.

By the 1970s, with few exceptions, pronunciation materials reflected three essential priorities of the field at that time. First, there was a primary focus on segmentals as opposed to suprasegmentals. Second, consideration of suprasegmentals was limited to utterance-level patterns and the attitudinal and grammatical functions of intonation. Finally, there was no consideration of prosodic level discourse patterns that might contribute to the structure of text such as pitch-based or temporal phenomena.

Discourse perspectives

During the 1970s, theoretical interest began to shift towards the analysis of discourse. Linguists such as Labov (1972) and Gumperz and Hymes (1972) prioritized naturally occurring language, and the investigation of spoken language extended to include structural analysis of units such as conversations and narratives. Conversation analysis (Sacks and Schegloff, 1979) focused on talk-in-interaction and examined the role of prosodic devices in conversation management in detail. Increasingly, our understanding of the role of pitch and pause structure expanded to include not only grammatical and attitudinal functions but also discourse functions. These comprised both informational functions such as marking boundary strength (e.g. distinguishing an utterance boundary versus a paragraph boundary), discerning topic structure at the local (utterance) and global (discourse) levels (Cutler, Dahan & Donselaar, 1997; Swerts, 1997), and interactional functions including the use of pitch variation to regulate turn-taking, to communicate sociolinguistic information such as status differences and to contribute to relationship-building between participants (Chun, 2002).

It was understood that prosodic features played a crucial cohesive function in spoken texts. Pitch and temporal cues contributed independently to the structure of the discourse and could not be circumvented without a reduction in comprehensibility or interactional effectiveness.

Arguably, the model that best reflects these developments with respect to intonation is Brazil's (1985/1997) discourse intonation model in which intonation patterns are viewed as essentially pragmatic in nature and as contributing primarily to the communicative message of the discourse. In Brazil's view, there is a fundamental flaw in equating pitch structures with grammatical function or emotional expression. While intonation clearly correlates with these components in the discourse, the meaning of intonation features are not located in the grammatical structure or emotive content of language; thus, they are not predictable based on what is happening in these domains of the language system. Rather, by focusing on these domains we are essentially picking out pieces of the intonation system and trying to make sense of them individually rather than looking at the system as a whole in a discourse context.

In addition to these important theoretical developments, the past 20 years have seen an increased use of instrumental analysis to support research findings in prosody where previously researchers had relied exclusively on auditory impressions. Freely downloadable programs such as WASP (Huckvale, 2003) and Praat (Boersma & Weenick, 2002), and commercially available hardware such as the Computerized Speech Laboratory by Kay Pentax are now used to provide objective and detailed measures of a range of acoustic variables including fundamental frequency, amplitude and temporal features such as pause length. With these data, it is possible to create a complete profile of a given speaker's spoken discourse production. The following sections of the chapter outline the creation of one such profile and what we know about how these features develop in L2 learner discourse.

Features of discourse pronunciation

A comprehensive list of measurable features of discourse pronunciation was created by Pickering in 2007 as part of an ETS grant project.[1] This comprised a total of 26 temporal measures (aspects of speech rate and pause structure) and pitch measures (aspects of stress and fundamental frequency structure). These features were selected and operationalized largely on the basis of precedent in prior research (Brazil, 1997; Derwing, 1990; Derwing & Munro, 2001; Hincks, 2005; Kormos & Denes, 2004; Levis & Pickering, 2004; Pickering, 2001, 2004; Vanderplank, 1993; Wennerstrom, 2001; Wichmann, 2000). The complete list of measures is given in Table 26.1.

The two sets of temporal measures, rate and pause, include seven sub-measures that can be calculated for any given sample of spoken discourse. Rate measures comprise the number of syllables per second, articulation rate (the number of syllables per second excluding silent pause time), mean length of runs in which a run is operationalized as a stretch of speech bounded by pauses of 100 milliseconds or longer, and phonation time ratio (percentage of time spent speaking as a proportion of the total time of the speech sample). Three additional measures address pause structure. The number of silent pauses is calculated based on pauses of 100 milliseconds or longer; filled pauses are defined as including any non-prominent, non-lexical fillers such as *um* or *uh*; and the mean length of pauses is calculated using the total number of silent pauses.

Using instrumental means of analysis, these temporal sub-measures are straightforward to analyse; however, there is continued methodological debate regarding what inter-unit pause length should be considered as linguistically significant as this determines the length of runs and directly impacts numerical assessments of fluency. Currently, the choice of cut-off time

Table 26.1 Summary of discourse pronunciation measures

Measure	Sub-measure
Rate	Syllables per second
	Articulation rate
	Mean length of run
	Phonation time ratio
Pause	Number of silent pauses
	Number of filled pauses
	Mean length of pauses
Stress	Number of prominent syllables per run
	Proportion of prominent syllables
	Prominence characteristics
Pitch	Overall pitch range
	High, mid and low falling, rising and level tone choices
	Pitch on (non-)prominent syllables
	Pitch on new and given lexical items
Paratone	Number of low terminations
	Average height of onset pitch
	Average height of terminating pitch
	Average paratone pause length

Source: Adapted from Kang and Pickering (2011)

varies among researchers typically from 0.1 second (Anderson-Hsieh and Venkatagiri, 1994; Griffiths, 1991; Pickering, 2001, 2004) to 0.2 (Krivokapić, 2007) or 0.25 (Freed, 2000; Riggenbach, 1991).

Operationalizing stress and pitch measures requires a different approach as a theoretical framework is needed in order to determine significance. Fundamental frequency (F0), the acoustic correlate of pitch, is a gradient characteristic, and thus a determination must be made regarding what comprises a linguistically meaningful change for speakers and hearers and how that maps onto F0 values. In this sense, 'every attempt at transcription is an attempt at categorization' (Muller and Ball, 2009, p. 306). As is true of any model where a fit is attempted between theoretical categories and actual data, particularly where this involves gradient characteristics, the analyst must decide whether a given phonetic realization constitutes a variation within one category or a change of category. The addition of instrumental data in the form of F0 traces is invaluable in this process, and the measures combine both auditory and instrumental analysis.

For these measures, Brazil's (1985/1997) discourse intonation model was used. The model comprises 13 pitch features, which form four basic systems: division of speech into units; choice of pitch height on the first and last prominent syllable in each unit (termed key and termination); and choice of pitch melody or tone on the unit's tonic syllable or focus (these include possible fall, rise–fall, rise, fall–rise and level tones). Each of these is exemplified below.

Within Brazil's model, at least one, but usually two prominent syllables will occur in each tone unit and they are divided into two categories based on where they appear in the unit. The first prominent syllable in the unit is the onset and carries key choice (syllable is CAPITALIZ) and the last is the tonic syllable and carries termination choice (syllable is CAPITALIZ and underlined).[2] In cases where there is only one prominent syllable in the unit, both key and termination choice fall on the same syllable. Both possibilities are shown in (1) below. In the first tone unit, '*took*' carries the key choice and '*exam*' carries the termination choice. In the second tone unit '*failed*' carries both key and termination:

(1) //he TOOK the ex<u>AM</u>// and <u>FAILED</u>//

Key and termination are three term systems (high ($\Uparrow$), mid ($\Rightarrow$), and low($\Downarrow$)) and derived based on relative pitch height of prominent syllables within the discourse of any given speaker. Both key and termination pitch choices are also glossed with the same communicative values. Choice of high pitch on the prominent syllable denotes the constituent as either *contrastive* or *particularized* as shown in (2):

(2) //he $\Rightarrow$ TOOK the $\Rightarrow$ ex<u>AM</u>// and $\Uparrow$<u>FAILED</u>//

He did not pass, as you might have expected: *contrastive* (Sinclair & Brazil, 1982, p. 144).

Mid pitch choices have an additive function and denote the constituent as an *expansion* or *enlargement* of the information in previous units, as shown in (3):

(3) //he $\Rightarrow$TOOK the $\Rightarrow$ex<u>AM</u>// and $\Rightarrow$<u>FAILED</u>//

He did both: *additive* (Sinclair & Brazil, 1982, p. 144).

Finally, a low pitch choice signifies an *equative* value in relation to previous units, which carries with it an additional restrictive function, as shown in (4):

(4) he $\Rightarrow$TOOK the $\Rightarrow$ex<u>AM</u>// and $\Downarrow$<u>FAILED</u>//

As you would expect from what you know of him, you will assume that taking it involves failing it: *equative* (Sinclair & Brazil, 1982, p. 144).

The system of tone is also realized on the tonic syllable. It is the maximum, sustained pitch or F0 movement in any unit, and it may be a rising ($\nearrow$; $\searrow\nearrow$), falling ($\searrow$;$\nearrow\searrow$) or sustained level ($\rightarrow$) movement. Although tone choice also appears on the tonic syllable, unlike termination choice tone is concerned with *pitch movement* as opposed to *pitch level*. Tone is chosen by speakers based on their assessment of whether the information in the tone unit is likely to be perceived as *new* or *given* with the context of a specific interaction. Tones that end in a falling movement signify that the content is new, i.e. not recoverable from the preceding discourse, or is asserted, i.e. as a necessary or incontrovertible truth or fact. Rising tones signify that the information is already recoverable in some way. This might be from the preceding discourse or the non-linguistic context that can be assumed to exist between the speaker and hearer. In the example below, a news announcer in Britain assumes that the name of the prime minister of Britain in (a) will be known to the audience (hence the rising tone) whereas the name of her French counterpart in (b) may not:

(a) // the prime $\searrow$<u>MIN</u>ister// mrs $\nearrow$<u>THAT</u>cher//

(b) //the prime $\searrow$<u>MIN</u>ister// Raymond $\searrow$<u>BARRE</u>//

(Brazil, Coulthard & Johns, 1980, p. 18)

The final tone is a level-pitched tone that can also be realized with a slight low rise. Unlike the falling and rising tone choices, the speaker can use this tone to present information as neither shared with nor new to the hearer but simply as a language specimen. Typically, this neutral tone is used for routinized language that is generic rather than specific to a particular interaction. A characteristic use of level tones from classroom discourse, for example, is a teacher's reiteration of well-established procedures or instructions (e.g. //stop →WRITing// put your pens →DOWN//). Level tones can also be indicative of the kinds of online production issues that typically occur in natural speech. Spontaneous utterances frequently contain increased hesitation phenomena or fillers such as //→UH. . .// as speakers negotiate real-time speech production.

The three stress sub-measures focus on prominence structure. Prominent syllables are distinguished from the syllables around them by significant fundamental frequency peaks or valleys, higher volume, and longer duration than non-prominent syllables. These measures calculate the number of prominent syllables per unit (pace), the proportion of prominent syllables as a fraction of syllable production overall (space) and the number of complete units (i.e. units that exhibit a tonic syllable). Four additional pitch measures provide a picture of the speaker's overall pitch range and movement. Key, termination and tone measures provide a comprehensive measure of the use of rising, falling and level pitch choices and placement in the speaker's register (high, mid or low). Fundamental frequency differences are also calculated for the average pitch differences between prominent and non-prominent syllables and new versus given lexical items for each speaker.

The final set of sub-measures address larger structural units in speech. Paratones are variously described in the literature as pitch sequences, speech paragraphs or intonational paragraphs (Barr, 1990; Lehiste, 1979; Tench, 1996; Thompson, 2003; Yule, 1980). Within Brazil's model, a pitch sequence comprises a stretch of consecutive tone units that fall between two low termination choices. It may be uttered by one speaker or shared between two participants in an exchange. It typically delimits longer sections of speech that are related in topic structure, and in this way is analogous to the concept of written paragraph. For example, within one paratone a speaker is likely to use a high pitch to initiate a new topic, a mid pitch level at points of continuation and a low pitch level at the closing of the topic or for any asides or digressions (Brown, Currie & Kenworthy, 1980; Wennerstrom, 2001; Wichmann, 2000). Example (5) below shows a single pitch sequence from a business presentation. It begins with a high key start, steps down to a mid key and closes with a low termination:

(5) //⇑LET'S look at the competition// ⇒Our main competitor, Benton, entered the market 10 years later than us// ⇒But since then they have grown more rapidly and are now the biggest in terms of market share// ⇒Their products are better, sold at lower prices and presented more ⇓attractively//

Example (6) shows a shared pitch sequence between a teacher and student. This is a typical teacher-student initiation-response-feedback (IRF) interaction that might be found in the classroom. The teacher opens the pitch sequence with a high key frame 'so', and the mid termination question 'what's the final answer?' The student responds with a mid key and termination on 'twelve' and the teacher uses a mid agreement key to confirm that the student is correct and then closes the pitch sequence with the low termination evaluative 'good'.

(6) T: //⇑SO// ⇒WHAT'S the final ⇒ANSwer//
    S: //⇒ TWELVE //
    T: //⇒TWELVE ⇓GOOD//

In a given sample of speech, the paratone sub-measures indicate the average pitch height of opening and closing pitches and the average length of the pauses that appear between them.

Discourse pronunciation features in L2 discourse

This set of measures can function as a checklist to allow us to create a more detailed picture of L2 spoken discourse production (Kang, Rubin & Pickering, 2010) and draw together many of the findings regarding prosodic development in second language learners of English, specifically within an English as a second language (ESL) context. Temporal measures are currently the most thoroughly investigated with regard to L2 speech. Research suggests that speaking rates are highly variable across proficiency levels (Anderson-Hsieh & Koehler, 1988; Anderson-Hsieh & Venkatagiri, 1994; Munro & Derwing, 1998).

Munro and Derwing (2001) find a curvilinear relationship between speaking rates and assessments of comprehensibility by native speaker (NS) listeners of L2 speech. In other words, listener ratings were at their worse when the speakers were either too fast *or* too slow; thus, there was an optimal speaking rate. The researchers report that the precise number is very difficult to estimate due to the complex factors involved in that assessment; however, they report that optimal rates were 'somewhat faster than those actually used by the L2 speakers and somewhat slower than rates typical of native speakers of English' (p. 466).

With regard to pause structure, both pause length and placement have been shown to affect perceptions of fluency (Pickering, 1999). Riggenbach (1991) and Anderson-Hsieh and Venkatagiri (1995) found that there were more non-lexical fillers and unfilled pauses in lower-level L2 speech and that long 'empty' pauses frequently appeared within intonation units (Rounds, 1987). This is supported by both Kormos and Denes (2004) and Iwashita, Brown, McNamara & O'Hagan (2008), who show that lower-proficiency speakers tend to pause more often, for longer durations, and within rather than between tone units.

Features of stress also differentiate L2 discourse production. Field (2005) shows that the production of non-standard lexical stress (i.e. word stress) diminishes comprehensibility. Hahn (2004) reports similar findings for primary stress (i.e. final tonic prominence). Wennerstrom (1994, 1997) found that L2 speakers used significantly less pitch variation to signal new or contrastive lexical items and to distinguish prominent from non-prominent syllables. A particularly significant issue in a discourse context is the over-production of acoustically stressed syllables, which are then perceived by the listeners as designated as prominent. This can obscure meaningful patterns of onset and tonic prominence. Findings suggest that lower-proficiency learners often stress virtually every content word within a tone unit (Pickering, 1999; Wennerstrom, 2000).

Turning to pitch measures, researchers are increasingly moving away from asking listeners to rate intonation as a general category as it is very difficult to assess precisely what features of the pitch structure a given rater is focused on (Hayes-Harb & Hacking, 2015). Instead, instrumental measures of F0 have been used to identify significant differences in discourse production. One important area concerns overall pitch range production. Both Mennen (1998) and Pickering (2004) report demonstrably narrower pitch ranges in L2 learner discourse when compared to NS production. This has important implications for paratone structure as it is hampered by an overall compression of pitch range. For example, Pickering (2004) showed that the overall pitch range of teaching presentations given by native speakers was between 50 and 250 hertz (the unit of measurement used to calculate pitch). In contrast, L2 speakers varied their range between only 100 and 200 Hz, and their pitch level structure correlated less systematically with topic structure.

Mennen (2007) also found significant differences in pitch range characteristics between native English speakers and German speakers of English. She suggests that native German speakers exhibit a narrower pitch range in their own language and that this may be transferred to L2 production. At least one study of the fundamental frequency in Arabic learners of English (Abu-Al-Makarem & Petrosino, 2007) has observed that the mean fundamental frequency for spontaneous speech samples of Arabic speakers was 'significantly higher' than for Euro-American, African-American and Polish samples (p. 576). In addition to possible transfer issues, however, it is also the case that pedagogical literature on the subject of pitch paragraphing is rare, and a lack of focus on this area in the classroom may contribute to the problem.

Finally, tone and key choices have also been examined in L2 discourse. Wennerstrom (1994, 1997) reported that Japanese, Thai and Chinese speakers used low, falling tones at boundaries between related propositions where the expectation would be rising or mid-level tones, thus impacting intelligibility for NS listeners. Pirt (1990) found the same for Italian learners, and Pickering (2001) reported equivalent findings for Chinese speakers of English in academic discourse. Tone and key choices also negatively impacted social convergence between NS and NNS participants. Hewings (1995) found a preference for the use of falling tones in the discourse of advanced L2 learners from Korea, Greece and Indonesia in contexts in which NSs would use rising or level tones to mitigate their contradiction or disagreement. Koester (1990) found that German learners of English frequently used a low termination pitch where a mid 'agreement' termination was expected by the listener prompting the first speaker to confirm their partner's agreement. Similarly, Anderson (1990) reports an interaction between an English speaker and a Dutch speaker of English in which the use of high pitch choices by the L2 speaker project conflict and result in a failed interaction. Pickering and Levis (2002) found that, overall, lower-proficiency learners were less able to manipulate key and termination patterns both within and between tone units.

Pedagogical applications

With the exception of a few publications (Bradford, 1988; Brazil, 1994; Cauldwell, 2003, 2013; Dalton & Seidlhofer, 1994; Gorsuch, Meyers, Pickering & Griffee, 2010), features of discourse pronunciation do not commonly appear in pronunciation textbooks, for two reasons. First, the phonological system still tends to be taught piecemeal rather than through larger spoken texts in which discourse features acquire their full significance. Second, there has consistently been little connection between the research and the pedagogical materials developed in this area (Derwing & Munro, 2005). According to Levis (1999), this has resulted in outdated descriptions of suprasegmental structure:

> Because underlying assumptions have not changed, many current textbook treatments of intonation are startlingly similar to each other in scope, in the kinds of exercises offered, and in descriptions of intonational meaning and function. Even more startling is that many current textbooks strongly resemble materials used 50 years ago, differing mostly in typesetting and page layout but not in content and philosophy.
>
> (p. 46)

Although research findings continue to outpace teaching materials, an increase in empirical research, often undertaken by practitioner-researchers (Murphy & Baker, 2015) and assisted by the rapid developments in digital speech processing, has created some synergy between the laboratory and the classroom. As an example, Levis and Pickering (2004) used speech visualization technology to demonstrate how a discourse context affects intonational choices. Four readers read lists of sentences, and the same sentences were read again as a coherent text. In both cases, the onset pitches were measured. In all cases, the onset pitches used to mark each paragraph opening were the highest in the paragraph, and the closing pitch for each paragraph was followed by an extra-high pitch reset to mark the opening of the following paratone or pitch sequence. Thus, the paratone or pitch sequence structure created by the reader was consistently coterminous with the paragraph structure of the written text. In contrast, the onset pitch of each paratone was significantly higher than the equivalent onset pitch from the list reading. Thus, the lack of a genuine discourse context in the list reading disrupted patterns of systematic pitch change that would normally be seen in discourse. This suggests that discourse-level pedagogical treatment is critical for development of these features. Hincks (2005) developed a pitch variation quotient (PVQ) in order to measure the liveliness of speech in presentations by Swedish learners of English. The PVQ measure samples the F0 of speakers at 10-second intervals and adds speech rate and mean length of runs to produce the quotient. Overall, her results suggest that this method of pitch variation feedback could be used as a pedagogical tool to encourage learners to vary their pitch range more effectively and to improve spoken fluency.

With regard to assessment in a pedagogical context, this continues to be conducted largely through impressionistic analysis. One computerized test battery that has been used to profile intonation in L2 learners is Profiling Elements of Prosody for Speech and Communication (PEPS-C) (Peppé & McCann, 2003). Setter, Stojanovik and Martinez-Castilla (2010) examined Chinese and Arabic learners of English focusing on tonality (division into tone units) and tonicity (placement of the focus or tonic). They found some differences in aspects of the production and perception of intonation, particularly in the area of assessing function as opposed to form such as in the ability of learners to assess likes versus dislikes. The authors suggest that the test could be used as a basic diagnostic tool for L2; however, the battery was originally designed to assess pathological speech and participants produce only single words or short phrases. One productive area of investigation may be in the development of more detailed rubrics such as the one described above and shown in Table 26.1. Multiple measures could be tested in a discourse context, and the results used to produce a prosodic competency scale. In any event, the suggestion made by Chun (1988, p. 65) that we integrate acoustic-phonetic analysis with discourse-level analysis is now well on its way.

Future directions

In addition to the development of materials and assessment of discourse pronunciation features for ESL/EFL environments, the continued growth of English as a global language requires that we extend our interest to contexts of world Englishes and English as a lingua franca. World Englishes can be narrowly defined within Kachru's (1985) model as 'outer circle Englishes', i.e. those that derived largely from colonization in Asia and Africa. Early work in Indian English (IE) phonology (Gumperz, 1982; Mohanan, 1986) suggested that spoken discourse was divided into sub-contours that created short prosodic pieces lacking a unified intonational contour. There were also differences in the phonetic realization of prominence that caused misinterpretation of lexical stress patterns. This was verified by Pickering and Wiltshire (2000), who found a 'dip' in F0 on prominent syllables and irregular amplitude changes in contexts in which speakers of inner circle Englishes (e.g. British or American English) would raise both their pitch and their volume.

More recently, this work has been supplemented by research into the pronunciation features of Hong Kong English (Cheng, 2004; Cheng and Warren, 2005), Singaporean English (Sg E; Ling and Grabe, 1999; Low 2006), Malaysian English (My E; Goh, 2001) and Filipino English (Pickering, Menjo & Bouchard, 2012). When compared to inner circle Englishes, differences in discourse features of prosody include the phonetic realizations of prominence patterns and nucleus placement.

Low (2006) and Setter (2006) report that Hong Kong Englissh speakers and Singapore English speakers show little evidence of prosodically attenutating syllables that would be 'deprominenced' in British (or other inner circle) Englishes as they were unstressed or weakened syllables or appeared on what would be considered given information. Example (7) is from SgE in which 'mark' is highlighted in the final unit despite its status as given information.

(7) //it is NOT ONly the asSIGNments// you have to MARK// but ALso// the NUMber of assignments// you have to MARK//

(Goh, 2001, p. 94)

This pattern is particularly striking when the final stress is a usually unstressed pronominal, as shown in Example (8) from MyE:

(8) //NOT this ONE// that SMALL ONE//

(p. 95)

Both Setter and Low note that these characteristics may have important implications for intelligibility when these speakers are interacting with speakers of inner circle varieties. Setter advocates classroom work in the area of rhythm, and Low suggests a pronunciation syllabus that should highlight aspects of nuclear and contrastive stress placement. However, Low also emphasizes that these areas are the result of differences, not of errors. She suggests, for example, that teachers encourage students who speak these varieties to paraphrase the conversations with their own words. Teachers can then observe how students make distinctions between new and given information and use this information to inform their classroom instruction.

Finally, the field has recently begun to address discourse pronunciation in English as a lingua franca (ELF) interaction. The investigation of intonational resources in ELF interaction is in its earliest stages. Deterding and Kirkpatrick (2006) investigated ELF interaction between ASEAN speakers (L2 speakers of English from Brunei, Malaysia, the Phillipines, Singapore, Cambodia, Indonesia, Laos, Myanmar, Thailand and Vietnam). They found 'heavy end stress' (i.e. placement of the nucleus on the final word) to be a common feature of the interaction. Pitzl (2005) analysed extracts from ELF business meetings and reported that the combination of tonic placement and rising intonation were used by participants to signal that there was a need for feedback. Similarly, Pickering (2009) and Pickering and Litzenberg (2011) established that ELF interlocutors employ intonational cues meaningfully throughout their interactions. Examples of such cues included the use of tonic stress to assign information value, the use of rising tones to signal negotiation, the use of falling tones to indicate completion and the use of high key to indicate surprise or astonishment. However, although prosodic resources played a role in the production of intelligible and successful interaction in ELF, use of these features did not mirror NS-based interaction. This was particularly the case with regard to social or interactional uses of intonation. For example, there was no evidence of ELF interlocutors employing the face-saving function of rising tones that would be anticipated in NS-based interaction to mitigate disagreement or contradiction.

Although it is as yet unclear how representative these findings are of the broad spectrum of ELF interaction, this more recent research suggests we may want to incorporate additional intonational features into those currently contained in proposals for a lingua franca core (Jenkins, 2000), which typically comprise only tonic stress and unit division.

Appendix: Transcription conventions

// //	Tone unit boundaries
CAPS	Prominence
UNDERLINE	Tonic syllable
High key	⇑
Mid key	⇒
Low key	⇓
Rising tones	↗; ↘↗
Falling tones	↘; ↗↘
Level tone	→

Notes

1   TOEFL COE Grant, ETS (2006–07), Don Rubin, Okim Kang and Lucy Pickering. Relative Impact of Rater Intercultural and Language Background, Rater Language Attitudes, Rater Training, and Measurable Elements of Pronunciation on TOEFL iBT Speaking Proficiency Scoring.
2   Transcription conventions are given in full in the Appendix.

Further reading

Brazil, D. (1997). *The communicative value of intonation in English*. Cambridge: Cambridge University Press. This is a republished manuscript that was originally published in 1986 as a research monograph by the University of Birmingham, which was David Brazil's home institution. It comprises the most readily available and complete exposition of the discourse intonation model that is described in this chapter.

Cauldwell, R. (2013). *Phonology for listening: Teaching the stream of speech*. Birmingham: Speech in Action. In this volume, Cauldwell provides a framework for the description and teaching of spontaneous speech. It is inspired by Brazil's work, and a number of the principles and terminology derive from the discourse intonation model. However, Cauldwell expands well beyond these issues to present a comprehensive model of spontaneous speech and how it can be used to improve listening skills.

Derwing, T., & Munro, M. (2015). *Pronunciation fundamentals: Evidence-based perspectives for L2 teaching and research*. Philadelphia, PA: John Benjamins. Authored by two of the leading scholars in the field of L2 pronunciation over the past 30 years, this volume surveys much of the foundational and cutting-edge empirical work that underlies the current work in pronunciation in discourse, and which has been included in this chapter.

Pickering, L. (in press). *Discourse intonation: A discourse-pragmatic approach to intonation in English for ESL/EFL teacher*s. Ann Arbour, MI: Michigan University Press. Designed for both pre-service and in-service teachers, this volume uses Brazil's model of discourse intonation as the foundation of a comprehensive overview of the intonation system in English. It highlights the importance of intonation in intercultural communication and includes discussion of world Englishes and English as a lingua franca.

Trouvain, J., & Gut, U. (2007). *Non-native prosody: Phonetic description and teaching practice*. Berlin: Mouton de Gruyter. The first part of this edited volume comprises studies of a number of prosodic features in L2 speech including intonation, rhythm and temporal patterns. The second part focuses on research specifically designed to test teaching practices in L2 prosodic instruction. This unique volume demonstrates the important synergy between experimentally and pedagogically based research.

References

Abu-Al-Makarem, A., & Petrosino, L. (2007). Reading and spontaneous speaking fundamental frequency of young Arabic men for Arabic and English languages: A comparative study. *Perceptual & Motor Skills, 105*(2), 572–580.

Anderson, L. (1990). Intonation, turn-taking and dysfluency: Non-natives conversing. In M. Hewings (Ed.), *Papers in discourse intonation* (pp. 102–113). Birmingham: University of Birmingham, English Language Research.

Anderson-Hsieh, J., Koehler, K. (1988). The effect of foreign accent and speaking rate on native speaker comprehension. *Language Learning, 38*, 561–613.

Anderson-Hsieh, J., & Venkatagiri, H. (1994). Syllable duration and pausing in the speech of Chinese ESL speakers. *TESOL Quarterly, 28*. 807–812.

Barr, P. (1990). The role of discourse intonation in lecture comprehension. In M. Hewings (Ed.), *Papers in discourse intonation* (pp. 5–21). Birmingham: University of Birmingham, English Language Research.

Bloomfield, L. (1933). *Language*. New York, NY: Henry Holt.

Boersma, P. and Weenick, D. (2002). Praat. [Computer software]. Amsterdam: Institute of Phonetic Sciences, University of Amsterdam.

Bradford, B. (1988). *Intonation in context: Intonation practice for upper-intermediate and advanced learners of English – teacher's book*. Cambridge: Cambridge University Press.

Brazil, D. (1985/1997). *The communicative value of intonation in English*. Cambridge: Cambridge University Press.

Brazil, D. (1994). Pronunciation for advanced learners of English. New York, NY: Cambridge University Press.

Brazil, D., Coulthard, M., & Johns, C. (1980). *Discourse intonation and language teaching*. London: Longman.

Brown, G., Currie, K. L., & Kenworthy, J. (1980). *Questions of intonation*. Baltimore, MD: University Park Press.

Cauldwell, R. (2003). *Streaming speech*. Birmingham: Speech in Action.

Cauldwell, R. (2013). *Phonology for listening*. Birmingham: Speech in Action.

Cheng, W. (2004). //→ Did you TOOK // from the miniBAR//: What is the practical relevance of a corpus-driven language study to practitioners in Hong Kong's hotel industry? In U. Connor & T. A. Upton (Eds), *Discourse in the professions: Perspectives from corpus linguistics* (pp. 141–166). Amsterdam: Benjamins.

Cheng, W., & Warren, M. (2005). //↗CAN i help you //: The use of rise and rise-fall tones in the Hong Kong corpus of spoken English. *International Journal of Corpus Linguistics, 10*(1), 85–107.

Chomsky, N., & Halle, M. (1968). *The sound pattern of English*. Cambridge, NY: MIT Press.

Chun, D. M. (1988). The neglected role of intonation in communicative competence and proficiency. *Modern Language Journal, 72*, 295–303.

Chun, D. (2002). *Discourse intonation in L2: From theory and research to practice*. Amsterdam: Benjamins.

Cutler, A., Dahan, D., & Donselaar, W. (1997). Prosody in the comprehension of spoken language: A literature review. *Language and Speech, 40*, 141–201.

Dalton, C., & Seidlhofer, B. (1994). *Pronunciation*. Oxford: Oxford University Press.

Derwing, T. (1990). Speech rate is no simple matter: Rate adjustment and NS-NNS communicative success. *Studies in Second Language Acquisition, 12*, 303–313.

Derwing, T., & Munro, M. (2001). What speaking rate do non-native listeners prefer? *Applied Linguistics, 22*, 324–337.

Derwing, T. M., & Munro, M. J. (2005). Second language accent and pronunciation teaching: A research-based approach. *Tesol Quarterly, 39*(3), 379–397.

Deterding, D., & Kirkpatrick, A. (2006). Emerging South-East Asian Englishes and intelligibility. *World Englishes, 25*(3/4), 391–409.

Field, J. (2005). Intelligibility and the listener: The role of lexical stress. *TESOL Quarterly*, *39*, 399–424.

Freed, B. F. (2000). Is fluency, like beauty, in the eyes (and ears) of the beholder? In H. Riggenbach & R. Schmidt (Eds), *Perspectives on fluency* (pp. 243–265). Ann Arbor, MI: University of Michigan Press.

Goh, C. C. M. (2001). Discourse intonation of English in Malaysia and Singapore: Implications for wider communication and teaching. *RELC Journal*, *32*(1), 92.

Gorsuch, G., Meyers, C. M., Pickering, L., & Griffee, D. T. (2010). *English communication for international teaching assistants* (1st ed.). Long Grove, IL: Waveland.

Griffiths, R. (1991). Pausological research in an L2 context: A rationale, and review of selected studies. *Applied Linguistics*, *12*(4), 345–364.

Gumperz, J. J. (1982). *Discourse strategies*. New York, NY: Cambridge University Press.

Gumperz, J. J. H., & Hymes, D. (1972). *Directions in sociolinguistics: The ethnography of communication*. New York, NY: Holt.

Hahn, L. D. (2004). Primary stress and intelligibility: Research to motivate the teaching of suprasegmentals. *TESOL Quarterly*, *38*, 201–223.

Halliday, M. A. K. (1967). *Intonation and grammar in British English*. The Hague: Mouton.

Hayes-Harb, R., & Hacking, J. (2015). Beyond rating data: What do listeners believe underlies their accentedness judgments? *Journal of Second Language Pronunciation*, *1*, 1, 43–64.

Hewings, M. (1995). Tone choice in the English intonation of non-native speakers. *The International Review of Applied Linguistics*, *33*(3), 251–265.

Hincks, R. (2005). Measures and perceptions of liveliness in student oral presentation speech: A proposal for an automatic feedback mechanism. *System*, *33*, 575–591.

Huckvale, M. (2003). *SFS/WASP Version 1.41*. Retrieved from www.phon.ucl.ac.uk/resource/sfs/wasp.htm.

Iwashita, N., Brown, A., McNamara, T., & O'Hagan, S. (2008). Assessed levels of second language speaking proficiency: How difficult? *Applied Linguistics*, *29*, 24–49.

Jenkins, J. (2000). *The phonology of English as an international language*. Oxford: Oxford University Press.

Kachru, B. (1985). Standards, codification, and sociolinguistic realism: The English language in the outer circle. In R. Quirk & H. Widdowson (Eds), *English in the world: Teaching and learning the language and literature* (pp. 11–30). Cambridge: Cambridge University Press.

Kang, O., & Pickering, L. (2011). The role of objective measures of suprasegmental features in judgments of comprehenisibility and oral proficiency in L2 spoken discourse. *Speak Out!*, *44*, 4–8.

Kang, O., Rubin, D., and Pickering, L. (2010). Suprasegmental measures of accentedness and judgments of language learner proficiency in oral English. *The Modern Language Journal*, *94*(4), 554–566.

Kenstowicz, M. (1994). *Phonology in generative grammar*. Cambridge: Blackwell.

Koester, A. (1990). The intonation of agreeing and disagreeing in English and German. In M. Hewings (Ed.), *Papers in discourse intonation. Discourse analysis monograph*, *16* (pp. 83–101). Birmingham: University of Birmingham, English Language Research.

Kormos, J. and Denes, M. (2004). Exploring measures and perceptions of fluency in the speech of second language learners. *System*, *32*, 145–164.

Krivokapić, J. (2007). Prosodic planning: Effects of phrasal length and complexity on pause duration. *Journal of Phonetics 35*(2), 162–179.

Labov, W. (1972). *Sociolinguistic patterns*. Philadelphia, PA: University of Pennsylvania Press.

Lehiste, I., 1979. Perception of sentence and paragraph boundaries. In B. Lindblom & S. Ohman (Eds), *Frontiers of speech perception* (pp. 191–201). London: Academic Press.

Levis, J. M. (1999). Intonation in theory and practice, Revisited. *TESOL Quarterly*, *33*(1), 37–64.

Levis, J., & Pickering, L. (2004). Teaching intonation in discourse using speech visualization technology. *System: An International Journal of Educational Technology and Applied Linguistics*, *32*(4), 505–524.

Lieberman, P. (1966). *Intonation, perception, and language*. Cambridge, NY: MIT Press.

Ling, L. E., & Grabe, E. (1999). A contrastive study of prosody and lexical stress placement in Singapore English and British English. *Language & Speech*, *42*, 39–56.

Low, E. L. (2006). A cross-varietal comparison of deaccenting and 'given' information: Implications for international intelligibility and pronunciation teaching. *TESOL Quarterly*, *40*(4), 739–761.

Mennen, I. (1998). *Can language learners ever acquire the intonation of a second language*. Paper presented at the ESCAL Workshop on Speech Technology in Language Learning, International Speech Communication Association, Marholmen, Sweden.

Mennen, I. (2007). Phonological and phonetic influences in non-native intonation. In J. Trouvain & U. Gut (Eds), *Non-native prosody: Phonetic description & teaching practice* (pp. 131–176). Berlin: Mouton de Gruyter.

Mohanan, K. P. (1986). *The theory of lexical phonology*. Dordrecht: Reidel.

Muller, N., & Ball, M. (2009). Transcribing prosody. *International Journal of Speech-Language Pathology*, *11*(4), 305–307.

Munro, M. J., & Derwing, T. M. (1998). The effects of speech rate on the comprehensibility of native and foreign accented speech. *Language Learning*, *48*, 159–182.

Munro, M. J., & Derwing, T. M. (2001). Modelling perceptions of the accentedness and comprehensibility of L2 speech: The role of speaking rate. *Studies in Second Language Acquisition*, *23*(4), 451–468.

Murphy, J. M., & Baker, A. A. (2015). History of ESL pronunciation teaching. In J. Levis & M. Reed (Eds), *Wiley-Blackwell handbook of English pronunciation* (pp. 36–65). Hoboken, NJ: Blackwell.

O'Connor, J. D., & Arnold, G. F. (1961/1973). *Intonation of colloquial English* (2nd ed.). London: Longman.

Palmer, F. (1970). *Prosodic analysis*. Oxford: Oxford University Press.

Peppé, S., & J. McCann (2003). Assessing intonation and prosody in children with atypical language development: the PEPS-C test and the revised version. *Clinical Linguistics and Phonetics*, *17*(4–5), 345–354.

Pickering, L. (1999). *An analysis of prosodic systems in the classroom discourse of native speaker and nonnative speaker teaching assistants*. Unpublished dissertation, University of Florida.

Pickering, L. (2001). The role of tone choice in improving ITA communication in the classroom. *TESOL Quarterly*, *35*, 233–255.

Pickering, L. (2004). The structure and function of intonational paragraphs in native and non-native instructional discourse. *English for Specific Purposes*, *23*, 19–43.

Pickering, L. (2009). Intonation as a pragmatic resource in ELF interaction. *Intercultural Pragmatics*, *6*(2), 235–255.

Pickering, L., & Levis, J. (2002). *Assessing the intonation patterns of second language learners*. Paper presented at the 36th Annual TESOL Convention, Salt Lake City, Utah, 12 April 2002.

Pickering, L., & J. Litzenberg (2011). Intonation as a pragmatic resource, revisited. In A. Archibald, A. Cogo & J. Jenkins (Eds), *Latest trends in ELF*. Newcastle-upon-Tyne: Cambridge Scholars.

Pickering, L., Menjo, S., & Bouchard, J. 2012. *Are you telling me or asking me? International intelligibility in call center interaction and implications for EFL*. Colloquium paper presented at ACTA conference, Queensland, Australia.

Pickering, L., & Wiltshire, C. (2000). Pitch accent in Indian English TAs' teaching discourse. *World Englishes*, *19*, 173–183.

Pike, K. L. (1945). *The intonation of American English*. Ann Arbor, MI: University of Michigan Press.

Pirt, G. (1990). Discourse intonation problems for non-native speakers. In M. E. Hewings (Ed.), *Papers in discourse intonation* (pp. 145–155). Birmingham: English Language Research.

Pitzl, M.-L. (2005). Non-understanding in English as a lingua franca: Examples from a business context. *Vienna English Working Papers*, *14*(2), 50–51. Retrieved from www. univie.ac.at/Anglistik/Views0502mlp.pdf (accessed 26 June 2007).

Riggenbach, H. (1991). Toward an understanding of fluency: a microanalysis of nonnative speaker conversations. *Discourse Processes*, *14*, 423–441.

Rounds, P. L. (1987). Characterizing successful classroom discourse for NNS teaching assistant training. *TESOL Quarterly*, *21*(4), 643–671.

Sacks, H., & Schegloff, E. (1979). Two preferences in the organization of reference to persons in conversation and their interaction. In G. Psathas (Ed.), *Everyday language: Studies in Ethnomethodology* (pp. 15–21). New York, NY: Irvington.

Setter, J. (2006). Speech rhythm in world Englishes: The case of Hong Kong. *TESOL Quarterly*, *40*(4), 763–782.

Setter, J.,Stojanovik, V., & Martinez-Castilla, P. (2010). Evaluating the intonation of non-native speakers of English using a computerized test battery. *International Journal of Applied Linguistics*, *20*(3), 368–385.

Sinclair, J. M., & Brazil, D. (1982). *Teacher talk*. Oxford: Oxford University Press.

Stockwell, R. P. (1964). *Realism in historical English phonology*. Paper presented at the winter meeting of the Linguistics Society of America, University of California at Los Angeles.

Swerts, M. (1997). Prosodic features at discourse boundaries of different strength. *The Journal of the Acoustical Society of America, 101*, 514–521.

Tench, P. (1996). *The intonation systems of English*. London and New York, NY: Cassell.

Thompson, S. E. (2003). Text-structuring in metadiscourse, intonation and the signalling of organization in academic lectures. *Journal of English for Academic Purposes, 2*, 5–20.

Trim, J. (1975). *English pronunciation illustrated*. Cambridge: Cambridge University Press.

Trubetzkoy. N. (1969). *Principles of phonology*. Berkeley, CA: University of California Press.

Vanderplank, R., 1993. Pacing and spacing as predictors of difficulty in speaking and understanding English. *English Language Teaching Journal, 47*, 117–125.

Wennerstrom, A. (1994). Intonational meaning in English discourse: A study of non-native speakers. *Applied Linguistics, 15*(4), 399–420.

Wennerstrom, A. K. (1997). *Discourse intonation and second language acquisition: Three genre-based studies*. Unpublished dissertation, University of Washington.

Wennerstrom, A. (2000). The role of intonation in second language fluency. In H. Riggenbach (Ed.), *Perspectives on fluency* (pp. 102–127). Ann Arbor, MI: University of Michigan Press.

Wennerstrom, A. K. (2001). *The music of everyday speech: prosody and discourse analysis*. Oxford and New York, NY: Oxford University Press.

Wichmann, A. (2000). *Intonation in text and discourse: Beginnings, middles, and ends*. Harlow and New York, NY: Longman.

Yule, G. (1980). Speakers' topics and major paratones. *Lingua, 52*, 33–47.

Section 6

Future directions
of pronunciation

27

Innovations in pronunciation teaching

Donna M. Brinton

Introduction

With the transition in the late 1970s and early 1980s from direct method and audiolingual approaches to communicative language teaching (CLT), the field of second language (L2) pronunciation teaching entered an era of challenge. Pronunciation practitioners made concerted efforts to align their classroom practice with emerging communicative approaches to language teaching (e.g. Celce-Murcia, Brinton & Goodwin, 2010), as did materials developers such as Morley (1979) and Gilbert (1984). This alignment of theory and practice resulted in fundamental changes to pronunciation teaching.

The first of these changes involved revisiting the idea, central to the then prevailing contrastive analysis hypothesis (see Tarone, 2013), that interference from the learner's first language (L1) constituted the primary source of error in pronunciation (for example, the contrastive analysis hypothesis would attribute an Arabic speaker's difficulty producing the voiceless stop /p/ to interference from the L1 on the grounds that the native sound inventory of Arabic did not contain the voiceless stop /p/). Instead, there was awakened recognition that other factors (such as overgeneralization) also play a central role in L2 acquisition, including the acquisition of the L2 sound system (for example, a learner's pronunciation of the past tense inflectional ending –ed as /əd/ in words such as *walked*, *missed*, *robbed* and *moved* would be viewed as the learner's overgeneralizing the /əd/ pronunciation of past tense endings of verbs ending in /t/ or /d/ to all instances of past tense endings of regular verbs). Replacing the notion of L1 interference was that of L1 transfer, which could be either positive (i.e. in cases where the L1 and L2 share phonological features) or negative (i.e. in cases where the L1 lacks phonological features that are present in the L2). There were several important outcomes of this change in thinking. First, the primacy of the minimal pair drill in the pronunciation classroom – and its role in helping learners to eradicate the 'bad habits' deriving from their L1 – came under scrutiny. This in turn resulted in efforts to make drills more communicative in nature – e.g. via the Bowen technique (Bowen, 1972; see also Celce-Murcia et al., 2010), pronunciation bingo, minimal pair-focused dialogues and other ways of accomplishing communication-oriented minimal pair practice.

A second outcome of the move away from traditional teaching methods was a shift in focus away from segmentals to suprasegmentals, i.e. in recognition of the importance of the latter in communicating overall meaning (Celce-Murcia et al., 2010). A clear leader in this movement was Gilbert, whose first edition of *Clear Speech: Pronunciation and Listening Comprehension in American English* (1984) focused almost exclusively on suprasegmentals, thus breaking tradition with other current student texts on the market. Other authors of student pronunciation texts quickly followed suit, with the result that by the mid-1990s coverage of suprasegmental aspects became a standard feature in pronunciation course texts.

Other changes to pronunciation practice included the efforts of materials developers and classroom practitioners to balance work on accuracy with work on fluency, to enhance the authenticity of teaching materials, and in general to create tasks that engaged learners in interactive, meaningful exchanges of information. Also, in keeping with CLT practice, course developers sought to design student-centred pronunciation curricula in which learner needs drove decisions about what was to be included.

Equally significant in the evolution of pronunciation teaching has been the recognition that, in today's global culture and economies, preparing non-native English speakers (NNESs) to communicate with native English speakers (NESs) of the language is no longer the sole goal of pronunciation instruction – especially in contexts where the primary anticipated use of English is as a common language of communication among lingua franca speakers of the language (Walker, 2010).

Emerging innovations in pronunciation teaching

Today, almost four decades after the initial appearance of CLT on the scene, pronunciation teaching is emerging from its past history of rote drill and repetition. Influenced significantly by works on contemporary pedagogical practices – e.g. Avery and Ehrlich (1992), Celce-Murcia et al. (1996, 2010), Kenworthy (1987) – and by the growing body of empirical research into factors that directly impact learner intelligibility, pronunciation teaching has embraced numerous innovations in classroom practice. These innovations range from a focus on the role of suprasegmentals in communicating meaning to prioritizing learner intelligibility over achievement of a native-like pronunciation and to the use of instructional techniques such as mirroring and shadowing.

This chapter highlights the juncture of research and emerging innovative practices in pronunciation pedagogy. These practices include but are not limited to means of increasing learner motivation and autonomy, implementing multimodal approaches to pronunciation teaching, the increasing role of technology in today's pronunciation practice, pronunciation priorities when teaching the pronunciation of English as a lingua franca, and insights into the impacts of rhythm, stress, intonation and thought groups on learners' overall intelligibility. We will examine each of these innovations in turn.

Increasing learner motivation

Discussions of success in the acquisition of L2 pronunciation skills generally mention factors such as the learner's L1, age, exposure to the target language, amount and type of prior pronunciation instruction, language aptitude, individual differences, attitude towards the target language and, finally, type and degree of learner motivation (Celce-Murcia et al., 2010; Moyer, 1999). Of these, only the last three factors are ones that can potentially be addressed in the classroom and/or are influenced by classroom practices. Unfortunately, these factors are not only difficult to measure but also suffer from varying definitions and are thus difficult to operationalize. Although limited research into these factors exists, more is needed, and concrete suggestions in the pronunciation literature for how to individualize pronunciation instruction, help learners acquire a more positive attitude towards L2 pronunciation and increase their motivation are scant.

What we know from available research is that there is a significant correlation between learners' beliefs and attitudes towards L2 pronunciation and their ultimate attainment. Cenoz and Lecumberri (1999), for example, document learners' awareness of the important role that motivation plays in their acquisition of L2 pronunciation, while Baran-Lucarz (2014) demonstrates the negative effects that learner anxiety and low self-confidence in L2 skills have on learners' willingness to communicate. Moyer (2014), in her study of exceptional language learners, suggests that the factors that correlate most strongly with pronunciation success are both cognitive and sociolinguistic. In particular, she notes that learner factors such as identifying strongly with the L2, wanting to sound like an NES, having a socially outgoing orientation and using the language in a variety of domains figured strongly in success. And as McCrocklin and Link (2014) and Levis (2015) note, despite the overriding importance of social factors in L2 pronunciation acquisition, many learners remain unaware of the relation between identity and accent; they also appear confused as to which social factors play important roles in helping them to acquire L2 pronunciation skills. Thus it becomes incumbent upon the teacher to assist learners in understanding how social forces affect L2 pronunciation acquisition.

Turning to classroom suggestions that can support learners in this critical area of motivation and identity, Zielinski (2012) stresses the overriding importance of providing safe environments in the classroom for learners to practise as this can help them build confidence and be more willing to speak in the L2. Further, Brinton (2014) notes that, for L2 learners who may resist acquiring features of the target language, a possible technique is to adopt Dörnyei's (2014) notion of a possible self. Using this technique, learners envision an alternate L2 self without fear. This alternate self is seen as a long-term goal that teachers can help to nurture and which can be reinforced via learner contracts (e.g. Acton, 1984), motivation surveys, journal exchanges, out-of-class surveys of NESs and the like.

Encouraging learner autonomy

The desire by teachers to create a community of autonomous learners (i.e. learners who are more independent of the teacher and who can take charge of their own learning) is most certainly not restricted to the field of pronunciation teaching. And yet pronunciation requires a great deal of out-of-class effort. Thus helping learners to become more autonomous and stressing the importance of out-of-class practice remain top priorities in the pronunciation classroom.

Research underscores the importance of autonomy as leading to the successful acquisition of L2 pronunciation skills. For example, McCrocklin (2014) reports that autonomy has been shown as empowering and as leading to higher learning achievement and motivation. The problem comes with translating this finding into classroom practice, particularly in the pronunciation classroom. With respect to traditional L2 pronunciation teaching, the teacher served as a model for students to emulate, and thus students remained dependent on the teacher as a role model, provider of feedback and evaluator. As McCrocklin points out, this role of teacher as the sole model is antithetical to fostering autonomy in students.

Fortunately, in today's communicatively oriented classroom, the role of the teacher has expanded significantly, and the majority of teachers are able to find ways to create out-of-class learning opportunities – thus encouraging autonomous learning. Creating an archive of self-access materials is greatly facilitated by course management software (e.g. Moodle or Blackboard) that allows teachers to create direct links to authentic sources such as TED Talks, elevator pitches and Three Minute Thesis activities that can serve as motivational models for listening and pronunciation practice. Teachers can require students to dedicate a specified amount of out-of-class time (for example, two hours a week) to exploring the posted links and to keeping a journal of their reactions and progress. In a study of graduate students enrolled in a course for international teaching assistants, for example, Sardegna and McGregor (2013) report the successful use of scaffolded instruction accompanied by student self-regulated practice. In this course, students reflected on their strategy use and self-assessed their experiences with the provided out-of-class practice materials using pronunciation trackers. Study results indicated improvement in students' L2 production as well as evidence of effective teacher scaffolding.

A second technique providing for autonomous student practice is that of echoing, shadowing or mirroring – i.e. delivering a passage from a recorded speaker while imitating as exactly as possible the speakers' gestures, facial expressions and body movements (Acton, 1984; Rosse, 1999). Chung (2017) reports on a technique that is grounded in the theory of echoic memory. In this technique, students practise intensively with a two- to three-minute recorded passage accompanied by a written transcript. They listen to a succession of short clips, replaying each clip in their mind after hearing it (hence the name 'echo' method) and then repeating the echoed passage aloud. They continue this process until the entire passage becomes automatized. Students are encouraged to practise in this manner for up to 20 minutes a day, keeping a record of their practice time and perceived progress. They are also encouraged to seek feedback. Echo practice can later be augmented by other forms of shadowing or mirroring practice such as synchronous reading (in which students shadow a native speaker reading a text).

Goodwin (2004) and Meyers (2014) report loosely related alternatives to this practice, in which students first identify an area of speech with which they are struggling (e.g. thought groups, intonation, rhythm and stress). They then either self-select a speaker whom they wish to emulate or are assigned one, locate a relevant video clip, and transcribe a short passage from the clip. Once the passage has been transcribed, students mark it up to indicate thought groupings and otherwise annotate it (e.g. marking intonation contours, focus words, drawing in non-verbal cues) to assist them in the mirroring process. Following intensive practice, they record themselves (one or more times) 'mirroring' the speaker. They then view the product, conduct a self-assessment of their performance and consult with their instructor and/or peers for feedback. Overall, the authors claim that mirroring helps students improve their use of pausing, prominence and non-verbal communication as well as gain confidence in speaking.

A final related area of pronunciation research that has links to the pedagogy of learner autonomy involves the use of strategy instruction. Rokoszewska (2012) reports a strong correlation between instruction in pronunciation strategies and Polish L2 learners' perception and production of English vowels and diphthongs, while Smemoe and Haslam (2013) report a similar positive correlation between learners' strategy use and end-of-course increased comprehensibility. However, Sardegna (2012) cautions that, in addition to strategy use, other factors such as student engagement and sense of self efficacy play a role in pronunciation progress. Generalizing from these three studies, we can conclude that strategy instruction can be a useful tool for heightening student awareness of phonological features and motivating them to become more autonomous learners.

Multimodal approaches to pronunciation

Multimodal approaches (such as the use of visuals, gestures, sound and movement) are by no means new to the field of teaching pronunciation. Celce-Murcia et al. (2010) suggest that such approaches can help to break down ego boundaries, thereby increasing learners' receptivity towards acquiring L2 sound features. And Brinton (2014) notes that, since pronunciation teaching involves auditory, visual and kinesthetic modalities, best practice mandates that it be taught through a multimodal approach.

Visuals such as the vowel quadrant, the consonant chart and the sagittal diagram are our legacy from articulatory phonetics and the teaching practices of the 1960s and 1970s. Similarly, the use of audio recordings (today in the form of digitized sound files) comes to us via the audiolingual approach, which depended heavily on recorded passages of NESs reciting sentences, performing dialogues and reading narrative passages aloud. These recorded materials served as models for listen-and-repeat activities, which typically took place in language labs and were an integral part of audiolingualism.

A significant advance in the use of multimodal approaches, however, occurred in the early 1990s with the publication of a book chapter by Gilbert (1991) entitled 'Gadgets: Non-verbal tools for teaching pronunciation' (p. 308). There, Gilbert advocated using a variety of gadgets (e.g. rubber bands to illustrate vowel length; kazoos to demonstrate pitch rise in intonation) to illustrate features of English pronunciation.

Two more recent pioneers in the push to include multimodal approaches are Chan (2007) and Acton (2012). Chan's (2007) video 'Using Your Hands to Teach Pronunciation' underscores the importance of visual reinforcement when introducing speech features. On her YouTube channel, Chan (n.d.) also includes numerous 'pronunciation workout' exercises to heighten learners' awareness of their vocal apparatus, increase the strength and flexibility of their articulatory muscles, and enhance the automaticity of L2 sound production.

Influenced by work on embodied cognition and learning, Acton's (2012) blog post describes what he refers to as 'haptic' pronunciation teaching, a teaching system grounded in the coordinated use of movement, touch and gesture. Examples of haptic techniques include clapping the hands on primary stressed syllables of multisyllabic words, stepping or dancing in time to key words in a stretch of discourse, or holding an object and shaking it to the rhythm of a poem. Echoing pioneering theorists on the role and function of physical gesture in human communication such as McNeill (1992) and Wylie (1997), Acton maintains that the inclusion of body movement is critical to successful pronunciation teaching and that such physical engagement provides a viable pathway to more accurate L2 fluency. Students are introduced to various pedagogical movement patterns where the hands move across the visual field and make contact with other parts of the body. According to Acton, these movements are used to present, correct, practise and anchor new sound structures. Though supporting empirical evidence is slight, Acton and his colleagues posit that the system they describe enhances students' ability to anchor sounds, words, and phrases to movement and/or visuals (e.g. a phonemic vowel chart) and to facilitate students' recall and integration of the target features in spontaneous speech (Acton, Baker, Burri & Teaman, 2013).

Technological innovations

For those of us who began teaching pronunciation with a blackboard, audiotapes, flash cards (and perhaps an overhead projector), the most obvious advances in pronunciation teaching today are the countless applications of technology. Hardison (this volume) discusses current uses of technology in pronunciation in far more detail than is possible in this overview. However, given the direct link between technology and innovation, the following brief summary of tools and techniques is included here as well.

The influence of technology on pronunciation teaching includes the entire spectrum of digital technologies – from the simplest audio solutions such as Audacity (digital recording software) (http://web.audacityteam.org/) to Wimba's threaded voice boards (www.wimba.com/products/wimba_voice) to far more advanced technologies such as web-based applications and automatic speech recognition (ASR). With regard to web-based applications, preliminary evidence from Thomson (2011, 2012) indicates that learners exposed to high-variability phonetic training (in which multiple sounds are contrasted using multiple voices) improved not only their perception of unfamiliar English vowels but also, to a limited degree, the intelligibility of their production. For a comprehensive discussion of how ASR can impact pronunciation teaching, see McCrocklin (2014).

Today, even the least tech-savvy pronunciation teachers make use of at least a modicum of technology, such as having students upload audio file attachments for feedback, playing streaming video samples of authentic native speaker discourse, posting links to digital resources on the course website and the like (Godwin-Jones, 2009). Similarly, the rapid growth of international online tutoring (the focus of which is often on pronunciation issues) makes use of synchronous video conversations where tutors can view images of the learners' faces in real time as they acquire new sound features, providing both visual and audio feedback as needed. All of these techniques require a minimum of technological expertise yet show great promise as resources for enhancing the quality of classroom study and out-of-class work.

Before leaving the topic of technology behind, some mention should be made of recent advances in the availability and use of mobile technologies. Jarvis (2015) reports that there are currently 6.8 billion mobile phone subscribers worldwide (i.e. rapidly approaching the world's population of 7.1 billion) – an astounding statistic portending that soon mobile or smartphones will be in the hands of virtually everyone on earth. Given that far more learners have access to a cell phone than to a personal computer (especially in developing areas of the world), mobile technologies hold great promise for empowering literally billions of learners in their acquisition of English pronunciation skills. Huffman (2011) provides a comprehensive discussion of uses to which mobile technologies can be put, starting with synchronous voice chat apps such as Skype and progressing to more interactive apps such as MobiLearn – a talking phrasebook that provides instant feedback to learners (www.mobilearn.net) – and videoconferencing software such as NetMeeting (www.microsoft.com/en-us/download/details.aspx?id=23745) that allows tutors and instructors to hear and speak to one another while attending real-time virtual classrooms. As Huffman concludes, mobile technologies not only empower learners and encourage learner autonomy but also enable learning to extend beyond the classroom.

Pronunciation priorities for English as a lingua franca communication

One area of research that has had tremendous impact on the field concerns teaching the pronunciation of English as a lingua franca (ELF) – i.e. to NNESs who opt to use English as a language of wider communication when speaking with other NNESs from different L1 backgrounds. Based on the premise that the NES is no longer the sole target interlocutor, ELF pedagogy concludes that our job as pronunciation teachers is to prepare ELF users of the language to communicate effectively and intelligibly with other ELF speakers, prioritizing those pronunciation features that will best prepare them for this goal.

First identified and discussed by Jenner (1989), the concept of a 'common core' (i.e. the minimal inventory of pronunciation features needed for successful interaction among ELF speakers) to guide the design of pronunciation curricula was further promoted by applied linguists such as Jenkins (2000, 2006) and Walker (2010). Based on continuing research on NNES–NNES interactions (in particular of instances where communication breakdown occurs as the result of non-target-like usage), these researchers are seeking to establish a basis for ELF pronunciation syllabus design. In direct contrast to the traditional pronunciation syllabus, with its focus on NES target forms, the ELF pronunciation syllabus omits those features that are deemed peripheral to intelligible NNES–NNES communication. To illustrate, features such as aspiration following /p, t, k/, word-initial and word-medial consonant clusters, long/short vowel contrasts, and nuclear or tonic stress are deemed essential to include in an ELF pronunciation syllabus, while other features that have traditionally been stressed in the English as a second/foreign language pronunciation curriculum are not. A partial list of these omitted features includes vowel reduction, schwa, and weak or reduced forms (such as /kən/ for *can*); features of connected speech such as linking and palatalization; stress-timing; pitch movement; and certain consonant phonemes such as /θ/, /ð/, and dark /l/, along with the General American flap /ɾ/. The end goal of a common core approach to pronunciation syllabus design is a significantly reduced (and thus assumedly a more attainable) set of ELF pronunciation goals.

Groundbreaking as the concept of a common core ELF pronunciation syllabus has been, several issues bear mentioning. First, there is as yet no complete consensus as to which features constitute an ELF common core (Brinton & Goodwin, 2006). Additionally, an ELF approach to pronunciation teaching is most appropriate in certain settings (i.e. in settings where learners are most likely to be using English as a lingua franca). In other settings where near-native pronunciation plays an important role, the ELF approach to pronunciation syllabus design is less appropriate. (Examples of such learners include immigrant students in English-speaking countries whose goal is to assimilate into the culture, professionals who attend and present at international conferences, service personnel who deal with native English-speaking clientele, actors etc.) In both cases, the identification of learners' needs helps in establishing what type of approach to syllabus design is in order.

The impact of rhythm, stress, intonation and thought groups on learners' overall intelligibility

Despite the overriding focus on segmentals in the pronunciation teaching of the 1960s and 1970s, there were notable exceptions. One of these involved the three-volume publication of *Drills and Exercises in English Pronunciation* (English Language Services, 1967), which devoted two volumes to work on stress and intonation. Intended for use with adult learners of English as a second language, the content was influenced by the work of the linguist Kenneth Croft and contained exercises at both word level and discourse level. As for student texts, as noted in the introduction of this article, the first work to clearly break tradition with texts that were almost exclusively focused on segmentals was Gilbert (1984). Finally, in terms of teacher reference works, Kenworthy (1987) and Wong (1987) in particular constituted early, very rich compendiums of sources and activities for teachers seeking to champion and emphasize the importance of suprasegmentals.

From a purely linguistic perspective, there remain numerous disagreements among applied linguists concerning English suprasegmentals. What is the relation between grammatical structures and intonation (if any)? Which system of marking intonation is the most appropriate for teaching purposes? (See, for example, Levis, 2013). What about the so-called stress-timing characterization of the rhythm of spoken English? Is this a fiction that only pronunciation teachers and course texts seek to maintain, despite abundant evidence from linguists that the concept of stress-timing does not adequately represent the rhythm of English? See, for example, Cauldwell (2002) and Dickerson (2014); for a contrastive view, see Barrera-Pardo (2008). Further, as summarized in Saito (2014), research shows that the overall intelligibility of a message (i.e. the ability of a listener to understand its content) is based somewhat disproportionately on certain of these phonetic features – most notably (on the phrasal level) on correctly placed prominence on the focus word within a thought group and (on the word level) on correctly placed lexical stress.

As for practical suggestions pertaining to these research findings, Derwing and Munro (2014) remind us that the concepts of intelligibility and comprehensibility are of critical importance to what we do in the classroom. Reiterating the findings reported by Saito above, the authors suggest focusing classroom time on issues of stress at both the word and phrase level. Further, Murphy (2013) contends that thought grouping is essential to most other aspects of English pronunciation and that, consequently, it should be prioritized over other aspects of pronunciation teaching – especially when classroom time devoted to pronunciation is limited. Murphy further maintains that features such as prominence, intonation, linking, assimilation and deletion can be taught more efficiently once learners are familiar with the process of thought grouping.

Other techniques and approaches

One of the more curious phenomena in teaching is the extent to which previously popular and well-received classroom practices or methods resurface in a later time period and are pedagogically re-envisioned (or in some cases simply 'repackaged') under new labels or with new enhancements to better appeal to contemporary learners and teachers. As an example, one need only think of the phonics approach to teaching reading, which first appeared on the scene in the nineteenth century but continually reappears as an alternative to whatever other approach is currently in favour. This phenomenon of reappearing trends has been excellently captured by the metaphor of the methods pendulum (Celce-Murcia, 2014), which swings from one extreme to the other, yet always returns to its original position.

A number of popular approaches to pronunciation teaching appear to fit under this category. In a recent webinar offered through Electronic Village Online (2015), several of the practices that were introduced to participants included teaching articulatory settings, using abdominal musculature to produce stressed elements and employing silent way practices such as a sound/colour chart, fidels and Cuisenaire rods. Strictly speaking, none of these practices can be considered novel or innovative since they have been widely discussed in the literature and are by no means new practices in the field. However, the seminar leaders note that, in terms of the articulatory approach, they have integrated the element of speech breathing (Messum, 2010), which they contend has a positive effect on learners' acquisition of stress and reduction in English. With respect to the silent way, they also report having substantially revised the materials to better reflect the sound system of English and have created a new set of word charts (fidels) for non-beginners (see Young & Messum, 2013). To learn more about Messum and Young's work, visit Pronunciation Science: www.pronunciationscience.com.

Reminiscent of Gattegno's (1963) sound colour chart, as well as similar colour coding charts in Finger (1989) and Celce-Murcia et al. (1996, 2010), is Taylor and Thompson's (2012) Color Vowel Chart (CVC), a tool for teaching the vowels of English. Aimed especially at those teachers who feel that a phonetic alphabet is irrelevant to their students' needs, the CVC uses colours to signal vowel sounds (e.g. *green* for the high-front-tense vowel /iy/; *black* for low-front /æ/) along with key words (e.g. *red dress* for mid-front-lax /ɛ/; *blue moon* for high-back-tense /uʷ/) as additional hooks for learners to recall each sound. Taylor and Thompson maintain that, compared with other colour charts, their CVC more accurately portrays the vocal tract and assists learners in mastering linking via the prominent placement of the glides /y/, /w/ and liquid /r/ at the top of the CVC. Additionally, they claim, the colour coding of the CVC facilitates its use with even low-literacy or younger learners, who can refer to vowels in stressed syllables by naming their associated 'colour' rather than using metalanguage. (For example, learners would refer to the word *raisin* is as a 'grey' word based on the stressed syllable's vowel /ey/.) Other CVC enhancements include an accompanying booklet with sample lesson plans along with a website and social media site containing additional resources (e.g. printable wall charts, a webinar describing how to use the CVC and a video illustrating a corollary of the CVC known as Color Yoga).

Challenges and future directions

This chapter has highlighted the direct relation between pronunciation research and innovations in pronunciation pedagogy. Topics covered involved increasing learner motivation and autonomy, multimodal approaches, the increasing role of technology, pronunciation priorities for lingua franca communication, and insights into the impact of stress, rhythm and intonation, as well as the process of thought grouping, on learners' overall intelligibility.

Research and practice are not always in perfect synchrony, and this certainly holds true in the case of L2 pronunciation teaching. One challenge faced when dealing with teaching methodology in general (and practical phonetics in particular) concerns the time lag between the implementation of a new classroom practice and its validation via empirical research. In fact, many of the ideas that we espouse as 'best practices' in pronunciation teaching are based on teacher experiences and successes in the classroom, rather than on a direct link to research (see Murphy and Baker, 2015).

This challenge can, however, serve a facilitative role in defining the future direction of innovation. As Levis and LeVelle (2010) observe, we are in the process of rebuilding (brick by brick) a professional space for L2 pronunciation teaching and learning. In this rebuilding process, we need to ensure that our foundations (L2 pronunciation research, teachers' reflections on their experiences) are sound and that the architects (researchers, materials developers, classroom teachers, course developers) design a structure that provides a constructive and stimulating living environment for as many teachers and language learners as possible. In terms of the future of L2 pronunciation research, more studies are needed concerning which aspects of pronunciation most impact learner intelligibility and lead to noticeable or significant improvement in learners' output. As well, the learners' L1 and setting variables need to be taken into account as anything like a 'one-size-fits-all' pronunciation curriculum is definitely a thing of the past. Finally, pronunciation research must continue to delve into matters of learner variability so that teachers can more effectively deal with issues of learner motivation, autonomy and strategy use.

When my co-authors and I published the first edition of *Teaching Pronunciation* (Celce-Murcia et al., 1996), we included a chapter entitled 'New Directions in the Teaching of Pronunciation'. Its subsections included: fluency-building activities, multisensory modes of teaching pronunciation, the use of authentic materials, techniques from psychology, theatre arts and other disciplines, and the role of instructional technology. Some of the activities we described included: board games (e.g. values topics, discussion wheel); tools for visual and tactile reinforcement (e.g. rubber bands, drinking straws, ice lolly sticks, kazoos); kinesthetic reinforcement (e.g. using the fingers or hands to demonstrate stress placement or position of the articulators); auditory reinforcement (e.g. clapping or tapping out stress patterns); the use of limericks, poetry, jazz chants or other authentic materials (e.g. advertising copy); guided imagery and visualization or relaxation exercises; drama techniques (e.g. the use of voice modulation techniques or mirroring, tracking and shadowing); and finally applications of instructional technology to the teaching of pronunciation (e.g. audio journals, video feedback and speech spectrographic devices).

At the time, most of the activities we described seemed relatively groundbreaking and thus constituted appropriate inclusions under the chapter title. However, when we published the text's second edition in 2010, we were hard-pressed to identify a sufficient number of innovative techniques to feature under the same chapter heading. We therefore re-envisioned the chapter as 'Techniques, Tools, and Technology' (featuring many of the same techniques described in the initial edition's 'innovations' chapter).

In writing the present chapter, I have wrestled with what constitutes genuine innovation in pronunciation teaching. In the course of so doing, I have come to believe that true innovation connects directly to research findings. As Murphy and Baker (2015) observe, the fourth wave of pronunciation teaching is still in progress. This wave is dedicated to emerging ways of teaching pronunciation as informed by contemporary empirical research; it is defined by researchers in the field who have posed foundational questions that bear a direct relation to classroom pronunciation teaching. In the fourth wave, empirical research is beginning to have more of an impact on the teaching of pronunciation while methodological 'bandwagons' of past decades are receiving diminished attention from teachers, materials developers and curriculum designers. As recent volumes by Derwing and Munro (2015), Grant (2014) and Reed and Levis (2015) illustrate, research specialists and instructional practitioners can and are collaborating to forge an invigorating professional space – a space where research on the acquisition and teaching of L2 pronunciation can inform instructional practices and where researchers and practitioners can work together to improve the quality of L2 pronunciation teaching. Given these very promising circumstances, this is a very exciting time indeed for all those interested in either researching or teaching the pronunciation of English as a second, foreign or international language.

Further reading

Brown, A. (Ed.). (1991). *Teaching English pronunciation: A book of readings*. New York, NY: Routledge. This classic anthology presents groundbreaking articles that significantly impacted the shape of pronunciation pedagogy today. Among the articles included in the volume are discussions by Esling and Wong on voice quality settings, by Gilbert on the use of gadgets, by Kachru on appropriate models of English for the third world, by Brown on functional load, and by Dickerson on orthography as a pronunciation resource. The volume also contains a useful bibliography.

Brown, J. D. (Ed.). (2012). *New ways in teaching connected speech*. Alexandria, VA: TESOL. This edited volume in TESOL's New Ways series is aimed at classroom teachers. Divided into 14 sections, each focusing on a particular aspect of connected speech (e.g. contractions and blendings, sentence stress and timing), the volume presents a wide variety of innovative teaching ideas in lesson plan format. Each section begins with a brief description by the editor of the connected speech feature.

Grant, L. (Ed.). (2014). *Pronunciation myths: Applying second language research to classroom teaching*. Ann Arbor, MI: University of Michigan Press. This edited volume in the University of Michigan Press's 'myths' series is devoted to the link between research in the field of pronunciation and classroom pedagogy. Seven commonly held misconceptions about pronunciation teaching are examined and dispelled based on research evidence. A prologue by the author defines key terminology; a useful epilogue sums up best practices and innovations in pronunciation teaching.

Walker, R. (Ed.). (2014). *Speak Out! The Newsletter of the IATEFL Pronunciation Special Interest Group, 50* (Special issue). In this fiftieth issue of IATEFL's pronunciation special interest group (PronSIG), pronunciation specialists from around the world reflect on the state of the art of English pronunciation teaching by looking both back to the past and forward to new and innovative practices. Among the many issues examined are: the relation between accent and intelligibility, grapheme/phoneme correspondence, consonant cluster simplification, intonation signaling new vs. given information, the nature of spontaneous speech and challenges for pronunciation teacher training.

References

Acton, W. (1984). Changing fossilized pronunciation. *TESOL Quarterly, 18*, 71–85.

Acton, W. (23 October 2012). *Explaining the EHIEP 'haptic' system to students and colleagues.* [blog post]. Retrieved from http://hipoeces.blogspot.ca/2012/10/explaining-ehiep-to-students-and.html.

Acton, W., Baker, A., Burri, M., & Teaman, B. (2013). Preliminaries to haptic-integrated pronunciation instruction. In J. Levis & K. LeVelle (Eds), *Proceedings of the 4th Pronunciation in Second Language Learning and Teaching Conference* (pp. 234–244). Ames, IA: Iowa State University.

Avery, P., & Ehrlich, S. (1992). *Teaching American English pronunciation.* Oxford: Oxford University Press.

Baran-Lucarz, M. (2014). The link between pronunciation anxiety and willingness to communicate in the foreign-language classroom: The Polish EFL context. *The Canadian Modern Language Review, 70*(4), 445–473.

Barrera-Pardo, D. (2008). The reality of stress-timing. *English Language Teaching Journal, 62*, 11–17.

Bowen, J. D. (1972). Contextualizing pronunciation practice in the ESOL classroom. *TESOL Quarterly, 6*(1), 83–94.

Brinton, D. M. (2014). Epilogue to the myths: Best practices for teachers. In L. Grant (Ed.), *Pronunciation myths* (pp. 225–242). Ann Arbor, MI: University of Michigan Press.

Brinton, D. M., & Goodwin, J. (with Celce-Murcia, M.). (2006, December). World English, intelligibility, and pronunciation standards: What pronunciation specialists think. *Speak Out!, 36*, 26–32.

Cauldwell, R. (2002). The functional irrhythmicality of speech: A discourse view of speech rhythms. *Journal of Applied Language Studies, 2*(1), 1–24.

Celce-Murcia, M. (2014). An overview of language teaching methods and approaches. In M. Celce-Murcia, D. M. Brinton, & M. A. Snow (Eds), *Teaching English as a second or foreign language* (4th ed.) (pp. 2–14). Boston, MA: Cengage/National Geographic Learning.

Celce-Murcia, M., Brinton, D. M., & Goodwin, J. M. (1996). *Teaching pronunciation: A reference for teachers of English to speakers of other languages.* New York, NY: Cambridge University Press.

Celce-Murcia, M., Brinton, D. M., & Goodwin, J. M. (with Griner, B.). (2010). *Teaching pronunciation: A course book and reference guide* (2nd ed.). New York, NY: Cambridge University Press.

Cenoz, J., & Lecumberri, L. G. (1999). The acquisition of English pronunciation: Learners' views. *International Journal of Applied Linguistics, 9*(1), 3–17.

Chan, M. (n.d.). *Pronunciation doctor: Pronunciation workout videos.* [Video file]. Retrieved from www.youtube.com/playlist?list=PLqCkG27JV0f1PqfV7pVrBxwew94WM2D0U.

Chan, M. (2007). *Using your hands to teach pronunciation* [Instructional DVD]. Retrieved from www.sunburstmedia.com.

Chung, K. S. (2017). Teaching pronunciation to adult learners of English. In H. Widodo, A. Wood, D. Gupta, & W. Cheng (Eds), *Asian English language classrooms: Where theory and practice meet.* New York, NY: Routledge.

Derwing, T., & Munro, M. J. (2014). Myth 1 Once you've been speaking a language for years, it's too late to change your pronunciation. In L. Grant (Ed.), *Pronunciation myths* (pp. 34–55). Ann Arbor, MI: University of Michigan Press.

Derwing, T. M., & Munro, M. J. (2015). *Pronunciation fundamentals: Evidence-based perspectives for L2 teaching and research.* Philadelphia, PA: Benjamins.

Dickerson, W. (2014, September). *A nail in the coffin of stress-timed rhythm*. Paper presented at the 6th Annual Conference on Pronunciation in Second Language Teaching and Learning, Santa Barbara, CA.

Dörnyei, Z. (2014). Motivation in second language learning. In M. Celce-Murcia, D. M. Brinton & M. A. Snow (Eds), *Teaching English as a second or foreign language* (4th ed.) (pp. 518–531). Boston, MA: Cengage/National Geographic Learning.

Electronic Village Online. (2015). Teaching pronunciation differently [Webinar]. Retrieved from http://evosessions.pbworks.com/w/page/90060791/2015_Teaching_Pronunciation_Differently.

English Language Services. (1967). *Drills and exercises in English pronunciation* (Vols. 1–3). New York, NY: Collier Macmillan.

Finger, J. (1989). Teaching pronunciation with the vowel colour chart. *TESL Canada Journal, 2*(2), 43–50.

Gattegno, C. (1963). *Teaching foreign languages in schools: The silent way*. New York, NY: Educational Solutions.

Gilbert, J. B. (1984). *Clear speech: Pronunciation and listening comprehension in American English*. New York, NY: Cambridge University Press.

Gilbert, J. B. (1991). Gadgets: Non-verbal tools for teaching pronunciation. In A. Brown (Ed.), *Teaching English pronunciation: A book of readings* (pp. 308–322). London: Routledge.

Godwin-Jones, R. (2009). Emerging technologies—Speech tools and technologies. *Language Learning & Technology, 13*(3), 4–11.

Goodwin, J. (2004). The power of context in teaching pronunciation. In J. Frodesen & C. Holten (Eds), *The power of context in language teaching and learning* (pp. 225–236). Boston, MA: Thomson/ Heinle.

Grant, L. (2014). *Pronunciation myths: Applying second language research to classroom teaching*. Ann Arbor, MI: University of Michigan Press.

Huffman, S. (2011). Using mobile technologies for synchronous CMC to develop L2 oral proficiency. In. J. Levis & K. LeVelle (Eds), *Proceedings of the 2nd Pronunciation in Second Language Learning and Teaching Conference* (pp. 122–129). Ames, IA: Iowa State University.

Jarvis, H. (2015). From PPP and CALL/MALL to a praxis of task-based teaching and mobile assisted language use. *TESL-EJ, 19*(1), 1–9.

Jenkins, J. (2000). *The phonology of English as an international language*. Oxford: Oxford University Press.

Jenkins, J. (2006). Current perspectives on teaching world Englishes and English as a lingua franca. *TESOL Quarterly, 40*(1), 157–181.

Jenner, B. (1989). Teaching pronunciation: The common core. *Speak Out!, 4*, 2–4.

Kenworthy, J. (1987). *Teaching English pronunciation*. London: Longman.

Levis, J. (2013). Intonation. In C. A. Chapelle (Ed.), *The encyclopedia of applied linguistics*. New York, NY: Blackwell.

Levis, J. (2015). Learners' views of social issues in pronunciation learning. *Journal of Academic Language and Learning, 9*(1), A42–A55.

Levis, J., & LeVelle, K. (2010). Rebuilding a professional space for pronunciation. In J. Levis & K. LeVelle (Eds), *Proceedings of the 1st Pronunciation in Second Language Learning and Teaching Conference* (pp. 1–9). Ames, IA: Iowa State University.

McCrocklin, S. M. (2014). *The potential of automatic speech recognition for fostering pronunciation learners' autonomy*. Unpublished doctoral dissertation, Iowa State University, Ames, IA.

McCrocklin, S., & Link, S. (2014). What is identity? ELL and bilinguals' views on the role of accent. In J. Levis & S. McCrocklin (Eds), *Proceedings of the 5th Pronunciation in Second Language Learning and Teaching Conference* (pp. 137–144). Ames, IA: Iowa State University.

McNeill, D. (1992). *Hand and mind: What gestures reveal about thought*. Chicago, IL: University of Chicago Press.

Messum, P. (2010). Understanding and teaching the English articulatory setting. *Speak Out!, 43*, 20–24.

Meyers, C. (2014). Intelligible accented speakers as pronunciation models. In J. Levis & S. McCrocklin (Eds), *Proceedings of the 5th Pronunciation in Second Language Learning and Teaching Conference* (pp. 172–176). Ames, IA: Iowa State University.

Morley, J. (1979). *Improving spoken English*. Ann Arbor, MI: University of Michigan Press.

Moyer, A. (1999). Ultimate attainment in L2 phonology: The critical factors of age, motivation and instruction. *Studies in Second Language Acquisition, 21*, 81–108.

Moyer, A. (2014). Exceptional outcomes in L2 phonology: The critical factors of learner engagement and self regulation. *Applied Linguistics, 35*(4), 418–440.

Murphy, J. (2013). *Teaching pronunciation.* Alexandria, VA: TESOL.

Murphy, J. M., & Baker, A. A. (2015). History of ESL pronunciation teaching. In M. Reed & J. Levis (Eds), *The handbook of English pronunciation* (pp. 36–65). Hoboken, NJ: Wiley Blackwell.

Reed, M., & Levis, J. (Eds). (2015). *The handbook of English pronunciation.* Hoboken, NJ: Wiley Blackwell.

Rosse, M. (1999). Tracking: A method for teaching prosody to ESL learners. *Prospect: An Australian Journal of TESOL, 14*(1), 53–61.

Rokoszewska, K. (2012). The influence of pronunciation learning strategies on mastering English vowels. *Studies in Second Language Learning and Teaching, 2*(3), 391–413.

Saito, K. (2014). Experienced teachers' perspectives on priorities for improved intelligible pronunciation: The case of Japanese learners of English. *International Journal of Applied Linguistics, 24*(2), 250–277.

Sardegna, V. G. (2012). Learner differences in strategy use, self-efficacy beliefs, and pronunciation improvement. In. J. Levis & K. LeVelle (Eds), *Proceedings of the 3rd Pronunciation in Second Language Learning and Teaching Conference* (pp. 39–53). Ames, IA: Iowa State University.

Sardegna, V. G., & McGregor, A. (2013). Scaffolding students' self-regulated efforts for effective pronunciation practice. In J. Levis & K. LeVelle (Eds), *Proceedings of the 4th Pronunciation in Second Language Learning and Teaching Conference* (pp. 182–193). Ames, IA: Iowa State University.

Smemoe, W. B., & Haslam, N. (2013). The effect of language learning aptitude, strategy use and learning context on L2 pronunciation learning. *Applied Linguistics, 34*(4), 435–456.

Tarone, E. (2013). Interlanguage. In C. A. Chapelle (Ed.), *The encyclopedia of applied linguistics.* New York, NY: Blackwell.

Taylor, K., & Thompson, S. (2012). *Color vowel chart: A visual tool for teaching the sounds of English.* Santa Fe, NM: English Language Training Solutions.

Thomson, R. I. (2011). Computer assisted pronunciation training: Targeting second language vowel perception improves pronunciation. *Calico Journal, 28*(3), 744–765.

Thomson, R. I. (2012). Improving L2 listeners' perception of English vowels: A computer-mediated approach. *Language Learning, 62*(4), 1231–1258.

Walker, R. (2010). *Teaching the pronunciation of English as a lingua franca.* New York, NY: Oxford University Press.

Wong, R. (1987). *Teaching pronunciation: Focus on English rhythm and intonation.* Englewood Cliffs, NJ: Prentice-Hall Regents.

Wylie, L. (1997). *Beaux gestes. A guide to French body talk.* Cambridge, MA: Undergraduate Press.

Young, R., & Messum, P. (2013, May–June). Gattegno's legacy. *IATEFL Voices, 232,* 8–9.

Zielinski, B. (2012). The social impact of pronunciation difficulties: Confidence and willingness to speak. In. J. Levis & K. LeVelle (Eds), *Proceedings of the 3rd Pronunciation in Second Language Learning and Teaching Conference* (pp. 18–26). Ames, IA: Iowa State University.

28

Applying a cognitive linguistic framework to L2 pronunciation teaching

Graeme Couper

Introduction

The aim of this chapter is to review the theory of Cognitive Linguistics (CL) and explain its relevance to pronunciation teaching. It begins by defining CL and mapping the development of the theory and the role of phonology from this perspective. It then explains how CL provides a theory of both language and language learning before focusing in on its role in pronunciation learning. This is followed by consideration of what sorts of insights CL may offer and how these can be applied in practice. It will be seen that a number of other disciplines offer perspectives on teaching and learning that are in harmony with CL and can also be drawn upon in considering classroom practice, namely educational psychology, sociocultural theory and L2 speech research. Having considered the potential of CL, a series of five studies undertaken by the author is reviewed, which provides evidence for the relevance of CL and in particular for its power in helping to define type-of-instruction in ways that make pronunciation teaching effective.

Historical and current conceptualizations

Defining Cognitive Linguistics

Cognitive Linguistics (CL) does not provide a unified single theory of language but, rather, it represents a number of similar and related views as to the nature of language. Perhaps the most central aspect is the focus on 'the analysis of the conceptual and experiential basis of linguistic categories' (Geeraerts & Cuyckens, 2007, p. 3). That is, language 'is seen as a repository of world knowledge, a structured collection of meaningful categories that help us deal with new experiences and store information about old ones' (p. 5). This draws on the idea of the embodied mind allowing us to make sense of the socio-physical world that we are a part of, that is cognitive, physical and social factors influence how we construct meaning (Rohrer, 2007). CL sees language as consisting of meaning (semantic structures), phonological structures and symbolic structures that link meaning and form (Langacker, 1987,

2008). Semantics is seen as central to language and not in need of an additional structural level in order to explain the relationship between world knowledge and linguistic forms. It is also understood that language does not reflect objective reality but rather is the result of conceptualization and categorization resulting from individual and collective experiences (Taylor & Littlemore, 2014).

Cognitive Linguistics is thought of as being cognitive because it starts with our cognitive ability to conceptualize the world around us based on our experience. It is generally capitalized to distinguish it from other cognitive approaches that more broadly focus on language as a mental phenomenon. CL is also a usage-based model of language, that is, it emerges from engagement with the real world: 'acquisition proceeds on the basis of encounters with actual data, it is not driven by the setting of parameters of a supposedly Universal Grammar' and 'what is grammatical in a language is determined by conformity with schemas and patterns extracted by previous usage, not by reference to abstract innate principles' (Taylor & Littlemore, 2014, p. 15). Ellis and Robinson (2008) note that CL has much in common with functional linguistics, both being usage-based approaches and seeing language structure as being shaped by 'the processing conditions of language performance, and the communicative goals and intentions of language users' (p. 4). However, as they point out, CL goes further because it attempts to relate conceptual structure to its phonological representation through language, that is, the construction of form–meaning relationships. While Nuyts (2007) notes some difficulties in drawing a clear distinction between the two, CL is more interested in a theory of how the embodied mind conceptualizes and categorizes the world around it, whereas functional linguistics, as the name implies, focuses on the functions of language.

Historical perspectives

Cognitive Linguistics is a relatively recent theoretical perspective on language, expressed originally through the work of Langacker (1987) and Lakoff (1987). It grew largely out of dissatisfaction with the Chomskyan approach, which viewed language as a system encapsulated within its own part of the brain that was quite separate from our embodied minds and the society in which we live (Taylor & Littlemore, 2014). Lakoff (1987) challenged the idea that sentence meaning could be related directly and objectively to reality, arguing instead that it was mediated by individuals' perceptions of the world, i.e. construal, conceptualization and categorization are the key to understanding language use. Lakoff is of course most well-known for his work on metaphor and bringing the understanding of the importance of metaphor to language and thought (Tay, 2014).

Langacker is perhaps the key figure in CL through the fundamental contribution he made to its advancement with his development of cognitive grammar, which defines language and analyses it in terms of the relationship between phonology (the form) and meaning (Bennett, 2014; Langacker, 1987, 2007; Taylor, 2002). Cognitive grammar also led to the specification of which cognitive abilities might be involved in the development of language (Langacker, 2000; Taylor, 2002). These abilities will be discussed in the section on the implications of CL for teaching. Bybee has made a major contribution in developing what it means to have a usage-based approach (Bybee, 2001; Sanford, 2014). Unlike generative phonology, which starts from the fundamental assumption that categories are determined by the presence or absence of distinctive features (voicing, for example), a usage-based approach focuses on how structure arises from use. That is, pronunciation is inextricably entwined with the construction of meaning. Others such as Fauconnier were important for bringing the focus to categories and concepts and leading to an increased understanding of the role they play in language (Birdsell, 2014). As CL has developed it has tended to research a number of aspects of cognition.

Phonology in CL

CL has tended to focus on semantic issues rather than phonology. While this is not surprising given the centrality of meaning, phonology is itself dependent on concepts and therefore open to conceptual analysis (Taylor & Littlemore, 2014). Aspects of phonology such as phonemes, syllables and stress are language-specific concepts; consequently, pronunciation is a cognitive phenomenon involving cognitive abilities such as categorization, perception and forming mental representations of sounds (Taylor, 2002). Mompean (2014) argues that CL has two main contributions to make to phonology. The first is that phonology draws on the same cognitive abilities as other faculties of the mind. He focuses on categorization, perception and conceptual combination. The second contribution is the embodiment thesis, which is that language, including phonology, is rooted in experience: physical, social and cultural. In the case of pronunciation, our bodies have a role to play in physically producing and hearing sounds, and this exists within the broader physical, social and cultural space of all our experiences. A further feature of embodiment is that pronunciation and gesture is the physical representation of our identities and ourselves as members of society.

Nathan (2007) sees phonology as representation of our knowledge of bodily experience and describes phonemes as mental sound images. He supports arguments for the importance of categorization and conceptualization in phonology with evidence from the way we perceive sounds phonemically without being aware of the physical variations. For example, the /p/ in <pot> and the /p/ in <top> are both thought of as being the same sound, a /p/ phoneme, yet the aspiration of the former and the lack of release on the latter makes them acoustically quite different. Nathan argues that CL views around categorization can be applied to phonology.

Nathan (2008) argues that phonological representations should not be viewed as merely abstract symbols that different languages organize according to abstract rules, as proposed by generative phonology, but rather that they are mental images of physical reality. That is, phonology is a mental phenomenon based on the categorization of speech sounds. These phonological categories are thought of as exemplar-based, that is, concepts are formed through a collection of experiences that slowly go to represent a particular category (Medin & Schaffer, 1978). For example, we form a picture of the English phoneme /t/ through hearing it from many different speakers in many different contexts.

Mompean (2006) explores the nature of phoneme classification using a CP (cognitive phonology) approach, discussing the radial nature of phoneme categories, along with other views such as the network model. Fraser (2006a, p. 59) says that CP theory 'suggests that a category can be defined in terms of a prototype, with "prototypical" members at the centre of the category and more "peripheral" members around an often "fuzzy" boundary'. Mompean (2014) argues that classical definitions of categories such as phonemes that rely on sets of features determining them are not in line with their psychological reality. He suggests an instance-schema network view in which there are prototypes and many allophones, which, while being seen as belonging to a particular category, these categories are in fact overlapping. Mompean also focuses on the importance of perception in cognition. In particular, this involves the ability to perceive similarity and difference and to manipulate figure-ground perspective in understanding categorization. Figure-ground perspective refers to our ability focus on what is salient to making the figure meaningful and draw that to the foreground and to push those features that are not critical to understanding the category into the background. Conceptual combination is also a relevant cognitive capacity in phonology as we are able to combine different phonological concepts when speaking, leading for example to changes of sounds in context.

CL and language learning

The central tenet of CL that language draws on the same cognitive faculties as we draw on for cognition in general has obvious implications for language learning. Within a CL framework, we are not concerned about whether or not it is possible to access universal grammar and a language acquisition device in order to be able to acquire language implicitly or to convert explicit knowledge to implicit knowledge. Rather, the focus is on how we can use our general cognitive faculties to learn the language. Taylor (2002) discusses a wide range of cognitive capacities that may be involved in language. Some examples of capacities of relevance to pronunciation learning include the ability to categorize, to perceive figure-ground organization and to focus on form.

Langacker (2000) proposes five underlying psychological constructs that are particularly relevant to understanding the learning process:

(a) entrenchment (sometimes called routinization, automatization or habit formation): 'through repetition even a highly complex event' can become easy, i.e. it becomes a 'unit' (ibid, p. 93);
(b) multiple experiences lead to abstraction and the development of schemata;
(c) the ability to compare two structures and detect discrepancy;
(d) composition: an ability to combine simpler structures to form more complex ones;
(e) association, especially symbolization of concepts to form mental representations.

There has still been only a limited amount of research into the practical application of CL to language teaching. Achard and Niemeier (2004) edited a special edition that considered the implications of CL for language acquisition and pedagogy. Eight of the papers focused on pedagogy, largely on issues related to semantics, teaching vocabulary and grammar. They considered how CL can assist in learning difficult culture-specific concepts. They also considered how the symbolic nature of grammatical constructions leads to a kind of instruction congruent with communicative language teaching, and the implications of viewing grammar and lexis as a continuum for the teaching of both grammar and vocabulary. Articles focused on the relevance of cultural and linguistic relativity, metaphor awareness, categorization and teaching vocabulary, and what the figure-ground distinction means for syllabus design. Traditional SLA suggests a discrete item syllabus, however CL suggests such a syllabus would not work because categories are overlapping and not discrete.

In their handbook, Ellis and Robinson (2008) pick up the theme of implications for pedagogy, in particular through Langacker (2008), who considers the implications of cognitive grammar for language teaching, and then Achard (2008) and Tyler (2008), who develop related pedagogical proposals. Littlemore and Juchem-Grundmann (2010) edited an AILA review on CL and L2 learning and teaching. They present five key cognitive processes and consider how they relate to language learning and teaching: (a) Construal; we perceive things from different angles in different ways so nothing is neutral. So to learn another language we need to learn how speakers of that language construe the world and language.

(b) Construction of categories; the categories of our first language become entrenched, making it difficult to change them for a second language. We have to learn to divide the world up differently. CL suggests categories are radial with prototype effects. (c) Identifying constructions and relationships between them; chunks of language are more lexical than grammatical. Associating certain words with certain constructions is the process of contingency learning. (d) Metaphor and (e) metonymy have less relevance to pronunciation teaching.

Holme (2012) draws a number of relevant conclusions regarding the practical classroom application of CL. He traces what four principles, 'embodied learning, conceptualization, the lexico-grammatical continuum, and usage' (p. 6) mean for classroom practice. In terms of pronunciation, he considers how the embodied learning principle is represented though the relationship between physical movement and meaning.

CL and pronunciation learning

CL is able to provide a productive theoretical basis from which to analyse and explain the teaching and learning of L2 pronunciation, leading to a theoretically motivated definition of type-of-instruction. This can be achieved by considering which cognitive capacities one might need to employ, such as perception, conceptualization and categorization. From a CL perspective, the goal of pronunciation instruction would be to assist in the formation of new phonological concepts as effective pronunciation relies on these concepts (Fraser, 2006b). These concepts include both segmental and suprasegmental concepts such as phonemes, syllables, stress, rhythm and intonation.

Fraser (2009) suggests critical listening (CritL) as one way in which teachers can help learners to form new concepts. The idea is that learners compare two forms of the same statement, their own one, which was not easily understood, with another, easily understood, one. A CL framework would suggest that learners can draw on cognitive skills to discern differences and through multiple exemplars of what is and is not perceived by the target language (TL) speaker as belonging to the particular category they can learn how to categorize the target sounds correctly. This leads to the formation of phonological concepts. Fraser's (2001) teacher handbook provides an in-depth guide as to how teachers can apply CL in the classroom. Fraser (2009) conducted an /r/ and /l/ experiment in which she found strong evidence for the ability to form new categories when the appropriate feedback was provided to be able to build up the category boundaries.

The idea that pronunciation learning involves learning new ways of categorizing sounds is not limited to CL. Flege (1995), working in the field of L2 speech research, proposed a speech learning model to explain how adults could form new categories. L2 speech research (e.g. Lively, Logan & Pisoni, 1993) has provided a considerable amount of evidence that perceptual training can facilitate category formation. This sometimes takes the form of identification training (Rvachew & Jamieson, 1995), which has led to the development of discrimination and or identification classroom exercises as proposed and implemented by Gilbert (2005) and Celce-Murcia, Brinton and Goodwin (2010), among others.

Sometimes we can learn the phonological concepts of a new language implicitly as the result of a great deal of exposure to multiple exemplars of the target categories. While this can occur naturally in some learning contexts, targeted training may help to speed up the process. Research in the area of speech perception has found that high-variability phonetic training (HVPT), which attempts to provide this exposure along with feedback on the accuracy of the learner's perception, can be effective (Thomson, 2012). CL suggests that, where these concepts are not formed easily, corrective feedback of both perception and production is required, along with awareness and explicit analysis of what is involved in a particular concept. Here, the teacher has a major role to play. In the first instance, the learner needs to be aware that there is a problem. Very often, we don't notice that there is a difference between what we are saying and what the native speaker is saying. This is normal as when we speak we naturally focus on meaning and not form. The teacher has to set up conditions so that the learner is able to notice that relationship between meaning and form. Once the learner has realized that something is wrong they then have to work out exactly where the problem is before they can establish its precise nature. This is a matter of perception.

A CL framework brings our focus to understanding linguistic and cultural differences in perception. For the teacher, it raises the issue of understanding that our perceptions of the TL concepts are not based on objective reality but rather on concepts of categories. Then the learner has to understand that their L1 perceptions of categories are not based on objective reality but rather on L1 concepts of categories. The teacher and the learner have to find ways to bring this together. This places a high premium on the need for the teacher and learner to successfully communicate about these concepts and how they are different in different languages. As will be seen in the second half of this chapter, a careful focus on this process in the first two studies led to the definition of what is described as socially constructed metalanguage (SCM).

Other approaches have also involved socially constructing meaning. Swain's *languaging* (2006) focuses on dialogue with students, as does Gibbons's (2006) discussion of the bridging role of talk between teachers and students as co-constructed discourse. Clearly, sociocultural theory (SCT) and other ideas from educational psychology also have a lot to say about the social nature of learning and the social construction of meaning. Indeed, Lantolf (2011) suggests that SCT and CL complement each other in the development of a comprehensive theory of language learning.

The use of SCM implies an explicit approach based on helping learners to understand figure-ground relationships, that is, to see what is salient in the mind of the TL speaker. However, this does not suggest that it is in line with the classic distinctions drawn between implicit and explicit instruction and focus on form, focus on forms and focus on meaning, which are generally made in mainstream SLA literature referring to type-of-instruction. As Lee, Jang and Plonsky (2015) note in their meta-analysis, these sorts of distinctions did not enable them to engage in a fine-grained analysis of what is happening in the classroom. Thomson and Derwing (2015) in the same issue undertook a narrative review of the same research and remark on the general lack of a theoretical explanation as to why instruction may or may not have been effective. The evidence from the five studies in the second half of this chapter suggests that CL is able to offer a theoretical explanation and a much more useful way of defining type-of-instruction.

CL does clearly draw on a number of general cognitive capacities that have been represented in studies into the role of language awareness, consciousness raising, attention and noticing. It provides a theoretical basis for helping to solve the difficulties noted by Nearey and Hogan (1986) and Munro and Bohn (2007) in directing learners' attention to finer phonetic detail and making sure they focus on the right cues. However, others have found it was possible to change selective attention (Guion & Pederson, 2007; Rochet, 1995). Kennedy and Blanchet (2014) report a link between awareness and explicit instruction on perception (Kennedy & Blanchet, 2014) and Svalberg (2012) suggests explicit instruction in general can be more effective the more learners engage with language.

	Study 1	Study 2	Study 3	Study 4	Study 5
Focus	Use a range of oft-used techniques to see if explicit instruction can work, noting what does or doesn't work	Within a CL framework, explore learners' perceptions and how the teacher can help them to understand TL phonological concepts	Testing the conclusions of the first two studies, the effects of SCM and CritL	Apply this type of instruction to teaching word stress: focus on learners' perception of stress and cross-linguistic comparisons	Replicating Study 4 and applying this approach to tonic stress: focus on awareness and perception
Pronunciation focus	Syllable codas: Absence and epenthesis	Syllable codas: Absence and epenthesis	Syllable codas: Epenthesis	Word stress: Begin with syllable stress, concept of stress	Tonic stress + word stress
Method	Quant. and qual. N = 21 and N = 50 in baseline group. 12 30-minute sessions included in normal teaching. Pre-/post-/delayed tests, interviews and question-naires	Ethnographic N = 4. Six 90-minute classes in addition to normal teaching. Analysis of classroom interactions, pre-/post-/delayed interviews and tests	Quant.: N = 24. One 50-minute lesson to test immediate effect of CritL and SCM. Four groups: CritL+/SCM– CritL–/SCM+ CritL–/SCM– Pre-/post-tests	Qual.: Ethnographic N = 9. 12 hours of instruction in addition to normal teaching. Analysis of classroom interactions, question-naires, teacher journals, pre-/post-tests	Qual.: Ethnographic N = 7. 16 hours of instruction in addition to normal teaching. Analysis of classroom interactions, questionnaires, teacher journals, pre-/post-tests
Findings	Explicit instruction helps where problem entrenched. Success when teaching helps form new concepts. TL orientation, e.g. syllable structure does not help	CL type activities improve awareness, perception and production, defined through two key variables: SCM and CritL	CritL and SCM lead to gains. CritL improved perception, SCM improved production, CritL + SCM improved both	CritL and SCM increased awareness, and qualitative evidence of progress in concept formation. Value of cross-linguistic and cross-cultural discussion	Replication of Study 4, similar findings regarding perception and increases in awareness Value of cross-linguistic and cross-cultural discussion

Figure 28.1 Overview of five studies

Notes: Abbreviations: SCM: socially constructed metalanguage. CritL: critical listening. CL: Cognitive Linguistics. TL: target language

In choosing which pedagogical techniques to use, one needs to consider how they will contribute to the development of phonological concepts. This will include work on perception and production with multiple exemplars and feedback to determine category boundaries, as found in HVPT. While HVPT focuses mainly on form, CL also suggests work on understanding the relationship between form and meaning. It promotes a social approach based on the embodied mind, meaningful dialogue and exploration of linguistic and cultural differences, and opportunities for further practice and feedback in order to entrench new concepts. The five studies discussed in the second half of the chapter explore how the teacher can do this, identifying CritL and SCM as two key variables representative of this sort of approach.

Illustrations and examples

This chapter now considers five studies that have variously explored and tested type-of-pronunciation-instruction within a CL framework. The evidence provides examples of how CL can be successfully translated into different types of activities so that new concepts are formed. An overview of these studies is provided in Figure 28.1. Owing to space limitations, and because these studies have been reported elsewhere, I will focus mainly on the role that CL played in explaining success or otherwise in these studies. The participants in all these studies came from similar populations. The first three studies involved participants studying full-time at a high-intermediate level of English in Auckland, New Zealand. The fourth and fifth studies involved participants with a slightly higher level of English who were on a degree preparation course in Auckland, New Zealand. The majority of participants were from East Asian countries such as China, Korea and Japan. They were all adults with ages ranging from 18–57.

Study 1

This study (Couper, 2006, 2009) was not explicitly guided by a CL framework but rather it aimed to test whether or not explicit pronunciation teaching was effective, both immediately and over time. It also aimed to explore the effect of a range of different teaching methods and techniques. The pedagogical focus was on the pronunciation of syllable codas, as previous assessment had revealed that these caused problems for the majority of participants. Pronunciation deviations involved epenthesis, the inappropriate addition of a vowel sound, and/or absence, the inappropriate omission of a consonant sound.

The study involved two groups, a quasi-experimental group (N = 21) consisting of an intact class that was taught by the researcher, and a baseline group (N = 50) drawn from three parallel classes at the same level. Data were collected from pre- and post- and delayed tests as well as interviews (N = 5), questionnaires (N = 17) and teacher observations and reflections. Those in the quasi-experimental group made significant gains, which were maintained 12 weeks later. By way of comparison, those in the baseline group made no progress.

Reflections and observations of teaching revealed that during teacher explanations a number of learners expressed their understandings of how they thought particular words were meant to be pronounced and they also tried to convey how some of these syllable codas sounded to them. This led to a number of insights into their perceptions. For example, many participants thought that words such as <and> should always be pronounced in the strong form and consequently they tended to use epenthesis. The weak form was easily demonstrated and the problem resolved. Also, after CritL practice, listening to appropriate versus inappropriate models of final consonants, participants showed signs of hearing the difference between what they said and what the TL speaker said. They would often refer to making the consonant shorter or lighter. Those who appeared to be dropping the final consonant often felt they were pronouncing those final consonant sounds. Once they realized the TL speaker couldn't hear them they found ways of what they described as making the final consonant stronger or longer.

It was clear that communicating about pronunciation could help, as did CritL activities. It was also found that many participants had a concept of the syllable that was different from the English concept. The class in which syllables were explained according to the English concept of a syllable with the potential for up to three consonants in the onset and four in the coda was not successful. For example when asked how many syllables there were in the word <strengths>, answers ranged from one to five. The interviews backed these observations up, with four of the five interviewees saying syllable explanations were not useful. It became clear that they did not understand the connection between syllables and correctly pronouncing consonant clusters and they did not see the value in learning about it. The fifth interviewee claimed to already understand syllable structure, and while she was able to use the metalanguage she was not able to apply it in practice so knowing about it didn't help either. Interviews and questionnaires (Couper, 2009) also revealed that prior to the course the participants had minimal awareness of pronunciation and that this had increased. It was found that participants believed they had improved and that teachers should always include some focus on pronunciation.

These findings pointed to some interesting observations around the potential value of CritL and the importance of the dialogue between the teacher and student in developing understanding. It also pointed out that more abstract things such as analysing syllable structure did not seem to translate into understanding on the part of the students. It was in analysing what seemed to work best and worst in this study that the value of CL as an explanatory tool for teachers became obvious. By thinking about what the students were doing in terms of concept formation, the way seemed to become clearer in terms working out how to teach pronunciation. These conclusions led to the development of materials for Study 2.

Study 2

The second study (Couper, 2013) was based explicitly on a CL framework. This involved exploring participants' perceptions of syllable codas in order to create dialogue about the concepts of the TL. It meant using CritL activities and developing practice activities that would allow for multiple exemplars and feedback in mapping out category boundaries and forming new concepts. This led to the isolation and definition of two variables: SCM and CritL.

This study involved four participants, allowing for a more ethnographic approach and a much more in-depth probing of their understanding of phonological concepts. There were tests of pronunciation and perception pre-instruction, after the second, fourth and final lessons and then again eight months later, although in one case this occurred 18 months later.

The teaching typically involved presenting a listening text before honing in on pronunciation difficulties, that is, pronunciation was explored within a meaningful context. This exploration included a focus on the difference between the participants' pronunciation and the teacher's interpretation of it. Explicit instruction was then typically followed with listen-and-repeat practice and CritL activities. There were also information-gap activities designed to provide further practice and discovery activities in which participants looked for patterns in the pronunciation of syllable codas. This was then followed up with pair work and ongoing corrective feedback. Information-gap activities (Couper, 2012) were particularly effective as they required accurate pronunciation to successfully communicate and win the game.

The participants all made progress both immediately and eight months (in one case 18 months) later. They also remembered some of the ways we had talked about pronunciation. They noted that they still sometimes made the same mistakes but not as often, and when they did make them they were aware of them and were able to correct them quickly. There was increased awareness and indications of having made progress in forming the concept of English syllable codas. This progress was also reflected in gains on tests of pronunciation and perception.

An analysis of classroom interactions revealed just how different the participants' concepts of syllables were from those of the English L1 speaker. It noted how a dialogue between the teacher and the participants, along with CritL activities and a great deal of practice and feedback, enabled the participants to increase their understanding of the target concept. A number of stages were observed, beginning with participants' understanding that there is a problem, then realizing precisely where it is, before being able to listen carefully and actually hear that there is a difference. The next step was to understand the difference and why it is.

Reflection on this led to defining socially constructed metalanguage (SCM) as a key variable in effective pronunciation teaching. CritL was also recognized as a key variable in relation to this. SCM was defined as:

> the kind of metalanguage needed for effective communication about language. Such cross-cultural communication relies on both parties having a common understanding of the concepts being discussed. SCM requires the teacher and the learners to work together to construct ways of talking about these concepts. This will involve the teacher in understanding how the learners interpret the sounds of the target language. This can be achieved by providing a contrast of the differences between the learners' productions and the target language equivalents and asking the learners how those differences sound to them. The teacher then needs to explain to the learners how the target language sounds to an L1 speaker and also how their productions sound to an L1 speaker. . . . The choice of the word 'social' for this term has been made to highlight that the metalanguage co-constructed in the classroom is owned by the class as a group and once developed it can be used throughout the course for quick and effective feedback.
>
> (Couper, 2013, p. 12)

CL played a dominant role in my analysis of these classroom interactions as well as in development of information-gap activities. By thinking about pronunciation in terms of the conceptualization of sounds it becomes clear how teachers can assist learners in the development or formation of these L2 phonological concepts. It leads to the conclusion that students can draw on their cognitive skills and with guidance work out the salient figure-ground configurations of the target concept. In conclusion concepts are formed with the assistance of CritL and SCM and a great deal of practice and ongoing feedback. This leads to a testable type-of-instruction.

Study 3

The first two studies allowed the isolation, definition and operationalization of two key variables that CL would predict to play a key role in the success of pronunciation teaching. Study 3 (Couper, 2011) was quasi-experimental and aimed to test for the role of SCM and CritL in improving both perception and production in relation to syllable codas.

The participants were drawn from the same population as for the first two studies. There were 24 participants who were pre-tested on both perception and production and invited to participate on the basis of results showing they had significant problems with epenthesis. They were assigned to one of four groups, as far as possible based on their test scores such that each group was equal. All participants were also post-tested for perception and production immediately after training.

Four different 50-minute lessons were devised to represent the four possible permutations of CritL(±) and SCM(±), that is, SCM–/CritL+, SCM+/CritL+, SCM–/CritL– and SCM+/CritL–. The group that received the SCM–/CritL– treatment was then invited to receive the SCM+/CritL+ lesson.

The CritL+ groups both improved in terms of perception but the SCM–/CritL+ group did not improve significantly on production. The SCM+/CritL+ group improved significantly on both production and perception. The SCM–/CritL– group made no significant improvement in either perception or production. This group then received the SCM+/CritL+ treatment and on further testing was found to have improved significantly on both the production and perception tests.

These findings led to the conclusion that both these variables played an important role, at least in achieving temporary gains in production and perception. They don't answer questions as to the relationship between perception and production other than to note that it is a rather complex one requiring further research.

In defining these variables (SCM and CritL) in terms of their contribution towards concept formation, the distinction has been drawn between two types of explicit instruction: one that attempts to assist learners in building up their concepts of L2 perception of syllable codas, and the contrasting approach, which focuses on using linguistic metalanguage to provide descriptive rules for the pronunciation of syllable codas. The results here support the validity of this distinction and provide strong empirical support for SCM and CritL as representing a type-of-instruction that is relevant to actual classroom practice and has a sound theoretical base. Because this type-of-instruction focuses on using general learning faculties to form new concepts, it also leads to more effective corrective feedback. By focusing on meaning in the context in which errors occur it helps learners recognize the correction and notice their errors, and it helps learners compare the correct form with their own production.

Study 4

This study (Couper, 2012) represents an exploratory extension of the previous three studies, which focused on syllable codas. It focused on word stress and aimed to find out whether the same variables of SCM and CritL might also help with this aspect of pronunciation.

A series of classes were developed based on the use of CritL and SCM. They started by focusing on participants' perceptions of my name <Graeme> and then comparing it with the Maori transliteration, <Kereama>. This led to discussion of linguistic differences across all the participants' languages followed up with CritL activities, computer lab practice (listening, recording, comparing and getting feedback from peers and the teacher) and role plays. The classes involved 12 hours of instruction across three days during the mid-semester break.

It was found that the participants did not understand the English concept of the syllable initially, but after discussion and comparison with other languages their understanding and awareness had increased. It was noted that some participants focused on the consonant in the onset when trying to mark the stressed syllable and they tended to think about syllables in terms of a consonant followed by a vowel. This was especially so for those with CV languages and is in line with the observations made in earlier studies. Once they became aware of the stressed syllable they described it as being <long> and . They noticed a change of tone in some cases and referred to <accent> and <stress>. They also demonstrated increased awareness of how stress changes in context. One of the difficulties they had was that they tended to stress all the syllables. It took quite a lot of CritL practice to help them understand how to de-stress syllables. Here a strong literary bias was observed as participants were influenced by the spelling. They also became more aware of the nature of stress and how it was realized differently in different languages. Overall, classroom dialogue led to greater conceptual understanding: bringing together current concepts and adjusting them to line up with those of the L2.

In this study, SCM and CritL helped to raise awareness of stress and the participants became better at hearing it. The study provides further evidence for the value of CL in analysing what is happening in the classroom and in devising activities that are most likely to assist in pronunciation improvement. There was a great deal of evidence of increased awareness and some indications of an improvement in production. CL explains how new concepts were formed as the learners used their abilities to compare and contrast and discern new category boundaries and to conceptualize the L2 in different ways.

Study 5

The fifth study in this series (Couper, 2014) involved some replication of Study 4, but extended the focus to include tonic stress. The participants were drawn from the same population as in Study 4 and they received 16 hours of instruction over four days. The classes were video and audio-recorded. The teacher/researcher also kept a diary after each day's teaching. Data were also collected from recordings participants made during computer lab sessions and from written questionnaires completed by students at the end of each day's teaching. A pre-post-test of perception was also undertaken.

The same materials were used as with Study 4, but with the addition of extra sections on tonic stress. As with Study 4, it was found that speakers of CV languages tended to focus on the consonant rather than the vowel when asked to count syllables. It was also observed that spelling interfered with participants' ability to focus on sounds. The Study 4 results were also replicated in that learners had some concept of word stress but did not realize how important it was for English speakers. As in the earlier study, they also struggled to understand the importance of weak forms in creating stress. It was found the participants had difficulty in perceiving tonic stress. Some also tended to put tonic stress on pronouns and inadvertently created an unintended contrastive stress.

The participants explored the relationship between form and meaning and compared and contrasted this relationship in other languages. This helped them to understand the perceptual and conceptual nature of speech and they could use this to work out where and how category boundaries were set. The SCM they established during this process helped to think through this process and to notice and attend to the salient differences. The work they did in CritL and other practice helped to reinforce this learning as did the more communicative role play type tasks.

These observations are what one might expect from a CL perspective as the participants engage various cognitive capacities in comparing and contrasting, in developing different concepts of what is salient through exploring figure-ground relationships, and in practising and receiving feedback. The two variables of SCM and CritL help to define type-of-instruction in such a way as to help in understanding what is leading to its success. This is in contrast to the less productive distinctions commonly used as seen in the meta-analysis by Lee et al. (2015).

One could interpret these results as engagement with language helping to make explicit instruction more effective (Svalberg, 2012) and of course this engagement relies on drawing on the cognitive faculties within the context of learner's socio-physical world has proposed by CL's embodiment thesis (Mompean, 2014).

In this study, I was also able to map changes of perception and observe participants' increased awareness of the category differences between L1 and L2. The participants drew on a number of cognitive capacities in comparing and contrasting in order to determine what was salient through focusing on the figure and learning what was ground.

New directions and recommendations

All five studies revealed different aspects of the learning process while supporting the value of two key variables, critical listening and socially constructed metalanguage. They also demonstrated the role of Cognitive Linguistics in gaining these insights and exemplified how a CL framework can be applied in practice. For the teacher this means helping learners to form new concepts. The starting point is the learner's L1 concepts and comparing them with the TL, and possibly with other languages too. Once it is clear to both the teacher and the learner that these are concepts and not objective reflections of reality the process of analysing the differences can begin. What is important, of course, is to understand which differences are salient to establishing category membership. For example, when is a final consonant in English perceived as being epenthesized, or when is a syllable perceived as being stressed? In the case of stress, there will be some learners who have a great deal of difficulty in hearing the difference between stressed and unstressed syllables. In such cases, CritL practice will be required to establish that there is a difference before moving on to locate exactly where the difference is and how it is indicated. SCM is a key factor in the success of helping learners understand how concepts are perceived by TL speakers. Once an initial, often only partial, understanding of these concepts has been achieved, practice and feedback through SCM are required to further develop and entrench them. Activities used are likely to include explicit discussion, listening and training learners to use their ears, recording and comparing, information-gap activities and role plays. It can be seen then that these are things teachers already know about, but the difference is the focus on using such activities to support learners in the formation of new concepts.

The studies surveyed here have developed a description of pronunciation instruction types based on CL. The next step is to undertake larger-scale studies, using teachers other than the researcher, to provide more quantitative evidence of the validity of this approach. So far, syllable codas, syllables and stress have been explored. An exploration of teaching other features of pronunciation would further round out the picture. It is also hoped that these examples will encourage cognitive linguists to look at this aspect of language learning more closely and provide still more evidence to support this approach.

References

Achard, M., & Niemeier, S. (2004). Cognitive linguistics, language acquisition, and pedagogy. In M. Achard & S. Niemeier (Eds), *Cognitive linguistics, second language acquisition, and foreign language teaching* (pp. 1–12). Berlin: Mouton de Gruyter.

Achard, M. (2008). Teaching construal: Cognitive pedagogical grammar. In P. Robinson & N. Ellis (Eds), *Handbook of cognitive linguistics and second language acquisition* (pp. 432–455). New York, NY: Routledge.

Bennett, P. (2014). Langacker's cognitive grammar. In J. Littlemore & J. Taylor (Eds), *Bloomsbury companion to cognitive linguistics* (pp. 29–48). London: Bloomsbury.

Birdsell, B. (2014). Fauconnier's theory of mental spaces and conceptual blending. In J. Littlemore & J. Taylor (Eds), *Bloomsbury companion to cognitive linguistics* (pp. 72–90). London: Bloomsbury.

Bybee, J. (2001). *Phonology and language use.* Cambridge: Cambridge University Press.

Celce-Murcia, M., Brinton, D., & Goodwin, J. (2010). *Teaching pronunciation* (2nd ed.). Cambridge: Cambridge University Press.

Couper, G. (2006). The short and long-term effects of pronunciation instruction. *Prospect, 21*(1), 46–66.

Couper, G. (2009). *Teaching and learning L2 pronunciation: Understanding the effectiveness of socially constructed metalanguage and critical listening in terms of a cognitive phonology framework.* Unpublished PhD thesis, University of New England, Armidale, Australia.

Couper, G. (2011). What makes pronunciation teaching work? Testing for the effect of two variables: Socially constructed metalanguage and critical listening. *Language Awareness, 20*(3), 159–182.

Couper, G. (2012). Teaching word stress: Learning from learners' perceptions. *TESOL in Context Special Edition S3: November 2012.* Retrieved from www.tesol.org.au/Publications/Special-Editions

Couper, G. (2013). Talking about pronunciation: Socially constructing metalanguage. *English Australia, 29*(1), 3–18.

Couper, G. F. (2014). Teaching concepts of pronunciation: Syllables, stress and drunk snails. *Speak Out!, 50,* 46–50.

Ellis, N., & Robinson, P. (2008). Introduction. In P. Robinson & N. Ellis (Eds), *Handbook of cognitive linguistics and second language acquisition* (pp. 3–24). New York, NY: Routledge.

Flege, J. (1995). Second language speech learning: Theory, findings, and problems. In W. Strange (Ed.), *Speech perception and linguistic experience: Issues in cross-language research* (pp. 233–277). Baltimore, MD: York.

Fraser, H. (2001). *Teaching pronunciation: A handbook for teachers and trainers.* Canberra: TAFE Access Division.

Fraser, H. (2006a). Phonological concepts and concept formation: Metatheory and application. *International Journal of English Studies, 6,* 55–75.

Fraser, H. (2006b). Helping teachers help students with pronunciation: A cognitive approach. *Prospect, 21*(1), 80–96.

Fraser, H. (2009). Pronunciation as categorization: The role of contrast in teaching English /r/ and /l/. In A. Mahboob & C. Lipovsky (Eds), *Studies in applied linguistics and language learning* (pp. 289–306). Newcastle upon Tyne: Cambridge Scholars.

Geeraerts, D., & Cuyckens, H. (2007). Introducing cognitive linguistics. In D. Geeraerts & H. Cuyckens (Eds), *The Oxford handbook of cognitive linguistics* (pp. 3–21). New York, NY: Oxford University Press.

Gibbons, P. (2006). *Bridging discourses in the ESL classroom.* London and New York, NY: Continuum.

Gilbert, J. (2005). *Clear speech: Teacher's resource book.* New York, NY: Cambridge University Press.

Guion, S., & Pederson, E. (2007). Investigating the role of attention in phonetic learning. In O. Bohn & M. Munro (Eds), *Language experience in second language speech learning* (pp. 57–78). Amsterdam and Philadelphia, PA: John Benjamins.

Holme, R. (2012). Cognitive linguistics and the second language classroom. *TESOL Quarterly, 46*(1), 6–29.

Kennedy, S., & Blanchet, J. (2014). Language awareness and perception of connected speech in a second language. *Language Awareness, 23*(1–2), 91–105. doi:10.1080/09658416.2013.863904.

Lakoff, G. (1987). *Women, fire and dangerous things: What categories reveal about the mind.* Chicago, IL: University of Chicago Press.

Langacker, R. (1987). *Foundations of cognitive grammar. Vol. 1. Theoretical prerequisites.* Stanford, CA: Stanford University Press.

Langacker, R. (2000). *Grammar and conceptualisation*. Berlin and New York, NY: Mouton de Gruyter.

Langacker, R. (2007). Cognitive grammar. In D. Geeraerts & H. Cuyckens (Eds), *The Oxford handbook of cognitive linguistics* (pp. 421–462). New York, NY: Oxford University Press.

Langacker, R. (2008). Cognitive grammar as a basis for language instruction. In P. Robinson & N. Ellis (Eds). *Handbook of cognitive linguistics and second language acquisition* (pp. 66–88). New York, NY: Routledge.

Lantolf, J. (2011). Integrating sociocultural theory and cognitive linguistics in the second language classroom. In E. Hinkel (Ed.), *Handbook of research in second language teaching and learning: Volume 2* (pp 303–318). Hoboken, NJ: Routledge.

Lee, J., Jang, J., & Plonsky, L. (2015). The effectiveness of second language pronunciation instruction: A meta-analysis. *Applied Linguistics, 36*(3), 345–366. doi:10.1093/applin/amu040.

Littlemore, J., & Juchem-Grundmann, C. (2010). Introduction to the interplay between cognitive linguistics and second language learning and teaching. *AILA Review, 23*, 1–6.

Lively, S., Logan, J., & Pisoni, D. (1993). Training Japanese listeners to identify English /r/ and /l/ 2: The role of phonetic environment and talker variability in learning new perceptual categories. *Journal of The Acoustical Society of America, 94*, 1242–1255.

Medin, D., & Schaffer, M. (1978). Context theory of classification learning. *Psychological Review, 85*, 207–238.

Mompean, J. (2006). Introduction: Cognitive phonology in cognitive linguistics. *International Journal of English Studies, 6*: vii–xii.

Mompean, J. (2014). Cognitive linguistics and phonology. In J. Littlemore & J. Taylor (Eds), *Bloomsbury companion to cognitive linguistics* (pp. 253–276). London: Bloomsbury.

Munro, M., & Bohn, O. (2007). The study of second language speech. In O. Bohn & M. Munro (Eds), *Language experience in second language speech learning* (pp. 3–11). Amsterdam and Philadelphia, PA: John Benjamins.

Nathan, G. (2007). Phonology. In D. Geeraerts & H. Cuyckens (Eds), *The Oxford handbook of cognitive linguistics* (pp. 611–631). New York, NY: Oxford University Press.

Nathan, G. (2008). *Phonology: A cognitive grammar introduction*. Amsterdam: John Benjamins.

Nearey, T., & Hogan, J. (1986). Phonological contrast in experimental phonetics: Relating distributions of production data to perceptual categorization curves. In J. Ohala & J. Jaeger (Eds), *Experimental phonology* (pp. 141–161). London: Academic Press.

Nuyts, J. (2007). Cognitive linguistics and functional linguistics. In D. Geeraerts & H. Cuyckens (Eds), *The Oxford handbook of cognitive linguistics* (pp. 543–565). New York, NY: Oxford University Press.

Rochet, B. (1995). Perception and production of second-language speech sounds by adults. In W. Strange (Ed.), *Speech perception and linguistic experience: Issues in cross language research* (pp. 379–410). Timonium, MD: York.

Rohrer, T. (2007). Embodiment and experientialism. In D. Geeraerts & H. Cuyckens (Eds), *The Oxford handbook of cognitive linguistics* (pp. 25–47). New York, NY: Oxford University Press.

Rvachew, S., & Jamieson, D. (1995). Learning new speech contrasts: Evidence from adults learning a second language and children with speech disorders. In W. Strange (Ed.), *Speech perception and linguistic experience: Issues in cross language research* (pp. 411–432). Timonium, MD: York.

Sanford, D. (2014). Bybee's usage-based models of language. In J. Littlemore & J. Taylor (Eds), *Bloomsbury companion to cognitive linguistics* (pp. 103–114). London: Bloomsbury.

Svalberg, A. (2012). Thinking allowed: Language awareness in language learning and teaching: A research agenda. *Language Teaching, 45*(3), 376–388. doi:10.1017/S0261444812000070.

Swain, M. (2006). Languaging, agency and collaboration on advanced language proficiency. In H. Byrnes (Ed.), *Advanced language learning: The contribution of Halliday and Vygotsky* (pp. 95–108). London: Continuum.

Tay, D. (2014). Lakoff and the theory of conceptual metaphor. In J. Littlemore & J. Taylor (Eds), *Bloomsbury companion to cognitive linguistics* (pp. 49–59). London: Bloomsbury.

Taylor, J. (2002). *Cognitive grammar*. Oxford: Oxford University Press.

Taylor, J., & Littlemore, J. (2014). Introduction. In J. Littlemore & J. Taylor (Eds), *Bloomsbury companion to cognitive linguistics* (pp. 1–26). London: Bloomsbury.

Thomson, R. (2012). Improving L2 listeners' perception of English vowels: A computer-mediated approach. *Language Learning, 62*(4), 1231–1258. doi:10.1111/j.1467–9922.2012.00724.x.

Thomson, R., & Derwing, T. (2015). The effectiveness of L2 pronunciation instruction: A narrative review. *Applied Linguistics, 36*(3), 326–344. doi:10.1093/applin/amu076.

Tyler, A. (2008). Cognitive linguistics and second language instruction. In P. Robinson & N. Ellis (Eds), *Handbook of cognitive linguistics and second language acquisition* (pp. 456–488). New York, NY: Routledge.

29

Computer-assisted pronunciation training

Debra M. Hardison

Introduction

In the classic award-winning film *My Fair Lady* (Warner & Cukor, 1964), adapted from G. B. Shaw's play *Pygmalion*, one of the main characters was Eliza Doolittle, a poor Cockney girl in London in the early 1900s who sought the assistance of Professor Henry Higgins to change her English accent. Much of his training focused on her vowel production, which she agonizingly practised using a kymograph (an instrument invented in the mid-1800s to measure medically related time-varying events such as blood pressure). In its application to speech, the kymograph was used to produce tracings on a rotating cylinder that 'was capable of registering details of articulation and phonation such as changes in nasal and oral airflow' (Collins & Mees, 1999, p. 246). The tracings were completely uninformative to Eliza, guidance was absent unless Higgins chose to intervene and the question of improvement attributable to this technique remained open. Eliza, the participant in that experiment, did not perceive a benefit at the time. Many years later, as we consider the potential advantages of computer-assisted pronunciation training (CAPT), these issues are still among those at the forefront of the discussion: interpretability of the displays as feedback on learners' speech production, role of an instructor, demonstration of improvement, and perceptions of the efficacy of training by the participant.

This chapter will examine the use of CAPT for second language (L2) learners. In the field of L2 speech perception and production, CAPT is a relatively recent development, an outgrowth of advances in digital technology. The following sections in this chapter include some of the issues in CAPT, contributions made by research studies to address them, methodological issues and recommendations for practice.

Historical perspectives

In a contemporary laboratory, the kymograph and other instruments used by Professor Higgins would likely be replaced by digital technology and various types of signal analysis software capable of producing displays that, in some cases, are interpretable with relatively minimal instruction. Displays of fundamental frequency illustrate pitch movement in either the short temporal domain of lexical tone (Chun, Jiang, Meyr & Yang, 2015) or the longer domain of an intonation phrase (e.g. Chun, Hardison & Pennington, 2008; Hardison, 2004), waveforms demonstrate segmental duration (e.g. Motohashi-Saigo & Hardison, 2009; Okuno & Hardison, 2016), and spectrograms display formant characteristics of sounds, each formant representing a concentration of acoustic energy around a particular frequency (e.g. Olson, 2014).

CAPT has benefited from two avenues of speech research over the past 25 years: successful perception training and bimodal speech input (i.e. visual and auditory). The perception training studies that yielded significant improvement in identification accuracy of sounds generally incorporated the following features in training: (a) multiple talkers producing sufficient exemplars in natural speech to represent the variability of the target sounds; (b) feedback during training, which is especially important in cases where the stimulus shows considerable variability; and (c) an identification task to promote observation of within-category similarities and between-category differences versus a discrimination task, which relies on low-level acoustic-phonetic input. Findings revealed that perception training significantly increased identification accuracy of sounds such as American English (AE) /r/ and /l/ for L2 learners whose first language (L1) was Japanese (e.g. Lively, Logan & Pisoni, 1993), with transfer to production improvement and retention of improved abilities (e.g. Bradlow, Akahane-Yamada, Pisoni & Tohkura, 1999). In addition, a second channel of visual input, such as cues from a talker's face further increased perceptual accuracy and production improvement for /r/ and /l/ for L1 Japanese and Korean speakers (Hardison, 2003), with transfer to earlier word recognition (Hardison, 2005b). From a theoretical perspective, research findings that have emphasized the context- and talker-variable nature of learner perceptual performance are compatible with exemplar or episodic models of speech processing. In these models, the attended details of perceptual events become part of long-term memory storage (e.g. Hardison, 2012; Lively, Logan & Pisoni, 1993).

CAPT has also benefited from the increasing interest in the use of technology in learning, development of web-based tools for signal analysis such as Praat (Boersma & Weenink, 2014), their accessibility within and outside the classroom, and their applicability to the study of any language. In addition, the development of automatic speech recognition (ASR) technology may offer learners language tutoring with feedback on errors and the possibility of simulating interactions in a less stressful environment (Strik, Neri & Cucchiarini, 2008), especially in a foreign language environment where interaction with target language speakers may not be readily available (Seferoğlu, 2005), although target language input may be accessible via the Internet on sites such as YouTube and Ted Talks. The next section discusses some of the issues involved in implementing CAPT.

Critical issues and topics

If one follows the old adage that a picture is worth a thousand words, then CAPT has the potential to make a substantial contribution to learning as visual displays can make more salient some of the features of learner speech. However, determining how to incorporate that picture into the learning process and make it informative raises several issues for researchers and teachers to consider:

- assessment of improvement following training and consideration of its potential to generalize beyond the experimental setting;
- speech perception–production link, suggested by research demonstrating a transfer of perception training to production improvement;
- issue of variability in training (e.g. number of stimuli, phonetic contexts);

- role and interpretability of the display in training. (Is a native speaker (NS) model presented for learners to imitate or is it used in a feedback role after learners have produced their own utterances?);
- role of an instructor/tutor;
- learners' perceptions of the efficacy of the training.

Current contributions and research

This section presents some of the contributions made by various studies to an understanding of the issues noted above. It is organized according to the primary focus of the research: suprasegmental (e.g. pitch) and segmental (i.e. consonants or vowels).

Suprasegmental focus

Several early reports advocated the use of computerized pitch displays to improve L2 learners' intonation (e.g. Anderson-Hsieh, 1992; de Bot, 1983; Leather, 1990; Molholt, 1988; Pennington & Esling, 1996). For example, de Bot (1983) investigated visual pitch feedback with L2 learners of English whose L1 was Dutch. In a pre-test/post-test design, auditory-visual (AV) was compared to auditory-only (A-only) input in relatively brief training sessions (45 versus 90 minutes). After a target sentence was presented auditorily, the pitch display appeared on a computer screen, learners imitated the sentence and then their pitch contours appeared. They were allowed to repeat the process a non-specified number of times. Production ratings indicated a significant advantage for AV input. In a follow-up study with Dutch learners of English imitating NS sentence models, Weltens and de Bot (1984) investigated whether the duration of feedback delay (i.e. the period of time between the speech signal and pitch display) affected improvement. The potential influence of such a delay is an issue in CAPT for programs that do not provide real-time displays. No significant difference was found in that study for delays of 40 ms, 250 ms or appearance of the display at the end of the speech signal.

Leather's (1990) study investigated two approaches to the learning of four Chinese lexical tones by Dutch speakers. One group received computer-based auditory perception training with subsequent testing of their production ability; the other group used computer-based visual feedback to produce the tones with subsequent testing of their perception. Findings revealed that training in one modality was sufficient to allow the learner to perform better in the other. This research served several important roles. It focused on a language (i.e. Chinese) that was less commonly the target of research at that time, drew attention to a link between perception and production and emphasized the importance of understanding the role of variability in training. The participants who received production training benefited from the acoustic-phonetic variability in the graphic representations of tone.

Across recent training studies using computerized displays, participants have reported positive attitudes to the inclusion of visual feedback in training. In a study focusing on the acquisition of L2 French prosody, native speakers of American English showed significant improvement in both prosody and segmental accuracy after training using real-time pitch displays of their sentence productions followed by displays of native speaker (NS) productions of the same sentences (Hardison, 2004). Training generalized to production of novel sentences. Participants also reported that they became more aware of the pitch variation in native speaker speech because they could see it, and more confident in their ability to produce it in their own speech.

In a recent study, 35 first-year learners of Mandarin were taught to create pitch displays of their productions of two-syllable words using Praat (Boersma & Weenink, 2014) and compare them with those of NSs (Chun et al., 2015). The focus was the acquisition of tone (four Mandarin tones plus a neutral tone), which contrasts meaning in Mandarin. Training was carried out over a period of nine weeks involving 20–25 minutes per week as a part of regular classroom instruction. Students were instructed on how to view a gender-matched NS model utterance as input, record their own productions and compare their pitch displays to those of the NS. They practised one tone each week followed by practice using the words in sentences. Native-speaking raters were asked to determine correctness of tone, the nature of the problem for incorrect tones (i.e. pitch height and/or contour), and which of the randomized pre-test and post-test samples was better. Ratings revealed more problems with pitch height versus pitch contour. Of the incorrect productions of tone in the pre-test, Tone 1 (relatively high and level) and Tone 4 (beginning high and falling) showed the largest improvement in ratings. In addition to auditory ratings, acoustic measurements were conducted that revealed both pitch height and/or contour problems with all five tones in the pre-test. Following training, improvement was noted in pitch height for Tone 3 (falling then rising) and pitch contour for Tone 4. Post-study surveys indicated that 68 per cent of respondents felt that the pitch visualizations had been helpful. This was particularly true of 12 participants who demonstrated the greatest improvement between pre-test and post-test. Some students suggested more dedicated class time for this type of training.

Following Chun's (2002) and Levis and Pickering's (2004) discussions of the value of pitch displays at the discourse level of speech, Hardison (2005a) explored the training potential of pitch displays synchronized with the video of the oral presentations of advanced L2 speakers of English whose L1 was Chinese. Anvil (Kipp, 2001), a web-based tool, was used to integrate segments of the learners' video-recorded oral presentations with the associated pitch visualization. Some participants received training input using Anvil and practised with the Real-time Pitch program (KayPentax), which included NS feedback; others used only the pitch program. While both groups improved over several weeks, the presence of the synchronized video was the most helpful especially when used with discourse-level input.

An alternative type of intonation feedback was developed by Hincks and Edlund (2009) consisting of flashing lights to show learners how much pitch variation they had produced. Flat speech produced yellow lights while more expressive speech that used pitch to give focus to a part of an utterance produced green lights. This type of feedback significantly improved the pitch variation made by L1 Chinese learners of English in their oral presentations.

Segmental focus

To demonstrate contrasts in segmental duration, waveforms, requiring only minimal instruction, were used to compare AV and A-only web-based training in consonant duration for beginning-level learners of L2 Japanese whose L1 was American English (Motohashi-Saigo & Hardison, 2009). Segmental duration is a contrastive feature in Japanese and, thus, important for comprehension and production. A geminate or a long vowel constitutes a special type of mora, which is a unit of timing in the language (Kubozono, 1999). Each geminate or long vowel represents two morae and has a longer duration than its singleton counterpart. In the study, stimuli were singleton and geminate /t/, /k/ and /s/, followed by /a/ or /u/ (produced in Japanese as a high-back unrounded vowel with lip compression) in two conditions: isolated words and carrier sentences. Results revealed significant improvement in perceptual identification accuracy following training, especially for learners who were given waveforms as feedback. A test of generalization to novel stimuli revealed only a 5 per cent decline in accuracy for the AV group compared to 14 per cent for A-only. Production of geminates also showed significant improvement, especially for the AV group that saw waveforms in training.

Waveforms were again used as visual feedback in the training of L2 Japanese vowel duration for 48 learners whose L1 was American English (Okuno & Hardison, 2016). These vowels have two phonologically distinctive features: duration and pitch accent. In Tokyo Japanese, accent is realized as a high pitch followed by a low pitch (Haraguchi, 1999). In the case of a long vowel, only the first mora carries the high pitch so that a high-low pitch contour occurs within the long vowel.

A pre-test-training–post-test design was used to compare AV training, A-only and no training (controls). Within-group variables were vowel type (/a, u/), preceding consonant (/k, s/), pitch pattern, and the syllabic position of the long vowel (i.e. in the first and/or second syllable of a word), and, for training, talker's voice (four NSs of Japanese). Testing and training materials involved two-syllable words. Perception tests using a forced-choice identification task assessed the effects of training on accuracy and response time (RT). Between pre- and post-test, there were eight sessions of perception training including feedback.

Results indicated significant improvement in identification accuracy for both the AV and A-only groups with generalization to novel stimuli; however, the AV group demonstrated a greater rate of improvement in perception, which also transferred to improvement in production. Vowel type, preceding consonant, pitch pattern and training talker's voice also significantly affected learners' perception of vowel duration. Prior to training, learners exhibited more accurate perception for stimuli that had a long vowel in the first syllable with a pitch pattern that began low and remained high after rising. The next best performance was for words with a long vowel in the second syllable with a consistently high pitch. These findings are compatible with English-based prosodic preferences for a rising intonation, and the salience created by a high pitch. In the post-test, there was generally less variability in accuracy across stimulus types; however, the best performance still tended to be for rising pitch patterns.

In contrast, RTs for both groups were slower after training. In post-study interviews, participants, especially in the AV group that saw waveforms, reported that they were more confident in their post-test accuracy, but this came at a processing cost. Having a greater awareness of durational cues following training and the variable stimulus set meant that they had more information on which to evaluate input and this increased the amount of time they took to respond. The potential benefits of variability in creating robust perceptual categories may be influenced by the duration of training; that is, longer periods offer a greater opportunity for some learners to sort out the stimulus differences, but may initially add to response time and possibly to participant fatigue, which may result in attrition.

Other types of visual feedback have been used in the training of L2 Japanese vowel duration. In an earlier study, Hirata (2004) used pitch contours as visual representations for both the pitch accent system and vowel duration (as indicated by the length of the contour). Participants were four learners of Japanese whose L1 was American English. They were instructed to imitate the pitch and duration of utterances produced by NSs of Japanese. Utterances consisted of minimal pairs in a variety of contexts. Results indicated significant improvement in production and perception.

Using the specialized software program Sona-Match (KayPentax), Carey (2004) found that Korean learners of L2 English were able to improve their production of the vowel [æ] in citation form, but not in continuous speech. Sona-Match uses the first and second formant frequencies of a speaker's vowel production to plot it in a vowel space on the computer screen.

While segmental duration is an important contrastive feature in some languages such as Japanese, L2 learners of English are often confused about its role in English vowel production where duration varies but does not create meaningful differences between words. Wang and Munro (2004) used synthesized speech to train L2 English learners who were L1 Chinese speakers to ignore duration, and focus on vowel quality differences between the members of the vowel pairs [i]–[ɪ], [u]–[ʊ] and [ɛ]–[æ]. Learners used a self-paced procedure and showed significant improvement on all three vowel contrasts after two months of training, and retained performance levels three months later.

A different approach was taken by Thomson (2011) in a study training 22 beginning-level ESL learners (L1 Mandarin) to improve the intelligibility of their production of 10 Canadian English vowels. In the pre-test and post-test, learners participated in an elicited imitation task involving the target vowels in /bV/ and /pV/ syllables. Training stimuli were produced by 20 NSs in the same consonant–vowel syllable frames. Half of the learners were trained on a stimulus set in which the vowel length was digitally doubled with the objective of allowing them to attend to vowel quality. The other half were trained with the stimuli determined to be the least acoustically similar to L1 Mandarin. Learners were trained to associate a distinctive nautical flag image on the computer screen with each of the 10 English vowel categories, and received visual and auditory feedback. Results showed significant improvement of vowel intelligibility for both training group types. Improvement was also found in novel /zV/ and /sV/ contexts but not in the /gV/ and /kV/ contexts.

In addition to the use of pitch tracking, waveforms and other graphical images, two studies have investigated the use of spectrograms to improve L2 pronunciation. In a study comparing AV and A-only input, Ruellot (2011) used side-by-side spectrograms of French /u/ and /y/ (a high front rounded vowel that does not exist in English) as visual feedback for English-speaking learners of French in a third-year phonetics course to help them differentiate these vowels in their pronunciation. To focus the attention of the AV group, the primary formants of each vowel were colour-coded to correspond to the information they provide (i.e. degree of mouth aperture/vowel height, backness of tongue position and degree of lip rounding). Learners were given instruction on articulation differences and told that their task in production was to approximate the distances between the formants in the NS examples. Findings revealed significant improvement for both A-only and AV groups with no additional benefit for those who received the spectrographic displays.

In contrast, Olson (2014) reported that spectrograms generated in Praat were helpful for 26 intermediate-low-proficiency learners of L2 Spanish who were L1 English speakers in raising awareness to the differences between stop consonants /b, d, g/ and their intervocalic alternations in Spanish as approximants (following Hualde (2005), these are represented as [β, ð, ɣ]). The approximants were placed in isolated words and in words embedded in longer utterances. Prior to the study, participants received a brief tutorial in the L2 on the use of Praat to record and produce the display. On a spectrogram, the approximants are visually distinguishable by the relative darkness of the image compared to the silence of the closure period for stops (see later discussion of Figure 29.3). Each training session focused on a single sound and consisted of the following procedure: a self-recording outside class, guided visual analysis in class of the spectrograms this produced, practice, comparison of learners' productions with those of a native Spanish speaker, and re-recording. Findings revealed significant improvement and more native-like productions of the target sounds with visual feedback.

With the goal of exploring the pedagogical effectiveness of ASR technology, Cucchiarini, Neri and Strik (2009) developed and tested the capability of Dutch-CAPT to provide corrective feedback on L2 Dutch pronunciation errors. Six criteria were set for the types of errors that the system should address. Errors should be (a) common across speakers of different L1s, (b) perceptually salient, (c) potentially disruptive to communication, (d) frequent in occurrence, (e) persistent and (f) suitable for robust automatic detection. The 11 Dutch segments that were selected for the experiment were embedded in units, which included a video of a daily communicative situation along with words and expressions for oral practice. There were simulated dialogues in which the user chose a role to play and pronounced the character's lines. Other exercises included individual words to be pronounced on the basis of a model utterance recorded by NSs.

The performance of Dutch-CAPT to detect errors was tested with three groups of immigrants who varied in terms of age, occupation and length of residence in the Netherlands; all were enrolled in a beginner course in Dutch. One group recorded their utterances and could compare them to NS examples but did not receive any feedback. A second group used the same system but received automatic feedback on the quality of their productions of the above segments. Feedback was in the form of a green face with a smile (correct utterance) or a red face with a frown (incorrect utterance); detection of an error was also accompanied by an orthographic presentation of the utterance with the problem area in a red font. A third group did not receive this extra training. All groups improved in terms of global segmental quality based on raters' scores. Although the group receiving the ASR-based corrective feedback improved the most, this group began with a pre-test score that was lower than that of the others, allowing more room for improvement. There was no statistically significant difference across the groups. The participants who worked with the system generally believed the training was useful and enjoyed working with it; those who received feedback said that it made them aware of pronunciation problems. The authors point out that the system was not 100 per cent accurate in its error detection, and, because the training was focused on a generalized list of problematic sounds for L2 Dutch learners, individual participants could not receive feedback on a large number of problem areas.

Cucchiarini et al. (2009) commented that their choice of feedback presentation was based on information from other studies (published from 2001 to 2003) on 'negative user experience effects: other feedback forms such as digital waveform plotting (which is readily available in most signal processing software), spectrograms . . . are often found incomprehensible and/or uninformative by users' (2009, p. 856). However, the findings of more recent studies (e.g. Motohashi-Saigo & Hardison, 2009; Okuno & Hardison, 2016; Olson, 2014) using waveforms and spectrographic displays do not support that assertion.

Main research methods and issues

As the name implies, CAPT involves training, which generally is part of a pre-test/treatment (e.g. training)/post-test design, often with an appropriate control group. Another element may also be added to this design description, specifically tests of generalization following the post-test, which challenge the participants' abilities beyond the confines of the experiment materials. In addition, many studies have examined the transfer of improvement in one domain (e.g. perception) to improvement in another (e.g. production). Investigating a transfer to production involves a production pre-test and post-test before the respective perception tests. Ideally, one would also explore the issue of retention of improved abilities (e.g. Bradlow et al., 1999; Wang & Munro, 2004). This has perhaps been the most difficult element to evaluate as participants may not be available beyond the initial study period.

Other challenges include the attrition that often impacts multiple-session research approaches such as training studies, and the lack of comparability across studies owing to differences in sample sizes, participant backgrounds, materials, procedures, length of training, statistical analyses and so forth. This lack of comparability affects researchers' ability to make informed choices based on previous research when setting up an experimental design. As in many areas of research in the field of second language acquisition, other challenges for CAPT studies include establishing an adequate sample size and controlling numerous participant variables such as L1, age at the time of initial exposure to the target language, residence in the target language environment, language use, interaction opportunities, language instruction and so forth. Participant fatigue is also a consideration. Although a session of 25 minutes may not seem long to the researcher, it can be perceived as much longer by participants in a research design that is somewhat repetitive in nature, as is the case in many training studies. Treatment sessions that include breaks and studies that provide participants with feedback on their performance may discourage attrition. Participation may also be encouraged by the opportunity to improve a skill to some degree within a relatively short period of time (i.e. the participant's perception of efficacy of training), especially through the convenience of web-based delivery, even though this removes some of the researcher's control.

Issue of variability

Finally, but of critical importance, is the role of variability in selecting materials for a study. The following statement goes to the heart of variability in perception and/or production training and the dilemma it poses for researchers and teachers: 'Too much or too little variability at too early a stage may prevent the learner from discovering with sufficient accuracy the prototypical forms that exemplars expound' (Leather, 1990, p. 96). Since the successful auditory training studies of the early 1990s, other researchers have adopted a so-called high-variability paradigm (e.g. the use of multiple exemplars and, in some cases, stimuli produced by multiple voices). Variability is thought to contribute to robust perceptual category development and to generalization of performance to novel stimuli (Lively et al., 1993). However, it is important to note that laboratory variability is strategically controlled and, in training, it may not be beneficial for all learners at all interlanguage stages.

The most effective degree of variability may well depend upon the focus of training, duration of training and learner tolerance. For AE /r/ and /l/, variability in training mirrors the variability exhibited by these sounds in different phonetic contexts in naturalistic speech. The benefit of training with multiple voices versus a single talker's voice is still unclear. Lively et al. (1993) reported that Japanese speakers receiving single talker training in the perception of AE /r/ and /l/ showed poor performance in generalization to novel words spoken by a familiar talker, and failed to generalize to new tokens produced by an unfamiliar talker. Hardison (2003) compared the two training group types for Korean learners of English and found only a marginally significant benefit of multiple-talker versus single-talker training on performance in a test of generalization when AV information was present. It is possible that performance in generalizing to familiar and unfamiliar talkers is influenced by other variables such as a talker's intelligibility and, in bimodal contexts, the discernibility of articulatory gestures.

In terms of CAPT studies, variability has included the use of different vocalic contexts and stimulus conditions (i.e. a stimulus presented as an isolated word or placed in a carrier sentence) to investigate the influence of these factors on the training of learners to identify L2 Japanese geminates (Motohashi-Saigo & Hardison, 2009). Findings in that study revealed that the geminate-vowel sequence of /s/ followed by /u/ was the most challenging for learners and showed the greatest improvement over the course of training; however, no significant effect of stimulus condition was noted. In two other studies, variability was introduced in the form of multiple pitch patterns and talker voices to create stimuli for the improvement of learners' perception and production of duration contrasts in L2 Japanese vowels (Hirata, 2004; Okuno & Hardison, 2016). In addition, Okuno and Hardison manipulated the preceding consonant and syllabic position (i.e., first and/or second syllable) of the vowels under test. In that study, perceptual accuracy for stimuli during training produced by one of the four talkers was consistently lower compared to stimuli produced by the other three talkers. While the precise source of the lower accuracy for that particular talker is not known, a possible explanation lies in the variability that was found in the degree of pitch movement by examining the pitch tracking in all of the training talkers' productions. For example, in the non-word <kaakaa>, there are two syllables and a long vowel in each one. One of the pitch patterns assigned to this token began high and then declined within the first long vowel, and remained low throughout the second syllable. Measurements indicated that the talkers' productions of these long vowels showed comparable duration but there was a difference in terms of overall pitch range. The stimuli produced by the training talker whose voice showed the least amount of pitch movement elicited the lowest perceptual accuracy scores. This talker was male; however, talker gender alone is unlikely to have accounted for the accuracy difference as one of the other training talkers was also male and his productions elicited an overall perceptual accuracy that was comparable to the accuracy found for one of the female training talkers. Although all auditory stimuli had been accurately identified by NSs of Japanese prior to their use in the study, the variability in the acoustic characteristics of the talkers' voices, including the degree of pitch movement, may have affected the learners' perceptual accuracy of duration.

There have been other sources of variability. Researchers have investigated the use of relatively large stimulus sets: nine AE vowels for L1 Japanese speakers (Nishi & Kewley-Port, 2007) and 10 Canadian English vowels for L1 Mandarin speakers (Thomson, 2011). Yet, this stimulus variability is still more controlled than that which might strike the perceiver's ear within a short period of time in the natural language environment. Laboratory-created stimuli are usually recorded under sound-attenuated conditions, choices are made in terms of phonetic contexts for target sounds, and rate of speech and amplitude are controlled.

Some studies have suggested that the benefits of variability in training vary with participants' initial abilities. Perrachione, Lee, Ha and Wong (2011) trained participants to use lexical tone to identify simulated foreign words under one of two conditions, which varied according to the degree of variability in the training tokens. High-variability training enhanced learning only for those participants who had higher pre-test scores in terms of pitch perception. In another study involving perception of Mandarin lexical tone, Shih, Lu, Sun, Huang and Packard (2010) used four groups of participants, who were classified according to the type of training stimuli they received: (a) control group – no training; (b) training with similar stimuli (minimal variability); (c) training with varied stimuli, that is, a combination of 'exaggerated' speech (recorded at a greater speaker–listener distance), normal speech, and speech with reduced clarity; and (d) training with varied stimuli using an adaptive approach. The stimulus types were based on the assumption that speech produced with exaggerated articulation would be clearer and easier to understand. The speaker–microphone distance and volume were held constant across stimulus types. Findings revealed that participants performed best when they received training with a varied stimulus set through an adaptive training approach, scaffolding them from a greater to a lesser degree of exaggeration, according to their performance. With the same varied stimulus set but without the adaptive approach, some participants improved but the performance of two actually declined.

Adaptive and fixed training were also compared in the perception of AE /r/ and /l/ by adult Japanese speakers (McClelland, Fiez & McCandliss, 2002). Participants were trained in one of four conditions, two of which involved adaptive training using synthesized speech stimuli that exaggerated the critical cue (third formant) differentiating AE /r/ and /l/. Adaptive training involved progressive reductions in exaggeration based on a participant's success on eight tokens in a row. Fixed training involved the use of good examples of /r/ and /l/. Within each training type, one group received feedback and one did not. Results indicated the following ranking from best to worst in terms of overall perceptual accuracy: fixed training with feedback, adaptive training with or without feedback, and fixed training without feedback (little improvement).

The adaptive approach is reminiscent of the perceptual fading technique used to train Canadian francophones to identify the interdental fricatives /θ/ and /ð/, which are not present in French, by exaggerating the amount of frication (Jamieson & Moroson, 1986). In that study, after 90 minutes of training, identification accuracy improved with generalization to natural speech and new voices but not to other positions of the sounds in a word nor to identifying /ð/ versus /d/ (Moroson & Jamieson, 1989). On the one hand, adaptive training techniques may draw attention to critical cues by making them more perceptually salient; on the other, natural speech cues offer the stimulus variability that is closer to the perceptual challenge of the natural language environment. The ability of learners to generalize training broadly likely requires training with a broad stimulus set that encompasses the variability of the feature in question in the learners' ambient language environment.

Role of the display

Another methodological issue involves the presentation of displays for imitation purposes. While this approach may be appreciated by and easier for some learners, it raises two concerns as to when it should be used and how the display should be interpreted. Failing to imitate a NS model precisely may suggest erroneously that a learner's production is unsatisfactory even though a native listener may perceive it as an acceptable utterance in the target language. Learners may also focus on a feature of the display that is not the target of training such as trying to match the rate of speech of the NS model instead of the overall intonation pattern. In addition, the quality of this type of feedback will depend on sustained phonation. In the early stages of learning, the imitation approach may also be discouraging to learners and may be less successful in terms of the generalizability of training. However, learners may respond well to seeing a comparison of their pre-test and post-test productions at the end of a training period. Figure 29.1, adapted from Hardison (2004), shows the pre-test and post-test pitch contours of a sentence produced by an L2 learner of French, which were shown to the learner at the end of the study. The added text follows the corresponding areas of the contour. For reference purposes, the display on the bottom shows an overlay of the learner's post-test production with a NS production of the same sentence.

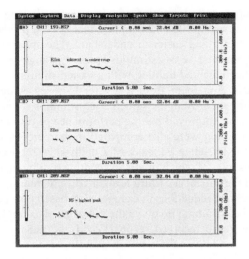

Figure 29.1

Top image: learner's pre-test pitch contour for *Elles adorent la couleur rouge* 'They love the color red'. Second image: same learner's post-test production. Bottom image: learner's post-test production with NS overlay. These images are from Figures 2 and 3 from the article 'Generalization of Computer-assisted Prosody Training: Quantitative and Qualitative Findings', by D. M. Hardison in *Language Learning & Technology*, 8, 2004, pp. 34–52, and were used with permission. Retrieved from http://llt.msu.edu/vol8num1/pdf/hardison.pdf

Recommendations for practice

From the earlier list of critical issues in the field of CAPT, the last two will be the focus of this section: interpretability of visual displays and the role of the instructor, and learner perception of the efficacy of visual feedback. Pitch displays have generally been considered the most user-friendly and learners have been able to interpret them with guidance (e.g. Chun et al., 2015; Hardison, 2004). Chun et al. (2015) pointed out that the use of tools such as Praat needs to be accompanied by clear instructions, including guidance on where to focus attention in interpreting the displays.

For more advanced learners, pitch displays can make clearer the relationship between focal stress, intonation, and meaning in English. A word that carries the focal stress in a sentence shows a corresponding rise in pitch. For example, in the sentence *Sam found a grey dog*, if a speaker wanted to emphasize the color of the dog, *grey* would be the focal element and would show the pitch peak in the sentence. However, if it were more important to emphasize *dog* in a particular context (e.g., to emphasize the type of animal), the speaker's sentence production would show a pitch rise on *dog*. Vocal pitch could be similarly manipulated on the other words in the sentence with corresponding changes in the pitch display. It is worth noting, too, that the value of such displays is not limited to use with second language learners; they are also informative in language teacher training (Hardison 2014). Prospective teachers, even native speakers of English, are not necessarily aware of the relationships among stress, intonation and meaning.

In contrast to pitch displays, waveforms and spectrograms may present different challenges. Some researchers have questioned the interpretability of this information provided by signal analysis systems (e.g. Cucchiarini et al., 2009; Strik et al., 2008), and studies have provided some conflicting results on this issue. Participants in two L2 Japanese studies on segmental duration (for geminates, Motohashi-Saigo & Hardison, 2009; for vowels, Okuno & Hardison, 2016) found waveforms interpretable following about five minutes of instruction, including demonstrations of how waveforms looked for consonants or vowels of different durations. As shown in Figure 29.2, differentiating the duration of closure (i.e. silence) for the stop consonant /k/ in the bottom pair of waveform displays is visually (and auditorily) easier than for the fricative /s/ in the top pair of waveforms.

During interviews following the geminate study, the participants, who were beginning learners on a study-abroad programme in Japan, commented that such training would be helpful as a regular part of language instruction. In addition, taking web-based training outside regular classes was convenient and they enjoyed the immediate feedback on their perception accuracy. Interestingly, these participants were neither language nor linguistics majors and were at a beginning level of proficiency.

The relative complexity of spectrograms has suggested the need for a trained individual at some point in the learning process (Neri, Cucchiarini & Strik, 2002). In Ruellot's (2011) study, participants received a six-minute introduction to spectrographic displays, plus

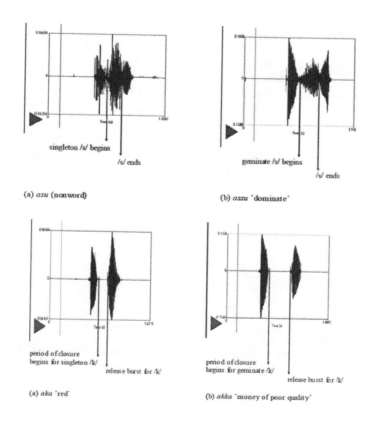

Figure 29.2

Waveform displays for singleton /s/ (upper left) and geminate /s/ (upper right); singleton /k/ (lower left) and geminate /k/ (lower right). These images are Figures 1 and 2 from the article 'Acquisition of L2 Japanese Geminates: Training with Waveform Displays', by M. Motohashi-Saigo and D. M. Hardison in *Language Learning & Technology*, *13*(2), 2009, 29–47, and were used with permission. Retrieved from http://llt.msu.edu/vol13num2/motohashisaigohardison.pdf

18 minutes in which to become familiar with the displays and interact with a trained instructor who guided their interpretations and practice sessions before they participated in two 50-minute training sessions. Both the A-only and AV groups showed improvement, but with no advantage for the spectrographic displays provided to the AV group. Participants favourably rated the experience with visual feedback in terms of their production and perception. They also appreciated the human component, which included presentation of the articulatory characteristics of French /u/ and /y/, explanations of the displays and interaction with the instructor. The author noted that it took longer for some learners to feel comfortable with this type of display as feedback.

In contrast, Olson (2014) found that only brief tutorials on the use of Praat to record speech and generate spectrograms were required for participants in that study to make use of this tool, and much of the pronunciation practice in the study was assigned as homework. Participants were also given spectrograms produced by native and non-native (L1 English) speakers of Spanish and were guided in the interpretation of areas of difference. Guidance included questions directing learner attention to auditory features and the visual characteristics shown in the spectrogram of the target sound in the learners' productions compared to those of the NS. These characteristics included the relative darkness of the image and the ability to visually distinguish the target from surrounding sounds. As shown in Figure 29.3, the NS's approximant (transcribed as [ð]) in the production of <vivido> 'lived' on the left is darker and more difficult to distinguish from surrounding vowels than the corresponding segment in the learner's production of the target on the right, which shows the relative silence associated with a stop closure ([d]).

The contrasting findings associated with spectrographic displays are notable as they remind us of the variability among individuals in their rates of learning, learning styles, and feedback preferences. Some forms of feedback such as spectrograms may require a greater tolerance for ambiguity than others such as intonation contours where upward and downward movements correspond to the variations in the pitch of the voice. As Olson (2014) noted, some features of sounds such as duration and intensity may be more suitable for this type of visual feedback than others. In addition to learner perceptions of the feedback, we must also consider the teachers' perceptions. Teachers may not be adequately trained to use technological tools to assist learners and may not feel comfortable interpreting the displays.

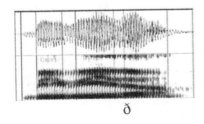
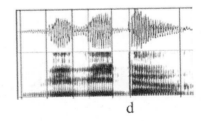

ð   d

Figure 29.3 Spectrograms

The left image corresponds to *vivido* 'lived' produced by a native Spanish speaker; the right image corresponds to *vivido* produced by a native English speaker. This image was adapted from Figure 3 from the article Benefits of Visual Feedback on Segmental Production in the L2 Classroom, by Daniel J. Olson in *Language Learning & Technology*, *18*(3), 2014, pp. 34–52, and was used with permission. Retrieved from http://llt.msu.edu/issues/october2014/olson.pdf

Future directions

In CAPT, as with the L2 speech field in general, a key word that has been emerging from research is variability – in language learner needs, the features that impact speech processing, selection of materials for training, learners' abilities and preferences, and so forth. There is variability, too, in the interpretability of pitch visualizations, waveforms and spectrograms by language teachers and learners, and the amount of guidance that is required for the use of such technological tools. Recent studies that have incorporated instruction on the use of signal analysis software have reported generally positive responses from their participants. These studies have also demonstrated significant improvement in one skill (e.g. perception), and often with generalization to novel stimuli and transfer to another skill (e.g. production). These findings are encouraging as CAPT research continues. The tools can be a valuable additional component in the language learning curriculum to supplement the human component. It is important that we continue to explore CAPT for segmental and suprasegmental features in a variety of languages using sound methodology. It is equally important that we add to the teacher training curriculum a component on the use of CAPT to increase the teachers' knowledge and comfort level in using these tools to help their learners. Studies should also incorporate post-study questionnaire and/or interview sessions with participants to determine their perceptions of the efficacy of the training and their suggestions on how it might aid classroom instruction. Their positive perceptions of any training protocol are crucial to successful implementation.

There appears to be a consensus among researchers that ASR features need further refinement and precision for broader implementation (e.g. Chun et al., 2015; Strik et al., 2008); however, considering how much progress has been made in digital technology over a relatively short period of time, the potential exists for continued development in this area. For those learners who do not have access to sufficient target language input or guidance, ASR-based feedback holds some promise for the future.

Further reading

Chun, D. M. (2002). *Discourse intonation in L2: From theory and research to practice.* Amsterdam: Benjamins. This book covers stress, rhythm and intonation from the perspective of theories, research and teaching. It includes numerous screen shots showing displays of pitch contours and waveforms. The companion CD-ROM plays these examples with a cursor that moves through the display, aligned in time with the audio. Examples of different intonation patterns that occur in utterances such as tag questions or simple words such as 'oh' provide a visually salient link between intonation and meaning.

Engwall, O., & Bälter, O. (2007). Pronunciation feedback from real and virtual language teachers. *Computer Assisted Language Learning, 20*(3), 235–262. Interviews with L2 learners and language teachers, and classroom observations were used to create a list of criteria for providing pronunciation feedback. These features were implemented in a short-term test of a virtual teacher providing feedback on articulatory positions and movements for L2 Swedish learners. The authors concluded that CAPT could be improved by studying how feedback occurs in teacher-learner classroom interaction.

Godwin-Jones, R. (2009). Emerging technologies: Speech tools and technologies. *Language Learning & Technology, 13*(3), 4–11. Available at http://llt.msu.edu/vol13num3/emerging.pdf. This column summarizes developments in several areas pertinent to technology and second-language speech: visualization of speech (e.g. through pitch contours), automatic speech recognition, speech analysis and language learning software (both commercial and non-commercial tools) and standards and outlook (providing directions for future development). In each section, discussion includes procedures, user concerns, advantages and shortcomings. The column concludes with a list of speech analysis tools and language learning software.

Liakin, D., Cardoso, W., & Liakina, N. (2014). Learning L2 pronunciation with a mobile speech recognizer: French /y/. *CALICO Journal, 32*(1), 1–25. This study reported significant improvement in the production of the French vowel /y/ by a group of elementary learners of French who used automatic speech recognition (ASR)-based pronunciation instruction on a mobile device. Activities, consisting of reading aloud target words and phrases, were accompanied by immediate orthographic feedback from an ASR dictation system. Learners provided positive evaluation of its use. The authors suggest the use of mobile technology as a complement to classroom instruction.

Massaro, D. W., & Light, J. (2003). Read my tongue movements: Bimodal learning to perceive and produce non-native speech /r/ and /l/. In *Proceedings of Eurospeech (Interspeech), 8th European Conference on Speech Communication and Technology*, Geneva, Switzerland. Baldi, a talking (computer-animated) head was used to train L1 Japanese learners of English to perceive /r/ and /l/ using a normal view and a view showing the movement of internal articulators such as the tongue. Both approaches resulted in improvement in perception and production; however, there was no additional benefit from seeing the articulators.

References

Anderson-Hsieh, J. (1992). Using electronic visual feedback to teach suprasegmentals. *System, 20*(1), 51–62.

Boersma, P., & Weenink, D. (2014). Praat: Doing phonetics by computer. [Computer program]. Available at www.fon.hum.uva.nl/praat.

Bradlow, A., Akahane-Yamada, R., Pisoni, D. B., & Tohkura, Y. (1999). Training Japanese listeners to identify English /r/ and /l/: Long-term retention of learning in perception and production. *Perception & Psychophysics, 61*, 977–985.

Carey, M. (2004). CALL Visual feedback for pronunciation of vowels: Kay Sona-Match. *CALICO Journal, 21*, 1–32.

Chun, D. M. (2002). *Discourse intonation in L2: From theory and research to practice*. Amsterdam: Benjamins.

Chun, D. M., Hardison, D. M., & Pennington, M. C. (2008). Technologies for prosody in context: Past and future of L2 research and practice. In J. H. Edwards & M. Zampini (Eds), *Phonology and second language acquisition* (pp. 323–346). Amsterdam: Benjamins.

Chun, D., Jiang, Y., Meyr, J., & Yang, R. (2015). Acquisition of L2 Mandarin Chinese tones with learner-created tone visualizations. *Journal of Second Language Pronunciation, 1*(1), 86–114.

Collins, B., & Mees, I. M. (1999). *The real Professor Higgins: The life and career of Daniel Jones*. Berlin: Mouton de Gruyter.

Cucchiarini, C., Neri, A., & Strik, H. (2009). Oral proficiency training in Dutch L2: The contribution of ASR-based corrective feedback. *Speech Communication, 51*, 853–863.

de Bot, K. (1983). Visual feedback of intonation I: Effectiveness and induced practice behavior. *Language and Speech, 26*(4), 331–350.

Haraguchi, S. (1999). Accent. In N. Tsujimura (Ed.), *The handbook of Japanese linguistics* (pp. 1–30). Malden, MA: Blackwell.

Hardison, D. M. (2003). Acquisition of second-language speech: Effects of visual cues, context and talker variability. *Applied Psycholinguistics, 24*, 495–522.

Hardison, D. M. (2004). Generalization of computer-assisted prosody training: Quantitative and qualitative findings. *Language Learning & Technology, 8*(1), 34–52. Retrieved from http://llt.msu.edu/vol8num1/hardison/

Hardison, D. M. (2005a). Contextualized computer-based L2 prosody training: Evaluating the effects of discourse context and video input. *CALICO Journal, 22*, 175–190.

Hardison, D. M. (2005b). Second-language spoken word identification: Effects of perceptual training, visual cues, and phonetic environment. *Applied Psycholinguistics, 26*, 579–596.

Hardison, D. M. (2012). Second-language speech perception: A cross-disciplinary perspective on challenges and accomplishments. In S. Gass & A. Mackey (Eds), *The Routledge handbook of second language acquisition* (pp. 349–363). London: Routledge.

Hardison, D. M. (2014). Phonological literacy in L2 learning and teacher training. In J. M. Levis & A. Moyer (Eds), *Social dynamics in second language accent* (pp. 195–218). Boston, MA, and Berlin: Mouton de Gruyter.

Hincks, R., & Edlund, J. (2009). Promoting increased pitch variation in oral presentations with transient visual feedback. *Language Learning & Technology, 13*(3), 32–50. Retrieved from http://llt.msu.edu/vol13num3/hincksedlund.pdf

Hirata, Y. (2004). Computer assisted pronunciation training for native English speakers learning Japanese pitch and durational contrasts. *Computer Assisted Language Learning, 17*(3–4), 357–376.

Hualde, J. I. (2005). *The sounds of Spanish*. New York, NY: Cambridge University Press.

Jamieson, D. G., & Moroson, D. E. (1986). Training non-native speech contrasts in adults: Acquisition of the English /ð/-/θ/ contrast by francophones. *Perception & Psychophysics, 40*, 205–215.

Kipp, M. (2001). *Anvil—A generic annotation tool for multimodal dialogue*. In *Proceedings of the 7th European Conference on Speech Communication and Technology* (pp. 1367–1370). Aalborg: Eurospeech.

Kubozono, H. (1999). Mora and syllable. In N. Tsujimura (Ed.), *The handbook of Japanese linguistics* (pp. 31–61). Malden, MA: Blackwell.

Leather, J. (1990). Perceptual and productive learning of Chinese lexical tone by Dutch and English speakers. In J. Leather & A. James (Eds), *New Sounds 90* (pp. 72–97). Amsterdam: University of Amsterdam.

Levis, J. M., & Pickering, L. (2004). Teaching intonation in discourse using speech visualization technology. *System, 32*, 505–524.

Lively, S. E., Logan, J. S., & Pisoni, D. B. (1993). Training Japanese listeners to identify English /r/ and /l/. II: The role of phonetic environment and talker variability in learning new perceptual categories, *Journal of the Acoustical Society of America, 94*, 1242–1255.

McClelland, J. L., Fiez, J. A., & McCandliss, B. D. (2002). Teaching the /r/–/l/ discrimination to Japanese adults: Behavioral and neural aspects. *Physiology & Behavior, 77*, 657–662.

Molholt, G. (1988). Computer-assisted instruction in pronunciation for Chinese speakers of American English. *TESOL Quarterly, 22*(1), 91–111.

Moroson, D. E., & Jamieson, D. G. (1989). Evaluation of a technique for training new speech contrasts: Generalization across voices, but not word-position or task. *Journal of Speech and Hearing Research, 32*, 501–511.

Motohashi-Saigo, M., & Hardison, D. M. (2009). Acquisition of L2 Japanese geminates: Training with waveform displays. *Language Learning & Technology, 13*(2), 29–47. Retrieved from http://llt.msu.edu/vol13num2/motohashisaigohardison.pdf.

Neri, A., Cucchiarini, C., & Strik, H. (2002). Feedback in computer assisted pronunciation training: Technology push or demand pull? In J. H. L. Hansen & B. Pellom (Eds), *ICSLP 2002* (pp. 1209–1212).

Nishi, K., & Kewley-Port, D. (2007). Training Japanese listeners to perceive American English vowels: Influence of training sets. *Journal of Speech, Language, and Hearing Research, 50*, 1496–1509.

Okuno, T., & Hardison, D. M. (2016). Perception-production link in L2 Japanese vowel duration: Training with technology. *Language Learning & Technology, 20*, 61–80. Retrieved from http://llt.msu.edu/issues/june2016/okunohardison.pdf

Olson, D. J. (2014). Benefits of visual feedback on segmental production in the L2 classroom. *Language Learning & Technology, 18*(3), 173–192. Retrieved from http://llt.msu.edu/issues/october2014/olson.pdf.

Pennington, M. C., & Esling, J. H. (1996). Computer-assisted development of spoken language skills. In M. C. Pennington (Ed.), *The power of CALL* (pp. 153–189). Houston, TX: Athelstan.

Perrachione, T. K., Lee, J., Ha, L., & Wong, P. (2011). Learning a novel phonological contrast depends on interactions between individual differences and training paradigm design. *Journal of the Acoustical Society of America, 139*, 461–472.

Ruellot, V. (2011). Computer-assisted pronunciation learning of French /u/ and /y/ at the intermediate level. In J. Levis & K. LeVelle (Eds), *Proceedings of the 2nd Pronunciation in Second Language Learning and Teaching conference* (pp. 199–213). Ames, IA: Iowa State University.

Seferoğlu, G. (2005). Improving students' pronunciation through accent reduction software. *British Journal of Educational Technology, 36*(2), 303–316.

Shih, C., Lu, H-Y D., Sun, L., Huang, J-T., & Packard, J. (2010, May). Paper presented at the *Speech Prosody 2010* conference, Chicago, IL. Retrieved from http://speechprosody2010.illinois.edu/papers/100981.pdf.

Strik, H., Neri, A., & Cucchiarini, C. (2008, February). Speech technology for language tutoring. In the *Proceedings of Lang Tech*, Rome. Retrieved from http://voice.fub.it/conferences/2008_langtech/en/poster/14_STRIK.pdf.

Thomson, R. I. (2011). Computer assisted pronunciation training: Targeting second language vowel perception improves pronunciation. *CALICO Journal, 29*(3), 744–765.

Wang, X., & Munro, M. J. (2004). Computer-based training for learning English vowel contrasts. *System, 32*, 539–552.

Warner, J. (Producer), & Cukor, G. (Director) (1964). *My Fair Lady*. [Motion picture]. United States: Warner Brothers.

Weltens, B., & de Bot, K. (1984). Visual feedback of intonation II: Feedback delay and quality of feedback. *Language and Speech, 27*(1), 79–88.

30

Pronunciation future in the twenty-first-century English-speaking world

Context, choice and consultation

Ivor Timmis

The exponential growth in the international use of English in recent years has thrown into question the status of native speaker norms in contemporary English language teaching. The specific question which has arisen is, 'In a world where English is increasingly spoken by non-native speakers, is it possible or desirable for native speaker norms to be the target for learners of English?' The debate has been particularly intense in the field of pronunciation teaching, arguably because pronunciation is such an obvious emblem of identity. An early proposal for a move away from native speaker norms in English language teaching (ELT) was Jenkins's (1998) proposal for a lingua franca core (LFC), which argued for a pedagogic focus on sounds that appear central to international communication rather than the full array of native speaker norms. It was a seminal contribution to the debate and a rallying cry for those proposing a shift away from native speaker norms on sociocultural grounds. Critics, however, have argued that the LFC represents an impoverished syllabus and may not meet learners' aspirations.

This chapter reviews the main lines of the debate with regard to the diverse pronunciation needs of learners in a diverse English-speaking world before focusing on a specific proposal to meet these needs: the LFC. The chapter then reviews the empirical studies that have been carried out both into learners' and teachers' attitudes to the debate and into the key pronunciation features that seem to affect intelligibility in international communication. Finally, the chapter outlines how an ELT pronunciation syllabus might be framed that reflects both a need for realistic goals and a need to acknowledge learners' aspirations. The concluding argument is that context, choice and consultation are the key factors in addressing the issue.

Introduction

In 1998, Jennifer Jenkins wrote a seminal article on the future of pronunciation teaching in ELT, beginning with the following striking observation about learners' pronunciation needs and goals:

> The recent growth in the use of English as an International Language (EIL) has led to changes in learners' pronunciation needs and goals. The acquisition of a native-like accent is no longer the ultimate objective of the majority of learners, nor is communication with native speakers their primary motivation for learning English.
>
> (Jenkins 1998, p. 119)

In current parlance, it was a game-changer: though it was not the first proposal that pronunciation teaching should move away from native speaker norms, it was more specific as to the direction of change. It was also more empirically based than previous proposals in that it arose from experimental research into sounds that appeared to cause miscommunication between non-native speakers. As it stands, the quotation above makes three claims:

(a) learners' pronunciation needs and goals have changed;
(b) a native-like accent is no longer the objective of the majority of learners;
(c) communicating with native speakers is no longer learners' primary motivation for learning English.

Controversy arose because of the nature of these three claims as, while there may be a prima facie case for all three declarations, none of them is actually self-evident and none of the claims was supported by empirical evidence: it is important to note that, while there was empirical evidence about intelligibility, there was none relating to learners' attitudes. What is presented as fact in relation to attitudes is actually a set of assumptions, perhaps even a set of desiderata. It is true that later in the same article Jenkins (1998) acknowledged that learners who aspired to native speaker norms had the right to aim for them, but in the overall tone of the article the line between pedagogic proposal and polemic appeared blurred, and, it may be argued, has remained so ever since. Whether we see it as pedagogic proposal or polemic, it is clear that Jenkins's article promoted vigorous debate about appropriate pronunciation norms in an era of world Englishes and increasing use of English as a lingua franca, a debate that, it is important to note, widened to include discussion of appropriate grammatical, lexical and pragmatic norms. Such has been the vigour of the debate that it has at times generated more heat than light: this chapter strives to turn down the heat and turn up the light.

In the chapter, I first sketch the changing landscape of the English-speaking world as it is the backdrop that has framed the debate. I then consider the theoretical arguments that have been made both for and against changing priorities in relation to target pronunciation norms. This leads to a survey and discussion of the empirical work that has arisen from and contributed to the debate: both attitudinal research and empirical work on intelligibility. Finally, we consider principled and practical proposals for classroom pronunciation work that arise from the discussion of the theoretical issues and empirical data.

The English-speaking world: a changing landscape

To contextualize the debate about pronunciation norms, it will be useful to revisit briefly Kachru's (1982) categorization of the English-speaking world into three circles: the inner circle, the outer circle and the expanding circle. The three circles are generally characterized thus:

(a) The inner circle refers to the traditional bases of English, where it is the primary language. Included in this circle are the USA, the UK, Ireland, Canada, Australia and New Zealand. The varieties used here have traditionally been seen as 'norm-providing'.

(b) The outer circle includes countries and territories where English has long been established and plays an important institutional role and an important 'lingua franca' role in a multi-lingual setting. India, Pakistan, Singapore, Nigeria and over 50 other territories are included in this circle. The varieties in this circle are not 'norm-providing' but 'norm-developing'.

(c) The expanding circle includes countries that recognize the current importance of English as an international language. However, these countries were not colonized by inner circle countries and English has no special status within the country itself. These varieties are 'norm-dependent'.

Kachru's model has the merit of describing in very broad terms the way English language use developed pre-1982 and the (almost unquestioned) status of inner circle countries as 'norm-providing' prior to that date. The model has, however, come in for criticism: Graddol (1997), for example, sees the three-circle model as essentially a static view of a dynamic landscape:

> This [Kachru] model, however, will not be the most useful for describing English usage in the next century. Those who speak English alongside other languages will outnumber first-language speakers, and, increasingly, will decide the global future of the language.

> (Graddol 1997, p. 10)

As well as being descriptively inaccurate, it is also, Graddol (1997) argues, ideologically unsound in privileging the traditional native speakers of the language:

> One of the drawbacks of this terminology is the way it locates the 'native speakers' and native-speaking countries at the centre of global use of English and, by implication, the source of models of correctness, the best teachers and English-language goods and services consumed by those in the periphery.

> (Graddol, 1997, p. 10)

A further criticism of the three circles model is that it overgeneralizes, obscuring differences within each circle and labelling varieties as non-native that some speakers may have used from birth: Indian English and Malaysian English, for example, may both be included in the outer circle, but it is arguable that Indian English is more deeply rooted in Indian society and that India has more people who would regard themselves as native speakers of English. McArthur (2001, pp. 8–10) outlined a number of developments that, he argues, undermine and will continue to undermine the validity of the three-circle model:

- the growth of multilingualism in inner circle countries;
- a greater awareness of variety among inner circle Englishes;
- growing controversy about appropriate standards and norms for the classroom;
- controversy about the definition of the native speaker;
- the growing codification of other native and non-native varieties of English;
- conflicts in national language policy between the promotion of English and the protection of local languages;
- increasing awareness of the phenomenon of 'hybridization'.

Such developments have led to questions about the ownership of English and the right of native speakers (henceforward NESs, and NNESs for non-native speakers) to legislate over its use, a view trenchantly, perhaps even provocatively, expressed by Widdowson (1994):

> How English develops in the world is no business whatever of native speakers in England, the United States, or anywhere else. They have no say in the matter, no right to intervene or pass judgment. They are irrelevant.
>
> (Widdowson 1994, p. 385)

Widdowson's (1994) verdict is dismissed rather intemperately by Sobkowiak (2008) as 'highly emotional, even hysterical', a response that in itself is an indication of the intensity of the debate about native speaker norms over the years. What we can say more temperately, I feel, is that Widdowson (1994) is presenting his own ideological judgement rather than fact. At the time of writing, the continuing dominance of British and American interests in the ELT market for teaching materials, reference books and teacher training courses indicates that native speakers, and in particular native speakers in the UK and the USA, continue, whether we like it or not, to exert a powerful influence on ELT and hence on the development of English. An ideologically motivated move away from native speaker norms leaves open the question, as Sewell (2013) notes, of what learners and teachers should move to:

> The challenge for language teaching is to theorize and implement approaches that acknowledge the variability of language while still making it accessible and acceptable for actual contexts, classrooms, and learners. There needs to be an awareness of communicative processes, as well as products. Norms of some kind will still be required for teaching and learning, but these should not be adopted in an uncritical fashion.
>
> (p. 9)

The lingua franca core – a response to a changing landscape

Intelligibility and nativeness

One response to this challenge in specific relation to pronunciation teaching was Jenkins's (1998) notion of a lingua franca core (LFC), which recommended a focus on an inventory of sounds and suprasegmental features believed to be crucial for intelligibility in international communication. As it has proved to be a focal point for the debate about appropriate ELT pronunciation in the contemporary world, we need at least to recapitulate its main features and rationale. Before we examine this proposal in more detail, however, we need to consider the notions of intelligibility and nativeness that are crucial to arguments concerning the pronunciation future of ELT. Although these terms may seem fairly self-evident, they require brief elaboration to highlight their relevance to the current debate. Both terms have their roots in an era when it was largely assumed that NNESs learned English for the purposes of communication with native speakers. The 'nativeness principle' operated on the assumption that NESs were the model for pronunciation teaching and learning and that attaining this putative ideal would guarantee intelligibility. The concomitant of this argument was that being mistaken for a native speaker would be the ultimate achievement and this, perhaps, also confers prestige on the L2 speaker. It is also worth noting that the native speakers in question at this stage were presumed to be those of BANA (Britain, America, New Zealand, Australia) countries and, in particular, those from Britain and the USA. The 'intelligibility principle', by contrast, allows for the retention of an L1 accent – this can be justified either on the grounds of realism (Murphy 2014) or idealism: realistically, it is generally acknowledged that a native speaker accent is very difficult to acquire without substantial exposure in formative years; in terms of ideals, even if it were possible for learners to 'lose' their L1 accent, the retention of an L1 accent can be seen far more positively as a badge of identity. We need here to draw attention to an assumption underpinning both the 'nativeness principle' and the 'intelligibility principle' as traditionally conceived (i.e. in both cases), there is an expectation that a one-size-fits-all L2 accent will suffice in all circumstances. We are faced then with a long-standing tension between the nativeness principle and the intelligibility principle, to which a new factor has been added: the exponential growth of English language use involving non-native speakers, in particular communication between non-native speakers.

Describing the lingua franca core

The LFC elevates the intelligibility principle and subordinates the nativeness principle. Drawing on Jenkins (1998, 2000), Levis (2005) and Walker (2010), we can summarize the LFC as follows. The LFC arose from changing patterns of English language use globally leading to the conclusion that 'the primary goal of teaching pronunciation must now be to make learners intelligible to the greatest number of speakers possible, and not just to the native speakers of the language' (Walker 2010, p. 19). In pursuit of this goal, Jenkins (1998) carried out research to establish which features of pronunciation significantly impeded or facilitated communication in English between non-native speakers. One significant finding was that individual phonemes rather than suprasegmentals were of greater importance in facilitating NNES–NNES communication. A logical follow-up was to establish which phonemes from the traditional native speaker inventory played a greater or lesser role in intelligibility between non-native speakers. Accordingly, Jenkins (1998) recommended a productive focus on a core of sounds and suprasegmental features. The core suprasegmental features were (Dauer 2005, p. 545):

- correct placement and production (lengthening) of nuclear stress and contrastive stress (e.g. <You deserve to be **SACKED**> versus <You de**SERVE** to be sacked>);
- division of the speech stream into word groups.

The core sounds of the LFC (Jenkins 1998) were:

(a) individual consonant sounds: The main exception here is [θ] and [ð], which are excluded on the grounds that the two interdental phonemes are 'inherently difficult to pronounce, notoriously resistant to classroom teaching, and unnecessary for ELF intelligibility' (Walker 2010, p. 30);
(b) consonant clusters;
(c) vowels: the recommended focus in the LFC is on vowel and diphthong *length* rather than native speaker quality, providing the vowel quality produced by the learner is consistent (Walker 2010);
(d) nuclear stress placement.

Jenkins (1997) argues that nuclear stress – the main stress in a word group – is crucial to intelligibility:

> Nuclear stress, whether unmarked ... or contrastive ... is the most important key to the speaker's meaning. It highlights the most salient part of the message, indicating where the listener should pay particular attention. And contrastive stress is particularly important in English as it does not have the morphological and syntactic resources that many other languages have to highlight contrasts.
>
> (p. 18)

These recommendations are clear enough, but sometimes, as we know from 'the dog didn't bark' in the Sherlock Holmes story 'The Curious Incident of the Dog in the Night-Time', it is omission rather than presence that can be crucial in a case. And noticeably absent from the LFC, as Walker (2010) points out, are many staples of the ELT pronunciation syllabus that have long been featured in teacher training courses and ELT materials:

- exact vowel quality;
- pitch movement (tone);
- word stress;
- stress-timing;
- vowel reduction, schwa and weak forms;
- certain features of connected speech – linking, assimilation, coalescence.

If I can be anecdotal for a moment, my own teaching experience suggested that the cost-benefit analysis for many of these features in terms of classroom teaching was negative, so I am quite glad to see these intuitions apparently validated, except in the case of word stress, which, from experience, I considered to be both teachable and crucial to clear communication. It is interesting, then, that Jenkins (2000) argued that word stress seemed to be more important in NNES–NES communication than in NNES–NNES communication. It is the perceived omissions from the LFC of the six features listed above that led to accusations of 'dumbing down' the pronunciation syllabus, and even of teaching an artificial Esperanto-type variety of the language (e.g. Sobkowiak, 2008).

We need to keep in mind, however, that the LFC was only the initial stage in what Jenkins (2000) envisaged as a five-stage programme, though the above features remain absent at all stages from a productive point of view:

(a) addition of core items to the learner's productive and receptive repertoire;
(b) addition of a range of L2 English accents to the learner's receptive repertoire;
(c) addition of accommodation skills;
(d) addition of non-core items to the learner's receptive repertoire;
(e) addition of a range of L1 English accents to the learner's receptive repertoire.

Partly as a result of the LFC proposal, confusion has arisen as to whether ELF (including grammatical, lexical and pragmatic norms) is to be regarded as a codified new variety of English or simply a mode of communication. This confusion is underlined by Sowden (2012, pp. 90–91), who cites Seidlhofer's (2004) statement that 'ELF is a natural language and can thus be expected to undergo the same processes that affect other natural languages, especially in contact situations'. In response to this statement, Sowden (2012) remarks:

> This would suggest that ELF can be viewed as an identifiable, discrete entity, yet this idea is called into question by the pronouncements of other writers in the field. Jenkins

(2007: 41) is clear that it does not refer to a monolithic construct which will merely replace traditional native-speaker norms with new but equally inflexible standards. Instead, it would consist of 'a variety of local versions of English', each influenced by the local native language.

(pp. 90–91)

In similar vein, Sewell (2013) refers to a lingering tendency among ELF scholars to refer to ELF as if it were a defined and uniform entity despite protestations to the contrary – it is not mere pedantry to point this out; it is crucial to the argument.

The LFC: pedagogic issues

The pedagogic arguments in favour of the LFC, while contested by many, can easily be summarized: the LFC presents a lighter and more focused pronunciation workload than the traditional procession towards native speaker norms by focusing on what is teachable and learnable and of proven value in NNES–NNES intelligibility. Learners faced with a manageable and practical target will gain in motivation and in self-esteem and probably feel empowered to express their own identity through their accent. From a teaching point of view, traditional activities can be adapted and harnessed to the cause of the LFC – there is no requirement for LFC-specific pronunciation techniques and activities (Walker, 2010). Both communicative activities and more traditional activities such as drills and minimal pairs can be applied to the LFC in the same way as they can to the traditional native speaker inventory of sounds (Walker, 2010). In a multilingual classroom, activities such as information gaps or learner-to-learner dictations can be useful in highlighting areas of difficulty and in offering opportunities for accommodation strategies to be applied (Walker, 2010). In fact, the full range of some of the more innovative teaching techniques being explored by pronunciation teaching specialists such as Brown (2012) and Marks and Bowen (2012) can be applied in modified form to LFC instruction.

An achievable and effective range of sounds that can be taught through established teaching procedures is a seductive proposition. Critics of the LFC, however, can point to the very light and limited research base that underpins the LFC, and to a certain optimistic vagueness in notions such as 'accommodation skills'. Dauer (2005) draws attention to the limited empirical base for the LFC:

it is important to note that Jenkins's data are based on a small number of well-educated, motivated nns [NNES] whose proficiency in written English, which they learned first, is at the intermediate to advanced level. (They were practicing for the Cambridge Certificate in Advanced English.) It is not clear whether these results can be generalized to a larger population of less literate learners or to more formal extended discourse.

(p. 549)

Among the specific reservations about the LFC expressed by Dauer (2005, pp. 547–548) are the following:

- The recommended substitution of [θ] and [ð] with /f/ and /v/ will not be helpful for the many groups of learners who have a problem with /v/: /t/ and /d/ might be better substitutions.

- The omission of word stress is incongruous for two reasons: first, there is no reason to suppose that word stress is unteachable as basic word stress rules account for 85 per cent of polysyllabic words. Second, aspects of pronunciation that are part of the LFC are closely related to word stress:

  > it is hard to understand how to teach aspiration, vowel length, or nuclear stress (all of which are part of the LFC and are associated with word stress) without students having been taught which syllable to stress in a word.
  >
  > (Dauer 2005, p. 548)

- While vowel reduction may not be so important for intelligibility, it is important for fluency.

With regard to teachability, Scheuer's (2005) experiment suggested that, contrary to Jenkins's argument, [θ] and [ð] are teachable, whereas the distinction between /I/ and /iː/ is not.

A further reservation about the LFC, I would argue, is the extent to which accommodation skills or strategies (Stage 3 in Jenkins's five-stage programme above), often stressed in ELF literature, can be taught. They seem to be largely a product of natural disposition and inventiveness, not necessarily the most teachable qualities. We also need to bear in mind that, while accommodation skills are clearly important, they are, just like communication strategies, a way of deploying existing resources to best effect, not a substitute for resources. At classroom level, we need to be able to answer basic questions from learners such as 'How do you pronounce this word in English?' One response would be to treat the 'you' as singular and give your own pronunciation, provided you are convinced your own accent is widely intelligible.

Pronunciation goals: a classroom view

The need for attitudinal surveys

It could be argued that we do not need attitudinal surveys on the issue of pronunciation norms: the debate is ideological and should be resolved in the debating chamber. However, we need to keep in mind that language and language teaching are *complex human* activities and are difficult to account for in a unified theory. As Cook and Seidlhofer (1995) argue:

> language teaching, being . . . a social and often institutional activity, brings theories of language and language learning into contact with practical constraints: the whims of governments, the availability of resources, the social conditions of those involved, and the ideological climate in which they live.
>
> (p. 8)

One of the 'practical constraints' facing language teaching theorists is the attitudes of teachers and learners to an issue, especially when a theoretical argument runs counter to long-established practice.

Learners' attitudes to native speaker pronunciation norms

I begin this section on attitudinal research with reference to my own attitudinal survey (Timmis, 2002). This is not out of any desire to promote my own work (I have been as surprised as anyone by the shelf life of this rather unsophisticated survey); it was, however, an early attempt to elicit a classroom view and has been referred to in a number of subsequent studies. The rather stark question presented to the students in Timmis (2002) is reproduced below:

Student A: 'I can pronounce English just like a native speaker now. Sometimes people think I am a native speaker.'

Student B: 'I can pronounce English clearly now. Native speakers and non-native speakers understand me wherever I go, but I still have the accent of my country.'

7.   Please underline one answer. Would you prefer to be like Student A or Student B?

Student A   Student B

The 'approval rating' for Student A (the native speaker option) was around 70 per cent. Perhaps surprisingly, the survey also revealed that respondents' views did not seem to be much affected by whether they felt they currently used or would in future use English more with non-native speakers than native speakers. The overall figures did not support Jenkins's (1997) assertion that 'the majority express a desire to retain something of their L1', except in the case of students from the 'outer circle' countries of South Africa, Pakistan and India. Despite the limitations of the survey, it seemed robust enough to support the following modest conclusion that you can't rule out learners' attachment to native speaker pronunciation norms. Let us now consider more recent and more localized studies of learners' attitudes to pronunciation norms. We begin in Iran, where Jodai, Pirhadi and Taghavi (2014) applied an adapted version of the Timmis (2002) questionnaire to 102 adult EFL learners at an English language institute in Teheran, finding (apparently to their regret) that a 'relatively high number' of the respondents had a desire to conform to native speaker pronunciation norms. In a Greek context, Kanellou (2011) surveyed 327 upper-intermediate and advanced students and found an 'overwhelming preference' as a target for RP (received pronunciation, i.e. the British 'standard' form) or GA (General American, i.e. the North American 'standard' form). Not all surveys, of course, put the question so starkly: Buckingham (2015) was interested in the relationship between students' ability to identify accents as native or non-native and their evaluation of accents as suitable for teaching purposes. In a study involving 327 Omani university students she found a 'moderate to strong correlation' between students' perception of a native speaker accent and their evaluation of an accent as suitable for teaching purposes (although it is important to note the students were not always successful in identifying a native speaker accent). This relationship between perception of a native speaker accent and positive evaluation of teaching ability is reflected in the study carried out by Kelch and Santana Williamson (2002), a study that involved 56 intermediate and upper-intermediate students at a community college in South Carolina. The results signalled that, while respondents were not reliably able to distinguish between NES and NNES accents, they favoured the perceived NES accents for teaching purposes.

The research carried out by Episcopo (2009) at the University of Texas had a slightly different focus: the 41 respondents were asked to rate different NNES accents and Episcopo concludes that the 'nativelikeness' of the accent was a more important factor than intelligibility in the rating. The question of whether non-native speakers (and also native speakers) can actually distinguish between native speaker and non-native speaker accents is also raised by Ballard's (2013) study, which involved 94 non-native speakers and 38 native speakers. Ballard found that non-native speakers were significantly less able than native speakers to distinguish between NS and NNS accents and that 'familiarity with an accent correlated with comprehensibility and acceptability'.

Teachers' attitudes to native speaker pronunciation norms

To begin our review of teachers' attitudes we must return briefly to Timmis (2002). The teachers in the survey were presented with a similar question to the learners (see above) designed to establish whether they saw native speaker norms or 'accented intelligibility' as the goal they were aiming for with their learners. However, the teachers were also allowed a no-preference option on the grounds that you don't need to have a preference on somebody else's behalf. The resulting question was as below:

Please read the comments by Student A and Student B and then answer the question below by circling one answer.

Student A: 'I can pronounce English just like a native speaker now. Sometimes people think I am a native speaker.'

Student B: 'I can pronounce English clearly now. Native speakers and non- native speakers understand me wherever I go, but I still have the accent of my first language.'

Which of these students represent(s) for you the ideal long-term outcome of your teaching?

Student A   Student B   neither Student A nor Student B

The 'headline' finding was that the results showed a stronger preference among teachers than learners for Student B (i.e. more teachers than learners regarded 'accented intelligibility' as a more desirable goal than native speaker norms). Somewhat in contrast, more localized studies of teachers' attitudes have shown that teachers have a strong preference for native speaker norms as a pronunciation target. Campos (2011, p. 213), for example, in a Chilean context, interviewed 15 trainee teachers and concluded that 'highly stereotypical beliefs prevail with regard to varieties and accents and that knowledge about the spread of English is meagre'. It is all too easy for researchers to dismiss results that confound their expectations as the product of ignorance or naivety. In a very large scale survey, Sifakis and Sougari canvassed the views of 421 Greek teachers of English and observed that their attitudes to pronunciation were predominantly native speaker 'norm-bound'. Again, the choice of language to report the results is interesting as 'bound' has a slightly negative sense of limitation and restriction. Also in a Greek context, Kanellou (2011) reports that the 47 teachers she surveyed had an 'overwhelming preference' for RP or GA, though, in an echo of Timmis (2002), she notes that teachers were happier than students to accept 'accented intelligibility'. A qualitative study was carried out by Jenkins (2005) using in-depth interviews to explore the views of eight non-native speaker teachers of varied nationalities. The qualitative dimension is particularly valuable and in this respect could provide an exemplar for future research. Her conclusion, however, is most interesting in the way it is expressed (Jenkins, 2005):

The most important point is that it cannot be taken for granted that teachers (let alone all speakers) from the expanding circle wish unequivocally to use their accented English to express their L1 identity or membership in an international (ELF) community.

(p. 541)

It is the tone of surprise which is particularly interesting here: in my view there is no reason at all to presuppose that the NNES teachers would prefer their accented English and, therefore, no need to be surprised. Indeed, there is no reason to presuppose that teachers even consider identity an issue in relation to L1/L2 accent or consciously wish to be a member of an ELF community or even recognize the ELF community as an entity. These are simply assumptions sometimes made on their behalf by academic researchers. While Jenkins's research methodology is exemplary, it has to be said that the reporting of an inconvenient result could not be more tendentious.

There are, however, more concrete indications that a preference for native speaker norms is not universal: Buss's (2015) study with 60 Brazilian EFL teachers indicated that over 80 per cent thought that a native speaker teacher was not necessarily best for teaching pronunciation and that just over 50 per cent considered that native speaker pronunciation need not be the target for learners.

The complexity of attitudes

To illustrate the complexity of learners' attitudes, I would like to describe an interview I carried out with a Nigerian woman for my PhD research.

'R' lives in Nigeria, where she is a women's group leader. Her work involves leading seminars and workshops in different parts of the country. She conducts the seminars and workshops in English, so she is effectively using English as a lingua franca for professional purposes. Her stated motivation for coming to England, however, was to 'improve her pronunciation', 'to learn how words are said'. It emerged that the people in her workshop groups had no problems understanding her, but she felt the need to improve her pronunciation because the workshops were sometimes attended by Nigerian doctors and lawyers. It is interesting that, though she came to England to improve her pronunciation, she had no particular desire to 'sound like these people'. On the other hand, she admitted to being quite gratified when a neighbour remarked that she was making progress and beginning to sound like 'one of us'. When I put it to her that adopting a native speaker accent might compromise her cultural identity, she was quite emphatic: 'I know I'm black, I know I'm African, I just want to speak English like you'.

This interview then highlighted a number of themes that are relevant to the pronunciation debate:

- the weak link between stated motivation and actual aspiration as a language learner;
- the idea that there is, somewhere, one correct way to speak English (the use of the passive in 'to learn how words are said' is interesting in this respect);
- the notion that native speaker English confers prestige;
- the notion that acquiring native speaker proficiency is a benchmark of achievement;
- the fact that it is difficult to disentangle the prestige notion from the benchmark notion;
- the fact that students seem to be less worried about and less sensitive to issues of cultural identity than teachers and specialist commentators are on their behalf.

(Timmis, 2003)

All of these views, whether we regard them as reasonable or not, present challenges for ELF scholars. I would like to draw particular attention to two challenges:

(a) There appears to be an underlying assumption in ELF literature that learners have a clear overriding motivation for learning English and can predict their future interaction patterns in English. There is a further assumption that these factors will determine the kind of English learners want to speak (e.g. a student learning English to conduct business with fellow non-native speakers will incline towards the LFC). I would argue that these rather large assumptions are unsafe: Timmis (2003) shows that motivation is frequently multifaceted and that learners' goals are rarely *purely* pragmatic, illustrating the argument with specific examples:

  (i) We cannot assume that a student whose motivation is professional does not also need to prepare for contact with native speakers (e.g. 'I need English for my job and at this moment I'm living in England.' (Spanish student)).

  (ii) We cannot assume that a student whose motivation is idealistic does not also have a utilitarian motive (e.g. 'Because I think it is a beautiful language. Nowadays it makes part of our lifes and we can't survive without it.' (Brazilian student)).

  (iii) We cannot assume that a student whose motivation is intranational does not also have an international motive (e.g. 'I am learning English because I think it will help me to communicate with the average people in my country and moreover because of its globalization which no other language is able to achieve.' (Indian student)).

  (iv) We cannot assume that a student who has international and intranational motives does not also have an idealistic motive (e.g. 'For good communication internationally and countrywide. And to help the growing mind.' (South African student)).

  (v) We cannot assume that a student who needs English for communication with non-native speakers does not want to be able to speak English like a native speaker (e.g. 'I'm fascinated by this language and I'd really like to be able to communicate like Student E and I need it for communication with non-native speakers.' (Czech student)).

(b) In the case of adult learners at least, there is no reason to suppose that their cultural identity is threatened by the adoption of a native speaker accent. They are surely capable of making their own choices.

Empirical work on intelligibility

As Jenkins, Cogo and Dewey (2011) note, remarkably few empirical replication or follow-up studies have been carried out to test the notion of the LFC. This, they argue, is perhaps because attention has shifted from 'an orientation to features and the ultimate aim of some kind of codification to an interest in the processes underlying and determining the choice of features used in any given ELF interaction' (p. 287). We can, however, consider one or two examples of empirical research into the LFC. Osimk (2009) focused on the following features: aspiration, realizations of [θ] (e.g. the 'th' in bath) and [ð] (e.g. the 'th' in bathe) and /r/. Aspiration was chosen because Jenkins's (2000) study indicated that it was important for intelligibility; [θ] and [ð] were chosen because, despite often being the focus of classroom attention, the LFC indicates that accurate realization is not important in NNS–NNS interactions. /r/ was chosen because of the rationale for including it in the LFC: teachability and reduced redundancy rather than intelligibility (Osimk 2009). The study confirmed that aspiration was important for mutual intelligibility whereas [θ] and [ð] were not. The case in relation to teaching rhotic /r/ seemed less conclusive.

Da Silva (1999) carried out an experiment in which three of his Brazilian students communicated with 12 students from nine different countries and with nine different first languages. Again the relative unimportance of [θ] and [ð] was confirmed. However, da Silva (1999) points to features of the Brazilian students' speech that are not included in the LFC but that did seem to impair intelligibility:

- the change in the quality rather than the quantity of the diphthong /əʊ/ (the vowel sound in <know>, <go>, <so> and <low>);
- the strong reduction of final syllable vowels by the Brazilian speakers (e.g. <coff> instead of <coffee>, <offs> instead of <office>, <happ> instead of <happy>

(da Silva, 1999, p. 2)

On the other hand, a violation of the LFC did not seem to cause problems: while the Brazilian students shorted the length of vowels in words such as *<read>*, *<speak>* and *<sort>*, this did not seem to affect intelligibility. While the above studies indicate a need to 'road-test' the LFC, a need acknowledged by Jenkins, Cogo and Dewey (2011), other studies cited in Jenkins, Cogo and Dewey (2011, p. 289) have tended, in their view, to support the LFC.

The scholars who have replicated the ELF pronunciation research, by contrast, have found that their findings in the main support those of Jenkins (e.g. da Silva, 1999; Deterding & Kirkpatrick, 2006; Rajadurai, 2007; Osimk, 2009; Kirkpatrick, 2010), although they have also identified occasional areas in which the LFC needs a degree of 'fine-tuning' (Walker 2010, pp. 43–44). For example, Pickering (2009) produces experimental evidence demonstrating that pitch cues may have a role to play in ELF communication.

Attitudes and intelligibility: blurring the boundaries

Thus far we have treated attitudes to accent and intelligibility as if they are separate issues, but it is arguable that they are not. To begin anecdotally, when I worked in Italy I noticed that the ticket clerk at the local railway station set his face into an attitude of incomprehension at least three metres before I actually reached the counter. It is this link between attitude and perceived intelligibility that Lindemann (2002) set out to investigate. In her experiment, 12 American students were paired with 12 Korean students and asked to complete an information-gap task based on a map. Lindemann (2002, p. 419) drew two interesting conclusions from this research:

- 'Some but not all of those who had been assessed as having negative attitudes toward Koreans were found to use either strategies that were described as problematizing their partners' utterances, or strategies that were described as avoidance.'
- 'There appeared to be a direct relationship between attitude and perceived success of interactions, which may ultimately have the same consequences for interactants as if the relationship were between attitude and actual success.'

The effect of attitudes on perceived intelligibility was also the focus of Rubin's (1992) study. In Rubin's (1992) experiment, listeners in one group were asked to listen to a few minutes of a lecture given by a native speaker of American English and shown a picture of a Caucasian as the lecturer. Listeners in another group were shown a picture of an Asian delivering the same lecture: this second group attributed a foreign accent to the speaker and achieved lower scores in a recall cloze test than the group, which perceived more of a native accent: it is important to underline that the actual content of what the two groups heard was identical.

Conclusion

In this chapter, we have reviewed the ideological arguments in relation to the future of pronunciation in an era of international use of English. We have also considered learners' and teachers' attitudes to the issue and referred to empirical work on intelligibility, noting that intelligibility can never be totally separated from attitudes. The focal point of the argument has been the notion of a lingua franca core. My own view is that, stripped of its ideological baggage and bolstered by further research, the LFC represents a promising basis from which learners and teachers can make informed choices about further goals. The LFC is, after all, fundamentally a starting point for syllabus development that reflects the main principles of communicative syllabus design: a focus on elements likely to be of most communicative value to learners and a focus on what is teachable and learnable.

By stripping the LFC of its ideological baggage, I leave myself open to the accusation, to use Campo's (2011) term, of being an 'apolitical relativist' (p. 71), particularly as the sociolinguistic issues are not trivial. Attitudes can be influenced by prejudice, for example, and prejudice can have unwanted social and economic consequences for its victims. I prefer (of course) to see myself as democratic. The views of learners and teachers may seem, at least to some, to be ill-informed, inconsistent and/or contradictory. Their views are certainly complex and may also be resistant to campaigning, though, as in any democratic enterprise, campaigning can sometimes be a legitimate endeavour. The evidence from a number of studies over recent decades indicates that learners and teachers are in no hurry to abandon the (perhaps quixotic) quest for native speaker norms. This may be an inconvenient research finding, but, if we want to maintain a democratic approach, we have to accept that, at least for the time being, many NNESs aspire to NES pronunciation norms and we have to accept this aspiration without necessarily impugning the motives of those who hold such views. Views may be slow to change, but they are not immutable to change; I would be very surprised if we were having this same discussion in 50 years' time.

References

Ballard, L. (2013). Student attitudes toward accentedness of native and non-native speaking English teachers. *MSU Working Papers in SLS*, *4*, 47–73.

Brown, J. D. (2012). *New ways in teaching connected speech*. Alexandria, VA: TESOL.

Buckingham (2015). Recognising English accents in the community: Omani students' accent preferences and perceptions of nativeness. *Journal of Multilingual and Multicultural Development*, *36*(2), 182–197.

Buss, L. (2015). Beliefs and practices of Brazilian EFL teachers regarding pronunciation. *Language Teaching Research*, *12*, 1–19.

Campos, M. (2011). A critical interrogation of the prevailing teaching model(s) of English pronunciation at teacher-training college level: A Chilean evidence-based study. *Literatura y Lingüística*, *23*, 213–236.

Cook, G., & Seidlhofer, B. (1995). An applied linguist in principle and practice. In G. Cook & B. Seidlhofer (Eds), *Principle and practice in applied linguistics* (pp. 1–26). Oxford: Oxford University Press.

da Silva, R. (1999). A small-scale investigation into the intelligibility of the pronunciation of Brazilian intermediate students. *Speak Out!*, *23*, 19–25.

Dauer, R. (2005). The lingua franca core: a new model for pronunciation instruction? *TESOL Quarterly*, *39*(3), 543–550.

Deterding, D., & Kirkpatrick, A. (2006). Intelligibility and an emerging ASEAN English lingua franca. *World Englishes, 25*(3), 391–410.

Episcopo, S. (2009). Non-native speaker attitudes toward non-native English accecnts, Unpuvliched MA theses. University of Texas.

Graddol, D. (1997). *The future of English?* London: British Council.

Jenkins, J. (1997). Changing priorities for successful communication in international contexts. In A. MacLean (Ed.), *SIG Selections 1997 Special Interests in ELT* (pp. 73–79). Whitstable: IATEFL.

Jenkins, J. (1998). Which pronunciation norms and models for English as an international language? *ELT Journal, 52*(2), 119–126.

Jenkins, J. (2000). *A phonology of English as an international language.* Oxford: Oxford University Press.

Jenkins, J. (2005). Implementing an international approach to English pronunciation: The role of teacher attitudes and identity. *TESOL Quarterly, 39*(3), 535–543.

Jenkins, J. (2007). *English as a lingua franca: Attitude and identity.* Oxford: Oxford University Press.

Jenkins, J., Cogo, A., & Dewey, M. (2011). Review of developments in research into English as a lingua franca. *Language Teaching, 44*(3), 281–315.

Jodai, H., Pirhadi, J., & Taghavi, M. (2014). Attitudes to native speaker norms: Evidence from an Iranian context. *Procedia – Social and Behavioral Sciences, 98,* 789–798.

Kachru, B. (1982). *The other tongue – English across cultures.* Urbana, IL: University of Illinois Press.

Kanellou, V. (2011). *The place and practice of pronunciation teaching in the context of the EFL Classroom in Thessaloniki, Greece.* Unpublished PhD thesis, University of Cardiff.

Kelch, K., & Santana Williamson, E. (2002). ESL students' attitudes towards native- and non-native speaker instructors' accents. *CATESOL Journal, 14*(1), 58–72.

Kirkpatrick, A. (2010). Researching English as a lingua franca in Asia: The Asian Corpus of English (ACE) project. *Asian Englishes, 31*(1), 4–18.

Levis, J. (2005). Changing contexts and shifting paradigms in pronunciation teaching. *TESOL Quarterly, 39*(3), 369–376.

Lindemann, S. (2002). Listening with an attitude: A model of native-speaker comprehension of non-native speakers in the United States. *Language in Society, 31,* 419–441.

Marks, J., & Bowen, T. (2012). *The book of pronunciation: Proposals for a practical pedagogy.* Peaslake: Delta.

McArthur, T. (2001). World English and world Englishes: Trends, tensions, varieties and standards. *Language Teacher, 34,* 1–20. Retrieved from http://ltsc.ph-karlsruhe.de/McArthur.pdf.

Murphy, J. M. (2014). Intelligible, comprehensible, nonnative models in ESL/EFL pronunciation teaching. System, *42,* 258–269.

Osimk, R. (2009). Decoding sounds: An experimental approach to intelligibility in ELF. *Vienna English Working Papers, 18,* 64–89.

Pickering, L. (2009). Intonation as a pragmatic resource in ELF interaction. *Intercultural Pragmatics, 6*(2), 235–255.

Rajadurai, J. (2007). Intelligibility studies: A consideration of empirical and ideological issues. *World Englishes, 26*(1), 87–98.

Rubin, D. L. (1992). Non-language factors affecting undergraduates' judgments of non-native English-speaking teaching assistants. *Research in Higher Education, 33,* 511–531.

Scheuer, S. (2005). L1 transfer in a PC world: why not LFC again? *Poznan Studies in Contemporary Linguistics, 40,* 197–207.

Seidlhofer, B. (2004). Research perspectives on teaching English as a lingua franca. *Annual Review of Applied Linguistics, 24,* 209–239.

Sewell, A. (2013). English as a lingua franca: ontology and ideology. *ELT Journal, 67*(1), 3–10.

Sifakis, N., & Sougari, A-M. (2005). Pronunciation issues and EIL pedagogy in the periphery: A survey of Greek State School teachers' beliefs. *TESOL Quarterly, 39*(3), 467–488.

Sobkowiak, W. (2008). Why not LFC? In: K. Dziubalska-Kołaczyk and J. Przedlacka (Eds), *English pronunciation models. A changing scene* (pp. 131–176). Frankfurt am Main: Peter Lang.

Sowden, C. (2012). ELF on a mushroom: the overnight growth in English as a lingua franca. *ELT Journal, 66*(1), 89–96.

Timmis, I. (2002). Native speaker norms and international English: a classroom view. *ELT Journal, 56*(3), 240–249.

Timmis, I. (2003). *Corpora, classroom and context: The place of spoken grammar in ELT.* Unpublished PhD thesis, University of Nottingham. Retrieved from eprints.nottingham.ac.uk/12246.

Walker, R. (2010). *Teaching the pronunciation of English as a lingua franca.* Oxford: Oxford University Press.

Widdowson, H. (1994). The ownership of English. *TESOL Quarterly, 28*(2), 377–389.

31

Assessment in second language pronunciation

Okim Kang and Alyssa Kermad

Introduction

With the growing number of non-native speakers (NNSs) preparing for overseas opportunities to study, teach or work abroad, oral performance has become a subject of critical assessment as evaluators attempt to determine adequate proficiency levels for targeted abilities. High-stakes, standardized tests of English proficiency may even establish the benchmark of proficiency for NNSs to be considered for international teaching assistant positions in American universities. Employment positions may also require a certain proficiency to verify that the NNS candidate can fulfill the particular duties of that position. With all of these contexts for assessing non-native-speaking ability, the validity of pronunciation assessment is of great importance and concern.

Research has unearthed trait-relevant features that are capable of informing pronunciation dimensions on which NNSs should be assessed as an outcome of pronunciation criteria, yet it has also exposed trait-irrelevant features, such as rater background, which should not be a factor in NNS speech assessment. Furthermore, given that defining a norm is problematic in the era of English as a lingua franca, assessing L2 pronunciation faces more challenges now than ever before. It is far from simple to define objective rating criteria to distinguish proficiency levels among English language learners, yet still maintain widely accepted principles that prioritize intelligibility and successful communication for use of English in different contexts. Furthermore, using a technology-based approach to speech analysis, pronunciation assessment is becoming more informed by features that are known to impact pronunciation, and less reliant on impressionistic judgements of speech. Rater training is becoming more solicited as a means of reducing rater bias. However, there is still much to be done to ensure that oral assessment continuously becomes more refined with evidence-based operationalizations of important speech constructs.

The current chapter will cover critical issues related to pronunciation assessment, beginning first with a brief historical overview. Current issues will be described in depth including topics of reliability and validity, measurement of pronunciation constructs, rating scales and criteria, rater background characteristics, classroom-based pronunciation assessment, assessment in the context of world Englishes, and automated pronunciation assessment. We will then discuss selected current contributions and research particularly related to rubric design and scales, human analysis versus machine analysis, and pronunciation priorities, followed by recommendations for practice and future directions.

Historical perspectives

Before the quasi-independent distinctions of accentedness, comprehensibility and intelligibility came to be, pronunciation assessment often fluctuated with the times in ways comparable to the field of L2 pronunciation itself (Levis, 2005). Oftentimes in isolation, pronunciation assessment has focused on the approximation of imitation or the accuracy of segmentals, and historical perspectives and methods of language learning and teaching have often held great influence over these foci. For example, because imitation was key to the direct method (which began in the late 1800s and still continues today), successful imitation of a native speaker model was the focus of assessment. Having similar native speaker priorities, accuracy was vital to the reform movement in the 1890s, especially as Henry Sweet (1899) promoted the phonetic training of teachers and learners with the idea that the teaching and learning of sound accuracy would lead to more intelligible speech.

Again, with a focus on accuracy, during the 1940s and 1950s the overseas deployment of American soldiers and diplomats gave birth to the oral proficiency interview (OPI), highly influenced by proficiency scales from the Foreign Service Institute, which measured accent and prioritized native-like pronunciation. This time period was followed by the rise of the audiolingual method (1950s–early 1960s), in which segmental features and articulatory phonetics were predominantly emphasized until, gradually, a major change took place with the rise of the cognitive approach in the 1960s. The notion emerged that native-like pronunciation is unattainable. Around this time, Lado's (1961) work on language testing comprehensively covered pronunciation assessment, including perception and production of sound segments, stress and intonation, as well as a full incorporation of phonemics. However, even then, Lado recognized the controversial role of pronunciation in that it was either completely ignored in language testing, only valued if native-like, or adopted as intelligibility. Soon after Lado's inclusion of pronunciation assessment, communicative language teaching (1980s) turned the focus to overall successful communication skills, especially with Canale and Swain's (1980) model of communicative competence. However, pronunciation became marginalized into this model and, for many years after, it was not of primary concern.

Transforming the direction of assessment, Derwing and Munro (2005) defined the constructs of intelligibility, comprehensibility and accentedness. *Intelligibility* is 'the extent to which a listener actually understands an utterance', *comprehensibility* is 'a listener's perception of how difficult it is to understand an utterance' and *accentedness* is 'a listener's perception of how different a speaker's accent is from that of the L1 community' (p. 385). Before these independent definitions, rating scales often construed these constructs together or even equated them with accentedness.,

Gradually, native-like pronunciation began to be seen as unattainable, and an increasing amount of attention was placed on global intelligibility. Coupled with the *nativeness versus intelligibility* principle (Levis, 2005) and its prioritization of mutual intelligibility, notions of these separate constructs would pave the way for pronunciation researchers and assessors to explore more valid and reliable operationalizations of their measurements. Accuracy and native-like pronunciation have seemingly lost their ground in the pronunciation literature, and researchers are now encouraged to prioritize successful communication through global intelligibility.

Critical issues and topics

Reliability and validity of pronunciation assessment

One of the critical issues involved in assessing pronunciation is determining to what extent pronunciation methods are valid and reliable. For example, it may be possible to obtain reliability in numbers, or inter-rater reliability, but, if these conclusions cannot be extended to real-word practicalities of how these constructs play a role in one's overall pronunciation, the validity of the measures is compromised. Isaacs (2008) examined intelligibility as a criterion of pronunciation proficiency for NNS graduate students and found that, although intelligibility was an adequate assessment criterion in which raters' and researchers' ratings corresponded, it was not enough to sufficiently assess pronunciation, indicating a threshold of intelligibility.

Furthermore, while internal reliability may be attained within a certain population of listener raters, this reliability should be reported with caution. Isbell (2018) describes the weakness of using reliability coefficients, such as Cronbach's alpha, with scalar listener judgements. In his argument, a high reliability coefficient does not ensure that listeners are using the scales in the same way; it simply measures rankings of speakers across listeners. In addition, reliability may also be a function of the listener group. The listener group from which a reliability coefficient is obtained may not be a valid assessment of second language speech, for listener groups may be subject to their own biases (Lindemann & Subtirelu, 2013). Because comprehensibility and intelligibility are a 'jointly achieved effort', researchers should not fail to 'indicate to whom speech is intelligible or comprehensible and in what situations or contexts' (Lindemann & Subtirelu, 2013, p. 583). Speech that may not be intelligible or comprehensible to one group of listeners in a certain context may be perceived differently by another group of listeners in a different context. Even in 1961, Lado recognized this issue with intelligibility, describing it as a standard that is difficult to define due to listener relativity. Many factors are at play in speech assessment, including both speaker- and listener-related issues. In other words, although validity cannot be argued without measures of reliability, reliability alone is still insufficient for validity (Lindemann & Subtirelu, 2013).

Tasks can also be a concern in obtaining validity in results. The speech stimuli involved in most experimental studies do not necessarily represent authentic interaction, in that there is an absence of communication properties (such as negotiation of meaning or typical conversation repair) that occur regularly in naturally occurring conversation (Lindemann & Subtirelu, 2013). Findings have also shown that listener judgements of accentedness, comprehensibility and proficiency vary across task, with more negative judgements on more difficult tasks (Kermad & Kang, 2016). Additionally, linguistic performance also seems to vary with the task itself (Kermad & Kang, 2016). For Crowther, Trofimovich, Isaacs and Saito (2015), task was an important variable in comprehensibility ratings, with speakers receiving higher comprehensibility scores on less cognitively demanding tasks. The effect of the task should thus be a serious consideration in any assessment study.

Isaacs and Trofimovich (2012) speak of the shortcomings in reliability in regards to the way pronunciation is assessed in many high- and low-stakes speaking scales. Not only are measures of pronunciation inconsistent, but they are often too vague, unclear from relativistic wording, or a misrepresentation of distinct constructs. Overlapping at times, intelligibility, accentedness and comprehensibility are partially independent speech constructs with definable properties (Isaacs & Trofimovich, 2012; Thomson & Derwing, 2015). More detailed accounts need to be provided to determine how these constructs should be measured, including which scales of segmentals and suprasegmentals are needed, the number or points on the scale, the number of subscales, and the descriptors.

Overall, Harding (2018) mentions that issues of validity and general speaking proficiency apply to pronunciation assessment and further emphasizes that pronunciation has its own, unique issues to be grappled with as well. The validity of overall speaking performance must be ensured by clear, construct scoring criteria, administrative and scoring conditions that do not interfere with the examinee's performance, appropriate tasks to measure speaking performance, and positive end results for both the examinee and society. However, Harding stresses issues of validity that are specific to pronunciation assessment. They include defining pronunciation constructs with world Englishes in mind, using human raters as judges of intelligibility, extending scores of automated scoring systems to real-world contexts of the target language and maintaining the fine balance between pronunciation and speaker identity. All of these issues must be simultaneously entertained while acknowledging the status of English as a lingua franca.

Measuring pronunciation constructs

The first step towards being able to measure a pronunciation construct is to be able to define it (Harding, 2018) and, in turn, utilize operationalized definitions designed to measure aspects of that construct. Accentedness and comprehensibility are often measured on a rating scale while intelligibility is a bottom-up measure of meaning comprehension (see Thomson, in press, for a review). However, in general, there has been a lack of agreement in the best method for measuring them (Munro & Derwing, 1995a). *Fluency*, yet another construct with overlapping definitions, is often conflated with comprehensibility and accentedness because of its superficial similarities, but fluency is distinct from these constructs (Thomson, 2015). A criterion that makes fluency so different from intelligibility, comprehensibility and accentedness is that the latter three rely on listener's judgement: intelligibility is operationalized by how much of a speaker's intended utterance a listener is able to understand; comprehensibility is operationalized by the facility in which a listener understands a speaker; and accentedness is operationalized by how different a speaker sounds from a listener. Fluency, on the other hand, although allowing listener judgements, concerns itself with more internal cognitive processes, such as speaker planning and production, on which these judgements are based (Thomson, 2015). On that note, these constructs should be measured separately in order to make more valid assessments of one's pronunciation, not conflating degree of accetendess per se with intelligibility or comprehensibility.

Instrumental and auditory analyses have been quite successful in determining precise, quantifiable estimators of these constructs. Although fluency is often a product of listener judgements, it is highly reflective of more temporal features. Derwing, Rossiter, Munro and Thomson (2004) found that the measure of standardized pruned syllables (measure calculated after removing all types of dysfluencies) accounted for 65 per cent or more of the variance in fluency judgements. Other measures of fluency analysed in this study included the mean length of the run, filled and unfilled pauses, speech rate and syllable counts (including self-corrections, self-repetitions, false starts, non-lexical filled pauses and asides). Fluency measured in part by speech rate has also been found to have an important impact on the overall assigned score of test-takers' speech production (Iwashita, Brown, McNamara & O'Hagan, 2008). Kormos and Dénes (2004) found that, for both native and non-native listeners, speech rate, mean length of the utterance, phonation time ratio (defined in this study as the proportion of speaking time to the time spent preparing the speech sample) and the number of stressed words per minute were the best indicators of fluency scores. Kang and Pickering (2013) confirm that the best predictors of L2 performance judgements often include some or all of the following features: syllables per second, articulation rate, phonation time ratio and mean length of run.

Advanced acoustic measures in combination with native speakers' overall judgements of proficiency have been productive in elucidating the relationship between linguistic features and other pronunciation constructs. Using spectrograms, pitch/fundamental frequency (F_0) and intensity indices, Kang, Rubin and Pickering (2010) analysed 29 suprasegmental features of rate, pause, stress, pitch and paratone (i.e. low termination tones, average height of onset pitch, average height of terminating pitch and average paratone pause length). They found that suprasegmental features jointly predicted 50 per cent of the variance in listener judgements of oral proficiency and comprehensibility. Similarly, further acoustic analyses revealed that listener ratings of accent for international teaching assistants' speech were best predicted by pitch range and word stress measures, and comprehensibility scores were mostly associated with speaking rates (Kang, 2010). Differences in speech measures related to accentedness and comprehensibility have been noted by Trofimovich and Isaacs (2012). They found that accentedness is largely related to rhythm and segmental accuracy, but grammatical and lexical features are tied more to comprehensibility. Word stress is a feature common to both of these constructs.

Acoustic and auditory research has also informed intelligibility. Lexical stress placement, for example, has been found to be important to a speaker's intelligibility (Field, 2005) along with prominence (also known as 'primary sentence stress') (Hahn, 2004). Segmental accuracy has also been strongly linked to a speaker's intelligibility (Fayer & Krasinski, 1987). In a more exploratory approach, Kang, Moran and Thomson (2015b) used a combination of five different measures (i.e. true/false sentences, nonsense sentences, filtered sentences, scalar judgement and transcription) to assess the intelligibility of English speakers from three circles of the English-speaking world (see Kachru, 1992). Of the five measures (true/false statements, scalar judgements, nonsense sentences, filtered sentences and transcription), nonsensical sentences were the best predictor of the speakers' intelligibility. However, segmental, supra-segmental and temporal fluency features predicted intelligibility scores differently, depending on the task measure. That is, the nonsense sentences, filtered sentences and transcription method mostly involved the listeners' attention to the phonemic level sound recognition, whereas the true/false statements required the listeners' global processing of the utterance so that fluency and prosody were more important than sounds. Scalar judgement seemed to be the measure in which listeners made a more impressionistic, subjective rating of the speaker's intelligibility. Important to keep in mind, however, is that these linguistic relationships with intelligibility were closely tied to the operationalization method.

Rating scales and criteria

Rating scales: Rating scales have often been used to measure listener judgements for speech dimensions such as proficiency, accent or comprehensibility – constructs that can rely on impressionistic judgement. Oral proficiency, for example, has been measured on a composite scale with high reliability by Kang (2012). Scalar (interval or sliding) judgements are especially common operationalizations of accentedness and/or comprehensibility (Kang, 2010; Kang, Moran & Thomson, 2015a; Munro & Derwing, 1995a, 1995b, 2001; Saito, Trofimovich & Isaacs, in press; Saito, Trofimovich & Isaacs, 2016; Southwood & Flege, 1999) with a variety of scalar points. These scales are appropriate for these constructs when they are defined as the representation of the continuum on which listeners make impressionistic judgements.

Ratings scales for measuring intelligibility, however, are not so common when intelligibility is considered a binary phenomenon (i.e. all-or-nothing). Other methods have more commonly measured intelligibility including transcription methods (Derwing & Munro, 1997; Gass & Varonis, 1984; Kang, Moran & Thomson, 2015a, 2015b; Munro & Derwing, 1995a; Munro, Derwing & Morton, 2006), comprehension questions (Hahn, 2004), cloze tests (Smith, 1992), true/false questions (Kang, Moran & Thomson, 2015b), nonsense sentences (Kang, Moran & Thomson, 2015b), and pause group boundaries (Zielinski, 2008). Yet, at the same time, scalar operationalizations have been justified on a five-point scale (Fayer & Krasinski, 1987), on a seven-point scale (Anderson-Hsieh, Johnson & Koehler, 1992), or even a scale of 1–100 for the percentage of words understood (Isaacs, 2008; Kang, Moran & Thomson, 2015b). These studies indicate that the criteria of ratings scales are closely aligned to a construct's operationalization, yet because of intelligibility's complex operationalization there is a lack of agreement on how best to measure this construct (Munro & Derwing, 1995a).

Rating criteria: Current standardized tests of English proficiency use speaking rubrics from which raters evaluate non-native speech. Although pronunciation has at last permeated these rubrics, there are still some weaknesses with the rubrics themselves. Ghanem and Kang (2018) compared and contrasted rubrics from CELA (Cambridge English Language Assessment), the Test of English as a Foreign Language (TOEFL) IBT (Internet-based test), and the International English Language Testing System (IELTS) to evaluate how research-informed phonological features of important pronunciation constructs are used in these rubrics. Some issues with the rubrics are that the descriptors are either too vague or too general, fluency remains highly semantic (i.e. defined by definitions using terms such as speech flow instead of phonological features), and prosody (i.e. intonation, stress and prominence) is under-represented. In their review, the authors provide recommendations for future rubric improvement.

Rater background characteristics

Although automated speech recognizers (ASR) and computer-assisted instrumental analyses are becoming well-integrated and established within the field of pronunciation research, human raters are still the most common means of assessing pronunciation. However, human raters are not without bias. Matched-guise studies and studies on linguistic stereotyping have illustrated that human listeners make moral, intellectual and aesthetic choices based on pictures of speakers (Kang & Rubin, 2009). This type of linguistic stereotyping becomes even more prevalent when the speakers are members of stigmatized groups, or when listeners think that speakers are members of these groups. Kang and Rubin (2009) found that listeners' attitudinal and background factors accounted for 18–23 per cent of the variance in listeners' judgements. As these attitudes can be quite profound, Subtirelu and Lindemann (2016) propose several approaches to improve communication between L1 English speakers and those from other English varieties.

Gass and Varonis (1984) found that listener variables of topic familiarity, familiarity with non-native speech in general, a specific non-native accent or a particular non-native speaker can all predict the comprehensibility of non-native speech. Gass and Varonis call these values and beliefs about the world 'belief spaces' (p. 81) because they allow listeners to interpret utterances based on their notions of the real world. The issue of shared L1s has been shown to both improve and impede listener comprehension. When listeners share characteristics of the speakers' L1, comprehension can be improved. In an analysis of differential item functioning, Harding (2012) found evidence of listener bias in shared L1s. This shared L1 effect can be applied to humans as raters in that shared L1s may contribute to mutual intelligibility. Not only can shared L1s contribute to mutual intelligibility, but more familiar native languages may affect listeners' judgements of test-takers' speech (Fayer & Krasinski, 1987; Harding, 2012; Major, Fitzmaurice, Bunta & Balasubramanian, 2002; Scales, Wennerstrom, Richard & Wu, 2006). Winke, Gass and Myford (2013) added to this body of research with their findings that raters were much more lenient with test-takers when raters had learned the test-takers' L1. On the other hand, Fayer and Krasinski (1987) found that English listeners of Spanish L1 speakers of English were significantly more tolerant and less annoyed than Spanish listeners of Spanish L1 speakers of English. Using TOEFL listening comprehension tests, Ockey and French (2014) noted that when accents were noticeable but did not require listeners to concentrate on listening any more than usual they did not significantly affect comprehension scores regardless of their L1s. Listener bias can thus stem from many different factors, and when choosing humans as raters to measure non-native speech these issues must be taken into consideration in order to inform the process of rater training and reduce trait-irrelevant variance.

Classroom-based pronunciation assessment

When the assessment of pronunciation is brought to the everyday classroom, modes and methods of assessment take on different forms. Classroom assessment occurs regularly and the turnover is rapid. In a classroom context, teachers are often alone at regularly assessing numerous speaking samples, in-class speaking productions, role play activities, pronunciation logs and the like. The goal then of classroom-based assessment is to utilize and adapt methods of assessment informed by relevant research in the field.

Classroom assessment often needs to assess several facets of pronunciation, including perception (e.g. listening discrimination), production (e.g. speaking) and the application of relevant phonological rules (Celce-Murcia, Brinton, Goodwin & Griner, 2010). Celce-Murcia et al. present several methods of assessing pronunciation, including diagnostic procedures, ongoing evaluation with feedback, and classroom achievement tests.

Diagnostic measures are a part of the needs assessment process in which teachers holistically evaluate the perception and production at the class and individual levels. Diagnostic measures of perception can include consonant–vowel discrimination, recognition of word stress, prominence, intonation and reduced speech. However, when engaging in diagnostic procedures for both perception and production, it is central to maintain focus on segmental features that are important to intelligibility (see Brown, 1991; Catford, 1987). Suprasegmental features are also important for overall discourse and connected speech purposes (Levis & Grant, 2003).

For diagnostic measures of production, it is most comprehensive to obtain both a standardized read aloud sample as well as a spontaneous speech sample. The read aloud sample allows teachers to assess aspects of pronunciation that may not occur often in free speech, such as certain consonant clusters or intonation patterns. On the other hand, read aloud tasks may not be as natural as free speech, and they may induce more errors. Kermad and Kang (2016) found that speakers had significantly more segmental deviations on the read aloud task compared with other tasks. Free speech samples, however, allow teachers to assess meaning over form.

Classroom-based assessment should also include ongoing evaluation with feedback in which the teacher's role becomes crucial (Celce-Murcia et al., 2010). Based on the diagnostic measures and needs assessment analysis, the teacher then has two roles in the process of ongoing assessment: (a) to determine the progress of students in order to individualize the curriculum and (b) to provide continuous feedback on individual progress.

As Morley (1991) explained, the role of the student is to adjust his/her pronunciation, but, before a student can do this, the educator's role becomes very important. It is an educator's role to diagnose students' pronunciation and assign certain areas in which students can begin to self-monitor and adjust their pronunciation. One way in which teachers can go about assessing these areas is to incorporate Morley's dual-focus framework (1991, 1994). This is a framework in which both micro and macro levels of focus are included in pronunciation instruction and assessment. Macro levels of assessment focus on the communicative use of segmental and suprasegmental features, while the micro level hones in on specific points of speech production.

Pronunciation assessment in the context of world Englishes

In the context of world Englishes, the orientation of pronunciation assessment shifts to reflect current notions of intelligibility for speakers in English as an international language (EIL) or English as a lingua franca (FLF) settings. NNSs now outnumber NSs of English (Jenkins, 2000). What this means is that NNSs of English are, more often than not, communicating with other NNSs of English. These NNSs around the world have adapted the language for their own uses, creating a variety of world Englishes. Accordingly, language assessment scholars (e.g. Hamp-Lyons & Davies, 2008; Taylor, 2006) argue that English proficiency tests should now adopt an EIL approach over reference to traditionally standard varieties in order to recognize EIL's greater heterogeneity of norms. Jenkins (2006) further adds that there is no longer a rationale for speakers from non-traditional English-speaking contexts to defer to native speakers and their particular standards of English. Given the increasing acceptance of world Englishes and its resulting consequences for language assessment, L2 pronunciation also faces different directionality.

Jenkins and Leung posit that languages testers need to 'assess whether ELF users' English is fit for ELF use' (2013, p. 8). Language testers can begin to implement this usage-based testing. Testers could, for example, acknowledge ELF variants, give credit to the use of successful ELF accommodation strategies and penalize native English forms that result in unsuccessful ELF communication (Jenkins, 2006). Standardized tests such as the academic Pearson Test of English, the International English Language Testing System, the TOEFL, and the Test of English for International Communication (TOEIC) claim to have international status, yet they all test competence in English as a 'foreign language', which implies that the test-taker is learning the target language in order to communicate in the target community with native speakers of English. To this end, deviations from the standard (inner circle) varieties are considered errors. Research in the area of ELF is thus advocating for participant-driven language testing for 'English as a linguistic resource in English as a Lingua Franca contemporary conditions' (Jenkins & Leung, 2013, pp. 8–9).

It is important to consider the end goal of the assessment. If TOEIC and TOEFL are being used for admission to American universities, would ELF norms be appropriate? Considering the wide range of accents present in the United States, it would seem that ELF patterns may be acceptable, yet biases towards accented English still exist (Kang & Rubin, 2009). On the other hand, considering English-medium universities in other countries where students from many different language backgrounds are often admitted, perhaps ELF norms are more relevant and should be accepted without penalty in these assessment contexts. Speaking assessment will eventually need to grapple with these issues, considering the different contexts in which English is used. Although standardized tests have begun to incorporate more standard English varieties, testers must also come to terms with the fact that learners may encounter other non-standard English varieties.

Speech technology and automated pronunciation assessment

Speech technology, including computer-assisted instrumental analysis programs and automated scoring systems, is becoming much more common in pronunciation assessment owing to 'the possible subjective nature of listener comprehension, the complexity of rater reliability, and the validity of the performance itself' (Kang & Pickering, 2013, p. 1047). With the advancements of speech science, computer-assisted instruments are being used to visualize and quantify acoustic (e.g. fundamental frequency, amplitude and spectral behaviour of intonation) and temporal (voice time and duration) aspects of human speech. Computer-assisted speech analysis is primarily conducted through the freeware program Praat (www.praat.org), but also through the KayPentax Computerized Speech Laboratory (CSL) (www.kayelemetrics.com) (see Kang et al., 2010; Pickering, 2004). Through both of these programs, speech can be analysed at the segmental (e.g. measures of consonants, voice onset times (VOTs) and vowel formants) and suprasegmental (e.g. speaking rates, intonation and various prosodic features) levels. This technology is being used in research to quantify human ratings; it is also beginning to be implemented in the classroom.

Using similar instrumentally defined measures as those used in Praat or CSL, automated scoring technology is being used in language testing for the speaking components of some standardized tests. Ordinate Corporation's Versant (otherwise known as PhonePass) and the Educational Testing Service's SpeechRater are two examples of automated scoring programs that are used to automatically detect accented speech. What is not known, however, is how valid these programs are in assigning test scores or how exactly these scores are assigned (Chapelle & Chung, 2010).

Some important issues of concern for those involved in internal processes of ASR are (a) the reference model which the system regards as the standard, well-defined model, which is different enough from learner speech, (b) whether the model is speaker-dependent or -independent, or (c) whether the speech assessed by the model is constrained or unconstrained. These issues are important in establishing how the model functions and assesses non-native speech.

Current contributions and research

Rubric design and rating scales

Defined by Isaacs and Thomson (2013), rating scales 'provide the framework within which human raters score second language (L2) performance, which is taken to be an indicator of L2 learners' ability on the construct being measured' (p. 135). However, shortcomings with pronunciation rating scales include how they are informed and how they are designed. Rating scales are often informed by theory, and because the role of pronunciation has failed to be recognized and incorporated in existing models of communicative competence, ratings scales have often neglected pronunciation as a rating criterion (Isaacs, 2014). The rating scales that do include representations of pronunciation are often too vague to articulate a clear construct (Ghanem & Kang, 2018; Isaacs, 2014). This vagueness makes it difficult for raters to assign scores, not knowing exactly what features are associated with a definition. Finally, rating scales are often known to conflate what should be distinguishable constructs.

An attempt at depicting pronunciation constructs in a pronunciation assessment rubric is the strength of accent scale by Ockey and French (2014). Having five bands (Band 5 as the highest level and Band 1 as the lowest), this rubric measured the strength of one's accent, in addition to the effect on comprehensibility and intelligibility. A possible concern of this approach is that Ockey and French's band descriptors tap into accentedness, comprehensibility and intelligibility all at once, even though these constructs are known to be partially independent. For example, a speaker's accent can be noticeably different from what someone is used to, but it does not necessarily lead to more difficulty in processing the speech or decreased understanding. Detailed rubrics informed by research with construct-relevant phonological features itemized for each separate construct are needed to validate rater judgements of non-native speech.

Another common concern researchers must face when assessing any given construct or sub-construct concerns the optimal number of points on a given rating scale (e.g. five-point, seven-point, nine-point etc.). Isaacs and Thomson (2013) examined this issue directly. Twenty novice and experienced raters were assigned at random a five-point or nine-point rating scale in order to assess the comprehensibility, accentedness and fluency of second language speakers in Canada. Results showed no differences in mean scores between the five-point and nine-point scales, although Rasch probability plots indicated scale category overlap most often when the nine-point scale was utilized. The seven-point scale has also been used to rate comprehensibility and fluency and has produced strong inter-rater reliability (intraclass correlation coefficients issued .95 for comprehensibility and .97 for fluency) (see Derwing, Munro & Thomson, 2008). What research has shown, however, is that, despite the number of scalar points, novice listeners have difficulty using numerical scales (Isaacs & Thomson, 2013; Isbell, 2018).

Human analysis versus machine analysis

Novice raters are often used in pronunciation research for the reason of giving instantaneous, global judgements, and also because findings have indicated that they can make judgements on inherent speech properties (Derwing et al., 2004). Trained raters have also been quite successful in minimizing trait-irrelevant variance in listener judgements (Kang, Rubin & Kermad, in preparation. However, bias, severity, consistency and fatigue are all potential issues that may arise from using humans as raters.

Instrumental analyses, on the other hand, help to avoid subjectivity to some extent. However, even computer-assisted quantitative measures must be interpreted and coded by human researchers, and in L2 assessment these measures are often compared to native speakers in order to quantify deviations from the 'norm' (Kang & Pickering, 2013; Lindemann & Subtirelu, 2013). Nowadays, it is common to not necessarily replace human judgements with computer-assisted quantifiable analyses but to use these two in conjunction (see Derwing, Munro, Thomson & Rossiter, 2009; Kang, 2010; Kang et al., 2010; Kang et al., 2015b; Kormos & Dénes, 2004). This methodology can be quite effective in looking at properties of the speech stream to better understand the relationship between linguistic measures and human judgements.

Automated speech recognizer (ASR) systems are attempting to support the assessment of human raters. These system ratings are first being compared to human ratings in order to establish human–computer correlations (see de Jong and Wempe, 2007). Zechner, Higgins, Xi and Williamson (2009) presented SpeechRater, a speech recognizer that was trained on non-native English speech data to score fluency-based measures for the Internet-based test TOEFL IBT. The .57 human–machine rating correlation score was high enough to warrant the use of SpeechRater in TOEFL practice online speaking tests since 2006. In more recent studies, using test-takers' responses to spoken test prompts in the Cambridge English Language Assessment (CELA), Johnson, Kang and Ghanem (2016) demonstrated that the correlation between the computer's calculated proficiency levels and the official CELA proficiency levels was .72. What is particularly interesting in this study is that the correlation improved substantially by solely incorporating 35 suprasegmental features (i.e. speech rate, pausing, stress and intonation).

The decision regarding whether or not to use humans or machines as raters should not be an 'all-or-nothing' decision. According to Kang and Pickering (2013), there are possible solutions to overcome the limitations of this dilemma: (a) using a combination of auditory and instrumental analysis and (b) checking inter-/intra-analyst reliability to ensure the consistency of the analyses. The instrumental analysis can be subject to perceptual subjectivity, so it 'should not be the sole basis for objective interpretation of candidates' scores in pronunciation assessment, but instead a useful methodology to identify information about a candidate's speech that would contribute to scoring decision-making or to assessment rubric development' (Kang & Pickering, 2013, p. 1048). In other words, there is still no perfect assessment method, and triangulation of data analysis can lead to the most rounded conclusions about properties of non-native speech.

Pronunciation priorities

In the production of L2 speech, researchers have studied at length the relative impact of suprasegmentals and segmentals on listeners' judgements of NNSs' speech. It is now known that suprasegmentals account for 50 per cent of the variance in NS ratings of oral proficiency (Kang et al., 2010) and segmentals are also quite influential (Fayer & Krasinkski, 1987). However, not all pronunciation features carry equal importance for intelligibility purposes. The hierarchy of segmental importance is called the functional load (Brown, 1991; Catford, 1987). Segmental errors at the top of the hierarchy are more critical than others, putting speakers at a higher risk of not being understood, whereas those with a reduced functional load are less severe. The functional load theory is relatively well established; however, few studies have considered the functional load in pronunciation judgements. In 2006, Munro and Derwing empirically tested and confirmed the notions of the functional load theory and found that high functional load errors had a significant impact on listeners' ratings of accentedness and comprehensibility, more so than low functional load errors. Kang (2013) and Kang and Moran (2014) made further efforts to advance the field by classifying functional load deviations with respect to how they affected L2 speech assessment across proficiency levels. Findings of these studies indicated that high functional load deviations caused significant differences across proficiency levels, but not so much with low functional load deviations. Implications from these studies should inform not only L2 instruction but L2 pronunciation assessment as well.

Recommendations for practice and future directions

Although pronunciation assessment has advanced a great deal, especially in how it has been recognized by standardized testing companies and incorporated into their speaking rubrics, assessors still need to grapple with the role of assessment under the nativeness and intelligibility principles (see Levis, 2005). Although evidence suggests that instruction should be guided by the intelligibility principle, accuracy still permeates facets of teaching and assessment. Yet, when these two dimensions (teaching and assessment) are not in congruence, learners can be unprepared for testing situations of oral performance with unfamiliar benchmarks. However, it is not fathomable to assume that all English learners worldwide have similar classroom situations that make them ideally prepared for the demands of standardized testing situations. Some parts of the world may have dominant teaching paradigms (e.g. the grammar translation method, the audiolingual approach or the communicative method), which makes universal teaching consistency unattainable. Furthermore, some approaches to teaching have either prioritized pronunciation teaching or completely ignored it (Levis, 2005). When pronunciation teaching is a focus of classroom instruction, the variety of instruction (e.g. inner/outer/expanding circle varieties, see Kachru, 1992) also becomes an issue. In this respect, pronunciation assessment rubrics must become more refined and evidence-based so that they can be more valid in establishing pronunciation thresholds applicable to learners from diverse native language backgrounds and classroom experiences. Future research may also investigate the effect of the classroom focus in different English contexts on assessment outcomes.

Whether or not there can be values assigned to pronunciation thresholds is also a question future research might answer. Work is already under way in exploring potential thresholds of intelligibility. Isaacs (2008) has found implications that a threshold exists for NNS graduate students in a Canadian, English-medium university, but what exactly corresponds to that threshold has much potential. Kang et al. (2015a) reported on an exploratory study seeking to determine what specific features of accented speech make it difficult for global listeners to process. Results indicate that it is possible to identify particular features of English speech varieties that can most likely lead to a breakdown in communication, and that the number of such features present in a particular speakers' speech can predict intelligibility. Implications of the existence of the threshold can be of importance to assessing pronunciation, but having actual values assigned to this cut-off point can be even more informative in influencing rubrics and rating scales. Future research may also explore thresholds of accentedness and comprehensibility and how a threshold for one of these dimensions might have positive or negative consequences for other pronunciation dimensions.

Understanding the role of listeners in speech assessment has also become quite critical, especially as research has exposed more of the listener biases that exist in speech perception and assessment contexts. Although rater training has dramatically decreased the variance from these variables (Kang, Rubin & Kermad, in preparation), more linguistic precision in speaking rubrics is needed, not only to clearly separate and maintain consistency of distinct pronunciation dimensions (such as accentedness, comprehensibility and intelligibility) but also to increase the objectivity of speech assessment. Attention to high and low functional load segmentals can also be of great value in this respect.

The future of assessment will become strongly influenced by the development and success of machines being trained to mimic the accuracy of human ratings of accented speech through automated scoring systems. Efforts have been made to combine the skills of phonetician experts and computer scientists to create an automated scoring system that can establish high correlations with human ratings (r = .68) (Johnson & Kang, 2016; Kang & Johnson, 2015) or (r = .72) (Johnson et al., 2016). The SpeechRater version (deployed) reached r = .55 human–computer correlations. Evanini and Wang (2013) reached the correlation of r = .62 by assessing the spoken English responses given by non-native children in an English proficiency assessment (TOEFL Junior Comprehensive Assessment) of middle school students. Developments in speech recognition programs such as these can certainly advance the course of pronunciation assessment history. Now that linguistic features are being more widely researched and attributed to speech constructs, machines can be developed by these different sets of features in order to obtain more reliable estimates of NNSs' speaking scores. The improvement of this ASR approach to speech assessment is certainly necessary.

On a final note, the utmost goal of pronunciation assessment is to ensure that listeners' ratings of pronunciation performance are valid and a true reflection of NNSs' English proficiency level. The above areas of future research are only select paths that may lead to this goal, yet there are many more. What is encouraging is that researchers, assessors and educators have gleaned a renewed interest in pronunciation, and, as their contributions become more in sync, assessment methods can become more precise and valid.

Further reading

Isaacs, T., & Trofimovich, P. (2017). *Second language pronunciation assessment: Interdisciplinary perspectives*. Bristol: Multilingual Matters.

Kang, O., & Ginther, A. (in press). *Assessment in second language pronunciation*. New York, NY: Routledge.

References

Anderson-Hsieh, J., Johnson, R., & Koehler, K. (1992). The relationship between native speaker judgments of nonnative pronunciation and deviance in segmentals, prosody, and syllable structure. *Language Learning, 42,* 529–555.

Brown, A. (1991). Functional load and the teaching of pronunciation. In A. Brown (Ed.), *Teaching English pronunciation: A book of readings* (pp. 211–224). New York, NY, and London: Routledge.

Canale, M., & Swain, M. (1980). Theoretical bases of communicative approaches to second language teaching and testing. *Applied Linguistics, 1,* 1–57.

Catford, J. C. (1987). Phonetics and the teaching of pronunciation: A systemic description of English phonology. In J. Morley (Ed.), *Current perspectives on pronunciation: Practices anchored in theory* (pp. 87–100). Washington, DC: TESOL.

Celce-Murcia, M., Brinton, D. M., Goodwin, J. M., & Griner, B. (2010). *Teaching pronunciation: A course book and reference guide*. Cambridge: Cambridge University Press.

Chapelle, C. A., & Chung, Y. R. (2010). The promise of NLP and speech processing technologies in language assessment. *Language Testing, 27,* 301–315.

Crowther, D., Trofimovich, P., Isaacs, T., & Saito, K. (2015). Does a speaking task affect second language comprehensibility? *The Modern Language Journal, 99,* 80–95.

Derwing, T. M., & Munro, M. J. (1997). Accent, intelligibility, and comprehensibility: Evidence from four L1s. *Studies in Second Language Acquisition, 19,* 1–16.

Derwing, T. M., & Munro, M. J. (2005). Second language accent and pronunciation teaching: A research-based approach. *TESOL Quarterly, 39,* 379–397.

Derwing, T. M., Munro, M. J., & Thomson, R. I. (2008). A longitudinal study of ESL learners' fluency and comprehensibility development. *Applied Linguistics, 29,* 359–380.

Derwing, T. M., Munro, M. J., Thomson, R. I., & Rossiter, M. J. (2009). The relationship between L1 fluency and L2 fluency development. *Studies in Second Language Acquisition, 31,* 533–557.

Derwing, T. M., Rossiter, M. J., Munro, M. J., & Thomson, R. I. (2004). Second language fluency: Judgments on different tasks. *Language Learning, 54,* 655–679.

Evanini, K., & Wang, X. (2013). Automated speech scoring for non-native middle school students with multiple task types. In *INTERSPEECH-2013* (pp. 2435–2439).

Fayer, J. M., & Krasinski, E. (1987). Native and nonnative judgments of intelligibility and irritation. *Language Learning, 37*, 313–326.

Field, J. (2005). Intelligibility and the listener: The role of lexical stress. *TESOL Quarterly, 39*, 399–423.

Gass, S. M., & Varonis, E. M. (1984). The effect of familiarity on the comprehensibility of nonnative speech. *Language Learning, 34*, 65–89.

Ghanem, R., & Kang, O. (2018). Pronunciation features in rating criteria. In O. Kang & A. Ginther (Eds), *Assessment in second language pronunciation*, pp. 115–136. London: Routledge.

Hahn, L. D. (2004). Primary stress and intelligibility: Research to motivate the teaching of suprasegmentals. *TESOL Quarterly, 38*, 201–223.

Hamp-Lyons, L., & Davies, A. (2008). The English of English tests: Bias revisited. *World Englishes, 27*, 27–39.

Harding, L. (2012). Accent, listening assessment and the potential for a shared-L1 advantage: A DIF perspective. *Language Testing, 29*, 163–180.

Harding, L. (2018). Validity in pronunciation assessment. In O. Kang & A. Ginther (Eds), *Assessment in second language pronunciation*, pp. 30–48. London: Routledge.

Isaacs, T. (2008). Towards defining a valid assessment criterion of pronunciation proficiency in non-native English speaking graduate students. *Canadian Modern Language Review, 64*, 555–580.

Isaacs, T. (2014). Assessing pronunciation. In A. J. Kunnan (Ed.), *The companion to language assessment* (vol. 1, pp. 140–155). Hoboken, NJ: Wiley-Blackwell.

Isaacs, T., & Thomson, R. I. (2013). Rater experience, rating scale length, and judgments of L2 pronunciation: Revisiting research conventions. *Language Assessment Quarterly, 10*, 135–159.

Isaacs, T., & Trofimovich, P. (2012). Deconstructing comprehensibility. *Studies in Second Language Acquisition, 34*, 475–505.

Isbell, D. R. (2018). Assessing pronunciation for research purposes with listener-based numerical scales. In O. Kang & A. Ginther (Eds), *Assessment in second language pronunciation*, pp. 89–111. London: Routledge.

Iwashita, N., Brown, A., McNamara, T., & O'Hagan S. (2008). Assessed levels of second language speaking proficiency: How distinct? *Applied Linguistics, 29*, 24–29.

Jenkins, J. (2000). *The phonology of English as an international language*. Oxford: Oxford University Press.

Jenkins, J. (2006). The spread of EIL: A testing time for testers. *English Language Teaching Journal, 60*, 42–50.

Jenkins, J. and Leung, C. (2013). English as a lingua franca. *The companion to language assessment*. IV:13:95, 1605–1616.

Johnson, D., & Kang, O. (2016). Automatic prosodic tone choice classification with Brazil's intonation model. *International Journal of Speech Technology, 19*(1), 95–109.

Johnson, D., Kang, O., & Ghanem, R. (2016). Language proficiency rating: Human versus machine. *Proceedings of the Pronunciation in Second Language Learning and Teaching, 9*, 119–129.

de Jong, N. H., & Wempe, T. (2007). Automatic measurement of speech rate in spoken Dutch. *ACLC Working Papers, 2*, 49–58.

Kachru, B. B. (1992). *The other tongue: English across cultures*. Urbana, IL: University of Illinois Press.

Kang, O. (2010). Relative salience of suprasegmental features on judgments of L2 comprehensibility and accentedness. *System, 38*, 301–315.

Kang, O. (2012). Impact of rater characteristics and prosodic features of speaker accentedness on ratings of international teaching assistants' oral performance. *Language Assessment Quarterly, 9*(3), 249–269.

Kang, O. (2013). Relative impact of pronunciation features on ratings of non-native speakers' oral proficiency. In J. Levis & K. LeVelle (Eds), *Proceedings of the 4th Pronunciation in Second Language Learning and Teaching Conference, August 2012* (pp. 10–15). Ames, IA: Iowa State University.

Kang, O., & Johnson, D. O. (2015). Comparison of inter-rater reliability of human and computer prosodic annotation using Brazil's prosody model. *English Linguistics Research, 4*, 58–68.

Kang, O., & Moran, M. (2014). Functional loads of pronunciation features in non-native speakers' oral assessment. *TESOL Quarterly, 48*, 176–187.

Kang, O., Moran, M., & Thomson, R. (2015a). *Intelligibility of different varieties of English: The effects of incorporating 'accented' English into high-stakes assessment*. Paper presented at the American Association for Applied Linguistics conference, Toronto, Canada.

Kang, O., Moran, M., & Thomson, R. (2015b). *Measures of intelligibility in different varieties of world Englishes*. Paper presented at the Pronunciation in Second Language Learning and Teaching conference, Dallas, TX.

Kang, O., & Pickering, L. (2013). Using acoustic and temporal analysis for assessing speaking. In A. J. Kunnan (Ed.), *The companion to language assessment* (pp. 1047–1062). Hoboken, NJ: Wiley-Blackwell.

Kang, O., & Rubin, D. (2009). Reverse linguistic stereotyping: Measuring the effect of listener expectations on speech evaluation. *Journal of Language and Social Psychology, 28*, 441–456.

Kang, O., Rubin, D., & Kermad, A. (in preparation). The effect of training on reducing rater bias in oral proficiency assessment.

Kang, O., Rubin, D., & Pickering, L. (2010). Suprasegmental measures of accentedness and judgments of language learner proficiency in oral English. *The Modern Language Journal, 94*, 554–566.

Kermad, A., & Kang, O. (2016). The validity of pronunciation measures: Relative Impact of assessment methods on learners' pronunciation. Paper presented at Second Language Research Form (SLRF). New York, NY.

Kormos, J., & Dénes, M. (2004). Exploring measures and perceptions of fluency in the speech of second language learners. *System, 32*, 145–164.

Lado, R. (1961). *Language testing: The construction and use of foreign language tests*. London: Longman.

Levis, J. M. (2005). Changing contexts and shifting paradigms in pronunciation teaching. *TESOL Quarterly, 39*, 369–377.

Levis, J. M., & Grant, L. (2003). Integrating pronunciation into ESL/EFL classrooms. *TESOL Journal, 12*, 13–19.

Lindemann, S., & Subtirelu, N. (2013). Reliably biased: The role of listener expectation in the perception of second language speech and its implications for research and pedagogy. *Language Learning, 63*, 567–594.

Major, R. C., Fitzmaurice, S. F., Bunta, F., & Balasubramanian, C. (2002). The effects of nonnative accents on listening comprehension: Implications for ESL assessment. *TESOL Quarterly, 36*, 173–190.

Morley, J. (1991). The pronunciation component in teaching English to speakers of other languages. *TESOL Quarterly, 25*, 481–520.

Morley, J. (1994). A multidemensional curriculum design for speech-pronunciation instruction. In J. Morley (Ed.), *Pronunciation pedagogy and theory: New views, new directions*. Alexandria, VA: TESOL.

Munro, M. J., & Derwing, T. M. (1995a). Foreign accent, comprehensibility, and intelligibility in the speech of second language learners. *Language Learning, 45*, 73–97.

Munro, M. J., & Derwing, T. M. (1995b). Processing time, accent, and comprehensibility in the perception of native and foreign-accented speech. *Language and Speech, 38*, 289–306.

Munro, M. J., & Derwing, T. M. (2001). Modeling perceptions of the accentedness and comprehensibility of L2 speech the role of speaking rate. *Studies in Second Language Acquisition, 23*, 451–468.

Munro, M. J., & Derwing, T. M. (2006). The functional load principle in ESL pronunciation instruction: An exploratory study. *System, 34*, 520–531.

Munro, M. J., Derwing, T. M., & Morton, S. L. (2006). The mutual intelligibility of L2 speech. *Studies in Second Language Acquisition, 28*, 111–131.

Ockey, G. J., & French, R. (2014). From one to multiple accents on a test of L2 listening comprehension. *Applied Linguistics*, 1–14.

Pickering, L. (2004). The structure and function of intonational paragraphs in native and nonnative speaker instructional discourse. *English for Specific Purposes, 23*, 19–43.

Saito, K., Trofimovich, P., & Isaacs, T. (2016). Second language speech production: Investigating linguistic correlates of comprehensibility and accentedness for learners at different ability levels. *Applied Psycholinguistics, 37*, 217–240.

Saito, K., Trofimovich, P., & Isaacs, T. (2017). Using listener judgments to investigate linguistic influences on L2 comprehensibility and accentedness: A validation and generalization study. *Applied Linguistics*.

Scales, J., Wennerstrom, A., Richard, D., & Wu, S. H. (2006). Language learners' perception of accent. *TESOL Quarterly, 40,* 715–737.

Smith, L. E. (1992). Spread of English and issues of intelligibility. In B. B. Kachru (Ed.), *The other tongue: English across cultures* (2nd ed., pp. 75–90). Urbana, IL: University of Illinois Press.

Southwood, M. H., & Flege, J. (1999). Scaling foreign accent: Direct magnitude estimation versus interval scaling. *Clinical Linguistics & Phonetics, 13,* 335–349.

Subtirelu, N. C., & Lindemann, S. (2016). Teaching first language speakers to communicate across linguistic difference: Addressing attitudes, comprehension, and strategies. *Applied Linguistics, 37,* 765–783.

Sweet, H. (1899). *The practical study of languages: A guide for teachers and learners.* London: Dent.

Taylor, L. (2006). The changing landscape of English: Implications for language assessment. *English Language Teaching Journal, 60,* 51–60.

Thomson, R. I. (2015). Fluency. In M. Reed & J. Levis (Eds), *The handbook of pronunciation* (pp. 209–226). Hoboken, NJ: Wiley.

Thomson, R. (2018). Measurement of pronunciation constructs. In O. Kang & A. Ginther (Eds), *Assessment in second language pronunciation.* London: Routledge.

Thomson, R. I., & Derwing, T. M. (2015). The effectiveness of L2 pronunciation instruction: A narrative review. *Applied Linguistics, 36,* 326–344.

Trofimovich, P., & Isaacs, T. (2012). Disentangling accent from comprehensibility. *Bilingualism: Language and Cognition, 15,* 905–916.

Winke, P., Gass, S., & Myford, C. (2013). Raters' L2 background as a potential source of bias in rating oral performance. *Language Testing, 30,* 231–252.

Zechner, K., Higgins, D., Xi, X., & Williamson, D. M. (2009). Automatic scoring of non-native spontaneous speech in tests of spoken English. *Speech Communication, 51,* 883–895.

Zielinski, B. W. (2008). The listener: No longer the silent partner in reduced intelligibility. *System, 36,* 69–84.

32

Suprasegmental aspects of pronunciation in New Englishes

Ee Ling Low

Introduction

This chapter will begin with a definition of the term NE and offer a historical perspective on its development. The term 'New Englishes' (henceforth 'NE') is used to describe the non-native varieties of Englishes of post-colonial countries in South Asia, South East Asia, West Africa and East Africa. These NEs, which coincide with Kachru's (1985) outer circle Englishes, have developed into localized varieties of English that serve a functional purpose in the official, administrative, educational and social domains. Schneider's (2003, 2007) dynamic evolutionary model of NEs postulates that all emergent and emerging NEs have been and are continually being shaped by a uniformed pattern resulting from the interaction between the colonial government and the indigenous population. Over time the varieties of these NEs have been influenced by local languages and cultures and become localized through the process of incorporating particular distinctive linguistic features of their own, including features of pronunciation, such that unique varieties of English are developed. These NEs have thus reached a stage in which an endonormative orientation to the use of local varieties of English has developed.

This chapter provides examples of three suprasegmental features (i.e. stress, rhythm and intonation) from four NEs, namely Hong Kong English ('HKE'), Indian English ('IndE'), Nigerian English ('NigE') and Singapore English ('SingE'). These NEs represent the more stabilized phases in Schneider's (2003, 2007) diachronic model, which describes the different phases of development of post-colonial Englishes comprising foundation, exonormative stabilization, nativization, endonormative stabilization and differentiation. An in-depth review of research on suprasegmental features in these NEs serves to outline and compare the development and change in the suprasegmental features of pronunciation. For example, current research on SingE and HKE has led to the suggestion that some NEs can be considered tone languages, as opposed to the description of old varieties of English as a stress/intonation language (Lim, 2011) owing to the influence of contact languages that exists in multilingual contexts such as in Singapore. In terms of rhythm, African Englishes show a tendency towards being stress-based (Schmied, 2006), while HKE and SingE have regularly been posited as syllable-based (Low, 2010; Low, Grabe & Nolan, 2000; Setter, 2006). This chapter ends with a discussion of implications for pronunciation teaching including a discussion of the possible consequences of differences in suprasegmentals of speakers from different varieties of English and suggests directions for future research.

Before proceeding to describe the suprasegmental features of these varieties, it is important to define what suprasegmentals are.

Defining suprasegmentals

Suprasegmental features extend beyond the domain of a single segment, i.e. a vowel or consonant, over larger domains of speech such as syllables, words, phrases and utterances. Typically, they describe stress, rhythm and intonation in different languages or varieties of the same language.

As Couper-Kuhlen (1986, p. 19) states, stress is 'nothing more than the fact that in a succession of spoken syllables or words some will be perceived as more salient or prominent than others'. While stress is responsible for making one syllable more prominent than the other, prominence distinctions cannot ignore the contributions of rhythm and intonation. As Cruttenden (1997, p. 7) asserts, the alternation of prominent and non-prominent syllables produces rhythmic effects that serve to characterize different languages and that these rhythmic patterns in turn form the backbone of intonation patterning of different languages. Thus, the consideration of suprasegmental features of speech should cover its stress, rhythm and intonation. I will now attempt brief working definitions of stress, rhythm and intonation.

Stress

Stress is the more forceful production of a particular syllable that is caused by any or all of the parameters of increased length, loudness, higher pitch and the syllable possessing a full vowel quality. In terms of the linguistic treatment of stress, one can distinguish between word (or lexical) stress and sentence stress (or utterance-level prominence). Utterance-level prominence marks the most prominent syllable in an utterance and usually carries the focal point of information in an utterance. In varieties of English where many prominent syllables occur and it is hard to decipher the most prominent syllable, nuclear stress is taken to be the last stressed syllable in the utterance. Nuclear stress can be neutral and unmarked or emphatic (contrastive). If it is intended to be neutral and unmarked, one expects the last content word to receive the nuclear stress. If, however, emphatic or contrastive stress is intended, then the stress can be placed on any content word depending on the choice of the speaker in order to draw the listener's attention to a particular syllable within a word. Owing to the limited availability of research on prominence, this chapter will mainly focus on lexical (word) stress in four varieties of NE.

Rhythm

In speech, the perception of rhythm occurs as a result of the occurrence of timing regularity of similar or like events and this gives rise to the notion of isochrony. Laver (1994, p. 253) acknowledges that isochrony is a pervasive attribute of all languages and defines it as 'the regular occurrence in time of some given unit of speech rhythm'. What constitutes this given unit of speech rhythm then forms the basis of the rhythmic classifications of languages. The earliest proponents of rhythm classified languages that have stresses recur at regular intervals as stress-based and languages that have syllables recurring at regular intervals as syllable-based, and Japanese, which has recurring mora, was considered to be mora-based.

Most researchers no longer accept absolute stress- or syllable-timing but consider languages to vary along a rhythmic continuum that is stress-based on one end, syllable-based on the other or somewhere in between i.e. rhythmically mixed (e.g. Cauldwell, 2013; Dauer, 1983, 1987). This is the view also taken in this chapter. Even when stress- or syllable-based tendencies are mentioned in the comparison, they are used as convenient reference points adopted by the researchers but this does not imply that the view of rhythmic typology undertaken in this chapter is based on this dichotomous classification only. The past decade or so of rhythmic research has concentrated on the use of rhythmic indices in an attempt to find the durational acoustic correlates for the perception of different rhythmic patterns found in world languages or varieties of a language.

Intonation

Intonation involves 'pitch variations/fluctuations in an utterance or stretch of speech' (Low, 2015, p. 115). These pitch variations are important because they help establish prominence distinctions between syllables that are functionally meaningful, especially for inner circle varieties. According to the British contour-based model of intonational analysis, the first step in studying intonation is the identification of distinctive contours in an utterance. Low & Brown (2005, p. 164) define the distinctiveness in terms of either grammar (where intonation serves to demarcate speech into smaller chunks) or semantics (how intonation is used to signal meaning). Intonational forms (tone or breath groups with distinctive tones) can be used to characterize the first type of distinctiveness while intonation functions can be used to describe tones that are used to signal different types of meaning in utterances. Differences in intonation forms and functions between NEs and inner circle varieties can lead to issues of intelligibility and it is thus important to study the differences in intonation (forms and functions) in NEs.

The next few sections will focus specifically on outlining the latest research on stress, rhythm and intonation in four varieties of NEs, namely HKE, IndE, NigE and SingE.

Stress in New Englishes

Stress in Hong Kong English

Both word stress and utterance-level prominence have been investigated in HKE, most of which are through perceptual analysis (see, for example, Bolton & Kwok, 1990; Hung, 2000, 2012; Deterding, Wong & Kirkpatrick, 2008). Although, as Hung (2012) points out, more studies are needed in order to yield comprehensive findings about suprasegmental features of HKE, there is some evidence that HKE places stresses both at word and utterance level.

Hung (2012) finds that the lexical stress placement in HKE depends much more on metrical conditions of the words such as the number of syllables than on morphological factors such as the suffixes used. In other words, for words with suffixes, the stress placement in HKE depends on the length of a word. For the three-syllable words, the stress is regularly placed on the first syllable, e.g. 'angelic and 'terrific. On the other hand, the stress for four-syllable words (or those with more syllables) in HKE tends to be placed on the penultimate syllable (e.g. photo'graphic). According to this general rule, there exist some words whose stress is placed in the way that coincides with that of inner circle varieties such as British English (BrE) and American English (AmE), as in words peri'odic and ener'getic.

However, this rule also results in the stress placement following the HKE pattern rather than that of BrE or AmE, as shown in the words *infor'mative* and *communi'cative* in HKE. In addition, unlike BrE or AmE speakers, HKE speakers normally do not use this stress placement to distinguish between the verb-noun pairs such as *in'crease* (v.) and *'increase* (n.), which are both pronounced with the stress placed on the second syllable in HKE.

With respect to utterance-level prominence, research available points to two features, namely the absence of de-accenting and the unexpected stress placed on pronouns both used as participants and as possessive determiners. It is reported in Bolton and Kwok (1990) that HKE speakers tend to place nuclear stress on the end of an utterance irrespective of the fact that the focus of information may have been placed on a certain emphatic word elsewhere in the sentence. They also report that repeated information tends not to be de-accented in HKE. For example, in the dialogue 'How many *dogs* did you see?' 'Four *dogs*.' (Bolton & Kwok, 1990, p. 158; author's italics), prominence tends to be given to the repeated word 'dogs' in HKE. Another feature concerning nuclear stress is that HKE speakers sometimes put stress on pronouns such as *we* and possessive determiners such as *my* and demonstrative determiners such as *this* in contexts in which inner circle speakers would not. The endo-normative use of prominence and stressing of pronouns and determiners are also reported in the studies of SingE (see Low, 1998; Goh, 2000; Levis, 2005; Deterding, 2007) and English in the ASEAN countries (see Deterding & Kirkpatrick, 2006).

Stress in Indian English

Stress in IndE has received interest in previous research (e.g. Chaudhary, 1993; Pandey, 1994; Nair, 1996), which notes that stress in some IndE words is placed on different syllables than it is in the same words in other varieties of English and that this type of stress placement in IndE can be a source of misunderstanding when IndE speakers communicate with speakers of other varieties of English. A study by Wiltshire and Moon (2003) showed no significant differences in phonetic realizations of stress between the two groups of IndE speakers (the Indo-Aryan group and the Dravidian group) but did show differences between IndE and AmE both in terms of lexical stress placement position and phonetic realizations. The study revealed that, compared with AmE, IndE seemed to have significantly less prominent cues for stress. For example, in terms of amplitude, the study showed that the AmE speakers averaged a 3.27 dB increase, whereas the IndE speakers averaged only a 0.15 dB increase for the stressed syllable.

There have also been studies investigating the rules of stress in varieties of IndE, for example, Vijayakrishnan's (1978) study of Tamil English, Pandey's (1994) study of general IndE, Nair's (1996) study of Malayalee English and Das's (2001) study of Tripura Bangla English. Vijayakrishnan (1978), for instance, suggested some rules for stress showing that a penultimate or final syllable containing a tense vowel (i.e. long vowel) or a lax vowel (i.e. short vowel) followed by a consonant cluster tends to be stressed (e.g. *amplitude*, *voltage* and *frequency*). However, there have been a small number of studies dedicated to the measurement of the phonetic properties of stress in IndE (see Vijayakrishnan, 1978; Pickering & Wiltshire, 2000). Vijayakrishnan's (1978) study of Tamil English stress indicates that increased duration is the primary cue for the phonetic correlates of stress. Pickering and Wiltshire's (2000) study, on the other hand, suggests that IndE speakers used pitch accent as the primary cue.

A relatively small number of studies have attempted to give a general description of IndE as a whole, for example those done by Chaudhary (1989), Wiltshire and Moon (2003) (as mentioned above) and Gargesh (2004). It is suggested in most of these studies that the weight of the syllable (i.e. whether it is a light, heavy or extra-heavy syllable, as explained below) is the determining factor for stress placement in IndE. These studies distinguish three types of syllables, namely light syllable (one that contains just one short vowel or when preceded by consonants, also expressed as V or CV, for example the first syllable in the word *taboo*), heavy syllable (one that contains a long vowel or a vowel followed by a consonant, also expressed as V: or VC, for example the second syllable in the word *taboo*), and extra-heavy syllable (one that contains either a long vowel preceding at least one consonant or a short vowel preceding at least two consonants, also expressed as V:C or VCC, for example the second syllable in the word *amass*) (see Sailaja, 2009). Based on these, Gargesh's (2004) simplified version of rules of stress is explained as:

(a) Two-syllable words. IndE speakers tend to place the stress on the first syllable if the second syllable is not extra heavy, e.g. ′taboo, ′mistake, ′monsoon, ′concrete (Gargesh, 2004, pp. 1000–1001; Sailaja, 2009, p. 30).
(b) Three-syllable words. In IndE, the stress is placed on the first syllable if the second syllable is not heavy; the stress falls on the second syllable if it is heavy, e.g. mo′desty, cha′racter, mi′nister, ′terrific (Gargesh, 2004, pp. 1000–1001; Sailaja, 2009, p. 30).

Gargesh's rules, as pointed out in Sailaja (2009), fail to explain a number of variations that exist in IndE. For example, they are unable to account for the different ways in which some IndE speakers place stress for the same words, e.g. ta′boo, mis′take, ′modesty. This phenomenon may suggest that, once a dynamic and complex language group such as IndE begins to transition away from an exonormative orientation towards more of an endonormative orientation, it undergoes a process of change. This change, however, takes time and may occur inconsistently. For some speakers, the process of change is incomplete and in a state of flux. In some contexts of interaction the exonormative rules may still be in operation.

In addition to the foregoing features of stress, Sailaja (2009) also provides useful demonstrations of the lexical stress placement, some of which are summarized as follows:

(a) Acronyms. IndE speakers tend to place stress on the first letter of these acronyms (whereas stress is placed on the last letter in BrE): ′BBC, ′TV, ′ECG.
(b) Compound words. In IndE, these words receive stress on the first word but on the second in BrE: ′loudspeaker, ′bad-tempered, ′headquarters. It must be noted, however, that North American English speakers would stress the first word for *loudspeaker* and *headquarters*.
(c) Morphological distinction through stress. In non-standard IndE, this function of stress is lost. Thus the stress tends to fall on the first syllable of the words ′insult, ′abstract, ′import, and ′conduct regardless of their part of speech.

There has been a scarcity of research on prominence in IndE. Research available seems to suggest that prominence is of more unpredictable nature than word stress. There appears to be a tendency in IndE that a sentence often has stress placed on 'all the content words' (Sailaja, 2009, p. 32). In addition, Sailaja (2009, p. 33) observes that in the speech of some IndE speakers in news channels, stress is placed on words such as *will* even when they are used to express purely routine information rather than to express contrast.

Stress in Nigerian English

Existing research on stress in NigE mainly focuses on word stress (see, for example, Kujore, 1985; Jowitt, 1991; Simo Bobda, 1995, 2000; Adedimeji, 2007; Sunday, 2011). According to Kujore (1985), 'delayed primary stress' is the most noticeable feature of NigE. Specifically, this encompasses the following sub-features (see Kujore, 1985, pp. 2ff; Simo Bobda, 1995, p. 255, 2000):

- There is a tendency for the NigE speakers to move the stress to the right, for example, *col'league* and *pe'trol*.
- There is a tendency for the stress to move to the right in compounds with final obstruents, for example, *fire'wood* and *proof'read*.
- Certain suffixes tend to attract stress to themselves, for example, the verb suffixes *–ate* (*indi'cate*), *-ize* (*recog'nize*) and *-fy* (*diversi'fy*).
- There is a tendency for the stress to move to the preceding syllable before some suffixes such as the adjective suffixes *-able* (*indo'mitable*) and *-ible* (*e'ligible*).
- The primary and secondary stresses are reversed in some words, such as *'education* and *'federation*.

It should be noted that this existing research mainly focuses on the lexical stress placement on words in citation forms. It would be interesting to learn how the stress placement may be impacted when such words occur in connected speech. For inner circle English (e.g. BrE and AmE), such citation forms may undergo changes in connected speech; for example, stress locations may shift or even disappear. This would indeed be an interesting topic for future research.

Stress in Singapore English

Studies on stress in SingE have been extensively reviewed in Low (2015). In a much earlier study, Low (2000) found differences in lexical stress placement between BrE and SingE for compounds and noun phrases. For BrE speakers, stress on compounds occurs on the first element, while stress for noun phrases tends to occur on the second element (e.g. the stress falls on the first word of the compound *'greenhouse* but on the second word of the noun phrase *green 'house*). However, for SingE speakers, stress for compounds and noun phrases is not distinguished and tends to occur on the second element, for example, SingE speakers tend to place stress on the second word in both cases (i.e. *green'house* and *green 'house*). Another interesting finding from Low's (2000) experimental investigation was that polysyllabic words were not stressed differently in SingE compared to BrE when the words were placed in medial position. Only in utterance-final position did the words have syllable-final stress. Deterding (2007) observed that when Singaporean speakers assign stress to the second syllable of two-syllable words like *colLEAGUE*, there appears to be a phonological rule that motivates the assignment of stress to the second syllable, i.e. when the second syllable contains a long vowel. Peng and Ann (2001) also observed that the principles of lexical stress assignment for Singapore, Nigerian and Spanish English were based on the phonological rule of syllable weight, where long vowels and diphthongs attracted stress. Given that the existing research on word stress in SingE tends to focus on words in citation forms, it remains to be investigated as to whether the lexical stress placement in these words will be affected (e.g. shifted) in connected speech.

Rhythm in New Englishes

Rhythm in Hong Kong English

HKE, like SingE, is said to fall closer to the syllable-based rather than stress-based end of the speech rhythm continuum owing to its relative absence of reduced vowels (see Deterding, Wong & Kirkpatrick, 2008; Hung, 2012; Low, Grabe & Nolan, 2000; Setter, 2003). Deterding, Wong and Kirkpatrick (2008) support this by providing some clear instances that demonstrate syllable-based rhythm in their HKE data. However, citing Crystal (1995), who notes that, even in the stress-based BrE syllable-based rhythm sometimes occurs in speech such as parent–infant talks and television slogans, Deterding and his colleagues point out that classification of HKE rhythm requires an in-depth study using rhythmic indices such as Low et al.'s (2000) pairwise variability index (PVI).

It is also noted in Hung (2012) that the mother tongue of HKE speakers (e.g. Cantonese or some other Chinese dialects) is syllable-based. HKE has little liaison or sound linking between words and, unlike inner circle varieties, there is a lack of vowel reduction in function words in HKE. These may be some of the factors that contribute to the syllable-based timing of HKE. In addition, owing to the fact that the substrate languages of HKE speakers are Cantonese or other Chinese dialects, which belong to tonal languages, HKE has some markedly tonal quality, i.e. a high tone is usually assigned to stressed syllables and a low tone to unstressed syllables (Hung, 2012).

Rhythm in Indian English

Owing to the vast number of substrate languages spoken in India, there seems to be little consensus on the general rhythmic patterning of IndE. While the rhythm of IndE is said to be syllable-based, which arises from the syllable-based rhythm of Indian languages (see Gargesh, 2004), this statement is not without controversy. Sailaja (2009), for example, points out that this claim is not fully verified as it is not true that there are no weak syllables or weak forms in IndE. In fact, it is maintained by some scholars in the field that IndE rhythm is not syllable-based. Prabhakar Babu (1971a, 1971b), for example, found that IndE is neither stressed- nor syllable-based, suggesting that it may fall along a continuum between stress- and syllable-based timing. In addition, owing to the existence of weak forms in connected IndE speech, it is clear that IndE is unlikely to be syllable-based (Sailaja, 2009). For example, in the sentence *I am thinking of you*, Gargesh (2004) claims that all words are stressed and all syllables are given prominence. However, Sailaja (2009) argues that, in Standard IndE pronunciation *I am* would certainly be reduced to *I'm*.

Sirsa and Redford's (2013) study, based on their analyses on global rhythm metrics and speech rate, indicates that the IndE rhythm patterning is clearly different from both Hindi and Telugu, leading them to conclude that IndE speakers' rhythm, which is significantly different from that of BrE, receives negligible influences from their native languages. Krivokapić (2013), however, reports that the rhythm of the IndE speaker in the study is observed to be more stress-based when conversing with an AmE speaker, which may be explained via speech accommodation when communicating with a speaker of a stress-based variety. More studies, therefore, are needed on investigating the rhythm of IndE before any definitive conclusions can be reached.

Rhythm in Nigerian English

NigE has been described to be a syllable-based variety of English owing to the influence from the syllable-based timing of Nigerian languages (see Adetugbo, 1977). This categorization is supported by Bamgbose (1982) and Jowitt (1991). It is, however, disputed by Jibril (1982, as cited in Udofot, 2003), who argues that the notion of syllable- versus stress-based timing does not fairly account for the important difference between NigE and inner circle Englishes, where the latter avoid having two stressed syllables occurring consecutively in an utterance. Eka (1993, pp. 1–11) does not subscribe to classifying NigE as a syllable-based variety. This is because NigE tends to have more prominent syllables than inner circle varieties and the greater number of prominent syllables in NigE makes it unable to 'squeeze in' or 'stretch out' the syllables as inner circle English speakers do (Eka 1993, pp. 1–11; Udofot, 2003).

Udofot (1993) investigated some rhythmic patternings of English spoken by the final-year secondary school students whose English approximates non-standard NigE, i.e. the reference here is between a standard and a colloquial non-standard variety of NigE. The results of the study confirmed that there is a preponderance of prominent syllables in NigE and that its rhythm veers towards the syllable-based end rather than wholly syllable-based. In Udofot (1997), the large number of prominent syllables in NigE spoken by Nigerians with varied educational and socio-economic backgrounds is also found, suggesting that there exists a tendency for long and short vowels to be pronounced with equal duration in NigE. It is concluded in Udofot (1997) that in terms of rhythm, NigE is 'heard as rhythmic, but hardly varying its tempo' (p. 203).

Rhythm in Singapore English

The rhythm of standard SingE was described by early scholars as possessing a staccato-effect. Brown (1988) explains what gives rise to this perception. First, there is an absence of reduced vowels in unstressed words. Second, there is a lack of linking between adjacent words in connected speech. Third, there is an absence of distinction between long and short vowels. The evidence provided in acoustic studies such as Low, Grabe and Nolan (2000) and Grabe and Low (2002) supports earlier claims that, in terms of rhythm, standard SingE lies at the syllable-based end of the rhythmic continuum. Low et al. (2000) investigated the observation by Taylor (1981) and Brown (1988) about the perceived lack of reduced vowels in SingE by designing two sentence sets: one comprising only full vowels and the other an alternation of full and reduced vowels if uttered by a BrE speaker. She measured the successive vowel durations and used the pairwise variability index (PVI) to calculate the degree of variability between these successive vowels. A low PVI denotes little variability in duration between successive vowels in an utterance, while a high PVI indicates that there is a high degree of variability between successive vowels in an utterance. The results showed that SingE had significantly lower PVI values for the full and reduced sentence sets compared to BrE but that no significant difference existed between the full vowel sentence sets between the two varieties. Thus, results provided evidence that, indeed, SingE does not appear to have reduced vowels, at least in the durational domain. Low et al. (2000) also measured the first and second formants of all potentially reduced vowels in both varieties and calculated the distance from the central point of a speaker's vowel quadrilateral known as 'the distance from the centroid'. Results showed more significantly peripheral realizations of the potentially reduced vowels in SingE compared to BrE, once again suggesting that the potentially reduced vowels in SingE were realized with more full vowel-like qualities.

Deterding (2001) measured successive syllable durations in SingE and BrE and used a variability index (VI) to calculate whether there was high or low variability between successive syllables in an utterance. His findings also pointed to the fact that SingE had a significantly lower VI compared to BrE, thus providing empirical evidence to support the classification of SingE as being syllable-based. Heng and Deterding (2005) investigated the presence or absence of reduced vowels in the first syllable of polysyllabic words in SingE. From their perceptual experiments, it was found that SingE speakers tended to have fewer reduced vowels than their BrE counterparts.

Intonation in New Englishes

Intonation in Hong Kong English

Bolton and Kwok (1990) describe some characteristic features of intonation in HKE. These include the following four features. The first and most noticeable feature is that HKE speakers tend to use a high-rising intonation for all types of questions, including *wh-* questions. The second feature relates to the prominence given to function words, though they receive no emphasis, suggesting the levelling of distinction between strong and weak syllables or between content and function words in terms of prominence distinctions. The third feature has to do with the tonic syllable, which is placed on repeated items in HKE. This is in contrast to BrE, in which repeated words are normally not given prominence or pitch accent. The fourth feature is related to accent shift, which is adopted in BrE to achieve emphasis by shifting accent from the normal position to where a different lexical item needs to receive prominence. This is, however, lacking in HKE. In addition, Wee (2008, p. 488) observes that a high or high-falling tone would occur in at least one syllable in any well-formed phonological word in HKE.

Intonation in Indian English

Little research has been done on the intonation in IndE and the works available are mostly based on impressionistic observation (e.g. Wiltshire & Harnsberger, 2006; Sailaja, 2009; Puri, 2013). Sailaja (2009) summarizes some features of IndE intonation. First, falling and rising intonations are in general more commonly seen than other intonations in IndE. Second, while the falling intonation is generally used for the *wh-* question, rising intonation is also commonly used for this type of question when IndE speakers talk to newcomers or strangers to show politeness, e.g. *Where do you live?* Third, it is common that announcements (e.g. in the airport and railway station) tend to end in rising intonation. Thus the sentence *The plane is taking off shortly* may end with a rising intonation. It is noted in Shuja (1995) that Urdu English speakers use falling, rising and fall–rise intonations more often than other intonations, which is also true for most IndE varieties. This feature is also observed in the speech files in Prabhakar Babu's (1971a) study.

Intonation in Nigerian English

In a study involving participants who were final-year undergraduates speaking different Nigerian languages, Jowitt (2000) investigated the intonation patterns of educated NigE speakers, focusing on the form and frequency. The study identified some main characteristic NigE intonation patterns including using falling intonation for statements, commands and *wh-* questions; using the rising intonation for yes/no questions and tag questions; the use of fall–rise intonation for non-final subordinate clauses and rise–fall for strong emphasis. Low (2015, p. 124) noted that

> end or final word stress is found for tone units and lexical words are assigned with pitch accents that are quite high and the main pattern found for the heads in the tone unit is initial high pitch followed by a downward drift before the start of the nucleus while the main pattern for the nucleus is one with a low-falling tone.

Some impressionistic descriptions (see Jowitt, 1991; Wells, 1982) note that the intonation of NigE is a reflection of the prosody of African tone languages, in which a high tone is used for stressed syllables and low tone for unstressed ones. This conforms to Leben's (1996) study, which noted that the stressed syllable in English loanwords in Hausa is pronounced with a high or falling tone.

Intonation in Singapore English

Some main findings on intonation patterns in SingE are summarized in Low (2012, 2015). Low's (2000) acoustic study, measuring the pitch range of the early marker in BrE (a high pitch accent used to signal new information) and the early booster of extreme high pitch in utterances in SingE, found that the early booster had the pitch range significantly greater than the early marker. However, disregarding the early booster and early marker, Low (2000) found no evidence to support that SingE had a pitch range greater than BrE. Two studies based on a spoken corpus of SingE, the Grammar of Spoken Singapore English Corpus (GSSEC), note that phrase-final prominence occurs in SingE (see Lim, 2004) and that syllable-final lengthening and lack of pitch variation (narrower pitch range) are found to be common in SingE (see Wee, 2004). In a study comparing the percentage of prominent syllables in SingE with that of AmE, Levis (2005) found that the prominent syllables in SingE were 46 per cent more than those in AmE. Goh's (2005) study, investigating the intonational tones in SingE, found that there was a tendency for the level tone to occur in the final position serving important communicative purposes. Low and Brown (2005), however, noted the difficulty in the application of the British intonation model to describing the intonation of SingE, the reason being that it is harder to distinguish between stressed, unstressed and pitch-accented syllables in SingE than those in BrE owing to the fact that many syllables in SingE seemed to be equally stressed. The lack of de-accenting in SingE was acoustically evidenced in Low (2006), who found in SingE a rise in peak fundamental frequency for repeated lexical items signalling old (or repeated) information in contrast to a step down in peak fundamental frequency for the same lexical items in BrE. Similarly, in a detailed analysis of the speech of an educated young Singaporean, Deterding (2007) also uncovered that the speaker tended to place the stress on function words such as pronouns, tended not to de-accent old or given information and tended to use an early booster.

That some differences exist in the functions of intonational tones in SingE and BrE is noted in Low and Brown (2005) and Deterding (2007). The main difference lies in the use of the rising and rise–fall tones. Unlike BrE speakers, SingE speakers may use the rising intonation to indicate that they have completed speaking. More recently, Ng (2011) found in the data of Chinese speakers of colloquial SingE that the word-final high tone was not used for the purpose of stress but to signal the word-final position. Explaining this phenomenon, Ng suggested that this feature might be attributable to Malay, in which phrase-final rising tone tends to be used.

Recommendations for practice

Low (2010) discusses the pedagogical implications of findings on SingE pronunciation for pronunciation syllabus design for the purpose of promoting international intelligibility. Combining the suggestions of a lingua franca core from Jenkins (2002), Low (2010, p. 248) suggests the specific features of SingE pronunciation that might interfere with international intelligibility and should therefore receive priority in the pronunciation syllabus of a variety of NEs.

In terms of the Jenkins lingua franca core, weak forms and stress-based rhythm do not affect intelligibility and should therefore not be the focus of instruction. However, it is arguable whether word stress does affect intelligibility and it is difficult to teach. Recent research has surfaced the teachability of primary stress placement. Pennington and Ellis (2000), for example, found that explicit instruction helped learners to significantly improve lexical word stress production. This is a view upheld by Dalton and Seidlhofer (1994), who advocated that primary word stress is both teachable and valuable for communicative purposes. Derwing, Munro and Wiebe (1998) provided empirical evidence to show that ESL students receiving just 20 minutes per day of instruction in suprasegmentals (including primary word stress) significantly improved in their comprehension and fluency in performing a narrative speaking task.

The critical feature that Jenkins has highlighted that interferes with intelligibility is nuclear or sentence-level stress. This is a feature that does seem to pose a problem for the international intelligibility of SingE since the last stress accent is taken to be the nuclear stress. This is the same feature found in the NEs reviewed in this chapter. If intelligibility is an issue, then sentence-level prominence has to be carefully considered in the design of a pronunciation syllabus that promotes international intelligibility.

McNerney and Mendelsohn (1992, p. 132) assert strongly that 'a short term pronunciation course should focus first and foremost on suprasegmentals as they have the greatest impact on the comprehensibility of the learner's English' and that 'giving priority to the suprasegmental aspects of English not only improves learners' comprehensibility but is also less frustrating for students because greater change can be effected'. Chun (1988, p. 295) also notes the importance of intonation to achieve discoursal competence, and argues that

> Intonation is fundamental to genuine communication because communicative competence is the ability not only to formulate grammatically correct utterances, but also to signal interactional strategies, such as interrupting, asking for clarification, taking the floor, changing the subject, concluding an argument, or constraining a hearer to reply.

More importantly, Chun states the importance of suprasegmentals in contributing to the overall mastery of sociolinguistic competence since intonational patterning has implications on the overall interpretations of a speaker's politeness or impoliteness.

In terms of rhythmic instruction, it is important to realize that the pedagogical relevance and usefulness of stress-based and syllable-based timings are still a point of continuing controversy and disagreement among scholars. Cauldwell (2002) found that the use of these rhythmic classifications hampered understanding of spontaneous speech and should be abandoned when designing pronunciation teaching and learning materials on rhythm. Marks's (1999, p. 198) view about rhythmic instruction considers the relevance of rhythmic typology research and pronunciation instruction, as he states that

> the pedagogic use of rhymes and verse, which are more likely to have a strictly stress-timed rhythm . . . provides a convenient framework for the perception and production

of a number of characteristic features of English pronunciation which are often found to be problematic for learners: stress/unstress (and therefore the basis for intonation), vowel length, vowel reduction, elision, compression, pause (between adjacent stresses).

Future directions

It is important to move beyond intelligibility in our consideration of what matters in terms of standards and norms in pronunciation (Low, 2010). For instance, achieving overall communicative competence is critical. According to the definitions provided by Canale and Swain (1980), communicative competence includes (a) *grammatical*: knowledge of linguistic rules of a language; (b) *sociolinguistic*: how to use language appropriately according to whom one is communicating with, when, where etc.; (c) *discoursal*: where both cohesion (how a text links) and coherence (whether the text is logical) are important; and (d) *strategic*: how to appropriately use communicative strategies to achieve communicative goals or to help repair breakdowns in communication. To this end, it is clear from the preceding sections that suprasegmentals play an important role in helping a speaker to achieve overall communicative competence and require attention in the pronunciation classroom that aims to achieve international intelligibility.

Apart from communicative competence, other factors that should concern us would be the identities that speakers of NEs want to portray. If, indeed these NEs are norm-developing and, in the endonormative stabilization phase of Schneider's (2003, 2007) dynamic model, then sounding local might be a deliberate and important aspect that allows a speaker to express their cultural identity.

Focusing on just these two aspects above for a start, future research on the suprasegmentals of NEs should move beyond features-based descriptions to focusing on the effect of pronunciation on overall communicative competence, possibly even breaking down the research focal areas according to each of the four dimensions of communicative competence. Next, conducting attitudinal surveys of speakers of NEs is extremely important before one can chart future directions for using, teaching and learning English.

In the final analysis, the study of NEs has to be considered against the context of English as a global language in an increasingly interconnected world and its implications for language policy, planning, implementation and educational purposes cannot be over-emphasized.

References

Adedimeji, M. A. (2007). *The linguistic features of Nigerian English and their implications for 21st century English pedagogy.* Paper presented at the 24th Annual Conference of the Nigeria English Studies Association (NESA), 'English in the Nigerian Environment: Emerging Patterns and New Challenges', held at the CBN Auditorium, University of Uyo, Akwa Ibom state, 18–21 September 2007.

Adetugbo, A. (1977). Nigerian English: Fact or fiction? *Lagos Notes and Records*, 6, 128–141.

Bamgbose, A. (1982). Standard Nigerian English: Issues of identification. In B. B. Kachru (Ed.), *The other tongue: English across cultures* (pp. 99–109). Urbana, IL: University of Illinois Press.

Bolton, K., & Kwok, H. (1990). The dynamics of the Hong Kong accent: Social identity and sociolinguistic description. *Journal of Asian Pacific Communication*, 1, 147–72.

Brown, A. (1988). The staccato effect in the pronunciation of English in Malaysia and Singapore. In J. Foley (Ed.), *New Englishes: The case of Singapore* (pp. 115–128). Singapore: Singapore University Press.

Canale, M., & Swain, M. (1980). Theoretical bases of communicative approaches to second language teaching and testing. *Applied Linguistics*, 1, 1–47.

Cauldwell, R. (2002). The functional irrythmicality of spontaneous speech: A discourse view of speech rhythms. *Apples*, *2*(1), 1–24.

Cauldwell, R. (2013). *Phonology for listening: Teaching the stream of speech*. Birmingham: Speech in Action.

Chaudhary, S. C. (1989). *Some aspects of the phonology of Indian English*. Ranchi: Jayaswal.

Chaudhary, S. C. (1993). Issues on Indian English phonology: A rejoinder. *World Englishes*, *12*, 375–383.

Chun, D. M. (1988). Teaching intonation as part of communicative competence: Suggestions for the classroom. *Die Unterrichtspraxis*, *21*, 81–88.

Couper-Kuhlen, E. (1986). *An introduction to English prosody*. London: Edward Arnold.

Cruttenden, A. (1997). *Intonation* (2nd ed.). Cambridge: Cambridge University Press.

Crystal, D. (1995). Documenting rhythmical change. In J. W. Lewis (Ed.), *Studies in general English and phonetics: Essays in honour of Professor J. D. O'Connor* (pp. 174–179). London and New York, NY: Routledge.

Dalton, C., & Seidlhofer, B. (1994). *Pronunciation*. Oxford: Oxford University Press.

Das, S. (2001). *Some aspects of the prosodic phonology of Tripura Bangla and Tripura Bangla English*. Unpublished PhD thesis, CIEFL, Hyderabad, India.

Dauer, R. M. (1983). Stress-timing and syllable-timing re-analysed. *Journal of Phonetics*, *11*, 51–62.

Dauer, R. M. (1987). Phonetic and phonological components of language rhythm. *Proceedings of the 11th International Congress of Phonetic Sciences* (pp. 447–450).

Derwing, T., M., Munro, M. J., & Wiebe, G. (1998). Evidence in favor of a broad framework for pronunciation instruction. *Language Learning*, *48*, 393–410.

Deterding, D. (2001). The measurement of rhythm: A comparison of Singapore English and British English. *Journal of Phonetics*, *29*, 217–230.

Deterding, D. (2007). *Singapore English*. Edinburgh: Edinburgh University Press.

Deterding, D., & Kirkpatrick, A. (2006). Emerging South-East Asian Englishes and intelligibility. *World Englishes*, *25*, 391–409.

Deterding, D., Wong, J., & Kirkpatrick, A. (2008). The pronunciation of Hong Kong English. *English World-Wide*, *29*(2), 148–175.

Eka, D. (1993). Timing in educated spoken Nigerian English. *Journal of Humanities*, *3*, 1–11.

Gargesh, R. (2004). Indian English: Phonology. In E. W. Schneider, K. Burridge, B. Kortmann, R. Mesthrie & C. Upton (Eds.), *The handbook of varieties of English*, vol. 1, Phonology (pp. 993–1002). Berlin: Mouton de Gruyter.

Goh, C. C. M. (2000). A discourse approach to the description of intonation in Singapore English. In A. Brown, D. Deterding & E. L. Low (Eds.), *The English language in Singapore: Research on pronunciation* (pp. 35–45). Singapore: Singapore Association for Applied Linguistics.

Goh, C. C. M. (2005). Discourse intonation variants in the speech of educated Singaporeans. In D. Deterding, A. Brown & E. L. Low (Eds.), *English in Singapore: Phonetic research on a corpus* (pp. 104–114). Singapore: McGraw-Hill.

Grabe, E., & Low, E. L. (2002). Durational variability in speech and the rhythm class hypothesis. In C. Gussenhoven & N. Warner (Eds.), *Laboratory phonology 7* (pp. 515–546). Berlin: Mouton de Gruyter.

Heng, M. G., & Deterding, D. (2005). Reduced vowels in conversational Singapore English. In D. Deterding, A. Brown & E. L. Low (Eds.), *English in Singapore: Phonetic research on a corpus* (pp. 54–63). Singapore: McGraw-Hill.

Hung, T. (2000). Toward a phonology of Hong Kong English. *World Englishes*, *19*(3), 337–356.

Hung, T. (2012). Hong Kong English. In E. L. Low & Azirah Hashim (Eds.), *English in Southeast Asia: Features, policy and language in use* (pp. 113–133). Amsterdam: John Benjamins.

Jenkins, J. (2002). A sociolinguistically based, empirically researched pronunciation syllabus for English as an international language. *Applied Linguistics*, *23*(1), 83–103.

Jibril, M. (1982). *Phonological variation in Nigerian English*. Unpublished PhD thesis, University of Lancaster, UK.

Jowitt, D. (1991). *Nigerian English usage: An introduction*. Lagos: Longman Nigeria.

Jowitt, D. (2000). Patterns of Nigerian English intonation. *English World-Wide*, *21*(1), 63–80.

Kachru, B. B. (1985). Standards, codification, and sociolinguistic realm: The English language in the outer circle. In R. Quirk & H. G. Widdowson (Eds.), *English in the world* (pp. 11–30). Cambridge: Cambridge University Press.

Krivokapić, J. (2013). Rhythm and convergence between speakers of American and Indian English. *Laboratory Phonology*, *4*(1), 39–65.

Kujore, O. (1985). *English usage: Some notable Nigerian variations*. Ibadan: Evans.

Laver, J. (1994). *Principles of phonetics*. Cambridge: Cambridge University Press.

Leben, W. (1996). Tonal feet and adaptation of English borrowings into Hausa. *Studies in African Linguistics*, *25*, 139–54.

Levis, J. M. (2005). Prominence in Singapore and American English: Evidence from reading aloud. In D. Deterding, A. Brown & E. L. Low (Eds.), *English in Singapore: Phonetic research on a corpus* (pp. 86–94). Singapore: McGraw-Hill.

Lim, L. (Ed.). (2004). *Singapore English: A grammatical description*. Amsterdam: John Benjamins.

Lim, L. (2011). Revisiting English prosody: (Some) New Englishes as tone languages?. In L. Lim & N. Gisborne (Eds.), *Typology of Asian Englishes* (pp. 97–118). Philadelphia, PA: John Benjamins.

Low, E. L. (1998). *Prosodic prominence in Singapore English*. Unpublished PhD thesis, University of Cambridge, UK.

Low, E. L. (2000). Is lexical stress placement different in Singapore English and British English?. In A. Brown, D. Deterding & E. L. Low (Eds.), *The English language in Singapore: Research on pronunciation* (pp. 22–34). Singapore: Singapore Association for Applied Linguistics.

Low, E. L. (2006). A review of recent research on speech rhythm: Some insights for language acquisition, language disorders and language teaching. In R. Hughes (Ed.), *Spoken English, TESOL and applied linguistics: Challenges for theory and practice* (pp. 99–125). Houndmills: Palgrave Macmillan.

Low, E. L. (2010). The acoustic reality of the Kachruvian circles: A rhythmic perspective. *World Englishes*, *29*(3), 394–405.

Low, E. L. (2012). Singapore English. In E. L. Low & Azirah Hashim (Eds.), *English in Southeast Asia: Features, policy and language in use* (pp. 35–53). Amsterdam and Philadelphia, PA: John Benjamins.

Low, E. L. (2015). *Pronunciation for English as an international language: From research to practice*. London and New York, NY: Routledge.

Low, E. L., & Brown, A. (2005). *English in Singapore: An introduction*. Singapore: McGraw-Hill.

Low, E. L., Grabe, E., & Nolan, F. (2000). Quantitative characterizations of speech rhythm: Syllable-timing in Singapore English. *Language and Speech*, *43*, 377–401.

Marks, J. (1999). Is stress-timing real? *ELT Journal*, 53, 191–199.

McNerney, M., & Mendelsohn, D. (1992). Suprasegmentals in the pronunciation class: Setting priorities. In P. Avery & S. Ehrlich (Eds.), *Teaching American English pronunciation* (pp. 185–196). Oxford: Oxford University Press.

Nair, N. G. (1996). *Indian English phonology: A case study of Malayalee English*. New Delhi: Prestige.

Ng, E.-C. (2011). Chinese meets Malay meets English: Origins of Singaporean English word-final high tone. *International Journal of Bilingualism*, *16*(1), 83–100.

Pandey, P. K. (1994). On a description of the phonology of Indian English. In R. K. Agnihotri & A. L. Khanna (Eds.), *Second language acquisition: Socio-cultural and linguistic aspects of English in India* (pp. 198–207). London: Sage.

Peng, L., & Ann, J. (2001). Stress and duration in three varieties of English. *World Englishes*, *20*(1), 1–27.

Pennington, M. C., & Ellis, N. C. (2000). Cantonese speakers' memory for English sentences with prosodic clues. *The Modern Language Journal*, *84*, 372–389.

Pickering, L., & Wiltshire, C. (2000). The prosody of Indian-English TA's teaching discourse. *World Englishes*, *19*, 173–183.

Prabhakar Babu, B. A. (1971a). *Prosodic features in Indian English: Stress, rhythm and intonation*. Postgraduate research diploma project, Hyderabad, India: CIEFL.

Prabhakar Babu, B. A. (1971b). Prosodic features in Indian English: Stress, rhythm and intonation. *CIEFL Bulletin*, *8*, 33–39.

Puri, V. (2013). *Intonation in Indian English and Hindi late and simultaneous bilinguals*. Unpublished PhD thesis, University of Illinois at Urbana-Champaign, Urbana, Illinois, USA.

Sailaja, P. (2009). *Indian English*. Edinburgh: Edinburgh University Press.

Schmied, J. (2006). East African Englishes. In B. B. Kachru, Y. Kachru & C. L. Nelson (Eds.), *The handbook of world Englishes* (pp. 188–202). Oxford: Blackwell.

Schneider, E. W. (2003). The dynamics of New Englishes: From identity construction to dialect birth. *Language, 79*, 233–281.

Schneider, E. W. (2007). *Postcolonial English: Varieties around the world.* Cambridge: Cambridge University Press.

Setter, J. (2003). A comparison of speech rhythm in British and Hong Kong English. In S.-S., Josep Maria, D. R. Vives & J. Romero (Eds.), *Proceedings of the 15th International Congress of Phonetic Sciences* (pp. 467–470), Barcelona, 3–9 August 2003. Barcelona: Causal.

Setter, J. (2006). Speech rhythm in world Englishes: The case of Hong Kong. *TESOL Quarterly, 40*(4), 763–782.

Shuja, A. (1995). *Urdu-English phonetics and phonology.* New Delhi: Bahri.

Simo Bobda, A. (1995). The phonologies of Nigerian English and Cameroon English. In A. Bamgbose, A. Banjo & A. Thomas (Eds.), *New English: A West African perspective* (pp. 248–268). Ibadan: Mosuro.

Simo Bobda, A. (2000). Comparing some phonological features across African accents of English. *English Studies, 81*(3), 249–266.

Sirsa, H., & Redford, M. A. (2013). The effects of native language on Indian English sounds and timing patterns. *Journal of Phonetics, 41*, 393–406.

Sunday, A. B. (2011). Compound stress in Nigerian English. *English Today, 27*(3), 43–51.

Taylor, D. S. (1981). Non-native speakers and the rhythm of English. *International Review of Applied Linguistics in Language Teaching, 19*, 219–226.

Udofot, I. (1993). Rhythm and intonation: a study of performance by Ibibio speakers of English. *Journal of Humanities, 3*, 19–27.

Udofot, I. (1997). *The rhythm of spoken Nigerian English.* Unpublished PhD thesis, University of Uyo, Nigeria.

Udofot, I. (2003). Stress and rhythm in the Nigerian accent of English: A preliminary investigation. *English World-Wide, 24*(2), 201–220.

Vijayakrishnan, K. G. (1978). *Stress in Tamilian English: A study within the framework of generative phonology.* Unpublished MLitt thesis, CIEFL, Hyderabad, India.

Wee, L. (2004). Singapore English: Phonology. In E. W. Schneider, K. Burridge, B. Kortmann, R. Mesthrie & C. Upton (Eds.), *A handbook of varieties of English*, vol. 1: Phonology (pp. 1017–1033). Berlin: Mouton de Gruyter.

Wee, L.-H. (2008). Phonological patterns in the Englishes of Singapore and Hong Kong. *World Englishes, 27*(3/4), 480–501.

Wells, J. C. (1982). *Accents of English*, 3 vols. Cambridge: Cambridge University Press.

Wiltshire, C., & Moon, R. (2003). Phonetic stress in Indian English vs. American English. *World Englishes, 22*(3), 291–303.

Wiltshire, C., & Harnsberger, J. D. (2006). The influence of Gujarati and Tamil L1s on Indian English: A preliminary study. *World Englishes, 25*(1), 91–104.

33

Intelligibility in global contexts

Jagdish Kaur

Introduction

It remains an undisputed fact that intelligibility is key to successful and effective human communication. As Munro points out, 'Intelligibility is the single most important aspect of all communication' (2011, p. 13), upon which the success of spoken communication depends. The issue of intelligibility has been and continues to be the subject of much research inquiry in the context of the use of English by its non-native speakers (NNSs). However, as English continues to strengthen its foothold in international settings as *the* global lingua franca, the issue of mutual intelligibility has taken on greater significance.

English, when used in global contexts, presupposes the contact of different varieties of English used by speakers of varied linguacultural backgrounds. While providing speakers with the means to communicate in a medium common to all, the variability in the Englishes used and the diversity of its speakers and contexts of use raise the question of just how well these speakers understand each other. The extensive spread of English the world over has resulted in the rise of both established and emerging NNS varieties that are often characterized by norms and practices distinct and separate from each other and from native speaker (NS) varieties. Notwithstanding that variety is the very essence of a global language (Hung, 2002), questions of how intelligible speakers of different varieties of English are to each other provide the impetus for numerous studies on intelligibility. In order to ensure the continued utility of English as a global lingua franca, researchers are particularly keen to identify the factors that promote intelligibility among speakers of different varieties of English.

Traditional approaches to the subject regard intelligibility, as Bamgbose puts it, as 'a one-way process in which non-native speakers are striving to make themselves understood by native speakers whose prerogative it was to decide what is intelligible and what is not' (1998, p. 8). In global contexts, however, such an approach is of little relevance as a large proportion of interactions involve NNSs communicating with other NNSs in English (Smith, 1992; Jenkins, 2000). More recent studies on international intelligibility therefore are more inclined to take into account 'all combinations of speakers of English as potential participants in international communication' (Berns, 2008, p. 329), particularly interactions among its non-native speakers (NNS–NNS) and non-native speakers and native speakers (NNS–NS).

The present chapter provides a review of research on intelligibility that has been carried out in the fields of L2 pronunciation, world Englishes and English as a lingua franca. While studies from the latter two fields are directly pertinent to the subject of intelligibility in global contexts, the former has addressed various aspects of intelligibility in experimental settings that have provided equally insightful observations on the matter. Further, since it is in pronunciation that varieties of English are most notably different (Bamgbose, 1998), researchers have tended to focus on this area of linguistics in their study of intelligibility. The review therefore will to a large extent cover the work done on intelligible pronunciation; however, in attempting to provide a comprehensive overview of the research on intelligibility, the review will not be limited to matters of pronunciation only.

Defining 'intelligibility'

Bamgbose considers the subject of intelligibility 'a complex matter' (1998, p. 8). In part, this complexity derives from the difficulty encountered in pinning down the concept of intelligibility itself and in identifying the best means of assessing it (Field, 2005; Pickering, 2006; Rajadurai, 2007; Munro, 2011). Deterding and Kirkpatrick refer to the concept as being 'somewhat elusive' (2006, p. 392). The first problem seems to be in the use of the term in both a general sense as well as a more technical or specific one, and the tendency to switch between the two (Kirkpatrick, Deterding & Wong, 2008; Nelson, 2008). To complicate matters, 'terms such as *intelligibility* and *comprehensibility* are often used interchangeably' (Field, 2005, p. 400) to refer to the same thing. As the definition of intelligibility commonly associated with the different fields of research varies in the scope it covers, attempts to come away with a conceptualization that is universally accepted proves to be challenging, as illustrated below.

Smith and Nelson (1985), in a survey of the then state-of-the-art research on international intelligibility, examined 163 published items on the subject and found the terms intelligibility, comprehensibility and interpretability to be used interchangeably in many instances. In order to address the confusion in the use of these terms, they provided distinct and specific meanings for each: intelligibility to refer to word or utterance recognition, comprehensibility to word or utterance meaning, and interpretability to the purpose or intent behind the use of a word or utterance. Each notion constitutes part of the broader concept of understanding, or, as Smith puts it, 'as degrees of understanding on a continuum, with intelligibility being lowest and interpretability being highest' (1992, p. 76). While lack of interpretability or comprehensibility is said to lead to more serious communication problems, the absence of intelligibility can be expected to affect an interlocutor's ability to comprehend or interpret an utterance. Smith and Nelson's definitions have provided the theoretical basis for much of the research on the intelligibility of world Englishes.

In the field of L2 pronunciation, the definition provided by Munro and Derwing (1995; Derwing & Munro, 2005) is generally adopted. They provide a broader definition of intelligibility than Smith and Nelson (1985), whereby it refers to 'the extent to which a speaker's message is actually understood by a listener' (Munro & Derwing, 1995, p. 76). On the other hand, comprehensibility, the other term used in common with Smith and Nelson (1985), is defined as 'a listener's perception of how difficult it is to understand an utterance' (Derwing & Munro, 2005, p. 385). While Derwing and Munro consider their definition of intelligibility to 'correspond fairly closely' (1997, p. 2) to the one provided by Smith (1992; also Smith & Nelson, 1985), this is open to debate. Munro and Derwing's (1995) conceptualization of intelligibility as 'actual understanding' lacks the specificity of Smith's definition, which confines it to 'matters of form', distinct from 'matters of meaning' covered by the term comprehensibility (Pickering, 2006). Nelson also makes this point when he says that 'the differentiation between processing sound and meaning introduced by Smith has been conflated in "intelligibility"' (2008, p. 12). Notwithstanding the aforementioned difference, Munro and Derwing (1995) employ the transcription method to assess the intelligibility of utterances, which in essence measures the extent to which the listener is able to recognize the form of words and utterances produced by the speaker. Thus, rather than using a listening comprehension test or a written/oral summary to gauge how much was actually understood, the chosen method is similar to Smith's use of the cloze test in that the focus is on the recognition of words and utterances.

While the definitions of intelligibility put forward by the aforementioned scholars are generally adopted in their respective fields, individual researchers themselves may propose some variation in the scope of the definition. Bamgbose, a name associated with world Englishes, describes intelligibility as 'a complex of factors comprising recognizing an expression, knowing its meaning, and knowing what that meaning signifies in the sociocultural context' (1998, p. 8), thus returning to the general sense of the term rather than the specific one advocated by Smith. Field, who works in the area of L2 pronunciation, on the other hand, emphasizes the need for a narrower conceptualization of intelligibility than the one provided by Munro and Derwing (1995); he explains the notion as 'the extent to which the acoustic-phonetic content of the message is recognizable by a listener' (2005, p. 401).

In the area of ELF, research on the intelligibility of the speech of NNSs interacting with other NNSs was pioneered by Jenkins (2000). Although Jenkins adopts Smith and Nelson's (1985) definition of intelligibility in that it 'concerns the production and recognition of the formal properties of words and utterances' (2000, p. 78), it is the interactional aspect of intelligibility, i.e. the 'negotiation of intelligibility' (p. 79), that she focuses on. Intelligibility is considered an aspect of understanding that is co-constructed in interaction with both speakers and recipients employing various accommodation strategies in the process as they work their way towards becoming mutually intelligible. While Jenkins focuses on phonological intelligibility (see also Deterding & Kirkpatrick, 2006; Deterding, 2013), others such as Mauranen (2006), Pitzl (2005) and Kaur (2010) examine intelligibility in relation to pragmatics. As researchers in ELF work with naturally occurring spoken data, the intelligibility of words and utterances is determined on the basis of the responses of the participants in interaction.

The above illustrates the continued presence of some variability in the conceptualization of intelligibility not only across different fields of research but also across researchers working within the same field. This, together with the application of different methodologies and the use of different types of data, means that research findings are not always consistent. Any one type of data, as Munro, Derwing and Morton quite rightly point out, provides 'only one perspective on the intelligibility of an utterance or of a speaker' (2006, p. 113). The next three sections will provide an overview of some of the major studies on intelligibility carried out in the selected fields of research – L2 pronunciation, world Englishes and ELF – and their findings; each contributes in shedding light on one or more aspects of this multifaceted construct. The review will adopt the terminology used by the researchers themselves, thus alternating between intelligibility and comprehensibility as the case may be.

Intelligibility and L2 pronunciation research

Research conducted in the field of L2 pronunciation sets out in the main to identify the variables that may lead to more intelligible pronunciation among L2 learners of English in

English as a second language (ESL) contexts (what Kachru (1985) refers to as the inner circle where English is the native language (ENL)). Given that English is 'the primary language for communication' in such contexts, learners will be expected, in the main, to use the language to communicate with its majority NSs (Derwing and Munro, 2005, p. 380). As such, the research tends to focus on one particular combination of participants comprising non-native speakers and native listeners of English. In the context of L2 pronunciation teaching, Abercrombie is often cited for advocating the goal of 'comfortably intelligible pronunciation ... which can be understood with little or no conscious effort on the part of the listener' (1949, p. 120). Such a goal is considered to be far more achievable than one that focuses on the perfect mimicry of NS pronunciation.

In seeking to determine what makes speech intelligible, researchers have examined the effect as well as the relative contribution of various speaker and listener variables on intelligibility, with the former receiving greater attention. As pronunciation is considered to have a major impact on the intelligibility of speech, researchers are keen to identify the aspects of pronunciation that are critical in this regard. In order to examine the interrelatedness between a non-native accent and intelligibility, Munro and Derwing (1995) conducted a study in which NSs of English transcribed utterances produced by Mandarin NSs who, although considered proficient in English, had a moderate to heavy non-native accent. The NSs also rated the speech samples for degree of foreign-accentedness and comprehensibility. The study was extended to include four other first language (L1) groups, namely Cantonese, Japanese, Polish and Spanish, in a study by Derwing and Munro (1997). Findings from both studies point to non-native speech being highly intelligible despite the presence of a foreign accent. As Derwing and Munro put it, 'a strong foreign accent does not necessarily interfere with intelligibility, although NSs may require extra processing time to understand NNS speech' (1997, p. 4), as reflected by the lower perceived comprehensibility ratings compared to the intelligibility scores. Acknowledging the limitations of previous research based solely on NS judgements of NNS pronunciation, Munro et al. (2006) extended their earlier study (Derwing & Munro, 1997) to take into account the judgements of non-native listeners as well, i.e. those of Cantonese, Japanese and Mandarin L1 backgrounds. Not only did the study confirm previous findings but there were also 'striking similarities across listener groups in their comprehension and evaluation of non-native utterances' (2006, pp. 124–125). The phonological properties of speech appear to have a greater influence on the listener's understanding of foreign-accented speech than the linguistic background of the learners themselves. Munro et al. however failed to find conclusive evidence of an own accent advantage in understanding L2 speech.

Anderson-Hsieh and Koehler (1988) in an earlier study, however, found a non-native accent to have an impact on comprehensibility, particularly when heavily accented English was produced at a fast rate. The researchers examined the extent to which native listeners comprehended material read by NSs of Chinese ranging in their English pronunciation proficiency from poor through fair to good. The NS participants listened to both NS and NNS speech samples, the latter produced at different speaking rates, and answered listening comprehension questions. Scores were significantly higher in the case of the former and the differences between the two were largest at the fast rate and with the most pronounced of accents. They also found prosody to have a greater impact on comprehension than segmentals. In a later study, Anderson-Hsieh et al. (1992) pursued their inquiry into the relative contribution of prosody, segmentals and syllable structure to intelligible speech. Based on speech samples produced by speakers from 11 language groups with a wide range of proficiency, the researchers found further evidence of prosody having the strongest impact on pronunciation ratings – which corresponded with intelligibility and acceptability ratings – compared to segmentals and syllable structure.

While the aforementioned study used an overall prosody score, which reflects the raters' overall impression of intonation, rhythm, stress and phrasing, in the analysis of its data, Field (2005) emphasizes the need to consider the effect of the various aspects of prosody on intelligibility separately. As he explains, 'it seems probable that the various constituents of prosody . . . contribute to intelligibility in different ways' (2005, p. 403). Field chose to study the effect of lexical stress on intelligibility from the listener's perspective, that is, by contrasting both native and non-native listeners' responses. Listeners transcribed the single words they heard in their standard form, with a shift in lexical stress only, and with a shift in lexical stress and change in vowel quality. While stress shifting impacted intelligibility, the impact was greatest in the case of a rightward shift in stress without a change in vowel quality. Interestingly, not only were native listener and non-native listener responses remarkably alike, but non-native listeners from various L1 backgrounds were also found to respond similarly. In this case then the properties of the L2 speech signal appear to have a greater impact on intelligibility than the listeners' L1 background (see also Munro et al., 2006). Zielinski (2008) also addressed the subject of intelligibility from the listener's perspective, specifically looking at how native listeners process the speech of L2 speakers of English at 'sites of reduced intelligibility' (p. 71). Zielinski, who examined both the speech signal features that the listeners relied on to identify hard-to-make-out words and the non-standard features that led listeners to wrongly identify words, found syllable stress patterns and segments in strong syllables to have the greatest impact on intelligibility. Given that these features are considered 'important sources of information for native listeners' (2008, p. 80) when processing native phonology, the NS listeners in the study appear to be applying the same processing strategies to non-native speech signals. The absence of adjustment when listening to L2 speech could thus contribute to reduced intelligibility in NS–NNS interaction.

Other listener variables that have been subjected to inquiry concern the listener's familiarity with and attitudes towards a NNS accent. An early study on the effect of familiarity on NS comprehension by Gass and Varonis (1984) looked at several types of listener familiarity: with the topic, with non-native speech in general, with a particular NNS accent, and with the NNSs themselves. While all types of familiarity were found to increase the NS's comprehension of NNS speech, it was 'the listener's familiarity with the topic of discourse [that] greatly facilitates the interpretation of the entire message' (1984, p. 85). Derwing and Munro (1997) also examined the listener's ability to identify a speaker's accent. Not only did familiarity with an accent increase the listener's success at identifying a language but, more importantly, the researchers found 'a correlation between familiarity and intelligibility scores' (1997, p. 14), thus providing support for Gass and Varonis's (1984) findings. NS attitudes towards NNSs and non-native accents are also expected to have an effect on the intelligibility of NNS speech to NSs. Anderson-Hsieh and Koehler (1988), who used the questionnaire method to elicit information about the NS subjects' attitudes, found that a positive attitude towards non-native accent meant that the listener was more willing to make the effort to understand non-native speech. The role of a positive attitude was particularly pronounced 'when it becomes increasingly difficult to understand – at a faster rate with more errors' (1988, p. 587).

L2 pronunciation research of the kind examined above considers the effect of speaker and listener variables on the intelligibility of L2 speech in controlled settings. Findings suggest that accent has less of an impact on intelligibility than once thought and that suprasegmental features have a greater influence on intelligibility than segmentals. Also, while some findings point to listener factors having greater effect on the listener's success in understanding L2 speech, others suggest that the properties of the L2 speech are more important in this regard. While findings such as the above inform decisions on what and how to teach pronunciation in many ESL classrooms around the world, questions remain on the extent to which findings from experimental settings apply to real-world communication. The vastly different conditions present in spontaneous dyadic or multi-party talk, in often less than ideal listening conditions, mean that when addressing the subject of intelligibility in international communication these findings must be considered together with those from research concerned with the actual use of English in global settings.

Intelligibility of world Englishes

Deterding explains world Englishes (WE) as a research paradigm that 'investigates new varieties of English as independent, named, regional varieties . . . and it generally focuses on features of pronunciation, lexis, grammar and discourse that make each variety distinct from the others' (2013, p. 6). Given that the number of NNSs of English worldwide is estimated to outnumber those who speak it natively, and that NNSs are more likely to interact with other NNSs than they are with NSs (Crystal, 2003), researchers are keen to examine the intelligibility of NNS varieties of English not only from the perspective of the NS but also from the perspective of other NNSs. Smith asserts that 'native speakers are not the sole judges of what is intelligible, nor are they always more intelligible than non-native speakers' (1992, p. 76), a point of view particularly relevant in contexts where English is not the native language of its speakers (e.g. in Kachru's (1985) outer circle). This stance means that, unlike L2 pronunciation research, which relies in the main on NS judgements of NNS speech, WE researchers are equally keen to examine the intelligibility of NS speech to NNSs. Findings from intelligibility studies that adopt a WE perspective are expected to not only have pedagogical implications but also provide much-needed evidence to support the legitimizing of NNS varieties of English.

Not unlike research on L2 pronunciation, research on the intelligibility of world Englishes tends to focus on matters related to pronunciation (Nelson, 2008). This is unsurprising as it is in pronunciation that 'non-native Englishes differ substantially from native ones' (Bamgbose, 1998, p. 5). Further, Smith's conceptualization of intelligibility as the formal recognition of words and utterances is dependent on the successful processing of sound. Smith's framework forms the basis of many, if not most, of the intelligibility studies in WE. In an early study, Smith and Rafiqzad (1979) set out to compare the intelligibility of native and non-native varieties of English using speech samples of nine varieties of educated English, including American English: 1,386 listeners from 11 countries in Asia completed a cloze test as they listened to the recordings, and a listening comprehension questionnaire afterwards. The main finding of the study, that 'the native speaker was always found to be among the least intelligible speakers' (1979, p. 375), raises questions about widely held assumptions that NS varieties of English are always more intelligible than NNS varieties. Smith and Rafiqzad further noted that the listeners were highly consistent in how intelligible they found the nine speakers.

As previously stated, English when used in global contexts involves various combinations of interlocutors from different linguistic backgrounds. Investigating how understandable NSs are to NNSs as well as how well NNSs of different L1 backgrounds understand each other is an important aspect of Smith's work. In order to compare the comprehensibility of native and non-native varieties of English, Smith and Bisazza (1982) used speech samples representing three varieties of English – two non-native (Japanese English and Indian English) and one native (American English). The American speaker was found to be the most comprehensible followed by the Japanese and the Indian. Based on information obtained from personal data sheets, the researchers attribute the differences in the degree of comprehensibility of the three speakers to the amount of active exposure the listeners had to those varieties. The greater the exposure to a variety, the more familiar the listener was with the variety and the easier it was to understand the speaker (cf. Gass & Varonis, 1984; Derwing & Munro, 1997). Exposing learners of English to NS models only therefore is unlikely to prepare them for effective communication in global contexts when interactions involve other NNSs. Smith asserts that the use of non-native varieties of English for international communication 'need not increase the problems of understanding across cultures, if users of English develop some familiarity with them' (1992, p. 88).

Matsuura (2007) also addresses the subject of language familiarity and its effect on the intelligibility of speech. The researcher examined the role of several individual learner differences, including familiarity with different varieties of English, on the intelligibility of American English and Hong Kong English to a group of Japanese university students. Although to the Japanese listeners Hong Kong English was an unfamiliar variety, scores on a cloze dictation test indicated that they found Hong Kong English more intelligible than American English. Taking into account the participants' experience with different varieties of English, it appears that 'the more varieties students are exposed to, the better their understanding of a nonstandard variety' (2007, p. 301). This finding has important pedagogical implications as it underscores the need to make available to learners input from a variety of non-native Englishes to better prepare them for communication in global settings. Although Tauroza and Luk (1997), in an earlier study, found that Hong Kong ESL learners had better comprehension of English with an RP accent than with a Hong Kong accent, they too attribute this to the familiarity factor. While the expectation is that the learners would be more familiar with their own variety of English, the researchers explain that this is not the case in Hong Kong. Exposure to Hong Kong-accented English is limited as the L1 Cantonese speakers are more inclined to use their mother tongue when communicating with each other. On the other hand, learners have greater exposure to the RP accent in their surroundings, which explains their higher comprehension scores for RP-accented English. Thus while Tauroza and Luk's study does not provide support for the idea of an own accent advantage (cf. Munro et al., 2006), it provides evidence of a positive role for accent familiarity in understanding speech.

In a more recent study, Kirkpatrick et al. (2008) examined the intelligibility of educated Hong Kong English to listeners from Singapore and Australia. The listeners completed a listening comprehension test based on recordings of semi-authentic conversations between Hong Kong L1 speakers of Cantonese and their British national lecturer. Although all the speakers 'displayed typical features of Hong Kong pronunciation' (2008, p. 362), both native and non-native listeners from Singapore and Australia, respectively, found them to be highly intelligible. Kirkpatrick et al. (2008) conclude that lack of conformity to NS norms need not hamper the international intelligibility of non-native varieties of English. Findings of this nature support calls being made by WE scholars for greater acceptance of the new varieties of English in the language classroom.

Intelligibility studies of world Englishes complement research on L2 pronunciation in that they address a research gap present as a result of the latter's focus on NS judgements of L2 speech in ESL contexts (see Derwing & Munro, 2005). Given the present realities of the global spread and use of English, it is equally important to take into account the NNS's perspective on the subject of intelligibility. Findings that point to NS accents being less intelligible than NNS ones bring into question long-held beliefs about the superiority of NS varieties of English. As it appears, NNS varieties, despite the influence of L1 features, are equally if not more intelligible in some cases. Strict adherence to NS norms in the language classroom, in contexts where learners are likely to use the language to interact with other NNSs, therefore, appears unnecessary as it fails to guarantee improved understanding. As Smith and Bisazza assert, 'the assumption that nonnative students of English will be able to comprehend fluent non-native speakers if they understand native speakers is clearly not correct' (1982, p. 269). What actually transpires in interactions in global settings, however, is less clear as studies such as the aforementioned continue to be conducted in controlled settings. In the next section, research in the area of ELF is examined to delve into the issue of intelligibility in real-world settings.

Intelligibility in ELF interaction

Research in the area of English as a lingua franca is a relatively new development in applied linguistics that examines 'any use of English among speakers of different first languages for whom English is the communicative medium of choice, and often the only option' (Seidlhofer, 2011, p. 7). Given the emphasis on the use of English among speakers of varied L1 backgrounds, international communication in English is examined as it occurs in interaction. This approach to the study of intelligibility ties in well with the notion of intelligibility as being 'interactional between speaker and listener' (Smith & Nelson, 1985, p. 333). The study of ELF, although perhaps displaying some superficial commonalities with WE (Berns, 2008), is different in that 'research on ELF usually considers common patterns that are shared by speakers from disparate backgrounds' (Deterding, 2013, p. 6) rather than the specific features that distinguish the different varieties of non-native Englishes. Further, while WE research with its '"varieties-based" approach' (Sewell, 2010, p. 266) tends to be form-focused, ELF research concerns itself with the practices and processes involved in ELF communication and when forms are examined it is done with the aim of uncovering the processes underlying the use of those forms (Seidlhofer, 2011; Cogo, 2012).

Notwithstanding the current focus on function over form, early research by Jenkins (2000) examined the phonological features of ELF interaction considered essential for intelligible speech and effective communication. However, unlike the studies on L2 pronunciation and WE reviewed above, Jenkins examines the intelligibility of speech in relation to the occurrence of misunderstanding as well as accommodation in interaction. Owing to the absence of a shared background – social, cultural and linguistic – among speakers in lingua franca contexts, there is 'a far greater reliance on the acoustic signal' (2000, p. 81) when trying to achieve understanding. However, the English used in such contexts tends towards variability in form, both within and across speakers, which can threaten successful communication. Jenkins, who examined instances of communication breakdown in the interactions of Swiss and Japanese speakers, found L1 phonological transfer to be the leading cause of breakdown. Those phonological features identified as leading to the loss of intelligibility constitute what Jenkins refers to as the lingua franca core (LFC), a set of features considered crucial for international intelligibility. These include most consonant sounds, appropriate consonant cluster simplification, vowel length distinctions and nuclear stress (2000, p. 132). Contrary to findings in L2 pronunciation research, Jenkins finds segmentals to have a greater impact on intelligibility than suprasegmentals. Apart from taking into account the teachability factor, Jenkins argues that NS prosody, particularly the use of weak forms and stress-timed rhythm, may in fact impede intelligibility in NNS–NNS interactions.

Jenkins's LFC has been largely criticized owing to what has been perceived as 'insistence on a prescribed set of features' (Berns, 2008, p. 333) for learners in countries where the mother tongue is not English. In her defence, the LFC is not intended to be a pronunciation model or a prescribed set of norms, rather it is an attempt to provide learners with choices on the basis of the kinds of contexts in which they are likely to use English. As Jenkins explains, 'the LFC allows far greater individual freedom . . . by providing speakers with the scope both to express their own identities and to accommodate to their receivers' (2000, p. 158). Support for Jenkins's LFC and the relative importance of segmentals over suprasegmentals in ensuring intelligibility comes from studies by Deterding and Kirkpatrick (2006) and Deterding (2013). Using conversational data obtained from speakers from ASEAN (Association of Southeast Asian Nations) countries, Deterding and Kirkpatrick (2006) examined instances of non-standard pronunciation produced by the speakers and their impact on intelligibility. Although non-standard, shared features were not found to impede communication while features that were unshared contributed to misunderstanding. All the shared features were precisely those that had been excluded from Jenkins's LFC, while the problematic ones had been included owing to their crucial role in maintaining intelligibility. The researchers also noted that syllable-based rhythm, the result of using a full vowel in unstressed syllables, was a common feature of their data, which appeared to enhance intelligibility. Non-native prosody it seems need not create an obstacle to intelligible speech.

The design of the studies on L2 pronunciation and WE, examined in the above two sections, precludes their researchers from having access to the accommodation practices the speaker engages in as well as the listener's contribution to the negotiation of intelligibility in interaction. With their focus on the use of ELF in action, researchers are able to examine the kinds of adjustments speakers make to their pronunciation as they monitor on a moment by moment basis how much the listener is able to understand. Jenkins observed that speakers take the recipients' needs into account and 'tend to minimize the use of L1 phonological transfer when they are able to do so' (2000, p. 90). Matsumoto (2011), to further the inquiry into the subject of phonological accommodation and negotiation, looked specifically at 'sequences of repair of pronunciation' (2011, p. 98) in ELF interactions among international postgraduate students at an American university. The participants were seen to employ various repair strategies when their pronunciation seemed to cause difficulty in understanding for the recipient. These include replacing problematic sounds with what they considered more target-like sounds and repeating with greater care lexical items that contained anomalous sounds. Speakers generally make adjustments to their pronunciation in response to the recipients' request for repair (see also Deterding, 2013). Studies of this nature illustrate how 'even at the level of pronunciation, intelligibility is dynamically negotiable between speaker and listener, rather than statically inherent in a speaker's linguistic forms' (Jenkins, 2000, p. 79).

Research on the intelligibility of speech from an ELF perspective is not limited to pronunciation or, for that matter, to word and utterance recognition only. In actual interaction, merely being able to recognize the form of words and utterances is insufficient to ensure successful communicative outcomes. Rather, word/utterance recognition needs to be accompanied with the attribution of meaning and intent for speech to make sense. Given the interest in how speakers in global contexts arrive at shared understanding and taking into account the preference for the use of naturally occurring spoken data, the boundaries between intelligibility and comprehensibility are understandably blurred in much of ELF research (Pickering, 2006). Researchers are keen to uncover the strategies and practices participants employ to not only manage non-understandings and misunderstandings when they occur but to also pre-empt such problems from the outset (Pitzl, 2005; Mauranen, 2006; Kaur, 2010). Based on sequential analyses of talk at sites of reduced or impaired intelligibility and/or comprehensibility, commonly used interactional practices such as repetition, paraphrase, comprehension checks and confirmation and clarification requests, among others, have been identified as those that speakers make strategic use of to restore understanding. The use of these procedures in interaction illustrates the collaborative and negotiated nature of the process of enhancing the intelligibility and comprehensibility of speech. Elsewhere, Mauranen (2007) and Kaur (2011, 2012) examine speakers' use of explicitness strategies to make their communication intelligible and more accessible to the interlocutor. A simple and straightforward practice such as repetition, for instance, may be used in a multitude of ways – parallel phrasing, keyword repetition, combined repetition with reformulation and repetition of repaired segments of talk – to improve on the clarity and intelligibility of speech (Kaur, 2012).

By examining intelligibility in interaction, researchers are able to take into account the context of the talk, both local and beyond. Words, perceived as unintelligible in isolation or in decontextualized utterances, may in fact have their intelligibility improved when context is made available. As Suenobu, Kanzaki and Yamane (1992), who conducted an experimental study of the intelligibility of Japanese English, noted, context 'enhanced the understanding of the word even if the word was not properly pronounced' (1992, p. 148). Also, while many intelligibility studies generally have identified the features of NNS phonology that lead to improved intelligibility, from an ELF perspective intelligibility is enhanced in interaction as participants adjust and modify their speech based on feedback provided by the interlocutor on an ongoing basis. Just as the English used in global contexts is fluid and flexible, intelligibility too is dynamic and relative, and dependent on the contexts of use and the ever-changing constellation of speakers. While ELF is a relatively new area of research, findings suggest that it provides 'a much needed complementary or alternative methodology' (Rajadurai, 2007, p. 96) to the study of intelligibility.

Pedagogical implications

It is a given that learners of English in countries that do not speak English as a mother tongue, for the most part, 'will *always* speak English with an identifiable accent' (Hung, 2002, p. 7). Non-native accent, however, as Munro and Derwing (1995), Derwing and Munro (1997) and Munro et al. (2006) point out, is, although related, quite separate from intelligibility. For purposes of international communication, it is only those features of pronunciation that are likely to hamper mutual intelligibility that should be of concern. Studies that have identified the features of NNS phonology that promote international intelligibility have to date produced mixed findings. This, however, is unsurprising, for, as Seidlhofer reminds us, 'findings are always relative to the conditions under which they come about, always shaped to some extent by the research questions asked, and always of necessity partial' (2007, pp. 99–100). The verdict it appears is still out on the relative contribution segmentals and suprasegmentals make towards intelligible pronunciation.

Levis recommends that decisions on how pronunciation is taught take into account 'the context [and the purpose] of instruction' (2005, p. 376). While learners destined for education, employment or residence in English mother tongue-speaking countries will certainly benefit from exposure to NS models, such models are likely to prove 'inappropriate or unnecessary' (Levis, 2005, p. 376) in other contexts. Insisting that learners mimic NS sounds and prosody makes little sense if their future communications in English are likely to be limited to fellow NNSs from their region of the world. As Deterding and Kirkpatrick (2006) point out, speakers of English in South East Asia are likely to find stress-timed rhythm associated with NS varieties less intelligible than syllable-based rhythm, a shared feature of their Englishes. As such, expecting that learners adhere to stress-timed rhythm in the classroom is unlikely to do much for them in terms of developing intelligible pronunciation for communication with fellow ASEAN members.

The changing reality of the global use of English also means that learners of English are likely to benefit from greater exposure to a range of non-native varieties of English. There seems to be a general consensus on the facilitating effect that familiarity has on the intelligibility of the different varieties of English (e.g. Smith & Bisazza, 1982; Tauroza & Luk, 1997; Derwing & Munro, 1997; Matsuura, 2007). Exposure to non-native varieties is not only likely to improve the learner's ability to understand L2 speech better but also expected to have a positive effect on his or her attitude towards NNSs in general, and their speech in particular. Matsuda states that 'limited exposure to English varieties in the class-room may lead to confusion or resistance when students are confronted with different types of English users or uses outside of class' (2005, p. 721). Many learners, and their NNS teachers, in countries that do not speak English as a mother tongue equate native-like accent with a good command of the language (Jenkins, 2005). Not infrequently, non-native accents are looked down upon and stigmatized, and can even lead to perceptions of unintelligibility. As 'attitude and tolerance play a role in communicative success and failure' (Berns, 2008, p. 332), it is as important to develop in learners a greater awareness of the variability of English across contexts and communities as it is to develop their competence in the language.

Given that it is not always possible to anticipate all the NNS varieties learners are likely to encounter in the real world, findings from ELF research emphasize that developing in learners the ability to accommodate their pronunciation towards their interlocutor is key to intelligible communication in global contexts. Giles and Coupland (1991, p. 85) assert that 'increased intelligibility is a valuable byproduct of convergent acts and may on occasion be the *principal* motivation for accommodating' (cited in Jenkins 2000, p. 173). Jenkins adds that, in seeking 'to produce pronunciation that is intelligible for the particular interlocutor' (2000, p. 66), both adjustments towards or away from the standard may occur as the situation warrants. Promoting phonological accommodation therefore entails developing in learners the ability to adjust and modify their pronunciation in response to listener feedback through the use of meaningful communication tasks (Walker, 2005). In this regard, Matsumoto recommends that instances of successful ELF interactions also 'be included as legitimate and alternative teaching materials in ELT' (2011, p. 110). Researchers, regardless of their research perspective, generally agree on the interactional nature of intelligibility; however, efforts to promote particular phonological features over others 'may give the misleading impression that intelligibility derives from linguistic forms and is speaker-dependent' (Sewell, 2010, p. 265). If indeed intelligibility is interactional, then it has to be acknowledged that it is in and through interaction that intelligibility is jointly constructed in an ongoing manner, and it is also in and through interaction that intelligible pronunciation needs to be developed.

Future directions

Gass and Varonis quote a participant from their experimental study who said, 'I could understand the man speaking because I had a few seconds to think about what he said. I think it would be very difficult to carry on a conversation with him' (1984, p. 84). The quote brings to light the crucial need to examine the subject of international intelligibility in the context of interaction in global settings as speakers of different linguistic and cultural backgrounds negotiate meaning in English in pursuit of real communicative goals. The impact of both speaker and listener variables on intelligibility as well as the relative contribution of various speech properties are likely to be influenced, to a greater or lesser degree, by the context – sociocultural and interactional – in which the interaction takes place. Rajadurai reminds us that, 'people speak differently in different situations . . . and people react to speech differently in different settings' (2007, p. 90). The notion of intelligibility as a dynamic, interactional construct means that attempts to determine the intelligibility of speech based on the judgements of a group of listeners, native or otherwise, in an artificial setting devoid of the possibility of examining the process of negotiation and the use of accommodation strategies are likely to result in partial insights at best.

Smith and Nelson (1985) argue for intelligibility to be investigated separate from the related but distinct notions of comprehensibility and interpretability. However, in real-world settings it is conceivable that the three are intertwined in complex ways that deserve further investigation. The ability to recognize words and utterances, although necessary, is unlikely to be sufficient in interactional contexts driven by real communicative goals. If research on international intelligibility is to be relevant in today's globalizing world, it must consider how word/utterance recognition and the attribution of meaning and intent interconnect to allow speakers to accomplish mutual understanding in encounters marked by diversity and variability. Insisting on the separation of the constructs will result to a large degree in the continued use of methodologies that isolate one from the other in controlled settings. Perhaps the time has come to consider reconceptualizing 'intelligibility' so that the context-bound, interactional and dynamic nature of the construct is brought to the fore. While many research-ers adopt definitions that make reference to the interactional nature of intelligibility, the design of their studies reveals underlying assumptions of intelligibility as residing in the speaker and dependent on the degree to which they adhere to prescribed norms.

As a large proportion of international communication involves NNSs interacting with other NNSs, there is also a need to examine the effect of the participants' linguistic and com-municative competence on the intelligibility of their speech and their ability to negotiate and accommodate to their interlocutor. Much of the research being conducted from the ELF perspective works with data from speakers with fairly high levels of competence – university students and staff, business people and the like. While it is important to identify the features of successful international communication and the kinds of interactional strategies used by such participants, it is equally important to examine the same in the interactions of participants with lower levels of competence. Comparisons of the two may reveal the kinds and levels of competences required for talk to be intelligible. Given the co-constructed nature of intelligibility and the widespread use of accommodation strategies in this regard, the notion of competence must be extended to include the effective use of relevant strategies that enhance intelligibility in interaction. This will certainly have important implications for ELT pedagogy. While there is still much to uncover on the subject of intelligibility, what is needed is a concerted interdisciplinary endeavour that brings together scholars with different ideologies and stances to look more closely at international intelligibility in action.

Further reading

Levis, J. (Ed.). (2005). Reconceptualizing pronunciation in TESOL: Intelligibility, world Englishes and Identity. *TESOL Quarterly Special Issue*, *39*(3), 365–572. This special volume comprises contributions from well-known scholars working on intelligibility issues from a wide range of research areas.

References

Abercrombie, D. (1949). Teaching pronunciation. *English Language Teaching, 3*(5), 113–122.

Anderson-Hsieh, J., & Koehler, K. (1988). The effect of foreign accent and speaking rate on native speaker comprehension. *Language Learning, 38*(4), 561–592.

Anderson-Hsieh, J., Johnson, R., & Koehler, K. (1992). The relationship between native speaker judgements of nonnative pronunciation and deviance in segmentals, prosody and syllable structure. *Language Learning, 4*(4), 529–555.

Bamgbose, A. (1998). Torn between the norms: innovations in world Englishes. *World Englishes, 17*(1), 1–14.

Berns, M. (2008). World Englishes, English as a lingua franca, and intelligibility. *World Englishes, 27*(3), 327–334.

Cogo, A. (2012). English as a lingua franca: Concepts, use, and implications. *ELT Journal, 66*(1), 97–105.

Crystal, D. (2003). *English as a global language* (2nd Ed.). Cambridge: Cambridge University Press.

Derwing, T. M., & Munro, M. J. (1997). Accent, intelligibility, and comprehensibility. *Studies in Second Language Acquisition, 20*, 1–16.

Derwing, T. M., & Munro, M. J. (2005). Second language accent and pronunciation teaching: A research-based approach. *TESOL Quarterly, 39*(3), 379–397.

Deterding, D. (2013). *Misunderstandings in English as a lingua franca*. Berlin: Mouton de Gruyter.

Deterding, D., & Kirkpatrick, A. (2006). Emerging south-east asian Englishes and intelligibility. *World Englishes, 25*(3), 391–409.

Field, J. (2005). Intelligibility and the listener: The role of lexical stress. *TESOL Quarterly, 39*(3), 399–423.

Gass, S., & Varonis, E. M. (1984). The effect of familiarity on the comprehensibility of nonnative speech. *Language Learning, 34*(1), 65–87.

Giles, H., & Coupland, N. (1991). *Language: Contexts and consequences*. Milton Keynes: Open University Press.

Hung, T. T. N. (2002). English as a global language and the issue of international intelligibility. *Asian Englishes, 5*(1), 4–17.

Jenkins, J. (2000). *The phonology of English as an international language*. Oxford: Oxford University Press.

Jenkins, J. (2005). Implementing an international approach to English pronunciation: The role of teacher attitudes and identity. *TESOL Quarterly, 39*(3), 535–543.

Kachru, B. B. (1985). Standards, codification and sociolinguistic realism: The English language in the outer circle. In R. Quirk & H. Widdowson (Eds), *English in the world: Teaching and learning the language and literatures* (pp. 11–30). Cambridge: Cambridge University Press.

Kaur, J. (2010). Achieving mutual understanding in world Englishes. *World Englishes, 29*(2), 192–208.

Kaur, J. (2011). Raising explicitness through self-repair in English as a lingua franca. *Journal of Pragmatics, 43*(11), 2704–2715.

Kaur, J. (2012). Saying it again: Enhancing clarity in English as a lingua franca (ELF) talk through self-repetition. *Text&Talk, 32*(5), 593–613.

Kirkpatrick, A., Deterding, D., & Wong, J. (2008). The international intelligibility of Hong Kong English. *World Englishes, 27*(3–4), 359–377.

Levis, J. M. (2005). Changing contexts and shifting paradigms in pronunciation teaching. *TESOL Quarterly, 39*(3), 369–377.

Matsuda, A. (2005). Incorporating world Englishes in teaching English as an international language. *TESOL Quarterly, 39*(3), 719–729.

Matsumoto, Y. (2011). Successful ELF communications and implications for ELT: Sequential analysis of ELF pronunciation negotiation strategies. *The Modern Language Journal, 95*, 97–114.

Matsuura, H. (2007). Intelligibility and individual learner differences in the EIL context. *System, 35*, 293–304.

Mauranen, A. (2006). Signaling and preventing misunderstanding in English as lingua franca communication. *International Journal of the Sociology of Language, 177*, 123–150.

Mauranen, A. (2007). Hybrid voices: English as the lingua franca of academics. In K. Flottum (Ed.), *Language and discipline perspectives on academic discourse* (pp. 243–259). Newcastle upon Tyne: Cambridge Scholars.

Munro, M. J. (2011). Intelligibility: Buzzword or buzzworthy? In J. Levis & K. LeVelle (Eds), *Proceedings of the 2nd Pronunciation in Second Language Learning and Teaching Conference* (pp. 7–16). Ames, IA: Iowa State University.

Munro, M. J., & Derwing, T. M. (1995). Foreign accent, comprehensibility, and intelligibility in the speech of second language learners. *Language Learning, 45*(1), 73–97.

Munro, M. J., Derwing, T. M., & Morton, S. L. (2006). The mutual intelligibility of L2 speech. *Studies in Second Language Acquisition, 28*, 111–131.

Nelson, C. L. (2008). Intelligibility since 1969. *World Englishes, 27*(3–4), 297–308.

Pickering, L. (2006). Current research on intelligibility in English as a lingua franca. *Annual Review of Applied Linguistics, 26*, 219–233.

Pitzl, M-L. (2005). Non-understanding in English as a lingua franca: Examples from a business context. *Vienna English Working Papers, 14*, 50–71. Retrieved from: www.univie.ac.at/Anglistik/Views 0502mlp.pdf (accessed 28 January 2015).

Rajadurai, J. (2007). Intelligibility studies: A consideration of empirical and ideological issues. *World Englishes, 26*(1), 87–98.

Seidlhofer, B. (2007). Comment. *World Englishes, 26*(1), 99–100.

Seidlhofer, B. (2011). *Understanding English as a lingua franca.* Oxford: Oxford University Press.

Sewell, A. (2010). Research methods and intelligibility studies. *World Englishes, 29*(2), 257–269.

Smith, L. E. (1992). Spread of English and issues of intelligibility. In B. Kachru (Ed.) *The other tongue: English across cultures* (2nd ed., pp. 75–90). Urbana, IL: Illinois University Press.

Smith, L. E., & Nelson, C. L. (1985). International intelligibility of English: Directions and resources. *World Englishes, 4*(3), 333–342.

Smith, L. E., & Bisazza, J. A. (1982). The comprehensibility of three varieties of English for college students in seven countries. *Language Learning, 32*(2), 259–269.

Smith, L. E., & Rafiqzad, K. (1979). English for cross-cultural communication: The question of intelligibility. *TESOL Quarterly, 13*(3), 371–380.

Suenobu, M., Kanzaki, K., & Yamane, S. (1992). An experimental study of intelligibility of Japanese English. *IRAL, 30*(2), 146–153.

Tauroza, S., & Luk, J. (1997). Accent and second language listening comprehension. *RELC Journal, 28*(1), 54–69.

Walker, R. (2005). Using student-produced recordings with monolingual groups to provide effective, individualized pronunciation practice. *TESOL Quarterly, 39*(3), 550–557.

Zielinski, B. W. (2008). The listener: No longer the silent partner in reduced intelligibility. *System, 36*, 69–84.

34

Automatic speech recognition for second language pronunciation training

Catia Cucchiarini and Helmer Strik

Introduction

In the current chapter we discuss how automatic speech recognition (ASR) and related technologies can be employed in the context of second language (L2) pronunciation learning and teaching. Examples of such use of ASR-based technologies are commercial products such as Rosetta Stone (www.rosettastone.com). These offer pronunciation exercises in which students can practice perception and production of L2 speech and receive automatic feedback from the computer. The rationale behind this overview is that cooperation between speech technologists and L2 pronunciation researchers would benefit both research and practice. However, such a form of cooperation requires researchers from both fields to step outside their own discipline, show interest in each other's work, make an effort to understand each other's concerns and be prepared to work together to find solutions. In the case of ASR-based pronunciation teaching this is not trivial, because the expertise required is highly varied and language teachers will have to communicate with engineers and computer scientists. In this chapter, we try to present ASR research in terms that are accessible to language teachers, but a minimal use of technical jargon is unavoidable.

Since the literature on this topic is extensive, a number of criteria have been applied to select the work presented in this chapter. First, the overview is mainly focused on studies that employ ASR prior to further analysis of pronunciation errors. The phase of ASR that aims at identifying the words a learner is trying to produce, also known as utterance verification, is one important advantage of using ASR as opposed to L2 speech analysis without ASR. It guarantees, as much as possible, that analyses are conducted on pertinent aspects of learner speech and that feedback is provided on the utterance that was really produced by the learner. Even cooperative learners might end up producing different utterances from those elicited by a pronunciation training programme, for instance because they experience difficulties of different kinds, they might not understand what they should do and say 'Sorry, I do not understand' instead of the expected utterance, or they may produce different words interspersed with disfluencies (Cucchiarini, Strik & Boves, 2002). A system that analyses L2 speech without ASR runs the risk of providing feedback on a different utterance (the one prompted or expected) than the one actually produced by the learner and might thus mislead the learner and lose credibility. Second, although pronunciation assessment and pronunciation error detection are both mentioned and explained, the latter constitutes the central topic of this chapter. Third, the overview is limited to research on automatic pronunciation assessment and training at segmental level and does not address suprasegmental aspects. The reasons for this are that suprasegmental features are addressed elsewhere in this volume and that suprasegmentals have been involved in automatic pronunciation assessment (Chen & Zechner, 2011), but not so much in ASR-based systems for pronunciation error detection in the context of learning and teaching. Fourth, although there are numerous publications on the different approaches to pronunciation error detection and the metrics developed for this purpose, these have not been included because of their extremely technical nature, which is beyond the scope of the present volume. Consequently, this overview is focused on illustrative studies and research considered to be relevant for pronunciation instruction. In line with these choices the term ASR-based pronunciation training will be used in this chapter instead of computer-assisted pronunciation training (CAPT), which refers to a broader range of technologies beyond ASR.

This chapter is organized as follows. A brief historical perspective is first provided, followed by a discussion of critical issues and topics. Subsequently, various systems that have been developed for pronunciation error detection are presented. Finally, recommendations for pronunciation teaching practice and future perspectives are discussed.

Historical perspectives

Interest in the potential of ASR technology for L2 learning and especially for pronunciation instruction became particularly evident and grew significantly in the 1990s. There was an increasing demand for language lessons, especially for practising oral skills, which traditionally receive less attention in the language classroom, and for one-on-one tutoring, which is unaffordable for the majority of language learners. But arguably most important were advances in ASR technology and its application in dictation systems that became commercially available. These products inspired L2 researchers who thought this upcoming technology could provide the kind of individual, intensive, anxiety-free practice that was required for L2 pronunciation training. Studies were carried out to determine to what extent ASR technology was accurate in recognizing L2 learners' speech and in identifying pronunciation deviations (Coniam, 1999; Derwing, Munro & Carbonaro, 2000). The results were generally disappointing, which was not surprising. First, the dictation systems investigated were developed for native speakers and not for L2 learners. Second, dictation is essentially a different task from L2 pronunciation training. The aim in dictation applications is to convert an incoming speech signal into a string of words, while for pronunciation training ASR should do more than that: in addition to determining which words a student is trying to pronounce, it should also evaluate the quality of L2 speech and identify possible errors. Which errors should then be addressed in the ASR-based pronunciation training system depends on the aim of the study or application. In any case, identifying errors requires a more complex procedure in which ASR technology needs to be optimized for the specific purposes for which it will be employed.

In the same period, the ASR community also began to show interest in applying ASR technology to pronunciation learning (Bernstein, Cohen, Murveit, Rtischev & Weintraub, 1990; Cucchiarini, Strik & Boves, 1997; Ehsani & Knodt, 1998; Neumeyer, Franco, Weintraub & Price, 1996; Witt & Young, 1997). Early research on the use of ASR for pronunciation assessment and training was exploratory, and investigated the extent to which automatic pronunciation assessment and error detection were feasible. Initial studies were promising and revealed high correlations between ASR-based objective measurements and subjective judgements of L2 speech (Akahane-Yamada & McDermott, 1998; Cucchiarini, Strik & Boves, 2000a, 2000b; Neumeyer et al., 1996; Witt & Young, 1997). The ASR-based objective measurements were usually obtained by employing ASR technology in forced alignment mode. This means that in this case ASR technology is used to align phonemic representations of words that are known to have been uttered (for instance because the students have to read aloud words from the screen) with the corresponding speech signal. In this way it is possible to automatically establish which portions of the speech signal correspond to which phonemes and which phoneme realizations are deviant. To express the degree of deviation, various measures can be employed that indicate to what extent the acoustic values of a given phoneme deviate from those normally expected. These measures can be calculated for each individual instance of a phoneme, or can be averaged over the phonemes in a word or sentence. In general, it is more difficult to obtain high correlations between these objective measures and human scores when these are calculated at the level of individual phones than when they are averaged over words, sentences or even all speech of one speaker.

One of the first systems employing ASR-based technology to detect L2 pronunciation errors was the fluency pronunciation trainer, which used Carnegie speech recognition (Eskenazi & Hansma, 1998; Eskenazi, 1999) with forced alignment to provide information on individual phone durations. Precoda, Halverson and Franco (2000) studied the effectiveness of SRI's FreshTalk pronunciation scoring software to improve segmental pronunciation quality and fluency in L2 Spanish of 45 adult native American learners. Post-test ASR-generated scores showed that practice did not significantly improve segmental pronunciation and that focus on accuracy led to lower speech rate. The HearSay system (Dalby, Kewley-Port & Sillings, 1998) was based on the idea of phonological contrast training and used minimal pairs. Segmental errors were evaluated by native English speakers (NESs) based on intelligibility criteria (Rogers & Dalby, 1996) and recognition scores were used as a basis for segmental pronunciation scoring. The Interactive Spoken Language Education (ISLE) system (Menzel, Herron, Bonaventura & Morton, 2000b) addressed German and Italian learners of English and aimed at providing feedback on mispronunciations of specific sounds and word stress errors. ISLE achieved poor performance and the authors concluded that with those results 'students will more frequently be given erroneous discouraging feedback than they will be given helpful diagnoses' (Menzel et al., 2000b). The 'Pronunciation Learning via ASR' (PLASER) system (Mak et al., 2003) was aimed at detecting pronunciation errors and at providing information on how to correct them with Chinese learners of English. Although students were positive about the system and thought that it improved their pronunciation, robustness and error detection appeared to be problematic.

Criticism of early research on ASR-based pronunciation training was that it was more driven by the possibilities offered by the technology than by pedagogical requirements (Pennington, 1999; Neri, Cucchiarini, Strik & Boves, 2002). At the end of the 1990s and early 2000s companies also started to incorporate ASR technology in language learning products such as Tell me More by Auralog, TriplePlayPlus and Learn German Now! In general, reviewers were critical about the performance of such systems and sceptical about their usability for language learning (Wachowicz & Scott, 1999).

Critical issues and topics

ASR of learner speech

A critical issue in ASR-based pronunciation training is first of all determining which words the language learners are trying to pronounce, also known as utterance verification. This requires that ASR technology be available for the L2 in question, which is not always the case. For cases in which ASR technology is not available for the L2, alternative procedures for pronunciation error detection have been proposed that do not rely on ASR capabilities (Lee, Zhang & Glass, 2013). However, if available, using ASR and performing utterance verification are to be preferred for the reasons mentioned in the introduction, namely that this ensures, as much as possible, that analyses are conducted on the utterance that was really produced by the learner. The process of automatically recognizing speech is essentially a probabilistic procedure for which a number of information sources have to be obtained. This is done by first training the speech recognizer with speech corpora containing speech signals and corresponding annotations. During this training phase different models are derived that are subsequently used as sources of information in the recognition process: acoustic models for individual speech sounds and language models that indicate which words are likely to follow each other. In the recognition phase a search algorithm converts the incoming speech signal into a string of words by employing basically three 'knowledge sources', the two types of models mentioned above, which are developed during the training phase and a lexicon. The language model contains probabilities of words and word sequences, the acoustic models model how the speech sounds are realized, and the lexicon, a list of words that can be recognized, is the connection between the language model and the acoustic models.

L2 learners make pronunciation errors, tend to use different words and grammar from native speakers, and produce more disfluencies. These deviations concern all three knowledge sources used in ASR (the acoustic models, the lexicon and the language model), which have to be adapted when recognizing learner speech, for instance by using learner speech material (see below) for training or adaptation. In addition, to limit the difficulties in speech recognition, techniques can be applied to constrain the learner's speech output and make the task easier, for instance by resorting to reading aloud, shadowing or directing learners to pre-specified responses (van Doremalen, Cucchiarini & Strik, 2010; Peabody, 2011).

Pronunciation assessment and pronunciation error detection

For utterance verification, learner acoustic models are generally used, while for assessing the quality of L2 speech native acoustic models are employed to determine to what extent the learner's speech differs from native speech. As explained above, this is usually expressed by a score, which can be computed at different levels of detail: individual speech sounds, words, utterances or speaker level. Measures of pronunciation quality at the speaker or utterance level, also referred to as 'holistic pronunciation evaluation' (Peabody, 2011), can provide useful indications for testing and screening purposes or for assessing global progress in pronunciation quality, but are in general not detailed enough to form a good basis for pronunciation instruction and corrective feedback (Precoda et al. 2000). For pronunciation instruction, more detailed information is required so that feedback can be provided when the mispronounced words or speech sounds are still available in working memory and learners can more easily repair them.

Providing immediate feedback on segmental errors requires specialized algorithms for pronunciation error detection at a finer level of granularity (detail) than pronunciation scoring, to localize the errors and possibly identify them. Guaranteeing high degrees of accuracy at this level of detail is much more challenging, first of all because there is less information (data, signal) available. Instead of analysing several utterances or several realizations of the same phoneme, the score has to be computed based on observing one single instance of a phoneme (Strik, Truong, de Wet & Cucchiarini, 2009). Second, because human judgements are less reliable at this level of detail than at a less detailed level, such as whole utterances (Witt & Young, 2000). It is consequently more difficult to obtain high correlations between ASR-based metrics and human judgements at the level of individual speech sounds

A critical issue in developing successful algorithms for pronunciation error detection is the availability of suitable training material in the form of annotated learner speech corpora. These are databases containing speech recordings with corresponding orthographic and, possibly, phonological and phonetic annotations, as will be discussed in the following section.

Annotated learner speech corpora

Annotated corpora of native and learner speech are required to develop ASR-based systems for pronunciation learning and teaching. These corpora are used for various goals and at various stages in the procedure. First, the automatic speech recognizer should be properly trained so that it can recognize the utterances the learners produce and which are likely to deviate from those by native speakers in many respects. Second, annotated learner speech corpora are needed to obtain information about possible mispronunciations and their frequency, which is sometimes expressed in mispronunciation rules and used to generate mispronunciation lexicons. Third, annotated learner speech corpora can be used to evaluate the performance of algorithms for pronunciation error detection and establish to what extent they are able to identify the mispronunciations contained in the speech recordings.

Which criteria are adopted to annotate mispronunciations will depend on the approach chosen by the collectors of the corpus and the aim for which the corpus is going to be used. These criteria can be in line with either the intelligibility principle or the nativeness principle. This means that important choices have to be made when developing the annotation protocols. A first issue is therefore what the human annotations should represent, i.e. ratings of nativeness, intelligibility (Munro & Derwing, 1995a; Levis, 2005), or perceptual salience (Neri, Cucchiarini & Strik, 2006). Otherwise, annotators can be asked to transcribe the L2 speech at different levels of detail (phonetic or phonemic). The resulting annotations may thus vary in terms of the construct they represent and the level of granularity, which also has consequences for the subsequent analyses and potential for corrective feedback.

Obtaining sufficiently large corpora of learner speech with annotations is labour-intensive and costly. In addition, detailed transcriptions at segmental level are subjective and are likely to differ between transcribers (Cucchiarini, 1996; Precoda et al., 2000; Wester, Kessens, Cucchiarini & Strik, 2001; Franco, Ferrier & Bratt, 2012), thus posing problems for what should be considered the ground truth.

Since learner speech data are often limited or even non-existent, alternative procedures have been proposed to alleviate this problem. One of them consists in artificially creating mispronunciation data by inserting errors in native speech corpora (Witt & Young, 2000; Kanters, Cucchiarini & Strik, 2009). If the errors are simulated based on knowledge of which mispronunciations are likely to occur in the L2 speech under study, this procedure can work satisfactorily (Cucchiarini, Neri & Strik, 2009). Recently, new perspectives have been opened by resorting to crowdsourcing (Wang, Qian & Meng, 2013). This term refers to a procedure for obtaining data by asking a large group of people to provide them online. Even in this case, however, disagreements between human annotators have to be resolved.

Corrective feedback on pronunciation errors

The automatic measures of pronunciation quality obtained through ASR-based algorithms can be used as a basis for providing feedback. It is important to note though that detecting pronunciation errors and providing feedback are two distinct processes and that not all information that is obtained by the algorithms needs to be incorporated in the feedback. Conversely, feedback can incorporate more than the knowledge obtained through mispronunciation detection algorithms and include visual representations of articulator movements (e.g. see review in Kartushina, Hervais-Adelman, Frauenfelder & Golestani, 2015). Feedback can signal errors by highlighting the letters corresponding to the mispronunciations (Cucchiarini et al., 2009), or indicate a mismatch between what the system identified and what should have been pronounced, provide instruction on how to improve articulation (Eskenazi, Kennedy, Ketchum, Olszewski & Pelton, 2007) and suggest remedial exercises (Strik, Colpaert, Van Doremalen & Cucchiarini, 2012). The manner, modality and timing of feedback should possibly be based on the results of research on pronunciation instruction and what is known to be the most effective strategy. In addition, since research increasingly shows the importance of individual learner characteristics and preferences, also with respect to corrective feedback, ASR-based pronunciation training should ideally be implemented so that the feedback provided takes account of such individual features.

Current contributions and research

In general terms, two main goals can be identified in research on ASR-based mispronunciation detection: (a) investigating the accuracy of the algorithms and (b) determining their suitability to support pronunciation learning and teaching when embedded in a system. To achieve the first goal, algorithms can be tested on annotated learner speech corpora. This type of research is mainly conducted by engineers and speech technologists and has a very technical character. For this reason these studies will not be covered in the current overview. However, it is important to point out that this research holds enormous potential for pronunciation research and teaching. In particular, the more recent approaches that make use of deep neural networks are very promising. Given their relevance for pronunciation learning and teaching, efforts should be made by pronunciation researchers to come to grips with this literature so that cooperation between the fields of speech technology and L2 pronunciation research becomes feasible. A list of relevant publications has been included in the further reading section. The second goal requires whole systems to provide pronunciation practice and feedback. As will be explained in the final section, developing such complete systems is complex and requires different types of expertise that are not always available in one research centre. In addition, to be able to conduct evaluation experiments with students, a considerable amount of content has to be developed that allows sufficient amounts of practice. In this overview we focus on studies that employed complete systems.

Systems for ASR-based pronunciation training

This section presents a selection of ASR-based systems for pronunciation training for which evaluation data could be found in the literature. Some of these evaluations were conducted online, with language learners actually working with the system, while others took place offline and relied on annotations contained in speech corpora. This difference is indicated when presenting the results.

One of the ASR-based pronunciation training systems developed by the company Auralog, Talk to Me, was evaluated by Hincks (2005) to determine to what extent it helped improve pronunciation. The PhonePass test developed by Ordinate (Bernstein, Jong, Pisoni & Townshend, 2000) was used to measure progress, together with expert ratings. The results showed that Talk to Me was beneficial for students with strongly accented English, while intermediate students did not profit from practice and their pronunciation even worsened, possibly because they slowed down their speech in an attempt to increase production accuracy. Similar results had been obtained by Precoda et al. (2000).

The commercial product NativeAccent by CarnegieSpeech offers practice in oral skills and explicit feedback on the pronunciation errors identified in the learner's utterance, together with articulatory information. Eskenazi et al. (2007) evaluated NativeAccent with 43 employees of a company in India, randomly divided into 25 test subjects and 18 controls, who received no extra training but performed their jobs in which they spoke English regularly. The experimental subjects practised individual phones and prosody. Progress was measured through the company's employee assessment of English fluency with focus on 'accent training'. The results showed more accent improvement for the experimental group than for the controls. The authors discuss differences between the groups in starting levels (the experimental group started at a lower level and had more room for improvement) and time on task (the experimental group had 20 hours of NativeAccent extra training, while the control group had no additional training), which might have played a role.

A more comprehensive evaluation was conducted with the Dutch Computer-Assisted Pronunciation Training (Dutch-CAPT) system, which was developed to provide automatic feedback on segmental (phoneme) errors in Dutch L2. The pronunciation errors to be addressed had been selected through a data driven-approach based on criteria such as frequency, persistence and perceptual salience (Neri et al., 2006). The system featured dialogues and pronunciation exercises including minimal pairs, and errors were highlighted in red. Cucchiarini et al. (2009) present an evaluation of Dutch-CAPT from four different perspectives based on data of adult Dutch L2 learners with different L1s assigned to experimental and control groups. Mispronunciation identification accuracy was high. The measures calculated include precision (P, the proportion of real errors among the errors detected) and recall (R, the proportion of detected errors among all errors made), which turned out to vary between 75 per cent and 86 per cent. Student appreciation was positive. Overall segmental quality did not significantly improve after practice with Dutch-CAPT, probably owing to the short duration of the training (two sessions of about 30–60 minutes) and the limited number of errors addressed (11). However, detailed analyses of pronunciation showed that practice with Dutch-CAPT led to a significant decrease in the number of pronunciation errors.

The Development and Integration of Speech technology into COurseware for language learning (DISCO) system (Strik et al., 2012) was aimed at providing feedback on pronunciation, morphology, and syntax in Dutch L2. In the exercises, learners engage in dialogues that elicit constrained responses to questions. For the pronunciation exercises, they read aloud sentences that are prompted by the system. User evaluations by students (Strik et al., 2012) and teachers (Van Doremalen, 2014) revealed positive results for all three modules. Analyses of accuracy in PED were carried out on speech recordings of five students working with the system, which were scored by two annotators. Average precision was 75.5 per cent for correct reject and 99.7 per cent for correct accept, while recall rates of 97.4 per cent were found for correct reject and 96.0 correct for correct accept (Van Doremalen, 2014, p. 106).

Peabody (2011) developed and evaluated an ASR-based pronunciation training system based on unscripted dialogues on flight reservations and a simple web-based game. Crowdsourcing through Amazon Mechanical Turk was applied to obtain pronunciation annotations at word level, as Turkers were not considered experienced enough for phone-level judgements. The approach assumes that a correct transcription is available and compares individual phones with parallel sets of native and non-native acoustic models. Important choices in developing this system were: that (a) evaluation and feedback be performed after each task to enhance concentration on language and to base the evaluation on all the speech produced during the dialogue; and that (b) precision be prioritized because missing pronunciation errors is less important. Evaluations based on the collected speech corpus indeed show higher levels of precision (67 per cent) and lower recall rates (22 per cent). Although this is in line with the priorities set in this study, it would be interesting to know how students evaluate delayed feedback and the fact that so many pronunciations errors are missed by the system. Unfortunately, user evaluation data are not presented in this study.

The company Rosetta Stone has developed innovative language learning products for more than 20 languages, which employ ASR technology to allow speaking practice and to provide immediate pronunciation feedback, in addition to live practice with a tutor (Pellom, 2012). Learners engage in 'listen-and-repeat' exercises that address difficult speech sounds. Mispronunciations are modelled through a machine translation approach (Stanley, Hacioglu & Pellom, 2011) that learns from the annotated data and generates learner phone sequences for error detection. After utterance verification, phonological errors are identified based on a Viterbi alignment of the speech signal with the expected text. More comprehensive evaluations involving language learners are not available in the literature.

EduSpeak is a speech recognition and scoring toolkit developed by SRI StarLab (Franco, Neumeyer, Digalakis & Ronen, 2000) that can be used for pronunciation scoring and feedback on words and phrases. Various machine scores have been employed and evaluated for this purpose (Franco et al., 2010, 2012). Evaluations of phone-level mispronunciation detection based on a phonetically transcribed database of 130,000 phones in sentences by 206 non-native speakers showed that, for the speech sounds with reliable human scores, EduSpeak scoring reliability was slightly lower than for the human transcribers. An implementation of EduSpeak is presented in Walker, Cedergren, Trofimovich and Gatbonton (2011), where it was employed to provide pronunciation feedback at word level in a computerized L2 speech learning module for healthcare professionals.

In addition to the systems described above there are many other commercial products (see also Witt, 2012) for which no extensive evaluations of mispronunciation detection could be found in the literature. Among these are the Tactical Language Tutoring System (TLTS) by Alelo (alelo.com), web-based programs for experiential learning of language and culture that focus on practical communication skills, and English Central by englishcentral.com, a program for learning English that offers speaking exercises with instant feedback on pronunciation and fluency.

Conclusions on current contributions and research

The review of studies on ASR-based pronunciation training systems indicates that current systems offer more possibilities for practice and feedback and in general achieve better performance. For instance, while early systems were often limited to isolated words, current systems can handle continuous speech and dialogues and enable the embedding of pronunciation training in more communicative approaches. With respect to the specific conceptualization of pronunciation adopted in these systems, it seems that the majority tacitly assumes the nativeness principle (Levis, 2005) as native realizations are taken as the point of reference for evaluating L2 speech. This is in line with the general stance taken in research on pronunciation instruction (Thomson & Derwing, 2014), in spite of calls in the literature to focus on intelligibility rather than on nativeness (Munro & Derwing, 1995a; Levis, 2005; Field, 2005; Levis, 2007). Some ASR-based systems rely on previous analyses and prioritization of pronunciations errors to be addressed, which probably helps to bring focus and improve performance (Cucchiarini et al., 2009; Strik et al., 2012). According to Munro et al. (2015), the detailed analysis and selection of Dutch L2 pronunciation errors conducted in Neri et al. (2006) was 'a critical step towards a beneficial and efficient CAPT program'. Similar approaches have been adopted in following studies on Dutch–English (Cucchiarini, Heuvel, Sanders & Strik, 2011) and Spanish–Dutch ASR-based CAPT (Burgos, Cucchiarini, Van Hout & Strik, 2014), but have definitely not become common practice in the field. Most ASR-based systems do not align with a specific theoretical stance. Some just assume nativeness to be the goal of the training, but in general this information is not explicitly provided.

Overall, the research reviewed in this section shows that there are indeed many commercial systems that look very appealing and promising. It would be interesting to know more about their performance and about what practice and feedback they offer, which often differ considerably between the various products, and how they contribute to improving L2 pronunciation. A possible drawback with respect to research with commercial products might be that such systems have to be taken as they are, while for research purposes it is often more desirable to be able to manipulate some of the parameters. On the other hand, developing complete systems for research on ASR-based pronunciation training is complex, labour-intensive and expensive, as will be discussed below.

Recommendations for practice

Important findings for teaching practice that emerge from this review are that ASR-based pronunciation training algorithms have found their way into complete systems that can be used by language learners. A number of important features have been highlighted that can be taken into account when judging these products, such as the use of ASR technology, the conceptualization of pronunciation adopted, the nature of the algorithms and metrics employed, the levels of accuracy achieved and the underlying assumptions in evaluating accuracy. Unfortunately, extensive information on accuracy is not available for all systems, especially the commercial products. To put things in perspective, though, it may be useful to recall that also human raters are not completely consistent and accurate in identifying mispronunciations (Precoda et al., 2000; Munro et al., 2015) and that teachers' feedback to language learners is often erratic (Carroll & Swain, 1993; Iwashita, 2003). Considering that we evaluate automatized products by comparing their performance to that of human beings, this is definitely something that has to be taken into account when considering the contribution of ASR-based pronunciation training systems. Encouraging in this respect is the finding that systems that achieve high levels of accuracy in mispronunciation detection can still help reduce pronunciation errors in the L2 even if accuracy is not 100 per cent (Cucchiarini et al. 2009).

Particular attention should be paid to the pronunciation goals addressed by the various algorithms and systems. Many studies are not explicit about their reference schemes and whether the aim is to assess nativeness or intelligibility. The lack of explicitness points to a tacit assumption of nativeness, which seems to be at odds with the growing emphasis on intelligibility in the pronunciation instruction literature (Levis, 2005; Field, 2005; Munro et al., 2015), but is apparently in line with teaching practice (Thomson & Derwing, 2014). In the case of ASR-based pronunciation training, a focus on intelligibility is not necessarily problematic as long as speech corpora can be provided in which learner speech recordings have been scored for intelligibility. ASR-based systems rely on machine learning and can learn from data, but we do need to provide the right data.

A final important consideration with respect to the use of ASR-based systems in practice is that, even with the recent improvements, these still should not be viewed as substitutes for pronunciation instruction by teachers, but as valuable supplements. Important advantages are that they can draw attention to problematic aspects of pronunciation, offer additional, individual practice in a stress-free environment on skills that can never be sufficiently practised in the classroom, and are always available independently of time and place.

Future directions

The review presented in this chapter has highlighted a number of interesting developments and promising new avenues in ASR-based pronunciation training, but has also identified some important research gaps. More cooperation is needed between speech technologists and engineers on the one hand and L2 pronunciation researchers and teachers on the other. In addition to improving the technology to achieve higher accuracy, one of the requirements for further research concerns more comprehensive approaches to the assessment of ASR-based pronunciation training with whole systems that are tested by language learners, as such evaluations are still few and far between. There are various explanations for this state of affairs. First, developing such systems requires interdisciplinary expertise from speech technologists, L2 researchers, CALL designers and experts on pronunciation and pedagogy, who are seldom available in one research centre. Second, considerable resources are needed to develop the speech technology, collect and analyse the speech training data, design sufficient content for practice sessions and conduct evaluations that, among other things, are based on time-consuming annotations of learner speech. Third, the difficulties in obtaining funding for research that cuts across different disciplines and that requires considerable time to develop a fully fledged system and subsequently use it to conduct research and test its suitability and effectiveness.

Despite these difficulties, it is important to emphasize that such concerted actions are necessary to advance the state of the art in ASR-based pronunciation training so as to benefit research and practice. So far, most initiatives have come from the field of speech technology and engineering, while it seems that also the pronunciation instruction field could profit from this type of research. An ASR-based pronunciation training system can be used not only to investigate the effectiveness of the training and its potential for teaching practice, but also to be employed as a research instrument to conduct innovative studies on pronunciation acquisition. By adding logging capabilities research environments can be created in which important parameters such as input, output, feedback and learner behaviour can be controlled and varied (Cucchiarini, Bodnar, Penning de Vries, van Hout & Strik, 2014). In addition, such systems make it possible to study not only the ultimate outcomes of learning, but also the learning process and its intermediate results and allow more individualized investigations. Finally, if the systems studied in laboratory conditions appear to be effective, they can be applied in real learning situations, as a supplement to traditional lessons. In other words, the experimental conditions are ecologically valid.

Further reading

Harrison, A. M., Lau, W. Y., Meng, H., & Wang, L. (2008). Improving mispronunciation detection and diagnosis of learners' speech with context-sensitive phonological rules based on language transfer. In *Interspeech 2008* (pp. 2787–2790), Brisbane, Australia.

Harrison, A. M., Lo, W., Qian, X., & Meng, H. (2009). Implementation of an extended recognition network for mispronunciation detection and diagnosis in computer-assisted pronunciation training. In *Proceedings of SLaTE 2009* (pp. 45–48), Birmingham, UK.

Hu, W., Qian, Y., Soong, F. K., Wang, Y. (2015). Improved mispronunciation detection with deep neural network trained acoustic models and transfer learning based logistic regression classifiers. *Speech Communication, 67*, 154–166.

Lo, W. K., Zhang, S., & Meng, H. (2010). Automatic derivation of phonological rules for mispronunciation detection in a computer assisted pronunciation training system. In *Interspeech 2010* (pp. 765–768), Makuhari.

Qian, X., Meng, H., & Soong, F. (2012). The use of DBN-HMMs for mispronunciation detection and diagnosis in L2 English to support computer-aided pronunciation training. In *Interspeech 2012* (pp. 775–778), Portland, Oregon, USA.

Qian, X. Meng, H., & Soong, F. (2011). On mispronunciation lexicon generation using joint-sequence multigrams in computer aided pronunciation training (CAPT). In *Interspeech 2011*(pp. 865–868), Florence, Italy.

Stanley, T., & Hacioglu, K. (2012). Improving L1-specific phonological error diagnosis in computer assisted pronunciation training. In *Interspeech 2012* (pp. 827–830), Portland, Oregon, USA.

Wang, H., Qian, X., & Meng, H. (2013). Predicting gradation of L2 English mispronunciations using crowdsourced ratings and phonological rules. In *Proceedings of SLaTE 2013* (pp. 127–131), Grenoble, France.

Yoon, S.-Y., Hasegawa-Johnson, M., & Sproat, R. (2010). Landmark-based automated pronunciation error detection. In *Interspeech 2010* (pp. 614–617).

Related topics

Dimensions of pronunciation; pronunciation instruction and teaching; individual differences; Computer-assisted Pronunciation Teaching

References

Akahane-Yamada, R., & McDermott, E. (1998). Computer-based second language production training by using spectrographic representation and HMM-based speech recognition scores, *Proceedings of ICSLP* (pp. 1747–1750), Sydney, Australia.

Bernstein, J., Cohen, M., Murveit, H., Rtischev, D., & Weintraub, M. (1990). Automatic evaluation and training in English pronunciation. *Proceedings ICSLP 90* (pp. 1185–1188), Kobe, Japan.

Bernstein, J., Jong, J. D., Pisoni, D., & Townshend, B. (2000). Two experiments on automatic scoring of spoken language proficiency. *Proceedings INSTiL 2000* (pp. 57–61), Dundee, UK.

Burgos, P., Cucchiarini, C., Van Hout, R., & Strik, H. (2014). Phonology acquisition in Spanish learners of Dutch: Error patterns in pronunciation. *Language Sciences, 41*, 129–142.

Carroll, S., & Swain, M. (1993). Explicit and implicit negative feedback: An empirical study of the learning of linguistic generalizations. *Studies in Second Language Acquisition, 15*, 357–386.

Chen, M., & Zechner, K. (2011). Computing and evaluating syntactic complexity features for automated scoring of spontaneous non-native speech. In *Proceedings 49th Annual Meeting of the Association for Computational Linguistics: Human Language Technologies* (pp. 722–731).

Coniam, D. (1999). Voice recognition software accuracy with second language speakers of English. *System, 27*, 49–64.

Cucchiarini, C. (1996). Assessing transcription agreement: methodological aspects. *Clinical Linguistics and Phonetics, 10*(2), 131–155.

Cucchiarini, C., Bodnar, S., Penning de Vries, B., van Hout, R., & Strik, H. (2014). ASR-based CALL systems and learner speech data: new resources and opportunities for research and development in second language learning. In *Proceedings of LREC 2014* (pp. 2708–2714), Reykjavik, Iceland.

Cucchiarini, C., Heuvel, H. van den, Sanders, E. P., & Strik, H. (2011). Error selection for ASR-based English pronunciation training in 'My Pronunciation Coach'. In *Proceedings of Interspeech 2011* (pp. 1165–1168), Florence, Italy.

Cucchiarini, C., Neri, A., & Strik, H. (2009). Oral proficiency training in Dutch L2: The contribution of ASR-based corrective feedback. *Speech Communication, 51*, 10, 853–863.

Cucchiarini, C., Strik, H., & Boves, L. (1997). Automatic assessment of foreign speakers' pronunciation of Dutch. In *Proceedings of EuroSpeech'97* (pp. 713–716), Rhodes, 22–25 September 1997.

Cucchiarini, C., Strik, H., & Boves, L. (2000a). Different aspects of expert pronunciation quality ratings and their relation to scores produced by speech recognition algorithm. *Speech Communication, 30*(2–3), 109–119. doi:10.1016/S0167-6393(99)00040-0.

Cucchiarini C., Strik, H., & Boves, L. (2000b). Quantitative assessment of second language learners' fluency by means of automatic speech recognition technology. *Journal of the Acoustical Society of America, 107*(2), 989–999.

Cucchiarini, C., Strik, H., & Boves, L. W. J. (2002). Quantitative assessment of second language learners' fluency: Comparisons between read and spontaneous speech. *Journal of the Acoustical Society of America, 111*(6), 2862–2873.

Dalby, J. Kewley-Port, D., & Sillings, R. (1998). Language-specific pronunciation training using the hearsay system. In *Proceedings of STILL* (pp. 25–28), Marholmen, Sweden.

Derwing, T. M., Munro, & M. J., & Carbonaro, M. (2000). Does popular speech recognition software work with ESL speech? *TESOL Quarterly, 34*, 592–603.

Ehsani F., & Knodt, E. (1998). Speech technology in computer-aided learning: Strengths and limitations of a new call paradigm. *Language Learning and Technology, 2*, 45–60.

Eskenazi, M. (1999). Using automatic speech processing for foreign language pronunciation tutoring: some issues and a prototype. *Language Learning & Technology, 2*, 62–67.

Eskenazi M., & Hansma, S. (1998). The fluency pronunciation trainer. In *Proceedings of STILL* (pp. 77–80), Marholmen, Sweden.

Eskenazi, M., Kennedy, A., Ketchum, C., Olszewski, R., & Pelton, G. (2007). The NativeAccent pronunciation tutor: measuring success in the real world. In *Speech and Language Technology in Education*, Farmington, PA, USA, 1–3 October 2007.

Field, J. (2005). Intelligibility and the listener: The role of lexical stress. *TESOL Quarterly, 39*, 399–423.

Franco, H., Neumeyer, L., Digalakis, V., & Ronen, O. (2000). Combination of machine scores for automatic grading of pronunciation quality. *Speech Communication, 30*, 121–130.

Franco, H. Bratt, H., Rossier, R., Gadde, V. E., Shriberg, E. Abrash, V., & Precoda, K. (2010). EduSpeak: A speech recognition and pronunciation scoring toolkit for computer-aided language learning applications. *Language Testing, 27*(3), 401–418.

Franco, H. Ferrier, L. Bratt, H. (2012). Adaptive and Discriminative Modeling for Improved Mispronunciation Detection. In *Proceedings IS ADEPT* (pp. 53–58), Stockholm, Sweden.

Hincks, R. (2005). *Computer support for learners of spoken English*. Unpublished doctoral thesis, KTH, Stockholm, Sweden.

Iwashita, N. (2003). Negative feedback and positive evidence in task-based interaction: Differential effects on L2 development. *Studies in Second Language Acquisition, 25*, 1–36.

Kanters, S., Cucchiarini, C., & Strik, H. (2009). The goodness of pronunciation algorithm: a detailed performance study. In *Proceedings of the SLaTE-2009 workshop* (pp. 1–4), Warwickshire, England.

Kartushina, N., Hervais-Adelman, A., Frauenfelder, U. H., & Golestani, N. (2015). The effect of phonetic production training with visual feedback on the perception and production of foreign speech sounds. *Journal of the Acoustical Society of America, 138*(2), 817–832.

Lee, Y. Zhang, & J. Glass (2013). Mispronunciation detection via dynamic time warping on deep belief network-based posteriorgrams. In *Proceedings ICASSP 2013* (pp. 8227–8231), Vancouver, BC, Canada.

Levis, J. (2005). Changing contexts and shifting paradigms in pronunciation teaching. *TESOL Quarterly*, *39*(3), 369–378.

Levis, J. (2007). Computer technology in teaching and researching pronunciation. *Annual Review of Applied Linguistics*, *27*, 184–202.

Mak, B. Siu, M., Ng, M., Tam, Y.-C., Chan, Y.-C., & Chan, K.-W. (2003). PLASER: pronunciation learning via automatic speech recognition. In *Proceedings of the HLT-NAACL 2003 Workshop on Building Educational Applications using Natural Language Processing* (pp. 23–29), Edmonton, Canada.

Menzel, W., Herron, D., Morton, R., Pezzotta, D. Bonaventura, P., & Howarth, P. (2000a). Interactive pronunciation training. *ReCALL*, *13*, 1, 67–78.

Menzel, W., Herron, D., Bonaventura, P., & Morton, R. (2000b). Automatic detection and correction of non-native English pronunciations. In *Proceedings of InSTILL 2000* (49–56).

Munro, M. J., & Derwing, T. M. (1995a). Foreign accent, comprehensibility, and intelligibility in the speech of second language learners. *Language Learning*, *45*, 73–97.

Munro, M. J., & Derwing, T. M. (1995b). Processing time, accent, and comprehensibility in the perception of native and foreign accented speech. *Language and Speech*, *38*, 289–306.

Munro, M. J., Derwing, T. M., & Thomson, R. I. (2015). Setting segmental priorities for English learners: Evidence from a longitudinal study. *International Review of Applied Linguistics in Language Teaching*, *53*(1) (Mar 2015), 39–60.

Neri, A., Cucchiarini, C., Strik, H., & Boves, L. (2002). The pedagogy-technology interface in computer assisted pronunciation training. *Computer Assisted Language Learning*, *15*(5), 441–467. doi:10.1076/call.15.5.441.13473.

Neri, A., Cucchiarini, C., & Strik, H. (2006). Selecting segmental errors in L2 Dutch for optimal pronunciation training. *International Review of Applied Linguistics*, *44*, 357–404.

Neumeyer, L., Franco, H., Weintraub, M., & Price, P. (1996). Automatic text independent pronunciation scoring of foreign language student speech. In *Proceedings ICSLP 96* (pp. 1457–1460), Philadelphia, PA.

Peabody, M. (2011). *Methods for Pronunciation Assessment in Computer Aided Language Learning*. PhD thesis, Massachusetts Institute of Technology.

Pellom, B. (2012). Rosetta Stone ReFLEX: Toward improving English conversational fluency in Asia, In *Proceedings IS ADEPT*, Stockholm, Sweden.

Pennington, M. C. (1999). Computer-aided pronunciation pedagogy: Promise, limitations, directions, *Computer Assisted Language Learning*, *12*, 427–440.

Precoda, K., Halverson, C. A., & Franco, H. (2000). Effects of speech recognition-based pronunciation feedback on second-language pronunciation ability. In *Proceedings of InSTIL 2000* (pp. 102–105).

Rogers, C., & Dalby, J. (1996). Prediction of foreign-accented speech intelligibility from segmental contrast measures, *Journal of the Acoustical Society of America*, *100*(2), 2725 (A).

Stanley, T., Hacioglu, K., & Pellom, B. (2011). Statistical machine translation framework for modeling phonological errors in computer assisted pronunciation training system. *SLaTE 2011* (pp. 125–128), Venice, Italy.

Strik, H., Colpaert, J., Van Doremalen, J., & Cucchiarini, C. (2012). The DISCO ASR-based CALL system: practicing L2 oral skills and beyond. In *Proceedings LREC 2012* (pp. 2702–2707), Istanbul, 2012.

Strik, H., Truong, K. de Wet, F., & Cucchiarini, C. (2009). Comparing different approaches for automatic pronunciation error detection. *Speech Communication*, *51*, 10, 854–852.

Thomson, R. I., & Derwing, T. (2014). The effectiveness of L2 pronunciation instruction: A narrative review. *Applied Linguistics*, doi:10.1093/applin/amu076.

Van Doremalen, J. (2014). *Developing automatic speech recognition-enabled language learning applications: from theory to practice. Evaluating automatic speech recognition-based language learning systems: a case study*. PhD thesis, Radboud University, Nijmegen.

Van Doremalen, J., Cucchiarini, C., & Strik, H. (2010). Optimizing automatic speech recognition for low-proficient non-native speakers. *EURASIP Journal on Audio, Speech, and Music Processing*, *2010*, 1–13. doi:10.1155/2010/973954.

Wachowicz, K., & Scott, B. (1999). Software that listens: It's not a question of whether, it's a question of how, *CALICO Journal 16*, 253–276.

Walker, N. R., Cedergren, H., Trofimovich, P., & Gatbonton, E. (2011). Automatic speech recognition for CALL: A task-specific application for training nurses. *The Canadian Modern Language Review*, *67*(4), 459–479.

Wang, H., Qian, X., & Meng, H. (2013). Predicting gradation of L2 English mispronunciations using crowdsourced ratings and phonological rules. In *Proceedings of SLaTE 2013* (pp. 127–131), Grenoble, France.

Wester, M., Kessens, J. M., Cucchiarini, C., & Strik, H. (2001). Obtaining phonetic transcriptions: A comparison between expert listeners and a continuous speech recognizer. *Language and Speech*, *44*(3), 377–403.

Witt, S. (2012). Automatic error detection in pronunciation training: Where we are and where we need to go. In *Proceedings IS ADEPT* (pp. 1–8), Stockholm, Sweden, 2012.

Witt S., & Young, S. (1997). Language learning based on non-native speech recognition. In *Proceedings Eurospeech 1997* (pp. 633–636).

Witt S., & Young, S. (2000). Phone-level pronunciation scoring and assessment for interactive language learning. *Speech Communication 30*(2/3), 95–108.

35

Fully automated speaking assessment

Changes to proficiency testing and the role of pronunciation

Talia Isaacs

Introduction

Technology has revolutionized capability in assessing speaking, making it possible to record, quantify and score test-takers' oral performances outside of live testing conditions. Technology has also opened the door to new possibilities in terms of the delivery and scoring of tests, resulting in greater choices for test-users in the second language (L2) speaking assessments available on the market in the twenty-first century. The focus of this chapter is on fully automated assessments of L2 speech – that is, operational test delivery and scoring of speech production without any human intervention, achieved through both automatic speech recognition (ASR) technology, and an algorithmic score generator to optimize approximation to human ratings. As a preface to discussing how technology has transformed the L2 speaking assessment terrain and the centrality of pronunciation (particularly segmental features) to the state of the art in machine scoring, it is important to situate automated assessment in its broader historical context. After outlining how age-old concerns about the lack of objectivity in human ratings of L2 speech have been addressed through the use of technology, the chapter will focus on operational machine scoring systems used for L2 speaking assessment, including feedback on segmental errors for low-stakes (e.g. research or pedagogical) purposes. The discussion will be underpinned by debates on trade-offs in using fully automated assessments, highlighting concerns about technological constraints dictating the nature of the assessment. Future directions will then be discussed, one of which is ways that technology can be used to prioritize the factors that are most important for intelligibility (i.e. being easily understandable to listeners), instead of simply promoting accent reduction (i.e. mastery of all L2 pronunciation features when some are more consequential for communication than others). Finally, the chapter will conclude with the possibility of using hybrid machine–human scoring systems.

Historical and current conceptualizations of the topic

The L2 assessment literature has long distinguished between three modes of speaking assessment that are foundational to a discussion of the topic. A 'direct test' refers to a spoken assessment conducted face-to-face with an interlocutor (e.g. interviewer, examiner, test-taker), whereas a 'semi-direct test' is machine administered (e.g. computer- or phone-based), with the test-taker speaking into a recording device. Finally, an 'indirect test' denotes assessing speaking without eliciting any form of spoken production (Ginther, 2013). An example of an indirect test item is the following multiple-choice question:

Which of the following words is unlike the others in terms of how the underlined sound is pronounced?

(a) trea<u>s</u>ure   (b) phy<u>s</u>ics   (c) ca<u>s</u>ual   (d) le<u>s</u>ion

All words in the example include /ʒ/ except for choice 'b', which is pronounced [z]. This discrete-point item is modelled on a prototype item proposed by Lado (1961), an exponent of structural testing, in the most comprehensive practical guide to constructing, administrating and scoring L2 pronunciation tests that exists today (Isaacs, 2014). Lado's contention that indirect testing could be used as an alternative to direct or semi-direct testing was predicated on his assumption that written responses of the type exemplified above would strongly correlate with test-takers' actual L2 pronunciation productions. However, subsequent research confirmed that indirect testing bears little if any relation to test-takers' oral outputs on the same task, and the statistical associations were even weaker with sentence- and discourse-level speaking tasks (Buck, 1989). Indirect testing is currently not regarded as a valid form of L2 speaking assessment because it strays from the seemingly common-sense assertion that 'the best way of assessing how well a learner speaks a language is to get him or her to speak' (He & Young, 1998, p. 1).

Although this major reservation should not be overlooked, indirect testing of speech is attractive for at least two reasons that draw parallels with modern arguments promoting fully automated assessments. First, as Lundeberg (1929) stated, individual oral assessment is 'cumbersome and time-consuming' (p. 195), particularly with large numbers of test-takers – a point that motivated Lado's (1961) suggestion for using indirect tests. To elaborate, human scoring often requires employing and training teachers or examiners to elicit and rate oral productions, which can be resource-intensive in terms of costs and time. Like indirect testing, fully automated assessment is a cheaper option and can generate results more quickly. For example, in English proficiency testing for university entrance purposes, the direct speaking component of the IELTS (British Council, 2016) and semi-direct TOEFL iBT (ETS, 2016) mail score reports to test-takers within 13 calendar days of taking the test, with the TOEFL results available online three days earlier. By comparison, the fully automated (computer-mediated and scored) Pearson Test of English (PTE) Academic provides online results within five business days (Pearson, 2014). In fact, the automated scoring of a sentence-level speech sample takes only a few seconds for the machine to compute, but online file transmission from the test location to the e-scoring site can be subject to broadband issues and other technical challenges (Van Moere & Downey, 2016). Test-takers' testimonials on Pearson's website praise the rapid delivery of PTE Academic results within 24 or 48 hours of taking the test, revealing Pearson's use of quick processing time for marketing purposes.

However, initially developing an ASR and machine scoring system, depending on the purpose and stakes of the assessment, can be large-scale and costly. Sentence-level models that involve machine training to recognize a particular fixed sentence that corresponds to test-takers' likely spoken output, as elicited through a highly controlled task (e.g. sentence repetition), are much more expensive to develop than phoneme-level models (Bernstein, Cohen, Murveit, Rtischev & Weintraub, 1990). Both models use phonemes as the 'building block', sequencing sounds based on the probability of occurrence associated with each sound in an effort to decode speech from the soundwave as recognizable output (Franco et al., 2010). The distinction is that phoneme-level models, unlike sentence-level ones, are not tied to particular predetermined utterances and, thus, can be used with random or impromptu testtaker responses. Sentence-level models, however, are superior in aligning detected phones with the speech signal and approximating human ratings. Once the ASR system has been developed, the machine scoring system is calibrated using a large database of human ratings of a large volume of L2 test-takers' speech (e.g. thousands of responses produced by hundreds of test-takers in developing Pearson's automated scoring technology for English; Pearson, 2012), which will inevitably involve some expense. However, regardless of the specifics of the methodology used for test development, wide-scale implementation of the eventual test is likely to more than offset development costs, making it an attractive option for assessment organizations, who may choose to pass on cost savings to test-users.

Another parallel between indirect speaking tests and automated assessment relates to concerns about the inherent subjectivity of human scoring, in part owing to the intangible and transient nature of speech (Lundeberg, 1929). For example, the dichotomous task of evaluating whether English learners from a mixed L1 background produce /i/ and /ɪ/ in a target-like or untarget-like way is unlikely to always yield exact rater agreement. Nor is having raters assign each token to one of the two vowel categories that represent the closest target-like approximation (e.g. Thomson & Isaacs, 2009). As Lado (1961) underscored, intelligibility (however measured) is fraught by the issue of intelligible to whom. Finally, global ratings of pronunciation-relevant constructs (e.g. degree of foreign accent), although possibly yielding high inter-rater reliability, clearly lack the objectivity of scoring multiple-choice items. Fully automated scoring offers a solution to this subjectivity issue that Lado found so pressing, offering standardized delivery and reliable and objective scoring of L2 speech. In so doing, it allows the test developer to draw on some of the advantages of indirect testing, which are disqualifying owing to concerns about validity, without actually resorting to indirect testing. Instead, it allows for a semi-direct, automatically scored speaking test.

One advantage of automated scoring that ties into the objectivity argument is that it is impervious to the individual rater idiosyncrasies that are present in human ratings (Xi, 2012). That is, automated scoring eliminates sources of construct-irrelevant variance, which refers to variables extraneous to the L2 speaking ability being measured that could come into play in human ratings (Messick, 1990). For example, individual differences in rater familiarity with or attitudes towards test-takers' L1 accent could unduly influence their speech or pronunciation ratings. Machines, which cannot replicate human listening and scoring processes, are not susceptible to such rater effects (Van Moere & Downey, 2016). However, there are trade-offs to the reliability and efficiency that automation entails, which surface in the next section and permeate the rest of this chapter.

Limitations of ASR and automatic scoring

There are several challenges in undertaking ASR and fully automated scoring of L2 speech that need to be considered before critically evaluating the use of this technology for L2 assessment purposes. First, automated scoring of the spoken medium is much more challenging to implement than automated scoring of writing. This is mainly due to the first step and complicating factor of needing to recognize words from the speech signal (Bridgeman, Powers, Stone & Mollaun, 2011). Second, word recognition tends to be much better on highly controlled tasks that constrain test-takers' output than on extemporaneous speech tasks that yield relatively unpredictable test-taker output. This is because when the test-takers' speech is predictable or known the audio track can be forcibly aligned with the transcription of the utterance using pattern matching, with deviations between the expected and actual response more easily detected (Zechner, Higgins, Xi & Williamson, 2009). Compared to spontaneous speech tasks, automatic scoring of controlled or guided tasks (e.g. sentence read-alouds) result in much stronger correlations between machine scoring and human ratings. Although such tasks may be less authentic in light of the tasks that test-takers need to perform in real-world settings, strong statistical associations with human-rated measures are sometimes used by testing organizations as part of the validity argument to justify their use for high-stakes purposes (e.g. Bernstein, Van Moere & Cheng, 2010).

A third major challenge lies in decoding L2 learners' as opposed to native speakers' (NSs') utterances, particularly when test-takers are from mixed L1 backgrounds due to L1 influence (Isaacs, 2014). Determining a standard that the speech will be compared to, which often begins with a NS corpus, is premised on the notion that L2 speech differs from L1 speech in the pronunciation and sequencing of sounds and words. These deviations are treated as errors, and parameters need to be set so that the system can classify errors and provide learners with feedback on their production accuracy (Cucchiarini, Neri, de Wet & Strik, 2007; Cucchiarini & Strik, Chapter 34 this volume). However, state-of-the-art error detection algorithms are imperfect and occasionally provide learners with misleading feedback about the correctness of utterances (Eskenazi, 2009). More specifically, automatic detection systems for L2 learners sometimes produce false positives (i.e. the system scores the production of a correctly pronounced phone as an error) and false negatives (i.e. the system fails to detect an incorrect phone when one is uttered). Nonetheless, there is some evidence that learners in laboratory contexts can improve their production of targeted phonemes when they receive ASR-based feedback compared to learners who receive no such feedback (Cucchiarini, Neri & Strik, 2009), highlighting the potential of this technology for targeting segmental accuracy. Unfortunately, not all fully automated tests publish information on the error classification accuracy of their patented technologies, making it difficult to evaluate these systems (e.g. Wagner & Kunnan, 2015).

One remaining challenge and limitation in light of technological capability is that current automatically scored speaking assessments heavily rely on spectral (i.e. frequency-based) and durational (i.e. time-based) measures associated with segmental accuracy and temporal fluency. This is mostly at the exclusion of other measures, since machines are less adept at scoring higher-order features of L2 speaking performances, such as discourse organization, lexical resource, grammatical accuracy, prosody and content development (Bridgeman et al., 2011). For example, temporal measures (e.g. speech rate, silent pause duration per word), which the machine can ably automatically compute, fail to capture broader notions of fluency that humans may heed in scoring discourse-level tasks, such as coherence and argumentation (Ginther, Dimova & Yang, 2010). Thus, some aspects of the L2 speaking construct that test developers and examiners may value and take into account when scoring are currently not captured in automated scoring systems (Xi, Higgins, Zechner & Williamson, 2012). Before discussing the implications of these challenges and constraints, the next section will describe the basic operational processes involved in fully automated scoring by drawing on examples of L2 assessments that use the technology.

Illustrations and examples

Operational ASR and automated feedback and scoring systems

The innovation of fully automated L2 proficiency assessments has resulted in major shifts in the L2 assessment and research terrain in the twenty-first century. One effect is that the centrality of pronunciation in ASR and automated scoring has, in part, fuelled a resurgence of interest in pronunciation within the L2 assessment community following a lengthy period of neglect (Isaacs, 2014). In order to situate fully automated assessments within the L2 testing context more broadly, the 2 × 2 matrix in Figure 35.1 provides examples of stand-alone L2 speaking tests, speaking components of L2 proficiency tests or patented scoring systems (e.g. SpeechRater). Quadrant II shows direct L2 speaking tests or speaking components that are also human-scored, Quadrant I shows semi-direct tests that are human-scored and Quadrant IV shows machine-scored semi-direct tests (see also Galaczi, 2010). The tests listed in Quadrant IV are fully automated and, hence, the focus of this review. Notably, no tests have, as yet, been developed in Quadrant III. Producing tests that are human-administered and machine-scored would remove the advantage of having a more authentic interaction with a human interlocutor on an extemporaneous L2 speech task, as the type of task that could be used would need to be constrained considerably to make it easily machine scorable. The constraints in the design of such a test, the lack of standardization if different human raters administered even a scripted test compared to machine administration, and the lack of a practical advantage entailed in a human needing to test individually would seem to make it a less attractive and perhaps less intuitive option for test developers. On the other hand, it could be argued that test-takers in classroom contexts might prefer speaking tests (however inauthentic and regardless of how it is scored) to be administered by their L2 teacher, although this has yet to be established. An extension of this argument is that, in foreign language contexts that do not routinely teach L2 speaking (Wall & Horák, 2006), integrating speaking into the classroom, even in a way that is reminiscent of audiolingual (as opposed to communicative language) teaching, is better than no speaking focus at all. What is clear is that many more speaking assessments that use automated scoring will be developed in the future. It is important to note, however, that attractive, user-friendly, accessible applications do not mean that fully automated assessments are effective L2 learning tools, nor that they provide valid information about L2 speaking ability, whether the feedback is formal or informal. Automated tests, and particularly those intended for high-stakes purposes (i.e. consequential decision-making) need to be held to the same standard of providing robust validation evidence as traditional human-scored tests (see Wagner & Kunnan, 2015).

But what about the architecture of assessment-oriented ASR and scoring systems? They tend to consist of an automatic telephone response system (if the test is telephone-mediated; e.g. Versant), a digital storage bank for the recordings, a speech recognizer for decoding the speech, a speech analyser or computation model, which prepares the recognized speech for scoring using mathematical representations, and a score generator, which maps a selection of measures onto an L2 speaking score based on previous ratings by human raters (Pearson, 2011; Zechner et al., 2009). The speech samples on which the system is trained should be produced using professional-quality microphones in environments with little ambient noise and recorded with an adequate sampling rate (e.g. 8 kHz for telephonic systems; 16 kHz for computer-mediated systems) and resolution (e.g. 16-bit) to ensure reasonable sound quality. Where possible, operational testing conditions should also avoid noisy environments, provide suitable microphones, use the same sampling rate as was used to generate the acoustic model

		L2 test mode of delivery	
		Human	**Machine**
L2 test scoring	**Human**	II IELTS Cambridge English exams (e.g., CAE) Oral Proficiency Interview (OPI)	I TOEFL iBT Aptis SOPI, COPI (tape- or computer-based OPI)
	Machine	III NONE	IV PTE (Academic, General) Versant tests ETS's SpeechRater

Figure 35.1 Matrix of L2 speaking assessment administration and scoring (i.e. human- or machine-mediated), with examples in each category

for audio recording and conduct sound checks prior to the assessment to ensure adequate volume levels (Chengalvarayan, 2009).

It is practical to illustrate how the technology works by drawing on some examples. EduSpeak, a pronunciation-focused computer-assisted language learning (CALL) application (Franco et al., 2010), was reportedly developed using a similar approach to the patented technology used for Pearson's automated speaking tests, providing some information about the development of the ASR technology than is not currently available in Pearson's validation manuals (e.g. Pearson, 2012). Franco et al. (2010) summarize three steps in scoring pronunciation on sentence reading or repetition tasks:

- phonetic segmentation (i.e. identifying the boundaries between phones) using the speech recognizer;
- machine generation of scores by comparing a learner's speech to the training database using probabilistic models;
- calibration of the scores using an algorithm to combine automatic measures that best map onto scores assigned by human listeners from the training database.

As with other ASR systems, EduSpeak was developed using statistical modelling that derives probabilities of sounds occurring within words and, in turn, within sentences. A hierarchical structure is imposed, with sentences modelled as word sequences that, in turn, are modelled as phone sequences that vary in their acoustic realization according to their phonetic context. The system combines data trained on both NSs and non-native speakers (NNSs) of North American English by assigning them different statistical weightings. Scores are computed by averaging the automatically derived scores for each phone in that sentence based on the likelihood of occurrence. Other computed measures are fluency-related (e.g. speech rate, length of phones uttered), normalized over the duration of the sentence or over all of the speaker's utterances. These measures are then compared to measures from the NS corpus to estimate probability distributions. Final scores for reporting purposes are assigned using statistical modelling to classify the set of scores obtained from the automated system into ratings that approximate predicted human scoring based on the training corpus. Information on the machine's error rates for phone-level mispronunciation is reported for each phone by comparing the machine scoring with the same speech manually transcribed by human listeners schooled in phonetics (Franco et al., 2010). For comparison purposes, in terms of sentence repetition scoring on Pearson's Versant English Test (2011), word error frequency is operationalized as the smallest number of segmental substitutions, deletions or insertions required to modify the test-taker's output to find the best string match. An utterance that matches the referent speech is scored as error-free, with dysfluencies disregarded in scoring this task type. However, machine misclassification rates (e.g. of individual phones or aggregate measures) are not reported in Pearson's test validation manuals, suggesting a degree of underreporting.

It is worthwhile discussing Pearson's Versant English Test (originally developed as PhonePass in the 1990s) in some depth, since this was the first fully automated L2 speaking test available in the high-stakes assessment market, revolutionizing the field (Isaacs & Harding, 2017). Versant tests, which are telephone- or computer-delivered (duration: 15–20 minutes), are currently available in six languages in addition to an aviation English test (Bernstein et al., 2010). Drawing on Levelt's (1989) speech production model, the Versant English Test validation manual defines the speaking construct as the 'facility' or 'ability to understand spoken English on everyday topics and to respond appropriately at a native-like conversational pace in intelligible English' or, stated differently, the 'ease and immediacy in understanding and producing appropriate conversational English' (Pearson, 2011, p. 8). Test items were initially developed for American English, were subsequently sent to NSs of other inner circle varieties for checking (e.g. British and Australian English) and were retained only when over 90 per cent of educated NSs responded appropriately to them. Five of six Versant item types are currently operational for machine scoring: reading, repeating and unscrambling short sentences, providing word length responses to short-answer questions, and retelling a story. The other item type, which elicits an opinion or explanation about a defined topic, is, as yet, too unpredictable for the machine to cope with in a way that sufficiently replicates the numerical ratings that humans assign.

The Versant targets 'phonological fluency, sentence construction and comprehension, passive and active vocabulary use, listening skill, and pronunciation of rhythmic and segmental units' (Pearson, 2011, p. 3). Score reporting includes four five-point analytic subscores that, together, comprise test-takers' 'facility' reported in an overall score (p. 18). The sentence mastery (syntactic processing) and vocabulary (lexical comprehension and production) subscales are derived based on the presence of expected lexical items in the expected order. The fluency subscale captures rhythm, phrasing and timing (e.g. response latency, speech rate, stops and starts), whereas the pronunciation subscale refers to 'the ability to produce consonants, vowels, and stress in a native-like manner' at the sentence level using everyday vocabulary (p. 12). What is said, which relates to the first two measures, and how it is said, which relates to the latter two, each account for half of the total score, although different subscales are used depending on the task.

Fluency and pronunciation subscores, which are strongly correlated with the total score (.88 and .86, respectively), are also highly intercorrelated (.80), suggesting that they are measuring a similar construct, compared to much lower intercorrelations between pronunciation and both sentence mastery (.55) and vocabulary (.51). Correlations between human and machine scoring are lower for pronunciation (.88) than for the other and overall subscores (.94–.97), but still acceptably high. In terms of concurrent validity, correlations with TOEFL iBT speaking and IELTS speaking are around .75 (Pearson, 2011). The resulting scores are aligned with the Common European Framework of References for Languages (CEFR) levels (Council of Europe, 2001). However, the CEFR global scale excludes pronunciation as a criterion from its descriptors (Isaacs, 2014) – a factor that heavily features in Pearson's automated scoring. Presumably for this reason, Versant scores are also related to a scale that the assessment team reportedly adapted from the CEFR oral interaction scale descriptors (de Jong & Bernstein, 2001), although published details about the adapted scale are scarce.

Word recognition is based on acoustic models solely trained on L2 speech. These are aligned with or compared to an acoustic model trained on NSs from a range of age and native accent varieties and roughly balanced across gender (Bernstein et al., 2010). Conversion to scores occurs by scaling based on the likelihood of the occurrence of the given feature in the NS model built for that specific task. For example, the algorithm scales silent pauses based on the locus of its occurrence and the probability of a NS pausing that long in that environment (e.g. within a clause). Another example is voice onset time (VOT). Aspiration of the [t^h] sound in the word 'take' (voiceless aspirated alveolar stop), for instance, would yield a positive voice onset time (long lag VOT), since voicing occurs only after the release of the aspiration. A lack of aspiration [t], which would diverge from most NS norms, would have a voice onset time of roughly zero (short lag VOT). Thus, the test-taker could be penalized based on divergence from NS norms tied to such durational or spectral measurements. Next, using a non-linear statistical model, parameter weights are assigned to the resulting values that best approximate estimated human ratings of fluency and pronunciation (Bernstein et al., 2010). The PTE Academic score guide, which uses similar tasks as the Versant, states that

> the machine does not need to be told what features of the speech are important; the relevant features and their relative contributions are statistically extracted from the massive set of data when the system is optimized to predict human scores.
>
> (Pearson, 2012, p. 52)

This is how the stochastic system works. However, the precise combination of measures selected in non-linear models to result in the score that best approximates the human ratings is opaque even to the test developers.

Although, in traditional ASR scoring and feedback systems, segmental measures dominate, and pronunciation clearly plays a central role in Pearson's approach to automated scoring, this is not ubiquitous (Van Moere & Downey, 2016). Educational Testing Service (ETS), a global competitor to Pearson in the English standardized testing industry, models a markedly different approach. For example, SpeechRater 1.0 was developed to help TOEFL iBT applicants with test preparation through informal feedback on their speaking performances. Owing to the complex nature of extemporaneous discourse-level speaking tasks on the TOEFL iBT, SpeechRater's job of recognizing and automatically scoring the speech is much more challenging than would be the case with the highly constrained word- or sentence-level Pearson-style tasks (Xi et al., 2012). Using variable sets of test-takers' responses in terms of L2 speaking proficiency level, correlations between trained TOEFL raters' operational ratings and SpeechRater's scores were between .65 and .69 (Bridgeman et al., 2011). This is much lower than the correlations obtained for Pearson tests with human raters, as reported above (Pearson, 2011). In several outputs centring on test validation and issues such as construct coverage (e.g. Xi et al., 2012), ETS researchers argue that, until SpeechRater's performance is more optimal, which would necessitate major improvements in the technological capability of the state of the art in ASR and automatic scoring, the intended uses of SpeechRater will remain low-stakes, which they deem appropriate. This is in contrast to Pearson tests, which are currently used for high-stakes purposes (e.g. government visas, academic admissions, professional certification).

Notably, Pearson (2012) does not publish a list of possible machine-generated measures that the algorithm could draw from (there could plausibly be hundreds or thousands) to optimize measurement and automatically derive test scores. In contrast, ETS provides a list of 29 automated speech measures that were candidates for selection for two statistical scoring models explored for use with SpeechRater 1.0. Eleven of these were ultimately selected in a final multiple regression model that was chosen, with fixed weights assigned for different measures as pre-specified by a panel of experts (Zechner et al., 2009). This advisory group took into account factors such as statistical efficiency, approximation to human scoring, and construct coverage, as reflected in the link between the automated measures, and the descriptors used in the TOEFL iBT speaking scoring rubrics (Educational Testing Service, 2009). Seven of the 11 included measures are fluency-related (e.g. mean duration of long pauses; silent pause duration per word) and two are lexical richness measures (types), expressed over the duration of the word or speech sample. The remaining measures are the 'language model', related to grammatical accuracy, and the 'acoustic model', related to segmental errors identified using phoneme sequence probabilities (p. 890). With the exception of the language model measure, all included measures can be related to the descriptors in the TOEFL iBT delivery subscale, which is one of three subscales contributing to overall TOEFL speaking scores. Conversely, features related to the language use subscale (i.e. lexical and grammatical resource) are only partially represented in the scoring model, and none of the measures links to topic development (e.g. content relevance, coherence) owing to current technological limitations (Zechner et al., 2009). Therefore, although automated scoring eliminates sources of construct-irrelevant variance that play into human ratings, resulting in more objective and efficient scoring, there are trade-offs. SpeechRater only measures a portion of the related features that make up the multifaceted TOEFL speaking construct, failing to assess the full range of construct-relevant linguistic features reflected in the scales (Bridgeman et al., 2011). It also does not encapsulate the breadth of linguistic properties that human raters reportedly heed in their scoring decisions, including prosody, task completion and discourse-level features (Brown, Iwashita & McNamara, 2005). The sections below will refer to this and other practical challenges and ways forwards.

New directions and recommendations

This chapter has described technological advances in machine recognition and scoring of speech. These innovations have resulted in new ways of assessing L2 speaking, removing long-standing concerns about subjective element of rating (e.g. Lundeberg, 1929), since the machine, once trained, will always reach the same result. The introduction of fully auto-mated assessment of L2 proficiency has resulted in major shifts in the L2 assessment market, accentuating differences between products (e.g. direct versus fully automated speaking tests). It is difficult to predict how technology will push the assessment field forward in the generations to come. Perhaps the growing use of interactive spoken dialogue systems will lead to tests involving test-takers creating avatars of themselves and interacting with a virtual teacher or interlocutor, who would be pre-programmed to respond to their spoken responses, providing feedback or leading simulated interactions (Wik & Hjalmarsson, 2009). The possibilities may appear limitless. For example, it may be that ASR and scoring systems will one day move beyond monologic tasks to capture interactional activities involving multiple talkers and overlapping speech, locating interlocutors in time and space. Although machines are able to predict human scoring, they will never be able to replicate human processing. Humans will remain the ultimate arbitrators of whether and the extent to which communication has been successful in real-world settings, and there will always be constraints on what machines are able to do (Isaacs & Harding, 2017).

When fully automated assessments intended for high-stakes purposes began to be actively marketed to test-users on the global stage in the first decade of the twenty-first century, field-wide debates surrounding this development were initially heated and even acerbic. For example, critics from a sociocultural perspective decried the inauthenticity of Versant's decontextualized items (Chun, 2006). However, Pearson (2011) contends that, by using tasks that are not contextually embedded, the test excludes cultural schema and social factors from the assessment of L2 speaking ability. They argue that this is more efficient for assessing actual speaking ability by spending the time eliciting test-takers' speech samples rather than creating context. Further, the test correlates with context-dependent speaking tests (e.g. TOEFL, IELTS), supporting the claim that test scores are related to speaking ability on contextually richer speaking tasks (Van Moere & Downey, 2016). Despite these and other rebuttals from the test provider, including about the psycholinguistic nature of the test construct, concerns about validity and authenticity still resonate. In fact, most Versant tasks are more reminiscent of now-dated grammar translation and audiolingual style activities than they are of more contemporary style communicative tasks. These points aside, the language assessment community has now transitioned to a more pragmatic understanding that automated assessments are here to stay (Xi, 2012). The next section turns to the topic of setting pedagogical and assessment priorities in relation to features being targeted using automated scoring.

Defining pedagogical priorities

Not all errors are created equal, with some being more detrimental for communication than others (Derwing & Munro, 2015). This chapter has drawn mostly on segmental examples but would not be complete without reference to prosody. There is growing evidence that prosodic features are important for listener understanding of L2 speech (e.g. Kang, Rubin & Pickering, 2010). However, prosody is difficult for ASR to target. For example, comparing an L2 learner's pitch variation over time to that of referent speakers from a training corpus is more difficult than examining segmental features analysed segment by segment (Eskenazi, 2009). In addition, prosodic features tend to be amenable to sociolinguistic variables such as age, gender, social class or geographical variety, making it complicated to determine acceptable deviations from the norm (van Santen, Prud'hommeaux & Black, 2009). Thus, taking into account inter-speaker L2 prosodic variation, particularly in contexts that allow for different target NS varieties, is challenging. It is relatively easy to set cut-offs in terms of acoustic space for vowel formants (Deng & O'Shaughnessy, 2003), with more or less stringent criteria applied depending on the language varieties accepted and the desired difficulty or leniency of the automated system. However, identifying a similarly narrow range for prosodic features, even after normalizing for vocal tract size differences, is not currently feasible. Van Santen et al. (2009) suggest using prosodic minimal pairs or lexical items with particular stress patterns as tasks to avoid unwanted prosodic variation. However, this would necessitate even more constrained speaking prompts than are currently common for ASR. To summarize, minimal focus on prosody is a limitation of current automated scoring.

In terms of segmental errors, research on the sound contrasts that most impede communication can inform instructional and assessment priorities (Isaacs, 2014) and this extends to automated scoring. Carnegie Speech's commercial NativeAccent program for training purposes detects mispronunciations of phonemes (Pelton, 2012), including some consonant cluster strings and minimal pairs (e.g. /t/ substituted for /θ/) that are unlikely to actually interfere with intelligibility (see Derwing & Munro, 2015). The cautionary note is that linguistic features that are easy for a machine to detect and score may not be of much importance for communication. Therefore, claims by test providers about how the selected features affect intelligibility may be moot, unsubstantiated or even contradictory of existing evidence. In the case of NativeAccent, the tool's claim to 'teach students to speak the language intelligibly in less training time' (Pelton, 2012, p. 11) is likely both overstated and misleading. The element of accent reduction that the software is targeting may be incompatible with helping learners become intelligible (Levis, 2005), with time likely better spent giving learners feedback other pronunciation features.

It is useful to illustrate a related point in reference to a high-stakes automated test. In score reporting for the PTE Academic image (e.g. graph) description task, the proportion of uttered words detected as unintelligible is specified at the three lowest levels of the six-level pronunciation scale (0–5), with half of the words unintelligible at level 0, a third unintelligible at level 1 and over two-thirds intelligible at level 2 (Pearson, 2012). However, at the scalar extremes, the descriptors of 'native-like' (level 5) and 'non-English' pronunciation (level 0) suggest that what is being measured is not intelligibility but rather deviations from what human raters consider to be NS norms, which is reflected in the machine training and scoring methodology (p. 54). The issue here is that being more intelligible does not incrementally increase with sounding more native-like (Derwing & Munro, 2015). In sum, although automated speaking tests may claim to assess intelligibility, most of the emphasis tends to be placed on pronunciation accuracy or congruence with NS norms.

Cucchiarini et al. (2007) demonstrate one approach to preventing an ASR system from indiscriminately targeting all learner errors in an experimental CALL setting. They pre-define error types as 'relevant' (p. 2182) for learners of Dutch from different L1 groups using the following criteria:

- common to speakers from different L1 backgrounds;
- perceptually salient;
- potentially impede communication;
- frequent;
- persist over time.

After training the model on a NS passage, it was applied to detect segmental (substitution, epenthesis, deletion) errors in addition to using a silent pause model to detect undue dysfluencies. Measurement thresholds for each phone were derived by artificially introducing errors in the NSs' productions and comparing the manipulated speech to the error-free NS productions for the selected targets. The efficacy of model classifications and pre- and post-test results comparing targeted and untargeted sounds were reported.

Raux and Kawahara (2002) describe an alternative approach to pre-specifying segmental errors (target: 10 epenthesis, deletion and substitution errors) for Japanese learners of English using a probabilistic algorithm to relate intelligibility to error rates detected by their ASR system. A human rater scored learners' read aloud productions targeting each error type using a Likert-type intelligibility scale, with the ratings also used to derive an 'error priority function' suggesting the most crucial segmental errors for intelligibility (p. 737). They then evaluated the model by eliciting additional data. The model was trained by calculating the error rate distribution of the speech samples for each of the five intelligibility levels, with constraints applied to the formula in light of the assumption that error rates decrease with intelligibility gains (although see Harding (2017) for problems with this approach). Finally, they examined the difference between the error rate of each learner on the 10 pre-specified errors and the pooled performance of learners at that ability level, with underperformance relative to the mean for features deemed relevant suggesting that it could be a pedagogical focus. Despite the methodological shortcomings of this small-scale study, we can conclude that it is possible to develop an approach to scoring L2 segmental accuracy taking into account presumed pedagogical importance (Eskenazi, 2009).

Is hybrid machine–human scoring a way forward?

One of the issues that has permeated this chapter is that fully automated assessment can result in what Galaczi (2013) has termed a reductionist approach to L2 speaking and a narrowing of the construct. Such tests fail to capture, among other things, different interactional patterns that are typical of tests that adopt an expansive approach to assessing speaking, which is at the other end of the spectrum (e.g. Cambridge First Certificate of English). Bennett and Bejar (1998) articulate the potential risks to validity when constraints of automated scoring having to do with the mode of delivery dictate the way that the assessment is carried out:

> the interface helps set task and construct parameters. In the worst case, it can unintentionally distort the task and construct definition, either by making the mechanics of response entry so difficult that the responses gathered are not fully reflective of examinee competence or by constraining the substantive aspect of the task to the point that it no longer represents the original construct definition.

(p. 11)

One way of mitigating limitations in technology-driven assessment is by having automatic scoring operate in tandem with human ratings. ETS' Test of English-for-Teaching (TEFT), the assessment component of an online teacher professional development training programme, demonstrates one way of combining machine and human scoring (Zechner et al., 2015). In contrast to the relatively unpredictable discourse-level TOEFL iBT tasks, the TEFT uses controlled tasks more reminiscent of the Versant (Pearson, 2011). To address difficulties that arose in a pilot administration of SpeechRater when it was applied to the test, ETS researchers developed a system whereby test-takers' responses viewed as unscorable by human raters, owing either to poor recording quality (e.g. background noise, equipment issues) or to problematic responses (e.g. not in English, off topic), which would have resulted in lower reliability had they been automatically scored, were filtered out and rerouted to a human rater. In this way, all non-problematic items could be machine-scored and all screened problematic ones could be human-scored. Poorly recorded items raise questions about the validity of the assessment, with the intelligibility of the speech possibly confounded with poor sound quality (Munro, 1998). However, this example demonstrates that, rather than being an either/ or option, human and machine scoring could be used in complementary ways in assessing test-takers' performances. A hybrid human–machine scoring system could consist of the machine scoring the elements it does best, including segmental and fluency measures. This way, instead of human raters providing holistic scores on overall speaking ability or on all facets of the performance using detailed analytic scales, an alternative could be implemented. Raters could instead be asked to focus solely on and provide ratings for some elements of the performance not already being assessed (and not scored well, if at all) by the machine (e.g. cohesion, idea development, task execution). This could free up raters' attentional space to concentrate on discrete aspects of speech when rating, potentially simplifying some of the complexity of the rating task (see Lumley, 2005). In sum, one way of offsetting the limitations of technology-mediated assessment and allowing for greater construct coverage is by having automatic scoring complement human ratings – an area for future exploration.

Acknowledgements

Some of the ideas in this chapter arose through an automated speaking assessment project supported by the British Council. I gratefully acknowledge Fred Davidson for the push to explore this area, Judith Fairbairn, Jamie Dunlea and Barry O'Sullivan for the opportunity to do so, Evelina Galaczi for sharing her thinking on the topic, and the editors of this volume for their helpful comments on this chapter.

References

Bennett, R. E., & Bejar, I. I. (1998). Validity and automated scoring: It's not only the scoring. *Educational Measurement: Issues and Practice, 17*(4), 9–17.

Bernstein, J., Cohen, M., Murveit, H., Rtischev, R., & Weintraub, M. (1990). Automatic evaluation and training in English pronunciation. In *Proceedings of the International Conference on Spoken Language Processing (ICSLP) 1990*, Kobe, Japan.

Bernstein, J., Van Moere, A., & Cheng, J. (2010). Validating automated speaking tests. *Language Testing, 27*(3), 355–377.

Bridgeman, B., Powers, D., Stone, E., & Mollaun, P. (2011). TOEFL iBT speaking test scores as indicators of communicative language proficiency. *Language Testing, 29*(1), 91–108.

British Council. (2016). *IELTS results process*. Retrieved from http://takeielts.britishcouncil.org/find-out-about-results/results-process (accessed 6 July 2016).

Brown, A., Iwashita, N., & McNamara, T. F. (2005). *An examination of rater orientations and test-taker performance on English for academic purposes speaking tasks*. Monograph Series MS-29. Princeton, NJ: ETS.

Buck, G. (1989). Written tests of pronunciation: Do they work? *ELT Journal, 43*(1), 50–56.

Chengalvarayan, R. (2009). *Sampling rate independent speech recognition. United States Patent No. 2009/0012785 A1*. Naperville, IL: Patent Application Publication.

Chun, C. W. (2006). An analysis of a language test for employment: The authenticity of the PhonePass test. *Language Assessment Quarterly, 3*(3), 295–306.

Council of Europe. (2001). *Common European Framework of Reference for Languages: Learning, teaching, assessment*. Cambridge: Cambridge University Press.

Cucchiarini, C., Neri, A., de Wet, F., & Strik, H. (2007). ASR-based pronunciation training: Scoring accuracy and pedagogical effectiveness of a system for Dutch L2 learners. In *Proceedings of Interspeech 2007*, Antwerp, Belgium.

Cucchiarini, C., Neri, A., & Strik, H. (2009). Oral proficiency training in Dutch L2: The contribution of ASR-based corrective feedback. *Speech Communication, 51*(10), 853–863.

de Jong, J. H. A. L., & Bernstein, J. (2001). Relating PhonePass overall scores to the Council of Europe framework level descriptors. In *Proceedings of the European Conference of Speech Communication and Technology (EUROSPEECH) 2001*, Aalborg, Denmark.

Deng, L., & O'Shaughnessy, D. (2003). *Speech processing: A dynamic and optimization-oriented approach*. New York, NY: Marcel Dekker.

Derwing, T. M., & Munro, M. J. (2015). *Pronunciation fundamentals: Evidence-based perspectives for L2 teaching and research*. Amsterdam: John Benjamins.

Educational Testing Service. (2009). The official guide to the TOEFL test (3rd ed.). New York, NY: McGraw-Hill.

Eskenazi, M. (2009). An overview of spoken language technology for education. *Speech Communication, 51*(10), 832–844.

ETS. (2016). *Getting your TOEFL iBT test scores.* Retrieved from www.ets.org/toefl/ibt/scores/get (accessed 6 July 2016).

Franco, H., Bratt, H., Rossier, R., Gadde, V. R., Shriberg, E., Abrash, V., & Precoda, K. (2010). EduSpeak: A speech recognition and pronunciation scoring toolkit for computer-aided language learning applications. *Language Testing, 27*(3), 401–418.

Galaczi, E. D. (2010). Face-to-face and computer-based assessment of speaking: Challenges and opportunities. In L. Araújo (Ed.), *Proceedings of the computer-based assessment (CBA) of foreign language speaking skills* (pp. 29–51). Brussels: European Commission.

Galaczi, E. D. (2013). Speaking assessment: Evolving and adapting to a changing world. *Cambridge English centenary symposium on speaking assessment.* Cambridge: Cambridge English Language Assessment.

Ginther, A. (2013). Assessment of speaking. In C. A. Chapelle (Ed.), *The encyclopedia of applied linguistics.* Hoboken, NJ: Blackwell. doi:10.1002/9781405198431.wbeal0052.

Ginther, A., Dimova, S., & Yang, R. (2010). Conceptual and empirical relationships between temporal measures of fluency and oral English proficiency with implications for automated scoring. *Language Testing, 27*(3), 379–399.

Harding, L. (2017). What do raters need in a pronunciation scale? The users' view. In T. Isaacs & P. Trofimovich (Eds), *Second language pronunciation assessment: Interdisciplinary perspectives* (pp. 12–34). Bristol: Multilingual Matters.

He, A. W., & Young, R. (1998). Language proficiency interviews: A discourse approach. In R. Young & A. W. He (Eds), *Talking and testing: Discourse approaches to the assessment of oral proficiency* (pp. 1–24). Amsterdam: John Benjamins.

Isaacs, T. (2014). Assessing pronunciation. In A. J. Kunnan (Ed.), *The companion to language assessment* (pp. 140–155). Hoboken, NJ: Wiley-Blackwell.

Isaacs, T., & Harding, L. (2017). Research timeline: Pronunciation assessment. *Language Teaching, 50*(3), 347–366.

Kang, O., Rubin, D., & Pickering, L. (2010). Suprasegmental measures of accentedness and judgments of language learner proficiency in oral English. *Modern Language Journal, 94*(4), 554–566.

Lado, R. (1961). *Language testing: The construction and use of foreign language tests.* London: Longman.

Levelt, W. J. M. (1989). *Speaking: From intention to articulation.* Cambridge, MA: MIT Press.

Levis, J. (2005). Changing contexts and shifting paradigms in pronunciation teaching. *TESOL Quarterly, 39*(3), 369–377.

Lumley, T. (2005). *Assessing second language writing: The rater's perspective.* Frankfurt: Peter Lang.

Lundeberg, O. K. (1929). Recent developments in audition-speech tests. *The Modern Language Journal, 14*(3), 193–202.

Messick, S. (1990). *Validity of test interpretation and use.* Research Report 90–11. Princeton, NJ: Educational Testing Service.

Munro, M. J. (1998). The effects of noise on the intelligibility of foreign-accented speech. *Studies in Second Language Acquisition, 20*(2), 139–154.

Pearson. (2011). *Versant English test: Test description & validation summary.* Palo Alto, CA: Pearson Education.

Pearson. (2012). *PTE academic: Score guide.* Pearson Education.

Pearson. (2014). *PTE academic: Test centres and fees.* Retrieved from http://pearsonpte.com/test-takers/test-centres (accessed 6 July 2016).

Pelton, G. (2012). *Mining pronunciation data for consonant cluster problems.* Paper presented at the International Symposium on Automatic Detection of Errors in Pronunciation Training (IS ADEPT), Stockholm, Sweden. Retrieved from www.speech.kth.se/isadept/presentations/Garrett_Pelton.pdf (accessed 6 July 2016).

Raux, A., & Kawahara, T. (2002). Automatic intelligibility assessment and diagnosis of critical pronunciation errors for computer-assisted pronunciation learning. In *Proceedings of the International Conference on Spoken Language Processing (ICSLP)* (pp. 737–740), Denver, CO, USA.

Thomson, R. I., & Isaacs, T. (2009). Within-category variation in L2 English vowel learning. In *Proceedings of the annual conference of the Canadian Acoustics Association, Niagara-on-the-Lake, Ontario, Canada* (pp. 138–139).

Van Moere, A., & Downey, R. (2016). Technology and artificial intelligence in language assessment. In D. Tsagari & J. Banerjee (Eds), *Handbook of second language assessment* (pp. 341–358). Berlin: De Gruyter Mouton.

van Santen, J. P. H., Prud'hommeaux, E. T., & Black, L. M. (2009). Automated assessment of prosody production. *Speech Communication, 51*(11), 1082–1097.

Wagner, E., & Kunnan, A. J. (2015). The Duolingo English Test. *Language Assessment Quarterly, 12*(3), 320–331.

Wall, D., & Horák, T. (2006). *The impact of changes in the TOEFL examination on teaching and learning in Central and Eastern Europe: Phase 1, the baseline study.* TOEFL Monograph MS-34. Princeton, NJ: ETS.

Wik, P., & Hjalmarsson, A. (2009). Embodied conversational agents in computer assisted language learning. *Speech Communication, 51*(10), 1024–1037.

Xi, X. (2012). Validity and the automated scoring of performance tests. In G. Fulcher & F. Davidson (Eds), *The Routledge handbook of language testing* (pp. 438–451). Abingdon: Routledge.

Xi, X., Higgins, D., Zechner, K., & Williamson, D. (2012). A comparison of two scoring methods for an automated speech scoring system. *Language Testing, 29*(3), 371–394.

Zechner, K., Chen, L., Davis, L., Evanini, K., Lee, C. M., Leong, C. W., . . . Yoon, S.-Y. (2015). Automated scoring of speaking tasks in the Test of English-for-Teaching (TEFT). *ETS Research Report Series* (RR15–31). Princeton, NJ: Educational Testing Service.

Zechner, K., Higgins, D., Xi, X., & Williamson, D. M. (2009). Automatic scoring of non-native spontaneous speech in tests of spoken English. *Speech Communication, 51*(10), 883–895.

Index

Abercrombie, D. 142, 144, 233, 545
Abrahamsson, N. 293
absence errors 345
accent choice 54
accentedness 2, 413–416, 418–419, 420–428, 512
accents: comprehensibility and 284–286; folk linguistics and 400–406; modification of 287–290; pitch 50; reduction of 287–288, 290, 320; regional 189–202
Accents of English (Wells) 200
acceptability 343–344
accuracy: definition of 340; fluency versus 271–272
accuracy-focused techniques 280
Achard, M. 465
acoustics 58
active articulators 42
active listening 252, 258
activity recipe collections (ARCs) 303–304, 309–310, 322, 362
Acton, W. 453
Adamson, H. D. 393
affective variables 388–389
affricates 43, 102–103
age 386–387
age of arrival (AOA) 386, 391
age of onset (AO) 386–387, 389, 391–392
Algeo, J. 211
Allen, W. 272
allophony 12
allphones 47–48
alphabetic principle 170
Amalgam English 210, 234
Amazon Mechanical Turk 563
American Dictionary of the English Language, The (Webster) 205, 219
American Folklife Center 199
American Speech-Hearing Association (ASHA) *Leader* 287
analytic-linguistic approach 256, 338
Anderson, J. D. 64
Anderson, L. 439

Anderson-Hsieh, J. 139, 146, 438, 545, 546
Anisman, P. H. 394
Ann, J. 532
annotated learner speech corpora 560–561
Anvil 481
anxiety 388–389, 451
applications in L2 pronunciation research 419
approximants 43, 99, 104–106
approximation 99
aptitude 387–388
Archibald, J. 14, 15, 16, 18, 21
Arciuli, J. 145
Arnold, G. F. 140, 433
articulation: manner of 42–43, 99, 123; place of 42, 95–98, 123, 128, 129
articulators 42, 94–95
Arvaniti, A. 147
arytenoids 40
asides 161
aspiration 19, 106
assessment 511–526, 559–560, 570–584
associative memory 387
Asu, E. L. 147
Atkey, S. 15–16
Atlas of North American English, The (Labov, Ash & Boberg) 196, 199
attitudes: complexity of 505–506; intelligibility and 507–508; learner 388–389, 502–504; teacher 504–505
attitudinal research 502–505
attitudinal surveys 502
attractiveness 400, 406
Aubrey, S. 342
Audacity 454
audiolingualism 259, 287, 321
audiolingual method (ALM) 267, 338, 453, 512
audioperceptual (AP) assessment 417, 419
automated scoring *see* fully automated speaking assessments
automaticity 164–165
automatic speech recognition (ASR) 454, 479, 516, 519, 521, 556–569, 570, 571–573

rule use 172
Ryan, E. B. 401, 405, 417, 418

sagittal diagram 453
Sailaja, P. 531, 533, 535
Saito, K. 323, 342–343, 416, 418, 456, 513
Salbrina, S. 224
saliency 123
Santana Williamson, E. 503
Saraceni, M. 238–239
Sardegna, V. G. 452
Savignon, S. 272
Scheuer, S. 502
Schiavetti, N. 414, 419, 420, 424
Schmidt, A. M. 290
Schmitt, N. 373
Schneider, E. W. 527, 538
Schneiderman, E. I. 322–323
Scovel, T. 11
Sebastian, R. J. 405
secondary phonemes 433
second language acquisition (SLA): description
    of 11; field of 9
second language phonology 11
Segalowitz, N. 164–165
segments 14–15, 46
Seidlhofer, B. 303, 347, 500, 502, 537, 551
self-monitoring 278
Selinker, L. 10, 29
semi-direct tests 571, 574–575
semi-vowels 99, 105–106
sentence stress 137, 139, 155
Sethi, J. 242
Setter, J. 220, 235, 440, 441
Sewell, A. 498, 501
shadowing 345–346, 348, 452
Shearer, J. W. 254
Sheridan, T. 205, 219
Shih, C. 487
Shuck, G. 402
Shuja, A. 535
sibilants 43
Sicola, L. 329
Siegal, M. 393
Sifakis, N. 504
Sikorski, L. D. 287, 290
Silent Way 321–322
similarity differential rate hypothesis (SDRH)
    33
Simpson, B. S. 145
Singapore English 212, 214, 441, 527, 532,
    534–535, 536
Sirsa, H. 533
Sitler, R. W. 420
Situational Language Teaching 259
Skehan, P. 340
skill acquisition theory 78–80

Slomanson, P. 394
small group discussions 311–312
Smemoe, W. B. 452
Smit, U. 389, 401
Smith, G. 294
Smith, L. E. 220, 415, 543–544, 547, 547–548,
    549, 553
Sobkowiak, W. 498
socially constructed metalanguage (SCM) 467,
    469, 470, 471–474
social purpose 146
sociocognitive perspective, on pronunciation
    83–85
sociocultural perspective, on pronunciation
    81–82
sociocultural theory (SCT) 467
soft palate 40, 42
solidarity 400
Sona-Match 483
sonority 124–125, 126, 127, 129
Sosa, J. Y. 64
Sougari, A-M. 504
Sound Pattern of English, The (Chomsky
    & Halle) 433
sound shapes 150, 353–355, 357–359
sound-spelling correspondence 2
sound substance of speech 352–369
Southern Vowel Shift 196–197, 209
Southwood, M. H. 418, 420, 426
Sowden, C. 500–501
Spada, N. 272
speaking, pronunciation and 337–351
speech, representing 46–47
Speech Accent Archive 199
speech breathing 456
speech-language pathologists (SLPs) 287–288,
    289–290
speech learning model (SLM) 34, 77–78
speech measurement 417–418
speech production: description of 94–95;
    methods of 66–67; overview of 40–46;
    research on 63–64
speech rate *see* speed of speech
SpeechRater 521, 523, 577–578, 581
speech sound discrimination 60–61
speech technology 519
speech visualization technology 440
speed of speech 329, 358, 360–362, 438
spelling differences, US versus UK 207
spelling reform 170
Spencer, S. 303
spontaneous speech model (SSM) 353, 356,
    359–363, 367–368
Springall, J. 326
'squeeze zones' 150
stand-alone pronunciation course books
    277–278